Dictionary of Literary Biography

1. *The American Renaissance in New England,* edited by Joel Myerson (1978)
2. *American Novelists Since World War II,* edited by Jeffrey Helterman and Richard Layman (1978)
3. *Antebellum Writers in New York and the South,* edited by Joel Myerson (1979)
4. *American Writers in Paris, 1920–1939,* edited by Karen Lane Rood (1980)
5. *American Poets Since World War II,* 2 parts, edited by Donald J. Greiner (1980)
6. *American Novelists Since World War II, Second Series,* edited by James E. Kibler Jr. (1980)
7. *Twentieth-Century American Dramatists,* 2 parts, edited by John MacNicholas (1981)
8. *Twentieth-Century American Science-Fiction Writers,* 2 parts, edited by David Cowart and Thomas L. Wymer (1981)
9. *American Novelists, 1910–1945,* 3 parts, edited by James J. Martine (1981)
10. *Modern British Dramatists, 1900–1945,* 2 parts, edited by Stanley Weintraub (1982)
11. *American Humorists, 1800–1950,* 2 parts, edited by Stanley Trachtenberg (1982)
12. *American Realists and Naturalists,* edited by Donald Pizer and Earl N. Harbert (1982)
13. *British Dramatists Since World War II,* 2 parts, edited by Stanley Weintraub (1982)
14. *British Novelists Since 1960,* 2 parts, edited by Jay L. Halio (1983)
15. *British Novelists, 1930–1959,* 2 parts, edited by Bernard Oldsey (1983)
16. *The Beats: Literary Bohemians in Postwar America,* 2 parts, edited by Ann Charters (1983)
17. *Twentieth-Century American Historians,* edited by Clyde N. Wilson (1983)
18. *Victorian Novelists After 1885,* edited by Ira B. Nadel and William E. Fredeman (1983)
19. *British Poets, 1880–1914,* edited by Donald E. Stanford (1983)
20. *British Poets, 1914–1945,* edited by Donald E. Stanford (1983)
21. *Victorian Novelists Before 1885,* edited by Ira B. Nadel and William E. Fredeman (1983)
22. *American Writers for Children, 1900–1960,* edited by John Cech (1983)
23. *American Newspaper Journalists, 1873–1900,* edited by Perry J. Ashley (1983)
24. *American Colonial Writers, 1606–1734,* edited by Emory Elliott (1984)
25. *American Newspaper Journalists, 1901–1925,* edited by Perry J. Ashley (1984)
26. *American Screenwriters,* edited by Robert E. Morsberger, Stephen O. Lesser, and Randall Clark (1984)
27. *Poets of Great Britain and Ireland, 1945–1960,* edited by Vincent B. Sherry Jr. (1984)
28. *Twentieth-Century American-Jewish Fiction Writers,* edited by Daniel Walden (1984)
29. *American Newspaper Journalists, 1926–1950,* edited by Perry J. Ashley (1984)
30. *American Historians, 1607–1865,* edited by Clyde N. Wilson (1984)
31. *American Colonial Writers, 1735–1781,* edited by Emory Elliott (1984)
32. *Victorian Poets Before 1850,* edited by William E. Fredeman and Ira B. Nadel (1984)
33. *Afro-American Fiction Writers After 1955,* edited by Thadious M. Davis and Trudier Harris (1984)
34. *British Novelists, 1890–1929: Traditionalists,* edited by Thomas F. Staley (1985)
35. *Victorian Poets After 1850,* edited by William E. Fredeman and Ira B. Nadel (1985)
36. *British Novelists, 1890–1929: Modernists,* edited by Thomas F. Staley (1985)
37. *American Writers of the Early Republic,* edited by Emory Elliott (1985)
38. *Afro-American Writers After 1955: Dramatists and Prose Writers,* edited by Thadious M. Davis and Trudier Harris (1985)
39. *British Novelists, 1660–1800,* 2 parts, edited by Martin C. Battestin (1985)
40. *Poets of Great Britain and Ireland Since 1960,* 2 parts, edited by Vincent B. Sherry Jr. (1985)
41. *Afro-American Poets Since 1955,* edited by Trudier Harris and Thadious M. Davis (1985)
42. *American Writers for Children Before 1900,* edited by Glenn E. Estes (1985)
43. *American Newspaper Journalists, 1690–1872,* edited by Perry J. Ashley (1986)
44. *American Screenwriters, Second Series,* edited by Randall Clark, Robert E. Morsberger, and Stephen O. Lesser (1986)
45. *American Poets, 1880–1945, First Series,* edited by Peter Quartermain (1986)
46. *American Literary Publishing Houses, 1900–1980: Trade and Paperback,* edited by Peter Dzwonkoski (1986)
47. *American Historians, 1866–1912,* edited by Clyde N. Wilson (1986)
48. *American Poets, 1880–1945, Second Series,* edited by Peter Quartermain (1986)
49. *American Literary Publishing Houses, 1638–1899,* 2 parts, edited by Peter Dzwonkoski (1986)
50. *Afro-American Writers Before the Harlem Renaissance,* edited by Trudier Harris (1986)
51. *Afro-American Writers from the Harlem Renaissance to 1940,* edited by Trudier Harris (1987)
52. *American Writers for Children Since 1960: Fiction,* edited by Glenn E. Estes (1986)
53. *Canadian Writers Since 1960, First Series,* edited by W. H. New (1986)
54. *American Poets, 1880–1945, Third Series,* 2 parts, edited by Peter Quartermain (1987)
55. *Victorian Prose Writers Before 1867,* edited by William B. Thesing (1987)
56. *German Fiction Writers, 1914–1945,* edited by James Hardin (1987)
57. *Victorian Prose Writers After 1867,* edited by William B. Thesing (1987)
58. *Jacobean and Caroline Dramatists,* edited by Fredson Bowers (1987)
59. *American Literary Critics and Scholars, 1800–1850,* edited by John W. Rathbun and Monica M. Grecu (1987)
60. *Canadian Writers Since 1960, Second Series,* edited by W. H. New (1987)
61. *American Writers for Children Since 1960: Poets, Illustrators, and Nonfiction Authors,* edited by Glenn E. Estes (1987)
62. *Elizabethan Dramatists,* edited by Fredson Bowers (1987)
63. *Modern American Critics, 1920–1955,* edited by Gregory S. Jay (1988)
64. *American Literary Critics and Scholars, 1850–1880,* edited by John W. Rathbun and Monica M. Grecu (1988)
65. *French Novelists, 1900–1930,* edited by Catharine Savage Brosman (1988)
66. *German Fiction Writers, 1885–1913,* 2 parts, edited by James Hardin (1988)
67. *Modern American Critics Since 1955,* edited by Gregory S. Jay (1988)
68. *Canadian Writers, 1920–1959, First Series,* edited by W. H. New (1988)
69. *Contemporary German Fiction Writers, First Series,* edited by Wolfgang D. Elfe and James Hardin (1988)
70. *British Mystery Writers, 1860–1919,* edited by Bernard Benstock and Thomas F. Staley (1988)
71. *American Literary Critics and Scholars, 1880–1900,* edited by John W. Rathbun and Monica M. Grecu (1988)
72. *French Novelists, 1930–1960,* edited by Catharine Savage Brosman (1988)
73. *American Magazine Journalists, 1741–1850,* edited by Sam G. Riley (1988)
74. *American Short-Story Writers Before 1880,* edited by Bobby Ellen Kimbel, with the assistance of William E. Grant (1988)
75. *Contemporary German Fiction Writers, Second Series,* edited by Wolfgang D. Elfe and James Hardin (1988)
76. *Afro-American Writers, 1940–1955,* edited by Trudier Harris (1988)
77. *British Mystery Writers, 1920–1939,* edited by Bernard Benstock and Thomas F. Staley (1988)

78 *American Short-Story Writers, 1880–1910,* edited by Bobby Ellen Kimbel, with the assistance of William E. Grant (1988)

79 *American Magazine Journalists, 1850–1900,* edited by Sam G. Riley (1988)

80 *Restoration and Eighteenth-Century Dramatists, First Series,* edited by Paula R. Backscheider (1989)

81 *Austrian Fiction Writers, 1875–1913,* edited by James Hardin and Donald G. Daviau (1989)

82 *Chicano Writers, First Series,* edited by Francisco A. Lomelí and Carl R. Shirley (1989)

83 *French Novelists Since 1960,* edited by Catharine Savage Brosman (1989)

84 *Restoration and Eighteenth-Century Dramatists, Second Series,* edited by Paula R. Backscheider (1989)

85 *Austrian Fiction Writers After 1914,* edited by James Hardin and Donald G. Daviau (1989)

86 *American Short-Story Writers, 1910–1945, First Series,* edited by Bobby Ellen Kimbel (1989)

87 *British Mystery and Thriller Writers Since 1940, First Series,* edited by Bernard Benstock and Thomas F. Staley (1989)

88 *Canadian Writers, 1920–1959, Second Series,* edited by W. H. New (1989)

89 *Restoration and Eighteenth-Century Dramatists, Third Series,* edited by Paula R. Backscheider (1989)

90 *German Writers in the Age of Goethe, 1789–1832,* edited by James Hardin and Christoph E. Schweitzer (1989)

91 *American Magazine Journalists, 1900–1960, First Series,* edited by Sam G. Riley (1990)

92 *Canadian Writers, 1890–1920,* edited by W. H. New (1990)

93 *British Romantic Poets, 1789–1832, First Series,* edited by John R. Greenfield (1990)

94 *German Writers in the Age of Goethe: Sturm und Drang to Classicism,* edited by James Hardin and Christoph E. Schweitzer (1990)

95 *Eighteenth-Century British Poets, First Series,* edited by John Sitter (1990)

96 *British Romantic Poets, 1789–1832, Second Series,* edited by John R. Greenfield (1990)

97 *German Writers from the Enlightenment to Sturm und Drang, 1720–1764,* edited by James Hardin and Christoph E. Schweitzer (1990)

98 *Modern British Essayists, First Series,* edited by Robert Beum (1990)

99 *Canadian Writers Before 1890,* edited by W. H. New (1990)

100 *Modern British Essayists, Second Series,* edited by Robert Beum (1990)

101 *British Prose Writers, 1660–1800, First Series,* edited by Donald T. Siebert (1991)

102 *American Short-Story Writers, 1910–1945, Second Series,* edited by Bobby Ellen Kimbel (1991)

103 *American Literary Biographers, First Series,* edited by Steven Serafin (1991)

104 *British Prose Writers, 1660–1800, Second Series,* edited by Donald T. Siebert (1991)

105 *American Poets Since World War II, Second Series,* edited by R. S. Gwynn (1991)

106 *British Literary Publishing Houses, 1820–1880,* edited by Patricia J. Anderson and Jonathan Rose (1991)

107 *British Romantic Prose Writers, 1789–1832, First Series,* edited by John R. Greenfield (1991)

108 *Twentieth-Century Spanish Poets, First Series,* edited by Michael L. Perna (1991)

109 *Eighteenth-Century British Poets, Second Series,* edited by John Sitter (1991)

110 *British Romantic Prose Writers, 1789–1832, Second Series,* edited by John R. Greenfield (1991)

111 *American Literary Biographers, Second Series,* edited by Steven Serafin (1991)

112 *British Literary Publishing Houses, 1881–1965,* edited by Jonathan Rose and Patricia J. Anderson (1991)

113 *Modern Latin-American Fiction Writers, First Series,* edited by William Luis (1992)

114 *Twentieth-Century Italian Poets, First Series,* edited by Giovanna Wedel De Stasio, Glauco Cambon, and Antonio Illiano (1992)

115 *Medieval Philosophers,* edited by Jeremiah Hackett (1992)

116 *British Romantic Novelists, 1789–1832,* edited by Bradford K. Mudge (1992)

117 *Twentieth-Century Caribbean and Black African Writers, First Series,* edited by Bernth Lindfors and Reinhard Sander (1992)

118 *Twentieth-Century German Dramatists, 1889–1918,* edited by Wolfgang D. Elfe and James Hardin (1992)

119 *Nineteenth-Century French Fiction Writers: Romanticism and Realism, 1800–1860,* edited by Catharine Savage Brosman (1992)

120 *American Poets Since World War II, Third Series,* edited by R. S. Gwynn (1992)

121 *Seventeenth-Century British Nondramatic Poets, First Series,* edited by M. Thomas Hester (1992)

122 *Chicano Writers, Second Series,* edited by Francisco A. Lomelí and Carl R. Shirley (1992)

123 *Nineteenth-Century French Fiction Writers: Naturalism and Beyond, 1860–1900,* edited by Catharine Savage Brosman (1992)

124 *Twentieth-Century German Dramatists, 1919–1992,* edited by Wolfgang D. Elfe and James Hardin (1992)

125 *Twentieth-Century Caribbean and Black African Writers, Second Series,* edited by Bernth Lindfors and Reinhard Sander (1993)

126 *Seventeenth-Century British Nondramatic Poets, Second Series,* edited by M. Thomas Hester (1993)

127 *American Newspaper Publishers, 1950–1990,* edited by Perry J. Ashley (1993)

128 *Twentieth-Century Italian Poets, Second Series,* edited by Giovanna Wedel De Stasio, Glauco Cambon, and Antonio Illiano (1993)

129 *Nineteenth-Century German Writers, 1841–1900,* edited by James Hardin and Siegfried Mews (1993)

130 *American Short-Story Writers Since World War II,* edited by Patrick Meanor (1993)

131 *Seventeenth-Century British Nondramatic Poets, Third Series,* edited by M. Thomas Hester (1993)

132 *Sixteenth-Century British Nondramatic Writers, First Series,* edited by David A. Richardson (1993)

133 *Nineteenth-Century German Writers to 1840,* edited by James Hardin and Siegfried Mews (1993)

134 *Twentieth-Century Spanish Poets, Second Series,* edited by Jerry Phillips Winfield (1994)

135 *British Short-Fiction Writers, 1880–1914: The Realist Tradition,* edited by William B. Thesing (1994)

136 *Sixteenth-Century British Nondramatic Writers, Second Series,* edited by David A. Richardson (1994)

137 *American Magazine Journalists, 1900–1960, Second Series,* edited by Sam G. Riley (1994)

138 *German Writers and Works of the High Middle Ages: 1170–1280,* edited by James Hardin and Will Hasty (1994)

139 *British Short-Fiction Writers, 1945–1980,* edited by Dean Baldwin (1994)

140 *American Book-Collectors and Bibliographers, First Series,* edited by Joseph Rosenblum (1994)

141 *British Children's Writers, 1880–1914,* edited by Laura M. Zaidman (1994)

142 *Eighteenth-Century British Literary Biographers,* edited by Steven Serafin (1994)

143 *American Novelists Since World War II, Third Series,* edited by James R. Giles and Wanda H. Giles (1994)

144 *Nineteenth-Century British Literary Biographers,* edited by Steven Serafin (1994)

145 *Modern Latin-American Fiction Writers, Second Series,* edited by William Luis and Ann González (1994)

146 *Old and Middle English Literature,* edited by Jeffrey Helterman and Jerome Mitchell (1994)

147 *South Slavic Writers Before World War II,* edited by Vasa D. Mihailovich (1994)

148 *German Writers and Works of the Early Middle Ages: 800–1170,* edited by Will Hasty and James Hardin (1994)

149 *Late Nineteenth- and Early Twentieth-Century British Literary Biographers,* edited by Steven Serafin (1995)

150 *Early Modern Russian Writers, Late Seventeenth and Eighteenth Centuries,* edited by Marcus C. Levitt (1995)

151 *British Prose Writers of the Early Seventeenth Century,* edited by Clayton D. Lein (1995)

152 *American Novelists Since World War II, Fourth Series,* edited by James R. Giles and Wanda H. Giles (1995)

153 *Late-Victorian and Edwardian British Novelists, First Series,* edited by George M. Johnson (1995)

154 *The British Literary Book Trade, 1700–1820,* edited by James K. Bracken and Joel Silver (1995)

155 *Twentieth-Century British Literary Biographers*, edited by Steven Serafin (1995)

156 *British Short-Fiction Writers, 1880–1914: The Romantic Tradition*, edited by William F. Naufftus (1995)

157 *Twentieth-Century Caribbean and Black African Writers, Third Series*, edited by Bernth Lindfors and Reinhard Sander (1995)

158 *British Reform Writers, 1789–1832*, edited by Gary Kelly and Edd Applegate (1995)

159 *British Short-Fiction Writers, 1800–1880*, edited by John R. Greenfield (1996)

160 *British Children's Writers, 1914–1960*, edited by Donald R. Hettinga and Gary D. Schmidt (1996)

161 *British Children's Writers Since 1960, First Series*, edited by Caroline Hunt (1996)

162 *British Short-Fiction Writers, 1915–1945*, edited by John H. Rogers (1996)

163 *British Children's Writers, 1800–1880*, edited by Meena Khorana (1996)

164 *German Baroque Writers, 1580–1660*, edited by James Hardin (1996)

165 *American Poets Since World War II, Fourth Series*, edited by Joseph Conte (1996)

166 *British Travel Writers, 1837–1875*, edited by Barbara Brothers and Julia Gergits (1996)

167 *Sixteenth-Century British Nondramatic Writers, Third Series*, edited by David A. Richardson (1996)

168 *German Baroque Writers, 1661–1730*, edited by James Hardin (1996)

169 *American Poets Since World War II, Fifth Series*, edited by Joseph Conte (1996)

170 *The British Literary Book Trade, 1475–1700*, edited by James K. Bracken and Joel Silver (1996)

171 *Twentieth-Century American Sportswriters*, edited by Richard Orodenker (1996)

172 *Sixteenth-Century British Nondramatic Writers, Fourth Series*, edited by David A. Richardson (1996)

173 *American Novelists Since World War II, Fifth Series*, edited by James R. Giles and Wanda H. Giles (1996)

174 *British Travel Writers, 1876–1909*, edited by Barbara Brothers and Julia Gergits (1997)

175 *Native American Writers of the United States*, edited by Kenneth M. Roemer (1997)

176 *Ancient Greek Authors*, edited by Ward W. Briggs (1997)

177 *Italian Novelists Since World War II, 1945–1965*, edited by Augustus Pallotta (1997)

178 *British Fantasy and Science-Fiction Writers Before World War I*, edited by Darren Harris-Fain (1997)

179 *German Writers of the Renaissance and Reformation, 1280–1580*, edited by James Hardin and Max Reinhart (1997)

180 *Japanese Fiction Writers, 1868–1945*, edited by Van C. Gessel (1997)

181 *South Slavic Writers Since World War II*, edited by Vasa D. Mihailovich (1997)

182 *Japanese Fiction Writers Since World War II*, edited by Van C. Gessel (1997)

183 *American Travel Writers, 1776–1864*, edited by James J. Schramer and Donald Ross (1997)

184 *Nineteenth-Century British Book-Collectors and Bibliographers*, edited by William Baker and Kenneth Womack (1997)

185 *American Literary Journalists, 1945–1995, First Series*, edited by Arthur J. Kaul (1998)

186 *Nineteenth-Century American Western Writers*, edited by Robert L. Gale (1998)

187 *American Book Collectors and Bibliographers, Second Series*, edited by Joseph Rosenblum (1998)

188 *American Book and Magazine Illustrators to 1920*, edited by Steven E. Smith, Catherine A. Hastedt, and Donald H. Dyal (1998)

189 *American Travel Writers, 1850–1915*, edited by Donald Ross and James J. Schramer (1998)

190 *British Reform Writers, 1832–1914*, edited by Gary Kelly and Edd Applegate (1998)

191 *British Novelists Between the Wars*, edited by George M. Johnson (1998)

192 *French Dramatists, 1789–1914*, edited by Barbara T. Cooper (1998)

193 *American Poets Since World War II, Sixth Series*, edited by Joseph Conte (1998)

194 *British Novelists Since 1960, Second Series*, edited by Merritt Moseley (1998)

195 *British Travel Writers, 1910–1939*, edited by Barbara Brothers and Julia Gergits (1998)

196 *Italian Novelists Since World War II, 1965–1995*, edited by Augustus Pallotta (1999)

197 *Late-Victorian and Edwardian British Novelists, Second Series*, edited by George M. Johnson (1999)

198 *Russian Literature in the Age of Pushkin and Gogol: Prose*, edited by Christine A. Rydel (1999)

199 *Victorian Women Poets*, edited by William B. Thesing (1999)

200 *American Women Prose Writers to 1820*, edited by Carla J. Mulford, with Angela Vietto and Amy E. Winans (1999)

201 *Twentieth-Century British Book Collectors and Bibliographers*, edited by William Baker and Kenneth Womack (1999)

202 *Nineteenth-Century American Fiction Writers*, edited by Kent P. Ljungquist (1999)

203 *Medieval Japanese Writers*, edited by Steven D. Carter (1999)

204 *British Travel Writers, 1940–1997*, edited by Barbara Brothers and Julia M. Gergits (1999)

205 *Russian Literature in the Age of Pushkin and Gogol: Poetry and Drama*, edited by Christine A. Rydel (1999)

206 *Twentieth-Century American Western Writers, First Series*, edited by Richard H. Cracroft (1999)

207 *British Novelists Since 1960, Third Series*, edited by Merritt Moseley (1999)

208 *Literature of the French and Occitan Middle Ages: Eleventh to Fifteenth Centuries*, edited by Deborah Sinnreich-Levi and Ian S. Laurie (1999)

209 *Chicano Writers, Third Series*, edited by Francisco A. Lomelí and Carl R. Shirley (1999)

210 *Ernest Hemingway: A Documentary Volume*, edited by Robert W. Trogdon (1999)

211 *Ancient Roman Writers*, edited by Ward W. Briggs (1999)

212 *Twentieth-Century American Western Writers, Second Series*, edited by Richard H. Cracroft (1999)

213 *Pre-Nineteenth-Century British Book Collectors and Bibliographers*, edited by William Baker and Kenneth Womack (1999)

214 *Twentieth-Century Danish Writers*, edited by Marianne Stecher-Hansen (1999)

215 *Twentieth-Century Eastern European Writers, First Series*, edited by Steven Serafin (1999)

216 *British Poets of the Great War: Brooke, Rosenberg, Thomas. A Documentary Volume*, edited by Patrick Quinn (2000)

217 *Nineteenth-Century French Poets*, edited by Robert Beum (2000)

218 *American Short-Story Writers Since World War II, Second Series*, edited by Patrick Meanor and Gwen Crane (2000)

219 *F. Scott Fitzgerald's* The Great Gatsby: *A Documentary Volume*, edited by Matthew J. Bruccoli (2000)

220 *Twentieth-Century Eastern European Writers, Second Series*, edited by Steven Serafin (2000)

221 *American Women Prose Writers, 1870–1920*, edited by Sharon M. Harris, with the assistance of Heidi L. M. Jacobs and Jennifer Putzi (2000)

222 *H. L. Mencken: A Documentary Volume*, edited by Richard J. Schrader (2000)

223 *The American Renaissance in New England, Second Series*, edited by Wesley T. Mott (2000)

224 *Walt Whitman: A Documentary Volume*, edited by Joel Myerson (2000)

225 *South African Writers*, edited by Paul A. Scanlon (2000)

226 *American Hard-Boiled Crime Writers*, edited by George Parker Anderson and Julie B. Anderson (2000)

227 *American Novelists Since World War II, Sixth Series*, edited by James R. Giles and Wanda H. Giles (2000)

228 *Twentieth-Century American Dramatists, Second Series*, edited by Christopher J. Wheatley (2000)

229 *Thomas Wolfe: A Documentary Volume*, edited by Ted Mitchell (2001)

230 *Australian Literature, 1788–1914*, edited by Selina Samuels (2001)

231 *British Novelists Since 1960, Fourth Series*, edited by Merritt Moseley (2001)

232 *Twentieth-Century Eastern European Writers, Third Series*, edited by Steven Serafin (2001)

233 *British and Irish Dramatists Since World War II, Second Series*, edited by John Bull (2001)

234 *American Short-Story Writers Since World War II, Third Series*, edited by Patrick Meanor and Richard E. Lee (2001)

235 *The American Renaissance in New England, Third Series*, edited by Wesley T. Mott (2001)

236 *British Rhetoricians and Logicians, 1500–1660,* edited by Edward A. Malone (2001)

237 *The Beats: A Documentary Volume,* edited by Matt Theado (2001)

238 *Russian Novelists in the Age of Tolstoy and Dostoevsky,* edited by J. Alexander Ogden and Judith E. Kalb (2001)

239 *American Women Prose Writers: 1820–1870,* edited by Amy E. Hudock and Katharine Rodier (2001)

240 *Late Nineteenth- and Early Twentieth-Century British Women Poets,* edited by William B. Thesing (2001)

241 *American Sportswriters and Writers on Sport,* edited by Richard Orodenker (2001)

242 *Twentieth-Century European Cultural Theorists, First Series,* edited by Paul Hansom (2001)

243 *The American Renaissance in New England, Fourth Series,* edited by Wesley T. Mott (2001)

244 *American Short-Story Writers Since World War II, Fourth Series,* edited by Patrick Meanor and Joseph McNicholas (2001)

245 *British and Irish Dramatists Since World War II, Third Series,* edited by John Bull (2001)

246 *Twentieth-Century American Cultural Theorists,* edited by Paul Hansom (2001)

247 *James Joyce: A Documentary Volume,* edited by A. Nicholas Fargnoli (2001)

248 *Antebellum Writers in the South, Second Series,* edited by Kent Ljungquist (2001)

249 *Twentieth-Century American Dramatists, Third Series,* edited by Christopher Wheatley (2002)

250 *Antebellum Writers in New York, Second Series,* edited by Kent Ljungquist (2002)

251 *Canadian Fantasy and Science-Fiction Writers,* edited by Douglas Ivison (2002)

252 *British Philosophers, 1500–1799,* edited by Philip B. Dematteis and Peter S. Fosl (2002)

253 *Raymond Chandler: A Documentary Volume,* edited by Robert Moss (2002)

254 *The House of Putnam, 1837–1872: A Documentary Volume,* edited by Ezra Greenspan (2002)

255 *British Fantasy and Science-Fiction Writers, 1918–1960,* edited by Darren Harris-Fain (2002)

256 *Twentieth-Century American Western Writers, Third Series,* edited by Richard H. Cracroft (2002)

257 *Twentieth-Century Swedish Writers After World War II,* edited by Ann-Charlotte Gavel Adams (2002)

258 *Modern French Poets,* edited by Jean-François Leroux (2002)

259 *Twentieth-Century Swedish Writers Before World War II,* edited by Ann-Charlotte Gavel Adams (2002)

260 *Australian Writers, 1915–1950,* edited by Selina Samuels (2002)

261 *British Fantasy and Science-Fiction Writers Since 1960,* edited by Darren Harris-Fain (2002)

262 *British Philosophers, 1800–2000,* edited by Peter S. Fosl and Leemon B. McHenry (2002)

263 *William Shakespeare: A Documentary Volume,* edited by Catherine Loomis (2002)

264 *Italian Prose Writers, 1900–1945,* edited by Luca Somigli and Rocco Capozzi (2002)

265 *American Song Lyricists, 1920–1960,* edited by Philip Furia (2002)

266 *Twentieth-Century American Dramatists, Fourth Series,* edited by Christopher J. Wheatley (2002)

267 *Twenty-First-Century British and Irish Novelists,* edited by Michael R. Molino (2002)

268 *Seventeenth-Century French Writers,* edited by Françoise Jaouën (2002)

269 *Nathaniel Hawthorne: A Documentary Volume,* edited by Benjamin Franklin V (2002)

270 *American Philosophers Before 1950,* edited by Philip B. Dematteis and Leemon B. McHenry (2002)

271 *British and Irish Novelists Since 1960,* edited by Merritt Moseley (2002)

272 *Russian Prose Writers Between the World Wars,* edited by Christine Rydel (2003)

273 *F. Scott Fitzgerald's* Tender Is the Night: *A Documentary Volume,* edited by Matthew J. Bruccoli and George Parker Anderson (2003)

274 *John Dos Passos's* U.S.A.: *A Documentary Volume,* edited by Donald Pizer (2003)

275 *Twentieth-Century American Nature Writers: Prose,* edited by Roger Thompson and J. Scott Bryson (2003)

276 *British Mystery and Thriller Writers Since 1960,* edited by Gina Macdonald (2003)

277 *Russian Literature in the Age of Realism,* edited by Alyssa Dinega Gillespie (2003)

278 *American Novelists Since World War II, Seventh Series,* edited by James R. Giles and Wanda H. Giles (2003)

279 *American Philosophers, 1950–2000,* edited by Philip B. Dematteis and Leemon B. McHenry (2003)

280 *Dashiell Hammett's* The Maltese Falcon: *A Documentary Volume,* edited by Richard Layman (2003)

281 *British Rhetoricians and Logicians, 1500–1660, Second Series,* edited by Edward A. Malone (2003)

282 *New Formalist Poets,* edited by Jonathan N. Barron and Bruce Meyer (2003)

283 *Modern Spanish American Poets, First Series,* edited by María A. Salgado (2003)

284 *The House of Holt, 1866–1946: A Documentary Volume,* edited by Ellen D. Gilbert (2003)

285 *Russian Writers Since 1980,* edited by Marina Balina and Mark Lipovetsky (2004)

286 *Castilian Writers, 1400–1500,* edited by Frank A. Domínguez and George D. Greenia (2004)

287 *Portuguese Writers,* edited by Monica Rector and Fred M. Clark (2004)

288 *The House of Boni & Liveright, 1917–1933: A Documentary Volume,* edited by Charles Egleston (2004)

289 *Australian Writers, 1950–1975,* edited by Selina Samuels (2004)

290 *Modern Spanish American Poets, Second Series,* edited by María A. Salgado (2004)

291 *The Hoosier House: Bobbs-Merrill and Its Predecessors, 1850–1985: A Documentary Volume,* edited by Richard J. Schrader (2004)

292 *Twenty-First-Century American Novelists,* edited by Lisa Abney and Suzanne Disheroon-Green (2004)

293 *Icelandic Writers,* edited by Patrick J. Stevens (2004)

294 *James Gould Cozzens: A Documentary Volume,* edited by Matthew J. Bruccoli (2004)

295 *Russian Writers of the Silver Age, 1890–1925,* edited by Judith E. Kalb and J. Alexander Ogden with the collaboration of I. G. Vishnevetsky (2004)

296 *Twentieth-Century European Cultural Theorists, Second Series,* edited by Paul Hansom (2004)

297 *Twentieth-Century Norwegian Writers,* edited by Tanya Thresher (2004)

298 *Henry David Thoreau: A Documentary Volume,* edited by Richard J. Schneider (2004)

299 *Holocaust Novelists,* edited by Efraim Sicher (2004)

300 *Danish Writers from the Reformation to Decadence, 1550–1900,* edited by Marianne Stecher-Hansen (2004)

301 *Gustave Flaubert: A Documentary Volume,* edited by Éric Le Calvez (2004)

302 *Russian Prose Writers After World War II,* edited by Christine Rydel (2004)

303 *American Radical and Reform Writers, First Series,* edited by Steven Rosendale (2005)

304 *Bram Stoker's* Dracula: *A Documentary Volume,* edited by Elizabeth Miller (2005)

305 *Latin American Dramatists, First Series,* edited by Adam Versényi (2005)

306 *American Mystery and Detective Writers,* edited by George Parker Anderson (2005)

307 *Brazilian Writers,* edited by Monica Rector and Fred M. Clark (2005)

308 *Ernest Hemingway's* A Farewell to Arms: *A Documentary Volume,* edited by Charles Oliver (2005)

309 *John Steinbeck: A Documentary Volume,* edited by Luchen Li (2005)

310 *British and Irish Dramatists Since World War II, Fourth Series,* edited by John Bull (2005)

311 *Arabic Literary Culture, 500–925,* edited by Michael Cooperson and Shawkat M. Toorawa (2005)

312 *Asian American Writers,* edited by Deborah L. Madsen (2005)

313 *Writers of the French Enlightenment, I,* edited by Samia I. Spencer (2005)

Dictionary of Literary Biography Documentary Series

1 *Sherwood Anderson, Willa Cather, John Dos Passos, Theodore Dreiser, F. Scott Fitzgerald, Ernest Hemingway, Sinclair Lewis,* edited by Margaret A. Van Antwerp (1982)

2 *James Gould Cozzens, James T. Farrell, William Faulkner, John O'Hara, John Steinbeck, Thomas Wolfe, Richard Wright,* edited by Margaret A. Van Antwerp (1982)

3 *Saul Bellow, Jack Kerouac, Norman Mailer, Vladimir Nabokov, John Updike, Kurt Vonnegut,* edited by Mary Bruccoli (1983)

4 *Tennessee Williams,* edited by Margaret A. Van Antwerp and Sally Johns (1984)

5 *American Transcendentalists,* edited by Joel Myerson (1988)

6 *Hardboiled Mystery Writers: Raymond Chandler, Dashiell Hammett, Ross Macdonald,* edited by Matthew J. Bruccoli and Richard Layman (1989)

7 *Modern American Poets: James Dickey, Robert Frost, Marianne Moore,* edited by Karen L. Rood (1989)

8 *The Black Aesthetic Movement,* edited by Jeffrey Louis Decker (1991)

9 *American Writers of the Vietnam War: W. D. Ehrhart, Larry Heinemann, Tim O'Brien, Walter McDonald, John M. Del Vecchio,* edited by Ronald Baughman (1991)

10 *The Bloomsbury Group,* edited by Edward L. Bishop (1992)

11 *American Proletarian Culture: The Twenties and The Thirties,* edited by Jon Christian Suggs (1993)

12 *Southern Women Writers: Flannery O'Connor, Katherine Anne Porter, Eudora Welty,* edited by Mary Ann Wimsatt and Karen L. Rood (1994)

13 *The House of Scribner, 1846–1904,* edited by John Delaney (1996)

14 *Four Women Writers for Children, 1868–1918,* edited by Caroline C. Hunt (1996)

15 *American Expatriate Writers: Paris in the Twenties,* edited by Matthew J. Bruccoli and Robert W. Trogdon (1997)

16 *The House of Scribner, 1905–1930,* edited by John Delaney (1997)

17 *The House of Scribner, 1931–1984,* edited by John Delaney (1998)

18 *British Poets of The Great War: Sassoon, Graves, Owen,* edited by Patrick Quinn (1999)

19 *James Dickey,* edited by Judith S. Baughman (1999)

See also DLB 210, 216, 219, 222, 224, 229, 237, 247, 253, 254, 263, 269, 273, 274, 280, 284, 288, 291, 294, 298, 301, 304, 308, 309

Dictionary of Literary Biography Yearbooks

1980 edited by Karen L. Rood, Jean W. Ross, and Richard Ziegfeld (1981)

1981 edited by Karen L. Rood, Jean W. Ross, and Richard Ziegfeld (1982)

1982 edited by Richard Ziegfeld; associate editors: Jean W. Ross and Lynne C. Zeigler (1983)

1983 edited by Mary Bruccoli and Jean W. Ross; associate editor Richard Ziegfeld (1984)

1984 edited by Jean W. Ross (1985)

1985 edited by Jean W. Ross (1986)

1986 edited by J. M. Brook (1987)

1987 edited by J. M. Brook (1988)

1988 edited by J. M. Brook (1989)

1989 edited by J. M. Brook (1990)

1990 edited by James W. Hipp (1991)

1991 edited by James W. Hipp (1992)

1992 edited by James W. Hipp (1993)

1993 edited by James W. Hipp, contributing editor George Garrett (1994)

1994 edited by James W. Hipp, contributing editor George Garrett (1995)

1995 edited by James W. Hipp, contributing editor George Garrett (1996)

1996 edited by Samuel W. Bruce and L. Kay Webster, contributing editor George Garrett (1997)

1997 edited by Matthew J. Bruccoli and George Garrett, with the assistance of L. Kay Webster (1998)

1998 edited by Matthew J. Bruccoli, contributing editor George Garrett, with the assistance of D. W. Thomas (1999)

1999 edited by Matthew J. Bruccoli, contributing editor George Garrett, with the assistance of D. W. Thomas (2000)

2000 edited by Matthew J. Bruccoli, contributing editor George Garrett, with the assistance of George Parker Anderson (2001)

2001 edited by Matthew J. Bruccoli, contributing editor George Garrett, with the assistance of George Parker Anderson (2002)

2002 edited by Matthew J. Bruccoli and George Garrett; George Parker Anderson, Assistant Editor (2003)

Concise Series

Concise Dictionary of American Literary Biography, 7 volumes (1988–1999): *The New Consciousness, 1941–1968; Colonization to the American Renaissance, 1640–1865; Realism, Naturalism, and Local Color, 1865–1917; The Twenties, 1917–1929; The Age of Maturity, 1929–1941; Broadening Views, 1968–1988; Supplement: Modern Writers, 1900–1998.*

Concise Dictionary of British Literary Biography, 8 volumes (1991–1992): *Writers of the Middle Ages and Renaissance Before 1660; Writers of the Restoration and Eighteenth Century, 1660–1789; Writers of the Romantic Period, 1789–1832; Victorian Writers, 1832–1890; Late-Victorian and Edwardian Writers, 1890–1914; Modern Writers, 1914–1945; Writers After World War II, 1945–1960; Contemporary Writers, 1960 to Present.*

Concise Dictionary of World Literary Biography, 4 volumes (1999–2000): *Ancient Greek and Roman Writers; German Writers; African, Caribbean, and Latin American Writers; South Slavic and Eastern European Writers.*

Dictionary of Literary Biography® • Volume Three Hundred Thirteen

Writers of the French Enlightenment, I

Dictionary of Literary Biography® • Volume Three Hundred Thirteen

Writers of the French Enlightenment, I

Edited by
Samia I. Spencer
Auburn University

A Bruccoli Clark Layman Book

Detroit • New York • San Francisco • San Diego • New Haven, Conn. • Waterville, Maine • London • Munich

Dictionary of Literary Biography
Volume 313: Writers of the French Enlightenment, I
Samia I. Spencer

Editorial Directors
Matthew J. Bruccoli and Richard Layman

© 2005 Thomson Gale, a part of The Thomson Corporation.

Thomson and Star Logo are trademarks and Gale is a registered trademark used herein under license.

For more information, contact
Thomson Gale
27500 Drake Rd.
Farmington Hills, MI 48331-3535
Or you can visit our Internet site at
http://www.gale.com

ALL RIGHTS RESERVED
No part of this work covered by the copyright hereon may be reproduced or used in any form or by any means—graphic, electronic, or mechanical, including photocopying, recording, taping, Web distribution, or information storage retrieval systems—without the written permission of the publisher.

For permission to use material from this product, submit your request via Web at http://www.gale-edit.com/permissions, or you may download our Permissions Request form and submit your request by fax or mail to:

Permissions Department
Thomson Gale
27500 Drake Rd.
Farmington Hills, MI 48331-3535
Permissions Hotline:
248-699-8006 or 800-877-4253, ext. 8006
Fax: 248-699-8074 or 800-762-4058

While every effort has been made to ensure the reliability of the information presented in this publication, Thomson Gale does not guarantee the accuracy of the data contained herein. Thomson Gale accepts no payment for listing; and inclusion in the publication of any organization, agency, institution, publication, service, or individual does not imply endorsement of the editors or publisher. Errors brought to the attention of the publisher and verified to the satisfaction of the publisher will be corrected in future editions.

LIBRARY OF CONGRESS CATALOGING-IN-PUBLICATION DATA

Writers of the French Enlightenment / edited by Samia I. Spencer.
   p. cm. — (Dictionary of literary biography ; v. 313–314)
   "A Bruccoli Clark Layman book."
   Includes bibliographical references and indexes.
   ISBN 0-7876-8131-8 (hardcover : v. 1 : alk. paper)—ISBN 0-7876-8132-6 (hardcover : v. 2 : alk. paper)
   1. French literature—18th century—Bio-bibliography—Dictionaries.
2. Authors, French—18th century—Biography—Dictionaries.
3. French literature—18th century—Dictionaries.   I. Spencer, Samia I., 1943–   . II. Series.
PQ261.W75 2005
840.9'005--dc22
[B]   2005000219

Printed in the United States of America
10 9 8 7 6 5 4 3 2 1

Contents

Plan of the Series xiii
Introduction xv

Charlotte-Elisabeth Aïssé (1694?–1733) 3
   Valérie Lastinger

Jean Le Rond d'Alembert (1717–1783) 8
   John Pappas and Servanne Woodward

Charles Batteux (1713–1780) 18
   Cecile Nebel

Pierre Bayle (1647–1706) 25
   Karlis Racevskis

Pierre-Augustin Caron de Beaumarchais
(1732–1799) 33
   Pamela Gay-White

Mme de Beaumer (?–1766) 43
   Eva Martin Sartori

Françoise-Albine Puzin de La Martinière Benoist
(1731–circa 1809) 48
   Althea Arguelles Ling

Bernardin de Saint-Pierre (1737–1814) 52
   Malcolm Cook

Georges-Louis Leclerc de Buffon
(1707–1788) 59
   Jeff Loveland

Marthe-Marguerite de Caylus
(1671–1729) 68
   Gabrielle Verdier

Sébastien-Roch Nicolas de Chamfort
(1740?–1794) 74
   Isabelle C. DeMarte

Isabelle de Charrière (1740–1805) 81
   Ruth P. Thomas

Gabrielle-Emilie Du Châtelet
(1706–1749) 88
   S. Pascale Vergereau-Dewey

Etienne Bonnot de Condillac
(1714–1780) 97
   Lauren Pinzka and Steven Berry

Marie-Jean-Antoine-Nicolas Caritat,
marquis de Condorcet (1743–1794) 103
   Jeanne Hageman

Sophie Cottin (1770–1807) 113
   Samia I. Spencer

Claude-Prosper Jolyot de Crébillon *fils*
(1707–1777) 121
   Lisa Beckstrand

Claude-Prosper Jolyot de Crébillon *père*
(1674–1762) 127
   Servanne Woodward

Anne Le Fèvre Dacier (1647–1720) 133
   Caryl L. Lloyd

Marie de Vichy-Chamrond, marquise Du Deffand
(1696–1780) 139
   Caryl L. Lloyd

Denis Diderot (1713–1784) 145
   Servanne Woodward

Anne-Marie Du Boccage (1710–1802) 163
   Perry Gethner

Pierre Samuel Du Pont de Nemours
(1739–1817) 168
   Karyna Szmurlo

Louise d'Epinay
(Louise-Florence-Pétronille Tardieu d'Esclavelles,
marquise d'Epinay) (1726–1783) 183
   Michèle Bissière

Bernard Le Bovier de Fontenelle
(1657–1757) 192
   Jin Lu

Elie Catherine Fréron (1718–1776) 200
   Daniel Brewer

Contents

Stéphanie-Félicité Ducrest, comtesse de Genlis
(1746–1830) 206
Valérie Lastinger

Madeleine-Angélique Poisson de Gomez
(1684–1770) 213
Michele L. Heintz

Olympe de Gouges (1748–1793) 218
Gabrielle Verdier

Françoise d'Issembourg de Graffigny
(1695–1758) 231
Ruth P. Thomas

Frédéric Melchior Grimm
(1723–1807) 241
John Blair

Claude-Adrien Helvétius (1715–1771) 249
Katharine Ann Jensen

Paul-Henri Thiry, baron d'Holbach
(1723–1789) 256
Natania Meeker

Louise-Félicité de Kéralio-Robert
(1758–1822) 262
Carla Hesse

Pierre-Claude Nivelle de La Chaussée
(1692–1754) 267
Perry Gethner

Pierre-Ambroise-François Choderlos de Laclos
(1741–1803) 274
Michèle Bissière

Jean-François de La Harpe (1739–1803) 281
Christopher Todd

Anne-Thérèse de Lambert
(Anne-Thérèse de Marguenat de Courcelles,
marquise de Lambert)
(1647–1733) 289
Catherine Daniélou

Julien Offroy de La Mettrie
(1709–1751) 293
Mary McAlpin

Alain-René Lesage (1668–1747) 298
Francis Assaf

Julie de Lespinasse (1732–1776) 308
Felicia B. Sturzer

Marie-Charlotte-Pauline Robert de Lézardière
(1754–1835) 317
Mary McAlpin

Contributors 323
Cumulative Index 327

Plan of the Series

. . . Almost the most prodigious asset of a country, and perhaps its most precious possession, is its native literary product—when that product is fine and noble and enduring.

Mark Twain*

The advisory board, the editors, and the publisher of the *Dictionary of Literary Biography* are joined in endorsing Mark Twain's declaration. The literature of a nation provides an inexhaustible resource of permanent worth. Our purpose is to make literature and its creators better understood and more accessible to students and the reading public, while satisfying the needs of teachers and researchers.

To meet these requirements, *literary biography* has been construed in terms of the author's achievement. The most important thing about a writer is his writing. Accordingly, the entries in *DLB* are career biographies, tracing the development of the author's canon and the evolution of his reputation.

The purpose of *DLB* is not only to provide reliable information in a usable format but also to place the figures in the larger perspective of literary history and to offer appraisals of their accomplishments by qualified scholars.

The publication plan for *DLB* resulted from two years of preparation. The project was proposed to Bruccoli Clark by Frederick G. Ruffner, president of the Gale Research Company, in November 1975. After specimen entries were prepared and typeset, an advisory board was formed to refine the entry format and develop the series rationale. In meetings held during 1976, the publisher, series editors, and advisory board approved the scheme for a comprehensive biographical dictionary of persons who contributed to literature. Editorial work on the first volume began in January 1977, and it was published in 1978. In order to make *DLB* more than a dictionary and to compile volumes that individually have claim to status as literary history, it was decided to organize volumes by topic, period, or genre. Each of these freestanding volumes provides a biographical-bibliographical guide and overview for a particular area of literature. We are convinced that this organization—as opposed to a single alphabet method—constitutes a valuable innovation in the presentation of reference material. The volume plan necessarily requires many decisions for the placement and treatment of authors. Certain figures will be included in separate volumes, but with different entries emphasizing the aspect of his career appropriate to each volume. Ernest Hemingway, for example, is represented in *American Writers in Paris, 1920-1939* by an entry focusing on his expatriate apprenticeship; he is also in *American Novelists, 1910-1945* with an entry surveying his entire career, as well as in *American Short-Story Writers, 1910-1945, Second Series* with an entry concentrating on his short fiction. Each volume includes a cumulative index of the subject authors and articles.

Between 1981 and 2002 the series was augmented and updated by the *DLB Yearbooks*. There have also been nineteen *DLB Documentary Series* volumes, which provide illustrations, facsimiles, and biographical and critical source materials for figures, works, or groups judged to have particular interest for students. In 1999 the *Documentary Series* was incorporated into the *DLB* volume numbering system beginning with *DLB 210: Ernest Hemingway.*

We define literature as the *intellectual commerce of a nation:* not merely as belles lettres but as that ample and complex process by which ideas are generated, shaped, and transmitted. *DLB* entries are not limited to "creative writers" but extend to other figures who in their time and in their way influenced the mind of a people. Thus the series encompasses historians, journalists, publishers, book collectors, and screenwriters. By this means readers of *DLB* may be aided to perceive literature not as cult scripture in the keeping of intellectual high priests but firmly positioned at the center of a nation's life.

DLB includes the major writers appropriate to each volume and those standing in the ranks behind them. Scholarly and critical counsel has been sought in deciding which minor figures to include and how full their entries should be. Wherever possible, useful refer-

*From an unpublished section of Mark Twain's autobiography, copyright by the Mark Twain Company

ences are made to figures who do not warrant separate entries.

Each *DLB* volume has an expert volume editor responsible for planning the volume, selecting the figures for inclusion, and assigning the entries. Volume editors are also responsible for preparing, where appropriate, appendices surveying the major periodicals and literary and intellectual movements for their volumes, as well as lists of further readings. Work on the series as a whole is coordinated at the Bruccoli Clark Layman editorial center in Columbia, South Carolina, where the editorial staff is responsible for accuracy and utility of the published volumes.

One feature that distinguishes *DLB* is the illustration policy–its concern with the iconography of literature. Just as an author is influenced by his surroundings, so is the reader's understanding of the author enhanced by a knowledge of his environment. Therefore *DLB* volumes include not only drawings, paintings, and photographs of authors, often depicting them at various stages in their careers, but also illustrations of their families and places where they lived. Title pages are regularly reproduced in facsimile along with dust jackets for modern authors. The dust jackets are a special feature of *DLB* because they often document better than anything else the way in which an author's work was perceived in its own time. Specimens of the writers' manuscripts and letters are included when feasible.

Samuel Johnson rightly decreed that "The chief glory of every people arises from its authors." The purpose of the *Dictionary of Literary Biography* is to compile literary history in the surest way available to us–by accurate and comprehensive treatment of the lives and work of those who contributed to it.

The *DLB* Advisory Board

Introduction

Samia I. Spencer
Auburn University

Attempting to capture the essence of the French Enlightenment in two volumes is a daunting undertaking, perhaps an impossible one. While the purpose of the present study is modest, it also seeks to achieve what few if any eighteenth-century references have attempted to date.

If asked to name authors of the Enlightenment, most respondents would be able to cite only the illustrious figures whose fame has endured the test of time: Charles-Louis de Secondat, baron de Montesquieu; Voltaire; Jean-Jacques Rousseau; Denis Diderot; and Jean Le Rond d'Alembert. Scholars would add such writers as Pierre Bayle, Bernard Le Bovier de Fontenelle, Etienne Bonnot de Condillac, and Claude-Adrien Helvétius, who may not be remembered by many among the educated public. A volume on the Enlightenment should focus on these and other well-known authors and devote ample space to their writings on such topics as government, religion, justice, the monarchy, ancient and modern philosophy, social issues, liberty, and human rights.

In the present study, however, writers not often included in literary anthologies—such as Pierre-Louis de Maupertuis, Charles Batteux, Jacques de Turgot, André Morellet, and Pierre Samuel Du Pont de Nemours—also find a place next to their more renowned contemporaries. Their inclusion provides the broadest possible perspective on the social, economic, literary, political, and intellectual issues that animated public debates and salon discussions, as well as offers a glimpse of the scientific progress achieved during that era. Readers will thus find many references to such controversial topics as taxation, free trade, or the commerce of grain and its impact on the price and availability of bread—in other words, concerns affecting the daily lives of French citizens at all levels.

This volume, however, does not claim to give voice to all authors who contributed to the promotion or vilification of the Enlightenment—no single volume can. Likewise, readers looking for information on such important matters as education, cosmopolitism, the Quarrel of the Ancients and the Moderns, the Expulsion of the Jesuits, the phenomenal expansion of the press, the rise of public opinion, even the *Encyclopédie* (1751–1780), will have to look through various entries to satisfy their curiosity. Organized by author's names, the book includes no chapters devoted to specific genres or themes.

French women, who enjoyed unprecedented freedom and visibility during the age of Enlightenment and who were described by Edmond and Jules de Goncourt as "le principe qui gouverne, la raison qui dirige, la voix qui commande" (the principle that governs, the reason that directs, the voice that commands), are generally overlooked in literary anthologies. Their omission implies that eighteenth-century women did not produce a single work worthy of mention, since none of their writings can be found between those of Marie Madeleine de Lafayette in the seventeenth century and those of Germaine de Staël in the nineteenth. As recently as 1992, the *Dictionnaire historique de la langue française, Robert* (The Historical Dictionary of the French Language, Robert) defined the Enlightenment as the thought imposed "par référence au programme laïc des philosophes et hommes de sciences qui travaillaient selon l'expression employée par Descartes à la 'seule lumière naturelle' (non plus théologique et surnaturelle)" (by reference to the secular program of the philosophes [the noun is defined in the same publication as masculine] and the men of science who adopted Descartes's recommendation to follow only natural enlightenment [not religious or supernatural]). The statement suggests that men alone engendered this intellectual movement, women having no role in its creation.

When eighteenth-century women do appear in literary manuals, they are usually remembered for their roles as *salonnières*—gracious hostesses who opened their homes to the great intellectuals and artists of their time, making possible the debates leading to the Enlightenment and generously providing the social and financial support needed by the great men. Even scholars who tried to remedy the gender imbalance by focusing on the achievements of women did not escape the bias. For example, in volume two of his monumental *Histoire des Françaises* (1972, A History of French Women), Alain Decaux states that "les femmes, mieux que les hommes s'en font le porte parole [de cette civilisation]" (women, better than men, are the voice [of Enlightenment civilization]) and that "toutes ces femmes, qu'elles aient écrit elles-mêmes, qu'elles aient tenu des salons, qu'elles aient simplement échangé des correspondances, s'insèrent dans un temps qui, sans elles, n'eut pas été vraiment 'le siècle des lumières'" (all these women, whether they wrote, held salons, or engaged in correspondence, figured in a time that would not truly have been "the age of Enlightenment" without them). Yet, despite recognizing their crucial role and the popularity of their enormous output—Decaux estimates that between four and five thousand new novels were published between 1789 and 1814, most of them written by women—he, like others before him, denigrates the quality of their writings. After exalting them for the large number of their contributions, he asserts that "le curieux de l'affaire, c'est que ce foisonnement intellectuel ne va produire aucun grand écrivain féminin" (strangely, this abundance of intellectual activity will not produce a single great woman author).

More recently, in her seminal study, *The Republic of Letters: A Cultural History of the French Enlightenment* (1994), Dena Goodman demonstrates convincingly that equality among the sexes, the polite discourse of sociability, and the values imparted by the *salonnières* were critical elements in the development of modern Western civilization and its republican model of government. According to her, the French Enlightenment was grounded in a female-centered, mixed-gendered sociability that imprinted French culture, the Enlightenment, and civilization itself as feminine. Yet, while acknowledging this pivotal role, Goodman does not highlight the importance of women's literary production.

While studying French reading habits of the eighteenth century, Roger Chartier notes that, among authors whose books were most frequently printed and most extensively sold throughout the country, the first place goes to Marie Catherine d'Aulnoy, whose fairy tales continued to make the fortune of printing presses until the eve of the French Revolution. Aulnoy was not the only woman to enjoy such privilege. *L'Histoire de Jean de Calais* (1723, The History of Jean de Calais), a short story by Madeleine-Angélique Poisson de Gomez, was also among those in highest popular demand. Despite irrefutable proof of the importance of their literature and recognition of their significant role in the development of the Enlightenment, women writers continue to be omitted from widely used textbooks that provide basic education in eighteenth-century literature, such as *Les Grands Auteurs français. Anthologie et histoire littéraire* (1997, The Great French Authors. An Anthology and Literary History) by André Lagarde and Laurent Michard, and *Littérature française* (1987, French Literature) by Danièle Nony and Alain André. The present study seeks to remedy this oversight. For the first time, authors of both genders who contributed to the French Enlightenment are incorporated in the same work. Few scholars have recognized and commented on the double-gendered nature of eighteenth-century French literature. George Eliot was one of the first who did. She wrote, "In France alone woman has had a vital influence on the development of literature; in France alone the mind of woman has passed like an electric current through the language, making crisp and definite what is elsewhere heavy and blurred; in France alone, if the writings of women were swept away, a serious gap would be made in the national history."

Fiction was a favorite genre for many women of letters. Françoise d'Issembourg de Graffigny, Marie Jeanne Riccoboni, Isabelle de Charrière, and Sophie Cottin, who have been the subject of recent scholarly research, were among the most popular novelists of their time. They generally focused on social issues, especially family relations, and offered a broad range of perspectives on love, marriage, friendship, and the status of women. Translated into most European languages, their works delighted masses of readers throughout the Continent and beyond. However, they are not the only ones to be encountered in the pages to follow.

In Versailles, Paris, and throughout the country, queens, favorites of kings, grandes dames, even women of more modest stations, including nuns, were personally involved in all aspects of theatrical productions, not only as spectators, actresses, and benefactors, but also as dramatists, directors, and producers. Their activities and interests resulted in significant changes in that art form and led to a proliferation of private theaters, a marked preference for comedy, and the development of a theater for children. Angélique de Staal-Delaunay, Gomez, Graffigny, and Stéphanie-Félicité de Genlis are some of the dramatists examined in the present volume.

From the pinnacle of the court and the lodestone of salons to the streets of Paris during the French Revolution, women left their mark on public and private life. They were involved in social, political, intellectual, and economic activities as well, and wrote eagerly to express their opinions and relate their experiences. Their visibility and influence were the most striking and unusual distinction of French society—a feature that caught the attention of foreign visitors to France, who commented on it at great length, notwithstanding Montesquieu's astute Persian observer, Rica. Thus, approximately a third of the entries in the present volume are devoted to women authors, selected to mirror the breadth and diversity of contributions made by their gender to the republic of letters.

Anne La Fèvre Dacier was instrumental in the revival of interest in the classics, and in the ensuing debate known as the *Querelle des Anciens et des Modernes* (Quarrel of the Ancients and the Moderns). In the *Journal des Dames* (The Ladies' Journal), Madame de Beaumer (first name and dates unknown) reported on women's concerns, offered practical advice for daily life, and provided a forum for an exchange of ideas among its readers, thus contributing to the nascent feminist consciousness. The most faithful description of the inner workings of the court of Louis XIV was given by Marthe Marguerite de Caylus, whose *Souvenirs* (1770, Recollections) was published thanks to Voltaire. In *Théorie des lois politiques de la monarchie française* (1792, A Theory of the Political Laws of French Monarchy), printed the same year the French monarchy came to an end, Pauline de Lezardière took a scholarly approach to her early interest in the political origins of France. Emilie du Châtelet achieved prominence not only because of her close relationship to Voltaire, but also because of the excellence of her work. Her scientific work continues to be recognized and contributes to her reputation as the prime woman scientist of her age. She was not, however, the only one to have been profoundly interested in the sciences. Perhaps because she did not collaborate with a renowned philosophe, Marie Thiroux d'Arconville does not enjoy the broad name recognition of the more illustrious Châtelet; yet, she, too, devoted her long and productive life to scientific research on physics, anatomy, natural history, agriculture, botany, and chemistry, publishing more than seventy volumes, including sixteen dealing with medical issues.

One of the liveliest economic debates in mid-century concerned the business of printed textiles. Printed cottons from India were introduced in France by Portuguese merchants in the sixteenth century; soon, they became the craze, especially among aristocratic women, because of their bright colors and attractive designs. Massive imports had a disastrous impact on the French textile industry; under pressure from manufacturers of silk and wool fabrics, consequently, in 1686 the government not only made importing or selling cotton prints illegal, but also wearing them or using them in upholstery. In 1692 French citizens were further ordered to dispose of all clothing and furniture made of printed fabrics. Despite two edicts and more than eighty ordinances aiming at the eradication of illegal imports, the vogue continued, and contraband markets thrived.

Seventy-two years later, enlightened economists convinced the authorities to repeal the archaic law in order to allow the French economy to prosper. Permission was then granted to create printing shops using Indian techniques on domestic fabrics and on imported ones for which taxes had been paid.

In discussions of this important issue, texts by Frédéric Melchior Grimm, Morellet, and Vincent de Gournay are often quoted to illustrate the arguments in favor of free trade. Yet, one of the strongest and most relevant texts, written by one of the most successful businesswomen of her time, is never mentioned. A free-market capitalist, Marie Catherine de Maraise, manager of the textile printing manufacture in Jouy, the second-largest industrial enterprise of France, dared to challenge Commerce Secretary Montaran, giving him a lesson in liberal economics. With deference but assurance, she wrote,

> La théorie pratique peut seule apprécier le joug dont nous sommes menacés. Qu'à l'exemple de Pierre le Grand, les ministres n'ont-ils exercé tous les états, nous n'aurions pas à trembler en ce moment. Votre indulgence encourage ma franchise, je ne craindrai donc pas de vous rappeler un principe incontestable; c'est que la liberté est le grand ressort, le véhicule le plus actif du commerce, des talents, du génie et des arts. . . . Les succès de Jouy sont dûs au bon usage de cette précieuse liberté. Cette manufacture et le commerce des toiles peintes n'existeraient peut-être plus en France ou y seraient encore dans l'enfance, s'ils eussent été assujettis à l'inspection, pour ne pas dire à la sorte d'inquisition à laquelle on veut les soumettre.

> (Only those with practical experience can understand the yoke that threatens us. If, following the example of Peter the Great, government ministers had been required to be experienced in the professions, we would not have had reason to fear for our own. Your tolerance allows me to be frank, therefore I will not be afraid to remind you of a basic principle; freedom is the greatest and most important element in the development of commerce, of talent, of genius, and of the arts. . . . The success of the Jouy enterprise is a result of the wise use that we have made of this precious freedom. Our factory and the printed textile trade in general would probably not exist in France today, or would still be in infancy, if they had been subjected to inspection, or rather to the sort of inquisition that is now being considered.)

The revolutionary spirit of the 1780s spurred women to political action, with unprecedented passion. The best known among them today is Olympe de Gouges, celebrated for her famous *Déclaration des droits de la femme* (1791; translated as *Declaration of the Rights of Woman*, 1979). Indefatigable, she wrote with uncommon vigor and zeal, producing hundreds of plays, letters, articles, pamphlets, and memoirs; she even contemplated publishing a daily newspaper. Secretly, Louise-Félicité-Guyenment de Kéralio-Robert, also known as "the first professional woman historian," established a printing shop and launched a new career as pamphleteer and journalist. Clearly, citizens of both genders contributed to the dramatic change that swept through French society, eventually affecting the rest of the Western world. The present volume seeks to reflect this reality as closely as possible.

Two words are key to understanding the French Enlightenment: 'Lumières' (light) and 'philosophe.' The shift in their meanings between the seventeenth century and the eighteenth provides an interesting glimpse of the transformation that occurred during that period. Lumière, in the figurative sense, was originally used in the singular, referring to faith or the natural clarity of the thinking mind. In the eighteenth century, people started to use it in the plural, and it took on a philosophical slant. It then denoted a free spirit that rejected superstition, prejudice, religious dogma, and absolute monarchy–a person who believed in the importance of reason and the value of science as means to achieve progress and ensure the welfare and happiness of humanity.

Likewise, a significant shift occurred in the word designating the main promoters of the Enlightenment. According to the late-seventeenth-century *Dictionnaire de l'Académie* (1694, Dictionary of the Academy), a philosophe was a man "qui s'applique à l'étude des sciences et qui cherche à en connaître les effets par leurs causes et par leurs principes . . . un sage qui mène une vie tranquille et retirée, hors de l'embarras des affaires, [et qui] se met au-dessus des devoirs et des obligations ordinaires de la vie civile" (who applies himself to the study of science, who tries to derive effects from causes and principles . . . a learned man who leads a quiet and retired life, impassive to worldly matters, [and who] rises above ordinary concerns and obligations of public life).

Within half a century, the traditional image of the philosophe–as a scholar who lives in isolation, distances himself from others, and scorns public life– underwent a total change. In 1741 the *Encyclopédie* offered a completely revamped portrait of the modern philosophe. This new man was guided by reason, not by faith or ancient philosophy. He was attuned to the problems of his time, engaged in discussion of social and political concerns, and fully committed to improving the quality of human life. A sociable being, he was comfortable in the company of others, and sought to savor earthly pleasures: "Notre philosophe ne se croit pas en exil dans ce monde; il ne croit point être en pays ennemi; il veut jouir en sage économe des biens que la nature lui offre; il veut trouver du plaisir avec les autres" (Our philosophe does not believe that he is exiled in this world, and does not believe that he lives among enemies; he seeks to enjoy wisely the gifts available to him from nature, and derives pleasure from the company of others). In other words, the philosophe portrayed in the *Encyclopédie* is a mirror image of the philosophes themselves. Like Diderot, d'Alembert, Voltaire, and others, the ideal philosophe described in the *Encyclopédie* benefited from the intellectual stimulation provided by his peers in gracious social environments that promoted debate and exchange of ideas, and allowed his own opinions to develop and flourish. The image of this civilized and sociable scholar is further reinforced in Voltaire's well-known poem "Le Mondain" (1736, The Sociable Man). The author basks in the pleasure, comfort, and prosperity afforded by modern life; he feels blessed to live in an age of elegance, luxury, sophistication, and refinement, and concludes his piece by saying, "Le paradis terrestre est où je suis" (Terrestrial paradise is where I am).

Several factors contributed to the dramatic evolution of French thinking between the seventeenth and eighteenth centuries, and the emergence of new themes and concerns. The Edict of Nantes (1598), which ended the bloody religious wars of the Renaissance and allowed Protestants to practice their faith and enjoy civil rights, was revoked in 1685. A patent sign of mounting intolerance, it prompted many Huguenots to seek refuge in countries where their religion was accepted. The move deprived France of the important economic output of a skilled and productive workforce–estimated at two hundred thousand, or one-fifth of French Protestants–further intensifying the financial difficulties caused by the long involvement of the country in costly wars. Lamenting the dire consequences of the Revocation of the Edict of Nantes for France, which led to "la ruine la plus considérable du commerce" (the most considerable ruin of commerce), military leader Sébastien Le Prestre de Vauban went on to list the benefits that this population brought to other countries, including among others: "Il a grossi les flottes ennemies de huit à neuf mille matelots des meilleurs du royaume . . . et leurs armées de 5 à 6000 officiers et de 10 à 12,000 soldats beaucoup plus aguerris que les leurs" (It strengthened enemy fleets by about eight to nine thousand of the best sailors in the world . . . and their armies by about 5 to 6000 officers, and by 10 to 12,000 soldiers much tougher than their own).

Interest in all things French grew exponentially in the nations that hosted the immigrants, and throughout Europe in general. Books were printed in French in many cities, especially in Great Britain and the Netherlands. This publishing trend was bolstered further by the increasing power of the French censorship and the frequent use of lettres de cachet (arrest warrants) against critics of the authorities. Diderot was arrested and imprisoned in Vincennes. Threatened by a lettre de cachet, Voltaire fled to England where he discovered a more tolerant and more prosperous society and a more desirable type of government–constitutional monarchy. Also forced to seek refuge across the English Channel, abbé Antoine Prévost was introduced to British literature. Upon returning from exile, he made it available to French readers through his periodicals and his translations of Samuel Richardson's novels. England was now hailed in France as a social, political, and economic model, while France was idealized in the British Isles as a model of elegance, refinement, and good taste, and a paragon of arts and letters.

Furthermore, narratives by missionaries in Asia and the New World promoted interest in real and philosophical travel journals and reports; they piqued curiosity for languages and mores in distant parts of the world, inspired a sense of relativity, and promoted comparisons between French customs and habits and those of other nations. New and controversial themes—such as liberty, religion, slavery, colonialism, the nature of man and animal, the importance of passion for human fulfillment, and the impact of progress and modern civilization on mankind—gradually found their way into the writings of the philosophes.

In his *Discours sur les sciences et les arts* (1750; translated as *Discourse on the Arts and Science,* 1751), Rousseau attributed the corruption and decadence of contemporary society to progress and the development of the arts and sciences. He yearned for the simple and pure life of primitive men:

> Les hommes trouvaient leur sécurité dans la facilité de se pénétrer réciproquement; et cet avantage dont nous ne sentons plus le prix, leur épargnait bien des vices. . . . Plus d'amitiés sincères; plus d'estime réelle; plus de confiance fondée. Les soupçons, les ombrages, les craintes, la froideur, la réserve, la haine, la trahison, se cacheront sans cesse sous ce voile uniforme et perfide de politesse, sous cette urbanité si vantée que nous devons aux lumières de notre siècle.
>
> (Men found security in understanding each other easily, an advantage that we no longer appreciate, and which spared them many vices. . . . No longer are there sincere friendships, true esteem, and well-founded trust. Suspicion, misdeed, fear, indifference, reticence, hate, and treason will ceaselessly hide behind this uniform and perfidious veil of politeness, behind the cherished urbanity imposed upon us by the enlightenment of our century.)

Despite the diversity and range of their opinions, most philosophes did not share Rousseau's nostalgic view of the past. They tended to consider the course of human history as one of progression, looked toward the future with optimism, and supported the noble mission of the *Encyclopédie* with enthusiasm. They believed that by transmitting their knowledge to future generations they would ensure the happiness and welfare of their descendants. In the article "Encyclopédie," for the book by that title, Diderot asserted that

> le but d'une encyclopédie est de rassembler les connaissances éparses sur la surface de la terre, d'en exposer le système général aux hommes avec qui nous vivons, et de le transmettre aux hommes qui viendront après nous; afin que les travaux des siècles passés n'aient pas été des travaux inutiles pour les siècles qui succèderont; que nos neveux, devenant plus instruits, deviennent en même temps plus vertueux et plus heureux, et que nous ne mourions pas sans avoir bien mérité du genre humain.
>
> (the purpose of an encyclopedia is to gather the knowledge scattered on the surface of the earth, to explain its general system to the men with whom we live, and to transmit it to those who will follow us; so that the work of centuries past will not be lost for the centuries to come; so that our nephews, while becoming more knowledgeable, will also become happier and more virtuous; and we will not have died without having merited to be a part of the human kind.)

Voltaire expressed his contempt for Rousseau's ideas with his usual irony and sarcasm. Acknowledging receipt of the *Discours sur l'origine et les fondements de l'inégalité parmi les hommes* (1755; translated as *Discourse on the Origin and Foundations of the Inequality among Mankind,* 1762), the older philosophe thanked the author of the essay in those terms: "J'ai reçu, Monsieur, votre nouveau livre contre le genre humain, je vous en remercie. . . . On n'a jamais tant employé d'esprit à vouloir nous rendre bêtes. Il prend envie de marcher à quatre pattes, quand on lit votre ouvrage" (Monsieur, I have received your new book against the human kind, and I want to thank you. . . . Never has so much brilliance been used to make us look so stupid. One feels like walking on four legs, when reading your work).

While Parisian salons, governed by women, played an undeniable and well-known role in the spreading of Enlightenment philosophy, they were not the only vehicle for its advancement. Other groups, generally all male, also contributed to its expansion. Men's clubs conducted weekly meetings at which members could discuss topics ranging from diplomacy and law to economics. The most famous among them was the short-lived Club de l'Entresol (Club of the Entresol) founded in 1720 and most active between 1724 and 1731. Suspecting its members to be allied with Parlement and hostile to the throne, the authoritarian cardinal André-Hercule de Fleury ordered the club shut down. Less-aristocratic clubs flourished again in the 1780s and played a central role in the political debates preceding the Revolution; none, however, attained the fame of their predecessor.

Not to be overlooked in the spreading of Enlightenment spirit is the advent of an English import—Freemasonry. Appearing in Paris as early as 1725, it extended first to the south, before lodges were created throughout the entire kingdom. Despite its condemnation by the Pope and by both Catholic and Protestant monarchs, the movement continued to expand. In France, its membership is estimated to have reached fifty thousand by 1788, of whom thirty-five thousand were affiliated with the Grand Orient de France in Paris. Although its rituals remained secret, the brotherhood emphasized tolerance, agnostic principles, solidarity, and equality among members regardless of their social origin or economic status. Initially, Masonic constitutions explicitly excluded women; however, around 1760 pressure from a significant portion of brothers and from women themselves led to the creation of special lodges for women, called "lodges of adoption." These were not autonomous: they had different rules and were presided over by men.

One of the first philosophes to join the order, Montesquieu was inducted in London in 1730, prior to the founding of the Grande Loge de France in 1735 and the election of its first famous grand master, Louis Antoine de Pardaillan de Gondrin, duc d'Antin, in 1738. Voltaire accepted the invitation to membership in Freemasonry only a few months prior to his death in 1778; thus, he united himself in brotherhood to his archenemy, Elie Catherine Fréron. Invited the same year to join the lodge of the "Nine Sisters," Diderot, d'Alembert, and Marie-Jean-Antoine-Nicolas Caritat, marquis de Condorcet, declined the offer.

Fervor for progress and new ideas swept through the country, as evidenced by the creation of new provincial academies, following the establishment of the Académie française (1635) and the Académie des Sciences (renamed Académie des Inscriptions et Belles-Lettres in 1717). Between 1715 and 1760, twenty large and middle-sized cities—among them Cherbourg, Brest, Rouen, Marseille, Lyon, and Dijon—founded their own academies, in addition to another dozen that existed prior to those dates in such places as Bordeaux, Montpellier, Nîmes, and Avignon. Members of these bodies cut across a broad range of economic and social backgrounds. Of the six thousand academicians in his survey, Daniel Roche estimates that approximately 20 percent were ecclesiastic, 37 percent were noble, and 43 percent were of common birth. Patterned after the Parisian academy, provincial institutions organized yearly competitions and extended their activities to include discussion and instruction in science, physics, chemistry, mathematics, music, and the visual arts. In fact, some well-known literary pieces were drafted as entries in essay contests sponsored by provincial academies. For example, Rousseau wrote his 1750 award-winning *Discours sur les sciences et les arts* in response to a question proposed by the Academy of Dijon, asking if the revival of the arts and sciences had done more to corrupt or purify morals. A few years later, another topic proposed by the same academy inspired Rousseau to write his other famous essay, *Discours sur l'origine et les fondements de l'inégalité parmi les hommes,* which did not receive the prize. Following the publication of *Les Liaisons dangereuses* (1782; translated as *Dangerous Liaisons,* 1784), Pierre Choderlos de Laclos drafted a response to a competition launched by the Academy of Châlons-sur-Marne, inquiring, "Quels sont les moyens de perfectionner l'éducation des jeunes demoiselles?" (How could the education of young ladies be perfected?). It stirred his interest in the subject of women's education and inspired him to write another essay, *Des femmes et de leur éducation* (On Women and Their Education). Both pieces were published together for the first time in 1903, under the title *De l'Education des femmes* (On the Education of Women).

While most academicians were men, provincial and European establishments did not exclude women, although the Académie française (French Academy) itself denied them access until 1980. Charlotte Caumont de la Force and Dacier were members of the Academy of Padua; Françoise Benoist and Charlotte d'Ormoy belonged to that of Rome; Fanny de Beauharnais was admitted in Rome and Lyon; Henriette Bourdic-Viot enjoyed membership in Nîmes; and Kéralio-Robert in Arras. Undoubtedly, the most honored among academicians of her gender was Anne Marie du Bocage, elected in Bologna, Padua, Rome, Lyon, and Rouen.

D'Alembert submitted a request to the Académie française to reserve four of its forty seats for women: he wished to nominate Julie de Lespinasse for one of them. In fact, an offer was made to Genlis in light of her increasing popularity and the mounting opposition to the philosophes. If she would give up writing against them, she would be elected to the Académie. She chose instead to give up the seat and thus kept her gender excluded from the august institution for another two centuries.

In 1698 and again in 1724, government decrees required parishes to appoint male and female teachers and urged parents to send their children to school until age fourteen; thus, at least in theory, the principle of compulsory education was established. While these rules were never fully enforced, they led, nevertheless, to an increase in the level of literacy for all social groups, especially in urban areas, where nearly all of the elite were literate. Everywhere the percentage of literacy was higher for men than for women: estimates in the north and the northeast were 71 percent for males and 44 percent for females; the figures were much lower in the south, where they only reached 27 and 12 percent respectively. With increased education came a tremendous thirst for knowledge. The printing industry flourished, not only in Paris but also in other cities, especially Lyon, Troyes, and Rouen, where many inexpensive reprints and religious texts were produced.

Readers looked for information in a multitude of printed sources, including newspapers, posters, broadsides, chapbooks, news sheets, and journals. The periodical press experienced such phenomenal growth (from 80 titles in 1750 to nearly 250 by 1789) that eventually the first daily, *Le Journal de Paris* (The Paris Daily), was created in 1777. Its raison d'être stemmed from the need to satisfy the ever-increasing popular demand for news and information: "Si la scène des événements varie chaque jour, n'est-ce point satisfaire utilement la curiosité publique que de la reproduire chaque jour à ses yeux? Tel est l'objet du *Journal de Paris*. Il sera donc la correspondance familière et journalière des citoyens d'une même ville" (Since events change from day to day, isn't it a useful way to satisfy public curiosity to submit to readers these events on a daily basis? Such is the purpose of the *Journal de Paris*, which will thus be the familiar and daily link among Citizens living in the same city). The daily paper reported on commercial, industrial, and political activities, social events, the arts, obituaries, and weather in addition to devoting ample space to letters to the editor and debates among readers.

Specialized publications dealing with specific occupations—for example, agriculture and fashion—also came into being during that era. Other periodicals, such as *La Clef du Cabinet des Princes* (The Key to the Offices of Princes), focused exclusively on activities related to a particular department of government—in this case, foreign affairs. Literary journals had a wide readership and espoused a broad range of perspectives, some favorable to the philosophes *(Le Mercure de France)*, others cautiously supportive of their ideas *(Le Journal des Savants)*, or clearly hostile to them *(L'Année littéraire)*. Readers were also interested in the foreign press, especially in times of war, when they turned their attention to such publications as *La Gazette d'Amsterdam* or *La Gazette de Leyde*. Journals and periodicals reached a large audience throughout the country and were enjoyed across all economic classes. They were available through affordable group subscriptions or in reading chambers, literary clubs, and academies.

The philosophes and their ideas were enthusiastically embraced not only in France but also throughout the Continent and beyond. French intellectuals and artists were admired and welcomed in the most prestigious European circles, at court among kings and aristocrats, and in the most respected scientific institutions. Queen Christina of Sweden invited Dacier to join her royal entourage in Rome, and later King Gustavus III of Sweden started a literary correspondence with Jean-François de La Harpe. Graffigny received a pension from the emperor of Austria to write playlets for the education of the children in the Imperial Court in Vienna. Grimm's journal *Correspondance littéraire* was passionately read in France and eagerly awaited by elite subscribers throughout Europe. D'Alembert was offered the presidency of the Berlin Academy of Science and the position of tutor to the heir of the Russian throne–both of which he turned down. Frederick II of Prussia, whose mastery of French was better than that of his own native tongue, maintained an active correspondence with Voltaire for many years and hosted him in his palace. Maupertuis was appointed president of the Berlin Academy of Science and had easy access to the Prussian king and his inner circle. Catherine the Great charged Diderot with the establishment of an educational plan for her country and provided a generous stipend to him and his family. She invited her friend *salonnière* Marie-Thérèse Rodet Geoffrin to her court, sponsored artist Elisabeth Vigée-Lebrun to paint in Russia, and appointed La Harpe as literary correspondent to her son, Paul. The tsarina was so infatuated with French culture that she wrote more than thirty plays in French, which were performed at her Hermitage palace. Du Pont was invited by Polish statesman Prince Fryderyk Michał Czartoryski to serve as tutor of his son and as secretary of a commission on education. Du Pont did accept the offer and traveled to Poland, but his stay in that country was cut short when he was recalled to Paris by Turgot, newly appointed controller general of finance. Later, he was asked by his friend Thomas Jefferson for suggestions for the plans of a university in Virginia. In his response, Du Pont went beyond this limited task and offered a lengthy treatise on the American educational system, *Sur L'Education nationale dans les Etats-Unis d'Amérique* (1800; translated as *National Education in the United States,* 1923).

Considered the main—perhaps the only—intellectual movement of that era, the French Enlightenment is associated with the rise of liberal thought and the triumph of reason over prejudice and superstition, and it is generally acknowledged as the foundation of modern democracies. Few remember opposition to it, undoubtedly because of Voltaire's witty and satirical attacks against his enemies, which made light of their production and minimized their importance. Yet, as convincingly demonstrated by Darrin M. McMahon, resistance to the Enlightenment was a robust movement and a powerful cultural force, comprised of "lofty courtiers, influential ecclesiastics, and powerful parlementaires, as well as lowly administrative officials, minor abbés, and Grub street hacks." Describing their opponents as "destructive" and "diabolic," and denouncing their "scorn of religion and hatred of all authority" in the most vociferous terms, the "anti-philosophes" considered the Enlightenment as an "abomination," a disease, and viewed France as a country imminently threatened by religious, moral, and political decay. In their Manichaean vision, the world was bipolar, divided into good and evil. As defenders of the heritage of the past, they considered theirs as a combat to quench the corrosive effects of modern philosophy, one in which no compromise could be tolerated. According to McMahon, the condemnation and propaganda against the philosophes "took the form of hundreds of books, pamphlets, sermons, essays, and poems . . . and a buoyant anti-philosophe press." Desperate and unable to arrest the mounting popularity of publications by the philosophes, they organized public burnings of their satanic works, amidst rousing inflammatory sermons. Although French born and profoundly Catholic, the movement spread into predominantly Protestant countries, especially in the aftermath of the French Revolution, resulting in what McMahon calls a "Counter-Enlightenment International."

None of the "great" philosophes lived long enough to witness the Revolution and assess the impact of their writings on the events that changed the course of the history of their country. Although Montesquieu (1755), Voltaire (1778), Rousseau (1778), d'Alembert (1783), and Diderot (1784) were all dead by 1789, polemic continued over the influence their works may have had in causing the turmoil that followed. According to some, the values hailed by the philosophes—liberty, equality, and justice for all—had finally triumphed with the Revolution, since the "Déclaration des droits de l'homme et du citoyen" (Declaration of the Rights of Man and Citizen), accepted as a Preamble to the Constitution of 1791, guaranteed basic human rights to all citizens. Actually, while the philosophes had struggled for equality and human rights, they never advocated a universal right to education, because they believed the masses had to submit to enlightened authorities. In fact, Diderot thought that peasants would no longer accept their condition if they were educated.

On the other hand, enemies of the Enlightenment linked the bloody events of the Revolution to the philosophes. They were accused of having called down the wrath of God and opening the gates of hell by destroying the foundations of the ancien régime—the church and the monarchy. Indeed, the passage of the "Déclaration des droits de l'homme et du citoyen" did not ensure the public safety and protection they were intended to safeguard. Within two years, the Reign of Terror brought about unprecedented oppression and tyranny, all under the guise of defending the nascent Republic. The guillotine was set in motion, beheading sixteen thousand people, including many innocent peasants and workers. Rousseau would have been appalled to know that the man behind this carnage claimed to be one of his greatest admirers and a faithful reader of his works.

The polemic between the forces of the Enlightenment and the Counter-Enlightenment did not end with the French Revolution, nor will it end with the present generation. Having planted the seed of modern Western civilization, the French Enlightenment will continue to be studied and debated, and will remain a shining moment in the history of humanity.

–*Samia I. Spencer*

Acknowledgments

This book was produced by Bruccoli Clark Layman, Inc. Penelope M. Hope was the in-house editor. She was assisted by Tracy S. Bitonti.

Production manager is Philip B. Dematteis.

Administrative support was provided by Carol A. Cheschi and Lesia C. Radford.

Accountant is Ann-Marie Holland.

Copyediting supervisor is Sally R. Evans. The copyediting staff includes Phyllis A. Avant, Caryl Brown, Melissa D. Hinton, Philip I. Jones, Rebecca Mayo, Nadirah Rahimah Shabazz, and Nancy E. Smith.

Pipeline manager is James F. Tidd Jr.

Editorial associates are Jessica R. Goudeau, Joshua Shaw, and Timothy C. Simmons.

In-house vetter is Catherine M. Polit.

Permissions editor is Amber L. Coker.

Layout and graphics supervisor is Janet E. Hill. The graphics staff includes Zoe R. Cook and Sydney E. Hammock.

Office manager is Kathy Lawler Merlette.

Photography editors are Anthony J. Scotti Jr., Mark J. McEwan, and Walter W. Ross. Photography assistant is Dickson Monk.

Systems manager is Donald Kevin Starling.

Typesetting supervisor is Kathleen M. Flanagan. The typesetting staff includes Patricia Marie Flanagan and Pamela D. Norton.

Library research was facilitated by the following librarians at the Thomas Cooper Library of the University of South Carolina: Elizabeth Suddeth and the rare-book department; Jo Cottingham, interlibrary loan department; circulation department head Tucker Taylor; reference department head Virginia W. Weathers; reference department staff Laurel Baker, Marilee Birchfield, Kate Boyd, Paul Cammarata, Joshua Garris, Gary Geer, Tom Marcil, Rose Marshall, and Sharon Verba; interlibrary loan department head Marna Hostetler; and interlibrary loan staff Bill Fetty, Nelson Rivera, and Cedric Rose.

This book is dedicated to its authors, without whose commitment and expertise the volume could not have come to life. Throughout the five years of its creation, invaluable advice and encouragement were provided by many friends and colleagues, to all of whom I wish to extend my sincere thanks.

Warm gratitude goes particularly to Eva Martin Sartori who entrusted me with the editorship of the eighteenth-century section of *The Feminist Encyclopedia of French Literature,* and thus provided me a unique and most enriching educational experience. My work on that project has broadened my own vision of *The French Enlightenment,* and has consequently impacted the scope of the present volume.

Special recognition is also due to Valérie Lastinger, Caryl Lloyd, Catherine Montfort, Felicia Sturzer, and Ruth Thomas who developed an early interest in the project, committed to writing entries, and recommended potential contributors. I am in debt for their friendship, loyalty, and staunch support.

Last but not least, my husband, William A. Spencer, should also be recognized, not only for enduring the endless hours I spent working on the present essays, but also for providing much needed assistance with technology and computer issues.

As I add the closing lines of this enterprise on the eve of its going to press, it is my hope that readers will find as much pleasure and intellectual stimulation in discovering *The French Enlightenment* as its authors and editor have had in writing about it.

Dictionary of Literary Biography® • Volume Three Hundred Thirteen

Writers of the French Enlightenment, I

Dictionary of Literary Biography

Charlotte-Elisabeth Aïssé
(1694? - 13 March 1733)

Valérie Lastinger
West Virginia University

BOOK: *Lettres de Mademoiselle Aïssé à Madame C . . .* (Paris: La Grange, 1787); republished as *Lettres de Mesdames de Villars, de La Fayette, et de Tencin, et de mademoiselle Aïssé . . .* , edited by Louis-Simon Auger (Paris: L. Collin, 1805); revised and edited by M. J. Ravenel and Charles-Augustin Sainte-Beuve as *Lettres de Mademoiselle Aïssé à Madame Calandrini*, fifth edition (Paris: Gerdès, 1846); republished as *Lettres portugaises avec les réponses. Lettres de mlle Aïssé, suivies de celles de Montesquieu et de mme du Deffand au chevalier d'Aydie . . .* , edited by Eugène Asse (Paris: Charpentier, 1873).

Charlotte-Elisabeth Aïssé was a well-known figure in her day because of the sensational story of her origins. Rumors of her life before she was brought to France, including tales of royal parentage and rescues from both a massacre and a Turkish slave trader, made her a focal point for the wave of orientalism that swept early-eighteenth-century France. Aïssé became well acquainted with some of the most powerful and influential figures of her time—including Voltaire; Claudine de Tencin; Henry Saint John, Lord Bolingbroke; and Anne Thérèse de Lambert—and her presence in elite social circles in Paris during the Regency of Philippe d'Orléans stirred the imaginations of many.

Aïssé's significant place in literary history came about somewhat by accident. She barely knew spelling and had no literary ambition of any kind. As with most women in eighteenth-century France, her only writings were private letters to her friends and acquaintances. More than fifty years after her death, however, a descendant of one of her friends decided to publish some of Aïssé's letters. These letters are filled with details, valuable to historians, on everyday life during

Charlotte-Elisabeth Aïssé (from Ronald Grimsley, Jean D'Alembert, 1963; Thomas Cooper Library, University of South Carolina)

the Regency, including anecdotes about the stage, the *molinistes* (followers of the Spanish Jesuit, Luis Molina [1535–1600], who tried to reconcile the doctrine of grace with the freedom of the human will) and the *jansénistes* (followers of the Dutch theologian Cornelius Jansen [1585–1638] who were influential in the seventeenth and eighteenth centuries). Aïssé's life and letters are of importance to an in-depth study of eighteenth-century France, not simply for their historical value but also because she was an inspiration or model for important eighteenth- and nineteenth-century writers.

Aïssé's life is intertwined with that of the Ferriol family, one of the richest and most powerful families of the Regency. Charles-Augustin de Ferriol, baron d'Argental, was an eccentric man of the lesser nobility, but through his leadership, he and his siblings rose to prominent positions at the courts of Louis XIV, the Regent, and Louis XV. After successful military and diplomatic missions in Turkey between 1669 and 1698, Ferriol served as Louis XIV's ambassador to the Sublime Porte from 1699 until 1711. Because of his military and governmental positions, Ferriol spent the greater part of his life in Constantinople, where he became fascinated with the Orient and its way of life. During his years in Turkey he amassed not only a great fortune but also a large collection of art objects that he used to create an oriental ambience in the Paris mansion he acquired at the end of his diplomatic career.

Ferriol likewise exhibited a penchant for collecting exotic girls. In 1686, he brought to France a five-year-old girl, known as Julistanne, at the request of a friend who had saved her from a massacre. Ferriol had Julistanne baptized and brought up in France by Countess de Bautru-Nogent. Her story became well known in Paris. In 1698 Ferriol brought back from Turkey another girl, about four years old, named Haïdé. Ferriol had purchased her "freedom" from a seraglio, and his intentions were probably never pure. Haïdé, or Aïssé as she was called in France, seems to have been chosen by Ferriol because of her physical beauty. She was originally from Circassia, a province well known for the legendary beauty of its women. In his *Lettres philosophiques* (1732; translated as *Letters Concerning the English Nation*, 1733), Voltaire described the region as one where the traffic in women was thriving. Aïssé must have been of particular beauty, since her purchase price was £1,500, whereas the usual price for a Circassian girl of four was around £500. The actual circumstances under which Aïssé had come into the possession of a Turkish master are unknown. Apparently, Ferriol was told that she was a sultan's daughter who escaped a massacre and was subsequently sold to a Turkish slave trader, but the story is unconfirmed and suspicious. Aïssé's aristocratic origins may have been invented by the Turkish merchant to justify the inordinately high price he was asking for her, and the story of Aïssé's rescue was convenient for Ferriol, who used it to portray his purchase as altruistic.

In 1698 Ferriol arrived in France with his charge and proceeded directly to his hometown, Lyons, where Aïssé was baptized as Charlotte-Elisabeth, the only legal name she was ever to have, since she did not have a last name. Ferriol then traveled to Paris, where he placed Aïssé under the care of his brother, Augustin. Within a few months, Charles de Ferriol was back in Constantinople in his new capacity as ambassador to the Sublime Porte, while Aïssé remained at the home of the Ferriols in Paris.

As with many aristocratic families of the day, the household of Augustin de Ferriol exhibited scandalous behavior. Voltaire and other contemporaries alluded to Augustin's well-known homosexuality. His wife, Marie-Angélique, carried on an extramarital affair with the Marshall d'Uxelles, whose homosexual affairs were also well known and whose house was conveniently located at the end of the Ferriols' garden. When Aïssé joined the Ferriols' household, the couple already had a three-year-old son, Antoine de Pont-de-Veyle, who became her childhood companion. In 1700 a second son, Charles-Augustin d'Argental, completed the family.

In an environment in which the pursuit of money and powerful political ambitions were the highest priorities, Aïssé's education was, undoubtedly, of little importance to the Ferriols. When one-day-old d'Argental was baptized, Pont-de-Veyle and Aïssé stood for the absent godparents, and the seven-year-old girl, apparently unable to write, signed as witness with a cross. Aïssé probably did not receive a formal education beyond the few months she spent in a convent school preparing for her first communion in 1705–1706, for which purpose she was admitted as a day student at the Nouvelles Catholiques, which was directed by the famed pedagogue François de Salignac de la Mothe-Fénelon. This convent was reserved for women and children who had not been born in the Catholic faith, and it sometimes hosted children who had been bought from slavery and brought to France. In 1706, Aïssé received her first communion.

That same year, Pont-de-Veyle left home for the elite college of Clermont, a Jesuit school where he and his brother later befriended one of the best-known students of the school, Voltaire. Aïssé, meanwhile, became the companion of Marie-Angélique de Ferriol and participated in her salon, where Aïssé learned the refined art of conversation. In 1711, Charles de Ferriol, sick and out of diplomatic favor, returned to France, where he had purchased a magnificent Paris mansion adjacent to that of his brother. Ferriol did not come back alone: with him was a young Armenian woman known as Lucie-Charlotte de Fontana. The intimate nature of the relationship between the two traveling companions was well known throughout Paris circles. Neither a servant nor an adoptive daughter like Aïssé, Lucie-Charlotte led a solitary life, always ready to answer the call of her master.

In 1719 Aïssé fell deeply in love with Blaise-Marie d'Aydie, knighted in the Order of Malta. The two began a lifelong affair. In 1720, a suspicious Charles de Ferriol wrote a stern letter to Aïssé, reminding her that he had purchased her, in his words, in order to "pour disposer de vous à ma volonté, et pour en faire un jour ma file où ma maîtresse. Le . . . destin vent que vous soiés l'une et l'autre" (dispose of you according to my will, and to make you one day either my daughter or my mistress. . . . Fate has made you both one and the other). This letter made clear that the relationship between Charles de Ferriol and Aïssé was master and servant, not father and daughter. Indeed, although always expressing gratitude to the Ferriol family in her correspondence, Aïssé refers to Charles as her *Aga* (Master) or "the Turk." In all likelihood Ferriol sexually pursued Aïssé, but she consistently refused him. Meanwhile, in 1720 Ferriol married off de Fontana to a young nobleman, providing her with a substantial dowry.

In 1721, with the complicity of the Marquise de Villette, Lord Bolingbroke's second wife, Aïssé secretly delivered Aydie's daughter, who was baptized under the name Célénie Le Blond. The girl was brought up as one of Bolingbroke's distant cousins by a governess residing in a suburb of Paris. In 1722 Charles de Ferriol died. His will clearly indicated his dissatisfaction with Aïssé: he provided for her as he would have for a governess, not a daughter. Aïssé's financial and social arrangements were by far worse than those Ferriol had arranged for de Fontana. Too poor to maintain on her own the lifestyle she had led at the Ferriols', still single and without a fixed social identity, Aïssé remained in the company of Marie-Angélique de Ferriol for the rest of her life.

In 1722 Aïssé briefly met Julie Calandrini, the sister of Lord Bolingbroke's stepmother. Calandrini's irreproachable virtue and religious serenity made her the perfect mother figure for Aïssé, and their friendship began to blossom during a second meeting in 1725. After Calandrini returned to her home in Geneva, the two began a regular correspondence that continued until Aïssé's death. Their friendship was carried on almost exclusively through letters, since aside from the two brief encounters in 1722 and 1725, the women saw each other only once again, in 1727, when Aïssé visited Calandrini in Geneva.

Aïssé's letters to Calandrini are her only published work. They provide revealing insights into an aristocratic household of the period, including the shaping of domesticity and motherhood. They also reveal the two friends' convergent lifestyles and codes of

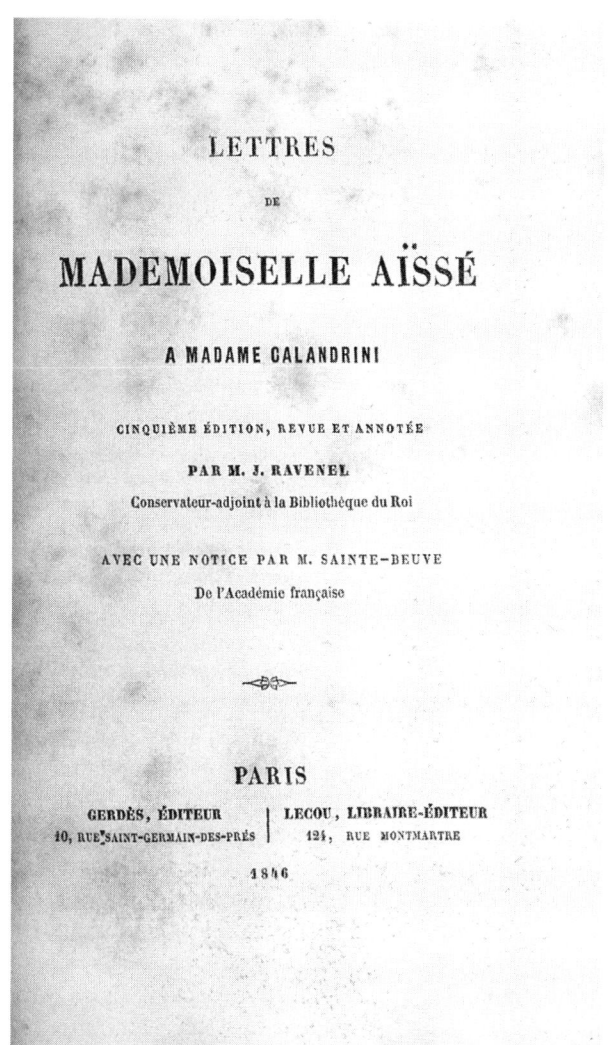

Title page for the fifth edition, 1846, of Aïssé's only published work, her letters to Madame Calandrini, edited by M. J. Ravenel and Charles-Augustin Sainte-Beuve (Ellis Library, University of Missouri at Columbia)

morality. Calandrini's moral standards called for Aïssé either to put an end to her relationship with Aydie or to marry him, but she would do neither. In contrast to Calandrini's conventional outlook, Aïssé's attitude toward her lifelong affair and her illegitimate daughter seems strikingly modern: she believed that the value of her daughter's life redeemed her sin of adultery. This attitude foreshadows that of characters in Félicité de Genlis's novels. Calandrini also objected to Aïssé's friendships with women she believed to be less virtuous than herself, such as the Marquise de Parabère, one of the Regent's former mistresses, and Marie du Deffand, who maintained a lifelong platonic relationship with Pont-de-Veyle. Although Aïssé could not embrace Calandrini's rigorous moral standards, she admired Calandrini's ideas about the benefits of a simple and austere lifestyle and the importance of morality in the achievement of personal happiness. Aïssé therefore continued to share the intimate details of her spiritual life with Calandrini.

In 1727 Célénie entered the convent where Bolingbroke's daughter served as abbess. Aïssé and Aydie worked diligently to constitute a dowry for their child. Aïssé often visited Célénie under various pretexts but never revealed to Célénie their biological relationship. Aïssé's struggle to maintain a personal friendship with her daughter sheds light on one way of coping with and caring for an illegitimate child in Enlightenment France. A striking contrast can be established between Aydie and Aïssé's attitude toward Célénie and that of Marie-Angélique de Ferriol's sister Tencin toward her own child, Jean Le Rond d'Alembert. Tencin, a defrocked nun, never acknowledged her distinguished son, even in adulthood; instead, his father took an interest in him and ensured that Jean was properly brought up. Aïssé, on the other hand, cared for her daughter and made every possible sacrifice so that Célénie would not have to spend her life in a convent. Aïssé resisted the temptation to reveal her identity to her daughter in order to protect Célénie from knowing her illegitimate status.

Aïssé's intense desire to help her daughter underscores her own feelings of alienation. Although she was brought up as the daughter of an aristocratic family, she remained, legally and socially, in a state of limbo. The law offered Aïssé nothing: adoption was not permitted in prerevolutionary France, and because slavery was not a common practice in France, no provision was made to recognize the status of slaves brought into the country. Marriage could have provided Aïssé legal status, as it did for de Fontana; however, even marriage might not have prevented prejudice, as evidenced by the case of Julistanne, who married into the aristocracy but remained a subject of mockery because of her status as a former slave. Her story is the best-known illustration of the ambiguous position of the French aristocracy toward slavery.

Aïssé died from tuberculosis on 13 March 1733. As her health began to fail, she—with the unlikely help of her friends Parabère and du Deffand—received last rites and renounced physical contact with Aydie. When Célénie finally came of age in 1740, Aydie took her out of the convent to live with him as his daughter and eventually married her off according to his social position.

Interest in Aïssé might not have lasted had the Calandrini family not published her letters to Calandrini in 1787, under the title *Lettres de Mademoiselle Aïssé à Madame C . . .* (Letters from Mlle Aïssé to Mme C . . .). In a letter to d'Argental dated 1758, Voltaire, a friend of Calandrini's grandson, commented on his reading of Aïssé's correspondence because he liked the friendship Aïssé had for d'Argental. The first edition of 1787 included Voltaire's notes and a biography of Aïssé as it was known to the Calandrini family. The accuracy of the published version of the letters is in doubt, as the original letters are lost, and in the eighteenth century published letters were often truncated or edited. In the early twentieth century, a few original letters from Aïssé to Aydie surfaced thanks to Célénie's descendants. These letters indicate that the 1787 text must have been significantly revised, since, although she had an excellent style, Aïssé had little knowledge of spelling.

Aïssé's letters were published approximately twelve times during the eighteenth and nineteenth centuries. Nineteenth-century literary critic Charles-Augustin Sainte-Beuve was fascinated by her and extensively researched her life. Although he had no access to Ferriol family documents, he strove to establish texts as close as possible to the original letters. He reestablished the internal chronology of the letters and corrected the names of some little-known people mentioned in them. His 1846 edition of the letters was preceded by a long biographical notice and followed by letters from Montesquieu and Marie du Deffand to or about Aydie. Despite biographical inaccuracies that have since been corrected, this edition remains valuable because of its scholarly integrity. It is also remarkable in what it reveals about Sainte-Beuve, who praises Aïssé's virtue even though she had an illegitimate child. Above all, the critic wanted to establish that Aïssé was not Charles de Ferriol's mistress, although this opinion is unlikely to be substantiated as fact and holds little importance to literary studies today. Overall, Sainte-Beuve appears to have found in Aïssé one of only a few acceptable women authors: subservient, as she was a slave; humble, as she never sought fame; virtuous although fallen; and beautiful with a "natural" sexual aura because of her exoticism.

Sainte-Beuve was not the only man whose imagination Aïssé unwittingly captured. As early as 1740, Antoine François Prévost d'Exiles' heroine of *Histoire d'une Grecque moderne* (translated as *The History of a Fair Greek who was Taken out of a Seraglio at Constantinople, and Brought to Paris by a Late Ambassador at the Ottoman Port: Interspersed with the Surprising Adventures of Several Other Slaves,* 1741) bore some striking resemblances to Aïssé, although Prévost always denied any connection. Several plays performed in the nineteenth century were also inspired by Aïssé's story and bore her name, including Marie Aycard's one-act comedy, *Mademoiselle Aïssé* (1832); Louis Bouilhet's *Mademoiselle Aïssé* (1872); Paul Foucher's *Mademoiselle Aïssé* (1884); and Louis Lantrey's *Aïssé* (1898).

Charlotte-Elisabeth Aïssé continues to draw the interest of historians and literary critics who are intrigued by her difficult, precarious place in eighteenth-century French society and who seek to understand her influence on those she encountered. Anne Soprani's thoroughly researched 1991 biography titled *Mademoiselle Aïssé* is the latest piece of scholarship to explore fully the life of Aïssé, an exotic woman whose eighteenth-century celebrity was carried forward by the chance posthumous publication of her private letters to a friend, letters that provide a window into one of the most interesting personal stories of Enlightenment France.

Biographies:

Elisabeth Guénard, *Mémoires historiques de Mlle Aïssé*, 2 volumes (Paris: L. Collin, 1808);

Robert Villatte des Prugnes, *Sur Mlle Aïssé* (Paris: Librairie Plon, 1903);

Evangeline Wilbour Blashfield, *Portraits and Backgrounds* (New York: Scribners, 1917);

Emile Boulan, *Figures du XVIIIe siècle: les amoureuses* (Groningue: Noordhoff, 1924);

Claude Ferval, *Mademoiselle Aïssé et son tendre chevalier* (Paris: A. Fayard, 1930);

Anne Soprani, *Mademoiselle Aïssé ou la nymphe de Circassie* (Paris: Fayard, 1991).

References:

Henri Courteault, *Mademoiselle Aïssé, le chevalier d'Aydie et leur fille* (Paris: Société des Bibliophiles Français, 1908);

Jeanne Fahmy-Bey, *L'étrange destin de Mademoiselle Aïssé* (Paris: Editions de la Nouvelle Revue Critique, 1935).

Jean Le Rond d'Alembert
(16 November 1717 - 29 October 1783)

John Pappas
Fordham University

and

Servanne Woodward
University of Western Ontario

BOOKS: *Traité de dynamique, dans lequel les loix de l' équilibre et du mouvement des corps sont réduites au plus petit nombre possible* . . . (Paris: Printed by Jean-Baptiste Coignard for Michel-Antoine David, 1743; revised and enlarged, 1758);

Traité de l'équilibre et du mouvement des fluides. Pour servir de suite au Traité de dynamique (Paris: David, 1744; revised and enlarged edition, Paris: Printed by J. Chardon for Briasson, 1770);

Réflexions sur la cause générale des vents . . . (Paris: David, 1747);

Recherches sur la précession des équinoxes et sur la mutation de l'axe de la terre, dans le système Newtonien (Paris: David, 1749);

Essai d'une nouvelle théorie de la résistance des fluides (Paris: David, 1752);

Elémens de musique théorique et pratique . . . (Paris: David, 1752; revised and enlarged edition, Lyon: Jean-Marie Bruyset, 1762);

Mélanges de littérature, d'histoire et de philosophie, 2 volumes (Berlin [Paris: Briasson], 1753)—volume 2 includes "Essai sur la société des gens de lettres avec les grands"; volume 3 (1758); 5 volumes (Amsterdam: Zacharie Chatelain & fils, 1759–1767)—volume 5 mostly completing the *Elémens de philosophie;* enlarged edition, 5 volumes (Amsterdam: Aux dépens de la Compagnie, 1760–1768); enlarged, 5 volumes (Amsterdam: Z. Chatelain, 1764–1773)—includes notes on the translation of excerpts from Tacitus; selectively translated as *Miscellaneous Pieces in Literature, History, and Philosophy* (London: Printed for C. Henderson, 1764);

Réflexions sur l'usage et sur l'abus de la philosophie dans les matières de goût (N.p., 1757); translated by Alexander Gerard in *An Essay on Taste, with Three Dissertations by*

Jean Le Rond d'Alembert (Ecole de la Tour, St. Quentin; from Ronald Grimsley, Jean d'Alembert, *1963; Thomas Cooper Library, University of South Carolina)*

Voltaire, d'Alembert and Montesquieu (New York: Garland, 1970);

Opuscules mathématiques, ou mémoires sur différents sujets de géométrie, de méchanique, d'optique, d'astronomie . . . , volumes (Paris: David Briasson, C.-A. Jombert, 1761-1780)–volume 2 includes "Réflexiones sur l'application du calcul des probabilités à l'inoculation de la petite vérole . . ."; translated by L. Bradley in *Smallpox Inoculation: An Eighteenth-Century Mathematical Controversy* (Matlock: University of Nottingham, 1971); volume 3 (1764); volumes 4 and 5 (1768); volume 6 (1773); volumes 7 and 8 (1780);

Sur la destruction des Jésuites en France par un auteur désintéressé, anonymous (N.p., n.d.; Edinburg: J. Balfour, 1765); translated as *An Account of the Destruction of the Jesuits in France . . .* (London: Printed for T. Becket & P. A. de Hondt, 1766);

Destruction des Jésuites en France. Seconde partie ou lettre à Mr *** conseiller au parlement de *** . . . , anonymous (N.p., 1765);

Nouvelles expériences sur la résistance des fluides, by d'Alembert, Marie-Jean-Antoine-Nicolas de Caritat, marquis de Condorcet, and l'abbé Bossut (Paris: Jombert, 1777);

Histoire des membres de l'Académie française morts depuis 1700 jusqu'en 1771 . . . , 6 volumes, edited by Condorcet–volume 1 (Paris: Panckouke & Moutard, 1779); volumes 2-6 (Paris: Moutard, 1785-1787); translated by J. Aiken as *Select Eulogies of Members of the French Academy, with notes by the late M. d'Alembert,* 2 volumes (London: Printed by A. Strahan, for T. Cadell jun. & W. Davies, 1799);

Morceaux choisis de Tacite. . . , 2 volumes (Paris: Moutard, 1784);

Esprit, maximes et principes de d'Alembert, de l'Académie française, published by Jean Chas (Paris & Geneva: Briand, 1789);

Œuvres posthumes de d'Alembert, 2 volumes, edited by Ch. Pougens (Paris: Pougens, 1799)–includes *Eloge de d'Alembert,* by Jean-François Marmontel;

Synonymes français, par Diderot, d'Alembert et de Jaucourt (Paris: Favre, an IX [1802]).

Edition and Collections: *Œuvres philosophiques historiques et littéraires de d'Alembert,* 18 volumes, edited by J. F. Sébastien (Paris: Bastien, 1805);

Œuvres [complètes] de d'Alembert, 5 volumes, edited by Bossange and Belin (Paris: Belin, Bossange, 1821-1822).

OTHER: Entries by d'Alembert from the *Encyclopédie, ou dictionnaire raisonné des sciences, des arts et des métiers par une société de gens de lettres; mis en ordre & publié par M. Diderot; & quant à la partie mathématique par M. d'Alembert,* 7 volumes (1751-1772):

"Discours préliminaire," in volume 1 of the Encyclopédie (1751); translated by Richard N. Schwab and Walter E. Rex as *Preliminary Discourse* (Indianapolis: Bobbs-Merrill, 1963);

"Eloge de Montesquieu," preface to volume 5 of the *Encyclopédie* (1755); translated by Thomas Nugent in Charles de Secondat, Baron de Montesquieu, *The Spirit of Laws, Including d'Alembert's Analysis of the Work,* 2 volumes (New York: Colonial Press, 1900);

"Genève," in volume 7 of the *Encyclopédie;* translated by Allan Bloom in Jean-Jacques Rousseau, *Politics and the Arts, Letter to M. d'Alembert on the Theatre* (Glencoe, Ill.: Free Press, 1960).

He signed his name Dalembert or D'Alembert. He transformed the name his family gave him when they sent him to college–Daremberg–to d'Alembert. "D'Alembert" now designates a principle he formulated in his *Traité de dynamique . . .* (1743, Treatise of Dynamics). Marie-Jean-Antoine-Nicolas de Caritat, Marquis de Condorcet explained that it reduced laws of motion to a question of equilibrium. It also includes the d'Alembert criterion: if $\lim_{\sup} u_n+1/u_n <1$, then the series of general positive term u_n converges. He contributed to the theorem of Gauss (or of d'Alembert-Gauss). Joseph Bertrand believes that d'Alembert helped to prepare Jean Kepler's work on the equinoxes. According to Pierre-Simon Laplace, d'Alembert was as important in astronomy as James Bradley. Throughout his life, d'Alembert contributed actively to the field of mathematics and geometry. With Denis Diderot, he codirected the first seven volumes of the *Encyclopédie, ou dictionnaire raisonné des sciences, des arts et des métiers* (1751-1772, A Detailed Dictionary of Sciences, Arts, and Crafts), in which he signed his entries with the letter *O*.

Whether the *Encyclopédie* worked toward the separation or unification of arts and sciences remains unclear. Roland Mortier evoked Johann Wolfgang von Goethe's indignation at one of Diderot's satires of d'Alembert, reducing his co-editor to the field of mathematics, thus denying his literary glory. Diderot counted on the inspired vision of the poet who worked on analogies that might direct the scientific man, while d'Alembert did not react well to the emotional outbursts and paradoxes of his friend. Both agreed on the project of extending reason to all realms of thought. Thomas Laurin Hankins notes that in quoting famous men of letters who were also mathematicians, such as Blaise Pascal and Bernard Le Bovier de Fontenelle, d'Alembert referred to the latter's vindication (1699) that an intellectual inclined to geometry could produce the best works of morals, literature, and criticism. Ernst Cassirer identified d'Alembert as a representative of the Enlightenment because of his enthusiasm for Sir Isaac Newton and because of his devotion to philosophy, even though expressed through letters and sciences. Hankins considers that d'Alembert's "role in the eighteenth century was more important than the sum of his specific literary and scientific accomplishments . . . , and [that] his participation in the 'philosophical' campaign of the 1760s, his domination of the Paris salons and academies, [and] his friendships . . . put him at the center of the intellectual turmoil."

When, in order to avoid scandal, d'Alembert's mother, former nun Claudine Alexandrine de Tencin, abandoned her newborn son in a wooden box at the door of Saint-Jean-Le-Rond (16 November 1717), the baptismal chapel of Notre Dame de Paris, she gave herself the means to identify him later. Since childhood, Tencin had consistently resisted the family pressure that forced her to become a nun. Relieved from her vows by the Pope, who also forbade her to marry (1712), she nevertheless lived in fear of being cloistered again. In this context she abandoned her child, who was baptized Jean Le Rond, thus bearing the name of the chapel where he was found. Upon returning from his journey to the Antilles six weeks later, the chevalier Louis-Camus Destouches-Canon identified his son, thanks to Tencin, and placed him with Madame Rousseau, the wife of a glazier, who gave the fragile child maternal love and care, according to the testimony of Amélie Suard. Destouches-Canon then enrolled his son in a pension under the tutelage of Bérée. Subsequently, with help from his father's family, Destouches-Canon obtained for his son a place at the Collège des quatre-nations, enrolling him as the chevalier Daremberg. Since students in that college were selected by the family of Cardinal Jules Mazarin—prime minister of Louis XIII—from among the sons of nobility, Tencin possibly used her influence to have her son accepted in that prestigious institution.

The chevalier Destouches-Canon never officially acknowledged his son. At his death in 1726, however, Destouches-Canon left his son an income, which may have included a donation by Tencin, and recommended him to his relatives, with whom d'Alembert always maintained a cordial relationship. According to the memoirs of Suard, during his pension days d'Alembert recalled receiving from his mother a single visit, which concluded with a statement that the place was not appropriate for her. Since the boy was not an aristocrat, he was not allowed to learn with his classmates the skills of horseback riding, fencing, or dancing, but he excelled in Latin, Greek, and rhetoric. Unlike most other institutions, this college devoted a whole year to the study of mathematics. However, d'Alembert's Jansenist teachers tried to discourage him from studying this science and from poetry reading. They wanted him to develop his gift for rhetoric in order to use it against their enemies, the Jesuits. When d'Alembert left the college in 1735, the quarrel between the Jansenists and the Molinists was raging. The Molinists, named after the Jesuit Molina, and the Jansenists, named after the Flemish Bishop, Cornelius Jansen, ignited a controversy regarding the extent of divine grace as opposed to free will. The quarrel aroused fanaticism on both sides and was complicated by personal dislikes. The Jansenists recognized the authority of their own conscience over church and state and became a threat to absolute monarchy. They were eventually viewed as heretics, though d'Alembert came to disregard both factions. In his "Memoir" found in the last volume of *Œuvres complètes* (1822) he concluded by defining his field of inquiry as "metaphysical geometry" and emphasized his hope that a culture based on science would eradicate the excesses of religion, as practiced by the Inquisition.

D'Alembert then enrolled in the Faculty of Law, graduating in 1738; however, he never practiced law but instead attempted medical studies. According to d'Alembert's own testimony (as there are no records of these studies), the profession offered a more lucrative perspective. In order to devote himself totally to these studies, he gave his mathematics books to a friend for safekeeping. Before long he gave up medical training in order to focus on his real passion, mathematics. In his early years, d'Alembert was essentially a self-taught mathematician remarkably gifted in the art of persuasive discourse. His first paper at the Académie Royale des Sciences de Paris (The Royal Academy of Sciences of Paris) in 1739 gained him some notice. The following year he solved the problem of the ricochet in the field of mechanics. Although respected by geometers, d'Alembert had not yet produced anything significant when he requested a position as associate at the Academy of Sciences in 1741 where most scientists started their careers as adjuncts. The promotion of Pierre Charles le Monnier to the post of associate left vacant his position as adjunct. D'Alembert applied for it, but Abbé de Gua de Malves, and then Abbé Nicolas Louis de la Caille, were preferred to him. A year later, however, at age twenty-four, d'Alembert was awarded the post of adjunct in the astronomy section. His *Traité de dynamique* was praised for the new methods he established and for his reduction of dynamics to mechanics; it was completed a year later with the *Traité de l'équilibre et du mouvement des fluides* (1744, Treatise on the Equilibrium and Motion of Fluids). The work caught the attention of Frederick II of Prussia, who offered patronage.

D'Alembert undertook as a mathematician the *Encyclopédie* project, proposed initially as a translation into French of Ephraïm Chambers's two-volume *Cyclopaedia, or Universal Dictionary of the Arts and Sciences* (1728). In 1745 d'Alembert replaced the Abbé de Gua as adviser and gradually became an important member of literary circles. In the salon of Marie du Deffand, guests found him entertaining, lighthearted, pleasant, and even seductive, as evidenced by his love correspondence with Renée-Caroline de Créqui. He eventually became an associate of geometry at the Paris Academy of Sciences in 1746, after receiving a prize from the Berlin Academy for his *Réflexions sur la cause générale des vents . . .* (1747, Reflection on the General Cause of Winds). By 1745 Daniel Bernoulli had already proposed d'Alembert's name for a position at the Berlin Royal Academy of Science, but he turned down an offer to direct it, alleging that he could not leave his friends behind. He may have been discouraged from living in Berlin. During this time he and Voltaire were exchanging frequent letters, and Voltaire had just been asked by his host, Frederick II, to leave Prussia, following an unfortunate fight with Pierre Louis Moreau de Maupertuis. That same year, 1746, a new scientific correspondence on logarithms was initiated with Leonhard Euler, while another regular exchange of letters on scientific and literary subjects continued with Gabriel Cramer of Geneva. Nearing thirty, d'Alembert was beginning to receive recognition for the 1747 publication of his essay on vibrating strings. He sent another work to the Berlin Academy for a competition it was proposing. However, the decision on the results was postponed for several years, thus giving Euler plenty of time to read the entries while he was working on the same subject. An ongoing competition ensued among d'Alembert, Alexis Clairaut, and Euler—each trying to beat the others to the solution of the same problems. D'Alembert came to mistrust Euler. In science, d'Alembert's tour de force is generally considered to be the *Recherches sur la précession des équinoxes* (Researches on the Precession of the Equinoxes), published in 1749, the same year Diderot wrote a memoir on mathematics, a circumstance that fed the competitiveness that the two developed with each other in later years. Meanwhile, Tencin died in 1749, leaving nothing to her son.

D'Alembert's relationship with Diderot, dating prior to 1745, was unstable. Jean-Jacques Rousseau and Etienne Bonnot de Condillac report encounters between d'Alembert and Diderot early on in their careers. In 1750, with the publication of the *Prospectus* for the *Encyclopédie* (with a Roger Bacon–inspired tree of knowledge), the two editors appeared to be on different scientific grounds, because they treated the fracture between deductive and inductive science differently. Diderot favored privileged experience and a Baconian accumulation of knowledge, while d'Alembert favored mental constructions issued from a rational order, proceeding harmoniously from one reasoning to the next. He was trained as a Cartesian, yet was strongly influenced by Nicolas de Malebranche and admired Newtonian scientific methodology. Some inherent incompatibilities, however, conflicted with the unification he proposed among all of the branches of old and new knowledge. Nevertheless, the "Discours prélimi-

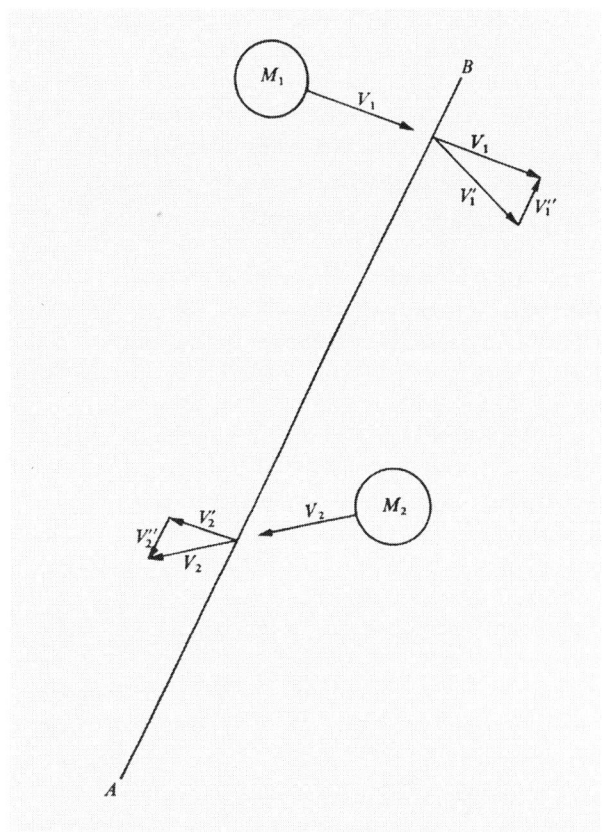

Illustration of "d'Alembert's Principle," the result of his attempt to describe mechanics in completely rational terms (from Thomas Laurin Hankins, Jean d'Alembert. Science and the Enlightenment, *1970; Thomas Cooper Library, University of South Carolina)*

naire" (1751; translated as *Preliminary Discourse,* 1963) in the first volume of the *Encyclopédie* is credited with revolutionizing science and considered the cornerstone of many philosophical reflections, including Michel Foucault's *Les Mots et les choses:* (1966; translated as The Order of Things, 1970). The "Discours préliminaire" strengthened d'Alembert's literary career and his reputation as a respected philosophe.

In 1752 the Abbé Jean de Prades wrote the article "Certitude" (certainty) in the second volume of the *Encyclopédie*. The thesis that Prades had defended at the Sorbonne included passages copied almost verbatim from d'Alembert's "Discours préliminaire." First, it was approved and then considered as heresy by the Faculty of Theology; consequently, the author took refuge in Holland. This action seemed to confirm the fears that the *Encyclopédie* was a plot against Church and State. Through the intercession of Marie Louise Denis, d'Alembert contacted her uncle, Voltaire, to request that the Abbé find refuge with him at Potsdam, where Frederic II held his court. The *Encyclopédie* was condemned by Christophe de Beaumont, the archbishop of Paris, on 31 January 1752 and suppressed by the Conseil d'état (Council of State). Instrumental in issuing this condemnation was a friend of the archbishop, Father Berthier, a Jesuit priest and the editor of the *Journal de Trévoux*—a publication that already had identified the work as impious. Another criticism was levied against the project. It claimed that despite their commendable scope and objective value, many articles were plagiarized. Meanwhile, the volumes were secured by Chrétien-Guillaume de Lamoignon de Malesherbes, who ensured the continued publication of the *Encyclopédie*. He was supported in his position by the mistress of the king, Jeanne-Antoinette Le Normand d'Etiolles, marquise de Pompadour, who greatly disliked the Jesuits, proponents of the attacks. Suppression of the volumes was also a financial disaster for the publishers, who argued that it would cause a great loss for the French economy. This fear may be one of the main reasons that the publication was allowed to continue, on condition that more severe censorship be exercised. The co-editors were asked to "resist all temptation to deal with religion and morality," and d'Alembert, who had resigned following the condemnation, was invited to return to the publication. The "Avertissement" preceding this third volume was written by d'Alembert. In it, he exults over the victory of the *Encyclopédie* and counterattacks Berthier and his *Journal de Trévoux* for their role in the suppression of the first two volumes.

The "Essai sur la société des gens de lettres avec les grands" (1753, Essay on the Association of Literary Authors with the Nobles) was published almost at the same time as the third volume of the *Encyclopédie* and sought to revolutionize the relationship between writers and their patrons. It exhorts artists to devote their writing to the truth rather than to commissioned ideas, even if doing so means living in poverty. Deffand commented that d'Alembert was a slave to his freedom. He wanted to elevate poetry as a true expression of rational philosophy, rather than as conventional pieces serving to amuse aristocrats. In 1754, d'Alembert obtained an exceptional status at the Paris Academy of Science out of public recognition for the excellence of his work, rather than through personal favors. That same year, Deffand used her influence to have him elected to the French Academy, where he attended the gatherings assiduously and participated in the discussions, although initially he may have been lukewarm about the honor. Condorcet describes d'Alembert's behavior at the French Academy as that of a cunning militant, most interested in gaining support for the ideas of the philosophes. D'Alembert was also noted for his lighthearted and brilliant rhetoric, which was appreciated by his fellow academicians and by the public as well.

The article "collège" (college), which came out in the third volume of the *Encyclopédie*, provoked the Tolomas "affair" in 1755. The Jesuits felt, with reason, that their educational programs were ridiculed. The article alluded to Molière's character Monsieur Jourdain in *Le Bourgeois gentilhomme* (1670), who is comically instructed in rhetoric. D'Alembert suggested that public schooling was in need of full reform. It should place less emphasis on rote learning and give more attention to scientific reflection, and it should reduce the teaching of religion as an institution in favor of stressing instruction in morality and ethics. This position led to personal attacks against d'Alembert by Father C. P. Tolomas, a teacher of rhetoric, a librarian at the Jesuit College of Lyon—a provincial academy—and a member of the Société Royale. Asking for an apology from the Société Royale and not receiving it, d'Alembert initiated a letter-writing campaign that not only resulted in the resignation of many members of the Société Royale, but also ultimately forced that academy to expel Tolomas. The public was generally outraged by Father Tolomas, who humiliated d'Alembert for being a foundling, an extremely touchy subject for the philosophe, one that might have inspired some of his disdain for the aristocracy and might have been his motivation for writing the "Essai sur la société des gens de lettres." During that period of his life d'Alembert was also developing important relationships, including one with Frederick II of Prussia. Their meeting in Wesel delighted them both.

Meanwhile, Diderot was negotiating a new contract with publishers of the *Encyclopédie*, and the fifth volume came out with "safe" articles by Voltaire, dealing with the less controversial subject of literary criticism. In the preface to that volume d'Alembert wrote an assessment of Charles Louis de Secondat de Montesquieu's work. The critical evaluation of "Eloge de Montesquieu" (1755; translated in *The Spirit of Laws, Including d'Alembert's Analysis of the Work,* 1900) unexpectedly brought d'Alembert closer to his mother in spirit, as Tencin was a strong supporter of Montesquieu's masterpiece. Ronald Grimsley suggests that d'Alembert may skillfully have used Montesquieu's name to associate him with the *Encyclopédie*, although the older philosophe always distanced himself from the younger group, despite complimenting d'Alembert on the "Discours préliminaire." The preface of the fifth volume was the object of continued and relentless attacks as well by Elie Catherine Fréron, whom d'Alembert had turned into an archenemy by preventing him from entering the Berlin Academy.

In 1756 d'Alembert received a small pension from the French government. He then went to Geneva and paid a visit to Voltaire. In 1757, after an attempt on Louis XV's life by Robert-François Damiens, a decree gave new strength to censorship. The Encyclopédistes along with the philosophes were targeted because of the public perception that their activities combated the regime. D'Alembert opened the seventh volume of the *Encyclopédie* with his "Eloge" of the grammarian César Chesneau Dumarsais. The piece was also anticlerical, and the volume included the article "Genève," inspired by d'Alembert's visit to Voltaire. This entry offended the Protestant ministers of Geneva, who were portrayed as Deists with a mitigated faith in Christ and as Socinians distant from Christian dogma. Among other suggestions, the article proposed that Geneva establish a theater, a proposal that thoroughly scandalized the local citizenry and caused Rousseau to respond with his famous *Lettre à M. d'Alembert sur les spectacles* (1758; translated as *A Letter from M. Rousseau, of Geneva, to M. d'Alembert, of Paris concerning the Effects of Theatrical Entertainments on the Manners of Mankind*, 1759). Both this letter and d'Alembert's reply to it were courteous, d'Alembert even pledging to love and honor Rousseau forever. D'Alembert felt somewhat dejected by the attacks he sustained for the article on Geneva and was inclined to sympathize with Rousseau's retreat from society. Diderot believed that "Genève" was overincendiary, causing the suspension of the *Encyclopédie* in 1759. Diderot suspected that d'Alembert might intentionally have caused the trouble, because he suggested that the work could be published outside France—for example, in Prussia. Since Frederick II did not like Diderot, such a development would have placed d'Alembert at the head of the new or renewed project.

Diderot was also disappointed that d'Alembert had published the *Mélanges de littérature, d'histoire et de philosophie* (Miscellaneous Pieces in Literature, History, and Philosophy) independently in 1753, using materials from the *Encyclopédie*. Indeed, d'Alembert was in the habit of referring to his own work, connecting his treatise on dynamics to the *Encyclopédie* and to his *Mémoires* (Memoirs) at the French Academy and at the Berlin Academy as well as to the *Recherches sur la précession des équinoxes*. In the *Traité de dynamique* he also compares himself to Bernoulli and Clairaut. Diderot was further disappointed with d'Alembert for quitting the editorship even before the project was suspended, and in light of what he suspected d'Alembert of doing, he was disheartened to see that Voltaire not only refused to provide new articles for the *Encyclopédie* but also withdrew the ones he had already submitted. D'Alembert had lent great credibility to the project and brought many contributors to it.

D'Alembert's *Elémens de philosophie* (Elements of Philosophy), published in volumes four and five of *Mélanges de littérature, d'histoire et de philosophie*, came out in 1759. It was part of an ongoing debate with Diderot, who had refuted part of the "Discours préliminaire" in his entry "Encyclopédie." Now that d'Alembert had been denied access to that publication except for mathematics, the only way he could refute Diderot was by writing the *Elémens de philosophie* separately, intending it to be a sort of

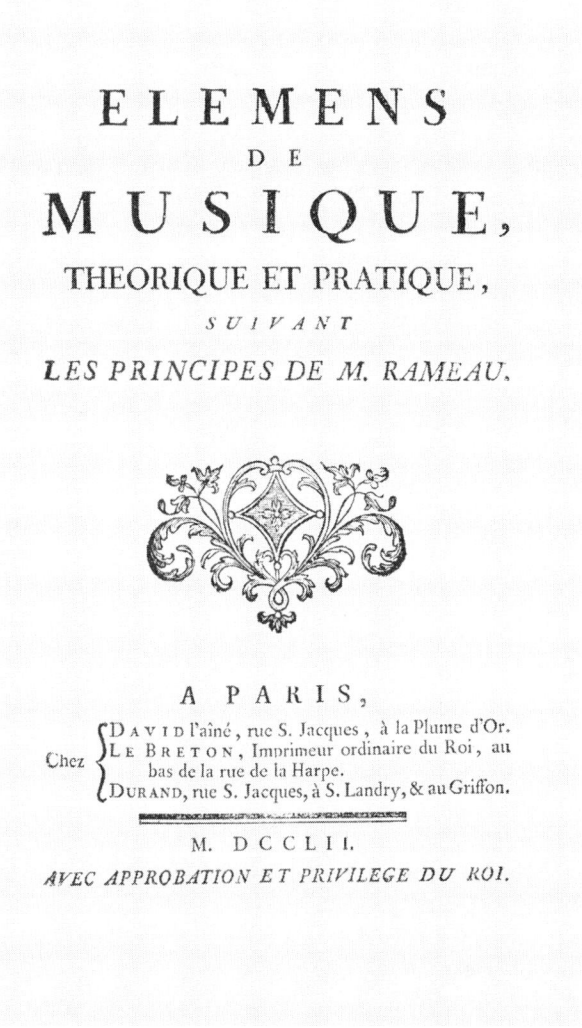

Title page of the first edition of d'Alembert's 1752 work applying mathmatical principles to the theory of music and harmony (from d'Alembert, Elemens de musique, theorique et pratique: A Facsimile of the 1752 Paris Edition, *1966; Thomas Cooper Library, University of South Carolina)*

introduction to the *Encyclopédie*. As d'Alembert explained to Voltaire, he also found that the editorship was distracting him from his own work and bringing him much negative attention.

Jean-Philippe Rameau originally admired d'Alembert for his mathematical approach to his theory of music and the principles of harmony outlined in *Elémens de musique* (1752, Elements of Music). Yet, Marie-Elisabeth Duchez believes that d'Alembert communicates only the "deductive skeleton" of Rameau's (Cartesian) theory in this work, as well as in the articles "Gamme" (Scale) and "Fondamental" (Fundamental) in the *Encyclopédie*. Eventually, Rameau saw the limits of d'Alembert's interpretation of harmony. As co-editor of the *Encyclopédie*, d'Alembert found himself in the awkward position of defending Rousseau's articles on music; yet, a few years later he considered laughable Rousseau's writing on music and opera in *Julie, ou la nouvelle Héloïse* (1761; translated as *Eloisa; or A Series of Original Letters . . .* , 1761), a novel he praised while pointing to its author's inconsistency in writing novels but condemning theater. Meanwhile, both Rousseau's and d'Alembert's musical entries were equally dissatisfying to Rameau. D'Alembert and Rameau made their fight public, answering each other's letters on the pages of the *Mercure de France* (1761, 1762). Meanwhile, d'Alembert was attempting to discourage Voltaire from vituperating publicly against Rousseau–Voltaire attributed his recent difficulties with the authorities in Geneva to the aftermath of Rousseau's *Lettre à d'Alembert*. By 1762, however, d'Alembert could no longer depend on Rousseau, who was, nevertheless, considered by the general public as one of the philosophes. Although the closeness of the philosophes suffered somewhat in these public disputes, the suppression of the Jesuits in 1762 brought some relief to the co-editors of the *Encyclopédie*.

D'Alembert left a "memoir" and a more intimate self-portrait addressed to "a lady" in *Œuvres Complètes*. The memoir indicates all his titles and his national and international memberships in the scientific academies of his time. It also includes a copy of a letter to him (1762), personally written by Catherine II of Russia, who asked that he become the tutor of her son. In 1763 d'Alembert visited Frederick II in Potsdam, and while d'Alembert refused once again the invitation to preside over the Berlin Academy of Science, he secured appointments in it for several of his countrymen and secured asylum at the court of Prussia for Frenchmen who were victims of censorship.

In 1764 d'Alembert contributed to the divisiveness between Deffand and her niece Julie de Lespinasse by leaving the salon of the former to join that of the latter. The love between d'Alembert and de Lespinasse may have been platonic, but their intellectual relationship was deeply rooted. He may also have benefited from the friendship, as de Lespinasse's salon was a compulsory passageway to the French Academy. She was the hostess, and he was the star. In Deffand's salon, he was also known as a man devoted to his friends and a financial benefactor for several dependents, including his foster mother. This devotion was the reason he gave for turning down the presidency of the Berlin Academy of Science and the offer to serve as the tutor of Catherine II's son. However, the true reason for not going abroad may have had to do with the abbé Canay's advice that when one becomes dependent on a monarch, as Voltaire had once done, one soon loses his freedom. The abbé recommended against the offer. D'Alembert dedicated his "Essai sur la société des gens de lettres" to Canay. In the foreword, d'Alembert begins by writing, "Recevez, mon cher ami, ce fruit de nos conversations philosophiques, qui vous appartient comme à moi" (Receive, my dear friend, this fruit of our philosophical conversations, which belongs to you as well as to me). In his self-portrait, d'Alembert adds a sentimental note on his love and gratitude for his first college mathematics professor and for his adoptive mother with whom he lived until 1765, when poor health required a move to healthier quarters.

D'Alembert's illness that year reconciled him with Diderot, who visited him. It occasioned Diderot's *Rêve de d'Alembert* (1769; translated as *D'Alembert's Dream*, 1966) and revealed that some of the dissent between the two friends involved the relationship between language and the real world, or the realm of theory and physical nature. In 1765, possibly because of the Franco-Prussian War, which had cut his incomes from both countries, d'Alembert resumed work on the *Encyclopédie*. By then, d'Alembert was identified with Diderot as an "encyclopédiste," and to work at what was considered his project was in his best interest. He proceeded to write articles on synonyms. The study of synonyms as a system of substitution among terms that are not perfectly equivalent, the forecasting of an evolution of language generated by the creative association of words, and even the creation of new words showed d'Alembert's keen interest in all aspects of language. That same year, d'Alembert reached the highest rank in the French Academy of Science, earning the title of *titulaire*. D'Alembert was then apparently avoiding controversy, although publishing anonymously on the Jesuits and easily identifiable as the author of his works. He signed his name to several pamphlets on this order and their persecution. *Sur la destruction des Jésuites en France* (1765) pleased Diderot immensely, and it was translated one year later as *An Account of the Destruction of the Jesuits in France* (1766).

D'Alembert also attended the salon of Marie-Thérèse Geoffrin, who gave him an annuity in the mid 1760s. As a regular guest, he admits to ignorance of finer "manners." His self-portrait indicates that his shrill voice lent itself to mockery and that his talent for mimicry was famous, as well as his unremarkable physique expertly described by Frederick Melchior Grimm and immortalized by Jean Antoine Houdon, Maurice Quentin de la Tour, Félix Lecomte, and Guillaume Francin.

D'Alembert was a friend of David Hume, who was a frequent visitor to France until 1766. Rousseau accused both of having written a letter that was actually composed by Horace Walpole. The accusation infuriated Hume, who had solicited a pension for Rousseau from the king of England. The quarrel became public knowledge in Paris. Until that time d'Alembert had defended Rousseau against Voltaire, but this latest incident "tempered" the friendship. Hume had been considering publishing Rousseau's correspondence; however, d'Alembert advised him to delay the project for fear that it would allow enemies of the philosophes to ridicule all concerned. On the other hand, Rousseau circulated a letter stating that Hume would never dare publish his letters. When Hume finally sent him his "Exposé succint" (1766, Brief Outline) on the affair, d'Alembert edited the French translation so it would do Rousseau the most harm. He had become the secret enemy Rousseau had fathomed.

D'Alembert's health started to deteriorate even further by the time he published the seventh volume of his *Mélanges* in 1770. He journeyed in the direction of Italy, where he hoped to lessen his ailments. Frederick II financed the voyage. Because of his weakness, d'Alembert rested at Voltaire's house on the way. He turned around and came back to Paris after the stay at Ferney, fearing that further traveling might prove too tiresome. Charles-Augustin Sainte-Beuve described d'Alembert's interaction with Voltaire as playing "on Voltaire's pet aversions" and nursing Voltaire's "resentments, designating his victims by name." On the other hand, the examination of the correspondence between the two philosophes led Anne-Marie Chouillet, François de Gandt, and Irène Passeron to believe that d'Alembert tempered Voltaire's feelings. Thomas Hankins hypothesizes that during the 1760s and 1770s, d'Alembert and Voltaire must have "joined a common cause against the materialists, Diderot and his friend [Paul Henri] d'Holbach."

In 1772 d'Alembert was elected permanent secretary of the French Academy. His predecessor, Fontenelle, excelled in writing the memoirs of previous fellow academicians. D'Alembert particularly admired his "éloges" (eulogies), having written some himself. The new post offered the opportunity to write the history of the institution and to revive the tradition of the memoirs. His article "Eloge" in the *Encyclopédie* recommends that such texts be founded on philosophical reflections and also be able to serve as circumstantial discourse to promote the ideas of the philosophes. This biographical work contributed to the spreading of Enlightenment thought to an appreciative audience that faithfully attended the meetings of the French Academy. D'Alembert was now at the center of the limelight, forcefully promoting the gospel of the philosophes.

Documents from 1989 not previously known may shed new understanding on d'Alembert's behavior. Jean-Noël Pascal believes that d'Alembert's unrequited love was the basis for his friendship for de Lespinasse. While some, including Rousseau, promoted a rumor of impotence, police reports of the time point to homosexuality. On the other hand, de Lespinasse claimed that some of the children for whom d'Alembert cared were his own. One of Diderot's servants, fired for refusing to reveal who had given him an antiphilosophe brochure, alleged that his former master had a relationship with one of the girls he sponsored.

Title page of the Paris edition of volume one of the Encyclopédie, *the first seven volumes of which were by d'Alembert and Denis Diderot (from John Lough,* The Encyclopédie, *1971; Thomas Cooper Library, University of South Carolina)*

In 1776 Julie de Lespinasse died. As the executor of her will, d'Alembert discovered documents relative to one of her passionate love affairs, of which he knew nothing. It provided him with material for his elegiac poem: "Sur la tombe de Mademoiselle de Lespinasse" (On the Tomb of Mademoiselle de Lespinasse). Geoffrin fell ill, closed her salon, and withdrew from social life. D'Alembert's morale was quite low, and Frederick II attempted to cheer him up with frequent letters. D'Alembert retreated to the apartment reserved for him at the Louvre, to which he was entitled because of his position as secretary of the French Academy. There he received many prestigious visitors, including actress Claire de la Tude, known as la Clairon, and one of his cousins, Charles Augustin Feriol Comte d'Argental.

In the academy, d'Alembert spearheaded charitable efforts, such as those aiming to help Pierre Corneille's great-nephew, who was living in misery as a playwright (1778). Ronald Grimsley suggests that these charitable efforts sought to show that the philosophes were also great humanitarians. In 1778 d'Alembert and Voltaire met for the third and last time when Voltaire returned to Paris shortly before his death. D'Alembert raised money to erect a monument to Voltaire's memory. In 1778 as well, the last volume of the *Supplément* to the *Encyclopédie* came out. By then d'Alembert was the sole editor of this portion of the project because of Diderot's absence at the court of Catherine II. The volumes were now as scientific as he had always wished them to be.

Biographers and witnesses tend to portray d'Alembert's last years as being melancholic and tainted by bittersweet remembrance of de Lespinasse; yet, he remained quite productive. He devoted himself to the translation of Tacitus, and, in an unpublished ninth volume of the *Opuscules mathématiques* (Volumes of Mathematics), acknowledged that Euler was correct on some points of contention. The volume was nearing completion at the time of his death, on 29 October 1783. D'Alembert had refused a bladder operation. Possibly under Condorcet's influence, he refused to meet with a priest on his deathbed; yet, he wanted a proper burial. His friends did their best to secure one, only after vespers were chanted for him at the church of Saint-Germain-l'Auxerrois. He was buried in the *fosse commune,* an unmarked common grave, at the Porcherons cemetery.

Hawkins concludes his study by writing, "His literary efforts have been overshadowed by those of Voltaire, Diderot and Rousseau; his philosophy lacks the thoroughness and penetration of Condillac . . . ; and his mathematical achievements seem insignificant compared to Euler's remarkable skill and productivity." D'Alembert is not often doubted as a scientist. Some people have inferred that his work pointed to several discoveries but that he did not come to the right conclusions because of his disregard for experimentation and a partiality for abstraction. Yet, the consensus is that d'Alembert was devoted to practical applications of science. For instance, he was interested in mechanics, hydrodynamics, and the lunar movement, for which he provided new tables. His work on the *Encyclopédie* was instrumental in the progress of philosophy, and his writings on language contributed to serious reflections.

Ernst Cassirer begins his study of the Enlightenment by calling it "the age of d'Alembert." D'Alembert enhanced the status of poets and writers and contributed to the spreading of Enlightenment thought, not only through his writings but also through his powerful position as a member of the Academy of Science and as permanent secretary of the French Academy. In the latter capacity, he became a legislator of language and letters, even on subjects beyond his competence. Thus, his declaration that the only good poem is one that comes closest to prose aroused indignation and protests, but it was the principle used in judging poems submitted to the French Academy during his tenure; furthermore, new members had to belong to his coterie in order to be admitted and respected. He was an organizer and ideologue and became what Grimm called "the visible head of the illustrious church of which Voltaire had been the founder and sustainer."

Letters:

"Lettre de M. d'Alembert à M. Rameau," *Mercure de France* (March 1762): 132–152;

"Correspondance inédite de d'Alembert avec Cramer, Lesage, Clairaut, Turgot, Castillon . . . ," edited by Charles Henry, *Bulletino di bibliografia e di storia delle scienze matematiche e fisiche,* 18 (September–December 1885): 507–570, 605–649;

Œuvres et correspondances inédites de d'Alembert, edited by Henry (Paris: Didier & Perrin, 1887);

John Pappas, "Inventaire de la correspondance de d'Alembert," *Studies on Voltaire and the Eighteenth Century,* 245 (1986): 131–276.

Biographies:

Joseph Dumas, *Eloge de d'Alembert, discours qui a concouru pour le prix extraordinaire proposé par l'Académie française pour l'année 1785* (London & Paris: P.-J. Duplain, 1789);

Joseph Bertrand, *d'Alembert* (Paris: Hachette, 1889);

Ronald Grimsley, *Jean d'Alembert 1717–1783* (Oxford: Clarendon Press, 1963);

Gilles Maheu, "La vie et l'œuvre de Jean d'Alembert: étude bio-bibliographique," 3 volumes, dissertation, Université de Paris, 1967.

References:

Antoine-Nicolas de Caritat de Condorcet, *Correspondance inédite de Condorcet et de Turgot 1770–1779,* edited by Charles Henry (Paris: Charavay frères, 1883);

de Caritat de Condorcet, *Œuvres,* 12 volumes, edited by A. Condorcet O'Connor and M. F. Arago (Paris: Didot frères, 1847–1849);

Ernst Cassirer, *Philosophy of the Enlightenment,* translated by Fritz C. A. Koeln and James P. Pettegrove (Boston: Beacon, 1955);

Anne-Marie Chouillet, François de Gandt, and Irène Passeron, "L'édition des œuvres complètes de d'Alembert (1717–1783)," *Gazette des mathématiciens,* 77 (1998): 59–71;

Roland Desné, ed., *d'Alembert,* special issue of *Dix-huitième siècle,* no. 16 (1984)—comprises an iconography, a review of recent works, and an article by

Jean-Noël Pascal, "Le rêve d'amour de d'Alembert," pp. 163–170;

Marguerite Dupont-Chatelain, *Les Encyclopédistes et les femmes* (Geneva: Slatkine Reprints, 1970);

Monique Emery and Pierre Monzani, eds., *Jean d'Alembert, savant et philosophe: portrait à plusieurs voix* (Paris: Edition des archives contemporaines, 1989)–includes the articles by Roland Mortier, "La place de d'Alembert dans la littérature des Lumières," pp. 17–40, and John Pappas, "Idées reçues contre évidences: problèmes pour un biographe de d'Alembert," pp. 85–110;

Dennis Fredrick Essar, "D'Alembert's Conception of Language and Their Implications in his Aesthetics and Epistemology," dissertation, University of Western Ontario, 1973;

Michel Foucault, *The Order of Things: An Archeology of the Human Sciences* (New York: Pantheon, 1970);

Martine Groult, *D'Alembert et la mécanique de la vérité dans l'Encyclopédie* (Paris: H. Champion, 1999);

Thomas Laurin Hankins, *Jean d'Alembert. Science and the Enlightenment* (Oxford: Clarendon Press, 1970; revised edition, London: Gordon & Breach, 1990);

Véronique Le Ru, *Jean Le Rond d'Alembert philosophe*, introduction by Maurice Clavelin (Paris: Librairie philosophique J. Vrin, 1994);

John Lough, *Essays on the* Encyclopédie *of Diderot et d'Alembert* (London: Oxford University Press, 1968);

John Pappas, *Berthier's* Journal de Trévoux *and the Philosophes* (Geneva: Droz, 1957)–monograph from *Studies on Voltaire and the Eighteenth Century*, 3 (1957);

Pappas, "D'Alembert et la nouvelle aristocratie," *Dix-huitième siècle*, 15 (1983): 335–343;

Pappas, "D'Alembert et *Le Fils naturel*," in *Essays on Diderot and the Enlightenment in Honor of Otis Fellows*, edited by Pappas (Geneva: Droz, 1974);

Pappas, "Diderot, d'Alembert et l'Encyclopédie," *Diderot Studies*, 4 (1963): 191–208;

Pappas, "L'esprit de finesse contre l'esprit de géométrie: un débat entre Diderot et d'Alembert," *Studies on Voltaire and the Eighteenth Century*, 89 (1972): 1229–1253;

Pappas, "La 'marâtre' Mme de Tencin, mère de d'Alembert," *2000 European Journal*, 3 (2002); 6–7;

Pappas, "The Role of the Poet in Eighteenth-Century French Society," *University of South Carolina French Literature Series*, 1 (1973): 97–115;

Pappas, "Rousseau and d'Alembert," *Publications of the Modern Language Association of America*, 75, no. 1 (March 1960): 46–60;

Pappas, *Voltaire and d'Alembert* (Bloomington: Indiana University Press, 1962);

Charles Pougens, *Lettres à Mme X sur divers sujets de morale et de littérature* (Paris, 1826);

Jean-Philippe Rameau, "Lettre de M. Rameau à M. d'Alembert," *Mercure de France*, 2 (April 1761): 124–126;

Jean-Jacques Rousseau, *Confessions*, translated by Angela Scholar, edited by Patrick Coleman (New York: Oxford University Press, 2000);

Charles-Augustin Sainte-Beuve, *Selected Essays*, translated by Francis Steegmuller and Norman Guterman (Garden City, N.Y.: Doubleday, 1963);

Amélie Suard, *Essai de mémoires sur M. Suard* (Paris: Lescure, 1881);

Glenn Joseph van Treese, *D'Alembert and Frederick the Great: A Study of their Relationship* (New York: Learned, 1974).

Papers:

The main body of Jean Le Rond d'Alembert's papers is at the Bibliothèque de l'Institut de France. More documents may be found in the archives of the Académie des Sciences, at the Bibliothèque nationale, at the Bibliothèque de l'Arsenal, and at the Bibliothèque de l'Académie de médecine.

Other libraries in France own some of his papers–the Bibliothèque de la ville, in Angers; the Bibliothèque municipale, in Arras; the Bibliothèque du Musée Calvet, in Avignon; the Bibliothèque de la ville, in Bayeux; the Bibliothèque publique, in Besançon; the Bibliothèque municipale, in Bordeaux; the Bibliothèque de Lyon; la Bibliothèque municipale, in Nantes; the Bibliothèque de la ville, in Poitiers; the Bibliothèque de la ville, in Reims; and the Bibliothèque municipale, in Rouen.

Papers may also be found in Germany, at the Deutschen Zentralarchiv, in Merseburg, and at the Thuringische Landesbibliothek, in Gotha. Some papers are held in Great Britain at the British Museum, Egerton. Other papers are in Russia, at the Academy of Sciences and in the Archives; still others are found in Switzerland, at the Bibliothèque de Genève. Some papers are in the United States–at the University of California, Berkeley; Columbia University; the Historical Society of Pennsylvania, Philadelphia; and the Pierpont Morgan Library in New York City.

Charles Batteux
(8 May 1713 - 14 July 1780)

Cecile Nebel
Hunter College of the City University of New York

BOOKS: *Les beaux-arts réduits à un même principe* (Paris: Durand, 1746); translated by John Miller as *The Polite Arts, or A Dissertation on Poetry, Painting, Musik, Architecture and Eloquence* (London: Printed for J. Osborn and T. Lownds, 1749); revised as *Cours de belles-lettres distribué par exercices*, 3 volumes (Paris: Desaint & Saillant, 1747–1748); revised as *Cours de belles-lettres; ou, principes de la littérature*, 4 volumes (Paris: Desaint & Saillant, 1753); translated by Miller as *A Course of the belles-lettres; or, The Principles of Literature*, 4 volumes (London: Sampson Low, 1761);

Parallèle de la Henriade et du Lutrin, avec des réflexions sur le remerciement de M. de Voltaire à l'Académie françaisè, et une dénonciation à la mesme Académie de l'Histoire de Louis XI, par Duclos (N.p., 1746);

La morale d'Epicure: tirée de ses propres écrits (Paris: Desaint & Saillant, 1758);

Traité de la construction oratoire (Paris: Desaint & Saillant, 1763);

Nouvel examen du préjugé sur l'inversion, pour servir de réponse à M. Beauzée (N.p., 1767);

Histoire des causes premières; ou, exposition sommaire des pensées des philosophes sur les principes des êtres (Paris: Saillant, 1769);

Cours d'études à l'usage des élèves de l'ecole royale militaire, 6 volumes (Paris: Nyon l'aîné, 1777);

Chefs-d'oeuvre d'éloquence poétique à l'usage des jeunes orateurs; ou, discours françois tirés des auteurs tragiques les plus célèbres... (Paris: Nyon l'aîné, 1780).

Editions and Collections: *Abrégé de l'histoire de France, à l'usage des élèves de l'Ecole militaire. Nouvelle édition, revue, corrigée et continuée jusqu'en 1811 par M. de Propriac*, 2 volumes (Paris: Patris, 1811);

Abrégé de l'histoire de France, à l'usage des élèves de l'Ecole militaire. Nouvelle édition, revue, corrigée, augmentée et continuée jusqu'à ce jour par M. Masselin, 2 volumes (Paris: Delalain, 1822);

Les beaux-arts réduits à un même principe: Edition critique, edited by Jean-Rémy Mantion (Paris: Aux amateurs de livres, 1989);

La Leçon de lecture: Textes de l'abbé Batteux choisis et présentés par Sonia Branca-Rosoff (Paris: Editions des Cendres, 1990).

OTHER: *Mémoires de littérature tirez des registres de l'Académie royale des inscriptions et belles-lettres:* "Conjectures sur le Système des Homéoméries, ou parties similaires, d'Anaxagore," 25 (1759): 48–67;

"Développement d'un principe fondamental de la physique des Anciens, d'où naissent les réponses aux objections d'Aristote, de Lucrèce, de Bayle, contre le système d'Anaxagore," 25 (1759): 68–98;

"Développement de la morale d'Aristippe, pour servir d'explication à un passage d'Horace," 26 (1759): 1–9;

"Réfléxions générales sur l'étude de la philosophie ancienne," 27 (1761): 153–163;

Mémoires historiques sur le principe actif de l'univers: "Premier Mémoire: Doctrine des Chaldéens, pensées des Perses sur le principe actif," 27 (1761): 233–252;

"Deuxième Mémoire: Doctrine des Egyptiens," 27 (1761): 187–211;

"Troisième Mémoire: Doctrine des Grecs dans les temps fabuleux," 27 (1761): 212–232;

"Quatrième Mémoire: La nuit et l'amour considérés comme principes," 27 (1761): 233–252;

"Cinquième Mémoire: Pensées de l'école de Thalès et de celle de Pythagore; traduction d'Ocellus Lucanus," 29 (1764): 229–294;

"Sixième Mémoire: Manière de raisonner de l'école d'Elée, Unité de Xénophane, Unité de Parménide et de Mélissus. De l'infinité mobile," 29 (1764): 295–324;

"Septième Mémoire: Sentiment de Socrate. Livre de Timée de Locre. Sentiment de Platon dans son Timée," 32 (1768): 1–53;

"Huitième Mémoire: Doctrine d'Aristote; Traduction du livre de Mundo," 32 (1768): 54–99;

"Neuvième Mémoire: Idées des Stoïciens sur la nature de Dieu et du destin," 32 (1768): 100–119;

"Dixième Mémoire: Idées de Straton et d'Epicure," 32 (1768): 120–136;

"Si les Païens ont jamais ignoré le vrai Dieu. Additions aux Mémoires sur le principe actif," 35 (1770): 171–188;

"Mémoires sur les nombres poétiques et oratoires (Du rythme considéré en lui-même, Du mètre considéré par rapport au rythme, De l'usage du rythme, et des mètres dans la prose oratoire ou soutenue)," 35 (1770): 413–431;

Mémoires de littérature tirez des registres de l'Académie royale des inscriptions et belles-lettres: "Mémoires sur la poétique d'Aristote: De la nature et des fins de la tragédie," 39 (1777): 54–70;

"Réponse à quelques objections de M. Rochefort contre le précédent Mémoire," 39 (1777): 71–90;

"De la nature et des fins de la comédie," 39 (1777): 91–105;

"De l'épopée comparée avec la tragédie et l'histoire," 39 (1777): 106–124;

"Observations sur l'*Hippolyte* d'Euripide et la *Phèdre* de Racine," 42 (1786): 452–472;

"Observations sur l'*Oedipe* de Sophocle," 42 (1786): 473–495;

Mémoires concernant l'histoire, les sciences, les arts, les moeurs, les usages des Chinois, par les missionnaires de Pékin (composés par PP. Amiot, Bourgeois, Cibo, Ko, Poirot . . .), 15 volumes, edited by Batteux (Paris: Nyon l'aîné, 1776–1791).

TRANSLATIONS: Horace, *Les Poésies d'Horace, traduites en françois,* 2 volumes (Paris: Desaint & Saillant, 1750);

Ocellus Lucanus, de la nature de l'univers; Timée de Locres, de l'âme du monde; Aristote, Lettre à Alexandre sur le système du monde, avec la traduction françoise et des remarques par M. l'abbé Batteux (Paris: Saillant & Nyon, 1768);

Les quatre poétiques d'Aristote, d'Horace, de Vida, de Despréaux, avec des remarques par M. l'abbé Batteux, 2 volumes (Paris: Saillant & Nyon, 1771);

Traité de l'arrangement des mots, traduit du grec de Denys d'Halicarnasse avec des réflexions sur la langue françoise comparée avec la langue grecque, et la tragedie de Polyeucte de P. Corneille, avec des remarques, par l'abbé Batteux (Paris: Nyon, 1788).

Charles Batteux was a Latinist, Hellenist, grammarian, rhetorician, commentator, translator, essayist, historian, critic, and professor. His first work, *Les beaux-arts réduits à un même principe* (1746; translated as *The Polite Arts, or A Dissertation on Poetry, Painting, Musik, Architecture and Eloquence,* 1749), firmly established his place as a founder of aesthetic theory in France.

Batteux was born in the small town of Allend'hui on 8 May 1713. His father, Jean Batteux, possibly a lawyer by profession, was an official who represented the government and the public in judicial proceedings in seigneurial courts. According to Batteux's short autobiographical sketch titled "A mes neveux" (1788, To My Nephews), his father lived satisfactorily on his revenues. Batteux's mother's name was Jeanne Stevenin. Batteux and his mother were close, and her influence on him was crucial in shaping his future.

Until his father's death in 1725, Batteux was tutored at home by his half brother, who was twenty-five years his elder. Batteux then entered the *collège* affiliated with the University of Reims, where he was placed in the *troisième* class—actually the ninth level—with other students his age. He studied Greek on his own and made such good progress that at the end of the year he was promoted to the first-year class, then called *la rhétorique*. Batteux completed the first-year class as well as two years of philosophy and a theology course by the time he was nineteen. Anonymously, he published a short essay on Voltaire's epic *La Henriade* (1728; translated as *The Henriade,* 1732), evidence of his admiration of that contemporary.

Batteux decided to become a priest because his mother, whom he adored, wanted him to follow in the footsteps of her late, beloved brother; however, he had to wait two years until he was old enough to enter a theological seminary. At the seminary affiliated with the University of Reims, one of his teachers offered him private lessons in Greek and Hebrew and gave him complete editions of the works of Homer and Cicero as well as a Hebrew Bible with a grammar and lexicon. Another teacher, Louis-Jean Lévesque de Pouilly, fostered Batteux's interest in literature, poetics, aesthetics, philology, and criticism and encouraged him to write a course in literature. Batteux studied the principles of literary genres, reading and comparing Greek, Latin, and French authors. The essay Batteux produced formed the basis for his first two published works.

At the age of twenty-three Batteux was ordained, and he accepted a professorship in rhetoric at the University of Reims. Soon, however, the young abbé became unhappy in Reims, where the working conditions were bad and his health was deteriorating. In 1743 Lévêque de Burigny, a scholar and the brother of Batteaux's teacher and mentor Louis-Jean Lévesque de Pouilly, wrote for Batteux a letter of recommendation to influential grammarian and translator Pierre-Joseph Thoulier d'Olivet, affiliated with the Académie française. D'Olivet helped Batteux obtain posts in Paris, first at the Collège de Lisieux, then at the Collège de Navarre, the latter considered to be one of the best schools in the country.

Frontispiece and title page for the 1747 edition of Charles Batteux's first book, translated as The Polite Arts, or a Dissertation on Poetry, Painting, Musik, Architecture, and Eloquence, *1749, which introduced aesthetic theory in France. The frontispiece shows Socrates and Phaedra reading a dissertation on beauty (Johnson reprint, 1970; Thomas Cooper Library, University of South Carolina).*

In *Les beaux-arts réduits à un même principe,* which Batteux published in 1746, he observes that over time critics have offered an array of opinions on art, beauty, and taste, but he claims that a lack of clear definitions for these concepts has made arriving at a clear understanding of aesthetic judgment impossible. In offering his theory about man's relationship with art, Batteux argues that the unifying principle common to all the arts is the imitation of beautiful nature, an imitation stemming from the love of order, a love that he ultimately defines as "taste." Batteux perceives taste as deriving from nature's beauty and having the greatest rapport with one's sense of perfection, and he believes that nothing matters more than striving for perfection. Thus, a work of art must be as exact an imitation of nature as possible in order to capture elements entirely in harmony with the soul and its needs. While Batteux is fully aware that being conscious of the imitation in art separates one from the ideal that art represents, he nevertheless insists that in good art the soul delights in its elevation and freedom and is transported to enchanted places of the imaginary. Just as the sciences aspire to truth, the arts aspire to beauty and goodness, concepts that Batteux conflates. Hence, while Batteux acknowledges that intelligence allows men to distinguish truth from falsehood, he insists that taste is vital, because it allows men to distinguish between good, mediocre, and bad without erring. Overall, Batteux sees the value, range, and power of art as making it irreplaceable—it is in essence another religion.

In terms of literature, Batteux insists that its study is more philosophical than is generally believed, because what pleases or displeases in art involves "toute la métaphysique de l'esprit et du coeur humain" (the entire metaphysics of the human heart and soul). Batteux soon felt that his discussion of literary genres needed to be expanded; he rewrote the section of *Les beaux-arts réduits à un même principe* dealing with literature, and this revision became *Cours de belles-lettres distribué par exercices* (1747–1748; translated as *A Course of the belles-lettres; or, The Principles of Literature,* 1761). Batteux's objective in this text was to make young people understand the importance of the principles of poetics and to show them how to apply these principles to different genres. He classifies and defines literary genres from the simplest to the most complex, discussing their origins, history, rules, forms, characteristics, and style. He then illustrates the principles and rules of each genre by using representative examples. In general, Batteux does not want to question or in any way alter traditional generic categories. If a work does not fit into a category, Batteux simply does not discuss it. This practice explains his silence concerning the novel. As Vivienne Mylne writes of eighteenth-century literary criticism:

> Because it was a genre which had not achieved greatness in Greek and Latin literature, the novel clearly could not merit the kind of serious theoretical discussion which was accorded to tragedy, the epic or the ode. And because it was not taken seriously by major critics and theorists, it acquired no body of explicit rules to define its essence and its form.

Consequently, that contemporary novelists were excluded from Batteux's analysis altogether is not surprising. As for contemporary writers of other genres, Batteux devotes one page to poet Jean-Baptiste Rousseau, whose poetry he admires with some reservations. Batteux also mentions favorably three tragedies by Voltaire—*Zaïre* (1732), *Mahomet* (1741), and *Mérope* (1743)—and he mentions the fabulist and essayist Houdar de la Motte. Batteux's silence on the work of other contemporaries might have resulted from his belief that the writings of living authors should only be judged by posterity, or he might have felt that none of them were equal to the great authors of the seventeenth century.

Batteux stated repeatedly that he wrote for young people, upperclassmen in the *collèges,* most of whom were, as Joan DeJean notes, "French male Christians." He wanted to impress upon young students that France had a distinguished literature, including many great writers whose works could be ranked with those of the Greeks and Romans. He felt to promote the work of French writers was important because during his own years at *collège* he had never heard anyone speak of Jean de la Fontaine, Pierre Corneille, Jean Racine, or Nicolas Boileau-Despréaux and had to discover these authors on his own.

Although Batteux's work was generally well received, the controversial philosopher Denis Diderot criticized *Les beaux-arts réduits à un même principe*. He strongly disagreed with a section of Batteux's *Cours de belles-lettres,* in which he makes comparisons between Latin and French syntax, poetics, and stylistics—much-debated topics of the period. Diderot's *Lettre sur les sourds et muets à l'usage de ceux qui parlent et entendent* (1751; translated as *Letter on the Deaf and Dumb for the Use of Those Who Speak and Hear,* in *Diderot's Early Philosophical Works,* 1916) includes a vitriolic attack on Batteux's work, claiming it does not show analogies between the beauty of poetry, painting, and music, nor explain how artists express the same image, nor capture the elusive form of these images. He believed the abbé did not show what each individual art represented or imitated nor what specific means each art had to represent or imitate. Diderot also claimed that the abbé did not give a definition of beautiful nature without which the book has no foundation and makes no sense. On the last point, Diderot seems to be mistaken, as Batteux does in fact define beautiful nature, and more than once. Jean Pommier claims that Diderot's sarcastic comments may well have been inspired by his displeasure at Batteux's appointment to the chair of Greek and Latin philosophy at the prestigious Collège de France in 1750.

In his mid forties, Batteaux felt that he knew little about life and had not explored its possibilities. On the recommendation of his friend, the abbé de Saint-Cyr, an assistant to the preceptor of the royal children, he was employed by the Dauphin or crown prince Louis (father of the future Louis XVI) and leader of the religious conservatives at Court. What Batteux's duties were is not clear; he may have been an assistant tutor or secretary. But he could not stand the subjection at Court, and worse, the machinations of jealous schemers whose hapless victim he immediately became. He resigned his post after six weeks, happy to return to his studies and writing, having learned firsthand a lesson about life.

In 1750 Batteux published a translation of the works of Horace. In 1747–1748 he published the first edition of the *Cours de belles-lettres distribuè par exercices.* In 1753 a new edition of the *Cours de belles-lettres* was published but with an addition to its title: *principes de la littérature* (later changed to *principes de littérature*). This addition marks a significant change in the author's thinking; the concept of "belles-lettres" emphasizing grammar, rhetoric, and eloquence was replaced by "littérature." This word indicates that his approach could now be far ranging and of greater depth. Batteux was elected to the Académie des Inscriptions et Belles-Lettres in 1754 and to the more prestigious Académie française in 1761. He was not aware at the time that he owed his election to the second learned society (and probably the first as well) to the abbé d'Olivet, a leader of one of two rival factions to whom he was already

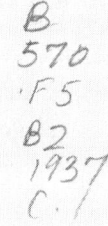

Front matter, with an illustration of Epicurus, from a modern version of Batteux's 1758 translation of Epicurus's apothegms and maxims (from Epicurus, Apophtegmes et Maximes d'Epicure, 1937; The Library, Johns Hopkins University)

indebted for his appointment at the Collège de Lisieux. Batteux felt he had incurred a burdensome obligation to d'Olivet, whose enemies at the Académie now considered Batteux their foe as well. The abbé d'Olivet was the leader of the ultra conservative religious part within the Académie whose partisans battled fellow academicians—those who believed in freedom, research, dissent, progress in the sciences, and the Enlightenment.

As befitted his status as chairman of Greek and Latin philosophy at the Collège de France, in 1758 Batteux published *La morale d'Epicure: tirée de ses propres écrits* (The Moral Philosophy of Epicurus: Drawn from His Own Writings). This text highlights the many similarities between the moral philosophies of Epicurism and Christianity. In his study *Mémoires historiques sur le principe de l'univers* (1761–1768, Historical Memoirs on the Principle of the Universe), Batteux traces first causes through works of ancient oriental philosophies, Greek philosophy, and the writings of René Descartes, Gottfried Wilhelm Leibniz, and Sir Isaac Newton. He finds among Greek philosophers a multitude of contrary opinions on the universe, causality, matter, being, soul, atoms, nature, mind, divinity, and order. He is dismayed by what he calls "un système d'incertitudes" (a system of uncertainties) in their philosophies. He questions the ideas of virtue and ethical principles that could result from such confusion, concluding that any ethics the Greeks had, resulted less from their metaphysical views than from man's natural sense of justice, truth, fairness, goodness, and beauty. According to Batteux, the morals available to the Greeks from their metaphysics would have led them at worst to a state of brutishness and war, and at best to lives driven by personal interest as it pertained to pleasures of the senses. He also discussed the philosophy of the ancient Chaldeans, Persians, Egyptians, and Phoenicians.

In 1763 Batteux returned to a topic of special interest when he published *Traité de la construction oratoire*

(Treatise on Oratory Structure). In 1771 he published *Les quatre poétiques d'Aristote, d'Horace, de Vida, de Despréaux* (The Four Poetics of Aristotle, Horace, Vida, and Despréaux), featuring translations of each writer's work with valuable notes and comments. Batteux was then asked to edit a series of memoirs by French missionaries in China and oversaw the publication of this collection, titled *Mémoires concernant l'histoire, les sciences, les arts, les moeurs, les usages des Chinois, par les missionaires de Pékin* (1776–1791, Memoirs Concerning the History, Sciences, Arts, Mores, and Customs of the Chinese by the Missionaries of Peking). Although Batteux gave up the editorship because of failing health, the collection remained in print until 1814. Around the year 1776 Batteux was also asked to provide an abridged version of his *Principes de littérature,* to be included in a multivolume textbook collection for students of the Royal Military School. The last work published during his lifetime, *Chefs-d'oeuvre d'éloquence poétique à l'usage des jeunes orateurs* (1780, Masterpieces of Eloquence for Young Orators), is an anthology of works by French dramatists.

Batteux died on 14 July 1780, laden with all the honors the Old Regime could bestow on its writers. Batteux's translation of Denys of Halicarnassus's *Traité de l'arrangement des mots* (Treatise on the Arrangement of Words), prefaced with his short autobiographical essay "A mes neveux," appeared posthumously in 1788.

Charles Batteux's work has recently experienced a revival among scholars and critics in France and Italy after many years of being labeled old-fashioned and rigidly simplistic. The many eighteenth- and nineteenth-century editions of Batteux's work give testimony to its importance in the history of ideas. Batteux enjoyed the respect and friendship of several distinguished contemporaries, at least one of whom, Lévesque de Burigny, was considered a freethinker. Batteux was instrumental in presenting and promoting Greek and Latin thought in aesthetics, philology, literature, and philosophy, but he also was convinced that France and its literature should no longer be considered of lesser importance than its renowned predecessors in antiquity. Hence, Batteux has an important place in the literary history of Enlightenment France as both a driving force in the theory of aesthetics and a champion of French culture in an age obsessed with antiquity.

Bibliography:
Fernando Bollino, *Teoria e sistema delle belle arti: Charles Batteux e gli esthéticiens del sec. XVIII* (Mantua: Istituto de filosofia dell'Università di Bologna, 1976).

Biographies:
Jean Baptiste Joseph Bouillot, "Batteux, Charles," in his *Biographie Ardennaise ou Histoire des Ardennais qui se sont fait remarquer par leurs écrits, leurs actions, leurs vertus ou leurs erreurs,* volume 1 (Paris: Chez l'éditeur, 1830), pp. 62–74;

Joseph Francis Michaud, "Batteux, Charles," in his *Biographie universelle ancienne et moderne; ou, Histoire, par ordre alphabétique, de la vie publique et privée de tous les hommes qui sont fait remarquer par leurs écrits, leurs actions, leurs talents, leurs vertues ou lures crimes. Nouvelle édition,* volume 3 (Paris: Delagrave, 1870–1873), pp. 265–267.

References:
Annie Becq, *Genèse de l'esthétique française moderne: De la raison classique à l'imagination créatrice, 1680–1814* (Paris: Albin Michel, 1994);

Mary Ellen Birkett, "Pictura, poesis and landscape," *Stanford French Review,* 2 (1978): 235–246;

Fernando Bollino, Angelo Calabrese, and Carlo Cipolli, "'Imitation' e 'Belle nature' nella poetica de Charles Batteux," *Lingua e stile,* 9 (1974): 437–487;

Michel Charles, "Quatorze remarques sur la *Poétique* d'Aristote suivi de *Littérature et Morale,*" *Poétique: revue de théorie et d'analyse littéraires,* 23 (1992): 477–511;

Charles, *Rhétorique de la lecture* (Paris: Seuil, 1977);

Jacques Chouillet, *L'Esthétique des lumières* (Paris: Presses universitaires de France, 1974);

Chouillet, *La Formation des idées esthétiques de Diderot, 1745–1763* (Paris: Colin, 1973);

Joan DeJean, *Tender Geographies: Women and the Origins of the Novel in France* (New York: Columbia University Press, 1991);

Denis Diderot, *Diderot's Early Philosophical Works,* translated and edited by Margaret Jourdain (Chicago & London: Open Court, 1916);

Diderot, *Lettera sui sordi et muti,* translated and edited by Bollino (Modena: Mucchi, 1984);

Diderot, *Lettre sur les sourds et muets à l'usage de ceux qui entendent et qui parlent* (N.p., 1751); republished in *Diderot Studies VII,* edited by Paul Hugo Meyer (Geneva: Droz, 1965);

Robert Finch, "Batteux: The Complexity of the Creative Act," in his *The Sixth Sense: Individualism in French Poetry, 1686–1760* (Toronto: University of Toronto Press, 1966), pp. 93–100;

Gérard Genette, "Blanc bonnet versus bonnet blanc," in his *Mimologiques: Voyage en Cratylie* (Paris: Seuil, 1976), pp. 183–226;

Genette, *Fiction et Diction* (Paris: Seuil, 1991);

Genette, *Figures I* (Paris: Seuil, 1966);

Genette, *Figures II* (Paris: Seuil, 1969);

Genette, *Figures III* (Paris: Seuil, 1972);

Genette, *Introduction à l'architexte* (Paris: Seuil, 1979);

Genette, "Rhétorique et enseignement" (Paris: Seuil, 1969), pp. 23–42;

Marion Hobson, "*La lettre sur les sourds et muets* de Diderot: labyrinthe et language," *Semiotica,* 16 (1976): 291–327;

W. G. Howard, "Burke Among Forerunners of Lessing," *PMLA,* new series 15, no. 4 (1907): 609–632;

Paul Oskar Kristeller, "The Modern System of the Arts," in his *Renaissance Thought and the Arts* (Princeton: Princeton University Press, 1980), pp. 163–227;

James S. Malek, "Literary Thievery: *The Polite Arts* and Batteux's *Les Beaux-Arts réduits à un même principe,*" *Notes and Queries,* 21 (1974): 257–260;

Jean-Rémy Mantion, "Batteux, Charles, 1713–1780, et les théories esthétiques," in *Dictionnaire universel des littératures,* volume 1, edited by Béatrice Didier (Paris: Presses universitaires de France, 1994), pp. 359–361;

Renata Mecchia, *Le teorie linguistiche e l'estetica di Diderot* (Rome: Carucci, 1980);

Ermanno Migliorini, *Studi sul pensiero estetico del Settecento: Crousaz, Du Bos, André, Batteux, Diderot* (Florence: Il Fiorino, 1966);

D. J. Mossop, *Pure Poetry: Studies in French Poetic Theory and Practice 1746–1945* (Oxford: Clarendon Press, 1971);

Vivienne Mylne, *The Eighteenth Century French Novel: Techniques of Illusion* (Manchester: Manchester University Press, 1965);

Alain Niderst, "*Beaux-Arts réduits à un même principe,*" in *Dictionnaire des oeuvres littéraires de langue française,* volume 1, edited by Jean-Pierre de Beaumarchais and Daniel Couty (Paris: Bordas, 1994), pp. 187–188;

Jean Pommier, "Autour de la *Lettre sur les sourds et muets,*" *Revue d'histoire littéraire de la France,* 51 (1951): 261–272;

Charles Porset and Frédéric Pousin, "Charles Batteux," in *Encyclopédie philosophique universelle,* volume 3, edited by André Jacob and Jean François Matté (Paris: Presses universitaires de France, 1992), pp. 957–958;

Johann Adolf Schlegel, *Batteux, Professors der Redekunst an dem königlichen Collegio von Navarra, Einschränkung der schönen Künste auf einen einzigen Grundsatz, aus dem Französischen übersetzt, und mit einem Anhange einiger Abhandlungen versehen* (Leipzig: Weidmann, 1751);

Jean-Paul Sermain, "Kanonbildung ou canonisation," in *Literarische Kanonbildung in der Romania: Beiträge aus dem Deutschen Romanistentag,* edited by Günter Berger and Hans-Jürgen Lüsebrink (Rheinfelden: Schäuble, 1987), pp. 103–127;

Tzvetan Todorov, *Théories du symbole* (Paris: Seuil, 1977).

Pierre Bayle
(18 November 1647 – 28 December 1706)

Karlis Racevskis
Ohio State University

See also the Bayle entry in *DLB 268: Seventeenth-Century French Writers.*

BOOKS: *Lettre à M.L.A.D.C., docteur de Sorbonne. Où il est prouvé par plusieurs raisons tirées de la philosophie, et de la théologie, que les comètes ne sont point le présage d'aucun malheur. Avec plusieurs réflexions morales et politiques, et plusieurs observations historiques; et la réfutation de quelques erreurs populaires* (Cologne: Pierre Marteau [i.e., Rotterdam: Reinier Leers], 1682); republished as *Pensées diverses, écrites à un docteur de Sorbonne à l'occasion de la comète qui parut au mois de décembre 1680,* 2 volumes (Rotterdam: Reinier Leers, 1683); translated as *Miscellaneous Reflections, Occasion'd by the Comet Which Appear'd in December 1680 Chiefly Tending to Explode Popular Superstitions. Written to a Doctor of the Sorbon,* 2 volumes (London: Printed for John Morphew, 1708);

Critique générale de l'histoire du calvinisme de Mr. Maimbourg (Ville-Franche: Pierre Le Blanc [i.e., Amsterdam: A. Wolfgang], 1682; revised and enlarged, 1683);

Recueil de quelques pièces curieuses concernant la philosophie de Monsieur Descartes, by Bayle, François Bernier, Nicolas Malebranche, and l'abbé de Lanion (Amsterdam: H. Desbordes, 1684);

Nouvelles lettres de l'auteur de la Critique générale de l'Histoire du calvinisme de Mr. Maimbourg. Première partie, où en justifiant quelques endroits de la Critique qui ont semblé contenir des contradictions, de faux raisonnemens et autres méprises semblables, on traite par occasion de plusieurs choses curieuses, qui ont du raport à ces matières, 2 volumes (Ville-Franche: Pierre le Blanc [i.e., Amsterdam: P. & J. Blaeu], 1685);

Ce que c'est que la France toute catholique, sous le règne de Louis-le-Grand (St. Omer [i.e., Amsterdam: A. Wolfgang], 1685);

Réponse de l'auteur des Nouvelles de la République des Lettres, à l'avis qui lui a esté donné sur ce qu'il avoit dit en faveur du P. Malebranche, touchant le plaisir des sens . . . , by Bayle and Malebranche (Rotterdam: Henri de Graef, 1686);

Pierre Bayle at age twenty-eight (frontispiece for the 1715, third edition, of his 1697 Dictionnaire historique et critique; *from George Havens,* The Age of Ideas, *1955; Thomas Cooper Library, University of South Carolina)*

Commentaire philosophique sur ces paroles de Jésus-Christ: Contrains-les d'entrer; où l'on prouve par plusieurs raisons démonstratives qu'il n'y a rien de plus abominable que de faire des conversions par la contrainte, et où l'on réfute tous les sophismes des convertisseurs à contrainte et l'apologie que S. Augustin a faite des persécutions. Traduit de l'anglais du Sieur Jean Fox de Bruggs par M.J.F., 2 volumes (Canterbury: Thomas Litwel [i.e., Amsterdam: A. Wolfgang], 1686);

Le Retour des pièces choisies: ou Bigarrures curieuses (Emmerich: Renoüard Varius, 1687);

Supplément du Commentaire philosophique sur ces paroles de Jésus-Christ, Contrains-les d'entrer. Où entre autres choses l'on achève de ruiner la seule échappatoire qui restoit aux adversaires, en démontrant le droit légal des hérétiques pour persécuter à celui des orthodoxes. On parle aussi de la nature et origine des erreurs (Hamburg [i.e., Amsterdam]: Thomas Litwel, 1688);

Réponse de M. *** ministre, à une lettre écrite par un catholique romain, sur le sujet des p. prophètes du Dauphiné et du Vivarets, attributed to Bayle (N.p., 1689);

Avis important aux refugiez, sur leur prochain retour en France donné pour estrennes à l'un d'eux en 1690, attributed to Bayle (Amsterdam: J. le Censeur, 1690);

La Cabale chimérique, ou Réfutation de l'histoire fabuleuse qu'on vient de publier malicieusement touchant un projet de paix, dans l'Examen d'un libelle . . . intitulé, Avis important aux refugiez sur leur prochain retour en France, attributed to Bayle (Rotterdam: Reinier Leers, 1691);

Entretiens sur le grand scandale causé par un livre intitulé, la Cabale chimérique (Cologne: Pierre Marteau, 1691);

Projet et fragmens d'un dictionnaire critique (Rotterdam: Reinier Leers, 1692);

Janua coelorum reserata cunctis religionibus, a . . . Petro Jurieu, as Carus Larebonius (Amsterdam: P. Chayer, 1692);

Addition aux pensées diverses sur les comètes, ou Réponse à un libelle intitulé, Courte revüe des maximes de morale et des principes de religion de l'auteur des Pensées diverses sur les comètes, . . . Pour servir d'instruction aux juges ecclésiastiques qui en voudront connoitre (Rotterdam: Reinier Leers, 1694);

Dictionnaire historique et critique, 2 volumes (Rotterdam: Reinier Leers, 1697; revised and enlarged, 1702); translated as *An Historical and Critical Dictionary: By Monsieur Bayle. Translated into English, with Many Additions and Corrections, Made by the Author Himself, That Are Not in the French Editions,* 4 volumes (London: Printed for C. Harper and others, 1710); French version revised and enlarged, 4 volumes (Rotterdam: Michel Bohm, 1720); translation revised and enlarged as *The Dictionary Historical and Critical of Mr. Peter Bayle. The Second Edition. To Which Is Prefixed the Life of the Author, Revised, Corrected, and Enlarged by Mr. Des Maizeaux,* 5 volumes (London: J. J. & P. Knapton, 1734–1738; New York: Garland, 1984);

Bibliothèque volante, ou, Elite de pièces fugitives. Par le Sr. J.G.J.D.M, attributed to Bayle and to J. G. Jolli (Amsterdam: Daniel Pain, 1700);

Réponse aux questions d'un provincial, 5 volumes (Rotterdam: Reinier Leers, 1704–1707);

Continuation des pensées diverses, écrites à un docteur de Sorbonne, à l'occasion de la comète qui parut au mois de Décembre 1680: ou Réponse à plusieurs difficultez que Monsieur *** a proposées à l'auteur, 2 volumes (Rotterdam: Reinier Leers, 1705);

Entretiens de maxime et de themiste; ou, Réponse à l'examen de la théologie de Mr. Bayle par Mr. Jaquelot (Rotterdam: Reinier Leers, 1707);

Oeuvres diverses de Mr. Pierre Bayle, professeur en philosophie, et en histoire, à Rotterdam: contenant tout ce que cet auteur a publié sur des matières de théologie, de philosophie, de critique, d'histoire, et de littérature; excepté son Dictionnaire historique et critique, 5 volumes, edited by Pierre Desmaizeaux (The Hague: P. Husson, T. Johnson, P. Gosse, J. Swart, H. Scheurleer, J. Van Duren, R. Alberts, C. Le Vier & F. Boucquet, 1727–1731).

Editions: *Oeuvres diverses,* 4 volumes, edited by Elisabeth Labrousse (Hildesheim: G. Olms, 1964–1968);

Oeuvres diverses, edited by Alain Niderst (Paris: Editions sociales, 1971);

Dictionnaire historique et critique, edited by Niderst (Paris: Editions sociales, 1974);

De la tolérance: commentaire philosophique sur ces paroles de Jésus-Christ "contrains-les d'entrer," edited by Jean-Michel Gros (Paris: Presses Pocket, 1992);

Personnages de l'affaire Abélard et considérations sur les obscénités, edited by Roland Oberson (Lausanne: L'Age d'homme, 2002);

Pensées sur l'athéisme, edited by Julie Boch (Paris: Desjonquères, 2004).

Editions in English: *A Philosophical Commentary on These Words of the Gospel, Luke XIV. 23. Compel Them to Come In, That My House May Be Full: In Four Parts,* 2 volumes (London: Printed by John Darby, sold by John Morphew, 1708)—comprises translations of *Ce que c'est que la France toute catholique, sous le règne de Louis-le-Grand, Commentaire philosophique sur ces paroles de Jésus-Christ,* and *Supplément du Commentaire philosophique sur ces paroles de Jésus-Christ Contrains-les d'entrer;*

The Life of Joseph Addison, Esq: Extracted from No. III and IV of the General Dictionary, Historical and Critical. To Which Is Prefixed the Life of Dr. Lancelot Addison, Dean of Litchfield, His Father (London: Printed for N. Prevost, 1733);

Selections from Bayle's Dictionary, edited by Elmer Adolph Beller and M. du P. Lee Jr. (Princeton: Princeton University Press, 1952);

Historical and Critical Dictionary: Selections, edited and translated by Richard H. Popkin and Craig Bush (Indianapolis: Bobbs-Merrill, 1965);

Pierre Bayle's Philosophical Commentary: A Modern Translation and Critical Interpretation, edited and translated by Amie Godman Tannenbaum (New York: Peter Lang, 1987);

Political Writings, edited by Sally L. Jenkinson (Cambridge: Cambridge University Press, 1999);

Various Thoughts on the Occasion of a Comet, translated, with notes and an interpretive essay, by Robert C. Bartlett (Albany: State University of New York Press, 2000).

OTHER: Gabriel Naudé and Guy Patin, *Naudæana et Patiniana, ou Singularitez remarquables,* compiled by Claude Lancelot or Louis Cousin, edited by Bayle (Paris: Florentin & Pierre Delaulne, 1701).

The thought and writings of Pierre Bayle were occasioned by events and circumstances that were central to the history of the seventeenth century, but the spirit in which they were composed seems to anticipate new ways of thinking. Bayle's influence on the eighteenth-century philosophes is evident; but to suggest, as scholars traditionally have, that he shared the views or concerns of the philosophes is misleading.

Bayle was born to Jean and Jeanne de Brugière Bayle on 18 November 1647 in the small town of Le Carla (now Carla-Bayle) in the county of Foix, near the Spanish border. His brother Jacob had been born in 1644; another brother, Joseph, was born in 1656. In this remote region in the foothills of the Pyrenees people still spoke Occitan, and many had turned to Protestantism; Bayle's grandparents were Huguenots from Montauban, and his father was the pastor of Le Carla. After elementary school, Bayle educated himself by reading everything he could find in his father's library. At eighteen he resumed his formal education at the Protestant Academy at Puylaurens; his studies were interrupted for a time by illness, but he continued to read voraciously. On 19 February 1669 he surprised his family by transferring to the Jesuit college of Toulouse. On 19 March he converted to Catholicism. He received his bachelor's degree on 7 August of the following year and formally abjured Catholicism on 19 August. These experiences had a formative role in Bayle's thought, showing him how one could give oneself over easily and completely to a belief that one would later come to regard as erroneous.

According to a recently passed law, relapsed Protestants were to be banished from France *in perpetuum.* Bayle moved to Geneva, where he worked as a tutor, attended the Protestant Academy, and assimilated new ideas—most notably those of the philosopher René Descartes. Returning clandestinely to France in 1674, he tutored in Rouen and in Paris. In 1675 he was named head of the philosophy department at the Protestant Academy of Sedan. There he immersed himself in the writings of contemporary philosophers such as Nicolas Malebranche, Benedict Spinoza, Pierre Gassendi, and François de La Mothe Le Vayer and those of the physician and librarian Gabriel Naudé. He established a friendship with the Protestant theologian Pierre Jurieu, who eventually became one of his bitterest enemies.

The academy was suppressed by royal decree in 1681. Many Huguenots were finding refuge in Holland from the intensifying persecutions in France, and in the fall Bayle was invited to teach philosophy and history at the newly founded Ecole Illustre in Rotterdam. He secured a post for Jurieu at the institution.

In 1682 Bayle published *Lettre à M.L.A.D.C., docteur de Sorbonne. Où il est prouvé par plusieurs raisons tirées de la philosophie, et de la théologie, que les comètes ne sont point le présage d'aucun malheur. Avec plusieurs réflexions morales et politiques, et plusieurs observations historiques; et la réfutation de quelques erreurs populaires* (Letter to M.L.A.D.C., Doctor of the Sorbonne. Wherein It Is Proved by Several Reasons Taken from Philosophy, and from Theology, that Comets Are Not the Portent of Misfortune. With Several Moral and Political Reflections, and Several Historical Observations; and the Refutation of Some Popular Errors). The work is mainly an attack on superstition. Bayle uses the occasion of the appearance of a particularly spectacular "blazing star" in 1680 to demonstrate that comets are natural phenomena and not miraculous signs portending disaster. The reflections on superstition lead him to raise the issue of beliefs in general and to conclude that people do not act according to their beliefs or principles but are motivated by self-interest. This theme was familiar to seventeenth-century readers; it was made popular most notably by François, duc de La Rochefoucauld, but Bayle gave it a new twist by arguing that religious belief may not be needed to ensure virtuous behavior: a community of atheists could lead lives that are just as edifying as those of Christians. Indeed, he says, the atheists might even be more virtuous, because history shows that Christians have a propensity for behaving in ways that belie the teachings of the Gospels.

Also in 1682 Bayle published *Critique générale de l'histoire du calvinisme de Mr. Maimbourg* (General Critique of the History of Calvinism by Mr. Maimbourg). Bayle's purpose in this work is to discredit the claim by the influential Jesuit historian Louis Maimbourg that Protestants are enemies of the state and one of the main causes of France's misfortunes. Louis XIV was preparing to revoke the freedoms that had been granted the Protestants by Henry IV's Edict of Nantes in 1598, and Bayle hoped to neutralize one of the more dangerous imputations aimed at his coreligionists. His book on

Facsimile of the opening page from the March 1684 first issue of Bayle's literary journal (from volume 1 of his Oeuvres diverses, edited by Elisabeth Labrousse, 1964; Thomas Cooper Library, University of South Carolina)

comets was republished in 1683 as *Pensées diverses, écrites à un docteur de Sorbonne à l'occasion de la comète qui parut au mois de décembre 1680* (translated as *Miscellaneous Reflections, Occasion'd by the Comet Which Appear'd in December 1680 Chiefly Tending to Explode Popular Superstitions. Written to a Doctor of the Sorbon,* 1708).

Bayle's brother Joseph died in 1684. That same year Bayle became the editor of a new journal, *Nouvelles de la République des Lettres* (News of the Republic of Letters); the first issue appeared in March, and the journal was banned in Paris the following year. Bayle's father died in May 1685, and his brother Jacob was jailed in June in retaliation for Pierre's publication of *Critique générale de l'histoire du calvinisme de Mr. Maimbourg.* Louis XIV revoked the Edict of Nantes on 22 October. Jacob Bayle died in prison the following month.

The revocation of the Edict of Nantes and the ensuing persecutions of Protestants provided the inspiration for two important writings by Bayle. In 1685 he published *Ce que c'est que la France toute catholique, sous le règne de Louis-le-Grand* (What Catholic France Really Is, under the Reign of Louis the Great). This indictment of the monarchy was followed by *Commentaire philosophique sur ces paroles de Jésus-Christ: Contrains-les d'entrer; où l'on prouve par plusieurs raisons démonstratives qu'il n'y a rien de plus abominable que de faire des conversions par la contrainte, et où l'on réfute tous les sophismes des convertisseurs à contrainte et l'apologie que S. Augustin a faite des persécutions. Traduit de l'anglais du Sieur Jean Fox de Bruggs par M.J.F.* (Philosophical Commentary on the Words of Jesus Christ: Compel Them to Come In; Wherein It Is Proved by Several Demonstrative Arguments That There Is Nothing More Abominable than Forced Conversions, and Wherein Are Refuted the Sophistries of the Converters by Force and the Apology that St. Augustine Made for the Persecutions. Translated from the English of Sir John Fox of Bruggs by M.J.F.), which appeared in two installments in October 1686 and June 1687; a supplement was published in 1688 (all of which were translated, along with *Ce que c'est que la France toute catholique, sous le règne de Louis-le-Grand,* as *A Philosophical Commentary on These Words of the Gospel, Luke XIV. 23. Compel Them to Come In, That My House May Be Full,* 1708). The well-known parable in the Gospel of Luke of the supper to which no one comes had provided Catholics with a justification for resorting to forced conversions. Bayle argues that the greatest evils result not from toleration but from intolerance and the persecutions to which it gives rise. Since reason is inadequate to establish the truth of religious beliefs, every individual has the right to an "erring" conscience, provided that the error is made in good faith.

Overcome by his personal tragedies as well as by a brutal workload, Bayle suffered a breakdown in 1687 and was forced to give up the editorship of his journal. At this time he broke with Jurieu over the *Commentaire philosophique sur ces paroles de Jésus-Christ: Contrains-les d'entrer;* the erstwhile friends thenceforth engaged in a prolonged and often rancorous polemic. Politically, Bayle sided with Holland's moderate bourgeois Republicans, the party of compromise, tolerance, and peaceful coexistence, while Jurieu was drawn to the radical populist ideology of the Party of Orange. In religion Bayle's strategy had always been to work toward an accommodation between Protestants and Catholics; for Jurieu, whose ideas reflected the mystical leanings and self-righteousness of John Calvin, the only acceptable goal was total victory over, and the eventual annihilation of, the papists. In 1693, in an attempt to have his colleague banished from the country—perhaps even hanged—Jurieu brought charges of treason against Bayle before the Rotterdam city council, accusing his former friend of secretly conspiring with French interests. The outcome was not as dramatic as Jurieu had hoped: Bayle lost his position at the Ecole Illustre.

Bayle had been hoping for some time to correct the errors and shortcomings in historical dictionaries of the time, especially those in one of the best-known and most influential such works: Louis Moréri's *Le Grand Dictionnaire historique, ou mélange curieux de l'histoire sacrée et profane* (1671, The Great Historical Dictionary, or Curious Miscellany of Sacred and Profane History). In 1692 the Rotterdam publisher Reinier Leers agreed to underwrite the project, and a proposal announcing the planned dictionary appeared. The end result went considerably beyond the initial plan. The *Dictionnaire historique et critique* (translated as *An Historical and Critical Dictionary,* 1710), which appeared in two volumes in 1697, is Bayle's most important achievement and the only work he published under his own name.

The dictionary was mainly inspired by Bayle's desire to expose the pretentiousness and partiality of Catholic interpretations of the Scriptures. One of his principal objections to Catholic tenets was what he considered their promotion of idolatry. This propensity was particularly evident, he thought, in the doctrine of transubstantiation, which had been established at the Council of Trent between 1545 and 1563. At the same time, Bayle did not want to replace one dogmatic approach with another but to present objective historical accounts of the topics he treated. The articles, organized alphabetically, mostly concern biblical characters and historical religious figures, many of the latter of Bayle's own time. If the dictionary has a unifying theme, it is the variety of sects and beliefs that make up the history of Christianity. By highlighting this great diversity, Bayle implicitly brings out the arrogance of any single claim to truth in matters of faith. Bayle thought that the best chance for the survival of Protestantism lay in peaceful coexistence with Catholicism, a view that was diametrically opposed to the schemes of violent overthrow and hope for a total victory over a sworn enemy promoted by Protestants such as Jurieu.

The dictionary is characterized by a markedly anti-Cartesian slant: Bayle's arguments rely on historical evidence, rather than on abstract reasoning. He explains in the preface, "I divided my composition in two parts: one is purely historical, a succinct narrative of the facts; the other is a long commentary, a mixture of proofs and discussions, in which I include criticism of several errors, and sometimes even a tirade of philosophical reflections." The main texts of the articles are relatively brief in comparison to the accompanying footnoted passages in which Bayle elaborates on and substantiates his arguments.

Another noteworthy aspect of the work is Bayle's hermeneutical approach to his subject matter: he treats the Scriptures as historical documents and endeavors to bring out contradictions and incoherences in the biblical narrative as he would in any other work produced by mortals. At the same time, his intention is not to discredit Christianity or religious practices as such: his skepticism is principally aimed at the attempt to resolve issues of faith by rational argumentation, and he proceeds by highlighting the limits to the human capacity for determining the truth about matters that are, by definition, beyond human comprehension. Recognition of these limits, Bayle hoped, would lead to the acceptance of toleration.

Jurieu attacked the dictionary soon after its publication—paradoxically echoing the condemnations pronounced by Catholic clerics, who saw to it that the work was banned in France. Not content with attacking Bayle in writing, Jurieu denounced him to the consistory of the Walloon Church of Rotterdam. The result was a fairly mild rebuke for the irreverent tone in which the author occasionally dealt with sacred matters: Bayle was not averse to discussing some of the more salacious passages in the Bible and often indulged in sarcastic and flippant remarks about subjects that were less than edifying. In a spirit of conciliation, he toned down his commentary and rewrote some of the more troubling passages in such articles as "David" and "Spinoza" for the second edition of the dictionary, which came out in 1702. Hoping to increase sales, however, Leers reproduced the original version of the entry on David as an appendix.

Bayle spent the last years of his life engaging in further polemical arguments and defending his views. In 1704 he published the first volume of *Réponse aux questions d'un provincial* (Response to the Questions of a Provincial), which concluded with a posthumous fifth volume in 1707. In August 1705 he brought out the two-volume *Continuation des pensées diverses, écrites à un docteur de Sorbonne, à l'occasion de la comète qui parut au mois de Décembre 1680: ou Réponse à plusieurs difficultez que Monsieur *** a proposées à l'auteur* (Continuation of the Miscellaneous Thoughts, Written to a Doctor of the Sorbonne, on the Occasion of the Comet That Appeared in the Month of December 1680: Or Response to Several Difficulties That Monsieur *** Has Proposed to the Author). Ill with tuberculosis, he continued to work almost until his death on 28 December 1706.

While Bayle was definitely a man of his century, his writings have frequently been interpreted as harbingers of the Age of Enlightenment. Emile Faguet and Ferdinand Brunetière, illustrious professors of the Third Republic, were instrumental in creating an image of Bayle that makes him a philosophe before his time. His aversion to dogmatic thought, his appeal to empirical evidence, and his skeptical bent have been invoked as reasons for seeing him as a precursor to the philosophes. It is true that in the eighteenth century his dictionary was to be found in the library of every important person in Europe and that it served the philosophes as a reference tool; Voltaire and Julien Offroy de La Mettrie made the most extensive use of Bayle's scholarship. Since the 1950s, however, scholars have done much to correct this simplistic rendering of Bayle's thought and have brought out the complexity of a writer whose ideas were both at odds with the reigning orthodoxies of his time and an example of the best his time could offer. As Paul Dibon pointed out in 1959, "during his lifetime he had been unable to find himself a place in his own century. They found him one in the following century." The monumental biography by Elisabeth Labrousse (1963, 1964) is especially effective in placing Bayle's work within the framework of the intellectual, political, and religious environment that shaped his mind; Bayle's oeuvre, she says, will appear anachronistic—"either ahead of its time or behind the times—unless it is situated in its true historical context." Thomas M. Lennon's *Reading Bayle* (1999) provides a detailed analysis of the religious dimension of Bayle's thought and its intricate and constant involvement with the theological controversies of his day.

To be sure, Pierre Bayle's writings did have consequences the author had never intended, and the history of his legacy is rife with irony in this sense. Alain Niderst and Pierre Rétat have shown that from the day it was published the *Dictionnaire historique et critique* was most often praised or attacked for the wrong reasons. At the same time, one can easily understand why Bayle's thought would have appealed to thinkers with agendas he could hardly have called his own: by questioning the premises underlying all claims to truth, he

Facsimile of a page from the first edition of Bayle's Dictionnaire historique et critique, *1697, his attempt to expose what he regarded as the pretentiousness of Catholic interpretations of the Scriptures (from Bayle,* Choix d'articles tirés du dictionnaire historique et critique, *edited by Elisabeth Labrousse, 1982; Thomas Cooper Library, University of South Carolina)* laid the groundwork for the French philosophes and English deists who opposed all forms of religion.

Letters:

Lettres choisies de Mr. Bayle: avec des remarques, edited by Pierre Desmaizeaux (Rotterdam: Frisch & Böhm, 1714);

Nouvelles lettres de Mr. Bayle: au sujet de sa Critique générale de l'histoire du calvinisme de Mr. Maimbourg (Amsterdam: D. Mortier, 1715);

Correspondance de Pierre Bayle: Tome 1, 1662-1674, lettres 1-65, edited by Elisabeth Labrousse, Edward James, Antony McKenna, Maria-Christina Pitassi, and Ruth Whelan (Oxford: Voltaire Foundation, 1999);

Correspondance de Pierre Bayle: Tome 2, novembre 1674- novembre 1677, lettres 66-146, edited by Labrousse, Eric-Olivier Lochard, Dominique Taurisson, Annie Leroux, and others (Oxford: Voltaire Foundation, 2001);

Correspondance de Pierre Bayle: Tome troisième, janvier 1678- fin 1683, lettres 147-241, edited by Labrousse, McKenna, Lochard, Taurisson, Leroux, and Laurence Bergon (Oxford: Voltaire Foundation, 2004).

Bibliography:

Elisabeth Labrousse, *Inventaire critique de la correspondance de Pierre Bayle* (Paris: Vrin, 1961).

Biography:

Elisabeth Labrousse, *Pierre Bayle,* 2 volumes (The Hague: Nijhoff, 1963, 1964).

References:

Olivier Abel and Pierre-François Moreau, eds., *Pierre Bayle: la foi dans le doute. Actes de la journée "Bayle" organisée par le C.E.R.P.H.I. de l'Ecole Normale Supérieure de Fontenay et la faculté de théologie protestante de Paris* (Geneva: Labor et Fides, 1995);

Hubert Bost, *Pierre Bayle et la religion* (Paris: Presses Universitaires de France, 1994);

H. Bracken, "Toleration Theories: Bayle vs. Locke," in *The Notion of Tolerance and Human Rights: Essays in Honour of Raymond Klibanski,* edited by Ethel Groffier and Michel Paradis (Ottawa: Carleton University Press, 1991), pp. 1-11;

Jean Delvolvé, *Essai sur Pierre Bayle: religion, critique et philosophie positive* (Paris: Alcan, 1906);

Paul Dibon, ed., *Pierre Bayle: le philosophe de Rotterdam* (Amsterdam: Elsevir / Paris: Vrin, 1959);

Michael Heyd, "A Disguised Atheist or a Sincere Christian? The Enigma of Pierre Bayle," *Bibliothèque d'Humanisme et Renaissance,* 39 (1977): 157-165;

Sally L. Jenkinson, "Bayle and Leibniz: Two Paradigms of Tolerance and Some Reflections on Goodness without God," in *Religious Toleration: The Variety of Rites from Cyrus to Defoe,* edited by John Christian Laursen (Basingstoke, U.K.: Macmillan, 1999), pp. 173-189;

Jean-Pierre Jossua, *Pierre Bayle ou l'obsession du mal* (Paris: Aubier Montaigne, 1977);

Elisabeth Labrousse, *Conscience et conviction: études sur le XVIIe siècle* (Oxford: Voltaire Foundation, 1996), pp. 139-208;

Labrousse, *Notes sur Bayle* (Paris: Vrin, 1987);

Edmond Lacoste, *Bayle: nouvelliste et critique littéraire* (Paris: Picart, 1929);

Thomas M. Lennon, *Reading Bayle* (Toronto: University of Toronto Press, 1999);

Michelle Magdelaine, Maria-Cristina Pitassi, Ruth Whelan, and Antony McKenna, eds., *De l'Humanisme aux Lumières: Bayle et le protestantisme. Mélanges en l'honneur d'Elisabeth Labrousse* (Paris: Universitas / Oxford: Voltaire Foundation, 1996);

D. F. Norton, "Leibniz and Bayle: Manicheism and Dialectic," *Journal of the History of Philosophy,* 2 (1964): 23-36;

S. G. O'Cathasaigh, "Scepticism and Belief in Pierre Bayle's *Nouvelles Critiques,*" *Journal of the History of Ideas,* 45 (1984): 421-433;

Richard H. Popkin, *The History of Scepticism from Erasmus to Spinoza* (Berkeley: University of California Press, 1979), pp. 38, 65, 77, 88, 90, 102, 138, 210, 215, 216;

Pierre Rétat, *Le Dictionnaire de Bayle et la lutte philosophique au XVIIIe siècle* (Paris: Les Belles Lettres, 1971);

Walter Rex, *Essays on Pierre Bayle and Religious Controversy* (The Hague: Nijhoff, 1965);

Karl C. Sandberg, *At the Crossroads of Faith and Reason: An Essay on Pierre Bayle* (Tucson: University of Arizona Press, 1966);

Amie Tannenbaum and Donald Tannenbaum, "John Locke and Pierre Bayle on Religious Toleration: An Enquiry," *Studies on Voltaire and the Eighteenth Century,* 303 (1992): 418-421;

B. Sher Tinsley, "Sozzini's Ghost: Pierre Bayle and Socinian Toleration," *Journal of the History of Ideas,* 57 (1966): 609-624;

"Two Concepts of Tolerance: Why Bayle Is Not Locke," *Journal of Political Philosophy,* 4 (1996): 302-322;

Luc Weibel, *Le Savoir et le corps: essai sur le Dictionnaire de Pierre Bayle* (Paris: L'Age d'homme, 1975);

Ruth Whelan, *The Anatomy of Superstition: A Study of the Historical Theory and Practice of Pierre Bayle* (Oxford: Voltaire Foundation, 1989).

Pierre-Augustin Caron de Beaumarchais
(24 January 1732 – 18 May 1799)

Pamela Gay-White
Alabama State University

BOOKS: *Eugénie: drame en cinq actes en prose, enrichi de figures en taille-douce; avec un Essai sur le drame sérieux* (Paris: Merlin, 1767);

Les deux amis, ou le négociant de Lyon, drame en cinq actes en prose . . . (Paris: Veuve Duchesne & Merlin, 1770); translated by C.H. as *The Two Friends; or, The Liverpool Merchant* (London: Baylis, 1800);

Mémoire à consulter, pour Pierre-Augustin Caron de Beaumarchais . . . accusé (Paris: C. Simon, 1773);

Supplément au Mémoire à consulter, pour Pierre-Augustin Caron de Beaumarchais . . . accusé en corruption de juge & calomnie (Paris: Quillau, 1773);

Addition au supplément (Paris: Jacques-Gabriel Clousier, 1773);

Mémoires de M. Caron de Beaumarchais, Ecuyer, Conseiller-Secrétaire du Roi, Lieutenant-Général des Chasses au Baillage & Captainerie de la Varenne du Louvre, grande Venerie & Fauconnerie de France, accusé de corruption de Juge. Contre: M. Goëzman, Conseiller de Grand'Chambre au Parlement de Paris, accusé de subornation et de faux. Mme Goëzman et le Sieur Bertrand, accusés. Le Sieur Marin, Gazetier de France, et le Sieur Darnaud-Bacular, Conseiller d'Ambassade, assignés comme Témoins (Paris: Ruault, 1773–1776);

Mémoires de M. Caron de Beaumarchais (Amsterdam: Merkus, 1775);

Le barbier de Séville, ou la précaution inutile (Paris: Ruault, 1775); translated by Elizabeth Griffith for W. B. Sheridan as *The Barber of Seville; or, The Useless Precaution* (London: Printed for the author by J. Bew, 1776);

Observations sur le mémoire justicatif de la Cour de Londres (London & Philadelphia, 1779); translated by Joseph-Mathias Gérard de Rayneval as *Observations on the Justificative Memorial of the Court of London* (Philadelphia: Bailey, 1781);

La folle journée, ou le mariage de Figaro (Au Palais-Royal [Paris]: Ruault, 1785); translated by Thomas Holcroft as *The Follies of a Day; or, The Marriage of Figaro* (London: G. G. J. & J. Robinson, 1785);

Pierre-Augustin Caron de Beaumarchais (engraving by Saint-Aubin in George Havens, The Age of Ideas, *1955; Collection of W. Ross)*

Tarare, opéra en trois actes, avec un prologue (Paris: P. de Lormel, 1787); translated by C. James as *Tarare, an Opera in Five Acts, with a Prologue* (London: R. Faulder, 1787);

L'autre Tartuffe, ou la mère coupable (Paris: Marcadan, l'an deuxième de la République Française [1793–1794]); translated by James Wild as *Frailty and Hypocrisy* (London: John Hayes, 1804).

Editions and Collections: *Oeuvres complètes de Pierre-Augustin Caron de Beaumarchais,* edited by Paul-Phillipe Gudin (Paris: Collin, 1809);

Oeuvres choisies de Beaumarchais, 3 volumes (Paris: Lecointe, 1832);

Théâtre de Beaumarchais, edited by L. S. Auger (Paris: Didot, 1846);

"Mémoires de Beaumarchais dans l'affaire Goëzman," précédés d'une appréciation tirée des Causeries du lundi par M. Sainte-Beuve (Paris: Garnier, 1857);

Oeuvres complètes, edited by F. Fournier (Paris: Laplace, Sanchez, 1876);

Théâtre complet de Beaumarchais, annotated by René d'Hermies (Paris: Magnard, 1952);

Théâtre complet (Paris: Gallimard, 1957);

Théâtre de Beaumarchais: Le barbier de Séville, Le mariage de Figaro, La mère coupable, edited by René Pomeau (Paris: Garnier Flammarion, 1965);

Parades, edited by Pierre Larthomas (Paris: Société d'édition et d'enseignement supérieur, 1977);

For the Good of Mankind: Pierre-Augustin Caron de Beaumarchais' Political Correspondence Relative to the American Revolution, compiled and edited by Antoinette Shewmake (Washington, D.C.: University Press of America, 1987);

The Barber of Seville; The Marriage of Figaro; and The Guilty Mother, translated by Graham Anderson (London: Oberon, 1993).

PLAY PRODUCTIONS: *Les Bottes de sept lieues,* Paris, Théâtre du Château d'Etoiles, 4 November 1760;

Léandre, marchand d'agnus, Paris, Théâtre du Château d'Etoiles, 26 July 1762;

Jean Bête à la foire, Paris, Théâtre du Château d'Etoiles, 4 November 1764;

Eugénie, The Hague, Comédiens français, 17 October 1767;

Les deux amis, Paris, La Comédie Française, 13 January 1770;

Le barbier de Séville, Paris, La Comédie Française, 23 February 1775;

La folle journée, ou le mariage de Figaro, Paris, Comédiens Français ordinaires du Roi, 27 April 1784;

Tarare, Paris, Théâtre de l'Académie Royale de la Musique, 8 June 1787;

L'autre Tartuffe, ou La mère coupable, Paris, Théâtre du Marais, 26 June 1792.

Pierre-Augustin Caron de Beaumarchais is known to modern scholars as the creator of a trilogy of plays in which the protagonist, Figaro, is representative both of the working class and the embodiment of the emerging man of the Enlightenment. Defending the aspirations of the eighteenth-century citizen, the character of Figaro the barber is portrayed as both a triumph over social constraints and an avenging alter ego for Beaumarchais. Representing class struggles and painful abuses of the ancien régime and prophesying social equality, *Le barbier de Séville, ou la précaution inutile* (first published 1775; translated as *The Barber of Seville; or, The Useless Precaution,* 1776) and *La folle journée, ou le mariage de Figaro* (first published 1785; translated as *The Follies of a Day; or, The Marriage of Figaro,* 1785), the first two dramatic works of Beaumarchais's trilogy, were quite successful. They were premiered in 1775 and 1784 respectively, by the prestigious Comédie Française. Throughout his life, Beaumarchais aspired to the increased social privilege and rank demonstrated in these two key dramatic works. In the third play of the trilogy, *L'autre Tartuffe, ou la mère coupable,* which premiered in 1792 (first published [1793–1794]; translated as *Frailty and Hypocrisy,* 1804), Beaumarchais affirmed the unity of the plays through the creation of a work lacking in gaiety but filled with strong moral overtones.

Throughout his varied careers as amateur musician, watchmaker, spy, arms dealer, and man of letters, Beaumarchais was constantly aware of the fine line between financial currents and politics, an acuity evidenced in his dramatic work. A celebrity because of his varied talents, Beaumarchais served as a harpist and music teacher to the daughters of Louis XV and excelled in precarious financial ventures. He also won many well-publicized lawsuits and was a secret agent and arms dealer for the fledgling American colonies. He satirized his society in *Mémoires de M. Caron de Beaumarchais* (1773–1776), directed against a certain Judge Goëzman, whom Beaumarchais accused of corruption as his defense while on trial for embezzlement. According to Charles-Augustin Sainte-Beuve in his introduction to the first edition of Beaumarchais's *Mémoires,* Beaumarchais was forced to plead to his judges while on short leaves from his incarceration at Fort-l'Evêque and was deceived by Madame Goëzman, who betrayed confidences concerning the case. Beaumarchais later defended his conduct during this period by recalling the marked capacity of women to feign emotion without changing their basic nature. The *Mémoires* consists of brilliant polemics, which formed his reputation as a writer and represented the apex of the growing appeal of writing as a career. The proliferation of the print culture and the rise of the legal profession further increased the social status of the writer himself as part of a new social order, as did his ability to drift from fashionable salons into the mainstream of public life. Although Beaumarchais did not identify himself principally as an author or "man of letters," his *Mémoires* recalls a life of adventures as an eighteenth-century citizen and *homme à tout faire* (jack of all trades).

Pierre-Augustin Caron was born 24 January 1732 in Paris, the only son in a family of five daughters of Huguenot watchmaker André-Charles Caron and Marie-Louise Pichon, daughter of a prominent Parisian bourgeois. He was apprenticed to his father, a watchmaker, from whose employ he was banished at age eighteen for failing to adhere to strict behavioral codes.

Resentment over his low social status engendered at an early age curiosity toward the emerging middle class. He was keenly aware that even the mistress of Louis XV, Madame de Pompadour, was a member of this class, newly titled "the bourgeoisie." At age twenty, he invented a watch escapement, showing it to his father's colleague, Jean-André LePaute, who appropriated the invention as his own. Beaumarchais then took the matter to court and won his case and enhanced his reputation through accounts reported in *Le Mercure de France*.

A certain Madame Madeleine-Catherine Franquet and her husband, clerk-controller of the king's household, befriended him, and in 1755 he became successor to the secretary of the royal kitchens following the death of Franquet, whose widow he married in 1756. Among the assets of Franquet was the village of Beaumarchais, a name he later added to his own. Ten months later his wife died, and he was left penniless by lawsuits alleging complicity in her sudden death, Beaumarchais clung to his position at court, seeking to augment his social circle by teaching music to the daughters of Louis XV. Beaumarchais's sudden ascent at court attracted the attention of the heir of a financial house, Joseph Pâris-Duverney, who taught him the intricate relationship between politics and trade. In turn, Beaumarchais won the king's favor with the bequest of legal status on Pâris-Duverney's enterprise, the prestigious *Ecole Militaire*. Against Pâris-Duverney's advice, Beaumarchais applied for the position of nobility "grand master of the rivers and forests," which he was denied because of his upbringing as a craftsman. Denied noble rank, he consoled himself by buying the title of lieutenant general of the hunt, a less remunerative position than the one he had failed to obtain, but one that was more aristocratic. In 1761, he was able to purchase a *brevet de la nobilité* (certificate of nobility), the title of secretary of the king, that gave him the legal right to bear the name Beaumarchais.

Beaumarchais's forays at court ushered in his first theatrical attempts, performed between 1760 and 1763 as short *parades,* popular forms of private entertainment dating from the seventeenth-century Italian comedy troupe Commedia dell'arte, in which crowds listened to masked performers shout commonplace dialogues from painted balconies. *Les Bottes de sept lieues* (first performed 1760; The Seven-League Boots), *Jean Bête à la foire* (first performed 1764; John the Beast at the Fair), and *Léandre, Marchand d'agnus* (first performed 1762; Leander, the Lamb Merchant) were three short farces performed at the Théâtre du Château d'Etioles. They became his first essays in a form of popular theater Beaumarchais later integrated into his major theatrical and operatic works. During this period he made several short trips to Madrid, where he became involved in legal proceedings

Beaumarchais at twenty-three (from Cynthia Cox, The Real Figaro, *1962; Thomas Cooper Library, University of South Carolina)*

against José de Clavijo, influential editor of the Spanish journal *Pensador,* who was then engaged to Beaumarchais's sister.

Defending the honor of his sister Lisette against Clavijo, Beaumarchais persuaded Clavijo on several occasions to honor his engagement, despite the fact that his sister eventually became engaged to a French merchant and noble of lesser standing. Although officially in Madrid to investigate Pâris-Duverney's Spanish holdings, Beaumarchais embarked on several literary pursuits, sketching first drafts of his plays *Les deux amis, ou le négociant de Lyon* (first performed and first published 1770; translated as *The Two Friends; or, The Liverpool Merchant,* 1800) and *Eugénie* (1767).

When he returned to Paris in 1764, Beaumarchais was attracted to the success of Michel-Jean Sedaine's *Le Philosophe sans le savoir* (1766, The Philosopher without Knowing It). Beaumarchais began to work in earnest on two short plays, using the new dramatic form advanced by Denis Diderot and Voltaire, known as *le drame bourgeois* (bourgeois drama). By this time, Beaumarchais was sensitive to the politics of playwriting and to the prestige of having one's play performed by the Comédie Française as a mark of success and recognition. Playwrights for the Comédie sought to associate themselves with this theater for public acclaim and honor, two domains that were often mutually exclusive. During this period, Beaumarchais, through a variety of means afforded by a newly established press–prefaces to printed editions, correspondence with troupes of actors, legal documents, and pamphlets–advanced the idea of creating a writers' union with other authors.

In 1768 Beaumarchais married Geneviève Madeleine Lévêque, the wealthy widow of a court official, who died two years later, causing his enemies to claim that he had poisoned his wives to gain their fortune, accusations Beaumarchais, of course, denied. Their first son, Augustin, died at the age of three. In 1774 Beaumarchais met Marie-Thérèse Willermaulaz, whom he married twelve years later. Their daughter, Eugénie, was born in 1777.

As both an aristocrat and a member of the bourgeoisie, Beaumarchais was interested in every stratum of society. Eagerly, he questioned the role of women, expressing compassion for them in his first play, *Eugénie*, a five-act drama that told the story of an English orphan, seduced and abandoned before finally being married by her seducer. In *Eugénie*, Beaumarchais countered the eighteenth-century ideas of women's essential weakness and their place in the domain of nature and of domesticity as opposed to public life, embodying superior moral strength and civility. In a century in which the male moralist of the classical age was replaced by the male philosophe, Beaumarchais argued that women had a civilizing influence. Indeed, during the Enlightenment, sentimentality issuing from the female gender became a means to touch and thereby persuade audiences to accept more readily the philosophical or social messages of the author. As the only writer who was not a philosophe to write in the genre *drame bourgeois*, which used simple dialogue and drew on scenes of everyday life, Beaumarchais was also the first to title his play a *drame* instead of the more prevalent term, *tragédie lyrique bourgeoise* (bourgeois lyric drama).

Although a failure commercially, Beaumarchais's second play, *Les deux amis*, dealt with the theme of rising financial speculation. The play asked if the employ of merit and hard work is victorious, and whether the goal of financial profit is beneficial to all members of society. It also questioned whether the prevalent business model implies a crime against the self and the sacrifice of public virtue. These and other issues intrigued the fledgling aristocrat. In this play, Beaumarchais took up the cause of venture capitalism, focusing on the right of the rising third estate to acquire wealth independent of birth or noble standing. Previously performed under the title *Les deux amis, ou le négociant de Lyon* (1770, The Merchant of Lyon), *Les deux amis* was the first play to represent a farmer-general onstage. It was a play about money invested, traded, and buried, but it was considered a fiasco because it depicted persons of modest means on the brink of ruin. In Beaumarchais's *drame bourgeois*, Cornelian dramatic principles of the previous century, which represented the etiquette of the court, were adapted to representations of everyday life. In presenting her paper on the genre at the 2001 convention of the Modern Language Association, Caroline Weber stated that the philosophes sought to "have it both ways," aspiring to reveal the discrepancies of private and public life under the ancien régime while making no attempt at social reform. Although the play failed in Paris, it paved the way for the author's later, more successful attempts at comedy, which did aim at reform.

Beaumarchais's literary success resulted from the publication of his *Mémoires* and the colorful events surrounding the performances of his plays *Le barbier de Séville* and *Le mariage de Figaro*. The premiere of *Le barbier de Séville* was delayed because of Beaumarchais's disgrace in Paris at the outset of the Goëzman trial. Its portrayal of Figaro as amateur philosopher and adviser to aristocrats in a world where good always triumphs foreshadowed a dawning age. The premiere of *Le mariage de Figaro* was heralded as the longest-awaited and perhaps most spectacular in the history of French theater. The patchwork of intrigues surrounding these premieres was itself indicative of Beaumarchais's enormous appeal, which resulted from his many and well-publicized lawsuits.

When financier Pâris-Duverney died in 1770, Beaumarchais was sued by his heir, the comte de la Blache, who accused Beaumarchais of falsifying papers in order to obtain a sum of 50,000 écus. When the case was ready for trial, Beaumarchais was then accused of bribing Judge Goëzman through his young wife. Beaumarchais defended himself by publishing a series of pamphlets with the intent to undermine the rapidly rising legal profession. As a result, he was censured, and his play, *Le barbier de Séville*, scheduled to premiere at last on 12 February 1774, could not be performed, since the authorities had banned it for a final time on 11 February 1774. Beaumarchais then left Paris for London.

Concurrent with his potential sentencing in the Goëzman case–one never formally pronounced–Beaumarchais's reputation was at stake. In London he was enlisted to serve as a spy for the French court with the mission to persuade a certain noble, Charles Théveneau de Morande, to withdraw publication of pamphlets known as *Le Chevalier cuirassé* (1784?), destined to disgrace the king's mistress, the duchesse du Barry. The pamphlets included scandalous anecdotes of the court and were intended to ruin the reputation of both du Barry and the king's ministers. Morande threatened

The remains of Beaumarchais's house as it appeared in the early nineteenth century, based on an etching by A. P. Martial in the Victoria and Albert Museum (from Cynthia Cox, The Real Figaro, *1962; Thomas Cooper Library, University of South Carolina)*

the court and extorted money from his victims to prevent publication. In a series of meetings, Beaumarchais succeeded in preventing the publication while maintaining influential contacts in London who could greatly influence future political strategy.

Although Beaumarchais had already won over public opinion by challenging the practices of Judge Goëzman, the case was not officially decided in Beaumarchais's favor until 1778. In his *Mémoires,* he included accounts of the Goëzman trial as well as those of previous affairs–that of Clavijo, for example–which earned him many financial revenues. The commercial success of his *Mémoires,* coupled with the 1775 premiere of *Le barbier de Séville,* enabled him to achieve success as a playwright.

Within *Le barbier de Séville* (as later with *Le mariage de Figaro*), Beaumarchais took every opportunity to denounce aristocrats for abuses of servants, to elucidate injustices in the treatment of women, and to challenge absurdities of the French state. In addition to the importance of these comedies in their denunciation of political power, Beaumarchais's use of comic procedures espoused by Molière enabled him to control the ebb and flow of intrigue. Such procedures as the use of nuanced characters and the apt depiction of social customs in diverse settings demonstrate an original dramatic style, one that allowed Beaumarchais to make new observations upon the changing relationship between the servant class and the aristocracy. At the same time, Beaumarchais filled his plot with new intrigues and changing social roles amid a burgeoning bourgeois economy, as when Figaro, in *Le barbier de Séville,* emphatically exclaims, "Me, spoil with a vile salary the good service that I do?"

In the subtitle *La précaution inutile,* the audience recognizes in Figaro the double of Beaumarchais. Encountering by chance his former master, Figaro recounts a tumultuous career as an apothecary, a secretary to a minister, and a failed writer. In the play, Figaro helps the aristocrat Count Almaviva marry his ward, Rosina, despite the advances of her aging tutor. First conceived as a comedy with songs, the theme for

Figaro's entrance, the song for Count Almaviva, and the arietta for Rosina were composed by Antoine Laurent Baudron, a first violinist and friend of Beaumarchais. Since the first performance of Molière's *Le Tartuffe* in 1664, no play had experienced such difficulties being performed. At its long-awaited premiere in Paris, many standees were present. After seeing the performance, those ready to criticize Beaumarchais forgave his attacks on Judge Goëzman. Because of many scandals involving the legal profession, the audience sided with Beaumarchais's denunciation of the upper classes even if they did not accept him as a writer because of his working-class beginnings. Beaumarchais's later addition of one more act between the third and the last was filled with references to Goëzman and included spicy dialogue. Despite the failure of the play on opening night, Beaumarchais listened to his critics and, in a period of three days, reduced it to four acts instead of five, resulting in the resounding success of the second performance. Recounting the premiere, eighteenth-century critic Frédéric Melchior Grimm noted in his *Correspondance* (1879) that Beaumarchais was "the horror of Paris a year ago, and everyone, based on neighborhood gossip, believed him capable of foulest crimes." And yet, he said, "the public raves about him today and defends him for what he has written. What a darling child is the French nation! When vexed, how spiteful it turns; when made to laugh, how good natured and well-behaved."

The performance of *Le barbier de Séville* served as a catalyst to precipitate legislation destined to benefit authors. According to a royal decree in effect since 1697, authors of the French state could receive one-ninth of profits for a five-act play and one-twelfth for a three-act play, derived from daily proceeds. Actors received additional sums if proceeds went below a certain figure. Furthermore, if a play were to fail because of lack of sufficient attendance, it was no longer considered as belonging to the author. If such were the case, following a brief period of "unsuccess," all proceeds could then be split among the actors, allowing them to control all of the profits. But with the premiere of *Le barbier de Séville,* which brought in a record 3,367 livres, Beaumarchais questioned the proportion that actors, financial backers, and authors were to receive.

Receipts for the premiere of *Le barbier de Séville* had set a record, of which only one-sixth went to Beaumarchais. In November 1776, following the thirty-first performance, Beaumarchais, as author, demanded a full share of the profits. After three months, he had received no response, until 3 January 1777, when the Comédie Française offered him 4,506 livres, which he refused. The theater then decided it would no longer perform the play. On 17 June 1777 Beaumarchais met with the Maréchal de Duras, one of four gentlemen of the King's Chamber charged with theater administration, and the basis of an authors' association for the arrangement of rights was formed, later known as La Société des Auteurs dramatiques (The Society of Men of Letters). Following this meeting, the Comédie Française was required to produce a list of receipts, which proved that Beaumarchais, as author, had received less than he was due. Although the problem of the rights to a work of art had been publicly broached by Diderot concerning literature, Beaumarchais was the first to apply the principle of fairness to dramatic works, an issue that was not completely resolved until December 1780. As a result of this new legislation, the eighteenth-century reader would have agreed with Figaro's own description of "men of letters" as being akin to Beaumarchais himself: "In Madrid, eying the Republic of Letters as one of wolves armed against each other scornfully led wherever this laughable addiction leads them. All insects, mosquitos, cousins, critics, flies, dipteres, envious, are attached to the flesh of these unhappy men." Between the premieres of his two plays, Beaumarchais enjoyed a career abounding in trials and intrigues and satirizing both the institutions and morals of the bourgeois class.

Following the death of Louis XV on 10 May 1774, Beaumarchais asserted his influence at the court of Louis XVI upon the news of the 13 December 1773 Boston Tea Party and the 4 July 1776 signing of the Declaration of Independence in Philadelphia. These events were the first steps of the American Revolution and the role that France played in it. Beaumarchais rallied support from the king. The marquis de Lafayette, who had received a special commission from the Continental Congress to serve as major general in the Continental Army, was then on the verge of battle at Brandywine Creek in the fall of 1777 and needed money to fund his army. Lafayette sought the help of Beaumarchais, who since 1774 had kept in contact with Morande. Beaumarchais and the younger brother of Morande undertook the transfer of funds for arms, horses, uniforms, equipment, and servants for the American insurgents. Following a visit to France by Connecticut merchant Silas Deane, Beaumarchais obtained from the American Congress a contract guaranteeing payment for arms on 16 April 1778. He wrote to Deane that he would send two hundred bronze four-pounders, two hundred thousand rounds of ammunition, twenty thousand muskets, a few bronze mortars, some cannonballs, sheets, tents, and gunlock plates. Although Beaumarchais did so, he was never repaid, despite Deane's many attempts to persuade the Congress on Beaumarchais's behalf.

Following a career as an arms negotiator, Beaumarchais saw his second play, *Le mariage de Figaro,* premiere in 1784; it excelled both as satire and as a plea for social justice. Figaro the barber, now risen to the rank of gatekeeper at the chateau of Count Almaviva, wishes to marry Suzanne, the countess's maid. Although the count agrees to this marriage, he also wishes the young woman's favors for himself, adhering to the long-standing droit de seigneur. Consumed by jealousy and infuriated by the escapades of the page Cherubin toward his wife, the count avenges himself in aiding the countess's servant, Marceline, in a lawsuit against Figaro. Through its many romantic intrigues, which link characters of diverse classes, *Le mariage de Figaro* can be considered a plea for social justice.

In both *Le barbier de Séville* and *Le mariage de Figaro* Beaumarchais's role as defender of morality of both sexes is offered through the representation of diverse views on love, money, and vanity, of concern to all classes in his society. Originally banned by Louis XVI, who stated that its performance would require the destruction of the Bastille, *Le mariage de Figaro* was first performed in private before the count of Artois, the king's brother. In 1784 the ban was lifted; first performances were both successful and scandalous, with Beaumarchais himself inciting groups of moralists and conservatives. Briefly imprisoned at the Bastille in 1785 for an impromptu diatribe against the king, Beaumarchais was then released and deemed worthy of praise by Louis XVI himself for having written a highly successful play.

Despite accusations of stealing important papers from the French court and of hoarding ammunition and weapons during the French Revolution, Beaumarchais continued to advocate for the profession of author and playwright. As part of a growing class of playwrights, he came from the newly created bourgeoisie and was at times at odds with standard protocols of court performance. Conversely, he needed the support of the royal court to identify with the newly emerging public. In founding La Société des Auteurs dramatiques, Beaumarchais had articulated the economic and social interests of a group of creative writers to the royal household and had influenced the Crown's regulation of their activity. Through this endeavor, the idea of "self-fashioning" on the part of an author gained credence as did Beaumarchais's relation to society as a whole.

The reader can perceive in Beaumarchais's only opera, *Tarare* (first performed and published, 1787; translated, 1787), written during his final years, the emerging textual space of the musical tableau. Beaumarchais resisted Jean-Jacques Rousseau's claim of the nonmusicality of French and created a polyvalent aes-

Event in act 1, scene 9 of Beaumarchais's La folle journée, ou le mariage de Figaro, *1785 (translated as* The Follies of a Day, or The Marriage of Figaro, *1785) (engraving by Liénard at the Bibliothéque nationale, from Cynthia Cox,* The Real Figaro, *1962; Thomas Cooper Library, University of South Carolina)*

thetic, wherein opera was presented as a sequence of strategic tableaux reflecting a series of outspoken texts. First performed to the music of Antonio Salieri, *Tarare* responded to the musical conception of Christophe Willibald Gluck, who held that music and drama could be welded into one central stage action. Using many forms of recitative, Beaumarchais established a hierarchy in which music was ranked third, following the beauty of the poem and the conception of the story. Like Gluck, Beaumarchais lamented excess, writing in the preface to *Tarare,* "Aux Abonnés de l'Opéra qui voudraient aimer l'opéra" (To Opera Subscribers Who Wish to Like Opera):

Writer of opera, I would say to my collaborator: "Friend you are a musician: translate this poem into music, but do not, as did Pindar, stray with your images and sing *Castor and Pollux* with the triumph of an athlete, because that is not what they are about." And if my musician possesses any talent, if he reflects before writing, he will know that his duty, his success consists in rendering my thoughts in a tongue only more harmonious, to give them stronger expression, not to make them a work apart.

As opera, *Tarare* was a fusion of literary and musical forms. Using the libretto *style ancien,* wherein the poem was conceived as a mixture of drama and ancient tragedy, the opera opened to acclaim. Grimm noted in December 1787: "Everywhere people spoke only of *Tarare.*" Yet, Beaumarchais was criticized by many, including critic Louis Petit de Bachaumont, who had written on 8 June 1787: "the libretto exemplifies unequaled barbarism." In the creation of *Tarare,* Beaumarchais profited from the musical quarrel between partisans of Gluck and those of the Italian composer Niccolò Piccinni. In his treatment of the libretto, Beaumarchais appropriated Gluck's theory concerning the subordination of the music to the poem, using as his source a Persian tale, privileging the genre favored by Gluck, *la tragédie lyrique* (the lyric tragedy).

Tarare was dedicated by Beaumarchais to Salieri. The prologue, an allegory in which the Genie of the Reproducer of Natural Beings is summoned to collaborate with the Genie of Fire to create main characters of the drama, uses special effects to reveal the turbulence and shock of creation depicted against a backdrop of primordial chaos.

In full-stage ensemble scenes of the first act, Tarare, a common citizen, is elected chief of the army. Settings and pantomimes decry the tragic aura of an ancient past casting a shadow over the strength and wisdom of the present. In the culminating scene of this first act, the final stages of the Revolution are foreshadowed by the demeanor and sorrow of the high priestess, Astasie. Falling on her knees, she prays before the choir for the salvation of Tarare. In the final act of the opera, as the death decree preparing the sacrifice of Tarare is signed, the plight of the people under the ancien régime is symbolized. The climax and final act of the opera heralds through lyric performance the themes of liberty and victory. The performance of *Tarare* demonstrated Beaumarchais's evolution as dramatist and as citizen aspiring to popular tastes.

During the French Revolution's darkest hours, Beaumarchais composed the third play of his trilogy, *L'autre Tartuffe, ou la mère coupable.* This play explores the proper comportment of women in society. Through the representation of guilt in the aristocratic figure of the Countess Almaviva, the play comes to terms with the new social order symbolized by the revolution, glorifying the rights and equal responsibilities of women.

This final play foreshadowed the twilight of the ancien régime and the impending sway of the revolution, as evidenced in the preface, "Un mot sur la mère coupable" (A Word About the Guilty Mother). Beaumarchais summons his audience to cast its eye on an aging Figaro, offering an apology for the vanity of youth and a plea for forgiveness: "convince yourselves along with us that, unless a man is born exceedingly wicked, he ends up being good."

Throughout his musical and dramatic works, Beaumarchais portrayed accurately the society of his period. In his comedies, he added a moral dimension, engendering a difference of point of view between playwright and principal protagonist and the audience of his plays through the creation of dramatic distance. The style of his comedies is varied, ranging from the serious *drame bourgeois* exemplified by *Eugénie,* to the humorous *parade* and satire exemplified in the final scenes of *Tarare.* In *Le mariage de Figaro,* Beaumarchais's use of satire makes light of serious issues of his time—class struggles or working for a salary—by means of the principal protagonists' frivolous vocabulary and witty remarks. Developing the broadest ranges of characterization in his final comedy, *L'autre Tartuffe,* Beaumarchais mixes comic intrigue with the pathos of drama, allowing serious characters to combine with those of farce.

In 1792 Beaumarchais was charged by the minister of war with treason against the French Republic for bringing to France guns that had been warehoused in Holland and intended to aid the French Revolution. He was accused and arrested; as a result, the first performance of his play *L'autre Tartuffe* failed. Beaumarchais was imprisoned, then released, thanks to the intervention of one of his mistresses. He was both criminal and commissioner of the Republic. Several attempts were made on his life, and he narrowly escaped being guillotined. In 1794 he sought exile in Hamburg, Germany. He was considered an émigré, so his possessions in Paris were confiscated, and his wife, daughter, and sister, Julie, were imprisoned. In 1796 he returned to France, ruined and in debt. He demanded that the French state pay him for ammunition supplied, but the case was never settled. On 18 May 1799 Beaumarchais died in Paris and was buried in the presence of friends in his garden, before his body was transferred in 1822 to the Père-Lachaise cemetery.

As spokesperson for the Enlightenment, Beaumarchais had considerable influence on eighteenth-century social institutions. Through dramatic, lyric, and autobiographical texts, he synthesized the spirit and fulfillment of his age into forms that relegated

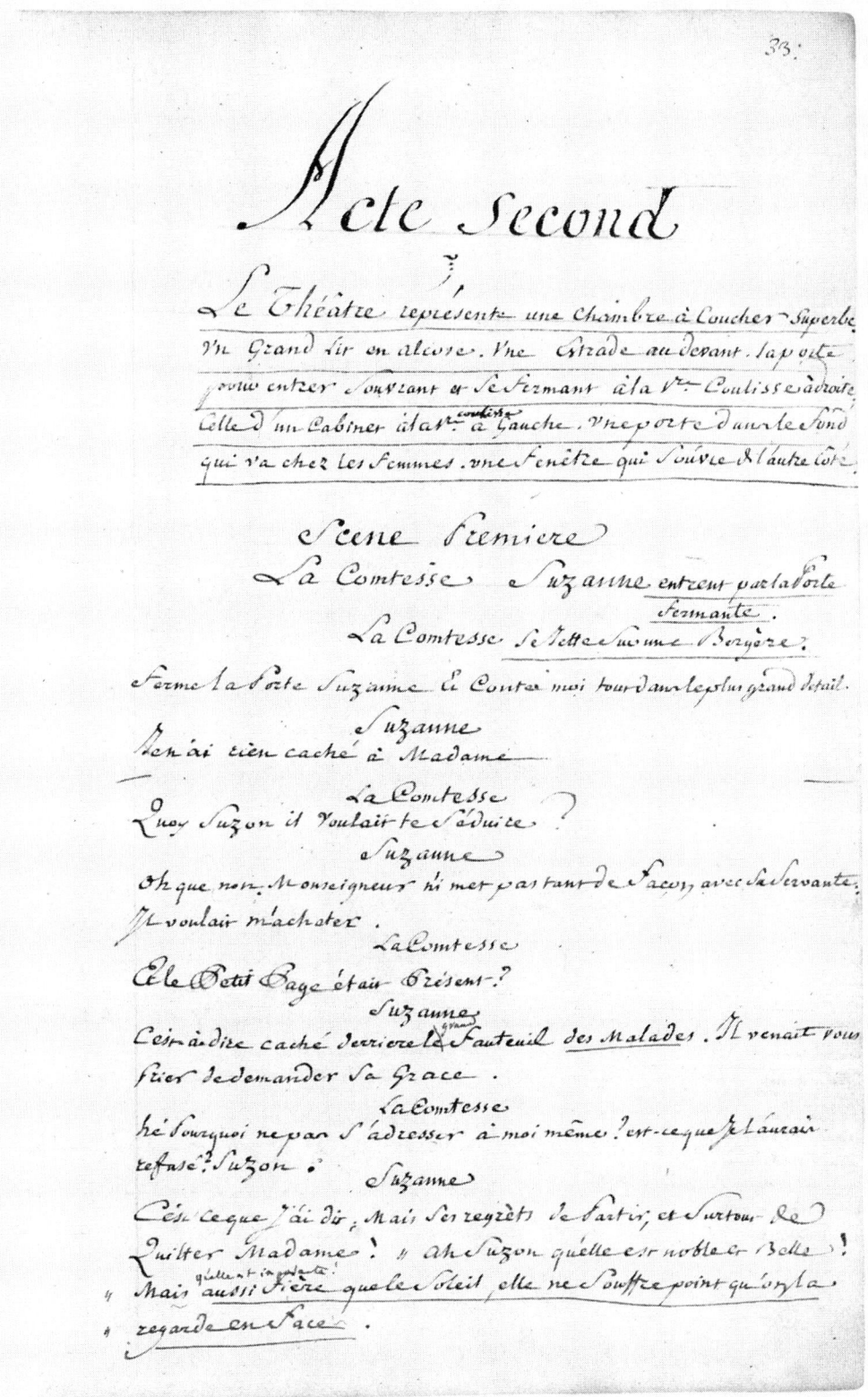

Page from the manuscript of La folle journée, ou le mariage de Figaro *(Bibliothèque Nationale; from Roselyn De Ayala and Jean-Pierre Gueno, eds.,* Belles Lettres: Manuscripts by the Masters of French Literature, *2001; BCL Archives)*

laughter to the service of characters. His drama was strikingly original in its portrayals of multifaceted characters and the social problems of the revolutionary period. Thus, he humanized stereotypes, according them the variety of social backdrops he himself had known. Relying on art, he displayed his public to itself, proclaiming through his wit essential preconditions for an aristocracy of merit and the advent of a new age.

Bibliography:

Brian N. Morton and Donald C. Spinelli, *Beaumarchais: Bibliography* (Ann Arbor, Mich.: Olivia & Hill Press, 1988).

References:

Maurice Descotes, *Les Grands Rôles dans le théâtre de Beaumarchais* (Paris: Presses Universitaires de France, 1974);

Béatrice Didier, *Beaumarchais ou la passion du drame* (Paris: Presses Universitaires de France, 1994);

Paul Frischauer, *Beaumarchais* (Port Washington, N.Y.: Kennikat Press, 1935);

Frédéric Melchior Grimm, Denis Diderot, and Jacques-Henri Meister, *Correspondance littéraire,* volume 10 (Paris: Garnier, 1879), p. 341;

René Guiet, "L'évolution d'un genre: le livret d'opéra en France de Gluck à la Révolution (1774–1793)," *Smith College Studies in Modern Languages,* 18 (October 1936–July 1937): 31–47;

Sophie Lecarpentier, *Le Langage dramatique dans la trilogie de Beaumarchais* (Saint Genouph: Librairie Nizet, 1997);

René Pomeau, *Beaumarchais ou la bizarre destinée* (Paris: Presses Universitaires de France, 1987).

Papers:

The Pierpont Morgan Library houses a collection of Pierre-Augustin Caron de Beaumarchais's correspondence.

Mme de Beaumer
(? – 1766)

Eva Martin Sartori
Five College Women's Studies Research Center

WORKS: *Oeuvres mêlées. Dialogue entre Charles XII, roi de Suède, et Mandrin, contrebandier* (The Hague, 1760); *Journal des dames,* edited by Beaumer, October 1761–April 1763.

Mme de Beaumer, a writer and journalist, was the first woman editor of the *Journal des dames,* the first periodical in France addressed specifically to women. Beaumer had expressed politically subversive views in her earlier writings, but as a journal editor she became an innovator, creating a serious organ of communication that focused on the aspirations and needs of women as a group. Between Marie de Gournay and Olympe de Gouges, no writer voiced feminist aspirations more forcefully and more insistently than Beaumer, maintaining that women were equal to men in all ways except physical strength. Although she appealed to men to treat women with respect and dignity, her strongest pleas were addressed to women, whom she praised, instructed, and lectured. She wanted women to assume responsibility for cultivating their minds and affirming their values. Her task as a journalist was to provide women with a forum in which they could express their concerns and the tools they needed to educate themselves, and she offered herself as a model they could emulate if they wished to participate in the public realm. She was the first woman to utilize the periodical as a tool in the service of women's rights.

Almost nothing is known of Beaumer's personal life, not even her first name or her place of birth. No documents exist that record her birth or marriage. According to abbé Joseph de La Porte, who included her in his *Histoire littéraire des femmes françaises* (1769, Literary History of French Women), she had strong ties to Holland, which she visited several times and where, according to La Porte, she died in miserable circumstances. Nina Rattner Gelbart, who has made the most extensive study of Beaumer's life and work, believes that Beaumer was probably a Huguenot. Her religion would account for her lack of official civil status, for Protestants preferred to record births and to marry clandestinely rather than to be branded illegitimate by the Catholic Church. That she was a Huguenot would also explain her attacks on Cardinal Richelieu in the *Journal des dames* and the protection after the attacks provided by the Huguenot Conti and Jaucourt families.

Shortly before taking on the editorship of the *Journal des dames,* Beaumer published a collection of brief literary works assembled under the title *Oeuvres mêlées* (1760, Miscellaneous Works), which includes poems, a mythological tale, and a dialogue. The most complete copy extant includes the "Dialogue entre Charles XII, roi de Suède, et Mandrin, contrebandier" (Dialogue between King Charles XII of Sweden and the brigand Mandrin), "Le triomphe de la fausse gloire" (The Triumph of False Glory), "La mort des héros" (The Death of the Heroes), "Le temple de la fortune" (Fortune's Temple), and the "Ode tirée du cantique que Moïse et les Israélites chantèrent . . . au passage de la Mer Rouge" (Ode Based on the Song that Moses and the Israelites Sang . . . as They Crossed the Red Sea). In these brief pieces, Beaumer focuses on the plight of the lower classes, on the misery and powerlessness of the *petit peuple* at the hands of power-hungry, self-centered, and glory-seeking rulers. The "Dialogue entre Charles XII, roi de Suède, and Mandrin, contrebandier" is the most openly subversive of these works. The conversation is set in the underworld before the judge Minos; it pits Mandrin, a Robin Hood–like figure hanged before a sympathetic crowd in 1755 and a symbol of opposition to the prevailing order, against Charles XII, a warrior ruler who had sought glory in warfare and brought misery to his people. Mandrin points out to the king that, although of low birth, he, Mandrin, was a self-made man whose exploits resulted from his own initiative and genius, whereas the king had managed to squander the vast resources he had inherited. Unlike the king, who sought empty glory, Mandrin was motivated by his desire to improve the lot of the poor and defenseless. Had he been born king, he asserts, he would not have tried to dominate others, as Charles had done, but would have provided for his people by improving commerce, protecting the arts and sciences, and bringing peace to the world. Charles agrees that the wars he conducted have brought misery to his people and blames historians for instilling in him the love of military glory by glamorizing such military figures as Alexander.

Like the "Dialogue," the allegory "Le triomphe de la fausse gloire" includes an attack on courtly behavior based on false values. Its heroine is Thincrèse, a stand-in for Queen Christina of Sweden, whom Beaumer admired greatly as embodying real princely virtues. Thincrèse has brought peace and prosperity to her people, but she abdicates in favor of her nephew Végatus (Gustavus). The goddess Magnanimity, who counsels Végatus, advises him to maintain a strong army but to keep peace at all costs, to be a mediator rather than a warrior, to be generous, and to act as a servant of his people. However, Végatus, like King Charles of Sweden, cannot resist the seduction of military glory, and like Charles, he is killed in battle.

"Les caprices de la fortune," originally part of the *Oeuvres mêlées* and later reprinted in the *Journal des dames* before Beaumer had taken over the editorship, is a transposition of a *fait divers* (an incident reported in the press). In it Beaumer takes up the cause of a young Dutch woman who had been seduced by a German prince. Beaumer saw her as a victim of the powerful and took the opportunity to plead her cause in a fictionalized work.

While still only a contributor to the journal, Beaumer submitted a proposal for a newspaper called the "Lettres de Magdelon Friquet." The proposal was rejected without explanation by the censor La Garde, perhaps because it was intended as an organ for populist grievances. Magdelon Friquet was a fictional character frequently used in low-class comedies. Gelbart believes that these letters were to have mixed "feminism and radical populism" and as such were viewed with disfavor by the authorities.

Beaumer's most significant achievement lay in the editorship of the monthly periodical, the *Journal des dames,* which she bought in 1761. Few women in France were journalists (Suzanne Van Dijk has identified 18 women out of the 450 journalists in France), and few periodicals were addressed specifically to women. As the first woman editor in France of a periodical aimed at a feminine public, Beaumer faced a difficult task, for she was operating in an essentially all-male profession, had little experience in publishing, and expressed unpopular views in a country that tightly controlled its press.

Beaumer was the third editor of *Journal des dames.* The periodical had been started in 1759 by a now forgotten novelist and essayist from Lyons, Thorel de Campigneulles, a staunch royalist who wished to make his way in the world by showing his devotion to the king and to the established order. He believed he would find a readership among women of leisure by offering amusing and inconsequential literature *(ces riens délicieux)* to fill their moments of boredom. Campigneulles's aim was to amuse–the literature he provided was meant to be read *à la toilette* (while dressing) and not to be pondered. Nor did he have a special interest in publishing the writings of women.

Campigneulles succeeded in obtaining for the paper a "tacit" permission to publish rather than a "privilège"–that is, it was screened by the royal censors but lacked financial and legal security. He published only four issues before abandoning the periodical. Publication resumed several years later under the editorship of Jean-Charles Relongue de La Louptière, whose aim was at the same time baser and loftier. In addition to literary ambitions, Louptière was in search of a suitable wife, and he hoped to find one among the readers of his periodical. Although he, too, aimed to amuse, he also felt an obligation to instruct. Louptière improved the prospects of the paper by securing the right to sell by subscription rather than by single issues only. Less conservative than his predecessor, Louptière succeeded in attracting women as contributors and in encouraging a dialogue with his readers through a letter column. In 1761 he announced that he was turning over the periodical to a *sçavante journaliste* (a learned woman journalist), Mme de Beaumer.

Beaumer had already published in the *Journal des dames* before taking over the editorship in October 1761. Although she had no experience as a publisher, she had a definite agenda and a fully formed program to implement it. With the first issue under her editorship the paper underwent a radical change in tone and content. Her opening statement in October 1761 declares that her mission is to convince the world that women are the equal of men and are equally capable of worthwhile deeds in all fields. She wants her audience to know that the voice of the paper is that of a woman and declares her solidarity with women, for she holds her sex in the highest esteem, as she asserts in the "Avant-propos," "Je n'ai d'autre mérite que celui de connoître tout ce que vaut mon sexe, et de vouloir contribuer à sa gloire et à son amusement. Que je serais heureuse de pouvoir le venger de cette idée injurieuse où sont encore quelques barbares parmi nos concitoyens qui ont de la peine à nous accorder la faculté de penser et d'écrire!" (My chief merit is to know the full worth of my sex and to want to contribute to its glory and its amusement. How happy I would be to rid the whole earth of the injurious notion still held by some barbarians among our citizens who have difficulty acknowledging that we can think and write!). Her program is unambiguously pedagogical. Because women are equal to men in intelligence, she will provide them with a full range of intellectual fare by publishing articles about science, politics, art, and literature, for a woman must be as familiar with Montesquieu and Jean Racine as with ribbons and pompons. Eager to provide her readership with role models, Beaumer announces plans to publish eulogies of queens and of talented and learned women such as classicist Anne Le Fèvre Dacier; writer Anne-Marie du Bocage; and scientist Emilie du Châtelet. Strong in her faith that women are capable of mastering all fields, Beaumer urges women from the provinces and from all of Europe to make their voices heard by sending her their works for publication and by reporting on the praiseworthy activities of other women. Hers is a call to action: she urges women to take an active role in their own emancipation. They must abandon their mirrors and spend time cultivating their minds. They will then become indispensable to men and will assert their influence in the world by shaping the character of their families. A few months later, in January 1762, caught up in the spirit of creating a universe parallel to that of men, she enthusiastically endorsed a suggestion by one of her readers that she adopt the words *autrice* (a woman author) and *éditrice* (a woman editor).

For the next several years Beaumer published excerpts from books, book reviews, announcements of new publications, plays, and art exhibitions, as well as original writings (often signed) consisting of poetry, letters, and stories. The book reviews dealt with a broad range of subjects, including agriculture and commerce, both because she observed that women were heavily involved in these areas and because she believed that for women to become acquainted with practical subjects was essential. Her emphasis was on the useful, on those works that would shape the character of women and make them participate more fully in the world. Whenever she could, she published notices of women in the trades—engravers, clock makers, lens grinders, taxidermists, weavers—as well as in the arts. The journal also published "anecdotes," stories that might have been taken from published books or that provided publicity for women in the trades. As an editor, Beaumer unequivocally favored the writings of women; men had to take second place. In addition to selections of new works by French women, she published translations of works by English and Italian women. Though she felt compelled to promise articles on fashion, those never appeared. She was clearly far more interested in instructing her female audience than in indulging in any frivolous inclinations.

In addressing her female readers, Beaumer created a sense of solidarity by addressing them in the sec-

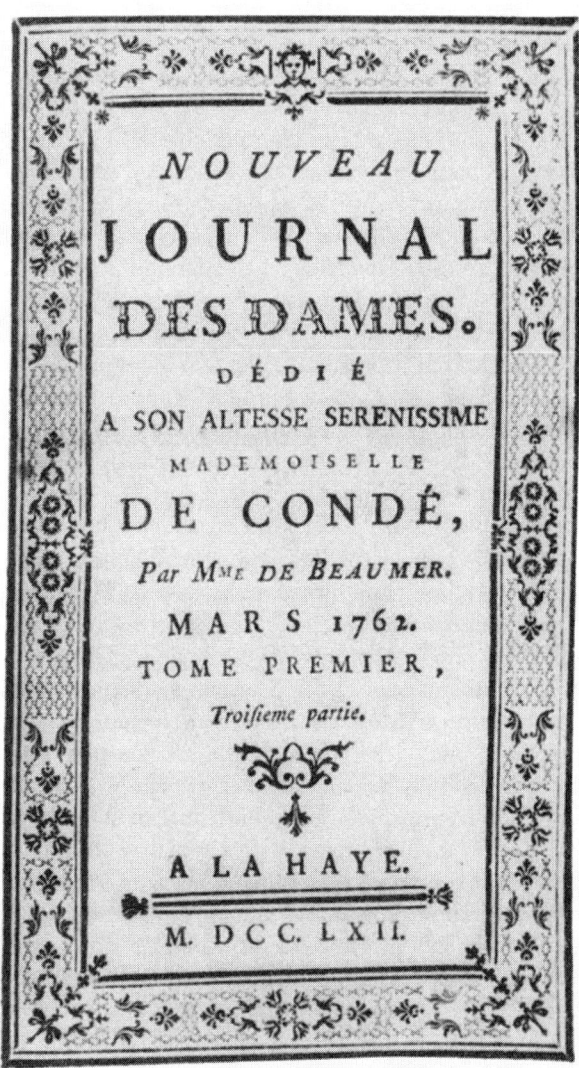

Title page for the March 1762 issue of the magazine for ladies, with an article by Mme de Beaumer. Later that year she purchased the magazine and became its first woman editor (Bibliothèque de l'Arsenal, Paris; from Nina Rattner Gelbart, Feminine and Opposition Journalism in Old Regime France, *1987; Thomas Cooper Library, University of South Carolina).*

ond person or even in the first person plural. She saw them as her natural allies in a society hostile to the aspirations of women. Men had thought her periodical would be insignificant, but in the March 1763 issue she claimed that she had shown it to be historical; she had demonstrated that women could successfully imitate male models. Women were her real judges and protectors, she declared in the May–July 1763 issue. By then, perhaps because her financial and political difficulties had become serious, her tone had become even more combative than earlier.

Beaumer's relationship with the royal censors was uneasy throughout her tenure as publisher of the *Journal des dames*. The degree of tension depended on the current political climate and on the identity of the particular censor who reviewed her periodical. In 1762, following a brief suspension in publication, the paper appeared under a slightly modified title, the *Nouveau Journal des dames* (The New Women's Journal). Gelbart believes Beaumer was allowed to continue publication and to maintain her feminist tone only if she demonstrated her patriotism in some way. Thus, she published in March a prospectus for a *Histoire militaire* (A Military History), a work at odds with the antiwar stance of the "Dialogue entre Charles XII, roi de Suède, et Mandrin, contrebandier," in which she proposed to extol the glory of King Louis XV and the bravery of his troops. That work was never published.

In 1762 the book-trade director, Chrétien Guillaume de Lamoignon de Malesherbes, and François Marin, the censor in charge of the *Journal des dames*, suspended its publication for reasons they never divulged. In desperate financial straits, Beaumer made the rounds of book-trade editor, censor, and chief of police; each sent her to one of the others. "Why are you punishing me?" she pitifully asked Malesherbes. She was finally allowed to resume publication, but a male editor, Pierre Barnabé Farmain de Rozoi, a young man with politics diametrically opposed to her own, as well as a new censor were imposed on her. Beaumer returned to Paris after a brief stay in Holland, dismissed de Rozoi, and reclaimed her position as editor. Her paper, she claimed, was known wherever French was spoken; it was essential for the survival of humanity. In March 1763 she bravely asserted that men were compelled to admit that the two sexes were equal in nature.

Publishing was a hard business, and Beaumer expressed her frustrations in the journal itself and in her correspondence with Malesherbes. She had problems with her subscribers, who often did not pay; with printers, who did not deliver on time; and with the censors, whose tolerance for opinions varied. Conflict with censors was a fact of life for both men and women. In Beaumer's case, however, her unorthodox opinions and behavior may have caused her additional difficulties.

In 1763 Marin suspended her paper again on the technical ground that she illegally sold it from home. The censor considered her a nuisance, if not a menace. In a letter to his superior, Malesherbes, Marin made fun of the title "autrice" she had adopted and ridiculed her physical appearance:

> un large chapeau sur la tête, une longue épée au coté, l'antérieur où il n'y a rien, le postérieur où il y a peu de choze couverts d'une longue culotte et le reste du corps préssé d'un habit noir, vieux, étroit et court.

> (a large hat on her head, a long sword at her side, her chest [where there is nothing] and her behind [where there is not much] covered by a long culotte, and the rest of her body squeezed into a worn, narrow, black habit.)

Asked why she dressed this way, she replied that since she ran her paper alone, relying only upon herself, she had to dress in this manner for reasons of economy and to be admitted to the (all male) parterre to review the latest play for 20 sous. In April 1763 she announced the sale of the periodical to Catherine-Michelle de Maisonneuve, after which Beaumer disappeared to Holland and was never heard from again.

How widely read was the *Journal des dames*? Beaumer sometimes made extravagant claims for its success. In the December 1761 issue, she published a list of eighty-one cities in which the journal was for sale, but so extensive a distribution was highly unlikely given her dire financial straits. To estimate how many subscribers the journal had and how many women read it is difficult. The periodical is mentioned in other publications, sometimes admiringly. In November 1761 the *Journal de Verdun* praised Beaumer: "cette sçavante a déjà donné trop de preuves de ses talents littéraires, pour qu'on puisse se permettre le moindre doute sur les success de son enterprise" (this learned woman has already given too many proofs of her literary talent for us to express the least doubt as to the success of her enterprise). In the same year the unnamed author of *Affiches, annonces, et avis divers* (Notices, Announcements, and Opinions), another periodical, expresses admiration for her talent, already visible in the *Oeuvres mêlées*. A journal destined for women could have no better editor. La Porte congratulated her for paying attention to women writers. These isolated statements, however, cannot give a true picture of the extent and influence of the readership. Nor can any data be found on her subscribers. Several volumes of the journal were found in Mme de Pompadour's library, although it is seldom mentioned in the correspondence of contemporary women.

Though Beaumer's tenure as a journal editor was brief, she introduced innovations on several fronts. Her political awareness extended beyond the plight of women to include other oppressed groups. She showed that a woman could act as a publisher in a male-dominated and politically hostile environment. Equally significant is the pioneering use she made of the medium, for she realized immediately that it constituted a powerful tool for feminist activism. Although women before her had argued the equality of women and men and had demanded access to education and to legal rights, theirs had been isolated voices. A journal provided women with a new way of communicating, because it allowed dialogue: not only did Beaumer speak (and often preach) to women, but she also heard from women and made their voices heard. She published their letters, responded to them in print, and publicized their concerns and their activities. Two of the subsequent editors of the *Journal des dames* were women: Mme de Maisonneuve edited the paper from 1763 to 1769 and Marie-Emilie de Montanclos from 1774 to 1775. In the hands of nineteenth-century activists the newspaper became an important tool in women's demands for equality.

References:

Nina Rattner Gelbart, *Feminine and Opposition Journalism in Old Regime France: Le Journal des dames, 1759–1778* (Berkeley: University of California Press, 1987);

Joseph de La Porte, *Histoire littéraire des femmes françaises, ou lettres historiques et critiques contenant un précis de la vie et une analyse raisonnée des ouvrages des femmes qui se sont distinguées dans la littérature française,* 5 volumes (Paris, 1769);

Jacques Rustin, "Romanesque et destin ou 'Les Caprices de la fortune' (Mme de Beaumer 1760)," *Travaux de linguistique et de littérature,* 4, no. 2 (1966): 59–73;

Suzanne Van Dijk, *Traces de femmes. Présence féminine dans le journalisme français du XVIIIe siècle* (Amsterdam & Maarssen: APA-Holland University Press, 1985).

Papers:

Madame de Beaumer's letters to the censors Malesherbes and Marin are at the Bibliothèque nationale in Paris.

Françoise-Albine Puzin de La Martinière Benoist

(3 October 1731 – circa 1809)

Althea Arguelles Ling
University of Sydney

BOOKS: *Journal en forme de lettres, mêlé de critiques et d'anecdotes* . . . (N.p., 1757);

Mes Principes, ou la Vertu raisonnée . . . (Amsterdam & Paris: Cuissart, 1759);

Elisabeth . . . (Amsterdam: Arkstée & Merkus, 1766);

Célianne, ou les amans séduits par leurs vertus . . . (Amsterdam & Paris: Lacombe, 1766);

Lettres du colonel Talbert . . . (Amsterdam & Paris: Durand, 1767); republished as *Paméla françoise, ou la vertu en célibat et en mariage, dépeinte dans les lettres de Messieurs de Talbert & Mozinge; rédigées dans le goût des lettres de Clarisse & Grandisson par Madame Riccoboni . . . Nouvelle édition*, 2 volumes (Amsterdam & The Hague: At the expense of the company, 1768);

Agathe et Isidore (Amsterdam & Paris: Durand, 1768);

Le Triomphe de la probité, comédie en deux actes et en prose; imité de l'Avocat, comédie de Goldoni (Paris: Le Jay, 1768);

La Supercherie réciproque, comédie en un acte et en prose (Amsterdam & Paris: Durand, 1768);

Sophronie, ou leçon prétendue d'une mère à sa fille (London & Paris: Duchesne, 1769);

L'Erreur des désirs (Paris: Veuve Regnard & Demonville / Lyon: Cellier / Rouen: Abraham Lucas, 1770);

Folie de la prudence humaine (Amsterdam & Paris: Regnard & Demonville, 1771);

Les Erreurs d'une jolie femme, ou l'aspasie françoise (Brussels & Paris: Duchesne, 1781); republished as *Les Aveux d'une jolie femme*, 2 volumes (Brussels & Paris: Duchesne, 1782);

Lettres sur le désir de plaire; suivies de, Ce que c'est que l'occasion: conte moral . . . (Amsterdam, 1786).

Edition: *Journal en forme de lettres, mêlé de critiques et d'anecdotes* and *Célianne, ou les amans séduits par leurs vertus*, introduction, biography, and bibliography by Olga B. Cragg (Saint-Etienne: Publications de l'Université de Saint-Etienne, 2002).

SELECTED PERIODICAL PUBLICATION–UNCOLLECTED: *Journal des dames* (February 1759): 80–86; (April 1759): 37–46; (July 1761): 53–66; (September 1761): 212–224.

The publication on 3 January 1766 of her novel *Elisabeth* caused a stir in Parisian society and in the life of Françoise-Albine Puzin de La Martinière Benoist. Louis Petit de Bachaumont mentioned this second novel by Benoist in his memoirs (6 July 1768), praising its natural style and exacting depiction of characters. Her novels were appreciated for their realism and the mise-en-scène of paradoxical situations comprising virtue and vice. Her confidence in *Elisabeth* and its evident public success encouraged her to send a copy (accompanied by a 15 December 1765 letter through his friend Nicolas Claude Thieriot) to Voltaire, who represented the epitome of literary accomplishment. Benoist's gesture demonstrates a certain daring and desire to be recognized. Voltaire responded in a letter that has been lost. Thieriot described Benoist as attractive and elegant, adding that she displayed wit and refinement (Letter 12172). The quality of her writing was recognized early in her career by the Accademia dell'Arcadia. (Academy of Arcadia) in Rome, which accepted her as a member. The *Mercure* (January 1766) notes that in Paris, dinners were given and verses composed in her honor to show appreciation of her talent and to celebrate the popularity of her novels. She publicly expressed her political opinions regarding women by writing articles for *Journal des dames* (1761), published by Charles de Champignol, treasurer of Lyon. She also showed a willingness to achieve her feminist goals by joining the *Francs-maçonnes* (Female Freemasons), who held the ideal of emancipation. The nineteenth and twentieth centuries did not share this appreciation of Benoist, and only through scholarship in the late twentieth century has interest in her work been renewed.

While most biographies indicate 1724 as the year of her birth, a birth certificate in Lyon states that "Françoise" was born 3 October 1731, at the parish of Saint-Nizier. Benoist has sometimes been confused with Marie-Guillemine Leroux-Delaville Benoist, painter and disciple of Elisabeth Vigée-Lebrun and later of Louis David. What is known of Benoist's family comes from her birth certificate, which relays that her father,

Simon Puzin, was a cloth shearer and her mother was named Blandine Lucquet. Nothing else is known of her early life. A marriage certificate dated 22 April 1754 attests a union between Françoise Puzin and established silk painter Jean Marie Benoit [sic] at the Collegiate and Parochial Church of La Platière in Lyon. Other sources identify her husband as Simon-Clement Benoist, who was accepted at the Academy of Saint-Luc in 1762, a neoclassical academy inspired by Queen Christina of Sweden and founded in Rome (1690). The couple may have gone to Rome after their marriage.

Benoist was already writing and publishing in Lyon during the late 1750s. Her popularity was marked in the 1760s when she participated in the vogue of the epistolary novel, writing works that were sentimental and introspective but also ironic. Her protagonists were primarily women, mother and daughter, or older and wiser confidante and young protégée. She signed them Benoist, Mde B***, or Mme ***, although *L'Erreur des désirs* (1770, Error of Desires) is signed Françoise de La Martinière Benoist, the name by which Voltaire designated her to Thieriot. She was referred to as Mde Benoist in the *Mercure* and in the journal of Marie Daniel Bourrée de Corberon, later a French diplomatic envoy to Russia, who initially wrote her name as Mde Benoît. Her first novel, *Journal en forme de lettres, mêlé de critiques et d'anecdotes* (Journal in the Form of Letters, Including Criticism and Anecdotes), was published in 1757, the same year as Marie-Jeanne Riccoboni's *Lettres de Mistriss Fanni Butlerd* (Letters of Mistress Fanni Butlerd) and ten years after Françoise de Graffigny's *Lettres d'une Péruvienne* (Letters of a Peruvian). The monophonic first person narrator describes to her friend in detail her occupations throughout the day, while critiquing events as an insider of society; she wittily comments on a performance of Molière's *Les Femmes savantes* (1672, The Learned Ladies) and on François Marie de Marsy's *Analyse raisonnée de Bayle* (1755), comments that displeased the Lyonnais. Joseph de La Porte, in his *Histoire littéraire des femmes françoises* (1769), surmises that Benoist left Lyon because readers there found "malicious allusions" where she only meant "moral observations."

By 1765 she was in Paris, a widow. In a letter to Voltaire, Thieriot recounts a visit he made to Benoist on which he found her living in opulence. The reason he gave was that her husband, a renowned painter of flowers and decoration for French royalty, had left her well off. Her second novel, *Elisabeth,* a novel that Thieriot incorrectly designated as her first, like its predecessor, is epistolary, consisting of letters written by the title character, "âgée de 24 ans, accoutumée à réfléchir, dont le coeur et le jugement sont formés" (twenty-four years of age, accustomed to thinking, and whose heart and judgment are mature), who writes to her friend Madame d'Albi about her feelings for Luzan, a member of the Knights of Malta. The novel was so popular that it was reprinted three times in one year. The *Mercure,* after its first announcement, ran a second, longer article describing the contents of the book. Its realism attracted readers, and the *Mercure* (February 1766) calls it "une peinture exacte de nos moeurs; d'où résulte un excellent traité de morale, propre à inspirer la vertu" (an exact painting of our mores; from which results an excellent moral treatise that inspires virtue), an opinion shared by Bachaumont (3 January 1766). Friendship, love, and virtue are the themes of the plot. The deep friendship between the two women is expressed by Elisabeth herself in the following terms: "Ma tendresse pour toi . . . a toujours été si vive depuis que je t'ai connue . . . que je n'ai respiré que pour t'aimer" (My feelings for you . . . have always been so strong since I've known you, . . . that I breathed only so I could love you). Even her love for Luzan is expressed in relation to the friendship between the two women: "Et devois-je attendre si tard pour te donner un rival?" (And did I have to wait so long to give you a rival?). Mme d'Albi counsels her young friend with an incongruous statement that is a recurring theme in Benoist's works: "l'enthousiasme de la vertu égare plus d'amans que la volupté n'en séduit" (enthusiasm for virtue leads astray more lovers than sensuality may seduce).

Later in the year 1766, Benoist published *Célianne, ou les amans séduits par leurs vertus* (Célianne, or Lovers Seduced by Their Virtues), a novel that plays on the tensions that arise between friends and lovers, virtue and vice. The title page identifies it as written by "l'auteur d'*Elisabeth,*" a phrase that attests to the wide reception of the latter novel. Two more editions followed in 1767 and 1768; in 1785 it was translated into Italian. In its preface the author states that the purpose of her novel is "de montrer . . . le danger d'une amitié trop intime entre des personnes engagées, conçue même avec les intentions les plus pures & formée sous les auspices de l'innocence" (to show . . . the danger of a too intimate friendship between persons otherwise attached, conceived even with the purest intentions and created under the auspices of innocence). The novel has been compared to Riccoboni's *Histoire d'Ernestine* (1762, Ernestine's Story) as well as to Jean-Jacques Rousseau's *La Nouvelle Héloïse* (1761, The New Heloise). Benoist imagines emotional variants and permutations of *amitié amoureuse* (romantic friendship) in the context of arranged marriages. The title character, who marries, in accordance with her parents' wishes, a man for whom she feels indifference, is described as "jeune, belle, aimable, vertueuse, mais coquette, avoit, sans s'en douter, un penchant extrême à l'amour: l'habitude de

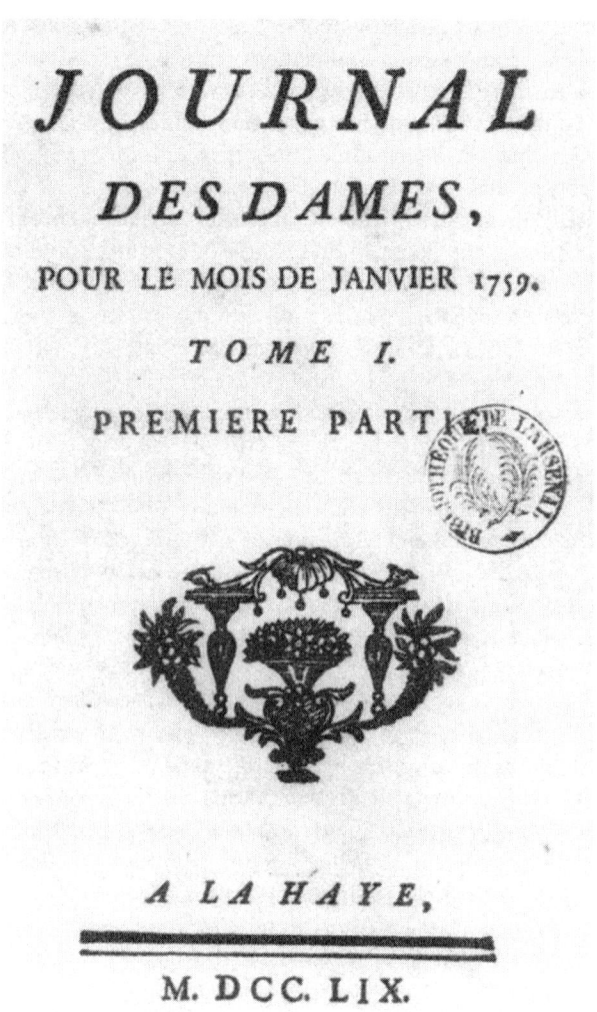

Title page for the first issue of the magazine in which Françoise-Albine Puzin de La Martinière Benoist expressed her political opinions about women (from Nina Rattner Gelbart, Feminine and Opposition Journalism in Old Regime France, 1987; Thomas Cooper Library, University of South Carolina)

réfléchir & un système de conduite, basé sur ses remarques plus que sur ses inclinations, lui faisoit maîtriser ses passions" (young, beautiful, amiable, virtuous, but coquettish, having, without a doubt, an extreme penchant for love without suspecting it: her habit of thinking and her system of behavior, based on her remarks more than on her inclinations, made her master her passions). The friend is the estimable and modest Mozime, introduced to her by her husband. The pleasure Célianne and Mozime take in each other's company soon becomes a danger, but their virtue saves them, and Mozime marries another. All complications are resolved, and both couples spend time together and take pleasure in each other's company.

In 1767, more than a decade before Pierre Choderlos de Laclos's *Les Liaisons dangereuses* (1782, Dangerous Liaisons), Benoist created a character who is a menacing libertine, Talbert in *Lettres du colonel Talbert* (Letters of Colonel Talbert), a novel that has been compared to Samuel Richardson's *Clarissa* (1747, 1748). Talbert reveals to Mozinge, his esteemed and moral correspondent, his plans and subsequent actions to seduce the virtuous Hélène. In her preface Benoist states her intention to "Imprimer l'horreur du vice, inspirer des sentimens d'humanité, faire naître le désir de devenir vertueux" (to imprint the horror of vice, inspire feelings of humanity, and engender the desire to become virtuous) while at the same time entertaining her readers and capturing their esteem. In doing so, she includes herself in the category of those she names *écrivain moral* (moral writer). To distance herself from the odious character to whom she gives words, she claims that she did not need to study real-life models in order to create him because "le seul secours de la mémorie suffit" (the sole recourse of memory suffices). Hélène refuses Talbert, thus reflecting the author's desire for her female character not to be a victim. However, Hélène dies after falling off a ladder in her effort to escape.

Theatricality in her novels was valued by readers of the time, as the critic of *Elisabeth* in the *Mercure* (February 1766) pointed out: "il faut lire dans l'ouvrage même une assemblée de parens qui forme une scène vraiment théâtrale" (the work itself shows an assembly of relations which form a truly theatrical scene). After producing a corpus of acclaimed novels, Benoist published two plays that were never produced, both of which deal with a young woman on the verge of inheritance or marriage or both. The first one, *Le Triomphe de la probité* (1768, The Triumph of Integrity), a comedy in two acts and in prose, adapted from Carlo Goldoni's *L'Avocat* (1749, The Lawyer), figures the lawyer Jersan, who is about to appear in court to appeal for the inheritance of his client, Sainvil. Jersan discovers too late that his beloved, Lucille, is the adversary. Sainvil, who knows of Jersan's infatuation and suspects that his lawyer may not defend his interests fully, already sees himself the loser. To cut his losses, he proposes to marry Lucille, who refuses him. Jersan comes back to declare that Sainvil has won his case and asks Lucille's hand in marriage. *La Supercherie réciproque* (1768, Mutual Trickery) a comedy in one act and in prose, features the story of Rosalie, who was raised in the house of the count of Orbac, her guardian and, though he does not want it revealed, her uncle. Diapason, under the name of the marquis de Fleville, is her music teacher, and he wants to marry her, but her uncle is opposed. Rosalie holds chivalric ideas regarding Diapason's identity—that is, she thinks he is of nobility—and this notion makes her vulnerable to his wiles.

To the end of the 1760s Benoist continued her experiments on the paradox of vice and virtue with *Sophronie, ou leçon prétendue d'une mère à sa fille* (1769, Sophronie, or Supposed Lesson of a Mother to Her Daughter), in which the title character, a thirty-one-year-old widow, attempts to give a lesson on virtue to her fifteen-year-old daughter, Adelle. Sophronie wants to demonstrate how to refuse a man's advances but at the same time tries to seduce her object, Valzan, who in reality is in love with her daughter. The plot concludes with Sophronie arranging Adelle's mariage to Valzan. *L'Erreur des désirs* focuses on the daughter who does not heed her mother's fearful intuitions about the man she wants to marry.

Benoist's production waned during the 1770s, but her reputation lingered. From 14 January 1775 to 20 June 1775 Corberon in his journal described Benoist and her young daughter, Josuel, whose date of birth was between 1755 and 1765. They lived in Paris on the rue Neuve St. Eustache, the same street as Madame l'Epine, whose concerts they frequented and where they encountered the young Manon Roland, in what one can surmise as the present-day Forum-des-Halles neighborhood. Corberon met with them often, for he shared an appreciation for poetry and writing with Benoist, drawing and painting with her daughter, and a certain attraction for the daughter as well. He was aware of Benoist's novels, such as *Colonel Talbert* and *L'Erreur des désirs*. He added that mother and daughter were freemasons, a circumstance that marked them as women who aspired to equality: 1774 was the year when lodges for women received official status.

The exact date and circumstances of Benoist's death are not known; Manon Roland remembers and writes about her on 28 August 1793 but does not indicate if she was still living. Some sources, such as the *Dictionnaire des journalistes* (1976), give the date of her death as 1789, but the commonly accepted one in early biographies is 1809, in Lyon. Benoist was a writer appreciated for her natural style and the realism of the characters and events she described, a reputation that did not continue, however, into the following centuries.

Letter:

François Marie Arouet dit Voltaire, *Correspondance* (Paris: Gallimard, Bibliothèque de la Pléiade, 1983), VIII: Letter 12172.

Biographies:

Joseph de La Porte, *Histoire littéraire des femmes françaises* (Paris, 1769), V: 309–379;

A. V. Arnault, A. Jay, E. Jouy, J. Norvins, and others, "Françoise-Albine Benoist," in *Biographie nouvelle des contemporains ou dictionnaire historique et raisonné, de tous les hommes qui, depuis la révolution française, ont acquis de la célébrité* (Paris: Librairie historique, 1824), II, 351;

Michel Gilot, "Françoise-Albine Benoist," in *Dictionnaire des journalistes (1600–1789),* under the direction of Jean Sgard (Grenoble: Presses universitaires de Grenoble, 1976), pp. 33–34;

Joan Hinde Stewart, "Françoise Albine Benoist," in *Feminist Encyclopedia of French Literature,* edited by Eva Martin Sartori (Westport, Conn.: Greenwood Press, 1999), pp. 49–50.

References:

Louis Petit de Bachaumont, *Mémoires secrets pour servir à l'histoire de la République des Lettres en France, depuis 1752 jusqu'à nos jours* (London: John Adamson, 1780), XIII: January 1766, p. 280; July 1766, p. 149;

Marie Daniel Bourrée de Corberon, *Journal* (A scientific cooperation of SHADYC, Sociologie, histoire et anthropologie des dynamiques culturelles UMR 8562-EHESS-CNRS, Marseille; Université Paul-Valéry, Montpellier III, with the support of revues.org, a Federation of University Revues), January–June 1775 <http://egodoc.revues.org/corberon/> [accessed on 18 January 2004];

Suzanna van Dijk, *Françoise-Albine Benoist (1724–1809)* (Igitur: Utrecht Publishing and Archiving Services) <http://www.roquade.nl/womenwriters/fr/publish/issues/Benoist_index.html> [accessed on 9 January 2004];

van Dijk, *Traces de femmes. Présence féminine dans le journalisme français du XVIIIe siècle* (Amsterdam: APA-Holland University Press, 1988);

M. M. Krings, *Madame Benoît, eine 'romancière oubliée' des 18 Jahrhunderts* (Aix-la-Chapelle, 1982);

"*Une personne, charmé du nouveau roman d'Elisabeth, donna une fête à Madame***, auteur de cet ouvrage,*" *Mercure de France* (January 1766): 71, 131;

Jeanne Marie ou Manon Phlipon Roland de la Platière, *Mémoires particuliers de Mme Roland,* introduced and annotated by Paul de Roux (Paris: Mercure de France, 1986), pp. 279–280;

Jeff Ravel, David Trott, and Mark Bannister, eds., *CESAR Calendrier Electronique des spectacles sous l'ancien régime* <http://cesar.org.uk/cesar2/home.php> [accessed on 18 January 2004].

Bernardin de Saint-Pierre
(19 January 1737 – 21 January 1814)

Malcolm Cook
University of Exeter, U.K.

BOOKS: *Voyage à l'Isle de France à l'Isle Bourbon, au Cap de Bonne-Espérance . . . avec des observations nouvelles sur la nature et les hommes,* 2 volumes (Amsterdam & Paris: Merlin, 1773); translated by John Parish as *A Voyage to the Island of Mauritius, or Isle of France, the Isle of Bourbon, the Cape of Good-Hope . . . With Observations and Reflections upon Nature and Mankind* (London: W. Griffin, 1775);

Etudes de la nature, 3 volumes (Paris: De l'Imprimerie de Monsieur, 1784); second edition corrected and enlarged as 4 volumes, 1787–1788–volume 4 comprises the first publication of *Paul et Virginie* and *L'Arcadie;* translated by Henry Hunter as *Studies of Nature,* 5 volumes (London: Printed for C. Dilly, 1796)–volume 5 comprises *Paul and Virginia* and *Arcadia;*

Paul et Virginie (Paris: De l'Imprimerie de Monsieur, 1789); translated by Daniel Malthus as *Paul and Mary: An Indian Story* (London: Printed for J. Dodsley, 1789);

Voeux d'un solitaire (Paris: De l'Imprimerie de Monsieur, Chez P. F. Didot jeune, 1789);

La Chaumière indienne (Paris: De l'Imprimerie de Monsieur, Chez P. F. Didot jeune, 1791); translated by R. A. Kendall as *The Indian Cottage* (London: Printed for John Bew, 1791);

La Mort de Socrate . . . précédé d'un essai sur les journaux, et suivi d'un discours académique (Paris: P. Didot, 1808).

Editions: *Oeuvres complètes,* edited by Louis Aimée-Martin (Paris: Méquignon-Marvis, 1818–1820);

Voyage à l'île de France: un officier du roi à l'île Maurice, 1768–1770, La Découverte, no. 69 (Paris: Maspéro, 1983);

Voyage à l'isle de France, edited by Robert Chaudenson (Rose-Hill, Mauritius: La Découverte/Maspéro, 1986);

Paul et Virginie, edited by Edouard Guitton, Classiques Garnier (Paris: Garnier, 1989);

Empsaël et Zoraïde, ou les blancs esclaves des noirs à Maroc, edited by Roger Little (Exeter: Exeter University Press, 1995);

Bernardin de Saint-Pierre (engraving from Marie-Therese Veyrenc, Edition critique du manuscrit de 'Paul et Virginie,' *1975; Thomas Cooper Library, University of South Carolina)*

Paul et Virginie, edited by Jean-Michel Racault (Paris: Livre de Poche, 1999).

Bernardin de Saint-Pierre is known to scholars today primarily as the author of a best-selling novel, *Paul et Virginie* (translated as *Paul and Virginia,* 1796), which first appeared in 1788 as part of volume four of the 1787–1788 edition of *Etudes de la nature* (1784; translated as *Studies of Nature*, 1796). The novel is the account of young love on an island in the Indian Ocean, a work that is often described as poetic because of its lyrical passages. A story of tragic love in which circumstances and events work against a happy outcome, *Paul et Virginie* has been called the first major exotic novel in France. A story rich in religious imagery, it prefigures the debate about republicanism during the French Revolution; it both seeks to address the ills of contemporary France and points to a solution in another world. Also a novel of education, it paints an idyllic picture of two young children raised in what seems to be an island paradise–but in this paradise the horrors of slavery become apparent to the children, and a wealthy population of French colonials thrives against a backdrop of poverty and misery. The novel had immense influence: quoted throughout the nineteenth century by writers as a formative text, it was much admired by the generation of writers that succeeded Bernardin. However, he was not simply the author of a single novel. His *Etudes de la nature* met with significant contemporary success and brought him to the attention of the intellectual public. He was a major literary figure of the final years of the ancien régime in France and was active in the French Revolution, both as an intellectual and as a significant element of the Parisian cultural landscape. No doubt the success of the *Etudes de la nature* was the reason behind the king's decision to offer him the intendance of the Jardin du Roi (Garden of the King) in July 1792, a post he occupied for a year until the position was suppressed by the National Convention. Because of Bernardin, the gardens acquired a menagerie and established a major museum that incorporated the museum from Chantilly, of which Bernardin supervised the physical move. During the later years of the revolution, Bernardin was active in the Ecole Normale Supérievre as professeur de morale républicaine (professor of republican morality).

Jacques-Henri Bernardin de Saint-Pierre was born in Le Havre on 19 January 1737 into a lower-middle-class household with noble ambitions; his father was Nicolas de Saint Pierre, and his mother was Catherine Godebout. The family claimed to have aristocratic status, and Bernardin used the title "chevalier," which suggested a noble background he did not have. In 1749 Bernardin accompanied his uncle on a sea voyage to the island of Martinique. The trip was not a success: Bernardin hated the voyage and suffered badly from seasickness and homesickness. He was similarly averse to the kind of education he received at the hands of the Jesuits in Caen and Rouen. However, in 1757 (or possibly 1755) he was awarded a prize for mathematics by the Académie de Caen, studied at the Université de Caen, and entered the Ecole des Ponts et Chaussées to train as an engineer. Although he did not finish his studies because of the outbreak of war, Bernardin was awarded a diploma, and he joined the army of the comte de Saint-Germain in Germany. He quarreled with his superiors, though, and returned to Versailles. He was offered the chance of joining other engineers who were being sent to Malta, then threatened by an invasion from the Turks. This proposition came to nothing; he was argumentative with his fellow engineers, and his complaints to the French ministry led them to believe that they were dealing with a difficult and unstable personality. The early 1760s were trying times for Bernardin; in 1762 he sold his few possessions and left for Holland, moving from there to St. Petersburg. In St. Petersburg he met a Swiss jeweler, Louis-David Duval, with whom he stayed in contact for many years. Few details about his period in Russia have survived, but he was made lieutenant and then captain and left St. Petersburg for Moscow. He then undertook a spying mission to Finland in order to assess the military status of the country, and he produced a report for Catherine II, the manuscript of which survives in Le Havre.

In 1764, encouraged by the baron de Breteuil, who was the French ambassador in Russia, Bernardin left Russia for Poland. The details of this period of his life are not clear; the correspondence suggests that he became a kind of secret agent working on behalf of the prince de Conti (grandson of François-Louis, elected king of Poland in 1697), working with the Radziwill faction against the Poniatowski faction backed by Russia. In 1765 Bernardin made his way to Berlin and sought an audience with Frederick the Great. In November 1765 Bernardin returned to France. Life in Paris was difficult as he sought employment. His correspondence from this period clearly indicates that he was working out the theories he later published in the *Etudes de la nature*. Eventually, he joined an expeditionary force, ostensibly going to the Ile de France (Mauritius) but actually intending to go to Madagascar. He left Lorient in February 1768 but argued with his superior, left the ship at Mauritius, and was employed as an engineer on the island. There he formed an acquaintance with a man called Poivre, a senior administrator on the island, for whose philosophy Bernardin had the greatest admiration. Bernardin crossed the island on foot and describes his journey and his stay on the island in his first publication, *Voyage à l'Isle de France à l'Isle Bourbon, au Cap de Bonne-Espérance* (1773, translated as *A Voyage to the Island of Mauritius, or Isle of France, the Isle of Bourbon, the Cape of Good-Hope,* 1775), published after his return to France in 1771. *Voyage à l'Isle de France à l'Isle Bourbon, au Cap de Bonne-Espérance* is a fascinating account of Bernardin's journey to the Indian Ocean, which also includes

First page of the manuscript of Bernardin's best-known work, about young love on an island in the Indian Ocean (from Marie-Therese Veyrenc, Edition critique du manuscrit de 'Paul et Virginie,' *1975; Thomas Cooper Library, University of South Carolina)* a brief description of Brittany. The journey led Bernardin into philosophical reflections about the relationship between poverty and liberty.

Bernardin left the island on 9 November 1770. The circumstances of his departure are not clear, and he spent many years asking the French authorities to recognize his service and give him a pension. While his pleas were not successful, he eventually managed to appeal to royal charity and for many years was given the kind of financial support that allowed him to write his major works and to offer assistance to his sister, Catherine, who was in a convent in Normandy. Bernardin's letters to her have not survived, but hers to him have, giving an account of her struggle with poverty in Normandy.

The baron de Breteuil, whom Bernardin had known in Russia, was at first supportive of Bernardin's claims for financial compensation, but the relationship did not last. During this period Bernardin became acquainted with the influential writers known as the philosophes. He was a visitor to the salon of Mlle de Lespinasse, where he met Jean Le Rond d'Alembert, an editor of the *Encyclopédie* (1751–1772). A year later, in 1772, Bernardin met and formed a friendship with Jean-Jacques Rousseau that, in spite of certain periods of coldness, lasted until Rousseau's death in 1778.

Tradition says that Bernardin first read extracts of his novel *Paul et Virginie* in the salon of Suzanne Necker in 1777. Clearly, the novel, based to a large extent on Bernardin's memory of Mauritius, was the result of many years of reflection and reworking. During the same year, Bernardin was writing a text that he entered into a competition organized by the Académie de Besançon on the following question: *Comment l'éducation des femmes pourrait contribuer à rendre les hommes meilleurs*. This essay, published posthumously in *Oeuvres Complètes*, shows Bernardin's admiration for women and points to themes of later works. These years were difficult ones for Bernardin, as he lived on the breadline in Paris and suffered from poor health. In 1779 he became involved in the affairs of his brother, Dutailli, who was accused of treason and locked up in the Bastille. Many surviving papers give details of this affair, and Bernardin argued for his brother's release in vain. He wrote a long text that describes the background of the accusation; indications show now that the brother was guilty of the crime of which he was accused–but evidence of madness finally led Bernardin to ask that his brother be locked up.

The next major event in Bernardin's life was the publication of the *Etudes de la nature*. Thanks to financial support from his friend Pierre-Michel Hennin, a career diplomat whom Bernardin had met on his travels, the *Etudes de la nature* appeared in June 1784. With the success of *Etudes de la nature* Bernardin was able to purchase a small house and to pay off all his debts. The 1787–1788 edition of the *Etudes de la nature* laid the foundation for Bernardin's enduring popularity, particularly since the fourth volume included *Paul et Virginie* and *L'Arcadie* (translated as *Arcadia*, 1796). Published as a single volume in 1789, *Paul et Virginie* became one of the literary phenomena of the age. In that same year, his *Voeux d'un solitaire* (Wishes of a Solitary Man) was published, which reflects his thoughts on the evolving politics of the French Revolution. Bernardin sought to achieve a certain respectability during these difficult times of the Revolution by claiming, with some justification, that he had always been a defender of the people, and *Voeux d'un solitaire* allowed him to express these thoughts in writing.

In 1791 he published a short philosophical novel, *La Chaumière indienne* (translated as *The Indian Cottage*, 1791), interpreted by some contemporaries as a satire of Catholic religion. Readers then and since have, on the whole, failed to sense the irony of the text, in which the author seeks to define the foundations of a life of happiness. Similarities between the message of *Paul et Virginie* and that of this short novel, based on an attempt originating in London to seek truth in the world, are remarkable. Bernardin is now considered a deist because of the message that emerges from the novel. Later, Bernardin commented on the relationship between the republic and religion–claiming that atheism had led to the destruction of morality and to political crimes.

In July 1792 Bernardin was, somewhat surprisingly, appointed by the king to be the intendant of the Jardin du Roi and of its museum. He also argued that the garden should have a menagerie. Bernardin had no formal horticultural training, and his appointment was not popular with the specialists who found themselves working under him. He kept the post for just one year, but he was compensated for his loss of it and for the considerable expenses that he paid out in order to live in the official residence. In July 1792 he published a pamphlet, *Invitation à la concorde pour la fête de la Confédération* (Invitation to Union for the Confederation), an appeal for moderation at a time when the political reality was about to change radically. Yet, it seems to have done Bernardin no damage, and he continued to live in Paris in relative freedom when others were imprisoned and executed. Bernardin could have participated in the National Convention, but he claimed that his health was not good enough. He claimed in a 1792 letter that he had worked for the republic by his writing and that he had defended the interests of people living in the country, sailors, soldiers, workers, slaves in the colonies, and all people who lived in wretched conditions.

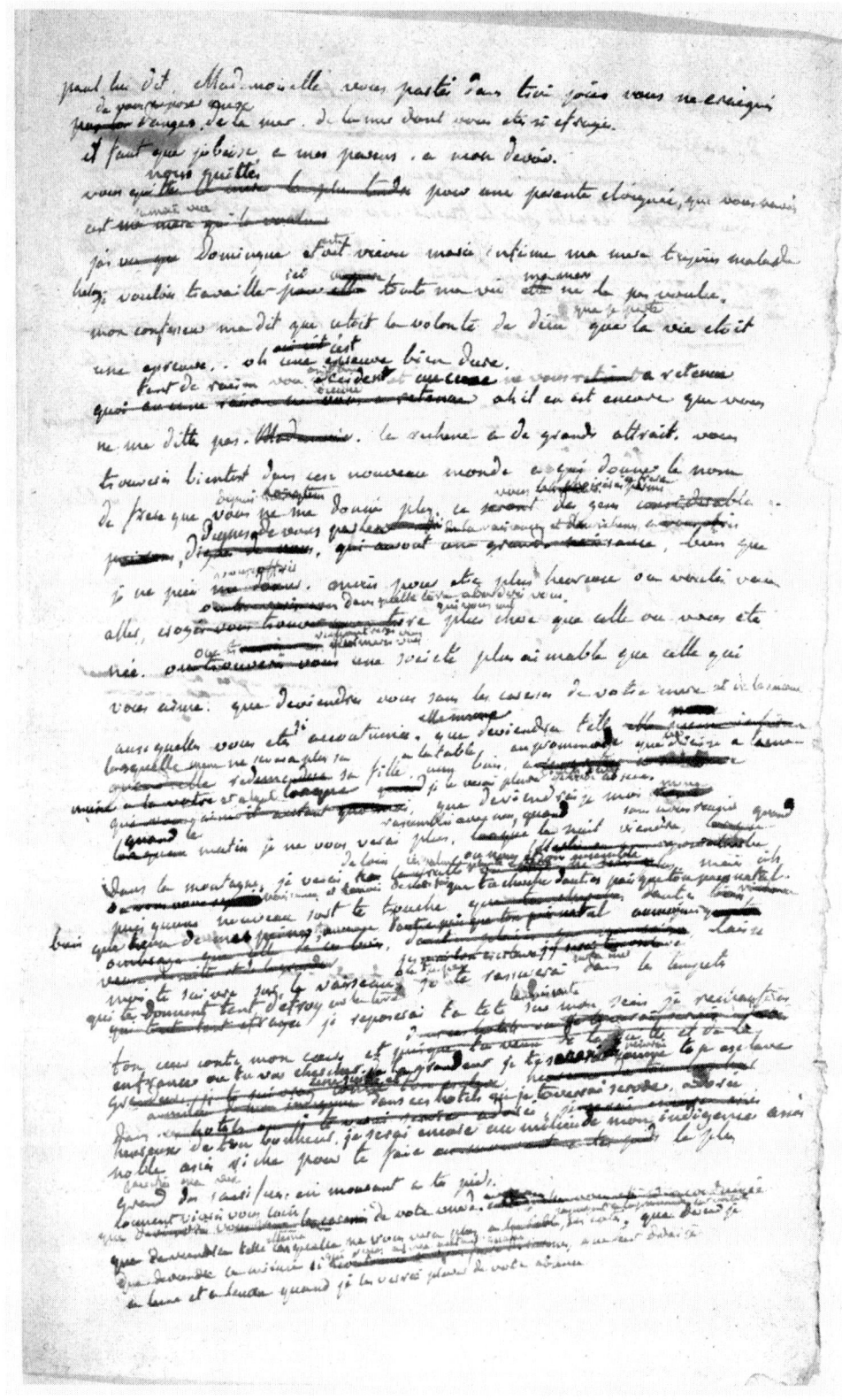

Page from the manuscript of Bernardin de Saint-Pierre's Paul et Virginie (1788), (Bibliotheque nationale; from Roselyn and Jean-Pierre Gueno, eds., Belles Lettres: Manuscripts by the Masters of French Literature, 2001; Bruccoli Clark Layman Archives)

Illustration by J. B. Huet; from the 1934 Paris edition of Bernardin's Paul et Virginie *(Thomas Cooper Library, University of South Carolina)*

He also pointed out that his role in the Jardin du Roi was further evidence of his work for the people and for the republic. He left Paris for the country and took up residence in Essonnes, just outside the capital. In 1793 he married a much younger woman, Félicité, the daughter of his printer, Didot. Their first child, Virginie, was born in 1794, the year Bernardin became professor of republican morality in the Ecole Normale Supérievre. Bernardin's emphasis on belief in the divinity and his somewhat bizarre scientific theories—for example, he maintained that tides were created not by the force of gravity but by the thawing and freezing of the polar ice caps—were not popular with his young audience. When the school was closed in 1795, Bernardin was made a member of the newly created Institut, where, again, his deist views were not well received. Nevertheless, throughout this period he continued to work on his literary production—much of it not published during his lifetime; the texts, which eventually were published posthumously by his secretary, Louis Aimée-Martin, were sometimes freely edited.

Bernardin's second child, Paul, was born in 1798, but a year later Bernardin's young wife died. A second marriage followed in 1800 when Bernardin, now aged sixty-three, married a young woman of just twenty. They had a son, Bernardin, in 1802, who died in early childhood. By this time, Bernardin was an old man, but he continued to be active in literary terms, entering the Académie française in 1803 and becoming its president in 1807. During this period he became a supporter of Napoleon, from whom he received a grant to educate his daughter, Virginie. Bernardin became a kind of elder statesman whom the state honored and feted.

In 1806 he completed work on the luxury quarto edition of his novel *Paul et Virginie;* although beautifully illustrated and presented, the edition was not a commercial success. In 1808 he published the play *La Mort de Socrate* (The Death of Socrates), in which the eponymous hero becomes a spokesman for Bernardin's philosophical views. Toward the end of his life, Bernardin retired to live in Eragny (Oise), where he seems to have come to terms with the Catholic church. He died on 21 January 1814, aged seventy-seven.

Bernardin de Saint-Pierre was a major figure of the late French Enlightenment. Once he became established as a writer in Paris, his views were respected. In spite of his early escapades, he was not a man of action but an intellectual with deep convictions. Although he is best remembered as the author of a short novel that has never been out of print, he was also recognized as perhaps the major intellectual of his age.

Letters:

Louis Aimée-Martin, ed., *Correspondance de J-H. Bernardin de Saint-Pierre,* 4 volumes (Paris: L'advocat, 1826).

Biographies:

Louis Aimée-Martin, *Essai sur la vie et les ouvrages de Bernardin de Saint-Pierre* (Paris: Méquignon-Marvis, 1820);

Arvède Barine, *Bernardin de Saint-Pierre* (Paris: Hachette, 1891);

Fernand Maury, *Essai sur la vie et les oeuvres de Bernardin de Saint-Pierre* (Paris: Hachette, 1892; Geneva: Slatkine Reprints, 1971);

Maurice Souriau, *Bernardin de Saint-Pierre d'après ses manuscrits* (Paris: Société française d'imprimerie et de librairie, 1905).

References:

"Bernardin de Saint-Pierre, Actes du colloque de la société littéraire de la France," *Revue d'histoire littéraire de la France,* 5 (September–October 1989);

Clifton Cherpack, "*Paul et Virginie* and the myths of death," *Publications of the Modern Language Association of America,* 90 (1975): 47–55;

Malcolm Cook, "Bernardin de Saint-Pierre: *Observations sur la Finlande,*" in *L'Invitation au voyage, Studies in Honour of Peter France,* edited by John Renwick (Oxford: Voltaire Foundation, 2000), pp. 119–139;

Cook, "Bernardin de Saint-Pierre: Unpublished Prose Fables," in *The Secular City, Studies Presented to Haydn Mason* (Exeter: Exeter University Press, 1994), pp. 154–169;

Cook, "Bernardin de Saint-Pierre, *Paul et Virginie:* Premier essai autographe de la conversation de Paul et du Vieillard," *Eighteenth-Century Fiction,* 9 (1997): 149–160;

Cook, "Bougainville and One Noble Savage," *Modern Language Review,* 89 (1994): 842–855;

Cook, "Childhood in the Works of Bernardin de Saint-Pierre," *Romance Studies,* 28 (1998): 17–27;

Cook, "Des moyens de vivre heureux en menant une vie naturelle: un texte inédit de Bernardin de Saint-Pierre," *Studies on Voltaire and the Eighteenth Century,* 358 (1998): 161–170;

Cook, "Discord and Harmony in *Paul et Virginie,*" *Eighteenth-Century Fiction,* 3 (1991): 205–216;

Cook, "Un inédit de Bernardin de Saint-Pierre: sur le nouveau dictionnaire de la langue française," *Revue d'histoire littéraire de la France,* 97 (1997): 119–125;

Cook, "La réception de *Paul et Virginie* dans la presse contemporaine," in *Journalisme et fiction au 18e siècle,* edited by Cook and Annie Jourdan (Bern: Peter Lang, 1999), pp. 189–195;

Cook, "Robinson Crusoe in Siberia: The Writing of a Novel in the Late Eighteenth Century," *Studies on Voltaire and the Eighteenth Century,* 317 (1994): 1–43;

Simon Davies, "*Paul et Virginie,* 1953–1991, The Present State of Studies," *Studies on Voltaire and the Eighteenth Century,* 317 (1994): 239–266;

Jean Fabre, "*Paul et Virginie,* pastorale," in his *Lumières et romantisme: énergie et nostalgie de Rousseau à Mickiewicz* (Paris: Klincksieck, 1980), pp. 225–227;

Richard A. Francis, "Bernardin de Saint-Pierre's *Paul et Virginie* and the Failure of the Ideal State in the Eighteenth-century French Novel," *Nottingham French Studies,* 13 (1974): 51–60;

Ingrid Kisliuk, "Le symbolisme du jardin et l'imagination créatrice chez Rousseau, Bernardin de Saint-Pierre et Chateaubriand," *Studies on Voltaire and the Eighteenth Century,* 185 (1980): 297–418;

Jean-Michel Racault, "*Paul et Virginie* et l'utopie. De la petite société au mythe collectif," *Studies on Voltaire and the Eighteenth Century,* 242 (1986): 419–471;

Racault, "Virginie entre la nature et la vertu: cohésion narrative et contradictions idéologiques dans *Paul et Virginie,*" *Dix-huitième siècle,* 18 (1986): 389–404;

Racault, ed., *Etudes sur 'Paul et Virginie' et l'oeuvre de Bernardin de Saint-Pierre* (Paris: Didier-Erudition, 1986);

Philip Robinson, *Bernardin de Saint-Pierre: 'Paul et Virginie,'* Critical Guides to French Texts, no. 51 (London: Grant & Cutler, 1986);

Robinson, "Virginie's Fatal Modesty: Thoughts on Bernardin de Saint-Pierre and Rousseau," *British Journal for Eighteenth-Century Studies,* 5 (1982): 35–48;

Paul Toinet, *'Paul et Virginie,' Répertoire bibliographique et iconographique* (Paris: Maisonneuve & Larose, 1963);

Kurt Wiedermeier, *La Religion de Bernardin de Saint-Pierre* (Fribourg: Editions universitaires, 1985).

Papers:

The majority of Bernardin de Saint-Pierre's papers—correspondence, drafts, and workbooks—are in the Bibliothèque Muncipale du Havre in France.

Georges-Louis Leclerc de Buffon

(7 September 1707 – 16 April 1788)

Jeff Loveland
University of Cincinnati

Georges-Louis Leclerc de Buffon (1777 engraving of a drawing by Andre Pujos; Bibliothèque centrale du Muséum national d'histoire naturelle, Paris; from Jean Piveteau, ed., Oeuvres philosophiques de Buffon, 1954, volume 41; Thomas Cooper Library, University of South Carolina)

BOOKS: *Histoire naturelle, générale et particulière*, 36 volumes, by Buffon, Louis-Jean-Marie Daubenton, and Philibert Guéneau de Montbeillard (Paris, 1749–1789)—comprises *Histoire naturelle, générale et particulière, avec la description du Cabinet du roi*, by Buffon and Daubenton, 15 volumes (Paris: Imprimerie royale, 1749–1767); *Histoire naturelle des oiseaux*, by Buffon and Montbeillard, 9 volumes (Paris: Imprimerie royale, 1770–1783); translated anonymously by Sir John Leslie as *The Natural History of Birds*, 9 volumes (London: A. Strahan, 1793); *Supplément à l'histoire naturelle*, 7 volumes (Paris: Imprimerie royale, 1774–1789)–includes "Epoques de la nature," in *Histoire naturelle des minéraux*, 5 volumes (Paris: publisher varies, 1783–1788);

Histoire naturelle, générale et particulière was translated and adapted in excerpt from at least 1751 onward; translated extensively but not completely by William Kenrick and J. Murdoch as *Natural History of Animals, Vegetables, and Minerals, with the Theory of the Earth in General*, 6 volumes (London: T. Bell, 1775–1776); by William Smellie as *Natural History, General and Particular, by the Count de Buffon*, 9 volumes (Edinburgh: William Creech, 1780–1785; the fourth, 1812 edition of this translation included Leslie's *Natural History of Birds*); by J. S. Barr as [Barr's Buffon]: *Buffon's Natural History, Containing a Theory of the Earth, A General History of Man, of the Brute Creation, and of Vegetables, Minerals, etc.*, 10 volumes (London: J. S. Barr, 1792).

Editions: *Oeuvres complètes de Buffon*, 14 volumes, edited by J.-L. [Jean-Louis] de Lanessan and H. Nadault de Buffon (Paris: Le Vasseur, 1884–1885);

Oeuvres philosophiques de Buffon, edited by Jean Piveteau (Paris: Presses universitaires de France, 1954).

TRANSLATIONS: Stephen Hales, *La statique des végétaux et l'analyse de l'air* (Paris: Debure, 1735);

Isaac Newton, *La méthode des fluxions et des suites infinies* (Paris: Debure, 1740).

Georges-Louis Leclerc de Buffon was one of the principal figures of the French Enlightenment, famous throughout Europe and North America as a philosopher-naturalist and a literary stylist. His *Histoire naturelle, générale et particulière* (1749–1789, Natural History, General and Particular), thirty-six volumes in the original edition in quarto, was one of the best-selling texts of the epoch. During Buffon's lifetime alone it appeared in nearly ten French editions and was translated incompletely into German, English, Italian, and Spanish. Reference works throughout Europe, from the *Encyclopédie* (1751–1772) to the *Encyclopaedia Britannica* (first edition, 1768–1771), copied Buffon's articles on animals, usually without naming him and sometimes supplementing them with nomenclature borrowed from his rival, Swedish classifier Carl Linnaeus. Buffon's theories of reproduction and geology, presented in the *Histoire naturelle,* were discussed if not accepted by almost everyone dealing with these subjects in the last half of the eighteenth century. A longtime member of the Académie Royale des Sciences and the Académie française, Buffon was most active institutionally in the Jardin du Roi, where he acted as intendant from 1739 onward. Thanks to Buffon's vision, audacity, and political connections, the Jardin du Roi doubled in size under his tenure. As intendant of this increasingly prestigious center for research, he wielded great scientific authority and nurtured the careers of several important naturalists–notably, Jean-Baptiste de Lamarck and Louis-Jean-Marie Daubenton.

Buffon–known originally as Georges-Louis Leclerc–was the oldest of five children born to Benjamin-François Leclerc and Anne-Cristine Marlin. Georges-Louis's first years were spent in Montbard, a small administrative center in Burgundy, where his father worked as a civil servant and tax collector. Thanks to an inheritance from Anne-Cristine's brother in 1717, Benjamin-François was able to buy his way into the lesser nobility and become a magistrate in the Burgundian *parlement*. The family moved to Dijon, where Georges-Louis studied at the Jesuit Collège des Godrans from 1717 to 1723 and then at the newly opened law school from 1723 to 1726. His father must have expected him to pursue a judicial, administrative career and ultimately inherit the position of magistrate, but Georges-Louis was already determined to explore other options. In 1727 he began exchanging letters on mathematical topics with Gabriel Cramer, a young professor at the Academy of Geneva. In 1728 he moved to Angers and studied mathematics, medicine, and botany, but his apparent involvement in a duel seems to have forced him to return to Dijon by 1730.

By the end of 1730, Buffon had embarked on the one extensive voyage he made in his life, accompanied by two Englishmen roughly his age, the second duke of Kingston and his preceptor, Nathan Hickman. Kingston and Hickman had already spent time in Dijon and Angers in 1729 and 1730, where Buffon must have met them. Like many sons of the British elite, Kingston had been sent abroad with his tutor to undertake a Grand Tour of France and Italy. With Buffon, between 1730 and 1732, he and Hickman passed successively through Nantes, Bordeaux, Toulouse, Montpellier, Lyon, Geneva, Turin, Milan, Genoa, Pisa, Florence, and Rome. In his letters Buffon described cities and their inhabitants, but nothing suggests he was interested in the natural history of the regions they passed through. At one time, scholars believed that Buffon traveled to England as Kingston's guest later in the 1730s, but Stephen Milliken has shown in his doctoral dissertation that this trip, though projected, never took place.

Buffon's mother died in 1731. In 1732, assisted by friends in the Dijon *parlement,* Buffon managed to defend his claim to her fortune against the bitter opposition of his now remarried father. This windfall enabled him to repurchase the village of Buffon–sold by his father in 1729–and thus justify his recent practice of calling himself Leclerc de Buffon. His wealth also gave him the leisure to pursue a career in the sciences. Established in Paris in 1732 at the residence of the chemist Gilles-François Boulduc, Buffon lost little time in making himself known to the Académie Royale des Sciences, the primary scientific institution of France. He was already familiar to several of its members–notably Boulduc, Alexis-Claude Clairaut (another correspondent of Cramer's on mathematical subjects), and Pierre-Louis de Maupertuis (a friend of Clairaut and a passionate defender of Isaac Newton's theory of gravity, as Buffon himself soon became). At the same time, Buffon won the attention and gratitude of powerful minister Jean-Frédéric Phélypeaux de Maurepas by responding to the latter's plea for studies of wood strength that would help the French navy. Buffon, a landowner with acres of forest, was able to step forth, whereas other academicians were forced to demur. In 1733 he began doing experiments on trees near Montbard. He remained involved in such studies, sometimes in collaboration with Henri-Louis Duhamel du Monceau, for the next forty years–though less and less after the 1730s.

During his travels, Buffon had maintained his mathematics correspondence with Cramer. In 1733 he presented his first paper, a memoir on probability theory, to the Académie Royale des Sciences. With it he is said to have inaugurated a new field of mathematics, geometrical probability. What he sought was the probability that a coin, a square token, or a needle dropped on a regularly tiled floor would come to rest on the lines. This problem is still known as "Buffon's needle problem." His solution shows both his strengths and his weaknesses as a mathematician: his bold synthesis was accompanied by a certain carelessness regarding details. The paper was favorably received in the Académie Royale des Sciences, and Buffon was invited to present another, this one examining the mechanics of a pendulum under particular circumstances. On the basis of these papers, not to mention his contacts and his favor with Maurepas, who oversaw appointments to the Académie Royale des Sciences, Buffon was appointed to the section on mechanics in 1734.

Through the 1730s Buffon's scientific interests ranged widely, from mathematics to such experimental sciences as arboriculture and chemistry. Emblematic of his breadth were the translations from English he undertook in this period. In 1735 he published a translation of Stephen Hales's *Vegetable Staticks* (1727), which dealt with the chemistry and physiology of plants from an experimental, Newtonian, mechanistic point of view. Then in 1740 he translated Isaac Newton's dated classic on calculus, *The Method of Fluxions and Infinite Series*, originally written in Latin but translated into English by John Colson in 1736. In his preface, Buffon repudiated his earlier, unproblematic acceptance of infinity and expressed caution about the use of ideas without concrete referents. Such concerns, which were amplified in the *Histoire naturelle*, may have pushed him to specialize in a more tangible field. In any case, he changed sections within the Académie Royale des Sciences in 1739, moving from mechanics to botany.

A few months later he was faced with the greatest opportunity of his life when the intendant of the Jardin du Roi, Charles de Cisternay du Fay, died unexpectedly of smallpox. Buffon began lobbying for the position at once and ultimately obtained it, thanks also to the efforts of his friends and patrons. Not only did the appointment come with a salary and a residence on the grounds of the Jardin du Roi, it also gave Buffon control over the policies and personnel of one of the most distinguished French centers for scientific research and teaching, especially in botany and pharmacy but also in chemistry, anatomy, and natural history in general. His appointment irked many in the Académie Royale des Sciences because of his lack of seniority relative to his main rival, Duhamel du Monceau. Even in the Jardin du Roi, brothers Bernard and Antoine Jussieu, both professors of botany, had supported Duhamel's candidacy.

From the mid 1730s onward, Buffon maintained a schedule that varied little to the end of his life. Extended summers were spent in Montbard, where he constructed a mansion and, on the bluff next to it, a park, a menagerie, a laboratory, and a study. Here he did experiments, made observations, and spent long hours writing and thinking, relatively protected from interference and distraction. During the winter he lived in Paris, attending meetings of the Académie des Sciences and grudgingly participating in the social life of the city. Even his new duties at the Jardin du Roi from 1739 onward did little to increase his time spent in

An illustration from Buffon's Histoire naturelle, *1749–1789 (from Jacques Roger,* Buffon, *1997; Thomas Cooper Library, University of South Carolina)*

Paris. Such independence was irritating to his more conventional colleagues.

At the time of his appointment to the Jardin du Roi, Buffon received a request from Maurepas to prepare a catalogue of the collections of the institution—a standard activity in early modern museums and gardens. Instead, around 1740, Buffon conceived the project of a multivolume natural history, only loosely based on the holdings of the Jardin du Roi, to be titled *Histoire naturelle, générale et particulière, avec la description du Cabinet du roi*. Not only did the title mention the proposed catalogue as an afterthought, but it also emphasized Buffon's ambition to cover not just particular natural history—the description of specific plants, animals, and minerals—but also general natural history, the theoretical aspect of the study of nature. René-Antoine

Ferchault de Réaumur, the leading naturalist in the Académie des Sciences, a man who had devoted decades to the detailed observation of insects, was immediately critical of Buffon's pretensions. Natural history, he argued, was not yet ready to advance to general truths. Around this time, Réaumur, probably also dismayed by Buffon's "conquest" of the intendancy of the Jardin du Roi, began to dislike his younger colleague, with whom he had been on good terms in 1735.

Though the first volumes of *Histoire naturelle* did not appear until 1749, Buffon was already preparing key texts by 1744. Still, his new dedication to natural history and the Jardin du Roi did not prevent him from engaging in other scientific matters. In 1747 he won a first taste of celebrity by assembling a network of "burning mirrors" capable of igniting targets through reflected sunlight at distances of up to two hundred feet—a variation on the weapon Archimedes was said to have designed to defend ancient Syracuse. Buffon's demonstrations of his mirrors, performed for audiences that included Louis XV among other notables, were all the more dramatic in that René Descartes had argued that such a feat was impossible. In 1748 Buffon entered a controversy over Newton's theory of gravity. The previous year Clairaut had "discovered" that the movements of the moon belied Newton's theory and had proposed slightly modifying it. Buffon reacted vehemently, citing mathematical, physical, and above all, metaphysical reasons for the necessity of the old law. In 1749 Clairaut found a mistake in his calculations and dropped his proposal, leaving Buffon to gloat over an unearned triumph. The episode may have reinforced his developing tendency to see Newtonian attraction as the key to explaining all of nature, not just gravitation.

In 1749 the first three volumes of *Histoire naturelle* were finally published. The title pages did not name an author, but Buffon co-signed the dedication to Louis XV with family friend Daubenton, whom he had brought from Montbard as an assistant in 1742. Daubenton fulfilled Maurepas's wish by describing the holdings of the Cabinet du Roi in volume three. Buffon, responsible for all of volumes one and two and much of volume three, limited himself to more theoretical matters. Volume one opened with a methodological essay, the "Premier Discours," in which Buffon condemned classification of natural history, especially Linnaeus's, which had been making inroads in France since around 1740. Most objectionable to Buffon was the practice of classifying plants and animals not by overall appearance but on the basis of a few chosen organs—a practice that could only lead to arbitrary results, he contended. The "Premier Discours" ended with a critique of mathematics, which Buffon argued was mere manipulation of symbols. As such, it could hardly be expected to be of much use in the "real" sciences, least of all natural history. Imperious in tone, aggressive in its claims, the "Premier Discours" was designed to be provocative, and so it was.

The "Premier Discours" grew out of an academic presentation Buffon made in 1744. Following it in volume one was another text written by Buffon in 1744, "Histoire et théorie de la terre" (History and Theory of the Earth). For one attempting as he was to write a general natural history, this subject was natural to turn to after methodology, since Earth could be seen as the cradle of the traditional kingdom of natural history. "Histoire et théorie" featured a description (a "history" in the language of eighteenth-century naturalists) of such terrestrial features as rivers, oceans, and mountains as well as a theory of the processes governing their formation. According to Buffon, water above all determined geography, whether through erosion or sedimentation, but he rejected as impious certain contemporaries' efforts to rationalize the biblical deluge—a momentous rejection because it effectively desacralized the study of the development of the Earth. In dismissing such rare, catastrophic events as earthquakes and volcanoes, not to mention the biblical deluge, as having little effect on the layout of the Earth, Buffon was following the methodology of the "Premier Discours," which made recurrent events the basis for physical truth. In an appendix to the main text, though, he went on to explain the formation of the planets by imagining the ultimate catastrophe—the near-collision of a comet with the sun, which tore out molten protoplanets. This famous "hypothesis" was crucial in establishing Buffon's reputation for bold speculation in the manner of Descartes.

Volume two set forth Buffon's theory of reproduction. By 1746, inspired by the ideas of Louis Bourguet and Maupertuis, Buffon had come to doubt the widely accepted doctrine of preformation, according to which offspring could be found fully formed before fertilization in the seeds of plants and the equivalent parts of animals. According to ovists, offspring were housed in eggs in the female, whereas animalculists placed them in the "animalcules" (spermatozoa) discovered by Antonie van Leeuwenhoek in 1687. Like Maupertuis, Buffon believed offspring developed only after fertilization—the doctrine of epigenesis—and that both males and females contributed materially. In his scheme, "organic molecules" from both parents' reproductive organs organized themselves into an embryo in virtue of microforces analogous to Newtonian gravity and an "internal mold" similar to the Aristotelian form. To verify his hypothesis, Buffon invited English microscopist John Turberville Needham to the Jardin du Roi in 1748. Among other things, they found that Leeuwenhoek's spermatozoa were unstable, energetic, often tailless globules and that females, too, had such structures in their Graafian follicles. Females, Buffon concluded, released spermatic fluid no less than males, and this fluid sustained combinations of active organic molecules, not preformed animalcules. Scholars have long assumed that these observations were simply faulty, despite Needham's expertise and the presence of witnesses, but Phillip R. Sloan has argued in his "Organic Molecules Revisited" (1992) that Buffon's microscope was so powerful that he was seeing beyond spermatozoa to smaller bodies, notably bacteria.

Buffon's treatment of reproduction, focused on animals, led into his examination of human beings in volumes two and three–a logical progression for an author who had been a materialist and perhaps an atheist for at least a decade already, but a problematic one for people of the eighteenth century, in that humans were supposed to transcend nature except in their bodies. To earn himself freedom to look at humans holistically, Buffon started the section with a half-Cartesian proof of the existence of an immaterial, immortal soul. Thereafter, he dealt with humans along both developmental and geographical axes, describing not only physical features but also behaviors and cultural practices. So broad was his view of the human species–he rejected the notion of races as species–that he is often counted among the founders of modern anthropology. His discussions of sexuality were frank and extensive, and so they remained throughout the series, offending certain readers but presumably titillating many more. To explain learning and thinking he turned to sensationism–a widespread doctrine making sensation the source of all knowledge–and illustrated it with a precious narrative showing how, as a just-created adult, he would have experienced his first day of life.

With the publication of the three volumes of 1749, *Histoire naturelle* became extremely popular and controversial. The sciences in general had been cultivated by the educated French public since the late seventeenth century. As a best-seller focused on natural history, the *Histoire naturelle* moved into territory already established by Noël-Antoine Pluche's *Spectacle de la nature* (1732–1750). As a multivolume compendium of natural knowledge, it rivaled the *Encyclopédie* (in which it was frequently copied and alluded to) through the 1750s and 1760s. Buffon's ideas on method, geology, and reproduction provoked vigorous rejoinders and were never much accepted by the scientific elite. On the other hand, his ideas formed a nearly obligatory point of reference in discussions of these subjects in the second half of the century, and nearly everyone appreciated the series as a source of information. Encouraged by the pious, the Sorbonne considered condemning *Histoire naturelle*, but Buffon negotiated an agreement by which the theological faculty would accept a fourteen-point retraction. In 1753, at the head of volume four, his retraction was printed, so unconditional and respectfully pious that many must have found it transparently hypocritical, especially insofar as he continued to publish the offending volumes without emendation and to display no less heterodoxy in subsequent volumes, albeit along with protests of faith. As this episode indicates, he preferred to placate the church rather than confront it in the style of many philosophes. With his critics in general, he avoided entangling himself in disputes, but he was not above seeking vengeance in subtle ways. After Réaumur helped a friend write a refutation of *Histoire naturelle*, Buffon avenged himself both by ridiculing entomology–Réaumur's specialty–in volume four and by championing Benjamin Franklin's electrical theory, which contradicted the views of one of Réaumur's favorite disciples.

In 1752 Buffon married twenty-year-old Marie-Françoise de Saint-Belin-Malain, who came from a poor but noble Burgundian family. With her he ultimately produced one child who survived infancy, Georges-Louis-Marie, nicknamed Buffonet, who had a difficult if privileged existence in the shadow of his celebrated father. After a disastrous marriage and a remarriage in 1793 to Betzy (Elisabeth-Georgette) Daubenton–Louis-Jean-Marie's grand-niece–he was guillotined in 1794, accused of betraying the French Revolution under mysterious circumstances.

Thanks to the perceived literary excellence of the first volumes, Buffon was admitted to the Académie Française in 1753. His inaugural speech, "Discours sur le style" as it came to be known, was published at once, to great acclaim, and also appeared in volume four of the *Supplément*. In "Discours sur le style" Buffon presented style as a matter of order and clarity more than of ornament. With typical self-assurance, he criticized the styles of others, without naming names, but in such a way as to implicate members of the listening Académie française. At one point he recommended using only the most general vocabulary. Citing this prescription, critics later argued that he was an imprecise writer, but beyond a small number of grandiose sections, *Histoire naturelle* is, in fact, rich in specific terminology. The most famous line of "Discours sur le style," "le style est l'homme même" (style is man himself), is often seen as anticipating Romantic, "personal" style, but Buffon was probably thinking of style as expressing authors' rational distinctiveness rather than their personality in the broad sense. Already in his lifetime, the "Discours sur le style" was sometimes interpreted as exalting style over substance. Certainly it provided ammunition for those disposed to dismiss him as a

Illustration for the hippopotamus from Buffon's Histoire naturelle
(from Jacques Roger, Buffon, *1997; Thomas Cooper Library, University of South Carolina)*

mere stylist. Buffon, for his part, was evidently happy to cultivate the myth of his style, for he increased the frequency and level of his renowned stylish passages starting with volume four in 1753.

In volume four, Buffon and Daubenton began examining animal species individually. In accordance with the antitaxonomical arguments of "Premier Discours," their treatment followed an order of European utility rather than any assumed order of nature. First came domestic animals, then animals traditionally hunted, then other Old World animals, and finally New World animals. Within this order, "similar" animals were frequently, and increasingly, treated together. Much of the zoological information in *Histoire naturelle* came from firsthand experience. Even exotic animals could sometimes be studied alive, whether in the royal menagerie or in a Parisian fair, but the authors were also forced to rely on informants and preserved specimens. Buffon described animals' appearances, habitats, food, reproduction, and habits. Then Daubenton, a physician retrained as a naturalist and anatomist, continued with a selective study of animals' anatomy—measuring organs, describing joints, comparing female and male anatomy, and so on. Evidently, Daubenton's sections were assumed to be of less interest to the public than Buffon's, for they were printed in smaller type—thirty lines per page rather than twenty-eight. Many, but not all, editions and translations of the series dropped Daubenton's anatomy, despite its acknowledged scientific value. Along with the texts prepared by Buffon and Daubenton, *Histoire naturelle* included plates showing animals in "natural" states as well as dissected. Jacques de Sève, the main artist, contributed more than 1,500 drawings to *Histoire naturelle*.

"Premier Discours" contends that classification is essentially arbitrary, but it is ambiguous enough to suggest that Buffon was already wondering if a "real" basis for taxonomy might be found. By 1751 he was doing experiments in his menagerie in Montbard to see if similar animals, such as the horse and the ass, could reproduce together. In accordance with a notion presented in volume two, he was considering defining species not by resemblance but by the capacity to produce fertile offspring together—the so-called "biological criterion" for species, previously countenanced by several other naturalists. Satisfied with this understanding of divisions in nature, Buffon proclaimed in 1753 that species—though not genera, classes, or families—were a real part of nature. Within species, he argued, degeneration brought on by climate, nutrition, and domestication created different varieties in the course of generations. In volume five he thus drew a map displaying genealogical and geographical relations among breeds of dogs. While recognizing that species could change over time, he insisted at this point that degeneration was circumscribed within narrow limits. By the end of his treatment of the quadrupeds, however, he saw degeneration as a more potent force. In 1766, in volume fourteen, he proposed that all quadrupeds had developed by degeneration from an original set of just thirty-eight species. Buffon's "transformism," restricted in scope and driven directly by environmental impingement rather than indirectly by natural selection, was never evolution in Charles Darwin's sense, despite the claims of certain commentators of the late nineteenth century. Darwin himself was more reasonable in merely citing Buffon in *The Origin of Species* (1859) as someone who had examined organic change "in a scientific spirit."

His quadrupeds finished, Buffon turned to birds. In so doing, he was not only respecting a vaguely anthropocentric logic but also taking advantage of his most recent acquisition. In 1757 Réaumur had died, and to the horror of his allies, the Jardin du Roi inherited his mineral samples, prepared insects, and stuffed animals, among them the largest collection of birds in Europe. Daubenton was not invited to write anatomy for *Histoire naturelle des oiseaux,* apparently because Buffon wanted the subseries completed quickly, and probably also because he first conceived it as being rich in illustrations and relatively light in description, but Buffon asked him to study whales for a projected subseries that Bernard-Germain-Etienne Lacépède finally published in 1804. Buffon suffered unexpected hardship in the course of *Histoire naturelle des oiseaux*. His wife died in 1769, and in 1771 he fell ill and came close to dying. Even before these crises, he had engaged a new collaborator to allow him more time for his new passion, mineralogy. Philibert Guéneau de Montbeillard, a Burgundian nobleman with an article in the *Encyclopédie*, imitated Buffon's style so effectively that readers assumed he was Buffon before the latter acknowledged his participation in 1775. From 1772 onward, Gabriel-Léopold Bexon also contributed, but Buffon never allowed him to sign any articles, perhaps because of the editing his drafts required. In the end, the subseries proceeded along lines similar to the previous one, but anatomy was minimized; birds were lumped together in fairly traditional genera; and special editions were published with hand-colored plates by François-Nicolas Martinet.

Even as he was directing *Histoire naturelle des oiseaux,* Buffon began issuing a series of *Suppléments*. Predictably, these volumes included updates, amendments, and addenda to previous material. They also featured reprints and reworkings of his earlier texts for the Académie des Sciences and the Académie française. One notable adaptation was his "Essai d'arithmétique morale," which synthesized his ideas on mathematics and methodology from the 1730s and 1740s. In this essay, elaborating on a key theme of the "Premier Discours," Buffon drew on probability theory to distinguish between mathematical, physical, and moral truth. Finally, the *Suppléments* provided him with a forum for exposing his recent, interconnected theories of chemistry, mineralogy, and geology. In chemistry, more than ever committed to rational elegance, he saw all forces, from electricity to heat, as deriving from Newtonian attraction. Life itself, he speculated, was a by-product of heat.

Heat was the determining factor in his revised theory of the development of Earth, too. In the more than thirty years since the publication of "Histoire et théorie de la terre," two discoveries had altered his view of the subject. In 1765 Jean-Jacques Dortous de Mairan presented a paper in the Académie des Sciences claiming to prove that the interior of the Earth was radiating a huge amount of heat unrelated to incident sunlight. Buffon thought that this heat could only be a vestige of the long-ago epoch in which the planets were torn out of the sun. To examine the speed with which heated spheres cool and thus date the origin of the Earth, he set up a foundry near the village of Buffon in 1767. After six years of experimentation with spheres of various sizes and compositions, he came up with results in the form of tables and heuristic mathematical formulas. They allowed him to estimate the age of Earth for his "Epoques de la nature," published in 1778 in volume five of the *Supplément*–roughly seventy thousand years in the printed text, but up to three million years in a series of adjustments he made in unpublished manuscripts. Since he now considered life self-generating within a broad range of temperatures, his schema allowed him to calculate that living beings originated some forty thousand years ago, already recognizable in form and destined to do little more than degenerate in size or become extinct in subsequent millennia. At the same time, his experiments made him notice that cooling left dimples on once molten spheres–a fact that persuaded him to attribute many of the mountains of Earth to its fiery origin, not to sedimentation as in "Histoire et théorie." His new theory was received skeptically by the scientific community, but his attempt to give the Earth a definite chronology inspired subsequent thinkers in a general way.

According to a prospectus of 1748, *Histoire naturelle* was to cover all three kingdoms of nature in just fifteen volumes. It soon became clear that the series would be much longer, but Buffon continued to hope it would be comprehensive. In 1771 he tried to arrange for Jean-Jacques Rousseau to write a subseries on plants, but to no avail. The best Buffon could do in botany was to promote the separate publication of Lamarck's non-Linnaean *Flore française* (1778). Meanwhile, with Daubenton, and especially Lacépède, working on such remaining animals as whales and reptiles, Buffon himself turned to his last subseries, *Histoire naturelle des minéraux,* aided this time by Barthélemy Faujas de Saint-Fond as well as Bexon. In this work, Buffon's use of grandiose style diminished, perhaps because minerals did not lend themselves to poetry, or perhaps because his view of his project had changed. Like the other subseries, this one was mostly organized around specific minerals, ordered according to their origin as described in "Epoques de la nature." Throughout the subseries, he focused on the place of minerals in his geological chronology, to the neglect, for example, of chemical analysis, which he saw as largely irrelevant to the way nature worked outside the laboratory.

George-Louis Leclerc de Buffon died in 1788 at the age of eighty. Read throughout Europe and elsewhere, he had exercised an enormous influence on his contemporaries, notably on such luminaries as Denis Diderot, Rousseau, and Immanuel Kant. So wide was the currency of his ideas that even the many who rejected them were obliged to take account of them. Perhaps his greatest legacy was the model he provided for historical thinking, which inspired scholars both inside and outside natural history. As a naturalist, he

Illustration from Buffon's Histoire naturelle *(from Jacques Roger,* Buffon, *1997; Thomas Cooper Library, University of South Carolina)*

helped move his subject away from theology, and in the several decades after his death, his example gave rise to an informal school of natural history premised on fine writing, far-reaching speculation, and openness to the public. Despite the disapproval of Georges Cuvier, the dominant French naturalist after Buffon's death, this approach survived well into the nineteenth century, as illustrated by the careers of Lamarck and Etienne Geoffroy de Saint-Hilaire, for example. When Darwin introduced his theory of natural selection, Buffon was inevitably touted as a precursor and even a preferred alternative, but his reputation was already declining. Historians of science in the positivistic mode were soon unable to find any definite discovery to attribute to him, while literary scholars found him pompous and unappealing in comparison with wittier, more volatile writers such as Voltaire and Diderot. J.-L. de Lanessan's edition of Buffon's complete works in 1884–1885 was the only critical edition of *Histoire naturelle* until 1954—and the last critical edition to include a substantial portion of the whole series. Even abridgments and anthologies of the *Histoire naturelle,* extremely popular in the early nineteenth century, had diminished in number by the late nineteenth century. Buffon has benefited from considerable serious scholarship, notably on the part of Lesley Hanks, Jacques Roger, and Sloan, but he will probably never again be seen as he was in his own time as the equal of Voltaire, Charles-Louis de Secondat, baron de Montesquieu, and Rousseau.

Letters:

Correspondance inédite, 2 volumes, edited by H. Nadault de Buffon, (Paris: Hachette, 1860);

Eugène Ritter, "Lettres de Buffon et de Maupertuis adressées à Jalabert," *Revue d'histoire littéraire de la France,* 8 (1901): 650–656;

Franck Bourdier and Yves François, "Lettres inédites de Buffon," in *Buffon* (Paris: Muséum National d'Histoire Naturelle, 1952), pp. 181–224;

Françoise Weil, "La Correspondance Buffon-Cramer," *Revue d'histoire des sciences et de leurs applications,* 14 (1961): 97–136;

Correspondance générale, 2 volumes, edited by Buffon (Geneva: Slatkine, 1971).

Interview:

Marie-Jean Hérault de Séchelles, "Voyage à Montbard contenant des détails très intéressants sur le caractère, la personne et les écrits de Buffon" (Paris: Solvet, 1801); translated by John Lyon as "Journey to Montbard," in *From Natural History to the History of Nature: Readings from Buffon and his Critics,* edited by Lyon and Phillip R. Sloan (Notre Dame, Ind.: University of Notre Dame Press, 1981), pp. 355–377.

Bibliographies:

E. Genet-Varcin and Jacques Roger, "Bibliographie de Buffon," in *Oeuvres philosophiques de Buffon,* edited by Jean Piveteau (Paris: Presses universitaires de France, 1954), pp. 513–575;

Marie-Françoise Lafon, "Bibliographie de Buffon (1954–1991)," in *Buffon 88: Actes du colloque international pour le bicentenaire de la mort de Buffon,* edited by Jean Gayon and others (Paris: Vrin, 1992), pp. 689–743.

Biographies:

Lesley Hanks, *Buffon avant l' "Histoire naturelle"* (Paris: Presses universitaires de France, 1966);

Otis E. Fellows and Stephen F. Milliken, *Buffon* (New York: Twayne, 1972);

Jacques Roger, *Buffon: A Life in Natural History,* translated by Sarah Lucille Bonnefoi (Ithaca, N.Y.: Cornell University Press, 1997).

References:

Scott Atran, *Cognitive Foundations of Natural History: Towards an Anthropology of Science* (Cambridge: Cambridge University Press, 1990);

Giulio Barsanti, "Buffon et l'image de la nature: de l'échelle des êtres à la carte géographique," in *Buffon 88: Actes du colloque international pour le bicentenaire de la mort de Buffon,* edited by Jean Gayon and others (Paris: Vrin, 1992), pp. 255–296;

Alain-Marie Bassy, "A l'heure des grandes synthèses: l'œuvre de Buffon à l'Imprimerie royale, 1749–1789," in *L'Art du livre à l'Imprimerie nationale* (Paris: Imprimerie nationale, 1973), pp. 170–189;

Pietro Corsi, *The Age of Lamarck,* translated by Jonathan Mandelbaum (Berkeley: University of California Press, 1988);

John H. Eddy Jr., "Buffon's *Histoire naturelle:* History? A Critique of Recent Interpretations," *Isis,* 85 (1994): 644–661;

Paul Lawrence Farber, "Buffon and the Concept of Species," *Journal of the History of Biology,* 5 (1972): 259–284;

Ana María Gómez Torres, *Las Ideas de Buffon sobre retórica y poética en los inicios de la teoría literaria moderna* (Málaga, Spain: AEDILE, 1996);

N. Jardine, J. A. Secord, and E. C. Spary, eds., *Cultures of Natural History* (Cambridge: Cambridge University Press, 1996);

Jeff Loveland, "Georges-Louis Leclerc de Buffon's *Histoire naturelle* in English, 1775–1815," *Archives of Natural History,* 31 (2004): 214–235;

Loveland, *Rhetoric and Natural History: Buffon in Polemical and Literary Context,* no. 3 (Oxford: Voltaire Foundation, 2001);

Stephen Milliken, "Buffon and the British," dissertation, Columbia University, 1965;

Louise E. Robbins, *Elephant Slaves and Pampered Parrots: Exotic Animals in Eighteenth-Century Paris* (Baltimore: Johns Hopkins University Press, 2002);

Jacques Roger, *The Life Sciences in Eighteenth-Century French Thought,* translated by Robert Ellrich (Stanford, Cal.: Stanford University Press, 1997);

Phillip R. Sloan, "Buffon Studies Today," *History of Science,* 32 (1994): 469–477;

Sloan, "From Logical Universals to Historical Individuals: Buffon's Idea of Biological Species," in *Histoire du concept d'espèce dans les sciences de la vie* (Paris: Fondation Singer-Polignac, 1987), pp. 101–140;

Sloan, "Organic Molecules Revisited," in *Buffon 88: Actes du colloque international pour le bicentenaire de la mort de Buffon,* edited by Jean Gayon and others (Paris: Vrin, 1992), pp. 415–438;

Emma C. Spary, *Utopia's Garden: French Natural History from Old Regime to Revolution* (Chicago: University of Chicago Press, 2000);

Dirk Stemerding, "How to Make Oneself Nature's Spokesman? A Latourian Account of Classification in Eighteenth- and Early Nineteenth-Century Natural History," *Biology and Philosophy,* 8 (1993): 193–223.

Papers:

Georges-Louis Leclerc de Buffon destroyed many of his personal papers. The largest collection of those remaining can be found in the Bibliothèque Centrale of the Muséum National d'Histoire Naturelle (Paris). Pertinent documents can also be found in the Archives de l'Académie Royale des Sciences (Paris), the Bibliothèque Publique et Universitaire (Geneva), and the Archives Départementales de la Côte-d'Or (Dijon), as well as in libraries and private collections throughout the world.

Marthe-Marguerite de Caylus

(17 April 1671 – 15 April 1729)

Gabrielle Verdier
University of Wisconsin–Milwaukee

BOOK: *Les Souvenirs de Madame de Caylus,* edited by Voltaire (Geneva: Jean Robert, 1769; Amsterdam: Marc-Michel Rey, 1770); translated by Elizabeth Griffith as *Memoirs, Anecdotes and Characters of the Court of Lewis XIV, translated from Les Souvenirs, or Recollections of Madame de Caylus, Niece to Madame de Maintenon . . . ,* 2 volumes (London: Printed for the editor and sold by J. Dodsley . . . J. Murray . . . Richardson & Urquhart, 1770).

Editions: *Souvenirs et correspondance de Madame de Caylus,* edited by Emile Raunié (Paris: Charpentier, 1881);

Souvenirs de Madame de Caylus, edited by Bernard Noël (Paris: Mercure de France, 1965);

L'estime et la tendresse: Correspondances intimes réunies et présentées par Pierre-E. Leroy et Marcel Loyau, edited by Pierre-E. Leroy and Marcel Loyau (Paris: Albin Michel, 1998).

Like many women who wrote before the French Revolution, Marthe-Marguerite de Villette, marquise de Caylus, was not a professional writer. An aristocrat whose life was primarily spent at the court of Louis XIV, she wrote hundreds of letters, some of which remain in manuscript, and recollections titled *Les Souvenirs de Madame de Caylus,* which were only published in 1769, forty years after her death. This slim volume was hailed as the first eyewitness account of the court of Louis XIV to be published. Indeed, Caylus, a niece of Françoise d'Aubigné who became Madame de Maintenon, the morganatic wife of Louis XIV, had privileged information that soon entered anecdotal history. Though overpowered by Louis de Rouvray, duc de Saint-Simon's massive memoirs published in 1830, *Les Souvenirs de Madame de Caylus* refutes his violent indictment of Maintenon as the evil power behind the throne. Caylus has been appreciated principally for her witty and charming style, described by nineteenth-century critic Charles-Augustin Sainte-Beuve as the perfect expression of classical "urbanity."

Marthe-Marguerite de Caylus (engraving by Jean Daullé, in Bibliothèque de l'Arsenal, Paris; from M. Le Comte d'Haussonville, ed., Souvenirs de Mme de Caylus, *n.d.; Zimmerman Library, University of New Mexico)*

Caylus's life was interwoven with that of her aunt. Her father, Philippe de Valois, marquis de Villette, and Maintenon were first cousins; their grandfather was Huguenot poet Agrippa d'Aubigné, author of *Les Tragiques* (1616), a powerful epic on the wars of religion. Villette's parents, Louise-Arthémise d'Aubigné and Benjamin de Valois, sieur de Villette, had cared for their niece Françoise d'Aubigné in their chateau at Mursay in the Poitou region of central France. They remained faithful to the Calvinist religion, as did their son, but Françoise had been forced by another relative to convert to Roman Catholicism at age fourteen. Marthe-Marguerite de Valois de Villette was born on 17 April 1671 to Villette and his wife, Marie-Anne de Châteauneuf. She spent her first years at Mursay, and was raised a Protestant by caring parents.

As Maintenon's favor increased, she attended to the interests of her relatives. She furthered Villette's career in the navy, where he rose to the rank of lieutenant general, and also promoted the army careers of his two sons. Embracing Louis XIV's campaign to extirpate heresy, she undertook her family's conversion. During Villette's absence at sea, Maintenon conspired with his sister, a Catholic convert, to kidnap Marthe-Marguerite, as she herself had been kidnapped, and to bring her to Paris. After shedding some tears, the nine-year-old girl was so dazzled by the king's mass that she agreed to convert on 23 December 1680. "C'est là toutes la controverse qu'on employa, et la seule abjuration que je fis" (it was the only argument made and my only abjuration), recalls Caylus in *Les Souvenirs de Madame de Caylus*. Forced conversions were, in fact, common practice at the time and applauded as acts of virtue. Despite Villette's protest, his two sons eventually abjured their faith as well. Villette himself finally converted on the eve of the Edict of Fontainebleau (17 October 1685), which revoked the freedoms granted to the Protestants by the Edict of Nantes (1598).

A born educator, Maintenon took charge of educating and establishing Mademoiselle de Mursay, the name by which her niece was known before her marriage. *Les Souvenirs de Madame de Caylus* praises the aunt's care in selecting tutors and giving writing exercises that "former ma raison et cultiver mon esprit" (formed my reason and cultivated my mind). On the other hand, Maintenon's letters to her cousins dwell on their daughter's intractable streak. According to Pierre-E. Leroy and Marcel Loyau, "un véritable incompatibilité d'humeur" (an incompatibility of temper) affected the relationship between the aunt and her niece. Because of her duties, Maintenon had to place her rebellious ward in the convent during certain periods. At court, Mursay attracted illustrious suitors, and her beauty, grace, expressive charm, and delightful wit were extolled by Saint-Simon and other memorialists. In 1681, the eleven-year-old duc du Maine–the illegitimate son of Louis XIV and Madame de Montespan–who was raised by Maintenon, declared his love to his governess's niece and remained her friend for the next fifty years. Maintenon, however, did not seek a glorious marriage for her relative, but a more modest one, befitting a girl from the minor nobility.

Caylus at age twenty-three (Bibliothèque nationale; from d'Haussonville, ed., Souvenirs de Mme de Caylus, *n.d.; Zimmerman Library, University of New Mexico)*

On 14 March 1686, at age fifteen, Mademoiselle de Mursay was wed to Jean-Anne de Tubières de Grimoard de Pestel de Levis, comte de Caylus. It was a disastrous match. In *Les Souvenirs de Madame de Caylus*, Madame de Caylus mentions her marriage only in passing. Though illustrious, the Caylus family was not prosperous. Yet, the twenty-year-old count seemed embarked on a glorious military career, as the dowry given to his wife by the king bought him the office of *menin* to the dauphin (a gentleman attached to the service of the dauphin). Soon, however, the young man revealed his true nature: a wild and brutal drunkard, he was unworthy of appearing at Versailles. Despite Maintenon's efforts to reconcile the spouses, the best solution was to keep the count busy at the front, far away from his young wife. Still, they had four children, of whom only two survived.

In January 1688, Maintenon persuaded the king to allocate an apartment at Versailles for Madame de Caylus and another niece and entrusted both of them to a chaperone–her old friend Madame de Montchevreuil. For the next six years Caylus lived at court. Some of the details of her life during that period are not mentioned in Les Souvenirs de Madame de Caylus—for example, a difficult pregnancy and the loss of her first child (July 1688), or the birth of a second son (1692), Anne-Claude Philippe de Tubières, comte de Caylus, who became a renowned antiquarian. She does dwell, however, on an important literary event that displayed her dramatic talents. In 1686 Maintenon founded a boarding school for poor girls of the nobility at Saint-Cyr and asked dramatist Jean Racine to write a play on a sacred subject suitable for performance by young girls. The result was Esther (1689), a tragedy based on the biblical story of the Jewish queen who wed the king of Persia and saved her people. Overhearing Racine read his verses, Caylus recited them so beautifully that the poet wrote for her the allegorical prologue in which Piety sings the praises of the king, Maintenon, and Saint-Cyr. Throughout the winter of 1688–1689, Caylus recited the prologue and served as understudy for all the parts of the play, even performing the title role before the deposed English monarchs, King James II and his wife. Caylus's acting created a sensation; memorialists and letter writers compared her favorably with Marie Desmares, known as La Champmeslé, the greatest interpreter of Racine's heroines. But, by mid February 1689, Caylus was so dangerously moving that she was replaced by a younger, more naive actress. Caylus's fun-loving nature caused her greater troubles. Despite her aunt's admonitions, she joined a circle of impertinent ladies gathered around Madame la duchesse, Louise-Françoise de Bourbon, a bastard daughter of Louis XIV and Montespan, married to Louis III, duc de Bourbon-Condé. Although Madame la duchesse had been raised by Maintenon, she had broken away and flouted the austerity that the aging king and Maintenon imposed at Versailles. Caylus, a born comedienne, joined la duchesse in composing satirical portraits of members of the court, including that of her own chaperone, Montchevreuil. Unable to sanction the royal princes and princesses easily, Louis XIV punished their entourage. The jokes "on y tronva de l'impiété" (he found impious) and banished Caylus, pregnant at the time, in May 1694. Saint-Simon believes another reason was responsible for this action, symptomatic of the dissipation among the younger generation at court: a liaison between Caylus and the duc de Villeroy, son of the Maréchal de Villeroy, one of Louis XIV's oldest friends. Often mentioned in Caylus's letters, the duke remained a friend for life.

Caylus's exile from the court lasted twelve years. She was allowed to stay in Paris, however, and lived on rue de Vaugirard, in the Saint-Sulpice parish. Contemporary letter writers report that despite her reduced means, she enjoyed the company of freethinking Parisians unfettered by the conformism of Versailles. In February 1698, she gave birth to another son, the chevalier de Caylus, nicknamed "Brindi"—an occasion that rekindled the correspondence with her aunt. Although a blessing, her husband's death in November 1704 left her with the responsibility of caring for her sons' futures. In the meantime, she devoted herself to good works and renewed her spiritual life under the direction of father Pierre François d'Arères de La Tour, vicar-general of the Oratoire congregation. As noted by Leroy and Loyau, Caylus had, at age thirty-three, finally reconciled the contradictory sides of her character: "La spontanéité enjouée et la gravité melancolique" (the lively spontaneity and the melancholic seriousness). But the Oratorians were sympathetic to the Jansenists—the religious dissidents considered to be a threat to the state—against whom negative sentiments flared up again in 1704. In view of this situation, Maintenon advised Caylus to leave Father de La Tour and find a more orthodox confessor, promising that if she conformed graciously to the king's will, her 6,000-livre pension would be raised to 10,000 livres. Caylus complied and soon returned to more balanced worldly pursuits. Maintenon continued to write, complimenting her niece, giving her advice, and asking for her opinion on domestic matters, with the intent of testing her before reintroducing her at court. Caylus's letters to her aunt between 1704 and 1708 were destroyed, probably when Maintenon left Versailles, following Louis XIV's death.

By 1707, Caylus was back in the king's good graces. On 23 October 1708, he reassigned her an apartment at Versailles, in the mezzanine, just below her aunt's apartment. However, because of Maintenon's enormous duties the two women did not see each other as often as Caylus had hoped. Between 1708 and 1714, she wrote many short letters to her aunt that have been preserved. Although undated, these gracious, yet at times melancholic, notes reveal Caylus's activities and preoccupations during those years: anxiety concerning her status and her aunt's affection, her fragile health, and the struggle to solicit positions and apartments for her sons. She joined a small group of ladies who called themselves "the cabal," united by their admiration for Maintenon. These women included the marquise de Dangeau, the marquise de Levis, the comtesse de Mailly, the marquise d'O, the marquise d'Heudicourt, and the duchesse de Noailles. Gathered in Maintenon's apartment, these ladies were the only people capable of distracting Louis XIV in his failing years. The lively, affectionate, and respectful letters exchanged between Caylus and Maintenon are a model of epistolary style, as they captured the art of conversation mastered by women of the period.

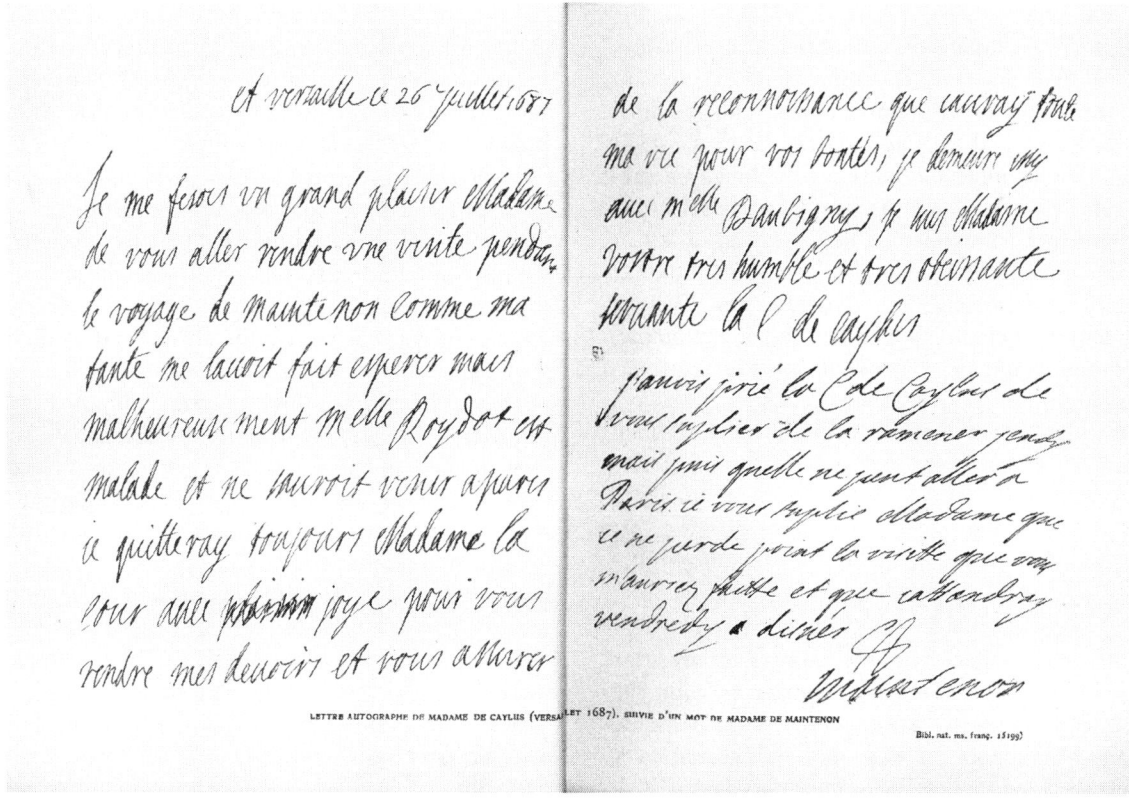

Letter (1687) from Caylus to her aunt, Madame de Maintenon, who added a postscript (Bibliothèque nationale; from d'Haussonville, ed., Souvenirs de Mme de Caylus, *n.d.; Zimmerman Library, University of New Mexico)*

Indeed, they illustrate "esteem and tenderness," the title of a recent edition of the letters exchanged by Caylus, Maintenon, and Dangeau. Tender concern also characterizes the letters Caylus wrote to her older son—nicknamed "the philosopher" and the "melancholic one"—which were published with the comte de Caylus's own *Souvenirs* in 1805. While touring Italy in 1715, the young count decided to abandon the army in order to devote himself to his lifelong passion for archaeology. While assuring him that she only wanted his happiness, Caylus pleaded with him not to make such a "singular" decision too hastily. Faced with the practical task of selling the military regiment she had bought for him, she showed real business acumen.

Louis XIV's death on 1 September 1715 radically altered the lives of the women who surrounded him. Maintenon retreated from the world to Saint-Cyr and devoted the remaining years of her life to her beloved school. Caylus moved to a pleasant little lodge she was awarded in the gardens of the Luxembourg palace, one that Maintenon fondly called Caylus's "votre ermitage au milieu de Paris" (your hermitage in the heart of Paris). Soon, her older son joined her there. Madame de Dangeau was a neighbor in the Saint-Sulpice parish and was one of the few women Maintenon continued to see. The distance between the three friends—Saint-Cyr was only thirty kilometers away from Paris but four hours by carriage—gave new meaning to the epistolary exchange. It became not only their principal means of communication but also their greatest pleasure and consolation in life. In the much longer letters of this period, Caylus, Dangeau, and Maintenon discussed political and religious matters, exchanged news about family and friends, and described their own daily lives. "vos letters font mon seul plaisir" (Your letters are my only pleasure), wrote Maintenon; "je vous sins dans toutes vos heures, je m'y transporte en esprit" (I follow your every hour at Saint-Cyr in spirit), replied Caylus. The first group of letters dwelled on the difficulty Caylus and Dangeau encountered in organizing their first visit to Saint-Cyr, postponed until December 1715 because of their illnesses and a smallpox epidemic. Subsequent letters evoke political issues of concern to the three women during the period of the regency—for example, the fate of James III, the pretender to the English throne, supported by France, and that of James II's widow, the exiled queen, a friend of Maintenon; the attacks by the legitimate princes against the privileges Louis XIV had granted his natural son, the duc du Maine, which led to his imprisonment; the religious controversy reignited by *Unigenitus Dei Filius,* the 1713 papal bull condemning the Jansenist teachings on predestination; and Madame de Dangeau's dangerous inclination toward Jansenism. The last group of letters follow the gradual decline of Maintenon's condition until her death at age eighty-three on 15 April 1719. In her two letters of consolation to her aunt's confidante, Marie-Jeanne d'Aumale, Caylus suggested a sequel to this most important chapter. She asked Aumale to save her letters to Maintenon and to write down the principal events of Maintenon's life so that the memories would console them.

Not much is known about Caylus's own last years. She continued to live quietly in her house in the Luxembourg gardens, surrounded by friends and admirers, such as the duc de Villeroy and her two sons—"the philosopher" and the more rambunctious chevalier. She did not retreat completely from the world. In 1727 she wrote a letter to the duc du Maine on behalf of his supporters, suggesting that he consider accepting the office of prime minister to Louis XV. Caylus's letter is lost, but Maine's polite refusal shows the great esteem that he continued to feel for the niece of his beloved governess. Plagued by ill health for many years, Caylus died in her fifty-eighth year, on 15 April 1729, ten years to the day after Madame de Maintenon.

Legend has it that Caylus dictated *Les Souvenirs de Madame de Caylus* to her older son, at his request, on her deathbed. What is certain is that the comte de Caylus, author of many books and collector of antiquities, possessed the manuscript of his mother's recollections and that he allowed selected friends to read it. In 1770, five years after his death, *Les Souvenirs de Madame de Caylus* officially appeared in Amsterdam but was actually printed clandestinely in Geneva in late 1769. The author of the anonymous preface and notes is reputed to be Voltaire. According to another legend, propagated by the royal censor Fr.-L.-Claude Marin to discredit the philosophes, Denis Diderot had copied the manuscript without permission and sold it to a book dealer. Research has shown, however, that Marin himself, a friend of the comte de Caylus, asked Voltaire to sell it for him to the Geneva publisher. Interested in conciliating the censor, Voltaire also thought that *Les Souvenirs de Madame de Caylus* complemented his own history of the Sun King's reign, *Le Siècle de Louis XIV* (1751), and discredited the popular, semi-apocryphal *Memoirs and Letters of Madame de Maintenon,* published in the 1750s by literary hack Laurent de La Beaumelle. *Les Souvenirs de Madame de Caylus* was reprinted twice in the eighteenth century, re-edited five times in the nineteenth, but only once in the twentieth. The 1965 edition, however, was the fifth text published in the popular series "le Temps retrouvé."

Voltaire presents *Les Souvenirs de Madame de Caylus* as one of the works that best reveal the "inner works" of Louis XIV's court. He admires the candid small details that capture the characters of people at the court, praises the natural conversational style characteristic of women of wit, but regrets the abrupt end of the recollections. On the other hand, a few editors have deplored the absence of chronology and apparent lack of order, although Caylus announced at the outset that hers are not memoirs but "des souvenirs sans ordre, sans exactitude, et sans autre prétention que celle d'amuser mes amis" (reminiscences without order or exactness, written merely to amuse her friends), at their own request. The recollections include events at court that she had heard about, as well as those she witnessed herself and that are often linked to the earlier ones by association. Battles described by official historians are generally less important than anecdotes about the king and his mistresses, and "bagatelles" (trifles) she knew from the inside shed light on important events. The hundred-page text is clearly unfinished. The longest part of the work is dedicated to the life of Madame de Maintenon and those who surrounded her. Caylus speaks of her ancestry, going back to Agrippa d'Aubigné; her difficult childhood, marriage, and widowhood; her conversion and that of her family; her friendship and subsequent rivalry with Madame de Montespan, whose children by the king she was asked to raise; the king's mistresses and illegitimate children; Montespan's family; Maintenon's appointment as second lady-in-waiting of the dauphine; the dauphine's maids of honor; the death of the queen and Maintenon's secret marriage to Louis XIV (1683); as well as Saint-Cyr and the performance of *Esther.* The last fourth of *Les Souvenirs de Madame de Caylus* recalls various members of the court related to the king: his children, his cousins of the house of Condé, his nephew the duc d'Orléans, his grandsons the ducs de Bourgogne and de Berry and their intrigues, and the mingling by marriage of legitimate and illegitimate family lines. The text ends abruptly with an anecdote about the duchesse de Burgundy, who died in 1712.

Challenging the tradition that highlights the oral, careless spontaneity "natural" to women who write, Rachel Sauvé discerns traces in *Les Souvenirs de Madame de Caylus* of a genuine literary project, which would have been completed in a second part leading to the king's death and the regency. The text is organized around clusters of portraits framed by anecdotes rather than by chronology. A fine psychologist, Caylus is able to reveal hidden moral dimensions of the illustrious people by painting dominant traits with a few incisive strokes. The thirty portraits, all but five of which are devoted to women, bring to light the extent of women's sphere of influence at the court, as well as the humiliation they suffered for the power they held. More than just a delightful complement to history, *Les Souvenirs de Madame de Caylus* thus creates a dialogue with male-authored memoirs and histories. The forthcoming reprint of *Les Souvenirs de Madame de Caylus* and the edition of some of Caylus's letters, coupled with the new perspectives on women's historical writings, should lead to a reevaluation of her slim but forceful body of writing.

Letters:

"Lettres inédites au Comte de Caylus," in *Les Souvenirs de M. le comte de Caylus* (Paris: Hubert, 1805).

Biographies:

A. Geffroy, *Madame de Maintenon d'après sa correspondance authentique. Choix de lettres et entretiens* (Paris, 1887);

Louis de Rouvray, duc de Saint-Simon, *Mémoires,* volume 2 (Paris: Gallimard, 1947–1961).

References:

Jean de Booy, "Diderot, Voltaire, et *Les souvenirs de Madame de Caylus,*" *Revue des Sciences humaines,* 109 (1963): 23–38;

Roland Mortier, "Diderot, le censeur Marin et les *Souvenirs* de la Marquise de Caylus," *Recherches sur Diderot et sur l'Encyclopédie,* 24 (1998): 151–153;

Charles-Augustin Sainte-Beuve, "Madame de Caylus et de ce qu'on appelle urbanité," *Causeries du lundi* (Paris: Garnier, 1852–1862), III: 56–77;

Rachel Sauvé, "*Les Souvenirs* de madame de Caylus: causerie écrite ou projet scripturaire?" *Dalhousie French Studies,* 47 (1999): 51–60.

Papers:

The letters of Marthe-Marguerite de Caylus to Madame de Maintenon are held in the Archives Mouchy and the Bibliotèque municipale de Versailles, Ms. G 327.

Sébastien-Roch Nicolas de Chamfort
(22 June 1740? – 13 April 1794)

Isabelle C. DeMarte
Lewis and Clark College

BOOKS: *La Jeune Indienne* . . . (Paris: Cailleau, 1764);
Epître d'un père à son fils sur la naissance d'un petit-fils . . . (Paris: Regnard, 1764);
Grand vocabulaire français, by Chamfort, Joseph Nicolas Guyot, Ferdinand Camille, and Duchemin de la Chesnaye (Paris: Panckoucke, 1767–1774);
Combien le génie des grands écrivains influe sur l'esprit de leur siècle . . . (Paris: Duchesne, 1768);
Eloge de Molière . . . (Paris: Regnard, 1769);
Le Marchand de Smyrne . . . (Paris: Delalain, 1770);
Eloge de La Fontaine . . . (Marseille: Favet, 1774; Paris: Ruault, 1774);
Mustapha et Zéangir . . . (Paris: Duchesne, 1778);
Des Académies . . . (Paris: Buisson, 1791);
Sébastien Chamfort à ses concitoyens, en réponse aux calomnies de Tobiesen-Duby (Paris, 1792);
Maximes et pensées, caractères et anecdotes, edited, with an introduction, by Pierre Louis Ginguené (London: Baylis, 1796); translated, with an introduction, by E. Powys Mathers as *Maxims and Considerations,* 2 volumes (Waltham Saint Lawrence, U.K.: Golden Cockerel Press, 1926).

Collections: *Oeuvres complètes, recueillies et publiées par un de ses amis,* 4 volumes, edited by Pierre Louis Ginguené (Paris: Imprimeries des Sciences et des Arts, 1795)–includes *Maximes et pensées,* translated by W. S. Mervin as "Maxims and Thoughts," in *Products of the Perfected Civilization,* edited by Mervin (Toronto: Macmillan, 1969), pp. 109–207; *Caractères et anecdotes,* translated in part by Mervin as "Characters and Anecdotes," in *Products of the Perfected Civilization,* edited by Mervin (Toronto: Macmillan, 1969), pp. 208–260; and *Petits dialogues philosophiques,* translated in part by Mervin as "Short Philosophical Dialogues," in *Products of the Perfected Civilization,* edited by Mervin (Toronto: Macmillan, 1969), pp. 261–264;
Oeuvres complètes, 5 volumes, edited by Pierre René Auguis, enlarged edition (Paris: Chaumerot jeune, 1824–1825).

Sébastien-Roch Nicolas de Chamfort (1805 painting by an unknown artist; from Claude Arnaud, Chamfort, *1992; Thomas Cooper Library, University of South Carolina)*

PLAY PRODUCTIONS: *La Jeune Indienne,* Paris, Comédie-Française, 30 April 1764;
Le Marchand de Smyrne, Paris, Comédie-Française, 26 January 1770;
Mustapha et Zéangir, Fontainebleau, Théâtre de Fontainebleau, devant LEURS MAJESTES, 1 November 1776; revised, Paris, Comédie-Française, 15 December 1777.

OTHER: Joseph de Laporte, *Dictionnaire dramatique, contenant l'histoire des théâtres, les règles du genre dramatique, les observations des maîtres les plus célèbres, & des réflexions nouvelles sur les spectacles, sur le génie & la conduite de tous les genres, avec les notices des meilleures pièces, le catalogue de tous les drames, & celui des auteurs dramatiques*, 3 volumes (Paris: Lacombe, 1776)—includes contributions by Chamfort;

Jean-Claude Richard de Saint-Non, *Voyage pittoresque, ou description des royaumes de Naples et de Sicile* (Paris: Clousier, 1781)—volume 1 includes "Précis historique des révolutions de Naples et de Sicile," by Chamfort, pp. 1–56;

Honoré-Gabriel Riquetti de Mirabeau, *Opinion du comte de Mirabeau sur la noblesse ancienne et moderne: considérations sur l'Ordre de Cincinnatus, ou imitation d'un pamphlet anglo-américain, suivies de plusieurs pièces relatives à cette institution: d'une lettre signée du général Washington, accompagnée de remarques par l'auteur français; et d'une lettre de feu M. Turgot, Ministre d'Etat en France, au Docteur Price, sur les législations américaines,* written by Chamfort (Paris, 1784); translated by Sir Samuel Romilly as *Considerations on the Order of Cincinnatus . . .* (Philadelphia: T. Seddon, 1785);

Tableaux historiques de la Révolution française ou collection de quarante-huit gravures illustrant les événements les plus remarquables qui ont eu lieu en France depuis la transformation des Etats-Généraux en Assemblée nationale, le 20 juin 1789, 3 volumes, by Chamfort, Claude Fauchet, Pierre-Louis Ginguené, and François-Xavier Pagès (Paris: Briffault de la Charprais et Madame L'Esclapart, 1791); translated as *Historical Pictures, Representing the Most Remarkable Events Which Occurred During the Early Period of the French Revolution . . .* (Paris: Charles, 1803)—tableaux 1–26 by Chamfort.

Compared to the celebrated moralists François de La Rochefoucauld, Jean de La Bruyère, or Blaise Pascal, Chamfort's name evokes little more than the genre of his posthumous work *Maximes et pensées, caractères et anecdotes* (1796; translated as *Maxims and Considerations,* 1926), cynical observations on the hierarchical nature of society and on the animal-like underpinnings of human interaction. Chamfort is a mysterious and contradictory figure, having gravitated toward aristocratic circles, written for the French Revolution, and vowed to stop writing altogether. For his opponents and supporters alike, "son destin est le terreau, le complement, Presque le second tome de son œuvre—le rêve pour un biographe" (his personal fate was the fertilizer, the complement, practically the companion volume of his writings—a biographer's dream), as Claud Arnaud states in his 1988 biography.

Chamfort was born Sébastien-Roch Nicolas, near Clermont-Ferrand, in central France. According to one birth certificate found after his death, he was born on 6 April 1740, the son of Thérèse Croiset and grocer François Nicolas. A local *Journal d'émigration*, however, indicates that he was the son of Françoise de Cisternes de Vinzelles and the local canon Nicolas, related to the grocer. Religiously, socially, and morally unacceptable, these circumstances allegedly spurred Françoise de Cisternes to give up Sébastien-Roch for adoption to Thérèse, whose own newborn died around the same time. This version, more widely accepted and more accurately documented, corroborates another birth certificate recording Sébastien-Roch as born of unknown parents on 22 June 1740.

Informed at age seven that his birth was illegitimate, Nicolas developed both a need for recognition from the nobility and a lasting contempt for them. His education was different from both the one typical in his social class and from the one his origins should have afforded him. Initially educated by a tutor, Sébastien-Roch went to Paris in 1754 and attended the Collège des Grassins, an institution for poor students. Unruly and defiant toward his teachers, he proved adept at English, Greek, Italian, Latin, and rhetoric and earned prizes in all five subjects. Failing in an attempt to escape from the college and sail across the Atlantic, he retreated to Paris, where, according to Ginguené, he was determined to drop out of school: "Je ne serai jamais prêtre; j'aime trop le repos, la philosophie, les femmes, l'honneur, la vraie gloire; et trop peu les querelles, l'hypocrisie, les honneurs et l'argent" (I'll never be a priest; I am too fond of sleep, philosophy, women, honor, and real fame; and not fond enough of quarrels, hypocrisy, honors, and money). Money was scarce, and during the early 1760s, "the best student of France"—as he was called in school—would not settle for any occupation, although he contributed to the *Journal encyclopédique* (Encyclopedic Journal) and wrote priestly sermons, as did many a would-be writer.

During his adolescence, Nicolas became increasingly antagonistic toward the nobility that later welcomed him in their circles without considering him one of their own. He tutored aristocratic youngsters, but, often seducing their mothers, was promptly dismissed. Much appreciated yet also feared for his feisty, incisive, and acerbic observations on the nobility, he grew popular among women, who created his reputation as Hercules and Adonis. Eager to remain independent from his patrons, he rejected financial opportunities that would limit his freedom. For example, hired to tutor the nephew of the comte de Van Eyck in May 1761, Nico-

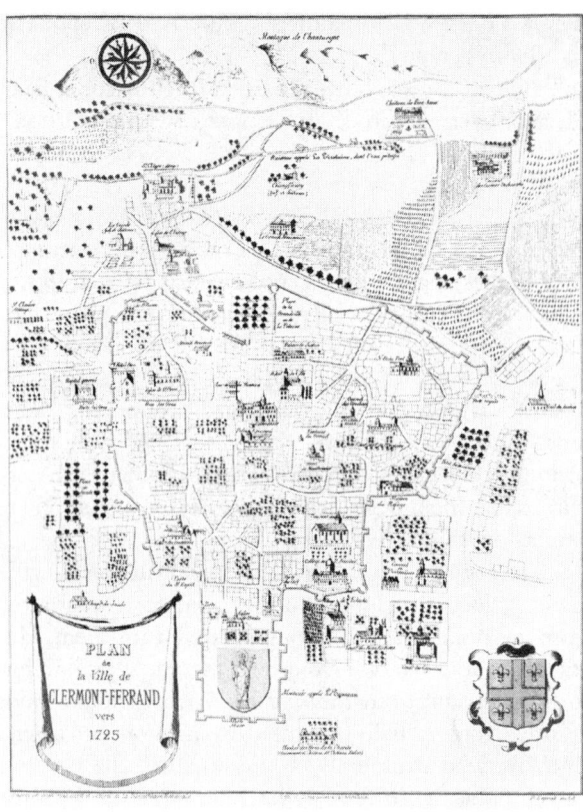

Map of Clermont-Ferrand, the city near where Chamfort was born (from Emile Dousset, Chamfort et son temps, *1974; Jean and Alexander Heard Library, Vanderbilt University)*

las resigned, allegedly in protest for his low wages, and returned to Paris more bitter about the nobility, yet more determined to attain true fame.

He began this search by entering the literary world under the pen name "Chamfort" preceded by the noble-like particle "de" and by participating in writing competitions held by various academies throughout France. A younger and more successful critic, Jean-François de La Harpe, was instrumental in Chamfort's first successes. In early 1764, La Harpe submitted Chamfort's new one-act comedy *La Jeune Indienne* (The Young Indian) to Voltaire, who found it promising. This first step opened the way to success in salons and playhouses: the play was soon scheduled at the Comédie-Française. Lucid and cynical, Chamfort expected fame and publicity, but little money, from a world he overtly despised. Premiering on 30 April, his play disappointed the critics and was dropped on 27 May after only nine performances. Reviews in Grimm and Meister's *Correspondance littérair* (Literary Correspondence) were harsh. Meanwhile, the poetry prize awarded by the Académie Française in Paris for his *Epître d'un père à son fils sur la naissance d'un petit-fils* (1764, Letter from a Father to His Son upon the Birth of a Grandson) validated Voltaire and Jean-Jacques Rousseau's support, while Chamfort's ideas were beginning to be associated with theirs, as well as with Charles-Louis de Secondat de Montesquieu's and Claude-Adrien Helvétius's.

With its setting in the English colonies, *La Jeune Indienne* explores the popular vein of exotic sentimentalism and the myth of the noble savage, and introduces political and religious relativism. Betti is a young native Indian who saves Belton, an Englishman stranded on her island in the West Indies. Four years later, Belton takes her back to the colonies, only to face a cruel dilemma: either he accepts the institutions and monetary values of his civilization and marries the daughter of his father's friend, or he becomes an outcast and embraces a life of mutual trust and happiness with Betti. Betti—who speaks like Racine's heroines rather than an eighteenth-century bourgeois or a native Indian—successfully uses her common sense to win Belton over and appeal to Mowbrai, a good-natured Quaker and Belton's would-be father-in-law. She counters the arbitrary principles of their society, pitting hierarchy and wealth against merit and intelligence. Criticized by contemporaries as imitating a story published in the *Spectator,* Chamfort deserves credit for the unprecedented introduction in *La Jeune Indienne* of a Quaker on the French stage. The play confirmed the popularity that Quakers had acquired thanks to Voltaire and Montesquieu and prompted the stereotype of Quaker communities as paragons of honesty, virtue, and merit—values that Chamfort desperately sought.

Unable to live by his writing, Chamfort had to rely on the generosity of friends and protectors. He bluntly denounced their patronage as the domination of asses over horses that are unable to compete in the social arena. His moderate success and lowly origins fostered the antagonism he felt toward social and academic institutions. To make matters worse, his growing popularity as Hercules-Adonis was cut short when a venereal disease left him disfigured and deprived of energy. He withdrew from society, alternating between actively seeking success and passively spurning it, and gradually he isolated himself by espousing Rousseau's mistrust of society. In 1765, he began a multivolume contribution to the *Grand vocabulaire français* (1767–1774, Great French Vocabulary). In January 1766, his "Ode sur la grandeur de l'Homme" (Ode on the Greatness of Man), which urged that geniuses are world citizens unbound by social status and capable of regenerating human nature, won a prize from the Académie des Jeux Floraux. That same year, Voltaire invited him to visit his estate at Ferney with La Harpe. Chamfort never went.

Whether La Harpe played a part in this mishap remains unclear. Yet, he hurt Chamfort's pride by revealing the well-kept secret of Chamfort's birth. This incident ended their friendship. It also fostered Chamfort's doubt that true friendship could exist while reinforcing his contempt for the rampant opportunistic behavior among writers. At the same time, Chamfort's remarkable talent for acerbic repartees and malicious sorties at the expense of the undiscriminating, undeserving aristocrats made his company both feared and sought-after in the salons. Upon meeting Chamfort in 1768, Denis Diderot pointedly portrayed him in a letter to Sophie Volland as "d'une figure très aimable, avec assez de talent, les plus belles apparences de la modestie et la suffisance la mieux conditionée. C'est un petit ballon dont une piqûre d'épingle fait sortir un vent violent" (a young poet of a rather amenable countenance, with sufficient talent, with the most handsome and humble appearance, yet with the most cultivated arrogance; a little balloon, that, stung by a needle, lets air out violently).

In 1769, Chamfort won a prize from the Académie Française for his *Eloge de Molière* (Praise of Molière), which extolled Molière's plays *Tartuffe* (1664) and *Le Misanthrope* (1666). Chamfort's essay was well received, especially by Voltaire, who had published a *Vie de Molière* (Life of Molière) in 1739. In 1770, Chamfort's *Le Marchand de Smyrne* (The Merchant of Smyrna), another one-act comedy, was performed thirteen times by the Comédiens français between January and March. Reminiscent of Voltaire's *Zaïre* (1732), set in the Orient against an historical background of religious strife, *Le Marchand de Smyrne* also dramatized criticism of French politics and society. Hassan is a wealthy Muslim. Grateful for having been freed from slavery the year before, he happens to free Dornal, the same Frenchman who, moved by Hassan's plea not to be separated from his bride, Zaïde, had released him. Coincidentally, Zaïde, now Hassan's wife, has secretly bought from the slave merchant a French slave woman who turns out to be Dornal's companion. Propelled by reversals of fortune, this plot of generous love and reciprocal friendship pits bourgeois characters against their aristocratic counterparts, depicted as morally and economically worthless slaves.

Weakened and disheartened by attacks of his disease, Chamfort was unable to enjoy his success. Thanks to the generosity of friends, he left Paris for spa treatments in Contrexéville (1771) and Barèges (1774). Vowing to remain independent and reclusive, he refused to accompany the influential baron de Breteuil (Louis-Auguste le Tonnelier) on a diplomatic mission. Nevertheless, he cultivated friendships with prominent individuals and intellectuals—Jaques Necker and his wife Suzanne Curchod de Nasse Necker and Anne-Catherine de Ligniville Helvétius, who, for example, provided him with living quarters. Sufficiently reconciled with social life, Chamfort returned to Paris. During these years, he continued to frequent high society, enjoying it some, criticizing it more, yet writing little. In 1774, he began making extensive contributions to Joseph de Laporte's three-volume *Dictionnaire dramatique* (1774–1776, Dictionary on Drama), which defined technical terms and gave synopses of plays and operas. In December 1774, Chamfort was elected associate of the Académie in Marseille, after his *Eloge de La Fontaine* (1774, Praise of La Fontaine) unexpectedly received its prize, winning over La Harpe's submission.

In 1776, the count Charles-Claude de la Billarderie d' Angivilller and his mistress Madam de Marchais used their influence at court to support the performance of *Mustapha et Zéangir* (first performed, 1776), a tragedy in verse, before the French king and queen at Fontainebleau. The tragedy merges various influences, from the Racinian set of characters and classic five-act development, through the title borrowed from a 1705 play by François Belin, to the sacrificial brotherly love between Mustapha and Zéangir, reminiscent of Diderot's serious drama. With Mustapha, the son of aging sultan Soliman's first marriage, away from court, Roxelane, the new sultana, plots against him and supports her son, Zéangir, as Soliman's successor. Her maneuver, which leads to Mustapha's death, fails because Zéangir remains loyal to Mustapha. Zéangir willingly sacrifices his claim to the throne, his love for Azémire—the daughter of Soliman's Persian enemy and lover of Mustapha—and his life by committing suicide on Mustapha's remains. Soliman orders Roxelane to live and expiate her acts in jail.

Despite royal financial and political support, the actors at the Comédie-Française demanded that Chamfort alter several roles and the denouement. These changes delayed performance by another year. Critics accused Chamfort of plagiarizing Belin, and ridiculed his ambitions. These statements affected him deeply. Reacting to the antagonism of the Comédiens français, Pierre Augustin Caron de Beaumarchais invited Chamfort to join other playwrights in founding the Société des Auteurs Dramatiques (Society of Dramatic Authors). Chamfort dubbed its manifesto—inspired by the American Declaration of Independence—"les Etats Généraux de l'art dramatique" (the States General of Dramatic Art). Unwilling to compromise his intellectual freedom by entertaining financial connections with the nobility, Chamfort declined to be appointed chief secretary to the prince de Condé—who subsidized him nonetheless—or to accept Charles-André Panckoucke's offer to write on "spectacles" for the *Mercure de France,* the

Etching by Jacques-Louis David of Jean-Paul Marat, assassinated on 13 July 1793 by Charlotte Corday. Upon being informed of his impending arrest for collusion, Chamfort shot himself in the head and cut his throat (Réunion des Musées Nationaux / Art Resource, New York).

readership of which included aristocrats. Similarly, despite succeeding in obtaining coveted membership in the Académie Française on 5 April 1781, Chamfort shunned its meetings. He consciously withdrew from society, perhaps weakened by his venereal disease. He retreated to Auteuil before going to Vaudouleurs, the residence of his new companion, Marthe-Anne Buffon, with whom he shared the happiest times of his life until her death in 1783–as attested in his poem "A celle qui n'est plus" (1824–1825 To the One No Longer Living). During that time, Chamfort collaborated on Jean-Claude Richard de Saint-Non's *Voyage pittoresque, ou description des Royaumes de Naples et de Sicile* (1781, Picturesque Voyage or Description of the Kingdoms of Naples and Sicily).

Within a year of Marthe-Anne Buffon's death, Chamfort's foster mother died in June 1784. Quite affected by these two losses, he threw himself into political activity, more than ever committed to denouncing social inequalities and questioning the foundations of the ancien régime. Having met the colorful and radical Honoré-Gabriel Riquetti de Mirabeau, Chamfort mentored him and corresponded with him. He proofread Mirabeau's radical pamphlet "Des lettres de cachet et des prisons d'états" (On 'Lettres de cachet' and state prisons) in 1783, and wrote most of his *Considérations sur l'ordre de Cincinnatus* (1785, Considerations on the Order of Cincinnatus). Commissioned by Benjamin Franklin, this work rejected the hereditary legitimacy of the nobility. Chamfort's friendship with Mirabeau degenerated, however, when the tribune printed as his own, polemical anecdotes and bons mots collected by Chamfort for future publication. Not unlike La Harpe's, Mirabeau's betrayal supported Chamfort's cynicism concerning friendship, as he stated in "Caractères et Anecdotes" in *Oeuvres complètes, recueillies par un de ses amis* (1795): "Il faut que le coeur se brise ou se bronze" (the heart must break or turn into bronze).

Although his service as chief secretary to Madame Elisabeth, sister of Louis XVI, and a royal pension rendered his intellectual autonomy and freedom of speech questionable, Chamfort lost neither. Rather, he took advantage of his position to defend democracy. In December 1788, his speech to the National Assembly, likely commissioned by his protector, Louis-Philippe de Rigaud Vaudreuil, pitted seven hundred thousand privileged aristocrats against the Third Estate, anticipating the French Revolution, which he blamed on the nobility's keeping the people illiterate–a recurrent theme in his later maxims on the period. In 1789, Chamfort, who then lived near the Palais-Royal, chronicled the growing unrest in Paris, hailed the fall of the Bastille on 14 July, and the abolition of aristocratic privileges in August. One of the first writers admitted into the Club des Jacobins (Jacobins' Club), dominated by representatives of the Third Estate, he drafted its minutes for their bulletin, *Journal des Etats généraux* (Journal of the Estates General). Chamfort embraced defending the people's plight enthusiastically, in keeping with his principles and despite the financial loss entailed by the abolition of governmental pensions and the massive exile of aristocrats abroad. On 26 August 1789, the Declaration of the Rights of Man and Citizen was ratified by the Constituent Assembly. It agreed with his belief in the value of merit and intelligence over birth and fortune.

Chamfort's fervent commitment to the Revolution helped to bring back *La Jeune Indienne* to the stage as an opening act for Marie-Joseph Chénier's *Charles IX* (1789). Chamfort now wrote frequently in the less aristocratic *Mercure*. Meanwhile, he contributed to many speeches by Emmanuel-Joseph Seyiès, Charles-Maurice de Talleyrand-Périgord, and Mirabeau, who died before he could read *Des académies* (1791, On Academies) at the National Assembly, a speech against the institution that ruled over language and literature. For Sieyès, whose religious stance Chamfort helped secularize, he wrote the memorable line: "What is the Third Estate? Everything. What does it have? Nothing!" Along with speeches and such mottos as "Guerre aux châteaux, paix aux chaumières" (War on castles, peace for cottages), Chamfort made a notable contribution to revolutionary historiography by writing half of the collective *Tableaux historiques de la Révolution* (1791; translated as *Historical Pictures, Representing the Most Remarkable Events Which Occurred During the Early Period of the French Revolution,* 1803). Although Louis XVI's cavalier attitude toward the newly constituted republic reinforced Chamfort's republicanism, his depiction of the Revolution targeted monarchical institutions rather than its representatives.

Chamfort's association with Mirabeau and other "opportunistic members of the constituent Assembly" fostered monarchist Antoine Rivarol's criticism of Chamfort as a republican. Solicited by interior minister Jean-Marie Roland in 1792, Chamfort reluctantly became administrator of the Bibliothèque nationale (French National Library). Like many revolutionary sympathizers, he dropped the "de" once attached to his name to avoid unwanted association with the nobility. His finances increasingly poorer, he soon moved from his quarters at the Bibliothèque nationale into a smaller apartment. When the Société de 1789 (Society of 1789), founded by Sieyès; Marie Joseph Paul Yves Roch Gilbert du Montier, marquis de Lafayette; Talleyrand; Marie-Jean-Antoine Nicolas de Caritat, marquis de Condorcet; Jacques-Pierre Brissot, Chamfort himself, and thirty other men, veered to the right, he decided to resign. Thus, Chamfort became even more suspect to the Jacobins as he now stood "against reaction and against insurrection,"–the motto for the Girondin faction (a group of Third Estate moderate representatives, a few of whom came from the southwestern Gironde area)–retreating away from the more radical stance of the Montaguards, named after the "Montagne" (mountain), that is, the higher benches in the room where extremist representatives would seat during sessions of the legislative Assembly. Throughout the Revolution, he never endorsed the recourse to the Terror, moving closer to Condorcet and away from action into reflection.

Brought before the Committee of General Safety in 1793, Chamfort was quickly released but went on to report openly on the excesses ordered by Jean-Paul Marat, Maximilien-François-Marie-Isidore de Robespierre, and others in power. Publicly denounced as an antirevolutionary traitor to the republic in July, he was arrested two weeks later, jailed at the Madelonnettes, released, but kept under house arrest by a ward whose expenses he had to pay. After Pierre-Anchor Tobiesen Duby, an opportunist coworker eager to inherit his librarianship, published accusations against him in the Jacobin *Journal de la Montagne,* Chamfort immediately resigned from the Bibliothèque nationale to better refute the accusations. But when his ward announced another arrest warrant, on 14 November 1793, Chamfort, terrified lest he might be headed for the guillotine, first shot himself–only blowing his eye out–then slashed his throat and chest. As the police were drafting a report on his suicide attempt, Chamfort found the strength to sign a declaration that he would rather kill himself than forfeit his freedom in prison. Having moved once more to smaller quarters, rue de Chabanais, he seemed to be recovering surprisingly well from his wounds. However, while he planned for a newspaper, *La Décade philosophique,* with his friend Pierre-Louis Ginguené, a virulent infection killed him on 13 April 1794.

Ginguené soon published Chamfort's *Oeuvres complètes* (1795, Complete Works), including his plays and his academic speeches, as well as material selected from the few files he salvaged after Chamfort's death. Ginguené suspected that governmental censors had managed to spirit away boxes of compromising notes he knew Chamfort had written over the previous thirty years. Chamfort's files, filled with fragmented observations on society, included *Maximes et pensées, caractères et anecdotes,* as well as a few lapidary *petits dialogues philosophiques* (short philosophical dialogues) thereafter published in various editions of Chamfort's works. Ginguené selected from this material and gathered it following an outline left by Chamfort while discarding Chamfort's original title, *Produits de la civilisation perfectionnée* (Products of the Perfected Civilization). Largely because of Ginguené's dogged efforts to publish them, Chamfort's works were reedited within a decade of their first appearance. They received wide attention well into the nineteenth century. Among several editors, Pierre René Auguis published an enlarged edition in 1824–1825, including poems and odes.

By the 1850s, Sébastien-Roch Nicolas de Chamfort's plays became second in importance to his *maximes, caractères, petits dialogues,* and *anecdotes* in the reception of his work. This collection of vignettes written in the style of a gossip column depicted a tongue-in-cheek vision of Parisian society as a pitiful spectacle in which all persons must play a hypocritical role lest they be excluded from it–hence, the preface to the *maximes,* in which Chamfort explained his decision to stop writing early so that he would not compromise his integrity by relying on fluctuating tastes and poor judgment and the arbitrarily maintained privileges of genealogy exposed. Plagued by the class distinctions defining the ruling aristocracy, society is thus framed historically. A mediocre imitation of its own ruins, it becomes a decadent arena perpetuating its inherent injustice at the expense of the poor and uneducated, ultimately making life a burden and an illness relieved only by death.

Chamfort's merciless portrayals of the wealthy and the great, of marriage and friendship, of literary and political institutions, and of France before and after the Revolution, have fostered two critical trends. André Pellisson and Emile Dousset, who somewhat rehabilitated Chamfort in the 1890s and 1940s, nevertheless represent the first dominant trend, an essentially biographical interpretation of Chamfort's writings. In contrast, the second trend shifted scholarly attention to Chamfort's texts and away from his biography. In his 1940 preface to the *Maximes,* for instance, Albert Camus contributed to Chamfort's reputation as a moralist, also highlighting the novelistic qualities in his style. He also singled out how the title metaphor of Chamfort's ode "Les Volcans" (Volcanoes), expressed both his explosive nature and his revolutionary view of society. Louis Kronenberg portrayed Chamfort as a "master aphorist" beside Friedrich Nietzsche who, discovering Chamfort after publishing *The Gay Science,* believed Chamfort embodied his ideas. Others have further shifted focus onto Chamfort's style (Katz and Poisson). Chamfort's aphoristic manner, contrasted with that of La Bruyère and La Rochefoucauld, appears less prescriptive and generalizing. Chamfort implicitly invites readers to participate in his observation and make up their minds, simultaneously calling for a critical and relativistic approach to the historical, social, and moral reality of his time. Finally, John Renwick's extensive critical bibliography (1986) and Claude Arnaud's acclaimed biography (1988, translated in 1992) offer broad access to Chamfort's life and production.

Bibliographies:

Pierre Grosclaude, *Chamfort: Produits de la civilisation perfectionnée. Maximes et pensées. Caractères et anecdotes* (Paris: Imprimerie nationale, 1953), pp. 51-65;

John Renwick, *Chamfort devant la postérité: 1794-1984* (Oxford: Voltaire Foundation, 1986).

Biographies:

Emile Dousset, *Sébastien-Roch-Nicolas Chamfort et son temps* (Paris: Fasquelle, 1943; Clermont-Ferrand: Editions Volcans, 1974);

Julien Teppe, *Chamfort, sa vie, son oeuvre, sa pensée* (Paris: Clairac, 1950);

André Pellisson, *Chamfort, étude sur sa vie, son caractère, ses écrits* (Geneva: Slatkine Reprints, 1970);

Claude Arnaud, *Biographie suivie de soixante-dix maximes, anecdotes, mots et dialogues inédits, ou jamais ré édités* (Paris: Laffont, 1988); translated by Deke Dusinberre as *Chamfort: A Biography* (Chicago: University of Chicago Press, 1992).

References:

Albert Camus, "Preface," in Chamfort, *Maximes et anecdotes* (Paris: Livre Club du Libraire, 1961);

Gilbert Chinard, Introduction, in *La Jeune Indienne* (Princeton: Princeton University Press, 1945), pp. 1-34;

René Doumic, "Deux moralistes 'fin de siècle': Chamfort et Rivarol," in *Etudes sur la littérature française: première série* (Paris: Perrin, 1896), pp. 155-179;

Jeannine Etiemble, "Chamfort," in *Encyclopaedia universalis,* volume 4 (Paris, 1990-1993), pp. 306-307;

Pierre Grosclaude, *Chamfort: produits de la civilisation perfectionnée. Maximes et pensées. Caractères et anecdotes* (Paris: Imprimerie nationale, 1953);

Eve Katz, "Chamfort," *Yale French Studies,* 40 (1968): 32-46;

Louis Kronenberger, "Chamfort," in *The Last Word: Portraits of Fourteen Master Aphorists* (New York: Macmillan, 1972), pp. 61-77;

W. S. Merwin, Introduction, in *Products of the Perfected Civilization: Selected Writings of Chamfort,* by Chamfort, translated by Merwin (New York: Macmillan, 1969);

Georges Pellissier, "Chamfort et Rivarol," in *Etudes de littérature contemporaine,* volume 1 (Paris: Perrin, 1898), pp. 337-352;

Jean-Marc Poisson, "Chamfort continuateur de La Rochefoucauld et de La Bruyère," dissertation, University of Wisconsin, 1999;

Georges Poulet, "Chamfort and Laclos," in *The Interior Distance,* translated by Elliott Coleman (Baltimore: Johns Hopkins University Press, 1959), pp. 45-55.

Papers:

Manuscripts by Sébastien-Roch Nicolas de Chamfort can be found in the Archives of the Bibliothèque nationale (Van Praet papers and Archive 47); in the Archives Nationales (Central Index); at the Bibliothèque nationale (Nouvelles acquisitions françaises, and Ginguené papers); in the Archives of the Comédie-Française; in the Archives of the Académie Française, and in the Archives de la Seine. Additional papers can be found in the Bibliothèque Historique de la Ville de Paris; in the Bibliothèque de l'Institut de France; and in the municipal libraries in Reims, Lille, and Paris (14th Arrondissement). Likewise, material by Chamfort can be found in Charavay, in the "Revue des autographes" (1866-1922). Papers can also be found in the Archives of the Puy-de-Dôme and in the private collection of Dr. Girard, in Clermont-Ferrand.

Isabelle de Charrière

(20 October 1740 - 26 December 1805)

Ruth P. Thomas
Temple University

BOOKS: *Le Noble, conte moral* (Amsterdam: Van Harrevelt, 1763); translated by Sybil Marjoie Cuffe Lubback as *The Noble,* in *Four Tales by Zélide* (London: Constable, 1925);

Lettres neuchâteloises (Amsterdam, 1784; Lausanne, 1784; revised edition, Geneva, 1784);

Lettres de Mistriss Henley, publiées par son amie (Geneva, 1784); translated by Lubback as *Mistress Henley,* in *Four Tales by Zélide* (London: Constable, 1925);

Lettres écrites de Lausanne (Geneva: Bonnant, 1785); translated by Lubback as *Letters from Lausanne,* in *Four Tales by Zélide* (London: Constable, 1925);

Caliste, ou suite des Lettres écrites de Lausanne (Geneva & Paris: Prault, 1787); translated as *Letters Written from Lausanne,* 2 volumes (Bath: Printed by R. Cruttwell and sold by C. Dilly, 1799);

Observations et conjectures politiques, 1787-1788 (Verrières: Witel, 1787-1788);

Bien-né: nouvelles et anecdotes: apologie de la flatterie (Paris, 1788);

Les Phéniciennes (Neuchâtel: Société typographique, 1788);

Lettres d'un évêque français à la nation (Neuchâtel: Fauche-Borel, 1789);

Plainte et défense de Thérèse Levasseur (Neuchâtel: Fauche-Borel, 1789);

Eclaircissemens relatifs à la publication des Confessions de Rousseau (Neuchâtel: Fauche-Borel, 1790);

Eloge de Jean-Jacques Rousseau (Paris: Grégoire, 1790);

Lettre à M. Necker sur son administration, écrite par lui-même; suivie d'Aiglonette et Insinuante, conte, par l'auteur de Bien-né; des Trois règnes, conte, par M. ***; et d'un décret sur la constitution civile du clergé (Neuchâtel: Fauche-Borel, 1791);

Lettres trouvées dans des porte-feuilles d'émigrés (Lausanne: Durand, 1793);

L'Emigré (Neuchâtel: Spineux, 1793);

Les Trois Femmes, 2 volumes (London: Baylis, 1796);

Réponse à l'écrit du colonel de La Harpe, attributed to Charrière by P. Godet (N.p., 1797);

Isabelle de Charrière (Geneva Museum of Art and History; from Dorothy Farnum, The Dutch Divinity, *1959; Thomas Cooper Library, University of South Carolina)*

L'Abbé de la Tour, ou recueil de nouvelles et autres écrits divers, 3 volumes (Leipzig: Pierre Philippe Wolf, 1798-1799)–volume 1, *Trois femmes* and *De l'Abbé De La Tour;* volume 2, *Honorine d'Userche* and *De l'Abbé De La Tour, suivie de Trois Dialogues;* volume 3, *Sainte Anne* and *Les Ruines de Yedburg;*

Sir Walter Finch et son fils William (Geneva: Paschoud, 1806).

Editions and Collections: *Lettres neuchâteloises, suivies de Trois Femmes,* afterword by Charly Guyot (Lausanne: Bibliothèque romande, 1971);

Caliste, ou lettres écrites de Lausanne, edited by Claudine Hermann (Paris: Des femmes, 1979);

Oeuvres complètes, 10 volumes, edited by Jean-Daniel Candaux, C. P. Courtney, Pierre H. Dubois, Simone Dubois-De Bruyn, Patrice Thompson, Jérôme Vercruysse, and Dennis M. Wood (Amsterdam: Van Oorschot, 1979–1984);

Isabelle de Charrière, une aristocrate révolutionnaire: écrits 1788–1794, edited by Isabelle Vissière (Paris: Des femmes, 1988);

Lettres neuchâteloises, edited by Isabelle and Jean-Louis Vissière, preface by Christophe Calame (Paris: La Différence, 1991);

Honorine d'Userche, nouvelle de l'abbé de la Tour (Toulouse: Editions Ombre, 1992);

Lettres trouvées dans des portefeuilles d'émigrés 1793, preface by Colette Piau-Gillot (Paris: Côté-femmes, 1993);

Lettres de Mistriss Henley publiées par son amie, edited by Joan Hinde Stewart and Philip Stewart (New York: Modern Language Association, 1993);

Trois Femmes, edited by Claire Jacquier (Lausanne: Editions L'Age d'Homme, 1996);

Lettres neuchâteloises, Lettres de mistriss Henley, Lettres écrites de Lausanne in *Romans de femmes du XVIIIe siècle,* edited by Raymond Trousson (Paris: Robert Laffont, 1996);

Sainte Anne, edited by Yvette Went-Daoust (Amsterdam & Atlanta: Rodopi, 1998);

Sir Walter Finch et son fils William, edited by Valérie Cossy (Paris: Editions Desjonquères, 2000).

TRANSLATION: Elizabeth Inchbald, *La Nature et l'art,* 2 volumes, translated by Charrière and Isabelle de Gélieu (Neuchâtel: Fauche-Borel, 1797).

Among her contemporaries, Isabelle de Charrière was known for her brilliant mind and her sharp wit. She was also celebrated for the company she kept: James Boswell, who courted her; Benjamin Constant, with whom she had a long and stormy relationship; and Constant's uncle, Constant d'Hermenches, with whom she exchanged letters for fourteen years. She was at the same time a prolific writer: in addition to her many letters—comprising six volumes of her complete works—she composed plays, librettos (and sometimes the music for them), verse, political pamphlets, and novellas. Many of her theatrical works, however, were left unfinished, and few were published; moreover, her later novels, in limited and sometimes foreign editions and translations, did not circulate widely. Her early novels brought her some fame and moderate success, but they were soon forgotten except for one, *Caliste* (1787; translated as *Letters Written from Lausanne,* 1799), which influenced Constant's *Adolphe* (1816) and Gemaine de Staël's *Corinne* (1807). Having spent most of her life in Holland and Switzerland, Charrière was kept from the literary mainstream by her distance from Paris, while her nontraditional novels with their simple plots, their focus on the vicissitudes of domestic life, and their inconclusive endings were out of step with the fictional conventions of the time.

Although nineteenth-century critics such as Charles-Augustin Sainte-Beuve praised her work and especially the beauty of her language, Charrière's life, particularly her relationship with Constant, continued to overshadow her writing until the last third of the twentieth century. New editions of her novels and a scrupulously edited collection of her complete works have made her writing more accessible to modern readers than to those of her own generation. Three Charrière societies—in Switzerland, the Netherlands, and France—collaborate on an annual bulletin dedicated to her life and work. The early novels, especially, have received critical attention: Charrière's break with tradition is hailed as the sign of her originality, and she is considered by many the Jane Austen of French letters.

Isabella Agneta Elisabeth van Tuyll van Serooskerken was born 20 October 1740 in the family château at Zuylen, not far from Utrecht. Her family had great wealth and social standing and a reputation for integrity. Her father, who belonged to the ancient Dutch nobility, was an inspector of dikes and public works and active in the local government, and her mother came from a wealthy merchant family of Amsterdam. Isabella, known to her contemporaries as Belle, was the eldest of five surviving children in a strict but loving and supportive family, for whom she felt great pride and loyalty. The family wintered at their mansion in Utrecht, where they often entertained royal guests and were close enough to The Hague to participate in the social events of aristocratic life.

Like many aristocratic families in that cosmopolitan country, the family spoke French along with their native Dutch, which was usually reserved for the servants. Belle's interest in French was sparked when she was ten when her Swiss governess, Jeanne-Louise Prevost, took her charge to Geneva, Prevost's native city, where Belle spent the year, with trips to Paris and Versailles; later, she wrote more easily and gracefully in French than in her native Dutch. The governess, who left when Belle was thirteen, corresponded with her for the next five years. Only Prevost's letters remain: they offer a portrait of the young Belle as highly intelligent and accomplished, artistically and musically talented, but excessively sensitive, with a penchant for melancholy.

Along with her many gifts, Belle was a free spirit who had little taste for the formalities of her class or the restrictions of provincial life. That she had been born

Dutch and a Tuyll astonished her. Her outspokenness, unconventional nature, and sharp wit—which set the tongues of The Hague wagging—hardly stood her in good stead for marriage, and while most young women of her social standing married in their twenties, Belle did not. Certainly she wanted to marry, have children, and leave the stifling provincial atmosphere. She was an attractive young woman and had many prospects and suitors—whom she called the *épouseurs* (would-be husbands)—including the prince of Orange himself. Her most famous suitor was Boswell, biographer of Samuel Johnson, who met her during a stay at Utrecht in 1763. Although the two corresponded until 1768, and Boswell even went so far as to write to her father of his intention to marry her, he wavered and finally decided that she was too intelligent, cultured, outspoken, and emancipated to make him a good wife.

The years before marriage, nevertheless, were not idle ones, and she filled them with the intellectual activity she found important for her peace of mind. She read the classical French writers, among them Michel de Montaigne, whose skepticism she shared; Jean de La Fontaine, whom she often quoted in her writing; and Marie de Sévigné, to whom she was later compared. Belle studied the philosophes—and later met Denis Diderot and Voltaire—and by age eighteen, she had already analyzed Charles-Louis de Secondat Montesquieu's *Esprit des lois* (1748, Spirit of the Laws). She learned physics and math and taught herself Italian. She also wrote. She composed verses and literary portraits, including her own, where under the name of Zélide—the name that Boswell used in his letters—she offered a provocative description of her virtues and her faults and noted that she was too sensitive to find lasting happiness.

Her first published work, *Le Noble* (published as a book in 1763, translated as *The Noble* in *Four Tales by Zélide*, 1925), first appeared in 1762 in *Le Journal étranger* (The Foreign Journal). An irreverent story in the tradition of Voltaire's *Candide* (1759), it satirizes her own noble class. When Julie wants to marry a fine young man of inferior nobility, her father refuses to allow the marriage. Julie elopes, using the family portraits as a platform as she flees from the family château. Belle's family was scandalized, and when an anonymous edition of *Le Noble* appeared the following year, her parents removed as many copies as they could from circulation. This scandal was but the first of many that her work created.

Her disregard of convention and independent cast of mind had also been apparent somewhat earlier on 28 February 1760 at The Hague at the Duke of Brunswick's ball when she approached David-Emmanuel Constant d'Hermenches; she wrote to him a month later. An officer in the Dutch army, d'Hermenches was eighteen years her senior, married, and had a reputation as a libertine. The first letter remained unanswered, but when they met two years later at The Hague at another official ball, she wrote to him again. Their correspondence, clandestine at first, continued for fourteen years. For the young woman, as Janet Whatley and Malcolm Whatley have noted in their introduction to the correspondence, d'Hermenches was the ideal reader to whom she wrote in total candor about her most intimate feelings and desires and with whom she could develop her mind. For d'Hermenches, Tuyll was not merely a kindred spirit but a "moral compass," guiding the middle-aged man of the world through his disillusions and disappointments. In these letters, which have been likened to a chaste *Liaisons dangereuses* (1782), she honed her skills for the epistolary novels she later wrote.

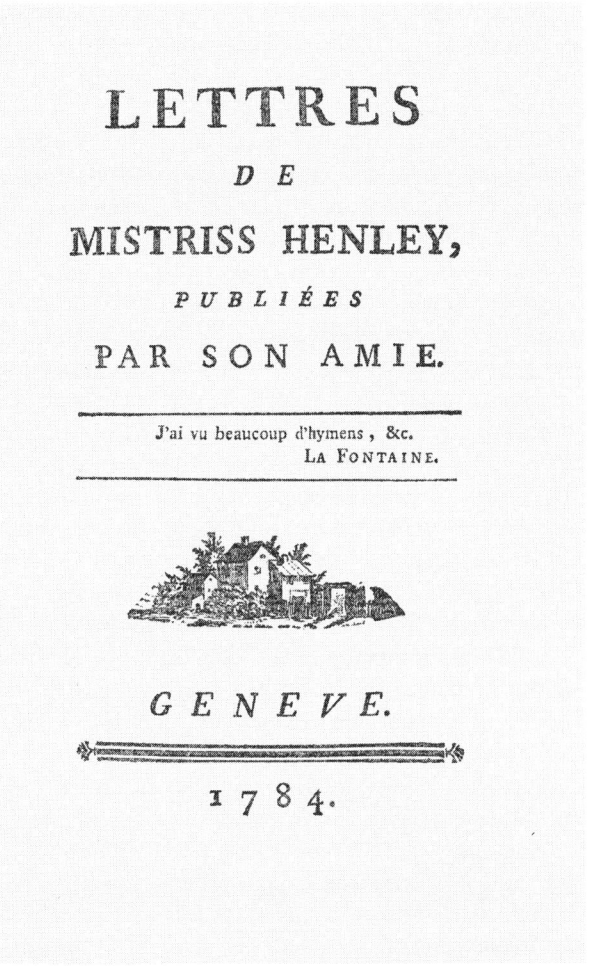

Title page for Charrière's epistolary novel about a wife who tries to resolve marital problems by adapting to her husband's personality (from C. P. Courtney, *A Preliminary Bibliography of Isabelle de Charrière*, 1980; Thomas Cooper Library, University of South Carolina)

Although d'Hermenches, who was estranged from his wife, would have liked to marry her himself, he tried to arrange her marriage with his friend the marquis de Bellegarde. Bellegarde was older, not too intelligent nor particularly rich, but such a marriage would bring her autonomy and children and also the chance to remain near d'Hermenches. But problems with the dowry, the need for a papal dispensation so that the Catholic Bellegarde could marry the Protestant Tuyll, and finally her own misgivings, ended the courtship. When she did at last settle on a husband in 1771, it was someone of her own choosing–Charles-Emmanuel de Charrière, a Swiss gentleman who had been her brothers' tutor. Bookish, quiet, sensitive, he was not her equal either financially or socially, and her reluctant father had to be persuaded to permit the marriage. D'Hermenches had reservations about the compatibility of the impetuous Tuyll and the phlegmatic Charrière, as did Charrière himself. Tuyll, however, was highly positive and certain of marital happiness.

With him she moved to Colombier, near Neuchâtel, into le Pontet, the house he shared with his elderly father and his two unmarried sisters. She tried to adapt to the routines of country life with its chores and gardening. She had time for books and letters, little parties, and short visits. Charles-Emmanuel de Charrière was a kind, loving, and supportive husband. Still, the marriage did not bring the happiness she expected. The children so desired did not come in spite of trips to spas for fertility treatments; she was not always in good health; and she was bored by the monotony of provincial life. Seemingly, tensions arose with her husband as well. As a distraction, she began to write.

At age forty-four, she published her first novel. *Lettres neuchâteloises* (1784) is a story of young love and courtship, closely linked to the social and economic realities of the time. In letters to their respective and silent friends, Henri Meyer, a young clerk newly arrived from Germany, and the noble but impoverished Marianne de la Prise confide their deepening feelings for one another. Henri's letters also include his– and Charrière's own–impressions of life in Neuchâtel. Their lives and letters become intertwined with those of Julianne C., the little seamstress with whom Henri has had a short fling and who is now pregnant. Marianne serves as the intermediary between Henri and the young woman and even makes arrangements for the baby's birth. Julianne's misfortunes–she must give up the baby and disappear–cement the relationship of Henri and Marianne, and the two finally acknowledge their love. The novel, however, has no resolution: Henri is called home.

Charrière chose the familiar setting of Neuchâtel to give greater reality to her fictional characters. The realism of the novel did not please all her readers. The prominent role of the working-class Julianne C., the impropriety of the well-born Marianne's even discussing Julianne's pregnancy with Henri, and the linguistic realism of Julianne's speech shocked some readers. Worse still, Charrière also included a character, aptly named *le caustique,* who made disparaging remarks about the people of Neuchâtel. Since the edition published in Lausanne (at Charrière's own expense) had many mistakes, Charrière traveled to Geneva to provide a corrected edition. In her second edition, she added an epigraph in verse to try to placate her readers.

While she was in Geneva, everyone was reading *Le Mari sentimental,* an "anonymous" novel by Samuel de Constant, a brother of Hermenches. M. de Bompré, a country gentleman of forty-six, tired of bachelor life, marries an intelligent and reasonable woman who turns his world upside down, makes his life a living hell, and drives him to suicide. Charrière decided to write her own version of the story, from the perspective of the wife, setting her novel in England but using Constant's monophonic epistolary form and many of the same details, and making the novel itself–which her heroine reads–a pretext for her own. In the *Lettres de Mistriss Henley* (1784, translated as *Mistress Henley,* 1925) the heroine, without family or fortune and pressed to marry, chooses a seemingly perfect husband–a handsome, cultured, and well-off country gentleman, widowed with a young daughter. But the differences in temperament and lifestyle between the phlegmatic, reasonable, and conservative Henley and his sensitive, imaginative, and sophisticated wife create marital tension in the trivial events of daily life. Faced with her husband's disapproval and his increasing insensitivity–he excludes her from important decisions in the marriage, including plans for the nurturing and care of their unborn child– she does not challenge his authority, in part perhaps because of her economic and social dependency. Instead, she resolves to conform and become more like her reasonable husband or die in the process.

Like her previous works, the novel created controversy. Published in Geneva, it reportedly split society in two, with men and women taking sides with the husband or the wife according to their sex. An anonymous *Justification de M. Henley* appeared soon afterward, written presumably by the now-widowed Mr. Henley. The *Justification,* along with Constant's and Charrière's novels, was published in Paris in 1785 in an unauthorized edition, much to the chagrin of Charrière, who quickly disclaimed authorship of the sequel. Some readers, struck by the realism of the characters, saw parallels between the fictional Henleys and the Charrières.

The *Lettres écrites de Lausanne* (1785, Letters from Lausanne) followed a year later. Another tale of young love and courtship, it was narrated this time by a widowed mother–noble but of insufficient fortune–concerned about the marriage prospects of her daughter. Although the heroine has several prospective suitors, only one, Edouard, a young lord in Lausanne on his grand tour of Europe, has clearly captured her heart. But the young man, enamored of Cécile as he seems to be, is unwilling or unable to make a commitment. So the mother and daughter leave Lausanne and the unresolved love affair.

The mother's perspective, as she writes a series of letters to a female relative, allowed Charrière to offer an unromanticized view of courtship and marriage and to lay bare the mechanisms and the strategies–the female education, the proper behavior, the role-playing–required by a young woman of limited economic means to find a suitable husband. But more than a mere primer of marriage codes, the book also permitted Charrière to offer an unusually positive image of the mother-daughter relationship, as the mother lovingly and frankly guides her daughter through her social, emotional, and sexual initiation. The novel was popular enough to be reedited in Paris the following year.

The creativity and productivity of these years–Charrière also composed sonatas, wrote an opera libretto and a comedy–did not cure Charrière of her despondency. At the beginning of 1786, after what may have been an unhappy love affair, she went alone to Paris (where her husband joined her in December). She continued to write music, and she also returned to the novel. Many readers wanted a sequel to the *Lettres de Lausanne,* but Charrière decided not to conclude the story of Cécile and Edouard but to focus instead on the experiences of William, Edouard's tutor. The novel *Caliste* was published in 1787 as the second part of *Lettres de Lausanne.* In a long "letter" to Cécile's mother, William recounts his love affair with Caliste–a beautiful, talented, and moral young woman tainted with a past. Caliste would gladly marry William, whom she loves, and erase the social stigma. But William hesitates, unwilling to face his father's disapproval and uncertain of his own feelings. Both make unhappy marriages, meet again briefly, and express their love. Caliste dies shortly afterward, much to William's chagrin.

Caliste was Charrière's most popular novel. The remorseful male narrator, the confessional form, and the unhappy love affair were conventions frequently used by male authors and familiar to eighteenth-century readers. The modern reader, however, is aware of the subtext of the novel. As Jean Starobinski has pointed out, Caliste's story is a more dramatic version of Cécile's, suggesting again the emotional and the material dependency of women. Caliste, moreover, differs from the traditional heroine: she is a desiring sub-

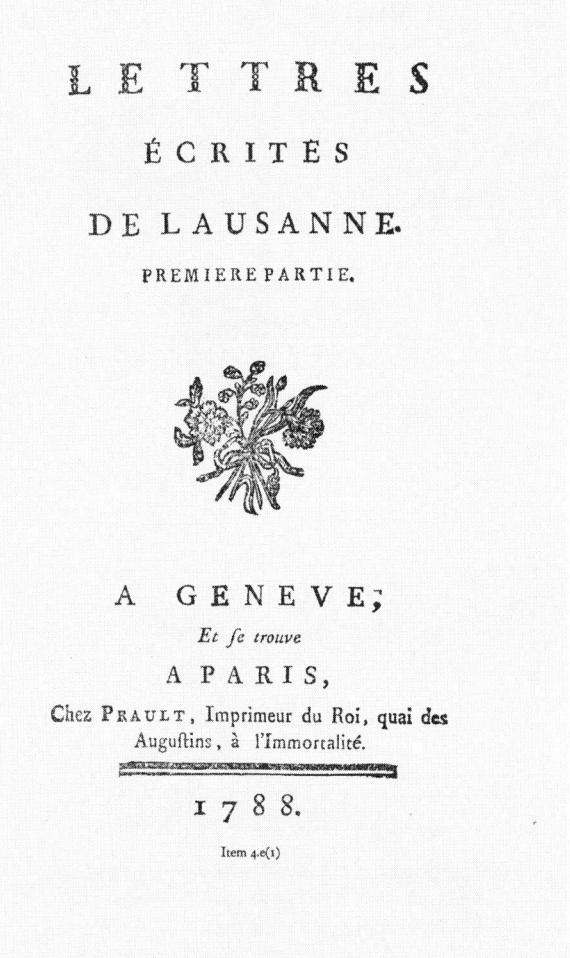

Title page for Charrière's 1788 corrected second edition of her epistolary novel first published in Geneva (from C. P. Courtney, A Preliminary Bibliography of Isabelle de Charrière, *1980; Thomas Cooper Library, University of South Carolina*)

ject, not a desired object, and the tale is told without the usual male bonding, since the intended reader is a woman. *Caliste* was perhaps Charrière's most personal novel. She said later that she wept as she wrote it and that she never had the courage to reread it.

During her year and a half in Paris, Charrière met, at the salon of Mme Suard, many of those who played a role in the French Revolution to follow. There also she met Benjamin Constant. He–the brilliant but already jaded twenty-year-old nephew of D'Hermenches–and Charrière were instantly drawn to one another, kindred spirits intellectually and emotionally, with similar republican ideals. During Constant's later visits to Pontet, they passed nights in animated conversation, drinking tea and dissecting ideas and prejudices, and they often wrote at great length to one another. As Constant's mentor (and perhaps his lover), Charrière

Bust of Charrière (Houdon, Museum of Art and History, Neuchâtel, Switzerland; from Dorothy Farnum, The Dutch Divinity, *1959; Thomas Cooper Library, University of South Carolina)*

helped the young man develop his intellect much as his uncle had helped develop hers. Although they remained lifelong friends—Charrière's last letter was written to Constant—their relationship was severely strained by Constant's love affair with Germaine de Staël and Charrière's jealousy.

In the fall of 1787 Charrière returned to Colombier, where she spent the rest of her life. As the political climate darkened in both the Netherlands and France, Charrière's works took on the cast of the contemporary scene. Disenchanted with the violence and the dogmatism of the revolutionary regimes, she composed pamphlets, in which she spoke out against the death penalty and lettres de cachet and in favor of tolerance and reform, and little tales that she addressed to the king and to the queen of France. To the former she counseled "sagesse" (wisdom) and to Marie Antoinette she advised "souplesse" (flexibility). Charrière also wrote on behalf of Thérèse Levassseur, Jean-Jacques Rousseau's companion (accused, among other things, of causing his death), and helped edit Rousseau's *Les Confessions* (1781–1788). Inspired by the plight of the émi-

grés who had come to Neuchâtel—she aided some financially and mentored others—she wrote *Lettres trouvées dans des porte-feuilles d'émigrés* (1793, Letters Found among the Émigrés' Papers), a story of love and friendship between those who supported the French Revolution and others who did not. Charrière, to be sure, was also annoyed by the arrogance of some of the émigrés, and they inspired her comedies, some of which she tried unsuccessfully to have performed. Other novels followed in which the personal stories, often of love and its obstacles, were linked to philosophical problems, moral and ethical dilemmas. *Les Trois Femmes* (1796, Three Women) dealt with good and evil and the changing notion of duty; *Honorine d'Userche* (1796), with faith and its loss; *Sainte-Anne* (1797), with education and the virtues of illiteracy. Some of these novels with their controversial subjects were difficult to publish, and they appeared first in German translations. In her last novel, *Sir Walter Finch et son fils William* (1806, Sir Walter Finch and His Son William), she returned to the theme of education, this time from the highly original perspective of the father writing a journal for his young son. In failing health, Charrière died of cancer on 26 December 1805.

In her works, as in her life, Isabelle de Charrière escapes classification. All her fiction deals with the heart and the mind; with relationships of gender, family, and social class; and with questions of education. But the early novels seem classical in theme and form while the later works, with their ideological basis, place her more in the tradition of the eighteenth-century philosophes. Charrière chafed under social and literary constraint, prized autonomy, distrusted dogma, and moved easily between different artistic forms and literary genres. Her subtle portraits of eighteenth-century life, while not in the popular tradition of the times, now enjoy a far broader public appreciation because they speak to the sensitivity of the modern reader.

Letters:

Lettres de Belle de Zuylen (Madame de Charrière) à Constant d'Hermenches, edited by Philippe Godet (Paris: Plon / Geneva: A. Jullien, 1909); translated, with an introduction and annotations, by Janet Whatley and Malcolm Whatley as *There Are No Letters Like Yours: The Correspondence of Isabelle de Charrière and Constant d'Hermenches* (Lincoln & London: University of Nebraska Press, 2000);

Boswell in Holland, 1763–1764, edited by Frederick A. Pottle (New York: McGraw-Hill, 1952);

Une Liaison dangereuse: correspondance avec Constant d'Hermenches 1760–1776, edited by Isabelle and Jean-Louis Vissière (Paris: La Différence, 1991);

Benjamin Constant, Isabelle de Charrière, Correspondance, 1787–1805, edited by Jean-Daniel Candaux (Paris: Desjonquères, 1996).

Bibliographies:

C. B. Courtney, *A Preliminary Bibliography of Isabelle de Charrière* (Oxford: Voltaire Foundation, 1980);

Courtney, *Isabelle de Charrière. A Secondary Bibliography* (Oxford: Voltaire Foundation / Paris: Jean Touzot, 1982).

Biographies:

Philippe Godet, *Madame de Charrière et ses amis, d'après de nombreux documents inédits (1740–1805),* 2 volumes (Geneva: A Jullien, 1906; Geneva: Slatkine Reprints, 1973);

Geoffrey Scott, *The Portrait of Zélide* (New York: Scribner, 1927);

C. P. Courtney, *Isabelle de Charrière (Belle de Zuylen): A Biography* (Oxford: Voltaire Foundation, 1993);

Raymond Trousson, *Isabelle de Charrière, un destin de femme au XVIIIe siècle* (Paris: Hachette, 1994).

References:

Jenene Allison, *Revealing Difference: The Fiction of Isabelle de Charrière* (Newark: University of Delaware Press, 1995);

Nadine Bérenguier, "From Clarens to Hollowpark, Isabelle de Charrière's Quiet Revolution," *Studies in Eighteenth-Century French Culture,* 21 (1991): 219–243;

Alix Deguise, *Trois Femmes: le monde de Madame de Charrière* (Geneva: Slatkine, 1981);

Beatrice Fink, ed., *Isabelle de Charrière/Belle de Zuylen,* special issue of *Eighteenth-Century Life,* 13 (February 1989);

Susan Jackson, "The Novels of Isabelle de Charrière, or, A Woman's Work is Never Done," *Studies in Eighteenth-Century French Culture,* 14 (1985): 299–306;

Kathleen Jaeger, *Male and Female Roles in the Eighteenth Century: The Challenge of Replacement and Displacement in the Novels of Isabelle de Charrière* (New York: Peter Lang, 1994);

Doris Jakubec and Jean-Daniel Candaux, eds., *Une Européenne: Isabelle de Charrière en son siècle: Actes du Colloque de Neuchâtel, 11–13 novembre 1993* (Hauterive-Neuchâtel: Gilles Attinger, 1994);

Marie-Paule Laden, "'Quel aimable et cruel petit livre': Madame de Charrière's *Mistriss Henley,*" *French Forum,* 11 (September 1986): 289–299;

Jacqueline Letzer, *Intellectual Tacking: Questions of Education in the Works of Isabelle de Charrière* (Amsterdam & Atlanta: Rodopi, 1998);

Elizabeth J. MacArthur, "Devious Narratives: Refusal of Closure in Two Eighteenth-Century Epistolary Novels," *Eighteenth-Century Studies,* 21 (Fall 1987): 1–20;

Sigyn Mimier, *Madame de Charrière: les premiers romans* (Paris: Champion / Geneva: Slatkine, 1987);

Monique Moser-Verrey, "Isabelle de Charrière en quête d'une meilleure entente," *Stanford French Review,* 11 (Spring 1987): 63–76;

Paul Pelckmans, "La fausse emphase de la 'mort de toi,'" *Neophilologus,* 72 (1988): 499–515;

Charles-Augustin Sainte-Beuve, "Madame de Charrière," in *Portraits de femmes* (Paris: Garnier, 1886), pp. 411–457;

Jean Starobinski, "*Les Lettres écrites de Lausanne* de Madame de Charrière: inhibition psychique et interdit social," in *Roman et Lumières au XVIIIe siècle* (Paris: Editions sociales, 1970), pp. 130–151;

Joan Hinde Stewart, "Designing Women," in *A New History of French Literature,* edited by Denis Hollier (Cambridge, Mass.: Harvard University Press, 1989), pp. 553–558;

Stewart, *Gynographs: French Novels by Women of the Late Eighteenth Century* (Lincoln: University of Nebraska Press, 1993);

Ruth P. Thomas, "The Teaching of the Fable: Mme de Charrière's Appropriation of 'Le Chêne et le roseau' in *Lettres de Mistriss Henley,*" in *Women Writers in Pre-Revolutionary France: Strategies of Emancipation,* edited by Colette H. Winn and Donna Kuizenga (New York: Garland, 1997), pp. 31–41;

Yvette Went-Daoust, ed., *Isabelle de Charrière (Belle de Zuylen): de la correspondance au roman épistolaire* (Amsterdam & Atlanta: Rodopi, 1995);

Janet Whatley, "Isabelle de Charrière," in *French Women Writers: A Bio-Bibliographical Source Book,* edited by Eva Martin Sartori and Dorothy Wynne Zimmerman (Westport, Conn.: Greenwood Press, 1991), pp. 35–46;

Whatley, "Letters to a Libertine: The Correspondence of Isabelle de Charrière and Constant d'Hermenches," in *Women Writers in Pre-Revolutionary France: Strategies of Emancipation,* edited by Winn and Kuizenga (New York: Garland, 1997), pp. 335–348.

Papers:

The papers of Isabelle de Charrière are located at the Bibliotheque publique de la ville de Neuchâtal, at the Bibliotheque universitaire in Geneva, and at the Bibliothèque cantonale et universitaire in Lausanne.

Gabrielle-Emilie Du Châtelet
(17 December 1706 – 10 September 1749)

S. Pascale Vergereau-Dewey
Kutztown University

BOOK: *Institutions de physique* (Paris: Prault, 1740).

OTHER: *Dissertation sur la nature et la propagation du feu,* in *Pièces qui ont remporté le prix de l'Académie Royale des Sciences en 1728: selon la fondation faite par feu Monsieur Rouillé de Meslay* . . . (Paris: Imprimerie Royale, 1739);
Doutes sur les religions révélées, adressés à Voltaire, ouvrage posthume (Paris, 1792);
La Fable des abeilles, in Ira Owen Wade, *Studies on Voltaire: With Some Unpublished Papers of Mme. du Châtelet* (Princeton: Princeton University Press, 1947);
Discours sur le bonheur, with an introduction by Robert Mauzi (Paris: Les Belles-Lettres, 1961).

TRANSLATIONS: Sophocles, *Œdipe Roi* (N.p., n.d.);
Isaac Newton, *Principes mathématiques de la philosophie naturelle par M. Newton,* translated by Châtelet with commentaries by Alexis de Clairaut, preface by Voltaire, 2 volumes (Paris: Desaint & Saillant, 1759).

Gabrielle-Emilie Du Châtelet (portrait by F.B. Lépicié; courtesy of Mme Thierry; from Nancy Mitford, Voltaire in Love, *1957; Thomas Cooper Library, University of South Carolina)*

An intellectual, eminent scientist, and accomplished singer and musician, Madame Du Châtelet is better known today as a translator and interpreter of Isaac Newton's works, which she helped make accessible in France. For a long time, biographers emphasized the role of Gabrielle-Emilie Le Tonnelier de Breteuil, marquise Du Châtelet-Laumont (or Madame "Newton-Pompon" Du Châtelet, as Voltaire affectionately called her) as Voltaire's "divine mistress." Recent criticism, however, has placed new focus on her own remarkable accomplishments as an independent thinker, endowed with a powerful intellect. In her time she was able to live almost as a law unto herself. Members of the scientific community treated her with respect, for, in fact, her own age recognized that her scientific and mathematical knowledge surpassed Voltaire's own.

Gabrielle-Emilie Le Tonnelier de Breteuil was born on 17 December 1706 in Paris. Her immediate ancestors had risen to power and wealth as magistrates of minor nobility. The second youngest of five children, Emilie was her father's favorite. Louis-Nicolas le Tonnelier, baron de Breteuil, had been involved in several scandals, but in 1697 he finally settled down at age forty-five and married Alexandra-Elisabeth de Froulay, a young woman of impeccable manners. He held the post of Master of Protocol for Ambassadors at Court, a position that required him to present foreign dignitaries to Louis XV at Versailles; in return, visitors paid him handsomely for the privilege. Nine years after his marriage, Breteuil retired from the court. Thanks to her father's support, Emilie received a superb education—a rare privilege at that time, even for a talented young lady. She grew up surrounded by talented tutors in the family's large Parisian home overlooking the Tuileries Gardens, where the Breteuils entertained lavishly. By age twelve, Emilie had mastered Latin and translated Aristotle's *Politics* and *Aesthetics* from classical Greek. A gifted linguist, she could read, write, and speak fluent English, Italian, and German. Torquato Tasso and John Milton were as familiar to her as Virgil. However, her real aptitude and long-lasting love was for mathematics and physical sciences. These interests made her the ideal partner and intellectual companion of the Anglophile Voltaire—a great admirer of Newton, John Locke, and Alexander Pope—and quite a match for his genius and biting wit. Châtelet was trained to think critically, a discipline she consistently pursued throughout her tumultuous life. She never flaunted her scholarship, and few ladies at court playing cards with her at the queen's table or watching her acting or singing at Cirey would have suspected that she was Newton's commentator. Growing up, she developed into a beautiful and extravagant lady of fashion who combined her passion for science with the feminine privileges of her time. She managed to earn recognition as an eminent scientist on a par with the most distinguished scholars of her age and as a philosophe in her own right. She belonged to an intellectual elite keenly interested in the cultural and political life of Europe. Châtelet was a lover of opera and theater; she was also a gifted singer and accomplished musician who gave recitals of works by Jean-Philippe Rameau. Yet, she did not confine herself to arts and sciences; she also enjoyed horseback riding and was a superb sportswoman who could beat most gentlemen in a duel. Throwing herself with abundant energy into every venue of life, she craved clothes and the finest gems; yet, she scorned money and lost vast sums at gambling. A gambler of high stakes, she was fascinated by games of chance and acquired great skill as a cardplayer. One night, she lost 80,000 livres playing a game of twenty-one. Enraged by her blunder, Voltaire quipped loudly in English that her partners were cheating. Such a public accusation required their immediate departure from Versailles to avoid arrest. The couple found refuge outside Paris at the Court of Sceaux until the scandal subsided. Châtelet did not concern herself much with others' opinions of her: she held a deep conviction of her own worth as a scientist, a mathematician, a classicist, a translator, and a feminist. In 1725, at age nineteen, she married the marquis Florent Claude Chastellet (the earlier spelling before being modernized by Voltaire), Seigneur de Cirey. Ten years her elder, this colonel of a regiment, the governor of Semur-en-Auxois in Burgundy, was the head of a great family of Lorraine who could trace their ancestry to the Crusades. She bore him three children, two sons and a daughter. Only interested in his military duties, the marquis was generally absent on garrison duty. According to aristocratic standards, the marriage was a success. News that the colonel had taken a mistress left his wife undisturbed and signaled that she also could take a lover, within limits of respectability. She had brief affairs but was only interested in her intellectual equals. She had a one-year liaison with dashing statesman and womanizer duc Louis de Richelieu; afterward they remained close friends whose correspondence, when published a century later, filled four volumes. Châtelet became famous as the mistress of Cirey-sur-Blaise, her husband's ancestral home, and as Voltaire's paramour from 1733 to 1749.

As a translator and interpreter of Newton's ideas, Châtelet made his work accessible in France and thus contributed to freeing French thought from its allegiance to the philosophy of René Descartes. Attraction to English thought and an empirical approach to philosophical questions divided intellectuals between the systems of Descartes and Newton. Since Descartes had been adequately expounded, Châtelet chose to give a wider scope to Voltaire's 1738 *Eléments de la philosophie de Newton* (Elements of Newton's Philosophy). In the twenty chapters of her *Institutions de physique* (1740, Institutions of Physics), she concerned herself with matter, gravity, weight, and equilibrium, but her interest soon shifted from her initial scientific description to philosophical argument. She was convinced that where scientific demonstration left off, reason should take over the demonstration. She decided, therefore, to find a form of formulaic calculation in metaphysics comparable to calculation in geometry. Pierre Louis Moreau de Maupertuis, a leading mathematician, astronomer, and flamboyant explorer of Lapland, helped her in the study of mathematics. A fellow of the English Royal Society and a member of the French Academy of Science, Maupertuis also served for a while as president of the Berlin Academy. This scholarly mathematician succeeded in making Newtonian ideas a modish topic of conversation in the great Parisian salons. In his company, high society protested the advantage of the law of gravity over Cartesian whirlwinds. Voltaire convinced Châtelet to translate Newton's works into French to make them available to French scholars.

Forced by Voltaire to choose between Maupertuis and social distractions in Paris or a quieter life of study with him in Cirey, Châtelet opted for the latter. She hosted Voltaire on her husband's estate at Cirey, where he escaped the king's arrest warrant following the unauthorized publication in 1734 of his *Lettres philosophiques sur les Anglais* (Letters Concerning the English Nation, 1733). Voltaire's *Lettres philosophiques* laid down a complete revolutionary program, and the result was a public burning of the book. Despite the light tone of the book, the

Title page for the 1742 Amsterdam edition of Châtelet's 1740 work (Institutions of Physics) on Isaac Newton's theories of matter, gravity, weight, and equilibrium, which includes her philosophical argument (from Esther Ehrman, Mme du Châtelet, 1986; Thomas Cooper Library, University of South Carolina)

ancien régime had reason to be threatened by such subversive writing. With the help of influential friends and the support of Louis de Richelieu, Châtelet made the necessary arrangements to guarantee Voltaire's personal freedom. The officer delivering the dreaded arrest warrant was told that Voltaire had left Paris to benefit from the curative waters in Lorraine. To be with Voltaire, Châtelet had to give up her meetings with Maupertuis and the exclusive clique of male philosophes and scientists at the café Gradot (among whom she had forced herself by cross-dressing) and the social whirl of Parisian salons, opera, theater, gambling, as well as friends such as the duchesse de Saint-Pierre. While the latter was a close friend, Marie du Deffand held a grudge against Châtelet for depriving Paris of Voltaire—the greatest and wittiest presence in literary circles. She left a vicious caricature of Châtelet describing her as a vain and shriveled creature, overdressed and untidy, wearing cheap undergarments, and covered with diamonds.

At Cirey in the summer of 1735, Châtelet began a highly productive intellectual life with Voltaire, who had already started to renovate the neglected estate, establishing a well-equipped laboratory and restocking and expanding the library acquisitions in science, philosophy, and history. According to Françoise de Graffigny's correspondence, Voltaire and Châtelet also built magnificently furnished wings for themselves, where they hosted friends and scientists from Paris and abroad, as well as many European literati and dignitaries. They included, for example, young Francesco Algarotti, son of a rich Venetian merchant, who was working on his 1737 *Il Newtonianismo per le dame* (Newton Made Easy for Ladies); well-known mathematicians Alexis-Claude Clairaut and Samuel Koenig; abbé de Bernis, the duc de Lorraine's chaplain; and President Charles Hénault, an influential member of the Parlement de Paris, the powerful judicial court. As did all who lived in the country, Voltaire and Châtelet depended on the mail. Knowing that Voltaire reacted strongly to many people and was prone to embroil himself in petty feuds, Châtelet secretly screened his mail. Literary critic abbé Pierre Desfontaines in particular remained abhorrent to Voltaire, who responded in kind to Desfontaines's vitriolic attacks. Châtelet involved herself in the quarrel, inundating her influential friends with letters of indignation. Although she resented Frederick of Prussia and suspected him of wanting to seduce Voltaire sexually, she wrote to ask him to put an end to the vicious libel campaign dubbed *La Voltairomanie*. Frederick, not particularly fond of her either, repeatedly invited Voltaire to join him in Berlin but never extended an invitation to her. She was suspicious every time Voltaire set off to escape the chief of police and maintained a strict censorship on his publications, keeping such subversive works as *Le Mondain* (1736, A Man of the World) and *La Pucelle* (1755, The Maid of Orleans) under lock and key.

Voltaire, on the other hand, delighted in reading excerpts of these irreverent works-in-progress to his guests. Graffigny, who was entertained at Cirey during the time of Voltaire's bitter quarrel with Desfontaines, gave a detailed daily account of the activities of her hosts to "Pampichon" (François Devaux), who was at the court of King Stanislas, in Lunéville, even quoting as much as she could remember from these improvised readings. In the habit of opening everyone's mail, Châtelet confronted the indiscreet guest and accused her of treachery. All of Voltaire's tact, apologies, and wit, as well as the other guests' efforts were needed to comfort Graffigny, who left Cirey precipitously and was so shaken that she could not describe the scene of December 1739 until one month later. She denied having copied excerpts of *La Pucelle* and made multiple gibes against Châtelet, even after she had gained fame and established her solid reputation as an author.

At Cirey, Voltaire and Châtelet worked together to produce critical works on Newton, English and German philosophy, and critical commentaries on the Bible. Practically all of Châtelet's writings were conceived during that time, when Voltaire, too, developed the scientific and philosophical content of his work. Distinguished scientist Clairaut, who had accompanied Maupertuis to the North Pole, agreed to tutor Châtelet in geometry. She made rapid progress but wished to explore questions that deism left unanswered. The philosophy of optimistic providentialism, inspired by Gottfried Wilhelm von Leibniz's religious rationalism and developed by his disciple Christian Wolff, satisfied her demand for rational demonstration. According to Leibniz and Wolff, God's providence would always rectify the evils resulting from the human exercise of free will, and justice would be rendered in a future life.

Châtelet turned to Germany and Leibniz's metaphysics to enlighten "the civilized men of the world" in *Institutions de physique*. She concerned herself with the necessary truth of the existence of God, the structure of matter as in the theory of monads (the existence of an ultimate entity), and the best of all possible worlds. Voltaire disagreed with her and ridiculed Leibniz's theory of optimistic providentialism in *Candide ou l'optimisme* (1759; *Candidus; or, All for the Best*, 1759). Voltaire believed that morality and religion must be separated. Reason provides empirical knowledge about the world around us. Humans can understand how the world functions but are unable to explain the reasons behind creation. Voltaire stressed that to understand the mechanism of a clock does not explain its purpose. Châtelet agreed with Voltaire that scientific investigation is an activity independent of metaphysics, but she explained that "sufficient reason" (what makes one thing preferable to another once all contradictions have been eliminated) makes ultimate certainty possible in the scientific explanation of the universe. She suggested that deductive hypotheses should not be underrated and admitted the existence of an immaterial level of reality that transcends the physical. "Sufficient reason," a concept of both science and logic, made demonstration and intellectual proof possible. Châtelet concluded that the ideas of neither the Leibnizians nor the Newtonians should be accepted exclusively; yet, she sought to introduce Wolff's thought to the French. Thanks to her, German rationalist philosophy and the theory of the monads received attention in France.

Since no secular philosophe in France would accept the validity of revealed doctrines, intellectual honesty demanded proof that divine revelation should be rejected. Châtelet and Voltaire studied the annotated Bible by Dom Augustin Calmet and commented on selected excerpts from this Bible. Châtelet outlined her thoughts in her "Examen de la Genèse" (Examination of the Genesis), in which she demonstrates the irrationality of various biblical tales. For instance, she wonders how there could have been a morning and an evening on the first day of creation since the sun and the moon were not created until the fourth day. No doubt because of her subversive criticism, the commentary was never published.

In 1738, the French Academy of Sciences held a competition for the best essay on the nature of fire. Voltaire had been working on this subject, but Châtelet disagreed with him. Having observed his experiments with much interest, she decided to enter the competition secretly, one month before the deadline. She wrote her 1739 essay, *Dissertation sur la nature et la propagation du feu* (Dissertation on the Phenomenon of Fire Propagation), at night, sleeping no more than one hour or so, plunging her hands into iced water, pacing up and down the house, and beating her arms to stay awake. Graffigny described this incredible feat to her correspondent Devaux, concluding that when women undertake serious scholarship they surpass men and musing on how many centuries it took to produce a woman such as Châtelet. Châtelet's essay presents cogent and original ideas. Her work anticipates the results of subsequent research by arguing that both light and heat are modes of motion; she also discovered that different colored rays do not produce an equal degree of heat. Although neither her entry nor Voltaire's won the competition, the academy printed both essays at its own expense. The prize went to Leonhard Euler for his essay on the velocity of heat waves. Voltaire's paper, however, came close to comprehending the phenomenon of oxidation, still unknown at that time.

Châtelet was a resolute scholar. Spectacularly healthy and demanding, she worked all day and the greater part of the night, sleeping only two or three hours and stopping briefly for a cup of coffee. In 1739, she quarreled over the subject of the infinitely small with Swiss mathematician Koenig, a disciple of Leibniz and Wolff, and abruptly ended their association. Koenig retaliated by telling acquaintances that her *Institutions de physique* was but a rehash of the private lessons he gave her at Cirey. Infuriated, she appealed to the Academy of Sciences and to Maupertuis, with whom she had discussed her ideas long before Koenig's lessons, and asked him to prove that the book was indeed her own. At that time, the classic physics textbook by

Château de Cirey, the provincial manor of Mme Du Châtelet, where she lived for a time with Voltaire (original in the Bibliotheque nationale; from Esther Ehrman, Mme du Châtelet, *1986; Thomas Cooper Library, University of South Carolina)*

Jacques Rohault was outdated; Châtelet believed it needed to be updated and supplemented. A textbook meant for her son, *Institutions de physique* dealt with the five principles of reasoning and the nature of matter and knowledge. She outlined physics in general terms of space, time, and extension, simultaneously describing the contributions of Descartes, Christian Huygens, Johannes Kepler, even the Greek atomists. She also introduced new materials by contemporary scientists such as James Bradley, Samuel Clarke, and Wolff and advocated the need for a better understanding of their achievements and the development of hypotheses. Despite Koenig's efforts to discredit her, the work established Châtelet's reputation among contemporaries such as Clairaut; Jean, Jacques, and Daniel Bernoulli; Jean-Jacques Dortous de Mairan; and Maupertuis. Although most scientists acknowledged her mastery of physics, Châtelet felt that she did not receive the respect she deserved because of her gender and Koenig's slander.

Châtelet also translated two important works: the first from English, *The Fable of the Bees* (1705) by Bernard Mandeville, translated as *La Fable des abeilles,* but not published until 1947); and the second from Latin, *Principia Mathematica* (1687) by Newton, translated as *Principes mathématiques de la philosophie naturelle* (1759). *The Fable of the Bees* upset accepted notions of morality with its thesis that private vice is public. It exposed the hypocrisy, greed, and cunning of the citizenry in every walk of life. More importantly, in her translator's preface Châtelet concludes with a powerful feminist manifesto, deploring women's apparent lack of achievement in the arts and sciences and calling for the elimination of prejudice against women and an end for the state of ignorance in which they are kept. She demands equal opportunity for her gender and pleads for proper education for women.

Principes mathématiques, published posthumously in 1759 with a preface by Voltaire, is considered Châtelet's most important work, for it led to the acceptance of Newtonian physics in France. It includes a set of her mathematical analyses of Newton's third book on his concept of the universe and materials on Clairaut's demonstration of Newton's theorem that all curves of the third order are projections of one of five parabolas. Although begun in 1745, only part of it was published in 1756 under the direction of Clairaut. Châtelet acknowledged her debt to commentaries by Algarotti, Clairaut, and the Bernoulli brothers, but the bulk of the work is her own. For many years it was the only translation of *Principia* available in French. Therefore, Châtelet deserves to be properly credited, together with Voltaire, for playing a significant role in winning an important intellectual battle. In fact, Voltaire's knowledge of Newton resulted primarily from her sharp grasp of mathematics. In turn, his interest in language may have inspired her to write "Grammaire raisonnée," of which only three chapters were found among Voltaire's papers in Leningrad. According to Châtelet, languages are based on a natural logic that all humans possess, while grammar describes the way mental processes operate. These are divided into three functions: perceiving, judging, and reasoning.

Moreover, her love of life and her need for self-fulfillment made her search for sources of happiness and prompted her in 1779 to write a short treatise on the subject, titled *Discours sur le bonheur* (1961, Essay on Happiness). It was probably written sometime between May 1746 and April 1748 but published long after her death. During those years, she was also working on the translation of Newton's *Principia*. According to René Vaillot, *Discours sur le bonheur* reflected the changing nature of her relationship with Voltaire, which she began to speak of as a "friendship." Châtelet's theory was personal: she pleaded for passion and illusion, thus underlining the ambivalence between the head and the heart and wondering which should dictate a woman's actions. She stresses the importance of good feelings and pleasant sensations, thus the need to avoid dwelling on past mistakes and thinking of death. Furthermore, since one cannot find happiness without passion, she invites her readers to disregard the advice of those who preach self-control. She claims that the only pleasures left to an older woman are gambling, study, and greed— if health allows. According to her, pleasure often derives from illusion, and gambling is instrumental for happiness, as the soul needs to be moved by hope and fear. Another passion she strongly recommends for women, deprived as they are of military and political ambitions, is a love for learning. Other forms of pleasure may include acquiring new furniture, snuffboxes, and pretty trinkets and keeping warm in extremely cold weather. On the subject of sensitivity, she shared the prevalent opinion of her time that a superior person is distinguished by the ability to be moved. She observed that stimuli depend on personality. Kings, who have a surfeit of possessions, need to find happiness elsewhere than in ownership and should strive to earn the respect and love of their subjects.

By 1744 Châtelet suffered from an underlying feeling of insecurity, making herself sick with anxiety when Voltaire traveled by himself to Paris or Berlin. When they traveled together to Belgium in 1739 to settle a long-standing lawsuit, they were frustrated by the boring and petty procedures it took to win the disputed property. They resented Brussels as a dull city, and Châtelet quarreled with her new tutor, Dortous de Mairan. In spite of her renewed effort to win for Voltaire a

Châtelet in middle age (portrait in the possession of Comte Charles de Breteuil; from Nancy Mitford, Voltaire in Love, *1957; Thomas Cooper Library, University of South Carolina)*

seat at the French Academy, he twice failed to be elected. Since Châtelet's protector at Versailles, Cardinal Hercule de Fleury, had died, she now tried to sway Jean-Frédéric de Maurepas in Voltaire's favor. In 1743 Voltaire returned from five months in Prussia, and they were happy, but their happiness did not last long. He insisted on repayment of the considerable sums of money he had lent her; moreover, he started to keep his finances separate from hers. He also fell in love with a dancer, Jeanne Catherine Gaussem, known as La Gaussin, and managed to keep secret his affair with his recently widowed niece, Marie-Louise Denis, the daughter of his sister Catherine. After nearly a decade and a half of almost-married life, Voltaire and Châtelet quarreled frequently. In the mid 1740s Voltaire enjoyed unprecedented success: he was appointed royal historiographer and finally won a seat at the French Academy. He now had an apartment in Versailles and a place in Paris where he spent much time with his new mistress, Denis. In 1746, Châtelet was granted the "privilege" (formal permission) to print her work on Newton, although it was far from being completed. She corresponded with Jesuit father François Jacquier, and her scholarship was gaining recognition in Italy, where the prestigious Bologna Institute made her a member. By

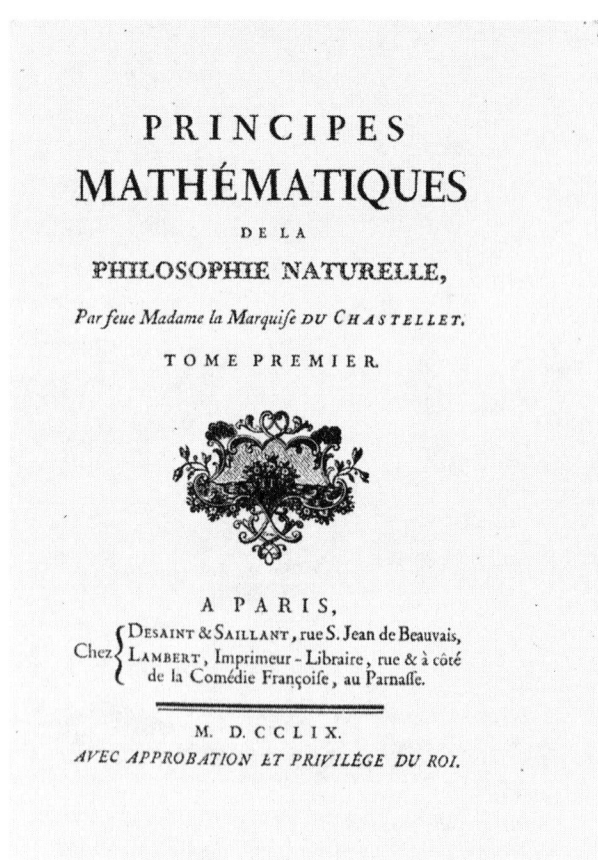

Title page for Châtelet's 1759 French translation of Isaac Newton's The Mathematical Principles of Natural Philosophy, published after her death, that led to the acceptance of Newton's physics in France (from Esther Ehrman, Mme du Châtelet, 1986; Thomas Cooper Library, University of South Carolina)

April 1747 she was reading proofs of the translation of Newton's *Principia* and working with Clairaut on a commentary; his commentary was incorporated into her work. In 1748, Voltaire and Châtelet accepted an invitation to visit Stanislas Leszczynski, the deposed king of Poland and Louis XV's father-in-law. As duke of Lorraine, Stanislas lived in his palace in Lunéville, graced by his mistress, Marie-Françoise, marquise de Boufflers—a close friend of Châtelet and one of only a few women who considered themselves her equal. The couple's intimacy waned, and Châtelet found solace with a young and handsome courtier of impeccable heritage but with rather feeble literary talent, Jean-François de Saint-Lambert. Although ten years his elder, Châtelet carried the passion to excess, for Voltaire caught them in a compromising situation. He was offended but did not let the infidelity destroy the friendship. When he found out that she was carrying Saint-Lambert's child, he was there to help Châtelet convince her husband that the child was his. That the marquis believed the child was his is doubtful, but he behaved with decorum, and her fears were alleviated. She could laugh at Voltaire's joke that since the baby had no claim to a father, it should find its place among her "miscellaneous works." Châtelet, pregnant at forty-three and more intent than ever to complete her work, gave up her social life and buried herself in her studies to finish her translation of Newton's complete works. Clairault came to assist her with abstract theories of mathematics. On 10 September 1749, six days after giving birth to a daughter at the court of Lunéville, Châtelet died. The infant soon followed her mother to the grave. In tears, Voltaire passed out when leaving the room in which she died.

No matter how frivolous or extravagant Gabrielle-Emilie Du Châtelet's personal and social life may appear to scholars today, her scientific and intellectual production was exceptional for a woman living in eighteenth-century France. If her work in mathematics was not as original as some critics contend, it was substantial, nevertheless, and that it was written at all was a remarkable feat.

Letters:

"Lettre sur les élements de la philosophie de Newton," *Journal des savants* (September 1738);

Lettre de Monsieur de Mairan, Secrétaire perpétuel de l'Académie royale des sciences, et correspondance à Madame la marquise du Chastellet (Paris, 1741); reprinted as *Lettre de Monsieur de Mairan, secrétaire perpétuel de l'Académie Royale des Sciences à Madame ***; sur la question des forces vives: en réponse aux objections qu'elle lui fait sur ce sujet dans ses' Institutions de physique'* (Paris: Jombert, 1980);

Réponse de Madame la marquise du Châtelet à la lettre que Monsieur de Mairan lui a écrite le 18 février 1741 sur la question des forces vives (Brussels: Foppens, 1741);

Lettres inédites de Madame la marquise du Châtelet à Monsieur le Comte d'Argental, auxquelles on a joint une dissertation sur l'existence de Dieu, les réflexions sur le bonheur par le même auteur, et deux notices historiques sur Madame du Chastelet et Monsieur d'Argental (Paris: Xhrouet, 1806);

Lettres inédites de Madame la marquise du Châtelet [à Maupertuis] et Supplément à la correspondance de Voltaire avec le Roi de Prusse . . . : on y a joint quelques lettres de cet écrivain, qui n'ont pas été recueillies dans les Oeuvres complètes . . . (Paris: Lefevre, 1818);

Correspondance autographe de Gabrielle-Emilie Le Tonnelier de Breteuil, marquise du Châtelet avec le Marquis de St Lambert et le Maréchal, duc de Richelieu (Paris: Antoine Serieys & Eckard, 1818; New York: Pierpont Morgan Library, 1998);

Lettres de la marquise du Châtelet réunies pour la première fois sur les autographes et les éditions originales, augmentées de trente-sept lettres entièrement inédites, de nombreuses notes, d'un index, edited by Eugène Asse (Paris: Charpentier, 1882);

Quelques lettres inédites de la marquise du Châtelet et de la duchesse de Choiseul: 1745–1775, edited by Ernest Jovy (Paris: Leclerc, 1906);

Lettres de la marquise du Châtelet, 2 volumes, edited by Théodore Besterman (Geneva: Institut et Musée Voltaire, 1958);

Lettres d'amour au marquis de Saint-Lambert, edited by Anne Soprani (Paris: Paris-Méditerranée, 1997).

Bibliographies:

Alexandre Cioranescu, *Bibliographie de la littérature française du dix-huitième siècle,* 3 volumes (Paris: CNRS, 1969);

Pierre M. Conlon, *Le Siècle des Lumières. Bibliographie chronologique,* 28 volumes (Geneva: Droz, 1983–2001).

Biographies:

Francis Hamel, *An Eighteenth-Century Marquise: A Study of Emilie du Châtelet and Her Times* (London: Stanley, 1910; New York: Pott, 1911);

André Maurel, *La Marquise du Châtelet, amie de Voltaire* (Paris: Hachette, 1930);

Samuel Edwards, *Divine Mistress* (New York: McKay, 1970; revised edition, London: Cassell, 1971);

René Vaillot, *Madame du Châtelet* (Paris: Albin Michel, 1978);

Gilbert Mercier, *Madame Voltaire* (Paris: Fallois, 2001).

References:

Francesco Algarotti, *Il Neutonianismo per le dame, ovvero dialoghi sopra la luce, I colori e l'attrazione* (Napoli, 1737); translated into French in *Oeuvres,* volume 1 (Berlin, 1772);

Lydia D. Allen, "Physics, Frivolity and 'Madame Newton-Pompon': The Historical Reception of the Marquise du Châtelet from 1750 to 1996," dissertation, University of Cincinnati, 1998;

Elisabeth Badinter, *Discours sur le bonheur de Gabrielle-Emilie du Châtelet* (Paris: Payot & Rivages, 1997);

Badinter, *Emilie, Emilie: l'ambition féminine au XVIIIe siècle* (Paris: Flammarion, 1983);

William Henry Barber, *Leibniz in France from Arnauld to Voltaire* (Oxford: Clarendon Press, 1955);

Barber, "Madame du Châtelet and Leibnizianism: The Genesis of the 'Institutions de physique' in the Age of the Enlightenment," in *The Age of the Enlightenment: Studies Presented to Théodore Besterman,* edited by Barber and others (Edinburgh & London: Oliver & Boyd, 1967);

Henri Bellugou, *Voltaire et Frédéric II au temps de la Marquise du Châtelet: un trio singulier* (Paris: Rivière, 1962);

Augustin Calmet, *Commentaire littéral sur tous les livres de l'ancien et du nouveau testament* (Paris: Pierre Emery, 1707–1717);

Jean-Baptiste Capefigue, *La Marquise du Châtelet et les amies des philosophes du XVIIIe siècle* (Paris: Amyot, 1868);

Bernard Cohen, "The French Translation of Newton's *Principia,*" *Archives internationales d'histoire des sciences,* 21 (1968): 261–290;

Esther Ehrman, *Madame du Châtelet: Scientist, Philosopher and Feminist of the Enlightenment* (Leamington Spa, Belgium: Berg, 1986);

Leonard Euler, "Dissertation sur le feu," in *De la Nature et de la propagation du feu, Cinq mémoires pour l'Académie des sciences 1738* (Wassy-en-Haute-Marne, France: édition de l'ASPM, 1995);

François de Gandt, *Cirey dans la vie intellectuelle: la réception de Newton en France,* volume 11 (Oxford: Voltaire Foundation, 2001);

Linda Janik Gardiner, "Searching for the Metaphysics of Science: The Structure and Composition of Madame du Châtelet's *Institution de physique* (1737–1740)," *Studies on Voltaire and the Eighteenth-Century,* 201 (1982): 85–113;

Gardiner, "Women in Science," in *French Women and the Age of Enlightenment,* edited by Samia I. Spencer (Bloomington: Indiana University Press, 1984), pp. 181–193;

Françoise d'Issembourg d'Happoncourt de Graffigny, *Correspondance de Madame de Graffigny,* edited by J. Alan Dainard, English Showalter, and others (Oxford: Voltaire Foundation, 1985–);

Graffigny, *Vie privée de Voltaire et de Madame du Châtelet pendant un séjour de six mois à Cirey; par l'auteur des Lettres péruviennes: suivie de cinquante lettres inédites, en vers et en prose, de Voltaire* (Paris: Treuttel & Wurtz, 1820);

Jean-Alexandre Harvard, *Voltaire et Madame du Châtelet; révélations d'un serviteur attaché à leurs personnes; manuscrit et pièces inédites avec commentaires et notes historiques* (Paris: Dentu, 1863);

Carolyn Iltis, "The Controversy over Living Force: Leibniz to D'Alembert," dissertation, University of Wisconsin, 1967;

Iltis, "Madame du Châtelet's Metaphysics and Mechanics," *Studies in History and Philosophy of Science,* 8 (1977): 29–48;

Keiko Kawashima, "Les Idées scientifiques de Madame du Châtelet dans ses 'Institutions de physique,'" *Historia Scientarum,* 3 (1993): 63–82;

Kawashima, "La participation de Madame du Châtelet et Madame Lavoisier à la querelle sur les forces vives," *Historia Scientarum,* 40 (1990): 9–28;

Gottfried Wilhelm Leibniz, *Monadologie* (Paris: Boutroux, 1966);

Georges Mangeot, "Les réflexions sur le bonheur," in *Mélanges Lanson* (Paris: Hachette, 1922);

Gaston Maugras, *La Cour de Lunéville au XVIIIe siècle: les marquises de Boufflers et du Châtelet, Voltaire, Devau, Saint Lambert . . .* (Paris: Plon-Nourrit, 1904);

Pierre Louis Moreau de Maupertuis, *Discours sur les différentes figures des astres* (1732);

Gilbert Mercier, *Bébé, le nain de Stanislas, ou, les amours mouvementées d'Emilie du Châtelet et de Voltaire à la cour de Lorraine* (Sarreguemines, France: Pierron, 1985);

Nancy Mitford, *Voltaire in Love* (London: Hamilton, 1957);

Lynn M. Osen, *Women in Mathematics* (Cambridge, Mass.: MIT Press, 1974);

Bertram Eugene Schwarzbach, "Une légende en quête d'un manuscrit: le Commentaire sur la Bible de Madame du Châtelet," in *De Bonne Main: la communication manuscrite au XVIIIe siècle,* edited by François Moureau (Paris: Universitas / Oxford: Voltaire Foundation, 1993), pp. 97–116;

Voltaire, *Elémens de la philosophie de Newton,* new edition (Neuchâtel & Paris: Panckoucke, 1772; revised edition, Oxford: Walters & Barber, 1992);

Voltaire, *Essai sur la nature du feu et sur sa propagation* (Aux deux-Ponts: chez Sanson, 1792);

Voltaire, *Lettres philosophiques* (Paris: Didier, 1964);

Voltaire, *Réponse à toutes les objections qu'on a faites en France contre la philosophie de Newton* (Amsterdam: Catuffe, 1740);

Ira Owen Wade, *The Intellectual Development of Voltaire* (Princeton: Princeton University Press, 1969), pp. 276–291;

Wade, *Studies on Voltaire with Some Unpublished Papers of Madame du Châtelet* (Princeton: Princeton University Press, 1947; New York: Russell & Russell, 1967);

Wade, *Voltaire and Madame du Châtelet. An Essay on Intellectual Activity at Cirey* (Princeton: Princeton University Press, 1941);

Judith Zinsser, "Emilie du Châtelet: Genius, Gender and Intellectual Authority," in *Women Writers and the Early Modern British Political Tradition,* edited by Hilda L. Smith (Cambridge & New York: Cambridge University Press, 1998), pp. 168–190.

Papers:

Gabrielle-Emilie Du Châtelet's manuscripts "Examen sur l'Ancien Testament" and "Examen sur le Nouveau Testament" are located in the Bibliothèque Royale Albert 1er, in Brussels, Belgium (MS 362).

Etienne Bonnot de Condillac
(30 September 1714 - 2 August 1780)

Lauren Pinzka
Yale University

and

Steven Berry
Yale University

BOOKS: *Essai sur l'origine des connaissances humaines,* 2 volumes (Amsterdam: Pierre Mortier, 1746); translated by Thomas Nugent as *An Essay on the Origin of Human Knowledge* (London: Printed for J. Nourse, 1756);

Les Monades, anonymous [attributed to Condillac by Laurence Bongie in 1980] (Berlin: Proceedings of the Academy of Berlin, 1747);

Traité des systèmes, 2 volumes (The Hague: Printed by Neaulme [false imprint], 1749); translated by Franklin Philip as *A Treatise on Systems,* volume 1 of *Philosophical Writings of Etienne Bonot, Abbé de Condillac* (Hillsdale, N.J.: Lawrence Erlbaum, 1982);

Traité des sensations (London & Paris: De Bure aîné, 1754); translated by Geraldine Carr as *Treatise on Sensations* (London: Favil, 1930);

Traité des animaux (Amsterdam & Paris: De Bure aîné, 1755);

Cours d'études pour l'instruction du prince de Parme, 16 volumes (Parma: L'Imprimerie royale [Deux-Ponts], 1775)—comprises volume 1, *Grammaire;* volume 2, *Art d'écrire;* volume 3, *Art de raisonner;* volume 4, *Art de penser;* volumes 5–10, *Introduction à l'étude de l'histoire ancienne;* and volumes 11–16, *Introduction à l'étude de l'histoire moderne;* introduction translated by Franklin Philip in volume 2 of *Philosophical Writings of Etienne Bonnot, Abbé de Condillac* (Hillsdale, N.J.: Lawrence Erlbaum, 1982);

Le Commerce et le gouvernement considérés relativement l'un à l'autre (Amsterdam & Paris: Jombert & Cellot, 1776); translated by Shelagh Eltis as *Commerce and Government Considered in Their Mutual Relationship* (Cheltenham, U.K. & Northhampton, Mass.: El Elgar, 1997);

La Logique ou les premiers développements de l'art de penser (Paris: L'Esprit et de Bure, 1780); translated by

Etienne Bonnot de Condillac (copy of a portrait by Van Lou; from Jean Piveteau, Oeuvres Philosophiques de Buffon, *1954, volume 33; Thomas Cooper Library, University of South Carolina)*

Joseph Neef as *The Logic of Condillac* (Philadelphia: Philadelphia printed, 1809);

Oeuvres de Condillac, revues, corrigées par l'auteur, imprimées sur ses manuscrits autographes et augmentées de la "Langue des calculs," 23 volumes (Paris: Charles Houel, 1798);

Dictionnaire des synonymes, volume 3 of *Oeuvres philosophiques de Condillac,* edited by Georges Le Roy, Corpus général des philosophes français (Paris: PUF, 1951);

Lettres inédites à Cramer, edited by Le Roy, Bibliothèque de philosophie contemporaine (Paris: PUF, 1953).

Edition: *Les Monades,* edited by Laurence L. Bongie, Studies on Voltaire and the Eighteenth Century, no. 187 (Oxford, U.K.: Voltaire Foundation, 1980).

Etienne Bonnot de Condillac is traditionally remembered as the father of French empiricism, expounding the ideas of British philosopher John Locke, who was in turn inspired by the rapid progress of Enlightenment science. Condillac eventually took an even more extreme position than Locke on "sensation" as the driver of human knowledge. He developed original ideas on the nature and role of language while also writing forward-looking work in economics. Condillac had a long intellectual friendship with both Denis Diderot and Jean-Jacques Rousseau. While Condillac did not directly contribute entries to the *Encyclopédie* (1751–1772), some entries, such as those on *système, analyse, axiome, logique,* and *analogie* (system, analysis, axiom, logic, and analogy), closely resemble Condillac's own writings. While Locke's ideas lived on in the tradition of British philosophy, Condillac's empiricism and his beliefs in "analysis" were largely swept away by contrary trends in Continental philosophy. In the last half of the twentieth century, however, his theories on the origin, role, and importance of language had a renewed impact on scholarly work.

Condillac was born Etienne Bonnot to Gabriel Bonnot, vicomte de Mably, and Catherine de la Coste on 30 September 1714, in Grenoble, France, the youngest of a prominent family. He supposedly was a frail child, of poor eyesight, who still did not know how to read at the age of twelve. He took on the title "de Condillac" from the name of family land purchased in 1720. After eventually receiving both a theological and a secular education, he was ordained a priest in 1741, seemingly without ever performing the functions of his position. Rousseau became the tutor to Condillac's younger brother in 1740, and afterward Rousseau and Condillac became well acquainted; Condillac and his family helped to introduce Rousseau to the Parisian intellectual society that Condillac had embraced. Independently wealthy, Condillac was able to devote himself to his writing and to intellectual salons, where he was sponsored by Claudine-Alexandrine Guerin de Tencin and Louis-Jules Mancini-Mazarini, duc de Nivernais.

Condillac first came to notice with his *Essai sur l'origine des connaissances humaines* (1746; translated as *An Essay on the Origin of Human Knowledge,* 1756). While Voltaire had already introduced Locke to France, Condillac's essay provides an exposition and extension of Lockean empiricism. Condillac argues that the advance of knowledge depends on empirical observation rather than on metaphysical introspection. Locke and Condillac were greatly impressed with the progress of science, particularly in physics, chemistry, and medicine. Locke had set out an intellectual agenda of capturing the methods of these successful sciences, which had relied to varying degrees on empirical observation and the development of formal language systems, either explicit mathematics and/or precise scientific jargons.

While disagreeing with the work of Locke on some points, Part 1 of the *Essai sur l'origine des connaissances humaines,* which focuses on the operations of knowledge and the mind, is typically read as the work of Locke's faithful disciple. In this work, Condillac generally accepts Locke's distinction between sensation originating outside the mind and the inner reflection of the mind acting on those sensations. Locke's concept of reflection accepts the notion that the mind has innate abilities, though no innate ideas. Condillac claims to differ from Locke—first, by emphasizing more strongly the importance of signs as a necessity for thought and, second, by underscoring the importance of an analytical method based on the "liaison" (connection or association) of ideas.

Part 2 of *Essai sur l'origine des connaissances humaines* focuses on language. A more original work, it was sometimes ignored by early commentators emphasizing Condillac's more purely Lockean contributions. Condillac has the reader imagine an early human family deprived of the ability of language. How is language invented? Condillac argues that language evolves through a process of social evolution. At first, people have only actions, such as reaching toward an out-of-reach object, thereby suggesting a desire for assistance, a gesture that is instinctively understood, or read, by others. The motion and the context create an obvious meaning. Eventually, gestures became codified in a kind of action language, which sometimes resembles the wordless rituals of ancient religions. Finally, a full language develops. However, naturally occurring language tends to associate complex ideas with names that obscure understanding; progress requires a thinker to redefine terms to refer more carefully to the simple ideas that make up more-complex thoughts. Although Condillac generally denies the existence of innate ideas, he here accepts the notion of an innate language of gestures that jump-starts the social process of language creation. He places language prior to thought.

Condillac, the family estate purchased by the Bonnot family in 1720 (photograph by Françoise Pascal, from Roger Lefèvre, Condillac, 1966; Thomas Cooper Library, University of South Carolina)

A brief departure from a pure Lockean system is found in the anonymously published work *Les Monades* (The Monads, 1747), which in the view of critics features some suspiciously metaphysical arguments, calling Condillac's consistency into question. However, this work, which was not attributed to Condillac until 1980 when Laurence Bongie exhumed it during careful archival research guided by a suggestive reference to its existence by Condillac in a later work, was submitted in response to a highly structured competition of Académie Royale des Sciences et Belles Lettres of Berlin (the Berlin Academy) and demonstrates Condillac's adherence to and rejection of Leibniz. Possibly, he published his work anonymously because he quickly altered his views in subsequent work.

Elected a member of the Berlin Academy in 1749, Condillac went on to write the *Traité des systèmes* (1749; translated as *A Treatise on Systems*, 1982), which returns to a Lockean point of view, critiquing the notion of innate ideas and metaphysical concepts as found in the works of René Descartes, Nicolas de Malebranche, and Gottfried Wilhelm Leibniz. Each of a series of chapters takes on a different metaphysician and his particular error, each stemming from a lack of understanding of the proper scientific principles of observation and analysis. In the first chapter Condillac harshly attacks the metaphysicians for the "uselessness" of their abstract systems and argues instead for the proposition that "des faits bien constatés peuvent seuls être les vrais principes des sciences" (only carefully established facts can be the true principles of the sciences).

Appointed the royal auditor of France in 1752, a position he held until his death, Condillac next further departed from Locke in his composition of the *Traité des sensations* (1754; translated as *Treatise on Sensations*, 1930), traditionally cited as his most important work, although modern critics often prefer the works on language. While Locke had argued for the importance of both outer sensation and inner reflection, Condillac now argues for a pure sensationism (or "sensationalism"), doing away with Locke's second mental process of inner reflection. To develop his argument, Condillac imagines a statue that is internally human but initially isolated from all sensation by its marble surface. In the beginning, the statue has no innate ideas and no knowledge. Condillac gradually grants it the various senses in a thought experiment designed to show how the statue's knowledge increases with the addition of each sense.

Condillac argues that not only ideas but also all mental processes can ultimately be traced back to "sensations transformées" (transformed sensations). When the statue is exposed only to smell, it is completely occupied with this one sense–to be so engaged with only one sensation is "attention" (attention). "La mémoire" (Memory) is but the sensation that remains after the object is gone. "La comparaison" (Comparison) is attending to two senses at once (perhaps one remembered and one present). In part 1 of chapter 2, Condillac says that eventually, a series of ideas thus formed are stored in the mind, and the "liaison de ces idées" (connection of ideas [frequently translated as "association of ideas"]) leads to further ideas, none of which would have been possible without the initial sensations. Only when touch is added at the end does the statue come to understand the distinction between itself and the exterior world; touch is therefore essential to the experience of individual identity and is a tutor to the other senses.

Once sensations are received, the resulting pain and pleasure lead to desire. Desire and habit produce "passions" (passions, in the sense of strong feelings); passion with an expectation of fulfillment is "la volonté" (will). Judgments are reactions to sensation: "la beauté" (beauty) is pleasure obtained from sight, sound, or touch, while "la bonté" (goodness) is pleasing to taste or smell. In this fashion, Condillac derives all emotions and judgment, beginning with sensation and driven by desire. Emotions and judgment, therefore, stem from an active process; this model contrasts with the earlier, more passive, metaphor of the statue receiving sensations.

Thus, Condillac extends Locke's position against innate ideas to deny any innate mental facilities. A question also arises of where sensation is perceived. Condillac does not necessarily assume the physical brain to be the location of the activities of transformed sensation. He thus reaffirms a possible mind-body duality and avoids a charge of pure materialism, which might have been awkward given his association with the church.

This argument is carried forward in the *Traité des animaux* (1755, Treatise on Animals). In this work Condillac attacks the Cartesian model of animal-machines. Man is superior to animals because of language, which allows for abstract thought and analytical reasoning; yet, Condillac affirms the animal's capacity for "sensations" (feelings), memory, acquisition of knowledge, and the ability to make comparisons and judgments. Condillac thus opposes the materialism of Diderot and affirms his adherence to spiritualism, the belief in the existence of a spirit and higher purpose for man's existence.

After his election to the Académie française in 1768, Condillac retired to the domaine de Flux, the château that belonged to his niece, Mme de Rouville, where he spent the rest of his life. He next published the *Cours d'études pour l'instruction du prince de Parme* (1775, The Course of Study for the Instruction of the Prince of Parma), which he composed as a curriculum for the grandson of Louis XV, for whom he served as tutor. It is a collection of Condillac's ideas on philosophy, history, and education. His theory of education predictably follows Locke's in arguing that children begin as a blank slate. In designing a curriculum for study, Condillac suggests that children should repeat the past stages of human mental development. This repetition begins with a child's natural talent for observation (not yet ruined by education) and to which then is added the analytic process of properly connecting ideas. Since so many mistakes have been made in the course of human knowledge, Condillac believes, one can easily take a child through many hundreds of years of human inquiry in a relatively short time. The *Cours d'études* suggests an emphasis on the teaching of history but includes a heavy dose of Condillac's own philosophical ideas.

Condillac's main work on economics, *Le Commerce et le gouvernement considérés relativement l'un à l'autre* (1776; translated as *Commerce and Government Considered in Their Mutual Relationship*, 1997), was published in the same year as Adam Smith's *Wealth of Nations,* and just two months before the minister and economist Anne-Robert-Jacques Turgot, who held economic theories similar to those of Condillac, was disgraced. In contrast to Smith's emphasis on cost as the basis of value, Condillac emphasizes a utilitarian approach in which value decreases or increases with the subjective needs of the consumer. Condillac also argues that subjective needs are likely to increase with the scarcity of the products, so that value is also attributed to scarcity. He argues that, ultimately, the final value of a good arises from a process of exchange. Condillac's ideas on economics are remarkably more similar to the late-nineteenth- and early-twentieth-century "supply and demand" ideas of Alfred Marshall and other economists of the "marginalist revolution" than to those of his French contemporaries, who emphasized either land or labor as the sole source of value. Condillac also emphasized the role of the risk-taking entrepreneur. His prescription of mathematics as the ideal model for scientific language is also reflected in the modern insistence that economic theory be expressible in the language of pure mathematics.

La Logique ou les premiers développements de l'art de penser (1780; translated as *The Logic of Condillac*, 1809), one of Condillac's most influential works, was commissioned by the Polish government as a textbook. In *La Logique ou les premiers développements de l'art de penser,* Condillac takes up where he ended *Traité des sensations,* continuing his theory of higher-order mental processes and returning to the discussion of language in the *Essai sur l'origine des connaissances humaines.* As in the *Essai sur l'origine des connaissances humaines,* Condillac presents thoughts as being composed of language. Once again, the innate language, the language of gesture and physical expression, is transformed into more-arbitrary signs. Every idea is capable of expression via the original language of gesture. However, to improve understanding, humans learn to decompose and systematize their own gestures and the gestures of others. Language thus develops into a "méthode analytique" (an analytic method), which is learned. Only later in human history are the pictures of ideas represented by "le geste" (gesture) replaced by the "signes arbitraires" (arbitrary signs) of words.

Once arbitrary signs replace the direct analogies of gesture, imprecision easily enters into language. For Condillac, the fundamental error is linguistic, as one has a tendency to use words without really knowing what they mean. As long as human inquiry is devoted to the satisfaction of immediate needs, such as hunger, human reasoning is closely disciplined by the need for careful observation and clear logic. However, when less-immediate concerns are investigated, the principles of observation and careful language are lost.

In response, each scientific discipline should develop a precise and exact language. Condillac believes that such a language can be created for all scientific inquiries and that all scientific questions—including those labeled "métaphysique" (metaphysical)—can become exact sciences. Algebra is held up as an example of an appropriate language. While a good scientific language need not literally be mathematics, it would share the analytic clarity of mathematics.

Condillac's interest in mathematics as language continues in his posthumously published *Langue des calculs* (1798, The Language of Arithmetic or Language of Numbers). He continues his study of algebra as a language, laying out the "grammaire" (grammar) of algebra as true language, as opposed to just a mathematical system. One advantage of algebra is the specificity of the numbers on which it is based. Condillac argues for languages that are specific to particular situations, including national languages, and dismisses calls for a single universal language.

Condillac, who died 2 August 1780, had a large impact on French Enlightenment philosophy and on the subsequent Idéologie (Ideology) movement that reigned in French schools for more than fifty years. The ideologues included such disciples as Destutt de

Title page for the first English translation, 1756, of Condillac's Essai sur l'origine des connaissances humaines, *1746, which explains and extends Lockean empiricism and first brought attention to the author (from* An Essay on the Origin of Human Knowledge, *edited by Robert Weyant, 1971; Thomas Cooper Library, University of South Carolina)*

Tracy, who were in turn followed by interested critics such as Maine de Biran. Antoine Laurent Lavoisier extensively quoted Condillac's *La Logique ou les premiers développements de l'art de penser* in his 1789 reform of chemical nomenclature. In "From Natural Philosophy to Scientific Discourse" (1989), Wilda Anderson asserts that the Ideologues' emphasis on depersonalized language in the school system "was intended to produce obedient, productive, and dedicated citizens for the new post-Revolutionary state." Critics found Condillac's extreme sensationism hard to accept and charged that he placed human learning in a passive context, ignoring the role of human will.

His account of the origin of language foundered on criticism that the invention of language seemed to require prior language. In his *Essai sur l'origine et les fondements de l'inégalité des hommes* (1755; translated as *Discourse on the Origin and Foundations of Inequality among Men,* 1984), Rousseau complained, as did later authors, that words could only be originally explained by other words. In *The Origin of Language: Aspects of the Discussion from Condillac to Wundt* (1987), G. A. Wells argues, however, that later critics—though not so much Rousseau—miss the role of the "original context" of gestures, which makes Condillac's argument more plausible. Condillac's ideas on language were generally ridiculed in the nineteenth century, and his empiricism was swept away in the face of German Romanticism and a renewed interest in spirituality, Cartesian philosophy, and eclecticism.

Condillac's writings on language are echoed in the works of twentieth-century philosophers of language such as Ferdinand de Saussure, who reflected the renewal of interest in eighteenth-century French linguistic theory at the end of the preceding century. Condillac's straightforward empiricism and analytic bent, however, are less pleasing to many twentieth-century Continental philosophers. In *L'Archéologie du frivole* (1973; translated as *The Archaeology of the Frivolous,* 1980), Jacques Derrida, for example, focuses on the apparent necessary circularity of Condillac's argument. Language constitutes thought, but imprecise language occurs when the word only vaguely matches the thought. Thus, on the one hand, thought precedes clear language, but on the other hand, language precedes all thoughts. Derrida is left with the "frivolity" of Condillac's imprecise, commonly used language, but without the promise of more precise scientific language (which would have to overcome somehow the circularity of thought being dependent on language and vice versa). Derrida's attack on and celebration of Condillac's contradictions also mocks Condillac's faith in plain language and scientific progress.

Aside from the Continental philosophers, others have argued that one can follow a path of influence from Locke through Condillac to the utilitarianism of Jeremy Bentham, to the writings of John Stuart Mill, and on through the British tradition of analytic philosophy, even though Mill disparaged Condillac's work. The largely British late-nineteenth-century "marginalist revolution" of economics, with its emphasis on utility and scarcity, clearly echoes Condillac, even though a strong counterargument claims that the various British traditions did not really need Condillac's work to continue on their paths.

Although the various disciplines of science and social science did not need Etienne Bonnot de Condillac's advice in order to become more empirical and more dependent on formal reasoning and on specialized languages of both a mathematical and nonmathematical nature, in practice most such disciplines did follow the path laid down for them, imperfectly, by the Enlightenment empiricists. Modern linguistics, for example, has returned with empirical evidence and specialized scientific language (the tools that Condillac advocated, but in practice lacked) to Condillac's questions of the innateness of language and the dependence of thought on language. New attention to the general method Condillac advocated for the "inexact sciences" indicates a lasting influence.

References:

Hans Aarsleff, "Condillac's Speechless Statue," *Studia leibnitiana,* supplement 15 (1972): 287–302;

Aarsleff, "The Tradition of Condillac," in *Studies in the History of Linguistics,* edited by Dell Hymes (Bloomington: Indiana University Press, 1974), pp. 93–156;

Wilda Anderson, "From Natural Philosophy to Scientific Discourse," in *A New History of French Literature,* edited by Denis Hollier (Cambridge, Mass. & London: Harvard University Press, 1989), pp. 460–465;

Sylvain Auroux, *La Sémiotique des encyclopédistes* (Paris: Payot, 1979);

Jacques Derrida, *L'Archéologie du frivole* (Paris: Editions du Galilée, 1990);

F. Duchesneau, "Condillac critique de Locke," *International Studies in Philosophy* (1974): 77–98;

Ellen McNiven Hine, *A Critical Study of Condillac's 'Traité des Systèmes'* (The Hague, Boston & London: Martinus Nijhoff, 1979);

Isabel F. Knight, *The Geometric Spirit, The Abbé de Condillac and the French Enlightenment* (New Haven & London: Yale University Press, 1968);

John Stuart Mill, *On Bentham and Coleridge* (New York: Harper Torchbooks, 1950);

Nicolas Rousseau, *Connaissance et langage chez Condillac* (Geneva: Droz, 1986);

Jean Sgard, ed., *Condillac et les problèmes du langage* (Geneva & Paris: Slatkine, 1982);

G. A. Wells, *The Origin of Language: Aspects of the Discussion from Condillac to Wundt* (La Salle, Ill.: Open Court, 1987).

Marie-Jean-Antoine-Nicolas Caritat, marquis de Condorcet
(17 September 1743 – 29 March 1794)

Jeanne Hageman
North Dakota State University

BOOKS: *Du Calcul intégral* (Paris: Imprimerie de Didot, 1765);

Essais d'analyse. Tome premier (Paris: Imprimerie de Didot, 1765–1768);

Du problème des trois corps (Paris: Imprimerie de Didot, 1767);

Sur le système du monde et sur le calcul intégral (Paris: Imprimerie de Didot, 1768);

Eloges des académiciens de l'Académie royale des sciences morts depuis 1666, jusqu'en 1699 (Paris: Hôtel de Thou, 1773; enlarged edition, Paris: Académie des Sciences, 1774; second enlarged edition, Paris: Vieweg et Fuchs, 1799);

Lettre d'un théologien à l'auteur du "Dictionnaire des trois siècles," anonymous (Berlin [i.e., France], 1774);

Lettre sur le commerce des grains (Paris: Couturier père, 1774);

Du commerce des bleds pour servir à la réfutation de l'ouvrage sur la législation & le commerce des grains (Paris: Grangé, 1775);

Lettre d'un laboureur de Picardie à M. N*** . . . (Paris, 1775);

Réflexions sur le commerce des bleds (London, 1776);

Eloge de Michel de L'Hôpital, chancelier de France: discours présenté à l'Académie française, en 1777 (Paris: Demonville, 1777);

Réflexions d'un citoyen catholique sur les lois de France relatives aux Protestants (Paris, 1778; London, 1788);

Dissertations sur les comètes, qui ont concouru au prix proposé par l'Académie royale des sciences et belles-lettres de Prusse pour l'année 1777, by Condorcet, G. F. Von Tempelhoff, and J. F. Hennert (Utrecht, Netherlands: Wild, 1780);

Un Ami de Voltaire à M. d'Eprémesnil, au sujet d'un plaidoyer qu'il a prononcé au parlement de Rouen contre le général Lally et contre son fils Mr. de Tolendal (Paris & London: L'Esprit, 1780);

Recueil de pièces sur l'état des Protestans en France (London: Dodsley, 1781);

*Marie-Jean-Antoine-Nicolas Caritat, marquis de Condorcet
(Hope Collection, Ashmolean Museum, Oxford; from
Jean-Pierre Schandeler,* Les Interprétations de
Condorcet, *2000; Thomas Cooper Library,
University of South Carolina)*

Réflexions sur l'esclavage des nègres (Neuchâtel, Switzerland: Société Littéraire-typographique, 1781);

Discours prononcés dans l'Académie française le jeudi XXI février M.DCC.LXXXII, à la réception de M. le Marquis de Condorcet, by Condorcet and Louis-Jules-Barbon Mancini-Mazarini Nivernais (Paris: Chez Demonville, 1782);

Eloge de M. le comte de Maurepas, ministre d'Etat, prononcé dans la séance publique de l'Académie royale des sciences, le 10 avril 1782 (Paris: Imprimerie royale, 1782);

Eloge de M. D'Alembert: lu dans l'assemblée publique de l'Académie des sciences, le 21 avril 1784 (Paris: Moutard, 1784);

Essai sur l'application de l'analyse à la probabilité des décisions rendues à la pluralité des voix (Paris: Imprimerie royale, 1785); translated by Keith Michael Baker as *An Essay on the Application of Mathematics to the Theory of Decision Making,* in *Condorcet: Selected Writings* (Indianapolis: Bobbs-Merrill, 1976);

Histoire des membres de l'Académie française, morts depuis 1700 jusqu'en 1771, pour servir de suite aux Eloges imprimés et lus dans les séances publiques de cette compagnie, 6 volumes, by Condorcet and Jean Le Rond d'Alembert (Paris: Moutard, 1785);

Vie de Monsieur Turgot (London [i.e., Paris], 1786); translated as *The Life of M. Turgot, Comptroller General of the Finances of France, in the Years 1774, 1775, and 1776* (London: Printed for J. Johnson, 1787);

Essai sur la Constitution et les fonctions des assemblées provinciales, 2 volumes (Paris, 1788);

Lettres d'un citoyen des Etat-Unis, à un Français, sur les affaires présentes (Philadelphia [i.e., Paris], 1788);

Réflexions d'un citoyen sur la révolution de 1788 (London, 1788);

Sentiments d'un républicain sur les assemblées provinciales et les Etats-généraux. Suite des Lettres d'un citoyen des Etats-Unis à un Français, sur les affaires présentes (Philadelphia [i.e., Paris], 1788);

Déclaration des droits (Versailles: Imprimerie de Pierres, 1789);

Examen de cette question, est-il utile de diviser une Assemblée nationale en plusieurs chambres? (Paris, 1789);

Instruction sur l'exercice du droit de souveraineté (Paris: Imprimerie nationale, 1789–1792?);

Mélanges (Paris: Philippe Pierres, 1789–1792);

Messieurs, à l'instant même où l'Amérique achevait de briser ses fers, les amis généreux de la liberté sentirent qu'ils aviliraient leur cause s'ils autorisaient par des lois la servitude des noirs (Paris, 1789);

Réflexion sur ce qui a été fait et sur ce qui reste à faire (Paris: Baudouin, 1789);

Réflexions de M. le marquis de Condorcet sur l'usufruit des bénéficiers (Paris, 1789);

Réflexions sur les affaires publiques (Paris, 1789);

Sur la fixation de l'impôt (Paris: Baudouin, 1789);

Sur la nécessité de faire ratifier la constitution par les citoyens, et sur la formation des communautés de campagne (Paris: Philippe Pierres, 1789);

Sur le choix des ministres (Paris: Imprimerie nationale, 1789);

Sur les fonctions des Etats-généraux et des autres assemblées nationales, 2 volumes (Paris, 1789);

Vie de Voltaire (Kehl, Germany: Société Littéraire-typographique, 1789); revised and enlarged as *Vie de Voltaire, suivie des avertissements et notes insérés par Condorcet dans l'édition complète,* edited by A. A. Barbier (Paris: Heinrichs, 1804); translated as *The Life of Voltaire* (London: Printed for G. G. J. and J. Robinson, 1790);

Bibliothèque de l'homme public, ou, analyse raisonnée des principaux ouvrages françois et étrangers: sur la politique en général, la législation, les finances, la police, l'agriculture, & le commerce en particulier, & sur le droit naturel & public, edited by Charles de Peyssonnel (Paris: Buisson, 1790–1792)–includes *Premier mémoire sur l'instruction publique* (1791); translated by Baker as *The Nature and Purpose of Public Instruction,* in *Condorcet: Selected Writings* (Indianapolis: Bobbs-Merrill, 1976);

Discours prononcé à l'Assemblée nationale (Paris: Baudouin, 1790);

Eloge de M. le comte de Buffon (Paris: Buisson, 1790);

Loi relative à l'établissement de nouvelles mesures pour les grains, suivie de la lettre du secrétaire de l'Académie des sciences, à M. le Président de l'Assemblée nationale, & de l'instruction de l'Académie des sciences, adressée aux directoires des quatre-vingt-trois départements du royaume (Paris: Imprimerie nationale, 1790);

Mémoires sur les monnoies (Paris: Baudouin, 1790);

Nouvelles réflexions sur le projet de payer la dette exigible en papier forcé (Paris: Baudouin, 1790);

Sur la forme des élections (Paris, 1790);

Sur la proposition d'acquitter la dette exigible en assignats (Paris: Baudouin, 1790);

Adresse aux Bataves (Paris, 1791);

De la République: ou, un roi est-il nécessaire à la conservation de la liberté? (Paris: Imprimerie du Cercle social, 1791);

Des Conventions nationales (Paris: Imprimerie du Cercle social, 1791);

Eloge de M. Franklin lu à la séance publique de l'Académie des Sciences, le 13 novembre 1790 (Paris: Pyre, 1791);

Opinion de M. Condorcet, député de Paris, sur les émigrants (Paris: Imprimerie nationale, 1791);

Rapport sur le choix d'une unité de mesure, lu à l'Académie des sciences le 19 mars 1791 (Paris: Imprimerie nationale, 1791);

Second projet de décret sur les émigrants auquel la priorité a été accordée par l'Assemblée nationale le 28 octobre 1791 (Paris: Imprimerie nationale, 1791);

Eloge historique de M. le comte de Buffon (Paris: Sanson, 1792);

Lettre de M. Condorcet, à M ***, magistrat de la ville de ***, en Suisse (Paris, 1792); enlarged and translated as *A Letter to a Magistrate in Swissserland [sic], Respecting the Massacree [sic] of the Swiss Guards on the 10th of August, &c. With a Letter from Thomas Paine to the Peo-*

ple of France, on his Election to the National Convention (New York: Printed for the book-sellers, 1793);

Aperçu des frais que coûtera le nouveau plan d'instruction publique (Paris: Imprimerie nationale, 1792);

Avis aux Espagnols (Paris: Imprimerie de la Gazette nationale de France, 1792);

Discours sur les finances (Paris: Imprimerie nationale, 1792);

Nouvelles réflexions sur le projet de payer la dette exigible en papier forcé (Paris: Baudouin, 1792);

Opinion . . . sur le jugement de Louis XVI (Paris: Imprimerie nationale, 1792); translated as *A narrative of the proceedings relating to the suspension of the King of the French on the 10th of August 1792* (Manchester, U.K.: Printed by Falkner, 1792);

Opinion . . . sur les mesures générales propres à sauver la patrie des dangers imminents dont elle est menacée, présentée à l'Assemblée nationale, le 6 juillet 1792 (Paris: Imprimerie nationale, 1792);

Rapport et projet de décret sur l'organisation générale de l'instruction publique présentés à l'Assemblée nationale législative au nom du Comité d'instruction publique, les 20 et 21 avril 1792 (Paris: Imprimerie nationale, 1792); revised and enlarged as *Rapport et projet de décret sur l'organisation générale de l'instruction publique, nouvelle édition,* edited by Gabriel Compayré (Paris: Hachette, 1883);

Réflexions sur la Révolution de 1688, et sur celle du 10 août 1792 (Paris, 1792); translated as *Reflections on the English Revolution of 1688, and that of the French, August 10, 1792* (London: Printed for J. Ridgeway, 1792);

Aux Citoyens français sur la nouvelle constitution (Paris, 1793);

Ce que les citoyens ont droit d'attendre de leurs représentants (Paris: Imprimerie des Sourds-Muets, 1793);

Exposition des principes et des motifs du plan présenté à la Convention nationale par le Comité de constitution (Paris, 1793);

Instruction sur l'exercice du droit de souveraineté (Paris: Imprimerie nationale, 1793);

Plan de constitution présenté à la Convention nationale les 15 et 16 février 1793, l'an 2e de la République (Paris: Imprimerie nationale, 1793); translated as *An Authentic Copy of the New Plan of the French Constitution, as Presented to the National Convention* (London: Printed for J. Debrett, 1793); republished as *Plan of the French Constitution and Declaration of Rights as Presented to the National Convention of France on the 16th of February, 1793* (London: Printed for J. S. Jordan, 1802);

Projet de déclaration des droits naturels, civils et politiques des hommes (Paris, 1793);

Rapport et projet de décret sur un nouveau système monétaire, présentés à la Convention nationale, au nom du Comité des finances, by Condorcet and Pierre Loisel (Paris: Imprimerie nationale, 1793);

Esquisse d'un tableau historique des progrès de l'esprit humain (Paris: Chez Agasse, 1795); translated as *Outlines of an Historical View of the Progress of the Human Mind* (London: Printed for J. Johnson, 1795);

Eloge des académiciens de l'Académie royale des sciences morts depuis l'an 1666 jusqu'en 1790 suivis de ceux de l'Hôpital et de Pascal (Paris: Frédéric Vieweg, 1799);

Moyens d'apprendre à compter sûrement et avec facilité. Ouvrage posthume de Condorcet (Paris: Moutardier, 1799); translated as *A Sure and Easy Method of Learning to Calculate* (Edinburgh, Scotland: Printed for W. Blackwood, 1815);

Eléments du calcul des probabilités et son application aux jeux de hasard, à la loterie, et aux jugemens des hommes (Paris: Royez, 1805).

Editions and Collections: *Oeuvres complètes,* 21 volumes (Paris: Frédéric Vieweg, 1804; Braunschweig, Germany: Henrichs, 1804);

Mémoires de Condorcet sur la Révolution française, extraits de sa correspondance et celles de ses amis, edited by Frédéric Gaëtan de la Rochfoucauld-Liancourt (Paris: Ponthieu, 1824);

Oeuvres, 12 volumes, edited by Arthur O'Connor and François Arago (Paris: Firmin Didot frères, 1847); reprinted in facsimile (Stuttgart-Bad Cannstatt, Germany: Frommann, 1968);

Condorcet: choix de textes et introduction, edited by J.-B. Séverac (Paris: L. Michaud, 1912);

Condorcet: Selected Writings, edited, with an introduction, by Keith Michael Baker (Indianapolis: Bobbs-Merrill, 1976);

Arithmétique politique: textes rares ou inédits (1767–1789), edited by Bernard Bru and Pierre Crépel (Paris: Presses universitaires de France, 1994);

Cinq mémoires sur l'instruction publique, edited by Charles Coutel and Catherine Kintzler (Paris: Flammarion, 1994);

Mémoires et discours sur les monnaies et les finances (1790–1792), edited by Bernard Courbis and Lucien Gillard (Paris: L'Harmattan, 1994);

De la Situation du Trésor public au 1er juin 1791, edited by Jean-Pierre Poirier (Paris: Editions du C.T.H.S., 1997).

OTHER: Blaise Pascal, *Pensées de Pascal,* corrected, augmented, and edited by Condorcet (Paris, 1776);

Leonhard Euler, *Lettres à une princesse d'Allemagne sur différentes questions de physique et de philosophie,* introduced, with a eulogy, by Condorcet (Paris, 1781);

"Mémoire sur le calcul des probabilités," in *Mémoires de l'Académie des sciences, année 1781* (Paris, 1784);

Voltaire, *Oeuvres complètes de Voltaire,* edited by Condorcet, Pierre Augustin Caron de Beaumarchais, and Jacques Joseph Marie Decroix (Paris: Société Littéraire-typographique, 1784–1789);

Journal de la société de 1789, edited by Condorcet, Pierre-Samuel DuPont de Nemours, C.-E. Pastoret, and others (5 June 1790–15 September 1790)–includes "Sur l'admission des femmes au droit de la cité," translated by Alice Drysdale Vickery as *The First Essay on the Political Rights of Women* (Letchworth, U.K.: Garden City Press, 1912);

Antoine Diannyère, *Notice sur la vie et les ouvrages de Condorcet, suivi de Conseils de Condorcet à sa fille,* contributions by Condorcet (Paris: Livre d'histoire, 1799);

Antoine Destutt de Tracy, *A Commentary and Review of Montesquieu's Spirit of Laws* (Philadelphia: Printed by William Duane, 1811)–includes observations by Condorcet on the thirty-first [twenty-ninth book]; French version published as *Commentaire sur l'esprit des lois de Montesquieu suivi d'observations inédites de Condorcet sur le vingt-neuvième livre du même ouvrage* (Paris: Delaunay, 1819).

In his *Esquisse d'un tableau historique des progrès de l'esprit humain* (1795; translated as *Outlines of an Historical View of the Progress of the Human Mind,* 1795), Marie-Jean-Antoine-Nicolas Caritat, marquis de Condorcet wrote,

Nos espérances sur les destinées futures de l'espèce humaine peuvent se réduire à ces trois questions: la destruction de l'inégalité entre nations; les progrès de l'égalité dans un même peuple; enfin le perfectionnement réel de l'homme. Toutes les nations doivent-elles se rapprocher un jour de l'état de civilisation où sont parvenus les peuples les plus éclairés, les plus libres, les plus affranchis de préjugés, les Français et les Anglo-Américains?

(Our hopes for the future condition of the human race can be subsumed under three important heads: the abolition of inequality between nations, the progress of equality within each nation, and the true perfection of mankind. Will all nations one day attain that state of civilization which the most enlightened, the freest and the least burdened by prejudices, such as the French and the Anglo-Americans, have already attained?)

This assessment of the state of French social and political development was written at the height of the Great Terror by a man who had been condemned to death by the leaders of the French government he lauds, a man hiding from Maximilien-François-Marie-Isidore de Robespierre's police, a man who died alone in prison only a short time later. Yet, this passage clearly reflects Condorcet's lifelong belief in man's perfectability and his optimism about the future of mankind. Throughout his life, Condorcet championed the causes of reason and science, and his belief in the positive progress of mankind toward a state of perfection formed the cornerstone of both his works and his actions.

Marie-Jean-Antoine-Nicolas Caritat de Condorcet was born on 17 September 1743 in Ribemont, in Picardie, in northern France. His father, Antoine de Condorcet, a captain in the Royal Army, came from a noble family with a long history of military service. While stationed in Ribemont, Condorcet's father met a young widow, Marie-Madeleine de Saint-Félix, whom he married in 1740. When Condorcet's father was killed during military exercises a few weeks after his son's birth, Condorcet's now twice-widowed mother focused all her attention on her son. A devout yet superstitious woman, her fear of losing him was so great that she had him consecrated to the Virgin and undertook to raise him alone. His isolation ended only when, at age nine, his paternal uncle, Jacques-Marie Caritat de Condorcet, bishop of Lisieux, took over the boy's education.

For the next two years, Condorcet's education was supervised by a Jesuit tutor, handpicked by his uncle. After Condorcet completed this rudimentary preparation, his uncle sent him to a Jesuit school in Reims, where he remained until the age of fifteen. Condorcet was an excellent student, and his studies progressed so well that in 1758 his uncle sent him to the University of Paris. He studied there for two years at the College of Navarre–a school with an outstanding reputation for scientific studies–where Condorcet discovered his love of mathematics.

In his final year at the college, Condorcet met Georges Girault de Kéroudou, an abbot and mathematics instructor who became not only a mentor but also a friend to the shy, introverted young man and who encouraged him to pursue his studies in mathematics, despite his family's wish that he should follow in his father's footsteps. In 1760, his studies completed, Condorcet returned to Ribemont to face a family adamantly opposed to his decision not to enter military service. For two years, Condorcet remained there, attempting to convince his family to allow him to become a mathematician, all the while continuing his solitary studies.

In October 1761 he presented the fruits of his labors in the form of a paper submitted to the Académie des Sciences (Academy of Sciences). His unpublished "Essai d'une méthode générale pour intégrer les equations différentielles à deux variables" (A Test of a General Method to Integrate Differential Equations with Two Variables), while appreciated by the academy, was deemed lacking in proofs and clarity. Still, he had made an impression on both the academicians and his family, and late in 1762, his family begrudgingly allowed him to return to Paris to live and study mathematics with Girault de Kéroudou.

Not to be dissuaded by the academy's initial rejection, Condorcet immediately embarked on a career of research and publication. He devoted himself entirely to the study of theoretical mathematics. In early 1764 he presented yet another paper to the academy. This time the article was reviewed by Jean de La Fontaine and Jean Le Rond d'Alembert, who commended the young man's promise in the field of infinitesimal calculus. This positive review marked the beginning of Condorcet's career as a mathematician, but more importantly, it marked the beginning of his lifelong friendship with d'Alembert, a leading mathematician and philosopher of the time.

Shortly after the academy's positive reception of his work, Condorcet published *Du Calcul intégral* (1765, On Integral Calculus). With this publication, he was acknowledged as one of the leading mathematicians of his time. This work was followed in quick succession by two more mathematical works: *Du Problème des trois corps* (1767, The Three-Body Problem) and *Sur le système du monde et sur le calcul intégral* (1768, On the System of the World and Integral Calculus).

In 1769, at the age of twenty-five, with the backing of d'Alembert, among others, Condorcet was elected to the French Academy of Sciences and promoted to the level of associate member the following year. Furthermore, he was elected in quick succession to the Academies of Sciences of Berlin, Turin, and St. Petersburg; thus, he made his name as a mathematician in fewer than ten years.

While d'Alembert's help had been instrumental to Condorcet's entry into the French academy, he also played a pivotal role in another area of Condorcet's life—his entry into the world of intellectual society and the world of the philosophes, for d'Alembert introduced Condorcet to salon society, especially the salon of Julie de Lespinasse. At these gatherings Condorcet met some of the most prominent and influential men and women of the Enlightenment. His acquaintances included Anne-Robert-Jacques Turgot, the future finance minister, as well as such American intellectuals as Thomas Paine and Thomas Jefferson. In these salons, with their intellectual discussions of both sciences and social issues, Condorcet began to expand the scope of his interests.

Since wit and the ability to converse were considered preeminent in the salons, Condorcet's lack of social graces and his innate shyness made his entry into this new milieu difficult, but under the guidance of Lespinasse, one of the leading *salonnières* (aristocratic and upper-bourgeoisie women who conducted salons in their homes) of the time, Condorcet began to blossom.

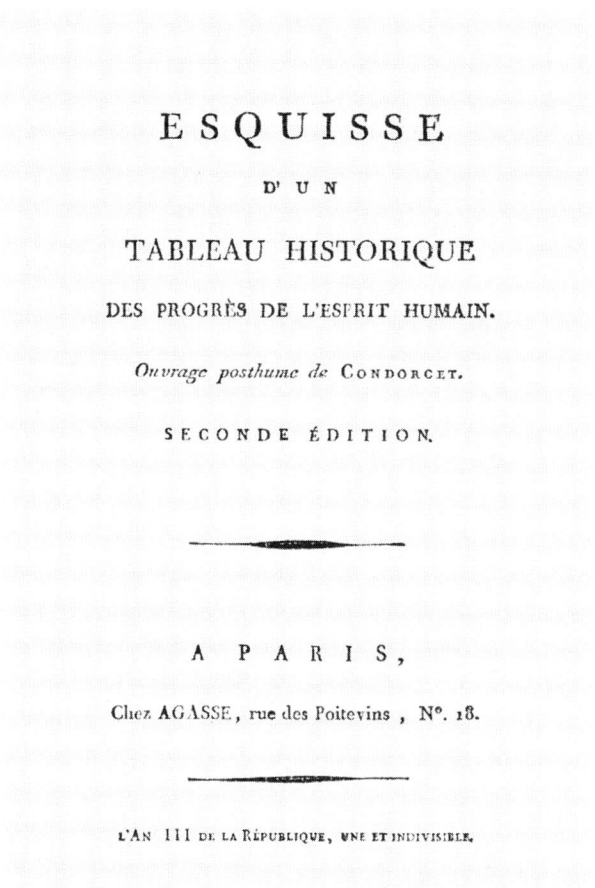

Title page for the second edition of Condorcet's 1795 work, translated as Outlines of an Historical View of the Process of the Human Mind *(from Jean-Pierre Schandeler,* Les Interprétations de Condorcet, *2000; Thomas Cooper Library, University of South Carolina)*

If d'Alembert had initiated the young Condorcet to the enlightened ideas of the era, Lespinasse, in her letters to her awkward protégé, suggested refinements in his manners as well as grooming and clothing that would improve his social standing. She appreciated the depth of his character, calling him her *bon* (good) *Condorcet*. She perhaps understood Condorcet better than anyone else, as evidenced by her 1775 portrait of Condorcet, in which she anticipates the revolutionary he became:

Cette âme calme et modérée dans le cours ordinaire de la vie, devient ardente et pleine de feu, s'il s'agit de défendre les opprimés, ou de défendre ce qui est plus cher encore, la liberté des hommes et la vertu des malheureux; alors son zèle va jusqu'à la passion; il en a la chaleur et le tourment, il souffre, il agit, il parle, il écrit avec toute l'énergie d'une âme active et passionnée.

(This soul, calm and moderate in the ordinary course of life, becomes ardent and full of fire if it is a question of defending the oppressed, or defending that which is even more dear, the freedom of men and the virtue of the less fortunate; then his zeal becomes passion; he is heated and tormented, he suffers, he acts, he speaks, he writes, and all with the energy of an active and passionate soul.)

The year 1770 marked a turning point in the young man's life. He had been accepted into the academy and was widely recognized as one of the preeminent mathematicians of his time. He could have remained just that, but at Lespinasse's request, he agreed to accompany his ailing friend d'Alembert on a convalescent trip to the south. The two men set off together on an extended voyage to Italy, but, in the end, they only made it as far as the Swiss border, where they stopped to visit the aging Voltaire. Instead of making a brief visit and moving on, the pair remained there, discussing philosophy with Voltaire. The host's warm welcome and his acceptance of Condorcet as a rising star of the Enlightenment encouraged Condorcet to enter the realm of political and social philosophy.

In 1771 Condorcet presented three more essays on integral calculus to the Academy of Sciences. He also began to work on probability theory, an interest that endured for the next fifteen years. In 1772, in an effort to gain the post of secretary of the Academy of Sciences, Condorcet began to write eulogies of its recently deceased members. The culmination of his work came in 1773 when he was elected to the position of assistant secretary of the academy and later the permanent secretary—a position he held until the abolition of the academies in 1793. Yet, even as his activity and duties within the academy increased, his interests in other areas blossomed. Although he never entirely abandoned his work in the field of mathematics, his publications and interests following the visit to Voltaire at Ferney became less and less oriented toward the study of pure mathematics. He now began to make his name as a social reformer.

In May 1774 Louis XV died of smallpox. A new king, Louis XVI, and a new regime encouraged the philosophes. Dreams of a new era and an enlightened world abounded. Condorcet became increasingly interested in the study of a nascent field, the "moral sciences," known today as the social sciences. Without abandoning mathematics entirely, Condorcet began to look at practical mathematics and set out to determine how to apply mathematical formulas to all aspects of man's existence. For Condorcet the mathematician and champion of rationalism, reason and logic governed all aspects of life; thus, all of man's actions could be explained if one were to determine and apply the vital natural laws underlying man's existence. By carefully observing humanity, one could determine the natural laws that governed all decisions and then define and describe them using mathematical formulas, which could then be used to predict human behavior. If scientists were presently unable to explain certain aspects of man's actions, Condorcet reasoned, it was not because they could not be explained using mathematics, but because the correct influences had not been determined or all of the facts influencing a decision had not been observed.

Condorcet's newly found interests in the social sciences led him to publish essays that sought to defend social justice and the superiority of the constant search for absolute truth, which could only be revealed through scientific study. His first attack on what he considered one of mankind's greatest ills, religion, was published anonymously and showed the extreme anti-clericalism of its author. Originally attributed to Voltaire, the *Lettre d'un théologien à l'auteur du "Dictionnaire des trois siècles"* (1774, Letter from a Theologian to the Author of the "Dictionary of Three Centuries") was a defense of the Enlightenment philosophes, who had been savaged by abbé Antoine de Sabatier de Castres in his *Dictionnaire* (1766–1815). Condorcet rejected the reliance of religion on tradition and mysticism and extolled the virtues of truth, reason, and research promoted by the philosophes. For Condorcet, the virtues of reason and logic rather than religion and emotion must govern all aspects of men's lives. He saw the Catholic Church as an enemy of these virtues and, perhaps more importantly, as an institution that misled the king and that condoned abuse of the masses as long as it received its share of the spoils.

With this radical and politically dangerous text, Condorcet entered the realm of politics and earned the wrath of many. Nevertheless, the new regime opened the door to new opportunities for the budding reformer. Until 1774, Condorcet had sought to improve society but had lacked the power. This situation changed when Louis XV appointed Turgot controller-general, a position that allowed Turgot to control the financial administration of the monarchy and to push through reform-minded legislation.

Condorcet the mathematician, now Condorcet the politician, allied himself closely with Turgot, writing in support of his friend's sweeping reforms, even in the face of stiff opposition from all directions. For Turgot, the most important reform of all was the abolition of all governmental controls on the commerce of grains. This idea was revolutionary, considering the long-standing governmental policies of interventionism and price supports that maintained grain prices at artificial levels. Since bread was the staple food of the majority of French citizens at the time, even minor fluctuations in the price of grain could be disastrous. Still, Turgot believed that, in the long run, free trade in grains would increase the amount of grain available and end the sporadic famines that ravaged the country. He was opposed by Jacques Necker, a conservative Swiss banker, who promoted the continuation of price controls on the trade of grain. Condorcet took the offensive against Necker, writing a series of scathing attacks, including *Lettre sur le commerce des grains* (1774, A Letter on the Grain Trade), *Lettre d'un laboureur de Picardie, à M. N**** (1775, Letter from a Laborer in Picardie to Mr. N*** [Necker]), and *Réflexions sur le commerce des bleds* (1776, Some Thoughts on Grain Trade), wherein he extolled the virtues of free trade and maintained that governmental intervention only benefited wealthy grain dealers.

Attempts to establish free trade in grains in 1774 coincided with a poor harvest. By spring 1775, bread had become scarce, and this problem, coupled with speculation and panic, caused prices to soar. Riots spread through Paris and the countryside. All the while, Condorcet defended Turgot's practices, even when they included the use of force to quell the riots. Condorcet thought the riots resulted from the masses' lack of education: they were unenlightened. If the people were enlightened, they, too, would see that free trade was beneficial to all, but since they were not, the government must do what was best for the people, regardless of the consequences. The theme of a public and enlightened education for all—one that became central to Condorcet's political philosophy and was often reiterated in his writings during the French Revolution—was beginning to take shape.

Even in the face of riots, Turgot continued to expand his reforms. If free trade in grain were to take place in a fair environment, he reasoned, France needed a uniform system of weights and measures. To accomplish this goal, he appointed Condorcet inspector of finances in 1775, and Condorcet immediately began to work on this task, monumental because of the many systems in existence at the time and the reticence of regions to relinquish their traditional systems of weights and measures. Furthermore, as a scientist, Condorcet was put in charge of modernizing the ancient system of canals in France, since they were key to alleviating existing transportation difficulties and facilitating free and open trade. Condorcet undertook all of these tasks with zeal and sought to find solutions based on mathematical principles.

With the fall of the Turgot government in 1776, the dream of creating an enlightened France governed by policies founded in logic came to an end, and a disillusioned Condorcet returned to his studies of mathematics. Once again he focused his efforts on the application of mathematics to the social sciences. His "Mémoire sur le calcul des probabilités" (1784, Dissertation on the Calculation of Probabilities) included not only probability theory but applications of probabilities to legal reform. For Condorcet, mathematics and social sciences were becoming inseparable.

In what became the centerpiece of his theory of political thought, the *Essai sur l'application de l'analyse à la probabilité des décisions rendues à la pluralité des voix* (1785; translated as *An Essay on the Application of Mathematics to the Theory of Decision Making*, 1976), Condorcet attempted to show that mathematics could be applied to all social sciences and moral decisions. For the scientist, politics must become a matter of reason. Reasonable and enlightened politicians must make sound decisions based on truth and science for the good of the society rather than for personal gain. Only then could citizens who had not voted upon every issue but who had instead elected representatives be expected to submit themselves to the laws enacted by their chosen delegates. The premise of Condorcet's work was to prove mathematically that this level of assurance could be guaranteed.

In addition to his work on probabilities, Condorcet returned to his work as secretary of the Academy of Sciences. Yet, even seemingly banal texts could be turned into social commentaries by Condorcet. He also worked tirelessly to defend and uphold the reputation of the scientific academies in the face of accusations of elitism and a burgeoning antiphilosophe movement. Condorcet thought the rational power of science could be used successfully to combat charlatanism, superstition, and prejudice, and such battles could best be waged in the academies. These themes were evident in his speech upon admission to the Académie française (French Academy) in 1782. Condorcet believed that human progress would come solely through scientific progress.

Condorcet the politician now turned to purely social issues. He wrote many pamphlets, continually taking the side of logic on such varied issues as the rights of Protestants in France and the abolition of slavery. In *Réflexions d'un citoyen catholique sur les lois de France relatives aux Protestants* (1778, Thoughts of a Catholic on the French Laws Governing Protestants), he reiterated his 1774 stance on religion, preaching tolerance and equality for all. He could see no possible logical justification for considering Protestants in France noncitizens, subject to condemnation and severe penalties, including imprisonment and death, simply for practicing their religion.

This same belief in the equality of all is evident in *Réflexions sur l'esclavage des nègres* (1781, Thoughts on Negro Slavery), in which Condorcet favored the abolition of slavery—a heinous crime, no matter the justification used. Even if the laws of a nation permitted it, slavery continued to be, by its nature, a crime that no human law could abrogate. Condorcet's adamantly abolitionist stance stemmed from his belief that all races are inherently equal. Consequently, no man could justify ownership of another. Condorcet went so far as to state that some slaves were superior to their owners:

> La nature vous a formés pour avoir le même esprit, la même raison, les mêmes vertus que les blancs. Je ne parle ici que de ceux d'Europe; car pour les blancs des colonies, je ne vous fais pas l'injure de les comparer avec vous; je sais combien de fois votre fidélité, votre probité, votre courage ont fait rougir vos maîtres. Si on allait chercher un homme dans les îles d'Amérique, ce ne serait point parmi les gens de chair blanche qu'on le trouverait.

> (Nature formed you with the same spirit, the same reason, and the same virtues as Whites. I am only speaking of those of Europe; as for the Whites in the colonies, I would not insult you by comparing them to you. I know how often your loyalty, your integrity and your courage have made your masters blush. If one went looking for a man in the islands of America, it would not be among the ones with white skin that one would look.)

Later, reflecting on a future society, one in which all slavery had been abolished, Condorcet foresaw a world with absolutely no differences between men. Following the emancipation of slaves would be a period during which the two societies would seem different, but Condorcet thought, "Au bout de quelques générations, à la vérité, les noirs se confondront absolument avec les blancs, et il n'y aura plus de différence que pour la couleur; le mélange des races fera ensuite disparaître, à la longue même, cette dernière différence" (After a few generations, in truth, Blacks would be mixed completely with Whites, and, except for skin color, there would be no remaining differences. Mixing of the races would, eventually, make even this last difference disappear). Condorcet believed such a world would be the ideal, the state of perfection.

While working on another social cause, the freeing of three peasants wrongly convicted of burglary, Condorcet met his future wife, Sophie de Grouchy. She was twenty-two; he was forty-three. After a whirlwind courtship, they were married in 1786, much to the dismay of many of Condorcet's contemporaries. Yet, his wife proved to be an intellectual in her own right, and theirs was a happy marriage. Their only child, Alexandrine-Louise-Sophie, was born in 1790.

With the advent of the French Revolution in 1789, Condorcet again returned to politics. Soon, this man who preached rational politics found himself faced with superstition, ignorance, and near anarchy. He produced many political pamphlets and essays, describing his opinion on the direction that the revolution should take. His first works emphasized the need for a declaration of the rights of men to serve as a basis for the future constitution. He encouraged voters to choose educated and enlightened politicians who could truly reform a nation and act in the best interests of its citizens. He preached the necessity of a single assembly in which voting would not be tied to class status, but this idea was rejected twice, along with Condorcet's candidacy for election to the nascent legislative assembly. Eventually, he was chosen to represent his district of Paris in the Electoral Assembly—as a nobleman, not simply as a member without class or rank.

As the revolution progressed, Condorcet continued to write on topics of contemporary significance. In 1790 he published an editorial in the *Journal de la Société de 1789* (Journal of the Society of 1789) titled "Sur l'admission des femmes au droit de la cité" (1790; translated as *The First Essay on the Political Rights of Women,* 1912), in which he decried the exclusion of women from the political process and reiterated his stance against slavery and religious discrimination:

> Or, les droits des hommes résultent uniquement de ce qu'ils sont des êtres sensibles, susceptibles d'acquérir des idées morales, et de raisonner sur ces idées. Ainsi les femmes ayant ces mêmes qualités, ont nécessairement des droits égaux. Ou aucun individu de l'espèce humaine n'a de véritables droits ou tous ont les mêmes; et celui qui vote contre le droit d'un autre, quels que soit sa religion, sa couleur ou son sexe, a dès lors abjuré les siens.

> (Now the rights of men result simply from the fact that they are sentient beings, capable of acquiring moral ideas and of reasoning concerning these ideas. Women, having these same qualities, must necessarily possess equal rights. Either no individual of the human species has any true rights, or all have the same. And he who votes against the rights of another, of whatever religion, color, or sex, has thereby abjured his own.)

Condorcet was also charged by the Electoral Legislative Assembly with the development of a program for public education. In his *Premier mémoire sur l'instruction publique* (1791; translated as *The Nature and Purpose of Public Instruction,* 1976), Condorcet preached the necessity of a free public education for all. Such an education was necessary not only to train workers but also to produce enlightened voters, a necessity in Condorcet's view of democracy. Furthermore, while he did accept certain social limitations on the education of women, he proposed that for the betterment of society as a whole, women should receive basically the same education as men. Perhaps most importantly, Condorcet's educational system was to be secular in nature, open to children of all faiths.

While he continued to publish and speak out on measures before the assembly, Condorcet also remained active at the Academy of Sciences. In early 1790 the academy was officially charged with developing a new system of weights and measures. Condorcet, who had begun working on just such a system under Turgot, immediately began working with other members to invent a uniform system predicated in science. Condorcet did not live to see the final definition of his "meter" (1799) nor its adoption in France as the sole legal form of measurement (1840).

Condorcet's political troubles began in early 1793, when he presented his version of the French constitution to the Assembly, a work he had been preparing since October 1792. His *Plan de constitution présenté à la Convention nationale les 15 et 16 février 1793, l'an 2e de la République* (1793; translated as *An Authentic Copy of the New Plan of the French Constitution, as Presented to the National Convention*, 1793) was rejected by the newly formed National Assembly. Condorcet refused to accept his removal from the committee and continued to publish pamphlets critical of the government and of the new committee now assigned to write another constitution.

In May 1793 the convention decreed the arrest of twenty-one members of the moderate Girondin Club. Although never a member of this political club, Condorcet associated closely with its members, sharing many of their ideas, including their belief that the existing extremism needed to end. Even though he barely escaped arrest in May, Condorcet continued to write and speak out against the Terror and its leaders. On 8 July 1793 an order was issued for his arrest—it was the equivalent of a death sentence. Condorcet immediately went into hiding at the home of Madame Vernet, a middle-class boardinghouse owner who was aware of his dangerous position. For eight months he remained in hiding, writing the work for which he is perhaps best known, *Esquisse d'un tableau historique des progrès de l'esprit humain*. This unfinished work, published posthumously, is a synthesis of Condorcet's ideas and beliefs. It is an historical study of the progress of mankind that emphasizes the perfectability of man. Each of its ten sections describes a stage of development of humanity, with each stage leading closer to a perfect state of being. Condorcet seeks to demonstrate that all progress has resulted from science and reason, not from superstition or divine intervention. He traces man's progress through its various stages, arriving at the French Revolution at the ninth level. The remaining stage represents

Illustration of the death of Condorcet, who was imprisoned in Bourg-la-Reine, on the outskirts of Paris. His death was attributed to self-poison or to a brain aneurysm (from Alphonse de Lamartine, Histoire des Girondins, *1865, 1866, in Jean-Pierre Schandeler,* Les Interprétations de Condorcet, *2000; Thomas Cooper Library, University of South Carolina).*

Condorcet's optimistic view of the future of mankind, even as he was in hiding, a state of equality and the true perfection of humanity. Many of the developments that Condorcet foresaw have come to pass: a form of social security for the protection of the elderly, a comprehensive system of public education, and increased agricultural production, all of which would lead, according to Condorcet, to an increased life expectancy.

In March 1794, fearing he would soon be betrayed and concerned for the safety of Madame Vernet, Condorcet left Paris and sought refuge at the home of his friends the Suards. Refused asylum, he sought food and shelter at a local inn, where his disheveled demeanor aroused suspicion. He was arrested and imprisoned on 27 March 1794 in Bourg-la-Reine on the outskirts of Paris. Having given his captors a fictitious name, he was being held until his identity could be established. Two days later he was found dead in his cell. The exact cause of death remains a mystery. Some maintain that he poisoned himself in order to avoid being returned to certain death in Paris, while others claim that he died of a brain aneurysm resulting from the stress and poor conditions he had endured. Condorcet was fifty years old.

As the last of the great Enlightenment philosophes, Marie-Jean-Antoine-Nicolas Caritat, marquis de Condorcet, cannot be defined simply as a mathematician, a politician, or a social scientist. His legacy is that of a visionary, a man ahead of his time. His revolutionary stance on women's equality, abolition of slavery, and democracy make many of his readings relevant today, more than two hundred years after his death. Condorcet's uncompromising personality forced him to live his beliefs, and his unwillingness to back down in the face of prejudice and opposition led to his untimely death. Yet, his positive attitude toward society and his altruism remained to the end, as can be seen when he wrote, while in hiding, to his young daughter in *Conseils de Condorcet à sa fille* (Condorcet's Advice to His Daughter), published in 1799 in *Notices sur la vie et les ouvrages de Condorcet suivi de Conseils de Condorcet a sa fille:* "Tu trouveras alors que . . . il est plus doux, plus commode, si j'ose le dire, de vivre pour autrui, et que c'est alors seulement que l'on vit véritablement pour soi-même" (You will find . . . that it is better, more convenient, to live for others, and it is only then that one lives for oneself).

Letters:

Correspondance inédite de Condorcet et de Turgot, 1770–1779, edited by Charles Henry (Geneva: Slatkine Reprints, 1970);

Correspondance inédite de Condorcet et Madame Suard, Monsieur Suard et Garat (1771–1791), edited by Elisabeth Badinter (Paris: Fayard, 1988);

Lettres à Condorcet, suivi du portrait de Condorcet rédigé par Julie de Lespinasse en 1774, edited by Jean-Noël Pascal (Paris: Presses universitaires de France, 1989).

References:

Elisabeth Badinter and Robert Badinter, *Condorcet (1743–1794): un intellectuel en politique* (Paris: Fayard, 1988; revised and enlarged, 1989);

Keith Michael Baker, *Condorcet: From Natural Philosophy to Social Mathematics* (Chicago: University of Chicago Press, 1975);

Janine Bouissounoux, *Condorcet: le philosophe dans la Révolution* (Paris: Hachette, 1962);

Anne-Marie Chouillet and Pierre Crépel, eds., *Condorcet: homme de Lumières et de la Révolution* (Fontenay-Saint-Cloud, France: Editions ENS, 1997);

Pierre Crépel and Christian Gilain, *Condorcet: mathématicien, économiste, philosophe, homme politique* (Paris: Minerve, 1989);

Hélène Delsaux, *Condorcet journaliste. 1790–1794* (Paris: Librairie ancienne Honoré Champion, 1931);

Edward Godell, *The Noble Philosopher: Condorcet and the Enlightenment* (Buffalo, N.Y.: Prometheus, 1994);

Kingsley Martin, *The Rise of French Liberal Thought: A Study of Political Ideas from Bayle to Condorcet,* edited by J. P. Mayer (New York: New York University Press, 1954; revised, 1956);

Iain McLean and Fiona Hewitt, *Condorcet: Foundations of Social Choice and Political Theory* (Brookfield, Vt.: Edward Elgar, 1994);

Colette Verger Michael, "Condorcet and the Inherent Contradiction in the American Affirmation of Natural Rights and Slaveholding," in *Transactions of the Fifth International Congress on the Enlightenment,* edited by Haydn Mason (Oxford: Voltaire Foundation, 1980), pp. 768–774;

John Pappas, "Condorcet, 'le seul' et 'le premier' féministe du 18e siècle?" *Dix-Huitième Siècle,* 23 (1991): 441–443;

Richard H. Popkin, "Condorcet, Abolitionist," in *Condorcet Studies I,* edited by Leonora Cohen Rosenfield (Atlantic Highlands, N.J.: Humanities Press, 1984), pp. 35–47;

Constance Rowe, "The Present-Day Relevance of Condorcet," in *Condorcet Studies I,* edited by Rosenfield (Atlantic Highlands, N.J.: Humanities Press, 1984), pp. 15–33;

J. Salwyn Schapiro, *Condorcet and the Rise of Liberalism* (New York: Octagon Books, 1963);

Schapiro, "The Esquisse of Condorcet," in *Essays in Intellectual History Dedicated to James Harvey Robinson by His Former Seminar Students,* edited by David Saville Muzzey (Freeport, N.Y.: Books for Libraries Press, 1929), pp. 165–185.

Papers:

Many of Marie-Jean-Antoine-Nicolas Caritat, marquis de Condorcet's manuscripts, those inherited by his daughter, can be found at the Bibliothèque de l'Institut de France (MSS 848–85). Additional manuscripts can be found at the Bibliothèque nationale (Fonds français, nouvelles acquisitions, MS 4586 and MS 23639).

Sophie Cottin
(22 March 1770 – 15 August 1807)

Samia I. Spencer
Auburn University

BOOKS: *Claire d'Albe* (Paris: Maradan, 1799); translated as *Dangerous Friendship; or The Letters of Clara d'Albe by a Lady of Baltimore* (Baltimore: Joseph Robinson, 1807);

Malvina (Paris: Maradan, 1801); translated by Elizabeth Gunning as *Malvina* (London: T. Hurst, 1803);

Amélie (Paris: Giguet & Michaud, 1802); translated as *Amelia Mansfield*, 4 volumes (London: Cox & Baylis, 1803);

Mathilde (Paris: Giguet & Michaud, 1805; London: Peltier, 1805); translated as *The Saracen* (London: R. Dutton, 1805);

Elisabeth, ou les exilés de Sibérie. Suivi de La Prise de Jéricho, poème (Paris: Giguet & Michaud, 1806); translated by Mary Meek as *Elizabeth, or The Exiles of Siberia: A Tale, Founded upon Facts* (London: Minerva Press, for Lane, Newman, 1807).

Editions and Collections: *Oeuvres complètes de Mme Cottin*, 7 volumes (Paris & London: Colburn, 1811)—preceded by memoirs of the author's life;

Oeuvres complètes de Madame Cottin avec une notice sur la vie et les écrits de l'auteur. Nouvelle édition révisée (Paris: Corbet, 1818);

Oeuvres complètes de Madame Cottin, edited by Joseph Michaud (Paris: Corbet, 1820);

Claire d'Albe: The Original French Text, edited by Margaret Cohen (New York: MLA, 2002);

Claire d'Albe: An English Translation, edited by Cohen (New York: MLA, 2002).

OTHER: "La Prise de Jéricho," in Jean-Baptiste Suard, *Mélanges de littérature* (Paris: Dentu, 1803).

Sophie Cottin (from Bureaux du Musee des Familles <www.chass.utoronto.ca/french/sable/recherche/banques/femmes/images/cottin2.jpg>)

A best-selling author of the late eighteenth century, Sophie Cottin was considered by many to be the foremost woman novelist, and Victor Hugo called her "le premier écrivain de l'époque" (the prime writer of the era). Her novels, *Claire d'Albe* (1799; translated as *Dangerous Friendship; or The Letters of Clara d'Albe by a Lady of Baltimore*, 1807), *Malvina* (1801; translated in 1803), *Amélie* (1802; translated as *Amelia Mansfield*, 1803), *Mathilde* (1805; translated as *The Saracen*, 1805), and *Elisabeth, ou les exilés de Sibérie: Suivi de La Prise de Jéricho, poèm* (1806; translated as *Elizabeth, or The Exiles of Siberia: A Tale, Founded upon Facts*, 1807), were immensely popular not only throughout Europe but also in the New World. Available to readers in Croatian, Danish, Dutch, English, German, Italian, Portuguese, Romanian, and Spanish, they were also adapted to the stage as plays and musicals. Evidenced by the frequency of their reprints, these novels delighted readers for nearly half a century after their author's premature death at age thirty-seven. In England, *Elisabeth, ou les exilés de Sibérie* was so popular that at least one publisher was confused about its national origin, printing it as a "British Pocket Classic" under the same cover as Oliver Goldsmith's *The Vicar of Wakefield* (1766). More astonishing, however, is the extraordinary fascination of the

American public with *Elisabeth, ou les exilés de Sibérie*, which started the year after its publication and lasted into the twentieth century, long after interest in Cottin's literary production had waned in Europe. It was printed simultaneously by several publishers, who produced many editions in New York, Baltimore, Chicago, Boston, Philadelphia, Rochester, and Poughkeepsie. Perhaps the most active among these publishers was Lockwood and Sons of New York, who printed twelve editions of the novel during a quarter of a century beginning in 1852. The many identical editions "with explanations of difficult words, phrases, and idiomatic expressions" that appeared in a twenty-five-year span (1856–1880), including a New York edition "with interlinear translation and French pronunciation of a few pages, accompanied by a vocabulary list of all the words in the text," indicate that the book may have been used as a manual in French classes.

Gradually, however, Cottin's works fell out of print until resurrected by feminist scholarship in the 1990s. Although rediscovered, Cottin has yet to find the place she deserves in French literature, in which some of her predecessors—such as Françoise de Graffigny, Marie-Jeanne Riccoboni, and Isabelle de Charrière—are now being recognized. Accurate biographical information on such basics as Cottin's name, date, place of birth, and place of death, is difficult to ascertain, as various spellings of her maiden name can be found (Restaud, Ristau, Ristaud, Restand, and Risteau). Sources list different places for her place of birth including Tonne, Tonneins, Bordeaux, and Paris; do not agree on the dates of the beginning (1770 and 1773) and end (April 1807, 15 August 1807, and 25 August 1807) of her life; and attribute her death to suicide, tuberculosis, or breast cancer.

According to her most reliable biographers, Marie Sophie Risteau was born in Paris on 22 March 1770 into a wealthy Bordelaise Protestant family. Her father, Jacques Risteau, a successful entrepreneur and later director of the famous trading company Companie des Indes (India Company), and his wife, Anne-Suzanne-Marie Lecourt, were married fourteen years earlier, in 1756. Childless for twelve years, their first daughter, Anne Marie Henriette, was born on 6 June 1768, followed by Marie Sophie two years later. When Sophie was two months old, the family returned to live in the Bordeaux region. The child often spent time with her mother on the maternal grandmother's property near Tonneins and grew up enjoying a peaceful provincial childhood. A cultivated woman, Madame Risteau provided her daughter a solid education at home and developed in her a love for reading. While close to her mother, Sophie also developed a strong bond to her father, who lavished affection on her. Such privileged father-daughter relationships are often reflected in Cottin's fiction.

As his health and fortune began to decline in the late 1780s, Jacques Risteau was anxious to find a suitable husband for Sophie. Business friends, the Jauges, found a suitor, Paul Cottin, a handsome and wealthy young banker of twenty-four, whose grandfather, like Jacques Risteau himself, had managed the Companie des Indes. Despite initial reluctance on both sides, the couple eventually developed a deep affection for each other and were married in Paris on 16 May 1789. However, the political turmoil that soon followed brought a quick end to the newlyweds' happiness.

In 1791 they fled the country, seeking refuge in the Pyrenees, in southern Spain, and in England. Returning to Paris for fear that all their possessions might be confiscated, they learned that Théodore Jauge, Paul's business associate and brother-in-law, had been guillotined and that Paul's own brother, André Cottin, had been incarcerated. Denounced as an aristocrat, Paul himself would have been arrested on 5 October 1793 had he not died two days earlier. Although most sources attribute the death to a heart attack, Colette Cazenobe finds it unlikely that a healthy young man under age thirty would suddenly succumb to a deadly massive attack. She suggests, instead, that death might have been self-inflicted to escape public humiliation and that his wife went along with the death of natural causes so as not to tarnish her husband's reputation. Cazenobe developed her hypothesis from inferences in various letters that Sophie Cottin wrote to friends, especially one letter in which she alluded to the burden of a secret she had been keeping to herself: "Le présent et l'avenir ont beau me présenter des sujets de tourments et de peine, j'y suis insensible, un triste souvenir me tient absolument subjuguée" (The present and the past try in vain to present me reasons for grief and torment, but I no longer react. A sad memory keeps me totally subjugated).

At age twenty-four, and within a two-year period, the young widow had lost not only her husband but also her father and her father-in-law, and she found herself near financial ruin. After the sealing of her house by the national guards who came to arrest her husband, she retired to their country estate in Champlan, a property that Paul Cottin had bought jointly with his brother-in-law and business partner, Antoine Louis Girardot, a few months prior to his death. Tragedy and financial difficulties nevertheless continued to plague Cottin's life. Joining her daughter in Champlan, Madame Risteau followed her son-in-law in death only four months later.

These tragic events exacerbated Cottin's feeling of grief and deep depression, leading her to implore death for relief. Writing to a friend in 1794, she told him: "la nuit la plus noire, lorsqu'elle m'enveloppe d'épaisses ténèbres est encore moins sombre que mon âme" (when the darkest night surrounds me with thickest gloom, it is still less somber than my soul). Later she added,

> J'ai des accès de tristesse noire, je suis habituellement inquiète; mes regards ont beau se fixer autour de moi, ils ne trouvent rien digne de les fixer. Le monde dans sa vaste étendue ne me paraît qu'une solitude stérile, il me semblre que je suis sur une terre étrangère où rien ne me convient. Je voudrais bien finir d'exister; non, il n'est point d'instants dans la journée où je ne reçusse la mort avec volupté.
>
> (I have spells of grave despair, and I live in a constant state of anguish. In vain do my eyes find anything worthy of being seen. The world in its vastness is nothing but a sterile solitude. I feel that I live in a strange land where nothing suits me. I would very much like for my life to end; or rather I should say that there is not a single moment in the day when I would not welcome death voluptuously.)

Cottin was able to overcome somewhat these deep feelings of despair through her love of nature and the warm and affectionate relationships she developed with close relatives and friends who went often to Champlan for extended visits. The most intimate among them were her cousins Félicité Lafargue and Julie Verdier, especially Julie, with whom she had developed an enduring friendship while growing up at their grandmother's estate and who remained her confidante and closest friend throughout her life. In fact, Cottin viewed herself as a second mother to Julie's three daughters and even considered adopting the youngest. When they were not together in Champlan, the cousins maintained a regular correspondence in which Cottin's talent as a writer was becoming evident. Other guests at Champlan included sister-in-law Sophie Girardot and close friends Fanny Soubies and Adélaïde de Pastoret.

Settled in her retreat, Cottin led a quiet and peaceful life. She painted, played music, welcomed visitors—including some of her husband's friends who remained loyal—and devoted herself to the education of Julie's daughters. She wrote detailed letters to her many correspondents, sharing her feelings and relating daily activities but avoiding comments on the troubling events affecting the country, whether through caution, fear of the authorities, or simply lack of concern about the world beyond the confines of her small inner circle.

While friendship with women was the most important element in Cottin's life, a few men also remained close. One, Joseph Michaud, a member of the

Sophie Cottin (monument located in Bagnères-de-Bigorre, France; photograph by Michael J. Call in his Infertility and the Novels of Sophie Cottin, *2002; Thomas Cooper Library, University of South Carolina)*

French Academy, was a cherished companion and later a valuable adviser, the editor of her novels, and her biographer—although some of the information in the introduction to the complete edition of her works he published in 1811 is inaccurate. Romantic relationships were not nearly as satisfying. The elder Etienne Gramagnac, one of her husband's business associates, played a crucial role in the early years of her widowhood, providing important financial advice on the management of her estate and her declining resources. However, when he extended a marriage proposal, she gently turned it down, preferring friendship. Other suitors followed, including Jacques Lafargue, the eighteen-year-old son of her cousin Félicité—a troubled young man who fell madly in love with her and eventually committed suicide on her property. Another cousin, Constant Lemarcis, a widower himself, also proposed in 1797. Like previous offers, his was rejected.

As was the case with most women writers of her era, Cottin did not intend to become an author, and even when her work was published, she preferred to remain anonymous: none of her first three novels bore her name. According to Michaud, Cottin strongly disapproved of women who sought authorship—naturally including herself in the group—and stated her thoughts on this subject forcefully in the first edition of *Amélie*. However, under pressure from friends, she reluctantly agreed to remove that passage from later editions. Some critics claim that she donated the profits from her book to charity in order to counter the guilt resulting from acting against her own convictions.

According to legend, Cottin's literary career began as a result of a casual incident, when a friend who feared for his life asked her to lend him money to flee the country. Since her dwindling resources did not allow such generosity, she thought of writing a novel and using the royalties to help the endangered man. She began immediately and within two weeks had completed a compact novel of approximately two hundred pages, *Claire d'Albe*. Published anonymously, the book was an instant success. It was immediately followed by four others: *Malvina* in 1801, *Amélie* in 1802, *Mathilde* in 1805, and *Elisabeth, ou les exilés de Sibérie* in 1806. Specific details concerning the composition and publication of a short piece inspired by the Bible, *La Prise de Jéricho* (The Fall of Jericho) are not well known. The work appeared for the first time in 1803, in a book by Jean-Baptiste Suard, and was printed thereafter in the same volume as *Elisabeth*. According to Michael J. Call, it may have been written before *Claire d'Albe*.

Like Jean-Jacques Rousseau's Julie in *Julie, ou La Nouvelle Héloïse* (1761), Claire d'Albe is married to a friend of her father, a man three times her senior. The couple live in an idyllic pastoral environment with their two children. Following the death of his mother, Frédéric, Monsieur d'Albe's nephew, is invited to join the family. Claire is instructed by her husband to become the young man's preceptor and substitute mother. As she fulfills her task with amusement and enthusiasm, the mentor and her protégé develop mutual respect and admiration, discover each other's noble characters and virtuous souls, and gradually fall in love. Their heightened feelings of mutual esteem and veneration add particular intensity to their physical encounter. Claire's soul, "confondue dans celle de son amant, nage dans un torrent de volupté" (lost in that of her lover, swims in a flood of voluptuousness). Love turns into a blazing and consuming passion, interlaced with guilt and remorse, eventually leading to death resulting from a plot by Claire's husband and her cousin Elise. Infidelity, however, in no way tarnishes Claire's virtue: she departs the world serenely, with a clear conscience, feeling comfortable as she prepares herself to "paraître devant Dieu" (appear before God).

The adulterous wife is still referred to as "une femme céleste" (a celestial woman) despite her transgression of social and moral laws. Clearly, the final message—tacit approval of infidelity—did not escape the attention of readers. Most vocal among Cottin's critics was Stéphanie de Genlis, who deplored "l'immoralité révoltante" (the revolting immorality) of the book and its description of "l'amour délirant, furieux et féroce" (delirious, furious, and ferocious love).

Aware of the turmoil caused by her first novel, Cottin, writing to her sister-in-law, apologized for "les couleurs un peu voluptueuses, [les] passions un peu vives" (the somewhat voluptuous colors, the somewhat lively passions) that she described in *Claire d'Albe* and vowed to do better in the second novel, *Malvina*. She kept her promise and avoided descriptions of erotic love scenes, focusing more on the inner conflict. Morality and social conventions were thus respected.

Like Cottin herself, Malvina is a young widow. She spent three unforgettable, happy years with her friend Clara and her English husband, Lord Sheridan. As she prepares to die, Clara does not trust her husband with the education of their daughter, Fanny; instead, she asks Malvina to devote her life exclusively to that mission and never to let herself be distracted from that responsibility by sharing her time or her affection with anyone but Fanny. Malvina agrees to honor her friend's wish. However, in the Scottish castle into which she moves to care for the child, the young woman encounters Sir Edmund Seymour, the nephew of her hostess, Mistress Birton, and both immediately fall in love.

Although in this case the protagonists are single, the relationship cannot develop into a happy ending, hindered as it is by different obstacles on each side. Malvina is bound by her "devoirs rigoureux" (rigorous duty) toward her dying friend. Sir Edmund, a notorious womanizer, must marry the rich Lady Sumerhill in order to obtain a seat in Parliament and make his aunt a "lady." Their love is described in enchanting terms, but without sensuality. Unlike Claire, Malvina does not succumb to her lover but remains chaste. Although Fanny frees Malvina from her vow and allows her to marry Sir Edmund, the novel does not have a happy ending. Sir Sheridan, Fanny's father, threatens to take his daughter from Malvina, who is forced to make a difficult choice between Fanny and Sir Edmund. She makes what she sees as the right decision, sacrificing love for duty. Following Claire d'Albe and Clara in death, Malvina sends that lesson as a final message to her adopted daughter: "Apprenez surtout à Fanny à ne jamais sacrifier le devoir à l'amour" (above all, teach Fanny never to sacrifice duty for love). *Malvina* appeared in early 1801 to tremendous public success.

Writing was now an important part of Cottin's life. She was sending her manuscripts to friends and family for comments and advice, although she still did not want her name to appear on her books. While completing *Malvina,* she had already started to work on her next novel, *Amélie,* and was considering a religious topic for the one to follow—a thought undoubtedly strengthened by her reading of François-René de Chateaubriand's *Atala* (1801). Early that year, while in Paris and caring for her cousin Julie's daughters, Cottin encountered Jean Devaines, an aging gentleman who offered not only literary advice on her writings but also friendship and a romantic relationship. She accepted the companionship along with some of the comments on her manuscript but did not fully trust Devaines's judgment on women writers. As for romance, it was totally discouraged.

Amélie, the main character in the new novel, mirrors her predecessor and resembles her own creator. Like Malvina and Cottin, she too is a young widow, but her life story is much more convoluted. As the novel begins, she recalls her marriage to Mansfield, a poet and musician to whom she was attracted because he embodied her father's love for the arts. The short-lived marriage was not, however, a happy one. After the couple's son was born, Mansfield proved to be a womanizer and was killed in a duel. The marriage not only had been a disappointment to Amélie but also had aroused the wrath of the family against her because her grandfather, the comte de Woldemar, had stipulated in his will that his title and wealth would go to his grandson Ernest only if he married his cousin Amélie. Instead, without consulting her family, Amélie had eloped with Mansfield, given birth to their child, and become a widow. The hard lesson she learned from her disappointing marriage led her to accept an offer from her late husband's uncle, Monsieur Grandson, to share his retired life in a distant place in Switzerland, far removed from her own relatives, and to become the older man's heir. Destiny, however, reunites the cousins; they fall in love, promise themselves to each other, and can thus execute the grandfather's will. But Madame de Woldemar, Ernest's mother, is adamantly opposed to this union and warns her son that marrying the renegade cousin will cause his mother's death and make him a matricide.

As in the previous two novels, love ultimately meets a tragic end, although in this instance the ending is more complex than those in the preceding books. Amélie, like Claire, gives herself to her lover, but the couple triumphs in death, fulfilling the grandfather's will despite Madame de Woldemar's opposition; they die within hours of each other. They have a magnificent funeral procession, and each year on the anniver-

Title page for an early English translation of Cottin's 1806 novel Elisabeth, ou les exilés de Sibérie, *which takes place in a small Siberian village for political exiles (Thomas Cooper Library, University of South Carolina)*

sary of their death, six couples are married in celebration of their love. Unlike her fictional predecessor, however, Amélie does not depart the world serenely and with a clear conscience. Filled with both pity and contempt, she refers to herself as "une pauvre créature bien criminelle" (a poor felonious creature) and dies victim of the love she could not resist. Henceforth, Cottin's life and novels take a different turn.

The author's only serious romantic liaison occurred in 1803–1804, during the months she spent in Bagnères-de-Bigorre with Julie and two of her three daughters, following the publication of *Amélie* and while she was working on her fourth novel, *Mathilde.* In the Soubies family, who hosted them, Cottin met Pierre-Hyacinthe Azaïs, the children's preceptor and a self-proclaimed philosophe. They spent hours discussing spirituality, metaphysics, and the scientific proof of the existence of God. Fascinated by his knowledge and captivated by their intellectual discussions, Cottin idealized a man unworthy of her, finding in him the incarnation of the romantic heroes she had created in her novels. Identifying with her own heroines, she fell in love with Azaïs, and thus life became an imitation of art, and reality a mirror of fiction. Against the advice of everyone in her entourage, she pursued the relationship and contemplated marriage during her brief recovery from an amenorrheic problem. The respite in the south was short-lived, for she suffered a relapse upon returning to Paris. Unable to bear children, she renounced her dream of becoming a wife and mother. With great difficulty, she wrote Azaïs to explain her infertility, thus her inability to fulfill his strong desire for family and children. As expected, the revelation brought the relationship to an end. Gradually, the illusion wore off, and she began to realize that this man was unworthy of her.

Faith provided the backdrop of her fourth and longest novel, *Mathilde*. For the first time, the author decided to publish under her own name, displaying her pride in being associated with her new religious-based story. Set in the twelfth century, the historical novel transports readers on a long journey throughout the Middle East. The action-filled story abounds with disguise, suspense, murder, kidnapping attempts, armed battles, and religious conflicts.

Raised in a convent, Mathilde is the pure and innocent sixteen-year-old sister of Richard the Lionheart, king of England. Just before taking the vow to become a nun, she begs to accompany her brother to the Holy Land, where he is about to engage in the third crusade. When Malek Adhel, Saladin's brother and "the most feared warrior in Asia," sees her, he immediately falls in love with her, intent on declaring his feelings. Meanwhile, Agnès, the Christian princess of Jerusalem, whose character contrasts with Mathilde's, is passionately enamored of Malek Adhel. When Agnès discovers that her lover plans to renounce all other women because of a new love, she attempts to kill Mathilde but strikes Malek Adhel instead. Gradually, the young virgin falls in love with her savior, but resisting her desire, she seeks refuge in a retreat in the desert. Malek Adhel follows her and, in awe of her moral strength, is tempted to adopt the religion that empowers her with extraordinary fortitude. The couple receives Saladin's blessings to marry, but an outraged Richard promises his sister's hand to whoever kills Malek Adhel. The lovers' ultimate encounter takes place near a tomb, but they remain chaste.

Malek Adhel is eventually killed in combat; however, just before dying, he is baptized and kisses the cross. The archbishop also joins the lovers' hands, declaring them husband and wife, as a majority of Muslims rally behind the funeral procession of their leader. When the heroine returns to convent life, she appears triumphant as she experiences the "beginning of eternity." According to Jean Gaulmier, "L'amores et la mort se confondent dans une immense apothéose" (love and death blend in boundless apotheoses). Like her predecessors Claire, Malvina, and Amélie, Mathilde, as Ruth P. Thomas states, discovers "the incompatibility between the real world and the ideal." Although, as in the other novels, the story ends with death, this love was not in vain, for God's cause is well served, and morality triumphs. Faith is the source of Mathilde's unfaltering moral strength and her ability to resist the temptations of love.

Sales of the book were phenomenal, and *Mathilde* brought Cottin both critical and public acclaim, inspiring in her even more enthusiasm for her skill, but the celebrity also resulted in unwelcome rumors about her religious commitment to the Protestant faith. While completing *Mathilde* in 1805, the author found the source of her new project, *Elisabeth*, in a true story reported in various publications.

The setting of this last novel is a remote Siberian village in which political exiles must live in isolation. An only child, Elisabeth is cherished by her father, Pierre Springer, and her mother, Phédora, and is unaware of their plight. No one knows where the family came from or the reason for their exile. The child grows up a great admirer of her father, inspired by the tales of courage and bravery that he relates to her. When she learns of her parents' situation, she resolves to go to St. Petersburg to meet the emperor and ask for their freedom. Her unusual courage and determination enable her to set out on a heroic journey of nearly two thousand miles.

Smoloff, the young man she meets along the way and who falls in love with her, also saved her father's life. Filial love and romantic love become intermingled, as Smoloff attempts to assist Elisabeth in reaching her goal. Religion plays a role in this novel as well; far from causing a conflict, it facilitates the reunion of lovers, whose encounters take place in a church. Like Mathilde's, Elisabeth's faith strengthens her will and resolve. The older man that Smoloff's father sends to protect the seventeen-year-old heroine on the trip to St. Petersburg is a Christian missionary. Although he dies on the way, he symbolically transmits his powers and blessings to the young woman. Recognizing her exceptional character, he gives her his cross and predicts that her uncommon virtue "aura sa récompense sur la terre avant de l'avoir dans le ciel" (will find its reward on earth before receiving it in heaven). Indeed, Elisabeth is the only protagonist in Cottin's novels to survive and accomplish her mission: she restores justice, frees her parents from exile, and will presumably marry Smoloff and find happiness.

Although a happy ending is implied, Cottin sheds doubt on the outcome in the final sentence of the book: "Arrêtons-nous ici, reposons-nous sur ces douces pensées. Ce que j'ai connu de la vie, de ses inconstances, de ses espérances trompées, de ses fugitives et chimériques félicités, me ferait craindre, si j'ajoutais une seule page à cette histoire, d'être obligée d'y placer un malheur" (Let's stop here, let's rest on these sweet thoughts. What I have known of life, its fickleness, its unfulfilled hopes, and its fleeting and chimeric felicity, makes me fear that if I added one more page to this story, it would certainly include a calamity).

In Cottin's fiction, love and marriage usually appear to be mutually exclusive. Claire's husband, although well intentioned, purposely engages in treachery and deceit, ultimately causing his wife's death. Lady Sheridan, Malvina's best friend, finds marriage unfulfilling: her husband is a womanizer. Shortly after Amélie's first marriage to Monsieur Mansfield, he loses interest in his wife and son and looks for pleasure with other women. Madame Simmeren, her older and more experienced friend, shares sobering thoughts with her: "Je vous dirai en grand secret (parce que c'est une vérité qu'il n'est pas bon de répandre) que l'amour ne vit qu'autant qu'il est libre; et qu'il n'est point qui puisse résister au mariage et que, si je devenais jeune, l'homme dont je voudrais le plus être aimée est celui que j'épouserai le moins" (I will tell you in private [because these thoughts cannot be stated openly] that love can only grow in freedom; it cannot flourish in marriage. If I were young again, the man that I would want most to love me would be the one I would want least to marry).

The unprecedented popularity and success of *Elisabeth* exceeded all expectations. Not only did the moral tale result in the printing of dozens of editions and immediate translations, it also brought compliments from Cottin's fiercest critic, de Genlis. Cottin did not live long beyond the publication of this novel. During the last year of her life, she accompanied a sick relative, Mélanie Lemarcis, to Italy. Upon returning from the long journey that took them through Switzerland and several Italian cities, Cottin began to feel the symptoms of the illness that ended her life. Nevertheless, she continued to write and started two new projects, but completed neither. Faith, which had provided solace and strength throughout her life, eased her pain during the final agony. Surrounded by loving relatives and friends, she died on 15 August 1807, most probably of breast cancer. She was only thirty-seven.

Cottin possessed unquestionable skill as a romantic writer; her remarkable descriptions of nature and human emotions were widely recognized and admired by such literary figures as Chateaubriand, Alphonse de Lamartine, Hugo, and Stendhal. Furthermore, in the first four novels, she succeeded in presenting complex moral issues from a controversial and original perspective. Important social and philosophical questions are raised concerning the concepts of love, marriage, and social conventions. According to Joan Hinde Stewart, the conclusions implied suggest an audacious new morality. *Claire d'Albe* in particular "is rich in symbolic detail, dramatizing the tensions and the revolt that characterize a tradition of novels by women and proposing a nuanced vision of female sexuality as integral to personality."

While Cottin's novels captivated and enthralled masses of readers throughout the Continent and beyond–including Napoleon, who read *Claire d'Albe* in exile–and inspired many writers of romance, literary critics of her own and following generations were less enthusiastic. Patronizing and scornful of women writers, nineteenth-century critic Charles-Augustin Sainte-Beuve granted that Cottin's works had met with unprecedented success but concluded that they were outdated and unreadable. Because of his enormous influence, he set the tone for generations of scholars, few of whom focused attention on Cottin's works; those who mentioned them did so only tangentially, as they discussed women authors in general. In 1972 Pierre Fauchery concurred with his nineteenth-century predecessor, noting that he saw no masterpieces among novels by women. He went on to conclude that women novelists were collectively inferior to the "incontestable masters"–Samuel Richardson, Henry Fielding, Laurence Sterne, Rousseau, and Johann Wolfgang von Goethe–who inspired them.

Contemporary scholars have expressed more interest in Cottin's writings, though her novels are not easily available, since the last edition of her complete works dates back to the mid nineteenth century. *Claire d'Albe* is the only novel available today to a broad United States readership, following the 2002 publication of two versions of that work, one in the original French and another in English translation. The 1976 edition published in France has long been out of print, and access to the other four novels remains limited.

Letters:

Henri de Latouche, "Deux lettres inédites de Mme Cottin," *La Revue de Paris,* 18 (1830): 144–149;

F. Soubies, "Deux lettres de Mme Cottin," *Petite Gazette de Bagnères-de-Bigorre,* 30 March 1865;

P. T. de Larroque, "Deux lettres inédites de Mme Cottin," *Revue d'Aquitaine,* 13 (1869): 463–468;

Leslie C. Sykes, "Choix de lettres de Madame Cottin et de ses correspondants" and "Les inédits de Madame Cottin," in *Madame Cottin* (Oxford: Blackwell, 1949), pp. 267–411.

References:

Arnelle, *Une Oubliée: Madame Cottin d'après sa correspondance* (Paris: Plon-Nourrit, 1914);

Michael J. Call, *Infertility and the Novels of Sophie Cottin* (Newark, Del.: University of Delaware Press, 2002);

G. Castel-Carriga, "Le roman de Mme Cottin," *La Revue des deux mondes* (May–June 1960): 120–137;

Colette Cazenobe, "Une préromantique méconnue, Madame Cottin," in *Travaux de littérature* (1988), I: 175–202;

David J. Denby, "Le thème des croisades et l'héritage des Lumières au début du 19e siècle," *Dix-Huitième Siècle,* 19 (1987): 411–421;

Pierre Fauchery, *La Destinée féminine dans le roman européen du dix-huitième siècle* (Paris: Armand Colin, 1972);

Jean Gaulmier, "Roman et connotations sociales: *Mathilde* de Mme Cottin," in *Roman et société,* edited by Michel Raimond (Paris: Colin, 1973), pp. 7–17;

Gaulmier, "Sophie et ses malheurs ou le romantisme du pathétique," *Romantisme,* 3 (1972): 3–16;

Caroline Stéphanie du Crest de Genlis, "Madame Cotin [sic]," in *De l'Influence des femmes sur la littérature française* (Paris: Maradan, 1811);

Pierre de Gorse, "Sophie, romancière oubliée," *Historia,* 353 (April 1976): 107–113;

André Le Breton, *Le Roman français du dix-neuvième siècle,* part 1, avant Balzac (Paris: Société française d'imprimerie et de librairie, 1901; reprinted, Geneva: Slatkine Reprints, 1982);

Alfred Marquiset, "Madame Cottin," in *Les Bas-Bleus du Premier Empire* (Paris: Champion, 1914), pp. 15–61;

T. M. Pratt, "The Widow and the Crown. Mme Cottin and the Limits of Neoclassical Epic," *British Journal for Eighteenth-Century Studies,* 9 (1986): 197–203;

Janine Rossard, "Passion et tensions pudiques dans *Claire d'Albe,*" in *Pudeur et romantisme* (Paris: Nizet, 1982), pp. 15–23;

Samia I. Spencer, "The French Revolution and the Early Nineteenth-Century Romantic Novel: The Case of Sophie Cottin," *Proceedings of the Western Society for French History,* 18 (1990): 498–504;

Spencer, "Reading in Pairs: *La Nouvelle Héloïse* and *Claire d'Albe,*" *Romance Languages Annual,* 7 (1996): 166–172;

Spencer, "Sophie Cottin," in *French Women Writers. A Bio-Bibliographical Source Book,* edited by Eva Martin Sartori and Dorothy Winne Zimmerman (Westport, Conn.: Greenwood Press, 1991), pp. 90–98;

Joan Hinde Stewart, *Gynographs. French Novels by Women of the Late Eighteenth Century* (Lincoln: University of Nebraska Press, 1993);

Leslie C. Sykes, *Madame Cottin* (Oxford: Blackwell, 1949);

Ruth P. Thomas, "The Death of an Ideal," in *French Women and the Age of Enlightenment,* edited by Spencer (Bloomington: Indiana University Press, 1984), pp. 321–331.

Papers:

Correspondence of Sophie Cottin is held by the Bibliothèque Nationale, Department of Manuscripts (western section).

Claude-Prosper Jolyot de Crébillon *fils*
(14 February 1707 – 12 April 1777)

Lisa Beckstrand
Montclair State University

BOOKS: *Le Sylphe, ou Songe de Madame de R*** écrit par elle-même à Madame de S**** (Paris: Delatour, 1730);

Lettres de la Marquise de M*** au Comte de R*** (N.p., 1732);

L'Ecumoire, histoire japonaise, 2 volumes (A Pékin [Paris]: Lou-Chou-Chu-La, le seul imprimeur de Sa Majesté chinoise pour les langues étrangères, 1733);

Les Egarements du coeur et de l'esprit, part one (Paris: Prault, 1736); parts two and three (The Hague: Gosse & Néaulme, 1738); translated by Barbara Bray as *The Wayward Head and Heart* (London: Oxford University Press, 1963);

Le Sopha, conte moral, 2 volumes (Paris: Prault, 1742); translated as *The Sofa: A Moral Tale* (London: Printed for T. Cooper, 1742);

Atalzaide (Paris, 1745);

Les Amours de Zéokinisul, roi des Kofirans (Amsterdam: Michel, 1747 [i.e., 1746]);

Les Heureux Orphelins, histoire imitée de l'anglais (Brussels: les Frères Vasse, 1754);

Ah, quel conte! conte politique et astronomique (Brussels: les Frères Vasse, 1754);

La Nuit et le moment, ou les matinées de Cythère (London [i.e., Paris]: B. Laville, 1755);

Le Hazard du coin du feu, dialogue moral (The Hague, 1763); translated by Wilfrid Jackson as "Fortunes in the Fire," in *Three Stories* (London: Routledge, 1927);

Lettres de la Duchesse de *** au Duc de *** (Paris: Merlin, 1769 [i.e., 1768]); translated as *A Lady of Quality: Dialogues Translated from the French of Crébillon Le Fils* (New York: Sheridan, 1928);

Lettres athéniennes, extraites du portefeuille d'Alcibiade, 4 volumes (London & Paris: Delalain, 1771).

Editions and Collections: *Collection complète des oeuvres de M. de Crébillon le fils* (London, 1772);

Collection complète des oeuvres de M. de Crébillon le fils (London, 1777);

Oeuvre complètes de monsieur de Crébillon, fils (Maastricht: J. E. Dufour & P. Roux, 1779);

(Engraving by Adolphe Lalauze; from Claude-Prosper Jolyot de Crébillon fils, Contes dialogués de Crébillon-fils, *1879; Thomas Cooper Library, University of South Carolina)*

Le Hazard du coin du feu (The Hague, 1880);

Oeuvres de Crébillon fils, edited, with a preface, by Pierre Lièvre (Paris: Le Divan, 1929–1930);

Crébillon fils, chosen texts edited, with a preface, by René Etiemble (Paris: Mercure de France, 1964);

Les Egarements du coeur et de l'esprit, edited, with a preface, by Etiemble (Paris: Gallimard, 1977);

Le Sopha, edited, with a preface, by Jean Sgard (Paris: Desjonquères, 1984);

Oeuvres, edited, with an introduction, by Ernest Sturm (Paris: François Bourin, 1992);

Oeuvres complètes. Claude Crébillon, edited, with a preface, by Sgard (Paris: Garnier, 1999).

While little is known about the personal life of Claude-Prosper Jolyot de Crébillon *fils,* the reception of his work until recent decades has been marked by controversy. Throughout the eighteenth and nineteenth centuries, his stories were repeatedly characterized as lascivious, and, as a result, his books were often poorly understood and banned from libraries. Not until the 1950s did René Etiemble introduce a new critical edition of one of Crébillon's novels, *Les Egarements du coeur et de l'espirit* (1736, 1738; translated as *The Wayward Head and Heart,* 1963), emphasizing the beauty of language and comparing the author to other great writers. Etiemble addressed the reader in the following way: "Aimez-vous les sentiments vifs, le beau langage, Stendhal, Courier, Paul Léautaud? Sinon inutile de vous égarer vers ces exquis égarements" (Do you like lively sentiments, beautiful language, Stendhal, Courier, Paul Léautaud? If not, it is useless to entertain yourself with these exquisite distractions). In 1992 Ernest Sturm introduced and edited a modern critical edition of the complete works of Crébillon *fils* that attributed pre-Freudian psychoanalytic elements to the author. These pioneering studies and editions underscoring Crébillon's linguistic ingenuity, his astute psychological portrayal of amorous relationships, and his representation of high-society gallantry have all contributed to a renewed interest in his work. More importantly, his work is valued for its role and function within libertine fiction of the eighteenth century. Such critics as Colette Cazenobe have pondered over why Crébillon's politico-erotic views did not retain the attention of his contemporaries, with the exception of Voltaire, who deemed Crébillon's work "wildly amusing." A closer look at Crébillon's life and work may illuminate these answers and give the reader a glimpse of an author who was raised in the shadow of his father–poorly understood by his contemporaries and ignored by generations to follow.

Crébillon *fils* was born in Paris on 14 February 1707 to the highly reputed author of classical tragedy and academician Claude-Prosper Jolyot de Crébillon *père.* His mother, Marie-Charlotte Péaget, died only four years after he was born, leaving him in the care of an eccentric, reclusive, and somewhat neglectful father. Crébillon *père* was known for his grandiose Racinian plays that evoked pity and used terror as a means to arrive at the sublime. Considered bourgeois by birth, his father added the ennobling element "de" to his name, giving him entry into aristocratic circles. A defender of monarchy and a rising playwright rivaling Voltaire, Crébillon *père* was a protégé of the king's court. In the salons of the upper classes, the son, even as a boy, became an observer of behavior in high society. However, unlike his father, Crébillon *fils* eschewed the idea of being or becoming "aristocratic" and mocked his father's insistence on it. In *Crébillon fils, ou la science du désir* (1995, Crébillon fils, or The Science of Desire), Sturm quotes a letter by Crébillon *fils* dated September 1750: "Ma famille est, dit-on fort ancienne, mais cela peut être, sans qu'elle en soit plus noble. Mon père se berce et compte me bercer aussi de je ne sais combien de grandes idées, que je crois plus poétique que vraies" (My family may be old and titled, but that does not mean that they are noble. My father deludes himself and tries to delude me with I don't know how many grandiose ideas that I believe are more poetic than true). As Sturm notes, this attitude is indicative of some of the essential differences between Crébillon *fils* and his father. While the father was an introverted misanthrope who reveled in the "tragic," the son was sociable, witty, and endowed with the ability to render "the serious" amusing. He found the genre of tragedy the greatest farce ever invented by man and claimed that one day he would read his father's tragedies for this reason.

After completing his studies at the Jesuit school, Louis-le-Grand, Crébillon *fils* was invited to enter the order as a monk but declined the offer, preferring instead to frequent the salons and to test his skills as a writer and observer of high-society Parisian life. At age twenty-three he published his first short story, *Le Sylphe* (1730, The Sylph), in which he showcased the themes and preoccupations that, as Sturm asserts, are prevalent throughout his work: sexuality, libertinage (profligacy), witty repartee between courtesans and lovers, and reflections about how to love in the Age of Reason. His predilection for psychological analysis becomes even more apparent in *Lettres de la Marquise de M*** au Comte de R**** (The Letters of the Marquise de M*** to the Count R***), an epistolary novel written in 1732, only two years after the publication of *Le Sylphe.* In this novel, Crébillon focuses on the reflections and inner thoughts of an intelligent, sensitive, and beautiful woman whose life is slowly destroyed by love. According to Cazenobe, the novel got a favorable review by critics, who compared the work to Gabriel-Joseph de Guilleragues's *Les Lettres portugaises* (1969, The Portuguese Letters) and to *Les Lettres* *d'Héloïse et Abélard* (collected in Latin in the 1130s; translated as *The Letters of Heloise and Abelard,* 1974). Sturm argues that this early work already exhibits a foreshadowing of realism, as it so precisely captures the psychological and erotic life of the imagination.

While little is known about Crébillon's love life, some critics think that he attempted a relationship with a certain actress, known as Mlle Gaussin, who accepted and then later rejected his marriage proposal. Not surprisingly, then, the female character satirized in *L'Ecumoire, histoire japonaise* (1734, The Skimmer, A Japanese Tale) is portrayed as a fickle, inconstant, and ignorant actress. While this work received praise from such critics as Voltaire, it also resulted in the author's imprisonment at Vincennes for political reasons. Set in the Orient, the story depicts the psychology of conjugal infidelity while satirizing a subject that was religiously and politically taboo: the papal edict known as the "Bulle Unigenitus." The Jansenists had been increasingly under attack for their resistance to this unpopular edict of the Pope, and the satire of it by Crébillon did not put him in good standing with the local authorities. One of the characters of the novel, Saugrénuto, urges the clergy to stand up to the Pope's abuses of power and states that wars have been inflicted by patriarchs of the past. Not only was this text insulting to political (the king) and religious (the Pope) authorities, but the nobles also were not depicted admirably either. Crébillon was officially arrested for his "licentious" portrayal of a prince in search of his lost virility; moreover, his mockery of the papal bull aroused suspicion and incited the anger of the French government against him. One of his admirers, the princesse de Conti, intervened on his behalf to get him released after only five days in prison. As Sturm notes, Voltaire praised *L'Ecumoire* and defended its author, writing, "L'histoire japonaise m'a fort réjoui dans ma solitude; je ne sais rien de si fou que ce livre, et rien de si sot que d'avoir mis l'auteur à la Bastille. Dans quel siècle vivons-nous donc? On brûlerait apparemment La Fontaine aujourd'hui?" (The Japanese story delighted me in my solitude; I don't know anything as crazy as this book and as stupid as having imprisoned its author at the Bastille. In what century are we living? Would we burn La Fontaine at the stake today?).

Though Crébillon dared to be critical of the abuses of the ancien régime in *L'Ecumoire,* his next novel was far removed from the politico-religious realm. *Les Egarements de l'esprit et du coeur* was set in the salons of the upper crust of Paris. The story, written in the form of a pseudomemoir, featured the thoughts of a mature man reflecting over his past life and adventures as a young adult in Paris. The reader becomes acquainted with the art of romance through the eyes of a naive seventeen-year-old protagonist who learns that achieving success with women in aristocratic circles will require dissimulation, pretense, and invulnerability. Sturm views this novel as a "masterpiece of elegance and discretion," an acerbic study of a young man's initiation into the corrupt world of adulthood. Anne Vila points out the importance of this novel with regard to sensibility and its communicative function in eighteenth-century high society. She argues that the protagonist's attempts at love require that he not only understand the differences between playfulness, seduction, and genuine feelings in the female characters, but that he also be able to communicate within that context. The protagonist and readers discover that acquiring these skills is critical to preserving one's place in the social hierarchy. The efforts of the author at writing a novel that would quiet suspicions and soothe angry public officials succeeded. Parisian audiences enjoyed the work and praised the author for his discretion, but his success was short-lived. He soon wrote another novel considered inflammatory and scandalous, *Le Sopha, conte moral* (1742; translated as *The Sofa: A Moral Tale,* 1742).

In this oriental tale, the protagonist, Almanzéi, is asked to entertain the sultan. He explains that he was condemned to remember earlier phases of his life through metempsychosis, and that in one of these, he was a sofa. Forced to remain in the state of a sofa until a man and woman lost their virginity together upon it, he underwent many adventures before finally returning to his human form. A series of questions by the sultan is followed by the narration of six titillating episodes of Almanzéi's experiences as a sofa. The sultan begins asking what it felt like to be a woman. Almanzéi remarks that as a woman he was often analyzed but never understood. Critics such as Clifton Cherpack have remarked that the inability of people to understand the real nature of others, even in the most intimate of situations, is the underlying theme running through the six episodes. Sturm argues that this setting allows for a detailed psychological analysis of the behavior of characters; they are examined by each other as well as by the voyeuristic third party, the sofa. While the frame of the novel was based on *Le Canapé couleur de feu* (The Fire-Colored Sofa), published anonymously in 1714, *Le Sopha* gives a greater psychological portrait of characters that was left out of earlier texts. Once again, Crébillon came under attack by authorities for having published a novel "contrary to good morals" without the king's permission. The cardinal de Fleury, who wished to use the case as an example to other authors, ordered Crébillon to be exiled from Paris. Crébillon fought the sentence for two months, arguing that *Le Sopha* had been published without his knowledge. With the help of a friend, the order was reversed, and the author reestablished residence in Paris.

At this time Crébillon met the woman who became his wife, Henriette-Marie Stafford. Though she was reputed to be extremely unattractive, dubious, poor, and without a connection to the world of arts and letters, some believe that she abandoned her native England to seek out an amorous relationship with this "licentious" author. In other accounts, as noted by Sturm, who cites Friedrich Melchior Grimm, she supposedly spent her youth in Saint-Germain-en-Laye, where she met her future husband. The pair courted for four years, during which time they had a son in 1746 and eventually signed a marriage contract in 1748. Unfortunately, their family life was short-lived, as their only son died at an early age, and Henriette-Marie died eight years after they were married.

During his liaison with Stafford, Crébillon wrote four works, the last of which was influenced and possibly even edited by her. *Atalzaide* was an oriental tale resembling *L'Ecumoire* and published in 1745. It had little success and was not included in further publications of his complete works. *Les Amours de Zéokinisul, roi des Kofirans* (1746, The Love Life of Zeokinisul, King of the Kofirans) was a satire of the private life of Louis XV. Like *Atalzaide,* it had a small circulation and was not included in later publications of the author's works. *Ah, quel conte! conte politique et astronomique* (Oh, What a Tale! An Astronomical and Political Tale), published in sequels from 1751 to 1754 and as a whole in 1754, was yet another satire of courtly life; in it the author transforms Louis XV, Queen Marie Leszczynska, Denis Diderot, and Diderot's mistress, Madeleine de Puisieux, into birds. These lively burlesque caricatures enabled the author to poke fun at his favorite political and literary targets. Finally, *Les Heureux Orphelins, histoire imitée de l'anglais* (The Happy Foundlings, A Story Adapted from the English) was published in 1754; it was considered mediocre at best. According to Cazenobe, abbé Guillaume-Thomas Raynal and Grimm insinuated that Henriette-Marie Crébillon must have had a hand in the publication of this little English story based on *The Fortunate Foundlings* (1744) by Eliza Haywood. The *Correspondance littéraire* (Literary Correspondence) gave it poor reviews, citing its "common characters" and "romanesque sentiments." Sturm finds some redeeming value in the last part of the story, which, after an exhausting accumulation of conventional sentimentality, finally introduces the libertine character, Chester, who became the prototype of the infamous Valmont in Pierre-Ambroise-François Choderlos de Laclos's *Les Liaisons Dangereuses* (1782, Dangerous Liaisons).

La Nuit et le moment, ou les matinées de Cythère (The Night and the Moment, or Cythera's Mornings), a small work that Crébillon began writing around 1737, was finally published in 1755, just one year before the death of his wife. It is a dialogue between two characters, Clitandre and Cidalise, who discuss their concepts of love and how they have behaved in their amorous liaisons. Clitandre's stories show that he is cruel, vicious, and contemptuous in his affairs with women. He pledges his love to each of them and shows his contempt by rejecting them and using them to get other favors. In spite of his behavior, he succeeds in seducing Cidalise, who, in the end, becomes aware of Clitandre's utter moral depravity and of her own defenselessness and weakness against his advances. Cherpack argues that Crébillon, rather than employing didactic moralizing, puts forth the idea that the two characters are simply the inevitable products of their society, "so that their conduct, given the age, the night, and the moment, is neither good, nor bad, nor pleasurable, nor distasteful. It is simply inevitable." After being treated so horrendously, the only conclusion Cidalise can come to is that she did what she felt compelled to do: "La seule chose que je puisse actuellement avoir quelque plaisir à croire, c'est que je ne pouvais faire que ce que j'ai fait" (The only thing that I can actually take pleasure in believing is that I could only do what I did).

In the years following his wife's death, Crébillon did not continue publishing new material; instead, he spent his time as the newly appointed royal censor—a position he had coveted and accepted in 1759. In spite of the controversy resulting from his earlier works (*Le Sopha* and *L'Ecumoire*), he was appointed to that office thanks to the assistance of Madame de Pompadour. The position, which had been held by his father for years, meant that he had to oversee and insure good morality in the publishable literary works of his contemporaries. However incongruous the position may seem in light of the nature and reception of his own work, Crébillon remained in office until his death in 1777.

During his tenure, he published three more works. *Le Hazard du coin du feu, dialogue moral* (1763; translated as "Fortunes in the Fire," in *Three Stories,* 1927) was written in the same vein as *La Nuit et le moment* and featured conversations between men and women about love and appropriate behavior and feelings for both sexes in amorous situations. *Lettres de la Duchesse de *** au Duc de **** (The Letters of the Duchess of *** to the Duke of ***) appeared in 1768 and seemed to show a departure from the author's typical themes. The central character and subject of the epistolary novel is a woman who, unlike other Crébillon characters, does not indulge her sexual desires. Cherpack has referred to this novel as a "purified" version of the author's early novel *Lettres de la Marquise de M*** au Comte de R****. In both stories, the heroine—who is pursued by a sophisticated, worldly man—becomes painfully aware of the pitfalls of love. In the latter story, she refuses to yield to her passion, finding satisfaction in her virtuous reputation. She thus keeps her suitor at a distance, making letters necessary and a physical relationship impossible.

As the century progressed, notions of sensibility, virtue, and morality defined and propagated by such popular authors as Jean-Jacques Rousseau and Samuel Richardson became increasingly important and ubiquitous. This development, coupled with his position as public censor, may have provided the impetus for Crébillon to depart from his rather licentious characters and to entertain ethical considerations. He even took care to mention Richardson in his preface, stating that admirers of Richardson's novels might be disappointed by his own rather thin plot with little drama, no adventures, and no tragic or exciting ending. Grimm's stinging critique of Crébillon six years earlier also may have contributed to the author's shift in his writing. Cazenobe cites Grimm, who wrote, "On ne peut s'empêcher de mépriser un homme qui a passé sa vie à écrire des ouvrages licencieux, à outrager les moeurs, et à fournir de l'aliment à la dépravation et à la corruption de la jeunesse" (One cannot help but to despise a man who spent his life writing licentious works, insulting morals, and furnishing food for the depravation and the corruption of youth).

Crébillon wrote his last novel in 1771 at age sixty-four. In contrast to his other works, *Lettres athéniennes* (Athenian Letters) is a lengthy epistolary novel set in ancient Greece and featuring twenty-three historical characters, including Alcibiades, Socrates, Plato, Aspasia, and Pericles. Although some of the action in the novel can be traced to real historic events, the life, lovers, and seductive games of the protagonist, Alcibiades, form the central subject of the story. His preoccupations resemble those of *petits maîtres* (flirtatious young men) and courtesans of Parisian society under the ancien régime. The return to libertine morals, the complex narrative, the theme, action, and multiple voicing of the novel may have served as a model for *Les Liaisons dangereuses*. However, the public's lessening interest in libertine fiction and growing desire for moral sentimentality resulted in a less than favorable appreciation of the novel. Sturm characterizes this polyphonic narrative and piecemeal plot as being

Title page for a work (translated as "Fortunes in the Fire") consisting of Crébillon fils's conversations between men and women about love (from the 1880 edition of Le Hazard du coin du feu; *Jean & Alexander Heard Library, Vanderbilt University)*

symptomatic of the lost stability and increased obsolescence of aristocratic society.

During the last six years of his life, Crébillon's responsibilities as public censor, coupled with the increasingly restrictive moral code, prevented him from writing any more licentious stories of libertines and lovers. He died in poverty at age seventy and was buried without a ceremony at the cemetery of Saint-Germain l'Auxerrois. Claude-Prosper Jolyot de Crébillon *fils* will be remembered for his contributions to the development of the novel. His astute understanding of the internal machinations of his characters, his psychological analysis of human behavior in amorous situations, and the exquisite beauty of his linguistic expression all give him an honored position among libertine novelists of the eighteenth century.

References:

Antoine-Alexandre Barbier, *Ouvrages anonymes* (Paris: P. Daffis, 1872–1879);

Colette Cazenobe, *Crébillon fils ou la politique dans le boudoir* (Paris: Honoré Champion, 1997);

Clifton Cherpack, *An Essay on Crébillon fils* (Durham, N.C.: Duke University Press, 1962);

Henri Coulet, *Le Roman jusqu'à la Révolution* (Paris: A. Colin, 1967), pp. 365–373;

Bernadette Fort, *Le Langage de l'ambiguité dans l'oeuvre de Crébillon fils* (Paris: Klincksieck, 1978);

Thomas Kavanagh, "The Libertine's Bluff: Cards and Culture in Eighteenth-Century France," *Eighteenth-Century Studies,* 33 (2000): 505–521;

Georges May, *Le Dilemme du roman au dix-huitième siècle: étude sur les rapports du roman et de la critique, 1715–1761* (New Haven: Yale University Press, 1963);

Stéphane Pujol, "Un meuble bavard," in *Oeuvres,* edited by Ernest Sturm (Paris: François Bourin, 1992), pp. 541–549;

Elena Russo, "La science du monde: The Double Tradition of *Honnêteté* in Marivaux and Crébillon," *Studies on Voltaire and the Eighteenth Century,* 319 (1994): 129–150;

Ernest Sturm, *Crébillon fils, ou la science du désir* (Paris: Nizet, 1995);

Sturm, "L'école du libertin," in *Oeuvres,* edited by Sturm (Paris: Francois Bourin, 1992), pp. 369–381;

Anne Vila, *Enlightenment and Pathology: Sensibility in the Literature and Medicine of Eighteenth-Century France* (Baltimore: Johns Hopkins University Press, 1998), pp. 113–119;

Voltaire, *Correspondance,* edited by Theodore Besterman (Geneva: Les Délices, 1954), p. 334.

Claude-Prosper Jolyot de Crébillon *père*
(13 January 1674 – 17 June 1762)

Servanne Woodward
University of Western Ontario

BOOKS: *Idoménée* (Paris: François le Breton, 1706);

Atrée et Thyeste (Paris: P. Ribou, 1709); translated and adapted by Edward W. Percy Sinnett as *Atreus and Thyestes* (London: C. & H. Baldwyn, 1822);

Electre (Paris: P. Ribou, 1709);

Rhadamiste et Zénobie (Paris: P. Ribou, 1711); translated and adapted by Arthur Murphy as *Zenobia* (London: Printed for W. Griffin, 1768)–includes an epilogue by David Garrick;

Sémiramis (Paris: P. Ribou, 1717);

Pyrrhus (Paris: Imprimerie de la veuve d'Antoine Urbain Coustelier, 1726);

Catilina (Paris: Prault fils, 1749);

Xerxès (The Hague & Paris: Prault fils, 1749);

Le Triumvirat, ou la mort de Cicéron (Paris: Charles Hochereau, 1755);

Cromwell, ou la mort de Charles Ier (Paris: Au Cabinet Bibliographique, 1790)–includes only Act 1.

Editions and Collections: *Les Oeuvres de M. de Crébillon. Quatre tragédies* (The Hague: T. Johnson, 1712);

Les Oeuvres de Monsieur de Crébillon (Paris: P. Ribou, 1716); enlarged and corrected as *Oeuvres,* 2 volumes (The Hague: Jean Van Duren, 1729);

Les Oeuvres de M. de Crébillon (2 volumes, Paris: P. Gandouin, 1737; augmented to 3 volumes, 1749);

Les Oeuvres de M. de Crébillon, revised and augmented, 3 volumes (Paris: Compagnie des Libraries, 1749);

Les Oeuvres de M. de Crébillon, revised, 3 volumes, 1749);

Les Oeuvres de Monsieur de Crébillon, 2 volumes (Paris: Imprimerie Royale, 1750); some volumes include the *Triumvirat* with different paper and characters, dated 1755;

Chef-d'oeuvre dramatiques de Crébillon, 2 volumes (Paris: Belin, 1791);

Théâtre français, répertoire complet Crébillon (Paris: Belin, 1821);

Chefs-d'oeuvre de Crébillon, avec les observations des anciens commentateurs et de nouvelles remarques, par Charles Nodier, P. Lepeintre, Lemazurier et autres gens de lettres, 2 volumes (Paris: Dabo-Butschert, 1825);

Claude-Prosper Jolyot de Crébillon père (*from* Oeuvres de Crébillon, *1828; Thomas Cooper Library, University of South Carolina*)

Oeuvres de Crébillon, avec les notes de tous les commentateurs, édition publiée par Pareille, 2 volumes (Paris: Lefèvre, Werdet, et Lequien fils, 1828);

Théâtre complet, nouvelle édition précédée d'une notice par M. Auguste Vitu (Paris: Garnier Frères, 1923);

Electre, édition critique par John Dunkley (Exeter: Exeter University Press, 1980).

PLAY PRODUCTIONS: *Idoménée,* Paris, Théâtre de la rue des Fossés, 29 December 1705;

Atrée et Thyeste, Versailles, Château de Versailles, 14 March 1707;

Electre, Paris, Théâtre de la rue des Fossés, 14 December 1708;

Rhadamiste et Zénobie, Paris, Théâtre de la rue des Fossés, 23 January 1711;

Xerxès, Paris, Théâtre de la rue des Fossés, 7 February 1714;

Sémiramis, Paris, Théâtre de la rue des Fossés, 10 April 1717;

Pyrrhus, Paris, Théâtre de la rue des Fossés, 21 April 1726;

Catilina, Paris, Théâtre de la rue des Fossés, 20 December 1748;

Le Triumvirat, ou la mort de Cicéron, Paris, Théâtre de la rue des Fossés, 20 December 1754.

Contemporaries compared Crébillon *père* to the best playwrights of seventeenth-century tragedies and considered him the best French literary artist of his century—the first poet in the highest genre, classical tragedy. His first tragedies showed blood on the stage, a feature the French associated with William Shakespeare. The Dutch translated Crébillon's plays throughout the century. In England, his most popular tragedy, *Rhadamiste et Zénobie* (1711), was translated and adapted by Arthur Murphy as *Zenobia* (1768). In France, Crébillon received many honors, including election to the French Academy and the position of censeur officiel (official censor) for literary works. His theater was judged extreme in its use of terror and found no imitators. His stellar reputation as a poet and tragedian was inflated as a result of court politics aiming at humiliating Voltaire, who vied for the same status as a playwright. Jean François de La Harpe, Jean Baptiste Le Rond d'Alembert, and Frédéric Melchior Grimm contended that as early as 1726 Crébillon was used in political maneuvers against his rival because he was a genuinely respectful and enthusiastic backer of Louis XV, whereas Voltaire was judged antagonistic to the king's regime because of his philosophical ideas. Crébillon, on the other hand, wrote plays opposed to the Enlightenment as well as plays promoting it. Despite his limited production of nine plays, he remained the most reputed poet of his time and employed the most destructive effect of passions.

Prosper Jolyot de Crébillon (or Crais-Billon) *père* was born 13 January 1674 in Dijon, the third of the ten children of Melchior Jolyot (or Joylot or Jolliot), notary in Dijon, and his wife Henriette Gagnard. Maurice Dutrait concludes that despite rumors to the contrary, the genealogy of the family did not include nobility: Melchior did not sign "Crais-Billon," nor did he use the title of esquire, because the purchase of the land of Crais-Billon did not confer any aristocratic title. In fact, at the time of Melchior Jolyot's death, the estate of Crais-Billon was not entirely paid for.

Prosper was educated by Jesuits, probably in Dijon. Around 1693–1700, he went to Paris, became a lawyer, and was accepted as a clerk in the study of Louis Prieur, a procurer who liked theater. In 1703, Crébillon may have met Bernard Le Bovier de Fontenelle, who was a tragedian before he became the well-known philosopher of fashionable literary salons, at the café Laurent, located near the Comédie française. Encouraged by his employer, Crébillon read his first tragedy, "La Mort des enfants de Brutus" (The Death of the Children of Brutus), before the actors of the Comédie française, who rejected it. The manuscript has either been lost or destroyed. Crébillon was not discouraged and went on to write the successful *Idoménée* (first performed, 1705; first published, 1706), performed thirteen times. The action takes place in Crete, where King Idoménée has killed a rebellious prince whose daughter, Erixène, he intends to wed. Prince Idamante, Idoménée's son, also falls in love with her. Erixène encourages the people to rebel and reveals an oracle that orders Idamante's death. As the unfortunate prince is about to be sacrificed, Erixène reveals her love for him, yet reiterates the impossibility of marrying into the family that killed her father. Idamante then commits suicide before his father's eyes.

Critics of the preview objected to the verses in the fifth and final act. Crébillon rewrote it, and the actors learned it in five days. *Idoménée* was successful as a novelty from a beginning playwright but was not shown again, although it attracted a fairly large audience during its thirteen performances. Following this play, Crébillon acquired a reputation as an author who relished horror, and Nicolas Boileau-Despréaux called him a "drunken Racine."

On 31 January 1707, against his father's will, Crébillon married Marie-Charlotte Péaget, who was already pregnant with his child. The same year, his tragedy *Atrée et Thyeste* (first performed, 1707; first published, 1709; translated as *Atreus and Thyestes,* 1822), inspired by Seneca's work, met with considerable success. Nonetheless, Crébillon decided to withdraw it after only ten performances so that the audience would not thin out, although no signs indicated that it would. The hero, Atrée, killed his wife, who had committed adultery with his brother Thyeste. Atrée raises Plisthène, son of his wife and brother, as his own for the sole purpose of making him a parricide. Plisthène falls in love with his cousin (really his sister) and is about to commit incest when Atrée reveals to him his true paternity. Peace between the two brothers appears to be sealed when Atrée and Thyeste drink from a sacred cup, although Atrée has not renounced his plans for revenge. Plisthène refuses to kill his father and is then executed under Atrée's order. Plisthène's blood is served as a drink to Thyeste, who, realizing his son's fate, commits suicide. The cup of blood that appeared in the closing act stunned the audience of the first performance. Clarence D. Brenner and Nolan A. Goodyear believe that with this play, Crébillon introduced "seeds of realism" to the classical French tragedy; thus, he can be considered a precursor to drama as theorized by Denis Diderot, melodrama, and Romantic drama.

Despite the notoriety and royalties he gained, Crébillon continued to experience financial difficulties throughout 1707. His father died later that year, leaving an inheritance that included debts. Crébillon and his two remaining brothers tried to salvage at least the money left by their mother and engaged in prolonged and costly legal appeals that took years to resolve and resulted in more expenses than benefits.

Inspired by the works of Sophocles, *Electre* was performed for the first time 14 December 1708 and published in 1709; it was acted fourteen times in Paris and once in Versailles. Elie Catherine Fréron and d'Alembert admired the roles of Electre and Palamède and agreed with the unanimous praises by censors, comedians, and spectators. Voltaire faulted the opening scene, although his criticism dignified rather than degraded it: he found it worthy of an opera, a genre that was growing in prestige. La Harpe objected to the lengthy descriptions interrupting the dialogues–a feature that John Dunkley believes is essential to the dramatic interest of the play.

Because of Crébillon's increased notoriety, some booksellers published unauthorized versions of his plays. When such a version, *Atrée,* appeared in Holland, the author decided to publish it himself in 1707 and again in 1709, along with *Electre,* to avoid further financial losses. Other problems also arose with the printing of these works. Despite Crébillon's protestation, readers believed that an author who invented such atrocities as depicted in these plays must share the evil character of the villains he created. He was then reviled by the public. No reprieve came to Crébillon's difficulties by the end of 1707: his second son, born extremely weak, was not expected to live.

According to d'Alembert, *Rhadamiste et Zénobie,* which was performed thirty times between 23 January 1711 and 19 March 1711, was Crébillon's masterpiece, an opinion that Voltaire shared, according to the eulogy he wrote for Crébillon. The play depicts Pharasmane, a king who sends his son Rhadamiste to kill the king of Armenia and marry his daughter, Zénobie. Believing that she had a role in her father's death, the Armenians chase the newlyweds to the edge of the city, where Rhadamiste attacks Zénobie and leaves her for

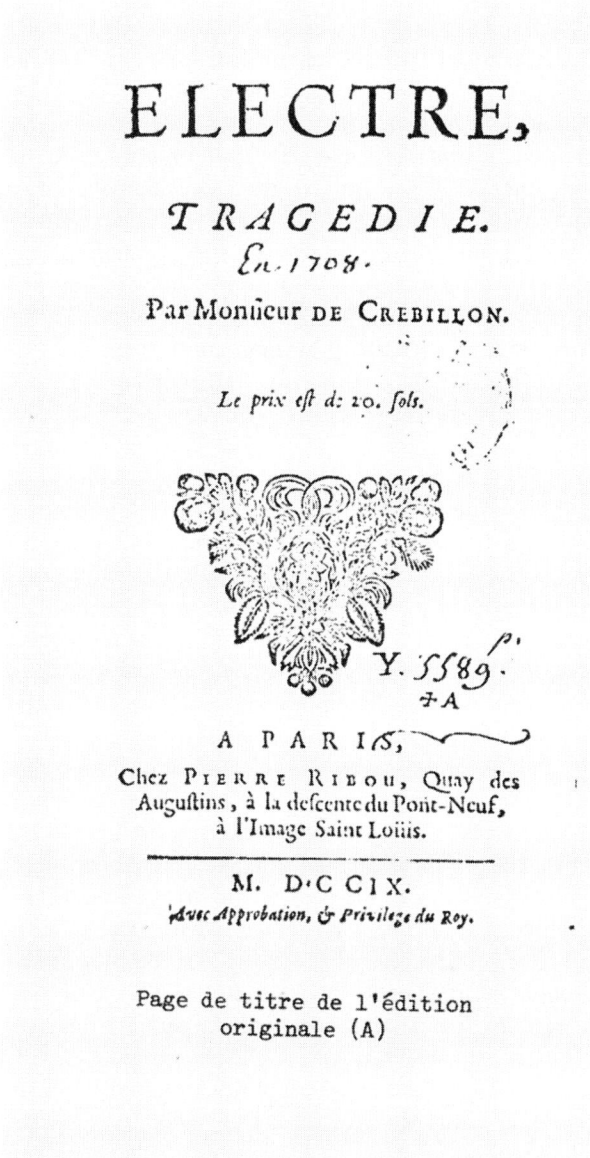

Title page for the first edition of Crébillon's play inspired by the works of Sophocles (from the 1980 edition of Electre; *Jean and Alexander Heard Library, Vanderbilt University)*

dead. However, she does not die, survives for ten years as a slave, until her home is destroyed by the conquering troops of King Pharasmane. Among King Pharasmane's spoils of war is Zénobie. Both the king and his younger son fall in love with her and neither knows her true identity. King Pharasmane is about to marry Zénobie despite her opposition to the wedding when Rhadamiste returns in disguise to his father's castle where, to his surprise, he finds his wife willing to elope and be reunited with him. The play was applauded in both Paris and Versailles, and its publication was a tremendous commercial success, with two editions selling out in eight days. Pierre Carlet de Chamblain de Marivaux declared that the character of Rhadamiste probed the depth of his soul in the realm of terrible passions. Crébillon's triumph and joy, however, were short-lived. His second son died at age four, and his wife died of consumption. Overcome by grief, Crébillon started to smoke compulsively.

Encouraged by his growing success, he hoped to be elected to the French Academy, but in vain. His failure to gain a seat in that body led him to write and circulate satiric verses caricaturing the academicians as animals. The mockery did not cause much backlash, though, except for the ire of Jean-Baptiste Rousseau. *Xerxès* (staged on 7 February 1714 but not published until 1749) met with so little enthusiasm that Crébillon withdrew the play after the first run, and it was never performed again. The author started to undertake works that he did not complete. His contemporaries refer to a new play on Oliver Cromwell that he read and recited around 1715. Although it was never staged, it may eventually have been completed as *Cromwell, ou la mort de Charles Ier* (Cromwell, or the Death of Charles the First), which was published under his name in 1790.

Unable to rely on the income from his floundering literary activities, Crébillon invested in the John Law scheme in 1715 and experienced a brief period of wealth. Law's investments benefited a few but ruined the vast majority of the people who invested with him. Crébillon found financial stability when he obtained a charge as tax collector through the Pâris de Marmontel brothers. Crébillon's play *Sémiramis* (1717) was performed only nine times, despite the support of such prestigious actors as Mademoiselle Desmares in the role of Sémiramis, Monsieur Beaubour as Agénor, Porteuil as Bélus, and Mademoiselle Dangeville as Ténésis. That Sémiramis appeared enamored with her own son was found by everyone to be in bad taste. The play was never performed again.

In a 1762 issue of the *Mercure de France*, abbé Joseph de La Porte and Charles Simon Favart speak of a two-hundred-line poem, *Maximes pour les rois* (Maxims for the Kings), that Crébillon presented to the regent as a piece of advice sometime in the 1720s. Favart doubts Crébillon's support for the monarchy; possibly, at this point in his career, Crébillon was tempted to emulate the philosophes, who sought to educate kings.

During that same period, the Pâris brothers paid the tuition in general education for Claude-Prosper Crébillon—who was then studying at the Collège Louis-le-Grand—because his father was penniless. In 1721, Crébillon's charge as tax collector was suppressed, and he was compensated with a check for 57,000 livres, which he did not cash immediately. Instead, he drew drafts against it and collected interest, eventually obtaining only 2,000 livres out of the original sum. After this period, Crébillon's biographers do not know his whereabouts until 21 April 1726, when he produced *Pyrrhus* (published, 1726), his best play, according to Dutrait, one in which virtue triumphs and no one dies. Five years in the making and dedicated to the elder of the Pâris brothers (who was facing disgrace and exile [1726–1729]), the tragedy played well to audiences in Paris and Versailles during its sixteen performances. Crébillon may have accompanied Pâris into exile, because the king's registers show no address for Crébillon until 1731, when he was elected to the French Academy. Then, for two years, he resided in the Palais du Luxembourg, home of his admirer Count Louis de Bourbon Condé, abbé de Clermont, who provided much-needed material comfort.

Crébillon disappointed the academicians with his reception piece and his eulogy for the marshal of Villars, Claude-Louis-Hector, but they admired the scenes he read from his new play, *Catilina* (first performed, 1748; first published, 1749). The author's new activities put an end to the novels he had reportedly been writing during his retirement from the stage. As a genre, the novel had influenced his plays, in which disguises, unlikely coincidences, and timely recognitions abound. Crébillon admired Gauthier de Costes de La Caleprenède's *Cléopâtre* (1647–1656), a novel that inspired *Rhadamiste et Zénobie;* and he also liked chivalric romances, as evident in the plot of *Electre*.

No novel was found among Crébillon's papers; his son Claude, however, who was pursuing a career as a novelist, ran into much trouble publishing novels. In 1734, for example, he was imprisoned for publishing a libertine novel, and in 1741 he was condemned to exile for the same reason. Not knowing that his son had fled to England, Crébillon worried for nearly two months until the authorities informed him of his son's whereabouts. Although Crébillon opposed his son's marriage to a British aristocrat in 1746, the wedding proceeded two years later.

Crébillon *père* devoted his time to his duties as academician and as censor—a position to which he was officially named in 1735, although some evidence shows that he was already fulfilling that function two years earlier. While providing him with steady income, the position brought unpopularity as well, particularly in 1743 when he refused to issue a privilege for Voltaire's *La Mort de César* (1735).

In 1748, Madame de Pompadour provided Crébillon with money and recalled him to the center of artistic life by promoting the completion of *Catilina*. Under her protection, the play premiered on 20 December 1748 and was performed twenty times to full houses. According to La Porte, Crébillon conceived *Catilina* while watching his own tragedy *Pyrrhus*.

Catilina became an affair of the State. It received the support of the king, who provided for the rich costumes. The actors competed so fiercely for the assignments of roles that Charles Collé (a dramatist and also reader and secretary to the duc d'Orléans) and Maurice de Saxe, marshal of France, marveled that the actors did not succeed in destroying the play. The role of Catilina was eventually played by Nicolas Racot de Grandval, although Crébillon preferred Quinault Dufresne; and Mademoiselle Gaussin managed to secure the role of Tullie for Mademoiselle Dumesnil (Marie-Françoise Marchand) instead of Claire de la Tude, known as La Clairon, who was assigned the lesser role of Fulvie hitherto filled by Gauthier. The substitutions occurred with Pompadour's diplomatic intercession. *Catilina* was greatly admired by many, especially by Charles-Louis de Secondat, baron de Montesquieu. When it was printed in 1749, it quickly sold five thousand copies in eight days.

This tremendous public success alerted debtors and claimants from his father's inheritance that Crébillon's plays were generating money. Their aggressive attempt to confiscate his earnings led the dramatist to plead with the state council for protection against financial disaster. In order to help him, the king passed a law prohibiting the seizure of "works of the mind" (21 March 1749); the playwright's revenues from his works were thus sheltered.

In 1750, Crébillon censored Voltaire's *Mahomet* (1742). Voltaire also feared that the manuscript of *Oreste* (1750) might be shredded to pieces by Crébillon's twenty-two dogs. According to Favart, by the 1750s, Crébillon collected stray animals. Toward the end of that decade, Louis Sébastien Mercier described the aging Crébillon as living among barren walls with a staircase littered with pet refuse. He described the playwright as a giant at six feet, sitting half naked among barking dogs, smoking a pipe, using a whip to free a chair, reciting "obscure verses" against gods and kings (perhaps from his new play "Cléomède"), and maintaining an intimate relationship with an old woman.

In 1750, Crébillon worked on *Le Triumvirat, ou la mort de Cicéron* (1755, The Triumvirate, or the Death of Cicero), staged for the first time on 20 December 1754 and continuing for ten performances. It was supposed to redeem the character of Cicero from the weak portrayal of him in *Catilina*. According to Voltaire, the first two acts of *Le Triumvirat* were recycled parts of *Cromwell*, a play Crébillon wrote in 1715. The author refuted that opinion.

In 1762, Crébillon was given the last rites because of the severity of his illness. During the past twenty

Crébillon as a young man (from Crébillon père, Théâtre complet, 1923; Thomas Cooper Library, University of South Carolina)

years, his legs had suffered from ulcers. His son came to tend to him, and they reconciled. Crébillon went into remission for a few months but eventually worsened; he died on 17 June 1762. He was buried at the Saint-Gervais church at a late hour, probably to prevent his actors from participating (who could not be buried in consecrated grounds or attend a solemn religious burial). The actors eventually resorted to the Order of Malta and settled for a ceremony at their church, Saint-Jean de Latran, during which eighty musicians played a "Mass for the Dead" (1700) by Jean Gilles (later sung also at Jean-Philippe Rameau's burial). The court planned to build a mausoleum in Crébillon's honor, designed by Jean-Baptiste Lemoyne. It was eventually carved in 1793; left unfinished, it has remained at the museum of Dijon.

Prosper Jolyot de Crébillon *père* was a lovable poet with a bohemian lifestyle in his youth and a careless, lazy, and rude man when he aged. He cultivated the image of a man gifted with a prodigious memory, who completed novels entirely in his head. Yet, he wrote only a few plays, and some people speculated that he could have given much more to the French stage. Because of his great reputation as a poet, the minor faults of his verses were imputed to his laziness.

His complete works were reedited regularly early in the nineteenth century, before eighteenth-century theater fell into permanent disfavor: Auguste Vitu speaks of unsuccessful attempts at reviving Crébillon's tragedies around 1864. Much of Crébillon's current reputation stems from studies comparing his theater to Voltaire's. Yet, Crébillon merits being studied for his own accomplishments, since he added a new "English" dimension to classical tragedies, precipitating the advent of melodrama and realism. His versification merits attention since it was respected by contemporary poets. He must be included in serious studies tracing the evolution of tragedy and theoreticians of the French Gothic style. Edgar Allan Poe concluded "The Purloined Letter" with French verses from *Atrée*–a quotation discussed in two works by literary theoretician Jacques Derrida, "The Purveyor of Truth" (1975) and the closing pages of *The Post Card* (1980; translated, 1987)–in passages pondering the status of writing over talking, and the stage of human destiny: "un destin si funeste / S'il n'est digne d'Atrée est digne de Thyeste" (such a gloomy destiny / If not worthy of Atrée is worthy of Thyeste).

Biographies:

Louis Sébastien Mercier, *Tableau de Paris*, 12 volumes (Amsterdam, 1738), X: 30–50;

Pierre-Antoine de la Place, "Eloge historique de M. De Crébillon, par M. de la Place," *Mercure de France*, 1 (July 1762): 149–201;

Joseph de la Porte, "Eloge historique de M. De Crébillon," in *Oeuvres de Crébillon, corrigée, revue augmentée de la vie de l'auteur, préface et éloge historique par l'abbé Joseph de la Porte*, 3 volumes (Paris: Chez les libraires associés, 1772);

C. M. Janvier, "Essai sur la vie et le théâtre de Crébillon," in *Oeuvres dramatiques de Crébillon, précédées d'un essai sur la vie et le théâtre de l'auteur, par C. M. Janvier* (Paris: Huet, 1796);

Charles Collé, *Journal et mémoires*, 3 volumes, edited by H. Bonhomme (Paris: Firmin Didot, 1868);

Voltaire, "Eloge de Crébillon," in *Oeuvres complètes, Mélange III* (Paris: Garnier, 1879), XXIV: 345–363;

Auguste Vitu, "Notice sur Crébillon sur sa vie et ses ouvrages," in *Théâtre complet, nouvelle édition, précédé d'une notice par M. Auguste Vitu* (Paris: Laplace, Sanchez et Cie, éditeurs, 1885), pp. 1–72;

Maurice Dutrait, *Etude sur la vie et le théâtre de Crébillon 1674–1762* (Bordeaux, 1895; Geneva: Slatkine Reprints, 1970).

References:

Clarence D. Brenner and Nolan A. Goodyear, eds., "Introduction," in *Eighteenth-Century French Plays* (New York & London: Century, 1927);

Jacques Derrida, *The Post Card: From Socrates to Freud and Beyond*, translated by Alan Bass (Chicago: University of Chicago Press, 1987);

Derrida, "The Purveyor of Truth," translated by Willis Domingo, Moshe Ron, and Marie-Rose Logan, *Yale French Studies*, 52 (1975): 31–114;

Charles Rivière Dufresny, "Réflexions sur la tragédie de *Rhadamiste et de Zénobie*," in *Oeuvres*, 4 volumes (Paris: Briasson, 1747), IV: 286–296;

Jean-François de La Harpe, *Lycée; ou cours de littérature*, 8 volumes (Paris: Agasse, 1813).

Papers:

Prosper Jolyot de Crébillon *père*'s papers may be found at the Bibliothèque Nationale, dossier Jolyot (registre 1586, Jolyot-Jore; cote 36397), and dossiers bleus: Jolyot, 9733; at the Bibliothèque de l'Arsenal; at the Bibliothèque de l'Institut; at the Bibliothèque de la Sorbonne; at the Bibliothèque Mazarine; at the Bibliothèque historique de la ville de Paris; at the archives at the Comédie française; and at the Archives nationales in the dossiers of the Papiers de l'Ordre du Temple and Lettres de M. de Marigny. A letter by Crébillon (1761) may be found at the Archives de la Côte d'Or. In Great Britain papers may be found at the libraries of the Universities of Oxford and Cambridge and at the library of the University College in London.

Anne Le Fèvre Dacier

(5 August 1647 – 16/17? August 1720)

Caryl L. Lloyd
University of West Georgia

BOOKS: *Lucii Annæi Flori Historia Romana, cum interpretatione et notis in usum Delphini* (Paris: Frédéric Léonard, 1674);

Callimachi Cyranæi Hymni, Epigrammata et Fragmenta (Paris: S. Mabre Chamoisy, 1675);

Lettres inédites . . . extraites de la correspondance de Huet, in Camille Henry, *Un Erudit homme du monde, homme d'église, homme de cour* (Paris: Hachette, 1679), pp. 40–48;

Dictys Cretensis de bello Troiano et Dares Phrygius de exidio Troiae (Paris: Frédéric Léonard, 1680);

Les Poésies d'Anacréon et de Sapho, traduites de grec en françois (Paris: D. Thierry et C. Barbin, 1681);

Sexti Aurelii Victoris Historiæ Romanæ compendium (Paris: Frédéric Léonard, 1681);

Comédie de Plaute, traduit en français avec des remarques et un examen selon les régles du Théâtre, 3 volumes (Paris: D. Thierry and C. Barbin, 1683);

Eutropii Historiæ Romanæ breviarium ab Urbe condita usque ad Valentinianum et Valentem Augustos (Paris: Cellier, 1683);

Le Plautus et les nuées d'Aristophane. Comédies greques traduites en françois Avec des Remarques & un Examen de chaque Piece selon les règles du théâtre (Paris: D. Thierry et C. Barbin, 1684);

Les Comédies de Terence, 3 volumes (Paris: D. Thierry et C. Barbin, 1688);

Réflexions morales de l'empereur Marc-Antonin, by Dacier and André Dacier, 2 volumes (Paris: C. Barbin, 1691);

L'Iliade d'Homère, traduite en françois avec des remarques (Paris: Rigaud, 1711); translated by Ozell, Broome, and Oldisworth as *The Iliad,* 5 volumes (London, 1712);

Des Causes de la corruption du goût (Paris: Rigaud, directeur de l'Imprimerie royale, 1714);

Homère défendu contre l'apologie du R. P. Hardoüin, ou suite des causes de la corruption du goust (Paris: Jean-Baptiste Coignard, 1716);

L'Odyssée d'Homère traduite en françois, 3 volumes (Paris: Rigaud, 1716).

Anne Le Fèvre Dacier (Bibliotheque nationale; from Fern Farnham, Madame Dacier, *1976)*

Prominent during her lifetime as a classical scholar, polemicist, and translator of Latin and Greek texts, Anne Le Fèvre Dacier has since faded into obscurity. While most educated men in the seventeenth century were able to read Latin, few of them had a similar knowledge of Greek. Even fewer women were competent in either language. Anne Dacier's father–a celebrated humanist, teacher, and classicist–helped prepare his talented daughter for her career as one of the most prolific translators in France. Widely praised for her editions of Sappho, Terence, Plautus, Aristophanes, and Florus, she achieved international fame for her editions of Homer. In fact, her translation of Homer's *Iliad* (*L'Iliade d'Homère,* 1711) set off a second phase of the Quarrel between the Ancients and the Moderns, in England called the Battle of the Books, a debate about the relative merits of classical versus modern letters. Her goal was to rescue classical works from obscurity and bring them broader readership within France.

Although born to a bourgeois family, Dacier was a significant participant in the culture of France's *Grand Siècle* (Grand Century). The reign of Louis XIV was a period of impressive artistic and intellectual activity, and Dacier was considered by many to be the most learned woman of her time. Hers was the world of the great thinkers of France: Voltaire, Jacques-Bénigne Bossuet, Nicolas Boileau-Despréaux and Jean Racine. Queen Christina of Sweden invited Dacier to be part of her royal entourage. She was a major contributor to the editing project designed to provide a library for the dauphin (the future Louis XV). Alexander Pope, whose English translation of Homer was based on Dacier's French version, praised her attentive scholarship. Dacier's obituaries, in France and abroad, described an esteemed woman scholar of considerable reputation.

Dacier published the authoritative version of many classical works not only for her generation but also for French readers throughout the eighteenth and early nineteenth centuries. Critics acknowledged her erudition, her understanding of Greek and Latin texts, and her knowledge of ancient history and cultures. Her position within the world of letters is one of general respect, although she was attacked by her enemies, the modernists, during her lifetime. Her primary antagonists were Houdar de la Motte, whose own verse translation of the *Iliad* followed hers, and Jean Hardoüin. They found fault with many aspects of Homer's poem as well as with Dacier's translations. French critic Charles-Augustin Sainte-Beuve, as late as 1854, lauded Dacier's versions for giving readers the specific flavor of Homer's world and the verve of his writing.

Some classicists then and now, such as Naomi Hepp, find fault with the way Dacier often made Homer's epic poetry too prosaic. They condemn her for the practice of eliminating violent or improper images in order not to offend her public. Modern readers of her translation of Sappho, such as Joan DeJean, also consider her emphasis on the Greek poet's heterosexuality an unfortunate distortion. Dacier biographer Fern Farnham suggests the most grievous fault for modern scholars is Dacier's failure to work from original manuscripts. Nonetheless, despite their limitations, her works still earn serious consideration among such modern scholars as Eric Foulon, Paul Mazon, and Giovanni Saverio Santangelo. Undeniably, for her time and well beyond, Dacier succeeded in her goal of creating widely read French and Latin versions of classical literature.

Dacier is perhaps best known today for her role in the debate between the Ancients and the Moderns. One work by DeJean on this polemical war in prerevolutionary Europe shows how the same battle has been fought many times throughout history. In fact, these "culture wars" include elements of this seemingly obscure argument and may contribute to a renewed interest in Dacier.

Twentieth-century scholars Santangelo and Louis Dubreuil-Chambardel agree that Anne Le Fèvre was born 5 August 1647 in the small town of Preuilly, in the province of Anjou, France. (Earlier biographers had given her birth date as 1651 or 1654.) Within two years of her birth, her father, Tanneguy Le Fèvre, moved his family to the town of Saumur on the Loire River, where five sons were subsequently born.

Tanneguy Le Fèvre was a famous Hellenist and teacher at the Protestant Academy in Saumur, a town Voltaire called "the Athens of Protestantism." He had converted prior to his daughter's birth and benefited from the relative religious tolerance that reigned in France until the Revocation of the Edict of Nantes (1685). A renowned humanist, he trained generations of Protestant ministers and classical scholars, among them his future son-in-law, André Dacier. Le Fèvre wrote a treatise on education, biblical commentaries, and editions of classical authors, including Terence and Horace. His daughter signed her first translation with the words *Tanaquilli Fabri Filla* (daughter of Tanneguy) and frequently quoted her father's publications in her own texts.

Le Fèvre was briefly married to a bookseller/publisher many years her senior named Jean Lesnier. They had a son who died in infancy, after which Le Fèvre returned to her parents' home. With the death of her father in 1672, Le Fèvre soon left the provincial town for Paris. She joined Dacier, whom she did not marry until 1683, eight years after Lesnier's death. Dacier's severest critics condemned her for leaving her first husband for her lover, but her reputation was not seriously damaged by this aspect of her private life.

In her early career Dacier greatly benefited from her acquaintance with her father's old friend Pierre-Daniel Huet (humanist, member of the French Academy, and bishop of Avranches), who became the young scholar's protector. He invited her to join André Dacier and others in an ambitious undertaking–the publication of new editions of major classical works. Ostensibly designed for the education of the dauphin, the collection came to be known as the Delphin series. Anne Dacier, the only woman, edited six of the sixty-four authors, including the work of the only Greek writer in the series.

Within a period of nine years Dacier published editions of five minor Latin historians: Florus (1674), Dictys of Crete/Dares of Phrygia (1680), Aurelius Victor (1681), and Eutropius (1683). Her father had written a pedagogical manual (*Méthode pour commencer les humanités grecques et latines,* 1672) in which he urged parents not to burden young scholars with difficult works but to offer them less difficult authors. This first scholarly effort on Dacier's part can thus be seen as a tribute to her parent. When the first volume appeared, noted critic Pierre Bayle commented in his *Nouvelles de la République des Lettres* (October 1684) that she was a credit to her gender and more diligent than her male collaborators. Modern classical scholar Enrica Malcovati praises Dacier's work on all four editions as still useful today.

These years were exciting for Dacier. In contact with the most prominent academicians and writers of her time, collaborating on an important project with André Dacier, Anne Dacier was well on her way to becoming one of the first professional women of letters in France. Unlike aristocratic women authors, Dacier had to earn a living, and her considerable productivity must be seen in part as a reflection of that necessity. In fact, in seven extant letters to Huet, Dacier tenaciously insists on prompt payment for her labors. At age thirty-two she was elected to the celebrated Academy of Padua (1679). At this time the queen of Sweden praised Dacier's erudition and unsuccessfully urged her to join her entourage in Rome.

While remaining one of the most productive members of the Delphin group, Dacier nonetheless found time for her own work. Her translation into Latin of the work of Greek poet Callimachus (circa 300–240 B.C.) appeared in 1675 with a dedication to Huet. Although not part of the original project, the work so impressed Huet that he included it in the Delphin series. In the preface to the work Dacier praises her father for educating her despite her being female. Favorably reviewed by the influential *Journal des Savants* (11 March 1675), this early work of scholarship further established Dacier's reputation.

The second independent project was more controversial, particularly for a woman mindful of the sensibilities of her contemporaries. While a revival of interest in Greek and Latin letters (neoclassicism) took place during the seventeenth century, it was also a period when readers insisted on discretion in matters of sexuality. Dacier rose to the challenge in 1681 with her translation into French of the Greek poets Anacreon and Sappho. Dedicated to her protector the duke of Montausier, the work is based on her father's Latin edition of these authors.

André Dacier, husband of Anne Le Fèvre Dacier and secretary of the French Academy (1713–1722) (from Fern Farnham, Madame Dacier, *1976; James A. Rogers Library, Francis Marion University)*

Dacier's presentation of Sappho differs significantly from her father's. One work on Sappho's reputation calls Le Fèvre's defense of Sappho "startling" for its time (DeJean). He accepted Sappho's homosexuality and made no mention of any male love interest. The daughter, for all her filial piety, chose another path. In her twenty-page preface she dismisses those who would tarnish Sappho's reputation (presumably by calling her a lesbian) and describes instead the Greek poet's heterosexual loves. Whatever the reasons for Dacier's "defense" of Sappho, her interpretation of the poet's life and work became the authoritative version for more than a century both in France and abroad. A second edition was published in 1696; two editions appeared in Amsterdam in 1699 and 1716. De la Motte, who became her enemy during the Quarrel between the Ancients and the Moderns, praised her translations. In England, Ambrose Philips published new translations based on hers, and the poet Joseph Addison acknowledged her talent in *The Spectator.*

The year 1683 was particularly productive for Dacier. She published a French edition of the comedies of the Latin writer Plautus and completed much of the work on *Plautus* and *The Clouds,* two plays by Greek author Aristophanes, which she published in 1684. The most popular genre in seventeenth-century France by far was the theater. This century was the time of the great dramatists Pierre Corneille, Racine, and Molière. The monarchy of Louis XIV showed increasing support for the theater with plays read at court and performed in the state theater, the Comédie française. Politically astute, Dacier dedicated her volume on Plautus to the king's influential minister Colbert. In her preface she expressed a preference for Plautus over Terence, who was a more popular Latin writer at the time. The work continued to be published well into the eighteenth century.

Dacier's translation of Aristophanes was the first to appear in French prose; yet, it received scant critical notice when it was published. The fashionable French public was unlikely to approve of this earthy Greek poet. While Dacier was no prude when it came to reading Aristophanes, she did soften many of the images to suit contemporary taste. At the end of the seventeenth century, critic Charles Perrault praised the work and called Dacier's command of Greek so impressive that it could be called her "paternal language." Her understanding of the differences between the Ancients' more robust culture and that of the late seventeenth century point to her future role as defender of Homer.

With the major part of Dacier's work on the Delphin series completed along with her independent translations, Anne Le Fèvre and André Dacier turned to their personal affairs. The couple possibly already had an illegitimate daughter, born in 1670 or 1671. In his will André Dacier recognized as his daughter a nun by the name of Marie at the Abbaye Royale in Longchamp. Prior to their marriage, the couple had been presented to the king, but their success was compromised both by their domestic life and their Protestant faith. On 4 November 1683, André and Anne married in the town of Charenton-le-Pont, thus solving the first problem. They lived quietly for two years, far from Paris and the court, in the town of Castres, André Dacier's family home. Their son, Jean-André, was born in 1684 and baptized a Protestant.

In September of the following year the Daciers took the second step toward conformity by converting to Catholicism. Protestant ministers and writers were outraged and unrelenting in their criticism of their motives. In truth, following the conversion, both Daciers were granted pensions (royal support). The Edict of Nantes was revoked in October 1685, and many French Protestants (Huguenots) fled abroad. Whatever the reasons for the conversion, it removed a significant obstacle from Dacier's career. One modern biographer, Emmanuel Bury, attributes the continuing importance of classical studies in France to this possibly sincere but certainly strategic change of faith.

In her next undertaking Dacier was not embarrassed to revise an earlier opinion. She decided to look at the comedies of Terence again and offered a decidedly more positive opinion of his merits relative to Plautus. She pointed out her new subject's wit, his subtlety, and his insight. Because of her enthusiasm Dacier typically found any criticism of the authors she had chosen unacceptable. In this case, she maintained that Terence had complied with Aristotle's basic rules of theater—the unities of action, time, and place. Seventeenth-century critics, on the other hand, interpreted Aristotle narrowly and felt that the actions depicted by Terence could not possibly take place within the limits prescribed by these rules. Despite minor disagreement about the unities, Dacier's translation was itself translated and remained the basis for future editions as late as 1771.

While both Daciers were classical scholars, they rarely collaborated on the same edition. In 1691, however, they produced such a volume, *Réflexions morales de l'empereur Marc-Antonin* (The Meditations of Marcus Aurelius). It has become a commonplace of eighteenth-century scholarship that the philosophes used the wisdom of the ancient world against the religious dogma of Christian Europe. The Daciers made quite the opposite use of the old texts. They found pre-Christian philosophy among the Latin and Greek writers. In their view, far from undermining a Christian philosophy, the great pagan writers prepare the way for it. Dacier finds Christian elements in the author's belief in a transcendent order and the importance of altruism.

After the remarkably productive decades of her late twenties through her forties, Dacier entered a quieter period. Her family life required much of her attention. Her son was only seven at this time, and in 1693 a second daughter, Henriette-Suzanne, was born. Although Dacier was known throughout Europe for her learning, she was also an accomplished hostess and attentive mother, according to her contemporaries (letter of Anne de Bellinzani Ferrand quoted in Santangelo). The tragic death of their son in 1694 was a deep loss for the Daciers. Jean-André had shown promise as a scholar and delighted his parents with his understanding of the ancient texts.

This period for the Dacier household, nonetheless, was successful. André Dacier, a prominent classicist in his own right, was elected to the French Academy in 1695. He progressed through a series of appointments, including that of royal censor in 1702.

André Dacier's career reached its apex in 1720 when he was named Bibliothécaire du Roi (Royal Librarian). The king had further granted the family a comfortable apartment in the Louvre. They lived there, entertained fellow writers, and both eventually died there. Despite her grief and her many social duties during this time, Anne Dacier was hardly idle. To the contrary, she began work on a project that was not completed until 1716–a translation and critical edition of Homer's *Odyssey* (*L'Odyssée d'Homère*), the crowning achievement of her career.

The *Iliad* appeared in 1711 with a lengthy preface in which Dacier justifies her prose translation in a rather startling image. Her work is like a mummy of the beautiful Helen of Troy; the features and the basic symmetry remain, but the life force is absent. As with her Marcus Aurelius, Dacier finds elements of Christianity in the pagan Greek writer. The notion of the gods as all-powerful manipulators of man's fate, the recognition of noble actions, the punishments meted out to evildoers, all become allegories for a Christian theology. Indeed, for Dacier the future of civilization depended on the values imparted by the classics: friendship, valor, love and awe of the gods. In an unusually personal reference appended to the preface Dacier informs her readers of the loss of her beloved seventeen-year-old daughter Henriette, in 1710. Henriette had been her constant companion, her confidante and helper. Dacier was inconsolable. She describes the solitude and horror of this event, humbly noting that a mother's loss may seem like nothing compared to the trials of Homer's heroes.

Reaction to the *Iliad* was mixed but predictable. De La Motte, Bernard Le Bovier de Fontenelle, and other modernists found fault; those in the Ancients' camp heaped praise on Dacier. In 1714 de la Motte, who did not know Greek, undertook his own translation in verse based on Dacier's prose version and glossed with critical comments. Dacier immediately responded to his criticisms with a lengthy polemic titled *Des Causes de la corruption du goust*. Others joined the fray, and soon much of educated Paris was divided between Ancients and Moderns. Pope used her translation in his own version of *The Iliad* and, although disagreeing with aspects of her work, complimented her on her learning. Having never learned English, Dacier misunderstood some of his comments and wrote a heated reply. She also published an answer to R. P. Hardouïn's arguments in a pamphlet *Homère défendu contre l'apologie du R. P. Hardouïn* (1716, A Defense of Homer against the Apology of R. P. Hardouïn). Thanks in part to the influential hostess the marquise of Lambert, the two sides were eventually reconciled and the quarrel died.

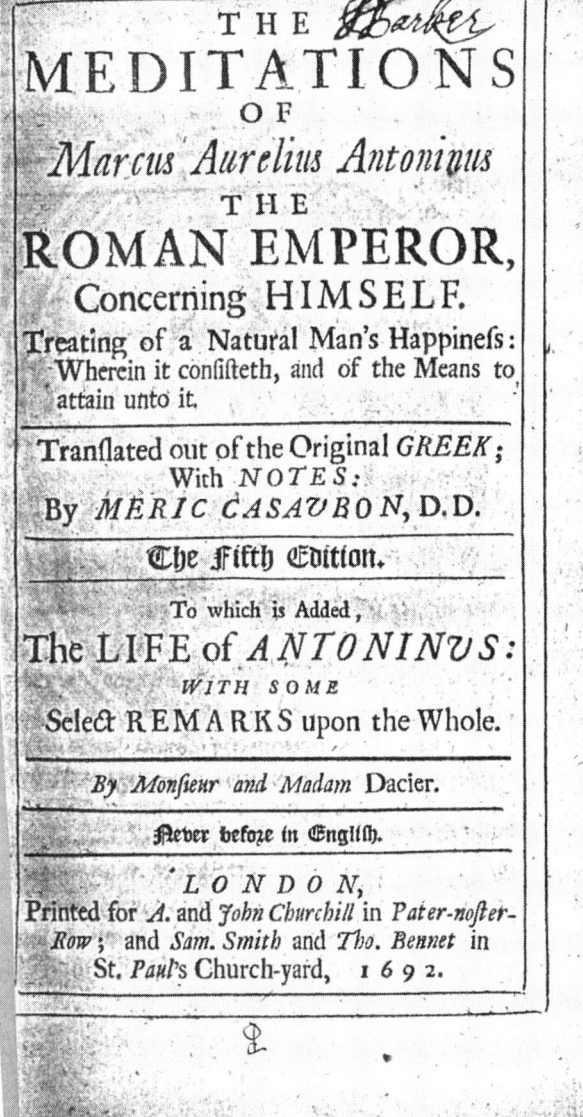

Title page from the fifth English edition of the 1691 Refléxions morales de l'empereur Marc-Antonin, by Dacier and André Dacier (Thomas Cooper Library, University of South Carolina)

By 1716 Dacier's translation of the *Odyssey* was ready for publication. Nearly seventy, Dacier was undoubtedly relieved that the work avoided the controversy of her *Iliad*. In her presentation of Homer's great epic she admires the simple virtues portrayed, the fidelity of Penelope, and the cleverness of Ulysses. She provides extensive notes about the dress, food, and customs of the Greeks. Although, as in her other translations, Dacier occasionally avoids translating vulgar actions that might displease her French audience, she manages to present a thorough rendition of the poem with few omissions.

Anne Le Fèvre Dacier died of a stroke in August 1720, and her husband died two years later. Both are buried near the Louvre in the church they attended, Saint Germain l'Auxerrois.

Although Dacier's devotion to the classics became forever associated with the Quarrel of the Ancients and the Moderns, it was also responsible for her greatest success. She translated into French for the first time the complete texts of many classical works. The prominent position of the classics within French education and culture is in part a result of her efforts.

Biographies:

Enrica Malcovati, *Madame Dacier: Una gentildonna filologa del gran secolo* (Florence: Sansoni, 1952);

Fern Farnham, *Madame Dacier: Scholar and Humanist* (Monterey, Cal.: Angel Press, 1976);

Giovanni Saverio Santangelo, *Madame Dacier, una filologa nella "crisi" (1672–1720)* (Rome: Bulzoni Editore, 1984).

References:

Emmanuel Bury, "Madame Dacier," in *Femmes savantes, savoirs des femmes,* edited by Colette Nativel (Geneva: Librairie Droz, 1999);

Joan DeJean, *Ancients against Moderns* (Chicago & London: University of Chicago Press, 1997);

DeJean, *Fictions of Sappho* (Chicago & London: University of Chicago Press, 1989);

Louis Dubreuil-Chambardel, "Notes sur le lieu de naissance de Madame Dacier," *Bulletin de la Société Archéologique de Touraine,* 12 (1900): 191–195;

Eric Foulon, "Madame Dacier: une femme savante qui n'aurait pas déplu à Molière," *Bulletin de l'Association Guillaume Budé,* 4 (1993): 357–379;

Jean Hardoüin, *Apologie d'Homère* (Paris, 1716);

Naomi Hepp, "L'ombre de Madame Dacier," in *Homère au XVIIème siècle* (Paris: Klincksieck, 1968), pp. 628–660;

Paul Mazon, *Madame Dacier et les traductions d'Homère en France* (Oxford: Clarendon Press, 1936);

Houdar de La Motte, *L'Iliade, poème, avec un discours sur Homère* (Paris, 1714);

Charles Perrault, *Parallèle des anciens et des modernes,* 4 volumes (Paris, 1692–1697), II: 248;

Arnaldo Pizzorusso, "La polemica di Madame Dacier: la tradizione e i principi della critica," *Revista Di Estetica,* 9 (1964): 161–183;

Alexander Pope, *The Poems of Alexander Pope,* Twickenham Edition (New Haven: Yale University Press, 1967);

Charles-Augustin Sainte-Beuve, "Madame Dacier," in *Causeries du lundi,* 11 volumes (Paris: Garnier, 1851–1856), IX: 379–410.

Marie de Vichy-Chamrond, marquise Du Deffand

(25 September 1696 – 23 September 1780)

Caryl L. Lloyd
University of West Georgia

BOOKS: *Letters of the Marquise Du Deffand to Horace Walpole,* 4 volumes, edited by Mary Berry (London: Longman, Hurst, Rees & Orme, 1810);

Correspondance complète de la Marquise du Deffand avec ses amies, le Président Hénault, Montesquieu, d'Alembert, Voltaire, Horace Walpole, 2 volumes, edited by Mathurin-François-Adolphe de Lescure (Paris: Henri Plon, 1865);

Correspondance de Mme Du Deffand avec la Duchesse de Choiseul, l'Abbé Barthélémy et M. Craufurt, 3 volumes, introduction by M. le Marquis de Sainte-Aulaire (Paris: Michel Lévy, 1866; revised and enlarged, 1877);

Lettres de la Marquise Du Deffand à Horace Walpole, 3 volumes, edited by Mrs. Paget Toynbee (London: Methuen, 1912);

Madame Du Deffand: lettres à Voltaire, edited by Joseph Trabucco (Paris: Bossard, 1922);

Letters to and from Madame Du Deffand and Julie de Lespinasse, edited by Warren Hunting Smith (New Haven, Conn.: Yale University Press, 1938);

Cher Voltaire: la correspondance de Madame Du Deffand avec Voltaire, edited by Isabelle and Jean-Louis Vissière (Paris: Des Femmes, 1987).

Madame Du Deffand is best remembered as a prolific *épistolière* (writer of letters). Throughout her long life, which spanned much of the eighteenth century, she wrote to her family, friends, and acquaintances, including many of the most important figures of the Enlightenment: Voltaire, Charles-Louis de Secondat Montesquieu, Jean Le Rond d'Alembert, English writer Horace Walpole, and important figures of the French court and salon society. These letters brought news of the court to those who were in the provinces or abroad and maintained a circuit of communication among members of the educated public. Politics, literature, court gossip, and personal relationships were the mainstays of discussion. Letters were often read aloud at

Marie de Vichy-Chamrond, marquise Du Deffand (from C.-A. Sainte-Beuve, Portraits of the Eighteenth Century, *1905; J. S. Mack Library, Bob Jones University)*

social gatherings; they were also copied and passed from hand to hand. Du Deffand was widely praised for her style and her insights. She often included short character sketches in which she analyzed the personalities and behavior of her subjects. Toward the end of her life, she conceived a passionate love for Walpole, and in her letters to him she revealed a more personal side of her life.

A recurrent theme of Du Deffand's letters is a kind of *ennui,* a sense of terror before the void, a constant pessimism about the purpose of life. She herself suffered from insomnia as well as from a condition she described as "black vapors," and which modern writers might call depression. Du Deffand also suffered from poor eyesight and was completely blind by the time she reached her mid fifties. Her physical condition reinforced her philosophical skepticism and sense of the futility of life. A dark personal side marks many of her letters and brings her closer to a contemporary audience. She seems to be describing an existential awareness that life has no predetermined meaning and no ultimate purpose.

Du Deffand was acquainted with many of the important minds of her time, in particular with those writers and thinkers who were challenging the beliefs of the Church and the French monarchy. Although she was friends with many of these philosophes, Du Deffand was nonetheless critical of aspects of their ideas. She was bored by their endless preaching about social justice and their criticism of those in power. Their demands for equality seemed to her little more than a desire to dominate the masses. She was especially critical of Jean-Jacques Rousseau, whose ideas, she feared, would lead France into anarchy. In fact, Du Deffand was at home in aristocratic France. Late in life she explained that politics bored her. This aspect of Du Deffand's writing most appealed to conservative critics after the French Revolution.

Du Deffand's contemporaries compared her to her well-known predecessor Marie de Rabutin Chantal, marquise de Sévigné (Madame de Sévigné). The art of letter writing, much admired in the seventeenth and eighteenth centuries, had a long and distinguished list of practitioners: Françoise d'Aubigne (Madame de Maintenon); Marie-Madeleine Pioche de La Vergne, comtesse de La Fayette (Madame de Lafayette); Roger de Rabutin, comte de Bussy (Bussy de Rabutin); and Sévigné, whose letters to her daughter were widely imitated. When she began to write in the style of Sévigné, Du Deffand's friends told her to trust in her own genius. Her wit and keen powers of observation were admired by her contemporaries. D'Alembert quoted her letters, and Voltaire urged her to continue writing but to eliminate the darker side of her analyses. Likewise, Walpole praised Du Deffand's mind and the cleverness of her character sketches. A first collection of her letters was published in 1810 and created a sensation. Napoléon Bonaparte took the volumes on his campaign into Russia. He later commented that he would only censor two words of the entire collection. In the nineteenth century, influential critic Charles-Augustin Sainte-Beuve admired the correspondence and placed Du Deffand among the classic letter writers of all time. He found her remarkably clear-minded and free of prejudice.

Successive editions of the letters inspired new evaluations of Du Deffand; the 1865 edition included previously unpublished letters to and from Walpole, Voltaire, d'Alembert, and Montesquieu. The volume also includes an appreciative essay by her editor, Mathurin-François-Adolphe de Lescure, who called her the most perfect literary and moral type of her century. He further placed her within the context of pre-Revolutionary France and said that she reflected its dual currents—a lack of religious faith and a libertine spirit. Lescure was considered the foremost authority on the details of Du Deffand's life. In the twentieth century, critic Gustave Lanson also saw Du Deffand as a representative of her time, both for her skepticism and for her late-blooming sentimentality. With the 1912 edition edited by Mrs. Paget Toynbee, the public could read more than five hundred new letters. In recent times, critics have focused their attention on two aspects of Du Deffand's work—the dark moods (especially noted by Wilhelm Klerks and Kurt Kloocke) and the genre of letter writing itself (such critics as Lionel Duisit and Judith Curtis). In fact, the revival of interest in the epistolary genre and the role of salons in general have rekindled discussion of Du Deffand and other eighteenth-century women such as Julie de Lespinasse.

Marie de Vichy-Chamrond, later marquise Du Deffand, was born in 1696 at her family's château in Burgundy. She was the third child of Anne Brûlart and Gaspard de Vichy. Although the family was aristocratic, it was far from wealthy, and the children were all aware of the importance of marrying well. Like many young women of her class, Marie was given a convent education, in her case at the Madeleine-Du-Traisnel Convent in Paris. Later in life, she wrote about the mediocrity of her education and her unfortunate lack of piety. Her priest, Father Massillon, admitted that the young girl was witty but said she was not particularly devout. The exact date of her arrival at the convent is not known, but she left when she was close to eighteen years of age and returned to her family in Chamrond.

She did not remain long with her family, however. Despite her small fortune, Du Deffand was married in 1718 to a distant cousin, Jean-Baptiste-Jacques Du Deffand, and soon became a leading figure of the Regency, the period after the death of Louis XIV and before the maturity of Louis XV. Her marriage was never central to Marie Du Deffand's concerns, and even before her separation from her husband less than five years later, Du Deffand led an independent life. As was widely known at the time, the young marquise had an affair with the regent himself, Philippe d'Orléans.

Du Deffand enjoyed the relaxed morality of the period and was reputed to have taken other lovers as well.

While Du Deffand's literary work consists primarily of her posthumously published correspondence and portraits of prominent contemporaries, she was widely quoted during her time as the author of parodies, notably a 1723 satire of Antoine Houdar de La Motte's popular play *Inès de Castro* (1723). Although her reputation was that of a spirited and witty woman of the world, Du Deffand describes herself in a self-portrait as intolerant of fools and subject to bouts of depression.

In the 1730s and 1740s she spent long periods of time at the estate of Anne Bénédicte Louise de Bourbon-Condé, duchesse de Maine. There she met Louise d'Epinay, marquise de Lambert (Madame de Lambert), and Claude Adrien Helvétius, as well as her lifelong friends and correspondents Voltaire and Charles-Jean-François d'Hénault. There she also learned about being a hostess and began the practice of writing down her observations about what was said at the many gatherings and sharing these observations with her acquaintances. Well before her letters were published, Du Deffand was considered the Madame de Sévigné of her century.

In 1747, six years before the death of the duchesse de Maine, Du Deffand was ready to join the ranks of the famous hostesses or *salonnières* of the eighteenth century. She had participated in such gatherings not only under the duchesse de Maine but also with Claudine-Alexandrine Guerin de Tencin (Madame de Tencin) and Madame de Lambert. Du Deffand's first independent experiments began in her small apartment at the rue de Beaune in Paris, but after she moved to larger quarters with her brother, the abbé at Sainte-Chapelle, she felt the need to find a larger, more permanent site for her new role. She chose a spacious apartment within the convent of Sainte-Joseph, where the large ensemble of buildings included an entire wing designed for rental to women living alone. It offered complete autonomy and housed many distinguished figures, including Princess Marie-Louise Jablonowska, wife of the Prince de Talmont (the Princess Talmont) and Stéphanie-Félicité Ducrest de Saint-Aubin, comtesse de Genlis, marquise Du Sillery (Madame de Genlis), pretender to the English throne. There she soon established herself as one of the best-known *salonnières* of the century. Those attending her gatherings included mathematician and encyclopedist d'Alembert, finance minister Anne-Robert-Jacques Turgot, geometrist Pierre de Maupertuis, and leading lights of the social and literary world in Paris.

Voltaire, increasingly concerned about Du Deffand's dark moods, urged her to write as a way of combating her depression. She could never aspire to be a Voltaire, she told him, and so preferred to write nothing at all. Ultimately, however, she changed her mind

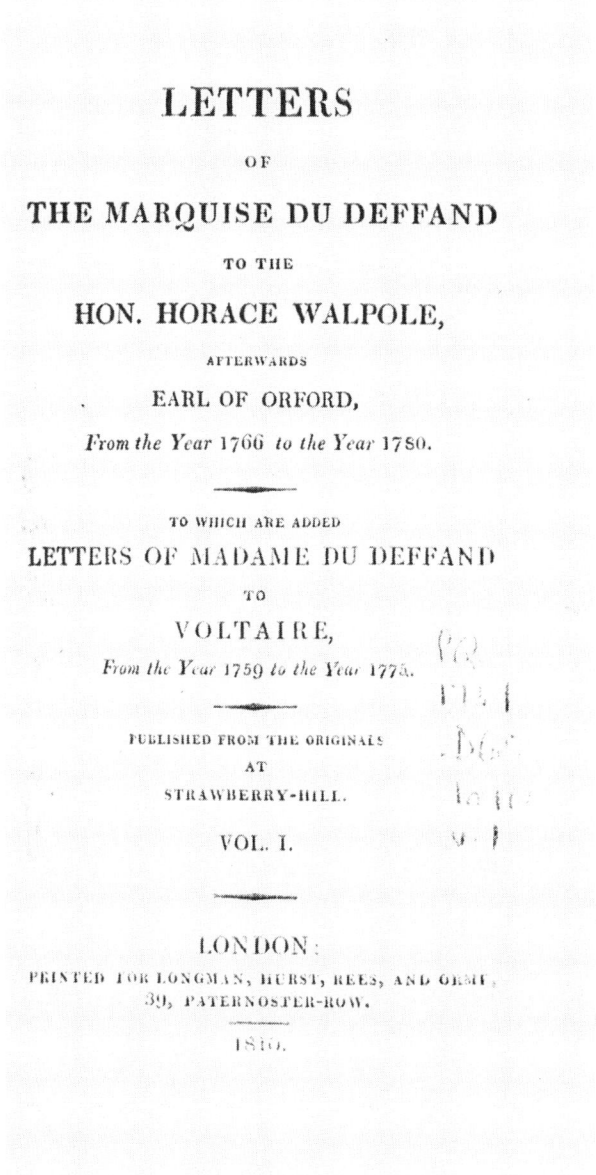

Title page for the first edition of Du Deffand's letters to Horace Walpole, with whom she was in love during the last years of her life (from Letters of the Marquise Du Deffand to the Hon. Horace Walpole, *1810; Thomas Cooper Library, University of South Carolina)*

and began a long career as an observer of her times. She admired the character analyses of seventeenth-century writer François duc de La Rochefoucauld. Less concerned with physical than psychological detail, Du Deffand drew character sketches that, although subtly phrased, were honest and uncompromising. Her ideal was that of the *honnête homme,* a cultivated man who is not worldly, with its emphasis on sociability, naturalness, and moderation.

In a portrait of her aunt, Anne Bénédicte Louise de Bourbon-Condé, duchesse de Luynes, Du Deffand describes a woman of reason and moderation who also loved freedom. But the duchesse, like many women, found that the loss of freedom in marriage was finally preferable to the anxieties of an unfettered life. In another portrait, Du Deffand describes Françoise de Neufville-Villeroy, duchesse de Chaulnes, as suffering from an overactive imagination; her mind, like a magic lantern, casts brilliant but fleeting images into the world. For the skeptical Du Deffand, imagination was strongest in the weakest minds. Religious zealots suffered from this tendency to distort reality. Like the philosophes, Du Deffand trusted in reason and was suspicious of both revealed religion and idle imaginings.

An important liaison in Du Deffand's life was one with Hénault, with whom she remained lifelong friends. Hénault was president of the Parlement de Paris and in 1723 was elected to the French Academy. She described the relationship with Hénault as an "affair of convenience" and ultimately enlisted him as a regular in her own salon in Paris, first at the rue de Beaune and, after 1747, at her apartment in the Saint-Joseph Convent. At this stage of her life, she rejected the well-worn path of Héloïse, the girl who fell in love with her tutor, Abélard, in the Middle Ages, and of the *Lettres portugaises* (1669) and their eighteenth-century descendant, *Lettres d'une Peruvienne* (1747). She was impatient with the image of an abandoned woman and made fun of what she called *rêvasserie* (daydreaming). She told Hénault that she was unsuited to emotional displays of feeling and explained that his absence was "delicious."

Completely blind by 1754, Du Deffand accepted her fate with dignity. To the duchesse de Luynes, who praised her courage in accepting her condition, Du Deffand protested that such acceptance is not courage, only an intelligent refusal of despair. During her earlier stay at the family estate of Chamrond, she had met Lespinasse, quite likely the illegitimate daughter of Du Deffand's brother. Du Deffand eventually established Lespinasse as her companion at the Saint-Joseph Convent. Lespinasse played an important role in Du Deffand's social career, as her style and interests complemented those of her mentor. Where Du Deffand was an acerbic, skeptical observer of her times, irreverent and disinterested in political talk, Lespinasse had a more youthful approach. She was fascinated by the future and talk of possible changes in both government and society. Her friends included academician Marie-Jean-Antoine-Nicolas Caritat, marquis de Condorcet, who played a part in the French Revolution; popular author Jean-François Marmontel; writer and critic Melchior Grimm; and, especially, d'Alembert. She encouraged discussions of government reform, economics, and political unrest.

The ten-year relationship between Du Deffand and Lespinasse, while mutually beneficial, came to a violent end in 1764 when Du Deffand discovered that her companion had been receiving visitors on her own. Already suspicious of the Encyclopedists, Du Deffand was reinforced in her criticism of them by the subsequent defection of both d'Alembert and Turgot. Of another well-known philosophe, Denis Diderot, she said simply that the two of them had no mutual attraction. In her letters to Lespinasse about their break, Du Deffand conveyed her deep sense of betrayal. The break between the two was immediate and absolute. Later Lespinasse described her mentor as a nasty child, the victim of her own bad character. Ultimately, Lespinasse was replaced by her faithful secretary Jean François Wiart, who remained with Du Deffand until her death.

In 1766, Du Deffand complained to Voltaire that she was increasingly isolated and that all of life appeared as an illusion to her. Her feeling of isolation, she suggests, might stem from a lack of self-knowledge. By the 1770s Du Deffand's depression became increasingly acute. She was terrified of the night and spent many long hours waiting for morning by composing and listening to letters read by Wiart. Yet, her dark moods were not all in vain; they helped her see man's dark condition (letter of 27 September 1773). Her insomnia revealed the barren landscape of life, its uncertainty, and its meaninglessness. Writing to Voltaire, she questioned whether all of life was an illusion and all thoughts pathways to a vast nothingness. Throughout her life Du Deffand suffered from her black vapors; yet, she was able to analyze the anxiety and continued to write and function.

In the last fifteen years of her life Du Deffand was obsessed with an unusual friendship with English novelist Walpole, to whom she wrote more than eight hundred letters. Walpole brought English literature to Du Deffand's attention, and her appreciation of William Shakespeare and Samuel Richardson illustrates an intellectual openness and vitality that was undiminished until her death in 1780. As much as she despised the *Lettres portugaises* and their imitators, Du Deffand was much less negative in her judgment of the English female protagonists Clarissa and Pamela. She was entertained by such "endless stories" and argued with Voltaire that these works made one desire virtue and believe it was attainable. While Richard III and King Lear were repulsive to her, the power and beauty in Othello and Henry VI convinced her that the French respect for formal rules was overrated. Although she was sixty-eight when Walpole made the first of five visits to Paris, Du Deffand experienced a profound and jealous love despite the twenty years' difference in their ages. Although he remained a close friend, Walpole constantly chided her about the intensity of her passion; he feared that the letters might be intercepted and cause him embarrassment. While she claimed to accept his rules limiting the number of letters and her talk about love, she continually found ways to reintroduce the subject closest to her heart.

Many critics find the letters to Walpole almost abject, because Du Deffand seems to have become the abandoned woman she so scorned in her early life. The woman who never allowed blindness to limit her told her reluctant correspondent to treat her like a servile animal, but not to ignore her. Undeniably, these letters are passionate analyses of the feelings of one who loves more than she is loved. Du Deffand once wrote to Voltaire that deathbed conversions do not redefine one's life but represent a reasonable giving in to the inevitability of death. One might perhaps situate in this philosophical perspective the final surrender to passionate love of a blind woman near the end of her life.

Along with her love of English literature, Du Deffand continued to admire French neoclassical playwright Pierre Corneille. She preferred his elaborate analyses of duty versus love to the passionate tirades of his rival Jean Racine. Two of the authors closest to her heart had a great deal in common with her own perspective on life: her contemporary Voltaire and sixteenth-century philosopher Michel de Montaigne. She admired Voltaire's style and his incisive descriptions of the contradictions of life, and described Montaigne as the only good philosopher who ever lived. Clearly, Montaigne's skepticism, his undermining of pious certainties, and especially his rejection of prideful systematizing, all made him an apt model for the independent Du Deffand.

In the last decade of her life Marie de Vichy-Chamrond, marquise Du Deffand, although increasingly despondent about Walpole's lack of affection, maintained an active circle of acquaintances at her Saint-Joseph apartment, including the ambassador from Naples; Danish envoy Baron Gleichen; Scottish philosopher David Hume; English historian Edward Gibbon; Marie-Charlotte de Campet de Saujon, comtesse de Boufflers (Madame de Boufflers); abbé Barthélémy; statesman Jacques Necker; and even Benjamin Franklin (during his frequent stays in Paris).

The last year of her life Du Deffand lived as she had since her youth, surrounded by influential friends and acquaintances and maintaining complex friendships, particularly through sustained correspondences with Walpole and Voltaire. She was acknowledged in

Portrait of Du Deffand at the time she was corresponding with Walpole (Strawberry Hill House in Twickenham, from Letters of the Marquise Du Deffand to the Hon. Horace Walpole, *1810; Thomas Cooper Library, University of South Carolina)*

her own time, as today, to be an insightful episolary writer, a participant in and critic of the rich social life of pre-Revolutionary France. She died 23 September 1780.

References:

Ursula Bohmer, "Konversation und Literatur: Zur Rolle der Frau im französichen Zalon des 18, Jahrhunderts," in *Die französische Autorin: Vom Mittelalter bis zur Gegenwart,* edited by Renate Baader and others (Wiesbaden: Athenaion, 1979), pp. 109–129;

Benedetta Craveri, *Mme Du Deffand et son monde,* translated by Sibylle Zavriew (Paris: Le Seuil, 1987);

Judith Curtis, "The Epistolières," in *French Women and the Age of Enlightenment,* edited by Samia I. Spencer (Bloomington: Indiana University, 1985), pp. 226–241;

Gerard Doscot, *Madame Du Deffand* (Lausanne: Editions Rencontres, 1966);

Lionel Duisit, *Madame Du Deffand, épistolière* (Geneva: Droz, 1963);

Duisit, "Madame Du Deffand et Voltaire: le mythe du progrès et la décadence du goût," *French Review*, 36 (1963): 284–292;

Victor Giraud, "La sensibilité de Madame Du Deffand," *Revue des Deux Mondes*, 8 (1 August 1933): 688–703;

Edmond and Jules de Goncourt, *La Femme au dix-huitième siècle* (Paris: Flammarion, 1838);

Jean-Yves Huet, "Madame de Sévigné: Horace Walpole et Madame Du Deffand," *La Nouvelle Revue Française*, 9 (January 1962): 404–435;

Wilhelm Klerks, *Madame Du Deffand: essai sur l'ennui* (Leiden: Universitaire Pers Leiden, 1961);

Kurt Kloocke, "Benjamin Constant et les débuts de la pensée nihiliste en Europe," in *Benjamin Constant, Madame de Staël et le groupe de Coppet*, edited by Etienne Hofman (Oxford: Voltaire Foundation, 1982), pp. 189–220;

Gustave Lanson, *Choix de lettres du XVIIIe siècle* (Paris: Hachette, 1908);

Jutta Lietz, "Madame Du Deffand und Voltaire im Briefwechsel," *Romantisches Jahrbuch*, 44 (1993): 164–193;

Caryl Lloyd, "Marie de Vichy-Chamrond, Marquise Du Deffand," in *French Women Writers*, edited by Eva Martin Sartori and Dorothy Wynne Zimmerman (Westport, Conn.: Greenwood Press, 1991), pp. 134–142;

Nicole Mallet, "Madame Du Deffand ou l'amitié par correspondance," *Women in French Studies*, 7 (1999): 46–56;

André Maurois, "Madame Du Deffand et Horace Walpole," in *Etudes anglaises* (Paris: Grasset, 1927), pp. 171–208;

Benoît Melançon, "La lettre *contre:* Mme Du Deffand et Belle de Zuylen," in *Penser par lettre* (Quebec City: Fides, 1998), pp. 39–62;

A. E. Naughton, "Some Literary Opinions of Madame Du Deffand," *Stanford Studies in Language and Literature* (1964): 157–274;

Charles de Remusat, "Horace Walpole," in *L'Angleterre au dix-huitième siècle,* volume 2 (Paris: Didier, 1856);

Charles-Augustin Sainte-Beuve, *Causeries du lundi*, volumes 2, 6, and 14 (Paris: Garnier, 1850–1857);

Sainte-Beuve, *Les Nouveaux Lundis*, volume 1 (Paris: Garnier, 1863–1873);

Sainte-Beuve, *Quelques Portraits féminins*, volume 11 (Paris: Garnier, 1927);

Fernando Savater, "Madame Du Deffand: Frivolidad y agonia," *Revista de Occidente*, 74–75 (July–August 1987): 88–102;

Edmond Scherer, "Le Roman de Madame Du Deffand," in *Etudes sur la littérature contemporaine,* volume 3 (Paris: Calmann Lévy, 1885), pp. 191–218;

Anne Waterman Sienkewicz, "Two Women of Letters: Mme de Sévigné and Mme Du Deffand," dissertation, Johns Hopkins University, 1978;

Lytton Strachey, *Biographical Essays* (New York: Harcourt, Brace & World, 1966), pp. 165–186;

Strachey, *Books and Characters* (New York: Harcourt, Brace, 1922), pp. 81–111.

Denis Diderot
(5 October 1713 – 31 July 1784)

Servanne Woodward
University of Western Ontario

BOOKS: *Pensées philosophiques* (The Hague [i.e., Paris]: Aux dépens de la Compagnie, 1746); translated as *Thoughts on Religion by M. Diderot* (London: Printed and published by R[obert] Carlile, 1819); augmented as *Thoughts on Religion by M. Diderot, with a Sketch of his Life and Writings* (London: Published by the Editors of Newgate Magazine, 1825);

Les Bijoux indiscrets, 2 volumes (Paris, 1748); translated as *The Indiscreet Toys . . . ,* 2 volumes (Tobago [i.e., London]: Reprinted for Pierrot Ragout, with the approbation of M-l S-xe. and sold by R. Freeman, near St. Paul's, 1749);

Mémoires sur différens sujets de mathématiques (Paris: Durand, Pissot, 1748)–includes *Principes généraux d'acoustique;*

Lettre sur les aveugles, à l'usage de ceux qui voient (London [Paris]: Durand, 1749); translated as *A Letter on Blindness. For the Use of Those Who Have their Sight* (London: Printed for William Bingley, 1770);

Lettre sur les sourds et muets, à l'usage de ceux qui entendent & qui parlent (N.p., 1751);

De l'Interprétation de la nature ([Paris], 1753); augmented and modified edition published as *Pensées sur l'interprétation de la nature* (N.p., 1754);

Le Fils naturel, ou les épreuves de la vertu [with *Conversations sur le fils naturel*] (Amsterdam [Paris: Prault], 1757); translated as *Dorval; or the Test of Virtue* (London: Printed for the Author and sold by J. Dodsley, 1767);

Le Père de famille, comédie en cinq actes avec un discours la poésie dramatique (Amsterdam [Paris: Pierre Lambert], 1758); translated as *The Father. A Comedy. Translated from the French of Monsieur Diderot, by the Translator of Dorval* ([London]: Printed for the Author and sold by W. Whittingham, R. Baldwin, 1770);

La Pièce et le prologue, ou celui qui les sert tous et qui n'en contente aucun (N.p., 1771); augmented and revised as "Est-il bon? Est-il méchant?" in *Mémoires, correspondance et ouvrages inédits,* edited by Frédéric Melchior Grimm (Paris: Paulin, 1830–1831);

Denis Diderot (portrait by Louis-Michel van Loo, Musée du Louvre; from Jeannette Rosso, Diderot et le portrait, *1998; Perkins Library, Duke University)*

Oeuvres philosophiques et dramatiques de M. Diderot, 6 volumes (London [Amsterdam], 1772);

Collection complete des oeuvres philosophique, littéraires et dramatiques de M. Diderot, 5 volumes (London [Amsterdam?], 1773);

Essai sur la vie et les écrits de Sénèque, in volume 7 of *Oeuvres de Sénèque,* translated by M. Lagrange (Paris: de Bure, 1778); revised and expanded in *Essai sur la vie de Sénèque le philosophe, sur ses écrits, et sur les règnes de Claude et de Néron* (Paris: de Bure, 1779);

La Religieuse (Paris: F. Buisson, 1796); translated as *The Nun* (London: G. G. & J. Robinson, 1797);

Jacques le fataliste et son maître, 2 volumes (Paris: F. Buisson, 1796, 1797); translated as *James the Fatalist and His Master,* 3 volumes (London: G. G. & J. Robinson, 1797);

Rameaus Neffe, first translated into German and published by Johann Wolfgang von Goethe (Leipzig: G. J. Göschen, 1805); first French edition, *Le Neveu de Rameau* (Paris: Delaunay, 1821; Paris: Brière, 1821 [i.e., 1823]); translated by John Morley as *Rameau's Nephew,* in volume 2 of *Diderot and the Encyclopedists* (London: Chapman & Hall, 1878);

Paradoxe sur le comédien, ouvrage posthume de Diderot (Paris: A. Sautelet, 1830); translated by Walter Herries Pollock as *The Paradox of Acting* (London: Chatto & Windus, 1883);

Eléments de physiologie, edited by Jean Mayer (Paris: Didier, 1964).

Collections: *Oeuvres,* 15 volumes, edited by Jacques-André Naigeon (Paris: Desray, Deterville, an VI [1798 or 1797]);

Oeuvres philosophiques de Denis Diderot, 2 volumes, edited by Charles-Frédéric Cramer (Paris: Cramer, 1798);

Frédéric Melchior Grimm, *Correspondance littéraire, philosophique et critique, adressée à un souverain d'Allemagne par le baron Grimm et par Diderot,* 16 volumes (Paris: Longchamps, F. Buisson, 1812–1813)–includes several articles by Diderot; revised as *Correspondance littéraire, philosophique et critique par Grimm et Diderot, depuis 1753 jusqu'en 1790* (Paris: Furne, 1829–1831);

Oeuvres complètes, 7 volumes (Paris: A. Belin, 1818–1819);

Oeuvres, 22 volumes (Paris: J. L. J. Brière, 1821–1823);

Oeuvres complètes, 20 volumes, edited by Jean Assézat and Maurice Tourneux, (Paris: Garnier, 1875–1877);

Salons, edited by Jean Seznec and Jean Adhémar (Oxford: Clarendon Press, 1957–1967);

Oeuvres complètes, 15 volumes, edited by Roger Lewinter (Paris: Club Français du Livre, 1969–1973).

Editions in English: *Diderot's Early Philosophical Works,* translated and edited by Margaret Jourdain (Chicago & London: The Open Court Publishing, 1916);

Rameau's Nephew and Other Works, translated by Mrs. Wilfrid Jackson (London: Chapman & Hall, 1926)–includes *A Supplement to Bougainville's Voyage, Regrets for my old Dressing-Gown,* and *Rameau's Nephew and Other Works;* translated by Jacques Barzun and Ralph H. Bowen (Garden City, N.Y.: Doubleday, 1956)–includes *D'Alembert's Dream, Supplement to Bougainville's Voyage, The Two Friends from Bourbonne, A Conversation Between a Father and his Children, The Encyclopedia, Regrets on Parting with my Old Dressing-Gown,* and *Diderot's Thoughts on Art and Style, with Some of his Shorter Essays,* selected and translated by Beatrix L. Tollemache (London: Remingtons, 1904);

Diderot Interpreter of Nature; Selected Writings, translated by Jean Stewart and Jonathan Kemp (London: Lawrence & Wishart, 1937);

Diderot's Selected Writings, selected and edited by Lester G. Crocker, translated by Derek Coltman (New York: Macmillan / London: Collier-Macmillan, 1966).

PLAY PRODUCTIONS: *Le Fils naturel ou les épreuves de la vertu, comédie en cinq actes en prose par Diderot,* Saint-Germain-en-Laye, at the home of the duc d'Ayen, 1757;

Le Père de famille, comédie en cinq actes en prose par Diderot, Marseille, Théâtre de Marseille, September 1760;

Madame de la Pommeraye, adapted by Paul Degouy from *Jacques le fataliste,* Paris, Théâtre de l'Odéon, 30 June 1901;

Est-il bon, est-il méchant? by Diderot, adapted by Paul Degouy, Paris, Théâtre de l'Odéon, 25 September 1913;

Le Paradoxe sur le comédien, adapted by Jacques Baillon, Paris, Théâtre de l'Odéon, 16 November 1976.

OTHER: *Encyclopédie, ou dictionnaire raisonné des sciences, des arts et des métiers, recueilli des meilleurs auteurs et particulièrement des dictionnaires anglais de Chambers, d'Harris, de Dyche & par une société de gens de lettres,* 35 volumes, edited by Diderot and Jean d'Alembert (Paris: Briasson, 1751–1780)–volume 1 includes "Prospectus" (1750) by Diderot.

*Note–Diderot had nothing to do with the publication of the *Encyclopédie* beyond 1780.

TRANSLATIONS: Temple Stanyan, *Grecian History,* translated by Diderot as *Histoire de la Grèce* (Paris: Briasson, 1743);

Antony Ashley Cooper Shaftesbury, *An Inquiry Concerning Virtue in Two Discourses,* translated by Diderot as *Principes de la philosophie morale, ou Essai . . . sur le mérite et la vertu* (Amsterdam [Paris]: Zacharie Chatelain, 1745); new edition titled *Philosophie morale réduite à ses principes ou Essai . . . sur le mérite et la vertu* (London, 1751).

A prominent philosopher, Diderot belongs to the radical branch of the Enlightenment–a distinction he could have done without. Because of his modest origin and his resistance to seeking patrons, he was less protected than most philosophes and endured a fair share of disgrace. Following Jean-François de La Harpe, many nineteenth-century critics vilified his memory, and the parliament of the Third Republic declined to erect monuments in his honor, although his contemporaries Voltaire and Jean-Jacques Rousseau attained this distinction. He is a precursor of Auguste Comte's positivism and an odd participant in German Romanticism because of his influence on several authors. Diderot once lent a copy of his *Jacques le fataliste* (1796, 1797; translated as *James the Fatalist and his Master,* 1797) to Johann Wolfgang Von Goethe on condition that he not take notes. Gotthold Ephraim admired Diderot's views on the pantomime. Other German authors were inspired by the French dramatist. In fact, *Le Père de famille* (1758; translated as *The Father,* 1770) inspired Friedrich Schiller's comedy *Kabale und Liebe* (1783, Cabal and Love), while Heinrich Heine modeled his style after Diderot's. Honoré de Balzac was impressed by Diderot's writings on art and manifestly recalled the *Salon de 1767* (Salon of 1767; collected in volumes 14 and 15 of *Oeuvres,* 1798 or 1797) while writing *Sarrasine* (1830). Likewise, Gustave Flaubert, Charles Baudelaire, Théophile Gautier, and Marie-Henri Beyle Stendhal praised Diderot and sought in him the antidote to François René de Chateaubriand and George Sand. Emile Zola and Claude Bernard were influenced by Diderot's *Eléments de physiologie* (1964, Elements of Physiology), while Jules Husson Champfleury admired *Ceci n'est pas un conte* (This Is Not a Story), which was published in volume 12 of Diderot's *Oeuvres* (1798). Since the late nineteenth century, Diderot has been considered the founder of the intellectual novel, and more recently as the forefather of late-twentieth-century authors of "anti-novels." His novels were adapted to the stage and the movie screen. For example, Paul Degouy's *Madame de la Pommeraye,* a comedy inspired by *Jacques le fataliste,* premiered at the Odéon Theater in Paris, on 30 June 1901, while *La Religieuse* (1796; translated as *The Nun,* 1797) was faithfully adapted to the screen by Jacques Rivette in 1966. Because of its daring portrayal of convent life, the movie was denied national and international distribution.

Denis Diderot was born in Langres on 5 October 1713. His father, Didier Diderot, was a master cutler, and his mother, Angélique Vigneron, was the daughter of a tanner. His sister Denise, nicknamed "soeurette" ("sis"), was born in 1715. Denis was godfather to Angélique, his second sister, born in 1720, two years before the youngest child in the family, Didier-Pierre. At age ten, Diderot was sent to the Jesuit college of Langres and submitted to the tonsure by the bishop of Langres at age thirteen. In 1728 his uncle died, leaving him his canonical position and prebend—his titles as a canon at the cathedral of Langres.

In 1729 Diderot's father accompanied him to Paris and signed him up at the college d'Harcourt, where rhetoric was emphasized. Diderot then went on to study at the University of Paris and for two years worked as a clerk for attorney Clément de Ris, originally from Langres. Actually, Diderot was interested neither in law nor in his uncle's religious titles; instead, he opted for a career in letters, much to his father's regret. By 1740 Diderot was befriending men of letters and attracted to the theater by beautiful actresses such as Jeanne-Catherine Gaussin and Maria Ana Botot, known as "la Dangeville." However, Anne-Toinette Champion, the daughter of a linen shopkeeper, developed a lasting relationship with him, and he ultimately married her.

Diderot and Rousseau met for the first time through Daniel Roguin. They enjoyed discussing music, a subject considered as a link between mathematics and the arts. In need of money, Diderot started to translate Temple Stanyan's *Grecian History* (1707), which was published by Antoine Claude Briasson as *Histoire de la Grèce* (History of Greece) in 1743. Returning to Langres to solicit a pension from his father in order to marry Anne-Toinette, Diderot was locked up in a monastery, as the older man was adamantly opposed to this union. Escaping through a window, Diderot joined his fiancée in Paris, and the couple finally married at night in a church known for performing clandestine marriages. Because their union was secret, Anne-Toinette could not adopt her husband's name—a situation that proved particularly embarrassing during her pregnancies. Ultimately, this relationship was not happy, and the couple fought frequently.

In addition to Rousseau, Diderot developed many friendships. He discussed music with abbé Mably and Bernard Le Bovier de Fontenelle, included Marc-Antoine Eidous and François-Vincent Toussaint in his translation contracts, and lunched weekly with mathematician Etienne Bonnot de Condillac, through whom he met Madeleine d'Arsant de Puisieux—the first intellectual woman he had encountered—who soon became his mistress. According to the memoirs of Diderot's daughter, Puisieux paid him fifty gold pieces for the *Pensées philosophiques* (1746; translated as *Thoughts on Religion,* 1819), written over the 1746 Easter weekend, following the completion of *Principes de la philosophie morale, ou Essai . . . sur le mérite et la vertu* (1745), the French translation of Antony Ashley Cooper Shaftesbury's *An Inquiry Concerning Virtue in Two Discourses* (1699). Since the *Pensées philosophiques* was published anonymously, it was attributed to Voltaire and Condil-

Arrest order for Diderot issued in July 1749. He was incarcerated in Vincennes, a fortress outside Paris, because in La Lettre sur les aveugles *(1749) he questioned that the cosmic order proved the existence of God, and possibly also because a reference in the book offended a woman friend of the minister of war and director of booksellers (Bibliothèque nationale; from John Lough,* An Introduction to Eighteenth-Century France, *1960; Thomas Cooper Library, University of South Carolina).*

lac and condemned by the Parliament of Paris in 1746. Undaunted by the setback, Diderot proceeded to write *La Promenade du sceptique* (1797, The Promenade of a Skeptic–inspired by Jonathan Swift's *A Tale of a Tub* [1710]), in which he revealed his doubts about religion. The manuscript, however, was seized by the police. Together with Rousseau and d'Alembert, Diderot intended to produce a magazine titled "Le Persifleur" (The Banterer). Although the project never materialized, the association proved beneficial when d'Alembert was called upon to translate Ephraim Chamber's *Cyclopaedia: or, Universal Dictionary of the Arts and Sciences* (1728).

Meanwhile, Diderot continued to pursue his interest in music and science. Jacques Chouillet believes that Diderot's *Principes généraux d'acoustique* (General Principles of Acoustics), which appeared in *Mémoires sur différens sujets de mathématiques* (1748, Memoirs on Different Subjects of Mathematics), is an important contribution, especially the part concerning the relationship between a vibrating chord and its tension. The piece appears to have been influenced by Leonhard Euler's *Tentamen novae theoriae musicae* (1739, New Musical Theory)–a reflection on music, acoustics, and physics–and the theoretical works of Jean-Philippe Rameau. Chouillet finds common references as well in Rameau's *Démonstration du principe de l'harmonie* (1750, Demonstration of the Principle of Harmony), appearances that suggest that Diderot may have discussed these topics with Rameau or even contributed to the drafting of his book. In *Principes généraux d'acoustique*, Diderot also develops René Descartes's *Compendium musicae* (1618, Compendium of Music).

Les Bijoux indiscrets (1748; translated as *The Indiscreet Toys*, 1749) was sold clandestinely by the publisher Durand. Its style is similar to that of Crébillon fils's *Le Sopha* (1739, The Sofa). It tells the story of a sultan's magic ring with the extraordinary power to provoke the intimate sexual confessions of women. In analyzing this work, Chouillet finds that, apart from the libertine genre, Diderot points to the differences between natural language and conventional language governed by social rules, while also capitalizing on the relationship between reality and dreams. Daniel Brewer notes that the fantasy of "speaking jewels" is deeply rooted in a Western concept of knowledge that links language to body; it was brought out for the first time by Michel Foucault in his discussion of Diderot in *Histoire de la sexualité* (1976, History of Sexuality). In the eighteenth century, readers considered *Les Bijoux indiscrets* a satire of Louis XV's liaison with the marquise de Pompadour. Following publication of the *Mémoires sur différens sujets de mathématiques*, which was favorably reviewed in the prestigious *Journal des Savants* (Journal of the Learned), Diderot undertook a most serious and demanding project–the *Encyclopédie*.

The year 1749 was a most dramatic one for Diderot. Demented and overworked, his younger sister died in a convent. (Undoubtedly, she must have inspired his heroine Suzanne Simonin when he later wrote *La Religieuse*.) In June, he published *Lettre sur les aveugles* (1749; translated as *A Letter on Blindness*, 1770), in which he questions the argument that cosmic order proves the existence of God. The essay was brought to the attention of the police by Pierre-Hardy de Levaré, the priest of Diderot's neighborhood church, and Diderot himself was denounced by booksellers Bonin and La Marche. Furthermore, *La Lettre sur les aveugles* refers to a cataract operation performed on a blind man who thus could see for the first time in his life. Diderot wished to attend the moment when the bandages were to be removed and the man suddenly acquired a new sense; however, the surgeon, René Antoine de Ferchault de Réaumur, did not honor Diderot's request and decided instead to invite Madame Dupré de Saint-Maur, described as "insignificant eyes" in *La Lettre sur les aveugles*. She was a good friend of Marc Pierre d'Argenson, the minister of war and director of booksellers, and she may have complained to him about the insult. Diderot's enemies succeeded in having him arrested and incarcerated in the prison of Vincennes, where he was to be kept for an indeterminate length of time by authority of a lettre de cachet, originating from an unknown source and for undisclosed charges.

Placed in the dungeon, deprived of visitors and communication with anyone, and interrogated by Nicolas René Berryer, Diderot denied authorship of any of the works he was known to have written. Berryer felt insulted by the obvious lies and found Diderot insolent. Eventually, the prisoner broke down and gave a detailed list of his publications, thus endangering his collaborators and his publishers. Many people consider Diderot's behavior in prison cowardly and despicable. Alice M. Laborde disagrees with those who attribute this behavior to fear, finding that his carefully crafted letters to the authorities do not reflect a terrorized man. Diderot's controlled use of rhetoric and name-dropping seem strategic and well planned. He speaks of Madeleine de Puisieux and of his friendship with Emilie du Châtelet, Voltaire's mistress and a family member of his warden, the marquis Du Châtelet. With time, Diderot was allowed to write his father, who was unaware that he had a daughter-in-law and a grandchild. The older man answered with a traditional reprimand, supporting the king's lettre de cachet, which he believed to be issued "by order of God." He, nevertheless, sent money and wished to be involved in

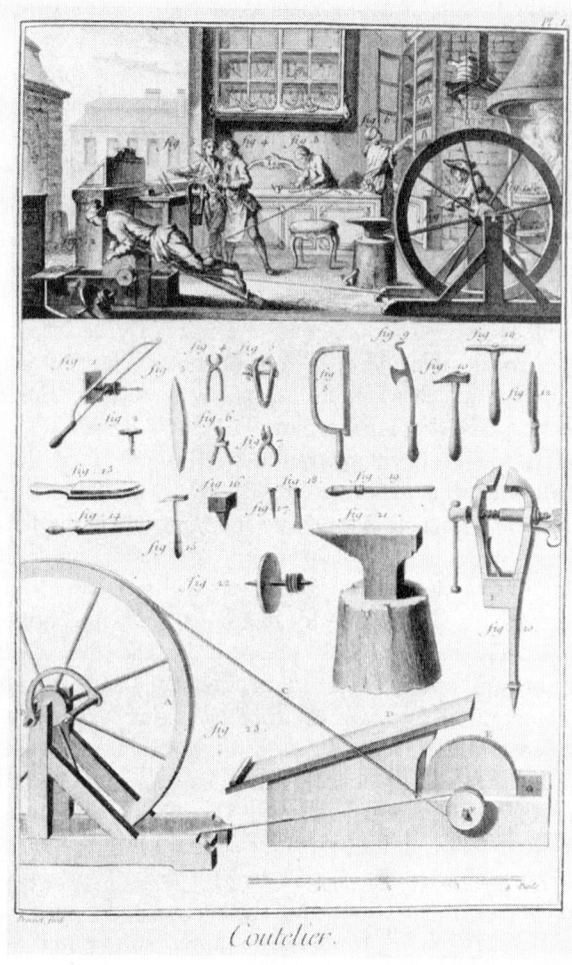

Illustration for Diderot's article on cutlery, which appeared in the Encyclopédie, 1751–1780 (from Arthur M. Wilson, Diderot, 1972; Collection of W. Ross)

his grandchild's life. This reaction was not the only positive outcome of Diderot's stay in prison.

In fact, the incarceration contributed to his reputation and designated him as a leader among the philosophes. Life as a prisoner was becoming less and less unpleasant, as friends often came to visit. Together with Puisieux, Diderot composed *L'Oiseau blanc* (included in volume 10 of the 1798 or 1797 *Oeuvres*), a transcription of a society game involving impromptu collective composition. For a while his wife was hosted in an adjacent room, and he even shared the table of his warden, the marquis Du Châtelet. During his spare time Diderot completed the translation of *L'Apologie de Socrate* (The Apology of Socrates; included in the 1978 *Oeuvres complètes*) by Plato and used the blank spaces in an edition of Milton's *Paradise Lost* to write with soot and a toothpick—at least so goes the myth of Diderot's confinement. Rousseau visited Diderot in October 1749, and apparently Diderot supported Rousseau's plan to answer the Academy of Dijon's call for an essay on the progress of sciences and the arts, and its impact on social mores. Apparently, Diderot suggested the direction of the argument that Rousseau was to follow in this essay. The sojourn in prison came to an end shortly thereafter, and Diderot wasted no time before meeting with Paul Henri Thiry, baron d'Holbach. By then, Diderot had achieved notoriety, his *Lettre sur les aveugles* having been praised by Voltaire.

Rousseau introduced Jesuit priest Louis Bertrand Castel and critic Frédéric Melchior Grimm to Diderot, who felt a close friendship with Grimm, although the feelings were not reciprocal. Rousseau, Diderot, and Grimm entertained the fantasy of traveling together to Italy and were eventually to be joined by another companion, Etienne-Noël Damilaville—a friend of Voltaire. While Diderot's public life was thriving, tragedy hit on the domestic front. On 30 June 1750, his four-year-old son, François-Jacques, died of a fever. Diderot's son Denis Laurent, born on 29 July, died as well in December of the same year when his godmother dropped him on the steps of the church where he was to be baptized.

By then, Diderot was devoting all his energy to the *Encyclopédie*. On 28 June 1751, the *Discours préliminaire* (Preliminary Discourse) appeared in the first volume of the *Encyclopédie*. Chouillet believes that Diderot was well-acquainted with David Hume's *Philosophical Essays Concerning Human Understanding* (1748) and was also influenced by Francis Bacon's *De dignitate et augmentis scientiarum, sive instaurationis magnae* (1623, Of the Advancement and Proficiency of Learning), as explained in his *Observations sur la division des sciences du chancelier Bacon* (Observations Upon the Division of Sciences by Chancellor Bacon)—an essay in volume 1 (1751) of the *Encyclopédie* that follows almost exactly d'Alembert's *Discours préliminaire*.

The first volume of the *Encyclopédie* was a tremendous success: 2,075 volumes were immediately sold. Diderot deposited the copies in the home of either Chrétien Guillaume de Lamoignon de Malesherbes—then in control of the publishing industry—or in that of his father, Lamoignon de Blancmesnil, the minister of justice. Diderot's contributions to the volume included several articles translated from Robert James's *A Medicinal Dictionary* (1743–1745) and other pieces borrowed from the Jesuit *Journal de Trévoux*. The second volume appeared in January 1752 but was suppressed the following month by the State Council. Diderot had contributed more than 3,500 entries to these first two volumes. The first one infuriated the most conservative people because d'Alembert's *Discours préliminaire* presented similarities to the controversial doctoral thesis of Jean-Martin de Prades. After a ten-hour examination, Prades was granted his degree on 18 November

1751 in the midst of a serious scandal caused by his discredit of some Bible passages. Prades was forced to flee to Berlin, where he defended himself by writing two "apologies." Yet, the *Encyclopédie* was tacitly allowed to continue until May 1752. Although the Royal Privilege had been officially revoked, the last formalities of its application were not fully completed for a while. Thus, the work did not become illegal immediately, although the editors were held more accountable.

The challenge of outwitting the censors and the police gave the *Encyclopédie* an unusual character. Michel Butor describes the *Encyclopédie* as a "gigantic mystification" destined to defuse the censorship—an omnipresent concern in most of Diderot's writings. Another feature common to the *Encyclopédie* and to other writings by Diderot is the notion of authorship as partial contribution to a collective multidirectional work in progress.

In May 1752 Diderot returned to Langres to see his father and to share with his relatives the many reports of his successes. A few months later, his wife joined him and was equally well received. In the summer of that year, the Royal Academy of Music presented Giovanni Battista Pergolesi's *La Serva padrona* (1733, The Mistress Maid), which caused the "Quarrel of the Buffoons"—a clash between two musical factions. One, known as "the corner of the Queen," defended Italian melody; the other, "the corner of the King," supported the French harmonic system. The best representative of the latter group was Jean-Philippe Rameau, who followed the aristocratic tradition of his precursor and rival, Jean-Baptiste Lulli. On the opposite side, Grimm, Rousseau, and Diderot were partial to the "Italians" and thus angered Rameau, who spotlighted the mistakes in the musical articles of the *Encyclopédie*.

The *Suite de l'apologie de M. de l'abbé de Prades* (Sequel to the Apology of the Abbé de Prades), written by Diderot signing as Prades, and critical of both the Jansenists and the Jesuits, was printed in October 1752 without permission. Shortly thereafter, Rousseau's *Le Devin du village* (1756, The Village Soothsayer), composed in simple melodic lines and praised by Diderot, caused the first disagreement between the two friends. *Le Devin* had so pleased the king that he wanted to reward its composer and offered him a pension, which he declined, to Diderot's dismay. Diderot believed that Rousseau owed accepting the income to his family. The conflict reflects the two men's opposite personalities. Unlike Rousseau, Diderot was intent on earning a steady income and gaining respectability.

Following the birth of Diderot's daughter, Angélique, on 2 September 1753, the third volume of the *Encyclopédie* came out. It was to be the culmination of Rousseau's contribution to its articles on music. Diderot immediately published *De l'Interprétation de la nature* (1753, On the Interpretation of Nature), inspired by articles from the *Encyclopédie* ("Animal," for instance). In this work, Diderot intended to complement and comment on the articles of the *Encyclopédie* in a manner that he could not have done as editor of the monumental work. From October until December 1753, he returned to his roots in Langres, where he held the newborn child of the Caroillon family during his baptism, already anticipating the marriage of his daughter to this baby. Back in Paris, Diderot threatened to resign from the *Encyclopédie* unless he received a higher payment from the publisher. While the reply was late in coming, Diderot suspected that d'Alembert was undercutting him. By then, Diderot's relationship with his family was cordial. He proudly sent the fourth volume of the *Encyclopédie* to his father and obtained the post of tobacco warehouse keeper for his close friend, Nicolas Caroillon. Diderot was clearly attempting to assert himself socially and to use his influence and his family ties to ensure his daughter's future.

Evidently, Diderot was unable to stay away from controversy. In early 1754 he published three pamphlets related to the Quarrel of the Buffoons—*Arrêt rendu à l'amphithéâtre de l'Opéra* (Verdict Issued at the Amphitheater of the Opera), *Au Petit Prophète de Boehmischbroda* (To the Little Prophet of Boehmischbroda), and *Les Trois Chapitres, ou la vision de la nuit du mardi-gras au mercredi des cendres* (The Three Chapters or The Vision of the Night from Mardi Gras to Ash Wednesday)—and an augmented edition of *De l'Interprétation de la nature* titled *Pensées sur l'interprétation de la nature* (Thoughts on the Interpretation of Nature), reprinted three times that year. In this work, he advocated the abandonment of the mathematical model and promoted the use of imagination, at the risk of displeasing even further his partner, d'Alembert, by proclaiming that mathematics was an exhausted science that had been brought to perfection but would now be dethroned by chemists, physicists, and naturalists. Enthusiastic about the sciences, Diderot undertook the study of chemistry with Guillaume François Rouelle for four years.

Better off financially now, Diderot moved to rue Taranne in 1755 and undertook to write *Histoire et secret de la peinture en cire* (1755? The History and Secret of Wax Painting). It revealed Jean-Jacques Bachelier's personal technique, which the latter had hoped to keep secret in the hope of selling it to other painters. Diderot justified this disservice to a friend on the grounds that secrecy is reprehensible and that the goal of the *Encyclopédie* was to spread knowledge. The fifth volume of that collective work crowned the effort of at least 142

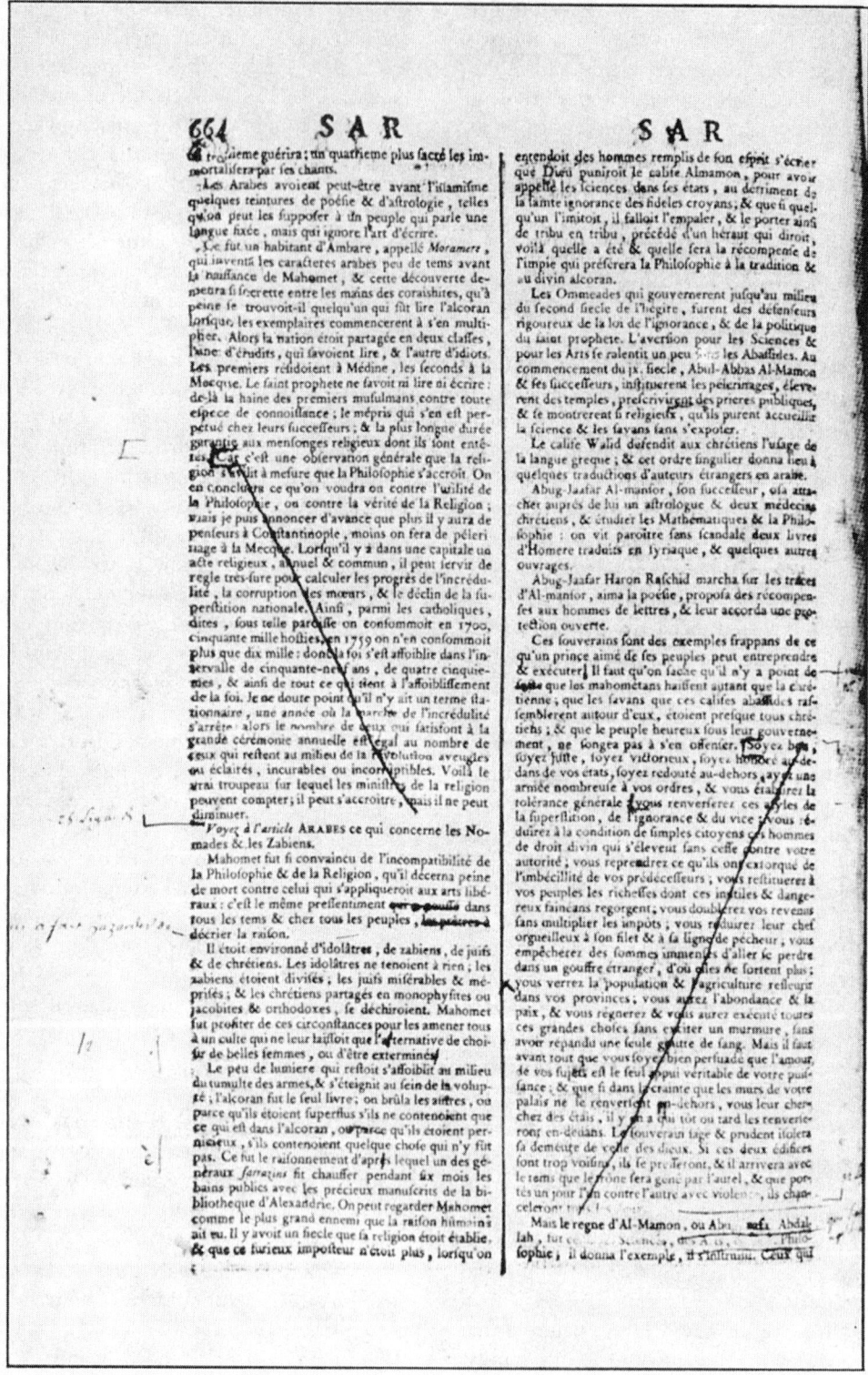

Diderot's article "Saracens" in the Encyclopédie, *from which André-François Le Breton, the publisher, had eliminated parts without Diderot's knowledge (from George Remington Havens,*
The Age of Ideas, *1955; Collection of W. Ross)*

contributors. Diderot wrote the article "encyclopédie" as a parallel to d'Alembert's *Discours préliminaire* in the first volume. He pointed to the weakness of the work and regretted that the topic of language had not been as expertly treated as the subject of grammar.

In late 1755 or early 1756, Diderot met for the first time Louise-Henriette Volland, better known as Sophie Volland. They started to see each other regularly, on Thursday and Sunday. Whether or not the relationship was sexual is not known. Meanwhile, work on the *Encyclopédie* was proceeding with the publication of the sixth volume in 1756, followed the next year by *Le Fils naturel, ou les épreuves de la vertu* (1757; translated as *Dorval; or The Test of Virtue*, 1767), a drama advocating that a father should recognize a child born to him by a woman other than his wife and should include him as one of his heirs. Such a claim brought Diderot a letter of reprimand from his own father and offended Rousseau. *Le Fils naturel* is probably based on Carlo Goldoni's play *Il vero amico* (1750, The True Friend), itself inspired by Molière's *L'Avare* (1668, The Miser). The illegitimate son recognized by his father is also a theme treated by Pierre Claude Nivelle de la Chaussée in *Mélanide* (1741). Grimm and other friends helped Diderot to revise his play. In the *Conversations sur le fils naturel,* which accompanied the publication of Diderot's first play, he proposed a new genre that combined both tragedy and comedy, two official genres devoted respectively to noble characters and bourgeois foibles. The "serious comedy" of Diderot has the moral vocation of a comedy, but instead of ridiculing ordinary people, it strives to elicit compassion in the audience by identifying with ordinary characters portrayed in a positive manner. Ken-ichi Sasaki describes the deep involvement that Diderot hoped to create in the spectators as "spontaneous participation," or a desire to intervene.

In October 1757, Louise d'Epinay traveled to Geneva with her husband and her son because Rousseau refused to accompany her on that trip. Instead, he was busy courting her sister-in-law, Sophie d'Houdetot, with whom he used to take afternoon promenades. This incident brought Diderot's relationship with Rousseau to an end, although both met once again in December of that year. In his memoirs, Jean-François Marmontel relates that shortly thereafter he encountered Diderot, who reportedly found the meeting with his former friend to be cordial. However, the same incident is described as confrontational in Louise d'Epinay's memoirs. The difference in viewpoints is undoubtedly a result of the influence of Grimm and Diderot, whose memory of the incident must have soured after the relationship between the two philosophes had deteriorated even further. Until then, Epinay had ably avoided getting involved in the disputes between Rousseau and Diderot, although Diderot discouraged Grimm from pursuing his relationship with Epinay and tended to avoid her himself. Other factors may have contributed to the strained relationship between the former friends. Rousseau was disappointed that Diderot preferred Grimm to him. On the other hand, Diderot objected to Rousseau's attempt to break up d'Houdetot's relationship with her lover, their mutual friend Jean-François de Saint-Lambert. Everyone agreed that Rousseau was morally reprehensible in courting the absent Saint-Lambert's mistress while he was on call in the army.

Other friendships of Diderot's youth were beginning to erode. Around mid November 1757, d'Alembert's article "Genève" in the *Encyclopédie* caused a scandal and offended Protestant ministers. D'Alembert attributed a philosophical tolerance to these ministers that they disavowed vehemently. Diderot had to apologize on behalf of his co-editor to his good friend Theodore Tronchin of Geneva, a pastor. A month later, Diderot's candidacy for a seat in the French Academy of Science was rejected by the king in favor of that of Jacques de Vaucanson—a decision that may have been influenced by the outrage caused by the article in question.

Wounded in battle, Saint-Lambert returned to Paris and visited Diderot. Evidently, Rousseau had complied with his friend's advice to temper the relationship with d'Houdetot and withdrew to new dwellings. Unwisely, but trustingly, Diderot reported the liaison to Saint-Lambert, resulting in d'Houdetot's immediate termination of her relationship with Rousseau. Now, the antagonism between the two philosophes peaked.

The rising discord among the many former friends contributed to increase the controversial reception of the *Encyclopédie* and the accusations against its editors. For instance, when Claude Adrien Helvétius published *De l'Esprit* (1758, On the Mind), its privilege was soon revoked among claims that Diderot had written the most objectionable parts. The thesis of an Encyclopedists' plot against government and religion was developed by Abraham Chaumeix. In September 1758, Rousseau denounced d'Alembert's article "Genève," maintaining that theater is an immoral genre that the Swiss had rightfully banned in their country. He also discredited Diderot's effort to create a moral theater in such plays as *Le Père de famille*. In October, Chaumeix published his *Préjugés légitimes contre l'Encyclopédie et essai de réfutation contre ce dictionnaire* (1758, Legitimate Prejudices against the Encyclopedia and Essay on the Refutation against this Dictionary). Within four months the *Préjugés* grew into an eight-volume

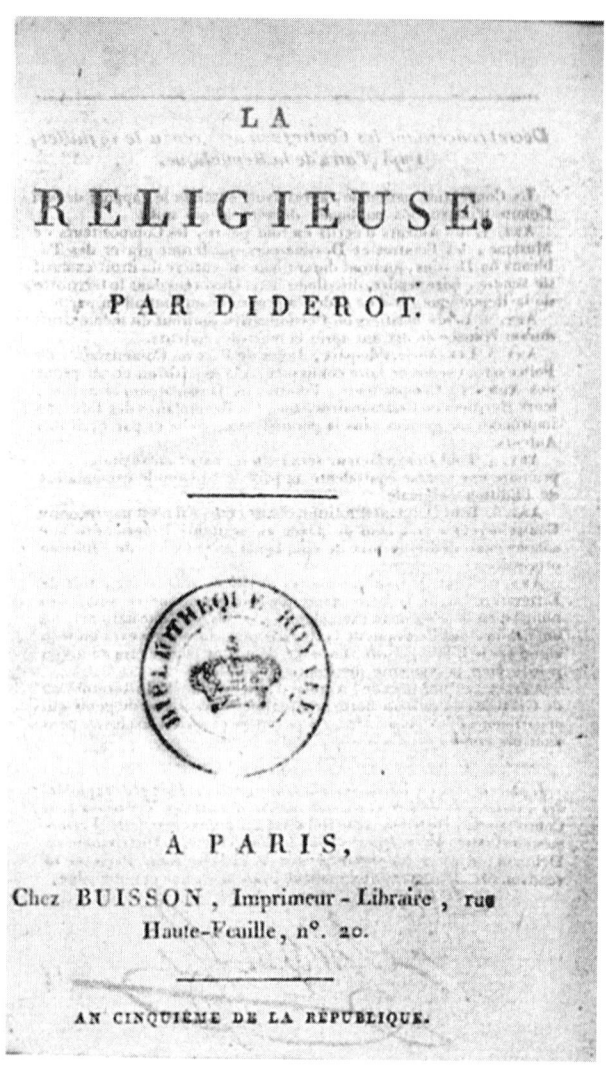

Title page from Diderot's posthumously published novel based on the life of his sister, a nun (Bibliothèque nationale; from Georges May, Diderot et "La Religieuse": Etude historique et littéraire, 1954; Thomas Cooper Library, University of South Carolina)

series. Soon thereafter the *Encyclopédie* was suspended by the Paris Parliament, condemned by the Pope, and its privilege revoked by the King's Council. Publication of the volumes of engravings continued, however, thanks to the protection of the lawyer Chrétien Guillaume de Lamoignon de Malherbes. Meanwhile, Diderot was developing a new interest. Encouraged by his friends baron d'Holbach and Grimm to visit the art exhibit sponsored by the king, he started to write his *Salons* series, which later inspired Beaudelaire's art criticism.

Complications with the *Encyclopédie* were endless. Elie Catherine Fréron accused the Encyclopedists of plagiarism and prompted the Academy of Sciences to launch an investigation in order to find out whether plates by naturalist René Antoine de Réaumur had been scavenged. The commission found the accusation false, and Fréron had to print the denial in his journal. The incident had some positive impact, though, as it led to much-needed support for Diderot from the authorities. Nevertheless, more accusations followed. Charles Palissot's popular play *Les Philosophes* (1760, The Philosophers), which parodied some of the most famous philosophers, was falsely attributed to Diderot and caused quite a stir. The counterattack by abbé André Morellet led to his imprisonment, while Diderot found disproving his authorship of the infamous play extremely difficult.

La Religieuse, perhaps Diderot's most famous and most controversial novel, inspired by the true story of his sister, was written in 1760, although not published until 1796 because of its subjects. From infidelity and abuse of parental authority to lesbianism and corruption in the convents, the issues discussed were shocking, although not unrealistic. That year was indeed a productive one for Diderot. He edited *Leçons de clavecin et principes d'harmonie* (1771, Lessons for the Harpsichord and Principles of Harmony) by German harpsichord composer Anton Bemetzrieder, maintained a prolific correspondence with Volland, and wrote a 1760 French adaptation of Edward Moore's 1753 domestic tragedy, *The Gamester,* which was turned down by the Comédie Française. According to Chouillet, the play was counter to French *bienséances* (decency rules) and may have prompted Diderot to remove Dorval's suicide scene from his own play, *Le Fils naturel.*

On the attack again, Fréron, pretending to be Goldoni, wrote a letter protesting Diderot's plagiarism (*Le Père de famille*), of his play by the same title, *Padre di famiglia* (1750, The Father of the Family), but on a different theme. Diderot asked two contributors to the *Encyclopédie,* Alexandre Deleyre and Francis Véron de Forbonnais, to translate Goldoni's plays into French in order to exonerate him.

The idea for *Le Neveu de Rameau* was probably conceived in April 1761, perhaps to overcome Diderot's sadness following his father's death. The character Lui may have been inspired by abbé Ferdinando Galiani. To recover from his many setbacks, Diderot and Volland undertook to read Samuel Richardson's *Clarissa* (1747) in English, and then played at composing a novel inspired by Richardson's through an exchange of letters that also involved Sophie's younger sister, Mme Le Gendre. Upon the death of Richardson on 14 July 1761, Diderot was inspired to write his well-known *Eloge de Richardson* (Praise of Richardson), which appeared the following year in the *Journal étranger*. At Grimm's behest, Diderot wrote the *Salon de 1761* (The 1761 Salon), which Grimm himself extensively revised. Not only did Grimm censor the piece–perhaps having found its tone either too free or insolent–but he also took the liberty to add to it and, furthermore, neglected to pay his friend in the name of friendship. Lack of income made 1761 a year of great financial difficulty for Diderot because of the suspension of the *Encyclopédie,* the final volumes of which appeared secretly. However, in January 1762 the first volume of engravings was published. Diderot considered this part of the enterprise one of its most valuable aspects because, for the first time, it demonstrated the complexity of manual and mechanical work.

On the private front, the relationship with Sophie Volland was beginning to take a turn for the worse, and the correspondence stopped for two and a half years. In the meantime, Diderot's wife became ill, and he received an invitation from the just-crowned Russian tsarina, Catherine II, which he turned down. On the literary front, activities continued, with the publication of the second volume of illustrations of engravings, and the *Salon de 1763,* published in the *Revue de Paris;* he was the only critic to admire young Joseph Marie Vien's paintings of "antiquities." He also wrote *La Lettre sur le commerce de la librairie* (Letter on the Commerce of Bookstores), published nearly a century later in 1861.

British presence in France increased following the signing of the peace treaty between the two countries in February 1763 and led to Diderot's encounters with several prominent Englishmen. Among others, he dined with Horace Walpole and met actor David Garrick, a guest of Helvétius; David Hume, whose writings he admired; and John Wilkes, a friend of Holbach. Diderot, having read Laurence Sterne's *Tristram Shandy* (1759–1767) the previous year and labeling him an "English Rabelais," particularly enjoyed hearing Sterne preach at the chapel of the English Embassy in Paris.

While reviewing one of his articles under the letter *s,* Diderot accidentally discovered that his good friend, publisher André-François Le Breton, had eliminated parts of the article. Upon further examination, Diderot found that the last ten volumes had been haphazardly censored. Diderot's disappointment was enormous; he had spent countless hours carefully editing the work of nearly 270 contributors, and he learned that the damage was permanent because Le Breton had burned the manuscripts. Grimm reported in the *Correspondance littéraire* in 1771 that Diderot worried seriously about complaints of authors and clients.

In 1765, Catherine II's friendship with Diderot led to the purchase of his library and later to an offer of additional money to acquire his manuscripts. Diderot declined the extra funds, believing that the manuscripts should go to the tsarina as part of the initial library purchase. Meanwhile, his circle of friends grew to include painters Louis-Michel Van Loo and Jean-Baptiste Greuze, whom he particularly admired, while he was working on the *Salon de 1765* under the guidance of sculptor Etienne Maurice Falconet. In this work, Diderot analyzed the dreamy imagination reflected in a painting by Jean Honoré Fragonard and incorporated notes on the young painter Philibert Benoît de La Rue. By then, Diderot had mastered the vocabulary of painting, as explained by Claude-Henri Watelet in the *Encyclopédie,* and was even able to invent new adjectives, such as "cotonneux" (cottony). By mid year, correspondence with Sophie Volland resumed, and a series of letters on posterity were exchanged with Falconet. In fact, identical passages can be found in the correspondence with both Volland and Falconet.

In January 1766, the last ten volumes of the *Encyclopédie* were delivered to foreign subscribers and covertly transmitted to Parisian clients. However, publisher Le Breton could not escape punishment for delivering the volumes in Versailles; he was locked up in the Bastille prison for a week. Puisieux's name is listed first among the contributors to the *Encyclopédie,* a common courtesy to women in that era. In February of that year, nineteen-year-old Jean-François de la Barre was tortured and executed for having kept his hat on while a religious procession was going by. This event triggered a campaign of persecution against the Encyclopedists that prompted Voltaire to advise Diderot to flee France. Diderot wrote back to express his appreciation for his friend's strong defense of chevalier de la Barre but decided to remain in the country and contributed to the funds collected for the victim's family.

Early in 1766 Diderot annotated Cesare Beccaria's *Traité des délits et des peines* (An Essay on Crimes and Punishments), and in July he finished the *Essais sur la peinture* (Essays on Painting), which were published in various issues of the *Correspondance littéraire.* On the last day of October, Catherine II issued Diderot a pension that was to last for the next fifty years. With great enthusiasm, Diderot sent her Falconet to sculpt an equestrian statue known as "the Bronze Horseman," which later inspired Aleksandr Pushkin's poem by the same title. With equal ardor, Diderot recommended Pierre Paul le Mercier de La Rivière as a man of great talent. However, accompanied by his wife and his mistress, de La Rivière behaved in odd ways and eventually left the Russian court in disgrace.

Following his brother's promotion as canon of the cathedral of Langres in 1767, Diderot became an associate at the Imperial Academy of Arts in St. Petersburg. Catherine II suggested that he direct a Russian encyclopedia. In September, Diderot wrote the *Salon de*

Page from the manuscript of Diderot's La Religieuse *(The Nun), 1796 (Bibliothèque nationale; from Roselyne De Ayala and Jean-Pierre Gueno, eds.,* Belles Lettres: Manuscripts by the Masters of French Literature, *2001; Collection of Matthew J. Bruccoli)*

1767, preceded by aesthetic considerations in which he claimed that illusion is essential to painting: it should represent nature with artistic truth. This idea contributed to a reevaluation of classic aesthetics because it suggested that art creates an ideal beauty not found in nature. Charles Batteux and Johann Joachim Winckelmann may have influenced Diderot along these lines. The *Salon de 1767* is well-known for Diderot's invitation to the onlookers to step into the painting and take a tour of the painted landscape. The poetic depiction of seven landscapes by Joseph Vernet is known as the "Vernet promenade." In his review of Hubert Robert's ruins, Diderot comments on the effect of time on human artifacts.

In December 1768, Charles Joseph Panckouke and Jean Dessaint, both Freemasons, purchased the right to publish future editions of the *Encyclopédie* from Le Breton. Even before the full publication of the first edition, they were already planning a new, revised, and augmented edition. The battle of the *Encyclopédie* was now becoming entirely commercial, with international ramifications concerning copies, summaries, and adaptations. Disillusionment followed with what Diderot once considered his most valuable contribution to posterity. He expressed his feelings in *Regrets sur ma vieille robe de chambre* (1772, Regrets for My Old Dressing-Gown), published in Grimm's *Correspondance littéraire*. Diderot claimed to be ill at ease in the new luxurious robe offered to him by his friend Marie-Thérèse Geoffrin, a symbol of his new hard-earned social status, and more comfortable in the old garment that more accurately fit his true identity.

In September 1769, Diderot completed *Le Rêve de d'Alembert* (D'Alembert's Dream; published in volume 4 of *Mémoires, correspondance et ouvrages inédits,* 1831), in which he affirmed that science is always evolving in a changing universe. It also gave a certain importance to the "truth" of dreams, which should be explored more seriously. The message did not carry over well with d'Alembert, who recommended the manuscript be burned. Diderot pretended to comply but obviously did not. In *Le Rêve de d'Alembert,* Diderot appears as a precursor to Jean-Baptiste Pierre Antoine de Monet de Lamarck and Charles Darwin.

Diderot also edited Galiani's *Dialogues sur le commerce des blés* (1770, Dialogues on the Commerce of Wheat), which forewarned of possible famine resulting from the application of Galiani's economic theory, then favored by the government. Galiani was expelled from France, but Diderot remained faithful to his friend and published his work. In a letter to Volland dated 31 August 1769, Diderot reports being visited by Panckouke, who proposed an offer to collaborate on future editions of the *Encyclopédie;* infuriated at such an idea, Diderot threw the publisher out.

Also in 1769 a legal procedure was launched against the *Encyclopédie* by Pierre Joseph François Luneau de Boisjermain, who was the only customer to have repeatedly sued on the ground that the work was "not what he expected." His action may have been prompted by his knowledge of Le Breton's manipulations of the text. The *Salon de 1769* and *Garrick ou les acteurs anglais* (Garrick or English Actors) were also written the same year. In August and September, Diderot traveled to Langres and on to Bourbonne in the company of Jeanne Catherine de Maux and her daughter, Cécile de Pruneveaux. During the trip, Diderot witnessed Maux's attraction to a new lover, thus signaling the end of his affair with her. These travels are described in *Voyage de Langres* (Voyage to Langres) and *Voyage de Bourbonne* (Voyage to Bourbonne), both of which were written in 1770 and published in 1831. He undertook to write *Les Deux Amis de Bourbonne* (1770, Two Friends from Bourbonne), meant to be read as a real exchange of letters between different people, and to contrast with Saint-Lambert's exotic fantasy *Les Deux Amis, conte iroquois* (1770, The Two Friends: A Tale of the Iroquois).

Diderot continued to devote himself mostly to writing by composing additions to the *Pensées philosophiques,* a tragedy in prose titled *Les Pères malheureux* (The Unhappy Fathers; collected in volume 8 of the 1875 reprint of *Oeuvres complètes,* edited by Jules Assézat and Maurice Tourneux) inspired by a drama by his Zurich friend Salomon Gessner, and *Entretien d'un père avec ses enfants* (1771, Conversation of a Father with his Children). In December 1770, Diderot and the English musicologist Charles Burney met with great reciprocal pleasure. A few days later, at the annual New Year's Eve party hosted by the Holbachs, Diderot presented "Les Eleuthéromanes" (1771, The Maniacs for Freedom, collected in volume 9 of the *Oeuvres complètes* [1875]), a text including strident words against priests and kings. Not long afterward, he wrote *L'Apologie de l'abbé Galiani* (In Praise of abbé Galiani), in response to Morellet's criticism of Galiani's work. This letter was published first in the February issue of the *Gazette littéraire des deux-ponts* (Literary Gazette of the Two-Bridges), then in the June edition of the *Mercure de France.* The September 1771 issue of the *Correspondance littéraire* included a review of the lessons for the harpsichord that Diderot had edited for Bemetzrieder. It followed the completion of *Principes philosophiques sur la matière et le mouvement* (Philosophical Principles on Matter and Motion), which was first published in volume 2 of the *Oeuvres complètes* (1875). A first version of *Jacques le fataliste* (Jacques the Fatalist) was also nearing com-

Diderot in old age (from Jeannette Rosso, Diderot et le portrait, *1998; Perkins Library, Duke University)*

pletion, as well as *Ceci n'est pas un conte* (This Is Not a Story). *De l'Inconséquence du jugement public* (On the Inconsistency of Public Opinion Regarding Our Private Actions) was about the fickleness of public opinion, and its role in establishing reputation, it was originally published in *Oeuvres,* edited by Jacques-André Naigeon (1797 or 1798).

The year 1772 brought relief with the publication of the last volumes of illustrations of the *Encyclopédie,* as Diderot no longer feared the censorship. He collaborated with the abbé Thomas François Raynal on *L'Histoire des deux Indes* (1977, The History of Both Indias), in which he expressed best his political thoughts, while preparing his daughter's wedding to Abel Caroillon. The contractual details of the marriage had been difficult and long in the making, from 1770 to 1772. Repeatedly, the future son-in-law aroused Diderot's indignation because of his resistance to share his fortune with his wife. Meanwhile, Diderot provided his daughter with a dowry of 30,000 livres, in addition to another 30,000 livres he was to receive from the Associated Book Sellers. Diderot worried over the haggling by his in-laws. He expressed his misgivings about the fate of married women in a letter to his daughter on 13 September 1772, while "Sur les femmes" (About Women), published in the *Correspondance littéraire* (1772) probably inspired by the events preceding the marriage, highlighted women's economic dependence on men and their ensuing submission to them. Diderot's wife was not well disposed toward the new couple, and Didier-Pierre Diderot disowned his niece for marrying a man he considered to be a "non-believer." Diderot maintained his relationship with the newlyweds and visited them so assiduously that he was ultimately advised to limit the visits. Perhaps he was somewhat jealous of his son-in-law.

Unpleasant developments ensued as texts he had not written were published under his name, while those he wrote were attributed to other writers. Among those including works claiming to be by Diderot are the six-volume *Oeuvres philosophiques de Mr D**** (1772, The Philosophical Works of Mr. D***), and the five-volume *Collection complète des oeuvres philosophiques, littéraires et dramatiques de M. D.* (1773, A Complete Collection of the Philosophical, Literary, and Dramatic Works of M.D.).

From April until June 1773, Diderot was preparing for his journey to Russia and entrusted his manuscripts to Naigeon. On 11 June, Diderot left Paris for The Hague, where he was hosted by Prince Dimitri-Alexievitch Galitzin at the Russian embassy. There, he completed the *Satire première* (First Satire; first published in the *Correspondance littéraire,* 1778), the *Réfutation de l'ouvrage d'Helvétius intitulé l'homme* (The Refutation of Helvétius's Work Called Man; first published in the *Correspondance littéraire* in 1750, and the first draft of *Paradoxe sur le comédien* (The Paradox of Acting), which was published for the first time in 1830. *Réfutation de l'ouvrage d'Helvétius intitulé l'homme* was inspired by Condillac. On 20 August 1773, Diderot left The Hague, visited the Dresden gallery on 3 September, and arrived in Saint Petersburg on 8 October, about twenty days after Grimm.

Diderot was admitted to speak daily with Catherine II, raising envy, suspicion, and coolness in the people he encountered at her court. Eventually, the visits with the tsarina became weekly, while Grimm met less publicly with her. Diderot experienced great difficulty while collecting minerals and talcum to take back to French scientists. He was able to obtain only the requests he had submitted in writing upon arrival. Elected to the St. Petersburg Academy of Science, he read a memoir concerning Siberia on 1 November, a few months before leaving Russia on 5 March 1774. During his return trip, Diderot nearly drowned in a river and changed carriages four times, as three broke along the way. In the spring of 1774, Grimm published the second installment of Diderot's *Supplément au voyage de Bougainville* (Supplement to the Voyage of Bougainville) in the *Correspondance littéraire,* after printing the first half in the previous fall issue. The piece is traditionally interpreted as a way of linking sexuality to politics. Diderot also expressed concern for reproduction—he falsely perceived a decline in the birth rate and feared a high rate of infant mortality. Conversely, he also feared overpopulation, which he thought fostered wars over territorial rights.

While in Hamburg on 30 March 1774, Diderot wrote to Carl Philipp Emanuel Bach, Johann Sebastian Bach's son, in order to obtain copies of the composer's music for his daughter. Again, he avoided Berlin as he had done on the way to Russia, and thus irritated Frederick II. From April until mid October, Diderot remained in Holland, where he wrote *Entretien d'un philosophe avec la Maréchale* (A Philosophical Conversation), signed "Crudeli," and published a year later in the *Correspondance littéraire,* and *Principes de politique des souverains* (Political principles of sovereigns; published in *Oeuvres complètes,* 1875–1877). He also started to draft *Observations sur le Nakaz* (1986, Observations on the Nakaz) and *Eléments de physiologie* (1960, Elements of Physiology), while taking notes for the *Voyage en Hollande* (Journey through Holland; first published in *Oeuvres inédites de D. Diderot,* 1821) and trying to establish a blueprint for a Russian encyclopedia. His hosts in Holland found him changed and melancholic. On 21 October, Diderot was back in Paris.

His legs and his chest were beginning to hurt after the long journey. He had lost his illusions about northern governments in Russia and Holland. In mid year, he sent to Catherine II his *Plan d'une université pour le gouvernement de Russie* (Outline of a University for the Government of Russia; published in volume 22 of his *Œuvres* [1798]), in which he recommended prizes and competitions to encourage excellence and expressed concern for the education of abandoned children and orphans. His education plans wavered between two poles: training of good workers and honest citizens, on the one hand, and fostering talent and genius on the other. *Salon de 1775* (published in the *Revue de Paris* [1857]) and *Pensées détachées sur la peinture, la sculpture, l'architecture, la poésie* (Thoughts on Painting, Sculpture, Architecture, and Poetry; published in *Oeuvres* [1798]) followed later that year.

In 1776, the *Principes de politique des souverains* appeared in *Correspondance secrète politique et littéraire* (Secret Political and Literary Correspondence) by François Métra. Diderot retired from Paris, where the philosophes seemed to be in favor with the new king and his government. Jacques Necker followed Anne-Robert-Jacques Turgot as minister of finance; Jean Baptiste Antoine Suard married Panckouke's sister and was elected to the French Academy; and Diderot's own daughter was now protected by Suzanne Necker. Diderot spent five months in Sèvres as the guest of jeweler Etienne Belle and one month at Grandval, hosted by the Holbachs. He compiled several texts that he intended to include in his novel *Jacques le fataliste et son maître,* inspired by Miguel de Cervantes and Sterne. The American Revolution hardened Diderot's political views, according to Philip Nicholas Furbank. Back in Sèvres the next year, he worked with Raynal on *L'Histoire des deux Indes* and on *La Pièce et le prologue* (1771, The Play and the Prologue), which later developed into *Est-il bon? Est-il méchant?* (1834, Is he Good? Is he Wicked?). In May 1777, Jean-Baptiste Pigalle unveiled a bust he had made of Diderot, attesting to the public recognition he had gained, and became the godfather of Diderot's granddaughter.

In November 1778 the Freemason lodge of "the nine sisters" invited Diderot, d'Alembert, and Antoine Nicolas de Condorcet to join its ranks. The three men declined, although Voltaire accepted this honor less than two months before his death. Meanwhile, Diderot continued to work on the *Essai sur la vie et les écrits de Sénèque* (1779, Essay on the Life of Seneca the Philosopher), which introduced the seventh volume of this ancient author's works to a French readership. He also reworked *Le Neveu de Rameau* (Rameau's Nephew), which became known first through Goethe's translation (*Rameaus Neffe,* 1805), prior to their being translated from German into French by Joseph Hern de Saur and Léonce de Saint-Geniès in 1821.

In 1780 Diderot shared some of his thoughts on his own works with Jakob Heinrich Meister, who had replaced Grimm as publisher of the *Correspondance littéraire.* Diderot viewed the digressions in *Jacques le fataliste et son maître* as a counterpart to *La Religieuse,* which was based on a Racinian model of tragedy, having only one main character. The *Lettre apologétique de l'abbé Raynal à M. Grimm* (Apologetic Letter from the abbé Raynal to Mr. Grimm) that Diderot wrote in 1781 was never sent to the baron because it revealed his deep resentment toward an ungrateful friend. In order to oppose its publication, Grimm feigned to ignore that Diderot co-authored *L'Histoire des deux Indes* with Raynal. In this book Diderot reflects on the evil of human nature, especially in its mass slaughter of colonized peoples. Resolutely anticolonial, *L'Histoire des deux Indes* was condemned by the Parliament of Paris, and Raynal was pursued by the police, actions that led him to flee to Switzerland. Its co-author, Diderot, was

Diderot's burial site, the Church of Saint-Roch, Paris. His body was displaced during the French Revolution (from Arthur M. Wilson, Diderot, *1972; Collection of W. Ross).*

recognized by the Antiquarian Society of Scotland and made one of its honorary members.

The triumph of Jacques-Louis David, who exhibited for the first time in the Royal Academic show, Salon de 1781, was a vindication for Diderot, who had expressed appreciation for the taste of the classics as early as 1763. Diderot's publication of the text titled *Salon 1781* was first published in the *Revue de Paris* in 1857. Consecration peaked when Diderot's bust sculpted by Jean Antoine Houdon was placed at the Langres city hall above a complete set of the *Encyclopédie*. Although the mayor's report of the ceremony deeply touched Diderot, Chouillet found evidence that the town had been deserted by uncooperative citizens that day, leading the authorities to bring a delegation of schoolchildren to fill the halls. While being honored in his hometown, Diderot was chastised by King Louis XVI in Paris for having published the *Essai sur les règnes de Claude et de Néron* (Essay on the Reigns of Claudius and Nero) in the *Mercure de France* collected in his *Oeuvres* in 1797 or 1798. Diderot completed his *Additions à la lettre sur les aveugles* (Additions to the Letter on the Blind, published in volume 1 of his *Oeuvres complètes* in 1875) and *Eléments de physiologie* (Elements of Physiology, published in volume 9 of his *Oeuvres complètes* in 1875) prior to the summer of 1781, when his wife's health and his own were deteriorating.

A revised version of *Essai sur les règnes de Claude et de Néron,* published in 1782, caused more problems with royal censorship. The chief of police, Jean Charles Pierre Le Noir, a good friend of Diderot, demanded that he write a letter disavowing the book's thesis and promising never to write controversial works for the remainder of his life. Meanwhile, Diderot paid a team of copyists to make triplicate copies of the final versions of his works to be kept in the care of his daughter, of Catherine II, and of the *Correspondance littéraire*.

In February 1784, Diderot suffered a stroke. A few days later, Sophie Volland died, followed two months later by Diderot's granddaughter, Marie-Anne Caroillon de Vandeul (Minette) at the age of eleven. This second death was not revealed to him because of his poor health and dejected state of mind following Volland's death. On 19 July 1784, Diderot moved to a hotel in Bezons to a room provided by Catherine II through Grimm. On the last day of that month he died while eating a compote of cherry and conversing with his wife. He was buried the next day according to Catholic rites in the church of Saint-Roch.

Despite efforts to safeguard his work for posterity, many of Diderot's manuscripts have been lost. He relied on his daughter and his friend and disciple Naigeon to preserve his works. His daughter eventually went through a mystical crisis, and the deteriorated "Vandeul manuscripts" were found years later in the home of descendants who, by then, had become part of the conservative establishment and were unwilling to publicize their ties to an embarrassing ancestor. Naigeon tried to control the damage to Diderot's reputation by withholding publication of several texts. *Les Pages contre un tyran* (1771) were discovered by Franco Venturi in 1937 in manuscript 6203 of the Bibliothèque Nationale. *L'Apologie de l'abbé Galiani* was found by Herbert Dieckman in 1948–1951 in the Vandeul collection. Despite his wavering fate throughout the years, Diderot remains a powerful symbolic figure of the Enlightenment.

Letters:

"Letters to Sophie Volland," in *Mémoires, correspondance et ouvrages inédits de Diderot* (Paris: Paulin, 1830–1831); augmented by André Babelon (Paris: Gallimard, 1930); translated by Peter France as *Diderot's Letters to Sophie Volland: A Selection* (London: Oxford University Press, 1972);

Correspondance inédite, 2 volumes, edited by André Babelon (Paris: Gallimard, 1931);

Correspondance, 16 volumes, edited by Georges Roth and Jean Varloot (Paris: Editions de Minuit, 1955–1970).

Bibliographies:

Herbert Dieckmann, *Inventaire du fonds Vandeul et inédits de Diderot* (Geneva: Droz / Lille: Giard, 1951);

Jean de Booy, "Inventaire provisoire des contributions de Diderot à la *Correspondance littéraire,*" *Dix-huitième Siècle,* 1 (1969): 353–397;

Alexandre Cioranescu, *Bibliographie de la littérature française du 18e siècle,* volume 1 (Paris: CNRS, 1969);

Frederick A. Spears, *Bibliographie de Diderot. Répertoire analytique international,* 2 volumes (Geneva: Droz, 1980);

Spears, *Bibliographie de Diderot: répertoire analytique international, 1976–1986* (Geneva: Droz, 1988);

Spears, "Bibliographie de Diderot, supplément no. 7," *Diderot Studies,* 27 (1998): 181–222;

David Adams, *Bibliographie des oeuvres de Denis Diderot 1739–1900,* 2 volumes (Paris & Ferney-Voltaire: Centre international d'études du XVIIIe siècle, 2000).

Biographies:

Charles Avzac-Lavigne, *Diderot et la société du baron d'Holbach* (Paris, 1875; Geneva: Slatkine Reprints, 1970);

Franco Venturi, *La Jeunesse de Diderot, 1713–1753,* translated from the Italian by Juliette Bertrand (Paris: Skira, 1939; Geneva: Slatkine, 1967);

André Billy, *Diderot* (Paris: Gallimard, 1943);

Charly Guyot, *Diderot par lui-même* (Paris: Le Seuil, 1966);

René Pomeau, *Diderot, sa vie, son oeuvre* (Paris: Presses universitaires de France, 1967);

Arthur M. Wilson, *Diderot* (New York: Oxford University Press, 1972);

Jacques Chouillet, *Diderot* (Paris: Société d'édition d'enseignement supérieur, 1977);

John Hope Mason, *The Irresistible Diderot* (London, Melbourne & New York: Quartet, 1982);

Alice M. Laborde, *Diderot et Mme de Puisieux,* Stanford French and Italian Studies, no. 36 (Saratoga, Cal.: Anma Libri, 1984);

Peter France & Anthony Strugnell, eds., *Diderot, les dernières années. 1770–1784* (Edinburgh: Edinburgh University Press, 1985);

Pierre Lepape, *Diderot* (Paris: Flammarion, 1991);

Philip Nicholas Furbank, *Diderot: A Critical Biography* (London: Secker & Warburg, 1992).

References:

Paul Benhamou, "La guerre de Palissot contre Diderot," in *Les Ennemis de Diderot,* edited by Anne-Marie Chouillet (Mayenne: Klincksieck, 1993), pp. 17–30;

Jean Th. de Booy, *Denis Diderot. Ecrits inconnus de jeunesse I: 1737–1744,* Studies on Voltaire and the Eighteenth Century, no. 119 (Oxford: Voltaire Foundation, 1974);

Daniel Brewer, *The Discourse of Enlightenment in Eighteenth-Century France. Diderot and the Art of Philosophizing* (Cambridge: Cambridge University Press, 1993);

Else Marie Bukdahl, "Diderot est-il l'auteur du Salon de 1771?" in *Diderot Salons,* volume 4 of "Héros et martyrs," text established by E.-M. Bukdahl, Michel Delon, D. Khan, and A. Lorenceau, 99 illustrations (Paris: Hermann, 1995), pp. 121–129;

Jacques Chouillet, *Diderot–Sophie Volland: un dialogue à une voix* (Paris: Champion, 1986);

Chouillet, *La Formation des idées esthétiques de Diderot, 1745–1763* (Paris: Armand Colin, 1973);

Lester G. Crocker, *The Embattled Philosopher* (New York: Free Press / London: Collier-Macmillan, 1966);

Charles Dédéyan, *Diderot et la pensée anglaise* (Florence, Italy: L. S. Olschki, 1987);

Herbert Dieckmann, "Les contributions de Diderot à la *Correspondance littéraire* et à *L'Histoire des deux Indes,*" *Revue d'Histoire littéraire de la France* (1951): 417–440;

Dieckmann, "L'Epopée du fonds Vandeul," *Revue d'Histoire littéraire de la France* (1985): 963–977;

Otis Fellows, *Diderot* (Boston: Twayne, 1977);

Peter France, *Rhetoric and Truth in France: Descartes to Diderot* (London: Oxford University Press, 1972);

George Remington Havens, *The Age of Ideas* (New York: Holt, 1955);

Michel Lioure, *Le Drame de Diderot à Ionesco* (Paris: Armand Colin, 1973);

Stéphane Lojkine, "*Le Fils naturel,* de la tragédie de l'inceste à l'imaginaire du continu," in *Diderot, l'invention du drame,* edited by Marc Buffat (Mayenne: Klincksieck, 2000), pp. 113–140;

France Marchal, *La Culture de Diderot* (Paris: Honoré Champion, 1999);

Georges May, *Diderot et "La Religieuse": Etude historique et littéraire* (New Haven: Yale University Press, 1954);

May, "Le Rêve de D'Alembert selon Diderot," *Diderot Studies,* 17 (1973): 25–39;

Robert Morin, *Les Pensées philosophiques de Diderot devant leurs principaux contradicteurs au XVIIIe siècle,* Annales littéraires de l'université de Besançon, no. 171 (Paris: Les Belles Lettres, 1975);

Merle Louis Perkins, "Community Planning in Diderot's *Supplément au Voyage de Bougainville*," *Kentucky Romance Quarterly,* 4 (1974): 399–417;

Maurice Posada, "An Introduction to the Textual Problems of Diderot-Falconnet Correspondence on Posterity," *Diderot Studies,* 16 (1973): 175–196;

Jacques Proust, *Diderot et l'Encyclopédie* (Paris: Armand Colin, 1962);

Proust, *Lectures de Diderot* (Paris: Armand Colin, 1974);

Jeannette Rosso, *Diderot et le portrait* (Pisa: Libreria Goliardica, 1998);

Ken-ichi Sasaki, "L'esthétique de l'intérêt, de d'Aubignac à Sulzer," *Journal of the Faculty of Letters,* 10 (1985): 29–50;

Udo Sautter, "Diderot Counselor of Catherine II," *Revue de l'université d'Ottawa* (January–March 1972): 108–132;

Anthony R. Strugnell, *Diderot's Politics. A Study of the Evolution of Diderot's Political Thought after the Encyclopédie* (The Hague: M. Nijhoff, 1973);

Maurice Tourneux, *Diderot et Catherine II* (Paris, 1899 / Geneva: Slatkine Reprints, 1970);

Paul Vernière, *Diderot, ses manuscrits et ses copistes: essai d'introduction à une édition moderne de ses oeuvres* (Paris: Klincksieck, 1967);

Francis Watson, "Diderot and Houdon: A Little-Known Bust," in *The Artist and the Writer in France. Essays in Honour of Jean Seznec,* edited by Francis Haskell, Anthony Levi, and Robert Shackleton (Oxford: Clarendon Press, 1974), pp. 15–20.

Papers:

Roland Girbal copied Denis Diderot's manuscripts so that at his death, Catherine II would receive Diderot's library and thirty-two volumes of manuscripts. They are now in St. Petersburg at the Library Saltikov-Shchedrin. Except for *Observations sur le Nakaz,* the collection is intact (cf. Paul Vernière). The seventy-three volumes of the Fonds Vandeul are in "Nouvelles acquisitions françaises" at the Bibliothèque nationale, in Paris. They include the manuscripts of Diderot's works and of a family collection left to his daughter. A manuscript of *Rameau's Nephew,* written by Diderot himself, is at the Pierpont Morgan Library in New York.

Anne-Marie Du Boccage
(22 October 1710 – 8 August 1802)

Perry Gethner
Oklahoma State University

BOOKS: *Le Paradis terrestre, poème imité de Milton* (Amsterdam, 1748; London, 1748; revised, London: [printed on the Continent], 1755);

Les Amazones ... (Paris: Mérigot, 1749); in *Femmes dramaturges en France (1650–1750), Pièces choisies,* volume 2 edited by Perry Gethner (Tübingen, Germany: Gunter Narr, 2002); selected scenes translated in *Writings by Pre-Revolutionary French Women,* edited by Anne R. Larsen and Colette H. Winn (New York & London: Garland, 2000);

La Colombiade, ou la foi portée au nouveau monde (Paris: Desaint & Saillant, 1756); republished with a foreword by Milagros Palma and a preface by Catherin Jardin (Paris: Côté-femmes, 1991);

Recueil des oeuvres ... , 3 volumes (N.p., 1762); enlarged to include travel letters, 3 volumes (Lyons: Périsse, 1764); enlarged again to include *l'Imitation en vers du poème d'Abel,* 3 volumes (Lyons: Périsse, 1770); letters translated as *Letters Concerning England, Holland and Italy,* 2 volumes (London: E. & C. Dilly, 1770);

La Mort d'Abel, poème imité de Gessner (N.p., n.d.).

PLAY PRODUCTION: *Les Amazones,* Paris, Comédie-Française, 24 July 1749.

TRANSLATION: Alexander Pope, *Le Temple de la renommée* ... (London, 1749).

Anne-Marie Du Boccage (from Grace Gill-Mark, Anne-Marie Du Boccage, 1927; Hayden Library, Arizona State University)

Anne-Marie Du Boccage is remembered today, if at all, as the most acclaimed French woman poet of the eighteenth century, a friend of Voltaire, and one of the rare women to attempt an epic poem. Anne-Marie Le Page—Marie to family and friends; some scholars call her Marie-Anne—was born in Rouen 22 October 1710. Her father, an affluent and well-connected businessman, was also a local dignitary, serving as consul-judge and as prior of the Rouen Chamber of Commerce. Marie received her schooling at the Convent of the Assumption in Paris, where she distinguished herself for her intelligence and seriousness of purpose. In 1727 she married Joseph Fiquet du Boccage (the spelling of the name most commonly found in the editions of her works published during her lifetime); in her letters she usually signed Duboccage as one word. Joseph du Boccage, the son of a Rouen financier, held a position as tax collector in Dieppe, and the young couple spent their first six years together in that city. The marriage was extremely happy: although the couple had no children, they had similar personalities and shared the same tastes. From the start, Joseph encouraged his wife in her reading and in her study of languages, and he later applauded her literary endeavors. He himself published translations of several English Restoration dramas, but anonymously.

In 1733 the couple moved to Paris, although they spent their summers in Rouen. Anne-Marie Du Boccage soon gathered around her a circle of friends with intellectual interests. Eventually, this gathering developed into a salon in which over the course of more than half a century she received many of the leading philosophers, poets, historians, scientists, and painters of her age. Some of these—such as Bernard Le Bovier de Fontenelle, Charles-Louis de Secondat de Montesquieu, Etienne Bonnot de Condillac, and Georges-Louis Leclerc de Buffon—became genuine friends. Fontenelle, who lived near her house in Paris, was more than ninety when he first met her. He liked her so well that he called her his adopted daughter and visited her regularly. She also welcomed women of letters and distinguished foreign intellectuals, including Carlo Goldoni and Benjamin Franklin. In accordance with the conventions of the ancien régime, she took care not to display her own erudition or, once she started writing, to advertise it. Thanks to her combination of good looks, elegance of manner, sweet and friendly personality, and genuine interest in the world of letters, her salon became not just one of the more brilliant in Paris but also one of the most relaxed and most amicable. In addition to being an exemplary hostess, she was considered to be a fine conversationalist, admired for her wit and sound judgment.

Although in her early years she tossed off several short poems, she never thought of herself as a serious writer. Around 1737 she began work on a translation of Alexander Pope's *The Temple of Fame* (1709, 1714, 1715), presumably encouraged by her mentor, Abbé Jean-François du Resnel, who had himself published translations of several other poems by Pope, but she was too unsure of herself to think of publishing it. Her attitude began to change in 1746 when a poem that she submitted anonymously to a contest sponsored by the Academy of Rouen won first prize. The topic was the mutual influence of the fine arts and the sciences. Her close friend Pierre-Robert de Cideville sent a copy of her poem to Voltaire, who was impressed and began to correspond with her.

She now started work on a far more ambitious project—a free adaptation of John Milton's *Paradise Lost* (1667). As she pointed out in her preface, a literal rendering was not needed, since a more faithful prose translation already existed. Her task, as she saw it, was to render the chief beauties of the English original into French, while eliminating or altering those elements unsuitable to French taste. She shortened Milton's poem from twelve books to six, reduced Satan to a secondary character who is merely sinister and is devoid of heroic energy, cut most of the scenes set in heaven or hell, and eliminated the lengthy descriptions of places other than Eden, as well as most of the prophecies. As for Milton's style, so alien to French classicism, she preserved only those passages that she deemed in good taste, always maintaining clarity and elegance, preferring abstract language to concrete, and virtually eliminating the epic sweep of the original. Anything in Milton that too closely followed the exact wording of Genesis was recast in more acceptable poetic diction, indicating the unease felt by Enlightenment writers when dealing with the Bible. In her biography of Du Boccage, Grace Gill-Mark provides a detailed textual comparison of the French poem and its English model. The success was huge and immediate: three editions followed in 1748, two more in 1755, and still another in 1760; an Italian translation from the French appeared in 1758.

Le Paradis terrestre (1748, The Earthly Paradise) should be read as an independent work of art, not as an inferior version of Milton's work. Elegant, graceful, and charming, it reveals much about French tastes and attitudes in the eighteenth century. Du Boccage retained only those parts of the great English poem that her readers could appreciate: the human drama of Adam and Eve, the exploration of primeval human innocence contrasting, in the angel's prophecy, with the corrupting power of society and prejudice, and the question of how humans acquire both scientific knowledge and moral virtues. Unconcerned with the cosmic drama, she presents the first humans as tender, innocent, loving, and lovable—led astray only because of the malice of an evil seducer. She goes so far as to insert, at the start of the fifth canto, an apology to her female readers for having to recall Eve's pivotal role in the fall of humankind, but points out that this same episode also displays the power of women's charms. The emphasis on pathos, rather than grandeur, links the poem more closely to the novels of worldliness and seduction, so popular in the eighteenth century, than to the epic world of Milton.

The following year, heartened by the huge success of *Le Paradis terrestre,* she published the Pope translation she had done some years before. *Le Temple de la renommée* (1749) likewise seems to have been well received, helped by French enthusiasm for all things English. By the standards of the age, her translation was faithful, and much of the time she reproduced

Pope's thoughts and images with considerable accuracy. However, since she and her contemporaries upheld the classical view that poems should be clear, logical, and easy to follow, she did not hesitate to eliminate digressions and descriptive passages that she deemed unnecessary. In other places she expanded the text to make smoother transitions or to explain an allusion or a complex image. Furthermore, because she was translating into verse rather than into prose, as her mentor had done, she had to conform to the many and complex rules of versification and poetic diction that French audiences continued to insist on; this requirement further limited her ability to be faithful to the English original.

Later that year Du Boccage made her only foray into drama with the tragedy *Les Amazones* (1749, The Amazons). Because the prejudice against women playwrights remained strong, she decided to let the play appear anonymously: it was the last tragedy by a woman publicly staged in Paris prior to the French Revolution. The Comédie-Française, at that time the only venue for tragedies, was the most prestigious theater in France but also the most conservative in its tastes and the most temperamental in its dealings with authors. The actors imposed several unfavorable conditions: they would stage the play in the summer—the off-season—and they insisted that she relinquish the normal payment made to an author. They also demanded a steady stream of textual changes, and after the eighth performance, they announced that they were stopping the run. Since the author had developed such a case of nerves that she had taken to her bed, her husband took charge of the negotiations, and the tragedy received three additional performances. It was never revived, and Du Boccage never again dared to try her luck on the stage, though her correspondence indicates that she began work on a second tragedy, only to abandon the project. She did, however, publish *Les Amazones* during the latter part of 1749. The reviews were mixed, ranging from wild adulation to contemptuous dismissal. The work attracted considerable international attention, since a detailed analysis, balancing favorable and critical comments, was published in Utrecht, and an Italian translation appeared in 1756.

In plot, structure, and style *Les Amazones* respects the conventions of French classical tragedy. The story deals with a love triangle—both Amazon rulers fall in love with the captured Athenian hero Thésée, who returns the love of the younger one. It also features a conflict between love and duty; since the Amazons reject love and allow sex only briefly and for the purpose of procreation, the heroines feel they are betraying the values of their society. The true originality of this play comes from Du Boccage's exploration of an all-female society. She seems to have felt a fundamental incompatibility between the two different meanings of the word *Amazon:* a poetic term for a female warrior and a member of a legendary all-female society. For the first meaning she had total admiration: her Amazons are glorious warriors and able rulers who prove themselves to be the equals of their male counterparts in both war and peace. However, she felt that the enforced separation of the sexes, plus the ban on love and on permanent marriage, was unnatural and unjust. Her play shows the Amazons at the apex of their fame, but at the brink of social disintegration. Following their defeat at the hands of Thésée and the dangerous examples set by Princess Antiope, who leaves her people to wed him, and by Queen Orithie, who commits suicide when she realizes that her love has been rejected, the Amazons seem unable to continue much longer, despite the remaining leader's final words of defiance. The playwright makes only a vague allusion to what will happen next, though she presumably expected her audiences to be familiar with the myth: the Amazons' revenge attack on Athens ended in defeat and heavy casualties, and the remnants merged with the neighboring Scythian people.

One of the most striking scenes in the play is the enthusiastic description of Amazon mores given by Ménalippe, the one Amazon leader who is totally impervious to love and feels nothing but contempt for men. However, even if she believes that Amazon ways are perfect, Orithie and Antiope are highly critical of their society. In good Enlightenment fashion, they think that unreasonable laws should be eliminated and that customs may be altered to fit changing conditions. They are especially uneasy about the custom of offering certain of their male captives as human sacrifices (a practice not found in any ancient account of the Amazons). By inventing a practice that she knew her audience would find abhorrent, Du Boccage may have been trying to suggest that any society that alters the basic laws of nature, either by keeping the sexes completely apart or by denying one sex its fundamental rights, is engaging in a kind of self-mutilation. Although her feminism may seem timid by standards of today, she deserves credit for raising basic questions about women's rights and abilities.

In 1750 the poet and her husband took their first foreign trip, spending several months in England and Holland. In a series of letters written to her sister, which she edited and published in 1764, she described her reactions to various facets of life in those countries, displaying a genuine interest in the monuments, the world of letters, and all facets of daily life. She was feted in some of the leading literary circles and was delighted to find that some of her hosts were familiar with her works. On their way home the couple took the waters at Forges, where she found the doctors ignorant and the patients lazy and foolish.

Du Boccage's second large-scale original work, the epic poem *La Colombiade* (The Columbiad), appeared in 1756. Presumably inspired by the esteem that Voltaire had garnered with his epic, *La Henriade* (1723), she hoped to fuse the conventions of an ancient genre with modern concerns. Although Du Boccage read voluminously in historical sources and provided many footnotes to explain the elements of local color that she included, such as the fauna and flora of America, her plot is almost entirely fictional. The character and exploits of Christopher Columbus are to a large extent grafted onto those of earlier epics, especially Virgil's *Aeneid* (19 B.C.), including a series of tempests stirred up by the pagan gods worshiped in the Indies, a pathos-filled love plot in which the hero is forced to abandon the Indian maiden whom he loves and who ultimately dies at the hands of an irate rival, and a protracted battle against a native kingdom that ends with the triumph of the more civilized side.

In this poem, Colomb is more a warrior and navigator than an explorer, but, most importantly, he is a spokesman for civilization and for Enlightenment ideas. The ideological heart of the work is an extended conversation between Colomb and the chief of the first Indian village he discovers. The latter is a perfect example of the noble savage, who gives an eloquent apologia for primitive and innocent mores. Since the protagonist takes this occasion to expound on the mores and accomplishments of the Europeans, Du Boccage can present both sides of one of the most hotly argued topics of her era. Significantly, although she gave the work the subtitle *la foi portée au nouveau monde* (The True Faith Carried to the New World), and dedicated it to the Pope, she displayed great sympathy for the pagan world of the Indians and did not suggest that their ignorance of Christianity would be held against them in the hereafter. Another passage linked to Enlightenment values is the prophecy of future discoveries to be made by the Italians, French, and English up through the author's own time. Her genuine desire to celebrate both scientific progress and the excitement involved in the quest for knowledge transcends the unconvincing plot and makes this poem something more than a laborious academic exercise. In any case, most of Du Boccage's contemporaries judged the work favorably. It went through three editions in Paris and was translated into Spanish, English, German, and Italian.

In 1757 she and her husband took their second and last foreign trip, visiting all the major cities in Italy. In letters to her sister that she later published, she again recorded her impressions, filled with judicious observations and a variety of colorful anecdotes. Unlike many travelers of her age, Du Boccage took an equal interest in the vestiges of ancient Rome and in modern-day Italy, conversed with people from all walks of life, and learned everything she could about local customs. Once again she was warmly received in cultivated circles, and many honors were bestowed on her, including a meeting with the Pope—who had accepted the dedication of her epic poem—and induction into three learned societies: the Academy of Padua, the Academy of Sciences and Letters in Bologna, and the Academy of the Arcadi in Rome. (The latter two ceremonies were held during her sojourn in those cities.) During the return journey, the couple made a pilgrimage to Voltaire's home in Switzerland, where the great man complimented her and placed a crown of laurels on her head. According to Frédéric Melchior Grimm, he also mocked her behind her back, though she never found out.

In 1760 she began work on her last major poem, *La Mort d'Abel* (Abel's Death). It was a free adaptation in verse of the Swiss poet Salomon Gessner's *Der Tod Abels* (1759), which he had written in a poetic prose. The appearance of a French prose translation that year inspired her to compose a work that formed a perfect sequel to her earlier poem about Adam and Eve. Once again Du Boccage toned down those elements of the foreign text that French taste might find unsuitable. Since she did not share Gessner's pre-Romantic interest in detailed descriptions of nature and in violent emotional states, she produced a gentle, graceful, and flowing narrative that emphasized pathos rather than terror. Her Cain, more unhappy and insecure than rebellious and violent, inspires a certain amount of pity, while her Abel is a model of sensibility, though less effusive than Gessner's hero in the way he expresses his devotion to God and his family.

In 1767 Joseph Du Boccage died, and Marie Du Boccage, devastated by the loss of the man she called her best friend, never remarried. His death also cost her half her fortune, and, as her income further dwindled in subsequent years, she was reduced to modest circumstances. However, she continued to receive friends until the end of her life. In 1768 the society of the Palinods in Rouen awarded a prize to her poem on the immaculate conception of the Virgin. From that point on, she composed little more than short occasional pieces, spending the bulk of her time on her preferred activities of reading and serious conversation. She seems to have been left alone during the turbulent years of the French Revolution, though she lost many of her friends to execution or exile. In 1790 two scurrilous pamphlets appeared in Brussels under her name in which she attacked a lady who had publicly insulted a Belgian minister. These works are totally out of character with everything else known about Du Boccage, and since there is no evidence that she ever left Paris in the final decades of her life, she probably did not write them.

Anne-Marie Du Boccage received many accolades and honors during her lifetime. In addition to those already mentioned, she was admitted to two local academies in France, Lyons and Rouen. In Rouen she was the first woman ever honored with membership. In 1801 the director of the Lycée des Arts held a celebration at which speeches were read praising her poetry and her character, and a bust of her was crowned. The aged poet modestly declined to attend. Her death the following year on 8 August 1802 attracted little notice: as a typical representative of the manners and ideas of the ancien régime, she seemed a mere historical relic in the age of Napoleon. Apart from a new edition of some of her poetry in 1825, she and her work quickly fell into oblivion.

Biography:

Grace Gill-Mark, *Une Femme de lettres au XVIIIe siècle: Anne-Marie Du Boccage* (Paris: Champion, 1927; Geneva: Slatkine Reprints, 1976).

References:

Jean-Charles Chessex, "Mme du Boccage ou la belle inconnue," *French Review,* 30 (1957): 297–302;

Frederick K. Turgeon, "Unpublished Letters of Mme Du Boccage," *Modern Philology,* 27 (1930): 321–338;

Roland Virolle, "Types sociaux en Normandie au XVIIIe siècle: Anne-Marie Du Boccage, la dixième muse," *Etudes normandes* (1979): 66–80;

R. Thomas Watson, "Forma Venus, Arte Minerva: Madame Du Boccage: A Simone de Beauvoir avant la lettre," *Simone de Beauvoir Studies,* 7 (1990): 3–13.

Pierre Samuel Du Pont de Nemours
(14 December 1739 – 7 August 1817)

Karyna Szmurlo
Clemson University

BOOKS: *Réflexions sur l'écrit intitulé, Richesse de l'Etat,* anonymous (Paris: Moreau, 1763);

Réponse demandée par M. le Marquis de *** à celle qu'il a faite aux Réflexions sur l'écrit intitulé: Richesse de l'Etat, anonymous (London, 1763);

De l'Exportation et de l'importation des grains (Soissons & Paris: P.-G. Simon, 1764);

De l'Administration des chemins (Pékin & Paris: Merlin, 1767);

De l'Origine et des progrès d'une science nouvelle (London & Paris: Desaint, 1768);

Lettre de M. de ***, Conseiller au Parlement de Rouen, à M. de M***, Premier Président. A . . . le 26 octobre 1768, anonymous [Limoges, 1768];

Objections et réponses sur le commerce des grains et des farines (Amsterdam & Paris: Delalain, 1769);

Du commerce et de la compagnie des Indes (Amsterdam & Paris: Delalain, Lacombe, 1769);

Observations sur les effets de la liberté du commerce des grains et sur ceux des prohibitions (Basel & Paris: Delalain, 1770);

Abrégé des principes de l'économie politique, by Du Pont, Honoré-Gabriel, comte de Mirabeau, and Carl Friedrich, Margrave of Baden (Karlsruhe & Paris: Lacombe, 1772);

Table raisonnée des principes de l'économie politique . . . 1773 (Karlsruhe: Macklot, 1775);

Mémoires sur la vie et les ouvrages de M. Turgot, ministre d'état, 2 parts (Philadelphia & Paris: Barrois, 1782); third revised edition in *Oeuvres de Turgot,* volume 1 (Paris: Belin, 1811);

Notice sur la vie de M. Poivre (Philadelphia & Paris: Moutard, 1786);

Idées sur les secours à donner aux pauvres malades dans une grande ville (Philadelphia & Paris: Moutard, 1786);

Mémoire sur les municipalités, by Du Pont and Jacques Turgot; published in *Oeuvres posthumes de M. Turgot, ou Mémoire de M. Turgot sur les administrations provinciales, mis en parallèle avec celui de M. Necker, suivi d'une Lettre sur ce plan, et des Observations d'un républicain sur ces mémoires* (Lausanne, 1787); edited by Du

Pierre Samuel Du Pont de Nemours (portrait by Rembrandt Peale, courtesy of Pierre S. Du Pont; from Ambrose Saricks, Pierre Samuel Du Pont de Nemours, *1965; Thomas Cooper Library, University of South Carolina)*

Pont in *Oeuvres de Turgot* (Paris: Belin, 1809–1811);

Lettre à M. le Comte Charles de Scheffer. Paris, le 20 août 1773, anonymous [N.p., 1788];

Lettre à la Chambre du commerce de Normandie sur le mémoire qu'elle a publié relativement au Traité de commerce avec l'Angleterre (Rouen & Paris: Moutard, 1788);

De la Meilleure Manière de délibérer et de voter dans une grande assemblée, anonymous (N.p., 1789);

De la Périodicité des Assemblées nationales . . . (Paris: Baudouin, 1789);

Analyse historique de la législation des grains depuis 1692, à laquelle on a donné la forme d'un rapport à l'Assemblée nationale (Paris: Petit, 1789);

De la Manière la plus favorable d'effectuer les emprunts, qui seront nécessaires, tant afin de pourvoir aux besoins du moment, que pour opérer le remboursement des dettes de l'Etat, dont les intérêts sont trop onéreux (Paris: Baudouin, 1789);

Première opinion sur les prétentions relatives à un droit de "veto," et sur les déclarations à faire par les députés des communes de France à ceux de l'ordre de la noblesse, exposée dans la séance du 29 mai 1789 (Paris, 1789);

Projets d'articles relatifs à la constitution de l'Assemblée nationale, à la forme de son travail, à la proposition, à la préparation et à la sanction des loix; remis sur le bureau de l'Assemblée nationale, dans la séance du vendredi 4 septembre (Paris: Baudouin, 1789);

Discours prononcé à l'Assemblée nationale sur les banques en général, sur la Caisse d'Escompte en particulier, et sur le projet du premier ministre des finances, relativement à cette dernière (Paris: Baudouin, 1789);

Principes et opinion sur la disposition que doit faire l'Assemblée nationale des biens ecclésiastiques en général, et de ceux des ordres religieux en particulier (Paris: Baudouin, [1789]);

Discours prononcé à l'Assemblée nationale sur l'état et les ressources des finances, avec pièces justificatives; le 24 septembre 1789 (Versailles: Baudouin, 1789);

Rapport sur le décret général, relatif aux départements du royaume, fait au nom du Comité de constitution; le 15 février 1790 (Paris: Imprimerie nationale, 1790);

Rapport du département du Barrois (Paris: Imprimerie nationale, 1790);

Observations sur les principes qui doivent déterminer le nombre des districts et celui des tribunaux dans les départements; le 15 février 1790 (Paris: Imprimerie nationale, 1790);

Principes et opinion sur la conduite constitutionnelle que doivent tenir les troupes en cas de sédition; le 22 février 1790 (Paris: Baudouin, 1790);

Rapport fait au nom du Comité des finances, sur les moyens de remplacer la gabelle, et de rétablir le niveau entre les recettes et les dépenses ordinaires de l'année 1790 (Paris: Baudouin, 1790);

Opinion sur les assignats, exposée à l'Assemblée nationale; le 15 avril 1790 (Paris: Baudouin, 1790);

Opinion sur le revenu public produit par la vente du tabac, prononcée à l'Assemblée nationale; le 23 avril 1790 [Paris: Baudouin, 1790];

Opinion sur l'exercice du droit de la guerre et de la paix, exposée à l'Assemblée nationale; le 19 mai 1790 (Paris: Imprimerie nationale, 1790);

Projet de décret proposé par M. Du Pont de Nemours; le 19 mai 1790 (Paris: Imprimerie nationale, 1790);

Réclamation faite par M. Du Pont de Nemours à l'Assemblée nationale; le premier juin 1790 (Paris: Imprimerie nationale, 1790);

Discours sur les écrits incendiaires prononcé á l'Assemblée nationale; le 3 août 1790 ([Paris]: Guillaume Jr., [1790]); translated by William F. Kelly as *Discourse of Monsieur Dupont de Nemours on Incendiary Writings, Delivered to the National Assembly on August 3, 1790* (Claymont, Del., 1967);

Rapport fait au nom du Comité des finances à l'Assemblée nationale . . . le 14 août 1790, sur la répartition de la contribution en remplacement des grandes gabelles, des petites gabelles, des gabelles locales et des droits de marque des cuirs, de marque des fers, de fabrication sur les amidons, de fabrication et de transport dans l'intérieur du royaume sur les huiles et savons (Paris: Baudouin, 1790);

Opinion sur le projet de créer pour dix-neuf cents millions d'assignats-monnaie sans intérêt, exposée à l'Assemblée nationale (Paris: Baudouin, 1790); translated by Edmond E. Lincoln as *Du Pont de Nemours on the Dangers of Inflation: An Address by Pierre Samuel du Pont, Deputy from Nemours, Made Before the National Assembly of France, September 25, 1790* (Boston: Harvard Graduate School of Business Administration, 1950);

Troisième rapport fait au Comité des finances sur le remplacement de la gabelle et des droits sur les cuirs, les fers, les huiles, les savons et les amidons; le 3 octobre 1790 (Paris: Baudouin, 1790);

Principes constitutionnels relativement au renvoi et à la nomination des ministres. Discours prononcé à la Société des amis de la liberté et de la constitution de 1789, dans leur séance du 20 octobre 1790 (Paris: Imprimerie nationale, 1790);

Rapport fait au nom du Comité de l'imposition sur les impositions indirectes en général et sur les droits, à raison de la consommation des vins et des boissons en particulier; le 29 octobre 1790 (Paris: Imprimerie nationale, 1790);

Examen et parallèle des différens projets de droits sur les boissons à l'Assemblée nationale (Paris: Imprimerie nationale, 1790);

Considérations sur la position politique de la France, de l'Angleterre et de l'Espagne à l'Assemblée nationale [N.p., 1790]; translated as *Considerations upon the Political Situations of France, Great Britain, and Spain, at the Present Crisis* (London: J. Bell, 1790);

Le Pacte de famille et les conventions subséquentes, entre la France et l'Espagne; avec des observations sur chaque article (Paris: Imprimerie nationale, 1790);

Idées sur la constitution politique la plus convenable à la ville de Paris formant seule un département (Paris: Baudouin, 1790);

De l'Etendue et des bornes naturelles de tester (Paris: Baudouin, 1790);

Projet de décret général sur les taxes à l'entrée des villes, le 11 février 1791 [Paris: Imprimerie nationale, 1791];

Réplique de M. Du Pont à M. Didelot au sujet de droits d'aides sur les boissons (Paris: Imprimerie nationale, 1791);

De Quelques Améliorations dans la perception de l'impôt et de l'usage utile qu'on peut faire des employés réformés (Paris: Imprimerie nationale, 1791);

Instruction pour les colonies françaises, contenant un projet de constitution, présentée à l'Assemblée nationale (Paris: Imprimerie nationale, 1791);

De la Loterie (Paris: Imprimerie nationale, 1791);

De la Position politique de la France. Moyen simple d'en écarter tout péril en lui conservant toute sa dignité (Paris: Du Pont, 1792);

Lettre de M. Du Pont à M. Pétion; le 13 avril de l'an IV ([Paris]: Imprimerie de l'auteur, [1792]);

Seconde lettre de M. Du Pont à M. Pétion; le 27 avril de l'an IV ([Paris]: Imprimerie de l'auteur, [1792]);

De l'Influence et de l'utilité des clubs par un ami de la constitution (Paris: [Du Pont], an IV de la liberté, 1792);

Sur une Opinion inconstitutionnelle que l'on cherche à répandre ([Paris]: Imprimerie de l'auteur, 1792);

Avant-dernier chapitre de l'histoire des Jacobins: lettre de M. Du Pont aux citoyens constitutionnaires; le 14 mai de l'an IV ([Paris]: Du Pont, 1792);

Traité d'alliance offensive entre les Français émigrans-aristocrates d'une part et les Français républicains, d'autre part, anonymous [Paris: Du Pont, 1792];

Vues sur l'éducation nationale par un cultivateur ou Moyen de simplifier l'instruction, de la rendre à la fois morale, philosophique, républicaine, civile et militaire, sans déranger les travaux de l'agriculture et des arts auxquels la jeunesse doit concourir (Paris: Du Pont, Imprimeur-Libraire, an II, 1793–1794);

Plaidoyer de Lysias contre les membres des anciens Comités de salut public et de sûreté générale (Paris: Du Pont, l'an III de la République, 1794–1795);

Observations sur la constitution proposée par la Commission des onze et sur la position actuelle de la France (Paris: Du Pont, l'an III de la République, 1795);

Constitution pour la République française. Du pouvoir législatif et du pouvoir exécutif, convenables à la République française (Paris: Du Pont, Imprimeur-Libraire, l'an III de la République, 1795);

Philosophie de l'univers (Paris: Du Pont, 1796; second revised edition, Paris, 1797; third enlarged edition, Paris: Goujon, 1799);

Rapport de la commission chargée d'examiner la résolution du 29 messidor, relative au paiement des fermages des domaines nationaux. Séance du 12 vendémiaire an V [Paris: Imprimerie nationale, an V, 1796];

Opinion sur la résolution relative à la loi du 3 brumaire. Séance du 27 brumaire an V [Paris: Imprimerie nationale, an V, 1796];

Opinion sur la résolution relative aux canaux d'Orléans et du Loing. Séance du 15 nivôse an V [Paris: Imprimerie nationale, an V, 1797];

Rapport sur les fonds à mettre à la disposition du ministre de la justice pour le trimestre de nivôse. Séance du 2 ventôse de l'an V [Paris: Imprimerie nationale, an V, 1797];

Opinion sur le projet d'un droit de passe. Séance du 9 ventôse an V [Paris: Imprimerie nationale, an V, 1797];

Opinion sur la contrainte par corps. Séance du 24 ventôse an V [Paris: Imprimerie nationale, an V, 1797];

Opinion sur les projets de loterie et sur l'état des revenus ordinaires de la République. Séance du 24 germinal an V [Paris: Imprimerie nationale, an V, 1797];

Rapport . . . sur l'organisation et les dépenses de la trésorerie nationale. Séance du 17 prairial an V [Paris: Imprimerie nationale, an V, 1797];

Opinion sur l'imprimerie de la République. Séance du 19 prairial an V [Paris: Imprimerie nationale, an V, 1797];

Opinion sur la résolution du 1er messidor, relative à l'urgence des paiements et aux négociations à faire par la trésorerie. Séance du 9 messidor an V [Paris: Imprimerie nationale, an V, 1797];

Opinion sur la résolution du 19 messidor, relative aux fugitifs du Haut et du Bas-Rhin. Séance du 11 fructidor [Paris: Imprimerie nationale, an V, 1797];

Rapport sur la résolution relative aux dépenses des relations extérieures. Séance du 15 fructidor, an V [Paris: Imprimerie nationale, an V, 1797];

Opinion sur la première résolution du 19 messidor relative aux transactions. Séance du 15 fructidor an V [Paris: Imprimerie nationale, an V, 1797];

Du Pont de Nemours à ses collègues [Paris: Du Pont, 1797];

Du Pont de Nemours à ses collègues sur les calculs de Vernier [Paris: Du Pont, 1797];

Compagnie d'Amérique. Mémoire qui contient le plan des opérations de la Société, anonymous (Paris, Thermidor de l'an VII, 1799);

Sur l'Education nationale dans les Etats-Unis d'Amérique (Philadelphia, 1800; second revised edition, Paris: Lenormant, 1812); translated by Bessie G. Du Pont as *National Education in the United States of America by Du Pont de Nemours* (Newark: University of Delaware Press, 1923);

Rapport fait à l'assemblée des créanciers de la Banque Territoriale, dans leur séance du 11 frimaire an XII (Paris: Goujon fils, 1803);

Rapport sur le droit de marque des cuirs, par un conseiller d'Etat (Paris: Veuve Goujon fils, 1804);

Sur la Banque de France, les causes de la crise qu'elle a éprouvée, les tristes effets qui en sont résultés et les moyens d'en prévenir le retour; avec une théorie des banques (Paris:

Delance, 1806; second edition, London: Hatchard, 1811);

Irénée Bonfils, sur la religion de ses pères et de nos pères (Paris: Didot, 1808); translated by Pierre S. Du Pont as *Irénée Bonfils* (Wilmington, Del.: Hambelton, 1947);

Lettre de M. Du Pont de Nemours, associé à l'Académie du Gard, sur l'ouvrage de M. Malthus, intitulé: "Essai sur le principe de population" [Nîmes: Blachier-Belle, 1811];

Notice sur la vie de M. Barlow, ministre plénipotentiaire des Etats-Unis d'Amérique auprès de S. M. l'Empereur et Roi; lue à la Société d'encouragement de l'industrie nationale, le 31 mars 1813 (Paris: Huzart, 1813);

Observations sur divers projets de changement dans l'organisation des administrations de finances, anonymous (Paris: Imprimerie de Lefebvre, 1814);

Examen du livre de M. Malthus sur le principe de population; auquel on à joint la traduction de quatre chapitres de ce livre supprimés dans l'edition française; et une lettre à M. Say sur son "Traité d'economie politique" (Philadelphia: Lafourcade, 1817);

Mémoires de Pierre Samuel Du Pont adressés à ses enfants, edited by Sophie Madeleine (Du Pont) and Eleuthera (Du Pont) Smith as *Extraits des lettres de Pierre Samuel du Pont de Nemours à ses enfants* (New York: Leypoldt & Holt, 1867); edited and annotated by Henry A. Du Pont as *L'Enfance et la jeunesse de Du Pont de Nemours, racontées par lui-même* (Paris: Plont-Nourrit, 1906); translated, with an introduction, by Elizabeth Fox-Genovese as *The Autobiography of Du Pont de Nemours* (Wilmington, Del.: Scholarly Resources, 1984);

Des courbes politiques, in *Carl Friedrichs von Baden Brieflicher Verkehr mit Mirabeau und Du Pont,* 2 volumes, edited by Carl Knies (Heidelberg: Carl Wintcr, 1892), II: 289–300; edited and translated by Henry W. Spiegel as *On Economic Curves: A Letter Reproduced in English Translation with the Original Diagram and an Introduction* (Baltimore: Johns Hopkins University Press, 1955).

Collections: *Observations sommaires et preuves sur le navire le New-Jersey et ses propriétaires,* with Joseph Delagrange [Paris: Delance, 1804];

Opuscules morales et politiques, retirées de différens journaux (Paris: Delance, an XIII, 1805);

Quelques mémoires sur différens sujets, lus ou communiqués à l'Institut (Paris: Delance, 1807); enlarged as *Quelques mémoires sur différens sujets, la pluspart d'histoire naturelle ou de physique générale et particulière* (Paris: Belin, 1813);

Collection des économistes et des réformateurs sociaux de la France: physiocrates, edited by Eugène Daire (Paris: Guillaumin, 1846);

L'Administration de l'agriculture au contrôle général des finances (1785 à 1787): Procès-verbaux et rapports, edited by Henri Pigeonneau and Alfred de Foville (Paris: Guillaumin, 1882);

Collection des économistes et des réformateurs sociaux de la France, edited by Auguste Dubois (Paris: Geuthner, 1910);

Collection de documents inédits sur l'histoire économique de la Révolution française: Procès-verbaux du comité des finances de l'Assemblée constituante, edited by C. Bloch (Rennes: Ministère de l'Instruction Publique, 1922–1923);

Oeuvres politiques et économiques, 10 volumes (Nendeln, Liechtenstein: KTO Press, 1979).

SELECTED BROADSIDES: *Lettre à Monsieur **** au sujet de la cherté des bleds en Guyenne. Paris, le 8 mai, 1764* (Soissons: Courtois, 1764);

Lettre sur la différence qui se trouve entre la grande et la petite culture (Soissons: Courtois, 1764);

Discours sur les biens ecclésiastiques (Paris: Baudouin, 1789);

Dessèchement des marais [N.p., 1790];

Discours au Roi, à l'occasion de sa fête, prononcé le 24 août 1790, par M. Du Pont, président de l'Assemblée nationale; avec la réponse du Roi (Paris: Baudouin, 1790);

Discours de M. Du Pont . . . à l'Assemblée nationale, sur la nécessité de la tranquilité publique, et décret rendu à ce sujet; le 7 septembre 1790 [N.p., 1790];

Effet des assignats sur le prix du pain, par un ami du peuple, le 10 septembre 1790 [Paris: Imprimerie nationale, 1790];

Imprimerie de Du Pont, député de l'Assemblée nationale (Paris: Du Pont, 1791);

De l'Amour de la constitution et celui de la liberté [Paris: Du Pont, 1791];

Sur l'Amnistie [Paris: Imprimerie de l'auteur, 1791];

Projet d'instruction pour les colonies (Paris: Imprimerie de la Feuille du Jour, 1791);

Opinion sur la manière dont les jurés doivent recevoir la déposition des témoins (Paris: Imprimerie nationale, 1791);

Motifs de ceux qui cherchent à engager la nation à faire une incursion sur les terres de l'Empire (Paris: Du Pont, [1792]);

Sur les Suisses de Château-vieux, as J. Eleuthere, Grenadier de la première Légion [Paris: Du Pont, 1792];

Le Pas de charge au lieu de la retraite [Paris: Du Pont, 1792].

OTHER: François Quesnay, *Physiocratie ou Constitution naturelle du gouvernement le plus avantageux au genre humain,* 2 volumes, edited by Du Pont (Leyde & Paris: Merlin, 1767);

Ephémérides du Citoyen, edited by Du Pont (1768–1772);

Journal de l'agriculture, du commerce et des finances, edited by Du Pont (1775);

Poésies diverses, anonymous (Paris: Chez les associés, 1779);

Essai de traduction en vers du Roland Furieux de l'Arioste, canto 1, anonymous (Paris: Jombert, 1781); enlarged as *Essai de traduction en vers du Roland Furieux de l'Arioste,* cantos 1–3 (Paris: Didot, 1812);

Procès-verbal de l'Assemblée baillivale de Nemours pour la convocation des Etats-Généraux, avec les cahiers des trois ordres, 2 volumes, edited by Du Pont (Paris: Duplain, 1789);

Déclaration des droits. Extrait du Cahier du Tiers-Etat du bailliage de Nemours (Paris: Baudouin, 1789);

Correspondance patriotique, edited by Du Pont (1791–1792);

L'Historien, edited by Du Pont (1796–1797);

Anne-Robert-Jacques Turgot, *Oeuvres de M. Turgot,* volumes 2–9, edited, with prefaces and notes, by Du Pont (Paris: Delance, 1808–1811).

SELECTED PERIODICAL PUBLICATIONS–UNCOLLECTED: "Réflexions sur le commerce de pure industrie," *Journal de l'agriculture, du commerce et des finances,* 3 October 1765, pp. 31–36;

"Situation actuelle du commerce anglais dans plusieurs de ses différentes parties," *Journal de l'agriculture, du commerce et des finances,* 3 December 1765, pp. 148–174;

"Catalogue des écrits composés suivant les principes de la science économique," *Ephémérides du citoyen,* 2 (1768): 191–202;

"Analyse des *Voyages d'un philosophe ou observations sur les moeurs et les arts des peuples de l'Afrique et de l'Asie,* par Poivre," *Ephémérides du citoyen,* 6 (1768): 166–217;

"Révolution dans le commerce de l'Inde," *Ephémérides du citoyen,* 7 (1769): 276–282;

"Réponse à la lettre de M.N., ingénieur des ponts et chaussées sur l'ouvrage de M. Du Pont qui a pour titre *De l'administration des chemins,*" *Ephémérides du citoyen,* 8 (1769): 93–135;

"Observations sur l'effet du dérangement des saisons depuis cinq années," *Ephémérides du citoyen,* 1 (1771): 68–88;

"Analyse des *Saisons,* poème par Saint-Lambert," *Ephémérides du citoyen,* 6 (1771): 163–246;

"Analyse de l'*Encyclopédie économique ou système général d'économie rustique* par la Société d'Economie Politique de Berne," *Ephémérides du citoyen,* 9 (1771): 59–144;

"Des divers moyens que l'on peut employer dans l'état actuel de l'Europe, pour procurer la construction et l'entretien des grands canaux de navigation," *Ephémérides du citoyen,* 10 (1771): 43–61;

"De l'aristocratie ou du pouvoir injuste usurpé par la minorité," *Correspondance patriotique,* 2, no. 10 (1791): 204–210;

"Causes très légitimes de la diversité des opinions relativement à l'usage que le roi a fait du veto sur le décret qui concernait les émigrés et sur celui qui regardait les prêtres non assermentés," *Correspondance patriotique,* 2, no. 12 (1791): 347–355;

"Sur la véritable et la fausse économie dans les dépenses publiques d'une nation," *Correspondance patriotique,* 4, no. 24 (1792): 269–285;

"Des gouvernements représentatifs en général. De la Constitution française en particulier," *Correspondance patriotique,* 4, no. 25 (1792): 337–352;

"De la position actuelle des colonies; de l'influence qui devait avoir sur elles la Révolution française; des moyens d'y amener et d'y assurer la paix," *Correspondance patriotique,* 5, no. 1 (1792): 265–276;

"De la manière dont la guerre doit être faite," *Correspondance patriotique,* 5, no. 29 (1792): 132–143;

"Lettre de M. du Pont aux citoyens constitutionnaires," *Correspondance patriotique,* 5, no. 32 (1792): 329–356;

"Sur les revenus de la France et les contributions possibles," *L'Historien,* 18 (1796): 282–285;

"Sur le serment du premier pluviôse," *L'Historien,* 63 (1796): 329–330;

"Pourquoi toutes les nations commencent aisément la guerre, et font difficilement la paix?" *L'Historien,* 73 (1796): 489–492;

"Sur la situation de la République et l'intérêt du gouvernement," *L'Historien,* 95 (1796): 49–55;

"De la force du Gouvernement actuel de la France, et de la nécessité de s'y rallier, par Benjamin Constant," *L'Historien,* 158 (1796): 325–333;

"Du goût," *Le Mois,* 6 (1798–1799): 259–262;

"Mémoire sur l'abus du mot 'nouveau' appliqué en histoire naturelle à des êtres anciens: lu à la classe des sciences physiques et mathématiques de l'Institut National, le 12 germinal an XIII," *Archives littéraires de l'Europe,* 12 (1806): 48–62;

"Sur la théorie des vents," *Transactions of the American Philosophical Society,* 6 (1809): 32–39.

Statesman, publicist, businessman, and writer, Pierre Samuel Du Pont de Nemours represents an authentic eighteenth-century *bourgeois conquérant* (conquering bourgeois) eager to act for the progress of humanity. His extensive body of works sheds light on various aspects of French society before, during, and after the French Revolution. The political economy, however, colored by a passionate propaganda of physiocracy, is the area of his most vital contributions. Despite tumultuous political and social changes, Du

Pont never wavered in his faith in the programs for reforming the depleted treasury of France nor in the power of knowledge communicated through public writing. He seized every opportunity—in treatises, pamphlets, memoirs, reports, speeches, letters, and editorials—to put forward physiocratic solutions to contemporary concerns.

Du Pont's versatile talents, which as Joseph A. Schumpeter notes, "were those of the pianist and not of the composer," reveal interpretative genius. With an astounding energy, Du Pont promulgated the ideas of the influential whom he admired. He became a disciple, collaborator, and later a custodian of the works of two celebrated economists—François Quesnay, physician to Louis XV, and Jacques Turgot, reforming minister of Louis XVI. Two other mentors, the comte de Vergennes and Charles Alexandre de Calonne—both ministers of Louis XVI—enabled him to perform increasingly important functions in trade and foreign affairs. The Revolution legitimized his voice, providing the social foundations for his own opinions and ambitions, already widely recognized by the international elite. Among Du Pont's correspondents and acquaintances, in addition to many enlightened European rulers, were Voltaire; Jean-Jacques Rousseau; Denis Diderot; Germaine de Staël; Honoré-Gabriel, comte de Mirabeau; Gilbert du Motier, marquis de Lafayette; Charles-Maurice de Talleyrand-Périgord; Benjamin Franklin; Thomas Jefferson; and James Madison.

Pierre Samuel Du Pont was born in Paris on 14 December 1739 to a Protestant couple, watchmakers Samuel and Anne Alexandrine de Monchanin. The liberal culture of the mother, raised by the Jaucourt family in the Encyclopedist milieu, strongly influenced Pierre's early education. At twelve, a pensioner at the reputable Viard's school, he could recite classical works, translate Latin, and debate logic, literary styles, and civil law. One of the public displays of his precocious abilities ended in a torchlight procession of his classmates celebrating the honor that he had conferred upon the establishment. The intensity of this triumph continued to resound in Du Pont's imagination all his life as a moment of happiness and high hopes.

Despite his son's achievements, the father, with no literary aspirations, removed the child from the school to place him at the workbench of a clockmaker. The child's mother, helped by Jean Le Rond d'Alembert, delayed the apprenticeship, extending her son's education in geometry, mathematics, and mechanical science. To escape horology and enter the upper classes through a military commission, Pierre contemplated a career in engineering. During these formative years, he had an opportunity to read a popular publication by engineer Sébastien Le Prestre de Vauban, *Dime royale*

Du Pont's parents, Samuel and Anne Alexandrine de Monchanin Du Pont, and Du Pont as a child (Henry Francis Du Pont Winterthur Museum; from Ambrose Saricks, Pierre Samuel Du Pont de Nemours, *1965; Thomas Cooper Library, University of South Carolina)*

(1707, Royal Tithe), and to reflect upon the serious conditions of French agriculture and finances.

In defiance of paternal prohibitions, Du Pont left the house shortly after the premature death of his mother and tried to make his way by writing. He composed a few tragedies and many poems but became more successful in economic studies, which gave him access to the court and circles of philosophers. At twenty-three, he acclaimed "la terre et les eaux" (the earth and the waters) as "les uniques sources des richesses" (the unique source of riches) and the sole taxable source of wealth; he devoted the rest of his life to the promotion and application of this simple truth of great importance for financial freedom. In a pamphlet that includes an interview with a countryside cook, *Réflexions sur l'écrit intitulé, Richesse de l'Etat* (1763, Reflections on a Piece Entitled: Wealth of the State), Du Pont replied to an unrealistic taxation proposal published by Roussel de La Tour and followed it up with a more detailed *Réponse demandée* (1763, Requested Reply).

Bust of Marie-Louise Le Dée de Roccourt, Du Pont's first wife, whom he married in 1775 (Eleutherian Mills Historical Library; from Ambrose Saricks, Pierre Samuel Du Pont de Nemours, 1965; Thomas Cooper Library, University of South Carolina)

Although personal and based on limited rural research, both pieces attracted the attention of Quesnay and Mirabeau, who were in the process of elaborating the entire system of social and political thought based on natural laws. Drawing on the pastoral tradition of the moral and political superiority of agriculture, they fought against market restrictions imposed on agricultural products, grain in particular, as violating the sacred law of property and impeding the realization of potential wealth.

Du Pont's first major work, *De l'Exportation et de l'importation des grains* (1764, On the Export and Import of Grains), was written at the request of Quesnay, who, according to Henry Du Pont's, became his "Maitré Instructeur et Père" (master, teacher, and father.) Introductory chapters supplemented with copious notes popularize the basic concepts of the natural-resource theory. The most fundamental is the valorization of the "productive" class of landowners as opposed to a "sterile" or "secondary" group of merchants and manufacturers who merely remold the products raised by agriculturists and depend upon the supply of food and raw materials. The capacity of agriculture to yield a disposable surplus over necessary costs, the net product, proves again the advantage of agriculture over more precarious occupations. In the rest of the work, Du Pont examines the production costs, fluctuations in grain prices, and statistical representations; in chapter 5, a table based on a nine-year period indicates predictable increases in agricultural productivity and revenues as a result of laissez-faire politics. The motif of oncoming opulence and expansion of foreign trade resonates through the final chapters and notes that include historical digressions, letters, and maxims. A meticulous résumé of the ideas discussed in each chapter closes the volume.

A milestone event for Du Pont's career, the study responded to a growing interest in statistics on governmental finances. It also brought him Turgot's friendship, commissioned assignments studying regional economies, and contacts with the Trudaine brothers (Charles-Louis Trudaine de Montigny and his brother, Charles-Michel Trudaine de la Sablière, sons of a wealthy financier), involved in drafting an edict on the internal/external freedom of grain. The editorship of the *Journal de l'agriculture, du commerce et des finances* (1775)–a monthly supplement to the *Gazette du commerce*–assured a much-needed income, and Du Pont could finally marry Marie-Louise Le Dée de Roccourt, whose family, aware of Du Pont's financial insecurity, strongly opposed the union for many years. The couple had two sons, Victor and Eleuthère-Irénée, named "in honor of liberty and peace." Marie-Louise Du Pont was a devoted wife, deeply involved in her husband's career. A few months after the wedding, Du Pont lost the editorship, mainly because of his authoritarian language in publicizing his convictions and in addressing opposing views. He then embarked on two new projects.

Quesnay's work that Du Pont edited, *Physiocratie ou Constitution naturelle du gouverment le plus avantageux au genre humain* (1767, Physiocracy or Natural Constitution of the Most Advantageous Government to Humankind), takes the doctrine in a direction of the progressive integration of economic theory with politics and philosophy. Placing Quesnay's article on "Natural Rights" at the head of the collection and, in his introduction, defining the right of property as presocial and unrestricted, Du Pont emphasized the philosophical character of the system. In a new publication, *De l'Origine et des progrès d'une science nouvelle* (1768, On the Origin and Progress of a New Science), he extended his ideas in light of a popular essay written by Mercier de La Rivière, *L'Ordre naturel et essentiel des sociétés politiques* (1767, The Natural and Essential Order of Political Societies). Du Pont's manifesto of the doctrine formally introduced the school founders and their contributions while focusing on the political system of hereditary monarchy as the best grantor of property rights.

These attempts at synthesis through consecutive restatements in simple language were aimed at reaching a general readership and were accompanied by the invention of the official name for the group, the "Physiocrats." The wider doctrine, "physiocracy," a name coined by Du Pont to stress natural rights and duties, as well as subordination to the universal and social order, dates only from 1767. The adherents and potential converts to the doctrine exchanged their views at Quesnay's regular entresol meetings or channeled them in their own journals.

During a four-year period of editorship (1768–1772), Du Pont produced forty-eight volumes of the *Ephémérides du Citoyen* and wrote 110 major articles in addition to 40 shorter pieces. His interests noticeably shifted from the promulgation of economic theories toward a direct involvement in administrative reforms. In addition to taxes and freedom of commerce, he insisted on the abolition of corvée (forced labor) and slavery in the French colonies; questioned the government allowances for charities and the relation of population to food supplies; and occasionally reviewed poetry, literature, and art. After the 1772 suppression of the journal, administrators continued to commission Du Pont's economic reports. In correspondence with Carl Friedrich, margrave of Baden, for example, Du Pont outlined governmental responsibilities toward the poor, debtors, and beggars. On another occasion, in his own lectures sent to Baden, *Des courbes politiques* (written circa 1774; published 1892; translated as *On Economic Curves*, 1955), he introduced the use of mathematics in economic laws. *Table raisonnée des principes de l'économie politique* (1775, Table of Principles of Political Economy)—inspired by Quesnay's *Tableau économique* (1758, Economic Table) and representing the economy as a circular flow is the most important tool of governance prepared for the hereditary margrave. The elaborated topology of Du Pont's chart gives visual support to the physiocratic system. In a sort of pyramid—created with finely printed groups of words—individual needs and property rights are placed prominently at the top to give rise to social duties and political institutions.

After reading some of Du Pont's works, Fryderyk Michal Czartoryski, a Polish statesman, invited Du Pont to tutor his son and serve as secretary for a commission on education. Du Pont arrived in Poland only to be recalled by Turgot, who had been elevated to controller-general of finances under Louis XVI. During his crucial twenty months in office as Turgot's private secretary (1774–1776), Du Pont worked expeditiously toward a general reform to bolster the king's treasury. In a piece written for Turgot in 1776, *Mémoire sur les municipalités* (1787, Essay on Municipalities), Du Pont reminded Louis XVI that the isolation of the social classes and the lack of a constitution were the basic weaknesses of the monarchy. Du Pont suggested that continuous clashes of private interests derive from a poor understanding of civic responsibilities. To enlighten citizens about the organic interrelations between social classes and the monarch, Du Pont recommended an aggressive policy of governmental schooling with emphasis on religious education, as well as the voiced participation in the business of the kingdom for property owners. The members of administrative bodies should take part in public affairs not as agents of the clergy, nobility, or the third estate but as deputies of landowners. *Ordre réel* (real order) must replace *ordre personnel* (personal order).

After Turgot's downfall in 1776 when he was asked to resign as Minister of Finance, Du Pont retired to his country estate, Bois-des-Fossés. Writing poetry was his preferred distraction from agricultural experiments and animal studies. His anonymously written *Essai de traduction en vers du Roland Furieux de l'Arioste* (1781, Essay in Verse Translation of Ariosto's *Orlando Furioso*), features the First Song only. Despite promising in the preface "an extremely literal" translation, Du Pont noticeably enriched the original. The notes for the First Song—as well as the Second and Third, published thirty-one years later (1812)—feature commentaries on the historical background of various parts of the poem. Punctilious about documentation, Du Pont familiarized readers not only with the original but also with possible sources.

Stricken by Turgot's death in 1781, Du Pont gathered documents on his mentor's career for the *Mémoires sur la vie et les ouvrages de M. Turgot, ministre d'état* (1782, Memoirs on Turgot's Life and Works). The first part focuses on Turgot's educational background and talents (foreign languages, literal translation, and works for the *Encyclopedie*); the second part presents a financial account of Turgot's ministry. Pages of transcribed statistical reports justify Turgot's resourceful maneuvers in reducing deficit. Furthermore, Du Pont presents a numerical assessment of what would have happened to the treasury if Turgot had not been dismissed from office. Du Pont finally draws a physical and moral portrait of the minister, devoted to governmental duties and the rights of citizens.

Du Pont embraced three principles of his master—to know the truth, to be useful, and to be loved. The 1783 *lettre de noblesse* acknowledged Du Pont's contributions to foreign commerce and gave him a coat of arms with the motto *Rectitudine sto* (Be upright). In 1784, Mme Du Pont, who managed the country estate while taking care of their sons' education, died unexpectedly at the age of forty-one. Du Pont struggled on a miserable salary, seldom paid, for his distinctive service as secretary of the Assembly of Notables (1787–1789). As a result,

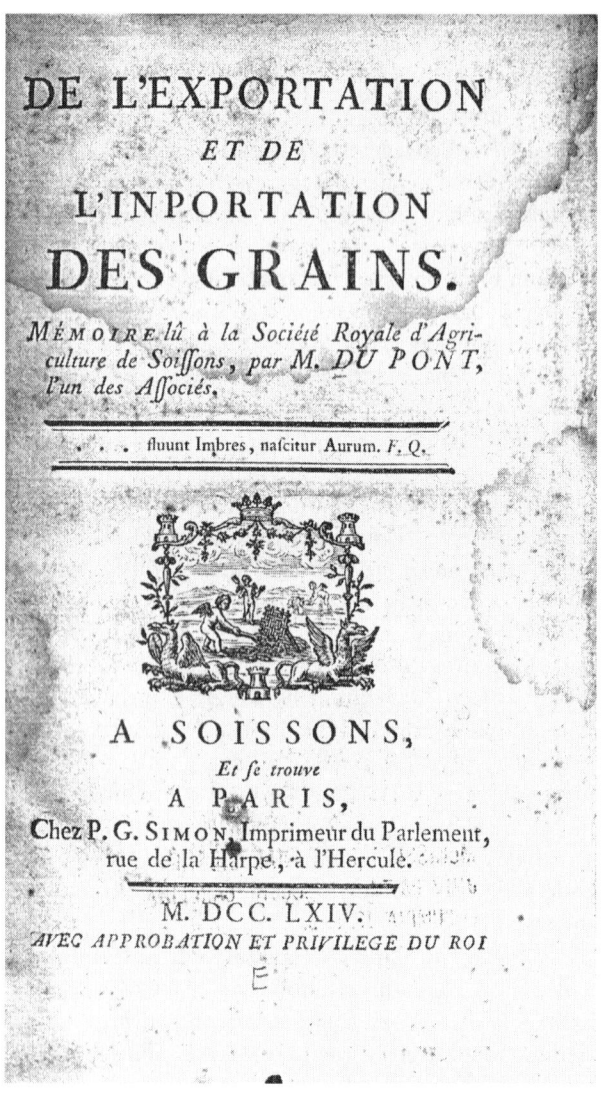

Title page for Du Pont's 1764 work (The Exportation and Importation of Grains), which presents his natural-resource theory that agriculturists are the most productive class of society (Thomas Cooper Library, University of South Carolina)

he discharged servants from Bois-des-Fossés, moved to a small apartment near the Bastille in Paris, and launched the careers of his sons. Victor, carrying a letter of introduction from Jefferson to Robert Livingston, United States minister to France, was sent to the United States for a career in diplomacy. Irénée went to Essone to study under Antoine Lavoisier, father of modern chemistry.

Du Pont's writings from this period deal with agricultural studies: flax culture, interdependence of production and market prices, and the *dîme* (tithe) as a negative tax factor. In a significant 1786 report, *Comparaison de l'état de l'agriculture en Angleterre avec celui de la France* (A Comparison of the State of Agriculture in England and France), Du Pont espoused the superiority of French agriculture. As a major player in the negotiations of the Anglo-French commercial treaty of 1786, he defended the treaty—against the voices of French merchants—to increase the wealth of the country through free trade as explained in his *Lettre à la Chambre du commerce de Normandie* (1788, Letter to the Normandy Chamber of Commerce).

In 1786 he published a eulogy for a Pierre Poivre, a well-known traveler and colonial administrator of the islands of Mauritus and Reunion who shared Du Pont's own interests in agriculture. The chronological summary of Poivre's life allowed Du Pont to list with evident pleasure the many exotic plants brought to France by his friend. That same year Du Pont published a brochure, *Idées sur les secours à donner aux pauvres malades dans une grande ville* (Ideas on Assistance for the Sick Poor in a Big City), in which he explains the deficiency of health care and funding of charitable hospitals and pleads for the creation of hospices for the homeless. For those who still had families, he demanded household relief. Later, as a member of the Association de bénéficence judiciaire, Du Pont advocated a free legal defense system for the needy.

The Revolution gave a new impetus to Du Pont's writing in the public interest. Before being elected deputy of the Third Estate from Nemours, where he owned property, he was restlessly preparing grievances for Chevannes and neighboring parishes. In the final draft of the 684–page manuscript, *Procès-verbal de l'Assemblée baillivale de Nemours pour la convocation des Etats-Généraux* (1789, Minutes of the Assembly of Nemours for the Convocation of the Estates General), Du Pont put forth a declaration of rights and thirty articles with precise reforms in civil/criminal law, finance, agriculture, and commerce.

The revolutionary symposia required an extraordinary capacity for work. During the two-year session of the National Assembly, Du Pont drafted hundreds of pages on economic policies, sat on twelve committees, and made 179 speeches, some of which were quite unpopular—for example, on the issue of assignats, which he vigorously opposed. In a major address on 4 September 1789 and in a 1789 pamphlet, *De la Périodicité des Assemblées nationales* (On the Periodicity of National Assemblies), Du Pont called for a social contract among the citizens whose union of will and intellect would increase national security and liberty, and preserve property. His other speeches denounced offensive wars as crimes and called for repressive actions against "agitators and anarchists," whose incendiary language misleads people. A moderate reformer, Du Pont became alarmed by the radicalization of Jacobins and was later stunned by the growing violence. He joined Lafayette,

Marie-Jean-Antoine-Nicolas Ceritat, marquis de Condorcet, and André-Marie de Chénier in organizing a short-lived moderate group publishing the *Journal de la Société de 1789*.

When the ordinance of the Assembly prohibited members from participating in the first legislature under the Constitution of 1791, Du Pont found another outlet for influencing public opinion. From his own print shop at the Hôtel Bretonvilliers on rue de l'Ile Saint-Louis, from 1791 to 1792 he published *Correspondance patriotique*, a weekly with the motto "Egalité, Liberté, Proprieté, Sécurite" (Equality, Liberty, Property, Security). During intense mob attacks, he organized a group of Grenadiers and Chasseurs of the Army of Paris, which came to the defense of the king trapped at the Tuileries on 10 August 1792. Du Pont's loyalty to the king—nourished by physiocratic beliefs in the natural basis of the monarchy—put his life in jeopardy. Accused of royalism, he went into hiding. In the shadow of the Revolution, Du Pont recorded his existence in a series of personal writings.

Drafted between 1792 and 1794 in epistolary format, *Mémoires de Pierre Samuel Du Pont adressés à ses enfants* (published as *Extraits des lettres de Pierre Samuel du Pont de Nemours à ses enfants*, 1867; translated as *The Autobiography of Du Pont de Nemours*, 1984) provides an account of his childhood, adolescence, and his first steps toward independence. This piece of social history records the life of the craftsmen under the ancien régime. It also depicts the social and economic advancement of a bourgeois. In a summation of his own existence, written at the age of fifty-three and supplemented with massive documentation, Du Pont describes the reality of his life and time in progressive terms. Education, prestigious friendships, publishing success, and above all, his own diligent labor, constituted the elements of a transition from a patronage system toward a formal career institutionalized by the Revolution.

Philosophie de l'univers (written circa 1792–1793; published 1796, Philosophy of the Universe), dedicated to Lavoisier, who had just been decapitated, is a poetic meditation on the secrets of nature. The introductory prose-poem, *Oromasis*, represents the two interconnected principles of good (Oromasis) and evil (Arimane) to show that a real appreciation of happiness would be impossible without the presence of destructive forces. Further in his cosmogonic work, Du Pont reflected upon the acts of the Creator and providential laws. While depriving men of immortality, the Creator gave them the passion of love and the ability to learn, two principles of species preservation. Among other stimuli discussed and occasionally compared to animal instincts are freedom, self-love, and sorrow. In the second and third editions of *Philosophie de l'univers*, the parallels between humans and animals were further elaborated because of Du Pont's growing interest in natural history and a "new religion"—the deistic cult of theophilanthropy. The leitmotiv of moral superiority, sympathy, and friendship penetrates the entire work; the invocation is to the "superior intelligence" of great men, who—even after death—can guide and protect the living. Despite the danger of being guillotined, Du Pont concluded with an enthusiastic passage against suicide.

Rushed to prison by the Jacobins on 22 July 1794, Du Pont was spared by Maximilien Robespierre's fall five days later. Still incarcerated, Du Pont wrote another optimistic work, *Vues sur l'éducation nationale par un cultivateur* (1793–1794, Views on National Education by a Farmer), to show how to teach writing and reading to young farmers and city youth. The pamphlet recommended natural training principles that promote morality and the new republican values.

After his release from the prison of La Force, Du Pont married Françoise Robin, his former colleague Poivre's widow, in 1795. Elected to the Council of Elders, he continued to champion the cause of moderation and order. Most of his interventions were printed in seventeen volumes of the journal under his editorship, *L'Historien* (1796–1797). He spoke in a new style of polite irony against the arbitrary actions of the Directory, the harsh laws against émigrés, and the sale of their property. He also addressed a disquieting imprecision in language—symptomatic of forthcoming tyranny—and recommended a civil code. The printed analysis of the revenues wasted by the Directory, in addition to recurring allusions to the shifty nature of Corsicans, led to Du Pont's arrest in the coup d'état of 18 Fructidor. The event muted his enthusiasm for politics and signaled a new phase in his life.

Before boarding the *American Eagle* for the United States, Du Pont wrote in 1799: "Le tour de l'Amérique est venu. Le gouvernement doux, modéré, judicieux et républicain des Etats-Unis offre à peuprès le seul asile où les persécutés puissent trouver du repos, où les fortunes puissent renaître par le travail, où la prudence des pères de familles puisse placer la réserve, le dernier magasin de la subsistance de leurs enfants" (It is now America's turn. The temperate, moderate, judicious and republican government of the United States offers almost the only asylum where persecuted men can find safety, where fortunes can be rebuilt through work, where the prudence of heads of families may invest their last savings, the last portion of the subsistence of their children). The natural right to property—already central to physiocracy as the basis of state prosperity—became a constant preoccupation in Du Pont's life. Landownership gradually emerged as a mark of distinction and endorsement of the right to vote and later as

Du Pont's country estate, Bois-des-Fossés, near Chevannes, which lack of money forced him to leave in 1784 after the death of his first wife (painting in Eleutherian Mills Historical Library; from Ambrose Saricks, Pierre Samuel Du Pont de Nemours, *1965; Thomas Cooper Library, University of South Carolina)*

material proof of individual values transferable in inheritance. For a land development project in Virginia, Du Pont collected subscriptions for his new stock company, mainly from Staël's circle of friends, between 1797 and 1799. The plan for an agricultural community, however, failed. The correspondence with Staël documents Du Pont's endless efforts to calm and repay his creditors.

As Du Pont grew older, education as the foundation of social life and advancement became the pivotal subject of his reflection. Asked by Jefferson for guidance in his plan for a state university in Virginia, Du Pont responded with a lengthy treatise on the entire system of American education. The fruit of lifelong reflections, *Sur l'Education nationale dans les Etats-Unis d'Amérique* (1800; translated as *National Education in the United States of America by Du Pont de Nemours,* 1923), emphasized the programs that should be fostered by government. He gave priority to the first years of schooling, the most crucial in the development of citizenship. The plan recommended prompt distribution of textbooks printed under the guidance of a Committee of Public Instruction and encouraged an award system for authors, instructors, and students. To form loyal members of society, such ethical values as liberty, property, justice, cooperation, sacredness of obligations, and compassion ranked first on the list of subjects to be taught.

He did not consider higher education and other "philosophical societies" among the most fundamental establishments and said they should serve only a small number of outstanding scholars. Instead of a traditional European "university" promoting abstract "universal" knowledge, Du Pont proposed a practical science center with four elitist institutions to teach medicine, mining, social science and legislation, and transcendental geometry.

To Du Pont's great regret, the English translation of this work was never completed in his lifetime. He asked Jefferson to undertake it, and Jefferson tried but finally said that "it would be easier to translate Homer" than Du Pont's philosophical writing. When the second French edition appeared in 1812, Du Pont had been living in Paris again for almost ten years and had high expectations for honors and new opportunities in the government. A nomination to the Senate, however–implied in the correspondence with Staël while Du Pont was still in America–never materialized. Du Pont exhausted his energy in trying to repay his shareholders and explaining his business difficulties in Virginia. Disappointed and filled with hatred for Napoleon Bonaparte, he found employment as a sublibrarian at the Arsenal, earning a humiliating salary of 200 livres per month. All the works he published thereafter were in response to the despotism of the empire.

The first modern edition of the nine-volume *Oeuvres de M. Turgot* (1808–1811, Turgot's Works) is a tribute to the minister who devoted his entire life to what he believed would result in the welfare of citizenry. The collection of manuscripts that were carefully protected and transported across the Atlantic features the volume of the *Mémoires sur la vie et les ouvreges de M. Turgot* published three decades earlier as an introduction and a variety of pieces compiled in chronological order, which included literature, miscellaneous papers, correspondence, and the documents related to Turgot's ministry. The last volume, with essays and translations of Virgil, Horace, and Alexander Pope, is literature oriented. It includes none of Turgot's letters to Du Pont. In a self-effacing gesture, the editor tried to point the spotlight at his master's achievements.

In prefaces, commentaries, and notes (reprinted in the 1844 edition of Turgot's works), Du Pont worked as an historian of economic thought. An overview of the various economic schools in a note in volume three reveals a change in his own perception. The works of economists now appeared primarily as complimentary, rather than antagonistic. The same tendency is found in Du Pont's 1805 commemorative "Notice historique sur M. Quesnay de Saint-Germain" (Historical Note on M. Quesnay de Saint-Germain), in which the old concepts of Physiocrats have been replaced with more-appropriate ones for an industrial society.

Du Pont's final critical contribution on economic theory was written in America, to which he hastily fled before Napoléon's return from Elba. Printed in Philadelphia, *Examen du livre de M. Malthus sur le principe de population* (1817, Analysis of Malthus's Book on the Principle of Population) provides an insightful analysis of British economist Thomas Robert Malthus and a French disciple of Adam Smith, Jean-Baptiste Say. Du Pont reworked his previously published reviews of the 1806 French translation of the *Principe de la population* and added his own translation of Malthus's four chapters, omitted from the French edition. According to Malthus, population increases faster than food supplies, thus causing most sinister miseries for mankind; however, these miseries can be prevented through moral constraints imposed by the government. Du Pont battled the idea of controlled reproduction and dismissed the pessimistic view of humanity's inability to increase food production. As evidenced by the example of the "happy" Cherokee Indians, an aggressive program to develop agriculture, combined with government assistance, can be a "productive" solution. Du Pont presented that idea in opposition to the British concept of industrial "transformation" of luxury products, which he claimed leads to poverty.

The last section is a piece of polemic bravery. Although Du Pont praised the 1815 popular edition of Say's *Traité d'économie politique* (Treatise of Political Economy), he disapproved of Say's arrogant representation of the Physiocrats as a "sect" of "good citizens" who made no contributions. In a tone of paternal rebuke, Du Pont advocates consideration for one's predecessors, with the help of maxims from Pierre Corneille, Voltaire, and Michel Eyquem de Montaigne. In retaliation, he pointed to Say's physiocratic heritage and named him "a grandson of Quesnay, a nephew of the great Turgot." He also questioned Say's principles of taxation, which included labor, machinery, and nature. Moving through time and space in historical examples–Egypt under the Pharaohs, Judea under the Hebrews, and France under Charlemagne–Du Pont enumerated the economic systems based on land taxation. The notes to this section also included an aggressive attack on Napoleon's politics. He also opposed Say's narrow definition of political economy as an experimental science of wealth. For Du Pont, judging by the paradigm of the past, the scope of political economy should embrace moral and scientific studies.

On the eve of David Ricardo's economic thought, Du Pont was still advocating the physiocracy that granted ontological order to moral, social, political, and economic phenomena and gave a remarkable unity to his own writings. His essays on theoretical and on applied economics, as well as his lyrical reflections on the universe, all called for social harmony and interaction. Formal changes in his texts, however, revealed the gradual maturation of a bourgeois individual. Whereas the volumes of propaganda exemplified boldness and discipline in argumentation, Du Pont's contributions as editor and translator were marked by intrusions and self-indulging addenda. He justified himself as "an artist," lacking precision and exactitude. The autobiographical series–overwritten, ecstatic, and chaotic, occasionally presented in the form of letters that included humor–reflects a growing need for personal expression.

Du Pont's fixation with the preservation of the autobiographical writings confirms not only a pre-Romantic sensibility but the awareness of private success. He was convinced that the *Philosophie de l'univers*–a recasting of his frustrated aspirations as a poet, scientist, and philosopher–would be the most important publication of his life. He also valued and impatiently awaited the translation of his work on education, based on his own experience as an immensely successful head of a

First page of a letter from Du Pont to Germaine de Staël, with whom he often corresponded about a failed agricultural venture in America. Most of the principal stockholders, whom he sought to repay, were her friends (Eleutherian Historical Library; from James Marshall, ed., De Staël-Du Pont Letters, *1968; Thomas Cooper Library, University of South Carolina).*

family, and later, as an industrial patriarch and founder of a prominent dynasty in America.

To the end, Pierre Samuel Du Pont de Nemours maintained his interests, writing for the National Institute and the American Philosophical Society, translating *Orlando Furioso,* corresponding with politicians, and preparing a manuscript on the Constitution for the Latin American republics. Amid all these projects, he was still planning to join his wife in Paris and secure the scattered manuscripts. He died in Delaware on 7 August 1817, with his sons at his bedside, and was buried near the site of the library that now shelters his papers. An embodiment of universal curiosity, Du Pont's contributions bring forth modern themes of property, family, education, and active citizenship as cornerstones of social order, while proclaiming faith in progress and the limitless possibilities of man.

Letters:

Charles Comte, ed., *Mélanges et correspondance d'économie politique: ouvrage posthume de Jean Baptiste Say* (Paris: Chamerot, 1833)—includes correspondence between Say and Du Pont, April 1815 to May 1816;

Bernhard Erdmannsdörffer, ed., *Politische Correspondenz Karl Friedrichs von Baden, 1783–1806,* 6 volumes (Heidelberg: Carl Winter, 1888–1901);

Carl Knies, ed., *Carl Friedrichs von Baden Brieflicher Verkehr mit Mirabeau und Du Pont,* 2 volumes (Heidelberg: Carl Winter, 1892);

Gustave Schelle, ed., "Lettres inédites de Du Pont de Nemours au Comte Chreptowicz," *Journal des economistes: revue mensuelle de la science économique et de la statistique,* sixth series, no. 14 (1907): 3–21;

Karl Obser, ed., *Lettres de Du Pont de Nemours à la Margrave Caroline-Louise de Bade sur les salons de 1773, 1777, 1779,* published by Obser with the assistance of Gaston Brière and Maurice Tourneux (Nogent-le-Rotrou: Daupeley-Gouverneur, 1909); from *Archives de l'art français,* receuil de documents inédits publiés par la Société de l'histoire de l'art français, nouvelle période (Paris: Jean Schemit, 1907–1908), II: 1–123; reprinted (Paris: Nobele, 1969);

B. G. Du Pont (Bessie Gardner), *Life of Eleuthère Irénée du Pont from Contemporary Correspondence,* 12 volumes (Newark: University of Delaware Press, 1923–1927);

Gustave Shelle, ed., *Lettres de Turgot à Du Pont de Nemours de 1764 à 1781; extraites de "Oeuvres de Turgot"* (Paris: F. Alcan, 1924);

Gilbert Chinard, ed., *Un Epilogue du neuf thermidor: Lettres de Du Pont de Nemours écrites de la prison de la Force; 5 thermidor–8 fructidor An II* (Paris: A. Margraff, 1929);

Dumas Malone, ed., *Correspondence between Thomas Jefferson and Pierre Samuel Du Pont de Nemours, 1798–1817,* translated by Linwood Lehman (Boston & New York: Houghton Mifflin, 1930); supplemented by Chinard with his "Jefferson and the Physiocrats" (New York: Da Capo Press, 1970);

Chinard, ed., *The Correspondence of Jefferson and Du Pont de Nemours, with an Introduction on Jefferson and the Physiocrats* (Baltimore: Johns Hopkins University Press, 1931);

Jean Léonor Le Marois, ed., "Du Pont de Nemours et Madame de Staël," *Cahiers de politique étrangère du Journal des nations américaines;* supplément bibliographique à *France-Amérique Magazine,* Nouvelle série, 40–41 (1946–1950): 499–512–includes sixteen letters and extracts from letters of Du Pont to Germaine de Staël, Jacques Necker, and Louis Necker dated from 8 February 1800 to 9 October 1810;

Chinard, ed., "Lettres de Du Pont de Nemours à Félix Faulcon; 12 mai 1795–25 octobre 1802," *French American Review,* 1 (1948): 174–183;

Raymond F. Betts, "Quelques lettres de Du Pont de Nemours à Talleyrand, 1815," *Cahiers d'histoire,* 6, no. 4 (1961): 457–465;

Arthur M. Wilson, "An Unpublished Letter of Diderot to Du Pont de Nemours (9 décembre 1775)," *Modern Language Review,* 58 (April 1963): 222–225;

James F. Marshall, ed. and trans., *De Staël-Du Pont Letters: Correspondence of Madame de Staël and Pierre Samuel Du Pont de Nemours and of Other Members of the Necker and Du Pont Families* (Madison: University of Wisconsin Press, 1968).

Biographies:

Denise Aimé-Azam, *Du Pont de Nemours, honnête homme* (Paris: Philippe Ortiz, [1933]);

Bessie Gardner Du Pont, *Du Pont de Nemours,* 2 volumes (Newark: University of Delaware Press, 1933);

Camille Streletski, *Pierre Samuel Du Pont de Nemours (1739–1817), étude historique, physiognomique et graphologique* (Nemours: Vaillot, 1936);

Ambrose Pierre Saricks, *Pierre Samuel Du Pont de Nemours* (Lawrence: University of Kansas Press, 1965).

References:

Marc Bouloiseau, *Bourgeoisie et Révolution: les Du Pont de Nemours 1788–1799* (Paris: Bibliothèque nationale, 1972);

Bouloiseau, "Du Pont de Nemours et l'éducation nationale," in *Actes du 96e Congrès national des Sociétés savantes* (Reims, 1970). Section d'histoire moderne et con-

temporaine (Paris: Bibliothèque nationale, 1974), I: 172–184;

Jeanine Dubuisson-Bertin, *Du Pont de Nemours et Napoléon,* Institut Napoléon: recueil de travaux et documents (Joigny: Imprimerie de Peyronnet, 1946);

Elizabeth Fox-Genovese, Introduction to *The Autobiography of Du Pont de Nemours* (Wilmington, Del.: Scholarly Resources, 1984), pp. 1–74;

Pierre Jolly, *Du Pont de Nemours, soldat de la liberté* (Paris: Presses universitaires de France, 1956); translated by Elise du Pont Elrick as *Du Pont de Nemours, Apostle of Liberty and the Promised Land* (Wilmington, Del.: Brandywine, 1977);

Georges Lioret, "Du Pont de Nemours député aux Etats généraux et à l'Assemblée constitutante," *Annales de la Société historique et archéologique du Gâtinais,* 32 (1914–1915): 1–77;

James J. McLain, *The Economic Writings of Du Dupont de Nemours* (Newark: University of Delaware Press, 1977);

Orville T. Murphy, "Du Pont de Nemours and the Anglo-French Commercial Treaty of 1786," *Economic History Review,* second series 19 (1966): 569–580;

Ambrose Saricks, "Du Pont de Nemours and the French Assembly (1789–1791)," *Historian,* 18, no. 2 (Spring 1956): 170–188;

Gustave Schelle, *Du Pont de Nemours et l'Ecole physiocratique* (Paris: Guillaumin, 1888); translated by Victor de Avenell as *Du Pont de Nemours and the Physiocratic School* ([Kennet Square, Pa.: Longwood Library], 1960);

Joseph A. Schumpeter, *History of Economic Analysis* (New York: Oxford University Press, 1954).

Papers:

The Hagley Library established by the Eleutherian Mills Foundation in Wilmington, Delaware, holds the most comprehensive collection of Pierre Samuel Du Pont de Nemours's papers, correspondence, books, pamphlets, periodicals, manuscripts, and manuscript collections. The Bibliothèque nationale in Paris is the second-largest depository of his papers. Among other sources of archival documentation, in addition to private collections, the following should be noted in France: Archives nationales, Institut de France, Archives de la Chambre de Commerce de Paris, and Archives du Ministère des Affaires Etrangères; and in Germany, Badische Generallandesarchiv and Badische Landesbibliothek.

Louise d'Epinay
(Louise-Florence-Pétronille Tardieu d'Esclavelles, marquise d'Epinay)
(11 March 1726 - 15 April 1783)

Michèle Bissière
University of North Carolina at Charlotte

BOOKS: *Mes Moments heureux* (Geneva: [Gauffecourt], 1758);

Lettres à mon fils (Geneva: Privately printed, 1759);

Les Conversations d'Emilie (Leipzig: Crusius, 1774; revised and enlarged edition, 2 volumes, Paris: Humblot, 1781); translated as *The Conversations of Emily*, 2 volumes (London: Marshall, 1787; Philadelphia: Carey, 1817);

Mémoires et correspondance de Madame d'Epinay, 3 volumes (Paris: Brunet, 1818); translated by J. H. Freese as *The Memoirs and Correspondence of Madame d'Epinay*, 3 volumes (London: Nichols, 1899; Paris: Société des Bibliophiles / New York: Merrill & Baker, 1903);

Histoire de Madame de Montbrillant; les pseudo-mémoires de Madame d'Epinay, 3 volumes, edited by Georges Roth (Paris: Gallimard, 1951).

Editions and Collections: *Mes Moments heureux,* edited by Challemel-Lacour (Paris: Sauton, 1869);

Les Contre-Confessions: Histoire de Madame de Montbrillant, edited by Elisabeth Badinter (Paris: Mercure de France, 1989);

Lettres à mon fils et Morceaux choisis, edited by Ruth Plaut Weinreb (Concord, Mass.: Wayside, 1989);

Qu'est-ce qu'une femme? edited by Badinter (Paris: P.O.L., 1989)—comprises A. L. Thomas, *Essai sur le caractère, les moeurs et l'esprit des femmes dans les différents siècles;* Denis Diderot, *Sur les femmes;* and Epinay, "Lettre de Madame d'Epinay à l'abbé Galiani sur le livre de Thomas";

Les Conversations d'Emilie, edited by Rosena Davison, Studies on Voltaire and the Eighteenth Century, no. 342 (Oxford: Voltaire Foundation, 1996).

OTHER: Fernandino Galiani, *Dialogues sur le commerce des bleds,* edited by Denis Diderot and Frédéric Melchior Grimm, contributions by Epinay (London [Paris?]: Merlin, 1770);

Louise d'Epinay (portrait by Jean-Etienne Liotard, Musée d'art et d'histoire, Geneva; from Arthur Wilson, Diderot, 1972; Collection of W. Ross)

Correspondance littéraire, philosophique, et critique, adressée à un souverain d'Allemagne par Grimm, Diderot, Raynal, Meister, 16 volumes, edited by Grimm, Diderot, Joseph-François Michaud, Guillaume-Thomas-François Raynal (abbé), Jacques-Henri Meister, and François Chéron (Paris: Longchamps, 1812–1813)—includes contributions by Epinay; translated as *Historical and Literary Memoirs and Anecdotes, Selected from the Correspondence of Baron de Grimm and Diderot, with the Duke of Saxe-Gotha,* 2 volumes (London, 1814).

Louise d'Epinay was a respected writer, critic, *salonnière*, and friend of the philosophes. Voltaire nicknamed her "ma belle philosophe" (my beautiful philosophe) and, recognizing her sharp mind, spoke of her as "un aigle dans une cage de gaze" (an eagle in a cage of gauze). Epinay is best known for her moral and pedagogical works and a partly autobiographical epistolary novel. She also wrote and edited articles on a variety of topics and maintained an extensive correspondence with the Neapolitan abbé Fernandino Galiani that provides rich information on the social, political, and intellectual developments in Paris during the second half of the eighteenth century.

Louise-Florence-Pétronille Tardieu d'Esclavelles was born in Valenciennes on 11 March 1726 to Baron Louis-Gabriel Tardieu d'Esclavelles, governor of the citadel of that small northeastern city, and to his wife, Florence Angélique Prouveur de Preux. After her father's death in 1736, Louise and her impoverished mother went to live with Marie-Josèphe Proveur, Madame de la Live de Bellegarde, a wealthy maternal aunt, married to a *fermier général* (tax farmer) and living in Paris, who treated them with condescension. Neither Bellegarde nor d'Esclavelles provided the child with the broad education that the father had envisioned for her. Louise's mother was a traditional woman who believed that members of her gender needed only minimal instruction.

A curious and intelligent child, Louise nevertheless managed to learn from her cousins' lessons, quickly outpacing her relatives, much to her aunt's chagrin. Louise and her mother eventually moved to a small apartment, and Louise completed her education at a convent school from 1737 to 1739. Upon completing her studies, she fell in love with her first cousin, Denis-Joseph Lalive d'Epinay, but her aunt was opposed to their union. They eventually married on 23 December 1745, two years after Madame de Bellegarde's death, and settled at the Château de La Chevrette, the Epinay estate near Paris. They led a rich social life, entertaining visitors with concerts, balls, and amateur theatrical productions. Their happiness was short-lived, however, because of their opposing views of marriage: she wished for a companionate marriage that focused on family life, while he preferred the more permissive aristocratic approach that tolerated the keeping of mistresses, on whom he squandered the family fortune. One of the couple's early disputes arose when Epinay forbade his wife to breast-feed their first child, Louis-Joseph, born 25 September 1746. The practice of nursing children was still rare among women of the bourgeoisie and aristocracy, and Epinay's husband shared the prevailing prejudice against this practice, which, he argued, interfered with his wife's social duties. The couple had another child, Suzanne-Françoise Thérèse, who was born 24 August 1747 and died 2 June 1748.

Unhappy in her marriage and angered by her husband's extravagant and dissolute lifestyle—having contracted syphilis from him—Epinay followed the advice of a female friend and started an affair with Claude-Louis Dupin de Francueil in 1748. A frequent visitor to La Chevrette, Francueil later became the grandfather of George Sand. With the support of her father-in-law, Louise obtained financial separation from her husband in 1749 and gave birth to a daughter by Francueil, Angélique-Louise-Charlotte, born on 1 August 1749, and a son, LeBlanc de Beaulieu, born in 1753. This period of her life was more rewarding, for Epinay was able to fulfill her earlier wish to breast-feed her children and enjoyed more freedom in their education, following the death of her father-in-law in 1751. Francueil, too, however, was unfaithful, and their relationship soon started to deteriorate. In 1755 Epinay started a lifelong relationship with Frédéric Melchior Grimm, a German intellectual who had moved to Paris in 1749 and befriended Jean-Jacques Rousseau and Denis Diderot.

Epinay's association with Francueil and Grimm added a new dimension to her life. Both men introduced her to their intellectual friends, and La Chevrette became a gathering place for artists and writers, including Diderot; Charles-Pinot Duclos; Paul-Henri Thiry, baron d'Holbach; Grimm; Galiani; Jean Le Rond d'Alembert; and Rousseau. Grimm, especially, revived her childhood interest in learning and encouraged her to write. Taking stock of her life in the mid 1750s, Epinay considered herself ignorant and vowed to become "une femme d'un grand mérite" (a woman of great merit). In 1755 she started to edit and write reviews and articles for the *Correspondance littéraire, philosophique, et critique, adressée à un souverain d'Allemagne par Grimm, Diderot, Raynal, Meister* (1812–1813; translated as *Historical and Literary Memoirs and Anecdotes, Selected from the Correspondence of Baron de Grimm and Diderot, with the Duke of Saxe-Gotha,* 1814), of which Grimm served as main editor from 1753 to 1773. The *Correspondance littéraire* was a private bimonthly newsletter designed to keep subscribers—mainly crowned princes of Europe—informed of political, literary, and social developments in Paris. It included extensive reviews of plays and exhibits, as well as salon discussions and witty repartee.

Epinay's initial contributions to the *Correspondance littéraire* dealt with home life—for example, "Lettre à la gouvernante de ma fille" (Letter to the Governess of My Daughter, 1 October 1756), and essays on education addressed to her son. These early works reveal the modernity of her pedagogical thought. Like Rousseau, Epinay believed that education should take into account the individuality of each person; unlike him, however, she believed that instruction should begin at an early age and stressed the need to improve women's education. "Lettre à la gouvernante de ma fille" was addressed to the governess of her seven-year-old daughter, Angélique, as Epinay was suffering from acute migraines and stomach pain at that time and could not personally supervise her daughter's education. In the letter, she emphasizes the need to occupy Angélique's mind by offering her such activities as writing; studying catechism, history, and geography; memorizing poetry; and observing the wonders of nature. She also encourages the use of a nondidactic method based on an accurate understanding of the child's personality. More importantly, she stresses the need to link instruction and character building in order to help Angélique develop into a compassionate and independent-minded human being.

In 1756 Epinay wrote ten essays on education addressed to her nine-year-old son, eight of which appeared in the *Correspondance littéraire* on 15 June 1756 and 1 January 1757 and were later published with two additional essays under the title *Lettres à mon fils* (1759, Letters to My Son). In the first letter, she details her own principles for her son's education. Until her separation from her husband and the death of her father-in-law in 1751, Epinay had had little input into the education of her son—a responsibility generally assumed by the father and his family. Her son had spent time at a boarding school but then was brought home to continue his education under his mother's supervision. The first letter of this group includes arguments against the *collèges*, or boarding schools, which were being increasingly criticized for their antiquated methods and curricula. Epinay believed the *collèges* were too despotic and was concerned that the stringent discipline to which her son was submitted would foster rebellion in him. She objected to the fierce intellectual competition in boys' schools, preferring instead to stimulate moral emulation through contact with wise and virtuous friends. As in "Lettre à la gouvernante de ma fille," *Lettres à mon fils* focuses on character building, but the tone is more urgent because Epinay was worried about her son's bad habits. Several of these letters were inspired by a particular event in her life or her son's and concentrate on a moral theme, such as "De la droiture" (On Righteousness) or "De la compassion" (On Compassion). Her son's response to praise, for example, led to a letter on flattery in which she encouraged him to judge his actions according to his own conscience and principles. His impending departure for Paris provided an opportunity to extol the simplicity and dignity of country life and to impress upon the young man the need to respect social inferiors. Epinay

Epinay as a young woman (Elisabeth Badinter, Emilie, Emilie, *1983; Sador Teszler Library, Wofford College)*

illustrated her moral teachings with parables and examples from history. One of the allegorical tales is the story of two young men—one deaf, the other blind—who stand for stubbornness and weakness. Too sure of themselves, they leave their father's house and meet with obstacles that cure them of their flaws. Epinay used the tale to teach her son the importance of knowing one's own strengths and weaknesses before venturing out on one's own.

Epinay's interest in educational matters was no doubt stimulated by her close relationship with Rousseau, whom Francueil introduced to her in 1747 and invited to stay at the country estate, the Hermitage, in 1756. Rousseau lived there for eighteen months with his companion, Thérèse, and her mother. At the Hermitage, he found inspiration to lay the groundwork for several of his major works, including *Du Contrat social* (1762; translated as *An Inquiry into the Nature of the Social Contract,* 1791), *Emile, ou de l'éducation* (1762; translated as *Emilius and Sophia; or, a New System of Education,* 1762), and *Julie, ou La Nouvelle Héloïse* (1761; translated as *Eloisa: or, A Series of Original Letters Collected and Published by J. J. Rousseau,* 1761). Rousseau and Epinay met fre-

Portrait of Denis-Joseph Lalive d'Epinay, husband of Epinay, whom she married 23 December 1745 (Collection of Lalive d'Epinay, comte G. de Bueil; from Francis Steegmuller, A Woman, a Man, and Two Kingdoms, *1991; Thomas Cooper Library, University of South Carolina)*

quently for walks and conversations. He advised her on her essays on education and shared with her his manuscript of *La Nouvelle Héloïse*. Although she did not particularly appreciate his style, she was strongly impressed by the novel and decided to start a story of her own. Their friendship, however, gradually started to deteriorate. According to Rousseau in book 9 of *Les Confessions* (written between 1765 and 1770, and published in 1782; translated as *The Confessions of J. J. Rousseau*, 1783), Epinay was an overly demanding hostess who interfered with his personal life and tried to monopolize him. While at the Hermitage, Rousseau also had a liaison with Sophie d'Houdetot, Epinay's sister-in-law, whose lover, poet Jean-François de Saint-Lambert, was away at war. Rousseau accused Epinay of stealing his correspondence with d'Houdetot and divulging the affair to Saint-Lambert, an accusation she denied. The discord was fueled by Epinay's friends, especially Grimm, who had their own difficulties with Rousseau over matters of authorship and reputation. The quarrel came to a head in 1757 when Epinay's health had deteriorated to the point that her friends feared for her life. She was advised to go to Geneva to consult Theodore Tronchin, a renowned Swiss doctor, and asked Rousseau to accompany her. He refused, hinting, moreover, that the reason for her trip was to hide a pregnancy. Epinay and her entourage were indignant at such ingratitude, and the friendship with Rousseau came to an end. He left the Hermitage, while Epinay traveled to Geneva under her husband's care.

Epinay lived in Geneva with her son Louis-Joseph from November 1757 until October 1759. She was impressed by the simplicity of Swiss life, which stood in stark contrast with the extravagance and frivolity of Parisian life, and appreciated people's respect for merit and virtue. She also approved of its participatory political system and its sumptuary laws. In Switzerland she wrote the last two essays of *Lettres à mon fils*. In letter 11, "Genève," Epinay laments that living in Geneva did not change her son, who remained weak, lazy, and vain, and she expresses concern for his future. Letter 12, "De la vertu et de la conscience" (On Virtue and Conscience), is a last reminder to him that, since he is not meant for heroic deeds, he should at least keep his self-respect and listen to his conscience to find happiness in life. Apart from her misgivings about her son, Epinay's life in Geneva was happy and productive. She collected her essays on education and printed them on a neighbor's printing press as *Lettres à mon fils*; she gathered a series of essays, letters, and self-portraits written over the previous ten years into a volume titled *Mes Moments heureux* (1758, My Happy Moments); she began writing her novel *Histoire de Madame de Montbrillant; les pseudo-mémoires de Madame d'Epinay* (1951, Story of Madame de Montbrillant; The Pseudo-Memoirs of Madame d'Epinay), published posthumously; and she also spent time with Voltaire, who lived in nearby Ferney and appreciated her company.

When Epinay returned to Paris, she resumed her work for the *Correspondance littéraire* and continued to write the first draft of her partly autobiographical novel, *Histoire de Madame de Montbrillant*, between 1756 and 1762. The book is in the tradition of the eighteenth-century epistolary genre with multiple correspondents. The action is introduced by a narrator who vouches for the authenticity of the story, explaining that it is published to legitimize the heroine's life and rehabilitate her reputation. A blend of letters, journal entries, and third-person commentary by the narrator, the story spans twenty-five years in the life of the protagonist, Emilie de Gondrecourt. Left fatherless at age ten, the young and submissive child is dominated by her aunt and her traditional mother. Emilie marries a libertine, remains oppressed, and seeks happiness in extramarital affairs. She gradually gains independence when she meets her second lover, who introduces her to the joys of reading, writing, and salon conversation. From that point on, she develops into a liberated, well-educated woman who dedicates herself to the education of her children. Clearly, the novel is based in part on the author's life up to 1762, but its ending is fiction. Emilie's health declines when her lover has to flee France, and she dies at age thirty-five. In fact, the end of the novel coincides with the death of Epinay's mother, Madame d'Esclavelles, in 1762.

In this multifaceted work, perhaps aided by Grimm and Diderot, Epinay experiments with new techniques. Her narrator is original compared to the more conventional narrator-editors of other eighteenth-century novels: he is actively involved in the plot as a letter writer, serves as confidant of the female protagonist, and comments on the events and characters. *Histoire de Madame de Montbrillant* also differs from contemporary epistolary novels in that it includes not only letters but also journal entries, in which the heroine records her innermost thoughts, thus making up for her lack of trustworthy friends. The letters begin when she breaks away from her mother's grip and decrease in number when she meets her lover, Volx. The novel is also original in its inclusion of details of daily life. The protagonist writes about her pregnancy, her family's reaction to the idea of breast-feeding her first child, and her thoughts on the education of children. She provides ample information on her financial situation and the proposals she made to her husband when she wanted to separate.

The novel has been interpreted as Epinay's attempt to measure her creative talents against that of Rousseau, whose manuscript of *La Nouvelle Héloïse* she had just read. Indeed, by focusing on the predicaments of a woman's life—her unhappy marriage and the difficulties she encounters while raising her children and trying to sustain female friendships—the novel offers a challenge to the idealized view of marriage, motherhood, and friendship found in Rousseau's novel. Moreover, *Histoire de Madame de Montbrillant* gives a positive view of facets of female life criticized in *La Nouvelle Héloïse,* such as extramarital affairs and literary and intellectual activities. Epinay did not publish her novel: she finished the original manuscript in 1762, continued to revise it until 1770-1771, and bequeathed a revised version with accompanying notes to Grimm. The untitled manuscript was found among his papers, and an abridged version was first published in 1818 as *Mémoires et correspondance de Madame d'Epinay* (translated as *The Memoirs and Correspondence of Madame d'Epinay,* 1899). Why she did not publish her novel is not clear. Perhaps she was reluctant to divulge her husband's immorality or lacked time because of involvement in other demanding projects.

In the early 1770s Epinay played a major role in the editing of the *Correspondance littéraire.* She and Diderot replaced Grimm when he was abroad on business, and she alone assumed most of the responsibilities during Grimm's extended absence in 1771-1772. In addition to performing administrative and financial duties, she wrote articles on politics and economics, as well as elaborate theater reviews. Her extensive contributions were minimized by editorial decisions when the *Correspondance littéraire* was published in the nineteenth century.

In the 1770s Epinay was also corresponding and collaborating with abbé Galiani, whom she met in Paris in 1759 while he was serving as secretary of the Neapolitan Embassy. When Galiani was recalled to Naples in 1769, he left her the manuscript of his *Dialogues sur le commerce des bleds* (1770, Dialogues on Grain Trade), a book that criticizes a 1764 edict allowing free trade of domestic grain and in which characters express opposing views on the question of government regulation of that trade. Grimm, Epinay, and Diderot edited the work, sought permission to publish it, and found a printer. Epinay also promoted the book, handled its distribution, and sued the printer to ensure that Galiani be paid. These business matters make up the bulk of their correspondence during the first two or three years. Like her contributions to the *Correspondance littéraire,* Epinay's work on the *Dialogues sur le commerce des bleds* was not properly credited in the first important edition of her correspondence with Galiani, *La Signora d'Epinay e l'Abate Galiani. Lettere Inedite, 1769-1772* (1929). The editor, Fausto Nicolini, deleted or shortened texts that highlighted Galiani's keen interest in financial matters. In addition to briefing Galiani on the latest developments concerning his book, Epinay's letters kept him informed of literary, cultural, and political events in Paris, with such extensive comments that he sometimes jokingly remarked that her letters were becoming an encyclopedia. The correspondence was also particularly personal: Epinay and Galiani shared their thoughts on music, love, and life in general, and discussed health-related concerns and home remedies. Epinay confided in him and shared her disappointment with the indifference of Grimm and the behavior of her son, who served several prison terms for the debts he accumulated. Epinay and Galiani also advised each other on the books or essays they were writing. In her letters, Epinay sometimes explored ideas that she later discussed in articles in the *Correspondance littéraire.*

One of her best-known letters to Galiani included a critique of Antoine-Léonard Thomas's *Essai sur le caractère, les moeurs et l'esprit des femmes dans les différents siècles* (1772; translated as *Essay on the Character, Manners, and Genius of Women in Different Ages,* 1774). In writing this essay, Thomas tried to prove that his female contemporaries had strayed from their natural call in life—

The Hermitage, a house on Epinay's country estate where she invited Jean-Jacques Rousseau to live for eighteen months and where he started several major projects (Marc-Vincent Howlett, L'Homme qui croyait en l'homme, *1989; Thomas Cooper Library, University of South Carolina)*

domesticity and motherhood—and were responsible for the moral decline of society. Through historical and cross-cultural examples, he demonstrated that women are by nature physically and intellectually inferior to men and should restrict their activity to the domestic sphere. In a letter to Galiani dated 14 March 1772, Epinay carefully refuted Thomas's points and argued that women's subordinate status in society was attributable instead to their inadequate education. Women's frivolity and superficiality, for example, resulted from the lack of serious responsibilities afforded them in society, not to nature. According to Epinay, social institutions had weakened women's minds and bodies in order to oppress them better. The imbalance had become such that to restore the original equality between the sexes was almost impossible. In the months following its publication, Thomas's essay also occasioned impassioned reactions from Grimm, Galiani, and Diderot in the *Correspondance littéraire*. Diderot responded in an essay titled *Sur les femmes* (On Women), published on 1 April 1772. Although Epinay did not share Galiani's traditional views on women, she published his response as well. This exchange of opinions was characteristic of the Enlightenment and showed that Epinay was a true participant in the major debates of her time. Unlike Diderot and Grimm, she believed that improved female education was key to restoring women to their original nature, and she dedicated her life and writings to that purpose.

Epinay's best-known work published during her lifetime was *Les Conversations d'Emilie* (1774; translated as *The Conversations of Emily*, 1787). The second edition (1781) received the Prix d'utilité of the Académie Française in 1783, awarded to the best work on pedagogy published in the year. *Les Conversations d'Emilie* is a series of conversations between a mother and her ten-year-old daughter and is based on Epinay's own experience as educator of her granddaughter Emilie de Belsunce, who came to live with her at age two. Emilie was the third child of Epinay's daughter Angélique. Following her husband's loss of his position as tax farmer, as a result of his debts and outrageous behavior, the impoverished Epinay had married off her daughter Angélique at age fourteen to Viscount Dominique de Belsunce, her senior by more than twenty years. The couple led an uneventful life in Navarre, in southwestern France, away from the center of culture. Epinay wrote to Galiani that her hope was to turn Emilie into a masterpiece, the first example of her kind in Paris, and that she was writing *Les Conversations d'Emilie* to share her knowledge about children's education with Angélique. The originality of the book lies in its relatively loose structure. The fictional mother follows no preconceived method. Rather, she takes advantage of Emilie's questions and certain circumstances to raise appropriate topics and to reinforce the values she seeks to instill in the child. She uses tales and examples inspired by nature, history, or daily life to develop Emilie's autonomy and self-reliance. The education given to Emilie is broad and progressive, especially if compared to traditional female education in the eighteenth century, which emphasized the teaching of religion and social graces. The fictional mother uses the Socratic approach, favors reflection over memorization, and proposes a broad curriculum that includes the sciences—a topic considered inappropriate for women. On the other hand, religious instruction is kept to a minimum, an aspect of the program for which Epinay was criticized. Realistic, the mother also stresses the importance of protecting one's reputation by hiding personal flaws from others, except from one's own mother.

Epinay believed that education was key to happiness for women, who had no outlet in society beyond motherhood. She raised her granddaughter according to that principle, which serves as a leitmotiv in all her writings. On 4 January 1771, for example, while still in charge of Emilie's education, she wrote her friend Galiani:

> Elle [la femme] a grande raison, les devoirs de mère, de fille, d'épouse une fois remplis, de se livrer à l'étude et au travail, parce que c'est un moyen sûr de se suffire à soi-même, d'être libre et indépendante, de se consoler des injustices du sort des hommes, et qu'on n'est jamais plus chérie, plus considérée d'eux que lorsqu'on n'en a pas de besoin.
>
> (She [woman] is well advised, once she has fulfilled her duties as daughter, wife, and mother, to dedicate herself to studying and working, because it is a sure means of being self-sufficient, free and independent, of finding solace for the injustices of her lot, and because men love and respect us best when we do not need them.)

Epinay intended to write an educational treatise in three parts: from birth to age ten, eleven to fourteen, and fifteen to marriage. She did not carry out that plan, but the 1781 revised edition of *Les Conversations d'Emilie* seems to have been the second stage of the project. This new edition includes changes in tone and content, and eight additional conversations, which address Emilie's needs as a young adolescent. It includes, for example, more anecdotes and conversations about marriage. When Emilie expresses her surprise at seeing a young bride cry on her wedding day, her mother impresses upon her that marriage is a solemn event that determines the quality of a woman's life. She warns her against a too romantic view of marriage by painting the disappointments that may come with it, and she advises Emilie to search for happiness elsewhere, especially in motherhood. The focus on motherhood is a notable addition to the 1781 edition. In the preface, Epinay explains that this new edition is designed for the mothers who want to follow Rousseau's advice and dedicate themselves to their children's education. Another reason for revising the book may have been to satisfy her literary ambition—especially after the positive comments she received for the first edition—and to express herself publicly on some of the educational debates of the time, particularly the one on the relative merits of private and public education, the subject of a large segment of the last conversation.

The ideas and methods detailed in *Les Conversations d'Emilie* were generally well received by contemporary readers, although some found the style and moral teachings above the level of understanding of a young child. Catherine the Great, a subscriber to the *Correspondance littéraire,* admired Epinay's Socratic approach and gave her—and later also gave her granddaughter—financial support. The book was also praised as "l'exécution la plus heureuse du catéchisme moral dont Jean-Jacques a tracé le projet dans son *Emile*" (the best execution of the moral catechism planned by Jean-Jacques in his *Emile*). Reviews of the second edition make even more references to *Emile*. Indeed, Epinay and Rousseau had common educational ideals. Both believed that children are fundamentally different from adults and must be educated according to their particular needs; both favored an education based on experience rather than on direct learning; and both stressed the importance of physical activity. Unlike Rousseau, however, Epinay believed that instruction should begin early. *Les Conversations d'Emilie,* like *Lettres à mon fils,* pokes fun at Rousseau's idea that intellectual education should be

Epinay at her desk (portrait by Louis Carmontelle, Musée Condé, Chantilly; from Jeannette Rosso, Diderot et le portrait, *1998; Perkins Library, Duke University)*

delayed. Modern critics have also highlighted parallels with Rousseau but have focused on Epinay's advanced views on female education compared to Rousseau's limited ideal for Sophie in book 5 of *Emile*.

Epinay remained productive in the last years of her life, despite suffering from stomach cancer. Her letters to Galiani in the late 1770s and early 1780s make increasing references to her deteriorating health, often with a humorous tone. They include many physiological details, as in a letter dated 12 May 1781, in which she describes herself as follows: "Ma main tremble, mes dents tombent, de sorte que je ressemble pas mal à la vieille de Candide, sauf les fesses" (My hand is shaking, my teeth are falling out, and I am beginning to look like the old woman in Candide, except for the buttocks). Louise d'Epinay died of her illness on 15 April 1783, three months after receiving the Prix d'utilité of the Académie Française for *Les Conversations d'Emilie*. Grimm ensured that her granddaughter Emilie was properly educated and possessed an adequate dowry, part of which came from Catherine the Great. The obituary that appeared in the *Correspondance littéraire,* possibly written by Grimm, downplays Epinay's contributions as a writer. The manuscript of her 1,550-page epistolary novel, for example, is described as "the outline of a long novel."

The history of the posthumous publication and reception of *Histoire de Madame de Montbrillant* illustrates the changing literary reputation of Louise d'Epinay from friend and foe of Rousseau to writer in her own right. The book was first published as authentic memoirs in 1818. Its publisher, J. C. Brunet, replaced fictional names with real ones: M. and Mme de Montbrillant, Formeuse, Volx, Garnier, and René became, respectively, Epinay and her husband, Dupin de Francueil, Grimm, Diderot, and Rousseau. Brunet substituted real letters written by or received by Epinay for fictional ones and removed other elements that he thought were not autobiographical. The book was popular in the nineteenth century because of growing interest in the ancien régime and in the conflict between Rousseau and the philosophes—one in which Epinay had played a central part as Rousseau's hostess at the Hermitage. Early readers believed Epinay's version of the story, and critics such as Charles-Augustin Sainte-Beuve and Louis Petit de Julleville praised the literary merits of the novel. The trend changed in the late nineteenth century when Frederika MacDonald, a Rousseau enthusiast, discovered the notes that Epinay had used to revise her original manuscript, some of which were in her own handwriting and others in Diderot's. She argued that Epinay, Grimm, and Diderot made changes in the novel after hearing that Rousseau was writing *Les Confessions* and especially when he started giving private readings of the book in 1770. According to MacDonald and later scholars, Epinay and her friends clouded Rousseau's character as an act of self-defense for his unflattering portrayal of the group in book 9 of *Les Confessions*. *Histoire de Madame de Montbrillant* was then considered untruthful memoirs and fell into oblivion until Georges Roth published an unabridged edition with notes in 1951. This new edition led to a revision of MacDonald's theory. Those who still tend to accept this interpretation now think that the changes in the portrayal of Rousseau were not major. More significantly, the 1951 edition and the 1989 edition by Elisabeth Badinter have shifted the attention onto the literary and historic merits of the novel. Together with recent studies and new editions of the *Correspondance littéraire* and Epinay's correspondence with Galiani, these works show that Epinay was an important educator, a fine critic, and a major writer of the Enlightenment.

Letters:

Eugène Asse, ed., *Lettres de l'Abbé Galiani à Mme d'Epinay, Voltaire, Diderot, Grimm, etc.,* 2 volumes (Paris: Charpentier, 1881);

Lucien Perey and Gaston Maugras, eds., *L'Abbé Galiani. Correspondance avec Madame d'Epinay, Madame Necker, Madame Geoffrin, etc.* (Paris: Calmann Lévy, 1881);

Fausto Nicolini, ed., *La Signora d'Epinay e l'Abate Galiani. Lettere Inedite, 1769–1772* (Bari: Laterza & Figli, 1929);

Nicolini, ed., *Gli ultimi anni della Signora d'Epinay. Lettere inedite all'abate Galiani, 1773–1782* (Bari: Laterza & Figli, 1933);

Georges Dulac and Daniel Maggetti, eds., *Correspondance de Fernandino Galiani et Louise d'Epinay,* 5 volumes (Paris: Desjonquères, 1992–1997).

Biographies:

Lucien Perey and Gaston Maugras, eds., *La Jeunesse de Madame d'Epinay* (Paris: Calmann Lévy, 1882);

Perey and Maugras, eds., *Une Femme du monde au XVIIIe siècle. Dernières années de Madame d'Epinay, son salon et ses amis d'après des lettres et des documents inédits* (Paris: Calmann Lévy, 1883);

Francis Steegmuller, *A Woman, a Man, and Two Kingdoms: The Story of Madame d'Epinay and the Abbé Galiani* (New York: Knopf, 1992).

References:

Elisabeth Badinter, *Emilie, Emilie, ou l'ambition féminine au XVIIIe siècle* (Paris: Flammarion, 1983);

Badinter, "Sur la mort de Mme d'Epinay: une lettre inédite de Grimm," *Dix-huitième siècle,* 22 (1990): 239–241;

Colette Cazenobe, "*L'Histoire de Madame de Montbrillant:* un laboratoire de formes romanesques," *Revue d'histoire littéraire de la France,* 96, no. 2 (1996): 229–245;

Rosena Davison, "Madame d'Epinay's Contribution to Girls' Education," in *Femmes savantes et femmes d'esprit,* edited by Roland Bonnel and Catherine Rubinger (New York: Peter Lang, 1994), pp. 219–241;

Martin Fontius, "Mozart chez Grimm et Madame d'Epinay," *Recherches sur Diderot et sur l'Encyclopédie,* 9 (1990): 95–108;

P. N. Furbank, "Diderot and the *Histoire de Madame de Montbrillant,*" *British Journal for Eighteenth-Century Studies,* 13, no. 2 (1990): 157–161;

U. Kölving and J. Carriat, "Inventaire de la *Correspondance littéraire,*" in *Studies on Voltaire and the Eighteenth Century,* edited by H. T. Mason (Oxford: Voltaire Foundation, 1984), pp. 225–227;

Alice Parker, "Louise d'Epinay's Account of Female Epistemology and Sexual Politics," *French Review,* 55, no. 1 (1981): 43–51;

Jean-Jacques Rousseau, *Les Confessions,* in *Oeuvres complètes,* 4 volumes, edited by Bernard Gagnebin and Marcel Raymond (Paris: Gallimard, 1961);

Leon Schwartz, "F. M. Grimm and the Eighteenth-Century Debate on Women," *French Review,* 58, no. 2 (1984): 236–243;

Samia I. Spencer, "Women and Education in Eighteenth-Century France," *Proceedings of the Annual Meeting of the Western Society For French History,* 10 (1984): 274–284;

Mary Trouille, "La Femme mal-mariée: Mme d'Epinay's Challenge to *Julie* and *Emile,*" *Eighteenth-Century Life,* 20, no. 1 (1996): 42–66;

Trouille, *Sexual Politics in the Enlightenment: Women Writers Read Rousseau* (Albany: State University of New York Press, 1997);

Trouille, "Sexual/Textual Politics in the Enlightenment: Diderot and d'Epinay Respond to Thomas's Essay on Women," *Romantic Review,* 85, no. 2 (1994): 191–210;

Pierre-Marie Tyl, *Madame d'Epinay (1726–1783): une femme au siècle des Lumières,* Exhibition catalogue (Epinay-sur-Seine, 1983);

Ruth Plaut Weinreb, "Double Vision: Jean-Etienne Liotard's Portraits of Louise d'Epinay," in *The Past as Prologue,* edited by Carla H. Hay and Syndy M. Conger-Syndy (New York: AMS, 1995), pp. 387–401;

Weinreb, *Eagle in a Gauze Cage: Louise d'Epinay, Femme de Lettres* (New York: AMS, 1993);

Weinreb, "Emilie or Emile? Madame d'Epinay and the Education of Girls in Eighteenth-Century France," in *Eighteenth-Century Women and the Arts,* edited by Frederick M. Keener and Susan E. Lorsch (New York: Greenwood Press, 1988), pp. 57–66;

Weinreb, "'Une femme toute nouvelle.' Louise d'Epinay in Geneva, 1757–1759," in *Femmes savantes et femmes d'esprit,* edited by Roland Bonnel and Catherine Rubinger (New York: Peter Lang, 1994), pp. 203–218;

Weinreb, "Madame d'Epinay's Contributions to the *Correspondance littéraire,*" *Studies in Eighteenth-Century Culture,* 18 (1988): 389–403.

Papers:

Louise d'Epinay's manuscripts and papers are found in Paris at the Bibliothèque nationale, the Bibliothèque de l'Arsenal, and the Archives Nationales. Part of her correspondence with Fernandino Galiani is at the Biblioteca della Società Napoletana di Storia Patria in Naples, Italy.

Bernard Le Bovier de Fontenelle

(11 February 1657 – 9 January 1757)

Jin Lu
Purdue University Calumet

See also the Fontenelle entry in *DLB 268: Seventeenth-Century French Writers.*

BOOKS: *Psyché,* by Fontenelle and Thomas Corneille (Paris: R. Baudry, 1678);

Bellérophon, by Fontenelle and Corneille (Paris: C. Ballard, 1679);

Nouveaux Dialogues des morts, anonymous, 2 volumes (Paris: Blageart, 1683); volume 1 translated as *New Dialogues of the Dead in Three Parts,* attributed to John Dryden (London, 1683); translated in complete form by John Hughes as *Fontenelle's Dialogues of the Dead, in Three Parts* (London: Tonson, 1708);

Lettres diverses de M. le chevalier d'Her . . . , anonymous, 2 volumes (Paris: Blageart, 1683, 1687); augmented and republished as *Lettres galantes de Monsieur le Chevalier d'Her . . .* (Paris: Brunet, 1699); translated by John Ozell as *Letters of Gallantry* (London: Brown & Watts, 1715);

Jugement de Pluton sur les deux parties des nouveaux dialogues des morts, anonymous (Paris: Blageart, 1684);

Doutes sur le système physique des causes occasionnelles, anonymous (Rotterdam: Acher, 1686);

Entretiens sur la pluralité des mondes, anonymous (Paris [Lyon]: T. Amaulry, 1686; Paris: Blageart, 1686)–comprises five evenings; translated by Sir W. D. Knight as *A Discourse of the Plurality of Worlds* (Dublin: Printed by Andr. Crook and Sam. Helsham, for William Norman, 1687); revised and augmented to comprise six evenings (Amsterdam: Pierre Mortier, 1689); second edition translated by William Gardiner as *Conversations on the Plurality of Worlds* (London: Bettesworth, 1715);

Histoire des oracles, anonymous (Paris: Luyne, 1686); translated by Aphra Behn as *The History of Oracles, and the Cheats of the Pagan Priests, in Two Parts* (London, 1688);

Poésies pastorales de M. D. F. (Paris: Guérout, 1688); revised and augmented as *Poésies pastorales: avec un traité sur la nature de l'églogue, une digression sur les*

Bernard Le Bovier de Fontenelle (from Ronald Grimsley, Jean d'Alembert, 1963; Thomas Cooper Library, University of South Carolina)

anciens, et les modernes, et un recueil de poésies diverses (The Hague: Gosse & Neaulme, 1728)–includes "Discours sur la nature de l'églogue," translated by Peter Anthony Motteux as "A Treatise upon Pastorals," in *Monsieur Bossu's Treatise of the Epic Poem* (London: Bennet, 1695); and "Digression sur les anciens & les modernes," translated by Leonard Mendes Marsak as "Discourse Concerning the Ancients and the Moderns," in *The Achievement of Bernard Le Bovier de Fontenelle* (New York: Johnson Reprint, 1970);

Thétis et Pélée (Paris: Ballard, 1689);

Enée et Lavinie (Paris: Ballard, 1690);

Histoire de l'Académie royale des sciences, 43 volumes (Paris: Imprimerie royale, 1702–1742); translated as *Memoirs of the Royal Academy of Science in Paris, epitomized* (London: Innys, 1721);

Histoire du renouvellement de l'Académie royale des sciences en 1699, et les éloges historiques de tous les académiciens morts depuis ce renouvellement, avec un discours préliminaire sur l'utilité des mathématiques et de la physique, par M. de Fontenelle . . . (Paris: J. Boudot, 1708; Amsterdam: Pierre de Coup, 1709–1720; Paris: Brunet, 1714; Paris: Brunet, 1724; The Hague: Isaac Vander Kloot, 1731);

Poésies, avec la statue de l'amour (Paris: Brunet, 1715);

Oeuvres diverses de M. de Fontenelle de l'Académie françoise, 3 volumes (Paris: Brunet, 1724);

Eléments de la géométrie de l'infini (Paris: Imprimerie royale, 1727);

Endymion (Paris: J. B. C. Ballard, 1731);

Oeuvres de M. de Fontenelle des Académies françoise, des sciences, des belles lettres, de la société royale de Londres, 6 volumes (Paris: Brunet, 1742; augmented to 7 volumes, 1751)–includes "Sur la poésie en général";

Théorie des tourbillons cartésiens, avec des réflexions sur l'attraction (Paris: Guérin, 1752);

Oeuvres, avec des lettres, des poésies (Paris: Brunet, 1761);

La République des philosophes, ou histoire des Ajaoiens (Geneva, 1768).

Editions and Collections: *Oeuvres complètes,* 3 volumes, edited by Georges-Bernard Depping (Paris: Belin, 1818);

Histoire des oracles, edited by Louis Maigron (Paris: Cornély, 1908);

De l'Origine des fables, edited by Jean-Raoul Carré (Paris: Alcan, 1932);

Entretiens sur la pluralité des mondes. Digression sur les Anciens et sur les Modernes, edited by Robert Shackleton (Oxford: Clarendon Press, 1955);

Lettres galantes, edited by Daniel Delafarge (Paris: Les Belles Lettres, 1961);

Entretiens sur la pluralité des mondes, edited by Alexandre Calame (Paris: Didier, 1966);

Nouveaux Dialogues des morts, edited by Jean Dagen (Paris: Didier, 1971);

Oeuvres complètes, 8 volumes, edited by Alain Niderst (Paris: Fayard, 1989–2000).

PLAY PRODUCTIONS: *Psyché,* libretto by Fontenelle and Thomas Corneille, music by Jean-Baptiste Lully, Paris, Académie Royale de Musique, 9 April 1678;

Bellérophon, libretto by Fontenelle, Nicolas Boileau-Despréaux, and Corneille, music by Lully, Paris, Palais Royal, Académie Royale de Musique, 31 January 1679;

Aspar, Paris, Académie Royale de Musique, 27 December 1680;

Thétis et Pélée, Paris, Académie Royale de Musique, 11 January 1689;

Enée et Lavinie, Paris, Académie Royale de Musique, 7 November 1690.

OTHER: Guillaume de L'Hôpital, *Analyse des infiniment petits,* preface by Fontenelle (Paris: Imprimerie royale, 1696).

Bernard Le Bovier de Fontenelle, best known to posterity as a precursor and representative of the Enlightenment and as secretary of the Académie des Sciences (Academy of Science), became well known in the late seventeenth century as a man of letters practicing a variety of literary genres: poetry, theater, opera, letters, and dialogues; as a popularizer capable of rendering science and erudition accessible to the general public; and as a polemist active in the literary and philosophical debates of his time. As a precursor of Enlightenment philosophy, he exemplified the spirit of independent critical thinking, fought against prejudice and superstition, and emphasized the importance of fact and observation. As secretary of the Academy of Science, he was the spokesman and interpreter of the best scientists of his time because of his exceptional ability to convey scientific ideas with precision and elegance. Although his achievements in poetry and theater were limited, his works in the genres of dialogue and popularization gained him immediate and enduring success. His literary theories, detailed in several important treatises, occupy an important place in the development of eighteenth-century aesthetics and criticism.

Fontenelle was born on 11 February 1657 in Rouen, in the province of Normandy. His father, François le Bovier de Fontenelle, belonged to an old aristocratic family and was a lawyer at the Parliament of Rouen, Fontenell and his mother, Marthe Corneille, was the sister of dramatist Pierre Corneille and his brother Thomas Corneille, also a well-known writer. Of extremely poor health but remarkable intelligence, Bernard was sent to the well-known Jesuit school Collège de Bourbon at age seven. A brilliant student, he received excellent literary training, although he was critical of the Jesuits' teaching of logic and physics. Upon completing his studies in 1674, he rejected the Jesuits' solicitation to become a member of their order and abandoned the legal career his family expected him to pursue. Rather than venturing into what he called the "lois arbitraires des hommes" (the arbitrary laws of men), he preferred to explore science and mathematics, especially geometry, the

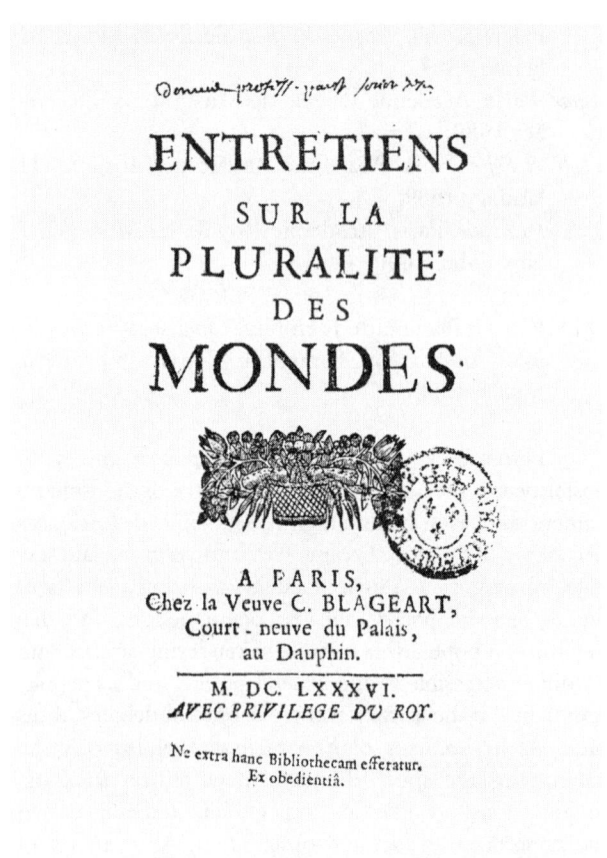

Title page for Fontenelle's most popular work, about Copernican-Cartesian cosmology (Bibliothèque nationale)

subjects that fascinated him. Of independent and balanced thought, he counted among his friends both moderate Jesuits and moderate Calvinists.

Fontenelle chose to pursue a literary career guided by his uncle Thomas Corneille, codirector of the *Mercure Galant* (Gallant Mercury), a prominent gazette founded in 1762 by Donneau de Visé. From 1677 until 1680, Fontenelle remained in Rouen most of the time while frequently staying with his uncles in Paris, where he was welcomed in prestigious salons and attended seminars by well-known scientists and scholars. His poems, published in the *Mercure Galant*, were graceful, witty, and ornate, full of personifications and hyperboles, and they fit well into a journal that boasted a large female readership. He was considered a skillful poet but not a great one. In his article "Description de l'empire de la poésie" (Description of the Empire of Poetry), in the January 1678 issue of the *Mercure Galant*, he used allegories to satirize different kinds of poetry and the classic aesthetics of imitation. He believed that the conflict between reason and rhyme was extremely difficult to resolve. Condemning both sublime pomposity and comical vulgarity, he valued the natural expression of thoughts but stated that it was difficult to achieve.

As the nephew of one of the most prestigious dramatists of his time, Fontenelle hoped to succeed his uncle as a great dramatist. He started to work with Corneille and produced two operas, *Psyché* (1678) and *Bellérophon* (1679), believed to be the result of their collaboration. The attribution of these two anonymous works to Fontenelle continues to be contested by some scholars and supported by others, including leading Fontenelle scholar Alain Niderst. In the case of *Bellérophon*, confirmation is provided by Fontenelle himself in a letter to the *Journal des Savants* (Journal of Savants) in 1741. While the first opera was disappointing, the second achieved a huge success. Fontenelle then wrote a tragedy—a genre considered superior to all others—which could have made him the equal of his renowned uncle. The complete failure of *Aspar* (1680), however, shattered his dream: he burned the manuscript and left Paris. Fontenelle's contemporaries as well as modern scholars find his versification weak and his style lacking in theatrics. The failure prompted him to seek new paths, better suited for his talent.

From 1681 until 1685, Fontenelle remained in Rouen, and while working seriously, he published nothing. Yet, those years of silence were among his most productive ones. Turning away from poetry and theater, he practiced instead the minor genres of dialogues and letters. Both forms allowed him to use his aptitudes to his advantage: his writings were subtle, witty, and satirical, capable of making serious reflections in conversational style; in other words, he excelled at short texts. *Nouveaux Dialogues des morts* (1683; volume one translated as *New Dialogues of the Dead in Three Parts*, 1683, and the complete work as *Fontenelle's Dialogues of the Dead, in Three Parts*, 1708), published anonymously when he was only twenty-six, was an immediate and lasting success. As suggested by its title, the work is an imitation of the *Dialogues of the Dead* (circa second century) by ancient Greek philosopher Lucian—an author known to French readers for his satirical and libertine writings and his lack of respect for nearly everything, including religion. Like Lucian, Fontenelle has the dead talk and moralize with each other, but his work is more creative than that of his predecessor, as his new themes and new ideas extend beyond Lucian's commonplace ones. Faithful to the libertine tradition of scepticism, Fontenelle constantly challenged the role of reason by arranging dialogues among people who had little in common and making those who initially appeared to be right always lose in the end. His art of the dialogue is consummate: brilliant and witty retorts, surprises, paradoxes, and irony are skillfully used in thought-provoking discussions. The aesthetics of *Nouveaux Dialogues des morts*, however, is opposed to that of French classicism, which values common sense and verisimilitude.

The first volume of *Lettres diverses de M. le chevalier d'Her . . .* (1683, Various Letters of the Chevalier d'Her . . .)

was published anonymously in 1683, while the second one came out in 1687. With the third enlarged edition in 1699, the title was changed to *Lettres galantes de Monsieur le Chevalier d'Her . . .* (translated as *Letters of Gallantry,* 1715). The publication of these fictional letters shocked Fontenelle's contemporaries, including Voltaire, who later wrote, "c'est une entreprise fort ridicule que de faire des lettres comme on fait un roman" (it is a rather ridiculous undertaking to make up letters as one writes a novel). The public was not ready to accept epistolary novels, a genre later popularized in the eighteenth century by Charles-Louis de Secondat de Montesquieu, Françoise de Graffigny, Jean-Jacques Rousseau, and Pierre Choderlos de Laclos. Fontenelle's work is halfway between a traditional collection of letters and an epistolary novel. Although the book has no central plot, letters including many anecdotes are collected in groups that form stories. Fontenelle is interested in types rather than in individuals, in reflection rather than narration, and in abstraction rather than experience. He offers no psychological development or concrete details. His art as author of these letters is not that of a novelist but that of a moralist: his reflections on the relationship between women and men are of central concern. Through satire, he criticizes social mores of his time and offers his own views on love: humans are inconstant, by nature. Fontenelle's concept of love is thus based on moderation with respect to nature, breaking with the classical association of reason, will, and passion. Defenders of classicism, including Voltaire, condemned his style, which they found strange and affected, while Fontenelle and his supporters believed it to be natural and similar to that of conversation. Fontenelle, who highly valued authenticity and lucidity, and whose mind was subtle and apt to grasp nuance, strove to use language that accurately expressed his thought. What he considered natural might have been perceived by others as affected and bizarre.

During his years in Rouen, Fontenelle was a close friend of the marquise Marguerite Rambouillet de la Mésangère and her family. He frequently went to her château and took long walks with her in the park. She inspired his most successful work, *Entretiens sur la pluralité des mondes* (1686; translated as *A Discourse on the Plurality of Worlds,* 1687), which went through thirty-three editions during his lifetime and was translated into all the major European languages. In fact, Fontenelle may not actually have spent as many as five evenings talking with her about Copernician-Cartesian cosmology. Like other works by Fontenelle during that period, *Entretiens sur la pluralité des mondes* appeared anonymously, but the *Mercure Galant* announced that it was by the author of *Nouveaux Dialogues des morts.* Fontenelle had long been interested in science, and his talent at popularizing it had already been recognized in the *Mercure Galant* as early as May 1677: "Il n'y a point de science sur laquelle il ne raisonne solidement; mais il le fait d'une manière aisée, et qui n'a rien de la rudesse des savants de profession. . . . Il n'aime les belles connaissances que pour s'en servir en honnête homme" (There is no science about which he cannot talk solidly, but he does it with ease, without the dryness of professional men of science. . . . He likes knowledge in order to use it only as a gentleman). In *Entretiens sur la pluralité des mondes,* Fontenelle's goal was twofold: for savants, he claimed to offer only entertainment; for ordinary women and men, he proposed both to educate and entertain them, while stating that truth and falsehood are mixed in the conversations; thus, readers were encouraged not to take his work as scientific fact. The dialogues were to be taken more as philosophical considerations rather than scientific lessons. From *Nouveaux Dialogues des morts* to *Entretiens sur la pluralité des mondes,* Fontenelle continued to criticize human stupidity, prejudice, credulity, and anthropocentrism. The plurality of worlds with their various inhabitants is not presented as a certainty, only as likelihood. He constantly warns humans of their tendency to rush to conclusion and recommends modesty and cautiousness, essential to a true philosopher, because, as he explains, "les vrais philosophes sont comme les éléphants, qui en marchant ne posent jamais le second pied à terre, que le premier ne soit bien affermi" (true philosophers are like elephants who, while walking, never put down the second foot before the first one is firmly in place). Even scientific progress is subject to caution, because new discoveries may modify current beliefs. In the conversations between the philosopher and the marquise, imagination compensates for the weakness of reason, while love, tenderness, and pleasure also find their place in the dialogues. Fontenelle demonstrates that science can be a pleasant subject of conversation while providing new material for literature. In other words, he sought to replace ancient mythology with a new kind of imagination inspired by science.

In 1686 Fontenelle also published, anonymously as well, *Doutes sur le système physique des causes occasionnelles* (Doubts on the Physical System of Occasional Causes), in which he refutes the theory of occasional causes invented by René Descartes and developed by Father Nicolas Malebranche. According to this theory, only God can be the real cause of a body's movement. Fontenelle agrees that God created the world and is the first cause of everything but refuses to believe that God acts continuously upon his creation, arguing that when God created bodies, he provided them with movement—a natural part of their being. Movement is therefore inherent in matter. Whether he accepts God's existence sincerely or tactfully, Fontenelle maintains that the Creator is remote and does not intervene in worldly affairs. Laws exist within nature itself and are independent from God. This scientific naturalism was adopted by many Enlightenment philosophers and marked a break with Cartesian metaphysics.

Fontenelle's art at the popularization of science is further demonstrated in *Histoire des oracles* (1686; translated as *The History of Oracles, and the Cheats of the Pagan Priests, in Two Parts,* 1688). He uses materials from the treatise *De Oraculis Ethnicorum Dissertationes duae* (Two Dissertations on the Subject of Pagan Oracles), published by Dutch scholar Antonius Van Dale in 1683. Van Dale's work was aimed at scholars, thus written in a dry style, full of erudite citations and scholarly discussions, confusing for the average reader. Fontenelle sought to inform and please men, and especially women, of polite society, who were curious about all matters, yet needed to be educated in elegant style with clear and concise presentation. The subject as treated by Fontenelle was similar to that of Van Dale: he wanted to prove that oracles were not rendered by demons and did not end with the coming of Jesus. The intentions of both authors, however, differ significantly: as a Protestant, Van Dale intended to deride Catholicism and remove superstition from religion; Fontenelle, on the other hand, did not wish to attack openly the established religion of his nation. While explicitly excluding practices authorized by the Catholic Church, his criticism of prejudice, which remained general, could potentially destroy all belief in the supernatural. By denouncing pagan superstitions, he inspired readers to doubt Christian miracles as well. He argued that oracles were not rendered by demons but were created by the imposture of priests and perpetuated by the credulity and ignorance of people. Fontenelle's belief in the universality of errors directly challenged the argument of universal consent, a major argument frequently used to strengthen belief in Christianity. Faced with the universality of errors, Fontenelle offers one solution: "Assurons-nous bien du fait, avant que de nous inquiéter de la cause" (Let us make sure of the fact, before worrying about the cause). This work, which influenced later generations of philosophers, including Voltaire, Montesquieu, and Denis Diderot, secured Fontenelle's reputation as a precursor of the Enlightenment.

Now a successful author, Fontenelle returned more often to Paris, while continuing to reside in Rouen. He became the protégé of Dauphine Victoire de Bavière and frequented the salon of Anne Thérèse de Marquenat de Courcelles, marquise de Lambert. The second edition of the *Entretiens sur la pluralité des mondes* was published in 1689 and achieved an even more dazzling success than the first one. Fontenelle corrected some errors in the first edition and added a new evening of conversation with the marquise, generally believed to be the marquise de Lambert. Science occupies a more important place in the sixth conversation, and the tone is more serious and measured.

As the nephew of Pierre and Thomas Corneille, both members of the prestigious Académie Française (French Academy), resting on his literary success and supported by Parisian salons and the progressive members of the court, Fontenelle sought to enter the Academy. It seemed an odd time for him to participate in the Quarrel of the Ancients and the Moderns, but the Ancients, supported by conservative members of the court and represented by Nicolas Boileau Despreéaux, Jean Racine, and Jean de La Bruyère, were already his enemies. Ever since the beginning of his literary career, Fontenelle had never ceased to insinuate his opposition to the imitation of ancient authors and believed that modern writers could surpass them. The salon of the marquise de Lambert was the central meeting place of the Moderns until her death in 1733. In 1688, Fontenelle's "Digression sur les anciens and les modernes" (translated as "Discourse Concerning the Ancients and the Moderns," 1970) appeared in the same volume as his *Poésies pastorales* (Pastoral Poems) and "Discours sur la nature de l'églogue" (translated as "A Treatise upon Pastorals," 1695). The poems illustrate Fontenelle's effort at innovating a genre in which the Ancients believed that Theocritus and Virgil had attained perfection. Fontenelle eliminates realistic details from his eclogues, believing that they are too coarse for a civilized and polite society. Eclogues, as he defined them, correspond to his own idea of happiness: a peaceful and innocent moment of life devoted to leisure and love, a love that is tender and sincere, without jealousy or betrayal. His opponents criticized his shepherds and shepherdesses for being too witty and brilliant, instead of being natural and simple. "Digression sur les anciens et les modernes" was based on two principles: throughout the ages, nature continues to have the same capacity to produce great men; and progress is the result of accumulated knowledge. Fontenelle claims the right to judge ancient Greek and Roman writers the same way he would judge his contemporaries. He finds flaws in the works of Homer and Virgil, declares that tragedy, comedy, and the novels of his century are superior to works of ancient Greece, and he especially praises the new genres created by his contemporaries. Antiquity was so venerated at the time that Fontenelle's writing provoked strong opposition. His involvement in the controversy made him the leader of the Moderns but also brought him powerful enemies who did everything they could to prevent him from being elected to the French Academy.

In January 1689, Fontenelle's opera *Thétis et Pélée* was performed with great success. It is a story of love overcoming obstacles and mortals triumphing over gods. A year later, however, *Enée et Lavinie,* an opera intended to flatter Louis XIV, was poorly received. It was Fontenelle's last attempt at opera.

A long tradition links Fontenelle to Catherine Bernard, both from the city of Rouen. Bernard, born in 1662 and five years younger than Fontenelle, is believed to be either Fontenelle's niece or cousin, but no evidence in their family's genealogies supports that claim. No historical document proves they were acquainted with each other, although certainly Fontenelle knew about Bernard, since he wrote favorable reviews of her work in the *Mercure Galant*. Fontenelle's relation to works published under Bernard's name in the late seventeenth century should be examined for possible connections: three novellas–*Eléonor d'Yvrée* (1687), *Le Comte d'Amboise* (1688), and *Inès de Cordoue* (1696)–and two tragedies, *Laodamie* (1689) and *Brutus* (1690). Suggestions of Fontenelle's role in these works appeared after 1730, thirty or forty years after their original publication and almost twenty years after Bernard's death. The exact nature of Fontenelle's contribution to these works is ambiguous; it ranges from help, advice, guidance, assistance, to possible collaboration. Unlike in modern scholarship, the source of these assertions is not identified by their authors, except in the case of abbé Nicolas-Charles-Joseph Trublet, who based his information on personal conversations with Fontenelle during his later years. One can understand why Fontenelle might not have wanted to recognize his role in the novellas when they were first published, because the genre was considered frivolous, but he would have had every reason to claim the two successful tragedies *Laodamie* and *Brutus* between their publication and the 1730s. Twentieth-century scholars remain divided on this case and others of involving Fontenelle authorship, contested partly because alleged collaboration with other writers and partly because of anonymous publications attributed to him.

Fontenelle finally won election to the French Academy in April 1691 after four failed attempts. Membership was the official consecration of his literary achievements, and it also was a triumph for the Moderns. In his acceptance speech Fontenelle exalted the name of his uncle Pierre Corneille and affirmed Corneille's superiority over any other tragic author. This praise was an offense to Racine and the Ancients. Thomas Corneille used the occasion to declare that the arts and sciences of the Moderns could be equal and even superior to those of the Ancients.

With his literary reputation secured, Fontenelle left Rouen to live in Paris with his uncle Thomas Corneille. All his life Fontenelle never had his own residence because he did not want to occupy himself with the details of everyday life. Intellectually, however, he was curious and open to new knowledge, and he enjoyed witty salon conversations of artists and scientists of his time. Between 1691 and 1696 he published no major works. In 1697 he became the permanent secretary of the Academy of Science, a position he successfully held for more than forty years, until 1740, when at age eighty-three, he asked to be retired. Although he made little original contribution to the sciences, he was sufficiently well informed and more capable than anyone else to write on abstract and difficult subjects with clarity, precision, and elegance. Without being a specialist, he had an excellent grasp of all disciplines of science. He was unanimously chosen by the best scientists of his time to be their spokesman and interpreter. Fontenelle viewed science as a powerful means to free the mind from the ignorance and errors that he combated throughout his life. His diligent work as secretary of the Academy of Science became his foremost priority and ensured that *Histoire de l'Académie des Sciences* (History of the Academy of Science)–a publication enjoyed by a wide readership among both the learned and the general public–appeared regularly from 1702 to 1742. He showed his ability to comprehend modern mathematics in *Eléments de la géométrie de l'infini* (1727, Elements of Infinitesimal Geometry) and started the tradition of writing *Eloges* (Eulogies) of deceased scientists–considered among his best works. Fontenelle no doubt contributed to the public's enthusiasm for science and the prestige enjoyed by scientists. In popularizing and spread-

Fontenelle in his middle years (portrait by Jacques-André-Joseph Aved; from George Havens, The Age of Ideas, *1955; Collection of W. Ross)*

Fontenelle in old age (portrait by Guillaume Voiriot; from Alain Niderst, Fontenelle à la Recherche de lui-même [1657–1702], 1972; Thomas Cooper Library, University of South Carolina)

ing scientific knowledge, Fontenelle was also fulfilling one of the major goals of the Enlightenment. More than just a popularizer of science, he also offered a philosophy of science. By praising scientists, he actually shaped the image of an ideal scientist–a person endowed with passion and dedication for research, as well as sincerity, modesty, simplicity, disinterestedness, and uprightness of character. Leonard Mendes Marsak believes that Fontenelle created a "secular sainthood" by portraying the scientist as the "hero of the age." Fontenelle remained a moralist because he believed that science elevates moral values.

His *Oeuvres diverses* (Various Works), published in 1724, included important essays. "De l'Origine des fables" (On the Origin of Fables), written between 1691 and 1699 according to Trublet, was a study of the human mind. Fontenelle continued to denounce mankind's tendency to believe in the marvelous, arguing that ignorance and lack of experience are the sources of marvels people claim to see. In primitive societies, humans created fables in order to explain phenomena they did not understand. Fontenelle is critical of mythologies and also religions, which are only sublimed versions of myths. His ideas in this work are consistent with his position in the Quarrel of the Ancients and the Moderns: the Moderns, possessed of more knowledge and enlightened by reason, are able to move beyond the state of ignorance that created and spread fables. In "Du Bonheur" (On Happiness), Fontenelle reveals his concept of happiness, one he also put into practice during his life. Born with poor health, Fontenelle lived to be almost one hundred. He believed that happiness cannot be enjoyed by everyone, since only a small part of it depends on us. Those born with a mild and moderate disposition, who can readily retain pleasant ideas and impressions and are endowed with lucidity and moderation, are more likely to be happy because they can think and act clearly. A bachelor for life, Fontenelle never had any violent passions and instead enjoyed the friendship and gallantry of polite society.

A new edition of his *Oeuvres* (Works) appeared in 1742, which included several new pieces written during the 1690s. In "Histoire du théâtre français jusqu'à M. Corneille" (History of French Theater until Mr. Corneille), he praised Corneille at the expense of his archrival, Racine. By tracing the origin of French theater as far back as the Middle Ages, Fontenelle, consistent with his stand in the Quarrel of the Ancients and the Moderns, shows how the human mind is able to create and develop art without inspiration from the ancient Greeks. In "Réflexions sur la poétique" (Reflections on Poetics), he presents his theory of aesthetics, in which he seeks to explain the mysterious *art de plaire* (art of pleasing) of French classicism and to search for principles for understanding the human mind and heart. His theory of aesthetics was further developed in "Sur la poésie en général" (On Poetry in General), published in the 1751 edition of *Oeuvres*. Fontenelle examines the relationship between poetry and philosophy, and declares that to be both a poet and a philosopher–as Antoine Houdar de La Motte was–is possible, even preferable. In the preface of the seven plays he wrote between 1710 and 1741, he developed a theory of dramatic scale and mixed genres. Between the two extremes of tragedy and comedy, he says an infinite number of nuances exist, similar to a scale of colors, unexplored as of yet, which offer great possibilities for new genres. In plays not intended for the stage, Fontenelle put into practice his own idea of theater and provides examples of plays in mixed genres. In writing *Idalie,* a tragedy in prose (collected in *Oeuvres,* 1751), Fontenelle made clear his position in one of the debates of the eighteenth century against those who believed that tragedy could only be written in verse.

In the *Entretiens sur la pluralité des mondes,* Fontenelle accepted the Cartesian theory of vortices and fought for it throughout his life. Opposed to Cartesian metaphysics, he had his own reason to defend the vortex in *Théorie des tourbillons cartésiens, avec des réflexions sur l'attraction* (1752, Theory of Cartesian Vortex, with Reflections on the Attraction). Fontenelle believed that matter is infinite, and since space was full of matter, void could not exist; consequently, locomotion should be caused by impulsion rather than by attraction. Fontenelle's rejection of attraction was based on its resemblance to the scholastic method—obscure and abstract—while he believed the Cartesian system to be founded on the principles of mechanics. This work was published at the time when Newtonian attraction, supported by many scientists, was firmly gaining ground in France. By defending the Cartesian vortex, Fontenelle was showing his independence of thought: he supported Newtonian optics and rejected many aspects of Cartesianism, such as animal automatism, innate ideas, and the radical separation of mind and body.

Bernard Le Bovier de Fontenelle, who enjoyed exceptional longevity and outlived all his enemies, became a venerable figure in France and in Europe toward the end of his life. Men of letters and those in high places in France and abroad paid him official homage, in verse and in prose, in the French Academy, and in the *Mercure Galant*. He remained popular in Parisian salons, and his witty remarks were spread by word of mouth. He was viewed alternatively as a model philosopher with legendary discretion and moderation, or as a perfect egoist who only cared about his own peacefulness and pleasure. He aged slowly and died peacefully on 9 January 1757 as a Christian, after receiving the sacraments. Throughout his life, he followed all the rituals of religion and never clearly expressed his personal religious position. Caution and skepticism, as well as aversion to the spirit of system, may be part of the reason. In his published works he openly supported the existence of a God who created the world and let it be governed by natural laws. But anonymous pamphlets that radically attacked Christianity were attributed to him. Was he a deist or an atheist? The best response comes from Fontenelle himself, in *Histoire des oracles:* "Faites comme les autres, et croyez ce qu'il vous plaira" (Do as others do, and believe whatever you fancy).

Despite the glory he enjoyed, contemporary critics maintained reservations on his talent as a writer. He was successful and influential; yet, the French literary canon never considered any of his works a masterpiece. While his contributions as secretary of the Academy of Science were unanimously praised, many believed his literary production lacked imagination, sentiment, and energy. Fontenelle's aesthetics, while opposing French classicism in favor of modernity, were not appreciated by Romantic writers, who tended to share Fontenelle's contempt for the rules and regulations of classicism but highly valued enthusiasm, imagination, and the sublime. They found Fontenelle's wit, intellectualism, and skepticism cold and dull. Admiration for Fontenelle as a philosopher and disregard for his literary talent continued in the twentieth century. As a result, except for a few texts, such as *Entretiens sur la pluralité des mondes* and *Nouveaux dialogues des morts,* many of his works have been neglected. Alain Niderst's *Fontenelle à la recherche de lui-même (1657–1702)* (1972, Fontenelle in Search of Himself) is a masterful study of Fontenelle's rich career in all its diverse aspects. However, many challenged his treatment of works whose attribution to Fontenelle is questionable. The publication of Fontenelle's *Oeuvres complètes* (Complete Works) by Editions Fayard (1989–2000) under the direction of Niderst, based on the 1751–1761 edition of *Oeuvres,* made some of his long-neglected texts available to the general public. One can hope that by facilitating the reading of the totality of Fontenelle's works, they will be reevaluated in the proper light.

Biographies:

Nicolas-Charles-Joseph Trublet, *Mémoires pour servir à l'histoire de la vie et des ouvrages de M. de Fontenelle* (Amsterdam: Rey, 1759);

Louis Maigron, *Fontenelle. L'homme, l'œuvre, l'influence* (Paris: Plon, 1906);

Alain Niderst, *Fontenelle* (Paris: Plon, 1991).

References:

Jean-Raoul Carré, *La Philosophie de Fontenelle ou le sourire de la raison* (Paris: Alcan, 1932);

John Cosentini, *Fontenelle's Art of Dialogue* (New York: King's Crown Press, 1952);

Jean Dagen, *L'Histoire de l'esprit humain dans la pensée française de Fontenelle à Condorcet* (Paris: Klincksieck, 1977);

Franz Grégoire, *Fontenelle, une "philosophie" désabusée* (Paris: Vrin, 1947);

Roger Marchal, *Fontenelle à l'aube des Lumières* (Paris: Champion, 1997);

Leonard Mendes Marsak, *Bernard de Fontenelle: The Idea of Science in the French Enlightenment* (Philadelphia: The American Philosophical Society, 1959);

Alain Niderst, *Fontenelle à la recherche de lui-même (1657–1702)* (Paris: Nizet, 1972);

Niderst, ed., *Fontenelle, Actes du colloque tenu à Rouen du 6 au 10 octobre 1987* (Paris: Presses Universitaires de France, 1989).

Papers:

All manuscripts of Bernard Le Bovier de Fontenelle's major works are now lost. Extant manuscripts and papers are scattered in various municipal libraries in France.

Elie Catherine Fréron
(18 January 1718 – 10 March 1776)

Daniel Brewer
University of Minnesota

BOOKS: *Histoire de Marie Stuart, reine d'Ecosse et de France,* by Fréron and François-Marie de Marsy, 2 volumes (London [i.e., Paris], 1742);

Opuscules de M. F***, 3 volumes (Amsterdam: Arkstée, 1753);

Histoire de l'empire d'Allemagne et principalement de ses révolutions, 8 volumes (Paris: Hérissant le fils, 1771);

Les Confessions de Fréron (1719–1776), sa vie, souvenirs intimes et anecdotiques, edited by Charles Barthélemy (Paris: Charpentier, 1876).

OTHER: *Observations sur les écrits modernes,* edited by Pierre François Guyot Desfontaines (1735–1743)–includes many contributions by Fréron;

Jugemens sur quelques ouvrages nouveaux, 11 volumes, edited by Desfontaines (1744–1746)–includes contributions by Fréron;

Lettres de Mme la comtesse de *** sur quelques écrits modernes, 19 volumes, edited by Fréron (1745–1746);

Lettres sur quelques écrits de ce temps, by Fréron and Joseph de La Porte, 13 volumes (1749–1754);

L'Année littéraire, 174 volumes, edited by Fréron (1754–1775);

Journal étranger, ouvrage périodique, by Fréron, Antoine François Prévost d'Exiles, François Arnaud, François Vincent Toussaint, Jean Pierre Moet, Alexandre Deleyre, Jean Baptiste Antoine Suard, and others, 45 volumes (1754–1762);

Les Deux Matrones; ou, les infidélités démasquées: ouvrage posthume de M. Fréron (Paris: Au Temple de la vérité, 1776)–part 1 is a translation of the *Widow of Ephesus* by Titus Petronius Arbiter; part 2 is a translation of a Chinese story on the same subject from *Description . . . de l'empire de la Chine,* by Jean-Baptiste Du Halde.

Elie Catherine Fréron (engraving based on drawing by Charles-Nicolas Cochin; from Arthur Wilson, Diderot, 1972; Collection of W. Ross)

Elie Catherine Fréron is chiefly known as a journalist and literary critic. He wrote for several influential periodicals, the most important of which, *L'Année littéraire* (The Literary Yearly), he founded in 1754 and directed until his death in 1776. He produced 174 volumes of commentary for the journal, reviewing approximately nine thousand books for a readership that extended throughout France and across Europe. Fréron maintained that the critic's role was not merely to supply information about authors and their works. Instead, he instructed writers and readers on matters involving literary taste, providing them with a system of principles designed to guide their individual aesthetic judgment. Fréron was tireless in his defense of belles lettres, the creative principles of which he took to be the imitation of natural beauty, moral instruction, and a purity of expression to be attained by remaining faithful to the literary models of classical antiquity and the literary masters of the preceding century.

L'Année littéraire is historically significant as a chronicle of the literary works and intellectual debates that defined elite cultural life in eighteenth-century Paris. Commentary in the periodical occasionally overstepped the bounds of opinion acceptable to the royal censor, who was favorably inclined toward the philosophes who were writers of the *Encyclopédie,* which Fréron constantly critiqued. These excessively critical remarks resulted in Fréron's spending several brief periods imprisoned in the Bastille. He has been caricatured as a hidebound, vindictive enemy of change, both intellectual and aesthetic; yet, that reputation was shaped by the philosophes, opponents in a cultural battle he ultimately lost. He was the bête noire of Voltaire, for whom he symbolized *l'infâme,* the infamous object of ignorance, superstition, and fanaticism that the Enlightenment patriarch labored so unrelentingly to crush. In the area of aesthetics, Fréron represents Enlightenment traditionalism, with all the tensions and contradictions that notion suggests. His periodicals illustrate the growing autonomy of the literary critic, as well as the increasingly significant role the press played in transforming public opinion in eighteenth-century France.

Elie Catherine Fréron was born in Quimper (Brittany) on 18 January 1718, the son of Daniel Fréron, a goldsmith, and Marie Anne Campion, his third wife. One of his father's fifteen children, Elie was raised in a Breton-speaking household. He received his education in Jesuit schools, first in Quimper and later at the prestigious Louis-le-Grand, a secondary school in Paris, where he was sent in 1734 to complete his education. In 1735 he entered the Jesuit novitiate and taught a year in Caen, following which time he returned to the teaching staff at Louis-le-Grand. His first published poetry dates from this time. After having been seen in borrowed lay clothes at the theater, which clerics were not permitted to attend, Fréron was sent out of Paris. He left the Jesuit order in 1739.

Fréron's career as a journalist began with his association with Pierre François Guyot Desfontaines, director of the journal *Observations sur les écrits modernes* (Observations on Modern Literature). *Observations sur les écrits modernes* began appearing in 1735 and ran until 1743, when its *privilège* was revoked because of a remark Desfontaines had made that irritated members of the Académie Française. Fréron continued his association with Desfontaines, contributing to the latter's *Observations sur les écrits modernes* and his *Jugemens sur quelques ouvrages nouveaux* (1744–1746, Judgments on some new works). Although formerly an associate of Voltaire, Desfontaines waged an acerbic battle with him in the pages of *Observations sur les écrits modernes.* In addition to his collaboration with Desfontaines, Fréron supplemented his income with occasional writing, revising François-Marie de Marsy's *Histoire de Marie Stuart* (1742, History of Mary Stuart) and writing a history of Germany. By 1745 he had published a few odes, including *Les Conquêtes du roi* (The King's Conquests), which celebrated royal victories. His talent at biting satire was already apparent in verses that poked jibes at several writers, including Voltaire.

In 1745 the first volume of Fréron's own journal appeared–*Lettres de Mme la comtesse de *** sur quelques écrits modernes* (1745–1746, Letters by Countess *** on Modern Literature). Subsequent issues included a sarcastic review of Voltaire's opera *Le Temple de la gloire* (The Temple of Glory), given in 1745 at Versailles and published in 1746, and cutting remarks concerning Bernard Le Bovier de Fontenelle and Alexis Piron. Critical remarks concerning two of Mme de Pompadour's protégés, abbé François-Joachim-Pierre de Bernis and abbé Jean-Bernard Le Blanc, won Fréron two months of imprisonment in the Bastille and four months of exile in Bar-sur-Aube outside Paris. The *Lettres de Mme la comtesse de *** sur quelques écrits modernes* was suppressed in 1746.

Fréron reestablished the review in 1749 as *Lettres sur quelques écrits de ce temps* (Letters on Writing of Our Times), which appeared until 1754 and comprised sixty-two letters. Abandoning the witty, bantering tone of earlier writing, Fréron aimed at producing serious criticism. An early letter included a harsh critique of the successful tragedy *Denys le tyran* (1748, Denis the Tyrant), written by Jean-François Marmontel, a protégé of Voltaire. Another letter attacked Voltaire himself, accusing him of being the author of an unsigned brochure that included extensive self-praise. Unable to defend himself without revealing his stratagem, Voltaire pressured the lieutenant of police, Nicolas-René Berryer, and chancellor Henri-François d'Aguesseau to revoke the tacit permission of the *Lettres sur quelques écrits de ce temps,* a tactic that led to a nine-month suppression of the review.

Fréron's criticism in the *Lettres sur quelques écrits de ce temps* exemplifies the engaged, at times polemical, intervention in the literary and cultural debates of Parisian society that was the hallmark of all of his later writing. In 1751, for instance, the event of the Parisian literary season was the publication of Jean-Jacques Rousseau's *Discours sur les sciences et les arts* (1750, Discourse on the Sciences and the Arts). In this short essay, Rousseau argued that literature was responsible for the

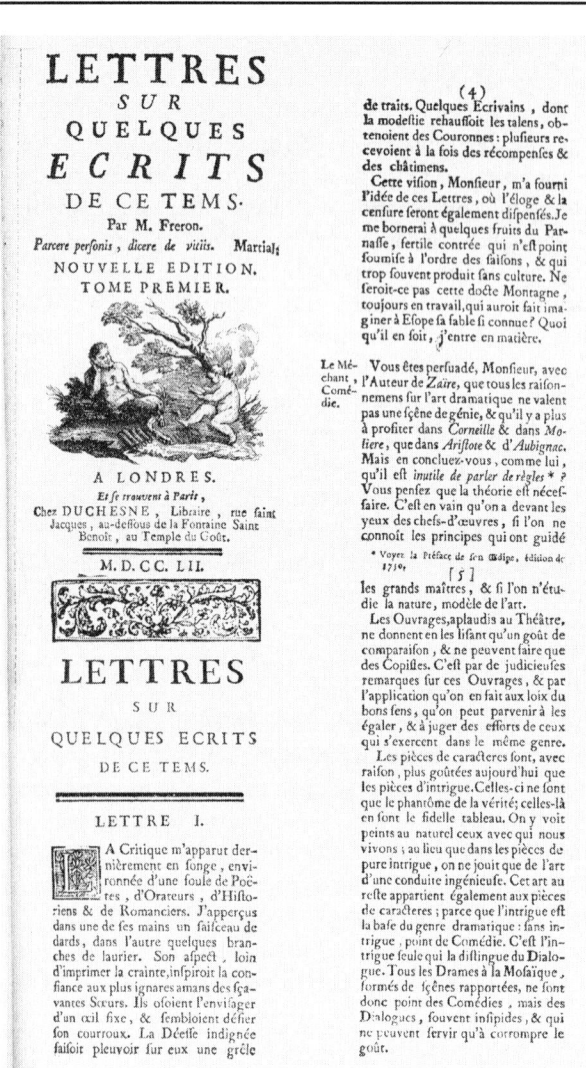

First page of the collected edition, begun in 1752, of Fréron's journal (Letters on the Writers of Our Times), published from 1749–1754. Because of Voltaire's opposition, the journal was suppressed for nine months in 1752 (from the facsimile edition by Salkine Reprints, 1966; Thomas Cooper Library, University of South Carolina)

corruption of contemporary society. Fréron joined the fray, taking the more worldly view that society was not at all as corrupt as Rousseau claimed, and that the sciences and the arts had the potential to perfect society, not pervert it. Marking a position to which he clung for a quarter of a century, Fréron argued that literature was indeed in crisis, but that the decadence of letters had resulted from social causes, not from intrinsically aesthetic ones. Authors of the previous century had been successful in combining genius and wit, he claimed, whereas present-day authors relied on wit alone. They rejected the classical values of the ancient Greeks and Romans and believed the power of reason and mathematical thought alone was sufficient to determine artistic creation. In another cultural debate of the time, partisans of French music, represented by the harmonically complex compositions of Jean-Baptiste Rameau, were pitted against partisans of Italian music, who included Rousseau, Jean Le Rond d'Alembert, and other writers associated with the *Encyclopédie* project of d'Alembert and Denis Diderot. Arguing in favor of French music on aesthetic grounds, Fréron did not fail to invoke nationalistic reasons for such arguments, thus anticipating many attacks he made against the philosophes during the Seven Years' War (1756–1763) for their idealist cosmopolitanism. In 1753 Diderot published a manifesto of the new scientific method, *Pensées sur l'interprétation de la nature* (Thoughts on the Interpretation of Nature). Fréron responded with a full-scale critical review, which took the work as symptomatic of a contagious madness caused by the clan of philosophes and their propaganda. The 'new philosophy,' represented by Etienne Bonnot de Condillac's *Traité des sensations* (1754, Treatise on Sensations), was rejected categorically by Fréron, who endorsed instead the classical philosophy of antiquity. The *Lettres sur quelques écrits de ce temps* was briefly suspended in 1752 on the order of the chief censor, Chrétien-Guillaume de Lamoignon de Malesherbes. This act was largely tactical, since with this order, Malesherbes wished to avoid the appearance that the censor's office was siding with conservative or even traditional forces, which were hostile to the Encyclopedists. Fréron enjoyed strong conservative support, both from the devout party at court and from the former king of Poland, Stanisław Leszczński, father-in-law of Louis XVI. Yet, by 1754 the *Encyclopédie* project he so fervently opposed had gained full strength, both intellectually and economically. Even the Jesuits' *Journal de Trévoux* had stopped opposing it.

In 1754 Fréron ceased publishing the *Lettres sur quelques écrits de ce temps*, but he did not remain silent. He contributed during the next eight years to the *Journal étranger, ouvrage périodique* (1754–1762, Foreign Journal, Periodical Journal), and contracted with a new publisher-bookseller, Michel Lambert, to found *L'Année littéraire*, which was devoted to reviews of recent writing. According to contemporary Jean-François de La Harpe, *L'Année littéraire* filled a gap between the uncritical *Mercure de France* and the learned *Journal des savants*. Its subject matter was more diverse than the Jesuits' *Journal de Trévoux*. After the disappearance of the *Gazette littéraire de l'Europe* in 1766, Fréron's periodical provided more coverage of foreign writing. Issues of *L'Année littéraire* included 72 pages and appeared every ten days. The review was continued after his death until 1786 by his son, Stanislas, and some assistants. At that time the periodical comprised 292 volumes of 260 pages each, and by the end of its thirty-two-year run it had published reviews of approximately twelve thousand books.

Fréron's influence reached its height when the philosophes came under greatest pressure from the defenders of traditional values. The *Encyclopédie* was suppressed briefly in 1759, and an assassination attempt on the life of Louis XV two years earlier only intensified the pressure brought to bear on the intellectual avant-garde. Fréron joined the attacks on d'Alembert, who had already been severely criticized for his encyclopedia article "Genève," in which he praised the doctrines and practices of Genevan protestant pastors. The publication of Claude-Adrien Helvétius's *De l'Esprit* (On Mind) in 1758 brought together Jesuits and Jansenists, as well as Crown and Parlement, in common denunciation of the doctrine of materialism. Fréron's own critique of Helvétius was unyielding. The philosophe, Fréron argued, had confused sensation and judgment, for he granted importance only to physical, not divine, causality. In equally harsh terms Fréron castigated the social and moral consequences of baron Paul-Henri Dietrich d'Holbach's *Système de la nature* (1771, System of Nature), another manifesto of materialist determinism. Holbach's work, he maintained, was the logical continuation of the philosophy of the century, which was leading to the disappearance of all religion and morality.

Fréron missed no opportunity to criticize the philosophes, pointing out obscurities in Diderot's writing, d'Alembert's lack of taste, Marmontel's verbosity, and the inadequacy of Voltaire's sense of the tragic. Several episodes of the battle between Fréron and the philosophes have gained a certain literary historical notoriety. In 1759, for instance, the *Année littéraire* published a letter by one of the engravers working on the *Encyclopédie* project, who accused Diderot of having commandeered the plates commissioned for the work of the Académie Royale de Sciences, its *Description des arts et métiers* (1761–1789, Description of Arts and Trades). The accusation was not entirely unfounded. The following year Voltaire created the comedy *Le Café ou l'Ecossaise* (1760, The Café, or The Scotswoman), which included a thinly disguised portrait of Fréron. In his preface to the play, Voltaire excoriated not only a so-called Frélon but also what he saw as an entire class of hack writers, third-rate journalists, and parasitic critics gnawing away at belles lettres. Fréron's publisher, Charles-Joseph Panckoucke, happened also to be the publisher of the *Encyclopédie*. Doubtless, for economic reasons, Panckoucke tried to bring about a reconciliation between Fréron and Voltaire, but their feud continued all the more vituperatively. By 1767 the philosophes were assuming control of the major cultural institutions in Paris, including the Comédie française and the Académie française. Living well at the time, Fréron enjoyed popularity among a group of younger writers. By 1770 *L'Année littéraire* had become a kind of anti-academy, and the considerable success of Fréron's review helped establish the respectability of the press. In 1771 and 1775 the Académie française inducted two journalists as members, an event unthinkable in 1740 when Fréron entered the world of journalism. Fréron's adversaries had taken the offensive, however. He was the target of Voltaire's barbs, launched from his home in Ferney, including the scurrilous *Anecdotes sur Fréron* (1770, Anecdotes about Fréron), and Fréron's journal was the object of machinations initiated by the Encyclopedists and the Holbach group in Paris. By the end of his life, Fréron had become an impoverished and all but solitary figure in the world of literature. *L'Année littéraire* was briefly suppressed a final time in 1776. Fréron died 10 March 1776 shortly after learning the news. His son, Stanisłas, continued to direct the periodical until 1786.

Fréron once described his objective as being to "veiller à la porte du Temple du Goût pour empêcher l'invasion de l'ignorance et du faux bel-esprit" (stand guard at the entrance to the Temple of Taste to ward off the invasion of ignorance and sham wit). He carried out that mission fervently in the pages of *L'Année littéraire;* in its reviews aesthetic concerns were always foremost. The picture of belles lettres that Fréron painted in the periodical grew increasingly somber. The sense of true aesthetic beauty has disappeared, he maintained, and clarity, precision, and elegance of expression have become rare. Everyone writes verse; yet, poetry itself is becoming increasingly impoverished. To view poetry simply as an ornament of rational thought, the versified expression of reason, he believed was a serious error. Poetry must be expressive, not simply didactic. It should translate a superior form of thought, one shaped by inspiration, feeling, and enthusiasm, not reason alone. While such arguments anticipate the aesthetic principles of pre-Romanticism, Fréron became increasingly prescriptive in the kind of poetic production he advocated. He invited authors not only to seek inspiration from such Greek and Latin authors as Horace, Virgil, and Pindar, but also to copy the genres these poets practiced in order to revivify French poetry. During the wave of epics that appeared during the Seven Years' War, Fréron called for a rebirth of epic poetry, to be produced by poets infused with a spirit of religion and patriotism. He praised the work of many foreign poets, including Edward Young, James Thomson, and Salomon Gessner, from whom one could draw valuable aesthetic lessons for rejuvenating French poetry.

Letter from Fréron to his friend Jacques Triboudet, counselor to the king (Bibliothèque nationale; from Jean Balcou,
Le Dossier Fréron, *1975; Thomas Cooper Library, University of South Carolina)*

For literary theoreticians of the eighteenth century, tragedy was the noblest theatrical genre. Yet, many of them believed, as Fréron did, that contemporary tragedies were unable to capture the imagination of theatergoers. Standards set in the previous century by an aristocratic public were being reshaped by a bourgeoisie, made up of writers and consumers alike, that saw in the art forms of high culture the means of expressing its own ideals, values, and aspirations. In his most polemical pronouncements on theater, Fréron castigated the philosophes for having turned the stage into a platform for the kind of propaganda found in the works of Diderot, Pierre-Auguste Caron de Beaumarchais, Louis-Sébastien Mercier, or Charles-Georges Fenouillot de Falbaire. Polemical objectives aside, Fréron was accurate in his assessment of the change of taste occurring in the mid eighteenth century, as the dramatic replaced the tragic in the works of authors whom Fréron saw as caught between an aristocratic and a bourgeois sensibility. His criticism of the tragedies of his time was not based on an inflexible faithfulness to the grand models of the seventeenth century. Blind subservience to theatrical rules (such as the three unities) had to be abandoned, he felt, if truly tragic situations were to be elaborated. Fréron's remarks on theater are shaped by this double objective—maintaining faithfulness to the great classical models and reworking these models to meet the requirements of a new sensibility and taste.

Fréron was not particularly well disposed toward the novel, a term that refers in *L'Année littéraire* to any form of prose fiction. He took the genre more seriously after the publication of Rousseau's immensely popular *La Nouvelle Héloïse* (1761, The New Heloise), which encouraged novelists to affirm that the novel could celebrate virtue and feeling. Yet, Fréron could rely on no established theoretical doctrine on which to base aesthetic judgment concerning novels, since the genre of the novel was undergoing constant transformation. His judgments of individual novels were founded on their degree of realism, on their capacity to provide moral instruction, and, increasingly, on their ability to evoke the reader's empathy and compassion. The sentimental novel, illustrated in large measure by women writers' works, thus represented for Fréron the direction that novelists' creations should take.

Although Fréron was religiously conservative and a proponent of Christian absolutism, his social policies were liberal, just as were those of his nemesis, Voltaire. Fréron called for religious toleration, the development of commerce, and inoculation. When commenting on the *Mémoires de l'Académie des sciences* (Reports of the Academy of Sciences), for instance, he sounded like a popularizer of Enlightenment science, espousing the belief that with change comes greater happiness. His intellectual curiosity was extremely wide-ranging, and he regularly reviewed works on agriculture, cartography, travel literature, economics, and medicine.

Elie Catherine Fréron is a figure through whom one can understand many of the major transformations taking place in the world of letters in eighteenth-century France. The foremost representative of eighteenth-century traditionalism, his aesthetic judgments did not favor forms and principles that came to define the literature of later periods. Yet, his literary reviews display an impressive erudition, an unflagging commitment to standards of taste and beauty, and an acute understanding of aesthetic form. His immensely influential publications provided a forum for public debate concerning cultural issues, and as a successful journalist he helped establish the respectability of the press. Fréron tirelessly denounced what he took to be the decadence of literature, which he attributed to a moral crisis of larger social dimensions. One of France's first modern critics and intellectuals of the Right, Fréron was an engaged journalist whose reputation was engulfed in the polemical battles he waged and was ultimately caught up in.

Fréron would not be well remembered by the literary history of the following two centuries. He would be portrayed, if mentioned at all, as a one-dimensional hidebound traditionalist, a reductive view of this complex figure that made it easier to portray a liberal, liberalizing, and ultimately triumphant Enlightenment. His direct influence on French literature was eclipsed in the nineteenth century by the Romantic literary historian, Charles-Augustin Sainte-Beuve. Little studied by historians or literary scholars, Fréron's life and writings nonetheless provide valuable insight concerning the place of literature and the literary critic in the complex dynamics of cultural change in eighteenth-century France.

Letters:

Le Dossier Fréron: correspondances et documents, edited by Jean Balcou (Geneva: Droz, [1975]).

References:

Jean Balcou, *Fréron contre les philosophes* (Geneva: Droz, 1975);

Balcou, ed., *Le Dossier Fréron: correspondances et documents* (Geneva: Droz, [1975]);

Paul Benhamou, *Index des "Lettres sur quelques écrits de ce temps" (1749–1754) d'Elie Catherine Fréron* (Geneva: Slatkine Reprints, 1985);

Jacqueline Biard-Millérioux, *L'Esthétique d'Elie Catherine Fréron, 1739–1776: littérature et critique au XVIIIe siècle* (Paris: Presses Universitaires de France, 1985);

Dante Lenardon, *Index de l'Année littéraire de Fréron, 1754–1790* (Geneva: Slatkine Reprints, 1979).

Stéphanie-Félicité Ducrest, comtesse de Genlis
(21 January 1746 – 31 December 1830)

Valérie Lastinger
West Virginia University

BOOKS: *La mère rivale* (Paris: Ruault, 1773);

Théâtre à l'usage des jeunes personnes, volume 1, anonymous (Paris: Panckoucke, 1779), volumes 2–4 (Paris: Lambert & Baudouin, 1780); translated as *Theater of Education,* 4 volumes (London: Cadell & Elmsley, 1781);

Théâtre de société, anonymous, 2 volumes (Paris: Lambert & Baudouin, 1781);

Annales de la vertu, ou cours d'histoire à l'usage des jeunes personnes, anonymous, 2 volumes (Paris: Lambert & Baudouin, 1782);

Adèle et Théodore, ou lettres sur l'éducation, anonymous, 3 volumes (Paris: Lambert & Baudouin, 1782); translated as *Adelaide and Theodore, or, Letters on Education* (London: Printed for C. Bathurst & T. Cadell, 1783);

Les Veillées du château, ou cours de morale à l'usage des jeunes personnes, anonymous, 3 volumes (Paris: Lambert, 1784); translated by Thomas Holcroft as *Tales of the Castle; or, Stories of Instruction and Delight* (London: Printed for G. Robinson, 1785);

Contes moraux (Paris, 1785); translated as *A New Method of Instruction for Children from Five to Ten Years Old* (London: Longman & Rees, 1800);

La Religion considérée comme l'unique base de bonheur et de la véritable philosophie (Paris: Imprimerie Polytype, 1787); translated as *Religion Considered as the Only Basis of Happiness, and of True Philosophy* (London: Printed for T. Payne & Son, 1787);

Discours sur l'éducation de M. le Dauphin et sur l'adoption (Paris: Onfroy, 1790);

Discours sur la suppression des convens de religieuses et de l'éducation publique des femmes (Paris: Onfroy, 1790);

Discours sur l'éducation publique du peuple (Paris: J. P. Roux, 1791);

Leçons d'une gouvernante à ses élèves, ou fragment d'un journal qui a été fait pour l'éducation des enfants de M. d'Orléans, 2 volumes (Paris: Onfroy, 1791); translated as *Lessons from a Governess to her Pupils; or, Journal of the Method adopted by Madame de Sillery-Brulart (formerly Countess de Genlis) in the Education of

Stéphanie-Félicité Ducrest, comtesse de Genlis (portrait by Antoine Vestier; Archives photographiques, Paris; from Violet Wyndham, Madame de Genlis, *1958; Thomas Cooper Library, University of South Carolina)*

the Children of M. d'Orleans, First Prince of the Blood Royal,* 3 volumes (London: G. G. J. & J. Robinson, 1792);

Discours sur le luxe et l'hospitalité (Paris: Onfroy, 1791);

Les Chevaliers du Cygne ou la cour de Charlemagne, 3 volumes (Hamburg: Fauche, 1795); translated as *The Knights of the Swan, or, the Court of Charlemagne,* 2 volumes (London: Printed for J. Johnson, St. Paul's Church-yard, 1796);

Epître à l'asile que j'aurai; Epître à Henriette de Sercey (Hamburg: Fauche, 1796);

Précis de la conduite de Madame de Genlis depuis la Révolution, suivi d'une lettre à M. de Chartres et de réflexions sur la critique (Hamburg: Hoffman / Paris: Cérioux, 1796); translated as *Short Account of the Conduct of Madame de Genlis Since the Revolution: To Which is Subjoined: A Letter to M. de Chartres, and the Shepherds of the Pyrennees, a Fragment* (Perth: Printed by R. Morison Jr. for R. Morison & Son, H. Mitchel, and Vernor & Hood, 1796);

Réflexions d'un ami des talens et des arts (Hamburg: Fauche, 1796);

Les Petits Emigrés ou correspondance de quelques enfants, 4 volumes (Paris: Onfroy / Berlin: Fr. de Lagarde, 1798); translated as *The Young Exiles; or, Correspondence of Some Juvenile Emigrants* (2 volumes, Dublin: Printed for V. Dowling & J. Stockdale, 1799; 3 volumes, London: Printed for J. Wright and H. D. Symonds, 1799);

Les Voeux téméraires ou l'enthousiasme, 2 volumes (Hamburg: Pierre Chateauneuf, 1798); translated as *Rash Vows, or, the Effects of Enthusiasm*, 3 volumes (London: Longman & Rees, 1799);

Manuel du voyageur (Berlin: F. T. de La Garde, 1799); translated as *The Traveller's Companion* (Paris: C. Barrois, 1810);

Herbier moral ou recueil de fables nouvelles et autres pièces fugitives, 2 volumes (Hamburg: Pierre Chateauneuf, 1799);

Nouvelle Méthode d'enseignement pour la première enfance (Besançon: Métayer, an VIII [1799]);

Le Petit La Bruyère ou caractères et moeurs de ce siècle (Hamburg: Fauche, 1799); translated as *La Bruyere the Less; or, Characters and Manners of the Children of the Present Age* (London: Printed by A. Strahan for Longman & Rees, 1800);

Les Mères rivales, ou la calomnie, 3 volumes (Berlin: F. T. de La Garde, 1800); translated as *Rival Mothers; or, The Calumny* (London: Longman & Rees, 1800);

Nouvelles heures à l'usage des enfants (Paris: Maradan, 1801);

Mademoiselle de Clermont. Nouvelle historique, 2 volumes (Paris: Maradan, 1802); translated as *Mademoiselle de Clermont* in *A Series of Novels by Madame de Genlis* (London: Longman & Rees, 1802);

Nouveaux Contes moraux et nouvelles historiques, 3 volumes (Paris: Maradan, 1802, 1805; enlarged, 6 volumes, 1819);

La Philosophie chrétienne (Paris: Maradan, 1802);

La Duchesse de La Vallière, 2 volumes (Paris: Maradan, 1804); translated as *The Duchess of La Vallière* (London: Printed for J. Murray, 1804);

L'Epouse impertinente par air, suivie du mari corrupteur et de la femme philosophe (Paris: Maradan, 1804); translated as *The Impertinent Wife* (London: Minerva Press, 1806);

Réflexions sur la miséricorde de Dieu par Mme de La Vallière (Paris, 1804);

[Les] Souvenirs de Félicie L*** (Paris: Maradan, 1804); translated as *Recollections of Felicia L**** (Dublin: Printed by T. Henshall, 1808);

Le Comte de Corke ou la séduction sans artifice, 2 volumes (Paris: Maradan, 1805); translated as *The Earl of Cork; or, Seduction Without Artifice*, 3 volumes (London: Printed for J. F. Hughes, 1808);

L'Etude du coeur humain (Paris: Maradan, 1805);

Les Monuments religieux, ou description critique et détaillée des monuments religieux, tableaux, statues, qui se trouvent actuellement en Europe et dans les autres parties du monde, 2 volumes (Paris: Maradan, 1805);

Alphonsine ou la tendresse maternelle, 2 volumes (Paris: Nicolle, 1806); translated as *Alphonsine; or, Maternal Affection*, 4 volumes (London: Hughes, 1806);

Madame de Maintenon pour servir de suite à l'histoire de Madame de La Vallière, 2 volumes (Paris: Maradan, 1806); translated as *Madame de Maintenon*, 2 volumes (London: M. Pelletier, 1806);

Le Siège de la Rochelle ou le malheur de la conscience (Paris: Nicolle, 1807); translated by Robert Charles Dallas as *The Siege of Rochelle; or, The Christian Heroine* (London: Printed by Cox, Son & Baylis, for B. Dulau, 1808);

Suite des souvenirs de Félicie L*** (Paris: Maradan & Nicolle, 1807); translated as *Recollections of Felicia L**** (Dublin: Printed by T. Henshall, 1808);

Bélisaire, 2 volumes (Paris: Maradan, 1808);

Sainclair ou la victime des sciences et des arts (Paris: Maradan, 1808); translated as *Sainclair; or, The Victim of the Arts and Sciences* (London: B. Dulau, 1808);

Alphonse ou le fils naturel (Paris: Maradan, 1809);

Arabesques mythologiques ou les attributs de toutes les divinités de la fable, 2 volumes (Paris: Charles Barrois, 1810);

La Maison rustique, 3 volumes (Paris: Maradan, 1810);

La Botanique historique et littéraire (Paris: Maradan, 1810);

De l'Influence des femmes sur la littérature française comme protectrices des lettres et comme auteurs (Paris: Maradan, 1811);

Les Bergères de Madian ou la jeunesse de Moïse (Paris: Galignani, 1812);

La Feuille des gens du monde ou le journal imaginaire (Paris: Eymery, 1813);

Mademoiselle de La Fayette ou le siècle de Louis XIII, 2 volumes (Paris: Maradan, 1813); translated as *Mademoiselle de La Fayette; or, The Century of Louis XIII*, 2 volumes (London: Colburn, 1813);

Les Hermites des Marais Pontins (Paris: Maradan, 1814);

Jeanne de France, 2 volumes (Paris: Maradan, 1814); translated as *Jane of France,* 2 volumes (Boston: Wells & Lilly, 1817);

Histoire de Henri le Grand, 2 volumes (Paris: Maradan, 1815);

[Les] Battuécas, 2 volumes (Paris: Maradan, 1816); translated by Alexander Jamieson as *Placide, a Spanish Tale,* 2 volumes (London: W. Simpkin & R. Marshall, 1817);

[Les] Tableaux du comte de Forbin, ou, la mort de Pline l'Ancien et Inès de Castro (Paris: Maradan, 1817);

Zuma ou la découverte du quinquina (Paris: Maradan, 1817); translated as *Zuma or, The Tree of Health* (New York: W. B. Gilley, 1818);

Dictionnaire critique et raisonné des étiquettes de la Cour, usages du monde, etc., 2 volumes (Paris: Mongie, 1818);

Voyages poétiques d'Eugène et d'Antonine (Paris: Maradan, 1818);

Pétrarque et Laure, 2 volumes (Paris: Ladvocat, 1819); translated as *Petrarch and Laura* (London: Colburn, 1820);

Catéchisme critique et moral de l'abbé Flévier de Reval, 2 volumes (Paris, 1820);

Palmyre et Flaminie, 2 volumes (Paris: Maradan, 1821);

Six Nouvelles morales et religieuses (Paris: Janet, 1821);

Les Jeux champêtres des enfants (Paris: Marc, 1821);

Les Dîners du baron d'Holbach (Paris: Trouvé, 1822);

Les Veillées de la chaumière (Paris: Lecointe & Durey, 1823);

Les Prisonniers (Paris: Bertrand, 1824);

De l'Emploi du temps (Paris: Bertrand, 1824);

Les Athées conséquents, ou mémoires du commander de Linanges (Paris: Trouvé, 1824);

Mémoires inédits sur le XVIIIe siècle et la Révolution française, 10 volumes (Paris: Ladvocat, 1825); translated as *Memoirs of the countess de Genlis: Illustrative of the History of the Eighteenth and Nineteenth Centuries* (New York: Wilder & Campbell, 1825–1826);

Thérésina ou l'enfant de la providence (Paris: Ladvocat, 1826);

Inès de Castro, nouvelle suivie de la mort de Pline, 2 volumes (Paris: Lecointe & Durey, 1826);

Le La Bruyère des domestiques, by Genlis and Jean de La Bruyère (Paris: Thiercelin, 1828);

Les Soupers de la maréchale de Luxembourg (Paris: Roux, 1828);

Le Dernier Voyage de Nelgis, ou mémoires d'un vieillard, 2 volumes (Paris: Roux, 1828);

Manuel de la jeune femme. Guide complet de la maîtresse de maison (Paris: Béchet, 1829).

Editions: *Oeuvres complètes,* 21 volumes (Maastricht: J. P. Roux, 1783–1792);

Nouvelle Méthode pour apprendre à jouer de la harpe (Geneva: Minkoff Reprints, 1974);

La Duchesse de La Vallière suivi de deux lettres de Mademoiselle de La Vallière (Paris: Librairie Lontaine, 1983);

Mademoiselle de Clermont (Paris: Editions Autrement, 1994);

Inès de Castro (Toulouse: Ombres, 1995);

De l'Esprit des étiquettes de l'ancienne cour et des usages du monde de ce temps (Paris: Mercure de France, 1996).

OTHER: *Les Lettres de Marie-Anne. La Feuille villageoise,* edited by Genlis (Paris, 1790–1795);

Jean-Jacques Rousseau, *Emile, ou de l'éducation,* 3 volumes, edited by Genlis (Paris: Maradan, 1820);

Voltaire, *Le Siècle de Louis XIV,* 3 volumes, edited by Genlis (Paris, 1820);

Marie Renée Marguerite, marquise de Bonchamps, *Mémoires de la marquise de Bonchamps,* edited by Genlis (Paris: Baudouin, 1823).

Stéphanie-Félicité de Genlis's long life spanned a particularly tumultuous period of French political and intellectual history. Her life and works were of great significance to her contemporaries for several reasons. Her longevity made her one of the few witnesses of eleven different political regimes. An avid reader and prolific writer, she published more than 140 titles—most of which were instant best-sellers—in a variety of genres. The importance of her work as a pedagogue with the Orléans children also made her an intellectual figure that dominated her time. Toward the end of her life, she was considered a national repository of the ancien régime and was often called upon to settle questions of etiquette and civility.

Despite this preeminence, Genlis's works remain largely forgotten today. With a few exceptions, most of her books have been out of print since the late nineteenth century, although critical interest in her works has increased since the mid 1980s. Knowledge of her work is important to an accurate understanding of the roots of modern France, since Genlis not only influenced people of her own time but also many nineteenth-century figures.

Genlis was born Caroline-Stéphanie-Félicité Ducrest in the small village of Issy-l'Evêque (Burgundy) on 21 January 1746. The Ducrests were an old military noble family, as poor as they were noble. Her father, who took the name of Pierre-César Ducrest de Saint-Aubin, was well educated, but his lack of financial savvy left the family in a difficult situation after his premature death in 1763. Félicité, together with her brother, received her first education from the village schoolteacher. Her mother soon moved to Paris with Félicité so that she could acquire the manners fit for her social standing. Though poor, the two women stayed with rich relatives and sampled the life of luxury afforded only by the most privileged. Félicité's teacher, a poorly educated young woman, limited her teaching to religious lessons. During her adolescence, Félicité began serious study of the harp and excelled in performing at private theaters. Her talent as an actress and an accomplished musician was soon recognized by professional musicians such as Jean-Philippe Rameau and such leading intellectuals as Jean Le Rond d'Alembert, who wanted to hear her play. In fact, Mme de Saint-Aubin soon reaped financial gain from her daughter's performances.

In 1763 Félicité secretly married Charles-Alexis Ducrest, comte de Genlis. Although, at first, the count's family was displeased with the match because of the bride's lack of fortune, her good humor and disposition soon won them over. Genlis found distinguished social mentors among her husband's relatives, who presented her at court. Although neither spouse was faithful, the couple maintained a good relationship and had three children, of whom only two daughters survived.

Through her aunt, Charlotte de Montesson—mistress, then wife, of the duc de Orléans—Genlis established a relationship with the Orléans family that defined the rest of her life. Montesson obtained for her niece a coveted position in the household of the duchess of Chartres, Orléans's daughter-in-law. Soon after the appointment, Genlis became the duc de Chartres's mistress, but more significantly, she earned his respect and intellectual admiration.

In 1779 Genlis began to publish the first volume of her *Théâtre à l'usage des jeunes personnes* (translated as *Theater of Education*, 1781), a series of plays she had begun to write for her daughters in 1777. Success was immediate, and critics (particularly, Frédéric Melchior Grimm and Jean-François de La Harpe) were unanimous in their praise. This first literary production caught the attention of such intellectuals as Denis Diderot and Voltaire and was followed by three more volumes in 1780. In 1779 Genlis was appointed governess to the Chartres' two-year-old twin daughters. In order to accomplish this task with utmost seriousness, Genlis retired with her pupils and her daughters to the small manor Bellechasse, built expressly for that purpose. She remained in charge of the education of the Orléans children until 1794.

In 1782 Chartres surprised everyone by sending his sons to be educated at Bellechasse with their sisters, giving Genlis the official masculine and more prestigious title of *gouverneur* (governor). This decision drew much negative attention to Genlis, since the position was generally given to high-ranking noblemen, although they did little for their pupils. Genlis ignored the criticism and, instead, continued to develop a full

Title page for Genlis's work that gives young people lessons on virtue based on history (from Genlis, Annales de la vertu, *1782; Thomas Cooper Library, University of South Carolina)*

educational program, organized every aspect of her pupils' lives, and stressed the importance of academics, physical activity, and hygiene. Dedicating herself to this pedagogical endeavor, she began to publish regularly on the topic of education. In 1782 she wrote *Annales de la vertu, ou cours d'histoire à l'usage des jeunes personnes* (The Annals of Virtue or, Historical Lessons for Young People), but, more importantly, *Adèle et Théodore, ou lettres sur l'éducation* (translated as *Adelaide and Theodore, or, Letters on Education*, 1783). In this famous treatise, she explained her ideas on education as implemented at Bellechasse—an experimental educational project inspired not only by John Locke and François de Salignac de la Mothe-Fénelon but also by Jean-Jacques Rousseau, although Genlis expressed reservations against the Encyclopedists. Her growing popularity and the general public's lack of support for the philosophes moved them to offer her a compromise: if she promised to stop writing about religion, she would be the first of four women invited to join the Académie française (French Academy). Genlis refused the offer, and the four seats were never granted to women.

The book also shares many of Louise d'Epinay's ideas in *Les Conversations d'Emilie* (1774; translated as *The Conversations of Emilie,* 1787), although Genlis's book stresses the importance of religion. Despite the inspiration she found in the ideas of the philosophes, the publication of *Adèle et Théodore* began Genlis's lifelong battle against them, for, unlike them, she believed that faith-based education would enable humanity to overcome the evils of society. Following a heated battle in 1783, Genlis lost the much coveted Montyon Prize of the French Academy to Epinay—the candidate supported by the philosophes—who won posthumously for the second volume of her *Conversations d'Emilie.*

In 1784 Genlis published *Les Veillées du château, ou cours de morale à l'usage des jeunes personnes* (translated as *Tales of the Castle; or, Stories of Instruction and Delight,* 1785), in which she pursued the liberal ideas that soon became her trademark: (A great birth is only an advantage; but it is education that establishes true inequality among men: a reasonable, learned, and enlightened person will not include in his inner circle an ignorant, rude, and careless person, full of prejudice). Again, the book met with instant success and was immediately translated into several languages, including English. The popularity of *Les Veillées du château* was probably even greater than that of *Adèle et Théodore* because it was both a treatise of education and one of the first French books written specifically for children. It continued to influence several generations of parents and children through the nineteenth and the early part of the twentieth centuries.

Les Veillées du château consists of independent tales framed in a narrative dialogue between a mother-teacher and her children-pupils. The theoretical aspects of education are developed in the narrative frame, whereas the tales, presented in ascending order of moral complexity, are directed at the children. In this work, Genlis defined the direction of fictional writings for children in France. She rejected the use of fantasy and fairy tales, and ambiguous moral fables, favoring instead the presentation of more realistic or historical characters acting in a plausible plot. The outcome of the stories is based on the protagonists' ability to use common sense and to demonstrate critical and analytical skills. The well-researched content of the tales contributes to the interest of the reader. Genlis was praised for the clarity and precision of her style, and many authors, such as George Sand, mention the influence of Genlis's books on their own educations. Among Genlis's many publications for children, one deserves a special mention—the 1810 *Arabesques mythologiques* (Mythological Arabesques), a book with pictorial riddles, in which she uses her talent as an educator and illustrator to teach mythology.

During the French Revolution, Genlis published essays about direly needed educational reforms and began to advocate a good education for women, one that would provide them with the necessary skills to survive in case of widowhood. Forced to go into exile in 1791, she left France with her youngest royal pupil, Adélaïde d'Orléans, the only one still in her care. During the Revolution, her position was a rather difficult one. Unwanted in France because of her ties to the monarchy, she was also rejected by fellow émigrés because of her early support for the Revolution and her former lover and protector's vote for the execution of his cousin, Louis XVI. She remained abroad until 1800. Because of her political position, she was often forced to hide while in exile and had no other income than the proceeds of her literary production. She used that time to publish several works, to continue to read extensively, and take notes that she used in later years. Also worthy of note is her 1799 *Manuel du voyageur* (translated as *The Traveller's Companion,* 1810), the first work of and a testimony to its author's creativity. An immediate success, it was soon imitated in all major European languages.

Upon her return to France, Genlis continued to live from money earned by her literary production and began to publish historical novels. *Mademoiselle de Clermont* (1802; translated, 1802) and *La Duchesse de La Vallière* (1804; translated as *The Duchess of La Vallière,* 1804) earned her even greater literary fame. Her thorough knowledge of the seventeenth century (nurtured by extensive readings on the period), her clarity of expression, and her personal knowledge of the characters she created earned her the praise of literary critics, who often compared her talent to that of Germaine de Staël. More importantly, these popular works enchanted their readership, including Napoleon. Once again, Genlis was in political favor, and in 1806 she became part of the large network of correspondents who wrote regularly to the emperor to keep him informed about the mood of the country. This effort was generously rewarded by a pension.

Following her return from exile, Genlis's productivity and creativity were remarkable. In addition to pioneering the historical novel in France, long before Sir Walter Scott made it a cornerstone of the Romantic movement, Genlis also wrote two volumes of personal anecdotes, [Les] Souvenirs de Félicie L*** (1804; translated as Recollections of Felicia L***, 1808), and several essays on religion. Furthermore, she found the time to return to music, this time as a musicologist and a harp teacher. She continued to develop her interest in school reform and wrote an essay on that subject for Napoleon.

Aside from her own literary production, Genlis continued to be an avid reader and an occasional literary critic while pursuing her battle with the Encyclopedists. Although most of them were dead by now, she resented their enduring influence and took it upon herself to correct their errors. Although her project of publishing a corrected version of Diderot and d'Alembert's Encyclopédie never came to fruition, she pursued her efforts in that direction and, in 1820, published a corrected edition of Rousseau's Emile, ou de l'éducation (1751; translated as Emilius; or, An Essay on Education, 1763) and also in 1820, Voltaire's Le Siècle de Louis XIV (1751; translated as The Age of Lewis XIV, 1752). Her arguments with the philosophes stemmed from the idea that intelligent and educated people of the Enlightenment were not necessarily atheists. For the main part, the philosophes' position had prevailed, and the polemical interest in Genlis's ideas was outdated. Nevertheless, she remained undeterred in her strong opinions. For example, in 1811, she was asked to write the biographical notices of famous French women for the ambitious Biographie universelle (1811, Universal Biography). Genlis set to work but withdrew her articles when she learned that several fellow contributors belonged to the Encyclopedist faction. She published the material she had written for the Biographie universelle along with Réflexions sur les femmes auteurs also in 1811, under the title De l'Influence des femmes sur la littérature française comme protectrices des lettres et comme auteurs (On the Influence of Women on Literature as Defenders of the Letters and as Authors). The role of women in society and the arts, and education of women were certainly not new topics for Genlis, as she had written essays, plays, and novellas on the subject for years.

During the Restoration, Genlis maintained political favor because of her ties with the Orléans family. Her former pupils came back to France, and the reunion with them was bittersweet. Once again, her literary style was much in demand, for her historical novels extolled the virtues of the great monarchs, starting with Henri IV in Histoire de Henri le Grand (Story of Henry the Great), published in 1815. At age seventy-three, Genlis reached the peak of her literary fame with the publication of a social novel, [Les] Parvenus, ou les aventures de Julien Delmour (1819; translated as The New Aera; or, Adventures of Julien Delmour Related by Himself, 1819), and another historical novel, Pétrarque et Laure (1819; translated as Petrarch and Laura, 1820). During

Portrait of Genlis in 1820 (engraving of a portrait by Mme Cheradame; from Violet Wyndham, Madame de Genlis, *1958; Thomas Cooper Library, University of South Carolina)*

the last ten years of her life, Genlis continued to publish, although her productivity declined somewhat. Her monumental ten-volume Mémoires inédits sur le XVIIIe siècle et la Révolution française was published in 1825 (translated as Memoirs of the countess de Genlis: Illustrative of the History of the Eighteenth and Nineteenth Centuries, 1825–1826). The first volumes of this work were met with enthusiasm and interest on the part of the readership; however, family members and literary critics were less pleased. Among others, in his Causeries du lundi (1850; translated as Monday-Chats, 1877), Charles-Augustin Sainte-Beuve was outraged that she chose to publish her memoirs while she was still alive.

In 1830 Genlis's health began to decline, just as her former pupil, Louis-Philippe d'Orléans, ascended to the throne and was crowned on 9 August of that year. Upon hearing the news, the former governor expressed the same reservations she had always had about her student's political abilities. On 31 December 1830, Genlis died in relative solitude, outliving most of her friends and contemporaries.

To assess the controversial life and works of Stéphanie-Félicité, comtesse de Genlis, marquise du Sillery, is difficult, although any study of that period is not complete without a full understanding of the importance and influence of her voluminous production. As an educator, she has always been praised, even by such critics as Sainte-Beuve, who otherwise despised her work. Her contributions to the fields of pedagogy and of children's literature alone have earned her a distinguished place in the history of French literature.

Overall, her literary interests reflect those of other eighteenth-century intellectuals—literature, music, history, botany, education, and social reform. Yet, she also truly belongs to the nineteenth century, as her contribution to the development of the historical novel in France was essential. Probably her personal actions and political choices have undermined the recognition she deserves. Her intrigues to gain fame often contradicted the image of virtue and self-effacement that she tried to convey. Her tiresome insistence to obtain favors for her relatives and protégés annoyed even her most ardent supporters. Today, however, modern scholars need to reevaluate her works, cast aside in the nineteenth and twentieth centuries because Genlis had often defended losing literary or political battles against the Encyclopedists or Romantic authors. Although she failed to recognize the genius of many contemporaries with whom she maintained a regular correspondence, her reasons for opposing their ideas were generally well argued and deserve to be incorporated for an understanding of the period.

Letters:

Henri Lapauze, ed., *Lettres inédites de Mme de Genlis à son fils adoptif Casimir Baecker 1802–1830* (Paris: Plon, 1902).

Biographies:

Violet Leverson Wyndham, *Madame de Genlis, a Biography* (London: Deutsch, 1958);

Gabriel de Broglie, *Madame de Genlis* (Paris: Perrin, 1985).

References:

Penny Brown, "La Femme Enseignante: Mme de Genlis and the Moral and Didactic Tale in France," *Bulletin of the John Rylands Library of the University Library of Manchester,* 76, no. 3 (1994): 23–42;

Jeanne Goldin, "Femme-auteur et réflexivité: Madame de Genlis," in *Masculin/féminin: le XIXe siècle à l'épreuve du genre,* edited by Chantal Bertrand-Jennings (Toronto: Centre d'Etudes du XIXe siècle Joseph Sable, 1999);

Alice Laborde, *L'Oeuvre de Madame de Genlis* (Paris: Nizet, 1966);

Marie Naudin, "Une Avocate des mères célibataires et des enfants naturels: Mme de Genlis," *Kentucky Romance Quarterly,* 30, no. 4 (1983): 349–358;

Naudin, "Stéphanie-Félicité, Comtesse de Genlis (1746–1830)," in *French Women Writers,* edited by Eva Martin Sartori and Dorothy Wynne Zimmerman (Westport, Conn.: Greenwood Press, 1991), pp. 178–187;

Bonnie Arden Robb, "Celestin/Celestine: Ambiguities of Identity chez Mme de Genlis," *Eighteenth-Century Fiction,* 12, no. 4 (1 July 2000): 549–571;

Charles-Augustin Sainte-Beuve, *Oeuvres,* 2 volumes (Paris: Gallimard, 1956);

Anne L. Schroder, "Going Public Against the Academy in 1784: Mme de Genlis Speaks Out on Gender Bias," *Eighteenth-Century Studies,* volume 32, no. 3 (Spring 1999): 376–383;

Samia I. Spencer, "Women and Education," in *French Women and the Age of Enlightenment,* edited by Spencer (Bloomington: Indiana University Press, 1984), pp. 83–96.

Madeleine-Angélique Poisson de Gomez

(22 November 1684 – 28 December 1770)

Michele L. Heintz
Tulane University

BOOKS: *Habis, tragédie* (Paris: P. Ribou, 1714);

Anecdotes, ou histoire de la maison Ottomane (Amsterdam: La Compagnie, 1722);

Les Journées amusantes . . . (Paris: G. Saugrain [Vve Guillaume, C. LeClerc], 1722); translated by Eliza Haywood as *La Belle Assemblée: Being a Curious Collection of Some Very Remarkable Incidents Which Happened to Persons of the First Quality in France* (London: Printed for D. Browne, 1724);

Histoire secrète de la conqueste de Grenade (Paris: LeClerc, 1723);

Les Epreuves (N.p., 1724);

Lettre sur le nouveau poème de Clovis, de Saint-Didier (Paris: Prault, 1725);

Anecdotes persanes (Paris: LeClerc, 1727; Paris: Prault, 1727); translated by Paul Chamberlen as *Persian Anecdotes; or, Secret Memoirs of the Court of Persia* (London: Printed for W. Bickerton, 1730);

Crémentine, reine de Sanga: histoire indienne (Paris: LeClerc, 1727);

Le Triomphe de l'eloquence (Paris: LeClerc, 1730);

Entretiens nocturnes de Mercure et de La Renommée au jardin des Tuilleries (Paris: LeClerc, 1731);

La Jeune Alcidiane (Paris: Guillaume-Denis David, 1733);

Les Cent Nouvelles nouvelles, 10 volumes (The Hague: Pierre de Hondt, 1733–1739); translated by Haywood as *L'Entretien des beaux esprits. Conversations, Comprising a Great Variety of Remarkable Adventures, Serious, Comic, and Moral* (London: Printed for F. Cogan & J. Nourse, 1734);

La Nouvelle Mer des histoires (Paris: Guillaume, 1733);

Histoire d'Osman premier du nom, XIXe empereur des Turcs, et de l'impératrice Aphendina Ashada (Paris: Prault, 1734);

Marsidie, reine des Cimbres, tragédie (Utrecht: Etienne Neaulme, 1735);

Histoires du comte d'Oxfort, de Miledy d'Herby; d'Eustache de St. Pierre et de Beatrix de Guines . . . (Paris: De Poilly, 1737);

Sémiramis, tragédie (Utrecht: Etienne Neaulme, 1737);

Clearque, tyran d'Héraclée, tragédie (The Hague: B. Gibert, 1738).

Collection and Editions: *Oeuvres mêlées . . . contenant des tragedies et différens ouvrages en vers et en prose* (Paris: André Morin, 1724);

Le Voleur amoureux (Lille: Cailleaux-Lecoq, 1811);

Le Scélérat trompé (Lille: Cailleaux-Lecoq, 1811).

Editions in English: *The Effects of Friendship. A Novel* (Dublin: Printed by and for O. Nelson & C. Connor, 1743);

The Memoirs of the Baron du Tan (New York: Garland, 1974).

PLAY PRODUCTIONS: *Habis, tragédie*, Paris, La Comédie française, 17 April 1714;

Sémiramis, tragédie en cinq actes et en vers, Paris, La Comédie française? 1716;

Cléarque, tyran d'Héraclée, tragédie, Paris, La Comédie française? 1717.

While virtually unknown today to students of French literature and modern French readers, Madeleine-Angélique Poisson de Gomez wrote prolifically and enjoyed literary success during her lifetime. Her novels were read on both sides of the English Channel; yet, her popularity and works virtually disappeared at the end of the eighteenth century. The opinion of Oliver Nelson and Charles Conner, two booksellers in Ireland in 1743, illustrates that Gomez's popularity had expanded beyond the confines of France and the French language. In the "Advertisement by the Editors" that precedes their first translated edition of her 1733 work *Des Effets de l'amitié*, *The Effects of Friendship. A Novel* (1743), which appeared in *Les Cent Nouvelles nouvelles* (1733–1739; translated as *L'Entretien des beaux esprits. Conversations, Comprising a Great Vartiety of Remarkable Adventures, Serious, Comic, and Moral*, 1734), Nelson and Conner wrote, "The celebrated Madame de Gomez is so well known by the productions with which she has favoured the world, that what drops from her pen needs no recommendation to raise the curiosity of the public." Nevertheless, her legacy did drop from the annals of literary history. The few modern scholars who have attempted to unearth and study her works have classified them mainly as romanesque productions: pseudohistorical and pseudoexotic romances and plays. Furthermore, scholars have frequently observed that she inherited from her older compatriot Marguerite de Navarre the commitment to discussions within her stories, thereby promoting debates of a moral as well as a sentimental nature. Such debates reflect the influence, popularity, and importance of discussions in the salon tradition and are most obviously reflected in the two works for which she is best known today–*Les Journées amusantes* (1722; translated as *La Belle Assemblée: Being a Curious Collection of Some Very Remarkable Incidents Which Happened to Persons of the First Quality in France*, 1724), and *Les Cent Nouvelles nouvelles*.

Madeleine-Angélique Poisson was born on 22 November 1684 in Paris. Her biographical details are quite sketchy: she claimed a genealogical connection to one of the more important families of the French theater; her father, Paul Poisson, her uncle François-Arnoul Poisson de Roinville, and her brother Philippe were all prominent actors on the Parisian stage. Her grandfather Raymond Poisson was a playwright. Surrounded by people involved in theater all of her life, she not only was drawn to the theater herself but also married a Spanish actor, Don Gabriel de Gomez. She began to write because her husband was neither wealthy nor successful. During her forty-odd years of writing she produced some twenty works of fiction, including letters, poems, songs, and hundreds of novellas, or *nouvelles*. Gomez eventually married a second time but never changed her name.

She turned first to writing plays. Her first tragedy, *Habis* (1714), having enjoyed an auspicious run, was acted at the Comédie française in 1714 and then revived in 1732. It was quite successful, as Henry Carrington Lancaster has pointed out in *Sunset: A History of Parisian Drama in the Last Years of Louis XIV, 1701–1715* (1945). He contended that for a new tragedy–defined roughly as anything not written by Pierre Corneille or Jean Racine–to survive was extremely difficult; to have it performed by the Comédie française was even more difficult. For example, during the fifteen-year time period that Lancaster studied, only seven out of thirty-two newly written tragedies survived beyond the first performance. The competition proved stiff, as the three most frequently acted tragedies during the same period were *Le Cid* (1636), *Phèdre* (1677), and *Andromaque* (1667). For any novice to the profession to attain success at the Comédie française was nearly impossible, but Gomez overcame the obstacles with *Habis*.

Habis, a tragedy of five acts, remains faithful to the classical unities (time, place, and action) and is written in verse. The tone is highly political, and the theme is the rejection of tyranny. Some modern scholars contend that Gomez achieved her first literary success with the publication of *Les Journées amusantes* in 1722; however, *Habis* won her the respect and confidence she needed to continue as a writer; this play was the third most popular new tragedy at the Comédie française between 1701 and 1715 and was performed twenty-nine times. In fact, Lancaster states that of all the plays written by women up through 1715, *Habis* was the most performed tragedy. This success undoubtedly encouraged Gomez to continue to write three more tragedies, all with the common theme of women who reject tyranny; however, they were judged to be failures. Two of the three plays written were, nonetheless, performed at the Comédie française: *Sémiramis* in 1716 and *Cléarque, tyran d'Héraclée* (Clearchus, Tyrant of Héraclée) in 1717. Gomez's final attempt at tragedy, *Marsidie, reine des Cimbres* (Marsidie, Queen of the Cimbri) did not attain any public success and does not seem to have appeared in print until 1735.

Gomez's next literary endeavor was exotic and historical fiction. A general consensus of critical opinion regarding her work in this area cannot be given because as yet not enough study and literary archaeology have been conducted. Her first two works in this area, *Anecdotes, ou histoire de la maison Ottomane* (1722, Anecdotes, or A History of the Ottaman Dynasty) and *Histoire secrète de la conqueste de Grenade* (1723, A Secret History of the Conquest of Grenada), both take place in far-off locations. The exotic setting is used as a means to discuss volatile, contemporary issues of a moral, political, and sentimental basis. *Les Journées amusantes,* her work that followed, exploits the use of discussions neatly woven between fictional stories. Navarre's influence is noticeable, for as in Navarre's *Heptaméron* (1559), a group of people come together–in this case, for two hours each day–to tell stories, listen, and discuss the moral and sentimental stakes in each tale. Instead of a great storm, which unites Navarre's ten storytellers, in Gomez's work boredom brings four women, Uranie the hostess, Félicie, Camille, and Florinde, and two men, Thélamon and Orophane, out to the country in search of untroubled happiness. For a total of eighteen days, the characters not only give autobiographical portraits of themselves, which expound mainly upon the negative effects of familial politics, but they also discuss such matters as instructions from mother to daughter on the general conduct of her life and on the fickleness of men. After the third day, the characters seem concerned with moral and sentimental issues. The tales are about such figures as Saladin, the sultan of Egypt; Jean de Calais; Amuray and the Princess Rakima; the count of Salmony; King Ethelred of England; and Donna Elvire de Zuares. The major themes of the tales are political intrigue and dissimulation, the dangers of religious life, honor, virtue, respect, lack of education, the importance of esprit and passion, love and marriage, and love in marriage.

Gomez's next literary enterprise, *Les Journées amusantes,* went through at least eight editions from 1722 through 1772 and was translated into English. That Eliza Haywood translated this work lends it a certain importance. In the history of British literature, Haywood was a pioneering novelist who, scholars contend, was the most prolific woman writer of the eighteenth century.

The next twelve years of Gomez's life seem quite industrious, although less remarkable than the years to follow. Besides attempting yet another play, this time a comedy called *Les Epreuves* (1724, The Trials), which was never performed, she undertook to publish a volume called *Oeuvres mêlées . . . contenant des tragedies et différens ouvrages en vers et en prose* (1724, Mixed Works . . . A Collection of Tragedies and Various Works of Poetry and Prose), which features various letters and poems. Five more exotically set short stories were also published, most notably her *Anecdotes persanes* (1727; translated as *Persian Anecdotes; or, Secret Memoirs of the Court of Persia,* 1730), and in 1733 a conclusion to the novel *La Jeune Alcidiane* (1651, Young Alcidiane) by seventeenth-century author and member of the Académie française, Marin Le Roy, sieur de Gomberville. Gomez employed a tried and true formula for success achieved in *Les Journées amusantes* to achieve notoriety, and to make money. In 1733 she published the first edition of her most ambitious project to date: the sequel to *Les Journées amusantes,* which she called *Les Cent Nouvelles nouvelles.* This substantial collection of tales, the title of which refers the reader once again to her predecessor Navarre, was in great demand through six years and multiple editions, as well as a subsequent English translation, again by Haywood.

In order to rekindle the enthusiasm of readers of the first part, *Les Cent Nouvelles nouvelles* begins with a familiar character, Célimène, who proposes to Uranie that they quit discussing moralizing and serious matters and instead tell amusing stories, ones that include gallantry, tenderness, and laughs; truth

Title page for the 1744 English translation of a work originally printed in Gomez's Les Cent Nouvelles nouvelles *(1733–1739) (from Madeleine Gomez,* The Memoirs of the Baron du Tan, *1974; Thomas Cooper Library, University of South Carolina)*

and *vraisemblance* (verisimilitude) were of secondary importance. Nonetheless, moralizing is once again the preferred method of operating for Gomez. Indeed, behind titles such as *Le Voleur amoureux* (The Amorous Thief), *La Fausse Prude* (The False Prude), *La Fidélité conjugale* (Conjugal Fidelity), *La Belle Hollandaise* (The Beautiful Dutchwoman), and *La Noce interrompue* (The Interrupted Wedding) lurks the suspicious odor of lessons to be learned. By and large, the major themes of this work involve tension—in love and in marriage, and in the privacy of families and in public society.

While roughly half of these tales take place within a different historical context from Gomez's time, her most successful use of history as a subversive narratological technique lies outside this particular text, two years later, with the publication of

Histoires du comte d'Oxfort, de Miledy d'Herby; d'Eustache de St. Pierre et de Beatrix de Guines (1737, The Histories of the Count of Oxford, of Lady Herby; Eustache of St. Pierre and Beatrix of Guines). In the second story, devoted to Eustache de St. Pierre and Beatrix de Guines, Gomez writes the private, personal love story of these two people while combining it with an actual public, historic event—that is, the siege of Calais of 1346.

The mélange of history and fiction dates back to the epic. In the past, authors exploited the power and credibility that history lent to a text because history had always been considered an important genre. What is at stake in this particular text is a rewriting of history. A group of women is inserted into a narrative about the founding of the French monarchy. The French chronicler Jean Froissart tells readers and listeners that in 1346, Edward III of England laid siege to the city of Calais; the city was closed off on all sides, and inhabitants died of starvation. The king of England agreed to end the siege in return for an act of submission—the sacrifice of the lives of six native Calaisians. Gomez rewrites the story so that Beatrix de Guines and her troop of Amazon women intervene to save the city.

The work is actually divided equally into two parts. The first is the private love story of Beatrix and Eustache. The major thrust of narration in the first part is the then-novel idea that two people must freely choose their partners in marriage. After Gomez gives a lengthy description of their courtship, Beatrix and Eustache announce to their fathers that they are in love and wish to marry. The patriarchs could not have been more delighted as in at least four scenes, they stress that they have no desire to force the young people to marry, a rather revolutionary idea in a traditional society that continued to arrange marriages based solely on social position. A wedding date and great feast are thus planned, but are interrupted by news that England has laid siege to the city of Calais, thus marking the movement and providing the link between private love and public war.

Eustache is sent off to lead the troops against English forces. Ill at ease with the idea that she is home doing nothing to help the cause, Beatrix dresses as an Amazon and fights alongside the troops, then rallies an Amazon army of the two hundred most capable women of the city, who fight with their men. Despite their great successes in battle, as well as the queen of England's (their enemy) great admiration for these women, the city of Calais is defeated when it is cut off from all supplies. True to history, Gomez writes that the king will lift the siege in exchange for the sacrifice of the six most important nobles of the city. Beatrix's husband and father volunteer for this sacrifice; however, unlike history, they and the other nobles are spared when Beatrix offers herself up instead. The queen though, having been most impressed by this woman warrior, begs for their lives to be spared. The king does not refuse; the war ends; and the marriage is able to proceed.

Modern students of French literature generally never read Madeleine-Angélique Poisson de Gomez's works. Fortunately, Jean-François de La Croix included her in his 1769 *Dictionnaire historique portatif des femmes célèbres,* as did Abbé Joseph de la Porte in *Histoire littéraire des femmes françaises* of the same year. The two entries provide hints as to where to find more clues to Gomez's life and how her production was evaluated by contemporary critics. Sabatier de Castres also included Gomez in his collection *Les Trois Siècles de la litterature française* (1774). Then, thirty-seven years later, in 1811, two more of her stories from *Les Cent Nouvelles nouvelles*—*Le Scélérat trompé* and *Le Voleur amoureux* (The Outwitted Scoundrel and The Amorous Thief)—reappeared separately, and the latest reprint attributed to Gomez, *Histoire de Jean de Calais* (History of Jean of Calais) dates back to 1861. Some of her works have even been translated into Spanish, Italian, German, and Dutch. Nonetheless, for almost one hundred years, virtually nothing was written about her until the 1960s, when Charles C. Mish wrote about Eliza Haywood's translation of Gomez and Spire Pitou attempted to resurrect and appraise her tragedy *Marsidie, reine des Cimbres* and to study her use of Cornelian techniques. Then in 1974, *The Memoirs of the Baron du Tan,* originally published as a chapter in *Les Cent Nouvelles nouvelles,* was reprinted. Georges May commented upon Gomez in his book *Le Dilemme du roman au XVIIIe siècle* (1963), and Shirley Jones-Day has added sophistication and depth to May's brief nod to Gomez. Thanks to such people, Gomez has been rediscovered as a writer who deserves to be recognized and resurrected from the forgotten world of eighteenth-century letters.

References:

Sabatier de Castres, *Les Trois Siècles de la litterature française,* 4 volumes (Paris: Chez de Hansy le jeune, 1774; Geneva: Slatkine Reprints, 1967);

Pascale Dewey, "Gomez, Madeleine-Angélique Poisson, Dame Gabriel de," in *The Feminist Encyclopedia of French Literature,* edited by Eva M. Sartori (Westport, Conn.: Greenwood Press, 1999), p. 237;

Jocelyn Godard, "Car Il n'y a ni homme, ni saint, ni ange: Marguerite d'Angoulême," in *Elles ont signé le temps. Anthologie biographique* (Paris: L'Harmattan, 1992), pp. 73–81;

Shirley Jones-Day, "Gomez, Madeleine-Angélique Poisson, Madame de," in *Dictionnaire des lettres françaises,* edited by François Moureau (Paris: Fayard, 1995), p. 543;

Jones-Day, "A Woman Novelist of the 1730s: Madame de Gomez," *Studies on Voltaire and the Eighteenth Century,* 304 (1992): 788–791;

Jones-Day, "A Woman Writer's Dilemma: Madame de Gomez and the Early Eighteenth-Century Novel," in *Femmes savantes et femmes d'esprit: Women Intellectuals of the French Eighteenth-Century,* edited by Roland Bonnel and Catherine Rubinger (New York: Peter Lang, 1994), pp. 78–98;

Jean François de La Croix, "Gomez, Madeleine-Angélique Poisson de," in *Dictionnaire historique portatif des femmes célèbres,* 2 volumes (Paris: L. Cellot, 1769), II: 469;

Henry Carrington Lancaster, *Sunset: A History of Parisian Drama in the Last Years of Louis XIV, 1701–1715* (Baltimore: Johns Hopkins University Press, 1945);

Abbé Joseph de La Porte, *Histoire littéraire des femmes françaises,* 5 volumes (Paris: Lacombe, 1769), IV: 470–471;

Georges May, *Le Dilemme du roman au XVIIIe siècle* (Paris & New Haven: Presses universitaires de France/ Yale University Press, 1963);

Spire Pitou, "Pierre Corneille and Mme de Gomez' Marsidie," *Romance Notes,* 13 (1971): 492–495.

Olympe de Gouges
(7 May 1748 – 3 November 1793)

Gabrielle Verdier
University of Wisconsin–Milwaukee

BOOKS: *Le Mariage inattendu de Chérubin* (Seville & Paris: Cailleau, 1786);

L'Homme généreux (Paris: Printed by the Author & Knapen, 1786);

Oeuvres de Madame de Gouges, 2 volumes (Paris: Printed by the Author & Cailleau, 1788)—comprises volume 1: *Le Mariage inattendu de Chérubin, Le Philosophe corrigé, ou le cocu supposé,* "Réminiscence"; and volume 2: *L'Homme généreux, Mémoire de Mme de Valmont sur l'ingratitude et la cruauté de la famille des Flaucourt envers la sienne, dont les sieurs de Flaucourt ont reçu tant de services, Dialogue entre mon esprit, le bons sens, et la raison, ou critique de mes oeuvres;*

Oeuvres de Madame de Gouges, volume 3 (Paris: Printed by the Author & Cailleau, 1788)—comprises "Réflexions sur les hommes nègres," translated by Sylvia Molta as "Reflections on Negroes," in *Translating Slavery: Gender and Race in French Women's Writing, 1783–1823,* edited by Doris Y. Kadish and Françoise Massardier-Kenney (Kent, Ohio & London: Kent State University Press, 1994), pp. 84–86; *Zamore et Mirza, ou l'heureux naufrage; Molière chez Ninon, ou le siècle des grands hommes; Bienfaisance, ou la bonne mère;* and *La Bienfaisance récompensée;*

Lettre au peuple ou projet d'une caisse patriotique, par une citoyenne (Vienne, France & Paris: Les marchands de nouveautés, 1788);

Remarques patriotiques, par la citoyenne auteur de la lettre au peuple (N.p., 1788);

Le Bonheur primitif de l'homme ou les rêveries patriotiques (Amsterdam & Paris: Royer, 1789);

Dialogue allégorique entre la France et la vérité, dédié aux Etats-Généraux (N.p., 1789);

Le Cri du sage, par une femme (N.p., 1789);

Avis pressant, ou réponse à mes calomniateurs (N.p., [ca. 1789]);

Pour sauver la patrie, il faut respecter les trois ordres (N.p., [ca. 1789]);

Discours de l'aveugle aux Français, par Mme de Gouges (N.p., [ca. 1789]);

Olympe de Gouges (medallion by Pierre Vidal; from Olympe de Gouges, Oeuvres, *1986; Thomas Cooper Library, University of South Carolina)*

Lettre à Monseigneur, le duc d'Orléans (N.p., [1789]);

Séance royale. Motion de Mgr le duc d'Orléans, ou Les songes patriotiques (N.p., 1789);

L'Ordre national, ou le comte d'Artois inspiré par Mentor, dédié aux Etats-Généraux (N.p., 1789);

Lettre aux représentants de la Nation ([Paris]: L. Jorry, [1789]);

Epitre dédicatoire à sa Majesté Louis XVI (N.p., [ca. 1789]);

Réponse au champion américain, ou colon très aisé à connaître (N.p., 1790); translated by Maryann DeJulio as "Response to the American Champion," in *Translating Slavery: Gender and Race in French Women's Writing, 1783–1823,* edited by Doris Y. Kadish and Françoise Massardier-Kenney (Kent, Ohio & London: Kent State University Press, 1994), pp. 120–124;

Lettre aux littérateurs françois, par Mme de Gouges (N.p., [1790]);

Les Comédiens démasqués, ou Madame de G. ruinée par la Comédie française, pour se faire jouer (Paris: Comédie française, 1790);

Les Démocrates et les aristocrates, ou les curieux du champ de mars (Paris, [ca. 1790]);

Départ de M. Necker et de Mme de Gouges, ou les adieux de Mme de Gouges aux Français et à M. Necker (Paris, 1790);

Projet sur la formation d'un tribunal populaire et suprême en matière criminelle, présenté par Mme de Gouges, le 26 mai 1790, à l'Assemblée Nationale (Paris: Patriote français, [1790]);

Oeuvres de Madame de Gouges (Paris, 1790)–comprises political texts 1788–1790;

Bouquet national dédié à Henri IV, pour sa fête (N.p., [1790]);

Mirabeau aux Champs-Élysées (Paris: Garnery, 1791);

Adresse au Roi, Adresse à la Reine, Adresse au Prince de Condé (N.p., [1791]);

Sera-t-il Roi, ne le sera-t-il pas? (N.p., [1791]);

Les Droits de la femme. A la Reine [14 September 1791] (N.p., [ca. 1792]); translated by Darline Gay Levy, Harriet Branson Applewhite, and Mary Durham Johnson as "The Declaration of the Rights of Woman," in *Women in Revolutionary Paris 1789–1795* (Urbana: University of Illinois Press, 1979), pp. 87–96;

Le Couvent, ou les voeux forcés (Paris: Duchesne, Bailly & Marchands de Nouveautés, 1792);

L'Esclavage des noirs, ou l'heureux naufrage (Paris: Duchesne, Bailly & Marchands de Nouveautés, 1792); translated by Maryann DeJulio as "Black Slavery, or The Happy Shipwreck," in *Translating Slavery: Gender and Race in French Women's Writing, 1783–1823,* edited by Doris Y. Kadish and Françoise Massardier-Kenney (Kent, Ohio & London: Kent State University Press, 1994), pp. 87–119;

[*L'*]*Esclavage des noirs, ou l'heureux naufrage, drame en trois actes, en prose* (Paris: Duchesne, Bailly & Marchands de nouveautés, 1792);

Le Prince philosophe (Paris: Briand, 1792);

L'Esprit français, ou le problème à résoudre sur le labyrinthe de divers complots, par Madame de Gouges (Paris: Duchesne, 1792);

Le Bon Sens français ou l'apologie des vrais nobles, dédié aux Jacobins (N.p., 1792);

Grande Eclipse du soleil jacobiniste et de la lune feuillantine, pour la fin d'avril, ou dans le courant du mois de mai; par la LIBERTÉ, L'An IVe de son nom; dédiée à la terre (N.p., 1792);

Oeuvres de Madame de Gouges, 2 volumes (Paris: Duchesne, 1792)–comprises political texts and revolutionary plays;

Lettres à la Reine, aux généraux de l'armée, aux amis de la constitution et aux françaises citoyennes. Description de la fête du 3 juin par Madame de Gouges (Paris: Société typographique, 1792);

Adresse au Don Quichotte du Nord (Paris: Imprimerie nationale, 1792);

Correspondance de la cour. Compte moral rendu et dernier mot à mes chers amis . . . à la Convention nationale et au peuple sur une dénonciation faite contre son civisme, aux Jacobins, par le sieur Bourdon (N.p., [ca. 1792]);

Avis pressant à la Convention, par une vraie républicaine (N.p., [ca. 1793]);

L'Entrée de Dumouriez à Bruxelles, ou les vivandiers (Paris: Reynaud & Lejay, 1793);

[*Les*] *Fantômes de l'opinion publique* (N.p., [ca. 1793]);

Testament politique d'Olympe de Gouges [4 juin 1793] (N.p., [1793]);

Oeuvres de Madame de Gouges, 2 volumes (Paris, 1793)–comprises political texts and plays 1791–1793;

Le Prélat d'autrefois, ou Sophie et Saint-Elme, fait historique mis en action, comédie en trois actes et en prose, par Pompigny et Degouges (Paris: Cailleau, 1795);

Le Philosophe corrigé ou le Cocu supposé, comédie en 5 actes et en prose (N.p., [ca. 1795]).

Editions and Collections: *Oeuvres,* edited by Benoîte Groult (Paris: Mercure de France, 1986);

L'Esclavage des noirs, ou l'heureux naufrage, preface by Eléni Varikas (Paris: Côté-femmes éditions, 1989);

Théâtre politique I, preface by Gisela Thiele-Knobloch (Paris: Côté-femmes éditions, 1992)–includes *Le Couvent, Mirabeau aux Champs-Elysées,* and *L'Entrée de Dumourier à Bruxelles;*

Théâtre, introduction by Félix-Marcel Castan (Montauban: Cocagne, 1993)–comprises the twelve extant plays, including two in manuscript;

Théâtre politique II, preface by Gisela Thiele-Knobloch (Paris: Côté-femmes éditions, 1993)–comprises *L'Homme généreux, Les Démocrates et les aristocrates, La Nécessité du divorce, La France sauvée ou le tyran détrôné,* and *Le Prélat d'autrefois, ou Sophie et Saint-Elme;*

Ecrits politiques, 1788–1791, volume 1, preface by Olivier Blanc (Paris: Côté-femmes éditions, 1993);

Ecrits politiques, 1792–1793, volume 2, preface by Blanc (Paris: Côté-femmes éditions, 1993);

Mémoire de Madame de Valmont, 1788, roman (Paris: Côté-femmes éditions, 1995);

Le Prince philosophe, conte oriental, 2 volumes (Paris: Côté-femmes éditions, 1995).

SELECTED BROADSIDES: *Mes voeux sont remplis ou le don patriotique,* as Mme de G. (N.p., [1789]);

Action héroïque d'une Française, ou la France sauvée par les femmes (Paris: Guillaume Junior, 1789);

Les Démocrates et les aristocrates, ou les curieux du champ de mars (Paris, [ca. 1790]);

Repentir de Mme de Gouges (N.p., [1791]);

Pacte national . . . adressé à l'Assemblée nationale (Paris: Société typographique, 1792);

La Fierté de l'innocence, ou le silence du véritable patriotisme (Paris: Imprimerie Nationale, 1792);

Réponse à la justification de Maximilien Robespierre, adressée à Jérôme Pétion, par Olympe Degouges (N.p, [ca.1792]); translated by Spencer as "Response to the Justification of Robespierre to Jérôme Pétion," in *Writings by Pre-Revolutionary French Women. From Marie de France to Elisabeth Vigée-Le Brun,* edited by Anne R. Larsen and Colette H. Winn (New York: Garland, 2000), pp. 565–568;

Pronostic sur Maximilien Robespierre, par un animal amphibie, signé Polyme [Olympe] (N.p., 1792); translated by Samia I. Spencer as "Prognosis for Maximilien Robespierre, by an Amphibious Animal: An Exact Portrait of that Animal," in *Writings by Pre-Revolutionary French Women. From Marie de France to Elisabeth Vigée-Le Brun* (New York: Garland, 2000), pp. 563–565;

Olympe de Gouges, défenseur officieux de Louis Capet (Paris: Valadé, 1792);

Arrêt de mort que présente Olympe de Gouges contre Louis Capet (N.p., [1793]);

Olympe de Gouges à Dumouriez, général des armées de la République française (N.p., 1793);

Complots dévoilés des sociétaires du prétendu théâtre de la République ([Paris]: Boileau, 1793);

Les Trois Urnes, ou le salut de la patrie, par un voyageur aérien (N.p., 1793);

Olympe de Gouges au tribunal révolutionnaire (N.p., 1793);

Une Patriote persécutée à la Convention nationale (N.p., 1793).

PLAY PRODUCTIONS: *[L']Esclavage des noirs, ou l'heureux naufrage,* Paris, Comédie française, 28 December 1789;

Le Couvent, ou les voeux forcés, Paris, Théâtre Comique et Lyrique, 4 October 1790;

Mirabeau aux Champs-Élysées, Paris, Comédie italien, 15 April 1791;

L'Entrée de Dumourier [sic] *à Bruxelles, ou les vivandiers,* Paris, Théâtre de la République, 23 January 1793;

Le Prélat d'autrefois, ou Sophie et Saint-Elme, Paris, Théâtre de la Cité-Variétés, 18 March 1795.

Olympe de Gouges was the first woman political analyst and the only woman guillotined for her political publications during the French Revolution. A prolific author, she wrote more than thirty plays, of which only thirteen have survived; a philosophical essay; an autobiographical memoir; an oriental tale; and more than sixty political pamphlets and posters, in addition to the well-known *Les Droits de la femme* (1791; translated as "The Declaration of the Rights of Woman," 1979), which has immortalized her name. She defied feminine decorum by proclaiming herself the author of her literary and political works. The object of both flattery and ridicule during her lifetime, she was condemned to death by the radical Montagnards, who viewed her as a delirious madwoman, a dangerous "virago" who fancied herself a "statesman" and trampled on the "virtues appropriate to her sex." These and subsequent attacks focusing on her unconventional behavior were reinforced by such contributions as the 1904 "medico-psychological" study by Alfred Guillois, who concluded that she suffered from gynecological disturbances and hysteria, leading to "paranoïa reformatoria." Despite attempts to study her life with more objectivity (beginning in 1840 with a biography by E. Lairtullier), she was confined to the margins of official history, and her written works were all but forgotten for nearly two hundred years. With the rediscovery of women writers beginning in the 1970s, Gouges's texts and ideas were reevaluated by Samia I. Spencer as "visionary"; indeed, many of the reforms Gouges had proposed between 1783 and 1793 had become a reality. She fought tirelessly for the rights of marginalized people, not just women but also black slaves, illegitimate children, the poor, and other victims of the ancien régime. Olivier Blanc's biography of Gouges (1989, substantially revised in 2003), based on extensive public and private archives and notarial records, opened the way for a thorough reconsideration of her extraordinary life and works. Most studies and reprints, however, appeared after 1989, the bicentennial of the French Revolution. Perhaps more than any other woman writer and participant in the Revolution, Gouges's fate exemplifies the position of her gender as outsider both in the public sphere and in the republic of letters.

Gouges was an outsider in many ways. Born in 1748 in the southern city of Montauban, near Toulouse, to Anne-Olympe Mouisset and her husband, Pierre Gouze, a butcher, Marie Gouze grew up speaking Occitan and immersed in its oral culture. On the eve of the Revolution half the population of France spoke dialects and languages other than French. Contrary to legend, Marie could read (although 65 percent of the girls in her parish were illiterate) and was probably schooled by Ursuline nuns. Like most of her contemporaries she did not write with ease, preferring instead to use secretaries. Sensitive, lively, and impatient, she dictated her ideas and feelings as they crossed her mind and rarely revised her prose. She claimed to have written some plays in less than twenty-four hours. As a provincial woman whose native language was not French, Marie Gouze was doubly stigmatized on the Parisian literary scene.

Her social origins were questionable as well. She was rumored to be the illegitimate daughter of Jean-Jacques Lefranc, marquis de Pompignan. Her mother's family, the Mouissets, were wealthy drapers who had close relations with the noble Lefranc de Pompignans. Her grandfather was Jean-Jacques's tutor, and her grandmother nursed his baby brother along with her own daughter, Anne-Olympe. At age five, Jean-Jacques became the godfather of Anne-Olympe; they grew up together and fell in love, but the Pompignans separated them. At age forty-eight, he wed the wealthy widow of a *fermier général* (tax collector), Marie-Antoinette de Caulaincourt, after the widowed Anne-Olympe remarried a man of her own rank. Pompignan had become somewhat of a celebrity, a renowned neoclassical poet and academician who fought the philosophes and was in turn ridiculed by them. Although forgotten by her father after his marriage, the illegitimate daughter (as Gouges apparently believed she was) often claimed that she inherited her literary talent from this illustrious father, a claim labeled delirious by her detractors. She waited until Pompignan's death in 1784 to write the *Mémoire de Madame de Valmont* (Memoirs of Madame de Valmont; published four years later in *Oeuvres*, 1788), a judicial memoir in the form of an epistolary novel, in which she reveals the cruelty of the so-called Flaucourt family. Flaucourt's pious widow, his brother (now an archbishop), and son vehemently reject her appeals for assisting her destitute mother—the goddaughter who had inspired a great passion. These characters reappeared in a subplot of her drama *L'Homme généreux* (1786, The Generous Man). The claim for the rights of illegitimate children is a recurrent theme in Gouges's writings. Eventually, the National Convention granted them some rights on 2 November 1793—on the eve of the execution of the woman who had fought so hard to be heard on that subject. However, these rights were short-lived, as they were revoked in the Civil Code of 1804.

Gouges's civil status during her adult years was also unconventional. At age seventeen she was married to a man she did not love, Louis-Yves Aubry, a successful caterer. Their son, Pierre, was born on 29 August 1766. Shortly thereafter, Louis-Yves Aubry died, perhaps during the floods that ravaged Montauban in November 1766. Marie Gouze Aubry changed her name to Marie-Olympe de Gouges, after her mother, Anne-Olympe, a name that, as she wrote in *Pronostic sur Maximilien Robespierre* (1792), evoked "something celestial." Gouges refused to remarry, even though she had

Gouges visiting a hospital at Nantes during the 1780s when she was crusading for maternity hospitals needed to reduce the high death rate of mothers and babies (Bibliothèque nationale; Olympe de Gouges, Oeuvres, *1986; Thomas Cooper Library, University of South Carolina)*

met Jacques Biétrix de Rosières, the man with whom she lived for several years. Later, in *Les Droits de la femme*, she explained that indissoluble marriage was the "tomb of trust and love." Biétrix de Rosières and his family had a monopoly on the transport of military supplies throughout France. He and Gouges may have met during an important deployment of troops in Montauban in 1767, or perhaps in Paris after she had joined her married sister, Jeanne Reynart. Over a period of ten years (1774–1784), Biétrix invested large sums of money in Gouges's name (totaling 70,000 livres), which brought her a comfortable annual income and ensured economic independence. She was able to rent a residence of her own, provide a good education for her son, and secure a pension for her mother. Gouges and Biétrix may have had a daughter who died at a young age. Gouges's critics insist that she was a *femme galante* ("loose woman," the closest translation of that expression, although it does not convey the complex nuances of the adjective *galante*). Contemporary testimony and portraits confirm that she was indeed beautiful; undoubtedly, she had many admirers and a few lovers, a common practice in a libertine century. However, she avoided scandal, since no evidence exists of notorious liaisons or financial support by anyone other than Biétrix.

Gouges did not remain marginal in Parisian society as some have asserted. Blanc's research confirms that she frequented salons and freethinking enlightened circles; moreover, she herself hosted writers, philosophes, artists, and scientists. In addition to Biétrix's connections, she may have gained entrance into this milieu through celebrities from her region, such as Jean-Baptiste du Barry, comte de Cérès, brother-in-law of Louis XV's last mistress, and Louis-Philippe-Joseph, duc de Chartres, the future duc d'Orléans, to whom she dedicated the first two volumes of her *Oeuvres* (Works). From 1774 until 1784 her name appeared in the "Almanach des adresses," a "Who's Who" of the two thousand most fashionable Parisians. In order to educate herself she subscribed to the Lycée, a learned academy where she attended lectures by writers, scientists, and philosophers. Among her close friends were playwright and journalist Louis-Sébastien Mercier; poet Michel de Cubières, whose brother was a confidant of Louis XVI; and dramatist Jean-François Cailhava. She maintained a friendly relationship with literary critic Jean-François La Harpe; philosophe Marie-Jean-Antoine-Nicholas Caritat, marquis de Condorcet; and politician Jacques-Pierre Brissot de Warville, founder of the abolitionist group Société des Amis des Noirs (Friends of the Blacks) in 1788, to which Gouges belonged. Her women friends were also prominent in enlightened circles and the arts. They included, for example, actress and playwright Julie Candeille, countess and dramatist Fanny de Beauharnais, and marquise de Montesson, the morganatic wife of the duc d'Orléans, the king's cousin. In the early 1780s, together with Candeille and Beauharnais, Gouges was probably initiated into a Masonic lodge for women associated with the Loge des Neuf Soeurs (Lodge of the Nine Sisters) founded by Cubières and his friends, or the Loge de la Candeur (Lodge of the Ingenuosness). Montesson was passionate about the theater; she had two private stages in her residences and wrote a dozen plays. She encouraged and protected Gouges, who for a while directed her own small acting troupe. Beauharnais's and Montesson's plays failed miserably when performed at the Comédie française, no doubt because of the hostility of actors and the public toward women playwrights.

Gouges's decision in 1784 to enter officially the male-dominated literary arena was thus not the sudden metamorphosis of an "aging" thirty-six-year-old *femme galante* into a woman of letters but rather the result of an understandable and courageous progression. Indignation at injustice inspired her to write plays and seek to have them performed by professional theaters. Although she states that by the 1780s she had written more than thirty plays, she also refers to *Zamore et Mirza, ou L'heureux naufrage* (1788; translated as "Black Slavery, or the Happy Shipwreck," 1994) as her first. This three-act "drame indien" (Indian drama) treats an incendiary issue, black slavery in the colonies, anticipating the founding of the abolitionist society in France by four years. In the French West Indies, the slave Zamore flees with his beloved Mirza after killing the white colonist who tried to rape her. Typical of contemporary melodramas, the plot is full of romance-like twists—a shipwreck, coincidences, recognitions, and the reunion of long-lost relatives. The slaves rescue Sophie and Valère from drowning, and in turn the young Frenchwoman and her husband plead for their saviors, who have been caught and are about to be executed. The conflict is resolved when the governor recognizes Sophie as his daughter (whom he had been forced to abandon in France) of a clandestine marriage. He can thus follow his heart and pardon Zamore, despite the fierce opposition of the colonists. The pardon of a slave who was a murderer was a scandalous violation of existing laws. Gouges's play and prefaces advocate gradual emancipation, since immediate abolition could lead to violence, which she dreaded above all. The characters' impassioned speeches, however, proclaim the humanity of black people unequivocally and condemn slavery as contrary to nature. Gouges gave the play a more provocative title, *L'Esclavage des noirs* (Black Slavery), when it was finally performed in 1789 and kept it in the revised version published in 1792. It was the first French play to condemn slavery, and Gouges is the only woman included among the abolitionists in abbé Henri Grégoire's *De la Littérature des nègres* (1808).

Gouges battled for five years with the imperious actors of the Comédie française to have her play performed, an event that finally occurred after the Revolution had begun. During that time Gouges wrote at least five additional plays, largely on social issues, while having to counter the accusation that her lovers were her ghostwriters—a claim regularly leveled at female playwrights. The triumphal performance of *The Marriage of Figaro* in April 1784 (after Pierre-Augustin Caron de Beaumarchais's own struggle with censorship and the Comédie française) inspired her to write a sequel, *Le Mariage inattendu de Chérubin* (1786, Chérubin's Unexpected Marriage; collected in *Ouevres*, 1788). At least a half-dozen other dramatists, including Beaumarchais himself in his 1792 *La Mère coupable* (The Guilty Mother), wrote sequels to his successful play. In Gouges's three-act comedy, the page Cherubin, having outgrown his infatuation with the countess and become a marquis, falls in love with the gardener's daughter, Fanchette. She turns out to be the daughter of noble parents whose clandestine marriage was broken off by their families. On 4 November 1784, the play was accepted by the Théâtre italien, which, along with the Comédie française, had a monopoly on the staging of all new plays. Without reading the play, Beaumarchais cried plagiarism, refused to meet Gouges, and got the Comédiens français to pressure the Italians not to perform it. Gouges recounts her struggles in the preface to the play, published in 1786, in which she proclaims, "I am a woman and an author." In an ironic letter, "Réminiscences" (1788), she challenges Beaumarchais to a "literary duel."

Thanks to Montesson's influence, the Comédiens français agreed to read *Zamore et Mirza* and accepted it with corrections on 8 July 1785. A 1781 ruling stipulated that the company had to perform plays in the order in which they were accepted. Anxious to have it performed and aware of the Comédie's hostility to women dramatists, Gouges showered the actors with gifts. But when the next play she presented, *Lucinde et Cardenio* (now lost), was badly read by them, deliberately no doubt, she criticized the company impetuously, particularly two actresses who had slandered her. Her war of words with the actors escalated to the point that they obtained a lettre de cachet to have her locked up in the Bastille. A friend (Montesson or Cubières) managed to have the order rescinded, but in revenge, the actors eliminated *Zamore et Mirza* from their repertoire. Impressed by Gouges's powerful protectors, however, they reinstated the play in November 1785, yet rejected *L'Homme généreux*, despite favorable critical reviews. In this five-act drama based on a true case, Gouges illustrates a crying injustice of the ancien régime, imprisonment for debt, and promised to give her box-office proceeds to the victimized family. Her next play, *Le Philosophe corrigé* (circa 1795, The Philosopher Chastised), a five-act comedy, refutes the age-old theme of women's inability to unite. Crossing social barriers, a countess, a middle-class governess, and a peasant girl plot to help the marquise prove to her "philosopher" husband, by setting a trap for him, that she is not guilty of adultery. Her next play, written when the Comédie française planned to stage one about Molière before *Zamore et Mirza*, is even more openly feminist. In the five-act *Molière chez Ninon, ou le siècle des grands hommes* (Molière at Ninon's, or the Century of Great Men; collected in *Oeuvres*, 1788), Ninon de Lenclos, famous courtesan and heroine of Gouges's play, overturns the double standard. Contrary to misogynist legend, she is able to reconcile philosophy, sexuality, and motherhood and protects a young woman–Olympe–against her tyrannical father. In February 1788, the actors of the Comédie française read the play badly and rejected it disdainfully. In the third volume of her 1788 *Oeuvres* Gouges published with the play lively prefaces and postfaces recounting her battle with the Comédie française. Despite her courteous objections, the company continued to produce other plays received after hers and attempted to sue her for defamation, although they retreated when the royal censors authorized the publication of Gouges's works in volume three of her *Oeuvres* (1788), including *Zamore et Mirza* and the strong denunciation of slavery in "Réflexions sur les hommes nègres" (translated as "Reflections on Negroes," 1994).

The theme of slavery in Gouges's play increased the company's hostility. The powerful lobby of aristocrats and colonial proprietors whose wealth depended on slavery pressured the Comédie not to perform the play, and then, in 1789, to make it fail. On 9 March 1789, after four years of waiting, Gouges threatened to sue the Comédie française for violating the 1781 regulation; then she sent a copy of the play to the National Assembly and wrote to the mayor of Paris, Jean-Sylvain Bailly, to request authorization for the performance. Engaged in a battle with Marie-Joseph Chénier over the 1789 performance of his controversial *Charles IX*, the Comédiens–some of whom, notably François-Joseph Talma, supported the Revolution–finally scheduled *L'Esclavage des noirs* for performance on 28 December 1789. Threatened by the abolition of the feudal regime (4 August 1789) by the National Assembly and the *Déclaration des droits de l'homme et du citoyen* (1789, Declaration of the Rights of Man and of the Citizen), the colonialist lobby increased its pressure on the Comédie française and its attacks on the Société des Amis des Noirs. Gouges responded to their anonymous brochure defaming her ("Lettre à Madame de Gouges," 25 December 1789) with the witty *Réponse au champion américain* (1790, Response to an American Champion), in which she insists that her drama does not preach insurrection in the colonies. Attacks continued, however, in the conservative newspaper *Actes des Apôtres* (Acts of the Apostles). The packed opening night was a tumultuous disaster. Actors in the role of slaves refused to color their faces black and performed their parts poorly while constantly booed by the colonists and their paid agitators. The rowdiness increased when someone announced that the author was a woman. The press reviews denounced the play as "immoral" and the hero as a murderer, and ridiculed the plot. Gouges offered to make changes, but the Comédiens, violating their own regulations, refused to postpone the second performance. After presenting it again on 31 December 1789 and 2 January 1790, they removed it from their repertoire, claiming that the receipts had not met the

Frontispiece of a brochure, showing Gouges delivering a patriotic speech to the French sovereigns (Bibliothèque nationale, Hennin collection; from Olympe de Gouges, Oeuvres, *1986; Thomas Cooper Library, University of South Carolina)*

even contemplated going to London, where her play could be performed. None of these actions brought her any result. In August 1790, however, a group of playwrights presented a petition to the Assembly requesting laws to protect the rights of authors and to free theaters from the tyranny of privileged ancien régime institutions. The Assembly then approved a decree to that effect on 13 January 1791. Furthermore, reacting to the 1791 slave revolt in Saint-Domingue, the Convention abolished slavery in February 1794, although it was reestablished by Napoleon Bonaparte in 1802.

Well before the French Revolution, Olympe de Gouges was distraught about France's mounting deficit and economic inequalities. She began to engage in social debate by writing and signing political pamphlets that she printed at her own expense—the only woman to do so. In 1789 she moved from Versailles to Paris in order to be closer to the center of literary and political action where she could react immediately by publishing her views on current events. If one were to attempt organizing her social and political texts written on various occasions, they would likely seem disorganized; however, one trait is constant: she fearlessly berated political figures for their failings. She even considered starting a newspaper, to be named appropriately *L'Impatient* (The Impatient), which would allow her to express on a daily basis her opinions on current events.

In her November 1788 *Lettre au peuple ou projet d'une caisse patriotique, par une citoyenne* (Letter to the People, or Project for a Patriotic Fund, by a Woman Citizen), she called for a voluntary contribution to the public coffers, proportionate to personal income—an idea adopted by the National Assembly a year later. Gouges contributed one-fourth of her annual income to the state's fund and exhorted all Frenchwomen to follow her example and that of dozens of generous patriotic women who donated their jewels. Her proposal, as well as the denunciation of the "calculating capitalists" ruining France, were outlined in *Action héroïque d'une Française, ou la France sauvée par les femmes* (1789, A Frenchwoman's Heroic Action, or France Saved by Women). In *Remarques patriotiques* (1788, Patriotic Remarks), she criticized the privileged classes, deplored the misery of ordinary people, and proposed a vast and original program of social reform. It included shelters for the poor in the winter, workshops for the unemployed, a special fund for natural disasters, and taxation of luxury items and activities such as gambling.

minimum requirement. According to the law at that time, such a play then became the property of the company and was banned from being performed on another stage. Gouges appealed the decision in vain and attempted to rally other playwrights to oppose the tyranny of the Comédie française in her *Lettre aux littérateurs françois* (1790, Letter to French Writers). She also addressed *Lettre aux représentants de la Nation* (1789, Letter to the Representatives of the Nation) to the National Assembly to denounce the colonialist cabal and published a scathing account of her treatment by the Comédiens, *Les Comédiens démasqués, ou Madame de G. ruinée par la Comédie française* (1790, The Comédiens Exposed, or Madame de. G. Ruined by the Comédie française). In *Départ de M. Necker et de Mme de Gouges* (1790, Departure of Monsieur Necker and Madame de Gouges), she

Although she supported Louis XVI and remained in favor of a constitutional monarchy until 1792, she urged the king to reform his administration. Her first political tracts made front-page news in the *Journal Général de France*. In *Dialogue allégorique entre la France et la vérité* (1789, Allegorical Dialogue between France and the Truth), she exhorted the upcoming Estates General to allow women to participate in public life and called for the establishment of maternity hospitals, since one out of four women died in childbirth. While agreeing with Jean-Jacques Rousseau that civilization corrupted the natural goodness of man, she argued in *Le Bonheur primitif de l'homme* (1789, The Primitive Happiness of Mankind) that morals would regenerate if women were granted greater equality, education, and responsibility. She called for the creation of a second national theater devoted exclusively to the performance of plays by women–a flagrant contradiction of both Rousseau's domestic ideal for women and his rebuke of the theater. While recognizing women's responsibility in their subservience in *Le cri du sage, par une femme* (1789, The Cry of a Sage, by a Woman), she challenged her gender to rise above petty vanity.

Before the Revolution she also wrote a long oriental political/philosophical tale, *Le Prince philosophe* (The Philosopher Prince), published in 1792, in which she outlined many of her ideas on the causes of hostility between the sexes. She imagined a mythical Siam where an energetic queen persuades women to develop their reason rather than their charm, thus demonstrating that education would make women equal to men in public life. Paradoxically, the queen is discredited in the plot, much as Gouges herself was slandered by her opponents.

Though socially progressive, she remained cautiously conservative in her politics, advocating in *Pour sauver la patrie, il faut respecter les trois ordres* (1789, To Save the Fatherland, the Three Orders Must Be Respected) peace and reconciliation between the Third Estate and the first two orders. Yet, when the Estates General proclaimed itself a "National Assembly" (9 July 1789) while the king remained passive, she urged him in *Epître dédicatoire à sa Majesté Louis XVI* (circa 1789, Letter Inscribed to His Majesty Louis XVI) to support the drafting of a Constitution and in *Séance royale* (1789, Royal Sitting) to consider abdicating during that process in favor of a regent. The proposal labeled her a partisan of the king's cousin, the duc d'Orléans; it led to a reprimand and the confiscation of the brochure. She denied being an Orléaniste and in *Lettre à Monseigneur, le duc d'Orléans* (1789, Letter to Monseigneur, the Duke of Orleans) hinted that Orléans was fomenting dissent. The letter resulted in the dismissal of her son from the duke's corps of engineers–an injustice she never forgot. To prevent civil war and promote national reconciliation, in *L'Ordre national* (1789, The National Order) she called upon the comte d'Artois–the king's brother who had emigrated to England to organize a counterrevolution– to return to France. Still accused of being an Orléaniste, she proclaimed in *Lettre aux représentants de la Nation* that she did not belong to any party but was a centrist patriot seeking middle-ground solutions. She was shocked by the violence during the October days, when unruly crowds marched on Versailles and forced the royal family to return to Paris; she feared that the Orléanistes had orchestrated it and that it would lead to bloodshed. In *Projet sur la formation d'un tribunal populaire* (1790, Project for the Formation of a People's Tribunal), she proposed the creation of criminal and appellate courts for ordinary citizens, where they would learn about the law by practicing it and be judged by their peers.

Engrossed in political debates, she attended the meetings of the Assembly from the gallery reserved for women and voiced her opinions in the cafés she frequented. In all likelihood she also attended the meetings of such groups as the "Friends of the Constitution" and the Masonic "Cercle social," open to women, which eventually became the "Amies de la vérité" (Women Friends of the Truth), presided over by Etta Palm d'Aëlders. Moving to the village of Auteuil in 1790, Gouges became a regular at the salon of Anne-Catherine de Ligneville d'Autricourt, widow of the philosophe Claude Adrien Helvétius. This enlightened "société d'Auteuil" included, among others, moralist Sébastien-Roch Nicolas de Chamfort, Benjamin Franklin, and Jean-Marie Roland de la Platière and his wife, Marie Jeanne Phlipon. Among her friends were also Condorcet and his wife, Sophie de Grouchy, who received the Talmas, revolutionary orator Honoré Gabriel Riqueti, the comte de Mirabeau, Mercier, Thomas Paine, and perhaps British feminist Mary Wollstonecraft. Gouges, together with the Condorcets, joined the Club de la Révolution when it was created in 1790.

Undaunted by the failure of *L'Esclavage des noirs*, she continued to write for the theater. In *Le Couvent, ou les voeux forcés* (performed 4 October 1790, The Convent, or the Forced Vows) and *La Nécessité du divorce* (1790, The Necessity of Divorce), she denounced two institutions that sealed women's fate and promoted vice: forced religious vocations and indissoluble marriage vows. Again, Gouges anticipated what was to happen in the near future. On 13 February 1790 the Constituent Assembly abolished religious orders, and, after much debate, the first law in the Western world authorizing divorce was passed in September 1792– although repealed a few years later in the Civil Code of 1804. The comedy on divorce was read and rejected by the Comédie italienne in early 1791 and was only rediscovered and republished in the 1990s. A modified but unauthorized version, *Le Couvent* (The Convent), was produced by the newly formed Théâtre National Comique et Lyrique in October 1790, after several other plays on similar themes had been successfully staged. By the time Gouges's work was published in 1792, it had had more than eighty performances. Her subsequent plays celebrated revolutionary events. Set during the Festival of Federation commemorating the first anniversary of the fall of the Bastille, the one-act revue *Les Démocrates et les aristocrates* (1790, The Democrats and the Aristocrats) makes fun of political extremists. Mirabeau's sudden death on 2 April 1791 inspired Gouges to write *Mirabeau aux Champs-Élysées* (1791, Mirabeau in the Elysian Fields), a four-act political drama, which was reduced to one act only when staged by the Comédie italienne on 15 April 1791. It was also successfully performed in Bordeaux in June 1791. Both serious and comical, the play revives dead leaders who welcome the hero of the National Assembly to the Elysian Fields. The Assembly includes Greek philosophers (Solon), French kings (Henry IV, Louis XIV), Enlightenment philosophes (Charles-Louis de Secondat, baron de Montesquieu, Voltaire, Rousseau), and contemporary political men (Franklin); however, the liveliest speeches are pronounced by Madame de Sévigné, Madame Deshoulières, and Ninon de Lenclos. The three great women of the ancien régime proclaim that the success of the Revolution depends on the "ascent" of women, which can only be achieved by allowing them to participate in political life.

In response to revolutionary events, Gouges not only advised and criticized political leaders but also proposed concrete ways to involve women in the public sphere. After the royal family's failed attempt to flee (22 June 1791), she proposed the creation of a national guard of women to surround the queen and urged the king in *Sera-t-il Roi, ne le sera-t-il pas?* (1791, Will He Be King, or Will He Not?) to replace his entourage of courtesans with patriotic citizens of both genders. She exulted when Louis XVI finally swore to uphold the constitution (15 September 1791) but was bitterly disappointed that the Constituent Assembly neglected women when it failed to mention them in the *Déclaration des droits de l'homme*. In order to remedy the gap, she drafted *Les Droits de la femme* and addressed it to the queen and indirectly to the newly formed Legislative Assembly. She challenged Marie Antoinette to end her intrigues with foreign powers and fight instead for a noble cause–the rights of her own gender. This powerful document parallels the seventeen articles of the *Déclaration des droits de l'homme,* in addition to other rights, such as the naming of fathers of children born out of wedlock, full citizenship, equal access to property and public office, and equal responsibility before the law. In the postfaces of that document, Gouges exhorts women, enslaved like blacks but sexually powerful, to rise above their petty intrigues and proposes that the indissoluble marriage vow be replaced with a limited-time "civil contract." This daring proposal went unheeded, although it become reality two centuries later. Conservative on matters of gender, radical Republicans were already hardening their position toward women, whom they considered born solely to be wives and bear children.

Gouges continued to make herself heard. She denounced the reported corruption of members of government and proposed regulations to control their salaries in *L'Esprit français* (1792, The French Spirit). When ridiculed by the Jacobins for her "feminine" obsession with peace, she responded strongly by warning against the extreme tendencies of such leaders as Maximilien Robespierre and predicted in *Le Bon Sens français* (1792, French Common Sense) and *Grande Eclipse du soleil jacobiniste* (1792, Full Eclipse of the Jacobin Sun) that the shedding of a single drop of blood could lead to massive bloodshed. When the mayor of Estampes was killed by a mob protesting the high price of food, the Legislative Assembly decided to honor him in a Festival of the Law on 3 June 1792. Gouges successfully petitioned the Assembly to allow women to participate in national festivals, following the example of Roman women. In charge of raising money to fund the women's procession, she went to the Tuileries to appeal to the queen but was rebuffed by her chief lady-in-waiting, Marie-Thérèse-Louise de Savoie Carignan, princesse de Lamballe–an incident that was later related in Gouges's unfinished play "La France sauvée, ou le tyran détrôné" (France Saved, or the Tyrant Dethroned). Eventually, Marie Antoinette instructed that Gouges be given 1,200 livres for the festival and offered a pension (to buy her off). In a brochure describing the procession, *Lettres à la Reine, aux généraux de l'armée, aux amis de la constitution et aux Françaises citoyennes* (1792, Letters to the Queen the Generals of the Army, the Friends of the Constitution, and French Women Citizens), she urged citizens and leaders of various factions to reconcile and led the women's procession as planned. However, the festival was marred by a sudden downpour, much to the delight of the Jacobin press. She also marched with Etta Palm d'Aëlders and Théroigne de Méricourt in the 14 July 1792 parade commemorating the third anniversary of the Revolution.

Tension between Louis XVI and the Assembly and among the various parties escalated in the summer of 1792. The king dismissed his Girondin ministers and refused to confirm certain decrees. On 20 June, working-class Parisians invaded the Tuileries and forced the king to wear the tricolor cockade and drink to the health of the nation. Gouges condemned the revolutionary event, arguing that the present government was "monstrous."

She thought that the Assembly should either abolish the monarchy as incompatible with new laws or respect it and work toward reconciliation, as she stated in the *Pacte national* (1792; National Covenant). Later, she approved of Louis XVI and Marie Antoinette's arrest and incarceration on 10 August 1792, after learning of their correspondence with France's enemies. Their intrigues were described in "La France sauvée." On the other hand, totally opposed to violence, in *La Fierté de l'innocence* (1792, The Pride of Innocence) she deplored the massacre of monarchists (including the princesse de Lamballe) and many innocent prisoners during the Paris Commune on 2–7 September.

On 22 September 1792, the new assembly, the National Convention, abolished the monarchy and proclaimed the first republic. Its president, Jérome Pétion, chose ministers belonging to the moderate Girondin faction that Gouges supported. Soon thereafter, however, the moderates clashed with the radical Montagnards, an occurence that prompted her in *Les Fantômes de l'opinion publique* (1793, The Ghosts of Public Opinion) to accuse Robespierre and Jean-Paul Marat of plotting anarchy. When the Girondin Louvet de Coudray accused Robespierre of preparing a dictatorship, Gouges plastered all over Paris a red poster lambasting Robespierre, *Pronostic sur Maximilien Robespierre* (1792, translated as "Prognosis on Maximilien Robespierre," 2000). Robespierre defended himself brilliantly, and one of his supporters denounced Gouges as an "aristocrat," the bastard daughter of Louis XV. Gouges replied in a impassioned brochure addressed to the Convention (*Correspondance de la cour;* 1792, Correspondence of the Court), which reviewed her patriotic words and deeds. By then, she had demonstrated her republican convictions again in *L'Entrée de Dumouriez à Bruxelles* (1793, Dumouriez's Entry Into Brussels), a play in which she celebrated the victory of General Charles-François Dumouriez and the French over the Austrian army about to invade France. The real heroes of this five-act play mixing battles and comic scenes are ordinary citizens—including two women soldiers, a cook, and a spy—ready to give their lives to fight tyranny and spread human rights to the rest of Europe. Disregarding warnings by her friends, Gouges intervened in politics again by writing to the Convention and offering to defend Louis XVI during his trial. As king, she argued, Louis was found guilty and dethroned; if executed, he would become a martyr and live on in the memory of the people. She exhorted the republic in *Olympe de Gouges, défenseur officieux de Louis Capet* (1792, Olympe de Gouges, Unofficial Defender of Louis Capet) to show magnanimity and exile Louis instead. Although she was not alone in opposing the king's execution, such argument from her met with jeers and attacks. On 21 January 1793, Louis was guillotined, following a majority vote of one voice in favor of execution. Two days later, after stalling for two months, the Théâtre de la République perfomed *L'Entrée de Dumouriez à Bruxelles,* badly, while agitators booed "Louis's advocate." In *Complots dévoilés* (1793, Plots Uncovered) Gouges accused the actors of sabotaging her play, but events soon overtook it. After losing the battle of Neerwinden in March 1793, Dumouriez defected to the Austrians.

As European countries declared war on France and the royalist Vendée region revolted against the revolutionary government, Gouges in *Avis pressant à la Convention* (1793, Urgent Warning to the Convention) beseeched the Convention to end its dissension and placarded her letter all over the city. After applauding the Girondins' denunciation of the Montagnards' rabble-rousing, she barely escaped physical violence. She expressed her anguish at the mounting fury in a letter accompanying the two volumes of her political writings that she addressed to Parisian journalists in April 1793. Wishing to get away from Paris, she visited her son in the Loire region, where she wanted to buy a retirement home. On 2 June, an armed crowd supported by the Montagnards invaded the Convention and forced the deputies to order the arrest of the twenty-nine Girondins. A law had been passed in March punishing with death anyone advocating a government other than republican. Despite the risk, Gouges defended the Girondins publicly and predicted her own death in *Testament politique* (1793, Political Testament). On 13 July Charlotte Corday killed Marat, an act further inflaming public opinion against women. As Bordeaux, Lyon, Marseille, and Toulon rebelled against Paris, Gouges prepared a poster proposing to end dissension by recommending self-determination in the various regions. *Les Trois Urnes, ou le salut de la patrie* (1793, The Three Ballot Boxes, or The Salvation of the Fatherland) proposed that French citizens choose among three forms of government—republican, monarchist, or federalist. The latter, favored by the Girondins, would give less power to Paris and the Convention and more to the rest of the country. She sent a copy to the Committee of Public Safety and waited for the placard to be posted.

On 20 July 1793, Gouges was arrested. Two days later the police took her on a thorough search of her apartment, where she readily led them to her papers, including play manuscripts, which they inventoried and confiscated. She was transferred to the Saint-Germain prison with an infected wound on her leg that added to her misery. Her case was referred to the Revolutionary Tribunal, and a letter to her influential friend Cubières intercepted. She protested against the unjust imprisonment but failed to convince Antoine Quentin Fouquier-

Illustration for Gouges's "Lettre au Peuple" (Letter to the People), Journal Générale de France (6 November 1788), in which she asks for personal donations for the country. She gave one-fourth of her own income (Bibliothèque nationale, Hennin collection).

Tinville, the prosecutor, that her intentions were not unpatriotic and that she had not violated the March law against difference of opinion. On the contrary, she claimed, *Les Trois Urnes* defended the sovereignty of the people. Although denied medical treatment, she took further risks by posting a placard, *Olympe de Gouges au tribunal révolutionnaire* (1793, Olympe de Gouges to the Revolutionary Tribunal) that described the terrible conditions of her detention, denounced the tyranny of Robespierre and the Jacobins, and argued that repression of opinion violated the Declaration of the Rights of Man. Fouquier-Tinville finally transferred her to the infirmary of the Petite Force, a prison for loose women, but delayed bringing her case to trial. Even as deputies voted in September "to put Terror on the agenda," Gouges courageously claimed *Les Trois Urnes* as additional proof of her service to the nation in *Une Patriote persécutée* (1793, A Persecuted Patriot Woman), in which she said, "Que l'on me juge donc! . . . La mort ou la liberté" (So let them judge me . . . Death or liberty). Members of moderate sections managed to have her moved to the Mahaye clinic, to which sick prisoners of both genders were admitted; she pawned her jewels to pay for medical care. The Terror accelerated in October when Marie Antoinette and twenty-one Girondins were guillotined. On 28 October, Fouquier-Tinville secretly transferred Gouges to the Conciergerie; two days later women's clubs were outlawed. Denied a lawyer, on 2 November Gouges was brought before the Revolutionary Tribunal and hundreds of spectators and charged with violation of the people's sovereignty in writing *Les Trois Urnes* and a display of treason in writing "La France sauvée." In vain, she responded that her character Marie Antoinette was the one making counterrevolutionary statements in the play, not herself. She was found guilty and sentenced to death, although she declared being pregnant–possibly resulting from her stay at the clinic. She wrote a moving last letter to her son and on 3 November was transported in an open cart to the Place de la Révolution, where several eyewitness accounts reported her calm and courageous. As she ascended the scaffold, she pronounced her last words: "Enfants de la Partie, vous vengerez ma mort" (Children of the fatherland, you will avenge my death!). Fearing for his future, her son, Pierre Aubry, who had been demoted from his rank of lieutenant general, disowned his mother and on 14 November 1793 called her execution justified. However, after the Terror, on 3 April 1795 he retracted his statement and petitioned the National Convention to rehabilitate her reputation. With the writer Maurin de Pompigny, he had *Le Prélat d'autrefois, ou Sophie et Saint-Elme*, a play probably based on one of his mother's manuscripts, successfully performed at the Théâtre de la Cité-Variétés (18 March 1795).

Olympe de Gouges remains a controversial figure, and much of her work remains neglected. To do her justice, studies of her writings must take into account many aspects of her extraordinary life and tumultuous times. Though rediscovered as a precursor of feminism, her ideas must be interpreted within her larger concern for all victims of unjust institutions. Scholarship generated by the bicentennial of the French Revolution hardly altered the misogynist legends perpetuated by two centuries of distorted history about her illiteracy and obsession with grandiose claims. Chantal Thomas labels her literary and political activities "lost causes," even though most of the reforms Gouges advocated have become a reality. Though fearless in risking her own life for the causes she championed, Gouges remained moderate politically, always advocating reconciliation. Her varied theatrical production, as a result of the research of Gisela Thiele-Knobloch and Gabrielle Verdier, has begun to emerge from oblivion, but thus far studies have focused mainly on *L'Esclavage des noirs*. Some critics—for example, René Tarin—interpret the contradictions in the play as her "guilty conscience," while others, such as Antoine Court and Catherine Masson, place them within her general message of nonviolence and study them from the perspective of dramatic conventions of her time while recalling her heroic struggle to have the play performed.

Gouges's most studied political text, "The Declaration of the Rights of Woman"—a radical vision of gender equality—has raised questions (as with Joan Wallach Scott and Mary Trouille) about Gouges's contradictions of Rousseau and the ambiguous meaning of "nature" in her political discourse. She identified with Rousseau as a "child of nature." On the other hand, she refused to marry, clearly expressed her "natural" literary talent, engaged in political activism, and left a complete public record of her thoughts and actions in her writings. Revolutionary discourse demonstrates that the argument of "rights" founded on "nature" led to a double bind that was used to confine women to their "natural" domestic role. Gouges's words and actions advocating full citizenship for women and involvement in political life have generated various responses. The habit of calling attention to herself in her writing has been described (by Gregory S. Brown and Lisa Beckstrand) as posturing and "fashioning" of a public self. By seeking to enter the male-dominated bastions of theater and politics, Gouges invented unscripted roles for women as self-proclaimed playwrights and active citizens. Going beyond criticism of her disorderly style, studies of her "voice," imagination, and the nature of her rhetoric, according to Janie Vanpee, is a promising approach to the much-needed reevaluation of Gouges's entire body of works. In spring 2004 the city of Paris finally paid tribute to the woman who prematurely proposed so many reforms, by naming a square in the third arrondissement "Place Olympe de Gouges."

Biographies:

E. Lairtullier, *Les Femmes célèbres de 1789 à 1795 et leur influence dans la Révolution, pour servir de suite et de complément à toutes les histoires de la Révolution Française,* 2 volumes (Paris: Librairie politique, 1840);

Léopold Lacour, *Les Origines du féminisme contemporain. Trois femmes de la Révolution* (Paris: Nourrit, 1901);

Edouard Forestié, *Olympe de Gouges (1748–1793)* (Montauban: Forestié, 1901);

Alfred Guillois, *Etude médico-psychologique sur Olympe de Gouges. Considérations générales sur la mentalité des femmes pendant la Révolution Française* (Lyon, 1904);

Olivier Blanc, *Une Femme de libertés, Olympe de Gouges* (Paris: Syros Alternatives, 1989); revised as *Marie-Olympe de Gouges, une humaniste à la fin du XVIIIe siècle* (Cahors: René Viénet, 2003);

Sophie Mousset, *Olympe de Gouges et les droits de la femme* (Paris: Félin, 2003).

References:

Lisa Beckstrand, "Olympe de Gouges: Feminine Sensibility and Political Posturing," *Intertexts,* 6 (Fall 2002): 185–202;

Gregory S. Brown, "The Self-Fashionings of Olympe de Gouges, 1784–1789," *Eighteenth-Century Studies,* 34 (Spring 2001): 383–401;

Henri Coulet, "Sur le roman d'Olympe de Gouges, *Le Prince philosophe,*" in *Les Femmes et la Révolution Française,* volume 2, edited by Marie-France Brive (Toulouse: Presses Universitaires du Mirail, 1990), pp. 273–278;

Antoine Court, "Un mélodrame d'Olympe de Gouges ou le noir impossible," in *Mélodrames et romans noirs, 1750–1890,* edited by Simone Bernard-Griffiths and Jean Sgard (Toulouse: Presses Universitaires du Mirail, 2000), pp. 67–82;

Marie-Pierre Le Hir, "Feminism, Theater, Race: *L'esclavage des noirs,*" in *Translating Slavery: Gender and Race in French Women's Writing, 1783–1823,* edited by Doris Y. Kadish and Françoise Massardier-Kenney (Kent, Ohio & London: Kent State University Press, 1994), pp. 65–83;

A. Lorrho, "Le théâtre politique d'Olympe de Gouges," M.A. thesis, Université de Paris III, 1985;

Catherine Masson, "Olympe de Gouges, anti-esclavagiste et non-violente," *Women in French Studies,* 10 (2002): 153–165;

Catherine Nesci, "La passion de l'impropre: lien conjugal et lien colonial chez Olympe de Gouges," in *Corps/décors: femmes orgie, parodie,* edited by Nesci and Gerald Prince (Amsterdam: Rodopi, 1999), pp. 45–56;

Guilia Pacini, "'Celle dont la voix publique vous a nommé le père': Olympe de Gouges's *Mémoire de Madame de Valmont,*" *Women in French Studies,* 9 (2001): 207–219;

Michèle Ratsaby, "Olympe de Gouges et le théâtre de la Révolution Française," dissertation, City University of New York, 1998;

Joan Wallach Scott, "French Feminists and the Rights of 'Man': Olympe de Gouges's Declarations," *History Workshop,* 28 (Autumn 1989): 1–21;

Scott, *Only Paradoxes to Offer: French Feminists and the Rights of Man* (Cambridge, Mass.: Harvard University Press, 1996), pp. 19–56;

Samia I. Spencer, "Olympe de Gouges," in *Feminist Encyclopedia of French Literature,* edited by Eva Martin Sartori (Westport, Conn.: Greenwood Press, 1999), pp. 238–239;

Spencer, "Olympe de Gouges," in *Writings by Pre-Revolutionary French Women. From Marie de France to Elisabeth Vigée-Le Brun,* edited by Anne R. Larsen and Colette H. Winn (New York: Garland, 2000), pp. 559–572;

Spencer, "Une remarquable visionnaire," *Enlightenment Essays,* 9 (1978): 77–91;

René Tarin, "L'esclavage des noirs, ou la mauvaise conscience d'Olympe de Gouges," *Dix-huitième siècle,* 30 (1998): 373–381;

Chantal Thomas, "Les causes perdues d'Olympe de Gouges," in *La Carmagnole des muses, l'homme de lettres et l'artiste dans la Révolution,* edited by Jean-Claude Bonnet (Paris: Armand Colin, 1988), pp. 308–312;

Mary Trouille, "Eighteenth-Century Amazons of the Pen, Stéphanie de Genlis and Olympe de Gouges," in *Femmes savantes, femmes d'esprit. Women Intellectuals of the French Eighteenth Century* (New York: Peter Lang, 1994), pp. 341–370;

Janie Vanpee, "*La Déclaration des droits de la femme:* Olympe de Gouges's Re-Writing of *La Déclaration des droits de l'homme,*" in *Literate Women and the French Revolution of 1789,* edited by Catherine R. Montfort (Birmingham, Ala.: Summa, 1994), pp. 55–79;

Vanpee, "Performing Justice: The Trials of Olympe de Gouges," *Theater Journal,* 51 (March 1999): 47–65;

Vanpee, "Revendications de la légitimité: les performances révolutionnaires d'Olympe de Gouges," in *Sexualité, mariage et famille au XVIIIe siècle,* edited by Olga B. Cragg and Rosena Davison (Quebec: Laval University Press, 1998), pp. 217–232;

Vanpee, "Taking the Podium: Olympe de Gouges's Revolutionary Discourse," in *Women Writers in Pre-Revolutionary France: Strategies of Emancipation,* edited by Colette H. Winn and Donna Kuizenga (New York: Garland, 1997), pp. 299–312;

Gabrielle Verdier, "From Reform to Revolution: The Social Theater of Olympe de Gouges," in *Literate Women and the French Revolution of 1789,* edited by Montfort (Birmingham, Ala.: Summa, 1994), pp. 189–221;

Verdier, "Olympe de Gouges et le divorce sur la scène révolutionnaire: adieu au mariage d'Ancien Régime?" *Dalhousie French Studies,* 56 (Fall 2001): 154–164;

Barbara Woshinsky, "Olympe de Gouges's *Declaration of the Rights of Woman* (1791)," *Mary Wollstonecraft Journal,* 2 (1973): 3–6.

Papers:

The manuscript for Olympe de Gouges's *La nécessité du divorce* is located in the Bibliothèque nationale, in Paris, FF 9280 (1790); the incomplete manuscript for "La France sauvée, ou le tyran détrôné" is in the Archives nationales, in Paris, W293, dossier 210.

Françoise d'Issembourg de Graffigny
(11 February 1695 – 21 December 1758)

Ruth P. Thomas
Temple University

BOOKS: *Lettres d'une Péruvienne,* anonymous ([Paris?]: Peine, [1747?]); translated as *Letters Written by a Peruvian Princess* (London: Brindley, 1748); revised as *Lettres d'une Péruvienne. Nouvelle édition. Augmentée de plusieurs lettres, et d'une introduction à l'histoire,* 2 volumes (Paris: Duchesne, 1752);

Cénie (Paris: Cailleau, 1751); translated as *Cenia, or, The Suppos'd Daughter* (London: Reeve, 1752);

La Fille d'Aristide (Paris: Duchesne, 1759);

Oeuvres posthumes de Madame de Graffigny, contenant: Ziman et Zenise, suivi de Phaza, comédies en un acte en prose (Amsterdam & Paris: Les libraires qui vendent les nouveautés, 1770); *Oeuvres complètes de Mme. de Graffigny* (Paris: Briand, 1821);

Les Saturnales, in English Showalter, "Madame de Graffigny and Rousseau: Between the Two Discours," *Studies on Voltaire and the Eighteenth Century* (Oxford: Voltaire foundation / Paris: Touzot, 1978).

Editions: *Lettres d'une Péruvienne,* edited by Gianni Nicoletti (Bari: Adriatica Editrice, 1967);

Lettres d'une Péruvienne, preface by Colette Piau-Gillot (Paris: Côté-Femmes, 1990);

Lettres d'une Péruvienne, introduction by Joan DeJean and Nancy K. Miller (New York: Modern Language Association, 1993);

Cénie, in *Femmes dramaturges en France (1650–1750): pièces choisies,* edited by Perry Gethner, *Papers on French Seventeenth-Century Literature* (Paris, Seattle & Tübingen: Biblio 17, 1993), pp. 317–372, 385–387;

Lettres d'une Péruvienne, in *Romans de femmes du XVIIIe siècle,* edited by Raymond Trousson (Paris: Robert Laffont, 1996), pp. 59–164;

Lettres d'une Péruvienne, edited and with an introduction by Jonathan Mallison (Oxford: Voltaire Foundation, 2002).

Edition in English: *Letters from a Peruvian Woman,* translated by David Kornacker (New York: Modern Language Association, 1993).

Françoise d'Issembourg de Graffigny (from English Showalter, ed., Correspondance de Mme de Graffigny, *1985; Thomas Cooper Library, University of South Carolina)*

PLAY PRODUCTIONS: *Cénie,* Paris, Comédie française, 25 June 1750;

La Fille d'Aristide, Paris, Comédie française, 29 April 1758.

OTHER: "La Nouvelle espagnole," in Caylus, Anne-Claude-Philippe, Comte de, and others, *Recueil de ces messieurs* (Amsterdam & Paris: Frères Westein, 1745);

"La Princesse Azerolle," in Caylus, *Cinq Contes de fées* (N.p., 1745).

When Françoise de Graffigny died in 1758, she was the best-known woman writer in France. In 1747 she had written *Lettres d'une Péruvienne* (translated as *Letters Written by a Peruvian Princess,* 1748), a best-selling and critically acclaimed novel, regularly republished, imitated, translated, and even adapted for the stage. She had followed this novel in 1750 with the play *Cénie* (translated as *Cenia, or, The Suppos'd Daughter,* 1752), a successful sentimental drama that many considered to be the model of the genre and that had an unheard-of first run of twenty-five performances. During the 1750s she had presided over a salon where she welcomed the great authors and public figures of her day. Yet, shortly after her death she was all but forgotten. When critic Charles-Augustin Sainte-Beuve spoke of her in the mid nineteenth century, it was not as a literary star but rather as a supporting player. What interested Sainte-Beuve was neither her novel nor her play but the more than thirty letters she had written during her ten-week stay at Cirey in 1738 and 1739 as the guest of Voltaire and Gabrielle Emilie Le Tonnelier de Breteuil, marquise Du Châtelet, which were published in 1820 under the title *Vie privée de Voltaire* (The Private Life of Voltaire). The title of Georges Noël's 1913 biography, *Une "Primitive" oubliée de l'école des coeurs sensibles* (A Forgotten "Primitive" Writer of the School of Sentimental Hearts), describes Graffigny's literary reputation at the beginning of the twentieth century. Within the last third of the twentieth century, however, she has clearly come into a more prominent position. The discovery in 1965 of the greater part of her papers—thousands of her letters to others, letters sent to her, unpublished manuscripts, and documents (many of which have since been scrupulously edited and published)—and the ongoing publication, beginning in 1985, of a complete edition of her correspondence provide a new perspective on the woman and the writer as well as an invaluable commentary on eighteenth-century public and private life. The renewal of interest in the eighteenth-century French novel starting in the 1960s and the subsequent reappraisal of women's fiction have focused attention on the originality of Graffigny's novel with its untraditional heroine, who chooses autonomy over marriage to a man she does not love. A similar scholarly interest in the contributions of women to the French stage of the eighteenth century, as well as new assessments of the sentimental drama, have drawn attention to *Cénie,* which has been reread as a protest against the patriarchal order. Perhaps no other eighteenth-century French woman writer has been so much in the public eye in the late twentieth and early twenty-first centuries.

Françoise d'Issembourg d'Happoncourt was born 11 February 1695 in the independent duchy of Lorraine. Although her father, François d'Issembourg du Buisson, a soldier whom his daughter once compared to the gruff but kind Squire Western in Henry Fielding's *Tom Jones* (1749), traced his nobility only as far back as the seventeenth century, the family was among the most prominent in Lorraine society. Françoise's mother, Marguerite Callot, came from a long-established Lorraine family and was related to Jacques Callot, a celebrated engraver. Little is known about Françoise's formative years, although when the heroine of her novel complains about the inadequate education offered to women, readers generally assume that the author is speaking of her own background: as a writer, Graffigny often required help with her grammar, punctuation, and spelling. She was not quite seventeen on 19 January 1712 when she married François Huguet, a minor noble attached to the ducal court, whose family was somewhat wealthier than hers. The couple took their name from his property of Graffigny. Huguet's fortune surely played a part in the marriage, since Françoise de Graffigny's father was constantly in debt. The marriage began to unravel almost from the beginning. Money—which remained a concern throughout her life and determined many of the directions she took—was an immediate problem because of Huguet's excessive spending: he turned to his wife's fortune after he had squandered his own. Worse still, Huguet was a jealous, violent, and brutal husband who abused his wife repeatedly both physically and mentally. The couple lived together only six years; in 1723 Graffigny asked for and was granted a legal separation. Huguet, who spent time in prison for some minor crimes, died two years later in an institution for the insane. The couple had three children, all of whom died in infancy.

Widowhood brought happier times than marriage to Graffigny. Without a husband or any family ties, she had freedom and some measure of financial stability since, like many impoverished nobles, she attached herself to the ducal court at Lunéville, where she had the protection of Princess Elisabeth-Charlotte d'Orléans. The court, which Voltaire compared to Versailles for its flowering of letters and arts and sciences, was a bustling center of cultural life. In addition to such illustrious visitors as Voltaire and the duchesse de Richelieu, Lunéville attracted young officers, students, artists, actors, poets, and writers, many of whom—such as poet Jean-François de Saint-Lambert and Claire Lebrun, a celebrated actress known as Mlle Clairon—became part of Graffigny's circle. The intellectual stimulation they provided may well have served to supplement her neglected education, for she had the reputation of being "une femme d'esprit" (a woman of wit) in her coterie. Graffigny spent fifteen years at Lunéville and formed two particularly significant attachments. Around 1730 she fell in love with Léopold

Desmarest, a young cavalry officer thirteen years younger than she and said to be her only true love. The liaison, although stormy, continued until 1743, even though Desmarest's regimental duties as well as family affairs often kept the two apart. He was a faithless lover whose sporadic affection caused her a great deal of pain, and his infidelity has echoes in her novel, in which the heroine is abandoned by the man she loves.

Graffigny's relationship with François-Antoine Devaux was different. She met Devaux, known familiarly as "Panpan," through Lebrun between 1730 and 1733. A young law student some seventeen years her junior and himself an aspiring writer and playwright, Devaux encouraged her literary efforts and participated in them. Her first works—a play, *L'Honnête Homme* (The Man of Honor); a dialogue, *La Réunion du bon sens et de l'esprit* (The Marriage of Good Sense and Wit); and a five-act tragedy in verse, *Héraclite*—were probably all written in collaboration with him. Whether these works were actually meant for publication or simply diversions to be read before friends is not certain. Nevertheless, Devaux tried later—unsuccessfully—to publish them. More importantly, Devaux was also a close friend and confidant, who wrote to her each time he left Lunéville, and when Graffigny herself left Lorraine, the two began a regular correspondence. For more than twenty years they exchanged almost daily letters informing, advising, and counseling one another—sharing opinions, gossip, problems, pleasures, and even the most intimate aspects of their lives. Their letters, about 2,500 written by Graffigny and 2,000 by Devaux, form the bulk of the correspondence.

The good life in Lunéville came to a close for Graffigny when, in 1736, the Treaty of Vienna ended the independence of Lorraine. It was made a province of France and ceded to the Polish crown. With the departure of the royal court came the end of Graffigny's financial resources, and she was obliged once again to depend on the protection and goodwill of others. In 1738 Graffigny set out for Paris to take a position as lady-in-waiting to the duchesse de Richelieu and stopped en route to accept the invitation of Voltaire to stay with him and Du Châtelet at Cirey. Graffigny had met Voltaire and his mistress during their visit to Lunéville in 1735, and Voltaire had even written a little poem to "cette veuve aimable et belle" (this beautiful and amiable widow). Life at Cirey was pleasant at the beginning. Graffigny's stay turned sour when Voltaire and Du Châtelet accused her of having sent a copy of his unedited *La Pucelle* (1762, The Maiden) to her friends at Lunéville to be copied and circulated. The accusation was false, fabricated by an overzealous Du Châtelet, who opened Voltaire's mail to protect her lover, known to be sensitive to criticism. Humiliated but

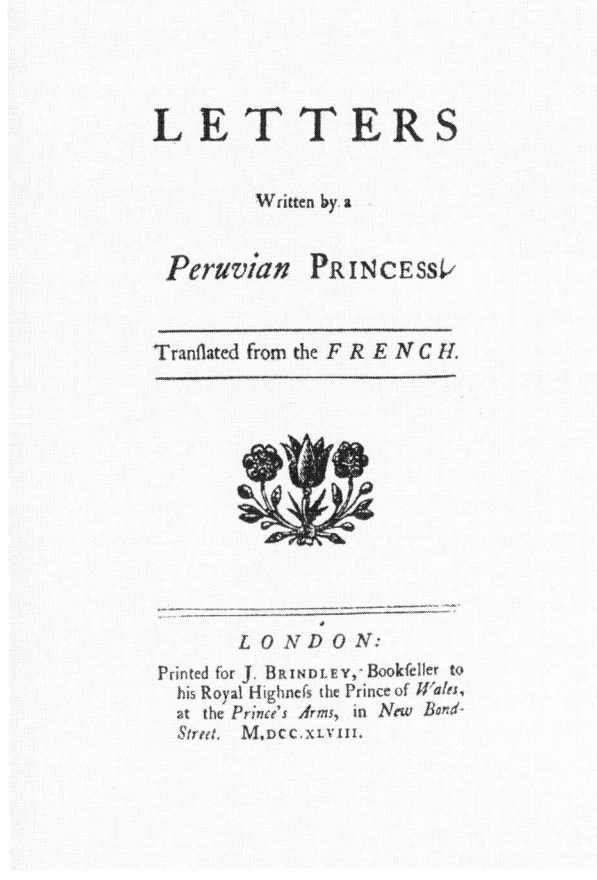

Title page for the first English translation in 1748 of Graffigny's Lettres d'une Péruvienne, 1747 (from Graffigny, Letters Written by a Peruvian Princess, 1974; Thomas Cooper Library, University of South Carolina)

without the financial means to leave, Graffigny remained at Cirey a virtual prisoner for more than a month, until Leopold Desmarets arrived to help her get to Paris. The incident had a lasting effect: not only did she distrust Voltaire and intensely dislike Du Châtelet, but, as a writer, from then on she feared public ridicule.

Paris was not the haven that Graffigny expected. The duchesse de Richelieu died in August 1740, and Graffigny found herself again alone, homeless, and in severe financial distress. In September she took a position as lady-in-waiting to the princesse de Ligue and lived with her in the convent of the Filles de Sainte-Elisabeth. When the princess left in February 1741, Graffigny remained there under the protection of Renée-Marguerite de Gouyon de Marcé Coutances de La Selle, marquise de Coutances, but that arrangement proved unsatisfactory, so she moved in July to another convent, the Filles du Précieux Sang, where she had the protection of Marie-Anne de Levis-Charlus, marquise de Chateaumorand, a relative of the princess.

Graffigny was expelled from this convent in May 1742 when she arranged the marriage of one of the *pensionnaires* (residents), Elisabeth de Melun, princess d'Epinoy, whose departure deprived the convent of a dowry; Graffigny then moved in with Lévis.

Graffigny's position was difficult not only because she was herself impractical about money but also because her birth and social status required that she maintain a certain standard of living. So, too, did her gender. A woman, as Graffigny pointed out to Devaux, needed expensive clothes and servants, a carriage, and a costly loge at the theater, while a man could get along with much less. Graffigny supplemented her meager income doing favors for friends; she also became involved in what were called her "châteaux" (castles)—moneymaking schemes, often proposed by her friends, that seemed to border on the illegal and that constantly came to nothing. Health was a concern as well, for she was afraid she might have breast cancer. In 1742, although she could scarcely afford it, she finally moved into an apartment of her own on the rue Saint-Hyacinthe. There she met one of her tenants, Pierre Valleré, a lawyer who was briefly her lover and remained throughout her life a loyal and devoted friend.

When Graffigny went to Paris, she probably did not intend to become a professional writer. Nor did she write the first three years she was there. Still, she was not totally absent from the literary scene. She read the new publications and literary gazettes, and as an agent for Devaux, who was in turn buying books for his patron, the Palatine elector, she had access to the latest publications. She often went to the theater and lobbied on behalf of her friends, Saint-Lambert and Devaux, both of whom had written plays, meeting with the actors and doing whatever else was necessary to get their works performed at the Comédie française. She was engaged in the mechanics of literature, sharpening her own skills in the process, when in the fall of 1742 she began helping the abbé Gabriel Louis de Calabre-Pérau with some of his editorial work. She read novels, corrected manuscripts, proofread, and helped Calabre-Pérau in the publication of the 1743 edition of Voltaire's works.

When she did resume writing, it was again a collaborative effort, this time in the literary group hosted by Mlle Quinault, an actress who had recently retired from the Comédie française, and her benefactor, distinguished archaeologist and member of the Académie des Inscriptions et des Belles-Lettres, Anne-Claude-Philippe, comte de Caylus. Graffigny met Quinault, also from Lorraine, in 1740 while trying to get Devaux's play produced, and the two became close friends. By the winter of 1743–1744 Graffigny was a regular member of the Quinault-Caylus circle, later known as the Société du Bout-du-Banc (The Company of the End of the Bench). The group, which at various times included such writers as Charles Pinot Duclos and Claude-Prosper Jolyot de Crébillon (fils), Jean-Baptiste Gresset, Pierre-Claude Nivelle de La Chaussée, and Alexis Piron, and such administrators as Claude-Arien Hélvetius and Pierre-Louis Moreau de Maupertuis, met weekly for informal suppers, lively and irreverent conversation, and occasional entertainment. Guests read their works in progress and contributed to collective projects. Caylus, who had already financed and published a collection of group *facéties* (jokes), mostly parodies of popular forms, assigned individual subjects, and the authors worked independently of one another. Quinault served as editor and critic and had the right of refusal for the collection. In January 1744 Graffigny was given her first exercise, "l'oraison funèbre d'un capucin" (the funeral oration of a Capucine monk), and when it was not accepted, Caylus in August gave her the outline of a Spanish tale. With the help of Calabre-Pérau and Devaux (to whom she submitted all her work) and after many revisions, "La Nouvelle espagnole" (The Spanish Novella) was completed in four months, and in March 1745 it appeared—without Graffigny's name—in a collection called *Recueil de ces messieurs* (Collection of These Gentlemen). Although the volume, which was little more than a joke, was not well received, friends gave Graffigny warm praise for her story, her first published work. In December, Caylus proposed another outline, this one for a fairy tale called "La Princesse Azerolle" (Princess Azerolle). More confident, Graffigny completed her parody almost entirely by herself in fewer than eight weeks. The intention was that the tale be published under the name of Mlle de Villeneuve, a writer of fairy tales, to earn some money for its author. Instead, it appeared in November 1745 in *Cinq contes de fées* (Five Fairy Tales). The Quinault-Caylus circle provided a supportive and nurturing atmosphere that facilitated Graffigny's literary debuts. But, as Judith Curtis has pointed out in "Anticipating Zilia: Madame de Graffigny in 1744" (1994), the collaborative process itself, in which the group taste dominates, imposed a kind of conformity that limited individuality and creativity.

In 1745, encouraged by the reception of her tales, Graffigny began to write a novel. It was the story of Zilia, a Peruvian princess engaged to Prince Aza and educated to rule alongside him. Kidnapped by the Spanish, she is taken from her homeland on the day she is to marry. Her boat is seized by the French, and she is brought to France by the gallant Déterville, who falls in love with her. With her she carries *quipos*, the colored thread with which she writes to her fiancé—recording her journey, her innermost feelings, and her impressions of French life. When she runs out of *quipos,* she must learn to read and write in French in order to continue her correspondence, and her journey becomes one of self-discovery. Déterville helps her locate Aza in Spain; Aza comes to France only to tell her that he has converted to Christianity and that he now loves someone else. Déterville, who has used the Peruvian spoils to provide her with a château of her own, proposes marriage, but she refuses. Instead, she offers friendship. She remains in France, knowing that her happiness will not come from love but from the simple pleasure of existing, a pleasure she invites Déterville to share with her.

Graffigny's novel was inspired by the *Lettres persanes* (1721; translated as *Persian Letters,* 1722), whose foreign visitors comment on French institutions; she specifically refers to its author, Charles-Louis de Secondat, baron de la Brède et de Montesquieu, in her preface. Zilia's letters also continue in the sentimental tradition of Gabriel-Joseph de Lavergne, vicomte de Guilleragues's *Lettres portugaises* (1669, Letters of a Portuguese Nun), whose heroine writes to an absent and unfaithful lover. Graffigny merged these two disparate traditions into a single work. Her reading of Garcilaso de la Vega's book on the Incas made her decide to create an Incan princess and to set her novel in Peru. Graffigny intended her heroine, unlike Montesquieu's Europeanized male visitors, to be much more of an outsider, an "other"—by virtue of her nation and her sex. And while Graffigny was aware of the anachronism of having a sixteenth-century Peruvian princess travel in eighteenth-century France, she did not believe it would jar the sensibilities of her readers, for whom plausibility was more important than historical truth. But her novel also, as she admitted, was based on personal memories. Zilia, poor and alone in France, has been considered a reflection of Graffigny's own circumstances, and the relationship with Aza is an echo of her liaison with the unfaithful Desmarets. The intellectual heroine's quest for knowledge and her critique of France express Graffigny's Enlightenment ideals. Zilia's being deprived of her *quipos* and then learning a new language has been compared by Nancy K. Miller to Graffigny's coming to writing and discovering her own female voice in a man's Enlightenment.

Graffigny worked on her novel for two years. She sent drafts to Devaux for comments and read it aloud and showed it to friends for editing and suggestions. She called it "l'ouvrage de Pénélope" (the handiwork of Penelope) because of its slow pace. She had originally planned a simple love story in which Zilia and Aza would be reunited by the good offices of Déterville, but, at Devaux's suggestion, she decided to make Aza unfaithful. She considered having Zilia and Déterville marry but decided that friendship could not be changed to love without violating Aristotle's rule on consistency of character. Devaux was among those who attempted to persuade her to make Aza and Zilia brother and sister, thereby rendering their incestuous marriage impossible and making Aza's behavior more excusable, but Graffigny did not wish to justify his infidelity.

Although Caylus had offered to help publish the novel even before it was finished, the publication did not go smoothly. Graffigny was unable to get official permission to publish her novel, and publishers were reluctant to pay much for such illegal novels because they could easily be pirated. Nor did she have the money to publish it at her own expense. With the help of Caylus and Calabre-Pérau, the novel was published in 1747 anonymously and without official approval. For all of her time and efforts, she received only 300 livres.

Since Graffigny was relatively unknown, the novel, as Janet Gurkin Altman has noted in "A Woman's Place in the Enlightenment Sun" (1991), took Paris by surprise. It was enthusiastically welcomed by the reading public and well received by the critics of the major literary journals, who immediately identified the anonymous author in their reviews. The abbé Guillaume-Thomas-François Raynal, Elie-Catherine Fréron, and Pierre de La Porte all praised the work for its originality and its blending of the sentimental and the philosophical. Although Anne-Robert-Jacques de Turgot, a well-known political economist, was unhappy with Zilia's critique of the French class system and private property (later the novel was accused of a socialist bias), he thought the work superior to the *Lettres persanes* because it integrated more skillfully the cultural criticism with the novel. Some critics—and readers—were disappointed with the untraditional ending, since the heroine does not die, enter a convent, or marry. Fréron and later La Porte would have preferred to have the novel end with the marriage of Aza and Zilia.

Shortly after its publication, the novel was followed by two sequels. One, an anonymous continuation, which Graffigny attributed to the chevalier de Mouhy, appeared in 1748. It included letters between Déterville, his sister Céline, and Zilia, but did not change the ending. A year later, Hugary de Lamarche-Courmont published his *Lettres d'Aza ou d'un Péruvien* (Letters of Aza or a Peruvian Man). In his sequel, which was frequently reprinted along with Zilia's letters, Aza writes to a friend, criticizes the Spaniards, and remains faithful to Zilia in spite of appearances. At the end, the two are about to marry. In 1797 another continuation, this one by a woman, Marie Renee-Elisabeth Choppin Morel de Vindé, had fifteen new letters, all by Zilia, and ended with the marriage of Zilia and Déter-

Letter from Graffigny to François-Antoine Devaux, a close friend who probably collaborated with her on her first literary endeavors (Pierpont Morgan Library; from English Showalter, ed., Correspondance de Mme de Graffigny, *1985; Thomas Cooper Library, University of South Carolina)* ville. As English Showalter Jr. has noted in "*Les Lettres d'une Péruvienne:* Composition, Publication, Suites," the identity of Zilia's potential husband—whether Aza or Déterville—was largely gender specific. Women preferred Déterville; men, Aza. While most of the critics were favorable, certain rumors claimed that Graffigny had not written the novel herself. Some suspected Devaux or Calabre-Perau, or Duclos, while Du Châtelet thought the author was Pierre Valleré.

In 1752 a second—and definitive—edition of the novel was published, this time with official permission, thanks to the support of Guillaume-Chrétien de Lamoignon de Malesherbes. Graffigny did not change the ending to please the critics. For Graffigny, however, Zilia's decision not to marry Déterville was less a matter of autonomy than a reflection of the heroine's moral code, which did not permit infidelity. The new edition added three letters—two entirely new, one reworked—to the original thirty-eight. The new letters were both critiques of French society: one on the French passion for the superfluous at the expense of what is really important and the other on the totally inadequate education of French women and its effect on married life. In the second version, as Vera Grayson has shown, Graffigny changed Zilia's character. No longer a "passive object of desire," she was better able to interact with the French and comment on their customs. Graffigny's motives for the second edition were less aesthetic than financial. By revising the novel, she made previous editions obsolete and the book salable again. Since two continuations to the novel had already been published, Graffigny was fearful of more. She received 3,000 livres—ten times the price of the first edition—but other rewards exceeded the monetary ones. The novel put her into the public eye and opened doors. It won her a pension to write morally edifying playlets to educate the children at the Imperial Court at Vienna where the former duc de Lorraine and his wife were now emperor and empress. She was also commissioned to buy luxury goods for the Imperial Court. The popularity of the novel continued, and Carlo Goldoni adapted it for the stage. His *La Peruviana* was peformed in Venice in 1754.

While Graffigny was still at work on *Lettres d'une péruviennes,* she began to compose a play. Neither a comedy nor a tragedy, it was in that mixed genre that Philippe Néricault Destouches and La Chaussée had made so popular and that was known as the "tragédie bourgeoise" (bourgeois tragedy) or "comédie larmoyante" (tearful comedy). In it, virtuous characters with whom the audience can identity find themselves in difficult and often pathetic family or social situations. They appeal directly to the emotions of the public through their misfortunes and offer moral lessons by their exemplary behavior and the maxims that they recite. Because of their often complicated plots, with mistaken identities and recognition scenes, and their maxims, they were sometimes considered closer to the novel than to drama.

Initially titled "La Gouvernante" (The Governess), Graffigny's play was the story of a governess who learns that she is the mother of the young woman in her care. Graffigny almost abandoned the project when she discovered that La Chaussée had written a "comédie larmoyante" with the same title. Devaux assured her the play was original, and others urged her to finish the work, although later she was unjustly accused of plagiarism. She had sent Devaux an outline of the play long before La Chaussée's play was performed. Graffigny's piece was planned as a three-act play in verse. She switched to prose at the suggestion of Quinault, who thought Graffigny's prose writing better than her verse, and because Graffigny herself felt that to write in verse as a woman might appear overly ambitious and unbecoming to her gender. She might be labeled a "femme savante" (a bluestocking). Graffigny finished a first version of the play in May 1749. It went through extensive revisions again with the help of Devaux and other friends to whom she read it. The play, now in five acts, was sent to the Comédie française in February 1750. The title was changed to *Cénie,* which, rumor had it, was an anagram of "niece" and referred to the life of her niece, Minette de Ligneville, who had come to live with her in 1746 and who remained until 1751 when she married Claude-Adrien Helvétius. Graffigny denied the rumor.

Cénie is the drama of a virtuous fifteen-year-old woman who has been raised by her governess, Orphise, as the daughter of Dorimond, a loving and wealthy nobleman, and his young wife, Mélisse, who has recently died. Cénie is courted by Dorimond's two nephews, Méricourt and Clerval. The first seeks Cénie's fortune; the second, her love. Cénie returns Clerval's love. Dorimond, who is unaware of Méricourt's character and his motives, gives him his blessing, and Méricourt proposes marriage. Orphise urges Cénie to be silent, obey her father, and marry Méricourt. But Cénie rejects the proposal, decries the injustice and tyranny of arranged marriages, and paints the happiness of a marriage of inclination. When Cénie refuses his proposal, Méricourt brings a deathbed letter from Mélisse in which she confesses that she faked motherhood to win Dorimond's affection and that Cénie is not Dorimond and Mélisse's real daughter. Méricourt offers to repair the shame of Cénie's birth by marrying her and keeping the truth from Dorimond. Cénie does neither, and Méricourt produces another letter, this one revealing that Orphise is the true mother of Cénie. Dorimond offers to adopt Cénie and thereby restore

Portrait of Graffigny by F. B. Lépicié; (from Nancy Mitford,
Voltaire in Love, *1957; Thomas Cooper Library,*
University of South Carolina)

her fortune and social position, but she refuses to accept his charity. Accompanied by Orphise, Cénie is about to go off to a convent, where she can hide her humiliation and shame, when a man whom Clerval had befriended turns out to be a nobleman who was unjustly exiled for an affair of honor and the husband of Orphise and the father of Cénie. Virtue is rewarded, and everyone except Méricourt is happy.

When Graffigny wrote her play, she was not sure it would be staged. The financial benefits for the playwright—royalties, performance privileges, and even membership in academies—were significant, and indeed Graffigny would earn much more for her play than for her novel, which may be why, after the *Lettres d'une Péruvienne,* she did not attempt another novel. But the benefits were outweighed by the difficulties involved in bringing a play to the stage, difficulties that Graffigny had experienced when she had tried to get the plays of Devaux and Saint-Lambert and later Palissot (Charles Palissot de Montenoy) produced. And, as Showalter has observed in "A Woman of Letters in the French Enlightenment: Madame de Graffigny," the staging of plays was especially difficult for women, who had to get the play read and cast, deal with the actors—some of whom could not be received in polite society—and supervise rehearsals, all of which ran counter to the proprieties and to the modesty expected of the female sex. Nor did she have any living role models. Between 1717 and 1789, she was the only woman to stage a play at the Comédie française. Cabals were also a problem and could make or break a play at a single performance; Graffigny was fearful of public ridicule, especially after her experience at Cirey. But friends such as Charles de Bourbon, comte de Clermont, encouraged her, sure that the play would be successful and financially rewarding. She agreed to having the play performed, but only on the condition that the comte de Clermont, on whose good offices she had to depend to get the play read and accepted, would say that *Cénie* was being staged without her knowledge or permission. She could not deny having written the play, because she had circulated her text and even held public readings. Still, when some of the actors attributed the play to Duclos, she was not at all unhappy.

The play was not performed immediately. Plays ran for as long as they were well received by the public, and Graffigny had to wait until a new tragedy by Jean-François Marmontel had its run. For a while she feared that Voltaire would insist on having his play staged before *Cénie.* He did not—perhaps because he wanted to make amends for the incident at Cirey, or because he planned to have it staged elsewhere. *Cénie* premiered 25 June 1750; it was a brilliant success. The audience was moved to tears, and so much applause and foot stomping took place that dust was raised in the theater. Graffigny, however, was not in the theater. She anxiously waited at home for her valet to return after the second act. He waited until the third to bring her the good news. In October the play was performed at Fontainebleau before an enthusiastic Madame de Pompadour. Critical reaction also was generally favorable, and several authors praised *Cénie* in verse. Reviewers insisted on the valuable moral lesson of the play and spoke of the glory of the female author and the triumph of the genre. Publishers were eager to print the play, which, probably with the help of Duclos, she sold for 2,000 francs. When the play appeared in print around the end of November 1751, the journals were lavish in their praise. If some detractors thought the plot too complex, the characters unreal, and the style too sententious, such critics as Fréron and Raynal did not. Even Jean-Jacques Rousseau, who was generally critical of women writers, praised Graffigny. But after 1754, critical reaction became more negative, as the genre itself lost favor. Conservative critics, including Voltaire (who had himself written a sentimental comedy), opposed the "comédie larmoyante" and its mixture of comic and tragic elements. Its admirable characters with bourgeois sensibilities were no longer in favor. The popular success of *Cénie* soon began to decline as well. Although nineteen editions of the play were published between 1751 and 1754, the play had only one long run after 1750. In June and July of 1754 it was performed ten times.

In 1751 the now famous Graffigny moved into larger and more comfortable quarters on the rue d'Enfer, which could better accommodate her wide circle of friends and the visitors who came in a steady stream. Officially, she began her career as the hostess of a salon. She modeled it after Quinault's, with the same informal atmosphere, conviviality, freedom of expression, and even many of the same guests. Like many a salon hostess, she had, at least for a while, a younger, prettier woman beside her—her niece. She could not afford regular dinners, since she had no benefactor, but she held open house, and guests were known to come and stay for long periods at a moment of crisis. Her gatherings were more social than literary. No group projects were initiated, nor were authors expected to read from their new works. As Showalter has observed in "A Woman of Letters," she never tried to impose her taste or to set a trend but saw herself simply as a mediator, bringing together her eclectic guests for good conversation. In her new living quarters she welcomed Diderot, Rousseau, and Hélvetius, whose marriage with her niece she arranged.

The salon was an important part of Graffigny's life. It gave her contacts and connections with people in administration, finance, and theater who could help her get on pension lists and get positions and contracts for friends. It also gave her the opportunity to mentor younger writers, to help them revise manuscripts, and to get their plays published or performed. But the constant demands of hospitality deprived her of her freedom. Her role as salon hostess took from her the time and energy that she might have devoted to writing. Graffigny wrote one more play, *La Fille d'Aristide* (1758, The Daughter of Aristide; published in 1759). It, too, was a sentimental drama, but set in ancient Greece, not in modern France. Its virtuous and persecuted heroine sells her freedom in an act of self-sacrifice to the interests of her surrogate father and is misjudged by the man she loves. Written earlier, the play was performed in 1758 but was withdrawn after only four performances. Although Graffigny had been in ill health for some time, the failure of the play is generally believed to have hastened her death on 21 December 1758.

Françoise d'Issembourg de Graffigny's novel, re-edited four times within the last twenty years alone and restored to canonic status, is a constant subject of critical inquiry, while her play, available in a modern edition, has also begun to attract critical attention. But it is her correspondence, revealing the writer's own view of herself as an artist and her craft, that may well provide the newest insight into the works themselves. While the correspondence has already led to important reappraisals of eighteenth-century life and culture, it has yet to be studied as a literary work. Much more needs to be said and written about Graffigny and her work.

Letters:

Lettres de Madame de Graffigny, suivies de celles de Mesdames de Staal, d'Epinay, du Boccage, Suard, du chevalier de Boufflers, du marquis de Villette . . . des relations de Marmontel, de Gibbon, du Chabanon, du prince de Ligne, de Grétry, de Genlis, sur leur séjour près de Voltaire, edited by Eugène Asse (Paris: G. Charpentier, 1879; Geneva: Slatkine Reprints, 1972);

Correspondance de Madame de Graffigny, edited by J. A. Dinard, English Showalter, and others (Oxford: Voltaire Foundation, 1985–).

Bibliographies:

David Smith, "The Popularity of Mme de Graffigny's *Lettres d'une Péruvienne:* The Bibliographical Evidence," *Eighteenth-Century Fiction,* 3 (October 1990): 1–20;

Smith, "Graffigny Rediviva: Editions of the Lettres d'une Péruvienne (1967–1993)," *Eighteenth-Century Fiction,* 7 (October 1994): 71–78;

Jo-Ann McEachern and Smith, "Mme de Graffigny's Lettres d'une Péruvienne: Identifying the First Edition," *Eighteenth-Century Fiction,* 9 (October 1996): 1–11;

Simon Davies, "*Lettres d'une Péruvienne,* 1977–1997: The Present State of Studies," *Studies on Voltaire and the Eighteenth Century,* (2000–2005): 295–324.

Biographies:

Georges Noël, *Une "Primitive" oubliée de l'école des coeurs sensibles: Mme de Graffigny 1695–1758* (Paris: Plon, 1913);

English Showalter Jr., "Sensibility at Cirey: Mme du Châtelet, Mme de Graffigny, and the *Voltairomanie,*" *Studies on Voltaire and the Eighteenth Century,* 135 (1975): 181–192;

Showalter, "The Beginnings of Mme de Graffigny's Literary Career: A Study in the Social History of Literature," in *Essays on the Age of Enlightenment in Honor of Ira O. Wade,* edited by Jean Macary (Geneva: Droz, 1977), pp. 293–304;

Showalter, "Mme de Graffigny and Her Salon," *Studies in Eighteenth-Century Culture,* 6 (1977): 377–391;

Showalter, "A Woman of Letters in the French Enlightenment: Mme de Graffigny," *British Journal for Eighteenth-Century Studies,* 1 (1978): 89–104.

References:

Janet Gurkin Altman, "Graffigny's Epistemology and the Emergence of Third-World Ideology," in *Writing the Female Voice: Essays on Epistolary Literature,* edited by Elizabeth C. Goldsmith (Boston: Northeastern University Press, 1989);

Altman, "Making Room for *Peru:* Graffigny's Novel Reconsidered," in *Dilemmes du roman: Essays in Honor of Georges May,* edited by Catherine Lafarge (Stanford, Cal.: Anma Libri, 1989), pp. 33–46;

Altman, "A Woman's Place in the Enlightenment Sun: The Case of F. de Graffigny," *Romance Quarterly,* 38 (August 1991): 261–272;

Centre d'étude des Lumières de l'Université de Strasbourg, *Vierge du soleil/Fille des Lumières: La Péruvienne de Mme de Graffigny et ses suites,* Travaux et Recherches, 5 (Strasbourg: Presses Universitaires, 1989);

Judith Curtis, "Anticipating Zilia: Madame de Graffigny in 1744," in *Femmes savantes et femmes d'esprit: Women Intellectuals of the French Eighteenth Century,* edited by Roland Bonnel and Catherine Rubinger (New York: Peter Lang, 1994), pp. 129–154;

Curtis, "Françoise d'Issembourg d'Happoncourt de Graffigny (1695–1758)," in *French Women Writers: A Bio-Bibliographical Source Book,* edited by Eva Martin Sartori and Dorothy Wynne Zimmerman (New York: Greenwood Press, 1991), pp. 208–217;

Curtis, "Mademoiselle Quinault and the Bout-du-banc: A Reappraisal," *Studies on Voltaire and the Eighteenth Century,* 8 (2000): 35–57;

Vera Grayson, "The Genesis and Reception of Mme de Graffigny's *Lettres d'une Péruvienne* and *Cénie,*" *Studies on Voltaire and the Eighteenth Century,* 336 (1996): 1–152;

Elizabeth J. MacArthur, "Devious Narratives: Refusal of Closure in Two Eighteenth-Century Epistolary Novels," *Eighteenth-Century Studies,* 21 (Fall 1987): 1–20;

Nancy K. Miller, "The Knot, the Letter and the Book: Graffigny's *Peruvian Letters,*" in *Subject to Change: Reading Feminist Writing* (New York: Columbia University Press, 1988), pp. 125–161;

English Showalter Jr., "Authorial Self-Consciousness in the Familiar Letter: The Case of Mme de Graffigny," *Yale French Studies,* 71 (1986): 113–130;

Showalter, "*Les Lettres d'une Péruvienne:* Composition, Publication, Suites," *Archives des bibliothèques de Belgique,* 54 (1983): 14–28;

Showalter, "Writing off the Stage: Women Authors and Eighteenth-Century Theater," *Yale French Studies,* 75 (1988): 95–111;

D. W. Smith, "La composition et la publication des contes de Mme de Graffigny," *French Studies,* 50 (1996): 275–284.

Papers:

Françoise d'Issembourg de Graffigny's papers are housed at the Beinecke Rare Book and Manuscript Library of Yale University.

Frédéric Melchior Grimm
(26 September 1723 - 19 December 1807)

John Blair
University of West Georgia

BOOKS: *Banise,* in *Die Deutsche Schaubühne: nach den Regeln und Exempeln der Alten,* volume 4 (Leipzig: Bernhard Christoph Breitkopf, 1740–1745), pp. 391–462;

De Historia Imperatoris Maximiliani I (Ratisbonne: Fratres Zunkelios, 1747);

Lettre de M. Grimm sur Omphale, tragédie lyrique, reprise par l'Académie royale de musique le 14 janvier 1752 (N.p., 1752);

Le Petit Prophète de Boehmischbroda (Paris, 1753);

Grimm and Denis Diderot, *Correspondance littéraire, philosophique et critique: adressée à un souverain d'Allemagne,* 3 parts in 16 volumes (Paris: Longchamps & Buisson, 1812–1813)—comprises Part 1, 1753–1769; [Part 2], 1770–1782; and Part 3, part of 1775–1776, and 1782–1790;

Supplément à la Correspondance littéraire, edited by Antoine-Alexandre Barbier (Paris: Potey, Buisson, Delaunay, 1814);

Correspondance inédite de Grimm et de Diderot et recueil de lettres, poesies, morceaux et fragmens retranchés par la censure imperiale en 1812 et 1813 (Paris: Furne, 1829);

Nouveaux mémoires secrets et inédits, historiques, politiques, anecdotiques et littéraires du Bon de Grimm, agent à Paris de la Cour de Russie et de Pologne, ou Chronique curieuse des personnages célèbres qui ont illustré le siècle dernier, suivie de la relation de ses voyages, 2 volumes (Paris: Lerouge-Wolf, 1834);

Gazette littéraire de Grimm, histoire, littérature, philosophie, 1753–1790. Etudes sur Grimm, edited by Charles-Augustin Sainte-Beuve and Paulin Limayrac (Paris: Eugène Didier, 1854);

La Correspondance littéraire, 1er janvier–15 juin 1760, 2 volumes, edited by Sigun Dafgård (Stockholm: Almqvist & Wiksell International, 1981).

Editions: *Correspondance littéraire, philosophique et critique par Grimm, Diderot, Raynal, Meister, etc., revue sur les textes originaux, comprenant outre ce qui a été publié à diverses époques les fragments supprimés en 1813 par la censure, les parties inédites conservées à la Bibliothèque*

Frédéric Melchior Grimm (Carmontelle, musée Condé, Chantilly; from Jeannette Rosso, Diderot et le portrait, *1998; Perkins Library, Duke University)*

ducale de Gotha et à l'Arsenal à Paris . . . , 16 volumes, edited by Maurice Tourneux (Paris: Garnier frères, 1877–1882).

Editions in English: *Historical & Literary Memoirs and Anecdotes, Selected from the Correspondence of Baron de Grimm and Diderot with the Duke of Saxe-Gotha, and Many Other Distinguished Persons, Between the Years of 1770 and 1790,* 2 volumes (London: Printed for H. Colburn, 1814);

Historical & Literary Memoirs and Anecdotes, Selected from the Correspondence of Baron de Grimm and Diderot with the

Duke of Saxe-Gotha, and Many Other Distinguished Persons, Between the Years of 1753 and 1790, 4 volumes (London: Printed for H. Colburn, 1815).

OTHER: "Du poème lyrique," in *Encyclopédie ou dictionnaire raisonné des sciences, des arts et des métiers par une sociéte de gens de lettres: mis en ordre & publié par M. Diderot; & quant à la partie mathématique, par M. d'Alembert* (Neufchâtel: Samuel Faulche, 1765), XII: 823–836.

SELECTED PERIODICAL PUBLICATIONS–UNCOLLECTED: *Lettres à l'auteur du Mercure sur la littérature allemande,* August 1750 and February 1751;
Préface du Journal étranger (Paris: Au Bureau du Journal étranger, 1754);
Mémoire historique sur l'origine et les suites de mon attachement pour l'impératrice Catherine II jusqu'au décès de sa Majesté Impériale; printed in *Correspondance littéraire* (Paris: Garnier frères, 1877–1882), I: 17–63.

Frédéric Melchior Grimm is best known for the *Correspondance littéraire, philosophique et critique* (1753–1790, Literary, Philosophical, and Critical Correspondence), a secret journal circulated in manuscript to a limited circle of prominent subscribers among the European nobility. In two issues monthly, it reported on events in Paris and reviewed performances and new works of all sorts–philosophical, political, and literary. It has been used by many scholars searching for background information on the second half of the eighteenth century and for the details of cultural discourse and literary life in Paris during that period. Although other secret journals from that time exist, the *Correspondance littéraire* is the most valuable and most often cited. Grimm was able to gain favor with Voltaire, Denis Diderot, Jean-Jacques Rousseau, Louise d'Epinay, and many other important cultural figures in Paris, and he was admitted to, and even courted at, literary salons almost from his arrival. He was on intimate terms with important philosophical and literary figures and could often count on them for submissions. In fact, because of the danger of publishing controversial works in France at that time, Diderot's *Jacques le fataliste* (1796; translated as *James the Fatalist and His Master,* 1797) was published in the *Correspondance littéraire*–where Johann Wolfgang von Goethe read it in one enthusiastic five-and-a-half-hour sitting–almost twenty years before it appeared in France. Several of Diderot's other works were also published in this manner, thereby establishing his reputation in Germany well in advance of that in France. Grimm's ideas and convictions made him an ally of the philosophes, and his regular support for the *Encyclopédie* (1751–1782) in the *Correspondance littéraire* helped to give it an international profile. His training, sensibility, and frankness brought innovation to opera and drama criticism. Perhaps most importantly, despite Grimm's access to insider information, he remained an outsider–a German who brought with him to Paris the senses of a stranger and an enthusiastic if critical interest in Parisian cultural life. Grimm is also well known for his connections to major political figures, particularly after he retired from editing the *Correspondance littéraire.* He visited Catherine the Great in Russia twice for extended periods and corresponded with her on a regular basis from 1774 until her death in 1796.

Grimm was born in Regensburg on 26 September 1723, the youngest of five brothers. His parents were respected members of the community despite their limited means. His father, Johann Melchior Grimm, was a Lutheran minister, and two of his brothers also became ministers. Grimm's mother, Sybilla-Margaretha, was long-lived, for she was in good mental and physical health at the age of eighty-five when Grimm visited her in 1769.

The German political and literary situation in the first half of the eighteenth century shaped Grimm's perspective on French literature and culture, and informed his later writings. Throughout that century, Germany existed as a nation, in the sense of a unified state, only in the minds of patriotic idealists. It was composed of more than three hundred independent principalities, a patchwork quilt the borders of which constantly shifted according to feuds, marriages, purchases, and treaties. Germany also lacked a consistent grammar, and many dialects were still competing to become the standard literary language. These problems are probably the reason that the French language and its philosophical and literary discourses exercised hegemonic power in German courts and literary circles. Frederick II was educated in French and preferred French literature and language; he hosted Voltaire many times in Potsdam at his castle Sans Souci.

As a young man, Grimm was already exposed to discussions of national literature and well aware of the relationship between literature and politics and national prestige. His oldest brother, who later became a senator of the imperial city of Regensburg, tutored the two sons of Count Johann Friedrich von Schönberg, a prominent nobleman in Saxony's political circles. This brother passed on recent literature and criticism to Grimm, who was particularly impressed with Johann Christoph Gottsched's *Versuch einer critischen Dichtkunst vor die Deutschen* (1730, Attempt at a Critical Art of Poetry for the Germans). Gottsched was a powerhouse of energy–editing periodicals and reforming the theater as well as German grammar and style. At age eighteen Grimm wrote to Gottsched, praising him for encouraging the

Germans to follow in the footsteps of the ancient Greeks and Romans, and the seventeenth-century French authors. Grimm was convinced that by following these models Germany would establish its own classical literature and would outshine that of its neighbors. Gottsched answered Grimm's letter, and his encouragement inspired the young man to write a tragedy according to Gottsched's principles. He chose a plot originating with Heinrich Anselm von Zigler's novel *Die asiatische Banise oder das blutig-doch mutige Pegu* (1689, Banise from Asia or the Bloody but Courageous Pegu). Because of its popularity (ten printings between 1689 and 1766), it spawned several theatrical productions, but they failed to follow the Aristotelian unities. Grimm revised his own dramatic version according to Gottsched's suggestions two years later while he was taking courses at the University of Leipzig. The play was successfully performed in Frankfurt and Strasbourg, and Gottsched published it in *Die deutsche Schaubühne: nach den Regeln und Exempeln der Alten* (1740–1745, The German Theater According to the Rules and Examples of the Ancients)—a six-volume collection of German plays and translations from other literatures meant as models for future German playwrights. At the university, Grimm studied poetry and philosophy with Gottsched, history and law with Johann Jacob Mascov, and Greek and Latin with Johann August Ernesti, all well-known scholars of the day.

Grimm left the university in 1745 to become a tutor for Schönberg, who conducted much of his professional and family life in French, as did many among the German upper aristocracy. This post forced Grimm to strengthen his knowledge of French. The relationship to this family proved an important part of his political education as well, for when the count represented Saxon electors and the king of Poland at the Diet of the Holy Roman Empire in Frankfurt, Grimm accompanied him. Despite his duties as tutor and political secretary, and despite a serious illness in 1746, Grimm finished his thesis, *De Historia Imperatoris Maximiliani I* (On the History of Emperor Maximilian I) in 1747, dedicating it to his friend Gottlob, Schönberg's eldest son. Grimm's political interests surfaced in this text, which describes the changes in public imperial law during the reign of Maximilian I. Soon thereafter, Gottlob left to become an officer in Count August Heinrich von Friesen's regiment in France. Before long, Grimm followed Gottlob to Paris as a companion of Adolf Heinrich, the count of Schönberg's youngest son.

Grimm must already have been considering a more independent future, since he remained with the Schönbergs only briefly before becoming a reader for Friedrich, the crown prince of Saxe-Gotha, at whose apartment he encountered Rousseau. Rousseau's *Confessions* (1782) indicate that this position was also temporary; Grimm was there "qui lui servait de lecteur en attendant qu'il trouvât quelque place, et dont l'équipage très mince annonçait le pressant besoin de la trouver" (only until he could find some other place, which his modest wardrobe betrayed his urgent need of so doing). Rousseau was quite taken by the young German: "je passais avec lui tous les moments que j'avais de libres, à chanter des airs italiens et debararolles sans trêve et sans relâche du matin au soir, ou plutôt du soir au matin" (I spent all my free moments with him, singing Italian airs and barcarolles, without pause or intermission from morning till evening, or rather from evening till morning). He introduced Grimm to many luminaries of Parisian literary life—including Diderot, Jean-Vincent Gauffecourt, Epinay, and Paul-Henri Thiry, baron d'Holbach. In 1749 Grimm found a better position as secretary for von Friesen, perhaps on Gottlob von Schönberg's recommendation. Other sources document Grimm's popularity in these circles: he was a favorite at both Suzanne Curchod Necker's and Epinay's salons. He acquired the respect of Voltaire and developed an especially deep and lasting friendship with Diderot.

By then, Grimm had established himself in Parisian salon circles that included many of the most famous people of the era. His first articles published in Paris were on German literature and appeared in the *Mercure de France*—an officially sanctioned and censored literary journal—in August 1750 and February 1751. In these *"Lettres à l'auteur du Mercure sur la littérature allemande"* (Letters to the Author of the *Mercure* on German Literature), Grimm introduced his native literature to the French public. Through references to France's *grand siècle* (great century)—the seventeenth—he suggests a relationship between political unity and cultural production. The German lack of unity and the absence of a great German cultural center such as Paris are the bases for the temporary mediocrity of German literature. A ruler such as Frederick II of Prussia could promote the development of German literature by encouraging the imitation of works of great cultural renaissances. However, despite his appreciation of French literature, he has failed to encourage its integration into German culture. According to Marilyn Sides, such a critic as Gottsched would have to be the one to invigorate the culture, "by borrowing the discoveries of and by inculcating a taste for the ancient *grands siècles*" and by creating "a public, a nation of educated and eager readers and writers." In his letters, Grimm also criticized the contemporary state of French culture as decadent, noting that other countries appreciated Molière, Pierre Corneille, and Jean Racine more than the French did. He urged Germany to imitate the artistic productions of

Grimm (left) in conversation with Denis Diderot (Carmontelle, musée Condé, Chantilly, Collection of Baron J. Le Vavasseur; from Arthur M. Wilson, Diderot, *1972; collection of W. Ross)*

the Greeks, the Romans, and seventeenth-century French authors and believed that contemporary French writers would benefit from doing likewise.

Grimm was well known in Parisian literary circles in part because of a celebrated and unrequited passion for Marie Fel, a popular opera singer. He made a name for himself among the reading public with his pamphlets during the *Querelle des Bouffons* (War of the Buffoons), a polemic between those who supported Italian opera buffa (opera of a light and amusing nature) and those who did not. This dispute over the relative merits of Italian and French opera had both musical and political bases. French opera of the time represented the power and authority of the monarchy. In pageants of pomp and circumstance, the kings of France were patriotically celebrated on the stage as gods and symbols of national superiority. When the Italian *opera buffo* troupe arrived in Paris in 1752, it performed shorter pieces either before or between the acts of French tragedies. The two competing genres could, as Rousseau notes, "entendues le même jour, sur le même théâtre" (be heard on the same day and in the same theater). Because of the political content of French opera and the recent suspension of the publication of the *Encyclopédie,* the philosophes supported Italian music, whereas the "L'un, plus puissant, plus numbreux, composé des grands, des riches et des femmes, soutenait la musique française" (more powerful and more numerous party, made up of the great, the rich, and the ladies, supported French music).

Grimm's first pamphlet, *Lettre de M. Grimm sur Omphale* (1752, Letter of Mr. Grimm on Omphale), was a response to an opera by André, Cardinal Destouches. At a time when opera criticism was a polite affirmation of the court's taste and negative criticism seen as disloyal and unpatriotic, Grimm suggested that taste should be guided by aesthetic principles and that intellectuals, particularly the philosophes, should strive to formulate and disseminate these principles. French opera had changed little since it was institutionalized by Louis XIV; and pieces by Jean-Baptiste Lully—who had been dead for sixty-five years—continued to dominate its repertoire. Despite Grimm's suggestion that the philosophes guide the public in matters of taste, he believed that the public (in direct comparison with the people of ancient Athens) should choose for themselves. He also noted that all the other countries had chosen the Italian opera because "ils ont préféré leur plaisir à leurs prétentions" (they preferred their pleasures to their pretensions). Grimm suggested that the real content of opera was the reactions and emotions of humans in extreme situations and that recitatives emphasizing the values of the court destroyed the effect of such moments.

Lettre de M. Grimm sur Omphale unleashed a flood of pamphlets from both camps, and Grimm followed in January 1753 with *Le Petit Prophète de Boehmischbroda* (The Little Prophet of Boehmischbroda), a fictional narrative parodying French musicals. A student in Prague is seized by the hair and transported to Paris where he sees visions and hears voices. He describes these sights in mock-biblical language, comparing a director's vigorous use of a baton trying to keep the violins together to both punishment (whipping the bad violins) and woodcutting. In fact, the student is amazed that the director does not dislocate his shoulder. The little prophet concludes that talent is often misplaced, that this director would have earned more money and respect as a woodcutter, and that despite his efforts, the musicians fail to stay together.

The voice heard by the little prophet complained that it had given France the greatest talents in the century of Louis XIV, but that France now seemed unable to hear it. It also said that the men who could continue this great tradition were the philosophes. Although the voice also wanted to give France musical genius in the *grand siècle,* the country had managed to create "un opéra qui m'ennuie depuis quatre-vingts ans, et qui fait la risée de l'Europe jusqu'à ce jour" (an opera that has bored me for the last eighty years and has been the laughingstock of Europe until this day). The voice threatens that if the French do not reform their opera, it will make them completely unable to distinguish good from bad in all the arts, and they will eventually succumb to complete moral and intellectual decay.

Le Petit Prophète des Boehmischbroda was enormously successful. Grimm bragged to Gottsched that it went through three editions in less than one month. Voltaire praised its Parisian wit, and it was translated into German in the same year (1753) by Luise Gottsched.

Grimm's fame opened new doors for him. He was offered the editorship of a new journal in 1754, *Le Journal étranger* (The Foreign Journal), dedicated to literatures from other countries. He wrote only the preface, however, in which he again criticized contemporary taste before deciding that he would prefer to spend more of his time working on French literature. He also felt an increasing drive to independence. In a letter to Gottsched dated 23 June 1753, he wrote that he was no longer Friesen's secretary but just living in his house; and a year later (2 May 1754), he requested that Gottsched avoid addressing him by rank or title, which are "ridicules en ce païs-ci où l'on trouve qu'un honnête homme ne peut rien porter de plus honorable que son nom tout court" (ridiculous in this country where one finds that an honorable man can carry nothing more honorable than his own name).

He began work with this attitude on the *Correspondance littéraire,* which he edited from 1753 to 1773 and for which he was also the predominant contributor. Some sources claim that Grimm took over and renamed abbé Guillaume Raynal's *Nouvelles littéraires,* but the overlap of more than a year suggests that the *Correspondance littéraire* was a completely independent project. The endeavor clearly involved internal tension and ambivalence. Grimm owed his current position to his family's connection to Schönberg and to a series of appointments resulting from the favors of various members of the nobility. The independence Grimm sought could only be partial, since he was to take a position as Louis-Philippe, duc d'Orléans's secretary when Friesen died in 1755. And the *Correspondance littéraire* was, after all, a secret journal subscribed to solely by sovereign kings and princes. Grimm no doubt noticed that public frankness was a dangerous occupation, since his friend Diderot was imprisoned in 1749; the publication, sale, and distribution of the *Encyclopédie* was suppressed by the Conseil du Roi (King's Council) in 1752; and Rousseau was also nearly imprisoned in 1752 for his pamphlet on Italian opera. A secret journal was undoubtedly the only outlet for a frank and outspoken critic, even though secrecy and limited circulation also reduced the influence Grimm hoped to exercise on contemporary culture.

Because the journal was secret and despite that the subscribers were all royalty, Grimm remained objective, even harsh, in the *Correspondance littéraire.* In the first issue, he described his intentions, dedicating the journal "à la vérité, à la confiance et à la franchise" (to truth, trust, and frankness). Although he set out to review only worthy works–especially theater and opera–and to avoid the many inferior ones, Grimm was inevitably forced to review a few of the latter kind and made good his claim to frankness. He described one work as "mal écrite, et d'un style puérilement précieux" (badly written in a childish precious style) and another as using "un jargon aussi fatigant qu'insipide" (a language as tiring as it is insipid).

Grimm's various nicknames suggest his critical stance. His friends called him *criticus, le tyran blanc,* and *le prophète* (critic, white tyrant, and prophet). Indeed, his absolutist tendency–the second nickname refers to a penchant for powdering his face–was justified by his critical endeavor and his negative vision of contemporary French literature. He saw himself in the role he earlier described for Gottsched, as a critic responsible for encouraging the reestablishment of a *grand siècle* by reawakening good taste in the public. Contemporary opera and theater productions only maintained a bored tranquility in the populace. Both genres were stylized and unrealistic; they entertained spectators rather than engaged them. Like Diderot, Grimm was an early advocate of a more realistic trend in French drama that gained strength as the century progressed. He was particularly interested in a more realistic presentation of human emotions and the depiction of grand passions. Grimm hoped that the shared experience of the audience reacting together to a human conflict on the stage would instill in them a sense of community or nation and that the power of real passion in the plays would encourage a moral strength that Grimm associated with the ancients, as opposed to a more facile concept of moral betterment closely linked to Enlightenment drama.

In his reviews, Grimm showed little interest in the function of a play as a medium for criticizing vice. He was interested in its concrete and realistic depiction of complex human relations, thus leading to a better understanding of human beings. One of Grimm's favorite techniques in his reviews was to remake a play, to show how it could be made more realistic and more moving. He often suggested making the characters more complex in order to make choices more difficult and thus increase the dramatic potential of the work. Visual aspects were also important to him: he recommended background action, effective placement of figures onstage, and appropriate gestures. In moments of high passion, he believed that action was more realistic than reasoned dialogue, and he found long and calm monologues ridiculous. For example, he thought that angry lovers should act in an agitated manner, and Cassandra could hardly be expected to speak reasonably and even optimistically about the fortunes of the Greeks while Troy was being destroyed in the background.

Although Grimm had the greatest respect for Racine and Corneille, he did not expect contemporary playwrights to follow exactly the same principles. In fact, from the outset of the *Correspondance littéraire,* he praised English theater, especially the works of William Shakespeare—complete anathema to neoclassical aesthetics—which he appreciated for the power of their language and their dramatic situations, just as Voltaire did in his *Lettres philosophiques* (1734, Philosophical Letters). Near the end of Grimm's tenure as editor, he described his great enjoyment while seeing *Romeo and Juliet* at Covent Garden in London.

In the *Correspondance littéraire,* Grimm's emphasis on rational argument, his regular support of the *Encyclopédie,* and his criticism of religion and the ancien régime all aligned him with the philosophes. In his criticism of theater and of opera, and his discussions of historiography, he appeared to be an early historicist with an appreciation for other peoples, their mores, and their cultures. Just as he encouraged French theater to evoke strong emotions, so he asked historical texts to inspire aesthetic appreciation and even identification with the most primitive cultures, rather than chronicle a series of events with an added moral. This awareness of context as a determinant carried over to his understanding of the position of women in society. In a reaction against Rousseau's *Discours sur l'origine de l'inégalité* (1755, Discourse on the Origin of Inequality), which posited women's complete inferiority and subordination as the result of their physiology, Grimm defended women at length, arguing that any inadequacies in their achievements resulted from the social context to which they were exposed and the limitations imposed on their education and activities. Grimm and Diderot's break with Rousseau occurred soon after this article, exacerbated further by Rousseau's questionable courtship of Sophie d'Houdetot and his lack of support of Epinay, Grimm's mistress from 1753 until her death in 1783. Grimm himself was appreciative and supportive of Epinay's literary career and entrusted her with the *Correspondance littéraire* for months at a time during his absences.

The twenty years that Grimm spent writing and editing the *Correspondance littéraire* were interrupted or complicated by several journeys and events that contributed to his political experience. From March until September 1757, he accompanied the duc d'Orléans on a military campaign against Frederick II during the Seven Years' War (1756–1763). Late in 1759, the city of Frankfurt was under French occupation and Grimm was appointed to the post of special ambassador—an influential and lucrative position. Unfortunately, he lost this post in early 1761, when the secret office of the postal service intercepted one of his letters to Germany and discovered criticism of French conduct in the war. He visited Louise-Dorothea, Duchesse of Saxe-Gotha, in September 1762 and thereafter served as her unofficial chargé d'affaires (business representative) in Paris.

The interest in music that Grimm exhibited during the *Querelle des Bouffons* also continued throughout the rest of his stay in Paris. In 1765, he published an article in the *Encyclopédie,* "Du poëme lyrique," which repeated many of the critical ideas already presented in *Lettre de M. Grimm sur Omphale* and *Le Petit Prophète des Boehmischbroda,* with additional theorizing on the origin of music and the potential utopian social function of a new opera—the establishment of a higher human community. On a more practical level, he met seven-year-old Wolfgang Amadeus Mozart and his family in Paris in 1763, recognized his talent, arranged concerts and salon appearances for the young prodigy, and supported the family in every possible way. Leopold Mozart, Wolfgang's father, wrote from Paris (1 April 1764) that "dieser mein großer Freund, von dem ich hier alles habe, dieser Mr. Grimm [. . .] hat Alles getan" (This, my great friend, from whom I have everything here, is Mr. Grimm [. . .], he has done everything). Grimm helped Mozart again in 1766 and in March 1778, when the young man and his mother traveled to Paris. After the mother's sudden death on 2 July 1778, Grimm and Epinay took Mozart into their home for several months. Eventually, the two men became estranged, and the young Austrian left hurriedly in early September.

After 1769, Grimm wrote less and less for the *Correspondance littéraire* and played more and more the role of a courtier. He visited several European courts and received many honors. In Vienna, he was awarded the title and diploma of baron of the Holy Empire; and in Gotha he was granted both the official title of Councilor and Legation for the Court of Saxe-Gotha and an annual stipend. In 1773, at Catherine the Great's request, Grimm accompanied Prince Louis of Hesse-Darmstadt to a wedding in St. Petersburg. On the way, they spent several weeks in Berlin and Potsdam visiting Frederick II, finally arriving in St. Petersburg in September 1773.

Grimm described his seven months in St. Petersburg in glowing terms. He saw Catherine on a daily basis, greatly enjoying their conversations. Yet, he managed to evade her offer of a position at the court, saying that he was too old at fifty to learn Russian well and that he could hardly abandon Epinay. After an illness Grimm attributed to the weather, he left in April 1774, promising to write regularly and to return for another visit after traveling to Italy. He returned to Paris in October 1774, after visiting King Stanislas August in Warsaw, Prince Henry of Prussia in Rheinsberg, and Frederick II in Berlin, and spending two months at a spa in Carlsbad.

A year later, in October 1775, Grimm traveled to Italy in the company of counts Nikolai and Sergei Rumiantzev, and then again to St. Petersburg, pausing at all of the major courts along the way. This time he spent almost an entire year with Catherine in extended daily contact, seeing her "au moins une fois par jour; passant pour l'ordinaire deux ou trois, quelquefois quatre et une fois jusqu'à sept heures de suite, tête à tête avec elle, sans que la conversation tarît un instant" (at least once a day, spending usually two or three hours, sometimes four and once even seven hours in private conversation with her without it ever flagging). Again, he declined a position in her government but accepted a post as her representative in Paris with an annual stipend of 2,000 rubles. From the end of Grimm's first visit in 1773 until Catherine's death in 1796, they maintained a prodigious correspondence about literature and their daily lives.

Since he had written almost nothing for the *Correspondance littéraire* since 1773, Grimm passed the editorship of the journal to Jacques-Henri Meister, who had been doing much of the work in his absence, with the help of Epinay and Diderot. Grimm's position as Catherine's factotum kept him busy. He arranged for the purchase of Diderot's and Voltaire's libraries, evaluated and purchased art collections, hired architects and actors, received visitors that Catherine sent from Russia, and asked her for favors for his friends. She gave Epinay a pension after French changes in government reduced and finally eliminated her income. Grimm lost his friend and mistress of thirty years in April 1783. That same year, with Catherine's financial assistance, Grimm arranged for the rent of a ground-floor apartment for Diderot, whose health was failing and who died a year later. Grimm continued to serve Catherine's interests in Paris and received the Great Cross of the Order of Saint Vladimir in 1785 for his exemplary service.

After Epinay's death, Grimm took on the responsibility for her granddaughter Emilie and arranged her marriage to count Louis Du Roux de Bueil, a young officer in the French guard. The couple and their three children became Grimm's adoptive family, with whom

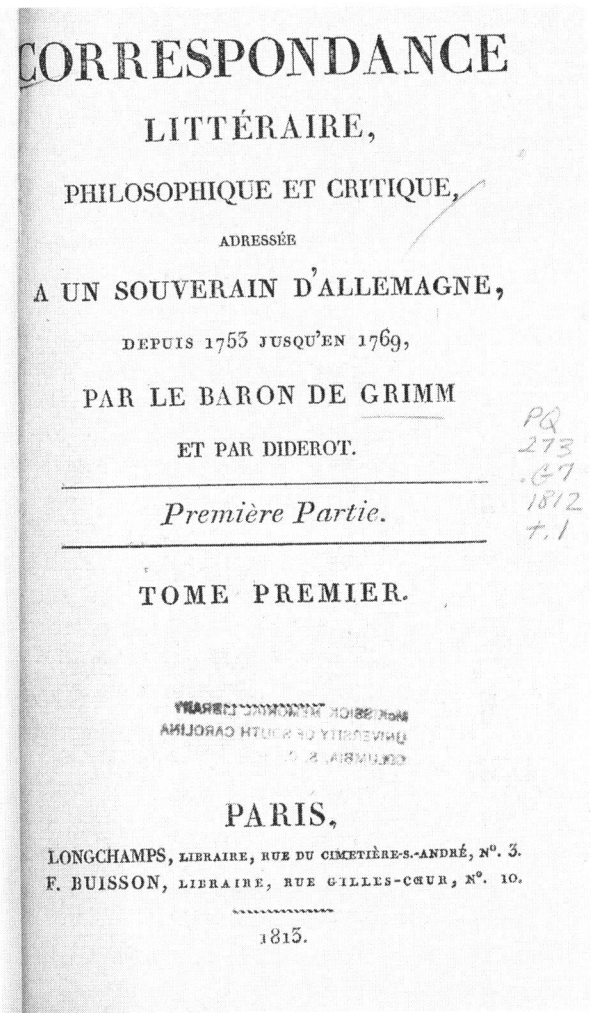

Title page for the first volume of the collected edition of Grimm and Diderot's secret journal, sent to subscribers among the royalty of Europe, reporting events and reviewing new literary works in France (Thomas Cooper Library, University of South Carolina)

he experienced the Revolution, its aftermath, and his final years. In 1791, the family decided to leave France. The count joined the European military campaign against France, and Emilie and the three children had to move from one city to the next as each city in turn expelled the émigrés fleeing revolutionary France. Johann Wolfgang von Goethe, who accompanied Karl August, duke of Saxe-Weimar, on a military campaign against the insurgents, describes it in "Campagne in Frankreich" (Campaign in France) and details meeting Grimm and "Frau von Bueil" in Pempelfort in November 1792. That December, despite difficult conditions, Grimm sent the family to Gotha and rejoined them in February 1793. Ernst II, duc de Saxe-Gotha, provided them with a house, and, two months before her death,

Catherine II named him her minister to Hamburg, thus ensuring him an adequate income. Ten years later, Grimm died on 19 December 1807, at age eighty-four.

Frédéric Melchior Grimm led a long and eventful life, in which he participated in the beginning of a cultural renaissance in Germany and brought his own enthusiasm for literature, culture, and politics with him to France. His views on opera, theater, and historiography helped to shape those of his era, while the reviews, reports, and anecdotes in the *Correspondance littéraire* give readers today an understanding of the Paris salons, the difficulties of publishing the *Encyclopédie,* and the literary problems and endeavors of the time. Grimm's monumental body of writings and letters has continued to be of interest to historians and literary scholars.

Letters:

Louise d'Epinay, *Mémoires et correspondance de madame d'Épinay: où elle donne des détails sur ses liaisons avec Duclos, J.-J. Rousseau, Grimm, Diderot, le baron d'Holbach, Saint-Lambert, Mme d'Houdetot, et autres personnages célèbres du dix-huitième siècle; ouvrage renfermant un grand nombre de lettres inédites de Grimm, de Diderot et de J.-J. Rousseau . . .* (Paris: Volland, 1818);

Lettres de Grimm à l'impératrice Catherine II (St. Petersburg, 1881);

Correspondance inédite (1794–1801) du baron Grimm au comte de Findlster, edited by André Cazes (Paris: Presses universitaires de France, 1934);

Correspondance inédite de Frédéric Melchior Grimm, edited by Jochen Schlobach (München: Fink, 1972).

Biographies:

Edmond Henri Adolphe Scherer, *Melchior Grimm, l'homme de lettres, le factotum—le diplomate, avec un appendice sur la correspondance secrète de Métra* (Paris: Lévy, 1887);

André Cazes, *Grimm et les Encyclopédistes* (Paris: Presses universitaires de France, 1933).

References:

Maurice Cranston, *The Solitary Self: Jean-Jacques Rousseau in Exile and Adversity* (Chicago: Chicago University Press, 1997);

George P. Gooch, *Catherine the Great and Other Studies* (Hamden, Conn.: Archon, 1966);

Anne Cutting Jones, *Frederick Melchior Grimm as a Critic of Eighteenth-Century French Drama,* dissertation, Bryn Mawr College, 1926;

Siegfried Jüttner, *Grundtendenzen der Theaterkritik von Friedrich-Melchior Grimm (1753–1773)* (Wiesbaden: Franz Steiner Verlag, 1969);

Emile Lizé, *Voltaire, Grimm et la Correspondance Littéraire* (Oxford: Voltaire Foundation, 1979);

Paul Nettl, *Der kleine Prophet von Böhmisch-Brod: Mozart und Grimm* (Esslingen: Bechtle Verlag, 1953)—includes a biographical introduction by Nettl, pp. 5–52, and a translation of *Le Petit Prophète* into German, pp. 53–87;

Jolanta T. Pekacz, "Gender as a Political Orientation: Parisian Salonnières and the Querelle des Bouffons," *Canadian Journal of History* (December 1997): 405–414;

John Pizer, "Friedrich-Melchior Grimm's Views on French Seventeenth Century Literature," *Papers on French Seventeenth Century Literature,* 11 (1984): 167–181;

Jeannette Rosso, *Diderot et le portrait* (Pisa: Libreria Goliardica, 1998);

Jean-Jacques Rousseau, *The Confessions of Jean-Jacques Rousseau,* translated, and with an introduction, by J. M. Cohen (London: Penguin, 1953);

Leon Schwartz, "F. M. Grimm and the Eighteenth-Century Debate on Women," *French Review,* 58 (1984): 236–243;

Schwartz, "Melchior Grimm on War and Peace," *French Review,* 40 (1967): 756–764;

Marilyn Sides, *The Fate of Culture: The Criticism of Frederick Melchior Grimm (1753–1772),* dissertation, Johns Hopkins University, 1984;

Joseph Royall Smiley, "Diderot's Relations with Grimm," *Illinois Studies in Language and Literature,* 34, no. 4 (1950);

Arthur M. Wilson, *Diderot* (New York: Oxford University Press, 1972).

Papers:

Frédéric Melchior Grimm's letters and manuscripts are scattered throughout Europe, Russia, and Sweden. Major collections may be found in Paris, at the Bibliothèque de l'Arsenal and the Bibliothèque Nationale; in Moscow, at the Archives d'actes anciens d'URSS; in Gotha, at the Forschungsbibliothek, Schloss Friedenstein; in Weimar, at the Staatsarchiv and the Goethe-Schiller-Archiv; in Stockholm, at the Royal Library; in Upsalla, at the University Library Carolina; in Zurich, at the Bibiothèque centrale; and in Dresden, at the Sächsische Landesbibliothek.

Claude-Adrien Helvétius

(26 December 1715 – 26 December 1771)

Katharine Ann Jensen
Louisiana State University

BOOKS: *De l'Esprit* (Paris: Durand, 1758); translated as *De l'Esprit: or, Essay on the Mind, and its Several Faculties* (London: Dodsley, 1759);

Le Bonheur, poëme en 6 chants, avec des fragments de quelques épîtres, ouvrages posthumes de M. Helvétius [Précédé de l'histoire de sa vie et de ses ouvrages, par Saint-Lambert] (London, 1772);

De l'Homme, de ses facultés intellectuelles et de son éducation. Ouvrage posthume (London: Société Typographique, 1773); translated by W. Hooper as *A Treatise on Man, His Intellectual Faculties and His Education*, 2 volumes (London: B. Law & G. Robinson, 1777);

Oeuvres complettes (4 volumes, Liège: Bassompierre, 1774; corrected and augmented edition, 5 volumes, Paris: Servière, 1795);

Les Progrès de la raison dans la recherche du vrai, ouvrage posthume (London, 1775).

Helvétius, one of the most radical philosophes, is best known for his sensationalist and materialist thought and its controversial reception. Building on works by John Locke, Thomas Hobbes, Bernard de Mandeville, Etienne Bonnot de Condillac, Julien Offroy de La Mettrie, and Morelly, he maintained that humans are born equal insofar as they are blank slates and neither good nor bad. All their ideas, faculties, feelings, and morality are produced from outside influences. Although education can channel their feeling in socially productive ways, they are continually subject to physical sensation, which produces a feeling either of pleasure or of pain. On the basis of these sensations, humans naturally–that is, automatically or mechanically–avoid pain while seeking pleasure. As a pleasure-seeking being or machine, man is motivated by self-interest. Through education and a legislative system of punishments and rewards, this self-interest can be socialized and trained to serve the public good.

Helvétius's synthesis of sensationalist and materialist philosophy in *De l'Esprit* (1758; translated as *De l'Esprit: or, Essay on the Mind, and its Several Faculties*, 1759) revealed the socially radical and antireligious implica-

Claude-Adrien Helvétius (portrait by van Loo, 1755; collection of Comte and Comtesse D'Andlau, from Ian Cumming, Helvétius, 1955; Thomas Cooper Library, University of South Carolina)

tions of these schools of thought, and this revelation unleashed the wrath of the Catholic church and the Parlement. Helvétius's right to publish *De l'Esprit*–its *privilège du roi*–was revoked in 1759, and he was obliged to retract his work three times, twice before the Jesuits at the Sorbonne and once before the Parlement. Mme de Pompadour, Louis XV's mistress, intervened on his behalf, however, and he was saved from personal harm. Meanwhile, as the target of such furor, *De l'Esprit* became a best-seller in clandestine editions.

Claude-Adrien Helvétius was born in Paris on 26 December 1715 to Geneviève-Noëlle de Carvoisin d'Armancourt and Jean Claude Adrien Helvétius, who was principal physician to the queen, Marie Leszczynska, wife of Louis XV. Claude's great-grandfather, Johan Schweitzer, a Catholic, had left Protestant Germany to seek refuge in Holland, where he studied medicine and changed his name to Helvétius. His son, Jean Adrien Helvétius–Claude's grandfather–settled in Paris and developed ipecacuanha as a cure for dysentery; he cured the Grand Dauphin of this ailment. Although the family had produced doctors for several generations, Claude's parents sought a financial career for him. He trained under a maternal uncle, who directed tax-farming in Caen, and in 1738, thanks to the queen's influence, Claude was appointed *fermier général* (Farmer General). *Fermiers généraux* were a group of financiers who, through an agreement with the Crown, had the right to collect indirect taxes and the income from the royal domain and to manage the royal monopolies (especially salt and tobacco). In return, the group paid the Crown a specified advance and annual sum. The position of *fermier général* was lucrative, and Helvétius gained a small fortune during the eleven years he held the position.

While he worked as a *fermier général*, traveling around various provinces, he also frequented several salons in Paris, notably those of Claudine de Tencin, Marie-Thérèse Geoffrin, and Françoise de Graffigny. In the literary and philosophical milieu of the salons, he composed a poem on happiness, *Le Bonheur* (1772, Happiness) and began writing *De l'Esprit* in the 1740s. At Graffigny's, he met Anne-Catherine de Ligniville d'Autricourt, a distant cousin of the *salonnière*, whom she had rescued from a bleak convent life in Lorraine and brought to Paris. Anne-Catherine came from a noble but impecunious family and struck Helvétius as a most pleasing young woman. She, in turn, was taken with him. They were married in 1751. By then, Helvétius had given up his position as *fermier général* and taken on the position of *maître d'hôtel ordinaire* (chief steward) to the queen. He also planned to devote time to thinking and writing and had bought, prior to his marriage, two country estates, Voré in Perche and Lumigny in Brie. He and Anne-Catherine spent the spring and summer at their country homes while wintering in Paris. They had four children, two of whom, both daughters, Elisabeth-Charlotte and Geneviève-Adélaïde, lived to adulthood.

The calm existence that Helvétius enjoyed as a philosopher and a family man was violently interrupted when he published *De l'Esprit* in 1758. He had great ambitions for this work, hoping it would make his reputation as a man of letters. Despite his sensationalist and materialist premises–he sought to treat morality like experimental physics–he was a rationalist rather than an experimental scientist and so never really adhered in a rigorous way to experimental methods. In fact, like René Descartes, Helvétius thought truth was fundamentally simple, and he eschewed complexity on principle as a sign of falsehood. This inclination toward the simple perhaps explains his naiveté, for he did not anticipate that *De l'Esprit* would provoke the crisis it did; he trusted in his influential social position and in having published his book through official channels. More to the point, earlier works on sensationalism, such as Condillac's *Traité des sensations* (1754, Treatise on Sensations), had escaped condemnation. On the other hand, Denis Diderot had been imprisoned in 1749 for his materialist *Lettre sur les aveugles* (1749, Letter on the Blind), while La Mettrie had fled to Holland three years earlier to escape punishment for his materialist *Histoire naturelle de l'âme* (1746, Natural History of the Soul). Furthermore, the first two volumes of the *Encyclopédie*, (1751–1780), with which *De l'Esprit* had clear ideological affinities, had been banned in 1752. Nonetheless, Helvétius was persuaded by a philosopher friend, Charles Georges Leroy, to proceed through official channels rather than publish abroad, as other writers of controversial works did in order to avoid Church and State censure and punishment. Leroy manipulated matters such that the censor, Jean-Paul Tercier, never read all of *De l'Esprit* and thus granted it his approbation as including nothing immoral or irreligious. A second, unknown, censor, appointed by the director of the book trade, Chrétien-Guillaume de Lamoignon de Malesherbes, demanded some revisions but recommended publication, and so *De l'Esprit* was published. Helvétius withheld his name from the publication, hoping that a supposedly anonymous work would protect him and his book from the Church's condemnation.

This attempt at anonymity did not protect him or his work. Indeed, the authorship of *De l'Esprit* was never in doubt, and the book ignited a conflict between the Church doctors at the Sorbonne and the Parlement, and between the Jansenists and Jesuits, who were traditional rivals over Catholic doctrine; in the end, Helvétius was held accountable for irreligious ideas. In some ways, Helvétius's book served as a pawn in political maneuvering, which had to do only superficially with the sensationalist and materialist content of the work. In other ways, this content was clearly understood by Catholic powers to endanger religion and, therefore, the clergy's control over its flock. Although censorship had been under the exclusive auspices of the Catholic Church since the early Middle Ages, by 1653 it had also come under the king's and Parlement's jurisdiction. From that time on, the Parlement slowly increased its censorship powers, consolidating its control over the Church and, consequently, over the ruling of the country. Indeed, by 1757, Parlement could put to death anyone whom it judged to be dangerous to Catholicism or the Crown. Led by Joly de Fleury, Parlement used *De l'Esprit* and the first seven volumes of the *Encyclopédie* to reveal the weakness in the Church's censorship system as a way to claim further censoring power for itself, which meant further power over the book trade. Parlement's condemnation forced the Jesuits at the Sorbonne to deal more harshly with *De l'Esprit* than they might otherwise have done. The Sorbonne demanded that Helvétius recant—as had Parlement and the queen, who also forced him to resign his position as her *maître d'hôtel ordinaire*—and drew up a list of dangerous premises taken from the various writers presumed to be Helvétius's sources. The premises consisted of "Soul," "Morality," "Religion," and "Government," and the suspect sources included La Mettrie, François Vincent Toussaint, David Hume, Mandeville, Locke, Charles-Louis de Secondat de Montesquieu, and the *Encyclopédie*. Like the Parlement, the Sorbonne stated clearly that it did not consider *De l'Esprit* a unique case but part of a much larger threat to the Church, which it was now determined to combat. In fact, most powerful Catholics, whether Jesuit or Jansenist, whether in the Parlement or the Sorbonne, were united in their desire to destroy, in particular, the antireligious *Encyclopédie*, which underneath its conservative, conformist appearance excoriated the Church as a bastion of prejudice, intolerance, and superstition. The Sorbonne had managed to suppress the first two volumes in 1752, but because it was such a great commercial success, supported by various powerful individuals, the Jesuits had not succeeded in taking away the right to publish it. In 1759, however, the impious *De l'Esprit* offered a new means to bring down the pernicious *Encyclopédie*. A month after Helvétius's work was banned and condemned to be burned, the right to publish the *Encyclopédie* was repealed.

Yet, the Catholics' united hope of dealing the *Encyclopédie* a mortal blow was dashed. Because of his and his wife's important connections, Helvétius himself was pardoned, which meant, according to "innocence by association," that the editors of the *Encyclopédie* could not be punished either. The printing of the vast work continued secretly in Paris. During the worst of the ordeal, Helvétius had called upon Malesherbes; the abbé Germain-Louis Chauvelin, who was a counselor in Parlement; Etienne-François, duc de Choiseul, who was the minister of foreign affairs and the cousin of Helvétius's wife; and most importantly, Mme de Pom-

Anne-Catherine de Ligniville d'Autricourt, whom Helvétius married in 1751 (portrait by Van Loo; from Peter Allan, ed., Correspondance générale d'Helvétius, *1981; Thomas Cooper Library, University of South Carolina)*

padour, the king's mistress. She persuaded the king to write letters to Joly de Fleury and to the Sorbonne on Helvétius's behalf, steps that resulted in his pardon.

Although Helvétius posed as a believer in Catholicism in *De l'Esprit*, his detractors could see that his materialist ontology was completely antagonistic to the Church on several grounds, primarily because it denied the existence of the soul. In Helvétius's system, all matter is potentially capable of sensitivity, while all thought processes are reducible to physical sensitivity. This theory means not only that all material beings (human, animal, vegetable, even mineral) might be capable of thought but also that the human is able to think even when conceived of as an exclusively material being. Thus, contrary to Catholic doctrine, no spiritual dimension is necessary for human thought, and no spiritual dimension distinguishes man from other material beings. By positing the exclusively material quality of the human, Helvétius implicitly renders all religious interest in the soul irrelevant, since the soul does not exist. Salvation, from his materialist standpoint, becomes meaningless, and the question of rewards in heaven or punishments in hell becomes moot. Since much of the Church's doctrine and power rested on the premise of the soul's immortality and the question of its fate after death, Helvétius's theories suggested that the Church played no valuable role in people's lives.

Moreover, Helvétius's sensationalist epistemology and ethics threatened the Church by denying free will. According to *De l'Esprit,* physical sensitivity is a passive characteristic; man receives impressions from his senses and seeks pleasure while avoiding pain. He has no control over this mechanical response to stimuli, and consequently his unchangeable nature is to pursue pleasure. This determinism challenged the Catholic belief in free will, according to which a human can choose to do good by favoring the spiritual over the material. By locating original sin in bodily desires, the Church held that the fallen nature of humans was reflected in their corporeality, while their free will was located in their soul. He maintained that all passions, whether simple—the need for food and sexual gratification—or social—envy, avarice, or pride—can contribute to the human drive for cultural accomplishment, whether the pursuit of knowledge or business or artistic creation. The key to virtue lies in harnessing human passions for the social good. No virtue exists apart from its social implementation. Helvétius's views fly in the face of the Catholic credo that virtue is an individual matter left to each human conscience regardless of the dictates of society. Virtue, in Helvétius's system, was strictly a secular, social issue, whereas the Church emphasized virtue as the path to eternal life. Helvétius thought that the only life that counted was the one on earth.

The key, meanwhile, to harnessing human passions for the social good lies in education and legislation. The human is completely malleable, and public education is the best way to train humans to produce a just society. Children should be separated from their parents (whose so-called love is just an interest in power) and educated communally by specialists. A legislative system of rewards and punishments would channel passions in the direction of the social good. Since the drive for sexual gratification is the strongest passion, the promise of sexual pleasure should be used by legislators as the ultimate reward. The institution of marriage, therefore, should be abolished, since it produces divided loyalties—a man is torn between serving family and state—and women should be owned by the state in order to best serve men's pleasure. Needless to say, this advocacy of sexual license (at least for men) and the abolition of marriage was anathema to the Church, which considered marriage a sacrament and sexual activity justifiable only in marriage and as procreative.

Helvétius even went so far as to represent religions "like" Christianity as their own unregulated egoistic fiefdoms, which looked after their own interests at the expense of the people's good. He considered that his ethical system based on physical sensation had never been adopted because of the selfish interests of the clergy and of the ruling class. Adoption of his system would inevitably come in time, he believed, once enough people were informed about it. Then, proper legislation would be developed to unseat the clergy and the rulers and to create a virtuous society.

Although the controversy over *De l'Esprit* was intense, it was resolved, at least on official levels, within a year after the first publication of the work. Whereas Helvétius's materialism and sensationalism alienated Church authorities, his naiveté and rationalism isolated him from most other philosophes, and they had an ongoing debate with him and his work. In practical terms, they resented him for naively publishing *De l'Esprit* through official channels, which thereby made the *Encyclopédie* vulnerable to the reprisals of Parlement and the Sorbonne, thus slowing down the spread of enlightenment. In philosophical terms, the rationalist conclusions of *De l'Esprit* appeared too extreme. Almost all philosophes accepted the sensationalist premises that Helvétius shared with Locke and Condillac. However, in his relentless, rationalist pursuit of simplicity, Helvétius drew the extreme conclusion that the human being was a mechanical processor of pleasure and pain, devoid of such noble qualities as compassion, friendship, or selflessness. The philosophes balked at such radicalism, for they believed in the fundamental goodness of man, in his moral capacity apart from social coercion, and they rejected Helvétius's reduction of all human faculties to sensation, according to which moral conduct was simply a function of feeling.

Both Jean-Jacques Rousseau and Diderot wrote works to counteract Helvétius's theories. Rousseau addressed them indirectly in sections of *Emile* (1762) and of *La Nouvelle Héloïse* (1761, The New Heloise), arguing, among other points, that an individual's internal organization affects how he processes and interprets sensory data. Humans are not born equal but with different temperaments, and education in morality must, therefore, take into account these individual temperaments. In response to Rousseau's critique, Helvétius defended his theories in part of his posthumously published *De l'Homme* (1773; translated as *A Treatise on Man,* 1777). In this work, which Helvétius intended to have published abroad—and only after his death—he clarified certain of his ideas from *De l'Esprit,* which he had tried to soften or obscure to escape censure. Condemned by

Parlement in 1774, *De l'Homme* is a bolder work than *De l'Esprit,* but it does not, in fact, include any new ideas. Diderot, nonetheless, took issue with Helvétius's extreme conclusions from the materialist premises that Diderot himself shared. In *Réfutation De l'Homme d'Helvétius* (1773, Refutation of Helvétius's *De l'Homme*), Diderot argues that thought cannot be reduced to sensation and the passive reception thereof, since the mind is able to combine and, through memory, actively compare feelings. Helvétius, Diderot contended, for fear of having recourse to the unexplainable, hence the mystical, erroneously limited himself in his theories to what was externally observable. He thus neglected the importance of the interior, notably the brain's capacity to combine, remember, and compare sensations and to make moral judgments.

After weathering the blows from Parlement and the Sorbonne for the irreligious implications of *De l'Esprit,* Helvétius spent the rest of his life in relative tranquillity, working on *De l'Homme* and on a dictionary of abstract ideas while enjoying the scholarly life of a man of letters. In the mid 1760s he traveled to England, where he became acquainted with David Garrick, Hume, Horace Walpole, and John Wilkes, a politician, and to Prussia, where he met Frederick the Great. In 1766 Helvétius founded a lodge for Freemasons of the Sciences.

On 26 December 1771, Helvétius died suddenly and unexpectedly from gout. Jean-François, marquis de Saint-Lambert, a friend of the philosophes and member of the Académie française, took charge of publishing Helvétius's lengthy poem *Le Bonheur,* which he had composed sometime during the 1740s. Written in the French classical style of alexandrine verse, *Le Bonheur* investigates the sources of human happiness. The poet asks Wisdom to guide him on his journey of exploration, and she shows him that happiness cannot be found in what men usually consider its provenance—sensual love, on the one hand, or ambitious wishes for fame, on the other. Instead, she explains, the happiest man is he who is least dependent on others and who has multiple sources for pleasure. Such a man is, in effect, a philosophe; his favorite activity is to study, and his preferred subjects are the natural and human sciences. While these intellectual pursuits afford him a desired independence, so, too, does his relationship to sensual pleasures, for he "masters" such pleasures by seeking them through sublimated forms: poetry, music, painting, sculpture, and architecture. In line with the philosophes' characteristic ideology, *Le Bonheur* ultimately argues that only the progress of knowledge will create happiness for society as a whole and for individuals, as well. Helvétius believed in an intrinsic connection between government and happiness. Enlightened

Title page for Helvétius's book (translated as Essay on the Mind and Its Several Faculties, *1759) combining sensationalist and materialist philosophy, with radical implications for both society and religion (Bibliothèque nationale; from Peter Allan, ed.,* Correspondance générale d'Helvétius, *1981; Thomas Cooper Library, University of South Carolina)*

rulers who have been instructed in the natural and human sciences will see that true pleasure lies in doing good for their subjects, while enlightened and well-governed subjects will find pleasure in contributing to the happiness of their fellow citizens. Since the world, far from having attained this ideal state, still labors under the oppressive forces of corrupt kings and priests, the wise man must seek to enlighten others as much as possible.

After Helvétius's death, his widow found herself with no significant property, since he had not left a will. By law, their daughters inherited Voré and Lumigny, and Anne-Catherine retained only what had been agreed upon in the marriage contract, about 60,000 livres and an additional 10,000 as long as she remained a widow. Within a year after her husband's death, she had arranged good marriages for both her daughters

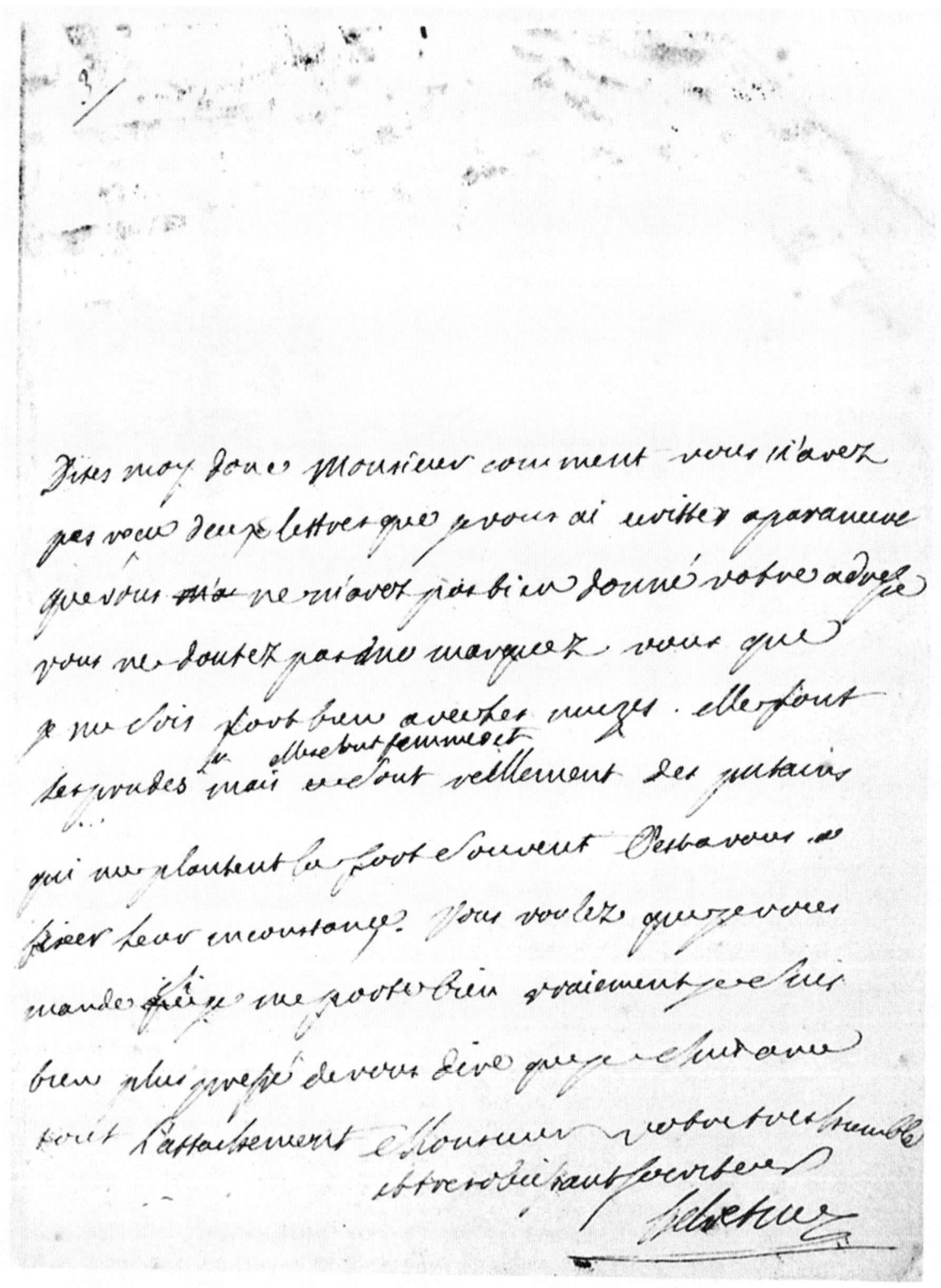

Letter from Helvétius to dramatist François-Thomas Baculard d'Arnaud, circa May 1739 (Université de Bâle; from Peter Allan, ed., Correspondance générale d'Helvétius, *1981; Thomas Cooper Library, University of South Carolina)*

and, thus unencumbered, bought a house in Auteuil, outside of Paris. There, she continued to preside over a salon, which she and her husband had established in the 1760s in Paris. But from the 1770s on, her salon became notable for its support of republican ideas. In fact, it is reputed to be the only ancien régime salon to pursue its intellectual-social activities through the Revolution and until the Terror. Initially, it also had a particular attraction for Freemasons, considering Helvétius's own membership in the group and Anne-Catherine Helvétius's work to establish the Lodge of the Nine Sisters (named for the nine Muses) in 1776, which, according to her husband's vision, would bring together philosophers, scholars, and artists of all sorts. The most famous member of the lodge was Benjamin Franklin, who, in a guarded fashion, professed love for Anne-Catherine Helvétius, while other lodge members included Pierre-Jean-George Cabanis, a doctor; Jean Antoine Roucher, a poet; and Sébastien-Roch-Nicolas Chamfort, a moralist. Marie-Jean-Antoine-Nicolas Caritat, marquis de Condorcet, also frequented Anne-Catherine Helvétius's salon.

Furthermore, she offered board, room, and intellectual sustenance to Jacques Fontaine, abbé de La Roche, who edited (and in some cases heavy-handedly rewrote) Helvétius's complete works; to the abbé André Morellet, who was a man of letters and known for his memoirs of late-eighteenth-century France; and to Cabanis, who sought to sustain Helvétius's theories through a rigorous physiological testing of them. During the 1789 Revolution, Morellet's conservatism alienated him from La Roche and Cabanis, who supported violence in the revolutionary and republican cause. As a result of this political rift, Morellet left Auteuil. In 1800 Anne-Catherine Helvétius died, leaving her property in Auteuil to La Roche and Cabanis.

Letters:
Correspondance générale d'Helvétius, 4 volumes, edited by David Smith, Peter Allan, Alan Dainard, Marie-Thérèse Inguenaud, and Jean Orsoni (Toronto: University of Toronto Press / Oxford: Voltaire Foundation, 1981–1998).

Biography:
Albert Keim, *Helvétius, sa vie et son oeuvre* (Paris: Alcan, 1907).

References:
C. B. A. Behrens, *The Ancien Régime* (London: Thames & Hudson, 1967; New York: Norton, 1989);

B. D'Andlau, *Helvétius Seigneur de Voré* (Paris: Sorlot, 1939);

Elizabeth Gardner, "The Philosophes and Women: Sensationalism and Sentiment," in *Women and Society in Eighteenth-Century France: Essays in Honor of John Stephenson Spink*, edited by Eva Jacobs, W. H. Barber, Jean H. Bloch, F. W. Leakey, and Eileen LeBreton (London: Athlone, 1979), pp. 19–27;

Marie-Thérèse Inguenaud, "Le Fermier Général Helvétius en Lorraine: un projet de réforme inédit (1744–1745)," *Dix-huitième siècle*, no. 18 (1986): 201–207;

Jean-Paul de LaGrave, ed., *Madame Helvétius et la société d'Auteuil* (Oxford: Voltaire Foundation, 1999);

David Raynor, "Hume's critique of Helvétius's *De l'Esprit*," *Studies on Voltaire and the Eighteenth Century*, 215 (1982): 223–229;

Jørn Schøsler, "Rousseau et Diderot, critiques de la philosophie égalitaire d'Helvétius," *Revue romane*, 15, no. 1 (1980): 68–83;

David Smith, *Helvétius, A Study in Persecution* (Oxford: Clarendon Press, 1965; Westport, Conn.: Greenwood Press, 1982);

Smith, "The Publishers of Helvétius's *De l'Homme:* The Société typographique de Londres," *Australian Journal of French Studies*, 30, no. 3 (1993): 311–323;

Gerhardt Stenger, "Diderot lecteur *De l'Homme:* une nouvelle approche de la *Réfutation d'Helvétius*," *Studies on Voltaire and the Eighteenth Century*, 228 (1984): 267–291.

Paul-Henri Thiry, baron d'Holbach
(8 December 1723 – 21 January 1789)

Natania Meeker
University of Southern California

BOOKS: *Lettre à une dame d'un certain âge sur l'état présent de l'opéra,* anonymous (N.p., 1752);

Le Christianisme dévoilé, ou examen des principes et des effets de la religion chrétienne, as "feu M. Boulanger" (London, 1756 [i.e., Nancy, 1766]); translated as *Christianity Unveiled* (New York: Columbian Gazetteer, 1795);

Théologie portative, ou dictionnaire abrégé de la religion chrétienne, by d'Holbach and Jacques-André Naigeon, as "M. l'abbé Bernier" (London, 1768 [i.e., 1767]);

La Contagion sacrée, ou histoire naturelle de la superstition, anonymous, 2 volumes (London, 1768);

Lettres à Eugénie, ou préservatif contre les préjugés, anonymous, 2 volumes (London [i.e. Amsterdam: Marc-Michel Rey], 1768); translated in Richard Carlile, *The Deist, or, Moral Philosopher,* 2 volumes (London: Published by the author, 1819);

L'Esprit du judaïsme, ou examen raisonné de la loi de Moïse et de son influence sur la religion chrétienne (London [i.e., Amsterdam: Marc-Michel Rey], 1770 [i.e., 1769]);

Essai sur les préjugés, ou de l'influence des opinions sur les moeurs et sur le bonheur des hommes, as "M. D. M." (London, 1770 [i.e., 1769]);

Histoire critique de Jésus-Christ, ou, analyse raisonnée des évangiles, anonymous (Amsterdam: Marc-Michel Rey, 1770); translated as *Ecce Homo! or, A Critical Inquiry into the History of Jesus Christ, Being a Rational Analysis of the Gospels* (London: Printed for the booksellers, 1799);

Système de la nature, ou des lois du monde physique et du monde moral, as Mirabaud, 2 volumes (London [i.e., Amsterdam], 1770); translated as *The System of Nature* (London: Printed for G. Kearsley, 1797);

Tableau des saints, ou examen de l'esprit, de la conduite, des maximes, et du mérite des personnages que le christianisme révère et propose pour modèles, anonymous, 2 volumes (London, 1770);

Le Bon Sens, ou idées naturelles opposées aux idées surnaturelles, as "l'auteur du *Système de la Nature*" (London, 1772); translated as *Common Sense* (New York, 1795);

Paul-Henri Thiry, baron d'Holbach (engraving after drawing by Charles-Nicolas Cochin, Photo Archives Photographiques–Paris; from Arthur Wilson, Diderot, 1972; Collection of W. Ross)

La Politique naturelle, ou discours sur les vrais principes du gouvernement, as "un ancien magistrat," 2 volumes (London [i.e. Amsterdam], 1773);

Système social, ou principes naturels de la morale et de la politique, avec un examen de l'influence du gouvernement sur les moeurs, anonymous, 3 volumes (London, 1773);

Ethocratie, ou le gouvernement fondé sur la morale, anonymous (Amsterdam: Marc-Michel Rey, 1776);

La Morale universelle, ou les devoirs de l'homme fondés sur sa nature, anonymous, 3 volumes (Amsterdam: Marc-Michel Rey, 1776);

Eléments de la morale universelle, ou catéchisme de la nature (Paris: de Bure, 1790).

Editions and Collections: *D'Holbach. Textes choisis,* edited by Paulette Charbonnel (Paris: Editions sociales, 1957);

Système de la nature, ou des lois du monde physique et du monde moral, edited by Yvon Belaval (Hildesheim: G. Olms, 1966);

D'Holbach portatif, edited by Georgette Cazes and Bernard Cazes (Paris: Pauvert, 1967);

Premières Oeuvres, edited by Charbonnel (Paris: Editions sociales, 1971);

Système de la nature, 2 volumes (Paris: Librairie Arthème-Fayard, 1990);

Système social (Paris: Librairie Arthème-Fayard, 1994);

La Politique naturelle (Paris: Librairie Arthème-Fayard, 1998);

Oeuvres philosophiques, 2 volumes, edited by J.-P. Jackson (Paris: Alive, 1999, 2000).

Editions in English: *The System of Nature,* 3 volumes, introduction by Robert D. Richardson Jr. (New York: Garland, 1984);

The System of Nature, volume 1, introduction by Michael Bush (Manchester, U.K.: Clinamen Press, 1999).

OTHER: *Encyclopédie, ou dictionnaire raisonné des sciences, des arts et des métiers, par une Société de Gens de lettres,* 28 volumes, edited by Denis Diderot and Jean Le Rond d'Alembert (Paris: Briasson and others, 1751–1772)–includes contributions by d'Holbach;

Nicolas-Antoine Boulanger, *Recherches sur l'origine du despotisme oriental,* edited by d'Holbach (Geneva, 1761); translated as *Origin and Progress of Despotism* (N.p., 1764);

Boulanger, *L'Antiquité dévoilée par ses usages, ou examen critique des principales opinions, cérémonies et institutions religieuses et politiques des différents peuples de la terre,* edited by d'Holbach (Amsterdam: Marc-Michel Rey, 1766);

Le Militaire philosophe, ou difficultés sur la religion, proposées au R. P. Malebranche, prêtre de l'Oratoire, edited by d'Holbach and Naigeon, as "un ancien officier" (London, 1768 [i.e., 1767]);

Lucretius, *De la Nature des choses,* edited by d'Holbach, Diderot, and Naigeon, translated by Brunet de La Grange (Paris: Bleuet, 1768);

J. Crellius, *De la Tolérance dans la religion, ou de la liberté de conscience,* edited by d'Holbach (London, 1769);

Recueil philosophique, 2 volumes, edited by Naigeon (London, 1770)–includes contributions by d'Holbach;

Thomas Hobbes, *Human Nature,* translated by d'Holbach as *De la Nature humaine* (London, 1772);

Seneca, *Oeuvres,* 7 volumes, edited by d'Holbach, translated by La Grange and Naigeon (Paris: de Bure, 1778–1779).

Although his works occasioned a series of public scandals, Paul-Henri Thiry, baron d'Holbach, has remained a somewhat obscure figure in the history of eighteenth-century French philosophy. After the onset of the French Revolution, he was rarely recognized for his contributions to the critique of the social, political, and religious institutions of the ancien régime. Nonetheless, the baron d'Holbach played a crucial role in the development of materialist thought during the latter half of the French Enlightenment. He was the author or editor of more than fifty books, and his circle of friends included some of the most important thinkers of his age. His radically atheist and materialist beliefs, as expressed in his most widely read writings, not only shocked theologians and devout Catholics but also earned the public condemnation of Voltaire. In addition to being a man of letters, well known for the breadth of his knowledge, d'Holbach hosted one of the most brilliant and intellectually daring salons of his age. His "coterie holbachique," as Jean-Jacques Rousseau derisively referred to the group of individuals gathered about d'Holbach, brought together intellectuals from across Europe. Yet, d'Holbach never achieved the renown of his friend and collaborator Denis Diderot, in part because so much of his writing was published anonymously.

D'Holbach's contribution to the development of the philosophy of the French Enlightenment is twofold. On the one hand, the lavish dinner parties he organized twice a week served to reunite the avant-garde of French letters. Diderot; Rousseau; Louise d'Epinay; Claude-Adrien Helvétius; Frédéric Melchior Grimm; Guillaume-Thomas-François, abbé Raynal; and Jean-François Marmontel all participated in these gatherings at d'Holbach's home in Paris and at his château, Grandval. Georges Louis Leclerc de Buffon, Jean Le Rond d'Alembert, David Hume, and Horace Walpole were also visitors to the d'Holbach salon. Reputations were made and destroyed at d'Holbach's parties, and conversation was carried out in what seems to have been an atmosphere of almost complete freedom of expression. These meetings not only allowed the philosophes to debate ideas that they were unable to voice in any other forum, but they also provided a meeting place for the contributors to Diderot's *Encylopedia* (1751–1780), a project for which d'Holbach wrote almost four hundred articles. He hosted these events for more than thirty-five years and thus became known as the "maître d'hôtel de la philosophie" (the master of the household of philosophy). In his preface to the works of La Grange, Jacques-André Naigeon wrote of d'Holbach that no one took a livelier and more sincere interest in the progress of reason.

On the other hand, d'Holbach's thought represents an important phase in the history of materialist philosophy. Although his work was neglected during the nineteenth century precisely because of the radical nature of his materialism, his denunciation of religious belief, resistance to the principles of the absolutist state, and thorough commitment to the rational, scientific examination of the material world as the foundation of human knowledge might be considered the ultimate development of many of the most significant ideas espoused by the philosophes of the French Enlightenment. D'Holbach was both a polemicist of great force and a writer of enormous range–the breadth of his learning was remarked upon even among thinkers who themselves were known for their command of a variety of disciplines. His *Système de la nature* (1770; translated as *The System of Nature,* 1797) was reedited many times in the years leading up to the French Revolution, and its powerful arguments in favor of physiology as the organizing principle of human behavior constituted an important defense of science and reason in the face of despotism.

Of German origin, Paul-Henri d'Holbach was born in Heidelsheim, in the Palatinate, on 8 December 1723. His uncle, Francis Adam d'Holbach, had made his fortune in Paris, where he was eventually ennobled. D'Holbach was brought to France at a young age and ultimately inherited the title and much of the wealth of his uncle, who had been his protector. From 1744 until about 1748, he studied at the University of Leiden in the Netherlands only to return to Paris in 1749; he spent the rest of his life in France, with the exception of a brief visit to England in 1765.

Upon his arrival in Paris, d'Holbach immediately set about putting in place the social networks that later played such an influential role in the history of eighteenth-century French thought and letters. He was young, rich, sociable, and given to hosting lavish dinner parties at his home. He married a close relative, Basile-Geneviève-Suzanne d'Aine, in 1750 and became acquainted with Diderot and Rousseau. Pierre Naville suggests that d'Holbach's love of music first brought him together with Diderot and Rousseau, who were also known for their interest in and work on this subject. (Although a protégé of d'Holbach's for a while, Rousseau later broke dramatically with the *encyclopédistes* and the man who had been his patron.) Indeed, d'Holbach's first published pamphlets consisted of commentaries on the fanaticism inspired by the heated mid-eighteenth-century debate over the relative merits of French and Italian music.

In the years following d'Holbach's arrival in Paris and his first encounters with the philosophes actively engaged in the production of the *Encylopedia,* he began translating a series of scientific works from the German, the majority of which focused on the sciences of mineralogy, geology, metallurgy, and chemistry. D'Holbach also began writing the collection of articles he published in the *Encylopedia,* which were for the most part related to the translations he was working on at that time–for example, "iron," "fossil," "lead," and "petrifaction." While d'Holbach was becoming known among his acquaintances for his materialist convictions as well as for his commitment to atheism, the majority of his work during this first part of his career involved the natural sciences. On the strength of his contributions to this discipline, he was eventually granted admission to the Imperial Academies of Berlin, St. Petersburg, and Mannheim in the Palatinate.

In 1754 d'Holbach became deeply depressed following the death of his wife, with whom he had had one son. The death of his father-in-law had occurred the same year, while his wealthy and generous uncle had died a year earlier. These events left d'Holbach grief-stricken for a time, but nonetheless served to consolidate both his fortune and his social position. Upon the death of his father-in-law he purchased the right of succession to the latter's office and acquired, as a result, entry into the French nobility. Around that time d'Holbach became assured of his status as a wealthy and respected protector to his friends and collaborators, even as he went on to publish, albeit under the cover of the strictest anonymity, a series of works that scandalized Europe. In 1756 d'Holbach married Charlotte-Suzanne d'Aine, the sister of his first wife. Over the course of the marriage, the couple had three children together (a son, born in 1757, and two daughters, born in 1758 and 1760).

Around 1760 d'Holbach shifted the focus of his intellectual work to the writing, publication, and translation of a series of critiques of religious doctrine and institutions. During this period, which lasted around a decade, the baron developed what became one of the most consistent and sweeping attacks on Christian thought and belief that the Enlightenment ever produced. In 1766 d'Holbach had his work *Le Christianisme dévoilé, ou examen des principes et des effets de la religion chrétienne* (translated as *Christianity Unveiled,* 1795) published under the name of philosopher Nicolas-Antoine Boulanger, a civil engineer and philosophe who had died in 1759 after writing a series of heretical essays. In this work d'Holbach argues for the separation of church and state. He claims that Christianity is harmful to both the sovereign and his subjects because it encourages fanaticism, obscures reason, and ultimately produces strife on both an individual and a national level. From d'Holbach's perspective, not the priest but the secular leader should take responsibility for the moral education of the citizenry. If the enlightened sovereign promotes freedom of thought and expression, not only will virtuous behavior become more widespread, but also

Grandval, the country estate of d'Holbach (from Arthur Wilson, Diderot, *1972; Collection of W. Ross)*

religious fanaticism and the troubles it causes will, in effect, dissolve of their own accord.

The publication of this tract was followed by several years of relative silence, although d'Holbach did continue to edit the writings of Boulanger. While he had certainly been known for his atheism in the years that preceded his most intense involvement in the publication and transmission of anti-Christian writings, both his visit to England in 1765 and the start of his thirty-year collaboration with Naigeon marked the real beginning of d'Holbach's remarkable devotion to the dissemination of atheistic texts. After 1765, not only did he translate and edit a wide variety of English pamphlets that were highly critical of Christian beliefs, but he was also responsible for the publication of many atheistic French manuscripts that had previously only circulated clandestinely. In fact, the time seemed right toward the middle of the decade for just such an initiative. The government had begun to relax its attitude toward the publication of "dangerous" texts even as d'Holbach had developed more-reliable networks for publishing his anonymous writings. Near the end of the 1760s, he produced a series of historical critiques of the origins of Christianity, including *La Contagion sacrée, ou histoire naturelle de la superstition* (1768, The Sacred Contagion, or the Natural History of Superstition). At the same time, he began to develop an analysis of the ways in which reason and enlightened philosophical thinking might function as remedies for the ills spread by religion.

In 1770 he published his best-known work, *Système de la nature,* in which he provided a comprehensive exposition of the principles of his materialist philosophy. This text has remained, along with *De l'Esprit* (1758) by Helvétius, one of the most significant and most scandalous eighteenth-century interventions in the debate regarding materialism. The work combines a detailed description of the materialist underpinnings of d'Holbach's understanding of the natural world and humanity's place therein with reflections on ethics, politics, theology, and pedagogy.

Système de la nature is remarkable for its rejection of Cartesian dualism–the separation between mind and matter–in favor of a radical monism. D'Holbach thought that matter–the substance or substances that produce perceptible effects on the senses–makes up the universe in its entirety. Everything that exists is, in essence, material. Accordingly, nothing in this universe is not matter nor should it be understood as somehow distinct from matter. Thought, life, spirit, emotions, beliefs–these abstractions are in reality nothing more than the product of chemical reactions. As d'Holbach writes in the first chapter of *Système de la nature,* "l'homme est un être purement physique" (man is a purely physical being).

Matter may take on a variety of forms, but d'Holbach believed it was always in motion. This motion is in effect caused by chemical interactions between the molecules that order the material world. Such molecular interactions are not only necessary, insofar as they are completely determined by the laws of attraction, but constantly changing even as they repeat themselves. Accordingly, d'Holbach's vision of the universe is both unified, in that all that exists is wholly material, and multiple, in that matter may exist in many different forms. He refuses any notion of divine or human will as an organizing principle. His universe is determinist, and thus not subject, in any sense, to the desires of human beings, who are, after all, nothing more than a collection of molecules. All thought—all consciousness—is the product of the movement of material substances according to chemical principles inherent in these substances.

D'Holbach's materialism is not without ethical consequences. In *Système de la nature* no distinction is made between "the moral man" and "the physical man": these terms simply represent different ways of referring to the same thing. Nonetheless, the outcome of d'Holbach's analysis of the primacy of matter is in no sense an abandonment of the notion of ethical responsibility. According to d'Holbach, "les mérites et la vertu sont fondés sur la nature de l'homme, sur ses besoins" (merits and virtue are grounded in the nature of man, in his needs). D'Holbach sees virtuous behavior as natural, in the sense that to act in a virtuous fashion is always in an individual's best interest. In a perfectly reasonable world, d'Holbach claims, nature would guarantee the morality of both the individual and the society in which he or she lives; the pursuit of happiness is linked, rationally and naturally, to the practice of virtue. D'Holbach said that the existence of vice does not prove that evil is necessary; rather, it indicates that human beings are likely to make mistakes in their attempts to understand their own interests. His hope is that these "mistakes" are subject to being rectified through the exercise of good scientific reasoning.

In the development of his ethics, d'Holbach emphasizes the significance of social groups to the attainment of individual happiness. He contends that, in order to maximize personal happiness, individuals must always be aware of the way in which they contribute to the well-being of society in general. Consequently, the utilitarianism of *Système de la nature* does not result in a glorification of individual self-interest. Instead, d'Holbach consistently discusses "man" in relation to the social context that, he argues, makes up a crucial part of the human experience. As he writes, "en un mot nul homme ne peut être heureux tout seul" (in a word, no man can be happy all alone).

A few months after the publication of d'Holbach's masterwork, the Parlement of Paris ordered the burning of *Système de la nature* along with at least four other texts written, edited, or translated by d'Holbach. The philosophes had much to say about the book: Voltaire excoriated it; d'Alembert disliked it; and Diderot praised it. In the midst of the turmoil, the baron continued to hold his salons on Thursday and Sunday of each week, as he had for the past twenty years, and relied for his anonymity on the discretion of his closest friends.

After finishing *Système de la nature,* d'Holbach went on to develop his analyses of ethical and political obligation in a series of works published throughout the 1770s and into the 1780s. In his writings of this period, d'Holbach produced a critique of absolutism accompanied by a defense of virtuous egalitarianism. In such works as *La Politique naturelle, ou discours sur les vrais principes du gouvernement* (1773, Natural Politics, or Discourse on the True Principles of Government), *Ethocratie, ou le gouvernement fondé sur la morale* (1776, Ethocracy, or Government Grounded in Morality), and *La Morale universelle, ou les devoirs de l'homme fondés sur sa nature* (1776, Universal Morality, or the Duties of Man Grounded in his Nature), d'Holbach seeks to reconcile the notion of moral obligation with that of natural inclination. He argues once again for the separation of church and state, as well as for the original authority of a "natural" morality whose claims on the individual exist prior to those made by religion or political and economic necessity. In the last years of his career, d'Holbach remained faithful to an ethical and political program that combined a secularist utilitarianism with what critics have often understood to be a radical altruism. He continued to press for both a constitutional monarchy and the right to more equal forms of political representation for the good of the many.

Fundamentally, d'Holbach's ideal of the rational atheist is also that of the virtuous citizen who works for the betterment of a society that guarantees him the opportunity to pursue his own happiness freely even as he pursues that of his compatriots. Ultimately, despite the harshness of his criticisms of the political and religious institutions of the ancien régime, d'Holbach maintained a kind of optimism in his political writing. For him, progress was not only desirable but quasi-inevitable. Only in extreme cases should outright rebellion be necessary. D'Holbach did not live to see the onset of the French Revolution.

He died at age sixty-five, in the first month of the year the Revolution began. He was buried in the church of St. Roch, a sign that he had successfully preserved his anonymity as a writer until the end. While his works were reprinted in the decades that followed, his influence on the history of French thought after the

Revolution is not always easy to evaluate. As the Revolution continued, French citizens had difficulty acknowledging an affiliation with the kind of extreme atheism that d'Holbach had come to represent. Nonetheless, radical thinkers in both Europe and North America continued to read *Système de la nature* throughout the first half of the nineteenth century.

Paul-Henri Thiry, baron d'Holbach's critique of Christianity and subsequent attempts to develop a consistently materialist philosophy of nature, man, and society have sometimes been considered by critics to have lost their political and philosophical resonance with the end of the Enlightenment. With his devotion to rationalism and his desire to construct a coherent ethical system not ultimately dependent on metaphysical abstractions, however, d'Holbach was both radical in his vision of matter as the organizing principle of all things and reformist in his efforts to portray a better world. Not only did his thought have an impact on the intellectual work and political activism of the philosophes who surrounded him, but his writing also remains a provocative elucidation of materialist philosophy as a constructive tool for social change.

Bibliography:

Jeroom Vercruysse, *Bibliographie descriptive des écrits du Baron d'Holbach* (Paris: Minard, 1971).

References:

Travis Gerald Benton, "Baron d'Holbach: A Materialist and his Salon," dissertation, University of Alabama, 1965;

Josiane Boulad-Ayoub, ed., *Corpus,* special d'Holbach issue, nos. 22–23 (1993);

Emile Callot, *La Philosophie de la vie au XVIIIe siècle, étudiée chez Fontenelle, Montesquieu, Maupertuis, La Mettrie, Diderot, d'Holbach, Linné* (Paris: Rivière, 1965);

Max Pearson Cushing, "Baron d'Holbach: A Study of Eighteenth-Century Radicalism in France," dissertation, Columbia University, 1914;

René Humbert, *D'Holbach et ses amis* (Paris: A Delpeuch, 1928);

Alan Charles Kors, *D'Holbach's Coterie: An Enlightenment in Paris* (Princeton: Princeton University Press, 1976);

Denis Lecompte, *Marx et le baron d'Holbach: aux sources de Marx, le matérialisme athée holbachique* (Paris: Presses universitaires de France, 1983);

Pierre Naville, *D'Holbach et la philosophie scientifique au XVIIIe siècle* (Paris: Editions Gallimard, 1943; revised and enlarged, 1967);

Georges Plékhanov, *Essais sur l'histoire du matérialisme: D'Holbach, Helvétius, Marx* (Paris: Editions sociales, 1957);

Ivan Sviták, *Baron d'Holbach, Philosopher of Common Sense* (Chico: California State University, 1976);

Jeroom Vercruysse, *D'Holbach et ses amis, 1760–1789* (New York: Clearwater, 1985);

W. H. Wickwar, *Baron d'Holbach: A Prelude to the French Revolution* (London: Allen & Unwin, 1935).

Louise-Félicité de Kéralio-Robert

(25 August 1758 – 1822)

Carla Hesse
University of California, Berkeley

BOOKS: *Adélaïde, ou mémoires de la marquise de M***. Ecrits par elle-même* (Neufchâtel: Société Typographique, 1782);

Histoire d'Elisabeth, reine d'Angleterre, 5 volumes (Paris: Lagrange et chez l'Auteur, 1786–1788);

Collection des meilleurs ouvrages français, composés par des femmes, dédiée aux femmes françaises, 12 volumes (Paris: Lagrange et chez l'Auteur, 1786–1789);

Les Crimes des reines de France, depuis le commencement de la monarchie jusqu'à Marie-Antoinette, publiées par L. Prudhomme, anonymous (Paris: au bureau des Révolutions de Paris, 1791; corrected and augmented, 1794);

Amélia et Caroline, ou l'amour et l'amitié, 5 volumes (Paris: L. Collin, 1808);

Alphonse et Matilde, ou la famille Espagnole, 4 volumes (Paris: L. Collin, 1809);

Rose et Albert, ou le tombeau d'Emma, 3 volumes (Paris: J.-G. Dentu, 1810).

OTHER: *Mercure national ou Journal de l'Etat et du Citoyen,* edited by Kéralio-Robert and others (1789);

Révolutions de l'Europe et Mercure national réunis, journal démocratique, edited by Kéralio-Robert and others (1790);

Mercure national et Révolutions de l'Europe, journal démocratique, edited by Kéralio-Robert and others (1790–1791).

TRANSLATIONS: John Gregory, *Essai sur les moyens de rendre les facultés de l'homme plus utiles à son bonheur, traduit de l'anglais de M. Jean Gregory par Mlle de Kéralio, sur la 6e édition* (Paris: Lacombe, 1775);

Riguccio Galluzzi, *Histoire du grand duché de Toscane sous le gouvernement des Médicis,* 9 volumes, translated by Kéralio and Lefebvre de Villebrune (Paris: rue et hotel Serpente, 1782–1784);

Henry Swinburne, *Voyages dans les deux Siciles, de M. Henri Swinburne, dans les années 1777, 1778, 1779 et 1780. Traduits de l'anglais par mademoiselle de Kéralio* (Paris: T. Barrois le jeune, 1785);

John Howard, *Etat des prisons, des hôpitaux et des maisons de force, par John Howard,* 2 volumes (Paris: Lagrange, 1788);

Sir John Carr, *Voyage en Hollande et dans le midi de l'Allemagne, sur les deux rives du Rhin, dans l'été de 1806* (Paris: L. Collin, 1806);

Carr, *L'Etranger en Irlande, ou Voyage dans les parties méridionales et occidentales de cette isle, dans l'année 1805, par Sir John Carr . . . Traduit de l'anglais par Me Kéralio-Robert,* 2 volumes (Paris: L. Collin, 1809).

Louise-Félicité de Kéralio-Robert was one of the most prominent and prolific women writers of the French revolutionary era. She published in a wide variety of genres, from novels and literary criticism to political history and revolutionary journalism, winning accolades under the Old Regime and stirring controversy during the Revolution and its aftermath. Her life and writings testify to the more general awakening of educated Frenchwomen to the ideas of the Enlightenment and to the political opportunities opened up by the revolutionary era for men and women alike.

Louise-Félicité Guinement de Kéralio was born on 25 August 1758 in Paris, into an old Breton noble family that exemplified the enlightened liberal aristocratic literati of the latter half of the eighteenth century. The intellectual world of Kéralio's parents was sharply delineated along gender lines. Her father, Louis-Félix Guinement de Kéralio, wrote military histories and was a member of the Royal Academy of Inscriptions and Belles-Lettres. Her mother, Marie-Françoise Abeille, wrote and translated fiction. As an only child, Kéralio struggled to come to terms with this dual intellectual inheritance of her father's historical erudition and her mother's passion for fiction.

Her father, rather than her mother, took charge of her education, and perhaps for this reason she was taught not only modern languages but also Latin, Greek, and classical history, an education that was with rare exception reserved for males. By the age of seventeen she had already been noticed within the world of letters for her linguistic virtuosity and her keen intellect. Her first published work, *Adélaïde, ou mémoires de la marquise de M**** (1782), was a memoir-novel–an unusual choice for a woman writer in the eighteenth century, especially one so young. It signaled the unusual intellectual independence that characterized Kéralio's literary endeavors throughout her life.

In writing a novel, Kéralio may have appeared to be emulating her mother, but *Adélaïde* proved to be a decidedly antimaternal novel. In the opening pages, the young heroine introduces her mother as a haughty and vain woman whose "l'orgueil de la naissance . . . le sentiment de ses lumières superieures avaient fortifies en elle des passions d'une extrême . . . et ma mere soumise à leur empire" (pride of birth . . . and sentiment of her superior enlightenment heightened her passions to an extreme . . . and my mother submitted to their empire.) The story of Adélaïde begins when she falls madly in love with a young count, Rofaure, who loves her in return. Her father delights in her choice, but he dies before the couple can be wed; and Adélaïde soon discovers that her mother has been secretly seeking Rofaure's affections for herself. Revealed as the thwarted rival, her mother determines never to allow the lovers to marry. The plot of mother-daughter rivalry ends tragically, with the triumph of the mother's will and an unbridgeable separation of the two lovers. Kéralio's first novel reveals two characteristics that she reworked continuously throughout her literary career: the creation of a body of work populated almost entirely by powerful and often tyrannical female figures, and a central preoccupation with the problem of female rivalry.

In 1786, four years after the publication of *Adélaïde,* Kéralio began publishing her two greatest intellectual projects: the five-volume *Histoire d'Elisabeth, reine d'Angleterre* (1786–1788, History of Elizabeth, Queen of England) and twelve of fourteen projected volumes of a *Collection des meilleurs ouvrages français, composés par des femmes* (1786–1789, Collection of the Best French Works Composed by Women). The *Collection des meilleurs ouvrages français composés par des femmes* and the *Histoire d'Elisabeth* were both historical works in the modern sense of the term, in that they aimed to offer a record of historical fact substantiated by sound evidence. Nonetheless, they represented two distinctive paths toward the creation of a public historical identity for women: one literary, the other political; one separatist, the other integrationist. The *Collection* was an explicitly feminist attempt to construct a separate literary tradition for women writers, from Héloïse to women of the eighteenth century. But as extraordinary as this work was, it was not especially innovative. Working strictly within the traditional conventions of historical writing about women established by the Renaissance histories of *femmes fortes* (worthy women), the *Collection des meilleurs ouvrages français composés par des femmes* presented a series of portraits of exceptional women, followed by a selection of each author's works.

The *Histoire d'Elisabeth,* by contrast, is both innovative and monumental. Kéralio departs radically from the *femme fortes* histories by situating Queen Elizabeth I's reign squarely within the history of male political sovereignty: "Sous Titus, Trajan, Marcus Aurelieus, Gustave Adolphus, Henri IV, et Elisabeth, la vertu reparaître" (Under Titus, Trajan, Marcus Aurelius, Gustavus Adolphus, Henry IV, and Elizabeth, virtue dared to reappear). The history of the queen is thus not specifically a history of a woman as such, but of a ruler among rulers. Moreover, citing John Locke and Charles-Louis de Secondat, baron de Montesquieu as her authorities, Kéralio wrote that her ultimate aim was to assess Elizabeth's contribution to the progress of the law. Her historiographic goal was to establish Elizabeth I's reign as a linchpin in the development of English constitutional law, the history of which had been written by David Hume and William Blackstone following the Revolution of 1688.

Kéralio argued that the real founder of the modern–by which she meant secular–constitutional state was not Henry VII, as past histories had claimed, but rather Elizabeth, because Elizabeth believed in religious tolerance and was the first ruler to successfully establish secular over religious rule. The reign of Elizabeth thus marked a critical turning point in the path toward secular constitutional monarchy, which would only be fully (or nearly; Kéralio hedged on this point) embodied by the liberal constitutional principles of 1688.

This critical, erudite, and magisterial synthesis of English constitutional history (including an entire volume of documentary references to substantiate its claims), written by a twenty-eight-year-old woman, became one of the literary sensations of the French pre-Revolution. A fourteen-page review by the eminent critic Jacques Mallet du Pan in the *Mercure de France* (23 June 1787) was not the only one to laud Kéralio as the "premier" woman historian of her era. In 1787 she became one of only three women ever elected to the Academy of Arras.

In these same years Kéralio expanded her participation in the republic of letters to include the roles of editor and publisher. Despite the laws prohibiting women from becoming publishers unless they were widows of guild masters, in 1785 she secretly launched a publishing business behind a man's name by providing capital to a Paris guild publisher, Jean Lagrange, who in effect served as her front man. In 1789, two weeks before the National Assembly officially declared

Frontispiece and title page for the 1794 corrected and augmented edition of Louise-Félicité de Kéralio-Robert's history of the queens of France up to Marie-Antoinette (from Carla Hesse, The Other Enlightenment, *2001; Thomas Cooper Library, University of South Carolina)*

freedom of the press in August, she threw herself openly into a new career as a revolutionary journalist-printer, founding her *Mercure national ou Journal de l'Etat et du Citoyen* (National Mercury or Journal of the State and Citizen). During the first few years of the Revolution (1789–1791), Kéralio used her writing and her presses in the service of the political and cultural vanguard of the Revolution, allying herself in pamphlets and journal articles with the most radical causes.

In her move from erudite history, written for an elite audience, to radical political activism, Kéralio encountered strong masculine prejudices against female participation in public life. By the end of October 1789 she found herself publicly characterized by radical journalists as a "phénomène politique" and as an "amazone." Moreover, by 1789 Kéralio was thirty-one years old and still single. She was thus also ridiculed as a "vieille fille" (old maid), "laide" (ugly), and "susceptible aux fureurs utérines" (prone to uterine hysteria). In 1790 she married François Robert, a Belgian Jacobin, and, in the face of this public vituperation, she began to withdraw not only from politics but from writing and publishing as well—at least in her own name.

In 1791 a new work of women's history, titled *Les Crimes des reines de France, depuis le commencement de la monarchie jusqu'à Marie-Antoinette* (Crimes of the Queens of France from the Beginnings of the Monarchy to Marie-Antoinette), appeared anonymously from the radical Parisian publisher Louis Prudhomme. It was immediately—and correctly—attributed to Kéralio-Robert. This work is frequently cited as part of the flurry of anonymous anti–Marie-Antoinette polemics of the early revolutionary period, and the publisher clearly intended the book for just this market. But because of its length and its substantive character, the book stands apart from the many porno-polemical tracts that attacked the queen. *Les Crimes des reines de France* is a work of history rather than a polemical tract. It was a generic inversion of

Kéralio's *Histoire d'Elisabeth*. And just as the *Histoire d'Elisabeth* had taken the genre of the *femme forte* and reworked it, transforming it from a series of portraits of exemplary queens into an institutional history of female sovereignty, so *Les Crimes des reines de France* attempted to perform a similar revision of the evil twin of the *femme forte* histories, the histories of bad queens.

There were earlier models for this kind of generic inversion, dating from earlier political crises such as the Wars of Religion (1650s–1680s) and the Fronde (1648–1650), when historical examples of bad queens were invoked to criticize the acts of strident regent queen mothers. While Kéralio-Robert's *Crimes des reines de France* drew upon these models, she broke with them in significant ways. Earlier "black" histories had been written with the purpose of restoring the monarchy to what the authors regarded as its proper course. The histories of bad examples put before Catherine de Medicis and Anne of Austria, in particular, were attempts to rein in these bad queens who had overstepped their authority and to "bring them back into order." They were reformist narratives. *Les Crimes des reines de France,* by contrast, had a revolutionary purpose: to condemn the institution of queenship itself. In the end, it implies, all queens, by the fact of being queens, are bad.

She advanced two different arguments against queenship. First she argued that the problem with queens was that they were women, and she deployed the traditional rhetoric about women's greater passions and their lesser capacity for self-control. She also advanced a corollary principle that as women deformed politics, so too did politics deform women: "une femme devenue reine change de sexe, se croit tout permis, et ne doute rien" (A woman who becomes a queen changes sex, she thinks everything is permitted to her, and defers to nothing), she wrote. This line of argument simply returned her to the problem of monarchy itself, with its absence of checks upon absolute power.

To get back to the problem of queens in particular she thus took another turn, this time toward a Rousseauian critique of the institution of queenship. French Salic law, which forbade women to rule in their own right, far from restraining them, made them worse than others because it put their power outside of the law and beyond the reach of public opinion. French queens ruled through deception because they were not allowed to rule in their own names.

It is difficult to read Kéralio-Robert's lines without wondering if she also meant to sound a warning to republicans who sought to exclude women from public life and who drove them to act through men. She momentarily strayed toward such musings, invoking an even earlier, premonarchical past under the Gauls, when she wrote, "plusieurs Gauloises prennaient place au Sénat, y votaient et délibéraient à l'instar des hommes" (several *gauloises* took seats in the senate and voted and deliberated the same as men). One wonders where this text might have gone in another political climate, or in the hands of a less misogynistic editor than Prudhomme. Perhaps Kéralio-Robert might have found an historical model for the inclusion of women in politics under the new regime, but she did not. She pursued the narrower, negative course taken by the broader revolutionary movement toward the queen: to write her out of public life.

The end to the historical era of queens spelled an end to the career of their greatest historian. After *Les Crimes des reines de France,* Kéralio-Robert ceased writing history, and during the course of the Terror and its aftermath she ceased writing at all. What little is known of her life during this period suggests that she devoted herself to family concerns, giving birth to a single daughter and occasionally intervening privately to help steer her husband's tenuous political career through the vicissitudes of revolutionary tumult. The family survived the Terror, and under the Napoleonic regime her husband, now tainted with regicide, was able to find an obscure post as a forest administrator responsible for supplying wood to the Napoleonic army.

In 1808 a five-volume novel titled *Amélia et Caroline, ou l'amour et l'amitié* (Amelia and Caroline, or Love and Friendship) was published under the signature of Kéralio-Robert. In the preface to the novel, the author reflected upon the distance that separated her from her prerevolutionary literary achievements and acknowledged having previously written a history of Queen Elizabeth. She said the success of that work gave her the courage to embark on publishing a collection of women writers, but the Revolution had forced her to abandon the project. Since the Revolution, she wrote, French literary taste *"allait s'égarer"* (has been deformed), leaving no market for women of the past. Nonetheless, the job of novelists was to capture the historical specificity of the era in which they wrote. Indeed, the novel, as she defined it, *"une histoire de la vie privée"* (is the history of private life.) Thus, in her hands, the novel became a pursuit of history by other means, and like many women writers of the postrevolutionary era, Kéralio-Robert began to use allegory as a fictional means to pursue her interest in political and historical themes.

Amélia et Caroline confronts the problem of historical writing and historical identity on several levels. First of all, it is set in the past, during the English Revolution of 1640–1660–clearly not an innocent choice of period. Contemporary readers would have recognized this setting immediately as an allegory for their own revolution, and Kéralio-Robert makes explicit the analogy between Oliver Cromwell and Maximilien Robespierre. The choice of period also had a particular resonance within her own work, for it would be difficult not to see this book as a continuation of her *Histoire d'Elisabeth* in its concern with a queen-like woman's machinations. Moreover, *Amélia et Caroline* is not simply a story of private lives set against an historical backdrop; rather, it unfolds as a double narrative, one recounting the public history of the English Revolution (replete with footnotes to authoritative sources and authentic documents), and the other detailing the fictional story of the private lives of its two heroines. The novel thus plays continuously with the double entendre of *histoire/ histoire,* history/story.

The dilemmas of postrevolutionary lineage and the determination of social identity offer the premise for the plot. Charles, the émigré son of a cavalier, rescues a girl named Caroline from robbers who have killed her guardian. Caroline does not know who she is, though she has retained a jewel box that she has been told contains the secret to her identity. Charles and Caroline fall in love, and his mother consents to their marriage. Suddenly, Cromwell's daughter, Adélina, and his granddaughter, Amélia, arrive at the neighboring château. The shrewish and vain Adélina becomes the young Caroline's persecutor, first attempting to seduce her beloved Charles, then, when that fails, trying to have the two lovers captured and put to death as counterrevolutionary traitors.

But Amélia becomes Caroline's best friend and protector. After volumes detailing the horrible persecutions of the two girls by the bad mother who, like a queen, manipulates her father's men and thus turns the whole political world against Caroline and Amélia, it is finally revealed that Caroline is, in fact, the daughter of the wicked Adélina's husband by his first marriage. Thus, Caroline and Amélia are not only friends but also half sisters. When the truth of their identities comes to light, Adélina attempts to kill first Caroline and then Amélia; failing in both these attempts, she finally kills herself.

The closing pages of the novel are concerned with the problem of settling the inheritance of the two half sisters. Their father announces that, by the terms of Caroline's mother's will, Caroline is to be the sole heir to the family fortune; but the girl rebels, insisting that she will not accept the inheritance unless it is divided equally between her half sister and herself. As two sisters, Caroline states, they "were united by unhappiness; wealth shall not have the deadly power to divide us." The revolt by the two daughters against the inequities of the maternal will at last puts an end to the deadly inheritance of maternal tyranny, female rivalry, and domination.

Amélia et Caroline was not only a thematic continuation of *Adélaïde,* nor of the *Histoire d'Elisabeth,* nor of *Les Crimes des reines de France.* It was a postrevolutionary rewriting of their female plots. Through fiction, Kéralio-Robert was able to write a truly revolutionary–indeed a utopian–plot, in which the problem of female rivalry is resolved through the suicide of the wicked queen-mother and the daughter's rebellion in the name of equality and sisterly love. In turning to fiction, Kéralio-Robert was able to move beyond the constraints of past models for writing women's history and to imagine them self-possessed actors, capable of making egalitarian judgments about the world.

Amélia et Caroline both thematically and artistically represented the culmination of Louise-Félicité de Kéralio-Robert's long and complex career in the revolutionary world of letters. She wrote two further minor novels, *Alphonse et Mathilde, ou la famille Espagnole* (1809, Alphonse and Mathilde or the Spanish Family) and *Rose et Albert, ou le tombeau d'Emma* (Rose and Albert, or Emma's Tomb), which was published in 1810, before she retired from writing and translating altogether. In 1815, with the restoration of the Bourbon monarchy, Kéralio-Robert's husband was sent into exile as a former regicide. She joined him in Brussels, where she died in 1822. Her work comprises one of the richest available documentaries of what it meant to undergo the revolutionary transformation from monarchist to republican from the perspective of a woman.

References:

L. Antheunis, *Le Conventionnel Belge François Robert (1763–1826) et sa femme Louise de Kéralio (1758–1826 [sic])* (Wetteren, Belgium: Editions Bracke, 1955);

Carla Hesse, "Revolutionary Histories: The Literary Politics of Louise de Kéralio-Robert, 1758–1821," in *Culture and Identity in Early Modern Europe, 1500–1800,* edited by Hesse and Barbara Diefendorf (Ann Arbor: University of Michigan Press, 1993), pp. 237–259;

Joseph-François Michaud and Louis-Gabriel Michaud, eds., *Biographie universelle, ancienne et moderne, nouvelle édition,* 45 volumes (Paris: Desplaces, 1843–1865), XXI: 535–536.

Pierre-Claude Nivelle de La Chaussée

(13 February 1692 – 14 March 1754)

Perry Gethner
Oklahoma State University

BOOKS: *Epître de Clio à M. de B . . . [Bercy], au sujet des nouvelles opinions répandües depuis peu, contre la poësie* (Paris: Foucault, 1732);
La Fausse antipathie (Paris: Prault père, 1734);
Le Préjugé à la mode (Paris: Le Breton, 1735);
L'Ecole des amis (Paris: Le Breton, 1737);
Maximien (Paris: Le Breton, 1738);
Mélanide (Paris: Prault fils, 1741);
Amour pour amour (Paris: Prault fils, 1742);
L'Ecole des mères (Paris: Prault fils, 1745); edited by Isabelle Bernard (Geneva: Droz, 1982);
Le Rival de lui-même (Paris: Prault fils, 1746);
La Gouvernante (Paris: Prault fils, 1747);
L'Amour castillan (Paris: Prault fils, 1747);
Oeuvres, edited by Sablier, 6 volumes (Paris: Prault petit-fils, 1762)–includes previously unpublished plays and verse tales.

PLAY PRODUCTIONS: *La Fausse antipathie,* Paris, Comédie française, 2 October 1733;
La Critique de la fausse antipathie, Paris, Comédie française, 11 March 1734;
Le Préjugé à la mode, Paris, Comédie française, 3 February 1735;
L'Ecole des amis, Paris, Comédie française, 25 February 1737;
Maximien, Paris, Comédie française, 28 February 1738;
Mélanide, Paris, Comédie française, 12 May 1741;
Amour pour amour, Paris, Comédie française, 16 February 1742;
Paméla, Paris, Comédie française, 6 December 1743;
L'Ecole des mères, Paris, Comédie française, 27 April 1744;
Le Rival de lui-même, Paris, Comédie française, 20 April 1746;
La Gouvernante, Paris, Comédie française, 18 January 1747;
L'Amour castillan, Paris, Théâtre italien, 11 April 1747;
L'Ecole de la jeunesse, ou le Retour sur soi-même, Paris, Comédie française, 22 February 1749;
Le Retour imprévu, Paris, Théâtre italien, July 1756.

Pierre-Claude Nivelle de La Chaussée (bust by Jean-Jacques Caffieri; Musée du Louvre; from <www.insecula.com/oeuvre/00010174.html>)

Pierre-Claude Nivelle de La Chaussée, remembered today as the father of *comédie larmoyante* (tearful comedy) in France, was born in Paris on 13 February 1692. Both sides of his family consisted of well-to-do merchants, some of whom were successful tax collectors. Although his father died when he was two, his affectionate mother took excellent care of her only child, who lived with her until her death in 1740. He studied at leading Jesuit schools, and never needing to worry about money, he passed up the chance to go into business so that he could cultivate the life of an elegant man of leisure. The letters he wrote during his only known business trip indicate that he found commercial matters boring. Even the loss of three-quarters of his fortune in the financial debacle of 1720 did not faze him. He retained enough to live comfortably for the rest of his days, with a home in Paris and a secondary residence in the suburbs. Having reached maturity during the notoriously riotous years of the Regency, La Chaussée tended to associate with nobles and men of letters who were witty, irreverent, and obscene in their conversation and often immoral in their behavior. His mordant wit and satirical bent made him a favorite in some of the more fashionable salons. However, his unwillingness to abide by the conventions of polite behavior, his mean-spirited character, and his inability to accept criticism prevented him from making many friends. He never married, but he had many affairs. His correspondence reveals him as callous, rude, and often contemptuous toward women, yet he owed his literary reputation to the idealized view of marriage and family presented in his plays.

La Chaussée's literary vocation was late in developing. He is generally believed to have been the author of an anonymous pamphlet, published in 1719, that attacked the fables of poet Antoine Houdar de La Motte, faulting that writer for a variety of linguistic and aesthetic sins. During the 1720s La Chaussée composed a group of licentious stories in verse, inspired by the *Contes* (Short Stories) of Jean de La Fontaine, but more vulgar and less entertaining. He also wrote short and indecent farces called *parades* for private performance by groups of friends, of which only one, *Le Rapatriage* (The Reconciliation), survives. These works, published posthumously in 1762, do nothing to suggest the heavily moralistic drama that he cultivated in his later years.

In 1732 La Chaussée published his first major work, the polemical poem *Epître de Clio à M. de B . . .* (Epistle from Clio to Mr. de B . . .), in which he again denounces the theory and practice of La Motte, who had died only a few months before. Allegedly written by one of the nine Muses to the poet Nicolas Boileau-Despréaux and drawing heavily from the latter's doctrines, the epistle lavishes praise on those writers who, in La Chaussée's judgment, uphold the highest traditions of French poetry, and condemns those who fall short. Clio preaches the superiority of verse over prose, the need to preserve linguistic purity against the dangers of preciosity and neologism, and the importance of careful craftsmanship. As a staunch conservative in matters of style, he failed to realize that the French language was evolving and that the Enlightenment required new means of expression.

La Chaussée's first play to be performed, *La Fausse antipathie* (1734, The Mistaken Antipathy), which premiered to great acclaim in 1733, was also the first full-fledged tearful comedy in France. Several previous works had anticipated this essentially new form in their use of pathos and heavy-handed moralizing, but the authors had seen themselves as continuing Molière's comedy of character. With La Chaussée, the link to traditional models of comic style, plots, and characterization is further weakened and ultimately severed. The tone is predominantly serious; the characters are excessively virtuous and constantly engage in moralizing; and the convoluted and artificial plot is calculated to make the audience weep profusely. In order to present the startling situation of two young people falling in love without realizing that they are already married to each other, he imagines a complex prehistory: the marriage was arranged; they had never met prior to the wedding; just after the ceremony the man is challenged to a duel, slays his opponent, and flees the country; both change their names; and the man does not return to France for some years. Despite the presence of two enterprising servants who try to assist the lovers, the play includes only a handful of moderately comic moments. Indeed, that laughter in the theater became unfashionable in the eighteenth century, while weeping came to be seen as both pleasurable and a sign of a good heart, was at the heart of La Chaussée's huge success.

Whether La Chaussée, who held conservative views about poetics, consciously set out to get noticed as an innovator or whether he was merely following what he correctly perceived as a shift in taste is uncertain. In any case, by the time of the premiere he had become aware of the radical nature of the work and tried to disarm the critics with a polemical prologue in the tradition of Molière. He satirized the different factions within the public and argued that proper comedy should be true to nature and aim to improve people's mores. The following spring he added an afterpiece, *La Critique de la fausse antipathie* (1734, The Critique of the Mistaken Antipathy). Having neglected in his prologue to raise the issue of the mixing of dramatic genres, La Chaussée imagines a quarrel between the Muses of comedy and tragedy, each of whom blames the other for invading her turf. Momus, the god of satire, is summoned to judge between them, but he finds theoretical discussions silly and insists that the main goal is to please. By failing to address the basic questions in a systematic way and by refusing to let Momus decide the quarrel, La Chaussée may have been admitting his own inability to formulate a coherent theory.

With *Le Préjugé à la mode* (The Fashionable Prejudice) in 1735, La Chaussée achieved his greatest success, and, perhaps not coincidentally, his best integration of tearful comedy with the school of Molière. The plot involves the marital difficulties of Durval and Constance. The young nobleman, though initially fond of his wife, has let himself be led astray by the low moral standards of the day; as a result, he has neglected her and taken mistresses. Having finally realized the futility of his liaisons and the genuineness of his love for his wife, he resolves to go back to her but is terrified by the ridicule that such an action would excite at court. Encouraging Durval on the path of virtue, in this case identical to personal happiness, are the characters in the subplot—his best friend, Damon, and Constance's cousin and best friend, Sophie. The obstacles come mainly from peer pressure, represented by the foppish courtiers Damis and Clitandre, and from the valet, who has received frequent tips during his master's love affairs. Unable to bring himself to admit his feelings directly to Constance, Durval finally changes place with Damon during a masked ball and is obliged to listen silently to her laments and grievances. Her dedication and nobility of character so deeply move him that he throws off his disguise and finally declares his love in public, an action that makes possible the union of Damon and Sophie. The plot, more believable than usual for La Chaussée, has energy and suspense. The characters, though they serve primarily as spokespersons for various attitudes or philosophical positions, are closer to being three-dimensional than in his other plays. The long-suffering Constance shows great dignity and restraint, though she is too saintly and masochistic for modern tastes; Sophie, who argues forcefully for women's rights in a society in which all the laws were obviously made by men, is forthright and self-assured; Durval—whose basic goodness is tainted by narcissism, jealousy, and a tyrannical streak—matures during the course of the play. The two foppish marquises, feebly copied from Molière, are only mildly amusing. The play remained in the repertoire of the Comédie française throughout the century.

The triumph of his first two plays was so great that La Chaussée was soon proposed for a seat in the Académie française, to which august body he was elected in 1736. So eager was he for this honor that he lobbied several of the playwrights who were already members for their support. In his inaugural speech he commended the académie as the guardian of the purity of the French language and the upholder of high aesthetic standards. He fulfilled his official duties with great diligence, almost never missing a meeting.

The following year he presented his third tearful comedy, *L'Ecole des amis* (1737, The School for Friends). The confusing plot concerns the misadventures of a naive young military officer who, in need of protection

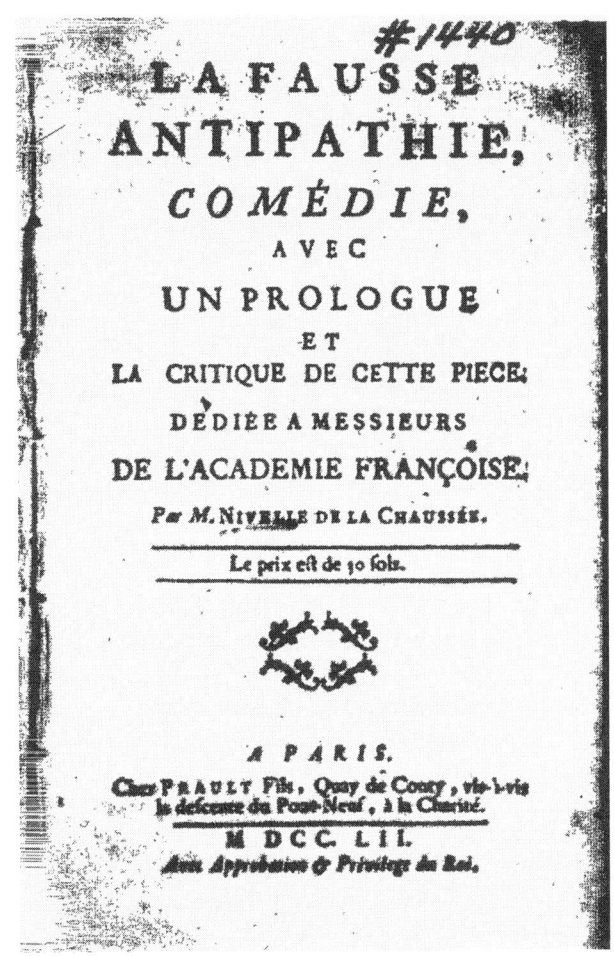

Title page for the 1752 edition of La Chaussée's 1733 play The Mistaken Antipathy, *the first French* comédie larmoyante, *or tearful comedy (Center for Research Libraries, Chicago)*

at court, relies on a pair of self-impressed, silly friends whose inept and unethical schemes invariably backfire. He is saved only because his late uncle's best friend, whom the young man tends to mistrust, secretly works on his behalf. La Chaussée could have developed the comic potential of the bungling friends but instead kept the tone of the play lugubrious and focused on the excessively timid and self-sacrificing lovers. Although the reception of the work was only lukewarm, it occasionally was revived.

In 1738 La Chaussée presented his one and only tragedy, *Maximien*. As with most men of letters of the time, he felt compelled to tackle the most prestigious of genres simply to prove his ability to do so. Since the heroic world of ancient Rome was clearly alien to him, his failure to bring it to life is hardly surprising. Although the style and construction are impeccable, the characters are two-dimensional and lack adequate motivation; the play lacks human interest; and the love component is unconvincing. Significantly, La Chaussée gave greatest prominence to the role of the empress Fausta, shown as the typical helpless lady in distress, saved in the nick of time from execution for a crime she did not commit. The work was well received, even garnering several performances at court and inspiring two dramatic parodies. Despite this initial success, the tragedy soon disappeared from the repertoire. La Chaussée, encouraged by its better-than-expected reception, composed a second tragedy, "Palmire," but he withdrew it when the Comédie française insisted on delaying the premiere until the off-season. The play has remained unpublished and unperformed.

La Chaussée achieved his next great success in 1741 with *Mélanide*, a tearful play in which for the first time pathos is dominant throughout and comic elements disappear. In part, this change occurred because La Chaussée eliminated the servant roles, but even the scene of the lovers' quarrel, probably based on Molière's works, is treated with an almost tragic tone. At the same time, La Chaussée reinforced the pathos of the plight of a long-separated married couple by adding a son of whose existence the father is unaware and by making the two men rivals in love. The plot, one of La Chaussée's more implausible, stems from a secret marriage, annulled by the young people's angry families. The man later inherits a fortune and title from an uncle, going on to have a distinguished military career. Mélanide raises her son, d'Arviane, whom she passes off as a nephew, in a remote area of Brittany, but she eventually moves to Paris, where they are welcomed into the home of the kindly widow Dorisée and her brother-in-law. Strangely, Mélanide never confides her story to either her son or her benefactors; they first learn the truth about her past during the course of the play. Meanwhile, d'Arviane has fallen passionately in love with Dorisée's daughter, Rosalie, who returns his affection but is too reserved and modest to reveal her feelings. However, the marquis has become acquainted with Dorisée and, despite a vow to remain true to the wife whom he believes to be dead, also falls in love with Rosalie. The girl's mother encourages his suit, despite the huge difference in ages, because her fortune is encumbered by debts and lawsuits. Since Mélanide makes a point to avoid contact with her hostess's visitors, she has never met the marquis, but once she sets eyes on him and recognizes him, the action moves toward the inevitable happy ending.

Mélanide, viewed by eighteenth-century audiences as a model of virtue in distress, strikes the modern reader as overly passive and self-sacrificing: she never does anything to promote her own interests or those of her son; she discourages her son in his love for Rosalie without giving him any real explanation; and she even assures the marquis, when they finally meet, that she will not stand in the way of his remarriage. This play treats no social problem, unless one considers parental power over children an abuse, and even on this issue no one challenges the system. The conflicts are purely internal: everyone is virtuous, and the marquis immediately returns to his duty once he is reunited with Mélanide. Audiences were especially moved to tears by the scene in which d'Arviane, suspecting that the marquis is his father, pleads for recognition and guidance, while the father, who knows the truth but hesitates to acknowledge his son, finally yields to the voice of nature.

La Chaussée next attempted a different type of comedy, one based on supernatural characters, in *Amour pour amour* (1742, Love for Love). The fairy queen, angered when Azor, one of her courtiers, spurns her love, banishes him and his best friend, Zaleg, to earth, gives them human form, and refuses to reinstate them until they have each inspired genuine love in a woman, who must declare her feelings even though the men are not allowed even to hint at the subject of love. Seeing Azor on the verge of success with the young and virtuous Zémire, the fairy queen disguises herself as a wealthy prince and tries to woo the girl for herself. The scheme backfires, since the prince's declarations provide the innocent girl the information she needs to identify her feelings and act on them, so true love triumphs. La Chaussée displays more grace and charm than usual in this work, though he makes surprisingly little use of his characters' magic powers. The fairy-tale dimension serves primarily to motivate the otherwise implausible test; otherwise, to have the ingenue be the first to proclaim her passion while the young man remains silent would be curious, considering the mutual love of the protagonists. La Chaussée was so nervous about the innovative nature of the play that he again tacked on a polemical prologue that satirizes inattentive spectators and malevolent critics. His fears turned out to be groundless, since the comedy enjoyed a moderate success and was revived several times.

In 1743 La Chaussée produced a dramatization of Samuel Richardson's *Pamela* (1740–1741), which had recently been translated into French and had quickly become a best-seller. The playwright, who did not read English and seemed to have had only minimal awareness of the tearful literature produced in England, could not resist the tale of a virtuous and long-suffering servant girl persecuted by a lustful and tyrannical young master. However, La Chaussée's uninspired adaptation, which eliminated both the local color and the religious dimension of the original, failed dismally. At its single performance, the audience repeatedly hissed it; according to some accounts, the actors could not even finish the play. The author withdrew the work and declined to publish it.

Apparently judging that the failure of *Paméla* (first published in the 1762 *Oeuvres*) stemmed from a decline in audience desire for sustained pathos, La Chaussée decided to reintroduce traditional comic material and limit the tearful component to scenes involving the persecuted heroine. In any case, his next play, *L'Ecole des mères* (1745, The School for Mothers) had a considerable success at its premiere in 1744 and became his third play to enter the standard repertoire. The mother, Madame Argant, is arguably his most convincing female role: she is self-assured, domineering, and fanatically devoted to the interests of her son but also intelligent enough to become disillusioned with his ungrateful behavior and tender-hearted enough to be touched by the goodness and humility of the girl who turns out to be her daughter. The daughter, Mariane, is the typical saint: placed in a convent at age two, she is removed by her father years later but told that she is his niece, that her parents are dead, and that her fortune depends on gaining the good graces of her aunt (really her mother). When the servants discover that the real niece died many years earlier, they and the other members of the household jump to the assumption that she is really Madame Argant's mistress and start to mistreat her. The recognition scene between mother and daughter, artificially postponed until the fifth act, is unusual in that Mme Argant's transformation requires her to yield to the voices of nature and reason simultaneously. Even though the plot is based on the practice of forced vocations, this social problem is never addressed as such. The dandified and selfish son, who has taken the title of marquis, is one of La Chaussée's liveliest comic characters: more conceited and silly than wicked, he is easily duped. The father, despite his noble birth, thinks and acts like a member of the bourgeoisie, strongly disapproving of his wife's snobbery and his son's aristocratic airs.

Le Rival de lui-même (1746, His Own Rival), the one traditional comedy that La Chaussée wrote for the Comédie française, deserved its feeble reception. He borrowed from himself the device of having a couple separated for many years because the man had to flee the country following a duel and changed his name upon his return. However, the man is a conceited fop who never loved the lady sincerely and who, when he finds her again, foolishly pretends to be someone else in order to see whether she will fall in love with him anew. Repulsed by his outrageous behavior, the heroine transfers her affections to his worthier rival. Despite some genuinely humorous situations, the comedy produces little laughter. At least La Chaussée showed that he could eliminate the pathos that he normally brought to the recognition scene; he also allowed the young heroine for once to get the upper hand and make her own decision.

The fourth of La Chaussée's plays to enter the standard repertoire, *La Gouvernante* (1747, The Governess), returns to the model of *Mélanide*. The character who seems to have most intrigued audiences and critics is a scrupulously honest judge who, upon discovering that he had, many years earlier, rendered an unjust verdict because his secretary had concealed a crucial document, resolves to reimburse out of his own pocket the innocent family that he had ruined. His son, Sainville, a philosophically minded youth who is just as fanatically devoted to honor and justice as his father, endorses the restitution, despite the financial loss to himself, but refuses to recoup his fortune by marrying a wealthy heiress. Needless to say, Angélique, whom he loves, turns out to be the daughter of the man ruined by his father, and the girl's governess is really her widowed mother, who has never revealed the truth to anyone. Despite the mother's masochistic refusal of the *président*'s offer and her determination to make Angélique enter a convent with her, the others finally persuade her to consent to the marriage of the lovers.

Only six weeks later, La Chaussée gave his first comedy specially written for the rival troupe, the Théâtre italien, which by this time was performing mostly French-language plays. Why he chose to work with the Italians at this juncture is uncertain, but he had periodically quarreled with the Comédie française, and this change may have been a gesture of defiance. *L'Amour castillan* (1747, Love Castilian Style), which is arguably his funniest play, derives its plot from a great comic novel, Alain-René Lesage's *Gil Blas* (1715, 1724, 1735), and its style and structure from the comedies of intrigue of the mid seventeenth century. In keeping with the tradition of the Italians, the play has characters with commedia dell'arte names, some risqué situations (the heroine dresses as a man to pursue her lover, pretends to be a swaggering man-about-town, and woos and humiliates the coquette with whom the lover has become infatuated), and some physical humor. Despite the poor reception of the play, La Chaussée felt convinced that he had talent for traditional comedy.

In 1749 La Chaussée returned to tearful comedy and the Comédie française with *L'Ecole de la jeunesse* (The School for Youth; first published in the 1762 *Oeuvres*), his last attempt to deal with real social problems. The play condemns the life of extravagant spending, drinking, gambling, and debauchery characteristic of fashionable young noblemen. However, instead of showing the rake's conversion to virtue, as suggested by the original title, "Le Retour sur soi-même" (Soul-Searching), he chose to show the difficulties encoun-

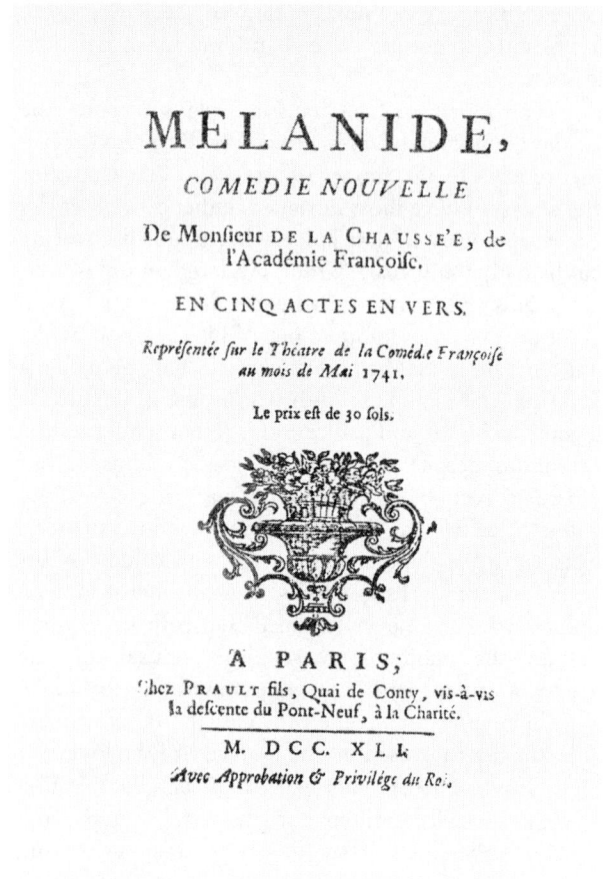

Title page for La Chaussée's first play in which pathos is dominant throughout and no comic elements are used (from W. D. Howarth, Mélanide, 1973; Thomas Cooper Library, University of South Carolina)

tered by the reformed libertine after he has changed his ways. Typically, the plot complications stem from the protagonist's changing his name: the disreputable count de Clairval, having seen combat and then inheriting a title and fortune upon the death of his uncle, becomes a paragon of virtue but must now combat his fiancée's family's bad memories of his previous identity. La Chaussée, blaming the troupe and hostile colleagues (especially his one-time friend Voltaire) for the failure of the play, severed relations with the Comédie française.

In 1751 he received a most prestigious commission: Madame de Pompadour, who had long championed his tearful comedies and enjoyed performing them at private theatricals, asked him to compose a work to inaugurate her new theater in the Château de Bellevue. Despite her support, *L'Homme de fortune* (The Millionaire; first published in the 1762 *Oeuvres*), La Chaussée's last tearful comedy, was a fiasco, since the amateur cast was inept and since some people at court claimed that the subject of the play constituted a slur on the royal mistress's family background. For his benefactress, La Chaussée provided a role laden with pathos: Méranie starts the play believing that she is the penniless child of an unknown father and, therefore, not good enough to wed the son of her rich benefactor; she later turns out to be the daughter of a wealthy nobleman who is now too highborn for a bourgeois financier's family. In the end, love and gratitude triumph.

Having decided to abandon tearful comedy once and for all, La Chaussée went on to compose two more plays for the Italians. *Le Retour imprévu* (The Unexpected Return; first published in the 1762 *Oeuvres*), staged posthumously in 1756 to little acclaim, recycles elements from previous plays, combining elements of comedy, social satire, and pathos. Though the last of these is less prominent, the play is not particularly funny. The troupe refused a comedy-ballet, *Les Tyrinthiens* (The People of Tiryns; first published in the 1762 *Oeuvres*), perhaps because it is weakly constructed and has only a few genuinely comic scenes. That a young woman is elected ruler and that she displays genuine leadership ability and good sense might suggest a feminist message were she not willing to hand over her power to her timid and self-absorbed fiancé. Curiously, Aristophanes briefly appears to condemn tearful comedy and insist that laughing comedy is the only valid kind, while a nameless second playwright objects to farces and ballets. If these characters were intended to represent La Chaussée's personal views, he was seriously questioning his own dramatic practice at the end of his life.

During his final years, La Chaussée also composed two comedies for the private theater of his main patron, the count de Clermont. *La Rancune officieuse* (The Obliging Grudge; first published in the 1762 *Oeuvres*), which received a posthumous premiere in November 1754, involves an overly timid young lover and a devoted friend who helps him win his beloved. Annoyed by d'Ormon's lack of trust, the friend tricks d'Ormon into believing that he (the friend) is wooing the lady for himself. The other comedy, *Le Vieillard amoureux* (The Old Man in Love; first published in the 1762 *Oeuvres*), was never performed. Mondor, a miserly old man who falls in love for the first time, may have been partly autobiographical. Although his passion is presented sympathetically, he loses the audience's esteem by his gratuitously cruel treatment of his virtuous nephew and niece. Another product of La Chaussée's final years, the tragicomedy *La Princesse de Sidon* (The Princess of Sidon; first published in the 1762 *Oeuvres*) was specifically intended for performance at court, but was rejected. This feeble work, presumably another of his attempts to demonstrate his dramatic versatility, tells a story of jealousy and betrayal during the time of the Crusades and features yet another passive lady in distress, falsely accused of adultery. The inclusion of a prologue with singing and ballet sequences suggests that the author hoped for a commission to write an opera libretto.

La Chaussée died 14 March 1754 of an internal hemorrhage brought on by overexertion while doing gardening work. He died calmly in the presence of his mistress. When La Chaussée's closest friend, Sablier, issued an edition of La Chaussée's complete works in 1762, he included the juvenilia and all the unpublished plays, except for his second tragedy, "Palmire," and a comedy titled "Le Véritable père de famille" (The True Head of the Household), which survive in manuscript.

Pierre-Claude Nivelle de La Chaussée's influence on French drama of the eighteenth century was considerable. His example prompted the two most gifted playwrights of the time, Voltaire and Pierre Carlin de Marivaux, to make several forays into tearful comedy, though neither adopted the model permanently. Even more indebted to him were those playwrights who went further in breaking with comedy and making what came to be termed the *drame* into a fully independent genre, especially Denis Diderot, Françoise de Graffigny, and Michel-Jean Sedaine, as well as Gotthold Ephraim Lessing in Germany. Several of La Chaussée's plays were translated into other languages.

Despite the high esteem in which critics of his own century held him, La Chaussée has received mostly scorn from those from later periods. His correct but undistinguished style, mostly wooden characters, implausible plots, pompous moralizing, and exploitation of pathos for its own sake have all contributed to his current disfavor. In addition, despite an occasional attempt at social criticism, he was not an original thinker and cannot be said to have played a major role in the development of Enlightenment thought. Still, his explorations of virtue in distress and his attempts to give a serious, even heroic, stage portrayal of the middle class (seen as the repository of reason, virtue, and stability) assure him a place in the history of drama.

Biographies:

Gustave Lanson, *Nivelle de La Chaussée et la comédie larmoyante* (New York: Burt Franklin, 1903; reprinted, 1971);

Catherine François-Giappiconi, "Des éléments nouveaux sur Nivelle de La Chaussée," *Revue de l'Histoire Littéraire de la France,* 102, no. 6 (2002): 907–919.

References:

Ernest Bernbaum, *The Drama of Sensibility* (Boston & London: Ginn, 1915);

Charles Lénient, *La Comédie en France au XVIIIe siècle,* 2 volumes (Paris: Hachette, 1888);

Deborah Steinberger, "A New Look at the comédie larmoyante," *Esprit créateur,* 39 (1999): 64–75;

Caroline Weber, "Overcoming Excess: *Jouissance* and Justice in Nivelle de la Chaussée's *Ecole des mères,*" *MLN,* 114 (1999): 719–742.

Papers:

The manuscripts of Pierre-Claude Nivelle de La Chaussée's unpublished plays, "Palmire" and "Le Véritable père de famille" are held at the Bibliotheque nationale in Paris.

Pierre-Ambroise-François Choderlos de Laclos
(18 October 1741 - 5 September 1803)

Michèle Bissière
University of North Carolina at Charlotte

BOOKS: *Les Liaisons dangereuses; ou, lettres recueillies dans une société et publiées pour l'instruction de quelques autres,* 4 volumes (Paris: Durand, 1782); translated as *Dangerous Connections; or, Letters Collected in a Society, and Published for the Instruction of Other Societies,* 4 volumes (London: T. Hookham, 1784);

"Lettre à Messieurs de l'Académie française sur l'éloge de M. le Maréchal de Vauban, proposé pour sujet du prix d'éloquence de l'année 1787" (Paris: Durand, 1786);

De l'Education des femmes (Paris: A. Messein, 1903);

Poésies de Choderlos de Laclos (Paris: Dorbon l'Aîné, 1908).

Editions and Collections: *Les Liaisons dangereuses* (N.p., 1787)–includes "Pièces fugitives" and Laclos's correspondence with Madame Riccoboni;

Oeuvres complètes, edited by Maurice Allem (Paris: Gallimard, Bibliothèque de la Pléiade, 1951)–includes Laclos's untitled review of *Voyage de La Pérouse autour du monde,* 1797;

Oeuvres complètes, edited by Laurent Versini (Paris: Gallimard, Bibliothèque de la Pléiade, 1979)–includes "De la guerre et de la paix";

De l'Education des femmes, edited by Chantal Thomas (Grenoble: Millon, 1991).

PLAY PRODUCTION: *Ernestine,* Paris, Comédie italienne, 19 July 1777.

SELECTED PERIODICAL PUBLICATIONS–UNCOLLECTED: "*Cécilia* ou les mémoires d'une héritière," *Mercure de France* (17 April 1784): 103–110; (24 April 1784): 152–165; (15 May 1784): 102–120;

"Third (untitled) essay on women's education," *Revue Bleue* (16 May 1908): 643–648.

Pierre-Ambroise-François Choderlos de Laclos (portrait in Bibliothèque nationale; from Ronald C. Rosbottom, Choderlos de Laclos, 1978; Thomas Cooper Library, University of South Carolina)

Pierre-Ambroise-François Choderlos de Laclos is remembered as the author of the classic epistolary novel *Les Liaisons dangereuses; ou, lettres recueillies dans une société et publiées pour l'instruction de quelques autres* (1782; translated as *Dangerous Connections; or, Letters Collected in a Society and Published for the Instruction of Other Societies,* 1784). He was also an artillery officer who dreamed of serving his country in battle and an inventor who sought to improve the military capabilities of France. Laclos shared his contemporaries' passion for politics and was involved in the French Revolution as secretary to the duc d'Orléans and a member of the Jacobin Club. In addition to *Les Liaisons dangereuses,* he wrote poetry, as well as reviews and essays on literature, politics, military topics, and women's education. Except for his well-known novel, most of his works were published posthumously.

Laclos was born in Amiens on 18 October 1741. He was the second son of Marie-Catherine Gallois and Jean-Ambroise Choderlos de Laclos, a member of the minor nobility who was secretary to the governor of Picardie. Little is known of Laclos's early life in Amiens. By all accounts, the family was close and led a simple life. They moved to the Marais district in Paris when Jean-Ambroise Choderlos de Laclos was transferred there in 1751. Because his father could not afford to buy positions for his sons, Laclos joined the army and was admitted to the Corps royal d'artillerie on 15 January 1762. He dreamed of military glory and asked to be sent to Canada to fight in the French and Indian War, but the Treaty of Paris in 1763 put an end to that hope. Instead, he spent most of his military career in provincial garrisons or was assigned to special fortification projects, rising through the ranks thanks to his skills and good conduct.

As an officer in peacetime, Laclos had a great deal of free time. He read and mingled with the intellectual circles in the cities where he was stationed. He also wrote poetry—not an uncommon practice among soldiers, one that led André-Marie de Chénier and Claude-Joseph Rouget de Lisle to fame. Some of Laclos's early poems were satirical—for example, "Epître à Margot" (1776, Epistle to Margot), a veiled attack against Louis XV's mistress, Madame du Barry (Jeanne Bécu du Barry). Because of the scandal it created, Laclos did not claim authorship until later.

In 1776 he was sent to Valence to organize the transfer of the artillery school from Besançon. While there, he wrote a play and a comic opera, *Ernestine* (1777), adapted from a best-selling novel by Marie-Jeanne Riccoboni. It flopped in the presence of Marie Antoinette at the Comédie italienne on 19 July 1777, so other performances were cancelled; this failure led Laclos to abandon the theater and write novels instead. Back in Besançon in 1778–1779, he began writing *Les Liaisons dangereuses,* a project he had conceived in the salons of the local aristocracy of Grenoble in 1769–1775.

In April 1779 Laclos was commissioned to fortify the island of Aix, off of Rochefort on the Atlantic coast, under the orders of Marc-René, marquis de Montalembert. War with Great Britain had resumed when France began to support the American colonies, and the island was key in maintaining communication with the overseas allies. While supervising the construction of the fort, Laclos also wrote treatises (in which he dissented from accepted theory) on how best to defend the island. He sent his work to military authorities, but it was ignored. Disappointed by this rejection and by the strengthening of aristocratic privilege in the army, Laclos resumed work on *Les Liaisons dangereuses* and requested temporary leaves of absence in 1780–1782 to finish the book.

Les Liaisons dangereuses, an epistolary novel, depicts the carefully planned seduction of a young girl and married woman by two libertines. It caused an immediate sensation when it appeared in April 1782; two thousand copies sold out in a few weeks, and twenty-five pirated editions appeared the same year. The epistolary genre was popular at that time; more than two hundred known French novels were written in that vein between 1707 and 1781—of which the best known were Charles-Louis de Secondat Montesquieu's *Les Lettres persanes* (1721; translated as *Persian Letters,* 1722), Françoise de Graffigny's *Les Lettres d'une Péruvienne* (1747; translated as *Letters Written by a Peruvian Princess,* 1748), and Jean-Jacques Rousseau's *Julie, ou la nouvelle Héloïse* (1761, Julie, or the New Eloise). Because of Laclos's skill in weaving together letters written by multiple correspondents, *Les Liaisons dangereuses* is considered unsurpassed in its genre.

The thread that unites the letters is the conflict between Valmont, a well-known libertine and seducer, and the marquise de Merteuil, who passes for a virtuous widow in society. Once lovers, the two maintain a friendship based on their perceptions of themselves as superior beings capable of seducing the most difficult adversaries while remaining immune to passion and feelings. The story begins with a challenge to Valmont from Merteuil, who wants to take revenge on the comte de Gercourt, a former lover who abandoned her when he became engaged to her cousin Cécile de Volanges. Merteuil asks Valmont to awaken and corrupt Cécile sexually in order to shock the groom on his wedding night. First, Valmont is offended by such an easy challenge, but he eventually agrees when he finds out that Cécile's mother is speaking against him to Madame de Tourvel, the virtuous married woman he has vowed to seduce. The setting for the double seduction plot is the country estate of Valmont's aunt, Madame de Rosemonde, where all the characters are gathered. The real mastermind is Merteuil, who has agreed to take Valmont as a lover again when he provides proof that Tourvel has yielded to him.

The story has to be reconstructed from the letters that the characters send to each other. Laclos adapted the style of the letters to the characters and gave the letters themselves a central role in the development of the plot. The letters make characters fall in love, reveal

Marie-Soulange Duperré, Laclos's wife (collection of M. Louis Chauvigny; portrait by Roger Roche; from Roger Vailland, Laclos par lui-même, *1953; Thomas Cooper Library, University of South Carolina)*

their writers' secrets to those who intercept them, or serve to blackmail one's enemies. Merteuil is particularly skillful at the art of writing and reading letters. She tells Valmont when his written declarations of love do not ring true, and she also understands from his letters that he is really in love with Tourvel, not just pretending. Jealous, she delays her favors and demands that he break off with Tourvel by sending her a cruel letter that Merteuil has written on his behalf. Valmont proceeds with the plan, but the change in their original agreement and Tourvel's ensuing illness and ultimate death make him turn against the marquise.

Letters play a major role in the *denouement:* Merteuil shows the young chevalier de Danceny the letters in which Valmont describes how he has corrupted Cécile; Danceny, who is in love with Cécile, challenges Valmont to a duel and kills him, but before he dies, Valmont entrusts Danceny with his correspondence. After Danceny publishes some of the letters incriminating Merteuil, the marquise is unmasked and punished: she loses her reputation and her fortune; she is disfigured by smallpox and loses the use of one eye; finally, she must flee abroad. Cécile enters a convent, and Danceny joins the Knights of Malta.

In addition to its complex structure, the novel is striking in its use of military and theatrical imagery. The act of seduction is described as a combat, and each step as a tactical maneuver. This metaphor has led to an interpretation of Laclos's novel as compensation for his never being called to battle. Another prominent image is that of acting and theater. Valmont and especially Merteuil are portrayed as cool, dispassionate actors whose success comes from an ability to act in a logical, tactical manner while keeping their emotions in check. A good example of such behavior is found in letter 81. In this letter, the marquise describes her efforts at "making herself" and building her image, thus rising above her station as a woman in a world in which men hold all the power. She tells how she learned to repress her feelings and compose herself, spending long hours studying people in books and in the salons, and forging a new identity that will keep others under her control. Her acting method is reminiscent of the one advocated by Denis Diderot in *Le Paradoxe sur le comédien* (written in 1773; published in 1830; translated as *The Paradox of Acting,* 1883). Merteuil, however, cannot remain completely detached. Rage and jealousy overwhelm her and eventually lead to her unmasking.

The question of Laclos's intentions has occupied readers and critics ever since the publication of the novel. *Les Liaisons dangereuses* was immediately judged scandalous and its author considered a libertine. Some of Laclos's contemporaries objected to his depiction of aristocratic life and argued that the action of the novel was inauthentic and immoral. Best-selling novelist Riccoboni considered his portrayal of the marquise de Merteuil an affront to her sex and to the French nation. In her correspondence with Laclos about *Les Liaisons dangereuses,* she urged him to promote virtue by depicting positive characters that could serve as role models rather than vicious individuals who are ultimately punished. The structure of the novel, with its multiple viewpoints and narrative detachment, precludes a definitive understanding of the author's viewpoint. Laclos added to the enigma by playing with the reader's expectations at the beginning of the novel. It opens with an "Avertissement de l'Editeur" (Letter from the Publisher), which warns the reader not to believe the "Préface du Rédacteur" (Editor's Preface), which guarantees that the letters are authentic. The "publisher" argues that the actions and characters are clearly fictional, because their perversity and immorality could not be found in real life. These contradictory statements—as well as the rest of the story—have led to a variety of interpretations. On the one hand, the book has been read as a manual for would-be seducers and on the other, as a denunciation of the immorality of contemporary life. It has also been interpreted as a tragedy of the rational man, as an appeal to sensibility, as an exercise in cynicism, and as a feminist novel.

After the publication of *Les Liaisons dangereuses,* Laclos returned to La Rochelle, where he fell in love with eighteen-year-old Marie-Soulange Duperré. Their relationship was kept secret for a while because of the bad reputation Laclos had acquired following publication of his novel. Meeting Duperré may have inspired Laclos to write an essay on a topic proposed by the Académie de Châlons-sur-Marne for a competition in 1783: "Quels sont les moyens de perfectionner l'éducation des jeunes demoiselles?" (What are the means to improve the education of young ladies?). In his notes on the subject, Laclos argues that to improve women's education in the present state of society is impossible, because women have been enslaved by men, and both sexes have grown comfortable with that enslavement. Unless women are willing to shake off their chains, he writes, they do not need to be educated. He did not finish this essay. He continued to reflect on the topic in his second essay on women, "Des femmes et de leur éducation" (Concerning Women and Their Education). Clearly influenced by Rousseau, Laclos described the beauty and strength of the natural woman, compared her to woman in society, and showed how institutions were responsible for the unfortunate change. These two essays were first collected and published as *De l'Education des femmes* (On the Education of Women) in 1903. In 1783–1784 Laclos also wrote literary criticism. In an extended review of Fanny Burney's *Cecilia* (1782) for the *Mercure de France* (17 April, 24 April, 15 May 1784), he offered a defense of the novel as a genre, then scorned by critics for its lack of rules. He argues that the novel is as valuable as history or theater because it is best suited for understanding human beings and for offering moral lessons. He praises the art of the novelist, which requires many skills, including the ability to "observer, sentir, et peindre" (observe, feel, and paint).

After gaining respectability with his election to the Académie de La Rochelle, Laclos was able to marry Duperré in May 1786 and to recognize their child, Etienne-Fargeau, born out of wedlock two years earlier. Shortly thereafter, he was ordered to leave La Rochelle as reprisal for his criticism of famous seventeenth-century military engineer Sébastien le Prestre de Vauban in his "Lettre à Messieurs de l'Académie française sur l'éoge de M. le Maréchal de Vauban" (1786, Letter to Members of the French Academy on the Praise of Vauban). In this letter, Laclos objects to the academy's choice of the topic "Eloge du maréchal de Vauban" (Praise of Vauban) for one of its essay competitions. He argues that Vauban does not deserve national fame because he merely improved on previous methods. Moreover, Vauban's forts imposed a financial burden on the country and were easily

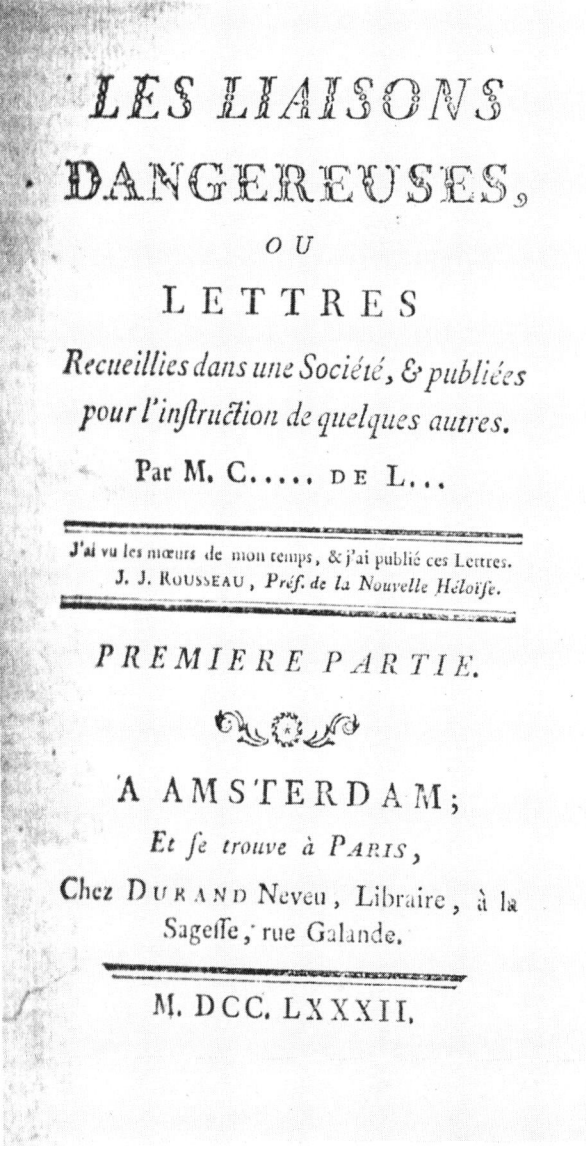

Title page for Laclos's best-known book, an epistolary novel about the planned seduction of a young girl and a married woman (Thomas Cooper Library, University of South Carolina)

taken over by the enemy. As punishment for his affront to the military establishment, Laclos was sent to the Ecole Militaire in La Fère, 150 kilometers from Paris, where his wife joined him six months later and where their second child, Catherine-Soulange, was born in 1787.

In 1788 Laclos requested a new leave of absence to accept a position as secretary to Philippe, duc d'Orléans, Louis XVI's cousin. Laclos's work in that capacity has raised much debate: contemporary pamphleteers and later critics accused him of conspiring to place Orléans on the throne in order to serve his own

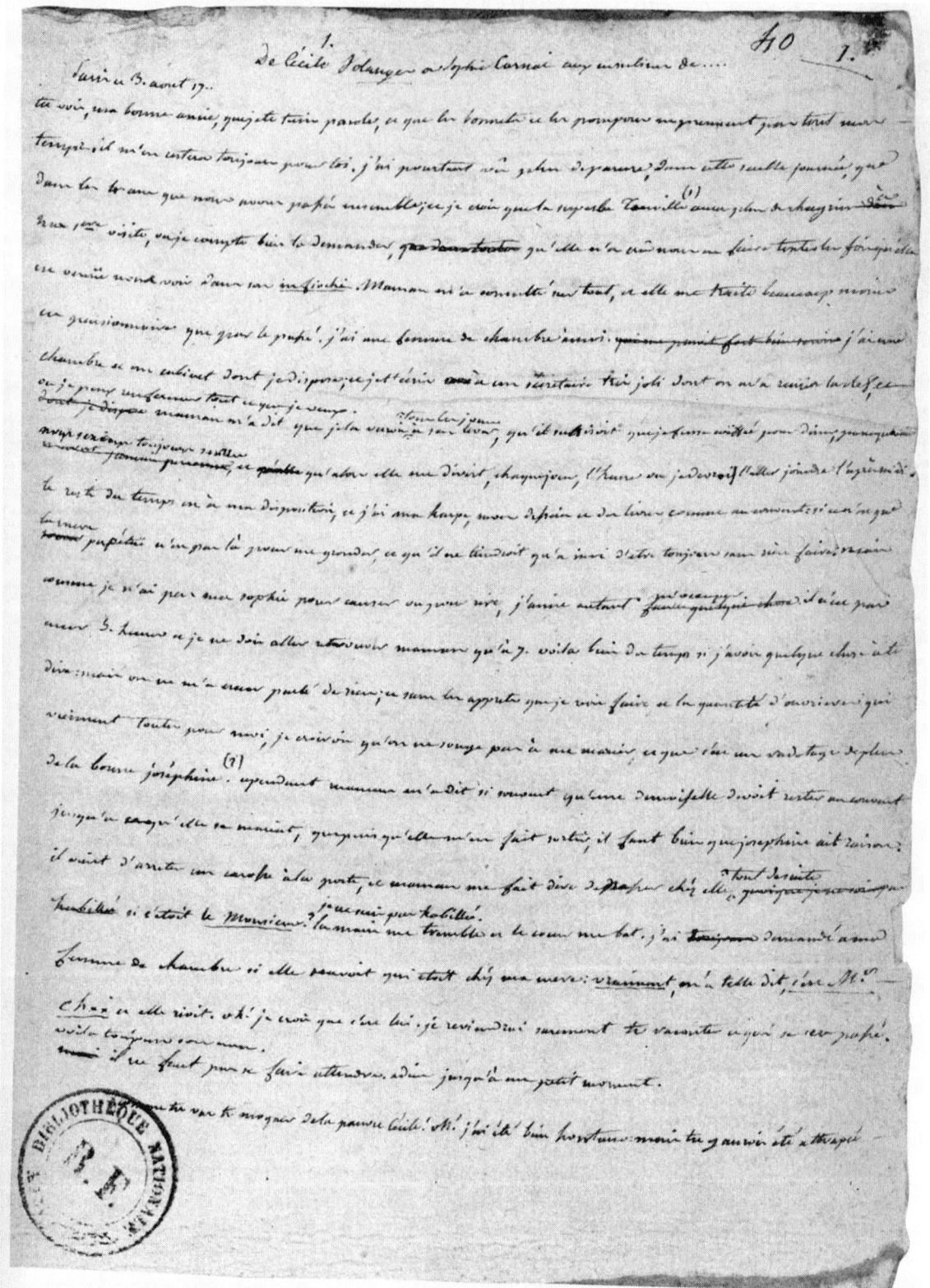

Page from the manuscript for Laclos's Les Liaisons dangereuses, 1782 (Bibliotheque nationale; from Roselyne De Ayala and Jean-Pierre Gueno, eds., Belles Lettres: Manuscripts by the Masters of French Literature, 2001; Bruccoli Clark Layman Archives)

political ambitions. Laclos was more likely acting out of principle. As secretary, he kept the duc informed of the political mood in Versailles, helped his supporters to get elected to the Estates-General, and wrote instructions that Orléans sent to those who drafted the *cahiers de doléances*–the lists of grievances to be discussed by the Estates-General. The duc's demands included freedom of the press, abolition of arbitrary arrests, privacy of correspondence, the right to private property, and equitable taxation. Laclos agreed with Orléans's progressive ideas but had little faith in his character and leadership ability. Laclos remained faithful to the duc, however, for lack of a better leader.

Laclos joined the Société des amis de la Constitution (Society of the Friends of the Constitution), also called the Jacobin Club, in 1790, was chosen editor of its newspaper and member of the correspondence committee, and participated in the many debates that followed the king's flight to Varennes in June 1791. To fill the void in the executive position while the new constitution for the country was being drafted, Laclos proposed to the Jacobin Club that Orléans be named regent to the throne. The events that led to the fall of the monarchy on 10 August 1792 put an end to Laclos's dream of a constitutional monarchy and left him isolated from both the Jacobins, who had now turned to radical republicanism, and from the ultraroyalists. Laclos was dismissed by the duc d'Orléans and resigned from his positions in the Jacobin Club. He was reinstated in the army and given the responsibility of organizing the defense against the Prussians.

During the Terror, Laclos was imprisoned twice for his ties to the Orléans faction and released, thanks to his previous contacts in the Jacobin Club and his technical expertise. In 1793 he was asked to experiment with the hollow cannonball that he had invented in 1786. While in prison the second time, he worked on a book on French grammar, tutored fellow prisoners, studied rural economy, and wrote encouraging letters to his wife, advising her to read the Stoics. He barely escaped the guillotine and was released in December 1794, shortly before the birth of his third child, Charles, the following year.

Laclos worked in the office of loans between 1795 and 1799, dedicating himself to writing and to caring for his family. By all accounts, he was a devoted husband and father. The works he wrote during that period–all published posthumously–include a treatise, "De la guerre et de la paix" (1979, *On War and Peace*), an untitled essay on the education of women, and a review of the publication of Jean-François de Galoup, comte de La Pérouse's travel diaries. Laclos's third essay on the education of women (1908), more practical than the first two, consists of reading recommendations for the comtesse de Gurson's daughter. As in letter 81 of *Les Liaisons dangereuses* and his review of *Cecilia*, he reiterates the importance of reading and annotating novels, and of studying works of morality and history, all necessary to lead a virtuous life, understand humanity, and improve one's style. He also recommends the study of Latin and science, and includes remarks on pedagogy, stressing the importance of gearing education to the needs and interests of the individual child. Laclos's untitled review of *Voyage de La Pérouse autour du monde*, written in 1797 and first published in 1951 (translated as *A Voyage Around the World*, 1798–1799), emphasizes his liberal egalitarian views. He cites an excerpt in which La Pérouse criticizes imperialism and focuses at length on La Pérouse's description of the advanced social development of a primitive-looking tribe. Based on La Pérouse's comments on peoples he met during his fateful travels, Laclos discusses the relative advantages of material and moral progress and, like Rousseau, reaches the conclusion that technological progress and moral decay go together. These later writings testify to Laclos's lifelong interest in literary, educational, and anthropological issues, and to his dedication to the improvement of humanity.

Like his brother, Laclos espoused the cause of Napoleon and was rewarded for his support by being named a general in the artillery on 16 January 1800 and serving in the army of the Rhine and in Italy. He died of dysentery in Taranto on 5 September 1803. His only novel, which is regularly reedited and adapted for the stage and the movie theater, continues to bring him the fame that he had expected to receive from his military career.

Letters:

Lettres inédites de Choderlos de Laclos (Paris: Société du Mercure de France, 1904).

Bibliographies:

Colette Verger Michael, *Choderlos de Laclos: The Man, His Works, and His Critics: An Annotated Bibliography* (New York: Garland, 1982);

David Coward, "Laclos Studies, 1968–1982," *Studies on Voltaire and the Eighteenth Century*, 219 (1983): 289–328;

Richard Frautschi, "Addenda to a Recent Bibliography on Laclos," *Romance Notes*, 25, no. 2 (1984): 153–159.

Biographies:

Emile Dard, *Un Acteur caché du drame révolutionnaire: le général Choderlos de Laclos, auteur des Liaisons dangereuses* (Paris: Perrin, 1905);

Georges Poisson, *Choderlos de Laclos, ou l' obstination* (Paris: Grasset, 1985).

References:

Charles Baudelaire, "Notes sur *Les Liaisons dangereuses*," in *Oeuvres complètes,* volume 2, edited by Claude Pichois (Paris: Gallimard, 1976), pp. 66–75;

Pierre Bayard, *Le Paradoxe du menteur: sur Laclos* (Paris: Minuit, 1993);

Jean Bloch, "Laclos and Women's Education," *French Studies,* 38, no. 2 (1984): 144–158;

Peter Brooks, *The Novel of Worldliness: Crébillon, Marivaux, Laclos, Stendhal* (Princeton: Princeton University Press, 1969);

Colette Cazenobe, "Le Système du libertinage de Crébillon à Laclos," *Studies on Voltaire and the Eighteenth Century,* 282 (1982);

Peter Conroy, *Intimate, Intrusive, and Triumphant: Readers in the Liaisons dangereuses,* Purdue University Monographs in Romance Languages (Philadelphia: Benjamins, 1987);

Joan DeJean, *Literary Fortifications: Rousseau, Laclos, Sade* (Princeton: Princeton University Press, 1984);

André Delmas and Yvette Delmas, *A la Recherche des Liaisons dangereuses* (Paris: Mercure de France, 1964);

Denis Diderot, *Les Paradoxe sur le Comédien,* in *Oeuvres,* edited by André Billy (Paris: Gallimard, 1951), pp. 1033–1088;

Film Forum: Les Liaisons dangereuses (1959, 1988 & 1989), special issue of *Eighteenth-Century Life,* 14, no. 2 (May 1990);

Lloyd R. Free, ed., *Laclos: Critical Approaches to Les Liaisons dangereuses* (Madrid: José Porrúa Turanzas, 1978);

Françoise de Graffigny, *Les Lettres d'une Péruvienne* (New York: MLA, 1993);

Madelyn Gutwirth, "Laclos and 'Le Sexe': The Rack of Ambivalence," *Studies on Voltaire and the Eighteenth Century,* 189 (1980): 247–296;

Emita B. Hill, "Man and Mask: The Art of the Actor in the *Liaisons dangereuses*," *Romanic Review,* 63 (1972): 111–124;

Brigitte E. Humbert, *De la Lettre à l'écran: Les Liaisons dangereuses* (Amsterdam: Rodopi, 2000);

Jean François de Galaup de La Pérouse, *Voyage de La Pérouse autour du monde,* 4 volumes, edited by L.-A. Millet-Mureau (Paris, 1797);

Paul-Edouard Levayer, "Les Ecrits politiques de Laclos," *Revue d'histoire littéraire de la France,* 69 (1969): 51–60;

André Malraux, *Le Triangle noir: Laclos, Goya, Saint-Just* (Paris: Gallimard, 1970);

Nancy K. Miller, *The Heroine's Text: Readings in the French and English Novel, 1722–1782* (New York: Columbia University Press, 1980);

Charles Secondat de Montesquieu, *Les Lettres persanes,* edited by Paul Vernière (Paris: Garnier, 1960);

René Pomeau and Laurent Versini, eds., *Laclos et le libertinage* (Paris: Presses Universitaires de France, 1983);

Revue d'histoire littéraire de la France, special Laclos issue, 82 (1982);

Ronald C. Rosbottom, *Choderlos de Laclos* (Boston: G. K. Hall, 1978);

Christine Roulston, *Virtue, Gender, and the Authentic Self in Eighteenth-Century Fiction: Richardson, Rousseau, and Laclos* (Gainesville: University Press of Florida, 1998);

Jean-Jacques Rousseau, *Julie, ou La Nouvelle Héloïse,* in *Oeuvres complètes,* volume 2, edited by Bernard Gagnebin and Marcel Raymond (Paris: Gallimard, 1961), pp. 1–793;

Jean-Luc Seylaz, *Les Liaisons dangereuses et la création romanesque chez Laclos* (Geneva: Droz, 1958);

Philip M. Thody, *Les Liaisons dangereuses* (London: Arnold, 1970);

Tzvetan Todorov, *Littérature et signification* (Paris: Larousse, 1967);

Laurent Versini, *Laclos et la tradition: essai sur les sources et la technique des Liaisons dangereuses* (Paris: Klincksieck, 1968);

Versini, "Laclos reconsidéré d'après sa correspondance," in *Approches des Lumières: mélanges offerts à Jean Fabre* (Paris: Klincksieck, 1974), pp. 547–560;

Versini, *"Le Roman le plus intelligent": les Liaisons dangereuses de Laclos* (Paris: Champion, 1998).

Papers:

Pierre-Ambroise-François Choderlos de Laclos's manuscripts and papers are found primarily at the Bibliothèque nationale, the Bibliothèque de l'Arsenal and the Archives nationales in Paris, and the Musée de Picardie in Amiens. Documents about his military life are also found at the archives of the Château de Vincennes and in the local archives of the cities where he was stationed.

Jean-François de La Harpe

(20 November 1739 – 11 February 1803)

Christopher Todd
Leeds University

BOOKS: *L'Aléthophile, ou l'ami de la vérité* (Amsterdam [i.e., Paris], 1758);

Héroïdes nouvelles, précédées d'un essai sur l'héroïde en général (Amsterdam & Paris: Cailleau, 1759);

Caton à César, et Annibal à Flaminius. Héroïdes (Paris, 1760);

L'Homme de lettres. Epître à Monsieur *** ([1760]);

Le Philosophe des Alpes, ode qui a concouru pour le prix de l'Académie françoise en 1762 (Paris: Brunet, 1762);

Le Comte de Warwik, tragédie (Paris: Duchesne, 1764);

Timoléon, tragédie en cinq actes et en vers (Paris: Duchesne, 1764);

Montézume à Cortez; Elisabeth de France, à Don Carlos; héroïdes nouvelles (Paris: Cailleau, 1764);

La Délivrance de Salerne et la Fondation du Royaume des Deux-Siciles. Poème couronné à l'Académie de Rouen le 25 août, jour de Saint-Louis (Paris: D'Houry, [1765]);

Mélanges littéraires, ou épîtres et pièces philosophiques (Paris: Duchesne, 1765);

Le Poète. Epître qui a remporté le prix de l'Académie françoise en 1766 (Paris: Regnard, 1766);

Eloge de Charles V, roi de France. Discours qui a remporté le prix de l'Académie françoise en 1767 (Paris: Regnard, 1767);

Des Malheurs de la guerre, et des avantages de la paix, discours qui a remporté le prix au jugement de l'Académie françoise, au mois de janvier 1767 (Paris: Regnard, 1767);

Les Douze Césars, traduits du Latin de Suétone, avec des notes et des réflexions, 2 volumes (Paris: Lacombe, 1770);

Mélanie, drame en trois actes et en vers (Amsterdam: Wan-Harrewelt, 1770);

Eloge de François de Salignac de La Mothe-Fénelon, archevêque de Cambrai, précepteur des enfans de France. Discours qui a remporté le prix de l'Académie françoise en 1771 (Paris: Demonville, 1771);

Des Talens dans leurs rapports avec la société et le bonheur. Pièce qui a remporté le prix de l'Académie françoise en 1771 (Paris: Regnard, 1771);

Eloge de Racine (Amsterdam & Paris: Lacombe, 1772);

Réponse d'Horace à M. de V** ([1772]);

Jean-François de La Harpe (Bibliothèque municipale de Lille; from Christopher Todd, Voltaire's Disciple: Jean-François de La Harpe, *1972; Thomas Cooper Library, University of South Carolina)*

La Navigation. Ode qui a remporté le prix de l'Académie françoise, en 1773 (Paris: Brunet & Demonville, 1773);

Eloge de La Fontaine, qui a concouru pour le prix de l'Académie de Marseille, en 1774 (Paris: Lacombe, 1774);

Vers à Sa Majesté Louis XVI, sur l'Edit du 31 mai (Paris: Morin, 1774);

Conseils à un jeune poète. Pièce qui a remporté le prix de l'Académie française en 1775 (Paris: Demonville, 1775);

Eloge de Nicolas de Catinat, Maréchal de France. Discours qui a remporté le prix de l'Académie Françoise, en 1775 (Paris & Avignon: Guichard, 1775);

Discours prononcés dans l'Académie françoise le jeudi 20 juin 1776, à la réception de M. de La Harpe (Paris: Demonville, 1776);

La Lusiade de Louis Camoëns, poème héroïque en dix chants, nouvellement traduit du portugais, avec des notes & la vie de l'auteur, 2 volumes (Paris: Nyon, 1776);

Oeuvres de M. de La H***, revues et corrigées par l'auteur, 3 volumes (Yverdon: Société littéraire et typographique, 1777);

Les Barmécides, tragédie en cinq actes et en vers, représentée pour la première fois par les Comédiens français le 11 juillet 1778 (Paris: Pissot, 1778);

Oeuvres de M. de La Harpe, de l'Académie française. Nouvellement recueillies, 6 volumes (Paris: Pissot, 1778);

Aux Mânes de Voltaire, dithyrambe qui a remporté le prix, au jugement de l'Académie françoise en 1779 (Paris: Demonville, 1779);

Les Muses rivales, ou l'Apothéose de Voltaire, en un acte, et en vers libres. Représentées pour la première fois, par les Comédiens français, le 1er février 1779 (Paris: Pissot, 1779);

Abrégé de l'Histoire générale des voyages, 21 volumes (Paris: Hôtel de Thou [Panckoucke], 1780);

Eloge de Voltaire (Geneva & Paris: Pissot, 1780);

Tangu et Félime, poème en IV chants (Paris: Pissot, 1780);

Menzicoff, ou les exilés, tragédie représentée devant leurs Majestés sur le Théâtre de Fontainebleau, au mois de novembre 1775 (Paris: Lambert & Baudouin, 1781);

Philoctète, tragédie, traduite du grec de Sophocle, en trois actes et en vers (Paris: Lambert & Baudouin, 1781);

Molière à la nouvelle salle, ou les audiences de Thalie, comédie en un acte et en vers libres. Représentée pour la première fois par les Comédiens français, sur le nouveau Théâtre du Faubourg Saint-Germain, le 12 avril 1782 (Paris: Lambert & Baudouin, 1782);

Jeanne de Naples, tragédie en cinq actes et en vers, représentée par les Comédiens français le 12 décembre 1781, au Palais des Tuileries; & à Versailles, devant leurs Majestés, le 20 du même mois; remise au nouveau Théâtre du Faubourg S. Germain, le 29 mai 1783 (Paris: Baudouin, 1783);

Coriolan, tragédie en cinq actes, et en vers, représentée pour la première fois, à Paris, par les Comédiens français le 2 mars 1784, & à Versailles, devant Leurs Majestés, le 11 du même mois (Paris: Belin & Brunet, 1784);

Adresse des auteurs dramatiques à l'Assemblée nationale, prononcée par M. de La Harpe dans la séance du mardi soir 24 août (Paris, [1790]);

Discours sur la liberté du Théâtre, prononcé par M. de La Harpe, le 17 décembre 1790, à la Société des Amis de la Constitution (Paris: Impr. Nationale, [1790]);

Réponse aux observations pour les comédiens français (Paris: [Bossange, 1790]);

Hymne à la liberté, récité à la séance de l'ouverture du Lycée, le lundi 3 décembre 1792 . . . imprimé aux frais de l'Administration du Lycée (Paris: Haener, [1792]);

Virginie, tragédie en cinq actes et en vers, représentée pour la première fois au Théâtre français du faubourg Saint-Germain, le 11 juillet 1786, et reprise sur le Théâtre de la République le 9 mai 1792 (Paris: Girod & Tessier, 1793);

Le Chant des Triomphes de la République française, ode. Musique de Le Sueur, de l'Institut national de musique (Paris: Au magasin de musique, [1794]);

Le Salut public, ou la vérité dite à la Convention par un homme libre (Paris: Migneret, an III [1794 or 1795]);

Acte de garantie pour la liberté individuelle, la sûreté du domicile, et la liberté de la presse (Paris: Migneret, an III [1795]);

"Leçons de littérature, prononcées à l'Ecole normale," in *Séances des Ecoles normales, recueillies par des sténographes et revues par les professeurs*, 5 volumes (Paris: Regnier, 1795), I: 170–188, II: 100–115, III: 180–227, IV: 201–222, 339–365, V: 151–173;

Lettres de Baudin à Laharpe, et de Laharpe à Baudin (Paris: Chevet, an III [1795]);

La Liberté de la presse, défendue . . . contre Chénier (Paris: Migneret, an III [1795]);

Oui ou non ([Paris: Migneret, 1795]);

Sections de Paris, prenez-y garde! discours prononcé dans la section de la Butte des Moulins ([Paris]: Chevet, an IV [1795]);

De la Guerre déclarée par nos derniers tyrans à la raison, à la morale, aux lettres et aux arts. Discours prononcé à l'ouverture du Lycée républicain, le 31 décembre 1794 (Paris: Migneret, an IV [1796]);

Sur la Déclaration exigée des prêtres catholiques (Paris & Brussels: Mornéweck, [1797]);

De l'Etat des lettres en Europe, depuis la fin du siècle qui a suivi celui d'Auguste, jusqu'au règne de Louis XIV. Discours prononcé à l'ouverture du Lycée républicain, le 1er décembre 1796 (Paris: Migneret, an V [1797]);

Du Fanatisme dans la langue révolutionnaire, ou de la persécution suscitée par les Barbares du dix-huitième siècle, contre la religion chrétienne et ses ministres (Paris: Migneret, an V [1797]);

Lettre de M. de La Harpe à La Revellière-Lépeaux (l'un des cinq directeurs de la République française) en faveur de la Religion et de ses ministres (London: Baylis, 1797);

Réfutation du livre de l'Esprit, prononcée au Lycée républicain, dans les Séances des 26 et 29 mars et des 3 et 5 avril (Paris: Migneret, an V [1797]);

Le Pseautier en français, traduction nouvelle, avec des notes pour l'intelligence du texte, et des argumens à la tête de chaque Pseaume; précédée d'un Discours sur l'esprit des livres saints et le style des prophètes (Paris: Migneret, an VI [1798]);

Lycée ou Cours de littérature ancienne et moderne, 16 volumes (Paris: Agasse, an VII [1799]–1805);

Correspondance littéraire, adressée à son altesse impériale, Mgr le Grand-Duc, aujourd'hui empereur de Russie, et à M. le comte André Schowalow, chambellan de l'impératrice Catherine II, depuis 1774 jusqu'à [1791], 6 volumes (Paris: Migneret, 1801–1807);

Oeuvres choisies et posthumes de M. de La Harpe, 4 volumes (Paris: Migneret, 1806);

"Commentaire sur le théâtre de Racine," in *Oeuvres completes de Jean Racine,* 7 volumes (Paris: Agasse, 1807);

Commentaire sur le théâtre de Voltaire . . . Imprimé d'après le manuscrit de ce célèbre critique et approprié aux différentes éditions de ce théâtre. Recueilli et publié par *** [L. P. Decroix] (Paris: Maradan, 1814);

Le Triomphe de la religion, ou le Roi martyr, poème épique (Paris: Migneret, 1814);

Prédiction de Cazotte, faite en 1788, et rapportée par La Harpe (Paris: Marchands de nouveautés / Montpellier: Seguin, 1817);

Mémoires du prince Menzicoff, favori de Pierre le Grand (Paris: Galignani / London: Iley, 1819);

Le Couvent des Camaldules, suivi de la Réponse d'un solitaire de La Trappe à l'abbé de Rancé (Paris: Sanson, 1826);

"Récit inédit de la mort de Voltaire," *Journal des débats,* 30 January 1869, pp. 2–3–published by Hippolyte Taine from a transcription sent to Catherine II by Ivan Bariatinsky;

"Two Lost Plays by La Harpe: *Gustave Wasa* and *Les Brames,*" edited by Christopher Todd, *Studies on Voltaire and the Eighteenth Century,* 62 (1968): 151–272;

"Un discours inédit de La Harpe: Les Sections et la Convention en 1795," présenté par David Adams, *Annales historiques de la Révolution française,* 50 (1978): 478–484.

Collection: *Oeuvres de La Harpe de l'Académie française,* 16 volumes (Paris: Verdière, 1820–1821).

PLAY PRODUCTIONS: *Le Comte de Warwik,* Paris, Comédie française, 7 November 1763;

Timoléon, Paris, Comédiens ordinaires du Roi, 1 August 1764;

Pharamond, Paris, Comédiens français, 14 August 1765;

Gustave Wasa, Paris, Comédiens français, 3 March 1766;

Menzicoff, ou les exilés, Théâtre de Fontainebleau, November 1775;

Les Barmécides, Paris, Comédiens français, 11 July 1778;

Les Muses rivales, ou l'Apothéose de Voltaire, Paris, Comédiens français, 1 February 1779;

Jeanne de Naples, Palais des Tuileries, Comédiens français, 12 December 1781;

Molière à la nouvelle salle, ou les audiences de Thalie, Théâtre du Faubourg Saint-Germain, Comédiens français, 12 April 1782;

Philoctète, Paris, Comédiens français, 16 June 1783;

Les Brames, Versailles, Comédiens français, 4 December 1783;

Coriolan, Paris, Comédiens français, 2 March 1784;

Virginie, Paris, Théâtre français, 11 July 1786;

Mélanie, Paris, Théâtre de La République, 7 December 1791.

OTHER: *Journal de politique et de littérature, contenant les principaux événemens de toutes le cours, les nouvelles de la république des lettres,* edited from 5 August 1776 onward by La Harpe and Joseph-Gaspard Dubois-Fontanelle, with the collaboration of Jean-Baptiste Antoine Suard and Louis Jean-Pierre de Fontanes (Bruxelles, Paris: Hôtel de Thou, 5 October 1774–15 June 1778);

Mercure de France, dédié au Roi par une société de gens de lettres, edited by La Harpe from June to November 1778 (Paris: Hôtel de Thou, June 1778–December 1789);

Mèmorial ou Receuil historique, politique et littèraire, edited by La Harpe, in collaboration with Imon Jèrome Bourlet de Vauxcelles et Louis Jean-Piere de Fontanes (20 May–4 September 1797);

SELECTED PERIODICAL PUBLICATION– UNCOLLECTED: "Ecrit qui devait précéder une édition épurée des œuvres de Laharpe," *Mercure,* 19 (5 January 1805): 126–130.

Many French writers in the nineteenth century found Jean-François de La Harpe's authority in matters of taste to be tyrannical. Stendhal said to Jean-Louis Guez de Balzac at least twice that he despised La Harpe's work, even though he had earlier suggested to his sister that she should read La Harpe's *Lycée ou Cours de littérature ancienne et moderne* ([1799]–1805, Lycée or the Course of Literature Ancient and Modern) as a primary introduction to literature. The many editions of this work that appeared throughout the first half of the nineteenth century demonstrate its continuing influence. Gustave Flaubert complained to Louise Colet that La Harpe still ruled them all from his tomb, though he felt that the true path for literary criticism lay somewhere between La Harpe's method of teaching established good taste through reference to the golden models of the past and the later fashionable habit of

La Harpe's house at Corbeil, where he hid to avoid arrest after the government was overthrown on 4 September 1797 (Bibliothèque nationale; from Christopher Todd, Voltaire's Disciple: Jean-François de La Harpe, 1972; Thomas Cooper Library, University of South Carolina)

weighing up the psychological background of the writer. Certainly, modern critics continue to stress the importance of La Harpe in the development of the art of literary history.

Judging La Harpe dispassionately has never been easy, as throughout much of his life and beyond, his character was a subject of controversy. Small in stature with a reputation for hubris and guile as well as having an eye for the ladies, he was a favorite target for the scandal sheets, and his combative journalism aroused such ire that in order to protect the other contributors, his editor forced him to take the then-unusual step of signing his articles in the *Mercure de France* (Mercury of France) from January 1771 on. In 1776, La Harpe's election to the Académie française (French Academy) was interpreted by many as the result of scheming by the Voltairean clique. At the same time La Harpe was criticized for taking advantage of the misfortune of others; for instance, when Simon Nicholas Henri Linguet was deprived of the profitable editorship of *Le Journal de Politique et de Littérature* (The Journal of Politics and Literature), La Harpe replaced him. In 1778 Marie-Jean-Antoine-Nicolas Caritat, marquis de Condorcet, and others accused La Harpe of ingratitude toward a man under whose shadow he had prospered when he dared to publish criticism of Voltaire's plays only weeks after the great man had died. In an oblique reference to how the former leading Voltairean converted to Christianity under the French Revolution and ended his days as a pillar of the Catholic church, attacking much of what the Enlightenment represented, the ever-hostile Stendhal called La Harpe a comical Tartuffe.

La Harpe's early career could almost have served as an archetype for that of any bright young man from a poor background anxious to gain success in the literary world of the day. Like Sébastien-Roch Nicolas de Chamfort and Jean-François Marmontel, La Harpe was rescued from poverty through his schooling before going on to seek success in prose and verse competitions at the Académie française and with a play at the Comédie française. The path to success was not, however, an easy one. La Harpe was born on 20 November 1739 in what is now the fifth arrondissement of Paris, the son of a former artillery captain of the same name from Rolle in Switzerland and of his wife, Marie-Louise Devienne. The family had fallen on hard times, and it became destitute when La Harpe's father died on 6 May 1749. The nine-year-old was taken in by some local nuns, and in the autumn of that year his parish priest presented him to the headmaster of the Collège d'Harcourt, who was so impressed by the boy that he granted him a scholarship. As a pupil, La Harpe worked hard and soon became adept at winning prizes while gaining a thorough grounding in the classics. He began his literary career while a somewhat desultory law student, publishing verse and soon choosing to which literary camp he should belong. He claimed to have quickly quarreled with Voltaire's enemy Elie Catherine Fréron, and La Harpe seems to have had some part at least in an attack on the latter called *L'Aléthophile* (friend of truth), published in January 1758.

In March 1760 he was reminded of the fragility of his position as a poor boy made good when he was accused of writing scurrilous verse against his former teachers. While friends and acquaintances used their influence to get out of trouble, he was imprisoned, somewhat arbitrarily, for more than two months. However, the experience only brought a momentary halt to the development of his literary career, and at the end of 1760 he strengthened his position as a follower of Voltaire with the publication of *L'Homme de lettres. Epître à Monsieur* *** (The Man of Letters. An Epistle to Monsieur ***), dedicated to Voltaire. La Harpe continued to publish other verse and even won an honorable mention for poetry from the Académie française in 1762. By this time he was already working hard on his first tragedy, *Le Comte de Warwik* (first performed 1763; first published 1764, The Count of Warwick), taking great care over it, only too aware, as Voltaire had been with *Oedipe* (1730, Oedipus), that success at the theater was the best key to a young author's making an early mark on the literary scene. The first performance of *Le Comte de Warwik* on 7 November 1763 marked the beginning of La Harper's association with the Comédie française, which made him the most performed author of his generation, even if he never again enjoyed quite the same degree of success.

With active support from Voltaire, La Harpe was now assured of his place in literary society, though he hardly improved his financial situation through marrying the daughter of a café owner, Marie-Marthe Monmayeux, on 22 November 1764. The gossip was that La Harpe was coerced into marrying Monmayeux, but whatever the case, the marriage did not prove to be a particularly happy one, and La Harpe was not the most faithful of husbands. He formed various liaisons with other women, of which the most publicized was with Stéphanie-Félicité, comtesse de Genlis, in 1779. Taking advantage of the new rules brought about by the Revolution, the childless La Harpe and his wife divorced on 29 March 1793, and she died at Saint-Germain-en-Laye on 11 November 1794.

From 1765 to 1768, La Harpe had mixed success in various academic competitions, and, to rescue him from his financial difficulties, Voltaire invited La Harpe and his wife to spend more and more time at his home at Ferney, where the young man worked slowly on new tragedies, acted in Voltaire's theater, and indulged in a mild flirtation with another guest. This peaceful routine came to an abrupt end in February 1768 when Voltaire accused La Harpe of circulating unauthorized copies of *La Guerre civile de Geneve* (1768, The Civil War of Geneva) among his Parisian friends. To what extent La Harpe had been led into this act by Voltaire's niece, Marie-Louise Mignot Denis, is still a subject of discussion, but in any case Voltaire was furious, particularly because La Harpe prevaricated. Voltaire sent La Harpe and nearly everybody else in the house back to Paris.

Voltaire did not bear a grudge against La Harpe for long, and the latter was soon defending Voltaire's cause in the pages of the *Mercure de France*. In 1774 Voltaire managed to improve La Harpe's financial situation when, with the help of Shuvalov, chamberlain to Catherine the Great, he obtained for La Harpe the post of literary correspondent to Paul, the heir to the Russian throne, a position that La Harpe kept until 1791. La Harpe also started a similar correspondence with King Gustavus III of Sweden. The drafts of his letters to Paul and to Shuvalov were later published in a highly revised form as his *Correspondance littéraire* (1801–1807, Literary Correspondance).

La Harpe was now also a prominent member of various Parisian salons and became an acquaintance if not a close friend of most of the well-known literary figures of the day, until the late 1770s when he quarreled most notably with those who preferred the music of Christoph Willibald Gluck to that of Giacomo Puccini. At many gatherings La Harpe read his verse and his plays, and he enjoyed considerable success in 1770 with recitations of a drama called *Mélanie* (1770), a work designed to strengthen further the tradition of antimonastic literature with its story of a young girl's being forced to become a nun against her will.

He was soon thinking that with the help of his powerful friends even the doors of the Académie française would be open to him before long. Such ambition was initially thwarted, however, when he was accused in 1770 of having written anonymous verse against Armand-Jean du Plessis, maréchal de Richelieu. In 1771 La Harpe won the prize for eloquence from the academy with his *Eloge de François de Salignac de La Mothe-Fénelon* (1771, Elegy of François de Salignac de La Mothe-Fénelon), but it was banned, and he was forced to submit to interrogation by theologians. He had become a source of contention between rival factions within the academy itself, and resistance to his election lasted until 1776. The year of glory for him at the academy was 1775, when, with undoubted help from Jean Le Rond d'Alembert, he won prizes for both eloquence and poetry. La Harpe was finally elected to the academy on 13 May 1776 and took his seat on 20 June. There he continued to defend the Voltairean cause, and in 1779 he even took part in a plot to ensure that Voltaire's memory would be celebrated by one of his own party by winning the poetry prize anonymously with his *Aux Mânes de Voltaire* (1779, To Voltaire's Departed Spirit), even though the rules hardly allowed for a member of the academy to take part in the competition himself.

As editor of *Le Journal de Politique et de Littérature,* La Harpe filled its pages with articles by his Voltairean friends and Voltaire himself, and when André Joseph Panckoucke combined the paper with the *Mercure de France* in June 1778, La Harpe became editor of the latter. However, his growing lack of popularity with the general public led to a loss in sales, and in November of the same year he lost his position. He had other work to fall back on, however, notably his editing of the

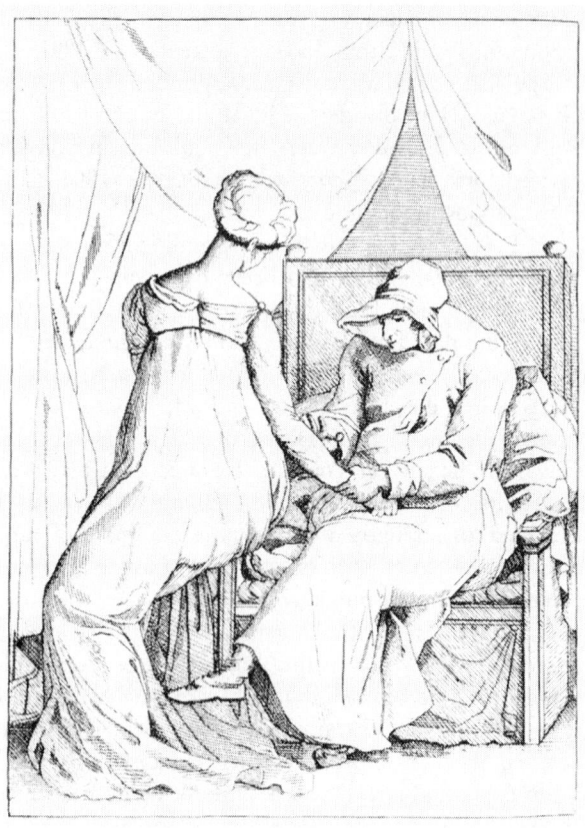

Jeanne-Françoise-Julie Bernard Récamier, salon hostess and friend, visiting La Harpe during his final illness (Brotherton Library, University of Leeds; from Christopher Todd, Voltaire's Disciple: Jean-François de La Harpe, *1972; Thomas Cooper Library, University of South Carolina)*

abridgment of *Histoire générale des voyages* (1746, General History of Voyages), by Antoine François Prévost d'Exiles (abbé Prévost), for which La Harpe had signed a lucrative contract with Panckoucke in 1775 and which was published in 1780. Although La Harpe still relied in traditional fashion on patronage and pensions for much of his income, to the further annoyance of some of his rivals, he was typical of what was a fairly new phenomenon at the time–a writer who managed to make a fair living out of what he produced, even if he sometimes had to descend to mere hackwork.

In addition, La Harpe fought hard to defend what he saw as his intellectual property. He was a founding member with Pierre-Augustin Caron de Beaumarchais and others in 1777 of the Bureau de législation dramatique (Office of Dramatic Legislation), the forerunner of Société des auteurs et compositeurs dramatiques (Society of Dramatic Authors and Composers), but he quarreled more and more frequently with the actors, whom he accused of wanting his plays to fail so that they could then claim ownership of the copyright. The struggle grew all the more bitter as time went on and continued into the Revolution.

On 13 January 1786, despite recurrent ill health, which had started around 1782, La Harpe embarked on a new career as professor of literature at the newly established Lycée in the rue de Valois. This institution, designed to occupy the leisure hours of the fashionable with instruction on a multitude of subjects, was a huge success, and La Harpe–with his good speaking voice and pleasing appearance–soon became one of its star attractions. In the years that followed, from the beginning of December to the end of August, twice a week La Harpe worked his way through the literary canon, from the writers of classical antiquity onward, building up the corpus for what became his most enduring work, *Lycée ou Cours de littérature ancienne et moderne*.

La Harpe's active involvement in the politics of the Revolution was limited to membership in the Paris Commune for a few weeks up to September 1789, but in November 1789 he was given a new outlet for expressing political as well as literary ideas when he returned to writing book reviews for the *Mercure de France*. In the early years of the Revolution, he cultivated the friendship of Honoré-Gabriel Riqueti, comte de Mirabeau, and became a member of the then-moderate Jacobin Club. Inevitably, La Harpe played a leading role in the ceremonies that accompanied the transferal of Voltaire's remains to the Panthéon on 11 July 1791.

To La Harpe's later chagrin, however, he was caught up in the increasing radicalization of the Revolution as it moved from a constitutional monarchy to a republican dictatorship: he wrote patriotic verse and publicly expressed approval for some of the worst excesses of the republic, even if–still in his heart a Voltairean elitist–he could scarcely bring himself to feel much sympathy for the uneducated masses. He was accused by some people of being unaware of the reality of what was going on around him, protected as he was by the ivory tower of literature. Others say that he finally fell into disfavor with the Terror through refusing to wear the Phrygian bonnet while at the Lycée, and a warrant for his arrest was issued on 16 March 1794.

Imprisonment was a chastening experience, even if it meant, because of his chronic ill health, transferal to a clinic after a short stay in the overcrowded Luxembourg. The threat of imminent execution remained real, and he turned for comfort to his fellow prisoners, who found solace in their Christian faith. La Harpe listened, and when he was finally freed on 1 August 1794, he was a changed man. Now ruined financially, he wanted to live quietly, but with a mission to preach in favor of religion. Tranquility was hardly in his nature, and apart from wanting to celebrate the post-Thermidorian spirit in verse, he now started to lecture on the Revolutionaries and their misuse of language: such words as *liberté* and *égalité* became meaningless, and a scant regard for form and linguistic etiquette reflected the attacks on social order and decency.

In the meantime, La Harpe not only defended his newfound faith but also started to be active in right-wing Royalist circles. Following the suppression of the popular uprising from the Left in May 1795, the government–always anxious to occupy the middle ground–sought to curb the right-wing press, a move that brought a stinging response from La Harpe. He also objected to the decision to allow two-thirds of the deputies of the new chambers created in 1795 to be chosen from among the members of the National Convention. Following his part in the abortive Vendémiaire uprising of October 1795, La Harpe had to hide for a little more than a year in a friend's house. While in hiding, he developed what he had said in his lectures and started work on a form of monumental dictionary later called "L'Esprit de la Révolution, ou commentaire historique sur la langue révolutionnaire." He never finished this work, though fragments were later published in various forms, and out of it grew one of the most polemic of his later works, the much reprinted *Du Fanatisme dans la langue révolutionnaire* (1797, On Fanaticism in the Language of the Revolution). In his lectures he started to attack those writers of the Enlightenment whom he held as responsible for undermining traditional moral values. He also returned to journalism and with Louis, marquis de Fontanes and abbé Simon-Jérôme Bourlet de Vauxelles on 20 May 1797 founded *Le Mémorial, ou recueil historique politique et littéraire* (The Memorial, an Historical, Political and Literary Miscellany), a daily paper designed to criticize the government.

Now the darling of the right-wing clubs, at the age of fifty-seven and not in the best of health, La Harpe was talked by Jacque and Jeanne Récamier into a disastrous marriage with a young girl aged twenty-three, Louise-Catherine Victoire de Hatte de Longuerue. They were married on 29 July 1797 and remained together for three weeks. In any case, the time was not right for domestic bliss. Fearing arrest following the sudden overthrow of the government on 4 September 1797, La Harpe fled from Paris and found refuge first near Dôle in the Jura and then nearer Paris in Corbeil, where he remained for more than two years. Again in hiding, he worked on an apologia of Christianity and, developing the theme of his recent lectures, wrote the *Histoire de la philosophie du XVIIIe siècle* (The Philosophical History of the Eighteenth Century), which eventually appeared as the final two volumes of his *Lycée ou Cours de littérature ancienne et moderne* and in which he separated those members of the Enlightenment such as Georges-Louis Leclerc de Buffon and Jean Le Rond d'Alembert, to whom he allowed some value, and those such as Claude-Adrien Helvétius and Denis Diderot, whom he now dismissed as sophists.

Jean-François de La Harpe finally returned to Paris on 16 January 1800 and took up lodgings in a small flat near Notre-Dame de Paris. By now in extremely poor health and impecunious, he returned to the Lycée in November to resume his attacks on the Enlightenment. Poverty probably forced him to bring out the first four volumes of his *Correspondance littéraire* in 1801 and thus resurrect old quarrels that had lain dormant for some years. Many people were struck by the incongruity of seeing La Harpe publish a text dating from a period that he now saw as a time of apostasy. While working on an expurgated edition of his works, in which he intended to remove all that might be deemed offensive to religion, he composed his last work, *Le Triomphe de la religion* (1814, The Triumph of Religion), an epic on the martyrdom of Louis XVI. In January 1803, La Harpe fell victim to an influenza epidemic, and he died on 11 February 1803, declaring, as *The Times* (London) reported 22 February 1803, "that he had a firm belief in the truth of the Christian religion, and solemnly retracted whatever may have appeared in his writings against its precepts and constitution."

Letters:

Richard Laurens Hawkins, "Unpublished French Letters of the Eighteenth Century," *Romanic Review*, 21 (1930): 1–15, 128–131, 209–217, 308–314;

Alexandre Jovicevich, *Correspondance inédite de J. F. de La Harpe* (Paris: Editions universitaires, 1965);

Christopher Todd, "La Harpe Quarrels with the Actors: Unpublished Correspondence," *Studies on Voltaire and the Eighteenth Century*, 53 (1967): 223–337;

Jovicevich, "Thirteen Additional Letters of La Harpe," *Studies on Voltaire and the Eighteenth Century*, 67 (1969): 211–228;

Todd, ed., *Letters to the Shuvalovs* (Banbury: Voltaire Foundation, 1973);

Rémy Landy, "La 'Correspondance suédoise' de Jean-François de La Harpe," *Studies on Voltaire and the Eighteenth Century*, 212 (1982): 225–310.

Bibliography:

Christopher Todd, *Bibliographie des oeuvres de Jean-François de La Harpe* (Oxford: Voltaire Foundation, 1979).

Biographies:

"La Harpe et les comédiens français," *Revue Retrospective,* 10 (1837): 296–302; 11 (1838): 191–192;

J. d'Hertault de Beaufort, *J. F. de La Harpe, littérateur français, 1739–1803* (Paris: 5, rue Bayard, 1904);

Louis de Préaudeau, "La Harpe et son bonnet rouge," *Revue hebdomadaire,* 9 (1911): 532–556;

"La Harpe robespierriste," *Révolution française,* 62 (1912): 546–549;

Louis Chardiny, "Aventure de La Harpe chez Mme Récamier, racontée par le bibliophile Coste," *Bulletin de la Société littéraire de Lyon,* 9 (1926): 62–69;

Christopher Todd, *Voltaire's Disciple: Jean-François de La Harpe* (London: M.H.R.A., 1972);

Alexandre Jovicevich, *Jean-François de La Harpe, adepte et renégat des Lumières* (South Orange: Seton Hall University Press, 1973);

Jovicevich, "Voltaire and La Harpe. L'Affaire des manuscrits. A Reappraisal," *Studies on Voltaire and the Eighteenth Century,* 76 (1979): 77–95.

References:

Theodore Besterman, "Le vrai Voltaire par ses lettres [La Harpe and the Stolen Manuscript Affair]," *Studies on Voltaire and the Eighteenth Century,* 10 (1959): 9–48;

Douglas Alan Bonneville, "La Harpe as Judge of his Contemporaries," dissertation, Ohio State University, 1961;

Daniel Brewer, "Political Culture and Literary History. La Harpe's 'Lycée,'" *Modern Language Queries,* 58 (1997): 163–184;

Pascal Caglar, "Deux précurseurs de l'histoire littéraire au XVIIIe siècle. La Harpe, Mme de Staël," *Ecole des Lettres II,* 85, no. 7 (1994): 7–17;

R. Chase, "La Harpe et Sainte-Beuve," *University of Toronto Quarterly,* 1 (1895): 11–20;

Jean-Marie Goulemot, "Le Cours de littérature de La Harpe ou l'émergence du discours de l'histoire des idées," *Littérature,* 6, no. 24 (December 1976): 51–62;

Andrew Hunwick, *La Critique littéraire de La Harpe* (Berne & Las Vegas: Peter Lang, 1977);

Hunwick, "La Harpe, the Forgotten Critic," *Modern Language Review,* 63 (1972): 282–290;

Rémy Landy, "Des Lumières à la contre-révolution. Un drame écartelé, la Mélanie de La Harpe," *Dix-huitième siècle,* 6 (1974): 143–152;

Landy, "Le prisme La Harpe," *Studies on Voltaire and the Eighteenth Century,* 63 (1976): 1255–1285;

Pierre Larthomas, "La Harpe critique de Beaumarchais et Gudin de la Brenellerie critique de La Harpe," *Dramaturgies, langages dramatiques. Mélanges pour Jacques Schérer* (Paris: Nizet, 1986), pp. 543–550;

Emile Malakis, "The First Use of Couleur Locale in French Literary Criticism," *Modern Language Notes,* 60 (1945): 98–99;

Hisayasu Nakagawa, "Une conclusion sur le temps des philosophes," *Etudes de langue et littérature française,* 66 (1995): 61–74;

Jean-Noël Pascal, "La mort de Mlle de Lespinasse dans les 'Correspondances littéraires' de Grimm et de La Harpe," in *Du Baroque aux Lumières. Pages à la mémoire de Jeanne Carriat* (Paris: Rougerie, 1986), pp. 176–179;

René Perin, *Esprit de J. F. de La Harpe, avec une notice sur cet académicien* (Paris: Hubert, 1814);

Alexis Pitou, "The authorship of La Harpe's 'Molière à la nouvelle salle' (1782)," *Australian Journal of French Studies,* 10 (1973): 326–333;

Pitou, "Les trois textes de la Mélanie de La Harpe," *Revue d'histoire littéraire de la France,* 16 (1909): 540–553;

William Reymond, *La Harpe et Sainte-Beuve* (Lausanne: Corbax et Rouiller fils, 1854);

Christopher Todd, "The Present State of La Harpe's Correspondence: A Provisional Catalogue," *Studies on Voltaire and the Eighteenth Century,* 94 (1972): 159–218;

Jacques Vier, "Le meurtre par les mots. La Harpe, 'Du Fanatisme dans la langue révolutionnaire,' 1797," in *Littérature à l'emporte-pièce* (Paris: Editions du Cèdre, 1976), pp. 161–171.

Anne-Thérèse de Lambert
(Anne-Thérèse de Marguenat de Courcelles, marquise de Lambert)
(25 September 1647 – 12 July 1733)

Catherine Daniélou
University of Alabama at Birmingham

BOOKS: *Lettre d'une dame à son fils. Sur la vraye gloire. Mémoires de littérature et d'histoire,* anonymous (Paris: Desmolets, 1726);

Réflexions nouvelles sur les femmes, par une dame de la Cour de France, anonymous (Paris: Le Breton, 1727);

Avis d'une mère à son fils et à sa fille, anonymous (Paris: Ganeau, 1728); translated as *Advice from a Mother to Her Son and Daughter* (London: Printed for Tho. Worrall, 1729);

Traité de l'amitié, par madame la marquise de ***, anonymous, in *Recueil de divers écrits sur l'amour et l'amitié* (Paris: Vve Pissot, 1736);

Oeuvres de Madame la Marquise de Lambert, avec un abrégé de sa vie, 2 volumes (Paris: Ganeau, 1742); translated as *The Works of the Marchioness de Lambert. Containing Thoughts on Various Entertaining and Useful Subjects, Reflections on Education, on the Writings of Homer and on Various Public Events of the Time* (London: Owen, 1749).

Collection: *Oeuvres,* edited by Robert Granderoute (Paris: Champion, 1990).

Anne-Thérèse de Lambert (from Paul Gazagne, Marivaux par lui, *1954; Thomas Cooper Library, University of South Carolina)*

Tuesdays were no ordinary days in early-eighteenth-century intellectual Parisian circles. Indeed, from 1698 until 1733, Tuesdays were well known for being the days when Anne-Thérèse, marquise de Lambert, hosted her famous literary and philosophical salon. When she died in 1733 at age eighty-five, Lambert had devoted nearly half her life to intellectual pursuits and social gatherings. Little in her early life indicated such a remarkable future.

Anne-Thérèse de Marguenat de Courcelles was born in Paris on 25 September 1647 to Monique Passart, who belonged to the rich middle class, and Etienne de Marguenat de Courcelles, whose family had risen from the upper middle class to acquired nobility. The young girl knew little of her father, who died in 1650. Her mother remarried quickly and secretly to François de Bachaumont, an Epicurean poet who initiated the convent-raised child into the world of letters, ideas, and refined discussions. In 1666 at age eighteen, Anne-Thérèse married Henri de Lambert, marquis of Saint-Bris–a brilliant thirty-five-year-old captain in the Royal Cavalry Regiment. After the 1684 siege of Luxembourg, Henri de Lambert became governor of the city and duchy of Luxembourg. Already sick when he and his wife moved to Luxembourg, Henri de Lambert died in 1686. Left with two children, Anne-Thérèse enjoyed a well-known name, a small royal pension, and a castle and land near Auxerre, but she possessed no liquid assets. Many legal and financial difficulties lay ahead for the widow, who waited until 1698 to inherit her paternal fortune—her mother having bequeathed it to her second husband. Anne-Thérèse de Lambert's two children, Monique-Thérèse, born in 1669, and Henri-François, born in 1677, were the focus of her life, and she devoted her first works to them. In Luxembourg, as the governor's wife in charge of a luxurious residence, she acquired a rich personal library, embraced a refined lifestyle, and represented the prestige of the French monarchy with grace and elegance. This experience proved useful when she moved back to Paris, where she fostered intellectual debates among the great minds and elite friends who gathered in her home.

In 1691 the forty-four-year-old widow, plagued by a long and difficult lawsuit she had brought against her mother, moved to rue de Richelieu. Seven years later, she finally inherited the fortune that was rightfully hers, and Lambert moved to a larger and more prestigious residence in the northern portion of the Hôtel de Nevers, located on the same street. Close to the Palais-Royal, it was part of the Mazarin palace that eventually became the Royal Library of France, later renamed Bibliothèque nationale.

Lambert lived in the Hôtel de Nevers until her death in 1733. For more than twenty years, especially after 1710, that residence became the most important and most renowned salon of the time. Functional, harmonious, solemn, rich, and well-lit, the interior design as well as the ceremonial were reminiscent of Catherine De Vivonne, marquise de Rambouillet's Chambre bleue (Blue Chamber)—the famous literary salon of the previous century that Lambert sought to emulate. In the early 1640s, when its reputation peaked, the Chambre bleue instituted new rules of purity of taste, urbanity, and social behavior. Its influence on the development of *préciosité*—a form of refined feminine wit and sensitivity—was enormous, as well as its impact on language, literature, and later salons. However, Lambert's salon did not become a pale imitation of Rambouillet's; it combined an aristocratic and précieux influence with the intellectual and rigorous ideal of *honnêteté*—the new code of politeness and grace of the second half of the seventeenth century, promoted by such moralists as François, duc de La Rochefoucauld. Although often compared to the Hôtel de Rambouillet, Lambert's salon welcomed the new ideals of modernity that eventually gave birth to the spirit of the Enlightenment.

Quite different in scope from the cafés and clubs of the time—whose customers did not have to follow any particular rules and enjoyed much greater freedom of expression and behavior—Lambert's salon was, indeed, ceremonious and more strictly organized. Its habitués could not be as free or audacious. Yet, despite the restrictions and stringent rules, it became the epicenter of literary and intellectual life, was open to modernity and progress, and fostered Enlightenment philosophy. In fact, it was instrumental in spreading a neoprécieux climate that continued to reign after Lambert's death. In turn, Lambert's salon served as a model for Claudine de Tencin's. Though different and less rigid, the latter became as influential as the former, especially after the death of Lambert, when Tencin switched her reception day to Tuesday.

So rigorously intellectual was the focus of Lambert's salon, it hardly had any room for entertainment, gambling, or games. The guests—intellectuals, writers, and influential personalities—first had lunch and then defined the agenda of the afternoon conversation. After determining the topics of discussion, the circle selected the manuscripts to be read and the order in which they would be presented. Soon, Lambert began to host a second weekly reception on Wednesdays. These gatherings were less rigorously planned and less intellectually stringent than those on Tuesdays. Wednesday receptions allowed Lambert to invite a larger group—not only her regular guests but also new or less prestigious ones, as well as foreign writers or intellectuals visiting Paris. Tuesday meetings, however, remained the most influential on Parisian intellectual and literary life during the late reign of Louis XIV and the Regency.

Topics discussed at Lambert's gatherings ranged from literary, philosophical, or moral themes, to happiness, friendship, love, education, women's status, science, and erudition. Books on utopia and education were also discussed, as Lambert was particularly interested in the works of Nicolas Malebranche, John Locke, and Charles-Louis de Secondat baron de Montesquieu. Her most prestigious guests included Bernard Le Bovier de Fontenelle; Montesquieu; Pierre Carlet de Chamblain de Marivaux; Antoine Houdar de La Motte; Anne Le Fèvre Dacier; René-Louis de Voyer de Paulmy, marquis d'Argenson; François-Joseph de Beaupoil de Sainte-Aulaire; Nicolas-Hubert, abbé Mongault; Henri de Boulainvilliers; Claude-Prosper Jolyot de Crébillon *père*; Louis de Sacy; and Anne-Bénédicte-Louise de Bourbon-Condé, duchesse du Maine. Although the full impact of these gatherings on the guests is difficult to assess, Lambert's overall legacy as hostess of these Tuesday reunions proved to be strong and enduring.

Debates in this salon were especially heated in the early part of the eighteenth century during the well-known Querelle des anciens et des modernes (Quarrel of the Ancients and Moderns), which had started decades earlier when Charles Perrault raised the issue in *Le Siècle de Louis le Grand* (1687, The Century of Louis XIV) and *Parallèle des Anciens et des Modernes* (1688–1697, A Parallel between Ancients and Moderns). He argued that the traditional veneration for ancient Greek and Latin writers and their imitators was taking its toll on modernity and new ideals. Almost three decades later, the dispute reached its final stage when de La Motte, one of Lambert's regular guests, published a 1714 "translation" of Homer's *Iliad*. He could not read Greek and had based his own interpretation on Dacier's translation. His preface, demystifying the Greek poet, triggered the last development of a conflict of civilization between humanist tradition and modernity, and eventually led the way to the Enlightenment. Having grown up with the "ancients," but a "modern" herself, Lambert acted as a referee, helped to foster a reconciliation by focusing on practical relativism, and thus brought closure to the long dispute.

Known as the antechamber to the Académie française (French Academy), the Tuesday salon at the Hôtel de Nevers exerted considerable influence over elections to the academy. Roger Marchal compiled numbers, indicating that one-fifth of the members elected between 1700 and 1733 were regular guests and friends of Lambert, who obtained their election through the cooperation of her influential circle. For example, Montesquieu owed her his election in 1727, difficultly won against the intrigues of prelates. Lambert's will, as well as her force of persuasion, gave her the extraordinary powers denied to her because of her gender. Prohibited from admission to the French Academy as a woman, Lambert nevertheless left her mark on this venerable institution.

No one knows exactly when Lambert started to write. As she read her manuscripts to her guests, she wished perhaps to be more than a mere spectator in the literary life she was fostering in Paris. First, she wrote as a mother, probably between 1690 and 1700, composing separate essays for her children, who were about to enter adulthood and aristocratic social circles. *Avis d'une mère à sa fille* (1728; translated as *Advice of a Mother to her Daughter*, 1749) was written for Monique-Thérèse, while *Avis d'une mère à sons fils* (1726; translated as *Advice of a Mother to her Son*, 1749) was intended for Henri-François. Never meant for publication, both essays were inspired by François de Salignac de la Mothe-Fénelon's treatise on the education of girls, *Education des filles* (1687; translated as *Treatise on the Education of Daughters*, 1805) and *Les Aventures de Télémaque* (1699; translated as *The Adventures of Telemachus*, 1701). Lambert focused on the personality of each of her children and the gender role assigned to him or her. She stressed the importance of civility, duty, and decent conduct in a frivolous and corrupt world. As adults, her children were expected to cultivate sociability and generosity, to live virtuously, to avoid selfishness, and to find happiness within themselves. Much in the vein of seventeenth-century moralists, Lambert attempted to define a moral philosophy. Above all, she wanted her children to be true to themselves. Although

Hôtel de Nevers, where Lambert conducted a salon for many years; it was part of the Mazarin palace (from Paul Gazagne, Marivaux par lui, *1954; Thomas Cooper Library, University of South Carolina)*

her other well-known works—*Réflexions nouvelles sur les femmes* (1727, New Reflections on Women), *Traité de l'amitié* (1736, Treatise on Friendship), *Traité de la viellesse* (1742, Treatise on Old Age), *Réflexions sur le goût* (1742, Reflections on Taste) and *Réflexions sur les richesses* (1742, Reflections on Wealth) focus on specific topics, they ultimately address the same issues developed in earlier writings.

Personal, yet strongly influenced by such moralists as Michel de Montaigne, Blaise Pascal, Pierre Nicole, Rochefoucauld, and Jean de La Bruyère, Lambert's works have often been described as lacking originality. Furthermore, while her contributions as a salonnière have always been acknowledged, her essays have often been dismissed as belonging neither to the seventeenth century nor to the eighteenth. Indeed, Lambert straddles both centuries: she owes to the former her analysis of the relationship between self and society; yet, she stands out in her own time as a singular and unusual voice, that of a Cartesian woman trying to achieve balance in the world and believing in the search for happiness.

Lambert's few and short works were written for her personal use, to be read only before guests at the Tuesday salon. When excerpts of *Advice from a Mother to Her Son* were published in 1726 as *Lettre d'une dame à son fils* (Letter of a Lady to Her Son) without her knowledge and against her will, and were soon followed by *Réflexions nouvelles sur les femmes* (1727, New Reflections on Women), she was utterly appalled and attempted to buy back the editions. The following year, both treatises to her children were also published without her consent. She felt disgraced by these acts, because she believed that a scholarly woman should be modest and humble, and should avoid the ridicule and discredit that befell the seventeenth-century *précieuses*.

Yet, in many ways, Lambert was leading the *précieuses* through her writings. With strength and determination, she denounced the condition of women, who were denied a proper education. She deplored that women lived in a society that exploited them, deprived them of knowledge, and kept them in intellectual, social, and moral servitude. She noted that women, left to themselves in a state of ignorance, could only find compensation in vain behavior, coquettishness, pleasure, and corruption. Like the *précieuses,* Lambert attacked injustice, claimed women's right to education, and believed that a woman's best way of influencing society derived from refined behavior. Her works emphasize personal solutions and redefine the role of women and men in their daily existence. In that respect, for instance, she encourages her daughter to remain independent and to hold steadfast to dignity, lucidity, and virtue. In her *Traité de la viellesse* (Treatise on Old Age), also dedicated to Monique-Thérèse, she sees the ideal old age as a mere continuation of a serene and generous existence of self-respect or a return to one's inner self following a life of worldly distractions.

Although inspired by earlier moralists and convinced of the benefits of a restrained and rigorous life of lucidity and discretion, Anne-Thérèse de Lambert indeed belonged to the Enlightenment, not only because of the influence of her extraordinary salon for thirty years but also because of her belief in reason, perfectibility, and the possibility of attaining happiness on earth.

Letters:

Jean-Bernard Le Blanc, ed., *Lettres de monsieur de La Motte [de la duchesse Du Maine et de la marquise de Lambert, publiées par l'abbé J.-B. Le Blanc] suivies d'un recueil de vers du même auteur . . .* (N.p., 1754);

Léopold Collin, ed., *Lettres de mademoiselle de Montpensier, de mesdames de Motteville et de Montmoranci, de mademoiselle Du Pré et de madame la marquise de Lambert . . .* (Paris: Collin, 1806).

References:

Faith Beasley, "Anne-Thérèse de Lambert and the Politics of Taste," *Papers on French Seventeenth Century Literature,* 37 (1992): 337–344;

Emmanuel de Broglie, "Les mardis et les mercredis de la Marquise de Lambert, 1710–1733," *Le Correspondant,* 179 (1895): 140–162, 319–345;

Catherine Daniélou, "'L'amour-propre éclairé': Pierre Nicole et Madame de Lambert," *Papers on French Seventeenth-Century Literature,* 42 (1995): 171–183;

Marie-José Fassiotto, *Mme de Lambert (1647–1733), ou le féminisme moral* (New York: Peter Lang, 1985);

Robert Granderoute, "De l'Education des filles aux Avis d'une mère à sa fille: Fénelon et Madame de Lambert," *Revue d'Histoire Littéraire de la France,* 87, no. 1 (1987): 15–30;

Granderoute, "Madame de Lambert et Montaigne," *Bulletin de la Société des Amis de Montaigne,* 7–8 (1981): 97–106;

Ellen McNiven Hine, "Madame de Lambert, her sources and her circle: on the threshold of a new age," *Studies on Voltaire and the Eighteenth Century,* 102 (1973): 173–190;

Paul Hoffmann, "Madame de Lambert et l'exigence de dignité," *Travaux de linguistique et de littérature,* 11 (1973): 19–32;

Ginette Kryssing-Berg, "La Marquise de Lambert ou l'ambivalence de la vertu," *Revue Romane,* 17 (1982): 35–45;

Roger Marchal, *Madame de Lambert et son milieu* (Oxford: Voltaire Foundation, 1991);

Corrado Rosso, "Madame de Lambert e lo spettro della meritocrazia," in *Mythe de l'égalité et rayonnement des Lumières* (Pisa: Goliardica, 1980), pp. 47–54;

Jeannette Geffriaud Rosso, "Madame de Lambert," in *Etudes sur la féminité aux XVIIe et XVIIIe siècles* (Paris, 1984), pp. 65–125;

J.-P. Zimmerman, "La morale laïque au commencement du dix-huitième siècle: Madame de Lambert," *Revue d'histoire littéraire de la France,* 24 (1917): 42–64, 440–466.

Julien Offroy de La Mettrie

(25 December 1709 - 11 November 1751)

Mary McAlpin
University of Tennessee

BOOKS: *Traité du vertige avec la description d'une catalepsie hystérique, et une lettre à M. Astruc dans laquelle on répond à la critique qu'il a faite d'une dissertation de l'auteur sur les maladies véneriennes, par M. de La Mettrie* (Rennes: Vve de P. A. Garnier, 1737);

Lettres de M. D. L. M., docteur en médecine, sur l'art de conserver la santé et de prolonger la vie (Paris: Prault père, 1738);

Nouveau traité des maladies véneriennes (Paris: Huart, 1739);

Traité de la petite vérole, avec la manière de guérir de cette maladie (Paris: Huart, 1740);

Essais sur l'esprit et les beaux esprits (Amsterdam: Bernard, 1740);

Vie de M. Hermann Boerhaave (Paris, 1740);

Observations sur quelques endroits du traité de M. Astruc, De morbis Venereis (Cartagena [i.e., Paris], 1741);

Observations de médecine pratique (Paris: Huart, 1743);

Saint Cosme vengé (Strasbourg: Doulseker & Pockle, 1744);

Histoire naturelle de l'âme, ou traité de l'âme (The Hague [i.e., Paris]: J. Néaulme, 1745; revised edition, Oxford [i.e., Paris?], 1747);

Politique du médecin de Machiavel, ou, le chemin de la fortune ouvert aux médecins (Amsterdam: Bernard, 1746);

La Faculté vengée, comédie en trois actes (Paris: Quillau, 1747); republished as *Les charlatans démasqués, ou Pluton vengeur de la société de médecine, comédie ironique en trois actes en prose* (Paris: Aux dépens de la Compagnie, 1762);

L'Ecole de la volupté: dans l'isle de Calypso, aux dépens des nymphes (Cologne: P. Marteau, 1747);

L'Homme-machine (Leiden: Luzac, 1748); translated as *Man a Machine* (London: W. Owen, 1749);

L'Homme-plante (Potsdam: Voss, 1748);

L'Homme plus que machine (Leiden, 1748);

Ouvrage de Pénélope, ou Machiavel en médecine, 3 volumes (Berlin, 1748-1750);

Anti-Sénèque, ou le souverain bien (Potsdam, 1750);

Mémoire sur la dysenterie (Leiden: Luzac, 1750);

Les Animaux plus que machines (Berlin, 1750);

Julien Offroy de La Mettrie (etching by George Friedrich Schmidt; from Raymond Boissier, La Mettrie, médecin, pamphlétaire et philosophe *[1709-1751], 1931; Thomas Cooper Library, University of South Carolina)*

Réflexions philosophiques sur l'origine des animaux (Berlin, 1750);

Oeuvres de médecine (Berlin: Froméry, 1751);

Oeuvres philosophiques, volume 1 (London [i.e., Berlin]: J. Nourse, 1751); volume 2 (Amsterdam, 1753);

L'Art de jouir (Berlin, 1751);

Vénus métaphysique, ou essai sur l'origine de l'âme humaine (Berlin: Voss, 1752).

Editions and Collections: *L'Homme-plante,* edited by Francis L. Rougier (New York: Columbia University Press, 1936);

Oeuvres philosophiques, edited by Francine Markovits (Paris: Fayard, 1987).

Editions in English: *L'Homme-machine: A Study in the Origins of an Idea,* edited by Aram Vartanian (Princeton: Princeton University Press, 1960);

Machine Man and Other Writings, edited and translated by Ann Thomson (Cambridge: Cambridge University Press, 1996).

TRANSLATIONS: *Système de M. Herman Boerhaave sur les maladies vénériennes, traduit en français par M. de La Mettrie* (Paris: Prault fils, 1735);

Aphorismes de M. Herman Boerhaave sur la connoissance et la cure des maladies (Rennes: Vve de P. A. Garnier, 1738; revised edition, Paris: Huart, 1745);

Traité de la matière médicale, pour servir á la composition des remèdes indiqués dans les Aphorismes par M. Herman Boerhaave; auquel on a ajouté les opérations chymiques du même auteur (Paris: Huart, 1739);

Institutions de médecine de M. Herman Boerhaave traduites du latin en français par M. de La Mettrie, 2 volumes (Paris: Huart, 1739, 1740; revised edition, 8 volumes, Paris: Huart, 1743–1750);

Abrégé de la théorie chymique, tiré des propres écrits de M. Boerhaave, par M. de La Mettrie (Paris: Huart/Briasson, 1741).

Julien Offroy de La Mettrie was the most infamous materialist philosopher of the French Enlightenment, a reputation caused in part by his unusual willingness to publish his atheistic philosophy. In his most important philosophical work, *L'Homme-machine* (1748; translated as *Man a Machine,* 1749), La Mettrie applies the Cartesian view of animals as soulless machine-like automata to human beings. Like the majority of his writings, *L'Homme-machine* was not published under La Mettrie's own name but under one of several pen names, a superficial precaution that did little to hide his identity. Banished successively from France and Holland, he settled in Berlin under the protection of Frederick the Great in 1748 and began to explore the moral consequences of his radical materialism. Having argued that all mental activity has its origin in sensation and that the existence of an immortal soul is a fanciful notion, La Mettrie concluded that human beings should make decisions based on their own potential happiness. He was subsequently denounced as a dangerous hedonist by both the French philosophes and their opponents. His works largely ignored, La Mettrie was generally viewed as an immoral and possibly unbalanced extremist until the 1960s. As critics began to rediscover his work, La Mettrie was rehabilitated as a daring innovator whose writings constitute an important step in the development of the modern scientific worldview.

La Mettrie was born on 25 December 1709 into a prosperous family in Saint-Malo. His father, a textile merchant, sent him to school to study for an ecclesiastical career, but La Mettrie chose instead to become a doctor. His training as a physician became a central component of his philosophical writings. La Mettrie had little respect for philosophers with no clinical training; in *L'Homme-machine* he goes so far as to declare that any writer without such training should avoid making pronouncements on the relationship between the mind and the body. Although his medical studies took place for the most part in Paris, for financial reasons he earned his final degree at Reims. His fascination with the mechanical functioning of the human body then led him to Leiden, where he became a disciple of Hermann Boerhaave, a natural philosopher influenced by the Cartesian notion that the soul receives sensations by means of animal spirits traveling through the nerves. While Boerhaave's iatromechanistic view of the body supposed a human automaton acting in a machine-like fashion, he ascribed the initial animation of this body to a conscious soul made in the image of God. La Mettrie claimed Boerhaave as the primary inspiration for his own work, translating Boerhaave's works into French as well as writing his biography, *Vie de M. Hermann Boerhaave* (1740, The Life of Mr. Hermann Boerhaave).

Other important influences on La Mettrie's philosophical writings include Abraham Trembley and Albrecht von Haller. Trembley's experiments on the polyp famously put into question the division between the animal and vegetable kingdoms, as detailed in his *Mémoires pour servir à l'histoire d'un genre de polypes d'eau douce* (1744, Memoirs for Preserving the History of a Type of Freshwater Polyp). This blurring of the boundaries dividing animals and plants, like that dividing human beings and animals, is an important theme in La Mettrie's works. Haller's relationship to La Mettrie was more combative. Although Haller's well-known experiments aimed at demonstrating a force inherent to animal muscle fibers, he was a Christian who proclaimed his belief in a divine soul. Haller objected to being the object of La Mettrie's dedicatory preface to *L'Homme-machine;* La Mettrie later claimed that by dedicating the work to Haller he had been attempting to hide his own authorship of the work.

Another important stimulus on La Mettrie's thought was the work of Voltaire, especially the critique of Blaise Pascal's Jansenism found in the *Lettres philosophiques* (1734, Philosophical Letters; translated as *Letters Concerning the English Nation,* 1733). During La

Mettrie's short career as a student of theology he had been quite influenced by Jansenism and may even have written a pro-Jansenist work that Frederick the Great mentioned in his eulogy, but it has never been found. La Mettrie admired Voltaire not only as a stylist but also as the greatest genius of the time, perhaps of all time. Although the two writers occasionally clashed, Voltaire returned La Mettrie's admiration, attempting (unsuccessfully) to have the philosopher's exile lifted.

The first extant works of La Mettrie's own writing career are treatises on medical questions, including *Traité du vertige avec la description d'une catalepsie hystérique* . . . (1737, Treatise on Dizziness with a Description of a Cataleptic Fit . . .), and *Traité de la petite vérole, avec la manière de guérir de cette maladie* (1740, Treatise on Smallpox, with a Means to Cure That Malady). Even in his early medical works La Mettrie demonstrates an unusual willingness to question received knowledge. During the pamphlet wars between the surgeons and the physicians of the late 1720s, he supported the surgeons in their efforts to challenge the authority of the doctors, even though he was a doctor himself. He championed the surgeons' practical experience over the bookish, antiquated training he had received during his medical studies. While such attacks on the established medical training of his day should be viewed as part of a general movement away from ancient authorities and toward clinical observation, as with his philosophical works La Mettrie was willing to go much further in his attacks than others who supported his opinion.

He also actively pursued a medical practice during this period of his life, first in Saint-Malo and later as personal physician to the duc de Gramont. He then assumed a medical post in the French military that led to a decisive experience in the development of his materialist philosophy. Convalescing from a wound received during battle that had caused a high fever, La Mettrie began to consider the interrelationship between physical and mental states. The result was the *Histoire naturelle de l'âme, ou traité de l'âme* (1745, Natural History of the Soul, or Treatise on the Soul), condemned by the Church and now considered the immediate precursor to *L'Homme-machine*. La Mettrie was permanently banished from Paris in 1746, as much for his medical writings as for his philosophy. His *Ouvrage de Pénélope, ou Machiavel en médecine* (1748–1750, Penelope's Work, or Machiavelli in Medicine), a reflection on his career as a medical satirist, was ordered burned, along with *La Faculté vengée, comédie en trois actes* (1747, The Faculty Avenged, a Comedy in Three Acts) and *Politique du médecin de Machiavel* (1746, Machiavelli's Politics for Doctors). La Mettrie had presented this last work to the public as a translation of an ancient Chinese text, but like the attribution of the *Histoire naturelle de l'âme* to an Englishman named Mr. Charp, this ruse did not offer adequate protection to the real author.

L'Homme-machine, written during La Mettrie's two-year exile in Holland, is a far bolder expression of theses already present in the earlier *Histoire naturelle de l'âme*. René Descartes had proposed that animals were mere bodies, capable of feeling and judging but essentially automata; in contrast, human beings were also endowed with an immortal, immaterial soul. As Descartes's critics had long warned, the conclusion that man was himself merely a "machine," that is, a purely physical mechanism, was the inevitable next step. While in the *Histoire naturelle de l'âme* La Mettrie proposes that human mental activity is controlled by physiological conditions (as when he himself was unable to think clearly in a feverish state) and argues that there is no proof of the existence of an immaterial soul, in *L'Homme-machine* he dismisses the immortal soul as a mere fantasy produced by a lack of scientific method. La Mettrie sees no logical justification for postulating two distinct substances in man. Followers of Descartes, La Mettrie writes, argue as if these two separate substances could be "seen and calculated"; his own philosophy is known as monism, based as it is on the belief that the world is composed of one sort of matter. Building on Haller's experiments with muscle fibers, La Mettrie argues that there is no need to suppose a second substance, for matter is clearly animated by its own inherent faculty of sensation. At the very least, he argues, there is no reason to assume otherwise, for there is no proof to the contrary.

La Mettrie excuses the limits of Cartesian reasoning as related to the historical moment of the philosopher's birth rather than to any defects in his genius, implying that Descartes would have supported the notion of man as machine had he been La Mettrie's contemporary. Despite this appeal to Descartes's authority, La Mettrie's brand of materialism is radically opposed to Cartesian principles. La Mettrie did not stop at a direct attack on Cartesian dualism; he also targeted the basis of the Cartesian method. In *L'Homme-machine* La Mettrie soundly denounces rationalism as a priori reasoning uninformed by intimate knowledge of the workings of the human body. As always, scientific observation is the only authority that he will allow as decisive. In an ironic echo of Pascalian humility before the vast natural universe, La Mettrie observes that to be blind and to believe oneself capable of walking without the cane of scientific observation is to be blind indeed. He declares himself ignorant of exactly how organized matter acquires the faculty of thought but argues that this awareness will at least keep him from reproducing the useless albeit impressive masterpieces of previous philosophers (Nicolas Malebranche is singled out for

Title page for La Mettrie's controversial 1748 philosophical work, translated in 1749 as Man a Machine, *in which he argues that man is a purely physical mechanism with no immortal soul (from a 1912 edition of* Man a Machine; *Thomas Cooper Library, University of South Carolina)*

ridicule). By grounding his own philosophy in observation, La Mettrie argues, he is guaranteed neither complete nor certain knowledge but rather a higher degree of probability concerning the true nature of man.

The scandal surrounding the publication of *L'Homme-machine* caused La Mettrie to flee Holland and to seek asylum in Prussia, where he served as doctor and court reader to Frederick II from 1748 until his death in 1751. He continued to publish medical treatises and again challenged received medical opinion in his *Vénus métaphysique, ou essai sur l'origine de l'âme humaine* (1752, Metaphysical Venus, or Essay on the Origin of the Human Soul), in which he presents a theory of human reproduction based on the attraction of elements in both male and female "seminal fluid." His philosophical writings during these last three years of his life became increasingly scandalous as he began to consider the moral consequences of his radical atheism. In works such as *Anti-Sénèque, ou le souverain bien* (1750, Anti-Seneca, or the Sovereign Good), La Mettrie proposes a natural morality based on the cultivation of pleasing sensations. Presenting himself as in the same line as Michel de Montaigne, La Mettrie argues that self-denial is contrary to reason. Since humans are born blank Lockean slates, they possess no innate awareness of natural law nor of transcendent good to guide their behavior. The relativity of social customs and mores in different countries demonstrates to La Mettrie that while education may be a highly effective manner of controlling human behavior, any particular system of training is based on arbitrary grounds. The very need for education demonstrates it to be a force that works against each individual's natural human impulse to maximize pleasure and minimize pain.

La Mettrie's insistence on the cultivation of pleasure drew sharp attacks from both sides of the philosophical divide in France. Denis Diderot and Paul-Henri Dietrich, baron d'Holbach, in particular attacked him as a dangerous extremist. Despite the intensity of their attacks on La Mettrie's work, the philosophes' quarrels with La Mettrie were to an extent a matter of style rather than content. Unlike Diderot and d'Holbach, La Mettrie had little inclination to compromise with public opinion. One unfortunate and unintended result of this attitude was that his works were often quoted in attacks aimed at more-moderate proponents of materialism. He did little to further the cause of the philosophes during his own lifetime; understandably, Diderot and d'Holbach viewed La Mettrie's extremism as working to undermine their own attempts to prove a nonreligious basis for morality. Even Frederick II ordered the suppression of La Mettrie's later philosophical works that treat morality, although La Mettrie himself was allowed to remain free.

In response to the attacks on his works, La Mettrie prepared a collected *Oeuvres philosophiques* (1751, 1753; Philosophical Works) prefaced by an important but typically uncompromising justification of his philosophy, the "Discours préliminaire" (Preliminary Discourse), a reworking of the earlier *Histoire naturelle de l'âme*. Whereas Diderot had accused him of ignoring the needs of society, La Mettrie responds that he writes for an enlightened elite, not for the common man. He gives as evidence his erudite medical references, although his works are accessible to a wider readership. A more important and telling objection to the claim that he poses a danger to society is La Mettrie's argument that religious fanatics are far more dangerous than philosophers. It is the denial of human nature that leads to fanaticism and unnatural behavior; philosophers, he argues, are concerned not with fantasies but rather with a dedicated search for truth. The main goal of the "Discours préliminaire" and of La Mettrie's work as a whole is to redefine philosophy as completely subject to nature. La Mettrie declares that along with true medical practice, philosophy must be limited to phenomena, causes, and effects—the science of things. He refuses categorically to admit that atheism in and of itself is a danger to society, as is clear in the long title to a subchapter of the "Discours préliminaire": "Le philosophe athée a toutes les qualités de l'honnête homme et toutes les vertus sociales" (The atheistic philosopher has all the qualities of an honorable man as well as all the social virtues).

La Mettrie's posthumous reputation was severely compromised by the long-standing influence of such powerful critics as Diderot. The author of *L'Art de jouir* (1751, The Art of Pleasure) has been presented as a carefree hedonist—his sudden death in 1751 after eating contaminated pâté is often cited—but La Mettrie's vision of the ideal social structure is far from anarchic. La Mettrie apologists have been especially successful at demonstrating that the philosopher's reputation for nihilism was exaggerated by his contemporaries. Materialist atheism is not a negative creed for La Mettrie. He does not base his philosophy on the absence of a loving God and the single-minded pursuit of physical pleasure. Having argued for radical materialism, La Mettrie insists that acceptance of the true state of nature is the only path to a sense of purpose in life.

There is a strong sense in La Mettrie's writings of empathy for the less fortunate as well. He argues for the common good and exhibits in particular a great deal of compassion for those individuals unable to live well among their fellow human beings. For La Mettrie, living for the present in a well-regulated society requires constraining the behavior of those few who are moved to harm others, but he insists that people have no right to make moral judgments about those born with a so-called criminal bent. If one believes that human conduct depends on physiology in a radically determined manner, it follows that those who exhibit abnormal behavior are acting according to the impulsions of their atypical makeup. No moralizing can prevent individuals from following their natural penchants, for in the end human beings can exercise little control over their innate physiological organizations.

In addition to the attacks of the philosophes, La Mettrie's stylistic failings have contributed to his negative reputation. The tone of his works is often grossly satirical or cynical; worse yet, his writing is at times quite confused in structure, leading some critics to question his sanity. Donatien-Alphonse-François, marquis de Sade did little to enhance La Mettrie's reputation when he admiringly, yet incorrectly, paraphrased the philosopher as advising humans to wallow in the mud of corruption in imitation of the natural behavior of pigs. La Mettrie's direct philosophical influence is better seen in the works of Pierre Jean Georges Cabanis, who further developed the relationship between the physical and moral realms. In another positive development, La Mettrie has been credited with enabling the development of evolutionary theory and laying the groundwork for behaviorism, in addition to his obvious importance to the history of modern materialism.

La Mettrie's most fervent admirer during his own lifetime may have been Frederick the Great. Although he censored La Mettrie's last works, Frederick delivered a touching eulogy emphasizing his subject's medical expertise and philosophical daring. He also mentions La Mettrie's wife, Louise-Charlotte Dréauno, and the couple's daughter, who was five at the time. Not quite forty-two when he died on 11 November 1751, La Mettrie was praised by Frederick for "un fond de gaîté naturelle intarissable" (a natural and inexhaustible gaiety). His impetuous nature is mentioned as a factor in the difficulties he faced as a physician, philosopher, and writer, but Frederick concluded his eulogy: "Tous ceux auxquels les pieuses injures des théologiens n'en imposent pos, regrettent en M. La Mettrie un honnête homme et un savant médecin" (All those who are not imposed upon by the pious insults of the theologians mourn in La Mettrie a good man and a wise physician).

Bibliography:

Roger E. Stoddard, *Julien Offray de La Mettrie, 1709–1751: A Bibliographical Inventory* (Cologne: Jürgen Dinter, 2000).

Biography:

Pierre Lemée, *Julien Offray de La Mettrie* (Mortain: Le Mortainais, 1954).

References:

Leonore Cohen Rosenfeld, *From Beast-Machine to Man-Machine: Animal Soul in French Letters from Descartes to La Mettrie* (New York: Oxford University Press, 1941);

Ann Thomson, *Materialism and Society in the Mid-Eighteenth Century: La Mettrie's 'Discours préliminaire'* (Geneva: Droz, 1981);

Kathleen Wellman, *La Mettrie: Medicine, Philosophy, and Enlightenment* (Durham, N.C.: Duke University Press, 1992).

Alain-René Lesage
(8 May 1668 - 17 November 1747)

Francis Assaf
University of Georgia

BOOKS: *Crispin rival de son maître* (Paris: Pierre Ribou, 1707);

Le Diable boiteux (Paris: Veuve Barbin, 1707; enlarged edition, 2 volumes, Paris: Veuve Ribou, 1726); translated as *Le Diable boiteux, or, The Devil Upon Two Sticks* (London: Jacob Tonson, 1708);

Turcaret. Comédie (Paris: Pierre Ribou, 1709);

Les Mille et un jours. Contes persans, traduits en français, par M. Pétis de la Croix, 5 volumes (Paris: Barbin, 1710–1712); translated by Dr. King and others as *The Persian and the Turkish Tales, Compleat. Translated Formerly from Those Languages into French,* 2 volumes (London: W. Mears & J. Brown, 1714);

L'Epreuve réciproque, comédie de R. Alain, by Lesage and Marc-Antointe Legrand (Paris: J. Le Febvre, 1711);

Histoire de Gil Blas de Santillane, volumes 1 and 2 (Paris: Pierre Ribou, 1715); volume 3 (Paris: Pierre Ribou, 1724); volume 4 (Paris: Pierre-Jacques Ribou, 1735); translated in part as *The History and Adventures of Gil Blas of Santillane* (London: Jacob Tonson, 1732); translated by Tobias Smollett in full as *The Adventures of Gil Blas of Santillane: A New Translation from the Best French Edition,* 4 volumes (London: J. Osborn, 1749);

Théâtre de la Foire, ou de l'Opéra comique, contenant les meilleures pièces qui ont été représentées aux Foires de Saint-Germain et de Saint-Laurent . . . Recueillies, revues et corrigées par Le Sage et d'Orneval, by Lesage, Louis Fuzelier, Jacques-Philippe d'Orneval, and Jean-Claude Gilliers, 10 volumes (Paris: Etienne Ganeau, 1721–1737);

Les Pélerins de la Mecque, pièce en 3 actes, by Lesage and d'Orneval (Paris: Flahault, 1726);

Histoire de Guzman d'Alfarache, nouvellement traduite et purgée des moralitez superfluës, 2 volumes (Paris: Etienne Ganeau, 1732); translated by Arthur O'Conner as *Pleasant Adventures of Gusman, of Alfarache. Taken from the History of His Life, and Translated from the Spanish into French, by M. Le Sage,* 3 volumes (London: Allen, 1812);

Alain-René Lesage (from a 1904 edition of The Adventures of Gil Blas; *Thomas Cooper Library, University of South Carolina)*

Les Aventures de Monsieur Robert Chevalier, dit de Beauchêne, capitaine de flibustiers dans la Nouvelle-France, 2 volumes (Paris: Etienne Ganeau, 1732); translated as *The Adventures of Robert Chevalier, call'd de Beauchesne, Captain of a Privateer in New-France,* 2 volumes (London: J. Gardner, R. Dodsley & M. Cooper, 1745);

Histoire d'Estévanille Gonzalez, surnommé le garçon de bonne humeur, tirée de l'espagnol, 2 volumes (Paris: Prault, 1734, 1741); translated as *The Comical History of*

Estevanille Gonzalez, surnamed the Merry Fellow. Translated from the original Spanish by Monsieur Le Sage. Done out of French (London: W. Mears, 1735);

Une Journée des Parques, divisée en deux séances (Paris: Pierre-Jacques Ribou, 1735); translated as *A Day's Work of the Fates* (London: Charles Bathurst, 1745);

Le Bachelier de Salamanque, ou les mémoires de Don Chérubin de la Ronda, tirés d'un manuscrit espagnol (Paris: Valleyre fils et Gissey, 1736); translated by Mr. Lockman as *The Bachelor of Salamanca; or, The Memoirs of Don Cherubin de la Ronda*, 2 volumes (London: A. Bettesworth, 1737, 1739);

Les Amours jaloux, comédie en trois actes (Paris: C. de Poilly, 1736);

Recueil des pièces mises au théâtre français, 2 volumes (Paris: J. Barsois fils, 1739);

La Valise trouvée (Paris: Prault, 1740);

Méslange amusant de saillies d'esprit et de traits historiques des plus frappants (Paris: Prault, 1743).

Collections: *Oeuvres choisies de Le Sage*, 15 volumes (Amsterdam: hôtel Serpente, 1783);

Histoire de Gil Blas de Santillane, edited by René Etiemble (Paris: Gallimard, 1966);

Histoire de Gil Blas de Santillane, 2 volumes, preface by Jean Digot (Lausanne: Editions Rencontre, 1968);

Le Diable boiteux, edited by Roger Laufer (The Hague: Mouton, 1970);

Histoire de Gil Blas de Santillane, edited by Laufer (Paris: Garnier-Flammarion, 1977);

Le Diable boiteux, edited by Laufer (Paris: Gallimard, 1984);

Les Aventures de Robert Chevalier, dit Beauchêne, capitaine de flibustiers dans la Nouvelle-France, preface by Roch Carrier (Quebec: Editions Alain Stanké, 1989).

PLAY PRODUCTIONS: *Le Point d'honneur*, Paris, Comédie française, 3 February 1702; revised as *L'Arbitre des différends*, by Lesage and Jacques-Philippe d'Orneval, Paris, Théâtre de la Foire Saint-Germain, 31 July 1725;

Crispin rival de son maître, Paris, Comédie française, 12 March 1707;

Don César Ursin, Paris, Comédie française, 15 March 1707;

Turcaret, Paris, Comédie française, 14 February 1709;

Arlequin baron allemand ou le triomphe de la folie, by Lesage, Louis Fuzelier, and d'Orneval (attributed to Lesage), Paris, Théâtre de la Foire Saint-Germain, 31 July 1712;

Arlequin et Mezzetin morts par amour, Paris, Théâtre de la Foire Saint-Germain, 31 July 1712;

Le Retour d'Arlequin à la foire, by Lesage, Fuzelier, and d'Orneval, Paris, Théâtre de la Foire Saint-Germain, 31 July 1712;

Les Petits-Maîtres, Paris, Théâtre de la Foire Saint-Germain, 31 July 1712;

Arlequin Thétis, Paris, Théâtre de la Foire Saint-Laurent, 27 June 1713;

Arlequin invisible chez le roi de Chine, music by Jean-Claude Gilliers, Paris, Théâtre de la Foire Saint-Germain, 31 July 1713;

L'Arbitre des différends, Paris, Théâtre de la Foire Saint-Germain, 31 July 1713;

Arlequin roi de Serendib, music by Gilliers, Paris, Théâtre de la Foire Saint-Germain, 31 July 1713;

Les Amours déguisés, opera-ballet, by Lesage, Fuzelier, and d'Orneval, music by Pierre-Philippe Saint-Sévin l'Abbé l'aîné, Paris, Théâtre de l'Opéra-Comique, 1713;

Arlequin colonel, Paris, Théâtre de la Foire Saint-Germain, 31 July 1714;

Arlequin Mahomet, music by Gilliers, Paris, Théâtre de la Foire Saint-Germain, 31 July 1714;

La Foire de Guibray, operetta, music by Gilliers, Paris, Théâtre de l'Opéra-Comique, 1714;

Le Tombeau de Nostradamus, Paris, Théâtre de la Foire Saint-Germain, 1714;

Arlequin et Mezzetin heureux pour un moment, operetta, Paris, Théâtre de l'Opéra-Comique, 1715;

Colombine Arlequin et Arlequin Colombine, operetta, music by Gilliers, Théâtre de l'Opéra-Comique, 1715;

La Ceinture de Vénus, operetta, music by Gilliers, Paris, Théâtre de l'Opéra-Comique, 1715;

Le Temple du Destin, Paris, Théâtre de l'Opéra-Comique, 25 July 1715;

Arlequin chatouilleux sur le point d'honneur, operetta, by Lesage and d'Orneval, Paris, Théâtre de l'Opéra-Comique, 1716;

Arlequin chirurgien de Barbarie, Paris, Théâtre de la Foire Saint-Germain, 31 July 1716;

Arlequin gentilhomme malgré lui ou l'amant supposé, operetta, music by Jacques Aubert, Paris, Théâtre de l'Opéra-Comique, 1716;

Arlequin-Hulla, ou la femme répudiée, operetta, by Lesage and d'Orneval, music by Aubert, Paris, Théâtre de l'Opéra-Comique, 1716;

L'Ecole des amants, operetta, by Lesage and Fuzelier, Paris, Théâtre de l'Opéra-Comique, 1716;

La Folie favorite de l'Amour et de Plutus, by Lesage and Fuzelier, Paris, Théâtre de la Foire Saint-Germain, ca. 31 July 1716;

Le Tableau du mariage, by Lesage and Fuzelier, Paris, Théâtre de la Foire Saint-Germain, 31 July 1716;

Les Arrêts de l'amour, operetta, Paris, Théâtre de l'Opéra-Comique, 1716;

Arlequin Orphée le Cadet, Paris, Théâtre de la Foire Saint-Germain, 31 July 1718;

Arlequin valet de Merlin, Paris, Théâtre de la Foire Saint-Germain, 31 July 1718;

La Princesse de Carizme, operetta, by Lesage and Joseph de La Font, music by Lacoste, Paris, Théâtre de l'Opéra-Comique, 1718;

La Querelle des théâtres, by Lesage and de La Font, music by Gilliers, Paris, Théâtre de l'Opéra-Comique, 1718;

Le Château des lutins, Paris, Théâtre de la Foire Saint-Germain, 31 July 1718;

Le Monde renversé, operetta by Lesage, d'Orneval, and de La Font, music by Gilliers, Paris, Théâtre de la Foire Saint-Germain, 31 July 1718;

Les Amours de Nanterre, operetta, by Lesage and d'Orneval, music by Gilliers, Paris, Théâtre de l'Opéra-Comique, 1718;

Les Filles ennuyées, Paris, Théâtre de la Foire Saint-Germain, 31 July 1718;

Les Funérailles de la foire, by Lesage, Fuzelier, and d'Orneval, music by Gilliers, Paris, Théâtre de la Foire Saint-Germain, 1718;

Arlequin roi des ogres ou les bottes de sept lieues, Paris, Théâtre de la Foire Saint-Germain, 31 July 1720;

L'Ane de Daggial, by Lesage and d'Orneval, Paris, Théâtre de la Foire Saint-Germain, 31 July 1720;

L'Ile de Gougou, by Lesage and d'Orneval, with *divertissement,* Paris, Théâtre de la Foire Saint-Germain, 31 July 1720;

L'Ile des Amazones, operetta, by Lesage and d'Orneval, operetta, music by Gilliers, Paris, Théâtre de l'Opéra-Comique, 1720;

L'Ombre de la foire, by Lesage and d'Orneval, Paris, Théâtre de la Foire Saint-Germain, 31 July 1720;

La Queue de vérité, by Lesage, Fuzelier, and d'Orneval, Paris, Théâtre de la Foire Saint-Germain, 31 July 1720;

La Statue merveilleuse, operetta, by Lesage, Fuzelier, and d'Orneval, music by Gilliers, Paris, Théâtre de l'Opéra-Comique, 1720;

Le Diable d'argent, by Lesage, Fuzelier, and d'Orneval, Paris, Théâtre de la Foire Saint-Germain, 31 July 1720;

Arlequin Endymion, by Lesage, Fuzelier, and d'Orneval, music by Gilliers, Paris, Théâtre de la Foire Saint-Germain, 31 July 1721;

L'Ombre d'Alard, by Lesage and d'Orneval, Paris, Théâtre de la Foire Saint-Germain, 31 July 1721;

La Boîte de Pandore, operetta, by Lesage and Fuzelier, Paris, Théâtre de l'Opéra-Comique, 1721;

La Fausse Foire, by Lesage, Fuzelier, and d'Orneval, Paris, Théâtre de la Foire Saint-Germain, 31 July 1721;

Le Rappel de la foire à la vie, operetta, by Lesage, Fuzelier, and d'Orneval, music by Gilliers, Paris, Théâtre de la Foire Saint-Germain, 31 July 1721;

Les Eaux de Merlin, operetta, music by Gilliers, Paris, Théâtre de l'Opéra-Comique, 1721;

Magotin, operetta, by Lesage and d'Orneval, Paris, Théâtre de l'Opéra-Comique, 1721;

Robinson, operetta, by Lesage and d'Orneval, Paris, Théâtre de l'Opéra-Comique, 1721;

L'Ombre du cocher poète, by Lesage, Fuzelier, and d'Orneval, music by Gilliers, Paris, Théâtre de l'Opéra-Comique, 1722;

L'Opéra-Comique assiégé, operetta, by Lesage and d'Orneval, music by Gilliers, Paris, Théâtre de l'Opéra-Comique, 1722;

La Foire des fées, by Lesage, Fuzelier, and d'Orneval, Paris, Théâtre de la Foire Saint-Germain, 31 July 1722;

La Force de l'amour, by Lesage, Fuzelier, and d'Orneval, Paris, Théâtre de la Foire Saint-Germain, 31 July 1722;

Le Dieu du hazard, by Lesage, Fuzelier, and d'Orneval, Paris, Théâtre de la Foire Saint-Germain, 31 July 1722;

Le Jeune Vieillard, by Lesage, Fuzelier, and d'Orneval, music by Jean-Joseph Mouret, Paris, Théâtre de l'Opéra-Comique, 1722;

Le Rémouleur ou de l'amour, by Lesage, Fuzelier, and d'Orneval, music by Gilliers, Paris, Théâtre de l'Opéra-Comique, 1722;

Pierrot Romulus ou le ravisseur poli, operetta, by Lesage, Fuzelier, and d'Orneval, music by Gilliers, Paris, Théâtre de l'Opéra-Comique, 1722;

Pierrot valet de magicien, by Lesage, Fuzelier, and d'Orneval, Paris, Théâtre de la Foire Saint-Germain, 31 July 1722;

Arlequin barbet, pagode et médecin, Paris, Théâtre de la Foire Saint-Germain, 31 July 1723;

Divertissement préparé pour le Roi à Chantilly, by Lesage and d'Orneval, Paris, Théâtre de la Foire Saint-Germain, 31 July 1724;

L'Oracle muet, Paris, Théâtre de la Foire Saint-Germain, 31 July 1724;

La Conquête de la Toison d'or, operetta, by Lesage and d'Orneval, Paris, Théâtre de l'Opéra-Comique, 1724;

La Forêt de Dodone, operetta, by Lesage, Fuzelier, and d'Orneval, music by Gilliers, Paris, Théâtre de l'Opéra-Comique, 1724;

La Matrone de Charenton, by Lesage and d'Orneval, Paris, Théâtre de la Foire Saint-Germain, 31 July 1724;

La Pudeur à la foire, by Lesage and d'Orneval, Paris, Théâtre de la Foire Saint-Germain, 31 July 1724;

Le Régiment de la calotte, operetta, by Lesage, Fuzelier, and d'Orneval, music by Gilliers and Aubert, Paris, Théâtre de l'Opéra-Comique, 1724;

Les Captifs d'Alger, Paris, Théâtre de la Foire Saint-Germain, 31 July 1724;

L'Enchanteur Mirliton, by Lesage and Fuzelier, music by Gilliers, Théâtre de l'Opéra-Comique, 1725;

Les Enragés, operetta, by Lesage, Fuzelier, and d'Orneval, music by Gilliers, Paris, Théâtre de l'Opéra-Comique, 1725;

Le Faux Prodige, operetta, by Lesage, d'Orneval, and Alexis Piron, Paris, Théâtre de l'Opéra-Comique, 1726;

Les Comédiens corsaires, by Lesage, Fuzelier, and d'Orneval, music by Gilliers, Paris, Théâtre de l'Opéra-Comique, 1726;

Les Pèlerins de la Mecque, operetta, by Lesage, Fuzelier, and d'Orneval, music by Gilliers, Paris, Théâtre de l'Opéra-Comique, 1726;

L'Obstacle favorable, operetta, by Lesage, Fuzelier, and d'Orneval, Paris, Théâtre de l'Opéra-Comique, 1726;

Les Débris de la foire Saint-Germain, by Lesage, Fuzelier, and d'Orneval, Paris, Théâtre de la Foire Saint-Germain, 31 July 1727;

Les Noces de Proserpine et de Pluton ou les Champs Elysées, operetta, by Lesage, Fuzelier, and d'Orneval, Paris, Théâtre de l'Opéra-Comique, 1727;

Achmet and Almanzine, operetta, music by Gilliers, Paris, Théâtre de l'Opéra-Comique, 1728;

L'Antre de Laverne, operetta, by Lesage and Fuzelier, Paris, Théâtre de l'Opéra-Comique, 1728;

La Pénélope moderne, operetta, by Lesage, Fuzelier, and d'Orneval, music by Gilliers, Paris, Théâtre de l'Opéra-Comique, 1728;

Les Amours de Protée, operetta, by Lesage, Fuzelier, and d'Orneval, Paris, Théâtre de l'Opéra-Comique, 1728;

La Noce anglaise, ballet-pantomime, Paris, Théâtre de la Foire Saint-Germain, 31 July 1729;

La Princesse de Chine, operetta, by Lesage and d'Orneval, music by Gilliers, Paris, Théâtre de la Foire Saint-Germain, 31 July 1729;

Le Corsaire de Salé, operetta, by Lesage and d'Orneval, music by Gilliers, Paris, Théâtre de l'Opéra-Comique, 1729;

Les Couplets en procès, by Lesage and d'Orneval, music by Gilliers, Paris, Théâtre de la Foire Saint-Germain, 31 July 1729;

Les Spectacles maladies, by Lesage and d'Orneval, music by Gilliers, Paris, Théâtre de la Foire Saint-Germain, 31 July 1729;

L'Amour marin, Paris, Théâtre de l'Opéra-Comique, 1730;

L'Impromptu du Pont-Neuf, operetta, by Lesage, d'Orneval, and Charles-François Pannard, music by Gilliers, Paris, Théâtre de l'Opéra-Comique, 1730;

L'Industrie, by Lesage, Fuzelier, and d'Orneval, music by Gilliers, Paris, Théâtre de l'Opéra-Comique, 1730;

Les Routes du monde, operetta, by Lesage, Fuzelier, and d'Orneval, music by Gilliers, Paris, Théâtre de la Foire Saint-Germain, 31 July 1730;

L'Espérance, operetta, by Lesage and Fuzelier, music by Gilliers, Paris, Théâtre de l'Opéra-Comique, 1731;

Roger de Sicile, surnommé le roi sans chagrin, operetta, by Lesage and d'Orneval, music by Gilliers, Paris, Théâtre de l'Opéra-Comique, 1731;

La Sauvagesse, operetta, by Lesage and d'Orneval, music by Gilliers, Paris, Théâtre de l'Opéra-Comique, 1732;

La Tontine, Paris, Comédie Française, 20 February 1732;

Les Désespérés, music by Gilliers, Paris, Théâtre de la Foire Saint-Germain, 31 July 1732;

Sophie et Sigismond, operetta, by Lesage and d'Orneval, music by Gilliers, Paris, Théâtre de l'Opéra-Comique, 1732;

La Première Représentation, music by Gilliers, Paris, Théâtre de la Foire Saint-Germain, 31 July 1734;

Le Rival dangereux, Paris, Théâtre de l'Opéra-Comique, 1734;

Les Deux Frères, operetta, Paris, Théâtre de l'Opéra-Comique, 1734;

Les Mariages du Canada, operetta, music by Gilliers, Paris, Théâtre de l'Opéra-Comique, 1734;

Les Noces de la folie, operetta, music by Gilliers, Paris, Théâtre de l'Opéra-Comique, 1735;

L'Histoire de l'Opéra-Comique ou les métamorphoses de la Foire, Paris, Théâtre de l'Opéra-Comique, 1736—comprised *Arlequin chirurgien de Barbarie; Le Mensonge véritable; Pierrot valet de magicien; Orphée; Ariane et Thésée; Les Ennemis réconciliés; L'Heureux Dénouement;* and *Le Mari préféré;*

Les Amants jaloux, Paris, Théâtre de la Foire Saint-Germain, 31 July 1737;

La Basoche du Parnasse (a revised version of *Couplets en procès*), operetta, Paris, Théâtre de l'Opéra-Comique, 1738;

Le Neveu supposé, operetta, by Lesage and Fromaget, Paris, Théâtre de l'Opéra-Comique, 1738;

L'Epreuve dangereuse ou le pot au noir, operetta, by Lesage and Fromaget, Paris, Théâtre de l'Opéra-Comique, 1740;

L'Ecole des amants, ballet, music by Niel, Théâtre de l'Opéra-Comique, 1744.

TRANSLATIONS: *Lettres galantes d'Aristénète, traduites du grec* (Rotterdam [Chartres]: De Graffe, 1695);

Le Théâtre espagnol, ou les meilleures comédies des plus fameux auteurs espagnols, traduites en français (Paris, 1700);

Nouvelles aventures de l'admirable Don Quichotte de la Manche, composées par le licencié Alonso Fernández de Avellaneda et traduites de l'espagnol en français pour la première fois, 2 volumes (Paris: par la Compagnie des libraires, 1716);

Matteo Maria Boiardo, *Nouvelle traduction de Roland l'amoureux . . .* , 2 volumes (Paris, 1717).

Alain-René Lesage was born on 8 May 1668 in Sarzeau (Brittany), the son of Claude Lesage, a minor court official, and Jeanne Brenugat. At fourteen, he was orphaned and left in a difficult financial position, as his father had contracted many debts. His court-appointed guardians sent him to the Jesuit school at nearby Vannes. There, the school principal recognized the boy's superior mind, which he began to develop. Consequently, Lesage became solidly grounded in the classics. As he neared graduation, he had to choose a career. His guardians reasoned that the son of a court officer should study law; thus, in 1692, he left to pursue law studies in Paris. When he began to practice, however, he realized that he did not like the profession and was not good at it.

In 1694 Lesage married Marie-Elisabeth Huyard, with whom he had three sons and a daughter. The eldest, René-André, born in 1695, became an actor and took the stage name of Montménil. He performed with great success at the Comédie française but was killed in a hunting accident on 8 September 1743. The youngest son, François-Antoine, born in 1700, also became an actor and took the stage name of Pittenec. After working in the provinces for several years, he returned to Paris in 1734, where he acted for a while, then vanished. The middle son, Julien-François, was a canon in the cathedral of Boulogne-sur-Mer. Lesage's fourth child, Marie-Elisabeth, born on 9 August 1702, lived her entire life with her parents and never married. She died on 30 January 1773, also in Boulogne-sur-Mer.

Although he spent almost all his adult life in Paris, Lesage never sought acceptance in Parisian upper circles. His collaborator Louis Fuzelier recounts an anecdote that summarizes the author's fierce independence. Prior to the staging of his most important comedy, *Turcaret*, in 1709, he had promised to read the play at the fashionable and well-attended salon of the duchess Marie-Anne de Bouillon; however, he was detained and arrived an hour late. When the duchess reproached him for wasting an hour of her time, he replied, "Well, Madam, I shall make you gain two," and he left. Nothing could make him come back to give the reading.

Lesage began his literary career in 1695, rather inauspiciously. His first published work was a translation into French of the Latin version of an obscure Greek treatise, the *Lettres galantes* (Amorous Letters) by Aristenetes, a fourth-century B.C. Greek epistolographer. The arrival of this book on the literary scene went largely unnoticed, so much so that no one realized, when Lesage published one of his last works, *La Valise trouvée* (1740, The Found Valise), that he had increased the size of the volume by adding the forty-two *Lettres galantes* to the thirty-one fictitious letters supposedly found in the mailbag of a murdered courier.

Also in 1695 he gained the patronage of the abbé Jules-Paul de Lyonne, son of Hughes de Lyonne, Louis XIV's secretary of state and architect of much of his foreign policy. Despite his title, the abbé was not a priest but had merely received the lower orders so as to become legally entitled to income from a Church establishment. He took a serious interest in Lesage: he opened his house to the author, provided him with a yearly pension of 600 francs, and allowed Lesage to participate in the Spanish tutoring he himself was receiving. That training proved invaluable when Lesage began to translate Spanish works into French. His major novels—*Le Diable boiteux* (1707; translated as *The Devil Upon Two Sticks*, 1708), *Histoire de Gil Blas de Santillane* (1715–1735; translated as *The History and Adventures of Gil Blas of Santillane*, 1732), and *Le Bachelier de Salamanque, ou les mémoires de Don Chérubin de la Ronda* (1736; translated as *The Bachelor of Salamanca; or, The Memoirs of Don Cherubin de la Ronda*, 1737, 1739)—are Spanish-themed and draw heavily upon his in-depth knowledge of that language and literature.

Lesage's theatrical debut in 1702 was as lackluster as the *Lettres galantes*. The plays he wrote, mostly translations or adaptations from major Spanish playwrights such as Francisco Rojas, Lope de Vega, or Calderón, failed to win the audiences' favor. Success did not come until 1707, with a double hit: a comedy in one act, *Crispin rival de son maître* (Crispin Rival of His Master), and his first novel, *Le Diable boiteux,* which borrows only its title and general theme from Luis Vélez de Guevara's 1641 novel *El Diablo cojuelo* (The Limping Devil).

Conventionally, the most important example of master-servant rivalry in French theater is considered to be Pierre-Augustin Caron de Beaumarchais's masterpiece *La Folle Journée ou le mariage de Figaro* (1784, The Marriage of Figaro). Yet, master-servant rivalry is already eloquently illustrated in *Crispin rival de son maître*, signaling that the era when valets merely served their masters' amorous or other schemes was over. An ambitious character, Crispin chafes against his status as a lackey and decides to assume another identity to compete against his master, an impecunious wastrel, for

Monsieur Oronte's daughter Angélique. The master wants Angélique's hand, not out of love, but to gain access to Oronte's money so as to continue to satisfy his gambling passion. In presenting assumed identity as a central dramatic device, the play also prefigures Pierre Carlet de Chamblain de Marivaux's best-known comedy, *Le Jeu de l'amour et du hasard* (1730, The Game of Love and Chance).

Le Diable boiteux was first published in 1707, with a considerably expanded edition following in 1726. The beginning of the novel conforms to the Guevara model: the hero, Cleofás Leandro Pérez Zambullo, is fleeing across the roofs of Madrid, ahead of a band of toughs intent upon doing him bodily harm for "excessively" wooing a young lady, when he notices, through the open window of an alchemist's attic, a strange-looking bottle on a shelf. When he slips into the room and uncorks the bottle, out comes Asmodeus, the limping devil who, in thanks for freeing him, endows Cleofás with the gift of seeing through the roofs of the city houses, which he renders magically transparent. What follows is a systematic character study based on what Cleofás sees inside each dwelling. Its interest for the modern reader lies in the incisive portraits and analyses by the author. Other than the story line, Lesage's work differs substantially from Guevara's: the former dispenses with any supernatural acts, such as the devil flying Cleofás through the air, and addresses more-contemporary and national concerns. The *Journal des Savants* (Journal of the Learned), the preeminent literary and scientific French periodical of the time, praised Lesage's work highly in the 26 September 1707 issue. The article also warns against a swarm of imitations such as *Le Diable borgne* (The One-Eyed Devil), *Le Diable aveugle* (The Blind Devil), and *Le Diable d'argent* (The Money Devil), which risk spoiling the distinctive qualities of Lesage's novel for the readership. Foreign periodicals, especially the Amsterdam-based *Nouvelles de la République des Lettres* (News from the Republic of Letters), also acknowledged the book, if more restrainedly.

In 1708 Lesage wrote another play, *La Tontine* (The Tontine), a scathing satire of medical incompetence; however, it was not performed until 1732. In 1709 he scored his biggest stage success with *Turcaret*, despite the efforts of a cabal of financiers to suppress the play. This five-act comedy mercilessly attacks tax farmers, a class of financiers universally hated by the common people for their ruthless greed and despised by intellectuals for their boorishness. Turcaret, the title character, is a wealthy tax contractor of low origin. His adulterous love interest, the baroness, is not much higher on the social scale. The widow of a middle-ranking officer, she is a financially ruined tease who is interested only in Turcaret's

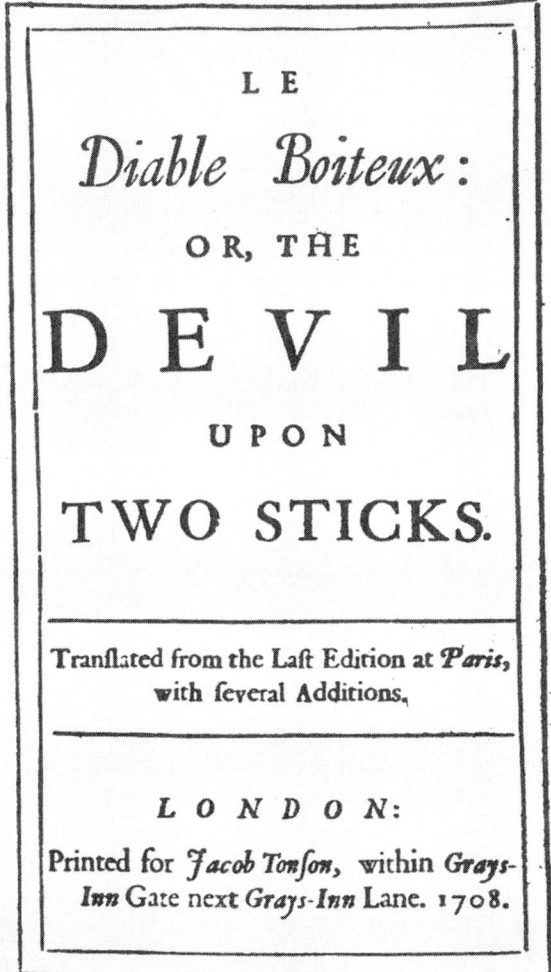

Title page from a 1972 facsimile edition of the first English translation of Lesage's 1707 novel, in which the hero is granted the ability to see through city roofs after freeing a devil from a bottle (Thomas Cooper Library, University of South Carolina)

money, while keeping on the side a gigolo, the chevalier, a gambling wastrel whom she subsidizes with the financier's largesse. These characters are surrounded by a bevy of scheming servants, thieving business agents, and sundry shady characters. The play ends with Turcaret's arrest for financial malfeasance. The only winner is the crooked valet, Frontin, who has embezzled enough money to marry the equally dishonest maid Lisette. The two will retire to "faire souche d'honnêtes gens" (start a bloodline of honest people).

In 1710 Lesage published the first volume of *Les Mille et un jours* (translated as *The Persian and the Turkish Tales*, 1714), followed by the second in 1712. This work is an imitation of *The Thousand and One Nights*, the classic of Arabic literature that had been translated into French by Antoine Galland in installments between 1704 and 1717. As soon as the first volume of Galland's translation appeared, a furor for all things Oriental seized the French literary scene, lasting practically throughout the century. Oriental-themed literature in France served both to satisfy the appetite for exoticism and to express political satire.

Lesage is not the original author of *Les Mille et un jours*. Rather, it is adapted from the work of the Orientalist François Pétis de la Croix, who traveled from Constantinople to Ispahan between 1670 and 1680, where he met the poet Cheikh-Zadeh, who had assembled and translated into Arabic a series of folktales culled from various Persian and Indian sources, giving it the collective Arabic title *Al-Faraj ba'ad al-shidda* (Solace After Hardship). Pétis in turn translated Cheikh-Zadeh's work into French under the title "La Sultane de Perse, ou les mille et un jours" (The Sultana of Persia, or, the Thousand and One Days). He presented it to a publisher who found it poorly written and asked Lesage to rewrite it.

Lesage's next major work was his masterpiece, *Histoire de Gil Blas de Santillane*. The first two volumes (books 1–6) appeared in 1715. It is the first novel of self-development in the nascent French eighteenth century, as well as the most elaborate example of the picaresque genre in French. Born in the small town of Santillana in northern Spain and raised in Oviedo, the hero leaves his home to study in Salamanca. He never reaches that city, at least not as a student, but instead has many adventures on the roads and throughout Spain. Told in the first person, the novel makes extensive use of secondary stories to enrich the main story line. The hero begins as a conventional *pícaro* (marginalized wanderer), going from town to town and master to master, meeting an assortment of characters from the virtuous to the unsavory to the downright criminal. Book 6 marks the nadir of Gil Blas's activities, when he participates, albeit halfheartedly, in a despicable scheme to intimidate and rob a Jewish merchant.

The yearly 600-franc pension that Jules-Paul de Lyonne had been providing to Lesage ended with Lyonne's death in 1715. With that patronage gone, Lesage had to rely more than ever on his writing talent for his income, which drove him to produce sequels. Appearing in 1724, the second volume of *Histoire de Gil Blas de Santillane* (books 7–9) shows the hero maturing, after many twists and turns, and settling down on an estate given to him by his friends and protectors, the Leyva family, near the town of Valencia. The novel could have ended there, but Lesage's creativity, coupled with his financial need, led him to produce the third and final volume (books 10–12) in 1735. Having become master of a prosperous estate, the former *pícaro* is retiring from his adventurous life. He holds letters patent of nobility and has married a lovely woman, much younger than he, from a penniless aristocratic family whose benefactor he becomes.

Although he was talented and in high demand, Lesage considered writing a job at which he had to work every day in order to put food on the family table. A critic for the French-language Dutch periodical *Journal littéraire* (Literary Journal), published in The Hague, remarked tartly in 1736 that Lesage could go on forever adding installments to *Histoire de Gil Blas de Santillane*, thus writing a history of the world.

The influence of *Histoire de Gil Blas de Santillane* on the genre of the picaresque novel is indisputable, however, both in France and in England. In French, the most obvious example of such influence is the anonymous sequel *La Vie de don Alphonse Blas de Lirias, fils de Gil Blas* (The Life of Don Alphonse Blas of Lirias, Son of Gil Blas), published in Amsterdam in 1744–a clear case of imitation being the most sincere form of flattery. In England, the works of Tobias Smollett (who translated *Histoire de Gil Blas de Santillane* into English), Henry Fielding, and William Makepeace Thackeray are among those that show this influence. Gil Blas differs from both Spanish *pícaros* and earlier seventeenth-century French ones by being a relatively well-educated bourgeois who eventually reaches a respectable social status, whereas his Spanish counterparts are lucky to rise barely above the dregs of society.

Lesage did not remain idle between sequels to the original six books of *Histoire de Gil Blas de Santillane*. He produced a constant stream of farces and operettas, as well as *pièces à écriteaux* for the Théâtre de la Foire Saint-Germain. The latter were musical comedies in which *écriteaux* (scrolls of canvas) bore in large print the couplets to be sung, along with the names of the characters supposed to sing them. The *écriteau* was unrolled downward as the orchestra played well-known popular tunes, while the audience sang the lines and the actors mimed the action. That performing method was used to bypass the royal edicts granting the right to pronounce the lines of a play onstage exclusively to royally sponsored acting companies, such as the Comédie française. In 1732 Lesage delivered his *Histoire de Guzman d'Alfarache* (History of Guzman d'Alfarache), an adaptation of the 1599 masterpiece by Mateo Alemán, *El Pícaro* (The Picaro), as the book was popularly known in Spain. It had been translated several times into French: in 1600, in 1619, and by Gabriel Brémond in 1732–the same year as Lesage's adaptation. The difference between Lesage's version and those of other translators is that he chose to eliminate completely the moral reflections, preserving only the main story line and the secondary tales. In 1732 he also published *Les*

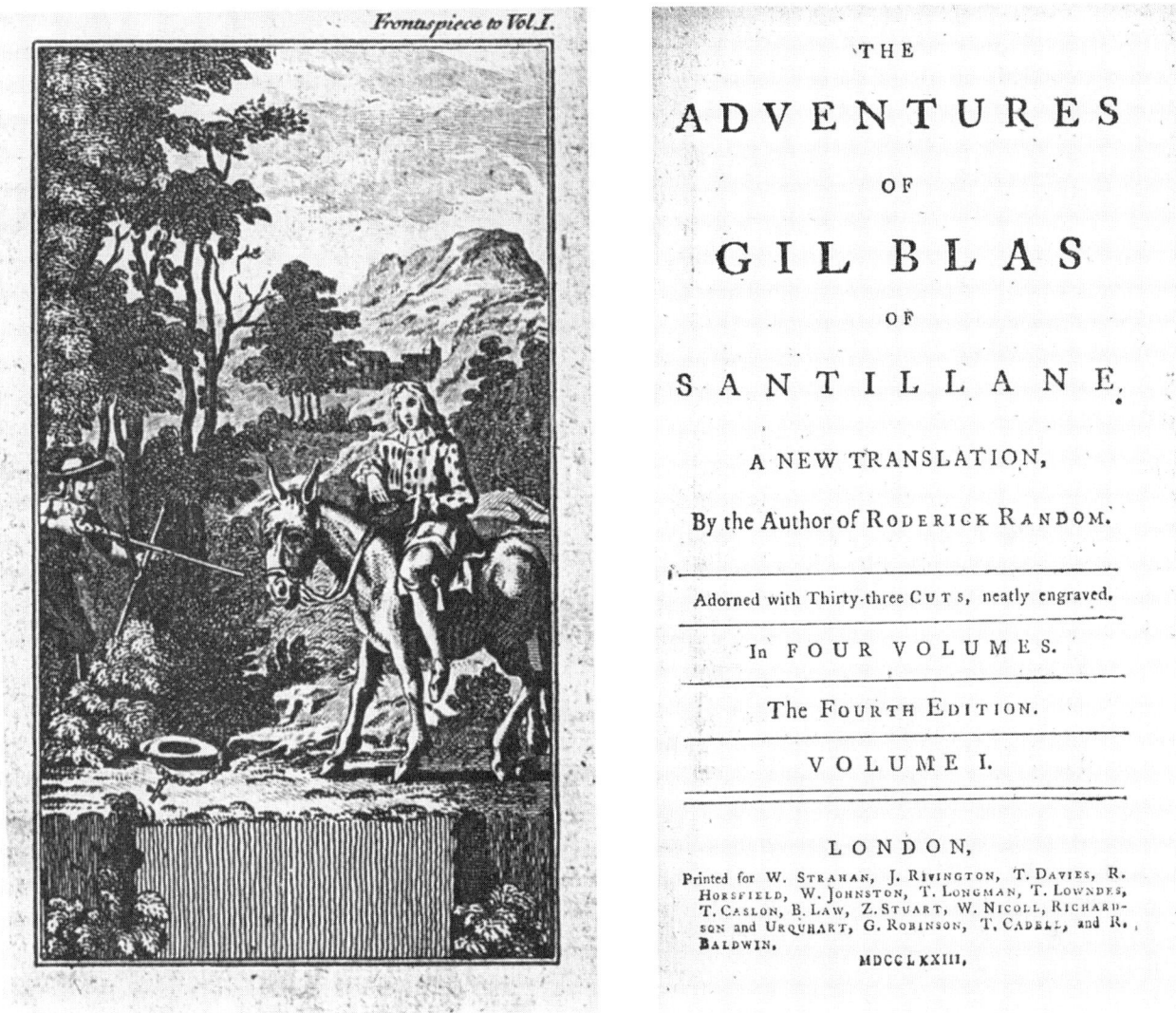

Frontispiece and title page for a 1773 edition of Tobias Smollett's 1749 translation of Lesage's multivolume novel
Histoire de Gil Blas de Santillane *(1715–1735), one of the most influential picaresque novels in
French literature (Thomas Cooper Library, University of South Carolina)*

Aventures de Monsieur Robert Chevalier, dit de Beauchêne, capitaine de flibustiers dans la Nouvelle-France (translated as *The Adventures of Robert Chevalier, call'd de Beauchesne, Captain of a Privateer in New-France*, 1745), a novel partially based on the memoirs of a real-life freebooter who was born on 26 April 1686 near Montreal and died on 11 December 1731 in Tours (France). His widow supposedly gave Lesage a small set of notes and sketches that he transformed into a story.

The structure of the novel is unusual: half of it is a long secondary tale containing an elaborate tertiary one. The story begins with Beauchêne's upbringing in seventeenth-century New France (Canada) and details his rebelliousness and subsequent running away from home to join a band of Iroquois; his adventures as a privateer, which take him from Canada to the coast of Angola via Jamaica and Haiti; and his encounter with the Count de Monneville, whose life story occupies the second half of the work. The ending is abruptly truncated; it is not even an open-ended conclusion to the tale. Nonetheless, this work is quite interesting, ranging across half the world, from the Caribbean to Ireland, where the hero is held prisoner for a while by the English.

Two years later, in 1734, the first volume of another Spanish picaresque adaptation came out: *Histoire d'Estévanille Gonzalez, surnommé le garçon de bonne humeur* (translated as *The Comical History of Estevanille Gonzales, surnamed the Merry Fellow*, 1735). It is largely based on the 1646 novel by Juan Eusebio Nieremberg,

La Vida y hechos de Estebanillo González, hombre de buen humor (The Life and Deeds of Estebanillo Gonzalez, a Man of Good Humor), one of the later examples of the genre in Spain. The second installment of Lesage's version followed in 1741. Meanwhile, in 1735, the year when the final volume of *Histoire de Gil Blas de Santillane* was published, Lesage also produced *Une Journée des Parques* (translated as *A Day's Work of the Fates*, 1745), a character study not unlike *Le Diable boiteux*, albeit much shorter, in which the three Fates—Clotho, Lachesis, and Atropos—comment elaborately upon the lives they spin out, measure, and cut.

Between 1736 and 1738 Lesage wrote *Le Bachelier de Salamanque, ou les mémoires de Don Chérubin de la Ronda*. Despite its subtitle, *tirés d'un manuscrit espagnol* (excerpted from a Spanish manuscript), it is entirely original. Much shorter and lacking the breadth and energy of *Histoire de Gil Blas de Santillane*, it follows a similar pattern. However, unlike Gil Blas's, Chérubin's adventures begin upon graduation from the University of Salamanca. He works for a while as a private tutor, meets assorted characters, tries various ways of making a living, and eventually marries. Having lost his wife to a seducer, he leaves Spain, first for Africa, then for Mexico and Central America. There, he observes life in the New World, remarking on the cruelty with which the Spanish colonial masters treat the natives. For the part concerning Guatemala, Lesage relied on the travel accounts of the English Dominican priest Thomas Gage, who traveled to Mexico and Central America in 1625 and lived there for twelve years. Upon his return to Europe, he had disputes with his superiors and converted to Anglicanism. Gage chronicled his experiences in Central America in *The English-American His Travail by Sea and Land; or A New Survey of the West India's, Containing a Journal of Three Thousand Miles Within the Main Land of America* (1648).

La Valise trouvée was published in 1740. Some critics have dismissed it as a hodgepodge, while others have compared it to *Le Diable boiteux* and *Une Journée des Parques* as another character study. In this allegedly random collection of scraps, one finds not only some valuable insights on human nature, society, and religion, but also enough clear references to Lesage's own works, literary tastes, and ideology to consider the work a literary testament. Lesage was seventy-three by then and perhaps felt the need to write a summary of his life's work and a literary and aesthetic manifesto.

Three years later, he published *Méslange amusant de saillies d'esprit et de traits historiques des plus frappants* (1743, An Entertaining Mix of Witticisms) and retired. Although profoundly deaf by then, he was not idle. He continued to work, and when he died in 1747 he had completed the definitive edition of *Histoire de Gil Blas de Santillane*. The famous periodical *Mercure de France* (Mercury of France) published an obituary praising his work, especially *Histoire de Gil Blas de Santillane*, which it predicted would become "immortal."

Lesage's works found a broad audience in eighteenth-century Europe. Many were quickly translated into English, German, and Spanish, and *Histoire de Gil Blas de Santillane* was brought to the stage in England. The most notorious Spanish translation of *Histoire de Gil Blas de Santillane* was by Padre José Francisco de Isla in 1763. It bore a rather inflammatory preface (likely added by the bookseller) claiming that Lesage had plagiarized a manuscript he had purchased during a trip to Spain, although there is no evidence that Lesage ever traveled abroad. The charge ignited the *Querelle de Gil Blas* (The Quarrel of Gil Blas) in 1824. Partially on the strength of a gratuitous assertion by Voltaire, the Spanish side was claiming that the novel had been entirely lifted from *Relaciones de la vida del escudero Marcos de Obregón* (circa 1582, An Account of the Life of the Squire Marcos de Obregón) by Vicente Espínel. On the French side, a group of academicians defended the opposite view; young Victor Hugo helped their side to win the argument.

In the nineteenth century, Lesage's works enjoyed more editions and additional translations into Danish, Russian, Polish, Portuguese, and Arabic. French editions abounded, including at least two editions of his complete works, minus the works for the Théâtre de la Foire. *Histoire de Gil Blas de Santillane* was also adapted to the stage, both in French and in English. Alexandre Dumas *père* gave Gil Blas's name to the main character in one of his minor novels set in gold-rush California. Toward the end of the century a famous periodical took the name *Gil Blas* and published literary and journalistic pieces by prominent authors and politicians.

Editions of *Histoire de Gil Blas de Santillane* and *Le Diable boiteux* have been published throughout the twentieth century. In April and May 2002, *Turcaret* was brought again to the stage in several locations in France. As of 2005, a team of French scholars is preparing a new edition of Alain-René Lesage's complete works, as none has been produced since 1828.

Bibliography:

Henri Cordier, *Essai bibliographique sur les œuvres d'Alain-René Lesage* (Paris: H. Leclerc, 1910; Geneva: Slatkine Reprints, 1970).

Biography:

Léo Claretie, *Lesage, romancier: d'après de nouveaux documents*, Le Roman en France au début du XVIIIe siècle (Paris: Colin, 1890; Geneva: Slatkine Reprints, 1970).

References:

Francis Assaf, "De *La Valise trouvée* aux textes retrouvés," in *Le Topos du manuscrit trouvé,* edited by Jan Herman, Fernand Hallyn, and Kris Peeters (Louvain: Peeters, 1999);

Assaf, *Lesage et le picaresque* (Paris: A.-G. Nizet, 1984);

Assaf, "Utopian Beginnings, Dystopian End: Mlle Duclos' Indian 'Nation' in Alain-René Lesage's Beauchêne," *Romanische Forschungen,* 98, nos. 1–2 (1986): 81–95;

Jenny H. Batlay, "L'Art du portrait dans *Gil Blas:* essai d'esthétique à travers le mouvement," *Studies on Voltaire and the Eighteenth Century,* 124 (1974): 181–189;

A. Benoit and G. Fontaine, eds., *The Picaresque Novel,* translated by Michael Woolff (London: Routledge, 2000);

Glen Campbell, "Domestic Alliances and Misalliances in Lesage's Novels," *Studies on Voltaire and the Eighteenth Century,* 305 (1992): 1710–1713;

Katharine Whitman Carson, "Aspects of Contemporary Society in *Gil Blas,*" *Studies on Voltaire and the Eighteenth Century,* 110 (1973);

Cécile Cavillac, "La dialectique du service dans l'*Histoire de Gil Blas de Santillane,*" *Revue d'Histoire Littéraire de la France,* 89, no. 4 (July–August 1989): 643–660;

Cavillac, *L'Espagne dans la trilogie "picaresque" de Lesage: emprunts littéraires, empreinte culturelle* (Talence: Presses universitaires de Bordeaux, 1984);

George Evans, "Lesage and d'Orneval's 'Théâtre de la foire', the *Commedia dell'arte* and Power," in *Studies in the Commedia dell'Arte,* edited by David J. George and Christopher J. Gossip (Cardiff: University of Wales Press, 1993);

Peter Fazziola, "Classical Allusions and Lesage's Comic Style," *Classical and Modern Literature: A Quarterly,* 2 (Winter 1993): 117–125;

Claude Filteau, "Un roman mineur d'Alain-René Lesage: *Les Aventures de Monsieur Robert Chevalier dit 'Beauchêne' capitaine de flibustiers en la Nouvelle-France,*" in *Pour une Esthétique de la littérature mineure,* edited by Luc Fraisse (Paris: Honoré Champion, 2000);

Philippe Garnier, *Retours et répétitions dans l'Histoire de Gil Blas de Santillane d'Alain-René Lesage* (Paris: L'Harmattan, 2002);

Jane Payne Kaplan, "Food as Structural Catalyst in *Gil Blas,*" *Food & Foodways,* 2, no. 4 (1988): 393–434;

Heinz Klüppelholz, *La Technique des emprunts dans* Gil Blas *de Lesage* (Frankfurt am Main & Bern: Peter Lang, 1981);

Marie-Paule Laden, "Lesage's *Gil Blas:* Double Imitation, Duplicitous Writing," *Degré Second: Studies in French Literature,* 7 (July 1983): 1–25;

Roger Laufer, *Lesage, ou le métier de romancier* (Paris: Gallimard, 1971);

Ronald D. LeBlanc, "Making *Gil Blas* Russian," *Slavic and East Europe Journal,* 30, no. 3 (Fall 1986): 340–354;

Mechele Leon, "La finance et la fiction: *Turcaret* d'Alain-René Lesage," in *L'Autre au XVIIe siècle,* edited by Ralph Heyndels and Barbara Woshinsky (Tübingen: Gunter Narr, 1999);

Isabelle Martin, "Une pièce manuscrite de Lesage: l'histoire de l'Opéra-Comique ou les métamorphoses de la foire. Un théâtre caméléon," *French Review,* 70, no. 2 (December 1996): 192–205;

Martin, "Usage et esthétique du miroir dans une pièce orientale: *La Statue merveilleuse* de Lesage," *L'Esprit Créateur,* 39, no. 3 (Fall 1999): 47–55;

Joellen Meglin, "Two Approaches to *Le Diable boiteux* and *La Cachucha:* French Society Behind a Spanish Façade," *Dance Chronicle,* 17, no. 3 (1994): 263–302;

Joseph G. Reish, "Lesage's Dramatization of a Social Cycle: The Ups and Downs of the Likes of *Turcaret,*" *French Literature Series,* 15 (1988): 31–40;

Roseann Runte, "Le rôle du théâtre dans *Gil Blas,*" *Dalhousie French Studies,* 38 (Spring 1997): 57–67;

Runte, "A Utopian Construct in the Canadian Desert: Lesage's Experiment in the Empowerment of the Female," *L'Esprit Créateur,* 34, no. 4 (Winter 1994): 18–33;

Jane Rush, "The Pricking of Balloons in Lesage's 'Théâtre de la Foire,'" *Eighteenth-Century Life,* 19, no. 3 (November 1995): 70–85;

Jacques Wagner, *Lectures du* Gil Blas *de Lesage. Etudes réunies et présentées par Jacques Wagner* (Clermont-Ferrand: Presses de l'université Blaise-Pascal, 2003);

Wagner, "L'orient voilé de Raphaël dans *Gil Blas,*" *Tangence,* 65 (Winter 2001): 33–51;

Wagner, ed., *Lesage, écrivain (1695–1735). Textes réunis, présentés et publiés par Jacques Wagner* (Amsterdam & Atlanta: Rodopi, 1997).

Julie de Lespinasse
(9 November 1732 – 22 May 1776)

Felicia B. Sturzer
University of Tennessee at Chattanooga

BOOKS: *Lettres de Mademoiselle de Lespinasse, écrites depuis l'année 1773, jusqu'à l'année 1776; suivies de deux chapitres dans le genre du Voyage sentimental de Sterne, par le même auteur*, 2 volumes, edited by Alexandrine de Courcelles, comtesse de Guibert, preface by Bertrand Barrère (Paris: L. Collin, 1809); enlarged as *Lettres de Mademoiselle de Lespinasse, écrites depuis l'année 1773, jusqu'à l'année 1776; suivies de deux chapitres dans le genre du Voyage sentimental de Sterne, par le même auteur, augmentées de son "Eloge" sous le nom d' "Eliza" par le comte de Guibert et deux opuscules d'Alembert*, 2 volumes, edited by Guibert (Paris: Longchamp, 1811; Paris: Menard & Desenne, 1815);

Nouvelles Lettres de Mademoiselle de Lespinasse, suivies du portrait de M. de Mora et d'autres opuscules inédits, attributed to Lespinasse (Paris: Maradan, 1820);

Lettres de Mademoiselle de Lespinasse, suivies de ses autres oeuvres et de lettres de Madame du Deffand, de Turgot, de Bernardin de Saint-Pierre, edited by Eugène Asse (Paris: Charpentier, 1876); enlarged as *Lettres de Mademoiselle de Lespinasse, suivies de ses autres oeuvres et de lettres de Madame du Deffand, de Turgot, de Bernardin de Saint-Pierre, augmentées des variantes, de nombreuses notes, d'un appendice comprenant les écrits d'Alembert, de Guibert, de Voltaire, de Frederic II sur Mlle de Lespinasse; d'un index et précédées d'une notice biographique et littéraire par Eugène Asse* (Paris: Bibliothèque-Charpentier, 1903);

Lettres inédites de Mademoiselle de Lespinasse à Condorcet, à d'Alembert, à Guibert, au comte de Crillon, publiées avec des lettres de ses amis, des documents nouveaux et une étude par M. Charles Henry, edited by Charles Henry (Paris: E. Dentu, 1887);

Correspondance entre Mlle de Lespinasse et le comte de Guibert, publiée pour la première fois d'après le texte original par le comte de Villeneuve-Guibert (Paris: Calmann-Lévy, 1906); translated by E. H. F. Mills as *Love Letters of Mademoiselle de Lespinasse to and from the Comte de Guibert* (London: Routledge, 1929);

Julie de Lespinasse (from Ronald Grimsley, Jean d'Alembert, *1963; Thomas Cooper Library, University of South Carolina)*

Lettres à Condorcet, suivies du Portrait de Condorcet rédigé par Julie de Lespinasse en 1774, edited by Jean-Noël Pascal (Paris: Editions Desjonquères, 1990).

Editions: *Lettres de Mademoiselle de Lespinasse, avec une notice biographique de Jules Janin* (Paris: Amyot, 1847);

Lettres de Mademoiselle de Lespinasse, précédées d'une notice de Sainte-Beuve (Paris: Garnier, 1893);

Lettres de Mademoiselle de Lespinasse (Paris: Garnier, 1925);

Les Plus Belles Lettres de Mademoiselle de Lespinasse, edited by Claude Roy (Paris: Calmann-Lévy, 1962);

Lettres de Mademoiselle de Lespinasse, précédées d'une notice de Sainte-Beuve, edited by Jean-Noël Pascal (Paris & Plan-de-la-Tour: Editions d'Aujourd'hui, 1978);

"La famille et les amis de Julie de Lespinasse: édition des lettres aux Vichy, à Devaines, et aux Suard," edited by Pascal, dissertation, Université de Montpellier III, 1988;

Lettres, edited by Jacques Dupont (Paris: La Table Ronde, 1997).

Editions in English: *Letters of Mademoiselle de Lespinasse. With Notes on Her Life and Character by d'Alembert, Marmontel, de Guibert, etc. and an Introduction by Sainte-Beuve,* translated by Katherine Prescott Wormeley (London: Heinemann, 1903; Toronto: George N. Morang, 1903);

Letters to and from Madame du Deffand and Julie de Lespinasse, edited by Warren Hunting Smith (New Haven: Yale University Press / London: H. Milford / Oxford: Oxford University Press, 1938).

Julie de Lespinasse was an *épistolière* (letter writer) who influenced the literary, social, and political culture that defined the French Enlightenment. The historical significance and cultural impact of her letters depend on the critical orientation of the reader. From a postmodern perspective, Lespinasse emerges not only as a romantic heroine whose death marked her entrance into literature but also as an accomplished intellectual whose salon attracted the leading writers, scholars, and politicians in Europe. Critics generally agree that Lespinasse glorified the art of witty conversation, encouraging her guests to express themselves freely and to use reason to debate all subjects and points of view. The gatherings she hosted became well known because they provided an atmosphere conducive to the spirit of reform nurtured by her friends the philosophes. Her role in facilitating the discussions and research that resulted in the publication of their work earned her the title "Muse of the Encyclopedia."

Julie-Jeanne-Eléonore de Lespinasse was born in Lyon on 9 November 1732 at the home of surgeon Louis Basiliac, her godfather, and his wife, Madeleine Ganinet, who represented the child's godmother, Julie Lechot. The parents of record were registered as Claude Lespinasse and Julie Navarre, neither of whom existed. Lespinasse's real mother was Julie-Claude-Hilaire d'Albon, a member of an old and illustrious aristocratic family, whose titles were princesse d'Yvetot, marquise de Saint-Forgeux, and comtesse d'Albon. The name Lespinasse refers to a property that belonged to the Albon family. Separated from her husband, the comtesse had little or no contact with him for several years. Possibly, the comte and comtesse had a formal judicial separation by which she was given control of her own estate. In any case, the comtesse had a secret lover who was the father of Lespinasse. At that time, she also had two other children by her husband, an eight-year-old son, Camille-Alexis, and a sixteen-year-old daughter, Marie-Camille-Diane. Little is known about another son, who became a monk. The comtesse was a loving and attentive mother who raised and educated Lespinasse in her château in Avauges. While the circumstances of her birth were not discussed, Lespinasse was regarded as the daughter of the comtesse, who provided her with a good education. Lespinasse acquired an excellent knowledge of English, particularly later in life. Her skill in English enabled her to read the novels of one of her favorite authors, Samuel Richardson, as well as the works of William Shakespeare, John Locke, and Laurence Sterne. She was also familiar with the works of Plutarch, Tacitus, Michel de Montaigne, and the principal works of French tragedy and comedy. Lespinasse's sheltered existence, however, ended abruptly when her mother died in 1748. Lespinasse inherited a small pension as well as a sum of money to be used as a dowry. In a selfless act that she lived to regret, Lespinasse gave the lump sum to her older brother, Camille. Her generosity left her essentially destitute. When she later appealed to her brother for financial help, he refused to give her the money that was rightfully hers.

Since her mother was still officially married when Lespinasse was born, the possibility existed that she might claim a right to an inheritance. She was taken, therefore, to the château of Champrond, where she was offered the position of governess to the three children of her older sister, who had married Gaspard-Nicolas de Vichy, comte de Champrond. During her stay at Champrond, Lespinasse supposedly learned the truth about her birth–Vichy, her brother-in-law, was also the secret lover whose name her mother had refused to reveal and thus her real father. Devastated by this knowledge, she now understood her precarious situation and the reason she was poorly treated by her family. Although Lespinasse was an excellent teacher, beloved by her nephews, she was unhappy with her situation and expressed her desire to enter a convent. In 1752, however, she met a woman who changed the course of her life.

Vichy had a sister, Marie de Vichy-Champrond, marquise Du Deffand, whose intellectual and physical attributes had earned her the admiration of powerful men and women who helped her establish one of the leading salons in Paris. On a rare visit to Champrond, Du Deffand was impressed by the charm and intellect of the young woman who was her niece. During their long conversations together, Du Deffand grew sympathetic to Lespinasse's plight and made a proposal that

Letter from Lespinasse to her close friend Marie-Jean-Antoine-Nicolas Caritat, marquis de Condorcet, mathematician and philosopher (top: address with Lespinasse's seal; bottom: letter) (from G. K. Fortescue, ed., Letters of Mlle. De Lespinasse, 1909; Thomas Cooper Library, University of South Carolina)

would benefit them both. Du Deffand was a middle-aged woman, almost blind, and needed a companion and reader to help her endure many sleepless nights. She invited the young woman to come live with her and fulfill these functions. To the dismay of the Vichy family, Lespinasse accepted the offer. Du Deffand, however, still had to overcome her family's fear that Lespinasse would claim part of the inheritance. Anxious to leave the Vichy household, Lespinasse entered a convent while Du Deffand informed her relatives of her intentions and eventually succeeded in making all the necessary arrangements.

In 1754 Lespinasse took up residence with her aunt in the convent of Saint-Joseph in Paris, where Du Deffand was renting an apartment. Lespinasse learned there the art of entertaining the greatest European minds of the century and how to coordinate the discussions of diverse and frequently controversial ideas. Du Deffand's salon was the center of a social circle that included Anne-Robert-Jacques Turgot, economist and close friend of Lespinasse, who was comptroller-general of France until 1766; writer Charles Jean-François Hénault, Du Deffand's former lover, who became president of the Chambre des Enquêtes and was elected to the French Academy in 1731; Jean-François Marmontel, writer and successor to d'Alembert as secretary of the Académie française (French Academy); Denis Diderot, philosopher, writer, and editor of the *Encyclopédie, ou dictionnaire raisonné des sciences, des arts et des métiers* (1751–1772, Encyclopedia, or a Descriptive Dictionary of the Sciences, Arts, and Trades); and Jean Le Rond d'Alembert, mathematician and co-editor of the *Encyclopédie*, whose life became closely linked with Lespinasse's. Accepted as an equal in this elite circle of friends, Lespinasse used her intelligence and social graces to cultivate her position among Du Deffand's guests. Initially happy and satisfied with this arrangement, the two women seemed to complement and support each other. Lespinasse, however, soon grew weary of the domineering aunt and mentor who controlled her life and who demanded absolute compliance with her wishes. Forced to stay up most of the night reading and limited in her activities during the day, Lespinasse soon complained of the constraints on her life to d'Alembert, with whom she had developed a warm friendship. D'Alembert, the star of Du Deffand's salon, became estranged from his hostess and sympathized with Lespinasse, whose relationship with her aunt grew increasingly tense and duplicitous.

Two events led to the eventual end of the association between the two women. One of the visitors to Du Deffand's salon was an Irish viscount, Nicholas Taaffe. He fell in love with Lespinasse and considered proposing marriage, an idea to which Du Deffand vigorously objected. She quickly put an end to the affair, much to the displeasure of her niece, who was forbidden to see him. Although she already occupied a social position of her own, Lespinasse nevertheless was financially dependent on her aunt and thus obligated to obey her. In an act of rebellion that affected not only her relationship with her mentor but also her subsequent health, Lespinasse took an overdose of opium and almost died. Remorseful, her aunt asked for forgiveness but never regained the affection she had previously enjoyed from her niece.

The second and more serious event resulted in the definitive separation of the two women. As Lespinasse became more popular with the habitués of the salon, Du Deffand began to regard her as a rival and grew increasingly jealous of her niece's social success. In 1764 Du Deffand discovered that several habitués, among them d'Alembert, Marmontel, and Turgot, were arriving an hour early to visit Lespinasse upstairs in her room. They engaged in discussions that should have taken place in the downstairs salon in the presence of Du Deffand. The older woman was furious and demanded that Lespinasse leave her house immediately. When many of her friends sided with her niece in the dispute, Du Deffand developed a hatred for the younger woman who had been her constant companion for ten years. Henceforth, she only spoke about Lespinasse in a derogatory and spiteful manner.

At the urging of her friends, Lespinasse decided to start her own salon. Her supporters, who were generous as well as faithful, subsidized this undertaking by paying for many of the expenses such an enterprise entailed. Marie-Thérèse Geoffrin, another famous *salonnière* and a rival of Du Deffand, was especially gracious in helping furnish the apartment that Lespinasse rented in rue Saint-Dominique, near the convent of Bellechasse. D'Alembert, forced by his hostess to choose between the two women, abandoned Du Deffand to become the magnet that attracted followers to the new and more progressive salon of Lespinasse. Among those who joined him were Marmontel, Turgot, chevalier François-Jean Chastellux (whose literary and scientific interests linked him to the philosophes) Marie-Jean-Antoine-Nicolas Caritat, marquis de Condorcet (a distinguished mathematician and philosopher who became a close friend and frequent correspondent of Lespinasse), and Madeleine-Angéline de Neufville, duchesse of Luxembourg, whose gifts also helped furnish the new salon. Regular guests included German-born writer Frédéric Melchior Grimm, who in 1753 became the principal editor of the *Correspondance littéraire,* a monthly newsletter sent to kings and princes throughout Europe; journalist Jean-Baptiste-Antoine Suard, who edited the *Gazette de France;* poet, literary critic, and playwright Jean-François de La Harpe; and memoir writer Charles-Pinot Duclos, who became the perpetual secretary of the French Academy in 1755.

D'Alembert's position was consolidated when in 1765, after a serious illness, he left his inadequate lodging in the house of Madame Rousseau, his foster mother, and moved from rue Michel-le-Comte to become a tenant in the same building as Lespinasse. He rented the spare rooms she had on the fourth floor of her suite. The two friends combined their expenses and were therefore able to live more easily within the limitations of their modest incomes. Rumors circulated about their impending marriage, but the event never took place. While they may have been romantically linked at the beginning, Lespinasse regarded d'Alembert as a close friend and colleague rather than a lover. He became her personal secretary, and they lived together until she died. By eighteenth-century standards, their association became socially acceptable, and they were generally regarded with admiration and respect. In later years, when she was overwhelmed with illness and emotionally distressed, Lespinasse sometimes took d'Alembert for granted, and he became the victim of her frustration and anger. D'Alembert, however, always entertained the idea of a more intimate relationship with her. He nursed his friend through many illnesses and remained deeply devoted to her throughout her life.

The revolutionary atmosphere of the new salon was matched by the exquisite but tasteful manner in which it was furnished, with busts of Voltaire and d'Alembert at its center. Unlike other *salonnières*, Lespinasse did not have the means to serve elaborate dinners at her gatherings, and glasses of sugar water sufficed to quench the thirsts of her guests. Every evening from five until nine o'clock, and sometimes later for intimate friends, from 1764 until just before her death in 1776, Lespinasse coordinated and facilitated the intellectual fervor that characterized these gatherings. Frequently, guests from abroad were included. This nightly routine was interrupted only when Lespinasse went to the opera, attended a special event, or accepted an invitation to dinner. One foreign visitor in particular, twenty-two-year-old Don José y Gonzaga, marquis de Mora, profoundly affected her life. When she met him in 1766, she was thirty-four years old.

The enlightened Mora, an aspiring philosopher and diplomat, was the son of the count de Fuentès, a member of the aristocratic house of Pignatelli of Aragon. He was the son-in-law of Count Aranda, the Spanish ambassador to Paris who had expelled the Jesuits from Spain and promoted the ideals of the Enlightenment. Recently widowed, Mora came to Paris to forget his sorrow in a round of social and diplomatic distractions. Soon after they met, he became infatuated with Lespinasse, who fell in love with this charming young intellectual from Spain. Although his military duties occupied much of his time, Mora visited Paris and spent nearly every evening with Lespinasse. When Mora seriously considered a proposal of marriage, his family strenuously objected and kept the lovers apart by increasing their demands on his time and energy. The length of the pair's separation was increased by his rapid physical deterioration from tuberculosis, a disease that also afflicted Lespinasse. Mora's passionate letters to his beloved helped sustain her during the convulsive coughing spells, migraines, and rheumatism that were symptoms of her illness. Mora left Paris for the last time in 1772. During this time the behavior of Lespinasse toward d'Alembert began to change, but he never suspected the reason for her ill humor.

On 21 June 1772, at the height of her liaison with Mora, Lespinasse met Count Jacques-Antoine-Hippolyte de Guibert at Moulin-Joli, a property that belonged to wealthy financier Claude-Henri Watelet. The twenty-nine-year-old colonel had commanded the Corsican Legion, served in the Seven Years' War, and was the author of the *Essai général de tactique* (1772, Essay on Tactics), a treatise on military strategy and reform that made him well known. The book was banned by the government for two years before it was published. Guibert's progressive ideas were considered brilliant and impressed everyone who read the work. Historians have claimed that even George Washington consulted it. Guibert was soon invited to all the literary and philosophic salons, where he read excerpts from his essay and his other works, including a play, *Le Connétable de Bourbon* (1775, The Constable of Bourbon), *Anne de Boleyn*, a tragedy that appeared in 1777, and *Défense du système de guerre moderne* (1779, In Defense of Modern Warfare). His correspondence with Lespinasse, however, brought him lasting fame and immortalized her name among the great *épistolières* of history.

Guibert, admired by all the women he met, became the confidant of Lespinasse and a regular guest at her salon. She revealed her love for Mora to him, her anxiety regarding his failing health, and the frustration she felt with his family's attempts to keep them apart. Guibert commiserated with her and voiced his own concerns regarding his mounting debts and his relationship with Madame de Montsauge, his current mistress. Guibert and Lespinasse discussed the latest literary works as well as the political events that defined eighteenth-century European society. Lespinasse soon realized she was in love with two men simultaneously—Mora and Guibert. The Lespinasse-Guibert correspondence began in May 1773 when Guibert traveled to Prussia, Austria, and Hungary before returning to

France at the end of October after visiting Voltaire. The correspondence lasted until Lespinasse's death in 1776. Although she corresponded with many other contemporaries, her passion for Guibert was what inspired her to write letters that have become classics of epistolary literature. To appreciate the complex and contradictory feelings revealed in these letters, one must understand their context.

Lespinasse and Guibert lived in an age when sensibility determined the code of behavior that defined polite society. Love was a game that people played in their public and private lives. The limits that separated genuine love from socially conventional expressions of friendship were hidden behind exaggerated language and behavior. Contemporary witnesses and his biographers describe Guibert as an intelligent, charming, but egocentric social climber with an inflated opinion of his literary talents. He was a skillful player in the game of love and sensibility, successful in manipulating men and women who helped him achieve the social and literary successes he enjoyed. Flattered by the attention he received from women, Guibert nevertheless avoided becoming involved in intimate relationships that might infringe on his social and military obligations or his literary aspirations. The biographers of Lespinasse agree that she, on the other hand, was a genuinely sensitive woman who searched for a deep and lasting relationship with a man who could reciprocate her feelings. Her sensitivity was heightened by the effects of tuberculosis. Consequently, Guibert was overwhelmed by a passion he did not understand and the sincerity of a woman he could not fully appreciate.

Mora, who was not aware of the relationship between Guibert and Lespinasse, wrote letters that expressed his love and made repeated attempts to see her. Constant travel, inadequate care, and excessive bleedings by incompetent doctors, however, contributed to his death. During a final effort to return to France, he died in Bordeaux on 27 May 1774. In his last letter to Lespinasse, dated 23 May, he expresses his regret that he will die before seeing her one more time. On 1 June 1774, when she found out that he had died, she became despondent. The knowledge that she had been unfaithful to a man who had loved her increased the bouts of depression that frequently incapacitated her. Subsequent letters from Lespinasse to Guibert reflect a pessimistic view of life, her disappointment in him, and guilt that she had betrayed Mora.

Guibert constantly traveled and attended to his military duties, social obligations, and literary endeavors. Lespinasse continued to write him letters, many of which he carelessly misplaced or lost. The longer he was absent, the more she was drawn to him until she became his mistress in February 1774. In her correspondence, she re-creates Guibert in her own idealized image of the perfect lover. Compared to the sensitive Mora, Lespinasse complains in her letters that Guibert fails to meet her expectations. Depending on her mood and his behavior, he is represented as both god and devil. In a state of desperation, Lespinasse continued writing to Mora, a lover who no longer existed, at the same time she wrote to Guibert. The comte, however, expressed his affection in ambivalent terms, which contributed to the sense of futility and isolation that overwhelmed Lespinasse. On 25 August 1774, a letter to Guibert provided an opportunity for her to write about Mora: "ma vie ne sera pas assez longue pour regretter et pour chérir l'homme le plus sensible et le plus vertueux qui exista jamais" (my life will not be long enough to regret and cherish the most sensitive and virtuous man who ever lived). It was not the memory of Mora, however, that had the power to calm her anxiety, but only Guibert himself, his letters, the music of Christoph Willibald Gluck's opera *Orphée* (1774), and opium.

While Lespinasse was jealous of Guibert's relationships with other women, she could not seriously consider marrying him. In spite of her political and social influence, her charm, and her intellectual superiority, she was not an eligible marriage partner. Although her family was aristocratic, she was too old, of illegitimate birth, and not wealthy enough to compete with her more attractive, younger, and wealthier rivals. Pressured by his family and burdened with debts, Guibert discussed with Lespinasse his need to marry a wealthy heiress. At first, she was sympathetic to his plight and offered to help him find a suitable wife. She was unaware, however, that he had been secretly visiting seventeen-year-old Alexandrine Louise Boutinon des Hays de Courcelles and negotiating the terms of a marriage contract with her family. On 1 June 1775 he married the young woman, much to the dismay of Lespinasse. Guibert attempted to convince her that the marriage was only for the sake of convenience. Based on comments made by his contemporaries and the entries he made in his journal, however, Guibert's biographers believe that the marriage was a love match. Lespinasse met the new bride and thought she was charming, but she resented the duplicity of the comte and never forgave him. She refused to remain his mistress after the wedding. They did, however, maintain a close relationship in which Guibert became more solicitous of his dying friend, and she used her influence to help him manage his personal affairs and promote his literary endeavors. She even read and critiqued his play, *Le Connétable de Bourbon*.

Throughout her long illness Lespinasse remained active in the rich intellectual life and social activities that surrounded her. She died at two o'clock in the morning

Lespinasse (painting by Louis de Carmontelle, Musée de Chantilly)

on 22 May 1776. She had requested a pauper's funeral and was buried at St. Sulpice, with d'Alembert and Condorcet as the chief mourners. D'Alembert was named executor of her will, in which she left modest sums to her servants and the poor. Among the friends who received her furniture and personal belongings were Guibert, d'Alembert, Condorcet, Suard, and Geoffrin. In a separate letter addressed to d'Alembert, Lespinasse thanked him for his devotion and asked that he burn all her letters from Mora, unread. He complied with her wishes, but much to d'Alembert's surprise and dismay, he found a document that left no doubt about her relationship with the Spaniard. In addition, despite the many years they spent together, he was not aware of her relationship with Guibert until he found the letters that the count had returned to her. D'Alembert, who felt betrayed, abandoned, and despondent over the loss of the only woman he had truly loved, died in 1783.

The first edition of the letters, *Lettres de Mademoiselle de Lespinasse, écrites depuis l'année 1773, jusqu'à l'année 1776; suivies de deux chapitres dans le genre du Voyage sentimental de Sterne, par le même auteur* (1809, Letters by Mademoiselle de Lespinasse, Written from the Year 1773 until 1776; Followed by Two Chapters in the Style of "The Sentimental Voyage" by Sterne, by the Same Author), was probably edited by Bertrand Barrère, with the cooperation of Guibert's widow. It consists of 180 letters from Lespinasse to the count. Based on this collection, many critics conclude that she was a romantic heroine victimized by the man she loved. The short text titled *Suite du Voyage Sentimental* (Continuation of the Sentimental Voyage), which consists of two additional chapters to Laurence Sterne's *A Sentimental Journey Through France and Italy* (1768), is also included in editions published in 1811 and 1815. In the nineteenth century, several other collections were published that focus on Lespinasse the literary heroine rather than the woman of intellect who associated with the most important writers, scientists, and politicians of her day. In 1820, a volume titled *Nouvelles Lettres de Mademoiselle de Lespinasse* (New Letters by Mademoiselle de Lespinasse) was published. Jean-Noël Pascal suggests in his article "De la lettre au roman: sur l'entrée en littérature de Julie de Lespinasse" that these letters are not authentic, but rather "une biographie épistolaire romancée" (a fictionalized epistolary biography) based on the letters in the 1809 edition. By selecting letters frequently taken out of context, critics have thus tended to romanticize Lespinasse's life. An authoritative edition of the Lespinasse-Guibert correspondence titled *Correspondance entre Mlle de Lespinasse et le comte de Guibert* (1906; translated as *Love Letters of Mademoiselle de Lespinasse to and from the comte de Guibert,* 1929) was published by Guibert's great-grandson. It comprises 201 letters, including 39 from Guibert beginning in July 1774. Pascal has studied the different editions of the Lespinasse correspondence. He suggests that the 1906 edition, which incorporates the voice of Guibert for the first time, best shows the contrast between his controlled language, characterized by conventional platitudes, and the sincere responses of a woman in love. The letters also reveal to what extent Lespinasse was involved in the intellectual and political events of her milieu. Pascal concludes that Guibert was a mediocre man loved by a superior woman who realized that her feelings for him were not reciprocated to her satisfaction. Critics have studied Lespinasse not only as a literary figure but as the author of an authentic text that has a cultural and historical significance.

The life of Lespinasse is also the subject of many biographies, beginning in the nineteenth century. The first authoritative work that provides readers with a more balanced account of her personality and the political and cultural context in which she lived was published by Pierre-Maurice-Henri, marquis de Ségur, and titled *Julie de Lespinasse* (1906). To provide a greater understanding of her contribution to literature and the history of ideas, her biographers have also increasingly focused on her correspondence with Condorcet, Turgot, and family members, as well as her relationship with the philosophes. Her letters to Condorcet, for example, express her solicitude for the young philosopher and offer him advice on his private and public life.

Critical investigation has also focused on the extensive commentary in the letters on tuberculosis and the medications used to treat its symptoms. References to signs of the disease, its effect on both mind and body, and the effectiveness of various treatments are significant sources of information on the philosophy and practice of medicine in eighteenth-century France. Lespinasse was already seriously ill when her relationship with Guibert began. In her letters to Condorcet as early as 1771 and continuing until just before her death, she complains about chronic insomnia, heart palpitations, coughing spells, high fevers, lethargy, digestive problems, fatigue, and depression. Among the remedies she tried were the milk of an ass for her digestion, opium to deaden her pain and calm her nerves, and "occimêle cilitique," an expectorant that included honey, vinegar, and shavings from white squills (sea onions that grow in the Mediterranean region). As her illness became hopeless and her disillusion with Guibert more acute, she stated that she expected nothing more from life; yet, she lacked the courage to end it, as she wrote to Condorcet in a letter dated 15 October 1774: "On sent tous les soirs qu'on serait bien heureux de ne pas se réveiller; alors, mon ami, on n'a plus le droit de juger rien" (one feels every evening that one would be very happy not to wake up, then, my friend, one no longer has the right to judge anything). She viewed death as a desired state, liberating her from the burden of life.

In her letters to Guibert, complaints regarding her health were as frequent as her expressions of love. As Lespinasse grew physically weaker and emotionally more vulnerable, her feelings toward him vacillated between love, hatred, friendship, and disillusion. Heaven was the recurring motif that represented her passion, while remorse for betraying Mora and anxiety over Guibert's absence were represented by images of hell. Her sensibility and self-pity were heightened by the effects of her rising and falling fever, characteristic of tuberculosis. In an early letter to Guibert, dated 1773, she compared her soul "au thermomètre qui est d'abord à la glace et peu de temps après au climat brûlant de l'équateur" (to the thermometer which at first indicates freezing and shortly thereafter the burning heat of the equator). The binary oppositions—love and hate, life and death—structure the letters to Guibert from 1773 until her death. Throughout the correspondence, life and love are linked to mental and physical suffering, death, and the overwhelming need to write. In a well-known letter to Guibert dated "De tous les instants de ma vie 1774" (At every instant of my life 1774), she wrote only the following message: "Mon ami je souffre, je vous aime, je vous attends" (My friend, I am suffering, I love you, I await you).

Guilt and remorse poisoned her feelings for Guibert, whom she regarded as both the savior who calmed her suffering and the executioner who could end her life. On 30 September 1774, she described the intense pleasure she derived from reading his letters. Such pleasure, however, was embittered by the memory of Mora, who, if he were alive, "m'aimerait, et je n'aurais plus ni remords ni malheur" (would love me, and I would have no more remorse or unhappiness). Her love for Guibert and her chronic bad health created a state of anxiety that influenced the exaggerated expressions of pain and pleasure in the letters. Even at the height of her affair with the count, in the midst of her social obligations, she described the despair that overwhelmed her. As she attempted to retreat from the world around her, life became a play, she claimed, in which she reluctantly participated. She begged Guibert to guide her in finding a new meaning in life, but all attempts to alleviate her suffering proved futile. Since contemporary medical opinion linked tuberculosis to emotional and nervous problems, she told Guibert in a letter dated 8 November 1775 that her doctors were unable to help her, claiming that they had no remedy for the soul and could only recommend therapeutic baths at a spa. She died on 22 May 1776.

Although Julie de Lespinasse wrote about the vicissitudes of love, she also commented on literature, politics, music, and art. While insisting that her life was more tragic and authentic than the fictional stories found in literature, she nevertheless compared herself to heroines in tragic plays and novels. The many literary references in her correspondence include the works of playwright Jean Racine, poet Jean de La Fontaine, novelist Honoré d'Urfé, Voltaire, poet and literary critic Nicolas Despréaux-Boileau, and novelist Antoine François Prévost. These references informed her lively and perceptive observations on the lives and political fortunes of her friends and acquaintances in France and abroad. In her private correspondence as in her public life, Lespinasse made an important contribution to the understanding of the events that shaped Enlightenment ideology and the Romantic sensibility that followed it.

Bibliography:

Charles Henry, "Bibliographie de Mademoiselle de Lespinasse," in his *Lettres inédites de Mademoiselle de Lespinasse à Condorcet, à d'Alembert, à Guibert, au comte de Crillon* (Paris: E. Dentu, 1887).

Biographies:

Pierre-Maurice-Henri, marquis de Ségur, *Julie de Lespinasse* (Paris: Calmann-Lévy, 1906); translated by P. H. Lee Warner as *Julie de Lespinasse* (New York: Holt, 1907);

Camilla Jebb, *A Star of the Salons: Julie de Lespinasse* (New York: Putnam, 1908);

J. Boisjolin and G. Mossé, *Julie de Lespinasse* (Paris, 1912);

Naomi Royde-Smith, *The Double Heart: A Study of Julie de Lespinasse* (New York: Harper, 1931);

Gonzague Truc, *Julie de Lespinasse, celle qui vécut et mourut d'amour* (Paris: A. Michel, 1942);

Janine Bouissounouse, *Julie de Lespinasse, ses amitiés, sa passion* (Paris: Hachette, 1958); translated by P. de Fontnouvelle as *Julie: The Life of Mademoiselle de Lespinasse* (New York: Appleton-Century-Crofts, 1962);

Margaret Mitchiner, *A Muse in Love: Julie de Lespinasse* (London: Bodley Head, 1962);

Jean Lacouture and Marie-Christine d'Aragon, *Julie de Lespinasse: mourir d'amour* (Paris: Ramsay, 1980);

René de La Croix, duc de Castries, *Julie de Lespinasse: le drame d'un double amour* (Paris: Michel, 1985).

References:

André Beaunier, "Julie, ou les périls de la sensibilité," *La Revue Universelle,* 18 (1924): 641–665;

Beaunier, *La Vie amoureuse de Julie de Lespinasse* (Paris: Ernest Flammarion, 1925);

Catherine Blondeau, "Lectures de la correspondance de Julie de Lespinasse: une étude de réception," *Studies on Voltaire and the Eighteenth Century,* 308 (1993): 223–232;

François Bott, *La Demoiselle des Lumières* (Paris: Gallimard, 1997);

Susan Lee Carrell, *Le Soliloque de la passion féminine ou le dialogue illusoire* (Tübingen: Gunter Narr / Paris: Jean-Michel Place, 1982);

Jacques Dupont, "De l'absence au chant: sur les lettres à Guibert de Julie de Lespinasse," *Dix-Huitième Siècle,* 10 (1978): 395–404;

Philippe Garcin, "L'amour et l'absence dans les Lettres de Mlle de Lespinasse," *Cahiers du Sud,* 302 (1950): 109–122;

Dena Goodman, "Julie de Lespinasse: A Mirror for the Enlightenment," in *Eighteenth-Century Women and the Arts,* edited by Frederick M. Keener and Susan E. Lorsch (New York, Westport, Conn. & London: Greenwood Press, 1988), pp. 3–10;

Eve Katz, "The Contradictions of Passion in the Love Letters of Julie de Lespinasse," *American Society Legion of Honor Magazine,* 43 (1972): 9–24;

Robert Mauzi, "Les maladies de l'âme au XVIIIe siècle," *Revue des Sciences Humaines* (1960): 459–493;

Gita May, "Julie de Lespinasse," in *French Women Writers—A Bio-Bibliographical Source Book,* edited by Eva Martin Sartori and Dorothy Wynne Zimmerman (New York, Westport, Conn. & London: Greenwood Press, 1991), pp. 296–304;

M. Melen, "Une salonnière au XVIIIe siècle: Mlle de Lespinasse et le mouvement philosophique," dissertation, Sorbonne, 1984;

Roland Mortier, "Julie de Lespinasse, femme savante et âme sensible," in *La Sensibilité dans la littérature française de l'Abbé Prévost à Madame de Staël,* Actes du Colloque international, 86 (N.p.: Biblioteca della ricerca, 1998), pp. 235–245;

Jean-Noël Pascal, "De la lettre au roman: sur l'entrée en littérature de Julie de Lespinasse," *Dix-Hutième Siècle,* 21 (1989): 381–393;

Pascal, "Une exemplaire mort d'amour, Julie de Lespinasse," in *Aimer en France 1760–1860,* edited by Paul Viallaneix and Jean Ehrard (Clermont-Ferrand: Association des Publications de la Faculté des Lettres, 1980), pp. 553–563;

Pascal, "Les maux et les mosts: de quelques confidencs de Mlle de Lespinasse a ses amis sur l'état de son ame," *Revue de L'AIRE, Récherches sur l'épistolaire,* 27 (Winter 2001): 39–53;

Pascal, "La muse de l'Encyclopédie: Julie de Lespinasse," in *Femmes savantes et femmes d'esprit,* edited by Roland Bonnel and Catherine Rubinger (New York: Peter Lang, 1994), pp. 243–265;

Pascal, "Quelque réflexions sur Julie de Lespinasse et la lettre d'amour: de la tragedie au roman," in *Femmes en toutes lettres–Les épistolières du XVIII siècle,* edited by Marie-France Girou Swiderski (Oxford: Voltaire Foundation, 2000), pp. 155–164;

A. F. Plicque, "Les tuberculeuses célèbres: Mlle de Lespinasse," *Chronique Médicale* (1901): 161–164;

Jürgen Siess, "Effusion amoreuse et échange intéllectual–La pratique épistolaire de Julie de Lespinasse," in *L'Epistolaire, Un Genre Feminin,* edited by Christine Plante (Paris: Honore Champion, 1998), pp. 117–131;

Siess, "L'épistolière comme auteur–Julie de Lespinasse femme de lettres," in *L'Auteur,* edited by Gabrielle Chamarat and Alain Goulet, Colloque de Cerisy-la-Salle (Caen: Presses Universitaires de Caen, 1996), pp. 61–73;

Felicia Sturzer, "Love and Disease: The Contaminated Letters of Julie de Lespinasse," *SVEC,* 9 (2000): 3–16.

Papers:

A reproduction of the manuscripts bequeathed by Julie de Lespinasse are on microfiche at the Voltaire Foundation, Taylor Institution, Oxford, England.

Marie-Charlotte-Pauline Robert de Lézardière

(25 March 1754 – 1835)

Mary McAlpin
University of Tennessee

BOOKS: *Esprit des lois canoniques et politiques qui ont régi l'Eglise gallicane dans les quatre premiers siècles de la monarchie*, 2 volumes (Paris: Nyon L'Aîné et Fils, 1791);

Théorie des lois politiques de la monarchie française (8 volumes, Paris: Nyon L'Aîné et Fils, 1792; augmented edition, 4 volumes, Paris: Comptoir des Imprimeurs-Unis, 1844);

Ecrits inédits de Mlle de Lézardière, edited by Ely Carcassonne (Paris: Presses universitaires de France, 1927).

Marie-Charlotte-Pauline Robert de Lézardière produced a monumental history of French political law, *Théorie des lois politiques de la monarchie française* (1792, Theory of the Political Laws of the French Monarchy), in an effort to counteract the absolutist tendencies of the French monarchy of her own day. Following the model of *Esprit des lois* (1748, Spirit of the Laws) by Charles-Louis de Secondat, baron de Montesquieu, Lézardière argued that modern French liberty originated in the primitive political structures of the Germanic tribes who "liberated" Gaul in the fifth century. Her most original contribution is the unwavering continuity and essential equity that she attributes to the French constitution, as an expression of the spirit of these original political structures. Early versions of the *Théorie des lois politiques de la monarchie française* were read in manuscript form by Louis XVI; seized in the raid on the Tuileries Palace in 1792, Lézardière's manuscripts became part of the body of evidence used against the king at his trial. Lézardière has been accused of confusing her ideals with history, as when she argues that the French people were happiest under a purely feudal regime; yet, her writing also reflects Enlightenment values, as illustrated by her profound faith in liberal monarchy. Proscribed by the Revolution, rehabilitated in the nineteenth century, Lézardière is known today primarily as a gifted disciple of Montesquieu.

Lézardière was born on 25 March 1754 in her family's ancestral castle of La Vérie, located in the Vendée, near the city of Challans. She was raised in relative isolation with her parents and four brothers in their manor house, La Proustière. According to Charles-Robert Lézardière, the brother who oversaw the reprinting of the *Théorie des lois politiques de la monarchie française* after her death, Lézardière's interest in writing history was initially opposed by her father, a former cavalry captain; he later relented and even served as intermediary in presenting his daughter's works to the king. In 1771, when Lézardière began writing, she was only seventeen but had access to the considerable collection of historical works in the library of La Proustière. She completed her first major work three years later: "Tableau des droits réels et respectifs du monarque et des sujets, depuis le fondement de la Monarchie française jusqu'à nos jours" (Tableau of the Real and Respective Rights of the Monarch and Subjects, from the Founding of the French Monarchy until the Present). Lézardière wrote this work in response to the suppression of the Parlements (high courts of justice). In her view, René-Nicolas-Charles-Augustin de Maupeou, chancellor of France, had taken advantage of the general public's ignorance of the French constitution in order to attack the Parlements for "dangerous innovations" that were in fact their ancient prerogatives. The Parlements were denied the right to reject or modify ordinances and limited to giving advice to the king and to following his orders. At Maupeou's instigation, Louis XV declared that he owed his crown to God alone, and that he alone in France possessed legislative authority. Lézardière's goal in the "Tableau des droits réels et respectifs du monarque et des sujets" was double: to support the rights that the Parlements were claiming for themselves, and to prevent future absolutist claims by the French monarchy.

The "Tableau des droits réels et respectifs du monarque et des sujets," sent to Louis XVI soon after his ascension to the throne, remained in manuscript form until the scholar Ely Carcassonne edited and published the *Ecrits inédits de Mlle de Lézardière* (1927, Unpublished Works of Mademoiselle de Lézardière).

Carcassonne also included in this volume two shorter pieces by Lézardière that, like the "Tableau des droits réels et respectifs du monarque et des sujets," had been sent, unsigned, to Louis XVI: "Essai sur le rétablissement possible de quelques points essentiels de la constitution politique de la France" (Essay on the Possible Reinstitution of Some Essential Points of the French Political Constitution), written in 1778, and "Idée générale . . . ou précis de la théorie" (General Idea . . . or Précis of the Theory), written circa 1788. The letter preceding the "Essai sur le rétablissement possible de quelques points essentiels de la constitution politique de la France" was written by Lézardière's father and was delivered to Louis XVI along with that work. In this letter, the baron de Lézardière insisted that the manuscript he was presenting to the king had been produced "dans ma maison par une très jeune main" (in my house, by a very young hand), and that despite the author's youth, the baron's own participation had been strictly limited to revision and correction. After describing the author's pleasure at hearing that Louis XVI had responded favorably to the "Tableau des droits réels et respectifs du monarque et des sujets," the baron reveals that this approbation–passed on by his brother-in-law, the marquis de Pezay, with a request for secrecy–had inspired the author to work ceaselessly on researching and writing a more developed version of that work (which became the *Théorie des lois politiques de la monarchie française*). The "Essai sur le rétablissement possible de quelques points essentiels de la constitution politique de la France" could not wait for inclusion in this larger work, however, as its content–a project for provincial assemblies, and a method to organize a national assembly–was of compelling interest to the monarchy in 1778.

The exact nature of this future national assembly is the central question of the "Essai sur le rétablissement possible de quelques points essentiels de la constitution politique de la France." As always, Lézardière examines the history of the French constitution in order to determine what type of national assembly would both remain true to the spirit of French political law and function practically to the advantage of the current monarchy and the nation as a whole. She explains that there had been historically two sorts of French national assemblies: the *placités* (general assemblies) and the *Etats généraux* (Estates General). The Salic Law and all other constitutive French laws had been drawn up by the king and the nation in the original or primitive *placités*. In these first assemblies, the king proposed laws that had no force until the national assembly approved them. The *placités*, held from the reign of Clovis (481–511) to that of Charles II (843–877), were not divided according to the three social orders, as were the *Etats généraux*.

Nor, significantly, were the *placités* ever formally dissolved; they simply ceased to be called when internal dissension caused the original national constitution to break down and to be replaced, in a rather haphazard manner, by a purely feudal constitution. Not until 1302, during the reign of Philip IV, did the *Etats généraux* first meet. Lézardière presents the *Etats généraux* as the only legitimate power, other than the *placités*, authorized to modify the ancient system of laws. She attributes many positive legal reforms to the *Etats généraux*, including the immovability of judges. Only after the Seance of Tours under Charles VIII did this type of national assembly cease to exercise supreme colegislative power. While continuing to meet on occasion, the *Etats généraux* dealt with fiscal matters and upheld laws already established, rather than creating new laws.

However, Lézardière is not advising the king to restore such authority to the *Etats généraux*. These had been a product of the feudal regime, with the three orders including only the inhabitants of the cities–noble, clerical, and bourgeois. The addition of the inhabitants of the countryside to the number of "French citizens" since the time of Philip IV meant that the *Etats généraux* were an untenable form of assembly for late-eighteenth-century France. Only with proper representation could the lesser clergy and the inhabitants of the countryside be expected to submit to new laws, especially ones concerning tax reform. Were Louis XVI to call any sort of national assembly, Lézardière argued, he would have to go back in French history to that ancient and original form, the *placités*, that were indeed never officially abolished. Only in this way, Lézardière concluded, would the king "réunir legalement les représentants de la totalité des citoyens de l'état" (legally unite representatives of the totality of the citizens of the state). At the same time, he would demonstrate respect for the essential constitution of the monarchy and regain the prerogative, reversed with the *Etats généraux*, of proposing laws himself, to be later approved by a national assembly. Lézardière pointed out yet another practical advantage of the *placités*: representatives of the population of the countryside would outnumber those of the city, a predominance that would overcome the serious divisions and animosities among the three traditional orders. As Lézardière prophetically pointed out, these divisions would be antithetic to the unanimity necessary for general deliberation.

The last of the three manuscripts published in 1927 by Carcassonne, the "Idée générale . . . ou précis de la théorie," is difficult to date precisely. Carcassonne speculates that Lézardière sent this outline of her unfinished *Théorie des lois politiques de la monarchie française* to the king as a result of a call to savants that he had issued in

1788, after resigning himself to the first meeting of the *Etats généraux* since 1614. Louis XVI was requesting information on what the *Etats généraux* had been and what they should be. Apparently, the king did not read or was not convinced by the details of Lézardière's "Essai sur le rétablissement possible de quelques points essentiels de la constitution politique de la France" in favor of the reestablishment of the *placités,* although her previous work had attracted the attention of several important political figures–including Chrétien Guillaume de Malesherbes, director of the King's Library–who had passed on their encouragement to the unknown author. With the help of these influential readers, Lézardière gained access to valuable archival resources, such as the holdings of the King's Library and those of the Benedictine monks of Poitiers, while revising the "Tableau des droits réels et respectifs du monarque et des sujets" into the *Théorie des lois politiques de la monarchie française*. Her use of these original materials did not cause much significant change in her argument; while the *Théorie des lois politiques de la monarchie française* includes considerably more citation than the "Tableau des droits réels et respectifs du monarque et des sujets," it retains the principal structure of the earlier work.

The eight-volume *Théorie des lois politiques de la monarchie française* was not published until 1792, although volumes 4 and 5 appeared separately in 1791 under the title *Esprit des lois canoniques et politiques qui ont régi l'Eglise gallicane dans les quatre premiers siècles de la monarchie* (Spirit of the Canonical and Political Laws that Governed the Gallican Church During the First Four Centuries of the Monarchy). Carcassonne speculates that this slightly premature publication was again occasioned by the immediacy of the question at hand, namely, the civil constitution of the French clergy. The *Théorie des lois politiques de la monarchie française* itself begins with the origins of the French monarchy, and while Montesquieu is the acknowledged authority whose work guides Lézardière on this subject, her version of events is also informed by her preoccupation with the legitimate authority of the Parlements and the colegislative power of the *placités*. As a result, she presents a more stable and linear vision of French political history than does Montesquieu. The French constitution, developing out of an original liberty enjoyed by the Germanic tribes, is presented as predating the nobility, just as the nobility predates the monarchy. This constitution is then seen as having come under the pressure of historical vicissitudes but also as maintaining its stable form and legal sovereignty over the centuries.

At the heart of the French constitution, as presented by Lézardière, are a few laws and structures that had governed the Frankish tribes before they left their

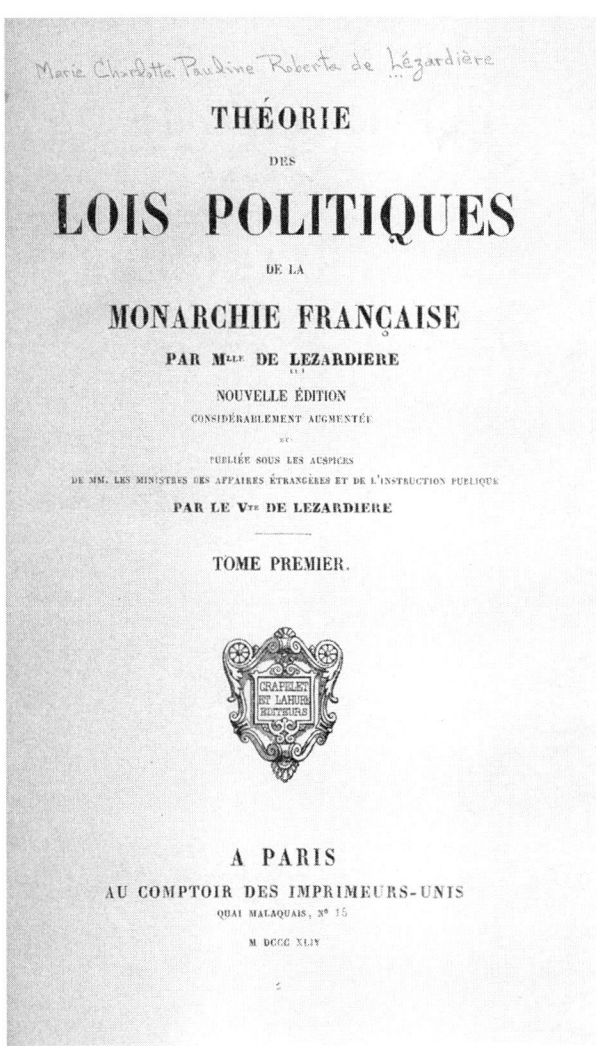

Title page for the first volume of a posthumous 1844 edition of Marie-Charlotte-Pauline Robert de Lézardière's landmark history of French political law, first published in 1792. This edition was augmented by her only surviving brother (Smith College Libraries).

native habitat in the woods. In the *Théorie des lois politiques de la monarchie française,* Lézardière specified that these tribes were governed by assemblies comprised of all free men of age able to bear arms. Magistrates were elected by this general assembly and charged with proposing laws, to be approved by that same assembly. These magistrates, the precursors of the nobility, were called princes by Tacitus, who points out as well the major problem with these assemblies: no particular person or entity was charged with calling these colegislative bodies together. This example of what Lézardière refers to as the too-extreme liberty enjoyed by the Franks was clearly chosen to reinforce Louis XVI's dominion over any form of national assembly he might

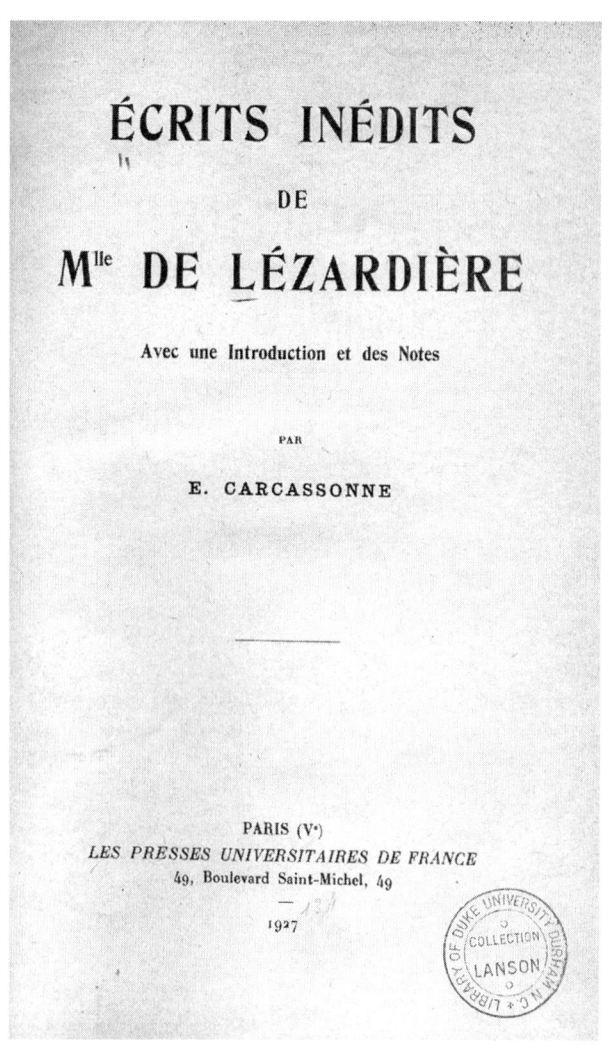

Title page from a collection of Lézardière's previously unpublished works, including her first major essay, "Tableau des droits réels et respectifs du monarque et des sujets" (Tableau of the Real and Respective Rights of the Monarch and Subjects), which she sent in manuscript form to Louis XVI in 1774 (Perkins Library, Duke University)

choose to call to order. Otherwise, the Germanic tribes are presented as enjoying a primitive yet well-balanced relationship to their princes. They wanted their independence to be well regulated, yet preserved for all time.

The French monarchy was established only by necessity when the Franks, having left their ancestral forests to conquer the Romans, became irremediably separated from the other Germanic tribes and needed a new form of government to ensure their safety. Legal reforms were necessary as well: under the old system, each citizen had the right to be judged by his peers, assembled as needed; now, under the monarchy, there was a Royal Court, the ancestor of the Parlements. Lézardière emphasized that the Franks chose their king as freemen from among their own number; thus the French king rules by divine right only in the most abstract sense, in which all that occurs is ordained by Providence. The king is the agent of God's plan. The constraints placed on the king's power by the Franks, Lézardière argued, were no less ordained by the nature of things than their choice of a monarchical form of government.

Lézardière's central goal is to prove that the spirit of French political laws resides in a respectful balance between king and nation, the latter being represented by an elite and well-chosen group of individuals exercising power in the Parlements as well as in the colegislative assemblies. While supporting the king's unquestioned right to rule and to exact obedience from his people, Lézardière provided a series of cautionary tales aimed at warning against absolutist tendencies. She addressed the issue of lettres de cachet in a manner that leaves no doubt as to her opinion on this particularly divisive abuse of royal authority. Kings are not judges, she noted, and have no right to judge individuals; nor are they sole legislators, their legislative power must be shared. No law authorizes the lettres de cachet, which are contrary to all the principles of the French constitution; therefore, "toute résistance contres elles de la part des déspotaires de cette constitution est permise, autorisée, commandée" (all resistance against them on the part of the inheritors of this constitution is permitted, authorized, commanded). Force is not to be used—as long as other paths of complaint remain open.

The *Théorie des lois politiques de la monarchie française*, as outlined in the "Idée générale . . . ou précis de la théorie," was to be divided into four epochs: the Gallo-Roman era, including the history of the Franks before the conquest of Gaul; from Clovis to the end of the reign of Charles II; from Charles II to Philip IV; and from Philip IV to the present. The eight volumes corresponding to the first two epochs appeared in 1792, just as the monarchy was abolished. They were immediately suppressed by the publisher or author out of prudence but became available for purchase again in 1801, when Lezardière's work received some praise; however, it was largely ignored. That same year, the author returned to the Vendée following her exile during the French Revolution, but she did not take up her writing again. The library on which she depended for her research had disappeared, along with the pertinence of the questions that she had addressed. Next to nothing is known about the last years of her life, except that she died a spinster. Her family had been decimated by the Revolution; three of her brothers had died, two guillotined, the third a victim of the September massacres:

during which crowds forced jailors to hand over their prisoners, who were then subjected to street "trials" and summarily executed. Only the youngest of her four brothers had been saved, owing in part to Lézardière's determined efforts, as detailed by Elie Fournier in his 1993 history of the family during this period.

In 1844, nine years after Lézardière's death at the age of eighty-one, this last surviving brother, Charles-Robert, oversaw the republication of the *Théorie des lois politiques de la monarchie française*. Produced under the auspices of the Ministry of Foreign Affairs and the Ministry of Public Instruction, this edition added a part of the third epoch; the fourth, although possibly well under way in 1791, was not included. If it ever existed, it is now lost. Despite the suppression of her erudite scholarly project covering fourteen centuries of French political law, Lézardière managed to participate through her manuscripts in the most telling and inflammatory debates of her time; through the efforts of scholars such as Carcassonne, she continues to occupy a place of distinction in the history of French political thought.

References:

Ely Carcassonne, *Montesquieu et le problème de la constitution française au XIIIe siècle* (Paris: Presses universitaires de France, 1927);

Octave Demartial, *Essai sur la théorie des lois politiques de la monarchie française par Mlle de Lézardière* (Poitiers, 1864);

Elie Fournier, *Une Famille vendéenne sous la Révolution* (Paris: Albin Michel, 1993);

George Grente, *Dictionnaire des lettres françaises* (Paris: Fayard, 1995);

Catherine Lafarge, "Lézardière," in *The Feminist Encyclopedia of French Literature,* edited by Eva Martin Sartori (Westport, Conn.: Greenwood Press, 1999), pp. 326–327;

Nouvelle Bibliographie générale (Paris: Firmin-Didot, 1862).

Contributors

Francis Assaf . . . . *University of Georgia*
Lisa Beckstrand . . . . *Montclair State University*
Steven Berry . . . . *Yale University*
Michèle Bissière . . . . *University of North Carolina at Charlotte*
John Blair . . . . *University of West Georgia*
Daniel Brewer . . . . *University of Minnesota*
Malcolm Cook . . . . *University of Exeter, U.K.*
Catherine Daniélou . . . . *University of Alabama at Birmingham*
Isabelle C. DeMarte . . . . *Lewis and Clark College*
Pamela Gay-White . . . . *Alabama State University*
Perry Gethner . . . . *Oklahoma State University*
Jeanne Hageman . . . . *North Dakota State University*
Michele L. Heintz . . . . *Tulane University*
Carla Hesse . . . . *University of California, Berkeley*
Katharine Ann Jensen . . . . *Louisiana State University*
Valérie Lastinger . . . . *West Virginia University*
Althea Arguelles Ling . . . . *University of Sydney*
Caryl L. Lloyd . . . . *University of West Georgia*
Jeff Loveland . . . . *University of Cincinnati*
Jin Lu . . . . *Purdue University Calumet*
Mary McAlpin . . . . *University of Tennessee*
Natania Meeker . . . . *University of Southern California*
Cecile Nebel . . . . *Hunter College of the City University of New York*
John Pappas . . . . *Fordham University*
Lauren Pinzka . . . . *Yale University*
Karlis Racevskis . . . . *Ohio State University*
Eva Martin Sartori . . . . *Five College Women's Studies Research Center*
Samia I. Spencer . . . . *Auburn University*
Felicia B. Sturzer . . . . *University of Tennessee at Chattanooga*
Karyna Szmurlo . . . . *Clemson University*
Ruth P. Thomas . . . . *Temple University*
Christopher Todd . . . . *Leeds University*
Gabrielle Verdier . . . . *University of Wisconsin–Milwaukee*
S. Pascale Vergereau-Dewey . . . . *Kutztown University*
Servanne Woodward . . . . *University of Western Ontario*

Cumulative Index

Dictionary of Literary Biography, Volumes 1-313
Dictionary of Literary Biography Yearbook, 1980-2002
Dictionary of Literary Biography Documentary Series, Volumes 1-19
Concise Dictionary of American Literary Biography, Volumes 1-7
Concise Dictionary of British Literary Biography, Volumes 1-8
Concise Dictionary of World Literary Biography, Volumes 1-4

Cumulative Index

DLB before number: *Dictionary of Literary Biography*, Volumes 1-313
Y before number: *Dictionary of Literary Biography Yearbook*, 1980-2002
DS before number: *Dictionary of Literary Biography Documentary Series*, Volumes 1-19
CDALB before number: *Concise Dictionary of American Literary Biography*, Volumes 1-7
CDBLB before number: *Concise Dictionary of British Literary Biography*, Volumes 1-8
CDWLB before number: *Concise Dictionary of World Literary Biography*, Volumes 1-4

A

Aakjær, Jeppe 1866-1930 . . . . DLB-214
Aarestrup, Emil 1800-1856 . . . . DLB-300
Abbey, Edward 1927-1989 . . . . DLB-256, 275
Abbey, Edwin Austin 1852-1911 . . . . DLB-188
Abbey, Maj. J. R. 1894-1969 . . . . DLB-201
Abbey Press DLB-49
The Abbey Theatre and Irish Drama,
　1900-1945 . . . . DLB-10
Abbot, Willis J. 1863-1934 . . . . DLB-29
Abbott, Edwin A. 1838-1926 . . . . DLB-178
Abbott, Jacob 1803-1879 . . . . DLB-1, 42, 243
Abbott, Lee K. 1947- DLB-130
Abbott, Lyman 1835-1922 . . . . DLB-79
Abbott, Robert S. 1868-1940 . . . . DLB-29, 91
'Abd al-Hamid al-Katib circa 689-750 . . . . DLB-311
Abe Kōbō 1924-1993 . . . . DLB-182
Abelaira, Augusto 1926- DLB-287
Abelard, Peter circa 1079-1142? DLB-115, 208
Abelard-Schuman DLB-46
Abell, Arunah S. 1806-1888 . . . . DLB-43
Abell, Kjeld 1901-1961 . . . . DLB-214
Abercrombie, Lascelles 1881-1938 . . . . DLB-19
　The Friends of the Dymock
　Poets Y-00
Aberdeen University Press Limited DLB-106
Abish, Walter 1931- DLB-130, 227
Ablesimov, Aleksandr Onisimovich
　1742-1783 . . . . DLB-150
Abraham à Sancta Clara 1644-1709 . . . . . . DLB-168
Abrahams, Peter
　1919- DLB-117, 225; CDWLB-3
Abramov, Fedor Aleksandrovich
　1920-1983 . . . . DLB-302
Abrams, M. H. 1912- DLB-67
Abramson, Jesse 1904-1979 . . . . DLB-241
Abrogans circa 790-800 . . . . DLB-148
Abschatz, Hans Aßmann von
　1646-1699 . . . . DLB-168
Abse, Dannie 1923- DLB-27, 245
Abu al-'Atahiyah 748-825? DLB-311

Abu Nuwas circa 757-814 or 815 . . . . DLB-311
Abu Tammam circa 805-845 . . . . DLB-311
Abutsu-ni 1221-1283 . . . . DLB-203
Academy Chicago Publishers DLB-46
Accius circa 170 B.C.-circa 80 B.C. DLB-211
Accrocca, Elio Filippo 1923-1996 . . . . DLB-128
Ace Books DLB-46
Achebe, Chinua 1930- DLB-117; CDWLB-3
Achtenberg, Herbert 1938- DLB-124
Ackerman, Diane 1948- DLB-120
Ackroyd, Peter 1949- DLB-155, 231
Acorn, Milton 1923-1986 . . . . DLB-53
Acosta, Oscar Zeta 1935?-1974? DLB-82
Acosta Torres, José 1925- DLB-209
Actors Theatre of Louisville DLB-7
Adair, Gilbert 1944- DLB-194
Adair, James 1709?-1783? DLB-30
Aðalsteinn Kristmundsson (see Steinn Steinarr)
Adam, Graeme Mercer 1839-1912 . . . . DLB-99
Adam, Robert Borthwick, II
　1863-1940 . . . . DLB-187
Adame, Leonard 1947- DLB-82
Adameșteanu, Gabriel 1942- DLB-232
Adamic, Louis 1898-1951 . . . . DLB-9
Adams, Abigail 1744-1818 . . . . DLB-183, 200
Adams, Alice 1926-1999 . . . . DLB-234; Y-86
Adams, Bertha Leith (Mrs. Leith Adams,
　Mrs. R. S. de Courcy Laffan)
　1837?-1912 . . . . DLB-240
Adams, Brooks 1848-1927 . . . . DLB-47
Adams, Charles Francis, Jr. 1835-1915 . . . . DLB-47
Adams, Douglas 1952-2001 . . . . DLB-261; Y-83
Adams, Franklin P. 1881-1960 . . . . DLB-29
Adams, Hannah 1755-1832 . . . . DLB-200
Adams, Henry 1838-1918 . . . . DLB-12, 47, 189
Adams, Herbert Baxter 1850-1901 . . . . DLB-47
Adams, James Truslow
　1878-1949 . . . . DLB-17; DS-17
Adams, John 1735-1826 . . . . DLB-31, 183
Adams, John Quincy 1767-1848 . . . . DLB-37
Adams, Léonie 1899-1988 . . . . DLB-48
Adams, Levi 1802-1832 . . . . DLB-99

Adams, Richard 1920- DLB-261
Adams, Samuel 1722-1803 . . . . DLB-31, 43
Adams, Sarah Fuller Flower
　1805-1848 . . . . DLB-199
Adams, Thomas 1582/1583-1652 . . . . DLB-151
Adams, William Taylor 1822-1897 . . . . DLB-42
J. S. and C. Adams [publishing house] DLB-49
Adamson, Harold 1906-1980 . . . . DLB-265
Adamson, Sir John 1867-1950 . . . . DLB-98
Adamson, Robert 1943- DLB-289
Adcock, Arthur St. John 1864-1930 . . . . . . DLB-135
Adcock, Betty 1938- DLB-105
　"Certain Gifts" DLB-105
　Tribute to James Dickey Y-97
Adcock, Fleur 1934- DLB-40
Addams, Jane 1860-1935 . . . . DLB-303
Addison, Joseph
　1672-1719 . . . . DLB-101; CDBLB-2
Ade, George 1866-1944 . . . . DLB-11, 25
Adeler, Max (see Clark, Charles Heber)
Adlard, Mark 1932- DLB-261
Adler, Richard 1921- DLB-265
Adonias Filho
　(Adonias Aguiar Filho)
　1915-1990 . . . . DLB-145, 307
Adorno, Theodor W. 1903-1969 . . . . DLB-242
Adoum, Jorge Enrique 1926- DLB-283
Advance Publishing Company DLB-49
Ady, Endre 1877-1919 . . . . . . DLB-215; CDWLB-4
AE 1867-1935 . . . . DLB-19; CDBLB-5
Ælfric circa 955-circa 1010 . . . . DLB-146
Aeschines circa 390 B.C.-circa 320 B.C. DLB-176
Aeschylus 525-524 B.C.-456-455 B.C.
　. DLB-176; CDWLB-1
Aesthetic Papers DLB-1
Aesthetics
　Eighteenth-Century Aesthetic
　　Theories DLB-31
African Literature
　Letter from Khartoum Y-90
African American
　Afro-American Literary Critics:
　　An Introduction DLB-33
　The Black Aesthetic: Background DS-8

The Black Arts Movement,
  by Larry Neal DLB-38
Black Theaters and Theater Organizations
  in America, 1961-1982:
  A Research List DLB-38
Black Theatre: A Forum [excerpts] ... DLB-38
Callaloo [journal] Y-87
Community and Commentators:
  Black Theatre and Its Critics..... DLB-38
The Emergence of Black
  Women Writers.............. DS-8
The Hatch-Billops Collection........ DLB-76
A Look at the Contemporary Black
  Theatre Movement DLB-38
The Moorland-Spingarn Research
  Center DLB-76
"The Negro as a Writer," by
  G. M. McClellan DLB-50
"Negro Poets and Their Poetry," by
  Wallace Thurman DLB-50
Olaudah Equiano and Unfinished Journeys:
  The Slave-Narrative Tradition and
  Twentieth-Century Continuities, by
  Paul Edwards and Pauline T.
  Wangman DLB-117
PHYLON (Fourth Quarter, 1950),
  The Negro in Literature:
  The Current Scene DLB-76
The Schomburg Center for Research
  in Black Culture DLB-76
Three Documents [poets], by John
  Edward Bruce DLB-50
After Dinner Opera Company Y-92
Agassiz, Elizabeth Cary 1822-1907...... DLB-189
Agassiz, Louis 1807-1873 .... DLB-1, 235
Agee, James
  1909-1955 .... DLB-2, 26, 152; CDALB-1
  The Agee Legacy: A Conference at
    the University of Tennessee
    at Knoxville................. Y-89
Aguilera Malta, Demetrio 1909-1981 .... DLB-145
Aguirre, Isidora 1919- DLB-305
Agustini, Delmira 1886-1914 .... DLB-290
Ahlin, Lars 1915-1997................ DLB-257
Ai 1947- DLB-120
Aichinger, Ilse 1921- DLB-85, 299
Aickman, Robert 1914-1981 .... DLB-261
Aidoo, Ama Ata 1942- DLB-117; CDWLB-3
Aiken, Conrad
  1889-1973........ DLB-9, 45, 102; CDALB-5
Aiken, Joan 1924- DLB-161
Aikin, Lucy 1781-1864 .... DLB-144, 163
Ainsworth, William Harrison
  1805-1882 .... DLB-21
Aïssé, Charlotte-Elizabeth 1694?-1733 ... DLB-313
Aistis, Jonas 1904-1973 ..... DLB-220; CDWLB-4
Aitken, George A. 1860-1917 .... DLB-149
Robert Aitken [publishing house]........ DLB-49
Aitmatov, Chingiz 1928- DLB-302
Akenside, Mark 1721-1770 .... DLB-109
Akhamatova, Anna Andreevna
  1889-1966 .... DLB-295

Akins, Zoë 1886-1958................. DLB-26
Aksakov, Ivan Sergeevich 1823-1826.....DLB-277
Aksakov, Sergei Timofeevich
  1791-1859...................... DLB-198
Aksyonov, Vassily 1932- DLB-302
Akunin, Boris (Grigorii Shalvovich
  Chkhartishvili) 1956- DLB-285
Akutagawa Ryūnosuke 1892-1927....... DLB-180
Alabaster, William 1568-1640 .... DLB-132
Alain de Lille circa 1116-1202/1203 ..... DLB-208
Alain-Fournier 1886-1914............... DLB-65
Alanus de Insulis (see Alain de Lille)
Alarcón, Francisco X. 1954- DLB-122
Alarcón, Justo S. 1930- DLB-209
Alba, Nanina 1915-1968............... DLB-41
Albee, Edward 1928- ... DLB-7, 266; CDALB-1
Albert, Octavia 1853-ca. 1889 .... DLB-221
Albert the Great circa 1200-1280 .... DLB-115
Alberti, Rafael 1902-1999............. DLB-108
Albertinus, Aegidius circa 1560-1620 .... DLB-164
Alcaeus born circa 620 B.C. DLB-176
Alcoforado, Mariana, the Portuguese Nun
  1640-1723..................... DLB-287
Alcott, Amos Bronson
  1799-1888................. DLB-1, 223; DS-5
Alcott, Louisa May 1832-1888
  ... DLB-1, 42, 79, 223, 239; DS-14; CDALB-3
Alcott, William Andrus 1798-1859.... DLB-1, 243
Alcuin circa 732-804................. DLB-148
Alden, Henry Mills 1836-1919 .... DLB-79
Alden, Isabella 1841-1930............. DLB-42
John B. Alden [publishing house] DLB-49
Alden, Beardsley, and Company DLB-49
Aldington, Richard
  1892-1962 ....DLB-20, 36, 100, 149
Aldis, Dorothy 1896-1966 .... DLB-22
Aldis, H. G. 1863-1919 .... DLB-184
Aldiss, Brian W. 1925- DLB-14, 261, 271
Aldrich, Thomas Bailey
  1836-1907...............DLB-42, 71, 74, 79
Alegría, Ciro 1909-1967 .... DLB-113
Alegría, Claribel 1924- DLB-145, 283
Aleixandre, Vicente 1898-1984......... DLB-108
Aleksandravičius, Jonas (see Aistis, Jonas)
Aleksandrov, Aleksandr Andreevich
  (see Durova, Nadezhda Andreevna)
Alekseeva, Marina Anatol'evna
  (see Marinina, Aleksandra)
d'Alembert, Jean Le Rond 1717-1783 .... DLB-313
Alencar, José de 1829-1877 .... DLB-307
Aleramo, Sibilla (Rena Pierangeli Faccio)
  1876-1960................. DLB-114, 264
Aleshkovsky, Petr Markovich 1957- ... DLB-285
Alexander, Cecil Frances 1818-1895..... DLB-199
Alexander, Charles 1868-1923 .... DLB-91
Charles Wesley Alexander
  [publishing house] DLB-49
Alexander, James 1691-1756 .... DLB-24

Alexander, Lloyd 1924- DLB-52
Alexander, Sir William, Earl of Stirling
  1577?-1640..................... DLB-121
Alexie, Sherman 1966- DLB-175, 206, 278
Alexis, Willibald 1798-1871 .... DLB-133
Alf laylah wa laylah
  ninth century onward DLB-311
Alfred, King 849-899 .... DLB-146
Alger, Horatio, Jr. 1832-1899.......... DLB-42
Algonquin Books of Chapel Hill DLB-46
Algren, Nelson
  1909-1981 ...... DLB-9; Y-81, 82; CDALB-1
  Nelson Algren: An International
    Symposium Y-00
'Ali ibn Abi Talib circa 600-661 .... DLB-311
Aljamiado Literature.................. DLB-286
Allan, Andrew 1907-1974 .... DLB-88
Allan, Ted 1916-1995 .... DLB-68
Allbeury, Ted 1917- DLB-87
Alldritt, Keith 1935- DLB-14
Allen, Dick 1939- DLB-282
Allen, Ethan 1738-1789................ DLB-31
Allen, Frederick Lewis 1890-1954 ....DLB-137
Allen, Gay Wilson 1903-1995 .....DLB-103; Y-95
Allen, George 1808-1876 .... DLB-59
Allen, Grant 1848-1899 .... DLB-70, 92, 178
Allen, Henry W. 1912-1991................ Y-85
Allen, Hervey 1889-1949 .... DLB-9, 45
Allen, James 1739-1808................ DLB-31
Allen, James Lane 1849-1925........... DLB-71
Allen, Jay Presson 1922- DLB-26
John Allen and Company.............. DLB-49
Allen, Paula Gunn 1939- DLB-175
Allen, Samuel W. 1917- DLB-41
Allen, Woody 1935- DLB-44
George Allen [publishing house]........ DLB-106
George Allen and Unwin Limited DLB-112
Allende, Isabel 1942- DLB-145; CDWLB-3
Alline, Henry 1748-1784............... DLB-99
Allingham, Margery 1904-1966 .... DLB-77
  The Margery Allingham Society Y-98
Allingham, William 1824-1889.......... DLB-35
W. L. Allison [publishing house] DLB-49
The *Alliterative Morte Arthure and the Stanzaic
  Morte Arthur* circa 1350-1400 .... DLB-146
Allott, Kenneth 1912-1973 .... DLB-20
Allston, Washington 1779-1843 ..... DLB-1, 235
Almeida, Manuel Antônio de
  1831-1861..................... DLB-307
John Almon [publishing house] DLB-154
Alonzo, Dámaso 1898-1990 .... DLB-108
Alsop, George 1636-post 1673 .... DLB-24
Alsop, Richard 1761-1815............. DLB-37
Henry Altemus and Company......... DLB-49
Altenberg, Peter 1885-1919 .... DLB-81
Althusser, Louis 1918-1990 .... DLB-242

Altolaguirre, Manuel 1905-1959 . . . . .DLB-108

Aluko, T. M. 1918- DLB-117

Alurista 1947- DLB-82

Alvarez, A. 1929- DLB-14, 40

Alvarez, Julia 1950- DLB-282

Alvaro, Corrado 1895-1956. . . . . .DLB-264

Alver, Betti 1906-1989. . . . . .DLB-220; CDWLB-4

Amadi, Elechi 1934- DLB-117

Amado, Jorge 1912-2001 . . . . .DLB-113

Amalrik, Andrei 1938-1980 . . . . .DLB-302

Ambler, Eric 1909-1998. . . . . .DLB-77

The Library of America. DLB-46

The Library of America: An Assessment After Two Decades Y-02

America: or, A Poem on the Settlement of the British Colonies, by Timothy Dwight DLB-37

American Bible Society
Department of Library, Archives, and Institutional Research Y-97

American Conservatory Theatre DLB-7

American Culture
American Proletarian Culture: The Twenties and Thirties DS-11

Studies in American Jewish Literature Y-02

The American Library in Paris Y-93

American Literature
The Literary Scene and Situation and . . . (Who Besides Oprah) Really Runs American Literature? Y-99

Who Owns American Literature, by Henry Taylor Y-94

Who Runs American Literature? Y-94

American News Company. DLB-49

A Century of Poetry, a Lifetime of Collecting: J. M. Edelstein's Collection of Twentieth-Century American Poetry Y-02

The American Poets' Corner: The First Three Years (1983-1986). Y-86

American Publishing Company. DLB-49

American Spectator
[Editorial] Rationale From the Initial Issue of the American Spectator (November 1932). DLB-137

American Stationers' Company. DLB-49

The American Studies Association of Norway. Y-00

American Sunday-School Union DLB-49

American Temperance Union DLB-49

American Tract Society DLB-49

The American Trust for the British Library . . Y-96

American Writers' Congress 25-27 April 1935 . . . . .DLB-303

American Writers Congress
The American Writers Congress (9-12 October 1981) Y-81

The American Writers Congress: A Report on Continuing Business Y-81

Ames, Fisher 1758-1808. . . . . .DLB-37

Ames, Mary Clemmer 1831-1884 . . . . .DLB-23

Ames, William 1576-1633 . . . . .DLB-281

Amiel, Henri-Frédéric 1821-1881. . . . . . . .DLB-217

Amini, Johari M. 1935- DLB-41

Amis, Kingsley 1922-1995
 . . . . . . DLB-15, 27, 100, 139, Y-96; CDBLB-7

Amis, Martin 1949- DLB-14, 194

Ammianus Marcellinus circa A.D. 330-A.D. 395 . . . . .DLB-211

Ammons, A. R. 1926-2001 . . . . .DLB-5, 165

Amory, Thomas 1691?-1788 . . . . .DLB-39

Anania, Michael 1939- DLB-193

Anaya, Rudolfo A. 1937- DLB-82, 206, 278

Ancrene Riwle circa 1200-1225 . . . . .DLB-146

Andersch, Alfred 1914-1980 . . . . .DLB-69

Andersen, Benny 1929- DLB-214

Andersen, Hans Christian 1805-1875 . . . .DLB-300

Anderson, Alexander 1775-1870 . . . . . . .DLB-188

Anderson, David 1929- DLB-241

Anderson, Frederick Irving 1877-1947 . . . .DLB-202

Anderson, Margaret 1886-1973 . . . . . . .DLB-4, 91

Anderson, Maxwell 1888-1959 . . . . . .DLB-7, 228

Anderson, Patrick 1915-1979 . . . . .DLB-68

Anderson, Paul Y. 1893-1938 . . . . .DLB-29

Anderson, Poul 1926-2001 . . . . .DLB-8

 Tribute to Isaac Asimov Y-92

Anderson, Robert 1750-1830. . . . . .DLB-142

Anderson, Robert 1917- DLB-7

Anderson, Sherwood 1876-1941 . . . . .DLB-4, 9, 86; DS-1; CDALB-4

Andrade, Jorge (Aluísio Jorge Andrade Franco) 1922-1984 . . . . .DLB-307

Andrade, Mario de 1893-1945. . . . . .DLB-307

Andrade, Oswald de (José Oswald de Sousa Andrade) 1890-1954 . . . . .DLB-307

Andreae, Johann Valentin 1586-1654 . . . .DLB-164

Andreas Capellanus flourished circa 1185. . . . . .DLB-208

Andreas-Salomé, Lou 1861-1937 . . . . .DLB-66

Andreev, Leonid Nikolaevich 1871-1919 .DLB-295

Andres, Stefan 1906-1970 . . . . .DLB-69

Andresen, Sophia de Mello Breyner 1919- DLB-287

Andreu, Blanca 1959- DLB-134

Andrewes, Lancelot 1555-1626 . . . . .DLB-151, 172

Andrews, Charles M. 1863-1943. . . . . .DLB-17

Andrews, Miles Peter ?-1814 . . . . .DLB-89

Andrews, Stephen Pearl 1812-1886 . . . . . .DLB-250

Andrian, Leopold von 1875-1951 . . . . . . .DLB-81

Andrić, Ivo 1892-1975 . . . . . .DLB-147; CDWLB-4

Andrieux, Louis (see Aragon, Louis)

Andrus, Silas, and Son. DLB-49

Andrzejewski, Jerzy 1909-1983 . . . . .DLB-215

Angell, James Burrill 1829-1916 . . . . .DLB-64

Angell, Roger 1920- DLB-171, 185

Angelou, Maya 1928- DLB-38; CDALB-7

 Tribute to Julian Mayfield. Y-84

Anger, Jane flourished 1589 . . . . .DLB-136

Angers, Félicité (see Conan, Laure)

The Anglo-Saxon Chronicle circa 890-1154. . . . . .DLB-146

Angus and Robertson (UK) Limited DLB-112

Anhalt, Edward 1914-2000 . . . . .DLB-26

Anissimov, Myriam 1943- DLB-299

Anker, Nini Roll 1873-1942. . . . . .DLB-297

Annenkov, Pavel Vasil'evich 1813?-1887 .DLB-277

Annensky, Innokentii Fedorovich 1855-1909 .DLB-295

Henry F. Anners [publishing house] DLB-49

Annolied between 1077 and 1081. . . . . . . .DLB-148

Anscombe, G. E. M. 1919-2001. . . . . . . .DLB-262

Anselm of Canterbury 1033-1109 . . . . . . .DLB-115

Anstey, F. 1856-1934. . . . . DLB-141, 178

'Antarah ('Antar ibn Shaddad al-'Absi) ?-early seventh century? DLB-311

Anthologizing New Formalism DLB-282

Anthony, Michael 1932- DLB-125

Anthony, Piers 1934- DLB-8

Anthony, Susanna 1726-1791. . . . . .DLB-200

Antin, David 1932- DLB-169

Antin, Mary 1881-1949 . . . . DLB-221; Y-84

Anton Ulrich, Duke of Brunswick-Lüneburg 1633-1714 .DLB-168

Antschel, Paul (see Celan, Paul)

Antunes, António Lobo 1942- DLB-287

Anyidoho, Kofi 1947- DLB-157

Anzaldúa, Gloria 1942- DLB-122

Anzengruber, Ludwig 1839-1889 . . . . . . .DLB-129

Apess, William 1798-1839 . . . . DLB-175, 243

Apodaca, Rudy S. 1939- DLB-82

Apollinaire, Guillaume 1880-1918. . . . . . .DLB-258

Apollonius Rhodius third century B.C. . . . DLB-176

Apple, Max 1941- DLB-130

Appelfeld, Aharon 1932- DLB-299

D. Appleton and Company DLB-49

Appleton-Century-Crofts. DLB-46

Applewhite, James 1935- DLB-105

 Tribute to James Dickey Y-97

Apple-wood Books. DLB-46

April, Jean-Pierre 1948- DLB-251

Apukhtin, Aleksei Nikolaevich 1840-1893 .DLB-277

Apuleius circa A.D. 125-post A.D. 164
 . . . . .DLB-211; CDWLB-1

Aquin, Hubert 1929-1977 . . . . .DLB-53

Aquinas, Thomas 1224/1225-1274 . . . . . .DLB-115

Aragon, Louis 1897-1982. . . . . .DLB-72, 258

Aragon, Vernacular Translations in the Crowns of Castile and 1352-1515. . . .DLB-286

Aralica, Ivan 1930- DLB-181

Aratus of Soli circa 315 B.C.-circa 239 B.C. DLB-176

Arbasino, Alberto 1930- DLB-196

Cumulative Index

Arbor House Publishing Company DLB-46
Arbuthnot, John 1667-1735 .... DLB-101
Arcadia House DLB-46
Arce, Julio G. (see Ulica, Jorge)
Archer, William 1856-1924 .... DLB-10
Archilochhus
   mid seventh century B.C.E. DLB-176
The Archpoet circa 1130?-? DLB-148
Archpriest Avvakum (Petrovich)
   1620?-1682 .... DLB-150
Arden, John 1930- DLB-13, 245
Arden of Faversham DLB-62
Ardis Publishers Y-89
Ardizzone, Edward 1900-1979 .... DLB-160
Arellano, Juan Estevan 1947- DLB-122
The Arena Publishing Company DLB-49
Arena Stage DLB-7
Arenas, Reinaldo 1943-1990 .... DLB-145
Arendt, Hannah 1906-1975 .... DLB-242
Arensberg, Ann 1937- Y-82
Arghezi, Tudor 1880-1967 .... DLB-220; CDWLB-4
Arguedas, José María 1911-1969 ...... DLB-113
Argüelles, Hugo 1932-2003 .... DLB-305
Argueta, Manlio 1936- DLB-145
'Arib al-Ma'muniyah 797-890 .... DLB-311
Arias, Ron 1941- DLB-82
Arishima Takeo 1878-1923 .... DLB-180
Aristophanes circa 446 B.C.-circa 386 B.C.
   ....DLB-176; CDWLB-1
Aristotle 384 B.C.-322 B.C.
   ....DLB-176; CDWLB-1
Ariyoshi Sawako 1931-1984 .... DLB-182
Arland, Marcel 1899-1986 .... DLB-72
Arlen, Michael 1895-1956 .... DLB-36, 77, 162
Arlt, Roberto 1900-1942 .... DLB-305
Armah, Ayi Kwei 1939- ...DLB-117; CDWLB-3
Armantrout, Rae 1947- DLB-193
Der arme Hartmann ?-after 1150 .... DLB-148
Armed Services Editions DLB-46
Armitage, G. E. (Robert Edric) 1956- .. DLB-267
Armstrong, Martin Donisthorpe
   1882-1974 .... DLB-197
Armstrong, Richard 1903- DLB-160
Armstrong, Terence Ian Fytton (see Gawsworth, John)
Arnauld, Antoine 1612-1694 .... DLB-268
Arndt, Ernst Moritz 1769-1860 .... DLB-90
Arnim, Achim von 1781-1831 .... DLB-90
Arnim, Bettina von 1785-1859 .... DLB-90
Arnim, Elizabeth von (Countess Mary Annette
   Beauchamp Russell) 1866-1941 .... DLB-197
Arno Press DLB-46
Arnold, Edwin 1832-1904 .... DLB-35
Arnold, Edwin L. 1857-1935 ....DLB-178
Arnold, Matthew
   1822-1888 .... DLB-32, 57; CDBLB-4
   Preface to *Poems* (1853) DLB-32

Arnold, Thomas 1795-1842 .... DLB-55
Edward Arnold [publishing house] DLB-112
Arnott, Peter 1962- DLB-233
Arnow, Harriette Simpson 1908-1986 ..... DLB-6
Arp, Bill (see Smith, Charles Henry)
Arpino, Giovanni 1927-1987 ....DLB-177
Arrebo, Anders 1587-1637 .... DLB-300
Arreola, Juan José 1918-2001 .... DLB-113
Arrian circa 89-circa 155 ....DLB-176
J. W. Arrowsmith [publishing house] DLB-106
Arrufat, Antón 1935- DLB-305
Art
   John Dos Passos: Artist Y-99
   The First Post-Impressionist
     Exhibition DS-5
   The Omega Workshops DS-10
   The Second Post-Impressionist
     Exhibition DS-5
Artaud, Antonin 1896-1948 .... DLB-258
Artel, Jorge 1909-1994 .... DLB-283
Arthur, Timothy Shay
   1809-1885 ....DLB-3, 42, 79, 250; DS-13
Artmann, H. C. 1921-2000 .... DLB-85
Artsybashev, Mikhail Petrovich
   1878-1927 .... DLB-295
Arvin, Newton 1900-1963 .... DLB-103
Asch, Nathan 1902-1964 .... DLB-4, 28
   Nathan Asch Remembers Ford Madox
     Ford, Sam Roth, and Hart Crane Y-02
Ascham, Roger 1515/1516-1568 .... DLB-236
Aseev, Nikolai Nikolaevich
   1889-1963 .... DLB-295
Ash, John 1948- DLB-40
Ashbery, John 1927- DLB-5, 165; Y-81
Ashbridge, Elizabeth 1713-1755 .... DLB-200
Ashburnham, Bertram Lord
   1797-1878 .... DLB-184
Ashendene Press DLB-112
Asher, Sandy 1942- Y-83
Ashton, Winifred (see Dane, Clemence)
Asimov, Isaac 1920-1992 ....DLB-8; Y-92
   Tribute to John Ciardi Y-86
Askew, Anne circa 1521-1546 .... DLB-136
Aspazija 1865-1943 .... DLB-220; CDWLB-4
Asselin, Olivar 1874-1937 .... DLB-92
The Association of American Publishers Y-99
The Association for Documentary Editing ... Y-00
The Association for the Study of
   Literature and Environment (ASLE) Y-99
Astell, Mary 1666-1731 .... DLB-252
Astley, Thea 1925- DLB-289
Astley, William (see Warung, Price)
Asturias, Miguel Ángel
   1899-1974 ....DLB-113, 290; CDWLB-3
Atava, S. (see Terpigorev, Sergei Nikolaevich)
Atheneum Publishers DLB-46
Atherton, Gertrude 1857-1948 .....DLB-9, 78, 186

Athlone Press DLB-112
Atkins, Josiah circa 1755-1781 .... DLB-31
Atkins, Russell 1926- DLB-41
Atkinson, Kate 1951- DLB-267
Atkinson, Louisa 1834-1872 .... DLB-230
The Atlantic Monthly Press DLB-46
Attaway, William 1911-1986 .... DLB-76
Atwood, Margaret 1939- DLB-53, 251
Aubert, Alvin 1930- DLB-41
Aubert de Gaspé, Phillipe-Ignace-François
   1814-1841 .... DLB-99
Aubert de Gaspé, Phillipe-Joseph
   1786-1871 .... DLB-99
Aubin, Napoléon 1812-1890 .... DLB-99
Aubin, Penelope
   1685-circa 1731 .... DLB-39
   Preface to *The Life of Charlotta
     du Pont* (1723) DLB-39
Aubrey-Fletcher, Henry Lancelot (see Wade, Henry)
Auchincloss, Louis 1917- DLB-2, 244; Y-80
Auden, W. H.
   1907-1973 .... DLB-10, 20; CDBLB-6
Audio Art in America: A Personal Memoir ... Y-85
Audubon, John James 1785-1851 .... DLB-248
Audubon, John Woodhouse
   1812-1862 .... DLB-183
Auerbach, Berthold 1812-1882 .... DLB-133
Auernheimer, Raoul 1876-1948 .... DLB-81
Augier, Emile 1820-1889 .... DLB-192
Augustine 354-430 .... DLB-115
Aulnoy, Marie-Catherine Le Jumel
   de Barneville, comtesse d'
   1650/1651-1705 ....DLB-268
Aulus Gellius
   circa A.D. 125-circa A.D. 180? DLB-211
Austen, Jane 1775-1817 ...... DLB-116; CDBLB-3
Auster, Paul 1947- DLB-227
Austin, Alfred 1835-1913 .... DLB-35
Austin, J. L. 1911-1960 .... DLB-262
Austin, Jane Goodwin 1831-1894 .... DLB-202
Austin, John 1790-1859 .... DLB-262
Austin, Mary Hunter
   1868-1934 ....DLB-9, 78, 206, 221, 275
Austin, William 1778-1841 .... DLB-74
Australie (Emily Manning)
   1845-1890 .... DLB-230
Authors and Newspapers Association DLB-46
Authors' Publishing Company DLB-49
Avallone, Michael 1924-1999 ......DLB-306; Y-99
   Tribute to John D. MacDonald Y-86
   Tribute to Kenneth Millar Y-83
   Tribute to Raymond Chandler Y-88
Avalon Books DLB-46
Avancini, Nicolaus 1611-1686 .... DLB-164
Avendaño, Fausto 1941- DLB-82
Averroës 1126-1198 .... DLB-115
Avery, Gillian 1926- DLB-161
Avicenna 980-1037 .... DLB-115

Ávila Jiménez, Antonio 1898-1965.......DLB-283

Avison, Margaret 1918-1987 ....DLB-53

Avon Books.......................DLB-46

Avyžius, Jonas 1922-1999 ....DLB-220

Awdry, Wilbert Vere 1911-1997 ....DLB-160

Awoonor, Kofi 1935- DLB-117

Ayckbourn, Alan 1939- DLB-13, 245

Ayer, A. J. 1910-1989................DLB-262

Aymé, Marcel 1902-1967..............DLB-72

Aytoun, Sir Robert 1570-1638 ....DLB-121

Aytoun, William Edmondstoune
1813-1865 ....DLB-32, 159

Azevedo, Aluísio 1857-1913............DLB-307

Azevedo, Manuel Antônio Álvares de
1831-1852 ....DLB-307

B

B.V. (see Thomson, James)

Babbitt, Irving 1865-1933 ....DLB-63

Babbitt, Natalie 1932- DLB-52

John Babcock [publishing house].......DLB-49

Babel, Isaak Emmanuilovich
1894-1940 ....DLB-272

Babits, Mihály 1883-1941 ...DLB-215; CDWLB-4

Babrius circa 150-200.................DLB-176

Babson, Marian 1929- DLB-276

Baca, Jimmy Santiago 1952- DLB-122

Bacchelli, Riccardo 1891-1985..........DLB-264

Bache, Benjamin Franklin 1769-1798......DLB-43

Bachelard, Gaston 1884-1962 ....DLB-296

Bacheller, Irving 1859-1950............DLB-202

Bachmann, Ingeborg 1926-1973.........DLB-85

Bačinskaitė-Bučienė, Salomėja (see Nėris, Salomėja)

Bacon, Delia 1811-1859............DLB-1, 243

Bacon, Francis
1561-1626 .....DLB-151, 236, 252; CDBLB-1

Bacon, Sir Nicholas circa 1510-1579 .....DLB-132

Bacon, Roger circa 1214/1220-1292 ......DLB-115

Bacon, Thomas circa 1700-1768.........DLB-31

Bacovia, George
1881-1957 ....DLB-220; CDWLB-4

Richard G. Badger and Company.......DLB-49

Bagaduce Music Lending Library Y-00

Bage, Robert 1728-1801................DLB-39

Bagehot, Walter 1826-1877.............DLB-55

Baggesen, Jens 1764-1826..............DLB-300

Bagley, Desmond 1923-1983............DLB-87

Bagley, Sarah G. 1806-1848?...........DLB-239

Bagnold, Enid 1889-1981...DLB-13, 160, 191, 245

Bagryana, Elisaveta
1893-1991 ....DLB-147; CDWLB-4

Bahr, Hermann 1863-1934 ....DLB-81, 118

Bailey, Abigail Abbot
1746-1815 ....DLB-200

Bailey, Alfred Goldsworthy 1905- DLB-68

Bailey, H. C. 1878-1961................DLB-77

Bailey, Jacob 1731-1808................DLB-99

Bailey, Paul 1937- DLB-14, 271

Bailey, Philip James 1816-1902 ....DLB-32

Francis Bailey [publishing house].........DLB-49

Baillargeon, Pierre 1916-1967 ....DLB-88

Baillie, Hugh 1890-1966 ....DLB-29

Baillie, Joanna 1762-1851...............DLB-93

Bailyn, Bernard 1922- DLB-17

Bain, Alexander
English Composition and Rhetoric (1866)
[excerpt] DLB-57

Bainbridge, Beryl 1933- DLB-14, 231

Baird, Irene 1901-1981 ....DLB-68

Baker, Augustine 1575-1641 ....DLB-151

Baker, Carlos 1909-1987 ....DLB-103

Baker, David 1954- DLB-120

Baker, George Pierce 1866-1935 ....DLB-266

Baker, Herschel C. 1914-1990 ....DLB-111

Baker, Houston A., Jr. 1943- DLB-67

Baker, Howard
Tribute to Caroline Gordon Y-81
Tribute to Katherine Anne Porter....... Y-80

Baker, Nicholson 1957- DLB-227; Y-00
Review of Nicholson Baker's *Double Fold:
Libraries and the Assault on Paper* Y-00

Baker, Samuel White 1821-1893........DLB-166

Baker, Thomas 1656-1740..............DLB-213

Walter H. Baker Company
("Baker's Plays")..................DLB-49

The Baker and Taylor Company DLB-49

Bakhtin, Mikhail Mikhailovich
1895-1975 ....DLB-242

Bakunin, Mikhail Aleksandrovich
1814-1876 ....DLB-277

Balaban, John 1943- DLB-120

Bald, Wambly 1902- DLB-4

Balde, Jacob 1604-1668 ....DLB-164

Balderston, John 1889-1954.............DLB-26

Baldwin, James 1924-1987
......DLB-2, 7, 33, 249, 278; Y-87; CDALB-1

Baldwin, Joseph Glover
1815-1864 ....DLB-3, 11, 248

Baldwin, Louisa (Mrs. Alfred Baldwin)
1845-1925 ....DLB-240

Baldwin, William circa 1515-1563.......DLB-132

Richard and Anne Baldwin
[publishing house] DLB-170

Bale, John 1495-1563..................DLB-132

Balestrini, Nanni 1935- DLB-128, 196

Balfour, Sir Andrew 1630-1694.........DLB-213

Balfour, Arthur James 1848-1930 ....DLB-190

Balfour, Sir James 1600-1657 ....DLB-213

Ballantine Books DLB-46

Ballantyne, R. M. 1825-1894..........DLB-163

Ballard, J. G. 1930- DLB-14, 207, 261

Ballard, Martha Moore 1735-1812......DLB-200

Ballerini, Luigi 1940-................DLB-128

Ballou, Maturin Murray (Lieutenant Murray)
1820-1895 .... DLB-79, 189

Robert O. Ballou [publishing house] DLB-46

Bal'mont, Konstantin Dmitrievich
1867-1942......................DLB-295

Balzac, Guez de 1597?-1654 ....DLB-268

Balzac, Honoré de 1799-1855 ....DLB-119

Bambara, Toni Cade
1939-1995 ....DLB-38, 218; CDALB-7

Bamford, Samuel 1788-1872 ....DLB-190

A. L. Bancroft and Company DLB-49

Bancroft, George 1800-1891 ...DLB-1, 30, 59, 243

Bancroft, Hubert Howe 1832-1918 ... DLB-47, 140

Bandeira, Manuel 1886-1968...........DLB-307

Bandelier, Adolph F. 1840-1914 ....DLB-186

Bang, Herman 1857-1912 ....DLB-300

Bangs, John Kendrick 1862-1922 .....DLB-11, 79

Banim, John 1798-1842 .... DLB-116, 158, 159

Banim, Michael 1796-1874 ....DLB-158, 159

Banks, Iain (M.) 1954- DLB-194, 261

Banks, John circa 1653-1706 ....DLB-80

Banks, Russell 1940- DLB-130, 278

Bannerman, Helen 1862-1946..........DLB-141

Bantam Books DLB-46

Banti, Anna 1895-1985 ....DLB-177

Banville, John 1945- DLB-14, 271

Banville, Théodore de 1823-1891 ....DLB-217

Baraka, Amiri
1934- DLB-5, 7, 16, 38; DS-8; CDALB-1

Barańczak, Stanisław 1946- DLB-232

Baranskaia, Natal'ia Vladimirovna
1908- DLB-302

Baratynsky, Evgenii Abramovich
1800-1844 ....DLB-205

Barba-Jacob, Porfirio 1883-1942 ....DLB-283

Barbauld, Anna Laetitia
1743-1825 ....DLB-107, 109, 142, 158

Barbeau, Marius 1883-1969.............DLB-92

Barber, John Warner 1798-1885 ....DLB-30

Bàrberi Squarotti, Giorgio 1929- DLB-128

Barbey d'Aurevilly, Jules-Amédée
1808-1889 ....DLB-119

Barbier, Auguste 1805-1882 ....DLB-217

Barbilian, Dan (see Barbu, Ion)

Barbour, John circa 1316-1395 ....DLB-146

Barbour, Ralph Henry 1870-1944 ....DLB-22

Barbu, Ion 1895-1961 ...... DLB-220; CDWLB-4

Barbusse, Henri 1873-1935 ....DLB-65

Barclay, Alexander circa 1475-1552......DLB-132

E. E. Barclay and Company DLB-49

C. W. Bardeen [publishing house].......DLB-49

Barham, Richard Harris 1788-1845 .....DLB-159

Barich, Bill 1943- DLB-185

Baring, Maurice 1874-1945 ....DLB-34

Baring-Gould, Sabine 1834-1924....DLB-156, 190

Barker, A. L. 1918- DLB-14, 139

Barker, Clive 1952- DLB-261

Cumulative Index

Barker, Dudley (see Black, Lionel)
Barker, George 1913-1991 .... DLB-20
Barker, Harley Granville 1877-1946 ...... DLB-10
Barker, Howard 1946- DLB-13, 233
Barker, James Nelson 1784-1858 .... DLB-37
Barker, Jane 1652-1727 .... DLB-39, 131
Barker, Lady Mary Anne 1831-1911 .... DLB-166
Barker, Pat 1943- DLB-271
Barker, William circa 1520-after 1576 ... DLB-132
Arthur Barker Limited DLB-112
Barkov, Ivan Semenovich 1732-1768 .... DLB-150
Barks, Coleman 1937- DLB-5
Barlach, Ernst 1870-1938 .... DLB-56, 118
Barlow, Joel 1754-1812 .... DLB-37
The Prospect of Peace (1778) DLB-37
Barnard, John 1681-1770 .... DLB-24
Barnard, Marjorie (M. Barnard Eldershaw)
 1897-1987 .... DLB-260
Barnard, Robert 1936- DLB-276
Barne, Kitty (Mary Catherine Barne)
 1883-1957 .... DLB-160
Barnes, Barnabe 1571-1609 .... DLB-132
Barnes, Djuna 1892-1982 .... DLB-4, 9, 45; DS-15
Barnes, Jim 1933- DLB-175
Barnes, Julian 1946- DLB-194; Y-93
 Notes for a Checklist of Publications Y-01
Barnes, Margaret Ayer 1886-1967 .... DLB-9
Barnes, Peter 1931- DLB-13, 233
Barnes, William 1801-1886 .... DLB-32
A. S. Barnes and Company DLB-49
Barnes and Noble Books DLB-46
Barnet, Miguel 1940- DLB-145
Barney, Natalie 1876-1972 ...... DLB-4; DS-15
Barnfield, Richard 1574-1627 .... DLB-172
Richard W. Baron [publishing house] DLB-46
Barr, Amelia Edith Huddleston
 1831-1919 .... DLB-202, 221
Barr, Robert 1850-1912 .... DLB-70, 92
Barral, Carlos 1928-1989 .... DLB-134
Barrax, Gerald William 1933- DLB-41, 120
Barrès, Maurice 1862-1923 .... DLB-123
Barreno, Maria Isabel (see The Three Marias:
 A Landmark Case in Portuguese
 Literary History)
Barrett, Eaton Stannard 1786-1820 ...... DLB-116
Barrie, J. M.
 1860-1937 ...... DLB-10, 141, 156; CDBLB-5
Barrie and Jenkins DLB-112
Barrio, Raymond 1921- DLB-82
Barrios, Gregg 1945- DLB-122
Barry, Philip 1896-1949 .... DLB-7, 228
Barry, Robertine (see Françoise)
Barry, Sebastian 1955- DLB-245
Barse and Hopkins DLB-46
Barstow, Stan 1928- DLB-14, 139, 207
 Tribute to John Braine Y-86

Barth, John 1930- DLB-2, 227
Barthelme, Donald
 1931-1989 .... DLB-2, 234; Y-80, 89
Barthelme, Frederick 1943- DLB-244; Y-85
Barthes, Roland 1915-1980 .... DLB-296
Bartholomew, Frank 1898-1985 .... DLB-127
Bartlett, John 1820-1905 .... DLB-1, 235
Bartol, Cyrus Augustus 1813-1900 .... DLB-1, 235
Barton, Bernard 1784-1849 .... DLB-96
Barton, John ca. 1610-1675 .... DLB-236
Barton, Thomas Pennant 1803-1869 .... DLB-140
Bartram, John 1699-1777 .... DLB-31
Bartram, William 1739-1823 .... DLB-37
Barykova, Anna Pavlovna 1839-1893 .... DLB-277
Bashshar ibn Burd circa 714-circa 784 ... DLB-311
Basic Books DLB-46
Basille, Theodore (see Becon, Thomas)
Bass, Rick 1958- DLB-212, 275
Bass, T. J. 1932- Y-81
Bassani, Giorgio 1916-2000 .... DLB-128, 177, 299
Basse, William circa 1583-1653 .... DLB-121
Bassett, John Spencer 1867-1928 .... DLB-17
Bassler, Thomas Joseph (see Bass, T. J.)
Bate, Walter Jackson 1918-1999 ...... DLB-67, 103
Bateman, Stephen circa 1510-1584 ..... DLB-136
Christopher Bateman
 [publishing house] DLB-170
Bates, H. E. 1905-1974 .... DLB-162, 191
Bates, Katharine Lee 1859-1929 .... DLB-71
Batiushkov, Konstantin Nikolaevich
 1787-1855 .... DLB-205
B. T. Batsford [publishing house] DLB-106
Batteux, Charles 1713-1780 .... DLB-313
Battiscombe, Georgina 1905- DLB-155
The Battle of Maldon circa 1000 .... DLB-146
Baudelaire, Charles 1821-1867 .... DLB-217
Baudrillard, Jean 1929- DLB-296
Bauer, Bruno 1809-1882 .... DLB-133
Bauer, Wolfgang 1941- DLB-124
Baum, L. Frank 1856-1919 .... DLB-22
Baum, Vicki 1888-1960 .... DLB-85
Baumbach, Jonathan 1933- Y-80
Bausch, Richard 1945- DLB-130
 Tribute to James Dickey Y-97
 Tribute to Peter Taylor Y-94
Bausch, Robert 1945- DLB-218
Bawden, Nina 1925- DLB-14, 161, 207
Bax, Clifford 1886-1962 .... DLB-10, 100
Baxter, Charles 1947- DLB-130
Bayer, Eleanor (see Perry, Eleanor)
Bayer, Konrad 1932-1964 .... DLB-85
Bayle, Pierre 1647-1706 .... DLB-268, 313
Bayley, Barrington J. 1937- DLB-261
Baynes, Pauline 1922- DLB-160
Baynton, Barbara 1857-1929 .... DLB-230

Bazin, Hervé (Jean Pierre Marie Hervé-Bazin)
 1911-1996 .... DLB-83
The BBC Four Samuel Johnson Prize
 for Non-fiction Y-02
Beach, Sylvia
 1887-1962 .... DLB-4; DS-15
Beacon Press DLB-49
Beadle and Adams DLB-49
Beagle, Peter S. 1939- Y-80
Beal, M. F. 1937- Y-81
Beale, Howard K. 1899-1959 .... DLB-17
Beard, Charles A. 1874-1948 .... DLB-17
Beat Generation (Beats)
 As I See It, by Carolyn Cassady DLB-16
 A Beat Chronology: The First Twenty-five
  Years, 1944-1969 .... DLB-16
 The Commercialization of the Image
  of Revolt, by Kenneth Rexroth ... DLB-16
 Four Essays on the Beat Generation .. DLB-16
 in New York City DLB-237
 in the West DLB-237
 Outlaw Days DLB-16
 Periodicals of DLB-16
Beattie, Ann 1947- DLB-218, 278; Y-82
Beattie, James 1735-1803 .... DLB-109
Beatty, Chester 1875-1968 .... DLB-201
Beauchemin, Nérée 1850-1931 .... DLB-92
Beauchemin, Yves 1941- DLB-60
Beaugrand, Honoré 1848-1906 .... DLB-99
Beaulieu, Victor-Lévy 1945- DLB-53
Beaumarchais, Pierre-Augustin Caron de
 1732-1799 .... DLB-313
Beaumer, Mme de ?-1766 .... DLB-313
Beaumont, Francis circa 1584-1616
 and Fletcher, John
 1579-1625 .... DLB-58; CDBLB-1
Beaumont, Sir John 1583?-1627 .... DLB-121
Beaumont, Joseph 1616-1699 .... DLB-126
Beauvoir, Simone de 1908-1986 .... DLB-72; Y-86
 Personal Tribute to Simone de Beauvoir ... Y-86
Beaver, Bruce 1928- DLB-289
Becher, Ulrich 1910-1990 .... DLB-69
Becker, Carl 1873-1945 .... DLB-17
Becker, Jurek 1937-1997 .... DLB-75, 299
Becker, Jurgen 1932- DLB-75
Beckett, Samuel 1906-1989
 .... DLB-13, 15, 233; Y-90; CDBLB-7
Beckford, William 1760-1844 .... DLB-39, 213
Beckham, Barry 1944- DLB-33
Bećković, Matija 1939- DLB-181
Becon, Thomas circa 1512-1567 .... DLB-136
Becque, Henry 1837-1899 .... DLB-192
Beddoes, Thomas 1760-1808 .... DLB-158
Beddoes, Thomas Lovell 1803-1849 ..... DLB-96
Bede circa 673-735 .... DLB-146
Bedford-Jones, H. 1887-1949 .... DLB-251
Bedregal, Yolanda 1913-1999 .... DLB-283

Beebe, William 1877-1962 . . . . DLB-275	Tribute to Isaac Bashevis Singer Y-91	Benson, Stella 1892-1933. . . . . DLB-36, 162
Beecher, Catharine Esther 1800-1878 . . . . DLB-1, 243	Belmont Productions DLB-46	Bent, James Theodore 1852-1897 . . . . DLB-174
	Belov, Vasilii Ivanovich 1932- DLB-302	Bent, Mabel Virginia Anna ?-? DLB-174
Beecher, Henry Ward 1813-1887 . . . . DLB-3, 43, 250	Bels, Alberts 1938- DLB-232	Bentham, Jeremy 1748-1832 . . . DLB-107, 158, 252
Beer, George L. 1872-1920 . . . . DLB-47	Belševica, Vizma 1931- DLB-232; CDWLB-4	Bentley, E. C. 1875-1956 . . . . DLB-70
Beer, Johann 1655-1700 . . . . DLB-168	Bely, Andrei 1880-1934 . . . . DLB-295	Bentley, Phyllis 1894-1977 . . . . DLB-191
Beer, Patricia 1919-1999 . . . . DLB-40	Bemelmans, Ludwig 1898-1962. . . . . DLB-22	Bentley, Richard 1662-1742 . . . . DLB-252
Beerbohm, Max 1872-1956 . . . . DLB-34, 100	Bemis, Samuel Flagg 1891-1973 . . . . DLB-17	Richard Bentley [publishing house] DLB-106
Beer-Hofmann, Richard 1866-1945 . . . . DLB-81	William Bemrose [publishing house] DLB-106	Benton, Robert 1932- and Newman, David 1937- DLB-44
Beers, Henry A. 1847-1926 . . . . DLB-71	Ben no Naishi 1228?-1271? DLB-203	
S. O. Beeton [publishing house]. DLB-106	Benchley, Robert 1889-1945 . . . . DLB-11	Benziger Brothers DLB-49
Begley, Louis 1933- DLB-299	Bencúr, Matej (see Kukučín, Martin)	*Beowulf* circa 900-1000 or 790-825 . . . . DLB-146; CDBLB-1
Bégon, Elisabeth 1696-1755 . . . . DLB-99	Benedetti, Mario 1920- DLB-113	
Behan, Brendan 1923-1964 . . . . DLB-13, 233; CDBLB-7	Benedict, Pinckney 1964- DLB-244	Berent, Wacław 1873-1940 . . . . DLB-215
	Benedict, Ruth 1887-1948 . . . . DLB-246	Beresford, Anne 1929- DLB-40
Behn, Aphra 1640?-1689 . . . . DLB-39, 80, 131	Benedictus, David 1938- DLB-14	Beresford, John Davys 1873-1947 . . . . DLB-162, 178, 197
Behn, Harry 1898-1973 . . . . DLB-61	Benedikt Gröndal 1826-1907 . . . . DLB-293	
Behrman, S. N. 1893-1973 . . . . DLB-7, 44	Benedikt, Michael 1935- DLB-5	"Experiment in the Novel" (1929) [excerpt] DLB-36
Beklemishev, Iurii Solomonvich (see Krymov, Iurii Solomonovich)	Benediktov, Vladimir Grigor'evich 1807-1873. . . . . DLB-205	
		Beresford-Howe, Constance 1922- DLB-88
Belaney, Archibald Stansfeld (see Grey Owl)	Benét, Stephen Vincent 1898-1943 . . . . DLB-4, 48, 102, 249	R. G. Berford Company DLB-49
Belasco, David 1853-1931 . . . . DLB-7		Berg, Elizabeth 1948- DLB-292
Clarke Belford and Company DLB-49	Stephen Vincent Benét Centenary Y-97	Berg, Stephen 1934- DLB-5
Belgian Luxembourg American Studies Association Y-01	Benét, William Rose 1886-1950 . . . . DLB-45	Bergengruen, Werner 1892-1964 . . . . DLB-56
	Benford, Gregory 1941- Y-82	Berger, John 1926- DLB-14, 207
Belinsky, Vissarion Grigor'evich 1811-1848 . . . . DLB-198	Benítez, Sandra 1941- DLB-292	Berger, Meyer 1898-1959 . . . . DLB-29
	Benjamin, Park 1809-1864. . . . . DLB-3, 59, 73, 250	Berger, Thomas 1924- DLB-2; Y-80
Belitt, Ben 1911- DLB-5	Benjamin, Peter (see Cunningham, Peter)	A Statement by Thomas Berger Y-80
Belknap, Jeremy 1744-1798 . . . . DLB-30, 37	Benjamin, S. G. W. 1837-1914. . . . . DLB-189	Bergman, Hjalmar 1883-1931 . . . . DLB-259
Bell, Adrian 1901-1980 . . . . DLB-191	Benjamin, Walter 1892-1940 . . . . DLB-242	Bergman, Ingmar 1918- DLB-257
Bell, Clive 1881-1964. . . . . DS-10	Benlowes, Edward 1602-1676 . . . . DLB-126	Berkeley, Anthony 1893-1971 . . . . DLB-77
Bell, Daniel 1919- DLB-246	Benn, Gottfried 1886-1956 . . . . DLB-56	Berkeley, George 1685-1753 . . . . DLB-31, 101, 252
Bell, Gertrude Margaret Lowthian 1868-1926 . . . . DLB-174	Benn Brothers Limited. DLB-106	The Berkley Publishing Corporation. DLB-46
	Bennett, Alan 1934- DLB-310	Berkman, Alexander 1870-1936. . . . . DLB-303
Bell, James Madison 1826-1902 . . . . DLB-50	Bennett, Arnold 1867-1931 . . . . DLB-10, 34, 98, 135; CDBLB-5	Berlin, Irving 1888-1989 . . . . DLB-265
Bell, Madison Smartt 1957- DLB-218, 278		Berlin, Lucia 1936- DLB-130
Tribute to Andrew Nelson Lytle. Y-95	The Arnold Bennett Society Y-98	Berman, Marshall 1940- DLB-246
Tribute to Peter Taylor. Y-94	Bennett, Charles 1899-1995. . . . . DLB-44	Berman, Sabina 1955- DLB-305
Bell, Marvin 1937- DLB-5	Bennett, Emerson 1822-1905. . . . . DLB-202	Bernal, Vicente J. 1888-1915 . . . . DLB-82
Bell, Millicent 1919- DLB-111	Bennett, Gwendolyn 1902-1981 . . . . DLB-51	Bernanos, Georges 1888-1948 . . . . DLB-72
Bell, Quentin 1910-1996 . . . . DLB-155	Bennett, Hal 1930- DLB-33	Bernard, Catherine 1663?-1712 . . . . DLB-268
Bell, Vanessa 1879-1961. . . . . DS-10	Bennett, James Gordon 1795-1872 . . . . DLB-43	Bernard, Harry 1898-1979. . . . . DLB-92
George Bell and Sons. DLB-106	Bennett, James Gordon, Jr. 1841-1918. . . . . DLB-23	Bernard, John 1756-1828 . . . . DLB-37
Robert Bell [publishing house]. DLB-49	Bennett, John 1865-1956 . . . . DLB-42	Bernard of Chartres circa 1060-1124? DLB-115
Bellamy, Edward 1850-1898 . . . . DLB-12	Bennett, Louise 1919- DLB-117; CDWLB-3	Bernard of Clairvaux 1090-1153 . . . . DLB-208
Bellamy, Joseph 1719-1790. . . . . DLB-31	Benni, Stefano 1947- DLB-196	Bernard, Richard 1568-1641/1642. . . . . . . DLB-281
John Bellamy [publishing house] DLB-170	Benoist, Françoise-Albine Puzin de La Martinière 1731-1809. . . . . DLB-313	Bernard Silvestris flourished circa 1130-1160 . . . . DLB-208
La Belle Assemblée 1806-1837 . . . . DLB-110		
Bellezza, Dario 1944-1996 . . . . DLB-128	Benoit, Jacques 1941- DLB-60	Bernardin de Saint-Pierre 1737-1814 . . . . DLB-313
Belli, Carlos Germán 1927- DLB-290	Benson, A. C. 1862-1925. . . . . DLB-98	Bernari, Carlo 1909-1992 . . . . DLB-177
Belli, Gioconda 1948- DLB-290	Benson, E. F. 1867-1940. . . . . DLB-135, 153	Bernhard, Thomas 1931-1989 . . . . DLB-85, 124; CDWLB-2
Belloc, Hilaire 1870-1953 . . . . DLB-19, 100, 141, 174	The E. F. Benson Society Y-98	
Belloc, Madame (see Parkes, Bessie Rayner)	The Tilling Society Y-98	Berniéres, Louis de 1954- DLB-271
Bellonci, Maria 1902-1986 . . . . DLB-196	Benson, Jackson J. 1930- DLB-111	Bernstein, Charles 1950- DLB-169
Bellow, Saul 1915- DLB-2, 28, 299; Y-82; DS-3; CDALB-1	Benson, Robert Hugh 1871-1914. . . . . DLB-153	Berriault, Gina 1926-1999 . . . . DLB-130
		Berrigan, Daniel 1921- DLB-5

Berrigan, Ted 1934-1983 . . . . DLB-5, 169

Berry, Wendell 1934- DLB-5, 6, 234, 275

Berryman, John 1914-1972 . . . . DLB-48; CDALB-1

Bersianik, Louky 1930- DLB-60

Berssenbrugge, Mei-mei 1947- DLB-312

Thomas Berthelet [publishing house] DLB-170

Berto, Giuseppe 1914-1978. . . . . .DLB-177

Bertocci, Peter Anthony 1910-1989 . . . . . .DLB-279

Bertolucci, Attilio 1911-2000. . . . . DLB-128

Berton, Pierre 1920- DLB-68

Bertrand, Louis "Aloysius" 1807-1841 . . . DLB-217

Besant, Sir Walter 1836-1901 . . . . . . DLB-135, 190

Bessa-Luís, Agustina 1922- DLB-287

Bessette, Gerard 1920- DLB-53

Bessie, Alvah 1904-1985. . . . . DLB-26

Bester, Alfred 1913-1987. . . . . DLB-8

Besterman, Theodore 1904-1976 . . . . DLB-201

Beston, Henry (Henry Beston Sheahan)
1888-1968 . . . . .DLB-275

Best-Seller Lists
An Assessment. Y-84

What's Really Wrong With
Bestseller Lists Y-84

Bestuzhev, Aleksandr Aleksandrovich
(Marlinsky) 1797-1837 . . . . DLB-198

Bestuzhev, Nikolai Aleksandrovich
1791-1855. . . . . DLB-198

Betham-Edwards, Matilda Barbara
(see Edwards, Matilda Barbara Betham-)

Betjeman, John
1906-1984 . . . . DLB-20; Y-84; CDBLB-7

Betocchi, Carlo 1899-1986 . . . . DLB-128

Bettarini, Mariella 1942- DLB-128

Betts, Doris 1932- DLB-218; Y-82

Beveridge, Albert J. 1862-1927 . . . . DLB-17

Beverley, Robert circa 1673-1722 . . . . . DLB-24, 30

Bevilacqua, Alberto 1934- DLB-196

Bevington, Louisa Sarah 1845-1895 . . . . . DLB-199

Beyle, Marie-Henri (see Stendhal)

Białoszewski, Miron 1922-1983 . . . . DLB-232

Bianco, Margery Williams 1881-1944 . . . DLB-160

Bibaud, Adèle 1854-1941 . . . . DLB-92

Bibaud, Michel 1782-1857. . . . . DLB-99

Bibliography
Bibliographical and Textual Scholarship
Since World War II Y-89

Center for Bibliographical Studies and
Research at the University of
California, Riverside Y-91

The Great Bibliographers Series Y-93

Primary Bibliography: A Retrospective . . . Y-95

Bichsel, Peter 1935- DLB-75

Bickerstaff, Isaac John 1733-circa 1808. . . . DLB-89

Drexel Biddle [publishing house] DLB-49

Bidermann, Jacob
1577 or 1578-1639 . . . . DLB-164

Bidwell, Walter Hilliard 1798-1881 . . . . . . DLB-79

Biehl, Charlotta Dorothea 1731-1788 . . . . DLB-300

Bienek, Horst 1930-1990 . . . . DLB-75

Bierbaum, Otto Julius 1865-1910 . . . . DLB-66

Bierce, Ambrose 1842-1914?
. . . . . . .DLB-11, 12, 23, 71, 74, 186; CDALB-3

Bigelow, William F. 1879-1966. . . . . DLB-91

Biggers, Earl Derr 1884-1933 . . . . DLB-306

Biggle, Lloyd, Jr. 1923- DLB-8

Bigiaretti, Libero 1905-1993 . . . . .DLB-177

Bigland, Eileen 1898-1970. . . . . DLB-195

Biglow, Hosea (see Lowell, James Russell)

Bigongiari, Piero 1914-1997 . . . . DLB-128

Bilac, Olavo 1865-1918 . . . . DLB-307

Bilenchi, Romano 1909-1989 . . . . DLB-264

Billinger, Richard 1890-1965 . . . . DLB-124

Billings, Hammatt 1818-1874 . . . . DLB-188

Billings, John Shaw 1898-1975 . . . . DLB-137

Billings, Josh (see Shaw, Henry Wheeler)

Binding, Rudolf G. 1867-1938 . . . . DLB-66

Bingay, Malcolm 1884-1953. . . . . DLB-241

Bingham, Caleb 1757-1817 . . . . DLB-42

Bingham, George Barry 1906-1988 . . . . . DLB-127

Bingham, Sallie 1937- DLB-234

William Bingley [publishing house] DLB-154

Binyon, Laurence 1869-1943 . . . . DLB-19

Biographia Brittanica DLB-142

Biography
Biographical Documents Y-84, 85

A Celebration of Literary Biography Y-98

Conference on Modern Biography Y-85

The Cult of Biography
Excerpts from the Second Folio Debate:
"Biographies are generally a disease of
English Literature" Y-86

New Approaches to Biography: Challenges
from Critical Theory, USC Conference
on Literary Studies, 1990 . . . . Y-90

"The New Biography," by Virginia Woolf,
New York Herald Tribune,
30 October 1927 . . . . DLB-149

"The Practice of Biography," in *The English
Sense of Humour and Other Essays*, by
Harold Nicolson DLB-149

"Principles of Biography," in *Elizabethan
and Other Essays*, by Sidney Lee . . DLB-149

Remarks at the Opening of "The Biographical
Part of Literature" Exhibition, by
William R. Cagle. Y-98

Survey of Literary Biographies Y-00

A Transit of Poets and Others: American
Biography in 1982. . . . . Y-82

The Year in Literary
Biography Y-83–01

Biography, The Practice of:
An Interview with B. L. Reid. Y-83

An Interview with David Herbert Donald . . Y-87

An Interview with Humphrey Carpenter . . . Y-84

An Interview with Joan Mellen Y-94

An Interview with John Caldwell Guilds Y-92

An Interview with William Manchester . . . Y-85

John Bioren [publishing house]. DLB-49

Bioy Casares, Adolfo 1914-1999 . . . . DLB-113

Bird, Isabella Lucy 1831-1904 . . . . DLB-166

Bird, Robert Montgomery 1806-1854 . . . DLB-202

Bird, William 1888-1963 . . . . DLB-4; DS-15

The Cost of the *Cantos*: William Bird
to Ezra Pound Y-01

Birken, Sigmund von 1626-1681 . . . . DLB-164

Birney, Earle 1904-1995. . . . . DLB-88

Birrell, Augustine 1850-1933 . . . . DLB-98

Bisher, Furman 1918- DLB-171

Bishop, Elizabeth
1911-1979. . . . . DLB-5, 169; CDALB-6

The Elizabeth Bishop Society. Y-01

Bishop, John Peale 1892-1944 . . . . . DLB-4, 9, 45

Bismarck, Otto von 1815-1898. . . . . DLB-129

Bisset, Robert 1759-1805 . . . . DLB-142

Bissett, Bill 1939- DLB-53

Bitov, Andrei Georgievich 1937- DLB-302

Bitzius, Albert (see Gotthelf, Jeremias)

Bjørnboe, Jens 1920-1976 . . . . DLB-297

Bjørnvig, Thorkild 1918- DLB-214

Black, David (D. M.) 1941- DLB-40

Black, Gavin (Oswald Morris Wynd)
1913-1998 . . . . .DLB-276

Black, Lionel (Dudley Barker)
1910-1980 . . . . .DLB-276

Black, Winifred 1863-1936. . . . . DLB-25

Walter J. Black [publishing house] DLB-46

Blackamore, Arthur 1679-? DLB-24, 39

Blackburn, Alexander L. 1929- Y-85

Blackburn, John 1923-1993 . . . . DLB-261

Blackburn, Paul 1926-1971. . . . . . . .DLB-16; Y-81

Blackburn, Thomas 1916-1977 . . . . DLB-27

Blacker, Terence 1948- DLB-271

Blackmore, R. D. 1825-1900 . . . . DLB-18

Blackmore, Sir Richard 1654-1729 . . . . . . DLB-131

Blackmur, R. P. 1904-1965. . . . . DLB-63

Blackwell, Alice Stone 1857-1950 . . . . DLB-303

Basil Blackwell, Publisher. DLB-106

Blackwood, Algernon Henry
1869-1951 . . . . .DLB-153, 156, 178

Blackwood, Caroline 1931-1996 . . . . .DLB-14, 207

William Blackwood and Sons, Ltd. DLB-154

Blackwood's Edinburgh Magazine
1817-1980. . . . . DLB-110

Blades, William 1824-1890. . . . . DLB-184

Blaga, Lucian 1895-1961 . . . . DLB-220

Blagden, Isabella 1817?-1873 . . . . DLB-199

Blair, Eric Arthur (see Orwell, George)

Blair, Francis Preston 1791-1876 . . . . DLB-43

Blair, Hugh
Lectures on Rhetoric and Belles Lettres (1783),
[excerpts] DLB-31

Blair, James circa 1655-1743 . . . . DLB-24

Blair, John Durburrow 1759-1823 . . . . DLB-37

Blais, Marie-Claire 1939- DLB-53

Blaise, Clark 1940- DLB-53

Blake, George 1893-1961 . . . . DLB-191

Blake, Lillie Devereux 1833-1913 . . . . DLB-202, 221

Blake, Nicholas (C. Day Lewis)
1904-1972 . . . . DLB-77

Blake, William
1757-1827 . . . . DLB-93, 154, 163; CDBLB-3

The Blakiston Company DLB-49

Blanchard, Stephen 1950- DLB-267

Blanchot, Maurice 1907-2003 . . . . DLB-72, 296

Blanckenburg, Christian Friedrich von
1744-1796 . . . . DLB-94

Blandiana, Ana 1942- DLB-232; CDWLB-4

Blanshard, Brand 1892-1987 . . . . DLB-279

Blaser, Robin 1925- DLB-165

Blaumanis, Rudolfs 1863-1908 . . . . DLB-220

Bleasdale, Alan 1946- DLB-245

Bledsoe, Albert Taylor
1809-1877 . . . . DLB-3, 79, 248

Bleecker, Ann Eliza 1752-1783 . . . . DLB-200

Blelock and Company DLB-49

Blennerhassett, Margaret Agnew
1773-1842 . . . . DLB-99

Geoffrey Bles [publishing house] DLB-112

Blessington, Marguerite, Countess of
1789-1849 . . . . DLB-166

Blew, Mary Clearman 1939- DLB-256

Blicher, Steen Steensen 1782-1848 . . . . . . DLB-300

The Blickling Homilies circa 971 . . . . DLB-146

Blind, Mathilde 1841-1896 . . . . DLB-199

Blish, James 1921-1975 . . . . DLB-8

E. Bliss and E. White
[publishing house] DLB-49

Bliven, Bruce 1889-1977 . . . . DLB-137

Blixen, Karen 1885-1962 . . . . DLB-214

Bloch, Ernst 1885-1977 . . . . DLB-296

Bloch, Robert 1917-1994 . . . . DLB-44

Tribute to John D. MacDonald Y-86

Block, Lawrence 1938- DLB-226

Block, Rudolph (see Lessing, Bruno)

Blok, Aleksandr Aleksandrovich
1880-1921 . . . . DLB-295

Blondal, Patricia 1926-1959 . . . . DLB-88

Bloom, Harold 1930- DLB-67

Bloomer, Amelia 1818-1894 . . . . DLB-79

Bloomfield, Robert 1766-1823 . . . . DLB-93

Bloomsbury Group DS-10

The Dreadnought Hoax DS-10

Bloor, Ella Reeve 1862-1951 . . . . DLB-303

Blotner, Joseph 1923- DLB-111

Blount, Thomas 1618?-1679 . . . . DLB-236

Bloy, Léon 1846-1917 . . . . DLB-123

Blume, Judy 1938- DLB-52

Tribute to Theodor Seuss Geisel Y-91

Blunck, Hans Friedrich 1888-1961 . . . . DLB-66

Blunden, Edmund 1896-1974 . . . DLB-20, 100, 155

Blundeville, Thomas 1522?-1606 . . . . DLB-236

Blunt, Lady Anne Isabella Noel
1837-1917 . . . . DLB-174

Blunt, Wilfrid Scawen 1840-1922 . . . . DLB-19, 174

Bly, Nellie (see Cochrane, Elizabeth)

Bly, Robert 1926- DLB-5

Blyton, Enid 1897-1968 . . . . DLB-160

Boaden, James 1762-1839 . . . . DLB-89

Boal, Augusto 1931- DLB-307

Boas, Frederick S. 1862-1957 . . . . DLB-149

The Bobbs-Merrill Company DLB-46, 291

The Bobbs-Merrill Archive at the
Lilly Library, Indiana University Y-90

Boborykin, Petr Dmitrievich
1836-1921 . . . . DLB-238

Bobrov, Semen Sergeevich
1763?-1810 . . . . DLB-150

Bobrowski, Johannes 1917-1965 . . . . DLB-75

Bocage, Manuel Maria Barbosa du
1765-1805 . . . . DLB-287

Bodenheim, Maxwell 1892-1954 . . . . . . DLB-9, 45

Bodenstedt, Friedrich von 1819-1892 . . . . DLB-129

Bodini, Vittorio 1914-1970 . . . . DLB-128

Bodkin, M. McDonnell 1850-1933 . . . . DLB-70

Bodley, Sir Thomas 1545-1613 . . . . DLB-213

Bodley Head DLB-112

Bodmer, Johann Jakob 1698-1783 . . . . DLB-97

Bodmershof, Imma von 1895-1982 . . . . . . DLB-85

Bodsworth, Fred 1918- DLB-68

Böðvar Guðmundsson 1939- DLB-293

Boehm, Sydney 1908- DLB-44

Boer, Charles 1939- DLB-5

Boethius circa 480-circa 524 . . . . DLB-115

Boethius of Dacia circa 1240-? DLB-115

Bogan, Louise 1897-1970 . . . . DLB-45, 169

Bogarde, Dirk 1921-1999 . . . . DLB-14

Bogdanov, Aleksandr Aleksandrovich
1873-1928 . . . . DLB-295

Bogdanovich, Ippolit Fedorovich
circa 1743-1803 . . . . DLB-150

David Bogue [publishing house] DLB-106

Bohjalian, Chris 1960- DLB-292

Böhme, Jakob 1575-1624 . . . . DLB-164

H. G. Bohn [publishing house] DLB-106

Bohse, August 1661-1742 . . . . DLB-168

Boie, Heinrich Christian 1744-1806 . . . . . . DLB-94

Boileau-Despréaux, Nicolas 1636-1711 . . . DLB-268

Bojunga, Lygia 1932- DLB-307

Bok, Edward W. 1863-1930 . . . . . . DLB-91; DS-16

Boland, Eavan 1944- DLB-40

Boldrewood, Rolf (Thomas Alexander Browne)
1826?-1915 . . . . DLB-230

Bolingbroke, Henry St. John, Viscount
1678-1751 . . . . DLB-101

Böll, Heinrich
1917-1985 . . . . DLB-69; Y-85; CDWLB-2

Bolling, Robert 1738-1775 . . . . DLB-31

Bolotov, Andrei Timofeevich
1738-1833 . . . . DLB-150

Bolt, Carol 1941- DLB-60

Bolt, Robert 1924-1995 . . . . DLB-13, 233

Bolton, Herbert E. 1870-1953 . . . . DLB-17

Bonaventura DLB-90

Bonaventure circa 1217-1274 . . . . DLB-115

Bonaviri, Giuseppe 1924- DLB-177

Bond, Edward 1934- DLB-13, 310

Bond, Michael 1926- DLB-161

Bondarev, Iurii Vasil'evich 1924- DLB-302

Albert and Charles Boni
[publishing house] DLB-46

Boni and Liveright DLB-46

Bonnefoy, Yves 1923- DLB-258

Bonner, Marita 1899-1971 . . . . DLB-228

Bonner, Paul Hyde 1893-1968 . . . . DS-17

Bonner, Sherwood (see McDowell, Katharine
Sherwood Bonner)

Robert Bonner's Sons DLB-49

Bonnin, Gertrude Simmons (see Zitkala-Ša)

Bonsanti, Alessandro 1904-1984 . . . . DLB-177

Bontempelli, Massimo 1878-1960 . . . . . . DLB-264

Bontemps, Arna 1902-1973 . . . . DLB-48, 51

The Book Buyer (1867-1880, 1884-1918,
1935-1938) DS-13

The Book League of America DLB-46

Book Reviewing
The American Book Review: A Sketch . . Y-92

Book Reviewing and the
Literary Scene Y-96, 97

Book Reviewing in America Y-87–94

Book Reviewing in America and the
Literary Scene Y-95

Book Reviewing in Texas Y-94

Book Reviews in Glossy Magazines Y-95

Do They or Don't They?
Writers Reading Book Reviews Y-01

The Most Powerful Book Review
in America [New York Times
Book Review] Y-82

Some Surprises and Universal Truths . . . Y-92

The Year in Book Reviewing and the
Literary Situation Y-98

Book Supply Company DLB-49

The Book Trade History Group Y-93

The Booker Prize Y-96–98

Address by Anthony Thwaite,
Chairman of the Booker Prize Judges
Comments from Former Booker
Prize Winners Y-86

Boorde, Andrew circa 1490-1549 . . . . DLB-136

Boorstin, Daniel J. 1914- DLB-17

Tribute to Archibald MacLeish Y-82

Tribute to Charles Scribner Jr. Y-95

Booth, Franklin 1874-1948 . . . . DLB-188

Booth, Mary L. 1831-1889 . . . . DLB-79

Booth, Philip 1925- Y-82

Booth, Wayne C. 1921- DLB-67

Booth, William 1829-1912 . . . . DLB-190

Bor, Josef 1906-1979 . . . . DLB-299
Borchardt, Rudolf 1877-1945 . . . . DLB-66
Borchert, Wolfgang 1921-1947 . . . . . . DLB-69, 124
Bording, Anders 1619-1677 . . . . DLB-300
Borel, Pétrus 1809-1859 . . . . DLB-119
Borgen, Johan 1902-1979 . . . . DLB-297
Borges, Jorge Luis
    1899-1986 . . . DLB-113, 283; Y-86; CDWLB-3
    The Poetry of Jorge Luis Borges Y-86
    A Personal Tribute. Y-86
Borgese, Giuseppe Antonio 1882-1952 . . . DLB-264
Börne, Ludwig 1786-1837 . . . . DLB-90
Bornstein, Miriam 1950- DLB-209
Borowski, Tadeusz
    1922-1951 . . . . DLB-215; CDWLB-4
Borrow, George 1803-1881 . . . . . DLB-21, 55, 166
Bosanquet, Bernard 1848-1923 . . . . DLB-262
Bosch, Juan 1909-2001 . . . . DLB-145
Bosco, Henri 1888-1976 . . . . DLB-72
Bosco, Monique 1927- DLB-53
Bosman, Herman Charles 1905-1951 . . . . DLB-225
Bossuet, Jacques-Bénigne 1627-1704 . . . . . DLB-268
Bostic, Joe 1908-1988 . . . . DLB-241
Boston, Lucy M. 1892-1990 . . . . DLB-161
Boston Quarterly Review DLB-1
Boston University
    Editorial Institute at Boston University . . . Y-00
    Special Collections at Boston University . . Y-99
Boswell, James
    1740-1795 . . . . DLB-104, 142; CDBLB-2
Boswell, Robert 1953- DLB-234
Bosworth, David. Y-82
    Excerpt from "Excerpts from a Report
    of the Commission," in *The Death
    of Descartes* Y-82
Bote, Hermann circa 1460-circa 1520 . . . . DLB-179
Botev, Khristo 1847-1876 . . . . DLB-147
Botkin, Vasilii Petrovich 1811-1869 . . . . . DLB-277
Botta, Anne C. Lynch 1815-1891 . . . . . DLB-3, 250
Botto, Ján (see Krasko, Ivan)
Bottome, Phyllis 1882-1963 . . . . DLB-197
Bottomley, Gordon 1874-1948 . . . . DLB-10
Bottoms, David 1949- DLB-120; Y-83
    Tribute to James Dickey Y-97
Bottrall, Ronald 1906- DLB-20
Bouchardy, Joseph 1810-1870 . . . . DLB-192
Boucher, Anthony 1911-1968 . . . . DLB-8
Boucher, Jonathan 1738-1804 . . . . DLB-31
Boucher de Boucherville, Georges
    1814-1894. . . . . DLB-99
Boudreau, Daniel (see Coste, Donat)
Bouhours, Dominique 1628-1702 . . . . DLB-268
Bourassa, Napoléon 1827-1916 . . . . DLB-99
Bourget, Paul 1852-1935 . . . . DLB-123
Bourinot, John George 1837-1902 . . . . DLB-99
Bourjaily, Vance 1922- DLB-2, 143

Bourne, Edward Gaylord 1860-1908 . . . . . DLB-47
Bourne, Randolph 1886-1918 . . . . DLB-63
Bousoño, Carlos 1923- DLB-108
Bousquet, Joë 1897-1950. . . . . DLB-72
Bova, Ben 1932- Y-81
Bovard, Oliver K. 1872-1945 . . . . DLB-25
Bove, Emmanuel 1898-1945 . . . . DLB-72
Bowen, Elizabeth
    1899-1973. . . . . DLB-15, 162; CDBLB-7
Bowen, Francis 1811-1890 . . . . . . DLB-1, 59, 235
Bowen, John 1924- DLB-13
Bowen, Marjorie 1886-1952 . . . . DLB-153
Bowen-Merrill Company DLB-49
Bowering, George 1935- DLB-53
Bowers, Bathsheba 1671-1718 . . . . DLB-200
Bowers, Claude G. 1878-1958 . . . . DLB-17
Bowers, Edgar 1924-2000. . . . . DLB-5
Bowers, Fredson Thayer
    1905-1991 . . . . DLB-140; Y-91
    The Editorial Style of Fredson Bowers . . . Y-91
    Fredson Bowers and
    Studies in Bibliography Y-91
    Fredson Bowers and the Cambridge
    Beaumont and Fletcher Y-91
    Fredson Bowers as Critic of Renaissance
    Dramatic Literature. Y-91
    Fredson Bowers as Music Critic. Y-91
    Fredson Bowers, Master Teacher Y-91
    An Interview [on Nabokov]. Y-80
    Working with Fredson Bowers Y-91
Bowles, Paul 1910-1999 . . . . . . DLB-5, 6, 218; Y-99
Bowles, Samuel, III 1826-1878 . . . . DLB-43
Bowles, William Lisle 1762-1850 . . . . DLB-93
Bowman, Louise Morey 1882-1944 . . . . . . DLB-68
Bowne, Borden Parker 1847-1919 . . . . . . .DLB-270
Boyd, James 1888-1944 . . . . DLB-9; DS-16
Boyd, John 1912-2002 . . . . DLB-310
Boyd, John 1919- DLB-8
Boyd, Martin 1893-1972 . . . . DLB-260
Boyd, Thomas 1898-1935 . . . . DLB-9; DS-16
Boyd, William 1952- DLB-231
Boye, Karin 1900-1941 . . . . DLB-259
Boyesen, Hjalmar Hjorth
    1848-1895 . . . . DLB-12, 71; DS-13
Boylan, Clare 1948- DLB-267
Boyle, Kay 1902-1992 . . . . DLB-4, 9, 48, 86; DS-15;
    . . . . Y-93
Boyle, Roger, Earl of Orrery 1621-1679 . . . DLB-80
Boyle, T. Coraghessan
    1948- DLB-218, 278; Y-86
Božić, Mirko 1919- DLB-181
Brackenbury, Alison 1953- DLB-40
Brackenridge, Hugh Henry
    1748-1816. DLB-11, 37
    The Rising Glory of America. DLB-37
Brackett, Charles 1892-1969 . . . . DLB-26
Brackett, Leigh 1915-1978 . . . . DLB-8, 26

John Bradburn [publishing house] DLB-49
Bradbury, Malcolm 1932-2000. . . . . . . DLB-14, 207
Bradbury, Ray 1920- DLB-2, 8; CDALB-6
Bradbury and Evans. DLB-106
Braddon, Mary Elizabeth
    1835-1915 . . . . .DLB-18, 70, 156
Bradford, Andrew 1686-1742 . . . . DLB-43, 73
Bradford, Gamaliel 1863-1932 . . . . .DLB-17
Bradford, John 1749-1830. . . . . DLB-43
Bradford, Roark 1896-1948 . . . . DLB-86
Bradford, William 1590-1657 . . . . DLB-24, 30
Bradford, William, III 1719-1791 . . . . . DLB-43, 73
Bradlaugh, Charles 1833-1891 . . . . DLB-57
Bradley, David 1950- DLB-33
Bradley, F. H. 1846-1924 . . . . DLB-262
Bradley, Katherine Harris (see Field, Michael)
Bradley, Marion Zimmer 1930-1999 . . . . . . DLB-8
Bradley, William Aspenwall 1878-1939 . . . . DLB-4
Ira Bradley and Company DLB-49
J. W. Bradley and Company DLB-49
Bradshaw, Henry 1831-1886 . . . . DLB-184
Bradstreet, Anne
    1612 or 1613-1672 . . . . DLB-24; CDALB-2
Bradūnas, Kazys 1917- DLB-220
Bradwardine, Thomas circa 1295-1349 . . DLB-115
Brady, Frank 1924-1986. . . . . DLB-111
Frederic A. Brady [publishing house] DLB-49
Braga, Rubem 1913-1990 . . . . DLB-307
Bragg, Melvyn 1939- DLB-14, 271
Brahe, Tycho 1546-1601 . . . . DLB-300
Charles H. Brainard [publishing house] . . . DLB-49
Braine, John
    1922-1986 . . . . DLB-15; Y-86; CDBLB-7
Braithwait, Richard 1588-1673 . . . . DLB-151
Braithwaite, William Stanley
    1878-1962. DLB-50, 54
Bräker, Ulrich 1735-1798 . . . . DLB-94
Bramah, Ernest 1868-1942 . . . . DLB-70
Branagan, Thomas 1774-1843 . . . . DLB-37
Brancati, Vitaliano 1907-1954 . . . . DLB-264
Branch, William Blackwell 1927- DLB-76
Brand, Christianna 1907-1988 . . . . .DLB-276
Brand, Max (see Faust, Frederick Schiller)
Brandão, Raul 1867-1930 . . . . DLB-287
Branden Press. DLB-46
Brandes, Georg 1842-1927 . . . . DLB-300
Branner, H.C. 1903-1966 . . . . DLB-214
Brant, Sebastian 1457-1521 . . . . .DLB-179
Brassey, Lady Annie (Allnutt)
    1839-1887 . . . . DLB-166
Brathwaite, Edward Kamau
    1930- DLB-125; CDWLB-3
Brault, Jacques 1933- DLB-53
Braun, Matt 1932- DLB-212
Braun, Volker 1939- DLB-75, 124

Brautigan, Richard
 1935-1984 . . . . DLB-2, 5, 206; Y-80, 84
Braxton, Joanne M. 1950- DLB-41
Bray, Anne Eliza 1790-1883. . . . . .DLB-116
Bray, Thomas 1656-1730. . . . . .DLB-24
Brazdžionis, Bernardas 1907- DLB-220
George Braziller [publishing house] DLB-46
The Bread Loaf Writers' Conference 1983 . . . Y-84
Breasted, James Henry 1865-1935. . . . . . . .DLB-47
Brecht, Bertolt
 1898-1956 . . . . DLB-56, 124; CDWLB-2
Bredel, Willi 1901-1964. . . . . .DLB-56
Bregendahl, Marie 1867-1940 . . . . .DLB-214
Breitinger, Johann Jakob 1701-1776 . . . . . .DLB-97
Brekke, Paal 1923-1993. . . . . .DLB-297
Bremser, Bonnie 1939- DLB-16
Bremser, Ray 1934-1998 . . . . .DLB-16
Brennan, Christopher 1870-1932. . . . . . . .DLB-230
Brentano, Bernard von 1901-1964. . . . . . . .DLB-56
Brentano, Clemens 1778-1842 . . . . .DLB-90
Brentano, Franz 1838-1917 . . . . .DLB-296
Brentano's DLB-49
Brenton, Howard 1942- DLB-13
Breslin, Jimmy 1929-1996 . . . . .DLB-185
Breton, André 1896-1966 . . . . .DLB-65, 258
Breton, Nicholas circa 1555-circa 1626 . . .DLB-136
The Breton Lays
 1300-early fifteenth century. DLB-146
Brett, Simon 1945- DLB-276
Brewer, Gil 1922-1983. . . . . .DLB-306
Brewer, Luther A. 1858-1933 . . . . .DLB-187
Brewer, Warren and Putnam. DLB-46
Brewster, Elizabeth 1922- DLB-60
Breytenbach, Breyten 1939- DLB-225
Bridge, Ann (Lady Mary Dolling Sanders
 O'Malley) 1889-1974. . . . . .DLB-191
Bridge, Horatio 1806-1893 . . . . .DLB-183
Bridgers, Sue Ellen 1942- DLB-52
Bridges, Robert
 1844-1930 . . . . .DLB-19, 98; CDBLB-5
The Bridgewater Library. DLB-213
Bridie, James 1888-1951 . . . . .DLB-10
Brieux, Eugene 1858-1932. . . . . .DLB-192
Brigadere, Anna
 1861-1933 . . . . .DLB-220; CDWLB-4
Briggs, Charles Frederick
 1804-1877 . . . . .DLB-3, 250
Brighouse, Harold 1882-1958 . . . . .DLB-10
Bright, Mary Chavelita Dunne
 (see Egerton, George)
Brightman, Edgar Sheffield 1884-1953 . . .DLB-270
B. J. Brimmer Company DLB-46
Brines, Francisco 1932- DLB-134
Brink, André 1935- DLB-225
Brinley, George, Jr. 1817-1875 . . . . .DLB-140
Brinnin, John Malcolm 1916-1998. . . . . . . .DLB-48
Brisbane, Albert 1809-1890 . . . . .DLB-3, 250

Brisbane, Arthur 1864-1936 . . . . .DLB-25
British Academy DLB-112
The British Critic 1793-1843 . . . . .DLB-110
British Library
 The American Trust for the
 British Library Y-96
 The British Library and the Regular
 Readers' Group Y-91
 Building the New British Library
 at St Pancras Y-94
British Literary Prizes DLB-207; Y-98
British Literature
 The "Angry Young Men" DLB-15
 Author-Printers, 1476-1599 . . . . .DLB-167
 The Comic Tradition Continued DLB-15
 Documents on Sixteenth-Century
 Literature DLB-167, 172
 Eikon Basilike 1649 . . . . .DLB-151
 Letter from London Y-96
 A Mirror for Magistrates DLB-167
 "Modern English Prose" (1876),
 by George Saintsbury DLB-57
 Sex, Class, Politics, and Religion [in the
 British Novel, 1930-1959] DLB-15
 Victorians on Rhetoric and Prose
 Style DLB-57
 The Year in British Fiction Y-99–01
 "You've Never Had It So Good," Gusted
 by "Winds of Change": British
 Fiction in the 1950s, 1960s,
 and After. DLB-14
British Literature, Old and Middle English
 Anglo-Norman Literature in the
 Development of Middle English
 Literature DLB-146
 The Alliterative Morte Arthure and the
 Stanzaic Morte Arthur
 circa 1350-1400. . . . . .DLB-146
 Ancrene Riwle circa 1200-1225 . . . . . .DLB-146
 The Anglo-Saxon Chronicle circa
 890-1154. . . . . .DLB-146
 The Battle of Maldon circa 1000 . . . DLB-146
 Beowulf circa 900-1000 or
 790-825. . . . . .DLB-146; CDBLB-1
 The Blickling Homilies circa 971. . . . .DLB-146
 The Breton Lays
 1300-early fifteenth century DLB-146
 The Castle of Perserverance
 circa 1400-1425. . . . . .DLB-146
 The Celtic Background to Medieval
 English Literature DLB-146
 The Chester Plays circa 1505-1532;
 revisions until 1575. . . . . .DLB-146
 Cursor Mundi circa 1300 . . . . .DLB-146
 The English Language: 410
 to 1500 . . . . .DLB-146
 The Germanic Epic and Old English
 Heroic Poetry: Widsith, Waldere,
 and The Fight at Finnsburg DLB-146
 Judith circa 930 . . . . .DLB-146
 The Matter of England 1240-1400 . . .DLB-146
 The Matter of Rome early twelfth to
 late fifteenth centuries DLB-146

Middle English Literature:
 An Introduction DLB-146
The Middle English Lyric. DLB-146
Morality Plays: Mankind circa 1450-1500
 and Everyman circa 1500 . . . . . . .DLB-146
N-Town Plays circa 1468 to early
 sixteenth century DLB-146
Old English Literature:
 An Introduction DLB-146
Old English Riddles
 eighth to tenth centuries DLB-146
The Owl and the Nightingale
 circa 1189-1199. . . . . .DLB-146
The Paston Letters 1422-1509. . . . . . . .DLB-146
The Seafarer circa 970 . . . . .DLB-146
The South English Legendary circa
 thirteenth to fifteenth centuries DLB-146
The British Review and London Critical
 Journal 1811-1825 . . . . .DLB-110
Brito, Aristeo 1942- DLB-122
Brittain, Vera 1893-1970 . . . . .DLB-191
Briusov, Valerii Iakovlevich
 1873-1924 . . . . .DLB-295
Brizeux, Auguste 1803-1858 . . . . .DLB-217
Broadway Publishing Company DLB-46
Broch, Hermann
 1886-1951 . . . . DLB-85, 124; CDWLB-2
Brochu, André 1942- DLB-53
Brock, Edwin 1927-1997 . . . . .DLB-40
Brockes, Barthold Heinrich 1680-1747 . . .DLB-168
Brod, Max 1884-1968 . . . . .DLB-81
Brodber, Erna 1940- DLB-157
Brodhead, John R. 1814-1873 . . . . .DLB-30
Brodkey, Harold 1930-1996 . . . . .DLB-130
Brodsky, Joseph (Iosif Aleksandrovich
 Brodsky) 1940-1996 . . . . DLB-285; Y-87
 Nobel Lecture 1987. . . . . .Y-87
Brodsky, Michael 1948- DLB-244
Broeg, Bob 1918- DLB-171
Brøgger, Suzanne 1944- DLB-214
Brome, Richard circa 1590-1652 . . . . .DLB-58
Brome, Vincent 1910- DLB-155
Bromfield, Louis 1896-1956 . . . . DLB-4, 9, 86
Bromige, David 1933- DLB-193
Broner, E. M. 1930- DLB-28
 Tribute to Bernard Malamud Y-86
Bronk, William 1918-1999 . . . . .DLB-165
Bronnen, Arnolt 1895-1959 . . . . .DLB-124
Brontë, Anne 1820-1849 . . . . .DLB-21, 199
Brontë, Charlotte
 1816-1855 . . . . . . .DLB-21, 159, 199; CDBLB-4
Brontë, Emily
 1818-1848 . . . . . . DLB-21, 32, 199; CDBLB-4
The Brontë Society Y-98
Brook, Stephen 1947- DLB-204
Brook Farm 1841-1847 . . . . . . .DLB-1; 223; DS-5
Brooke, Frances 1724-1789 . . . . .DLB-39, 99
Brooke, Henry 1703?-1783 . . . . .DLB-39

Brooke, L. Leslie 1862-1940 .... DLB-141

Brooke, Margaret, Ranee of Sarawak
  1849-1936 .... DLB-174

Brooke, Rupert
  1887-1915 .... DLB-19, 216; CDBLB-6

  The Friends of the Dymock Poets Y-00

Brooker, Bertram 1888-1955 .... DLB-88

Brooke-Rose, Christine 1923- DLB-14, 231

Brookner, Anita 1928- DLB-194; Y-87

Brooks, Charles Timothy 1813-1883 .. DLB-1, 243

Brooks, Cleanth 1906-1994 .... DLB-63; Y-94

  Tribute to Katherine Anne Porter Y-80

  Tribute to Walker Percy Y-90

Brooks, Gwendolyn
  1917-2000 .... DLB-5, 76, 165; CDALB-1

  Tribute to Julian Mayfield Y-84

Brooks, Jeremy 1926- DLB-14

Brooks, Mel 1926- DLB-26

Brooks, Noah 1830-1903 .... DLB-42; DS-13

Brooks, Richard 1912-1992 .... DLB-44

Brooks, Van Wyck 1886-1963 ... DLB-45, 63, 103

Brophy, Brigid 1929-1995 .... DLB-14, 70, 271

Brophy, John 1899-1965............. DLB-191

Brorson, Hans Adolph 1694-1764 ...... DLB-300

Brossard, Chandler 1922-1993.......... DLB-16

Brossard, Nicole 1943- DLB-53

Broster, Dorothy Kathleen 1877-1950.... DLB-160

Brother Antoninus (see Everson, William)

Brotherton, Lord 1856-1930........... DLB-184

Brougham, John 1810-1880 .... DLB-11

Brougham and Vaux, Henry Peter
  Brougham, Baron 1778-1868 ... DLB-110, 158

Broughton, James 1913-1999 .... DLB-5

Broughton, Rhoda 1840-1920 .... DLB-18

Broun, Heywood 1888-1939 .... DLB-29, 171

Browder, Earl 1891-1973 .... DLB-303

Brown, Alice 1856-1948 .... DLB-78

Brown, Bob 1886-1959 .... DLB-4, 45; DS-15

Brown, Cecil 1943- DLB-33

Brown, Charles Brockden
  1771-1810 .... DLB-37, 59, 73; CDALB-2

Brown, Christy 1932-1981 .... DLB-14

Brown, Dee 1908-2002 .... Y-80

Brown, Frank London 1927-1962 .... DLB-76

Brown, Fredric 1906-1972 .... DLB-8

Brown, George Mackay
  1921-1996 .... DLB-14, 27, 139, 271

Brown, Harry 1917-1986 .... DLB-26

Brown, Ian 1945- DLB-310

Brown, Larry 1951- DLB-234, 292

Brown, Lew 1893-1958 .... DLB-265

Brown, Marcia 1918- DLB-61

Brown, Margaret Wise 1910-1952 ...... DLB-22

Brown, Morna Doris (see Ferrars, Elizabeth)

Brown, Oliver Madox 1855-1874........ DLB-21

Brown, Sterling 1901-1989 ...... DLB-48, 51, 63

Brown, T. E. 1830-1897 .... DLB-35

Brown, Thomas Alexander (see Boldrewood, Rolf)

Brown, Warren 1894-1978............. DLB-241

Brown, William Hill 1765-1793 .... DLB-37

Brown, William Wells
  1815-1884 .... DLB-3, 50, 183, 248

Brown University
  The Festival of Vanguard Narrative Y-93

Browne, Charles Farrar 1834-1867....... DLB-11

Browne, Frances 1816-1879 .... DLB-199

Browne, Francis Fisher 1843-1913 .... DLB-79

Browne, Howard 1908-1999 .... DLB-226

Browne, J. Ross 1821-1875............. DLB-202

Browne, Michael Dennis 1940- DLB-40

Browne, Sir Thomas 1605-1682........ DLB-151

Browne, William, of Tavistock
  1590-1645 .... DLB-121

Browne, Wynyard 1911-1964 ..... DLB-13, 233

Browne and Nolan DLB-106

Brownell, W. C. 1851-1928 .... DLB-71

Browning, Elizabeth Barrett
  1806-1861 .... DLB-32, 199; CDBLB-4

Browning, Robert
  1812-1889 .... DLB-32, 163; CDBLB-4

  Essay on Chatterton DLB-32

  Introductory Essay: *Letters of Percy
  Bysshe Shelley* (1852) DLB-32

  "The Novel in [Robert Browning's]
  'The Ring and the Book'" (1912),
  by Henry James.................. DLB-32

Brownjohn, Allan 1931- DLB-40

  Tribute to John Betjeman.............. Y-84

Brownson, Orestes Augustus
  1803-1876.........DLB-1, 59, 73, 243; DS-5

Bruccoli, Matthew J. 1931- DLB-103

  Joseph [Heller] and George [V. Higgins] ... Y-99

  Response [to Busch on Fitzgerald] Y-96

  Tribute to Albert Erskine............. Y-93

  Tribute to Charles E. Feinberg......... Y-88

  Working with Fredson Bowers Y-91

Bruce, Charles 1906-1971.............. DLB-68

Bruce, John Edward 1856-1924

  Three Documents [African American
  poets].................... DLB-50

Bruce, Leo 1903-1979 .... DLB-77

Bruce, Mary Grant 1878-1958 .... DLB-230

Bruce, Philip Alexander 1856-1933 ...... DLB-47

Bruce-Novoa, Juan 1944- DLB-82

Bruckman, Clyde 1894-1955 .... DLB-26

Bruckner, Ferdinand 1891-1958 .... DLB-118

Brundage, John Herbert (see Herbert, John)

Brunner, John 1934-1995 .... DLB-261

  Tribute to Theodore Sturgeon.......... Y-85

Brutus, Dennis
  1924- DLB-117, 225; CDWLB-3

Bryan, C. D. B. 1936- DLB-185

Bryan, William Jennings 1860-1925..... DLB-303

Bryant, Arthur 1899-1985 .... DLB-149

Bryant, William Cullen 1794-1878
  .... DLB-3, 43, 59, 189, 250; CDALB-2

Bryce, James 1838-1922 .... DLB-166, 190

Bryce Echenique, Alfredo
  1939- DLB-145; CDWLB-3

Bryden, Bill 1942- DLB-233

Brydges, Sir Samuel Egerton
  1762-1837.................. DLB-107, 142

Bryskett, Lodowick 1546?-1612........ DLB-167

Buchan, John 1875-1940......... DLB-34, 70, 156

Buchanan, George 1506-1582 .... DLB-132

Buchanan, Robert 1841-1901........ DLB-18, 35

  "The Fleshly School of Poetry and
  Other Phenomena of the Day"
  (1872) DLB-35

  "The Fleshly School of Poetry:
  Mr. D. G. Rossetti" (1871),
  by Thomas Maitland.......... DLB-35

Buchler, Justus 1914-1991 .... DLB-279

Buchman, Sidney 1902-1975 .... DLB-26

Buchner, Augustus 1591-1661 .... DLB-164

Büchner, Georg
  1813-1837............ DLB-133; CDWLB-2

Bucholtz, Andreas Heinrich 1607-1671.... DLB-168

Buck, Pearl S. 1892-1973 .. DLB-9, 102; CDALB-7

Bucke, Charles 1781-1846 .... DLB-110

Bucke, Richard Maurice 1837-1902 ...... DLB-99

Buckingham, Edwin 1810-1833 .... DLB-73

Buckingham, Joseph Tinker 1779-1861 ... DLB-73

Buckler, Ernest 1908-1984 .... DLB-68

Buckley, Vincent 1925-1988............ DLB-289

Buckley, William F., Jr. 1925- DLB-137; Y-80

  Publisher's Statement From the
  Initial Issue of *National Review*
  (19 November 1955) DLB-137

Buckminster, Joseph Stevens
  1784-1812...................... DLB-37

Buckner, Robert 1906- DLB-26

Budd, Thomas ?-1698 .... DLB-24

Budrys, A. J. 1931- DLB-8

Buechner, Frederick 1926- Y-80

Buell, John 1927- DLB-53

Buenaventura, Enrique 1925-2003...... DLB-305

Bufalino, Gesualdo 1920-1996 .... DLB-196

Buffon, Georges-Louis Leclerc de
  1707-1788 .... DLB-313

Job Buffum [publishing house] DLB-49

Bugnet, Georges 1879-1981 .... DLB-92

al-Buhturi 821-897 .... DLB-311

Buies, Arthur 1840-1901 .... DLB-99

Bukiet, Melvin Jules 1953- DLB-299

Bukowski, Charles 1920-1994 ....DLB-5, 130, 169

Bulatović, Miodrag
  1930-1991 ....DLB-181; CDWLB-4

Bulgakov, Mikhail Afanas'evich
  1891-1940 ....DLB-272

Bulgarin, Faddei Veneediktovich
  1789-1859..................... DLB-198

Bulger, Bozeman 1877-1932 ....DLB-171

Bull, Olaf 1883-1933 ....DLB-297
Bullein, William between 1520 and 1530-1576 ....DLB-167
Bullins, Ed 1935- DLB-7, 38, 249
Bulosan, Carlos 1911-1956 ....DLB-312
Bulwer, John 1606-1656 ....DLB-236
Bulwer-Lytton, Edward (also Edward Bulwer) 1803-1873 ....DLB-21
"On Art in Fiction "(1838) DLB-21
Bumpus, Jerry 1937- Y-81
Bunce and Brother...................DLB-49
Bunner, H. C. 1855-1896 .... DLB-78, 79
Bunting, Basil 1900-1985...............DLB-20
Buntline, Ned (Edward Zane Carroll Judson) 1821-1886 ....DLB-186
Bunyan, John 1628-1688 ..... DLB-39; CDBLB-2
The Author's Apology for His Book....................DLB-39
Burch, Robert 1925- DLB-52
Burciaga, José Antonio 1940- DLB-82
Burdekin, Katharine (Murray Constantine) 1896-1963 ....DLB-255
Bürger, Gottfried August 1747-1794.......DLB-94
Burgess, Anthony (John Anthony Burgess Wilson) 1917-1993 ......DLB-14, 194, 261; CDBLB-8
The Anthony Burgess Archive at the Harry Ransom Humanities Research Center Y-98
Anthony Burgess's 99 Novels: An Opinion Poll Y-84
Burgess, Gelett 1866-1951 ....DLB-11
Burgess, John W. 1844-1931 ....DLB-47
Burgess, Thornton W. 1874-1965 ....DLB-22
Burgess, Stringer and Company DLB-49
Burgos, Julia de 1914-1953 ....DLB-290
Burick, Si 1909-1986 ....DLB-171
Burk, John Daly circa 1772-1808 ....DLB-37
Burk, Ronnie 1955- DLB-209
Burke, Edmund 1729?-1797 ....DLB-104, 252
Burke, James Lee 1936- DLB-226
Burke, Johnny 1908-1964 ....DLB-265
Burke, Kenneth 1897-1993...........DLB-45, 63
Burke, Thomas 1886-1945 ....DLB-197
Burley, Dan 1907-1962 ....DLB-241
Burley, W. J. 1914- DLB-276
Burlingame, Edward Livermore 1848-1922 ....DLB-79
Burman, Carina 1960- DLB-257
Burnet, Gilbert 1643-1715 ....DLB-101
Burnett, Frances Hodgson 1849-1924 .... DLB-42, 141; DS-13, 14
Burnett, W. R. 1899-1982 ....DLB-9, 226
Burnett, Whit 1899-1973 ....DLB-137
Burney, Fanny 1752-1840 ....DLB-39
Dedication, The Wanderer (1814) DLB-39
Preface to Evelina (1778)............DLB-39
Burns, Alan 1929- DLB-14, 194
Burns, Joanne 1945- DLB-289

Burns, John Horne 1916-1953............ Y-85
Burns, Robert 1759-1796 .....DLB-109; CDBLB-3
Burns and Oates DLB-106
Burnshaw, Stanley 1906- DLB-48; Y-97
James Dickey and Stanley Burnshaw Correspondence Y-02
Review of Stanley Burnshaw: The Collected Poems and Selected Prose........................ Y-02
Tribute to Robert Penn Warren Y-89
Burr, C. Chauncey 1815?-1883..........DLB-79
Burr, Esther Edwards 1732-1758 ....DLB-200
Burroughs, Edgar Rice 1875-1950 ....DLB-8
The Burroughs Bibliophiles Y-98
Burroughs, John 1837-1921 .... DLB-64, 275
Burroughs, Margaret T. G. 1917- DLB-41
Burroughs, William S., Jr. 1947-1981......DLB-16
Burroughs, William Seward 1914-1997 .... DLB-2, 8, 16, 152, 237; Y-81, 97
Burroway, Janet 1936- DLB-6
Burt, Maxwell Struthers 1882-1954 ....DLB-86; DS-16
A. L. Burt and Company...............DLB-49
Burton, Hester 1913- DLB-161
Burton, Isabel Arundell 1831-1896 ......DLB-166
Burton, Miles (see Rhode, John)
Burton, Richard Francis 1821-1890 ....DLB-55, 166, 184
Burton, Robert 1577-1640 ....DLB-151
Burton, Virginia Lee 1909-1968 ....DLB-22
Burton, William Evans 1804-1860........DLB-73
Burwell, Adam Hood 1790-1849 ....DLB-99
Bury, Lady Charlotte 1775-1861 ....DLB-116
Busch, Frederick 1941- DLB-6, 218
Excerpts from Frederick Busch's USC Remarks [on F. Scott Fitzgerald] Y-96
Tribute to James Laughlin Y-97
Tribute to Raymond Carver........... Y-88
Busch, Niven 1903-1991 ....DLB-44
Bushnell, Horace 1802-1876 .... DS-13
Business & Literature
The Claims of Business and Literature: An Undergraduate Essay by Maxwell Perkins................. Y-01
Bussières, Arthur de 1877-1913 ....DLB-92
Butler, Charles circa 1560-1647 ....DLB-236
Butler, Guy 1918- DLB-225
Butler, Joseph 1692-1752 ....DLB-252
Butler, Josephine Elizabeth 1828-1906 ....DLB-190
Butler, Juan 1942-1981 ....DLB-53
Butler, Judith 1956- DLB-246
Butler, Octavia E. 1947- DLB-33
Butler, Pierce 1884-1953 ....DLB-187
Butler, Robert Olen 1945- DLB-173
Butler, Samuel 1613-1680 ....DLB-101, 126
Butler, Samuel 1835-1902 .... DLB-18, 57, 174; CDBLB-5

Butler, William Francis 1838-1910 ......DLB-166
E. H. Butler and Company DLB-49
Butor, Michel 1926- DLB-83
Nathaniel Butter [publishing house]......DLB-170
Butterworth, Hezekiah 1839-1905........DLB-42
Buttitta, Ignazio 1899-1997 ....DLB-114
Butts, Mary 1890-1937 ....DLB-240
Buzo, Alex 1944- DLB-289
Buzzati, Dino 1906-1972 ....DLB-177
Byars, Betsy 1928- DLB-52
Byatt, A. S. 1936- DLB-14, 194
Byles, Mather 1707-1788.................DLB-24
Henry Bynneman [publishing house] DLB-170
Bynner, Witter 1881-1968...............DLB-54
Byrd, William circa 1543-1623 ....DLB-172
Byrd, William, II 1674-1744.........DLB-24, 140
Byrne, John Keyes (see Leonard, Hugh)
Byron, George Gordon, Lord 1788-1824 ....DLB-96, 110; CDBLB-3
The Byron Society of America Y-00
Byron, Robert 1905-1941 ....DLB-195

C

Caballero Bonald, José Manuel 1926- DLB-108
Cabañero, Eladio 1930- DLB-134
Cabell, James Branch 1879-1958 .... DLB-9, 78
Cabeza de Baca, Manuel 1853-1915 .....DLB-122
Cabeza de Baca Gilbert, Fabiola 1898- DLB-122
Cable, George Washington 1844-1925 .... DLB-12, 74; DS-13
Cable, Mildred 1878-1952 ....DLB-195
Cabral, Manuel del 1907-1999 ....DLB-283
Cabral de Melo Neto, João 1920-1999 ....DLB-307
Cabrera, Lydia 1900-1991 ....DLB-145
Cabrera Infante, Guillermo 1929- DLB-113; CDWLB-3
Cabrujas, José Ignacio 1937-1995........DLB-305
Cadell [publishing house]................DLB-154
Cady, Edwin H. 1917- DLB-103
Caedmon flourished 658-680 ....DLB-146
Caedmon School circa 660-899 ....DLB-146
Caesar, Irving 1895-1996 ....DLB-265
Cafés, Brasseries, and Bistros DS-15
Cage, John 1912-1992 ....DLB-193
Cahan, Abraham 1860-1951 .... DLB-9, 25, 28
Cahn, Sammy 1913-1993 ....DLB-265
Cain, George 1943- DLB-33
Cain, James M. 1892-1977.............DLB-226
Cain, Paul (Peter Ruric, George Sims) 1902-1966 ....DLB-306
Caird, Edward 1835-1908 ....DLB-262
Caird, Mona 1854-1932 ....DLB-197
Čaks, Aleksandrs 1901-1950 .... DLB-220; CDWLB-4

Caldecott, Randolph 1846-1886 . . . . DLB-163	Campbell, Thomas 1777-1844 . . . . . . DLB-93, 144	Carey and Hart DLB-49
John Calder Limited [Publishing house] DLB-112	Campbell, William Edward (see March, William)	Carlell, Lodowick 1602-1675 . . . . DLB-58
	Campbell, William Wilfred 1858-1918 . . . DLB-92	Carleton, William 1794-1869 . . . . DLB-159
Calderón de la Barca, Fanny 1804-1882 . . . . DLB-183	Campion, Edmund 1539-1581 . . . . DLB-167	G. W. Carleton [publishing house] DLB-49
Caldwell, Ben 1937- DLB-38	Campion, Thomas 1567-1620 . . . . DLB-58, 172; CDBLB-1	Carlile, Richard 1790-1843 . . . . DLB-110, 158
Caldwell, Erskine 1903-1987 . . . . DLB-9, 86	Campo, Rafael 1964- DLB-282	Carlson, Ron 1947- DLB-244
H. M. Caldwell Company DLB-49	Campton, David 1924- DLB-245	Carlyle, Jane Welsh 1801-1866 . . . . DLB-55
Caldwell, Taylor 1900-1985 . . . . DS-17	Camus, Albert 1913-1960 . . . . DLB-72	Carlyle, Thomas 1795-1881 . . . . DLB-55, 144; CDBLB-3
Calhoun, John C. 1782-1850 . . . . DLB-3, 248	Camus, Jean-Pierre 1584-1652 . . . . DLB-268	
Călinescu, George 1899-1965 . . . . DLB-220	The Canadian Publishers' Records Database . . Y-96	"The Hero as Man of Letters: Johnson, Rousseau, Burns" (1841) [excerpt] DLB-57
Calisher, Hortense 1911- DLB-2, 218	Canby, Henry Seidel 1878-1961 . . . . DLB-91	
Calkins, Mary Whiton 1863-1930 . . . . . . DLB-270	Cancioneros DLB-286	The Hero as Poet. Dante; Shakspeare (1841) DLB-32
Callaghan, Mary Rose 1944- DLB-207	Candelaria, Cordelia 1943- DLB-82	
Callaghan, Morley 1903-1990 . . . . DLB-68; DS-15	Candelaria, Nash 1928- DLB-82	Carman, Bliss 1861-1929 . . . . DLB-92
Callahan, S. Alice 1868-1894 . . . . . . DLB-175, 221	Canetti, Elias 1905-1994 . . . . DLB-85, 124; CDWLB-2	*Carmina Burana* circa 1230 . . . . DLB-138
Callaloo [journal] Y-87		Carnap, Rudolf 1891-1970 . . . . DLB-270
Callimachus circa 305 B.C.-240 B.C. DLB-176	Canham, Erwin Dain 1904-1982 . . . . . . DLB-127	Carnero, Guillermo 1947- DLB-108
Calmer, Edgar 1907- DLB-4	Canitz, Friedrich Rudolph Ludwig von 1654-1699 . . . . DLB-168	Carossa, Hans 1878-1956 . . . . DLB-66
Calverley, C. S. 1831-1884 . . . . DLB-35		Carpenter, Humphrey 1946- DLB-155; Y-84, 99
Calvert, George Henry 1803-1889 . . . . DLB-1, 64, 248	Cankar, Ivan 1876-1918 . . . . . DLB-147; CDWLB-4	
	Cannan, Gilbert 1884-1955 . . . . DLB-10, 197	Carpenter, Stephen Cullen ?-1820? DLB-73
Calverton, V. F. (George Goetz) 1900-1940 . . . . DLB-303	Cannan, Joanna 1896-1961 . . . . DLB-191	Carpentier, Alejo 1904-1980 . . . . DLB-113; CDWLB-3
Calvino, Italo 1923-1985 . . . . DLB-196	Cannell, Kathleen 1891-1974 . . . . DLB-4	
Cambridge, Ada 1844-1926 . . . . DLB-230	Cannell, Skipwith 1887-1957 . . . . DLB-45	Carr, Emily (1871-1945) DLB-68
Cambridge Press DLB-49	Canning, George 1770-1827 . . . . DLB-158	Carr, John Dickson 1906-1977 . . . . DLB-306
Cambridge Songs (Carmina Cantabrigensia) circa 1050 . . . . DLB-148	Cannon, Jimmy 1910-1973 . . . . DLB-171	Carr, Marina 1964- DLB-245
	Cano, Daniel 1947- DLB-209	Carr, Virginia Spencer 1929- DLB-111; Y-00
Cambridge University Cambridge and the Apostles DS-5	Old Dogs / New Tricks? New Technologies, the Canon, and the Structure of the Profession Y-02	Carrera Andrade, Jorge 1903-1978 . . . . . . DLB-283
		Carrier, Roch 1937- DLB-53
Cambridge University Press DLB-170	Cantú, Norma Elia 1947- DLB-209	Carrillo, Adolfo 1855-1926 . . . . DLB-122
Camden, William 1551-1623 . . . . DLB-172	Cantwell, Robert 1908-1978 . . . . DLB-9	Carroll, Gladys Hasty 1904- DLB-9
Camden House: An Interview with James Hardin Y-92	Jonathan Cape and Harrison Smith [publishing house] DLB-46	Carroll, John 1735-1815 . . . . DLB-37
		Carroll, John 1809-1884 . . . . DLB-99
Cameron, Eleanor 1912-2000 . . . . DLB-52	Jonathan Cape Limited DLB-112	Carroll, Lewis 1832-1898 . . . . . . DLB-18, 163, 178; CDBLB-4
Cameron, George Frederick 1854-1885 . . . . DLB-99	Čapek, Karel 1890-1938 . . . . DLB-215; CDWLB-4	
	Capen, Joseph 1658-1725 . . . . DLB-24	The Lewis Carroll Centenary Y-98
Cameron, Lucy Lyttelton 1781-1858 . . . . DLB-163	Capes, Bernard 1854-1918 . . . . DLB-156	The Lewis Carroll Society of North America Y-00
Cameron, Peter 1959- DLB-234	Capote, Truman 1924-1984 . . . . . . DLB-2, 185, 227; Y-80, 84; CDALB-1	
Cameron, William Bleasdell 1862-1951 . . . DLB-99		Carroll, Paul 1927- DLB-16
Camm, John 1718-1778 . . . . DLB-31	Capps, Benjamin 1922- DLB-256	Carroll, Paul Vincent 1900-1968 . . . . DLB-10
Camões, Luís de 1524-1580 . . . . DLB-287	Caproni, Giorgio 1912-1990 . . . . DLB-128	Carroll and Graf Publishers DLB-46
Camon, Ferdinando 1935- DLB-196	Caragiale, Mateiu Ioan 1885-1936 . . . . . . DLB-220	Carruth, Hayden 1921- DLB-5, 165
Camp, Walter 1859-1925 . . . . DLB-241	Carballido, Emilio 1925- DLB-305	Tribute to James Dickey Y-97
Campana, Dino 1885-1932 . . . . DLB-114	Cardarelli, Vincenzo 1887-1959 . . . . DLB-114	Tribute to Raymond Carver Y-88
Campbell, Bebe Moore 1950- DLB-227	Cardenal, Ernesto 1925- DLB-290	Carryl, Charles E. 1841-1920 . . . . DLB-42
Campbell, David 1915-1979 . . . . DLB-260	Cárdenas, Reyes 1948- DLB-122	Carson, Anne 1950- DLB-193
Campbell, Gabrielle Margaret Vere (see Shearing, Joseph, and Bowen, Marjorie)	Cardinal, Marie 1929-2001 . . . . DLB-83	Carson, Rachel 1907-1964 . . . . DLB-275
	Cardoza y Aragón, Luis 1901-1992 . . . . . DLB-290	Carswell, Catherine 1879-1946 . . . . DLB-36
Campbell, James Dykes 1838-1895 . . . . . DLB-144	Carew, Jan 1920- DLB-157	Cartagena, Alfonso de ca. 1384-1456 . . . . DLB-286
Campbell, James Edwin 1867-1896 . . . . . . DLB-50	Carew, Thomas 1594 or 1595-1640 . . . . DLB-126	Cartagena, Teresa de 1425?-? DLB-286
Campbell, John 1653-1728 . . . . DLB-43	Carey, Henry circa 1687-1689-1743 . . . . . DLB-84	Cărtărescu, Mirea 1956- DLB-232
Campbell, John W., Jr. 1910-1971 . . . . DLB-8	Carey, Mathew 1760-1839 . . . . DLB-37, 73	Carter, Angela 1940-1992 . . . . . . DLB-14, 207, 261
Campbell, Ramsey 1946- DLB-261	M. Carey and Company DLB-49	Carter, Elizabeth 1717-1806 . . . . DLB-109
Campbell, Robert 1927-2000 . . . . DLB-306	Carey, Peter 1943- DLB-289	Carter, Henry (see Leslie, Frank)
Campbell, Roy 1901-1957 . . . . DLB-20, 225		Carter, Hodding, Jr. 1907-1972 . . . . DLB-127
		Carter, Jared 1939- DLB-282

Carter, John 1905-1975 . . . . DLB-201
Carter, Landon 1710-1778 . . . . DLB-31
Carter, Lin 1930-1988 . . . . Y-81
Carter, Martin 1927-1997. . . . DLB-117; CDWLB-3
Carter, Robert, and Brothers DLB-49
Carter and Hendee DLB-49
Cartwright, Jim 1958- DLB-245
Cartwright, John 1740-1824. . . . . DLB-158
Cartwright, William circa 1611-1643. . . . . DLB-126
Caruthers, William Alexander
 1802-1846 . . . . DLB-3, 248
Carver, Jonathan 1710-1780 . . . . DLB-31
Carver, Raymond 1938-1988 . . DLB-130; Y-83, 88
 First Strauss "Livings" Awarded to Cynthia
  Ozick and Raymond Carver
  An Interview with Raymond Carver . . . Y-83
Carvic, Heron 1917?-1980 . . . . DLB-276
Cary, Alice 1820-1871 . . . . DLB-202
Cary, Joyce 1888-1957 . . . . DLB-15, 100; CDBLB-6
Cary, Patrick 1623?-1657 . . . . DLB-131
Casal, Julián del 1863-1893 . . . . DLB-283
Case, John 1540-1600 . . . . DLB-281
Casey, Gavin 1907-1964 . . . . DLB-260
Casey, Juanita 1925- DLB-14
Casey, Michael 1947- DLB-5
Cassady, Carolyn 1923- DLB-16
 "As I See It" DLB-16
Cassady, Neal 1926-1968 . . . . DLB-16, 237
Cassell and Company DLB-106
Cassell Publishing Company DLB-49
Cassill, R. V. 1919- DLB-6, 218; Y-02
 Tribute to James Dickey Y-97
Cassity, Turner 1929- DLB-105; Y-02
Cassius Dio circa 155/164-post 229 . . . . . . DLB-176
Cassola, Carlo 1917-1987 . . . . DLB-177
Castellano, Olivia 1944- DLB-122
Castellanos, Rosario
 1925-1974 . . . . DLB-113, 290; CDWLB-3
Castelo Branco, Camilo 1825-1890 . . . . . . DLB-287
Castile, Protest Poetry in DLB-286
Castile and Aragon, Vernacular Translations
 in Crowns of 1352-1515 . . . . DLB-286
Castillo, Ana 1953- DLB-122, 227
Castillo, Rafael C. 1950- DLB-209
The Castle of Perseverance
 circa 1400-1425 . . . . DLB-146
Castlemon, Harry (see Fosdick, Charles Austin)
Castro, Consuelo de 1946- DLB-307
Castro Alves, Antônio de 1847-1871 . . . . . DLB-307
Čašule, Kole 1921- DLB-181
Caswall, Edward 1814-1878. . . . . DLB-32
Catacalos, Rosemary 1944- DLB-122
Cather, Willa 1873-1947
 . . . . DLB-9, 54, 78, 256; DS-1; CDALB-3
 The Willa Cather Pioneer Memorial
  and Education Foundation Y-00

Catherine II (Ekaterina Alekseevna), "The Great,"
 Empress of Russia 1729-1796 . . . . DLB-150
Catherwood, Mary Hartwell 1847-1902 . . . DLB-78
Catledge, Turner 1901-1983 . . . . DLB-127
Catlin, George 1796-1872 . . . . DLB-186, 189
Cato the Elder 234 B.C.-149 B.C. DLB-211
Cattafi, Bartolo 1922-1979 . . . . DLB-128
Catton, Bruce 1899-1978 . . . . DLB-17
Catullus circa 84 B.C.-54 B.C.
 . . . . DLB-211; CDWLB-1
Causley, Charles 1917- DLB-27
Caute, David 1936- DLB-14, 231
Cavendish, Duchess of Newcastle,
 Margaret Lucas
 1623?-1673 . . . . DLB-131, 252, 281
Cawein, Madison 1865-1914 . . . . DLB-54
William Caxton [publishing house] DLB-170
The Caxton Printers, Limited DLB-46
Caylor, O. P. 1849-1897 . . . . DLB-241
Caylus, Marthe-Marguerite de
 1671-1729 . . . . DLB-313
Cayrol, Jean 1911- DLB-83
Cecil, Lord David 1902-1986 . . . . DLB-155
Cela, Camilo José 1916-2002 . . . . Y-89
 Nobel Lecture 1989 . . . . Y-89
Celan, Paul 1920-1970 . . . . . . DLB-69; CDWLB-2
Celati, Gianni 1937- DLB-196
Celaya, Gabriel 1911-1991 . . . . DLB-108
Céline, Louis-Ferdinand 1894-1961 . . . . . . DLB-72
Celtis, Conrad 1459-1508 . . . . DLB-179
Cendrars, Blaise 1887-1961 . . . . DLB-258
The Steinbeck Centennial Y-02
Censorship
 The Island Trees Case: A Symposium on
  School Library Censorship Y-82
Center for Bibliographical Studies and
 Research at the University of
 California, Riverside Y-91
Center for Book Research Y-84
The Center for the Book in the Library
 of Congress Y-93
 A New Voice: The Center for the
  Book's First Five Years Y-83
Centlivre, Susanna 1669?-1723 . . . . DLB-84
The Centre for Writing, Publishing and
 Printing History at the University
 of Reading Y-00
The Century Company DLB-49
A Century of Poetry, a Lifetime of Collecting:
 J. M. Edelstein's Collection of
 Twentieth-Century American Poetry Y-02
Cernuda, Luis 1902-1963 . . . . DLB-134
Cerruto, Oscar 1912-1981 . . . . DLB-283
Cervantes, Lorna Dee 1954- DLB-82
de Céspedes, Alba 1911-1997 . . . . DLB-264
Ch., T. (see Marchenko, Anastasiia Iakovlevna)
Cha, Theresa Hak Kyung 1951-1982 . . . . DLB-312
Chaadaev, Petr Iakovlevich
 1794-1856 . . . . DLB-198

Chabon, Michael 1963- DLB-278
Chacel, Rosa 1898-1994 . . . . DLB-134
Chacón, Eusebio 1869-1948 . . . . DLB-82
Chacón, Felipe Maximiliano 1873-? DLB-82
Chadwick, Henry 1824-1908 . . . . DLB-241
Chadwyck-Healey's Full-Text Literary Databases:
 Editing Commercial Databases of
 Primary Literary Texts Y-95
Challans, Eileen Mary (see Renault, Mary)
Chalmers, George 1742-1825 . . . . DLB-30
Chaloner, Sir Thomas 1520-1565 . . . . DLB-167
Chamberlain, Samuel S. 1851-1916 . . . . . . DLB-25
Chamberland, Paul 1939- DLB-60
Chamberlin, William Henry 1897-1969 . . . . DLB-29
Chambers, Charles Haddon 1860-1921 . . . DLB-10
Chambers, María Cristina (see Mena, María Cristina)
Chambers, Robert W. 1865-1933 . . . . DLB-202
W. and R. Chambers
 [publishing house] DLB-106
Chambers, Whittaker 1901-1961 . . . . DLB-303
Chamfort, Sébastien-Roch Nicolas de
 1740?-1794 . . . . DLB-313
Chamisso, Adelbert von 1781-1838 . . . . . . DLB-90
Champfleury 1821-1889 . . . . DLB-119
Chan, Jeffery Paul 1942- DLB-312
Chandler, Harry 1864-1944 . . . . DLB-29
Chandler, Norman 1899-1973 . . . . DLB-127
Chandler, Otis 1927- DLB-127
Chandler, Raymond
 1888-1959 . . . . DLB-226, 253; DS-6; CDALB-5
 Raymond Chandler Centenary Y-88
Chang, Diana 1934- DLB-312
Channing, Edward 1856-1931 . . . . DLB-17
Channing, Edward Tyrrell
 1790-1856 . . . . DLB-1, 59, 235
Channing, William Ellery
 1780-1842 . . . . DLB-1, 59, 235
Channing, William Ellery, II
 1817-1901 . . . . DLB-1, 223
Channing, William Henry
 1810-1884 . . . . DLB-1, 59, 243
Chapelain, Jean 1595-1674 . . . . DLB-268
Chaplin, Charlie 1889-1977 . . . . DLB-44
Chapman, George
 1559 or 1560-1634 . . . . DLB-62, 121
Chapman, Olive Murray 1892-1977 . . . . . DLB-195
Chapman, R. W. 1881-1960 . . . . DLB-201
Chapman, William 1850-1917 . . . . DLB-99
John Chapman [publishing house] DLB-106
Chapman and Hall [publishing house] . . . DLB-106
Chappell, Fred 1936- DLB-6, 105
 "A Detail in a Poem" DLB-105
 Tribute to Peter Taylor Y-94
Chappell, William 1582-1649 . . . . DLB-236
Char, René 1907-1988 . . . . DLB-258
Charbonneau, Jean 1875-1960 . . . . DLB-92
Charbonneau, Robert 1911-1967 . . . . DLB-68

Charles, Gerda 1914- DLB-14
William Charles [publishing house] DLB-49
Charles d'Orléans 1394-1465 .... DLB-208
Charley (see Mann, Charles)
Charrière, Isabelle de 1740-1805 .... DLB-313
Charskaia, Lidiia 1875-1937 .... DLB-295
Charteris, Leslie 1907-1993 .... DLB-77
Chartier, Alain circa 1385-1430 .... DLB-208
Charyn, Jerome 1937- Y-83
Chase, Borden 1900-1971 .... DLB-26
Chase, Edna Woolman 1877-1957 ..... DLB-91
Chase, James Hadley (René Raymond) 1906-1985 .... DLB-276
Chase, Mary Coyle 1907-1981 .... DLB-228
Chase-Riboud, Barbara 1936- DLB-33
Chateaubriand, François-René de 1768-1848 .... DLB-119
Châtelet, Gabrielle-Emilie Du 1706-1749 .... DLB-313
Chatterton, Thomas 1752-1770 .... DLB-109
  Essay on Chatterton (1842), by Robert Browning DLB-32
Chatto and Windus DLB-106
Chatwin, Bruce 1940-1989 .... DLB-194, 204
Chaucer, Geoffrey 1340?-1400 .... DLB-146; CDBLB-1
  New Chaucer Society Y-00
Chaudhuri, Amit 1962- DLB-267
Chauncy, Charles 1705-1787 .... DLB-24
Chauveau, Pierre-Joseph-Olivier 1820-1890 .... DLB-99
Chávez, Denise 1948- DLB-122
Chávez, Fray Angélico 1910-1996 .... DLB-82
Chayefsky, Paddy 1923-1981 ..... DLB-7, 44; Y-81
Cheesman, Evelyn 1881-1969 .... DLB-195
Cheever, Ezekiel 1615-1708 .... DLB-24
Cheever, George Barrell 1807-1890 ..... DLB-59
Cheever, John 1912-1982
  .... DLB-2, 102, 227; Y-80, 82; CDALB-1
Cheever, Susan 1943- Y-82
Cheke, Sir John 1514-1557 .... DLB-132
Chekhov, Anton Pavlovich 1860-1904 ... DLB-277
Chelsea House DLB-46
Chênedollé, Charles de 1769-1833 ...... DLB-217
Cheney, Brainard
  Tribute to Caroline Gordon Y-81
Cheney, Ednah Dow 1824-1904 ..... DLB-1, 223
Cheney, Harriet Vaughan 1796-1889 .... DLB-99
Chénier, Marie-Joseph 1764-1811 ...... DLB-192
Chernyshevsky, Nikolai Gavrilovich 1828-1889 .... DLB-238
Cherry, Kelly 1940 .... Y-83
Cherryh, C. J. 1942- Y-80
Chesebro', Caroline 1825-1873 .... DLB-202
Chesney, Sir George Tomkyns 1830-1895 .... DLB-190
Chesnut, Mary Boykin 1823-1886 ..... DLB-239

Chesnutt, Charles Waddell 1858-1932 .... DLB-12, 50, 78
Chesson, Mrs. Nora (see Hopper, Nora)
Chester, Alfred 1928-1971 .... DLB-130
Chester, George Randolph 1869-1924 ... DLB-78
The Chester Plays circa 1505-1532; revisions until 1575 .... DLB-146
Chesterfield, Philip Dormer Stanhope, Fourth Earl of 1694-1773 .... DLB-104
Chesterton, G. K. 1874-1936
  ... DLB-10, 19, 34, 70, 98, 149, 178; CDBLB-6
  "The Ethics of Elfland" (1908) DLB-178
Chettle, Henry circa 1560-circa 1607 .... DLB-136
Cheuse, Alan 1940- DLB-244
Chew, Ada Nield 1870-1945 .... DLB-135
Cheyney, Edward P. 1861-1947 .... DLB-47
Chiang Yee 1903-1977 .... DLB-312
Chiara, Piero 1913-1986 .... DLB-177
Chicanos
  Chicano History DLB-82
  Chicano Language DLB-82
  Chicano Literature: A Bibliography .. DLB-209
  A Contemporary Flourescence of Chicano Literature Y-84
  Literatura Chicanesca: The View From Without DLB-82
Child, Francis James 1825-1896 ... DLB-1, 64, 235
Child, Lydia Maria 1802-1880 ..... DLB-1, 74, 243
Child, Philip 1898-1978 .... DLB-68
Childers, Erskine 1870-1922 .... DLB-70
Children's Literature
  Afterword: Propaganda, Namby-Pamby, and Some Books of Distinction ... DLB-52
  Children's Book Awards and Prizes ... DLB-61
  Children's Book Illustration in the Twentieth Century DLB-61
  Children's Illustrators, 1800-1880 ... DLB-163
  The Harry Potter Phenomenon Y-99
  Pony Stories, Omnibus Essay on DLB-160
  The Reality of One Woman's Dream: The de Grummond Children's Literature Collection Y-99
  School Stories, 1914-1960 .... DLB-160
  The Year in Children's Books Y-92–96, 98–01
  The Year in Children's Literature Y-97
Childress, Alice 1916-1994 .... DLB-7, 38, 249
Childress, Mark 1957- DLB-292
Childs, George W. 1829-1894 .... DLB-23
Chilton Book Company DLB-46
Chin, Frank 1940- DLB-206, 312
Chin, Justin 1969- DLB-312
Chin, Marilyn 1955- DLB-312
Chinweizu 1943- DLB-157
Chitham, Edward 1932- DLB-155
Chittenden, Hiram Martin 1858-1917 .... DLB-47
Chivers, Thomas Holley 1809-1858 .. DLB-3, 248

Chkhartishvili, Grigorii Shalvovich (see Akunin, Boris)
Chocano, José Santos 1875-1934 .... DLB-290
Cholmondeley, Mary 1859-1925 .... DLB-197
Chomsky, Noam 1928- DLB-246
Chopin, Kate 1850-1904 ... DLB-12, 78; CDALB-3
Chopin, René 1885-1953 .... DLB-92
Choquette, Adrienne 1915-1973 .... DLB-68
Choquette, Robert 1905-1991 .... DLB-68
Choyce, Lesley 1951- DLB-251
Chrétien de Troyes circa 1140-circa 1190 .... DLB-208
Christensen, Inger 1935- DLB-214
Christensen, Lars Saabye 1953- DLB-297
The Christian Examiner DLB-1
The Christian Publishing Company DLB-49
Christie, Agatha 1890-1976 .... DLB-13, 77, 245; CDBLB-6
Christine de Pizan circa 1365-circa 1431 .... DLB-208
Christopher, John (Sam Youd) 1922- ... DLB-255
Christus und die Samariterin circa 950 ...... DLB-148
Christy, Howard Chandler 1873-1952 ... DLB-188
Chu, Louis 1915-1970 .... DLB-312
Chukovskaia, Lidiia 1907-1996 .... DLB-302
Chulkov, Mikhail Dmitrievich 1743?-1792 .... DLB-150
Church, Benjamin 1734-1778 .... DLB-31
Church, Francis Pharcellus 1839-1906 ... DLB-79
Church, Peggy Pond 1903-1986 .... DLB-212
Church, Richard 1893-1972 .... DLB-191
Church, William Conant 1836-1917 ..... DLB-79
Churchill, Caryl 1938- DLB-13, 310
Churchill, Charles 1731-1764 .... DLB-109
Churchill, Winston 1871-1947 .... DLB-202
Churchill, Sir Winston 1874-1965 .... DLB-100; DS-16; CDBLB-5
Churchyard, Thomas 1520?-1604 ...... DLB-132
E. Churton and Company DLB-106
Chute, Marchette 1909-1994 .... DLB-103
Ciardi, John 1916-1986 .... DLB-5; Y-86
Cibber, Colley 1671-1757 .... DLB-84
Cicero 106 B.C.-43 B.C. DLB-211, CDWLB-1
Cima, Annalisa 1941- DLB-128
Čingo, Živko 1935-1987 .... DLB-181
Cioran, E. M. 1911-1995 .... DLB-220
Čipkus, Alfonsas (see Nyka-Niliūnas, Alfonsas)
Cirese, Eugenio 1884-1955 .... DLB-114
Cīrulis, Jānis (see Bels, Alberts)
Cisneros, Antonio 1942- DLB-290
Cisneros, Sandra 1954- DLB-122, 152
City Lights Books DLB-46
Civil War (1861–1865)
  Battles and Leaders of the Civil War ... DLB-47
  Official Records of the Rebellion DLB-47
  Recording the Civil War DLB-47

Cixous, Hélène 1937- DLB-83, 242

Clampitt, Amy 1920-1994 ....DLB-105

    Tribute to Alfred A. Knopf Y-84

Clancy, Tom 1947- DLB-227

Clapper, Raymond 1892-1944.........DLB-29

Clare, John 1793-1864 ....DLB-55, 96

Clarendon, Edward Hyde, Earl of
    1609-1674 ....DLB-101

Clark, Alfred Alexander Gordon
    (see Hare, Cyril)

Clark, Ann Nolan 1896- DLB-52

Clark, C. E. Frazer, Jr. 1925-2001 .. DLB-187; Y-01

    C. E. Frazer Clark Jr. and
      Hawthorne Bibliography DLB-269

    The Publications of C. E. Frazer
      Clark Jr. DLB-269

Clark, Catherine Anthony 1892-1977 .....DLB-68

Clark, Charles Heber 1841-1915.........DLB-11

Clark, Davis Wasgatt 1812-1871 ....DLB-79

Clark, Douglas 1919-1993............DLB-276

Clark, Eleanor 1913- DLB-6

Clark, J. P. 1935- DLB-117; CDWLB-3

Clark, Lewis Gaylord
    1808-1873 ....DLB-3, 64, 73, 250

Clark, Mary Higgins 1929- DLB-306

Clark, Walter Van Tilburg
    1909-1971 ....DLB-9, 206

Clark, William 1770-1838 ....DLB-183, 186

Clark, William Andrews, Jr.
    1877-1934 ....DLB-187

C. M. Clark Publishing Company........DLB-46

Clarke, Sir Arthur C. 1917- DLB-261

    Tribute to Theodore Sturgeon Y-85

Clarke, Austin 1896-1974............DLB-10, 20

Clarke, Austin C. 1934- DLB-53, 125

Clarke, Gillian 1937- DLB-40

Clarke, James Freeman
    1810-1888 ....DLB-1, 59, 235; DS-5

Clarke, John circa 1596-1658............DLB-281

Clarke, Lindsay 1939- DLB-231

Clarke, Marcus 1846-1881...............DLB-230

Clarke, Pauline 1921- DLB-161

Clarke, Rebecca Sophia 1833-1906 ......DLB-42

Clarke, Samuel 1675-1729 ....DLB-252

Robert Clarke and Company DLB-49

Clarkson, Thomas 1760-1846 ....DLB-158

Claudel, Paul 1868-1955 ....DLB-192, 258

Claudius, Matthias 1740-1815 ....DLB-97

Clausen, Andy 1943- DLB-16

Claussen, Sophus 1865-1931 ....DLB-300

Clawson, John L. 1865-1933 ....DLB-187

Claxton, Remsen and Haffelfinger DLB-49

Clay, Cassius Marcellus 1810-1903.......DLB-43

Clayton, Richard (see Haggard, William)

Cleage, Pearl 1948- DLB-228

Cleary, Beverly 1916- DLB-52

Cleary, Kate McPhelim 1863-1905 ......DLB-221

Cleaver, Vera 1919-1992 and
    Cleaver, Bill 1920-1981.............DLB-52

Cleeve, Brian 1921- DLB-276

Cleland, John 1710-1789 ....DLB-39

Clemens, Samuel Langhorne (Mark Twain)
    1835-1910 ....DLB-11, 12, 23, 64, 74,
                 186, 189; CDALB-3

    Comments From Authors and Scholars on
      their First Reading of *Huck Finn*......Y-85

    Huck at 100: How Old Is
      Huckleberry Finn? Y-85

    Mark Twain on Perpetual Copyright Y-92

    A New Edition of *Huck Finn* Y-85

Clement, Hal 1922- DLB-8

Clemo, Jack 1916- DLB-27

Clephane, Elizabeth Cecilia 1830-1869 ...DLB-199

Cleveland, John 1613-1658 ....DLB-126

Cliff, Michelle 1946- DLB-157; CDWLB-3

Clifford, Lady Anne 1590-1676.........DLB-151

Clifford, James L. 1901-1978 ....DLB-103

Clifford, Lucy 1853?-1929.....DLB-135, 141, 197

Clift, Charmian 1923-1969 ....DLB-260

Clifton, Lucille 1936- DLB-5, 41

Clines, Francis X. 1938- DLB-185

Clive, Caroline (V) 1801-1873 ....DLB-199

Edward J. Clode [publishing house].......DLB-46

Clough, Arthur Hugh 1819-1861 ....DLB-32

Cloutier, Cécile 1930- DLB-60

Clouts, Sidney 1926-1982 ....DLB-225

Clutton-Brock, Arthur 1868-1924 ....DLB-98

Coates, Robert M.
    1897-1973............DLB-4, 9, 102; DS-15

Coatsworth, Elizabeth 1893-1986 ....DLB-22

Cobb, Charles E., Jr. 1943- DLB-41

Cobb, Frank I. 1869-1923 ....DLB-25

Cobb, Irvin S. 1876-1944.........DLB-11, 25, 86

Cobbe, Frances Power 1822-1904 ....DLB-190

Cobbett, William 1763-1835 ....DLB-43, 107, 158

Cobbledick, Gordon 1898-1969 ....DLB-171

Cochran, Thomas C. 1902- DLB-17

Cochrane, Elizabeth 1867-1922 ......DLB-25, 189

Cockerell, Sir Sydney 1867-1962 ....DLB-201

Cockerill, John A. 1845-1896...........DLB-23

Cocteau, Jean 1889-1963 ....DLB-65, 258

Coderre, Emile (see Jean Narrache)

Cody, Liza 1944- DLB-276

Coe, Jonathan 1961- DLB-231

Coetzee, J. M. 1940- DLB-225

Coffee, Lenore J. 1900?-1984...........DLB-44

Coffin, Robert P. Tristram 1892-1955.....DLB-45

Coghill, Mrs. Harry (see Walker, Anna Louisa)

Cogswell, Fred 1917- DLB-60

Cogswell, Mason Fitch 1761-1830 ....DLB-37

Cohan, George M. 1878-1942 ....DLB-249

Cohen, Arthur A. 1928-1986...........DLB-28

Cohen, Leonard 1934- DLB-53

Cohen, Matt 1942- DLB-53

Cohen, Morris Raphael 1880-1947 ......DLB-270

Colasanti, Marina 1937- DLB-307

Colbeck, Norman 1903-1987...........DLB-201

Colden, Cadwallader
    1688-1776 ....DLB-24, 30, 270

Colden, Jane 1724-1766 ....DLB-200

Cole, Barry 1936- DLB-14

Cole, George Watson 1850-1939 ....DLB-140

Colegate, Isabel 1931- DLB-14, 231

Coleman, Emily Holmes 1899-1974 ......DLB-4

Coleman, Wanda 1946- DLB-130

Coleridge, Hartley 1796-1849 ....DLB-96

Coleridge, Mary 1861-1907..........DLB-19, 98

Coleridge, Samuel Taylor
    1772-1834 ....DLB-93, 107; CDBLB-3

Coleridge, Sara 1802-1852.............DLB-199

Colet, John 1467-1519 ....DLB-132

Colette 1873-1954 ....DLB-65

Colette, Sidonie Gabrielle (see Colette)

Colinas, Antonio 1946- DLB-134

Coll, Joseph Clement 1881-1921 ....DLB-188

A Century of Poetry, a Lifetime of Collecting:
    J. M. Edelstein's Collection of
    Twentieth-Century American Poetry Y-02

Collier, John 1901-1980............DLB-77, 255

Collier, John Payne 1789-1883 ....DLB-184

Collier, Mary 1690-1762 ....DLB-95

Collier, Robert J. 1876-1918...........DLB-91

P. F. Collier [publishing house] DLB-49

Collin and Small DLB-49

Collingwood, R. G. 1889-1943 ....DLB-262

Collingwood, W. G. 1854-1932 ....DLB-149

Collins, An floruit circa 1653..........DLB-131

Collins, Anthony 1676-1729 ....DLB-252

Collins, Merle 1950- DLB-157

Collins, Michael 1964- DLB-267

Collins, Michael (see Lynds, Dennis)

Collins, Mortimer 1827-1876 ....DLB-21, 35

Collins, Tom (see Furphy, Joseph)

Collins, Wilkie
    1824-1889 ....DLB-18, 70, 159; CDBLB-4

    "The Unknown Public" (1858)
      [excerpt] DLB-57

    The Wilkie Collins Society Y-98

Collins, William 1721-1759 ....DLB-109

Isaac Collins [publishing house]..........DLB-49

William Collins, Sons and Company DLB-154

Collis, Maurice 1889-1973.............DLB-195

Collyer, Mary 1716?-1763? DLB-39

Colman, Benjamin 1673-1747 ....DLB-24

Colman, George, the Elder 1732-1794.....DLB-89

Colman, George, the Younger
    1762-1836 ....DLB-89

S. Colman [publishing house] DLB-49

Colombo, John Robert 1936- DLB-53

Colonial Literature DLB-307
Colquhoun, Patrick 1745-1820 . . . . DLB-158
Colter, Cyrus 1910-2002 . . . . DLB-33
Colum, Padraic 1881-1972 . . . . DLB-19
The Columbia History of the American Novel
    A Symposium on Y-92
Columella fl. first century A.D. DLB-211
Colvin, Sir Sidney 1845-1927 . . . . DLB-149
Colwin, Laurie 1944-1992 . . . . DLB-218; Y-80
Comden, Betty 1915- and
    Green, Adolph 1918- DLB-44, 265
Comi, Girolamo 1890-1968 . . . . DLB-114
Comisso, Giovanni 1895-1969 . . . . DLB-264
Commager, Henry Steele 1902-1998 . . . . . DLB-17
Commynes, Philippe de
    circa 1447-1511 . . . . DLB-208
Compton, D. G. 1930- DLB-261
Compton-Burnett, Ivy 1884?-1969 . . . . . . DLB-36
Conan, Laure (Félicité Angers)
    1845-1924 . . . . DLB-99
Concord, Massachusetts
    Concord History and Life DLB-223
    Concord: Literary History
      of a Town DLB-223
    The Old Manse, by Hawthorne DLB-223
    The Thoreauvian Pilgrimage: The
      Structure of an American Cult . . DLB-223
Concrete Poetry DLB-307
Conde, Carmen 1901-1996 . . . . DLB-108
Condillac, Etienne Bonnot de
    1714-1780 . . . . DLB-313
Condorcet, Marie-Jean-Antoine-Nicolas Caritat,
    marquis de 1743-1794 . . . . DLB-313
Congreve, William
    1670-1729 . . . . DLB-39, 84; CDBLB-2
    Preface to *Incognita* (1692) DLB-39
W. B. Conkey Company DLB-49
Conn, Stewart 1936- DLB-233
Connell, Evan S., Jr. 1924- DLB-2; Y-81
Connelly, Marc 1890-1980 . . . . DLB-7; Y-80
Connolly, Cyril 1903-1974 . . . . DLB-98
Connolly, James B. 1868-1957 . . . . DLB-78
Connor, Ralph (Charles William Gordon)
    1860-1937 . . . . DLB-92
Connor, Tony 1930- DLB-40
Conquest, Robert 1917- DLB-27
Conrad, Joseph
    1857-1924 . . . . DLB-10, 34, 98, 156; CDBLB-5
John Conrad and Company DLB-49
Conroy, Jack 1899-1990 . . . . Y-81
    A Tribute [to Nelson Algren] Y-81
Conroy, Pat 1945- DLB-6
Considine, Bob 1906-1975 . . . . DLB-241
Consolo, Vincenzo 1933- DLB-196
Constable, Henry 1562-1613 . . . . DLB-136
Archibald Constable and Company DLB-154
Constable and Company Limited DLB-112
Constant, Benjamin 1767-1830 . . . . DLB-119

Constant de Rebecque, Henri-Benjamin de
    (see Constant, Benjamin)
Constantine, David 1944- DLB-40
Constantine, Murray (see Burdekin, Katharine)
Constantin-Weyer, Maurice 1881-1964 . . . DLB-92
Contempo (magazine)
    Contempo Caravan:
      Kites in a Windstorm Y-85
The Continental Publishing Company DLB-49
A Conversation between William Riggan
    and Janette Turner Hospital Y-02
Conversations with Editors Y-95
Conway, Anne 1631-1679 . . . . DLB-252
Conway, Moncure Daniel
    1832-1907 . . . . DLB-1, 223
Cook, Ebenezer circa 1667-circa 1732 . . . . DLB-24
Cook, Edward Tyas 1857-1919 . . . . DLB-149
Cook, Eliza 1818-1889 . . . . DLB-199
Cook, George Cram 1873-1924 . . . . DLB-266
Cook, Michael 1933-1994 . . . . DLB-53
David C. Cook Publishing Company DLB-49
Cooke, George Willis 1848-1923 . . . . DLB-71
Cooke, John Esten 1830-1886 . . . . DLB-3, 248
Cooke, Philip Pendleton
    1816-1850 . . . . DLB-3, 59, 248
Cooke, Rose Terry 1827-1892 . . . . DLB-12, 74
Increase Cooke and Company DLB-49
Cook-Lynn, Elizabeth 1930- DLB-175
Coolbrith, Ina 1841-1928 . . . . DLB-54, 186
Cooley, Peter 1940- DLB-105
    "Into the Mirror" DLB-105
Coolidge, Clark 1939- DLB-193
Coolidge, Susan
    (see Woolsey, Sarah Chauncy)
George Coolidge [publishing house] DLB-49
Cooper, Anna Julia 1858-1964 . . . . DLB-221
Cooper, Edith Emma 1862-1913 . . . . DLB-240
Cooper, Giles 1918-1966 . . . . DLB-13
Cooper, J. California 19??- DLB-212
Cooper, James Fenimore
    1789-1851 . . . . . . DLB-3, 183, 250; CDALB-2
    The Bicentennial of James Fenimore Cooper:
      An International Celebration Y-89
    The James Fenimore Cooper Society Y-01
Cooper, Kent 1880-1965 . . . . DLB-29
Cooper, Susan 1935- DLB-161, 261
Cooper, Susan Fenimore 1813-1894 . . . . . DLB-239
William Cooper [publishing house] DLB-170
J. Coote [publishing house] DLB-154
Coover, Robert 1932- DLB-2, 227; Y-81
    Tribute to Donald Barthelme Y-89
    Tribute to Theodor Seuss Geisel Y-91
Copeland and Day DLB-49
Ćopić, Branko 1915-1984 . . . . DLB-181
Copland, Robert 1470?-1548 . . . . DLB-136
Coppard, A. E. 1878-1957 . . . . DLB-162
Coppée, François 1842-1908 . . . . DLB-217

Coppel, Alfred 1921- Y-83
    Tribute to Jessamyn West Y-84
Coppola, Francis Ford 1939- DLB-44
Copway, George (Kah-ge-ga-gah-bowh)
    1818-1869 . . . . DLB-175, 183
Copyright
    The Development of the Author's
      Copyright in Britain DLB-154
    The Digital Millennium Copyright Act:
      Expanding Copyright Protection in
      Cyberspace and Beyond Y-98
    Editorial: The Extension of Copyright . . . Y-02
    Mark Twain on Perpetual Copyright Y-92
    Public Domain and the Violation
      of Texts Y-97
    The Question of American Copyright
      in the Nineteenth Century
      Preface, by George Haven Putnam
      The Evolution of Copyright, by
        Brander Matthews
      Summary of Copyright Legislation in
        the United States, by R. R. Bowker
      Analysis of the Provisions of the
        Copyright Law of 1891, by
        George Haven Putnam
      The Contest for International Copyright,
        by George Haven Putnam
      Cheap Books and Good Books,
        by Brander Matthews DLB-49
    Writers and Their Copyright Holders:
      the WATCH Project Y-94
Corazzini, Sergio 1886-1907 . . . . DLB-114
Corbett, Richard 1582-1635 . . . . DLB-121
Corbière, Tristan 1845-1875 . . . . DLB-217
Corcoran, Barbara 1911- DLB-52
Cordelli, Franco 1943- DLB-196
Corelli, Marie 1855-1924 . . . . DLB-34, 156
Corle, Edwin 1906-1956 . . . . Y-85
Corman, Cid 1924- DLB-5, 193
Cormier, Robert 1925-2000 . . . DLB-52; CDALB-6
    Tribute to Theodor Seuss Geisel Y-91
Corn, Alfred 1943- DLB-120, 282; Y-80
Corneille, Pierre 1606-1684 . . . . DLB-268
Cornford, Frances 1886-1960 . . . . DLB-240
Cornish, Sam 1935- DLB-41
Cornish, William
    circa 1465-circa 1524 . . . . DLB-132
Cornwall, Barry (see Procter, Bryan Waller)
Cornwallis, Sir William, the Younger
    circa 1579-1614 . . . . DLB-151
Cornwell, David John Moore (see le Carré, John)
Cornwell, Patricia 1956- DLB-306
Coronel Urtecho, José 1906-1994 . . . . DLB-290
Corpi, Lucha 1945- DLB-82
Corrington, John William
    1932-1988 . . . . DLB-6, 244
Corriveau, Monique 1927-1976 . . . . DLB-251
Corrothers, James D. 1869-1917 . . . . DLB-50
Corso, Gregory 1930-2001 . . . . DLB-5, 16, 237
Cortázar, Julio 1914-1984 . . . . DLB-113; CDWLB-3
Cortéz, Carlos 1923- DLB-209
Cortez, Jayne 1936- DLB-41

Corvinus, Gottlieb Siegmund 1677-1746 ... DLB-168	Cox, James Middleton 1870-1957 ... DLB-127	William Creech [publishing house] ... DLB-154
Corvo, Baron (see Rolfe, Frederick William)	Cox, Leonard circa 1495-circa 1550 ... DLB-281	Thomas Creede [publishing house] ... DLB-170
Cory, Annie Sophie (see Cross, Victoria)	Cox, Palmer 1840-1924 ... DLB-42	Creel, George 1876-1953 ... DLB-25
Cory, Desmond (Shaun Lloyd McCarthy) 1928- ... DLB-276	Coxe, Louis 1918-1993 ... DLB-5	Creeley, Robert 1926- ... DLB-5, 16, 169; DS-17
Cory, William Johnson 1823-1892 ... DLB-35	Coxe, Tench 1755-1824 ... DLB-37	Creelman, James 1859-1915 ... DLB-23
Coryate, Thomas 1577?-1617 ... DLB-151, 172	Cozzens, Frederick S. 1818-1869 ... DLB-202	Cregan, David 1931- ... DLB-13
Ćosić, Dobrica 1921- ... DLB-181; CDWLB-4	Cozzens, James Gould 1903-1978 ... ... DLB-9, 294; Y-84; DS-2; CDALB-1	Creighton, Donald 1902-1979 ... DLB-88
Cosin, John 1595-1672 ... DLB-151, 213	Cozzens's *Michael Scarlett* ... Y-97	Crémazie, Octave 1827-1879 ... DLB-99
Cosmopolitan Book Corporation ... DLB-46	Ernest Hemingway's Reaction to James Gould Cozzens ... Y-98	Crémer, Victoriano 1909?- ... DLB-108
Cossa, Roberto 1934- ... DLB-305	James Gould Cozzens–A View from Afar ... Y-97	Crescas, Hasdai circa 1340-1412? ... DLB-115
Costa, Maria Velho da (see The Three Marias: A Landmark Case in Portuguese Literary History)	James Gould Cozzens: How to Read Him ... Y-97	Crespo, Angel 1926-1995 ... DLB-134
Costain, Thomas B. 1885-1965 ... DLB-9	James Gould Cozzens Symposium and Exhibition at the University of South Carolina, Columbia ... Y-00	Cresset Press ... DLB-112
Coste, Donat (Daniel Boudreau) 1912-1957 ... DLB-88		Cresswell, Helen 1934- ... DLB-161
Costello, Louisa Stuart 1799-1870 ... DLB-166	*Mens Rea* (or Something) ... Y-97	Crèvecoeur, Michel Guillaume Jean de 1735-1813 ... DLB-37
Cota-Cárdenas, Margarita 1941- ... DLB-122	Novels for Grown-Ups ... Y-97	Crewe, Candida 1964- ... DLB-207
Côté, Denis 1954- ... DLB-251	Crabbe, George 1754-1832 ... DLB-93	Crews, Harry 1935- ... DLB-6, 143, 185
Cotten, Bruce 1873-1954 ... DLB-187	Crace, Jim 1946- ... DLB-231	Crichton, Michael (John Lange, Jeffrey Hudson, Michael Douglas) 1942- ... DLB-292; Y-81
Cotter, Joseph Seamon, Jr. 1895-1919 ... DLB-50	Crackanthorpe, Hubert 1870-1896 ... DLB-135	Crispin, Edmund (Robert Bruce Montgomery) 1921-1978 ... DLB-87
Cotter, Joseph Seamon, Sr. 1861-1949 ... DLB-50	Craddock, Charles Egbert (see Murfree, Mary N.)	
Cottin, Sophie 1770-1807 ... DLB-313	Cradock, Thomas 1718-1770 ... DLB-31	Cristofer, Michael 1946- ... DLB-7
Joseph Cottle [publishing house] ... DLB-154	Craig, Daniel H. 1811-1895 ... DLB-43	Criticism
Cotton, Charles 1630-1687 ... DLB-131	Craik, Dinah Maria 1826-1887 ... DLB-35, 163	Afro-American Literary Critics: An Introduction ... DLB-33
Cotton, John 1584-1652 ... DLB-24	Cramer, Richard Ben 1950- ... DLB-185	The Consolidation of Opinion: Critical Responses to the Modernists ... DLB-36
Cotton, Sir Robert Bruce 1571-1631 ... DLB-213	Cranch, Christopher Pearse 1813-1892 ... DLB-1, 42, 243; DS-5	"Criticism in Relation to Novels" (1863), by G. H. Lewes ... DLB-21
Coulter, John 1888-1980 ... DLB-68	Crane, Hart 1899-1932 ... DLB-4, 48; CDALB-4	The Limits of Pluralism ... DLB-67
Cournos, John 1881-1966 ... DLB-54	Nathan Asch Remembers Ford Madox Ford, Sam Roth, and Hart Crane ... Y-02	Modern Critical Terms, Schools, and Movements ... DLB-67
Courteline, Georges 1858-1929 ... DLB-192	Crane, R. S. 1886-1967 ... DLB-63	
Cousins, Margaret 1905-1996 ... DLB-137	Crane, Stephen 1871-1900 ... DLB-12, 54, 78; CDALB-3	"Panic Among the Philistines": A Postscript, An Interview with Bryan Griffin ... Y-81
Cousins, Norman 1915-1990 ... DLB-137		
Couvreur, Jessie (see Tasma)	Stephen Crane: A Revaluation, Virginia Tech Conference, 1989 ... Y-89	The Recovery of Literature: Criticism in the 1990s: A Symposium ... Y-91
Coventry, Francis 1725-1754 ... DLB-39	The Stephen Crane Society ... Y-98, 01	The Stealthy School of Criticism (1871), by Dante Gabriel Rossetti ... DLB-35
Dedication, *The History of Pompey the Little* (1751) ... DLB-39	Crane, Walter 1845-1915 ... DLB-163	
Coverdale, Miles 1487 or 1488-1569 ... DLB-167	Cranmer, Thomas 1489-1556 ... DLB-132, 213	Crnjanski, Miloš 1893-1977 ... DLB-147; CDWLB-4
N. Coverly [publishing house] ... DLB-49	Crapsey, Adelaide 1878-1914 ... DLB-54	Crocker, Hannah Mather 1752-1829 ... DLB-200
Covici-Friede ... DLB-46	Crashaw, Richard 1612/1613-1649 ... DLB-126	Crockett, David (Davy) 1786-1836 ... DLB-3, 11, 183, 248
Cowan, Peter 1914-2002 ... DLB-260	Craven, Avery 1885-1980 ... DLB-17	
Coward, Noel 1899-1973 ... DLB-10, 245; CDBLB-6	Crawford, Charles 1752-circa 1815 ... DLB-31	Croft-Cooke, Rupert (see Bruce, Leo)
Coward, McCann and Geoghegan ... DLB-46	Crawford, F. Marion 1854-1909 ... DLB-71	Crofts, Freeman Wills 1879-1957 ... DLB-77
Cowles, Gardner 1861-1946 ... DLB-29	Crawford, Isabel Valancy 1850-1887 ... DLB-92	Croker, John Wilson 1780-1857 ... DLB-110
Cowles, Gardner "Mike", Jr. 1903-1985 ... DLB-127, 137	Crawley, Alan 1887-1975 ... DLB-68	Croly, George 1780-1860 ... DLB-159
	Crayon, Geoffrey (see Irving, Washington)	Croly, Herbert 1869-1930 ... DLB-91
Cowley, Abraham 1618-1667 ... DLB-131, 151	Crayon, Porte (see Strother, David Hunter)	Croly, Jane Cunningham 1829-1901 ... DLB-23
Cowley, Hannah 1743-1809 ... DLB-89	Creamer, Robert W. 1922- ... DLB-171	Crompton, Richmal 1890-1969 ... DLB-160
Cowley, Malcolm 1898-1989 ... DLB-4, 48; DS-15; Y-81, 89	Creasey, John 1908-1973 ... DLB-77	Cronin, A. J. 1896-1981 ... DLB-191
	Creative Age Press ... DLB-46	Cros, Charles 1842-1888 ... DLB-217
Cowper, Richard (John Middleton Murry Jr.) 1926-2002 ... DLB-261	Creative Nonfiction ... Y-02	Crosby, Caresse 1892-1970 and Crosby, Harry 1898-1929 and ... DLB-4; DS-15
	Crébillon, Claude-Prosper Jolyot de *fils* 1707-1777 ... DLB-313	
Cowper, William 1731-1800 ... DLB-104, 109		Crosby, Harry 1898-1929 ... DLB-48
Cox, A. B. (see Berkeley, Anthony)	Crébillon, Claude-Prosper Jolyot de *père* 1674-1762 ... DLB-313	Crosland, Camilla Toulmin (Mrs. Newton Crosland) 1812-1895 ... DLB-240
Cox, James McMahon 1903-1974 ... DLB-127		

Cross, Amanda (Carolyn G. Heilbrun) 1926-2003 .... DLB-306
Cross, Gillian 1945- DLB-161
Cross, Victoria 1868-1952 .... DLB-135, 197
Crossley-Holland, Kevin 1941- DLB-40, 161
Crothers, Rachel 1870-1958 .... DLB-7, 266
Thomas Y. Crowell Company DLB-49
Crowley, John 1942- Y-82
Crowley, Mart 1935- DLB-7, 266
Crown Publishers DLB-46
Crowne, John 1641-1712 .... DLB-80
Crowninshield, Edward Augustus 1817-1859 .... DLB-140
Crowninshield, Frank 1872-1947 .... DLB-91
Croy, Homer 1883-1965 .... DLB-4
Crumley, James 1939- DLB-226; Y-84
Cruse, Mary Anne 1825?-1910 .... DLB-239
Cruz, Migdalia 1958- DLB-249
Cruz, Sor Juana Inés de la 1651-1695.... DLB-305
Cruz, Victor Hernández 1949- DLB-41
Cruz e Sousa, João 1861-1898 .... DLB-307
Csokor, Franz Theodor 1885-1969 ..... DLB-81
Csoóri, Sándor 1930- DLB-232; CDWLB-4
Cuadra, Pablo Antonio 1912-2002 ...... DLB-290
Cuala Press DLB-112
Cudworth, Ralph 1617-1688 .... DLB-252
Cugoano, Quobna Ottabah 1797-? Y-02
Cullen, Countee 1903-1946 .... DLB-4, 48, 51; CDALB-4
Culler, Jonathan D. 1944- DLB-67, 246
Cullinan, Elizabeth 1933- DLB-234
Culverwel, Nathaniel 1619?-1651? DLB-252
Cumberland, Richard 1732-1811 .... DLB-89
Cummings, Constance Gordon 1837-1924 .... DLB-174
Cummings, E. E. 1894-1962 .... DLB-4, 48; CDALB-5
The E. E. Cummings Society Y-01
Cummings, Ray 1887-1957 .... DLB-8
Cummings and Hilliard DLB-49
Cummins, Maria Susanna 1827-1866 ..... DLB-42
Cumpián, Carlos 1953- DLB-209
Cunard, Nancy 1896-1965 .... DLB-240
Joseph Cundall [publishing house] DLB-106
Cuney, Waring 1906-1976 .... DLB-51
Cuney-Hare, Maude 1874-1936 .... DLB-52
Cunha, Euclides da 1866-1909 .... DLB-307
Cunningham, Allan 1784-1842 .... DLB-116, 144
Cunningham, J. V. 1911-1985 .... DLB-5
Cunningham, Michael 1952- DLB-292
Cunningham, Peter (Peter Lauder, Peter Benjamin) 1947- DLB-267
Peter F. Cunningham [publishing house] DLB-49
Cunqueiro, Alvaro 1911-1981 .... DLB-134
Cuomo, George 1929- Y-80

Cupples, Upham and Company DLB-49
Cupples and Leon DLB-46
Cuppy, Will 1884-1949 .... DLB-11
Curiel, Barbara Brinson 1956- DLB-209
Edmund Curll [publishing house]...... DLB-154
Currie, James 1756-1805 .... DLB-142
Currie, Mary Montgomerie Lamb Singleton, Lady Currie (see Fane, Violet)
Cursor Mundi circa 1300 .... DLB-146
Curti, Merle E. 1897-1996 .... DLB-17
Curtis, Anthony 1926- DLB-155
Curtis, Cyrus H. K. 1850-1933 .... DLB-91
Curtis, George William 1824-1892 .... DLB-1, 43, 223
Curzon, Robert 1810-1873 .... DLB-166
Curzon, Sarah Anne 1833-1898 .... DLB-99
Cusack, Dymphna 1902-1981 .... DLB-260
Cushing, Eliza Lanesford 1794-1886 .... DLB-99
Cushing, Harvey 1869-1939 .... DLB-187
Custance, Olive (Lady Alfred Douglas) 1874-1944 .... DLB-240
Cynewulf circa 770-840 .... DLB-146
Cyrano de Bergerac, Savinien de 1619-1655 .... DLB-268
Czepko, Daniel 1605-1660 .... DLB-164
Czerniawski, Adam 1934- DLB-232

D

Dabit, Eugène 1898-1936 .... DLB-65
Daborne, Robert circa 1580-1628 ...... DLB-58
Dąbrowska, Maria 1889-1965 .... DLB-215; CDWLB-4
Dacey, Philip 1939- DLB-105
"Eyes Across Centuries: Contemporary Poetry and 'That Vision Thing,'" DLB-105
Dach, Simon 1605-1659 .... DLB-164
Dacier, Anne Le Fèvre 1647-1720 ...... DLB-313
Dagerman, Stig 1923-1954 .... DLB-259
Daggett, Rollin M. 1831-1901 .... DLB-79
D'Aguiar, Fred 1960- DLB-157
Dahl, Roald 1916-1990 .... DLB-139, 255
Tribute to Alfred A. Knopf Y-84
Dahlberg, Edward 1900-1977 .... DLB-48
Dahn, Felix 1834-1912 .... DLB-129
The Daily Worker DLB-303
Dal', Vladimir Ivanovich (Kazak Vladimir Lugansky) 1801-1872 .... DLB-198
Dale, Peter 1938- DLB-40
Daley, Arthur 1904-1974 .... DLB-171
Dall, Caroline Healey 1822-1912 ..... DLB-1, 235
Dallas, E. S. 1828-1879 .... DLB-55
The Gay Science [excerpt](1866) DLB-21
The Dallas Theater Center DLB-7
D'Alton, Louis 1900-1951 .... DLB-10
Dalton, Roque 1935-1975 .... DLB-283

Daly, Carroll John 1889-1958 .... DLB-226
Daly, T. A. 1871-1948 .... DLB-11
Damon, S. Foster 1893-1971 .... DLB-45
William S. Damrell [publishing house].... DLB-49
Dana, Charles A. 1819-1897 ...... DLB-3, 23, 250
Dana, Richard Henry, Jr. 1815-1882 .... DLB-1, 183, 235
Dandridge, Ray Garfield DLB-51
Dane, Clemence 1887-1965 .... DLB-10, 197
Danforth, John 1660-1730 .... DLB-24
Danforth, Samuel, I 1626-1674 .... DLB-24
Danforth, Samuel, II 1666-1727 .... DLB-24
Daniel, John M. 1825-1865 .... DLB-43
Daniel, Samuel 1562 or 1563-1619 ...... DLB-62
Daniel Press DLB-106
Daniel', Iulii 1925-1988 .... DLB-302
Daniells, Roy 1902-1979 .... DLB-68
Daniels, Jim 1956- DLB-120
Daniels, Jonathan 1902-1981 .... DLB-127
Daniels, Josephus 1862-1948 .... DLB-29
Daniels, Sarah 1957- DLB-245
Danilevsky, Grigorii Petrovich 1829-1890 .... DLB-238
Dannay, Frederic 1905-1982 .... DLB-137
Danner, Margaret Esse 1915- DLB-41
John Danter [publishing house] DLB-170
Dantin, Louis (Eugene Seers) 1865-1945 .... DLB-92
Danto, Arthur C. 1924- DLB-279
Danzig, Allison 1898-1987 .... DLB-171
D'Arcy, Ella circa 1857-1937 .... DLB-135
Darío, Rubén 1867-1916 .... DLB-290
Dark, Eleanor 1901-1985 .... DLB-260
Darke, Nick 1948- DLB-233
Darley, Felix Octavious Carr 1822-1888 .... DLB-188
Darley, George 1795-1846 .... DLB-96
Darmesteter, Madame James (see Robinson, A. Mary F.)
Darrow, Clarence 1857-1938 .... DLB-303
Darwin, Charles 1809-1882 .... DLB-57, 166
Darwin, Erasmus 1731-1802 .... DLB-93
Daryush, Elizabeth 1887-1977 .... DLB-20
Dashkova, Ekaterina Romanovna (née Vorontsova) 1743-1810 ...... DLB-150
Dashwood, Edmée Elizabeth Monica de la Pasture (see Delafield, E. M.)
Daudet, Alphonse 1840-1897 .... DLB-123
d'Aulaire, Edgar Parin 1898- and d'Aulaire, Ingri 1904- DLB-22
Davenant, Sir William 1606-1668 ... DLB-58, 126
Davenport, Guy 1927- DLB-130
Tribute to John Gardner Y-82
Davenport, Marcia 1903-1996 .... DS-17
Davenport, Robert ?-? DLB-58
Daves, Delmer 1904-1977 .... DLB-26
Davey, Frank 1940- DLB-53

Davidson, Avram 1923-1993 . . . . DLB-8
Davidson, Donald 1893-1968 . . . . DLB-45
Davidson, Donald 1917- DLB-279
Davidson, John 1857-1909 . . . . DLB-19
Davidson, Lionel 1922- DLB-14, 276
Davidson, Robyn 1950- DLB-204
Davidson, Sara 1943- DLB-185
Davið Stefánsson frá Fagraskógi
  1895-1964 . . . . DLB-293
Davie, Donald 1922- DLB-27
Davie, Elspeth 1919-1995 . . . . DLB-139
Davies, Sir John 1569-1626 . . . . DLB-172
Davies, John, of Hereford 1565?-1618 . . . . DLB-121
Davies, Rhys 1901-1978 . . . . DLB-139, 191
Davies, Robertson 1913-1995 . . . . DLB-68
Davies, Samuel 1723-1761 . . . . DLB-31
Davies, Thomas 1712?-1785 . . . . DLB-142, 154
Davies, W. H. 1871-1940 . . . . DLB-19, 174
Peter Davies Limited DLB-112
Davin, Nicholas Flood 1840?-1901 . . . . DLB-99
Daviot, Gordon 1896?-1952 . . . . DLB-10
  (see also Tey, Josephine)
Davis, Arthur Hoey (see Rudd, Steele)
Davis, Benjamin J. 1903-1964 . . . . DLB-303
Davis, Charles A. (Major J. Downing)
  1795-1867 . . . . DLB-11
Davis, Clyde Brion 1894-1962 . . . . DLB-9
Davis, Dick 1945- DLB-40, 282
Davis, Frank Marshall 1905-1987 . . . . DLB-51
Davis, H. L. 1894-1960 . . . . DLB-9, 206
Davis, John 1774-1854 . . . . DLB-37
Davis, Lydia 1947- DLB-130
Davis, Margaret Thomson 1926- DLB-14
Davis, Ossie 1917- DLB-7, 38, 249
Davis, Owen 1874-1956 . . . . DLB-249
Davis, Paxton 1925-1994 . . . . Y-89
Davis, Rebecca Harding
  1831-1910 . . . . DLB-74, 239
Davis, Richard Harding 1864-1916
  . . . . DLB-12, 23, 78, 79, 189; DS-13
Davis, Samuel Cole 1764-1809 . . . . DLB-37
Davis, Samuel Post 1850-1918 . . . . DLB-202
Davison, Frank Dalby 1893-1970 . . . . DLB-260
Davison, Peter 1928- DLB-5
Davydov, Denis Vasil'evich
  1784-1839 . . . . DLB-205
Davys, Mary 1674-1732 . . . . DLB-39
  Preface to The Works of Mrs. Davys
    (1725) DLB-39
DAW Books DLB-46
Dawe, Bruce 1930- DLB-289
Dawson, Ernest 1882-1947 . . . . DLB-140; Y-02
Dawson, Fielding 1930- DLB-130
Dawson, Sarah Morgan 1842-1909 . . . . . . DLB-239
Dawson, William 1704-1752 . . . . DLB-31
Day, Angel flourished 1583-1599 . . . DLB-167, 236

Day, Benjamin Henry 1810-1889 . . . . DLB-43
Day, Clarence 1874-1935 . . . . DLB-11
Day, Dorothy 1897-1980 . . . . DLB-29
Day, Frank Parker 1881-1950 . . . . DLB-92
Day, John circa 1574-circa 1640 . . . . DLB-62
Day, Thomas 1748-1789 . . . . DLB-39
John Day [publishing house] DLB-170
The John Day Company DLB-46
Mahlon Day [publishing house] DLB-49
Day Lewis, C. (see Blake, Nicholas)
Dazai Osamu 1909-1948 . . . . DLB-182
Deacon, William Arthur 1890-1977 . . . . . . DLB-68
Deal, Borden 1922-1985 . . . . DLB-6
de Angeli, Marguerite 1889-1987 . . . . DLB-22
De Angelis, Milo 1951- DLB-128
Debord, Guy 1931-1994 . . . . DLB-296
De Bow, J. D. B. 1820-1867 . . . . DLB-3, 79, 248
Debs, Eugene V. 1855-1926 . . . . DLB-303
de Bruyn, Günter 1926- DLB-75
de Camp, L. Sprague 1907-2000 . . . . DLB-8
De Carlo, Andrea 1952- DLB-196
De Casas, Celso A. 1944- DLB-209
Dechert, Robert 1895-1975 . . . . DLB-187
Dedications, Inscriptions, and
  Annotations Y-01–02
Dee, John 1527-1608 or 1609 . . . . . . DLB-136, 213
Deeping, George Warwick 1877-1950 . . . . DLB-153
Deffand, Marie de Vichy-Chamrond,
  marquise Du 1696-1780 . . . . DLB-313
Defoe, Daniel
  1660-1731 . . . . DLB-39, 95, 101; CDBLB-2
  Preface to Colonel Jack (1722) DLB-39
  Preface to The Farther Adventures of
    Robinson Crusoe (1719) DLB-39
  Preface to Moll Flanders (1722) DLB-39
  Preface to Robinson Crusoe (1719) DLB-39
  Preface to Roxana (1724) DLB-39
de Fontaine, Felix Gregory 1834-1896 . . . . . DLB-43
De Forest, John William
  1826-1906 . . . . DLB-12, 189
DeFrees, Madeline 1919- DLB-105
  "The Poet's Kaleidoscope: The
  Element of Surprise in the
  Making of the Poem" DLB-105
DeGolyer, Everette Lee 1886-1956 . . . . . . DLB-187
de Graff, Robert 1895-1981 . . . . Y-81
de Graft, Joe 1924-1978 . . . . DLB-117
De Heinrico circa 980? DLB-148
Deighton, Len 1929- DLB-87; CDBLB-8
DeJong, Meindert 1906-1991 . . . . DLB-52
Dekker, Thomas
  circa 1572-1632 . . . . . . DLB-62, 172; CDBLB-1
Delacorte, George T., Jr. 1894-1991 . . . . . . DLB-91
Delafield, E. M. 1890-1943 . . . . DLB-34
Delahaye, Guy (Guillaume Lahaise)
  1888-1969 . . . . DLB-92

de la Mare, Walter 1873-1956
  . . . . DLB-19, 153, 162, 255; CDBLB-6
Deland, Margaret 1857-1945 . . . . DLB-78
Delaney, Shelagh 1939- DLB-13; CDBLB-8
Delano, Amasa 1763-1823 . . . . DLB-183
Delany, Martin Robinson 1812-1885 . . . . . DLB-50
Delany, Samuel R. 1942- DLB-8, 33
de la Roche, Mazo 1879-1961 . . . . DLB-68
Delavigne, Jean François Casimir
  1793-1843 . . . . DLB-192
Delbanco, Nicholas 1942- DLB-6, 234
Delblanc, Sven 1931-1992 . . . . DLB-257
Del Castillo, Ramón 1949- DLB-209
Deledda, Grazia 1871-1936 . . . . DLB-264
De León, Nephtal 1945- DLB-82
Deleuze, Gilles 1925-1995 . . . . DLB-296
Delfini, Antonio 1907-1963 . . . . DLB-264
Delgado, Abelardo Barrientos 1931- DLB-82
Del Giudice, Daniele 1949- DLB-196
De Libero, Libero 1906-1981 . . . . DLB-114
DeLillo, Don 1936- DLB-6, 173
de Lint, Charles 1951- DLB-251
de Lisser H. G. 1878-1944 . . . . DLB-117
Dell, Floyd 1887-1969 . . . . DLB-9
Dell Publishing Company DLB-46
delle Grazie, Marie Eugene 1864-1931 . . . . DLB-81
Deloney, Thomas died 1600 . . . . DLB-167
Deloria, Ella C. 1889-1971 . . . . DLB-175
Deloria, Vine, Jr. 1933- DLB-175
del Rey, Lester 1915-1993 . . . . DLB-8
Del Vecchio, John M. 1947- DS-9
Del'vig, Anton Antonovich 1798-1831 . . . DLB-205
de Man, Paul 1919-1983 . . . . DLB-67
DeMarinis, Rick 1934- DLB-218
Demby, William 1922- DLB-33
De Mille, James 1833-1880 . . . . DLB-99, 251
de Mille, William 1878-1955 . . . . DLB-266
Deming, Philander 1829-1915 . . . . DLB-74
Deml, Jakub 1878-1961 . . . . DLB-215
Demorest, William Jennings 1822-1895 . . . DLB-79
De Morgan, William 1839-1917 . . . . DLB-153
Demosthenes 384 B.C.-322 B.C. DLB-176
Henry Denham [publishing house] DLB-170
Denham, Sir John 1615-1669 . . . . DLB-58, 126
Denison, Merrill 1893-1975 . . . . DLB-92
T. S. Denison and Company DLB-49
Dennery, Adolphe Philippe 1811-1899 . . . DLB-192
Dennie, Joseph 1768-1812 . . . . . DLB-37, 43, 59, 73
Dennis, C. J. 1876-1938 . . . . DLB-260
Dennis, John 1658-1734 . . . . DLB-101
Dennis, Nigel 1912-1989 . . . . DLB-13, 15, 233
Denslow, W. W. 1856-1915 . . . . DLB-188
Dent, J. M., and Sons DLB-112
Dent, Lester 1904-1959 . . . . DLB-306
Dent, Tom 1932-1998 . . . . DLB-38

Cumulative Index

Denton, Daniel circa 1626-1703 .... DLB-24
DePaola, Tomie 1934- DLB-61
De Quille, Dan 1829-1898 .... DLB-186
De Quincey, Thomas
   1785-1859 .... DLB-110, 144; CDBLB-3
   "Rhetoric" (1828; revised, 1859)
     [excerpt] DLB-57
   "Style" (1840; revised, 1859)
     [excerpt] DLB-57
Derby, George Horatio 1823-1861 .... DLB-11
J. C. Derby and Company DLB-49
Derby and Miller DLB-49
De Ricci, Seymour 1881-1942 .... DLB-201
Derleth, August 1909-1971 ...... DLB-9; DS-17
Derrida, Jacques 1930- DLB-242
The Derrydale Press DLB-46
Derzhavin, Gavriil Romanovich
   1743-1816 .... DLB-150
Desai, Anita 1937- DLB-271
Desaulniers, Gonzalve 1863-1934 .... DLB-92
Desbordes-Valmore, Marceline
   1786-1859 .... DLB-217
Descartes, René 1596-1650 .... DLB-268
Deschamps, Emile 1791-1871 .... DLB-217
Deschamps, Eustache 1340?-1404 ..... DLB-208
Desbiens, Jean-Paul 1927- DLB-53
des Forêts, Louis-Rene 1918-2001 ...... DLB-83
Desiato, Luca 1941- DLB-196
Desjardins, Marie-Catherine
   (see Villedieu, Madame de)
Desnica, Vladan 1905-1967 .... DLB-181
Desnos, Robert 1900-1945 .... DLB-258
DesRochers, Alfred 1901-1978 .... DLB-68
Desrosiers, Léo-Paul 1896-1967 .... DLB-68
Dessaulles, Louis-Antoine 1819-1895 ..... DLB-99
Dessì, Giuseppe 1909-1977 .... DLB-177
Destouches, Louis-Ferdinand
   (see Céline, Louis-Ferdinand)
DeSylva, Buddy 1895-1950 .... DLB-265
De Tabley, Lord 1835-1895 .... DLB-35
Deutsch, Babette 1895-1982 .... DLB-45
Deutsch, Niklaus Manuel (see Manuel, Niklaus)
André Deutsch Limited DLB-112
Devanny, Jean 1894-1962 .... DLB-260
Deveaux, Alexis 1948- DLB-38
De Vere, Aubrey 1814-1902 .... DLB-35
Devereux, second Earl of Essex, Robert
   1565-1601 .... DLB-136
The Devin-Adair Company DLB-46
De Vinne, Theodore Low
   1828-1914 .... DLB-187
Devlin, Anne 1951- DLB-245
DeVoto, Bernard 1897-1955 ...... DLB-9, 256
De Vries, Peter 1910-1993 .... DLB-6; Y-82
   Tribute to Albert Erskine Y-93
Dewart, Edward Hartley 1828-1903 ..... DLB-99
Dewdney, Christopher 1951- DLB-60

Dewdney, Selwyn 1909-1979 .... DLB-68
Dewey, John 1859-1952 .... DLB-246, 270
Dewey, Orville 1794-1882 .... DLB-243
Dewey, Thomas B. 1915-1981 .... DLB-226
DeWitt, Robert M., Publisher DLB-49
DeWolfe, Fiske and Company DLB-49
Dexter, Colin 1930- DLB-87
de Young, M. H. 1849-1925 .... DLB-25
Dhlomo, H. I. E. 1903-1956 .... DLB-157, 225
Dhu al-Rummah (Abu al-Harith Ghaylan ibn 'Uqbah)
   circa 696-circa 735 .... DLB-311
Dhuoda circa 803-after 843 .... DLB-148
The Dial 1840-1844 .... DLB-223
The Dial Press DLB-46
Diamond, I. A. L. 1920-1988 .... DLB-26
Dias Gomes, Alfredo 1922-1999 .... DLB-307
Dibble, L. Grace 1902-1998 .... DLB-204
Dibdin, Thomas Frognall
   1776-1847 .... DLB-184
Di Cicco, Pier Giorgio 1949- DLB-60
Dick, Philip K. 1928-1982 .... DLB-8
Dick and Fitzgerald DLB-49
Dickens, Charles 1812-1870
   .... DLB-21, 55, 70, 159,
     166; DS-5; CDBLB-4
Dickey, Eric Jerome 1961- DLB-292
Dickey, James 1923-1997 .... DLB-5, 193;
   Y-82, 93, 96, 97; DS-7, 19; CDALB-6
   James Dickey and Stanley Burnshaw
     Correspondence Y-02
   James Dickey at Seventy–A Tribute Y-93
   James Dickey, American Poet Y-96
   The James Dickey Society Y-99
   The Life of James Dickey: A Lecture to
     the Friends of the Emory Libraries,
     by Henry Hart Y-98
   Tribute to Archibald MacLeish Y-82
   Tribute to Malcolm Cowley Y-89
   Tribute to Truman Capote Y-84
   Tributes [to Dickey] Y-97
Dickey, William
   1928-1994 .... DLB-5
Dickinson, Emily
   1830-1886 .... DLB-1, 243; CDALB-3
Dickinson, John 1732-1808 .... DLB-31
Dickinson, Jonathan 1688-1747 .... DLB-24
Dickinson, Patric 1914- DLB-27
Dickinson, Peter 1927- DLB-87, 161, 276
John Dicks [publishing house] DLB-106
Dickson, Gordon R.
   1923-2001 .... DLB-8
Dictionary of Literary Biography
   Annual Awards for *Dictionary of*
     Literary Biography Editors and
     Contributors Y-98–02
Dictionary of Literary Biography
   Yearbook Awards Y-92–93, 97–02
The Dictionary of National Biography DLB-144
Diderot, Denis 1713-1784 .... DLB-313

Didion, Joan 1934-
   .... DLB-2, 173, 185; Y-81, 86; CDALB-6
Di Donato, Pietro 1911- DLB-9
Die Fürstliche Bibliothek Corvey Y-96
Diego, Gerardo 1896-1987 .... DLB-134
Dietz, Howard 1896-1983 .... DLB-265
Digby, Everard 1550?-1605 .... DLB-281
Digges, Thomas circa 1546-1595 ...... DLB-136
The Digital Millennium Copyright Act:
   Expanding Copyright Protection in
   Cyberspace and Beyond Y-98
Diktonius, Elmer 1896-1961 .... DLB-259
Dillard, Annie 1945- DLB-275, 278; Y-80
Dillard, R. H. W. 1937- DLB-5, 244
Charles T. Dillingham Company DLB-49
G. W. Dillingham Company DLB-49
Edward and Charles Dilly
   [publishing house] DLB-154
Dilthey, Wilhelm 1833-1911 .... DLB-129
Dimitrova, Blaga 1922- DLB-181; CDWLB-4
Dimov, Dimitr 1909-1966 .... DLB-181
Dimsdale, Thomas J. 1831?-1866 ...... DLB-186
Dinescu, Mircea 1950- DLB-232
Dinesen, Isak (see Blixen, Karen)
Dingelstedt, Franz von 1814-1881 ...... DLB-133
Dinis, Júlio (Joaquim Guilherme
   Gomes Coelho) 1839-1871 .... DLB-287
Dintenfass, Mark 1941- Y-84
Diogenes, Jr. (see Brougham, John)
Diogenes Laertius circa 200 .... DLB-176
DiPrima, Diane 1934- DLB-5, 16
Disch, Thomas M. 1940- DLB-8, 282
Diski, Jenny 1947- DLB-271
Disney, Walt 1901-1966 .... DLB-22
Disraeli, Benjamin 1804-1881 .... DLB-21, 55
D'Israeli, Isaac 1766-1848 .... DLB-107
DLB Award for Distinguished
   Literary Criticism Y-02
Ditlevsen, Tove 1917-1976 .... DLB-214
Ditzen, Rudolf (see Fallada, Hans)
Dix, Dorothea Lynde 1802-1887 ..... DLB-1, 235
Dix, Dorothy (see Gilmer, Elizabeth Meriwether)
Dix, Edwards and Company DLB-49
Dix, Gertrude circa 1874-? DLB-197
Dixie, Florence Douglas 1857-1905 ..... DLB-174
Dixon, Ella Hepworth
   1855 or 1857-1932 .... DLB-197
Dixon, Paige (see Corcoran, Barbara)
Dixon, Richard Watson 1833-1900 ...... DLB-19
Dixon, Stephen 1936- DLB-130
DLB Award for Distinguished
   Literary Criticism Y-02
Dmitriev, Andrei Viktorovich 1956- .. DLB-285
Dmitriev, Ivan Ivanovich 1760-1837 ..... DLB-150
Dobell, Bertram 1842-1914 .... DLB-184
Dobell, Sydney 1824-1874 .... DLB-32
Dobie, J. Frank 1888-1964 .... DLB-212

Dobles Yzaguirre, Julieta 1943- DLB-283

Döblin, Alfred 1878-1957 ..... DLB-66; CDWLB-2

Dobroliubov, Nikolai Aleksandrovich
    1836-1861 .... DLB-277

Dobson, Austin 1840-1921 .... DLB-35, 144

Dobson, Rosemary 1920- DLB-260

Doctorow, E. L.
    1931- DLB-2, 28, 173; Y-80; CDALB-6

Dodd, Susan M. 1946- DLB-244

Dodd, William E. 1869-1940 .... DLB-17

Anne Dodd [publishing house] DLB-154

Dodd, Mead and Company DLB-49

Doderer, Heimito von 1896-1966 .... DLB-85

B. W. Dodge and Company DLB-46

Dodge, Mary Abigail 1833-1896 .... DLB-221

Dodge, Mary Mapes
    1831?-1905 .... DLB-42, 79; DS-13

Dodge Publishing Company DLB-49

Dodgson, Charles Lutwidge (see Carroll, Lewis)

Dodsley, Robert 1703-1764 .... DLB-95

R. Dodsley [publishing house] DLB-154

Dodson, Owen 1914-1983 .... DLB-76

Dodwell, Christina 1951- DLB-204

Doesticks, Q. K. Philander, P. B.
    (see Thomson, Mortimer)

Doheny, Carrie Estelle 1875-1958 .... DLB-140

Doherty, John 1798?-1854 .... DLB-190

Doig, Ivan 1939- DLB-206

Doinaş, Ştefan Augustin 1922- DLB-232

Domínguez, Sylvia Maida 1935- DLB-122

Donaghy, Michael 1954- DLB-282

Patrick Donahoe [publishing house] DLB-49

Donald, David H. 1920- DLB-17; Y-87

Donaldson, Scott 1928- DLB-111

Doni, Rodolfo 1919- DLB-177

Donleavy, J. P. 1926- DLB-6, 173

Donnadieu, Marguerite (see Duras, Marguerite)

Donne, John
    1572-1631 .... DLB-121, 151; CDBLB-1

Donnelly, Ignatius 1831-1901 .... DLB-12

R. R. Donnelley and Sons Company DLB-49

Donoghue, Emma 1969- DLB-267

Donohue and Henneberry DLB-49

Donoso, José 1924-1996 ..... DLB-113; CDWLB-3

M. Doolady [publishing house] DLB-49

Dooley, Ebon (see Ebon)

Doolittle, Hilda 1886-1961 ..... DLB-4, 45; DS-15

Doplicher, Fabio 1938- DLB-128

Dor, Milo 1923- DLB-85

George H. Doran Company DLB-46

Dorgelès, Roland 1886-1973 .... DLB-65

Dorn, Edward 1929-1999 .... DLB-5

Dorr, Rheta Childe 1866-1948 .... DLB-25

Dorris, Michael 1945-1997 .... DLB-175

Dorset and Middlesex, Charles Sackville,
    Lord Buckhurst, Earl of 1643-1706 .... DLB-131

Dorsey, Candas Jane 1952- DLB-251

Dorst, Tankred 1925- DLB-75, 124

Dos Passos, John 1896-1970
    .... DLB-4, 9; DS-1, 15; CDALB-5

    John Dos Passos: A Centennial
        Commemoration Y-96

    John Dos Passos: Artist Y-99

    John Dos Passos Newsletter Y-00

    U.S.A. (Documentary) DLB-274

Dostoevsky, Fyodor 1821-1881 .... DLB-238

Doubleday and Company DLB-49

Doubrovsky, Serge 1928- DLB-299

Dougall, Lily 1858-1923 .... DLB-92

Doughty, Charles M.
    1843-1926 .... DLB-19, 57, 174

Douglas, Lady Alfred (see Custance, Olive)

Douglas, Ellen (Josephine Ayres Haxton)
    1921- DLB-292

Douglas, Gavin 1476-1522 .... DLB-132

Douglas, Keith 1920-1944 .... DLB-27

Douglas, Norman 1868-1952 .... DLB-34, 195

Douglass, Frederick 1817-1895
    .... DLB-1, 43, 50, 79, 243; CDALB-2

    Frederick Douglass Creative Arts Center Y-01

Douglass, William circa 1691-1752 .... DLB-24

Dourado, Autran 1926- DLB-145, 307

Dove, Arthur G. 1880-1946 .... DLB-188

Dove, Rita 1952- DLB-120; CDALB-7

Dover Publications DLB-46

Doves Press DLB-112

Dovlatov, Sergei Donatovich
    1941-1990 .... DLB-285

Dowden, Edward 1843-1913 .... DLB-35, 149

Dowell, Coleman 1925-1985 .... DLB-130

Dowland, John 1563-1626 .... DLB-172

Downes, Gwladys 1915- DLB-88

Downing, J., Major (see Davis, Charles A.)

Downing, Major Jack (see Smith, Seba)

Dowriche, Anne
    before 1560-after 1613 .... DLB-172

Dowson, Ernest 1867-1900 .... DLB-19, 135

William Doxey [publishing house] DLB-49

Doyle, Sir Arthur Conan
    1859-1930 ... DLB-18, 70, 156, 178; CDBLB-5

    The Priory Scholars of New York Y-99

Doyle, Kirby 1932- DLB-16

Doyle, Roddy 1958- DLB-194

Drabble, Margaret
    1939- DLB-14, 155, 231; CDBLB-8

    Tribute to Graham Greene Y-91

Drach, Albert 1902-1995 .... DLB-85

Drachmann, Holger 1846-1908 .... DLB-300

Dracula (Documentary) DLB-304

Dragojević, Danijel 1934- DLB-181

Dragún, Osvaldo 1929-1999 .... DLB-305

Drake, Samuel Gardner 1798-1875 ...... DLB-187

Drama (See Theater)

The Dramatic Publishing Company DLB-49

Dramatists Play Service DLB-46

Drant, Thomas
    early 1540s?-1578 .... DLB-167

Draper, John W. 1811-1882 .... DLB-30

Draper, Lyman C. 1815-1891 .... DLB-30

Drayton, Michael 1563-1631 .... DLB-121

Dreiser, Theodore 1871-1945
    .... DLB-9, 12, 102, 137; DS-1; CDALB-3

    The International Theodore Dreiser
        Society Y-01

    Notes from the Underground
        of Sister Carrie Y-01

Dresser, Davis 1904-1977 .... DLB-226

Drew, Elizabeth A.
    "A Note on Technique" [excerpt]
    (1926) DLB-36

Drewitz, Ingeborg 1923-1986 .... DLB-75

Drieu La Rochelle, Pierre 1893-1945 ..... DLB-72

Drinker, Elizabeth 1735-1807 .... DLB-200

Drinkwater, John 1882-1937 ..... DLB-10, 19, 149

    The Friends of the Dymock Poets Y-00

Droste-Hülshoff, Annette von
    1797-1848 .... DLB-133; CDWLB-2

The Drue Heinz Literature Prize
    Excerpt from "Excerpts from a Report
    of the Commission," in David
    Bosworth's The Death of Descartes
    An Interview with David Bosworth Y-82

Drummond, William, of Hawthornden
    1585-1649 .... DLB-121, 213

Drummond, William Henry 1854-1907 ... DLB-92

Drummond de Andrade, Carlos
    1902-1987 .... DLB-307

Druzhinin, Aleksandr Vasil'evich
    1824-1864 .... DLB-238

Dryden, Charles 1860?-1931 .... DLB-171

Dryden, John
    1631-1700 ..... DLB-80, 101, 131; CDBLB-2

Držić, Marin
    circa 1508-1567 .... DLB-147; CDWLB-4

Duane, William 1760-1835 .... DLB-43

Dubé, Marcel 1930- DLB-53

Dubé, Rodolphe (see Hertel, François)

Dubie, Norman 1945- DLB-120

Dubin, Al 1891-1945 .... DLB-265

Du Boccage, Anne-Marie 1710-1802 ..... DLB-313

Dubois, Silvia 1788 or 1789?-1889 ..... DLB-239

Du Bois, W. E. B.
    1868-1963 .... DLB-47, 50, 91, 246; CDALB-3

Du Bois, William Pène 1916-1993 .... DLB-61

Dubrovina, Ekaterina Oskarovna
    1846-1913 .... DLB-238

Dubus, Andre 1936-1999 .... DLB-130

    Tribute to Michael M. Rea Y-97

Dubus, Andre, III 1959- DLB-292

Ducange, Victor 1783-1833 .... DLB-192

Du Chaillu, Paul Belloni 1831?-1903 ... DLB-189

Ducharme, Réjean 1941- DLB-60

Dučić, Jovan 1871-1943 ..... DLB-147; CDWLB-4

Duck, Stephen 1705?-1756 .... DLB-95

Gerald Duckworth and Company Limited...................... DLB-112

Duclaux, Madame Mary (see Robinson, A. Mary F.)

Dudek, Louis 1918-2001 .... DLB-88

Dudintsev, Vladimir Dmitrievich 1918-1998..................... DLB-302

Dudley-Smith, Trevor (see Hall, Adam)

Duell, Sloan and Pearce DLB-46

Duerer, Albrecht 1471-1528 ....DLB-179

Duff Gordon, Lucie 1821-1869 .... DLB-166

Dufferin, Helen Lady, Countess of Gifford 1807-1867..................... DLB-199

Duffield and Green.................. DLB-46

Duffy, Maureen 1933- DLB-14, 310

Dufief, Nicholas Gouin 1776-1834 ...... DLB-187

Dufresne, John 1948- DLB-292

Dugan, Alan 1923- DLB-5

Dugard, William 1606-1662........DLB-170, 281

William Dugard [publishing house] DLB-170

Dugas, Marcel 1883-1947.............. DLB-92

William Dugdale [publishing house]..... DLB-106

Duhamel, Georges 1884-1966 .... DLB-65

Dujardin, Edouard 1861-1949 .... DLB-123

Dukes, Ashley 1885-1959.............. DLB-10

Dumas, Alexandre *fils* 1824-1895 .... DLB-192

Dumas, Alexandre *père* 1802-1870..... DLB-119, 192

Dumas, Henry 1934-1968 .... DLB-41

du Maurier, Daphne 1907-1989 .... DLB-191

Du Maurier, George 1834-1896 .....DLB-153, 178

Dummett, Michael 1925- DLB-262

Dunbar, Paul Laurence 1872-1906........ DLB-50, 54, 78; CDALB-3

Introduction to *Lyrics of Lowly Life* (1896), by William Dean Howells....... DLB-50

Dunbar, William circa 1460-circa 1522 .... DLB-132, 146

Duncan, Dave 1933- DLB-251

Duncan, David James 1952- DLB-256

Duncan, Norman 1871-1916........... DLB-92

Duncan, Quince 1940- DLB-145

Duncan, Robert 1919-1988....... DLB-5, 16, 193

Duncan, Ronald 1914-1982 .... DLB-13

Duncan, Sara Jeannette 1861-1922 ..... DLB-92

Dunigan, Edward, and Brother DLB-49

Dunlap, John 1747-1812 .... DLB-43

Dunlap, William 1766-1839 ....DLB-30, 37, 59

Dunlop, William "Tiger" 1792-1848 ..... DLB-99

Dunmore, Helen 1952- DLB-267

Dunn, Douglas 1942- DLB-40

Dunn, Harvey Thomas 1884-1952...... DLB-188

Dunn, Stephen 1939- DLB-105

"The Good, The Not So Good" DLB-105

Dunne, Dominick 1925- DLB-306

Dunne, Finley Peter 1867-1936....... DLB-11, 23

Dunne, John Gregory 1932- Y-80

Dunne, Philip 1908-1992 .... DLB-26

Dunning, Ralph Cheever 1878-1930 .... DLB-4

Dunning, William A. 1857-1922........ DLB-17

Duns Scotus, John circa 1266-1308 ..... DLB-115

Dunsany, Lord (Edward John Moreton Drax Plunkett, Baron Dunsany) 1878-1957......... DLB-10, 77, 153, 156, 255

Dunton, W. Herbert 1878-1936 .... DLB-188

John Dunton [publishing house].........DLB-170

Dupin, Amantine-Aurore-Lucile (see Sand, George)

Du Pont de Nemours, Pierre Samuel 1739-1817..................... DLB-313

Dupuy, Eliza Ann 1814-1880 .... DLB-248

Durack, Mary 1913-1994 .... DLB-260

Durand, Lucile (see Bersianik, Louky)

Duranti, Francesca 1935- DLB-196

Duranty, Walter 1884-1957 .... DLB-29

Duras, Marguerite (Marguerite Donnadieu) 1914-1996 .... DLB-83

Durfey, Thomas 1653-1723 .... DLB-80

Durova, Nadezhda Andreevna (Aleksandr Andreevich Aleksandrov) 1783-1866 .... DLB-198

Durrell, Lawrence 1912-1990 .... DLB-15, 27, 204; Y-90; CDBLB-7

William Durrell [publishing house] DLB-49

Dürrenmatt, Friedrich 1921-1990 ....DLB-69, 124; CDWLB-2

Duston, Hannah 1657-1737............ DLB-200

Dutt, Toru 1856-1877................. DLB-240

E. P. Dutton and Company DLB-49

Duun, Olav 1876-1939............... DLB-297

Duvoisin, Roger 1904-1980 .... DLB-61

Duyckinck, Evert Augustus 1816-1878.................. DLB-3, 64, 250

Duyckinck, George L. 1823-1863 .... DLB-3, 250

Duyckinck and Company DLB-49

Dwight, John Sullivan 1813-1893..... DLB-1, 235

Dwight, Timothy 1752-1817............ DLB-37

America: or, A Poem on the Settlement of the British Colonies, by Timothy Dwight DLB-37

Dybek, Stuart 1942- DLB-130

Tribute to Michael M. Rea Y-97

Dyer, Charles 1928- DLB-13

Dyer, Sir Edward 1543-1607 .... DLB-136

Dyer, George 1755-1841.............. DLB-93

Dyer, John 1699-1757................ DLB-95

Dyk, Viktor 1877-1931............... DLB-215

Dylan, Bob 1941- DLB-16

E

Eager, Edward 1911-1964 .... DLB-22

Eagleton, Terry 1943- DLB-242

Eames, Wilberforce 1855-1937..................... DLB-140

Earle, Alice Morse 1853-1911 .... DLB-221

Earle, John 1600 or 1601-1665......... DLB-151

James H. Earle and Company DLB-49

East Europe
Independence and Destruction, 1918-1941 .... DLB-220

Social Theory and Ethnography: Language and Ethnicity in Western versus Eastern Man ... DLB-220

Eastlake, William 1917-1997......... DLB-6, 206

Eastman, Carol ?- DLB-44

Eastman, Charles A. (Ohiyesa) 1858-1939 ....DLB-175

Eastman, Max 1883-1969.............. DLB-91

Eaton, Daniel Isaac 1753-1814 .... DLB-158

Eaton, Edith Maude 1865-1914 .... DLB-221, 312

Eaton, Winnifred 1875-1954 ...... DLB-221, 312

Eberhart, Richard 1904- DLB-48; CDALB-1

Tribute to Robert Penn Warren Y-89

Ebner, Jeannie 1918- DLB-85

Ebner-Eschenbach, Marie von 1830-1916 .... DLB-81

Ebon 1942- DLB-41

E-Books' Second Act in Libraries Y-02

Ecbasis Captivi circa 1045 .... DLB-148

Ecco Press...................... DLB-46

Eckhart, Meister circa 1260-circa 1328... DLB-115

The Eclectic Review 1805-1868 .... DLB-110

Eco, Umberto 1932- DLB-196, 242

Eddison, E. R. 1882-1945............. DLB-255

Edel, Leon 1907-1997................ DLB-103

Edelfeldt, Inger 1956- DLB-257

A Century of Poetry, a Lifetime of Collecting: J. M. Edelstein's Collection of Twentieth-Century American Poetry Y-02

Edes, Benjamin 1732-1803 .... DLB-43

Edgar, David 1948- DLB-13, 233

Viewpoint: Politics and Performance DLB-13

Edgerton, Clyde 1944- DLB-278

Edgeworth, Maria 1768-1849...............DLB-116, 159, 163

The Edinburgh Review 1802-1929 .... DLB-110

Edinburgh University Press DLB-112

Editing
Conversations with Editors Y-95

Editorial Statements................DLB-137

The Editorial Style of Fredson Bowers ...Y-91

Editorial: The Extension of Copyright ...Y-02

We See the Editor at Work Y-97

Whose *Ulysses*? The Function of Editing .. Y-97

The Editor Publishing Company DLB-49

Editorial Institute at Boston University Y-00

Edmonds, Helen Woods Ferguson (see Kavan, Anna)

Edmonds, Randolph 1900-1983......... DLB-51

Edmonds, Walter D. 1903-1998......... DLB-9

Edric, Robert (see Armitage, G. E.)

Edschmid, Kasimir 1890-1966 .... DLB-56

Edson, Margaret 1961- DLB-266	Elin Pelin 1877-1949 ..... DLB-147; CDWLB-4	Ralph Waldo Emerson in 1982 ..... Y-82
Edson, Russell 1935- DLB-244	Eliot, George 1819-1880 ..... DLB-21, 35, 55; CDBLB-4	The Ralph Waldo Emerson Society Y-99
Edwards, Amelia Anne Blandford 1831-1892 ..... DLB-174	The George Eliot Fellowship Y-99	Emerson, William 1769-1811 ..... DLB-37
Edwards, Dic 1953- DLB-245	Eliot, John 1604-1690 ..... DLB-24	Emerson, William R. 1923-1997 ..... Y-97
Edwards, Edward 1812-1886 ..... DLB-184	Eliot, T. S. 1888-1965 ..... DLB-7, 10, 45, 63, 245; CDALB-5	Emin, Fedor Aleksandrovich circa 1735-1770 ..... DLB-150
Edwards, Jonathan 1703-1758 ..... DLB-24, 270	T. S. Eliot Centennial: The Return of the Old Possum Y-88	Emmanuel, Pierre 1916-1984 ..... DLB-258
Edwards, Jonathan, Jr. 1745-1801 ..... DLB-37	The T. S. Eliot Society: Celebration and Scholarship, 1980-1999 ..... Y-99	Empedocles fifth century B.C. DLB-176
Edwards, Junius 1929- DLB-33	Eliot's Court Press DLB-170	Empson, William 1906-1984 ..... DLB-20
Edwards, Matilda Barbara Betham 1836-1919 ..... DLB-174	Elizabeth I 1533-1603 ..... DLB-136	Enchi Fumiko 1905-1986 ..... DLB-182
Edwards, Richard 1524-1566 ..... DLB-62	Elizabeth von Nassau-Saarbrücken after 1393-1456 ..... DLB-179	Ende, Michael 1929-1995 ..... DLB-75
Edwards, Sarah Pierpont 1710-1758 ..... DLB-200	Elizondo, Salvador 1932- DLB-145	Endō Shūsaku 1923-1996 ..... DLB-182
James Edwards [publishing house] DLB-154	Elizondo, Sergio 1930- DLB-82	Engel, Marian 1933-1985 ..... DLB-53
Effinger, George Alec 1947- DLB-8	Elkin, Stanley 1930-1995 ..... DLB-2, 28, 218, 278; Y-80	Engel'gardt, Sof'ia Vladimirovna 1828-1894 ..... DLB-277
Egerton, George 1859-1945 ..... DLB-135	Elles, Dora Amy (see Wentworth, Patricia)	Engels, Friedrich 1820-1895 ..... DLB-129
Eggleston, Edward 1837-1902 ..... DLB-12	Ellet, Elizabeth F. 1818?-1877 ..... DLB-30	Engle, Paul 1908- DLB-48
Eggleston, Wilfred 1901-1986 ..... DLB-92	Elliot, Ebenezer 1781-1849 ..... DLB-96, 190	Tribute to Robert Penn Warren Y-89
Eglītis, Anšlavs 1906-1993 ..... DLB-220	Elliot, Frances Minto (Dickinson) 1820-1898 ..... DLB-166	English, Thomas Dunn 1819-1902 ..... DLB-202
Eguren, José María 1874-1942 ..... DLB-290	Elliott, Charlotte 1789-1871 ..... DLB-199	Ennius 239 B.C.-169 B.C. DLB-211
Ehrenreich, Barbara 1941- DLB-246	Elliott, George 1923- DLB-68	Enquist, Per Olov 1934- DLB-257
Ehrenstein, Albert 1886-1950 ..... DLB-81	Elliott, George P. 1918-1980 ..... DLB-244	Enright, Anne 1962- DLB-267
Ehrhart, W. D. 1948- DS-9	Elliott, Janice 1931-1995 ..... DLB-14	Enright, D. J. 1920- DLB-27
Ehrlich, Gretel 1946- DLB-212, 275	Elliott, Sarah Barnwell 1848-1928 ..... DLB-221	Enright, Elizabeth 1909-1968 ..... DLB-22
Eich, Günter 1907-1972 ..... DLB-69, 124	Elliott, Sumner Locke 1917-1991 ..... DLB-289	Epictetus circa 55-circa 125-130 ..... DLB-176
Eichendorff, Joseph Freiherr von 1788-1857 ..... DLB-90	Elliott, Thomes and Talbot DLB-49	Epicurus 342/341 B.C.-271/270 B.C. DLB-176
Eifukumon'in 1271-1342 ..... DLB-203	Elliott, William, III 1788-1863 ..... DLB-3, 248	d'Epinay, Louise (Louise-Florence-Pétronille Tardieu d'Esclavelles, marquise d'Epinay) 1726-1783 ..... DLB-313
Eigner, Larry 1926-1996 ..... DLB-5, 193	Ellin, Stanley 1916-1986 ..... DLB-306	Epps, Bernard 1936- DLB-53
Eikon Basilike 1649 ..... DLB-151	Ellis, Alice Thomas (Anna Margaret Haycraft) 1932- DLB-194	Epshtein, Mikhail Naumovich 1950- DLB-285
Eilhart von Oberge circa 1140-circa 1195 ..... DLB-148	Ellis, Bret Easton 1964- DLB-292	Epstein, Julius 1909-2000 and Epstein, Philip 1909-1952 ..... DLB-26
Einar Benediktsson 1864-1940 ..... DLB-293	Ellis, Edward S. 1840-1916 ..... DLB-42	Epstein, Leslie 1938- DLB-299
Einar Kárason 1955- DLB-293	Ellis, George E. "The New Controversy Concerning Miracles DS-5	Editors, Conversations with Y-95
Einar Már Guðmundsson 1954- DLB-293	Ellis, Havelock 1859-1939 ..... DLB-190	Equiano, Olaudah circa 1745-1797 ..... DLB-37, 50, CDWLB-3
Einhard circa 770-840 ..... DLB-148	Frederick Staridge Ellis [publishing house] DLB-106	Olaudah Equiano and Unfinished Journeys: The Slave-Narrative Tradition and Twentieth-Century Continuities DLB-117
Eiseley, Loren 1907-1977 ..... DLB-275, DS-17	The George H. Ellis Company DLB-49	Eragny Press DLB-112
Eisenberg, Deborah 1945- DLB-244	Ellison, Harlan 1934- DLB-8	Erasmus, Desiderius 1467-1536 ..... DLB-136
Eisenreich, Herbert 1925-1986 ..... DLB-85	Tribute to Isaac Asimov Y-92	Erba, Luciano 1922- DLB-128
Eisner, Kurt 1867-1919 ..... DLB-66	Ellison, Ralph 1914-1994 ..... DLB-2, 76, 227; Y-94; CDALB-1	Erdman, Nikolai Robertovich 1900-1970 ..... DLB-272
Ekelöf, Gunnar 1907-1968 ..... DLB-259	Ellmann, Richard 1918-1987 ..... DLB-103; Y-87	Erdrich, Louise 1954- DLB-152, 175, 206; CDALB-7
Eklund, Gordon 1945- Y-83	Ellroy, James 1948- DLB-226; Y-91	Erenburg, Il'ia Grigor'evich 1891-1967 ..... DLB-272
Ekman, Kerstin 1933- DLB-257	Tribute to John D. MacDonald Y-86	Erichsen-Brown, Gwethalyn Graham (see Graham, Gwethalyn)
Ekwensi, Cyprian 1921- DLB-117; CDWLB-3	Tribute to Raymond Chandler Y-88	Eriugena, John Scottus circa 810-877 ..... DLB-115
Elaw, Zilpha circa 1790-? DLB-239	Eluard, Paul 1895-1952 ..... DLB-258	Ernst, Paul 1866-1933 ..... DLB-66, 118
George Eld [publishing house] DLB-170	Elyot, Thomas 1490?-1546 ..... DLB-136	Erofeev, Venedikt Vasil'evich 1938-1990 ..... DLB-285
Elder, Lonne, III 1931- DLB-7, 38, 44	Emanuel, James Andrew 1921- DLB-41	Erofeev, Viktor Vladimirovich 1947- DLB-285
Paul Elder and Company DLB-49	Emecheta, Buchi 1944- DLB-117; CDWLB-3	Ershov, Petr Pavlovich 1815-1869 ..... DLB-205
Eldershaw, Flora (M. Barnard Eldershaw) 1897-1956 ..... DLB-260	Emerson, Ralph Waldo 1803-1882 ..... DLB-1, 59, 73, 183, 223, 270; DS-5; CDALB-2	Erskine, Albert 1911-1993 ..... Y-93
Eldershaw, M. Barnard (see Barnard, Marjorie and Eldershaw, Flora)		
The Electronic Text Center and the Electronic Archive of Early American Fiction at the University of Virginia Library Y-98		
Eliade, Mircea 1907-1986 ..... DLB-220; CDWLB-4		
Elie, Robert 1915-1973 ..... DLB-88		

At Home with Albert Erskine Y-00
Erskine, John 1879-1951 . . . . DLB-9, 102
Erskine, Mrs. Steuart ?-1948 . . . . DLB-195
Ertel', Aleksandr Ivanovich 1855-1908 . . . . DLB-238
Ervine, St. John Greer 1883-1971 . . . . DLB-10
Eschenburg, Johann Joachim 1743-1820 . . . . DLB-97
Escofet, Cristina 1945- DLB-305
Escoto, Julio 1944- DLB-145
Esdaile, Arundell 1880-1956 . . . . DLB-201
Esenin, Sergei Aleksandrovich 1895-1925 . . . . DLB-295
Eshleman, Clayton 1935- DLB-5
Espaillat, Rhina P. 1932- DLB-282
Espanca, Florbela 1894-1930 . . . . DLB-287
Espriu, Salvador 1913-1985 . . . . DLB-134
Ess Ess Publishing Company DLB-49
Essex House Press DLB-112
Esson, Louis 1878-1943 . . . . DLB-260
Essop, Ahmed 1931- DLB-225
Esterházy, Péter 1950- DLB-232; CDWLB-4
Estes, Eleanor 1906-1988 . . . . DLB-22
Estes and Lauriat DLB-49
Estleman, Loren D. 1952- DLB-226
Eszterhas, Joe 1944- DLB-185
Etherege, George 1636-circa 1692 . . . . DLB-80
Ethridge, Mark, Sr. 1896-1981 . . . . DLB-127
Ets, Marie Hall 1893-1984 . . . . DLB-22
Etter, David 1928- DLB-105
Ettner, Johann Christoph 1654-1724 . . . . DLB-168
Eudora Welty Remembered in Two Exhibits Y-02
Eugene Gant's Projected Works Y-01
Eupolemius flourished circa 1095 . . . . DLB-148
Euripides circa 484 B.C.-407/406 B.C. DLB-176; CDWLB-1
Evans, Augusta Jane 1835-1909 . . . . DLB-239
Evans, Caradoc 1878-1945 . . . . DLB-162
Evans, Charles 1850-1935 . . . . DLB-187
Evans, Donald 1884-1921 . . . . DLB-54
Evans, George Henry 1805-1856 . . . . DLB-43
Evans, Hubert 1892-1986 . . . . DLB-92
Evans, Mari 1923- DLB-41
Evans, Mary Ann (see Eliot, George)
Evans, Nathaniel 1742-1767 . . . . DLB-31
Evans, Sebastian 1830-1909 . . . . DLB-35
Evans, Ray 1915- DLB-265
M. Evans and Company DLB-46
Evaristi, Marcella 1953- DLB-233
Everett, Alexander Hill 1790-1847 . . . . DLB-59
Everett, Edward 1794-1865 . . . . DLB-1, 59, 235
Everson, R. G. 1903- DLB-88
Everson, William 1912-1994 . . . . . DLB-5, 16, 212
Ewald, Johannes 1743-1781 . . . . DLB-300

Ewart, Gavin 1916-1995 . . . . DLB-40
Ewing, Juliana Horatia 1841-1885 . . . . DLB-21, 163
The Examiner 1808-1881 . . . . DLB-110
Exley, Frederick 1929-1992 . . . . DLB-143; Y-81
Editorial: The Extension of Copyright Y-02
von Eyb, Albrecht 1420-1475 . . . . DLB-179
Eyre and Spottiswoode DLB-106
Ezera, Regīna 1930- DLB-232
Ezzo ?-after 1065 . . . . DLB-148

F

Faber, Frederick William 1814-1863 . . . . . DLB-32
Faber and Faber Limited DLB-112
Faccio, Rena (see Aleramo, Sibilla)
Facsimiles
  The Uses of Facsimile: A Symposium Y-90
Fadeev, Aleksandr Aleksandrovich 1901-1956 . . . . DLB-272
Fagundo, Ana María 1938- DLB-134
Fainzil'berg, Il'ia Arnol'dovich (see Il'f, Il'ia and Petrov, Evgenii)
Fair, Ronald L. 1932- DLB-33
Fairfax, Beatrice (see Manning, Marie)
Fairlie, Gerard 1899-1983 . . . . DLB-77
Faldbakken, Knut 1941- DLB-297
Falkberget, Johan (Johan Petter Lillebakken) 1879-1967 . . . . DLB-297
Fallada, Hans 1893-1947 . . . . DLB-56
Fancher, Betsy 1928- Y-83
Fane, Violet 1843-1905 . . . . DLB-35
Fanfrolico Press DLB-112
Fanning, Katherine 1927- DLB-127
Fanon, Frantz 1925-1961 . . . . DLB-296
Fanshawe, Sir Richard 1608-1666 . . . . . . DLB-126
Fantasy Press Publishers DLB-46
Fante, John 1909-1983 . . . . DLB-130; Y-83
Al-Farabi circa 870-950 . . . . DLB-115
Farabough, Laura 1949- DLB-228
Farah, Nuruddin 1945- . . . DLB-125; CDWLB-3
Farber, Norma 1909-1984 . . . . DLB-61
A Farewell to Arms (Documentary) DLB-308
Fargue, Léon-Paul 1876-1947 . . . . DLB-258
Farigoule, Louis (see Romains, Jules)
Farjeon, Eleanor 1881-1965 . . . . DLB-160
Farley, Harriet 1812-1907 . . . . DLB-239
Farley, Walter 1920-1989 . . . . DLB-22
Farmborough, Florence 1887-1978 . . . . . DLB-204
Farmer, Penelope 1939- DLB-161
Farmer, Philip José 1918- DLB-8
Farnaby, Thomas 1575?-1647 . . . . DLB-236
Farningham, Marianne (see Hearn, Mary Anne)
Farquhar, George circa 1677-1707 . . . . DLB-84
Farquharson, Martha (see Finley, Martha)
Farrar, Frederic William 1831-1903 . . . . . DLB-163

Farrar, Straus and Giroux DLB-46
Farrar and Rinehart DLB-46
Farrell, J. G. 1935-1979 . . . . DLB-14, 271
Farrell, James T. 1904-1979 . . . DLB-4, 9, 86; DS-2
Fast, Howard 1914- DLB-9
Faulkner, William 1897-1962
  . . . . DLB-9, 11, 44, 102; DS-2; Y-86; CDALB-5
  Faulkner and Yoknapatawpha Conference, Oxford, Mississippi Y-97
  Faulkner Centennial Addresses Y-97
  "Faulkner 100–Celebrating the Work," University of South Carolina, Columbia Y-97
  Impressions of William Faulkner Y-97
  William Faulkner and the People-to-People Program Y-86
  William Faulkner Centenary Celebrations Y-97
  The William Faulkner Society Y-99
George Faulkner [publishing house] DLB-154
Faulks, Sebastian 1953- DLB-207
Fauset, Jessie Redmon 1882-1961 . . . . DLB-51
Faust, Frederick Schiller (Max Brand) 1892-1944 . . . . DLB-256
Faust, Irvin
  1924- DLB-2, 28, 218, 278; Y-80, 00
  I Wake Up Screaming [Response to Ken Auletta] Y-97
  Tribute to Bernard Malamud Y-86
  Tribute to Isaac Bashevis Singer Y-91
  Tribute to Meyer Levin Y-81
Fawcett, Edgar 1847-1904 . . . . DLB-202
Fawcett, Millicent Garrett 1847-1929 . . . . DLB-190
Fawcett Books DLB-46
Fay, Theodore Sedgwick 1807-1898 . . . . . DLB-202
Fearing, Kenneth 1902-1961 . . . . DLB-9
Federal Writers' Project DLB-46
Federman, Raymond 1928- Y-80
Fedin, Konstantin Aleksandrovich 1892-1977 . . . . DLB-272
Fedorov, Innokentii Vasil'evich (see Omulevsky, Innokentii Vasil'evich)
Feiffer, Jules 1929- DLB-7, 44
Feinberg, Charles E. 1899-1988 . . . . DLB-187; Y-88
Feind, Barthold 1678-1721 . . . . DLB-168
Feinstein, Elaine 1930- DLB-14, 40
Feirstein, Frederick 1940- DLB-282
Feiss, Paul Louis 1875-1952 . . . . DLB-187
Feldman, Irving 1928- DLB-169
Felipe, Carlos 1911-1975 . . . . DLB-305
Felipe, Léon 1884-1968 . . . . DLB-108
Fell, Frederick, Publishers DLB-46
Fellowship of Southern Writers Y-98
Felltham, Owen 1602?-1668 . . . . DLB-126, 151
Felman, Shoshana 1942- DLB-246
Fels, Ludwig 1946- DLB-75
Felton, Cornelius Conway 1807-1862 . . . . DLB-1, 235

Mothe-Fénelon, François de Salignac de la
 1651-1715 ....DLB-268

Fenn, Harry 1837-1911 ....DLB-188

Fennario, David 1947- DLB-60

Fenner, Dudley 1558?-1587? DLB-236

Fenno, Jenny 1765?-1803 ....DLB-200

Fenno, John 1751-1798................DLB-43

R. F. Fenno and Company.............DLB-49

Fenoglio, Beppe 1922-1963 ....DLB-177

Fenton, Geoffrey 1539?-1608..........DLB-136

Fenton, James 1949- DLB-40

 The Hemingway/Fenton
  Correspondence Y-02

Ferber, Edna 1885-1968.......DLB-9, 28, 86, 266

Ferdinand, Vallery, III (see Salaam, Kalamu ya)

Ferguson, Sir Samuel 1810-1886 ....DLB-32

Ferguson, William Scott 1875-1954 ......DLB-47

Fergusson, Robert 1750-1774 ....DLB-109

Ferland, Albert 1872-1943 ....DLB-92

Ferlinghetti, Lawrence
 1919- DLB-5, 16; CDALB-1

 Tribute to Kenneth Rexroth Y-82

Fermor, Patrick Leigh 1915- DLB-204

Fern, Fanny (see Parton, Sara Payson Willis)

Ferrars, Elizabeth (Morna Doris Brown)
 1907-1995 ....DLB-87

Ferré, Rosario 1942- DLB-145

Ferreira, Vergílio 1916-1996 ....DLB-287

E. Ferret and Company DLB-49

Ferrier, Susan 1782-1854 ....DLB-116

Ferril, Thomas Hornsby 1896-1988......DLB-206

Ferrini, Vincent 1913- DLB-48

Ferron, Jacques 1921-1985.............DLB-60

Ferron, Madeleine 1922- DLB-53

Ferrucci, Franco 1936- DLB-196

Fet, Afanasii Afanas'evich
 1820?-1892 ....DLB 277

Fetridge and Company DLB-49

Feuchtersleben, Ernst Freiherr von
 1806-1849 ....DLB-133

Feuchtwanger, Lion 1884-1958 ....DLB-66

Feuerbach, Ludwig 1804-1872..........DLB-133

Feuillet, Octave 1821-1890.............DLB-192

Feydeau, Georges 1862-1921 ....DLB-192

Fibiger, Mathilde 1830-1872 ....DLB-300

Fichte, Johann Gottlieb 1762-1814 ......DLB-90

Ficke, Arthur Davison 1883-1945 ....DLB-54

Fiction
 American Fiction and the 1930s DLB-9
 Fiction Best-Sellers, 1910-1945 ....DLB-9
 Postmodern Holocaust Fiction DLB-299
 The Year in Fiction Y-84, 86, 89, 94–99
 The Year in Fiction: A Biased View Y-83
 The Year in U.S. Fiction Y-00, 01
 The Year's Work in Fiction: A Survey ...Y-82

Fiedler, Leslie A. 1917- DLB-28, 67

Tribute to Bernard Malamud Y-86

Tribute to James Dickey Y-97

Field, Barron 1789-1846...............DLB-230

Field, Edward 1924- DLB-105

Field, Eugene 1850-1895 .. DLB-23, 42, 140; DS-13

Field, John 1545?-1588 ....DLB-167

Field, Joseph M. 1810-1856 ....DLB-248

Field, Marshall, III 1893-1956..........DLB-127

Field, Marshall, IV 1916-1965 ....DLB-127

Field, Marshall, V 1941- DLB-127

Field, Michael (Katherine Harris Bradley)
 1846-1914 ....DLB-240

"The Poetry File" DLB-105

Field, Nathan 1587-1619 or 1620.........DLB-58

Field, Rachel 1894-1942..............DLB-9, 22

Fielding, Helen 1958- DLB-231

Fielding, Henry
 1707-1754........DLB-39, 84, 101; CDBLB-2

 "Defense of *Amelia*" (1752)...........DLB-39

 The History of the Adventures of Joseph Andrews
  [excerpt] (1742) DLB-39

 Letter to [Samuel] Richardson on *Clarissa*
  (1748) DLB-39

 Preface to *Joseph Andrews* (1742) DLB-39

 Preface to Sarah Fielding's *Familiar
  Letters* (1747) [excerpt]............DLB-39

 Preface to Sarah Fielding's *The
  Adventures of David Simple* (1744) ...DLB-39

 Review of *Clarissa* (1748) DLB-39

 Tom Jones (1749) [excerpt] DLB-39

Fielding, Sarah 1710-1768 ....DLB-39

 Preface to *The Cry* (1754) DLB-39

Fields, Annie Adams 1834-1915 ....DLB-221

Fields, Dorothy 1905-1974 ....DLB-265

Fields, James T. 1817-1881...........DLB-1, 235

Fields, Julia 1938- DLB-41

Fields, Osgood and Company DLB-49

Fields, W. C. 1880-1946 ....DLB-44

Fierstein, Harvey 1954- DLB-266

Figes, Eva 1932- DLB-14, 271

Figuera, Angela 1902-1984 ....DLB-108

Filmer, Sir Robert 1586-1653...........DLB-151

Filson, John circa 1753-1788...........DLB-37

Finch, Anne, Countess of Winchilsea
 1661-1720 ....DLB-95

Finch, Annie 1956- DLB-282

Finch, Robert 1900- DLB-88

Findley, Timothy 1930-2002 ....DLB-53

Finlay, Ian Hamilton 1925- DLB-40

Finley, Martha 1828-1909 ....DLB-42

Finn, Elizabeth Anne (McCaul)
 1825-1921 ....DLB-166

Finnegan, Seamus 1949- DLB-245

Finney, Jack 1911-1995 ....DLB-8

Finney, Walter Braden (see Finney, Jack)

Firbank, Ronald 1886-1926 ....DLB-36

Firmin, Giles 1615-1697................DLB-24

First Edition Library/Collectors'
 Reprints, Inc......................Y-91

Fischart, Johann
 1546 or 1547-1590 or 1591 ....DLB-179

Fischer, Karoline Auguste Fernandine
 1764-1842 ....DLB-94

Fischer, Tibor 1959- DLB-231

Fish, Stanley 1938- DLB-67

Fishacre, Richard 1205-1248 ....DLB-115

Fisher, Clay (see Allen, Henry W.)

Fisher, Dorothy Canfield 1879-1958 ...DLB-9, 102

Fisher, Leonard Everett 1924- DLB-61

Fisher, Roy 1930- DLB-40

Fisher, Rudolph 1897-1934 ....DLB-51, 102

Fisher, Steve 1913-1980...............DLB-226

Fisher, Sydney George 1856-1927 ....DLB-47

Fisher, Vardis 1895-1968............DLB-9, 206

Fiske, John 1608-1677 ....DLB-24

Fiske, John 1842-1901 ....DLB-47, 64

Fitch, Thomas circa 1700-1774..........DLB-31

Fitch, William Clyde 1865-1909 ....DLB-7

FitzGerald, Edward 1809-1883 ....DLB-32

Fitzgerald, F. Scott 1896-1940
 ....DLB-4, 9, 86; Y-81, 92;
  DS-1, 15, 16; CDALB-4

 F. Scott Fitzgerald: A Descriptive
  Bibliography, Supplement (2001)....Y-01

 F. Scott Fitzgerald Centenary
  Celebrations Y-96

 F. Scott Fitzgerald Inducted into the
  American Poets' Corner at St. John
  the Divine; Ezra Pound Banned.....Y-99

 "F. Scott Fitzgerald: St. Paul's Native Son
  and Distinguished American Writer":
  University of Minnesota Conference,
  29-31 October 1982 ....Y-82

 First International F. Scott Fitzgerald
  Conference Y-92

 The Great Gatsby (Documentary) DLB-219

 Tender Is the Night (Documentary)....DLB-273

Fitzgerald, Penelope 1916- DLB-14, 194

Fitzgerald, Robert 1910-1985...............Y-80

FitzGerald, Robert D. 1902-1987........DLB-260

Fitzgerald, Thomas 1819-1891..........DLB-23

Fitzgerald, Zelda Sayre 1900-1948..........Y-84

Fitzhugh, Louise 1928-1974 ....DLB-52

Fitzhugh, William circa 1651-1701........DLB-24

Flagg, James Montgomery 1877-1960 ....DLB-188

Flanagan, Thomas 1923-2002 ....Y-80

Flanner, Hildegarde 1899-1987 ....DLB-48

Flanner, Janet 1892-1978 ....DLB-4; DS-15

Flannery, Peter 1951- DLB-233

Flaubert, Gustave 1821-1880........DLB-119, 301

Flavin, Martin 1883-1967 ....DLB-9

Fleck, Konrad (flourished circa 1220) DLB-138

Flecker, James Elroy 1884-1915 ....DLB-10, 19

Fleeson, Doris 1901-1970...............DLB-29

Fleißer, Marieluise 1901-1974 ....DLB-56, 124

Fleischer, Nat 1887-1972 .... DLB-241
Fleming, Abraham 1552?-1607 .... DLB-236
Fleming, Ian 1908-1964 .. DLB-87, 201; CDBLB-7
Fleming, Joan 1908-1980 .... DLB-276
Fleming, May Agnes 1840-1880 .... DLB-99
Fleming, Paul 1609-1640 .... DLB-164
Fleming, Peter 1907-1971 .... DLB-195
Fletcher, Giles, the Elder 1546-1611 ..... DLB-136
Fletcher, Giles, the Younger
  1585 or 1586-1623 .... DLB-121
Fletcher, J. S. 1863-1935 .... DLB-70
Fletcher, John 1579-1625 .... DLB-58
Fletcher, John Gould 1886-1950 .... DLB-4, 45
Fletcher, Phineas 1582-1650 .... DLB-121
Flieg, Helmut (see Heym, Stefan)
Flint, F. S. 1885-1960 .... DLB-19
Flint, Timothy 1780-1840 .... DLB-73, 186
Fløgstad, Kjartan 1944- DLB-297
Florensky, Pavel Aleksandrovich
  1882-1937 .... DLB-295
Flores, Juan de fl. 1470-1500 .... DLB-286
Flores-Williams, Jason 1969- DLB-209
Florio, John 1553?-1625 .... DLB-172
Fludd, Robert 1574-1637 .... DLB-281
Flynn, Elizabeth Gurley 1890-1964 ..... DLB-303
Fo, Dario 1926- Y-97
  Nobel Lecture 1997: Contra Jogulatores
    Obloquentes Y-97
Foden, Giles 1967- DLB-267
Fofanov, Konstantin Mikhailovich
  1862-1911 .... DLB-277
Foix, J. V. 1893-1987 .... DLB-134
Foley, Martha 1897-1977 .... DLB-137
Folger, Henry Clay 1857-1930 .... DLB-140
Folio Society DLB-112
Follain, Jean 1903-1971 .... DLB-258
Follen, Charles 1796-1840 .... DLB-235
Follen, Eliza Lee (Cabot) 1787-1860 ... DLB-1, 235
Follett, Ken 1949- DLB-87; Y-81
Follett Publishing Company DLB-46
John West Folsom [publishing house] DLB-49
Folz, Hans
  between 1435 and 1440-1513 .... DLB-179
Fonseca, Manuel da 1911-1993 .... DLB-287
Fonseca, Rubem 1925- DLB-307
Fontane, Theodor
  1819-1898 .... DLB-129; CDWLB-2
Fontenelle, Bernard Le Bovier de
  1657-1757 .... DLB-268, 313
Fontes, Montserrat 1940- DLB-209
Fonvisin, Denis Ivanovich
  1744 or 1745-1792 .... DLB-150
Foote, Horton 1916- DLB-26, 266
Foote, Mary Hallock
  1847-1938 .... DLB-186, 188, 202, 221
Foote, Samuel 1721-1777 .... DLB-89
Foote, Shelby 1916- DLB-2, 17

Forbes, Calvin 1945- DLB-41
Forbes, Ester 1891-1967 .... DLB-22
Forbes, Rosita 1893?-1967 .... DLB-195
Forbes and Company DLB-49
Force, Peter 1790-1868 .... DLB-30
Forché, Carolyn 1950- DLB-5, 193
Ford, Charles Henri 1913-2002 .... DLB-4, 48
Ford, Corey 1902-1969 .... DLB-11
Ford, Ford Madox
  1873-1939 .... DLB-34, 98, 162; CDBLB-6
  Nathan Asch Remembers Ford Madox
    Ford, Sam Roth, and Hart Crane ... Y-02
J. B. Ford and Company DLB-49
Ford, Jesse Hill 1928-1996 .... DLB-6
Ford, John 1586-? DLB-58; CDBLB-1
Ford, R. A. D. 1915- DLB-88
Ford, Richard 1944- DLB-227
Ford, Worthington C. 1858-1941 .... DLB-47
Fords, Howard, and Hulbert DLB-49
Foreman, Carl 1914-1984 .... DLB-26
Forester, C. S. 1899-1966 .... DLB-191
  The C. S. Forester Society Y-00
Forester, Frank (see Herbert, Henry William)
Anthologizing New Formalism DLB-282
The Little Magazines of the
  New Formalism DLB-282
The New Narrative Poetry DLB-282
Presses of the New Formalism and
  the New Narrative DLB-282
The Prosody of the New Formalism DLB-282
Younger Women Poets of the
  New Formalism DLB-282
Forman, Harry Buxton 1842-1917 ..... DLB-184
Fornés, María Irene 1930- DLB-7
Forrest, Leon 1937-1997 .... DLB-33
Forsh, Ol'ga Dmitrievna 1873-1961 ..... DLB-272
Forster, E. M. 1879-1970
  ..DLB-34, 98, 162, 178, 195; DS-10; CDBLB-6
  "Fantasy," from Aspects of the Novel
    (1927) DLB-178
Forster, Georg 1754-1794 .... DLB-94
Forster, John 1812-1876 .... DLB-144
Forster, Margaret 1938- DLB-155, 271
Forsyth, Frederick 1938- DLB-87
Forsyth, William
  "Literary Style" (1857) [excerpt] DLB-57
Forten, Charlotte L. 1837-1914 ..... DLB-50, 239
  Pages from Her Diary DLB-50
Fortini, Franco 1917-1994 .... DLB-128
Fortune, Mary ca. 1833-ca. 1910 ...... DLB-230
Fortune, T. Thomas 1856-1928 .... DLB-23
Fosdick, Charles Austin 1842-1915 ..... DLB-42
Fosse, Jon 1959- DLB-297
Foster, David 1944- DLB-289
Foster, Genevieve 1893-1979 .... DLB-61
Foster, Hannah Webster
  1758-1840 .... DLB-37, 200

Foster, John 1648-1681 .... DLB-24
Foster, Michael 1904-1956 .... DLB-9
Foster, Myles Birket 1825-1899 .... DLB-184
Foster, William Z. 1881-1961 .... DLB-303
Foucault, Michel 1926-1984 .... DLB-242
Robert and Andrew Foulis
  [publishing house] DLB-154
Fouqué, Caroline de la Motte 1774-1831 ... DLB-90
Fouqué, Friedrich de la Motte
  1777-1843 .... DLB-90
Four Seas Company DLB-46
Four Winds Press DLB-46
Fournier, Henri Alban (see Alain-Fournier)
Fowler, Christopher 1953- DLB-267
Fowler, Connie May 1958- DLB-292
Fowler and Wells Company DLB-49
Fowles, John
  1926- DLB-14, 139, 207; CDBLB-8
Fox, John 1939- DLB-245
Fox, John, Jr. 1862 or 1863-1919 ... DLB-9; DS-13
Fox, Paula 1923- DLB-52
Fox, Richard Kyle 1846-1922 .... DLB-79
Fox, William Price 1926- DLB-2; Y-81
  Remembering Joe Heller Y-99
Richard K. Fox [publishing house] DLB-49
Foxe, John 1517-1587 .... DLB-132
Fraenkel, Michael 1896-1957 .... DLB-4
France, Anatole 1844-1924 .... DLB-123
France, Richard 1938- DLB-7
Francis, Convers 1795-1863 .... DLB-1, 235
Francis, Dick 1920- DLB-87; CDBLB-8
Francis, Sir Frank 1901-1988 .... DLB-201
Francis, Jeffrey, Lord 1773-1850 .... DLB-107
C. S. Francis [publishing house] DLB-49
Franck, Sebastian 1499-1542 .... DLB-179
Francke, Kuno 1855-1930 .... DLB-71
Françoise (Robertine Barry) 1863-1910 ... DLB-92
François, Louise von 1817-1893 .... DLB-129
Frank, Bruno 1887-1945 .... DLB-118
Frank, Leonhard 1882-1961 .... DLB-56, 118
Frank, Melvin 1913-1988 .... DLB-26
Frank, Waldo 1889-1967 .... DLB-9, 63
Franken, Rose 1895?-1988 .... DLB-228, Y-84
Franklin, Benjamin
  1706-1790 .... DLB-24, 43, 73, 183; CDALB-2
Franklin, James 1697-1735 .... DLB-43
Franklin, John 1786-1847 .... DLB-99
Franklin, Miles 1879-1954 .... DLB-230
Franklin Library DLB-46
Frantz, Ralph Jules 1902-1979 .... DLB-4
Franzos, Karl Emil 1848-1904 .... DLB-129
Fraser, Antonia 1932- DLB-276
Fraser, G. S. 1915-1980 .... DLB-27
Fraser, Kathleen 1935- DLB-169
Frattini, Alberto 1922- DLB-128

Frau Ava ?-1127...................DLB-148
Fraunce, Abraham 1558?-1592 or 1593...DLB-236
Frayn, Michael 1933- DLB-13, 14, 194, 245
Frazier, Charles 1950- DLB-292
Fréchette, Louis-Honoré 1839-1908.......DLB-99
Frederic, Harold 1856-1898....DLB-12, 23; DS-13
Freed, Arthur 1894-1973 ....DLB-265
Freeling, Nicolas 1927- DLB-87
   Tribute to Georges Simenon............Y-89
Freeman, Douglas Southall
   1886-1953.................DLB-17; DS-17
Freeman, Joseph 1897-1965 ....DLB-303
Freeman, Judith 1946- DLB-256
Freeman, Legh Richmond 1842-1915.....DLB-23
Freeman, Mary E. Wilkins
   1852-1930 ....DLB-12, 78, 221
Freeman, R. Austin 1862-1943 ....DLB-70
Freidank circa 1170-circa 1233..........DLB-138
Freiligrath, Ferdinand 1810-1876 ....DLB-133
Fremlin, Celia 1914- DLB-276
Frémont, Jessie Benton 1834-1902.......DLB-183
Frémont, John Charles
   1813-1890 ....DLB-183, 186
French, Alice 1850-1934 ....DLB-74; DS-13
French, David 1939- DLB-53
French, Evangeline 1869-1960..........DLB-195
French, Francesca 1871-1960 ....DLB-195
James French [publishing house] DLB-49
Samuel French [publishing house] DLB-49
Samuel French, Limited DLB-106
French Literature
   Epic and Beast Epic................DLB-208
   French Arthurian Literature DLB-208
   Lyric Poetry DLB-268
   Other Poets......................DLB-217
   Poetry in Nineteenth-Century France:
     Cultural Background and Critical
     Commentary DLB-217
   Roman de la Rose: Guillaume de Lorris
     1200 to 1205-circa 1230, Jean de
     Meun 1235/1240-circa 1305.....DLB-208
   Saints' Lives DLB-208
   Troubadours, *Trobaíritz,* and
     Trouvères....................DLB-208
French Theater
   Medieval French Drama DLB-208
   Parisian Theater, Fall 1984: Toward
     a New Baroque...................Y-85
Freneau, Philip 1752-1832 ....DLB-37, 43
   The Rising Glory of America DLB-37
Freni, Melo 1934- DLB-128
Fréron, Elie Catherine 1718-1776.........DLB-313
Freshfield, Douglas W. 1845-1934........DLB-174
Freud, Sigmund 1856-1939 ....DLB-296
Freytag, Gustav 1816-1895 ....DLB-129
Frída Á. Sigurðardóttir 1940- DLB-293
Fridegård, Jan 1897-1968 ....DLB-259
Fried, Erich 1921-1988..................DLB-85

Friedan, Betty 1921- DLB-246
Friedman, Bruce Jay 1930- DLB-2, 28, 244
Friedman, Carl 1952- DLB-299
Friedman, Kinky 1944- DLB-292
Friedrich von Hausen circa 1171-1190....DLB-138
Friel, Brian 1929- DLB-13
Friend, Krebs 1895?-1967? DLB-4
Fries, Fritz Rudolf 1935- DLB-75
Frisch, Max
   1911-1991 ....DLB-69, 124; CDWLB-2
Frischlin, Nicodemus 1547-1590 ....DLB-179
Frischmuth, Barbara 1941- DLB-85
Fritz, Jean 1915- DLB-52
Froissart, Jean circa 1337-circa 1404......DLB-208
Fromm, Erich 1900-1980................DLB-296
Fromentin, Eugene 1820-1876 ....DLB-123
Frontinus circa A.D. 35-A.D. 103/104 .....DLB-211
Frost, A. B. 1851-1928............DLB-188; DS-13
Frost, Robert
   1874-1963 ....DLB-54; DS-7; CDALB-4
   The Friends of the Dymock Poets.......Y-00
Frostenson, Katarina 1953- DLB-257
Frothingham, Octavius Brooks
   1822-1895 ....DLB-1, 243
Froude, James Anthony
   1818-1894 ....DLB-18, 57, 144
Fruitlands 1843-1844.........DLB-1, 223; DS-5
Fry, Christopher 1907- DLB-13
   Tribute to John Betjeman Y-84
Fry, Roger 1866-1934 ....DS-10
Fry, Stephen 1957- DLB-207
Frye, Northrop 1912-1991 ....DLB-67, 68, 246
Fuchs, Daniel 1909-1993 .....DLB-9, 26, 28; Y-93
   Tribute to Isaac Bashevis Singer Y-91
Fuentes, Carlos 1928- DLB-113; CDWLB-3
Fuertes, Gloria 1918-1998 ....DLB-108
Fugard, Athol 1932- DLB-225
The Fugitives and the Agrarians:
   The First Exhibition Y-85
Fujiwara no Shunzei 1114-1204.........DLB-203
Fujiwara no Tameaki 1230s?-1290s?.....DLB-203
Fujiwara no Tameie 1198-1275 ....DLB-203
Fujiwara no Teika 1162-1241 ....DLB-203
Fuks, Ladislav 1923-1994 ....DLB-299
Fulbecke, William 1560-1603?..........DLB-172
Fuller, Charles 1939- DLB-38, 266
Fuller, Henry Blake 1857-1929 ....DLB-12
Fuller, John 1937- DLB-40
Fuller, Margaret (see Fuller, Sarah)
Fuller, Roy 1912-1991 ....DLB-15, 20
   Tribute to Christopher Isherwood Y-86
Fuller, Samuel 1912-1997..............DLB-26
Fuller, Sarah 1810-1850.......... DLB-1, 59, 73,
             183, 223, 239; DS-5; CDALB-2
Fuller, Thomas 1608-1661.............DLB-151
Fullerton, Hugh 1873-1945 ....DLB-171

Fullwood, William flourished 1568......DLB-236
Fulton, Alice 1952- DLB-193
Fulton, Len 1934- Y-86
Fulton, Robin 1937- DLB-40
Furbank, P. N. 1920- DLB-155
Furetière, Antoine 1619-1688...........DLB-268
Furman, Laura 1945- Y-86
Furmanov, Dmitrii Andreevich
   1891-1926....................DLB-272
Furness, Horace Howard 1833-1912......DLB-64
Furness, William Henry
   1802-1896....................DLB-1, 235
Furnivall, Frederick James 1825-1910....DLB-184
Furphy, Joseph (Tom Collins)
   1843-1912....................DLB-230
Furthman, Jules 1888-1966 ....DLB-26
   Shakespeare and Montaigne: A
     Symposium by Jules Furthman.......Y-02
Furui Yoshikichi 1937- DLB-182
Fushimi, Emperor 1265-1317...........DLB-203
Futabatei Shimei (Hasegawa Tatsunosuke)
   1864-1909....................DLB-180
Fyleman, Rose 1877-1957...............DLB-160

G

Gaarder, Jostein 1952- DLB-297
Gadallah, Leslie 1939- DLB-251
Gadamer, Hans-Georg 1900-2002........DLB-296
Gadda, Carlo Emilio 1893-1973 ....DLB-177
Gaddis, William 1922-1998..........DLB-2, 278
   William Gaddis: A Tribute............Y-99
Gág, Wanda 1893-1946.................DLB-22
Gagarin, Ivan Sergeevich 1814-1882.....DLB-198
Gagnon, Madeleine 1938- DLB-60
Gaiman, Neil 1960- DLB-261
Gaine, Hugh 1726-1807................DLB-43
Hugh Gaine [publishing house]..........DLB-49
Gaines, Ernest J.
   1933- DLB-2, 33, 152; Y-80; CDALB-6
Gaiser, Gerd 1908-1976................DLB-69
Gaitskill, Mary 1954- DLB-244
Galarza, Ernesto 1905-1984.............DLB-122
Galaxy Science Fiction Novels..........DLB-46
Galbraith, Robert (or Caubraith)
   circa 1483-1544.................DLB-281
Gale, Zona 1874-1938 ....DLB-9, 228, 78
Galen of Pergamon 129-after 210 ....DLB-176
Gales, Winifred Marshall 1761-1839.....DLB-200
Medieval Galician-Portuguese Poetry DLB-287
Gall, Louise von 1815-1855..............DLB-133
Gallagher, Tess 1943- DLB-120, 212, 244
Gallagher, Wes 1911- DLB-127
Gallagher, William Davis 1808-1894......DLB-73
Gallant, Mavis 1922- DLB-53
Gallegos, María Magdalena 1935- DLB-209
Gallico, Paul 1897-1976 ....DLB-9, 171

Gallop, Jane 1952- DLB-246	Garrett, Almeida (João Baptista da Silva Leitão de Almeida Garrett) 1799-1854.................... DLB-287	Geddes, Gary 1940- DLB-60
Galloway, Grace Growden 1727-1782.... DLB-200		Geddes, Virgil 1897- DLB-4
Gallup, Donald 1913-2000 .... DLB-187	Garrett, George 1929- DLB-2, 5, 130, 152; Y-83	Gedeon (Georgii Andreevich Krinovsky) circa 1730-1763.................. DLB-150
Galsworthy, John 1867-1933 ...... DLB-10, 34, 98, 162; DS-16; CDBLB-5	Literary Prizes Y-00	Gee, Maggie 1948- DLB-207
Galt, John 1779-1839......... DLB-99, 116, 159	My Summer Reading Orgy: Reading for Fun and Games: One Reader's Report on the Summer of 2001...... Y-01	Gee, Shirley 1932- DLB-245
Galton, Sir Francis 1822-1911......... DLB-166		Geibel, Emanuel 1815-1884 .... DLB-129
Galvin, Brendan 1938- DLB-5	A Summing Up at Century's End Y-99	Geiogamah, Hanay 1945- DLB-175
Gambaro, Griselda 1928- DLB-305	Tribute to James Dickey Y-97	Geis, Bernard, Associates DLB-46
Gambit DLB-46	Tribute to Michael M. Rea Y-97	Geisel, Theodor Seuss 1904-1991 ...DLB-61; Y-91
Gamboa, Reymundo 1948- DLB-122	Tribute to Paxton Davis Y-94	Gelb, Arthur 1924- DLB-103
Gammer Gurton's Needle................ DLB-62	Tribute to Peter Taylor Y-94	Gelb, Barbara 1926- DLB-103
Gan, Elena Andreevna (Zeneida R-va) 1814-1842..................... DLB-198	Tribute to William Goyen Y-83	Gelber, Jack 1932- DLB-7, 228
	A Writer Talking: A Collage.......... Y-00	Gélinas, Gratien 1909-1999 .... DLB-88
Gandlevsky, Sergei Markovich 1952- .. DLB-285	Garrett, John Work 1872-1942......... DLB-187	Gellert, Christian Füerchtegott 1715-1769 .... DLB-97
Gannett, Frank E. 1876-1957 .... DLB-29	Garrick, David 1717-1779 .... DLB-84, 213	
Gao Xingjian 1940- Y-00	Garrison, William Lloyd 1805-1879....... DLB-1, 43, 235; CDALB-2	Gellhorn, Martha 1908-1998 .... Y-82, 98
Nobel Lecture 2000: "The Case for Literature".................... Y-00		Gems, Pam 1925- DLB-13
	Garro, Elena 1920-1998............. DLB-145	Genet, Jean 1910-1986 ....DLB-72; Y-86
Gaos, Vicente 1919-1980 .... DLB-134	Garshin, Vsevolod Mikhailovich 1855-1888 .... DLB-277	Genette, Gérard 1930- DLB-242
García, Andrew 1854?-1943........... DLB-209		Genevoix, Maurice 1890-1980.......... DLB-65
García, Cristina 1958- DLB-292	Garth, Samuel 1661-1719 .... DLB-95	Genis, Aleksandr Aleksandrovich 1953- DLB-285
García, Lionel G. 1935- DLB-82	Garve, Andrew 1908-2001 .... DLB-87	
García, Richard 1941- DLB-209	Gary, Romain 1914-1980 .... DLB-83, 299	Genlis, Stéphanie-Félicité Ducrest, comtesse de 1746-1830...................... DLB-313
García, Santiago 1928- DLB-305	Gascoigne, George 1539?-1577......... DLB-136	
García Márquez, Gabriel 1928- DLB-113; Y-82; CDWLB-3	Gascoyne, David 1916-2001 .... DLB-20	Genovese, Eugene D. 1930- DLB-17
	Gash, Jonathan (John Grant) 1933- DLB-276	Gent, Peter 1942- Y-82
The Magical World of Macondo........ Y-82	Gaskell, Elizabeth Cleghorn 1810-1865 ..... DLB-21, 144, 159; CDBLB-4	Geoffrey of Monmouth circa 1100-1155 .... DLB-146
Nobel Lecture 1982: The Solitude of Latin America Y-82		
A Tribute to Gabriel García Márquez.... Y-82	The Gaskell Society.................. Y-98	George, Elizabeth 1949- DLB-306
García Marruz, Fina 1923- DLB-283	Gaskell, Jane 1941- DLB-261	George, Henry 1839-1897 .... DLB-23
García-Camarillo, Cecilio 1943- DLB-209	Gaspey, Thomas 1788-1871 .... DLB-116	George, Jean Craighead 1919- DLB-52
Gardam, Jane 1928- DLB-14, 161, 231	Gass, William H. 1924- DLB-2, 227	George, W. L. 1882-1926..............DLB-197
Gardell, Jonas 1963- DLB-257	Gates, Doris 1901-1987 .... DLB-22	George III, King of Great Britain and Ireland 1738-1820 .... DLB-213
Garden, Alexander circa 1685-1756 ..... DLB-31	Gates, Henry Louis, Jr. 1950- DLB-67	
Gardiner, John Rolfe 1936- DLB-244	Gates, Lewis E. 1860-1924............. DLB-71	*Georgslied* 896?..................... DLB-148
Gardiner, Margaret Power Farmer (see Blessington, Marguerite, Countess of)	Gatto, Alfonso 1909-1976............. DLB-114	Gerber, Merrill Joan 1938- DLB-218
	Gault, William Campbell 1910-1995 .... DLB-226	Gerhardie, William 1895-1977 .... DLB-36
Gardner, John 1933-1982 .... DLB-2; Y-82; CDALB-7	Tribute to Kenneth Millar Y-83	Gerhardt, Paul 1607-1676 .... DLB-164
	Gaunt, Mary 1861-1942...........DLB-174, 230	Gérin, Winifred 1901-1981 .... DLB-155
Garfield, Leon 1921-1996............. DLB-161	Gautier, Théophile 1811-1872 .... DLB-119	Gérin-Lajoie, Antoine 1824-1882........ DLB-99
Garis, Howard R. 1873-1962 .... DLB-22	Gautreaux, Tim 1947- DLB-292	German Literature A Call to Letters and an Invitation to the Electric Chair DLB-75
Garland, Hamlin 1860-1940...DLB-12, 71, 78, 186	Gauvreau, Claude 1925-1971 .... DLB-88	
The Hamlin Garland Society........... Y-01	The *Gawain*-Poet flourished circa 1350-1400 .... DLB-146	
Garneau, François-Xavier 1809-1866..... DLB-99		The Conversion of an Unpolitical Man DLB-66
Garneau, Hector de Saint-Denys 1912-1943.................... DLB-88	Gawsworth, John (Terence Ian Fytton Armstrong) 1912-1970 .... DLB-255	The German Radio Play DLB-124
		The German Transformation from the Baroque to the Enlightenment.... DLB-97
Garneau, Michel 1939- DLB-53	Gay, Ebenezer 1696-1787 .... DLB-24	
Garner, Alan 1934- DLB-161, 261	Gay, John 1685-1732 .... DLB-84, 95	Germanophilism DLB-66
Garner, Hugh 1913-1979 .... DLB-68	Gayarré, Charles E. A. 1805-1895 .... DLB-30	A Letter from a New Germany Y-90
Garnett, David 1892-1981 .... DLB-34	Charles Gaylord [publishing house]...... DLB-49	The Making of a People........... DLB-66
Garnett, Eve 1900-1991 .... DLB-160	Gaylord, Edward King 1873-1974 ...... DLB-127	The Novel of Impressionism DLB-66
Garnett, Richard 1835-1906 .... DLB-184	Gaylord, Edward Lewis 1919- DLB-127	Pattern and Paradigm: History as Design.................... DLB-75
Garrard, Lewis H. 1829-1887 .... DLB-186	Gébler, Carlo 1954- DLB-271	
Garraty, John A. 1920- DLB-17	Geda, Sigitas 1943- DLB-232	Premisses DLB-66
		The 'Twenties and Berlin DLB-66

Wolfram von Eschenbach's *Parzival:* Prologue and Book 3 ....DLB-138

Writers and Politics: 1871-1918.......DLB-66

German Literature, Middle Ages
Abrogans circa 790-800 ....DLB-148

Annolied between 1077 and 1081 .....DLB-148

The Arthurian Tradition and Its European Context DLB-138

Cambridge Songs (Carmina Cantabrigensia) circa 1050 ....DLB-148

Christus und die Samariterin circa 950 ...DLB-148

De Heinrico circa 980?...............DLB-148

Ecbasis Captivi circa 1045 ....DLB-148

Georgslied 896?....................DLB-148

German Literature and Culture from Charlemagne to the Early Courtly Period...........DLB-148; CDWLB-2

The Germanic Epic and Old English Heroic Poetry: *Widsith, Waldere,* and *The Fight at Finnsburg* DLB-146

Graf Rudolf between circa 1170 and circa 1185 ....DLB-148

Heliand circa 850 ....DLB-148

Das Hildesbrandslied circa 820 ....DLB-148; CDWLB-2

Kaiserchronik circa 1147..............DLB-148

The Legends of the Saints and a Medieval Christian Worldview DLB-148

Ludus de Antichristo circa 1160.......DLB-148

Ludwigslied 881 or 882.............DLB-148

Muspilli circa 790-circa 850 ....DLB-148

Old German Genesis and *Old German Exodus* circa 1050-circa 1130 .....DLB-148

Old High German Charms and Blessings DLB-148; CDWLB-2

The *Old High German Isidor* circa 790-800..........DLB-148

Petruslied circa 854? DLB-148

Physiologus circa 1070-circa 1150......DLB-148

Ruodlieb circa 1050-1075............DLB-148

"*Spielmannsepen*" (circa 1152 circa 1500) DLB-148

The Strasbourg Oaths 842 ....DLB-148

Tatian circa 830 ....DLB-148

Waltharius circa 825 ....DLB-148

Wessobrunner Gebet circa 787-815......DLB-148

German Theater
German Drama 800-1280 ....DLB-138

German Drama from Naturalism to Fascism: 1889-1933 ....DLB-118

Gernsback, Hugo 1884-1967 ....DLB-8, 137

Gerould, Katharine Fullerton 1879-1944 ....DLB-78

Samuel Gerrish [publishing house] DLB-49

Gerrold, David 1944- DLB-8

Gersão, Teolinda 1940- DLB-287

Gershon, Karen 1923-1993 ....DLB-299

Gershwin, Ira 1896-1983 ....DLB-265

The Ira Gershwin Centenary Y-96

Gerson, Jean 1363-1429...............DLB-208

Gersonides 1288-1344 ....DLB-115

Gerstäcker, Friedrich 1816-1872 ....DLB-129

Gertsen, Aleksandr Ivanovich (see Herzen, Alexander)

Gerstenberg, Heinrich Wilhelm von 1737-1823.....................DLB-97

Gervinus, Georg Gottfried 1805-1871 ....DLB-133

Gery, John 1953- DLB-282

Geßner, Solomon 1730-1788 ....DLB-97

Geston, Mark S. 1946- DLB-8

Al-Ghazali 1058-1111.................DLB-115

Gibbings, Robert 1889-1958 ....DLB-195

Gibbon, Edward 1737-1794 ....DLB-104

Gibbon, John Murray 1875-1952.........DLB-92

Gibbon, Lewis Grassic (see Mitchell, James Leslie)

Gibbons, Floyd 1887-1939 ....DLB-25

Gibbons, Kaye 1960- DLB-292

Gibbons, Reginald 1947- DLB-120

Gibbons, William ?-? DLB-73

Gibson, Charles Dana 1867-1944 ....DLB-188; DS-13

Gibson, Graeme 1934- DLB-53

Gibson, Margaret 1944- DLB-120

Gibson, Margaret Dunlop 1843-1920 ....DLB-174

Gibson, Wilfrid 1878-1962............DLB-19

The Friends of the Dymock Poets.......Y-00

Gibson, William 1914- DLB-7

Gibson, William 1948- DLB-251

Gide, André 1869-1951 ....DLB-65

Giguère, Diane 1937- DLB-53

Giguère, Roland 1929- DLB-60

Gil de Biedma, Jaime 1929-1990 ....DLB-108

Gil-Albert, Juan 1906-1994 ....DLB-134

Gilbert, Anthony 1899-1973 ....DLB-77

Gilbert, Elizabeth 1969- DLB-292

Gilbert, Sir Humphrey 1537-1583 ....DLB-136

Gilbert, Michael 1912- DLB-87

Gilbert, Sandra M. 1936- DLB-120, 246

Gilchrist, Alexander 1828-1861 ....DLB-144

Gilchrist, Ellen 1935- DLB-130

Gilder, Jeannette L. 1849-1916 ....DLB-79

Gilder, Richard Watson 1844-1909....DLB-64, 79

Gildersleeve, Basil 1831-1924 ....DLB-71

Giles, Henry 1809-1882...............DLB-64

Giles of Rome circa 1243-1316 ....DLB-115

Gilfillan, George 1813-1878 ....DLB-144

Gill, Eric 1882-1940 ....DLB-98

Gill, Sarah Prince 1728-1771 ....DLB-200

William F. Gill Company DLB-49

Gillespie, A. Lincoln, Jr. 1895-1950 ......DLB-4

Gillespie, Haven 1883-1975 ....DLB-265

Gilliam, Florence ?-? DLB-4

Gilliatt, Penelope 1932-1993 ....DLB-14

Gillott, Jacky 1939-1980 ....DLB-14

Gilman, Caroline H. 1794-1888........DLB-3, 73

Gilman, Charlotte Perkins 1860-1935....DLB-221

The Charlotte Perkins Gilman Society...Y-99

W. and J. Gilman [publishing house].......DLB-49

Gilmer, Elizabeth Meriwether 1861-1951 ....DLB-29

Gilmer, Francis Walker 1790-1826 ....DLB-37

Gilmore, Mary 1865-1962.............DLB-260

Gilroy, Frank D. 1925- DLB-7

Gimferrer, Pere (Pedro) 1945- DLB-134

Gingrich, Arnold 1903-1976 ....DLB-137

Prospectus From the Initial Issue of *Esquire* (Autumn 1933) DLB-137

"With the Editorial Ken," Prospectus From the Initial Issue of *Ken* (7 April 1938) DLB-137

Ginsberg, Allen 1926-1997 ....DLB-5, 16, 169, 237; CDALB-1

Ginzburg, Evgeniia 1904-1977 ....DLB-302

Ginzburg, Lidiia Iakovlevna 1902-1990 ....DLB-302

Ginzburg, Natalia 1916-1991 ....DLB-177

Ginzkey, Franz Karl 1871-1963 ....DLB-81

Gioia, Dana 1950- DLB-120, 282

Giono, Jean 1895-1970................DLB-72

Giotti, Virgilio 1885-1957 ....DLB-114

Giovanni, Nikki 1943- DLB-5, 41; CDALB-7

Giovannitti, Arturo 1884-1959 ....DLB-303

Gipson, Lawrence Henry 1880-1971 .....DLB-17

Girard, Rodolphe 1879-1956 ....DLB-92

Giraudoux, Jean 1882-1944............DLB-65

Girondo, Oliverio 1891-1967...........DLB-283

Gissing, George 1857-1903 .....DLB-18, 135, 184

The Place of Realism in Fiction (1895)...DLB-18

Giudici, Giovanni 1924- DLB-128

Giuliani, Alfredo 1924- DLB-128

Gjellerup, Karl 1857-1919 ....DLB-300

Glackens, William J. 1870-1938.........DLB-188

Gladilin, Anatolii Tikhonovich 1935- DLB-302

Gladkov, Fedor Vasil'evich 1883-1958 ...DLB-272

Gladstone, William Ewart 1809-1898 ....DLB-57, 184

Glaeser, Ernst 1902-1963..............DLB-69

Glancy, Diane 1941- DLB-175

Glanvill, Joseph 1636-1680 ....DLB-252

Glanville, Brian 1931- DLB-15, 139

Glapthorne, Henry 1610-1643?..........DLB-58

Glasgow, Ellen 1873-1945.............DLB-9, 12

The Ellen Glasgow Society Y-01

Glasier, Katharine Bruce 1867-1950......DLB-190

Glaspell, Susan 1876-1948 ......DLB-7, 9, 78, 228

Glass, Montague 1877-1934 ....DLB-11

Glassco, John 1909-1981 ....DLB-68

Glauser, Friedrich 1896-1938 ....DLB-56

F. Gleason's Publishing Hall DLB-49

Gleim, Johann Wilhelm Ludwig
  1719-1803. . . . . DLB-97

Glendinning, Robin 1938- DLB-310

Glendinning, Victoria 1937- DLB-155

Glidden, Frederick Dilley (Luke Short)
  1908-1975. . . . . DLB-256

Glinka, Fedor Nikolaevich 1786-1880. . . . DLB-205

Glover, Keith 1966- DLB-249

Glover, Richard 1712-1785 . . . . DLB-95

Glover, Sue 1943- DLB-310

Glück, Louise 1943- DLB-5

Glyn, Elinor 1864-1943 . . . . DLB-153

Gnedich, Nikolai Ivanovich 1784-1833. . . DLB-205

Gobineau, Joseph-Arthur de
  1816-1882. . . . . DLB-123

Godber, John 1956- DLB-233

Godbout, Jacques 1933- DLB-53

Goddard, Morrill 1865-1937 . . . . DLB-25

Goddard, William 1740-1817 . . . . DLB-43

Godden, Rumer 1907-1998. . . . . DLB-161

Godey, Louis A. 1804-1878 . . . . DLB-73

Godey and McMichael. DLB-49

Godfrey, Dave 1938- DLB-60

Godfrey, Thomas 1736-1763 . . . . DLB-31

Godine, David R., Publisher. DLB-46

Godkin, E. L. 1831-1902 . . . . DLB-79

Godolphin, Sidney 1610-1643 . . . . DLB-126

Godwin, Gail 1937- DLB-6, 234

M. J. Godwin and Company DLB-154

Godwin, Mary Jane Clairmont
  1766-1841. . . . . DLB-163

Godwin, Parke 1816-1904 . . . . DLB-3, 64, 250

Godwin, William 1756-1836 . . . . DLB-39, 104,
  142, 158, 163, 262; CDBLB-3

  Preface to *St. Leon* (1799) DLB-39

Goering, Reinhard 1887-1936. . . . . DLB-118

Goes, Albrecht 1908- DLB-69

Goethe, Johann Wolfgang von
  1749-1832. . . . . DLB-94; CDWLB-2

Goetz, Curt 1888-1960 . . . . DLB-124

Goffe, Thomas circa 1592-1629 . . . . DLB-58

Goffstein, M. B. 1940- DLB-61

Gogarty, Oliver St. John 1878-1957 . . . DLB-15, 19

Gogol, Nikolai Vasil'evich 1809-1852 . . . DLB-198

Goines, Donald 1937-1974 . . . . DLB-33

Gold, Herbert 1924- DLB-2; Y-81

  Tribute to William Saroyan. Y-81

Gold, Michael 1893-1967 . . . . DLB-9, 28

Goldbarth, Albert 1948- DLB-120

Goldberg, Dick 1947- DLB-7

Golden Cockerel Press DLB-112

Golding, Arthur 1536-1606 . . . . DLB-136

Golding, Louis 1895-1958 . . . . DLB-195

Golding, William 1911-1993
  . . . . . . DLB-15, 100, 255; Y-83; CDBLB-7

Nobel Lecture 1993 . . . . Y-83

The Stature of William Golding Y-83

Goldman, Emma 1869-1940. . . . . DLB-221

Goldman, William 1931- DLB-44

Goldring, Douglas 1887-1960 . . . . DLB-197

Goldschmidt, Meïr Aron 1819-1887. . . . DLB-300

Goldsmith, Oliver 1730?-1774
  . . . . . . DLB-39, 89, 104, 109, 142; CDBLB-2

Goldsmith, Oliver 1794-1861 . . . . DLB-99

Goldsmith Publishing Company DLB-46

Goldstein, Richard 1944- DLB-185

Gollancz, Sir Israel 1864-1930 . . . . DLB-201

Victor Gollancz Limited DLB-112

Gomberville, Marin Le Roy, sieur de
  1600?-1674 . . . . DLB-268

Gombrowicz, Witold
  1904-1969 . . . . DLB-215; CDWLB-4

Gomez, Madeleine-Angélique Poisson de
  1684-1770 . . . . DLB-313

Gómez-Quiñones, Juan 1942- DLB-122

Laurence James Gomme
  [publishing house] DLB-46

Gompers, Samuel 1850-1924 . . . . DLB-303

Gonçalves Dias, Antônio 1823-1864 . . . . DLB-307

Goncharov, Ivan Aleksandrovich
  1812-1891 . . . . DLB-238

Goncourt, Edmond de 1822-1896 . . . . . DLB-123

Goncourt, Jules de 1830-1870. . . . . DLB-123

Gonzales, Rodolfo "Corky" 1928- DLB-122

Gonzales-Berry, Erlinda 1942- DLB-209

  "Chicano Language" DLB-82

González, Angel 1925- DLB-108

Gonzalez, Genaro 1949- DLB-122

Gonzalez, N. V. M. 1915-1999 . . . . DLB-312

González, Otto-Raúl 1921- DLB-290

Gonzalez, Ray 1952- DLB-122

González de Mireles, Jovita
  1899-1983 . . . . DLB-122

González Martínez, Enrique 1871-1952 . . DLB-290

González-T., César A. 1931- DLB-82

Goodis, David 1917-1967 . . . . DLB-226

Goodison, Lorna 1947- DLB-157

Goodman, Allegra 1967- DLB-244

Goodman, Nelson 1906-1998. . . . . DLB-279

Goodman, Paul 1911-1972 . . . . DLB-130, 246

The Goodman Theatre DLB-7

Goodrich, Frances 1891-1984 and
  Hackett, Albert 1900-1995 . . . . DLB-26

Goodrich, Samuel Griswold
  1793-1860. . . . . DLB-1, 42, 73, 243

S. G. Goodrich [publishing house] DLB-49

C. E. Goodspeed and Company. DLB-49

Goodwin, Stephen 1943- Y-82

Googe, Barnabe 1540-1594 . . . . DLB-132

Gookin, Daniel 1612-1687 . . . . DLB-24

Goran, Lester 1928- DLB-244

Gordimer, Nadine 1923- DLB-225; Y-91

Nobel Lecture 1991 . . . . Y-91

Gordon, Adam Lindsay 1833-1870 . . . . DLB-230

Gordon, Caroline
  1895-1981 . . . . DLB-4, 9, 102; DS-17; Y-81

Gordon, Charles F. (see OyamO)

Gordon, Charles William (see Connor, Ralph)

Gordon, Giles 1940- DLB-14, 139, 207

Gordon, Helen Cameron, Lady Russell
  1867-1949. . . . . DLB-195

Gordon, Lyndall 1941- DLB-155

Gordon, Mack 1904-1959 . . . . DLB-265

Gordon, Mary 1949- DLB-6; Y-81

Gordone, Charles 1925-1995 . . . . DLB-7

Gore, Catherine 1800-1861 . . . . DLB-116

Gore-Booth, Eva 1870-1926 . . . . DLB-240

Gores, Joe 1931- DLB-226; Y-02

  Tribute to Kenneth Millar Y-83

  Tribute to Raymond Chandler Y-88

Gorey, Edward 1925-2000 . . . . DLB-61

Gorgias of Leontini
  circa 485 B.C.-376 B.C. DLB-176

Gor'ky, Maksim 1868-1936 . . . . DLB-295

Gorodetsky, Sergei Mitrofanovich
  1884-1967 . . . . DLB-295

Gorostiza, José 1901-1979. . . . . DLB-290

Görres, Joseph 1776-1848 . . . . DLB-90

Gosse, Edmund 1849-1928 . . . . . DLB-57, 144, 184

Gosson, Stephen 1554-1624 . . . . DLB-172

  The Schoole of Abuse (1579). DLB-172

Gotanda, Philip Kan 1951- DLB-266

Gotlieb, Phyllis 1926- DLB-88, 251

Go-Toba 1180-1239 . . . . DLB-203

Gottfried von Straßburg
  died before 1230 . . . . . . .DLB-138; CDWLB-2

Gotthelf, Jeremias 1797-1854. . . . . DLB-133

Gottschalk circa 804/808-869 . . . . DLB-148

Gottsched, Johann Christoph
  1700-1766 . . . . DLB-97

Götz, Johann Nikolaus 1721-1781. . . . . . DLB-97

Goudge, Elizabeth 1900-1984 . . . . DLB-191

Gouges, Olympe de 1748-1793 . . . . DLB-313

Gough, John B. 1817-1886 . . . . DLB-243

Gould, Wallace 1882-1940 . . . . DLB-54

Govoni, Corrado 1884-1965 . . . . DLB-114

Govrin, Michal 1950- DLB-299

Gower, John circa 1330-1408 . . . . DLB-146

Goyen, William 1915-1983 . . . . .DLB-2, 218; Y-83

Goytisolo, José Augustín 1928- DLB-134

Gozzano, Guido 1883-1916 . . . . DLB-114

Grabbe, Christian Dietrich 1801-1836 . . . DLB-133

Gracq, Julien (Louis Poirier) 1910- DLB-83

Grady, Henry W. 1850-1889 . . . . DLB-23

Graf, Oskar Maria 1894-1967 . . . . DLB-56

Graf Rudolf between circa 1170 and
  circa 1185. . . . . DLB-148

Graff, Gerald 1937- DLB-246

Graffigny, Françoise d'Issembourg de
  1695-1758 . . . . .DLB-313
Richard Grafton [publishing house]. DLB-170
Grafton, Sue 1940- DLB-226
Graham, Frank 1893-1965. . . . . .DLB-241
Graham, George Rex 1813-1894. . . . . .DLB-73
Graham, Gwethalyn (Gwethalyn Graham
  Erichsen-Brown) 1913-1965 . . . . .DLB-88
Graham, Jorie 1951- DLB-120
Graham, Katharine 1917-2001. . . . . .DLB-127
Graham, Lorenz 1902-1989. . . . . .DLB-76
Graham, Philip 1915-1963. . . . . .DLB-127
Graham, R. B. Cunninghame
  1852-1936 . . . . DLB-98, 135, 174
Graham, Shirley 1896-1977 . . . . .DLB-76
Graham, Stephen 1884-1975 . . . . .DLB-195
Graham, W. S. 1918-1986. . . . . .DLB-20
William H. Graham [publishing house]. . . .DLB-49
Graham, Winston 1910- DLB-77
Grahame, Kenneth 1859-1932. . . DLB-34, 141, 178
Grainger, Martin Allerdale 1874-1941 . . . . .DLB-92
Gramatky, Hardie 1907-1979. . . . . .DLB-22
Gramcko, Ida 1924-1994. . . . . .DLB-290
Gramsci, Antonio 1891-1937. . . . . .DLB-296
Grand, Sarah 1854-1943 . . . . .DLB-135, 197
Grandbois, Alain 1900-1975. . . . . .DLB-92
Grandson, Oton de circa 1345-1397 . . . . .DLB-208
Grange, John circa 1556-? DLB-136
Granger, Thomas 1578-1627 . . . . .DLB-281
Granich, Irwin (see Gold, Michael)
Granin, Daniil 1918- DLB-302
Granovsky, Timofei Nikolaevich
  1813-1855 . . . . .DLB-198
Grant, Anne MacVicar 1755-1838. . . . . . .DLB-200
Grant, Duncan 1885-1978 . . . . DS-10
Grant, George 1918-1988 . . . . .DLB-88
Grant, George Monro 1835-1902 . . . . .DLB-99
Grant, Harry J. 1881-1963. . . . . .DLB-29
Grant, James Edward 1905-1966. . . . . .DLB-26
Grant, John (see Gash, Jonathan)
War of the Words (and Pictures): The Creation
  of a Graphic Novel Y-02
Grass, Günter 1927- . . . DLB-75, 124; CDWLB-2
  Nobel Lecture 1999:
    "To Be Continued . . ." Y-99
  Tribute to Helen Wolff. Y-94
Grasty, Charles H. 1863-1924. . . . . .DLB-25
Grau, Shirley Ann 1929- DLB-2, 218
Graves, John 1920- Y-83
Graves, Richard 1715-1804 . . . . .DLB-39
Graves, Robert 1895-1985
  . . . DLB-20, 100, 191; DS-18; Y-85; CDBLB-6
  The St. John's College
    Robert Graves Trust Y-96
Gray, Alasdair 1934- DLB-194, 261
Gray, Asa 1810-1888 . . . . .DLB-1, 235
Gray, David 1838-1861 . . . . .DLB-32

Gray, Simon 1936- DLB-13
Gray, Thomas 1716-1771 . . . . .DLB-109; CDBLB-2
Grayson, Richard 1951- DLB-234
Grayson, William J. 1788-1863 . . . .DLB-3, 64, 248
The Great Bibliographers Series Y-93
The Great Gatsby (Documentary). DLB-219
"The Greatness of Southern Literature":
  League of the South Institute for the
  Study of Southern Culture and History
  . . . . Y-02
Grech, Nikolai Ivanovich 1787-1867 . . . . .DLB-198
Greeley, Horace 1811-1872 . . . DLB-3, 43, 189, 250
Green, Adolph 1915-2002 . . . . .DLB-44, 265
Green, Anna Katharine
  1846-1935 . . . . .DLB-202, 221
Green, Duff 1791-1875. . . . . .DLB-43
Green, Elizabeth Shippen 1871-1954 . . . . .DLB-188
Green, Gerald 1922- DLB-28
Green, Henry 1905-1973 . . . . .DLB-15
Green, Jonas 1712-1767 . . . . .DLB-31
Green, Joseph 1706-1780 . . . . .DLB-31
Green, Julien 1900-1998 . . . . DLB-4, 72
Green, Paul 1894-1981 . . . . . . DLB-7, 9, 249; Y-81
Green, T. H. 1836-1882 . . . . .DLB-190, 262
Green, Terence M. 1947- DLB-251
T. and S. Green [publishing house] DLB-49
Green Tiger Press .DLB-46
Timothy Green [publishing house] DLB-49
Greenaway, Kate 1846-1901 . . . . .DLB-141
Greenberg: Publisher. DLB-46
Greene, Asa 1789-1838 . . . . .DLB-11
Greene, Belle da Costa 1883-1950. . . . . . .DLB-187
Greene, Graham 1904-1991
  . . . . .DLB-13, 15, 77, 100, 162, 201, 204;
  Y-85, 91; CDBLB-7
  Tribute to Christopher Isherwood Y-86
Greene, Robert 1558-1592. . . . . .DLB-62, 167
Greene, Robert Bernard (Bob), Jr.
  1947- DLB-185
Benjamin H Greene [publishing house] DLB-49
Greenfield, George 1917-2000 . . . . Y-91, 00
  Derek Robinson's Review of George
    Greenfield's *Rich Dust* Y-02
Greenhow, Robert 1800-1854 . . . . .DLB-30
Greenlee, William B. 1872-1953 . . . . .DLB-187
Greenough, Horatio 1805-1852. . . . . . .DLB-1, 235
Greenwell, Dora 1821-1882. . . . . . . .DLB-35, 199
Greenwillow Books DLB-46
Greenwood, Grace (see Lippincott, Sara Jane Clarke)
Greenwood, Walter 1903-1974 . . . . .DLB-10, 191
Greer, Ben 1948- DLB-6
Greflinger, Georg 1620?-1677 . . . . .DLB-164
Greg, W. R. 1809-1881 . . . . .DLB-55
Greg, W. W. 1875-1959. . . . . .DLB-201
Gregg, Josiah 1806-1850 . . . . .DLB-183, 186
Gregg Press DLB-46
Gregory, Horace 1898-1982 . . . . .DLB-48

Gregory, Isabella Augusta Persse, Lady
  1852-1932 . . . . .DLB-10
Gregory of Rimini circa 1300-1358. . . . . .DLB-115
Gregynog Press DLB-112
Greiff, León de 1895-1976 . . . . .DLB-283
Greiffenberg, Catharina Regina von
  1633-1694 . . . . .DLB-168
Greig, Noël 1944- DLB-245
Grekova, Irina (Elena Sergeevna Venttsel')
  1907- DLB-302
Grenfell, Wilfred Thomason
  1865-1940 . . . . .DLB-92
Gress, Elsa 1919-1988 . . . . .DLB-214
Greve, Felix Paul (see Grove, Frederick Philip)
Greville, Fulke, First Lord Brooke
  1554-1628 . . . . DLB-62, 172
Grey, Sir George, K.C.B. 1812-1898. . . . .DLB-184
Grey, Lady Jane 1537-1554 . . . . .DLB-132
Grey, Zane 1872-1939 . . . . .DLB-9, 212
  Zane Grey's West Society. Y-00
Grey Owl (Archibald Stansfeld Belaney)
  1888-1938 . . . . DLB-92; DS-17
Grey Walls Press. DLB-112
Griboedov, Aleksandr Sergeevich
  1795?-1829 . . . . .DLB-205
Grice, Paul 1913-1988 . . . . .DLB-279
Grier, Eldon 1917- DLB-88
Grieve, C. M. (see MacDiarmid, Hugh)
Griffin, Bartholomew flourished 1596. . . .DLB-172
Griffin, Bryan
  "Panic Among the Philistines":
    A Postscript, An Interview
    with Bryan Griffin Y-81
Griffin, Gerald 1803-1840 . . . . .DLB-159
The Griffin Poetry Prize Y-00
Griffith, Elizabeth 1727?-1793 . . . . .DLB-39, 89
  Preface to *The Delicate Distress* (1769) . . .DLB-39
Griffith, George 1857-1906 . . . . .DLB-178
Ralph Griffiths [publishing house]. DLB-154
Griffiths, Trevor 1935- DLB-13, 245
S. C. Griggs and Company DLB-49
Griggs, Sutton Elbert 1872-1930 . . . . .DLB-50
Grignon, Claude-Henri 1894-1976 . . . . . . .DLB-68
Grigor'ev, Apollon Aleksandrovich
  1822-1864 . . . . .DLB-277
Grigorovich, Dmitrii Vasil'evich
  1822-1899 . . . . .DLB-238
Grigson, Geoffrey 1905-1985 . . . . .DLB-27
Grillparzer, Franz
  1791-1872 . . . . DLB-133; CDWLB-2
Grimald, Nicholas
  circa 1519-circa 1562. . . . . .DLB-136
Grimké, Angelina Weld 1880-1958. . . .DLB-50, 54
Grimké, Sarah Moore 1792-1873 . . . . . . .DLB-239
Grimm, Frédéric Melchior 1723-1807 . . . .DLB-313
Grimm, Hans 1875-1959 . . . . .DLB-66
Grimm, Jacob 1785-1863 . . . . .DLB-90
Grimm, Wilhelm
  1786-1859 . . . . DLB-90; CDWLB-2

Cumulative Index

Grimmelshausen, Johann Jacob Christoffel von 1621 or 1622-1676 ..... DLB-168; CDWLB-2

Grimshaw, Beatrice Ethel 1871-1953 ..... DLB-174

Grímur Thomsen 1820-1896 .... DLB-293

Grin, Aleksandr Stepanovich 1880-1932 .... DLB-272

Grindal, Edmund 1519 or 1520-1583 .... DLB-132

Gripe, Maria (Kristina) 1923- DLB-257

Griswold, Rufus Wilmot 1815-1857 .... DLB-3, 59, 250

Gronlund, Laurence 1846-1899 .... DLB-303

Grosart, Alexander Balloch 1827-1899 .. DLB-184

Grosholz, Emily 1950- DLB-282

Gross, Milt 1895-1953 .... DLB-11

Grosset and Dunlap DLB-49

Grosseteste, Robert circa 1160-1253 ..... DLB-115

Grossman, Allen 1932- DLB-193

Grossman, David 1954- DLB-299

Grossman, Vasilii Semenovich 1905-1964 .... DLB-272

Grossman Publishers DLB-46

Grosvenor, Gilbert H. 1875-1966 .... DLB-91

Groth, Klaus 1819-1899 .... DLB-129

Groulx, Lionel 1878-1967 .... DLB-68

Grove, Frederick Philip (Felix Paul Greve) 1879-1948 .... DLB-92

Grove Press DLB-46

Groys, Boris Efimovich 1947- DLB-285

Grubb, Davis 1919-1980 .... DLB-6

Gruelle, Johnny 1880-1938 .... DLB-22

von Grumbach, Argula 1492-after 1563? DLB-179

Grundtvig, N. F. S. 1783-1872 .... DLB-300

Grymeston, Elizabeth before 1563-before 1604 .... DLB-136

Grynberg, Henryk 1936- DLB-299

Gryphius, Andreas 1616-1664 .... DLB-164; CDWLB-2

Gryphius, Christian 1649-1706 .... DLB-168

Guare, John 1938- DLB-7, 249

Guarnieri, Gianfrancesco 1934- DLB-307

Guberman, Igor Mironovich 1936- DLB-285

Guðbergur Bergsson 1932- DLB-293

Guðmundur Böðvarsson 1904-1974 ..... DLB-293

Guðmundur Gíslason Hagalín 1898-1985 .... DLB-293

Guðmundur Magnússon (see Jón Trausti)

Guerra, Tonino 1920- DLB-128

Guest, Barbara 1920- DLB-5, 193

Guèvremont, Germaine 1893-1968 ...... DLB-68

Guglielminetti, Amalia 1881-1941 ...... DLB-264

Guidacci, Margherita 1921-1992 .... DLB-128

Guillén, Jorge 1893-1984 .... DLB-108

Guillén, Nicolás 1902-1989 .... DLB-283

Guilloux, Louis 1899-1980 .... DLB-72

Guilpin, Everard circa 1572-after 1608? DLB-136

Guiney, Louise Imogen 1861-1920 ...... DLB-54

Guiterman, Arthur 1871-1943 .... DLB-11

Gumilev, Nikolai Stepanovich 1886-1921 .... DLB-295

Günderrode, Caroline von 1780-1806 .... DLB-90

Gundulić, Ivan 1589-1638 ... DLB-147; CDWLB-4

Gunesekera, Romesh 1954- DLB-267

Gunn, Bill 1934-1989 .... DLB-38

Gunn, James E. 1923- DLB-8

Gunn, Neil M. 1891-1973 .... DLB-15

Gunn, Thom 1929- DLB-27; CDBLB-8

Gunnar Gunnarsson 1889-1975 .... DLB-293

Gunnars, Kristjana 1948- DLB-60

Günther, Johann Christian 1695-1723 ... DLB-168

Gurik, Robert 1932- DLB-60

Gurney, A. R. 1930- DLB-266

Gurney, Ivor 1890-1937 .... Y-02

The Ivor Gurney Society Y-98

Guro, Elena Genrikhovna 1877-1913 .... DLB-295

Gustafson, Ralph 1909-1995 .... DLB-88

Gustafsson, Lars 1936- DLB-257

Gütersloh, Albert Paris 1887-1973 .... DLB-81

Guterson, David 1956- DLB-292

Guthrie, A. B., Jr. 1901-1991 .... DLB-6, 212

Guthrie, Ramon 1896-1973 .... DLB-4

Guthrie, Thomas Anstey (see Anstey, FC)

Guthrie, Woody 1912-1967 .... DLB-303

The Guthrie Theater DLB-7

Gutiérrez Nájera, Manuel 1859-1895 .... DLB-290

Guttormur J. Guttormsson 1878-1966 ... DLB-293

Gutzkow, Karl 1811-1878 .... DLB-133

Guy, Ray 1939- DLB-60

Guy, Rosa 1925- DLB-33

Guyot, Arnold 1807-1884 .... DS-13

Gwynn, R. S. 1948- DLB-282

Gwynne, Erskine 1898-1948 .... DLB-4

Gyles, John 1680-1755 .... DLB-99

Gyllembourg, Thomasine 1773-1856 .... DLB-300

Gyllensten, Lars 1921- DLB-257

Gyrðir Elíasson 1961- DLB-293

Gysin, Brion 1916-1986 .... DLB-16

H

H.D. (see Doolittle, Hilda)

Habermas, Jürgen 1929- DLB-242

Habington, William 1605-1654 .... DLB-126

Hacker, Marilyn 1942- DLB-120, 282

Hackett, Albert 1900-1995 .... DLB-26

Hacks, Peter 1928- DLB-124

Hadas, Rachel 1948- DLB-120, 282

Hadden, Briton 1898-1929 .... DLB-91

Hagedorn, Friedrich von 1708-1754 ..... DLB-168

Hagedorn, Jessica Tarahata 1949- DLB-312

Hagelstange, Rudolf 1912-1984 .... DLB-69

Hagerup, Inger 1905-1985 .... DLB-297

Haggard, H. Rider 1856-1925 .... DLB-70, 156, 174, 178

Haggard, William (Richard Clayton) 1907-1993 .... DLB-276; Y-93

Hagy, Alyson 1960- DLB-244

Hahn-Hahn, Ida Gräfin von 1805-1880 .. DLB-133

Haig-Brown, Roderick 1908-1976 .... DLB-88

Haight, Gordon S. 1901-1985 .... DLB-103

Hailey, Arthur 1920- DLB-88; Y-82

Haines, John 1924- DLB-5, 212

Hake, Edward flourished 1566-1604 .... DLB-136

Hake, Thomas Gordon 1809-1895 ...... DLB-32

Hakluyt, Richard 1552?-1616 .... DLB-136

Halas, František 1901-1949 .... DLB-215

Halbe, Max 1865-1944 .... DLB-118

Halberstam, David 1934- DLB-241

Haldane, Charlotte 1894-1969 .... DLB-191

Haldane, J. B. S. 1892-1964 .... DLB-160

Haldeman, Joe 1943- DLB-8

Haldeman-Julius Company DLB-46

Hale, E. J., and Son DLB-49

Hale, Edward Everett 1822-1909 .... DLB-1, 42, 74, 235

Hale, Janet Campbell 1946- DLB-175

Hale, Kathleen 1898-2000 .... DLB-160

Hale, Leo Thomas (see Ebon)

Hale, Lucretia Peabody 1820-1900 .... DLB-42

Hale, Nancy 1908-1988 .... DLB-86; DS-17; Y-80, 88

Hale, Sarah Josepha (Buell) 1788-1879 .... DLB-1, 42, 73, 243

Hale, Susan 1833-1910 .... DLB-221

Hales, John 1584-1656 .... DLB-151

Halévy, Ludovic 1834-1908 .... DLB-192

Haley, Alex 1921-1992 .... DLB-38; CDALB-7

Haliburton, Thomas Chandler 1796-1865 .... DLB-11, 99

Hall, Adam (Trevor Dudley-Smith) 1920-1995 .... DLB-276

Hall, Anna Maria 1800-1881 .... DLB-159

Hall, Donald 1928- DLB-5

Hall, Edward 1497-1547 .... DLB-132

Hall, Halsey 1898-1977 .... DLB-241

Hall, James 1793-1868 .... DLB-73, 74

Hall, Joseph 1574-1656 .... DLB-121, 151

Hall, Radclyffe 1880-1943 .... DLB-191

Hall, Rodney 1935- DLB-289

Hall, Sarah Ewing 1761-1830 .... DLB-200

Hall, Stuart 1932- DLB-242

Samuel Hall [publishing house] DLB-49

al-Hallaj 857-922 .... DLB-311

Hallam, Arthur Henry 1811-1833 .... DLB-32

On Some of the Characteristics of Modern Poetry and On the Lyrical Poems of Alfred Tennyson (1831) DLB-32

Halldór Laxness (Halldór Guðjónsson) 1902-1998 .... DLB-293
Halleck, Fitz-Greene 1790-1867 .... DLB-3, 250
Haller, Albrecht von 1708-1777 .... DLB-168
Halliday, Brett (see Dresser, Davis)
Halliwell-Phillipps, James Orchard 1820-1889 .... DLB-184
Hallmann, Johann Christian 1640-1704 or 1716? DLB-168
Hallmark Editions DLB-46
Halper, Albert 1904-1984 .... DLB-9
Halperin, John William 1941- DLB-111
Halstead, Murat 1829-1908 .... DLB-23
Hamann, Johann Georg 1730-1788 .... DLB-97
Hamburger, Michael 1924- DLB-27
Hamilton, Alexander 1712-1756 .... DLB-31
Hamilton, Alexander 1755?-1804 .... DLB-37
Hamilton, Cicely 1872-1952 .... DLB-10, 197
Hamilton, Edmond 1904-1977 .... DLB-8
Hamilton, Elizabeth 1758-1816 ..... DLB-116, 158
Hamilton, Gail (see Corcoran, Barbara)
Hamilton, Gail (see Dodge, Mary Abigail)
Hamish Hamilton Limited DLB-112
Hamilton, Hugo 1953- DLB-267
Hamilton, Ian 1938-2001 .... DLB-40, 155
Hamilton, Janet 1795-1873 .... DLB-199
Hamilton, Mary Agnes 1884-1962 ...... DLB-197
Hamilton, Patrick 1904-1962 .... DLB-10, 191
Hamilton, Virginia 1936-2002 ... DLB-33, 52; Y-01
Hamilton, Sir William 1788-1856 .... DLB-262
Hamilton-Paterson, James 1941- DLB-267
Hammerstein, Oscar, 2nd 1895-1960 ... DLB-265
Hammett, Dashiell 1894-1961 .... DLB-226; DS-6; CDALB-5
An Appeal in *TAC*. Y-91
The Glass Key and Other Dashiell Hammett Mysteries Y-96
Knopf to Hammett: The Editoral Correspondence Y-00
The Maltese Falcon (Documentary) DLB-280
Hammon, Jupiter 1711-died between 1790 and 1806 .... DLB-31, 50
Hammond, John ?-1663 .... DLB-24
Hamner, Earl 1923- DLB-6
Hampson, John 1901-1955 .... DLB-191
Hampton, Christopher 1946- DLB-13
Hamsun, Knut 1859-1952 .... DLB-297
Handel-Mazzetti, Enrica von 1871-1955 ... DLB-81
Handke, Peter 1942- DLB-85, 124
Handlin, Oscar 1915- DLB-17
Hankin, St. John 1869-1909 .... DLB-10
Hanley, Clifford 1922- DLB-14
Hanley, James 1901-1985 .... DLB-191
Hannah, Barry 1942- DLB-6, 234
Hannay, James 1827-1873 .... DLB-21
Hannes Hafstein 1861-1922 .... DLB-293

Hano, Arnold 1922- DLB-241
Hanrahan, Barbara 1939-1991 .... DLB-289
Hansberry, Lorraine 1930-1965 .... DLB-7, 38; CDALB-1
Hansen, Martin A. 1909-1955 .... DLB-214
Hansen, Thorkild 1927-1989 .... DLB-214
Hanson, Elizabeth 1684-1737 .... DLB-200
Hapgood, Norman 1868-1937 .... DLB-91
Happel, Eberhard Werner 1647-1690 .... DLB-168
Harbach, Otto 1873-1963 .... DLB-265
The Harbinger 1845-1849 .... DLB-1, 223
Harburg, E. Y. "Yip" 1896-1981 .... DLB-265
Harcourt Brace Jovanovich DLB-46
Hardenberg, Friedrich von (see Novalis)
Harding, Walter 1917- DLB-111
Hardwick, Elizabeth 1916- DLB-6
Hardy, Alexandre 1572?-1632 .... DLB-268
Hardy, Frank 1917-1994 .... DLB-260
Hardy, Thomas 1840-1928 .... DLB-18, 19, 135; CDBLB-5
"Candour in English Fiction" (1890) DLB-18
Hare, Cyril 1900-1958 .... DLB-77
Hare, David 1947- DLB-13, 310
Hare, R. M. 1919-2002 .... DLB-262
Hargrove, Marion 1919- DLB-11
Häring, Georg Wilhelm Heinrich (see Alexis, Willibald)
Harington, Donald 1935- DLB-152
Harington, Sir John 1560-1612 .... DLB-136
Harjo, Joy 1951- DLB-120, 175
Harkness, Margaret (John Law) 1854-1923 .... DLB-197
Harley, Edward, second Earl of Oxford 1689-1741 .... DLB-213
Harley, Robert, first Earl of Oxford 1661-1724 .... DLB-213
Harlow, Robert 1923- DLB-60
Harman, Thomas flourished 1566-1573 ... DLB-136
Harness, Charles L. 1915- DLB-8
Harnett, Cynthia 1893-1981 .... DLB-161
Harnick, Sheldon 1924- DLB-265
Tribute to Ira Gershwin Y-96
Tribute to Lorenz Hart Y-95
Harper, Edith Alice Mary (see Wickham, Anna)
Harper, Fletcher 1806-1877 .... DLB-79
Harper, Frances Ellen Watkins 1825-1911 .... DLB-50, 221
Harper, Michael S. 1938- DLB-41
Harper and Brothers DLB-49
Harpur, Charles 1813-1868 .... DLB-230
Harraden, Beatrice 1864-1943 .... DLB-153
George G. Harrap and Company Limited DLB-112
Harriot, Thomas 1560-1621 .... DLB-136
Harris, Alexander 1805-1874 .... DLB-230
Harris, Benjamin ?-circa 1720 .... DLB-42, 43
Harris, Christie 1907-2002 .... DLB-88

Harris, Errol E. 1908- DLB-279
Harris, Frank 1856-1931 .... DLB-156, 197
Harris, George Washington 1814-1869 .... DLB-3, 11, 248
Harris, Joanne 1964- DLB-271
Harris, Joel Chandler 1848-1908 .... DLB-11, 23, 42, 78, 91
The Joel Chandler Harris Association ... Y-99
Harris, Mark 1922- DLB-2; Y-80
Tribute to Frederick A. Pottle Y-87
Harris, William Torrey 1835-1909 ...... DLB-270
Harris, Wilson 1921- DLB-117; CDWLB-3
Harrison, Mrs. Burton (see Harrison, Constance Cary)
Harrison, Charles Yale 1898-1954 .... DLB-68
Harrison, Constance Cary 1843-1920 .... DLB-221
Harrison, Frederic 1831-1923 .... DLB-57, 190
"On Style in English Prose" (1898) DLB-57
Harrison, Harry 1925- DLB-8
James P. Harrison Company DLB-49
Harrison, Jim 1937- Y-82
Harrison, M. John 1945- DLB-261
Harrison, Mary St. Leger Kingsley (see Malet, Lucas)
Harrison, Paul Carter 1936- DLB-38
Harrison, Susan Frances 1859-1935 ...... DLB-99
Harrison, Tony 1937- DLB-40, 245
Harrison, William 1535-1593 .... DLB-136
Harrison, William 1933- DLB-234
Harrisse, Henry 1829-1910 .... DLB-47
The Harry Ransom Humanities Research Center at the University of Texas at Austin Y-00
Harryman, Carla 1952- DLB-193
Harsdörffer, Georg Philipp 1607-1658 .... DLB-164
Harsent, David 1942- DLB-40
Hart, Albert Bushnell 1854-1943 .... DLB-17
Hart, Anne 1768-1834 .... DLB-200
Hart, Elizabeth 1771-1833 .... DLB-200
Hart, Julia Catherine 1796-1867 .... DLB-99
Hart, Lorenz 1895-1943 .... DLB-265
Larry Hart: Still an Influence Y-95
Lorenz Hart: An American Lyricist Y-95
The Lorenz Hart Centenary Y-95
Hart, Moss 1904-1961 .... DLB-7, 266
Hart, Oliver 1723-1795 .... DLB-31
Rupert Hart-Davis Limited DLB-112
Harte, Bret 1836-1902 .... DLB-12, 64, 74, 79, 186; CDALB-3
Harte, Edward Holmead 1922- DLB-127
Harte, Houston Harriman 1927- DLB-127
Hartlaub, Felix 1913-1945 .... DLB-56
Hartleben, Otto Erich 1864-1905 .... DLB-118
Hartley, David 1705-1757 .... DLB-252
Hartley, L. P. 1895-1972 .... DLB-15, 139
Hartley, Marsden 1877-1943 .... DLB-54
Hartling, Peter 1933- DLB-75

Hartman, Geoffrey H. 1929- DLB-67

Hartmann, Sadakichi 1867-1944......... DLB-54

Hartmann von Aue
circa 1160-circa 1205 ... DLB-138; CDWLB-2

Hartshorne, Charles 1897-2000 .... DLB-270

Haruf, Kent 1943- DLB-292

Harvey, Gabriel 1550?-1631....DLB-167, 213, 281

Harvey, Jack (see Rankin, Ian)

Harvey, Jean-Charles 1891-1967 .... DLB-88

Harvill Press Limited DLB-112

Harwood, Gwen 1920-1995 .... DLB-289

Harwood, Lee 1939- DLB-40

Harwood, Ronald 1934- DLB-13

al-Hasan al-Basri 642-728 .... DLB-311

Hašek, Jaroslav 1883-1923 .. DLB-215; CDWLB-4

Haskins, Charles Homer 1870-1937 ...... DLB-47

Haslam, Gerald 1937- DLB-212

Hass, Robert 1941- DLB-105, 206

Hasselstrom, Linda M. 1943- DLB-256

Hastings, Michael 1938- DLB-233

Hatar, Győző 1914- DLB-215

The Hatch-Billops Collection DLB-76

Hathaway, William 1944- DLB-120

Hatherly, Ana 1929- DLB-287

Hauch, Carsten 1790-1872 .... DLB-300

Hauff, Wilhelm 1802-1827 .... DLB-90

Hauge, Olav H. 1908-1994............ DLB-297

Haugen, Paal-Helge 1945- DLB-297

Haugwitz, August Adolph von
1647-1706..................... DLB-168

Hauptmann, Carl 1858-1921 .... DLB-66, 118

Hauptmann, Gerhart
1862-1946 ....DLB-66, 118; CDWLB-2

Hauser, Marianne 1910- Y-83

Havel, Václav 1936- DLB-232; CDWLB-4

Haven, Alice B. Neal 1827-1863 .... DLB-250

Havergal, Frances Ridley 1836-1879 .... DLB-199

Hawes, Stephen 1475?-before 1529 ...... DLB-132

Hawker, Robert Stephen 1803-1875...... DLB-32

Hawkes, John
1925-1998 .... DLB-2, 7, 227; Y-80, Y-98

John Hawkes: A Tribute Y-98

Tribute to Donald Barthelme........... Y-89

Hawkesworth, John 1720-1773 .... DLB-142

Hawkins, Sir Anthony Hope (see Hope, Anthony)

Hawkins, Sir John 1719-1789 ..... DLB-104, 142

Hawkins, Walter Everette 1883-? DLB-50

Hawthorne, Nathaniel 1804-1864
... DLB-1, 74, 183, 223, 269; DS-5; CDALB-2

The Nathaniel Hawthorne Society....... Y-00

The Old Manse DLB-223

Hawthorne, Sophia Peabody
1809-1871................ DLB-183, 239

Hay, John 1835-1905 ....DLB-12, 47, 189

Hay, John 1915- DLB-275

Hayashi Fumiko 1903-1951 .... DLB-180

Haycox, Ernest 1899-1950............ DLB-206

Haycraft, Anna Margaret (see Ellis, Alice Thomas)

Hayden, Robert
1913-1980 .... DLB-5, 76; CDALB-1

Haydon, Benjamin Robert 1786-1846 ... DLB-110

Hayes, John Michael 1919- DLB-26

Hayley, William 1745-1820 .... DLB-93, 142

Haym, Rudolf 1821-1901............. DLB-129

Hayman, Robert 1575-1629 .... DLB-99

Hayman, Ronald 1932- DLB-155

Hayne, Paul Hamilton
1830-1886 ....DLB-3, 64, 79, 248

Hays, Mary 1760-1843 .... DLB-142, 158

Hayslip, Le Ly 1949- DLB-312

Hayward, John 1905-1965 .... DLB-201

Haywood, Eliza 1693?-1756 .... DLB-39

Dedication of *Lasselia* [excerpt]
(1723)..................... DLB-39

Preface to *The Disguis'd Prince*
[excerpt] (1723) DLB-39

The Tea-Table [excerpt] DLB-39

Haywood, William D. 1869-1928 ...... DLB-303

Willis P. Hazard [publishing house] DLB-49

Hazlitt, William 1778-1830 ....DLB-110, 158

Hazzard, Shirley 1931- DLB-289; Y-82

Head, Bessie
1937-1986......... DLB-117, 225; CDWLB-3

Headley, Joel T. 1813-1897 .. DLB-30, 183; DS-13

Heaney, Seamus 1939-.. DLB-40; Y-95; CDBLB-8

Nobel Lecture 1994: Crediting Poetry.... Y-95

Heard, Nathan C. 1936- DLB-33

Hearn, Lafcadio 1850-1904 ......DLB-12, 78, 189

Hearn, Mary Anne (Marianne Farningham,
Eva Hope) 1834-1909 .... DLB-240

Hearne, John 1926- DLB-117

Hearne, Samuel 1745-1792 .... DLB-99

Hearne, Thomas 1678?-1735 .... DLB-213

Hearst, William Randolph 1863-1951 .... DLB-25

Hearst, William Randolph, Jr.
1908-1993 .... DLB-127

Heartman, Charles Frederick
1883-1953 .... DLB-187

Heath, Catherine 1924- DLB-14

Heath, James Ewell 1792-1862 .... DLB-248

Heath, Roy A. K. 1926- DLB-117

Heath-Stubbs, John 1918- DLB-27

Heavysege, Charles 1816-1876.......... DLB-99

Hebbel, Friedrich
1813-1863 .... DLB-129; CDWLB-2

Hebel, Johann Peter 1760-1826.......... DLB-90

Heber, Richard 1774-1833 .... DLB-184

Hébert, Anne 1916-2000 .... DLB-68

Hébert, Jacques 1923- DLB-53

Hecht, Anthony 1923- DLB-5, 169

Hecht, Ben 1894-1964 ....DLB-7, 9, 25, 26, 28, 86

Hecker, Isaac Thomas 1819-1888 .... DLB-1, 243

Hedge, Frederic Henry
1805-1890 .... DLB-1, 59, 243; DS-5

Hefner, Hugh M. 1926- DLB-137

Hegel, Georg Wilhelm Friedrich
1770-1831...................... DLB-90

Heiberg, Johan Ludvig 1791-1860 ...... DLB-300

Heiberg, Johanne Luise 1812-1890...... DLB-300

Heide, Robert 1939- DLB-249

Heidegger, Martin 1889-1976.......... DLB-296

Heidish, Marcy 1947- Y-82

Heißenbüttel, Helmut 1921-1996........ DLB-75

Heike monogatari.................. DLB-203

Hein, Christoph 1944- DLB-124; CDWLB-2

Hein, Piet 1905-1996 .... DLB-214

Heine, Heinrich 1797-1856 ... DLB-90; CDWLB-2

Heinemann, Larry 1944- DS-9

William Heinemann Limited DLB-112

Heinesen, William 1900-1991 .... DLB-214

Heinlein, Robert A. 1907-1988........... DLB-8

Heinrich, Willi 1920- DLB-75

Heinrich Julius of Brunswick|
1564-1613 .... DLB-164

Heinrich von dem Türlîn
flourished circa 1230 .... DLB-138

Heinrich von Melk
flourished after 1160 .... DLB-148

Heinrich von Veldeke
circa 1145-circa 1190 .... DLB-138

Heinse, Wilhelm 1746-1803 .... DLB-94

Heinz, W. C. 1915- DLB-171

Heiskell, John 1872-1972 ....DLB-127

Hejinian, Lyn 1941- DLB-165

Helder, Herberto 1930- DLB-287

Heliand circa 850 .... DLB-148

Heller, Joseph
1923-1999 ......DLB-2, 28, 227; Y-80, 99, 02

Excerpts from Joseph Heller's
USC Address, "The Literature
of Despair" Y-96

Remembering Joe Heller, by William
Price Fox Y-99

A Tribute to Joseph Heller............ Y-99

Heller, Michael 1937- DLB-165

Hellman, Lillian 1906-1984 ..... DLB-7, 228; Y-84

Hellwig, Johann 1609-1674............. DLB-164

Helprin, Mark 1947- Y-85; CDALB-7

Helvétius, Claude-Adrien 1715-1771..... DLB-313

Helwig, David 1938- DLB-60

Hemans, Felicia 1793-1835 .... DLB-96

Hemenway, Abby Maria 1828-1890 .... DLB-243

Hemingway, Ernest 1899-1961 ...DLB-4, 9, 102,
210; Y-81, 87, 99; DS-1, 15, 16; CDALB-4

A Centennial Celebration Y-99

Come to Papa Y-99

The Ernest Hemingway Collection at
the John F. Kennedy Library........ Y-99

Ernest Hemingway Declines to
Introduce *War and Peace*........... Y-01

Ernest Hemingway's Reaction to
 James Gould Cozzens............Y-98
Ernest Hemingway's Toronto Journalism
 Revisited: With Three Previously
 Unrecorded Stories..............Y-92
Falsifying Hemingway................Y-96
A Farewell to Arms (Documentary)....DLB-308
Hemingway Centenary Celebration
 at the JFK Library..............Y-99
The Hemingway/Fenton
 Correspondence................Y-02
Hemingway in the JFK...............Y-99
The Hemingway Letters Project
 Finds an Editor.................Y-02
Hemingway Salesmen's Dummies......Y-00
Hemingway: Twenty-Five Years Later...Y-85
A Literary Archaeologist Digs On:
 A Brief Interview with Michael
 Reynolds.....................Y-99
Not Immediately Discernible... but
 Eventually Quite Clear: The *First
 Light* and *Final Years* of
 Hemingway's Centenary.........Y-99
Packaging Papa: *The Garden of Eden*......Y-86
Second International Hemingway
 Colloquium: Cuba...............Y-98
Hémon, Louis 1880-1913.............DLB-92
Hempel, Amy 1951-...................DLB-218
Hempel, Carl G. 1905-1997...........DLB-279
Hemphill, Paul 1936-...................Y-87
Hénault, Gilles 1920-1996............DLB-88
Henchman, Daniel 1689-1761..........DLB-24
Henderson, Alice Corbin 1881-1949.....DLB-54
Henderson, Archibald 1877-1963........DLB-103
Henderson, David 1942-...............DLB-41
Henderson, George Wylie 1904-1965.....DLB-51
Henderson, Zenna 1917-1983...........DLB-8
Henighan, Tom 1934-..................DLB-251
Henisch, Peter 1943-..................DLB-85
Henley, Beth 1952-....................Y-86
Henley, William Ernest 1849-1903......DLB-19
Henniker, Florence 1855-1923..........DLB-135
Henning, Rachel 1826-1914............DLB-230
Henningsen, Agnes 1868-1962..........DLB-214
Henry, Alexander 1739-1824...........DLB-99
Henry, Buck 1930-....................DLB-26
Henry, Marguerite 1902-1997..........DLB-22
Henry, O. (see Porter, William Sydney)
Henry, Robert Selph 1889-1970........DLB-17
Henry, Will (see Allen, Henry W.)
Henry VIII of England 1491-1547......DLB-132
Henry of Ghent
 circa 1217-1229 - 1293.........DLB-115
Henryson, Robert
 1420s or 1430s-circa 1505......DLB-146
Henschke, Alfred (see Klabund)
Hensher, Philip 1965-.................DLB-267
Hensley, Sophie Almon 1866-1946.....DLB-99
Henson, Lance 1944-..................DLB-175

Henty, G. A. 1832-1902.............DLB-18, 141
 The Henty Society................Y-98
Hentz, Caroline Lee 1800-1856......DLB-3, 248
Heraclitus
 flourished circa 500 B.C........DLB-176
Herbert, Agnes circa 1880-1960......DLB-174
Herbert, Alan Patrick 1890-1971.....DLB-10, 191
Herbert, Edward, Lord, of Cherbury
 1582-1648..............DLB-121, 151, 252
Herbert, Frank 1920-1986......DLB-8; CDALB-7
Herbert, George 1593-1633...DLB-126; CDBLB-1
Herbert, Henry William 1807-1858.....DLB-3, 73
Herbert, John 1926-..................DLB-53
Herbert, Mary Sidney, Countess of Pembroke
 (see Sidney, Mary)
Herbert, Xavier 1901-1984...........DLB-260
Herbert, Zbigniew
 1924-1998............DLB-232; CDWLB-4
Herbst, Josephine 1892-1969.........DLB-9
Herburger, Gunter 1932-.........DLB-75, 124
Herculano, Alexandre 1810-1877.......DLB-287
Hercules, Frank E. M. 1917-1996.......DLB-33
Herder, Johann Gottfried 1744-1803.....DLB-97
B. Herder Book Company.............DLB-49
Heredia, José-María de 1842-1905......DLB-217
Herford, Charles Harold 1853-1931.....DLB-149
Hergesheimer, Joseph 1880-1954......DLB-9, 102
Heritage Press......................DLB-46
Hermann the Lame 1013-1054.........DLB-148
Hermes, Johann Timotheu 1738-1821.....DLB-97
Hermlin, Stephan 1915-1997..........DLB-69
Hernández, Alfonso C. 1938-.........DLB-122
Hernández, Inés 1947-...............DLB-122
Hernández, Miguel 1910-1942........DLB-134
Herntón, Calvin C. 1932-............DLB-38
Herodotus circa 484 B.C.-circa 420 B.C.
 ....DLB-176; CDWLB-1
Heron, Robert 1764-1807............DLB-142
Herr, Michael 1940-..................DLB-185
Herrera, Darío 1870-1914...........DLB-290
Herrera, Juan Felipe 1948-...........DLB-122
E. R. Herrick and Company..........DLB-49
Herrick, Robert 1591-1674...........DLB-126
Herrick, Robert 1868-1938.......DLB-9, 12, 78
Herrick, William 1915-...............Y-83
Herrmann, John 1900-1959.............DLB-4
Hersey, John
 1914-1993...DLB-6, 185, 278, 299; CDALB-7
Hertel, François 1905-1985...........DLB-68
Hervé-Bazin, Jean Pierre Marie (see Bazin, Hervé)
Hervey, John, Lord 1696-1743.......DLB-101
Herwig, Georg 1817-1875............DLB-133
Herzen, Alexander (Aleksandr Ivanovich
 Gersten) 1812-1870.............DLB-277
Herzog, Emile Salomon Wilhelm
 (see Maurois, André)
Hesiod eighth century B.C...........DLB-176

Hesse, Hermann
 1877-1962.............DLB-66; CDWLB-2
Hessus, Eobanus 1488-1540...........DLB-179
Heureka! (see Kertész, Imre and Nobel Prize
 in Literature: 2002)...............Y-02
Hewat, Alexander circa 1743-circa 1824...DLB-30
Hewett, Dorothy 1923-2002............DLB-289
Hewitt, John 1907-1987...............DLB-27
Hewlett, Maurice 1861-1923........DLB-34, 156
Heyen, William 1940-..................DLB-5
Heyer, Georgette 1902-1974.........DLB-77, 191
Heym, Stefan 1913-2001...............DLB-69
Heyse, Paul 1830-1914................DLB-129
Heytesbury, William
 circa 1310-1372 or 1373........DLB-115
Heyward, Dorothy 1890-1961........DLB-7, 249
Heyward, DuBose 1885-1940...DLB-7, 9, 45, 249
Heywood, John 1497?-1580?...........DLB-136
Heywood, Thomas 1573 or 1574-1641....DLB-62
Hiaasen, Carl 1953-..................DLB-292
Hibberd, Jack 1940-..................DLB-289
Hibbs, Ben 1901-1975.................DLB-137
 "The Saturday Evening Post reaffirms
 a policy," Ben Hibb's Statement
 in *The Saturday Evening Post*
 (16 May 1942).................DLB-137
Hichens, Robert S. 1864-1950........DLB-153
Hickey, Emily 1845-1924.............DLB-199
Hickman, William Albert 1877-1957....DLB-92
Hicks, Granville 1901-1982..........DLB-246
Hidalgo, José Luis 1919-1947........DLB-108
Hiebert, Paul 1892-1987..............DLB-68
Hieng, Andrej 1925-..................DLB-181
Hierro, José 1922-2002..............DLB-108
Higgins, Aidan 1927-.................DLB-14
Higgins, Colin 1941-1988.............DLB-26
Higgins, George V.
 1939-1999...........DLB-2; Y-81, 98–99
 Afterword [in response to Cozzen's
 Mens Rea (or Something)]........Y-97
 At End of Day: The Last George V.
 Higgins Novel..................Y-99
 The Books of George V. Higgins:
 A Checklist of Editions
 and Printings..................Y-00
 George V. Higgins in Class........Y-02
 Tribute to Alfred A. Knopf.........Y-84
 Tributes to George V. Higgins......Y-99
 "What You Lose on the Swings You Make
 Up on the Merry-Go-Round"...Y-99
Higginson, Thomas Wentworth
 1823-1911..................DLB-1, 64, 243
Highsmith, Patricia 1921-1995.......DLB-306
Highwater, Jamake 1942?-........DLB-52; Y-85
Hijuelos, Oscar 1951-................DLB-145
Hildegard von Bingen 1098-1179......DLB-148
Das Hildesbrandslied
 circa 820................DLB-148; CDWLB-2
Hildesheimer, Wolfgang 1916-1991..DLB-69, 124

Cumulative Index

Hildreth, Richard 1807-1865... DLB-1, 30, 59, 235
Hill, Aaron 1685-1750 .... DLB-84
Hill, Geoffrey 1932- DLB-40; CDBLB-8
George M. Hill Company............... DLB-49
Hill, "Sir" John 1714?-1775 .... DLB-39
Lawrence Hill and Company,
   Publishers...................... DLB-46
Hill, Joe 1879-1915 .... DLB-303
Hill, Leslie 1880-1960................. DLB-51
Hill, Reginald 1936- DLB-276
Hill, Susan 1942- DLB-14, 139
Hill, Walter 1942- DLB-44
Hill and Wang DLB-46
Hillberry, Conrad 1928- DLB-120
Hillerman, Tony 1925- DLB-206, 306
Hilliard, Gray and Company DLB-49
Hills, Lee 1906-2000.................. DLB-127
Hillyer, Robert 1895-1961 .... DLB-54
Hilsenrath, Edgar 1926- DLB-299
Hilton, James 1900-1954............. DLB-34, 77
Hilton, Walter died 1396 .... DLB-146
Hilton and Company DLB-49
Himes, Chester 1909-1984 ....DLB-2, 76, 143, 226
Joseph Hindmarsh [publishing house] DLB-170
Hine, Daryl 1936- DLB-60
Hingley, Ronald 1920- DLB-155
Hinojosa-Smith, Rolando 1929- DLB-82
Hinton, S. E. 1948- CDALB-7
Hippel, Theodor Gottlieb von
   1741-1796...................... DLB-97
Hippius, Zinaida Nikolaevna
   1869-1945 .... DLB-295
Hippocrates of Cos flourished circa
   425 B.C. DLB-176; CDWLB-1
Hirabayashi Taiko 1905-1972.......... DLB-180
Hirsch, E. D., Jr. 1928- DLB-67
Hirsch, Edward 1950- DLB-120
"Historical Novel," The Holocaust...... DLB-299
Hoagland, Edward 1932- DLB-6
Hoagland, Everett H., III 1942- DLB-41
Hoban, Russell 1925- DLB-52; Y-90
Hobbes, Thomas 1588-1679... DLB-151, 252, 281
Hobby, Oveta 1905-1995 .... DLB-127
Hobby, William 1878-1964............. DLB-127
Hobsbaum, Philip 1932- DLB-40
Hobsbawn, Eric (Francis Newton)
   1917- DLB-296
Hobson, Laura Z. 1900- DLB-28
Hobson, Sarah 1947- DLB-204
Hoby, Thomas 1530-1566 .... DLB-132
Hoccleve, Thomas
   circa 1368-circa 1437 .... DLB-146
Hoch, Edward D. 1930- DLB-306
Hochhuth, Rolf 1931- DLB-124
Hochman, Sandra 1936- DLB-5
Hocken, Thomas Moreland 1836-1910 ... DLB-184

Hocking, William Ernest 1873-1966......DLB-270
Hodder and Stoughton, Limited......... DLB-106
Hodgins, Jack 1938- DLB-60
Hodgman, Helen 1945- DLB-14
Hodgskin, Thomas 1787-1869 .... DLB-158
Hodgson, Ralph 1871-1962 .... DLB-19
Hodgson, William Hope
   1877-1918 ....DLB-70, 153, 156, 178
Hoe, Robert, III 1839-1909 .... DLB-187
Hoeg, Peter 1957- DLB-214
Hoel, Sigurd 1890-1960 .... DLB-297
Hoem, Edvard 1949- DLB-297
Hoffenstein, Samuel 1890-1947 .... DLB-11
Hoffman, Alice 1952- DLB-292
Hoffman, Charles Fenno 1806-1884... DLB-3, 250
Hoffman, Daniel 1923- DLB-5
   Tribute to Robert Graves Y-85
Hoffmann, E. T. A.
   1776-1822............. DLB-90; CDWLB-2
Hoffman, Frank B. 1888-1958 .... DLB-188
Hoffman, William 1925- DLB-234
   Tribute to Paxton Davis Y-94
Hoffmanswaldau, Christian Hoffman von
   1616-1679...................... DLB-168
Hofmann, Michael 1957- DLB-40
Hofmannsthal, Hugo von
   1874-1929.........DLB-81, 118; CDWLB-2
Hofmo, Gunvor 1921-1995 .... DLB-297
Hofstadter, Richard 1916-1970.......DLB-17, 246
Hogan, Desmond 1950- DLB-14
Hogan, Linda 1947- DLB-175
Hogan and Thompson DLB-49
Hogarth Press............... DLB-112; DS-10
Hogg, James 1770-1835.........DLB-93, 116, 159
Hohberg, Wolfgang Helmhard Freiherr von
   1612-1688 .... DLB-168
von Hohenheim, Philippus Aureolus
   Theophrastus Bombastus (see Paracelsus)
Hohl, Ludwig 1904-1980 .... DLB-56
Højholt, Per 1928- DLB-214
Holan, Vladimir 1905-1980 .... DLB-215
d'Holbach, Paul-Henri Thiry, baron
   1723-1789 .... DLB-313
Holberg, Ludvig 1684-1754 .... DLB-300
Holbrook, David 1923- DLB-14, 40
Holcroft, Thomas 1745-1809 .... DLB-39, 89, 158
   Preface to Alwyn (1780)............ DLB-39
Holden, Jonathan 1941- DLB-105
   "Contemporary Verse Story-telling" .. DLB-105
Holden, Molly 1927-1981 .... DLB-40
Hölderlin, Friedrich
   1770-1843 .... DLB-90; CDWLB-2
Holdstock, Robert 1948- DLB-261
Holiday House DLB-46
Holinshed, Raphael died 1580 .... DLB-167
Holland, J. G. 1819-1881 ....DS-13
Holland, Norman N. 1927- DLB-67

Hollander, John 1929- DLB-5
Holley, Marietta 1836-1926 .... DLB-11
Hollinghurst, Alan 1954- DLB-207
Hollingsworth, Margaret 1940- DLB-60
Hollo, Anselm 1934- DLB-40
Holloway, Emory 1885-1977 .... DLB-103
Holloway, John 1920- DLB-27
Holloway House Publishing Company ... DLB-46
Holme, Constance 1880-1955 .... DLB-34
Holmes, Abraham S. 1821?-1908........ DLB-99
Holmes, John Clellon 1926-1988 .....DLB-16, 237
   "Four Essays on the Beat
   Generation"................... DLB-16
Holmes, Mary Jane 1825-1907..... DLB-202, 221
Holmes, Oliver Wendell
   1809-1894 .... DLB-1, 189, 235; CDALB-2
Holmes, Richard 1945- DLB-155
Holmes, Thomas James 1874-1959.......DLB-187
The Holocaust "Historical Novel"...... DLB-299
Holocaust Fiction, Postmodern DLB-299
Holocaust Novel, The "Second-Generation"
   .... DLB-299
Holroyd, Michael 1935- DLB-155; Y-99
Holst, Hermann E. von 1841-1904 ...... DLB-47
Holt, John 1721-1784 .... DLB-43
Henry Holt and Company......... DLB-49, 284
Holt, Rinehart and Winston............ DLB-46
Holtby, Winifred 1898-1935 .... DLB-191
Holthusen, Hans Egon 1913-1997 ...... DLB-69
Hölty, Ludwig Christoph Heinrich
   1748-1776 .... DLB-94
Holub, Miroslav
   1923-1998 .... DLB-232; CDWLB-4
Holz, Arno 1863-1929 .... DLB-118
Home, Henry, Lord Kames
   (see Kames, Henry Home, Lord)
Home, John 1722-1808................. DLB-84
Home, William Douglas 1912- DLB-13
Home Publishing Company............ DLB-49
Homer circa eighth-seventh centuries B.C.
   ....DLB-176; CDWLB-1
Homer, Winslow 1836-1910 .... DLB-188
Homes, Geoffrey (see Mainwaring, Daniel)
Honan, Park 1928- DLB-111
Hone, William 1780-1842..........DLB-110, 158
Hongo, Garrett Kaoru 1951- DLB-120, 312
Honig, Edwin 1919- DLB-5
Hood, Hugh 1928-2000 .... DLB-53
Hood, Mary 1946- DLB-234
Hood, Thomas 1799-1845 .... DLB-96
Hook, Sidney 1902-1989 ....DLB-279
Hook, Theodore 1788-1841 .... DLB-116
Hooker, Jeremy 1941- DLB-40
Hooker, Richard 1554-1600........... DLB-132
Hooker, Thomas 1586-1647 .... DLB-24
hooks, bell 1952- DLB-246

Hooper, Johnson Jones
  1815-1862 . . . . DLB-3, 11, 248
Hope, A. D. 1907-2000 . . . . DLB-289
Hope, Anthony 1863-1933 . . . . DLB-153, 156
Hope, Christopher 1944- DLB-225
Hope, Eva (see Hearn, Mary Anne)
Hope, Laurence (Adela Florence
  Cory Nicolson) 1865-1904 . . . . DLB-240
Hopkins, Ellice 1836-1904 . . . . DLB-190
Hopkins, Gerard Manley
  1844-1889 . . . . DLB-35, 57; CDBLB-5
Hopkins, John ?-1570 . . . . DLB-132
Hopkins, John H., and Son DLB-46
Hopkins, Lemuel 1750-1801 . . . . DLB-37
Hopkins, Pauline Elizabeth 1859-1930 . . . . DLB-50
Hopkins, Samuel 1721-1803 . . . . DLB-31
Hopkinson, Francis 1737-1791 . . . . DLB-31
Hopkinson, Nalo 1960- DLB-251
Hopper, Nora (Mrs. Nora Chesson)
  1871-1906 . . . . DLB-240
Hoppin, Augustus 1828-1896 . . . . DLB-188
Hora, Josef 1891-1945 . . . . . . DLB-215; CDWLB-4
Horace 65 B.C.-8 B.C. DLB-211; CDWLB-1
Horgan, Paul 1903-1995 . . . . . DLB-102, 212; Y-85
  Tribute to Alfred A. Knopf Y-84
Horizon Press DLB-46
Horkheimer, Max 1895-1973 . . . . DLB-296
Hornby, C. H. St. John 1867-1946 . . . . . . DLB-201
Hornby, Nick 1957- DLB-207
Horne, Frank 1899-1974 . . . . DLB-51
Horne, Richard Henry (Hengist)
  1802 or 1803-1884 . . . . DLB-32
Horne, Thomas 1608-1654 . . . . DLB-281
Horney, Karen 1885-1952 . . . . DLB-246
Hornung, E. W. 1866-1921 . . . . DLB-70
Horovitz, Israel 1939- DLB-7
Horta, Maria Teresa (see The Three Marias:
  A Landmark Case in Portuguese
  Literary History)
Horton, George Moses 1797?-1883? DLB-50
  George Moses Horton Society Y-99
Horváth, Ödön von 1901-1938 . . . . . DLB-85, 124
Horwood, Harold 1923- DLB-60
E. and E. Hosford [publishing house] DLB-49
Hoskens, Jane Fenn 1693-1770? DLB-200
Hoskyns, John circa 1566-1638 . . . . . DLB-121, 281
Hosokawa Yūsai 1535-1610 . . . . DLB-203
Hospers, John 1918- DLB-279
Hostovský, Egon 1908-1973 . . . . DLB-215
Hotchkiss and Company DLB-49
Hough, Emerson 1857-1923 . . . . DLB-9, 212
Houghton, Stanley 1881-1913 . . . . DLB-10
Houghton Mifflin Company DLB-49
Hours at Home DS-13
Household, Geoffrey 1900-1988 . . . . DLB-87
Housman, A. E. 1859-1936 . . . DLB-19; CDBLB-5

Housman, Laurence 1865-1959 . . . . DLB-10
Houston, Pam 1962- DLB-244
Houwald, Ernst von 1778-1845 . . . . DLB-90
Hovey, Richard 1864-1900 . . . . DLB-54
Howard, Donald R. 1927-1987 . . . . DLB-111
Howard, Maureen 1930- Y-83
Howard, Richard 1929- DLB-5
Howard, Roy W. 1883-1964 . . . . DLB-29
Howard, Sidney 1891-1939 . . . . . DLB-7, 26, 249
Howard, Thomas, second Earl of Arundel
  1585-1646 . . . . DLB-213
Howe, E. W. 1853-1937 . . . . DLB-12, 25
Howe, Henry 1816-1893 . . . . DLB-30
Howe, Irving 1920-1993 . . . . DLB-67
Howe, Joseph 1804-1873 . . . . DLB-99
Howe, Julia Ward 1819-1910 . . . . DLB-1, 189, 235
Howe, Percival Presland 1886-1944 . . . . . DLB-149
Howe, Susan 1937- DLB-120
Howell, Clark, Sr. 1863-1936 . . . . DLB-25
Howell, Evan P. 1839-1905 . . . . DLB-23
Howell, James 1594?-1666 . . . . DLB-151
Howell, Soskin and Company DLB-46
Howell, Warren Richardson
  1912-1984 . . . . DLB-140
Howells, William Dean 1837-1920
  . . . . DLB-12, 64, 74, 79, 189; CDALB-3
  Introduction to Paul Laurence
    Dunbar's Lyrics of Lowly Life
    (1896) DLB-50
  The William Dean Howells Society Y-01
Howitt, Mary 1799-1888 . . . . DLB-110, 199
Howitt, William 1792-1879 . . . . DLB-110
Hoyem, Andrew 1935- DLB-5
Hoyers, Anna Ovena 1584-1655 . . . . DLB-164
Hoyle, Fred 1915-2001 . . . . DLB-261
Hoyos, Angela de 1940- DLB-82
Henry Hoyt [publishing house] DLB-49
Hoyt, Palmer 1897-1979 . . . . DLB-127
Hrabal, Bohumil 1914-1997 . . . . DLB-232
Hrabanus Maurus 776?-856 . . . . DLB-148
Hronský, Josef Cíger 1896-1960 . . . . DLB-215
Hrotsvit of Gandersheim
  circa 935-circa 1000 . . . . DLB-148
Hubbard, Elbert 1856-1915 . . . . DLB-91
Hubbard, Kin 1868-1930 . . . . DLB-11
Hubbard, William circa 1621-1704 . . . . DLB-24
Huber, Therese 1764-1829 . . . . DLB-90
Huch, Friedrich 1873-1913 . . . . DLB-66
Huch, Ricarda 1864-1947 . . . . DLB-66
Huddle, David 1942- DLB-130
Hudgins, Andrew 1951- DLB-120, 282
Hudson, Henry Norman 1814-1886 . . . . . . DLB-64
Hudson, Stephen 1868?-1944 . . . . DLB-197
Hudson, W. H. 1841-1922 . . . . DLB-98, 153, 174
Hudson and Goodwin DLB-49
Huebsch, B. W., oral history Y-99

B. W. Huebsch [publishing house] DLB-46
Hueffer, Oliver Madox 1876-1931 . . . . . . DLB-197
Huet, Pierre Daniel
  Preface to The History of Romances
  (1715) DLB-39
Hugh of St. Victor circa 1096-1141 . . . . . . DLB-208
Hughes, David 1930- DLB-14
Hughes, Dusty 1947- DLB-233
Hughes, Hatcher 1881-1945 . . . . DLB-249
Hughes, John 1677-1720 . . . . DLB-84
Hughes, Langston 1902-1967 . . . . . DLB-4, 7, 48,
  51, 86, 228; ; DS-15; CDALB-5
Hughes, Richard 1900-1976 . . . . DLB-15, 161
Hughes, Ted 1930-1998 . . . . DLB-40, 161
Hughes, Thomas 1822-1896 . . . . DLB-18, 163
Hugo, Richard 1923-1982 . . . . DLB-5, 206
Hugo, Victor 1802-1885 . . . . . . DLB-119, 192, 217
Hugo Awards and Nebula Awards DLB-8
Huidobro, Vicente 1893-1948 . . . . DLB-283
Hull, Richard 1896-1973 . . . . DLB-77
Hulda (Unnur Benediktsdóttir Bjarklind)
  1881-1946 . . . . DLB-293
Hulme, T. E. 1883-1917 . . . . DLB-19
Hulton, Anne ?-1779? DLB-200
Humboldt, Alexander von 1769-1859 . . . . . DLB-90
Humboldt, Wilhelm von 1767-1835 . . . . . . DLB-90
Hume, David 1711-1776 . . . . DLB-104, 252
Hume, Fergus 1859-1932 . . . . DLB-70
Hume, Sophia 1702-1774 . . . . DLB-200
Hume-Rothery, Mary Catherine
  1824-1885 . . . . DLB-240
Humishuma
  (see Mourning Dove)
Hummer, T. R. 1950- DLB-120
Humor
  American Humor: A Historical
    Survey DLB-11
  American Humor Studies Association . . . Y-99
  The Comic Tradition Continued
    [in the British Novel] DLB-15
  Humorous Book Illustration DLB-11
  International Society for Humor Studies . . Y-99
  Newspaper Syndication of American
    Humor DLB-11
  Selected Humorous Magazines
    (1820-1950) DLB-11
Bruce Humphries [publishing house] DLB-46
Humphrey, Duke of Gloucester
  1391-1447 . . . . DLB-213
Humphrey, William
  1924-1997 . . . . DLB-6, 212, 234, 278
Humphreys, David 1752-1818 . . . . DLB-37
Humphreys, Emyr 1919- DLB-15
Humphreys, Josephine 1945- DLB-292
Hunayn ibn Ishaq 809-873 or 877 . . . . DLB-311
Huncke, Herbert 1915-1996 . . . . DLB-16
Huneker, James Gibbons 1857-1921 . . . . . DLB-71
Hunold, Christian Friedrich
  1681-1721 . . . . DLB-168

Cumulative Index DLB 313

Hunt, Irene 1907- DLB-52
Hunt, Leigh 1784-1859 .... DLB-96, 110, 144
Hunt, Violet 1862-1942 .... DLB-162, 197
Hunt, William Gibbes 1791-1833 .... DLB-73
Hunter, Evan (Ed McBain)
   1926- DLB-306; Y-82
   Tribute to John D. MacDonald Y-86
Hunter, Jim 1939- DLB-14
Hunter, Kristin 1931- DLB-33
   Tribute to Julian Mayfield Y-84
Hunter, Mollie 1922- DLB-161
Hunter, N. C. 1908-1971 .... DLB-10
Hunter-Duvar, John 1821-1899 .... DLB-99
Huntington, Henry E. 1850-1927 .... DLB-140
   The Henry E. Huntington Library Y-92
Huntington, Susan Mansfield
   1791-1823 .... DLB-200
Hurd and Houghton DLB-49
Hurst, Fannie 1889-1968 .... DLB-86
Hurst and Blackett DLB-106
Hurst and Company DLB-49
Hurston, Zora Neale
   1901?-1960 .... DLB-51, 86; CDALB-7
Husserl, Edmund 1859-1938 .... DLB-296
Husson, Jules-François-Félix (see Champfleury)
Huston, John 1906-1987 .... DLB-26
Hutcheson, Francis 1694-1746 ...... DLB-31, 252
Hutchinson, Ron 1947- DLB-245
Hutchinson, R. C. 1907-1975 .... DLB-191
Hutchinson, Thomas 1711-1780 ...... DLB-30, 31
Hutchinson and Company
   (Publishers) Limited DLB-112
Huth, Angela 1938- DLB-271
Hutton, Richard Holt
   1826-1897 .... DLB-57
von Hutten, Ulrich 1488-1523 .... DLB-179
Huxley, Aldous 1894-1963
   ..... DLB-36, 100, 162, 195, 255; CDBLB-6
Huxley, Elspeth Josceline
   1907-1997 .... DLB-77, 204
Huxley, T. H. 1825-1895 .... DLB-57
Huyghue, Douglas Smith 1816-1891 ..... DLB-99
Huysmans, Joris-Karl 1848-1907 ...... DLB-123
Hwang, David Henry
   1957- DLB-212, 228, 312
Hyde, Donald 1909-1966 .... DLB-187
Hyde, Mary 1912- DLB-187
Hyman, Trina Schart 1939- DLB-61

I

Iavorsky, Stefan 1658-1722 .... DLB-150
Iazykov, Nikolai Mikhailovich
   1803-1846 .... DLB-205
Ibáñez, Armando P. 1949- DLB-209
Ibáñez, Sara de 1909-1971 .... DLB-290
Ibarbourou, Juana de 1892-1979 ...... DLB-290
Ibn Abi Tahir Tayfur 820-893 .... DLB-311

Ibn Qutaybah 828-889 .... DLB-311
Ibn al-Rumi 836-896 .... DLB-311
Ibn Sa'd 784-845 .... DLB-311
Ibrahim al-Mawsili 742 or 743-803 or 804 DLB-311
Ibn Bajja circa 1077-1138 .... DLB-115
Ibn Gabirol, Solomon
   circa 1021-circa 1058 .... DLB-115
Ibn al-Muqaffa' circa 723-759 .... DLB-311
Ibn al-Mu'tazz 861-908 .... DLB-311
Ibuse Masuji 1898-1993 .... DLB-180
Ichijō Kanera
   (see Ichijō Kaneyoshi)
Ichijō Kaneyoshi (Ichijō Kanera)
   1402-1481 .... DLB-203
Iffland, August Wilhelm
   1759-1814 .... DLB-94
Iggulden, John 1917- DLB-289
Ignatieff, Michael 1947- DLB-267
Ignatow, David 1914-1997 .... DLB-5
Ike, Chukwuemeka 1931- DLB-157
Ikkyū Sōjun 1394-1481 .... DLB-203
Iles, Francis
   (see Berkeley, Anthony)
Il'f, Il'ia (Il'ia Arnol'dovich Fainzil'berg)
   1897-1937 .... DLB-272
Illich, Ivan 1926-2002 .... DLB-242
Illustration
   Children's Book Illustration in the
     Twentieth Century DLB-61
   Children's Illustrators, 1800-1880 ... DLB-163
   Early American Book Illustration DLB-49
   The Iconography of Science-Fiction
     Art DLB-8
   The Illustration of Early German
     Literary Manuscripts, circa
     1150-circa 1300 .... DLB-148
   Minor Illustrators, 1880-1914 ...... DLB-141
Illyés, Gyula 1902-1983 .... DLB-215; CDWLB-4
Imbs, Bravig 1904-1946 .... DLB-4; DS-15
Imbuga, Francis D. 1947- DLB-157
Immermann, Karl 1796-1840 .... DLB-133
Imru' al-Qays circa 526-circa 565 ..... DLB-311
Inchbald, Elizabeth 1753-1821 .... DLB-39, 89
Indiana University Press Y-02
Ingamells, Rex 1913-1955 .... DLB-260
Inge, William 1913-1973 ... DLB-7, 249; CDALB-1
Ingelow, Jean 1820-1897 .... DLB-35, 163
Ingemann, B. S. 1789-1862 .... DLB-300
Ingersoll, Ralph 1900-1985 .... DLB-127
The Ingersoll Prizes Y-84
Ingoldsby, Thomas (see Barham, Richard Harris)
Ingraham, Joseph Holt 1809-1860 .... DLB-3, 248
Inman, John 1805-1850 .... DLB-73
Innerhofer, Franz 1944- DLB-85
Innes, Michael (J. I. M. Stewart)
   1906-1994 .... DLB-276
Innis, Harold Adams 1894-1952 .... DLB-88
Innis, Mary Quayle 1899-1972 .... DLB-88

Inō Sōgi 1421-1502 .... DLB-203
Inoue Yasushi 1907-1991 .... DLB-182
"The Greatness of Southern Literature":
   League of the South Institute for the
   Study of Southern Culture and History
   .... Y-02
International Publishers Company DLB-46
Internet (publishing and commerce)
   Author Websites Y-97
   The Book Trade and the Internet Y-00
   E-Books Turn the Corner Y-98
   The E-Researcher: Possibilities
     and Pitfalls Y-00
   Interviews on E-publishing Y-00
   John Updike on the Internet Y-97
   LitCheck Website Y-01
   Virtual Books and Enemies of Books Y-00
Interviews
   Adoff, Arnold Y-01
   Aldridge, John W. Y-91
   Anastas, Benjamin Y-98
   Baker, Nicholson Y-00
   Bank, Melissa Y-98
   Bass, T. J. Y-80
   Bernstein, Harriet Y-82
   Betts, Doris Y-82
   Bosworth, David Y-82
   Bottoms, David Y-83
   Bowers, Fredson Y-80
   Burnshaw, Stanley Y-97
   Carpenter, Humphrey Y-84, 99
   Carr, Virginia Spencer Y-00
   Carver, Raymond Y-83
   Cherry, Kelly Y-83
   Conroy, Jack Y-81
   Coppel, Alfred Y-83
   Cowley, Malcolm Y-81
   Davis, Paxton Y-89
   Devito, Carlo Y-94
   De Vries, Peter Y-82
   Dickey, James Y-82
   Donald, David Herbert Y-87
   Editors, Conversations with Y-95
   Ellroy, James Y-91
   Fancher, Betsy Y-83
   Faust, Irvin Y-00
   Fulton, Len Y-86
   Furst, Alan Y-01
   Garrett, George Y-83
   Gelfman, Jane Y-93
   Goldwater, Walter Y-93
   Gores, Joe Y-02
   Greenfield, George Y-91
   Griffin, Bryan Y-81
   Groom, Winston Y-01
   Guilds, John Caldwell Y-92

Hamilton, Virginia	Y-01	
Hardin, James	Y-92	
Harris, Mark	Y-80	
Harrison, Jim	Y-82	
Hazzard, Shirley	Y-82	
Herrick, William	Y-01	
Higgins, George V.	Y-98	
Hoban, Russell	Y-90	
Holroyd, Michael	Y-99	
Horowitz, Glen	Y-90	
Iggulden, John	Y-01	
Jakes, John	Y-83	
Jenkinson, Edward B.	Y-82	
Jenks, Tom	Y-86	
Kaplan, Justin	Y-86	
King, Florence	Y-85	
Klopfer, Donald S.	Y-97	
Krug, Judith	Y-82	
Lamm, Donald	Y-95	
Laughlin, James	Y-96	
Lawrence, Starling	Y-95	
Lindsay, Jack	Y-84	
Mailer, Norman	Y-97	
Manchester, William	Y-85	
Max, D. T.	Y-94	
McCormack, Thomas	Y-98	
McNamara, Katherine	Y-97	
Mellen, Joan	Y-94	
Menaker, Daniel	Y-97	
Mooneyham, Lamarr	Y-82	
Murray, Les	Y-01	
Nosworth, David	Y-82	
O'Connor, Patrick	Y-84, 99	
Ozick, Cynthia	Y-83	
Penner, Jonathan	Y-83	
Pennington, Lee	Y-82	
Penzler, Otto	Y-96	
Plimpton, George	Y-99	
Potok, Chaim	Y-84	
Powell, Padgett	Y-01	
Prescott, Peter S.	Y-86	
Rabe, David	Y-91	
Rechy, John	Y-82	
Reid, B. L.	Y-83	
Reynolds, Michael	Y-95, 99	
Robinson, Derek	Y-02	
Rollyson, Carl	Y-97	
Rosset, Barney	Y-02	
Schlafly, Phyllis	Y-82	
Schroeder, Patricia	Y-99	
Schulberg, Budd	Y-81, 01	
Scribner, Charles, III	Y-94	
Sipper, Ralph	Y-94	
Smith, Cork	Y-95	

Staley, Thomas F.	Y-00
Styron, William	Y-80
Talese, Nan	Y-94
Thornton, John	Y-94
Toth, Susan Allen	Y-86
Tyler, Anne	Y-82
Vaughan, Samuel	Y-97
Von Ogtrop, Kristin	Y-92
Wallenstein, Barry	Y-92
Weintraub, Stanley	Y-82
Williams, J. Chamberlain	Y-84
Into the Past: William Jovanovich's Reflections in Publishing	Y-02
Ireland, David 1927-	DLB-289
The National Library of Ireland's New James Joyce Manuscripts	Y-02
Irigaray, Luce 1930-	DLB-296
Irving, John 1942-	DLB-6, 278; Y-82
Irving, Washington 1783-1859	DLB-3, 11, 30, 59, 73, 74, 183, 186, 250; CDALB-2
Irwin, Grace 1907-	DLB-68
Irwin, Will 1873-1948	DLB-25
Isaksson, Ulla 1916-2000	DLB-257
Iser, Wolfgang 1926-	DLB-242
Isherwood, Christopher 1904-1986	DLB-15, 195; Y-86
The Christopher Isherwood Archive, The Huntington Library	Y-99
Ishiguro, Kazuo 1954-	DLB-194
Ishikawa Jun 1899-1987	DLB-182
Iskander, Fazil' Abdulevich 1929-	DLB-302
The Island Trees Case: A Symposium on School Library Censorship An Interview with Judith Krug An Interview with Phyllis Schlafly An Interview with Edward B. Jenkinson An Interview with Lamarr Mooneyham An Interview with Harriet Bernstein	Y-82
Islas, Arturo 1938-1991	DLB-122
Issit, Debbie 1966-	DLB-233
Ivanišević, Drago 1907-1981	DLB-181
Ivanov, Viacheslav Ivanovich 1866-1949	DLB-295
Ivanov, Vsevolod Viacheslavovich 1895-1963	DLB-272
Ivaska, Astrīde 1926-	DLB-232
M. J. Ivers and Company	DLB-49
Iwaniuk, Wacław 1915-	DLB-215
Iwano Hōmei 1873-1920	DLB-180
Iwaszkiewicz, Jarosław 1894-1980	DLB-215
Iyayi, Festus 1947-	DLB-157
Izumi Kyōka 1873-1939	DLB-180

J

Jackmon, Marvin E. (see Marvin X)	
Jacks, L. P. 1860-1955	DLB-135
Jackson, Angela 1951-	DLB-41

Jackson, Charles 1903-1968	DLB-234
Jackson, Helen Hunt 1830-1885	DLB-42, 47, 186, 189
Jackson, Holbrook 1874-1948	DLB-98
Jackson, Laura Riding 1901-1991	DLB-48
Jackson, Shirley 1916-1965	DLB-6, 234; CDALB-1
Jacob, Max 1876-1944	DLB-258
Jacob, Naomi 1884?-1964	DLB-191
Jacob, Piers Anthony Dillingham (see Anthony, Piers)	
Jacob, Violet 1863-1946	DLB-240
Jacobi, Friedrich Heinrich 1743-1819	DLB-94
Jacobi, Johann Georg 1740-1814	DLB-97
George W. Jacobs and Company	DLB-49
Jacobs, Harriet 1813-1897	DLB-239
Jacobs, Joseph 1854-1916	DLB-141
Jacobs, W. W. 1863-1943	DLB-135
The W. W. Jacobs Appreciation Society	Y-98
Jacobsen, J. P. 1847-1885	DLB-300
Jacobsen, Jørgen-Frantz 1900-1938	DLB-214
Jacobsen, Josephine 1908-	DLB-244
Jacobsen, Rolf 1907-1994	DLB-297
Jacobson, Dan 1929-	DLB-14, 207, 225
Jacobson, Howard 1942-	DLB-207
Jacques de Vitry circa 1160/1170-1240	DLB-208
Jæger, Frank 1926-1977	DLB-214
Ja'far al-Sadiq circa 702-765	DLB-311
William Jaggard [publishing house]	DLB-170
Jahier, Piero 1884-1966	DLB-114, 264
al-Jahiz circa 776-868 or 869	DLB-311
Jahnn, Hans Henny 1894-1959	DLB-56, 124
Jaimes, Freyre, Ricardo 1866?-1933	DLB-283
Jakes, John 1932-	DLB-278; Y-83
Tribute to John Gardner	Y-82
Tribute to John D. MacDonald	Y-86
Jakobína Johnson (Jakobína Sigurbjarnardóttir) 1883-1977	DLB-293
Jakobson, Roman 1896-1982	DLB-242
James, Alice 1848-1892	DLB-221
James, C. L. R. 1901-1989	DLB-125
James, George P. R. 1801-1860	DLB-116
James, Henry 1843-1916	DLB-12, 71, 74, 189; DS-13; CDALB-3
"The Future of the Novel" (1899)	DLB-18
"The Novel in [Robert Browning's] 'The Ring and the Book'" (1912)	DLB-32
James, John circa 1633-1729	DLB-24
James, M. R. 1862-1936	DLB-156, 201
James, Naomi 1949-	DLB-204
James, P. D. (Phyllis Dorothy James White) 1920-	DLB-87, 276; DS-17; CDBLB-8
Tribute to Charles Scribner Jr.	Y-95
James, Thomas 1572?-1629	DLB-213
U. P. James [publishing house]	DLB-49
James, Will 1892-1942	DS-16

James, William 1842-1910 . . . . .DLB-270

James VI of Scotland, I of England
1566-1625 . . . . .DLB-151, 172

Ane Schort Treatise Conteining Some Revlis and Cautelis to Be Obseruit and Eschewit in Scottis Poesi (1584) DLB-172

Jameson, Anna 1794-1860. . . . . DLB-99, 166

Jameson, Fredric 1934- DLB-67

Jameson, J. Franklin 1859-1937 . . . . DLB-17

Jameson, Storm 1891-1986. . . . . DLB-36

Jančar, Drago 1948- DLB-181

Janés, Clara 1940- DLB-134

Janevski, Slavko 1920- . . . DLB-181; CDWLB-4

Janowitz, Tama 1957- DLB-292

Jansson, Tove 1914-2001 . . . . DLB-257

Janvier, Thomas 1849-1913 . . . . DLB-202

Japan
"The Development of Meiji Japan" . . DLB-180
"Encounter with the West" DLB-180

Japanese Literature
Letter from Japan. Y-94, 98
Medieval Travel Diaries DLB-203
Surveys: 1987-1995 . . . . DLB-182

Jaramillo, Cleofas M. 1878-1956. . . . . DLB-122

Jaramillo Levi, Enrique 1944- DLB-290

Jarir after 650-circa 730. . . . . DLB-311

Jarman, Mark 1952- DLB-120, 282

Jarrell, Randall
1914-1965. . . . . DLB-48, 52; CDALB-1

Jarrold and Sons DLB-106

Jarry, Alfred 1873-1907. . . . . DLB-192, 258

Jarves, James Jackson 1818-1888 . . . . DLB-189

Jasmin, Claude 1930- DLB-60

Jaunsudrabiņš, Jānis 1877-1962 . . . . DLB-220

Jay, John 1745-1829 . . . . DLB-31

Jean de Garlande (see John of Garland)

Jefferies, Richard 1848-1887 . . . . DLB-98, 141
The Richard Jefferies Society Y-98

Jeffers, Lance 1919-1985. . . . . DLB-41

Jeffers, Robinson
1887-1962 . . . . DLB-45, 212; CDALB-4

Jefferson, Thomas
1743-1826 . . . . DLB-31, 183; CDALB-2

Jégé 1866-1940 . . . . DLB-215

Jelinek, Elfriede 1946- DLB-85

Jellicoe, Ann 1927- DLB-13, 233

Jemison, Mary circa 1742-1833. . . . . DLB-239

Jen, Gish 1955- DLB-312

Jenkins, Dan 1929- DLB-241

Jenkins, Elizabeth 1905- DLB-155

Jenkins, Robin 1912- DLB-14, 271

Jenkins, William Fitzgerald (see Leinster, Murray)

Herbert Jenkins Limited DLB-112

Jennings, Elizabeth 1926- DLB-27

Jens, Walter 1923- DLB-69

Jensen, Axel 1932-2003 . . . . DLB-297

Jensen, Johannes V. 1873-1950. . . . . DLB-214

Jensen, Merrill 1905-1980. . . . . DLB-17

Jensen, Thit 1876-1957 . . . . DLB-214

Jephson, Robert 1736-1803. . . . . DLB-89

Jerome, Jerome K. 1859-1927 . . . . .DLB-10, 34, 135
The Jerome K. Jerome Society Y-98

Jerome, Judson 1927-1991. . . . . DLB-105
"Reflections: After a Tornado" DLB-105

Jerrold, Douglas 1803-1857 . . . . DLB-158, 159

Jersild, Per Christian 1935- DLB-257

Jesse, F. Tennyson 1888-1958 . . . . DLB-77

Jewel, John 1522-1571. . . . . DLB-236

John P. Jewett and Company DLB-49

Jewett, Sarah Orne 1849-1909 . . . .DLB-12, 74, 221

The Jewish Publication Society. DLB-49

Studies in American Jewish Literature Y-02

Jewitt, John Rodgers 1783-1821 . . . . DLB-99

Jewsbury, Geraldine 1812-1880 . . . . DLB-21

Jewsbury, Maria Jane 1800-1833 . . . . . . DLB-199

Jhabvala, Ruth Prawer 1927- DLB-139, 194

Jiménez, Juan Ramón 1881-1958 . . . . . . DLB-134

Jin, Ha 1956- DLB-244, 292

Joans, Ted 1928- DLB-16, 41

Jōha 1525-1602. . . . . DLB-203

Jóhann Sigurjónsson 1880-1919 . . . . DLB-293

Jóhannes úr Kötlum 1899-1972 . . . . DLB-293

Johannis de Garlandia (see John of Garland)

John, Errol 1924-1988 . . . . DLB-233

John, Eugenie (see Marlitt, E.)

John of Dumbleton
circa 1310-circa 1349 . . . . DLB-115

John of Garland (Jean de Garlande, Johannis de Garlandia)
circa 1195-circa 1272 . . . . DLB-208

The John Reed Clubs DLB-303

Johns, Captain W. E. 1893-1968 . . . . DLB-160

Johnson, Mrs. A. E. ca. 1858-1922. . . . . . . DLB-221

Johnson, Amelia (see Johnson, Mrs. A. E.)

Johnson, B. S. 1933-1973 . . . . DLB-14, 40

Johnson, Charles 1679-1748 . . . . DLB-84

Johnson, Charles 1948- DLB-33, 278

Johnson, Charles S. 1893-1956. . . . . . . DLB-51, 91

Johnson, Colin (Mudrooroo) 1938- . . . DLB-289

Johnson, Denis 1949- DLB-120

Johnson, Diane 1934- Y-80

Johnson, Dorothy M. 1905–1984. . . . . . . DLB-206

Johnson, E. Pauline (Tekahionwake)
1861-1913 . . . . .DLB-175

Johnson, Edgar 1901-1995 . . . . DLB-103

Johnson, Edward 1598-1672. . . . . DLB-24

Johnson, Eyvind 1900-1976 . . . . DLB-259

Johnson, Fenton 1888-1958 . . . . DLB-45, 50

Johnson, Georgia Douglas
1877?-1966. . . . . DLB-51, 249

Johnson, Gerald W. 1890-1980 . . . . DLB-29

Johnson, Greg 1953- DLB-234

Johnson, Helene 1907-1995 . . . . DLB-51

Jacob Johnson and Company DLB-49

Johnson, James Weldon
1871-1938. . . . . DLB-51; CDALB-4

Johnson, John H. 1918- DLB-137
"Backstage," Statement From the Initial Issue of *Ebony*
(November 1945 . . . . .DLB-137

Johnson, Joseph [publishing house] DLB-154

Johnson, Linton Kwesi 1952- DLB-157

Johnson, Lionel 1867-1902 . . . . DLB-19

Johnson, Nunnally 1897-1977 . . . . DLB-26

Johnson, Owen 1878-1952 . . . . Y-87

Johnson, Pamela Hansford 1912-1981 . . . . DLB-15

Johnson, Pauline 1861-1913 . . . . DLB-92

Johnson, Ronald 1935-1998 . . . . DLB-169

Johnson, Samuel 1696-1772 . . . DLB-24; CDBLB-2

Johnson, Samuel
1709-1784 . . . . DLB-39, 95, 104, 142, 213
Rambler, no. 4 (1750) [excerpt] DLB-39
The BBC Four Samuel Johnson Prize
for Non-fiction Y-02

Johnson, Samuel 1822-1882 . . . . DLB-1, 243

Johnson, Susanna 1730-1810 . . . . DLB-200

Johnson, Terry 1955- DLB-233

Johnson, Uwe 1934-1984 . . . . .DLB-75; CDWLB-2

Benjamin Johnson [publishing house]. DLB-49

Benjamin, Jacob, and Robert Johnson
[publishing house] DLB-49

Johnston, Annie Fellows 1863-1931 . . . . . . DLB-42

Johnston, Basil H. 1929- DLB-60

Johnston, David Claypole 1798?-1865 . . . DLB-188

Johnston, Denis 1901-1984. . . . . DLB-10

Johnston, Ellen 1835-1873 . . . . DLB-199

Johnston, George 1912-1970. . . . . DLB-260

Johnston, George 1913- DLB-88

Johnston, Sir Harry 1858-1927. . . . . .DLB-174

Johnston, Jennifer 1930- DLB-14

Johnston, Mary 1870-1936 . . . . DLB-9

Johnston, Richard Malcolm 1822-1898 . . . DLB-74

Johnstone, Charles 1719?-1800? DLB-39

Johst, Hanns 1890-1978 . . . . DLB-124

Jökull Jakobsson 1933-1978 . . . . DLB-293

Jolas, Eugene 1894-1952 . . . . DLB-4, 45

Jón Stefán Sveinsson or Svensson (see Nonni)

Jón Trausti (Guðmundur Magnússon)
1873-1918. . . . . DLB-293

Jón úr Vör (Jón Jónsson) 1917-2000 . . . . DLB-293

Jónas Hallgrímsson 1807-1845 . . . . DLB-293

Jones, Alice C. 1853-1933. . . . . DLB-92

Jones, Charles C., Jr. 1831-1893. . . . . DLB-30

Jones, D. G. 1929- DLB-53

Jones, David
1895-1974. . . . . DLB-20, 100; CDBLB-7

Jones, Diana Wynne 1934- DLB-161

Jones, Ebenezer 1820-1860. . . . . DLB-32

Jones, Ernest 1819-1868 . . . . DLB-32

Jones, Gayl 1949- DLB-33, 278

Jones, George 1800-1870 ....DLB-183
Jones, Glyn 1905-1995................DLB-15
Jones, Gwyn 1907- DLB-15, 139
Jones, Henry Arthur 1851-1929.........DLB-10
Jones, Hugh circa 1692-1760 ....DLB-24
Jones, James 1921-1977 ......DLB-2, 143; DS-17
    James Jones Papers in the Handy
      Writers' Colony Collection at
      the University of Illinois at
      Springfield..................... Y-98
    The James Jones Society Y-92
Jones, Jenkin Lloyd 1911- DLB-127
Jones, John Beauchamp 1810-1866 ......DLB-202
Jones, Joseph, Major
    (see Thompson, William Tappan)
Jones, LeRoi (see Baraka, Amiri)
Jones, Lewis 1897-1939 ....DLB-15
Jones, Madison 1925- DLB-152
Jones, Marie 1951- DLB-233
Jones, Preston 1936-1979 ....DLB-7
Jones, Rodney 1950- DLB-120
Jones, Thom 1945- DLB-244
Jones, Sir William 1746-1794 ....DLB-109
Jones, William Alfred 1817-1900 ....DLB-59
Jones's Publishing House................DLB-49
Jong, Erica 1942- DLB-2, 5, 28, 152
Jonke, Gert F. 1946- DLB-85
Jonson, Ben
    1572?-1637..........DLB-62, 121; CDBLB-1
Jonsson, Tor 1916-1951................DLB-297
Jordan, June 1936- DLB-38
Jorgensen, Johannes 1866-1956 ....DLB-300
Joseph, Jenny 1932- DLB-40
Joseph and George...................... Y-99
Michael Joseph Limited DLB-112
Josephson, Matthew 1899-1978 ....DLB-4
Josephus, Flavius 37-100................DLB-176
Josephy, Alvin M., Jr.
    Tribute to Alfred A. Knopf Y-84
Josiah Allen's Wife (see Holley, Marietta)
Josipovici, Gabriel 1940- DLB-14
Josselyn, John ?-1675 ....DLB-24
Joudry, Patricia 1921-2000..............DLB-88
Jouve, Pierre Jean 1887-1976 ....DLB-258
Jovanovich, William 1920-2001........... Y-01
    Into the Past: William Jovanovich's
      Reflections on Publishing Y-02
    [Response to Ken Auletta]............ Y-97
    The Temper of the West: William
      Jovanovich Y-02
    Tribute to Charles Scribner Jr. Y-95
Jovine, Francesco 1902-1950 ....DLB-264
Jovine, Giuseppe 1922- DLB-128
Joyaux, Philippe (see Sollers, Philippe)
Joyce, Adrien (see Eastman, Carol)
Joyce, James 1882-1941
    ....DLB-10, 19, 36, 162, 247; CDBLB-6

Danis Rose and the Rendering of *Ulysses*... Y-97
James Joyce Centenary: Dublin, 1982.... Y-82
James Joyce Conference Y-85
A Joyce (Con)Text: Danis Rose and the
    Remaking of *Ulysses*.............. Y-97
The National Library of Ireland's
    New James Joyce Manuscripts Y-02
The New *Ulysses* Y-84
Public Domain and the Violation of
    Texts............................ Y-97
The Quinn Draft of James Joyce's
    Circe Manuscript Y-00
Stephen Joyce's Letter to the Editor of
    The Irish Times Y-97
Ulysses, Reader's Edition: First Reactions.. Y-97
We See the Editor at Work........... Y-97
Whose *Ulysses*? The Function of Editing.. Y-97
Jozsef, Attila 1905-1937 .....DLB-215; CDWLB-4
Juarroz, Roberto 1925-1995...........DLB-283
Orange Judd Publishing Company DLB-49
Judd, Sylvester 1813-1853 ....DLB-1, 243
Judith circa 930 ....DLB-146
Juel-Hansen, Erna 1845-1922 ....DLB-300
Julian of Norwich 1342-circa 1420......DLB-1146
Julius Caesar
    100 B.C.-44 B.C.........DLB-211; CDWLB-1
June, Jennie
    (see Croly, Jane Cunningham)
Jung, Carl Gustav 1875-1961..........DLB-296
Jung, Franz 1888-1963................DLB-118
Jünger, Ernst 1895- DLB-56; CDWLB-2
Der jüngere Titurel circa 1275 ....DLB-138
Jung-Stilling, Johann Heinrich
    1740-1817......................DLB-94
Junqueiro, Abílio Manuel Guerra
    1850-1923 ....DLB-287
Justice, Donald 1925- Y-83
Juvenal circa A.D. 60 circa A.D. 130
    ....DLB-211; CDWLB-1
The Juvenile Library
    (see M. J. Godwin and Company)

K

Kacew, Romain (see Gary, Romain)
Kafka, Franz 1883-1924......DLB-81; CDWLB-2
Kahn, Gus 1886-1941 ....DLB-265
Kahn, Roger 1927- DLB-171
Kaikō Takeshi 1939-1989 ....DLB-182
Káinn (Kristján Níels Jónsson/Kristjan
    Niels Julius) 1860-1936 ....DLB-293
Kaiser, Georg 1878-1945 ....DLB-124; CDWLB-2
Kaiserchronik circa 1147 ....DLB-148
Kaleb, Vjekoslav 1905- DLB-181
Kalechofsky, Roberta 1931- DLB-28
Kaler, James Otis 1848-1912 ....DLB-12, 42
Kalmar, Bert 1884-1947 ....DLB-265
Kamensky, Vasilii Vasil'evich
    1884-1961 ....DLB-295

Kames, Henry Home, Lord
    1696-1782 ....DLB-31, 104
Kamo no Chōmei (Kamo no Nagaakira)
    1153 or 1155-1216 ....DLB-203
Kamo no Nagaakira (see Kamo no Chōmei)
Kampmann, Christian 1939-1988 ....DLB-214
Kandel, Lenore 1932- DLB-16
Kane, Sarah 1971-1999 ....DLB-310
Kaneko, Lonny 1939- DLB-312
Kang, Younghill 1903-1972 ....DLB-312
Kanin, Garson 1912-1999 ....DLB-7
    A Tribute (to Marc Connelly).......... Y-80
Kaniuk, Yoram 1930- DLB-299
Kant, Hermann 1926- DLB-75
Kant, Immanuel 1724-1804 ....DLB-94
Kantemir, Antiokh Dmitrievich
    1708-1744 ....DLB-150
Kantor, MacKinlay 1904-1977..........DLB-9, 102
Kanze Kōjirō Nobumitsu 1435-1516 .....DLB-203
Kanze Motokiyo (see Zeimi)
Kaplan, Fred 1937- DLB-111
Kaplan, Johanna 1942- DLB-28
Kaplan, Justin 1925- DLB-111; Y-86
Kaplinski, Jaan 1941- DLB-232
Kapnist, Vasilii Vasilevich 1758?-1823 ...DLB-150
Karadžić, Vuk Stefanović
    1787-1864............DLB-147; CDWLB-4
Karamzin, Nikolai Mikhailovich
    1766-1826 ....DLB-150
Karinthy, Frigyes 1887-1938 ....DLB-215
Karmel, Ilona 1925-2000 ....DLB-299
Karsch, Anna Louisa 1722-1791........DLB-97
Kasack, Hermann 1896-1966 ....DLB-69
Kasai Zenzō 1887-1927 ....DLB-180
Kaschnitz, Marie Luise 1901-1974........DLB-69
Kassák, Lajos 1887-1967 ....DLB-215
Kaštelan, Jure 1919-1990 ....DLB-147
Kästner, Erich 1899-1974................DLB-56
Kataev, Evgenii Petrovich
    (see Il'f, Il'ia and Petrov, Evgenii)
Kataev, Valentin Petrovich 1897-1986....DLB-272
Katenin, Pavel Aleksandrovich
    1792-1853 ....DLB-205
Kattan, Naim 1928- DLB-53
Katz, Steve 1935- Y-83
Ka-Tzetnik 135633 (Yehiel Dinur)
    1909-2001......................DLB-299
Kauffman, Janet 1945- DLB-218; Y-86
Kauffmann, Samuel 1898-1971 ....DLB-127
Kaufman, Bob 1925-1986 ....DLB-16, 41
Kaufman, George S. 1889-1961...........DLB-7
Kaufmann, Walter 1921-1980..........DLB-279
Kavan, Anna (Helen Woods Ferguson
    Edmonds) 1901-1968 ....DLB-255
Kavanagh, P. J. 1931- DLB-40
Kavanagh, Patrick 1904-1967 ....DLB-15, 20

Cumulative Index

Kaverin, Veniamin Aleksandrovich
  (Veniamin Aleksandrovich Zil'ber)
  1902-1989 .... DLB-272
Kawabata Yasunari 1899-1972 .... DLB-180
Kay, Guy Gavriel 1954- DLB-251
Kaye-Smith, Sheila 1887-1956 .... DLB-36
Kazakov, Iurii Pavlovich 1927-1982 ..... DLB-302
Kazin, Alfred 1915-1998 .... DLB-67
Keane, John B. 1928- DLB-13
Keary, Annie 1825-1879 .... DLB-163
Keary, Eliza 1827-1918 .... DLB-240
Keating, H. R. F. 1926- DLB-87
Keatley, Charlotte 1960- DLB-245
Keats, Ezra Jack 1916-1983 .... DLB-61
Keats, John 1795-1821 ... DLB-96, 110; CDBLB-3
Keble, John 1792-1866 .... DLB-32, 55
Keckley, Elizabeth 1818?-1907 .... DLB-239
Keeble, John 1944- Y-83
Keeffe, Barrie 1945- DLB-13, 245
Keeley, James 1867-1934 .... DLB-25
W. B. Keen, Cooke and Company DLB-49
The Mystery of Carolyn Keene Y-02
Kefala, Antigone 1935- DLB-289
Keillor, Garrison 1942- Y-87
Keith, Marian (Mary Esther MacGregor)
  1874?-1961 .... DLB-92
Keller, Gary D. 1943- DLB-82
Keller, Gottfried
  1819-1890 .... DLB-129; CDWLB-2
Keller, Helen 1880-1968 .... DLB-303
Kelley, Edith Summers 1884-1956 .... DLB-9
Kelley, Emma Dunham ?-? DLB-221
Kelley, Florence 1859-1932 .... DLB-303
Kelley, William Melvin 1937- DLB-33
Kellogg, Ansel Nash 1832-1886 .... DLB-23
Kellogg, Steven 1941- DLB-61
Kelly, George E. 1887-1974 .... DLB-7, 249
Kelly, Hugh 1739-1777 .... DLB-89
Kelly, Piet and Company DLB-49
Kelly, Robert 1935- DLB-5, 130, 165
Kelman, James 1946- DLB-194
Kelmscott Press DLB-112
Kelton, Elmer 1926- DLB-256
Kemble, E. W. 1861-1933 .... DLB-188
Kemble, Fanny 1809-1893 .... DLB-32
Kemelman, Harry 1908-1996 .... DLB-28
Kempe, Margery circa 1373-1438 .... DLB-146
Kempinski, Tom 1938- DLB-310
Kempner, Friederike 1836-1904 .... DLB-129
Kempowski, Walter 1929- DLB-75
Kenan, Randall 1963- DLB-292
Claude Kendall [publishing company] DLB-46
Kendall, Henry 1839-1882 .... DLB-230
Kendall, May 1861-1943 .... DLB-240
Kendell, George 1809-1867 .... DLB-43

Keneally, Thomas 1935- DLB-289, 299
Kenedy, P. J., and Sons DLB-49
Kenkō circa 1283-circa 1352 .... DLB-203
Kenna, Peter 1930-1987 .... DLB-289
Kennan, George 1845-1924 .... DLB-189
Kennedy, A. L. 1965- DLB-271
Kennedy, Adrienne 1931- DLB-38
Kennedy, John Pendleton 1795-1870 .. DLB-3, 248
Kennedy, Leo 1907-2000 .... DLB-88
Kennedy, Margaret 1896-1967 .... DLB-36
Kennedy, Patrick 1801-1873 .... DLB-159
Kennedy, Richard S. 1920- DLB-111; Y-02
Kennedy, William 1928- DLB-143; Y-85
Kennedy, X. J. 1929- DLB-5
  Tribute to John Ciardi Y-86
Kennelly, Brendan 1936- DLB-40
Kenner, Hugh 1923- DLB-67
  Tribute to Cleanth Brooks Y-80
Mitchell Kennerley [publishing house] DLB-46
Kenny, Maurice 1929- DLB-175
Kent, Frank R. 1877-1958 .... DLB-29
Kenyon, Jane 1947-1995 .... DLB-120
Kenzheev, Bakhyt Shkurullaevich
  1950- DLB-285
Keough, Hugh Edmund 1864-1912 ...... DLB-171
Keppler and Schwartzmann DLB-49
Ker, John, third Duke of Roxburghe
  1740-1804 .... DLB-213
Ker, N. R. 1908-1982 .... DLB-201
Keralio-Robert, Louise-Félicité de
  1758-1822 .... DLB-313
Kerlan, Irvin 1912-1963 .... DLB-187
Kermode, Frank 1919- DLB-242
Kern, Jerome 1885-1945 .... DLB-187
Kernaghan, Eileen 1939- DLB-251
Kerner, Justinus 1786-1862 .... DLB-90
Kerouac, Jack
  1922-1969 .. DLB-2, 16, 237; DS-3; CDALB-1
  Auction of Jack Kerouac's
    On the Road Scroll Y-01
  The Jack Kerouac Revival Y-95
  "Re-meeting of Old Friends":
    The Jack Kerouac Conference Y-82
  Statement of Correction to "The Jack
    Kerouac Revival" Y-96
Kerouac, Jan 1952-1996 .... DLB-16
Charles H. Kerr and Company DLB-49
Kerr, Orpheus C. (see Newell, Robert Henry)
Kersh, Gerald 1911-1968 .... DLB-255
Kertész, Imre DLB-299; Y-02
Kesey, Ken
  1935-2001 .... DLB-2, 16, 206; CDALB-6
Kessel, Joseph 1898-1979 .... DLB-72
Kessel, Martin 1901-1990 .... DLB-56
Kesten, Hermann 1900-1996 .... DLB-56
Keun, Irmgard 1905-1982 .... DLB-69
Key, Ellen 1849-1926 .... DLB-259

Key and Biddle DLB-49
Keynes, Sir Geoffrey 1887-1982 .... DLB-201
Keynes, John Maynard 1883-1946 .... DS-10
Keyserling, Eduard von 1855-1918 ..... DLB-66
al-Khalil ibn Ahmad circa 718-791 ..... DLB-311
Khan, Ismith 1925-2002 .... DLB-125
al-Khansa' flourished late sixth-mid
  seventh centuries DLB-311
Kharitonov, Evgenii Vladimirovich
  1941-1981 .... DLB-285
Kharitonov, Mark Sergeevich 1937- ... DLB-285
Khaytov, Nikolay 1919- DLB-181
Khemnitser, Ivan Ivanovich
  1745-1784 .... DLB-150
Kheraskov, Mikhail Matveevich
  1733-1807 .... DLB-150
Khlebnikov, Velimir 1885-1922 .... DLB-295
Khomiakov, Aleksei Stepanovich
  1804-1860 .... DLB-205
Khristov, Boris 1945- DLB-181
Khvoshchinskaia, Nadezhda Dmitrievna
  1824-1889 .... DLB-238
Khvostov, Dmitrii Ivanovich
  1757-1835 .... DLB-150
Kibirov, Timur Iur'evich (Timur
  Iur'evich Zapoev) 1955- DLB-285
Kidd, Adam 1802?-1831 .... DLB-99
William Kidd [publishing house] DLB-106
Kidde, Harald 1878-1918 .... DLB-300
Kidder, Tracy 1945- DLB-185
Kiely, Benedict 1919- DLB-15
Kieran, John 1892-1981 .... DLB-171
Kierkegaard, Søren 1813-1855 .... DLB-300
Kies, Marietta 1853-1899 .... DLB-270
Kiggins and Kellogg DLB-49
Kiley, Jed 1889-1962 .... DLB-4
Kilgore, Bernard 1908-1967 .... DLB-127
Kilian, Crawford 1941- DLB-251
Killens, John Oliver 1916-1987 .... DLB-33
  Tribute to Julian Mayfield Y-84
Killigrew, Anne 1660-1685 .... DLB-131
Killigrew, Thomas 1612-1683 .... DLB-58
Kilmer, Joyce 1886-1918 .... DLB-45
Kilroy, Thomas 1934- DLB-233
Kilwardby, Robert circa 1215-1279 .... DLB-115
Kilworth, Garry 1941- DLB-261
Kim, Anatolii Andreevich 1939- DLB-285
Kimball, Richard Burleigh 1816-1892 ... DLB-202
Kincaid, Jamaica 1949-
  .... DLB-157, 227; CDALB-7; CDWLB-3
Kinck, Hans Ernst 1865-1926 .... DLB-297
King, Charles 1844-1933 .... DLB-186
King, Clarence 1842-1901 .... DLB-12
King, Florence 1936- Y-85
King, Francis 1923- DLB-15, 139
King, Grace 1852-1932 .... DLB-12, 78
King, Harriet Hamilton 1840-1920 ..... DLB-199

King, Henry 1592-1669 . . . . DLB-126
Solomon King [publishing house] DLB-49
King, Stephen 1947- DLB-143; Y-80
King, Susan Petigru 1824-1875 . . . . DLB-239
King, Thomas 1943- DLB-175
King, Woodie, Jr. 1937- DLB-38
Kinglake, Alexander William
  1809-1891 . . . . DLB-55, 166
Kingo, Thomas 1634-1703. . . . . DLB-300
Kingsbury, Donald 1929- DLB-251
Kingsley, Charles
  1819-1875 . . . . DLB-21, 32, 163, 178, 190
Kingsley, Henry 1830-1876 . . . . DLB-21, 230
Kingsley, Mary Henrietta 1862-1900 . . . . . DLB-174
Kingsley, Sidney 1906-1995. . . . . DLB-7
Kingsmill, Hugh 1889-1949 . . . . DLB-149
Kingsolver, Barbara
  1955- DLB-206; CDALB-7
Kingston, Maxine Hong
  1940- . . DLB-173, 212, 312; Y-80; CDALB-7
Kingston, William Henry Giles
  1814-1880 . . . . DLB-163
Kinnan, Mary Lewis 1763-1848. . . . . DLB-200
Kinnell, Galway 1927- DLB-5; Y-87
Kinsella, Thomas 1928- DLB-27
Kipling, Rudyard 1865-1936
  . . . . DLB-19, 34, 141, 156; CDBLB-5
Kipphardt, Heinar 1922-1982 . . . . DLB-124
Kirby, William 1817-1906 . . . . DLB-99
Kircher, Athanasius 1602-1680 . . . . DLB-164
Kireevsky, Ivan Vasil'evich 1806-1856 . . . DLB-198
Kireevsky, Petr Vasil'evich 1808-1856 . . . DLB-205
Kirk, Hans 1898-1962 . . . . DLB-214
Kirk, John Foster 1824-1904 . . . . DLB-79
Kirkconnell, Watson 1895-1977 . . . . DLB-68
Kirkland, Caroline M.
  1801-1864 . . . . DLB-3, 73, 74, 250; DS-13
Kirkland, Joseph 1830-1893 . . . . DLB-12
Francis Kirkman [publishing house] DLB-170
Kirkpatrick, Clayton 1915- DLB-127
Kirkup, James 1918- DLB-27
Kirouac, Conrad (see Marie-Victorin, Frère)
Kirsch, Sarah 1935- DLB-75
Kirst, Hans Hellmut 1914-1989 . . . . DLB-69
Kiš, Danilo 1935-1989 . . . . . . DLB-181; CDWLB-4
Kita Morio 1927- DLB-182
Kitcat, Mabel Greenhow 1859-1922 . . . . . DLB-135
Kitchin, C. H. B. 1895-1967 . . . . DLB-77
Kittredge, William 1932- DLB-212, 244
Kiukhel'beker, Vil'gel'm Karlovich
  1797-1846. . . . . DLB-205
Kizer, Carolyn 1925- DLB-5, 169
Kjaerstad, Jan 1953- DLB-297
Klabund 1890-1928 . . . . DLB-66
Klaj, Johann 1616-1656 . . . . DLB-164
Klappert, Peter 1942- DLB-5
Klass, Philip (see Tenn, William)

Klein, A. M. 1909-1972 . . . . DLB-68
Kleist, Ewald von 1715-1759 . . . . DLB-97
Kleist, Heinrich von
  1777-1811. . . . . DLB-90; CDWLB-2
Klíma, Ivan 1931- DLB-232; CDWLB-4
Klimentev, Andrei Platonovic
  (see Platonov, Andrei Platonovich)
Klinger, Friedrich Maximilian
  1752-1831 . . . . DLB-94
Kliuev, Nikolai Alekseevich 1884-1937 . . . DLB-295
Kliushnikov, Viktor Petrovich
  1841-1892 . . . . DLB-238
Klopfer, Donald S.
  Impressions of William Faulkner Y-97
  Oral History Interview with Donald
    S. Klopfer Y-97
  Tribute to Alfred A. Knopf Y-84
Klopstock, Friedrich Gottlieb
  1724-1803 . . . . DLB-97
Klopstock, Meta 1728-1758 . . . . DLB-97
Kluge, Alexander 1932- DLB-75
Kluge, P. F. 1942- Y-02
Knapp, Joseph Palmer 1864-1951 . . . . DLB-91
Knapp, Samuel Lorenzo 1783-1838 . . . . . . DLB-59
J. J. and P. Knapton [publishing house] . . . DLB-154
Kniazhnin, Iakov Borisovich
  1740-1791 . . . . DLB-150
Knickerbocker, Diedrich (see Irving, Washington)
Knigge, Adolph Franz Friedrich Ludwig,
  Freiherr von 1752-1796 . . . . DLB-94
Charles Knight and Company DLB-106
Knight, Damon 1922-2002 . . . . DLB-8
Knight, Etheridge 1931-1992 . . . . DLB-41
Knight, John S. 1894-1981 . . . . DLB-29
Knight, Sarah Kemble 1666-1727 . . . . . DLB-24, 200
Knight-Bruce, G. W. H. 1852-1896 . . . . . . DLB-174
Knister, Raymond 1899-1932 . . . . DLB-68
Knoblock, Edward 1874-1945 . . . . DLB-10
Knopf, Alfred A. 1892-1984 . . . . Y-84
  Knopf to Hammett: The Editoral
    Correspondence Y-00
Alfred A. Knopf [publishing house] DLB-46
Knorr von Rosenroth, Christian
  1636-1689 . . . . DLB-168
Knowles, John 1926- DLB-6; CDALB-6
Knox, Frank 1874-1944 . . . . DLB-29
Knox, John circa 1514-1572 . . . . DLB-132
Knox, John Armoy 1850-1906 . . . . DLB-23
Knox, Lucy 1845-1884 . . . . DLB-240
Knox, Ronald Arbuthnott 1888-1957 . . . . . DLB-77
Knox, Thomas Wallace 1835-1896 . . . . . . DLB-189
Knudsen, Jakob 1858-1917 . . . . DLB-300
Kobayashi Takiji 1903-1933 . . . . DLB-180
Kober, Arthur 1900-1975 . . . . DLB-11
Kobiakova, Aleksandra Petrovna
  1823-1892 . . . . DLB-238
Kocbek, Edvard 1904-1981 . . . DLB-147; CDWLB-4
Koch, C. J. 1932- DLB-289

Koch, Howard 1902-1995 . . . . DLB-26
Koch, Kenneth 1925-2002 . . . . DLB-5
Kōda Rohan 1867-1947 . . . . DLB-180
Koehler, Ted 1894-1973 . . . . DLB-265
Koenigsberg, Moses 1879-1945 . . . . DLB-25
Koeppen, Wolfgang 1906-1996 . . . . DLB-69
Koertge, Ronald 1940- DLB-105
Koestler, Arthur 1905-1983 . . . . . . Y-83; CDBLB-7
Kohn, John S. Van E. 1906-1976 . . . . DLB-187
Kokhanovskaia
  (see Sokhanskaia, Nadezhda Stepanova)
Kokoschka, Oskar 1886-1980 . . . . DLB-124
Kolb, Annette 1870-1967 . . . . DLB-66
Kolbenheyer, Erwin Guido
  1878-1962 . . . . DLB-66, 124
Kolleritsch, Alfred 1931- DLB-85
Kolodny, Annette 1941- DLB-67
Kol'tsov, Aleksei Vasil'evich
  1809-1842 . . . . DLB-205
Komarov, Matvei circa 1730-1812 . . . . DLB-150
Komroff, Manuel 1890-1974 . . . . DLB-4
Komunyakaa, Yusef 1947- DLB-120
Kondoleon, Harry 1955-1994 . . . . DLB-266
Koneski, Blaže 1921-1993 . . . DLB-181; CDWLB-4
Konigsburg, E. L. 1930- DLB-52
Konparu Zenchiku 1405-1468? DLB-203
Konrád, György 1933- DLB-232; CDWLB-4
Konrad von Würzburg
  circa 1230-1287 . . . . DLB-138
Konstantinov, Aleko 1863-1897 . . . . DLB-147
Konwicki, Tadeusz 1926- DLB-232
Koontz, Dean 1945- DLB-292
Kooser, Ted 1939- DLB-105
Kopit, Arthur 1937- DLB-7
Kops, Bernard 1926?- DLB-13
Kornbluth, C. M. 1923-1958 . . . . DLB-8
Körner, Theodor 1791-1813 . . . . DLB-90
Kornfeld, Paul 1889-1942 . . . . DLB-118
Korolenko, Vladimir Galaktionovich
  1853-1921 . . . . DLB-277
Kosinski, Jerzy 1933-1991 . . . . . DLB-2, 299; Y-82
Kosmač, Ciril 1910-1980 . . . . DLB-181
Kosovel, Srečko 1904-1926 . . . . DLB-147
Kostrov, Ermil Ivanovich 1755-1796 . . . . DLB-150
Kotzebue, August von 1761-1819 . . . . DLB-94
Kotzwinkle, William 1938- DLB-173
Kovačić, Ante 1854-1889 . . . . DLB-147
Kovalevskaia, Sof'ia Vasil'evna
  1850-1891 . . . . DLB-277
Kovič, Kajetan 1931- DLB-181
Kozlov, Ivan Ivanovich 1779-1840 . . . . . . DLB-205
Kracauer, Siegfried 1889-1966 . . . . DLB-296
Kraf, Elaine 1946- Y-81
Kramer, Jane 1938- DLB-185
Kramer, Larry 1935- DLB-249
Kramer, Mark 1944- DLB-185

Kranjčević, Silvije Strahimir 1865-1908 . . DLB-147	Kunnert, Gunter 1929- DLB-75	Lagerlöf, Selma 1858-1940 . . . . DLB-259
Krasko, Ivan 1876-1958 . . . . DLB-215	Kunze, Reiner 1933- DLB-75	Lagorio, Gina 1922- DLB-196
Krasna, Norman 1909-1984 . . . . DLB-26	Kuo, Helena 1911-1999 . . . . DLB-312	La Guma, Alex 1925-1985 . . . . DLB-117, 225; CDWLB-3
Kraus, Hans Peter 1907-1988 . . . . DLB-187	Kupferberg, Tuli 1923- DLB-16	Lahaise, Guillaume (see Delahaye, Guy)
Kraus, Karl 1874-1936 . . . . DLB-118	Kuprin, Aleksandr Ivanovich 1870-1938 . . . . DLB-295	La Harpe, Jean-François de 1739-1803 . . . . DLB-313
Krause, Herbert 1905-1976 . . . . DLB-256	Kuraev, Mikhail Nikolaevich 1939- . . . DLB-285	Lahontan, Louis-Armand de Lom d'Arce, Baron de 1666-1715? DLB-99
Krauss, Ruth 1911-1993 . . . . DLB-52	Kurahashi Yumiko 1935- DLB-182	Laing, Kojo 1946- DLB-157
Kreisel, Henry 1922-1991 . . . . DLB-88	Kureishi, Hanif 1954- DLB-194, 245	Laird, Carobeth 1895-1983 . . . . Y-82
Krestovsky V. (see Khvoshchinskaia, Nadezhda Dmitrievna)	Kürnberger, Ferdinand 1821-1879 . . . . . DLB-129	Laird and Lee DLB-49
Krestovsky, Vsevolod Vladimirovich 1839-1895 . . . . DLB-238	Kurz, Isolde 1853-1944 . . . . DLB-66	Lake, Paul 1951- DLB-282
	Kusenberg, Kurt 1904-1983 . . . . DLB-69	Lalić, Ivan V. 1931-1996 . . . . DLB-181
Kreuder, Ernst 1903-1972 . . . . DLB-69	Kushchevsky, Ivan Afanas'evich 1847-1876 . . . . DLB-238	Lalić, Mihailo 1914-1992 . . . . DLB-181
Krėvė-Mickevičius, Vincas 1882-1954 . . . DLB-220		Lalonde, Michèle 1937- DLB-60
Kreymborg, Alfred 1883-1966 . . . . DLB-4, 54	Kushner, Tony 1956- DLB-228	Lamantia, Philip 1927- DLB-16
Krieger, Murray 1923- DLB-67	Kuttner, Henry 1915-1958 . . . . DLB-8	Lamartine, Alphonse de 1790-1869 . . . . DLB-217
Krim, Seymour 1922-1989 . . . . DLB-16	Kuzmin, Mikhail Alekseevich 1872-1936 . . . . DLB-295	
Kripke, Saul 1940- DLB-279	Kuznetsov, Anatoli 1929-1979 . . . . DLB-299, 302	Lamb, Lady Caroline 1785-1828 . . . . DLB-116
Kristensen, Tom 1893-1974 . . . . DLB-214		Lamb, Charles 1775-1834 . . . . . . DLB-93, 107, 163; CDBLB-3
Kristeva, Julia 1941- DLB-242	Kyd, Thomas 1558-1594 . . . . DLB-62	
Kristján Níels Jónsson/Kristjan Niels Julius (see Káinn)	Kyffin, Maurice circa 1560?-1598 . . . . . . DLB-136	Lamb, Mary 1764-1874 . . . . DLB-163
	Kyger, Joanne 1934- DLB-16	Lambert, Angela 1940- DLB-271
Kritzer, Hyman W. 1918-2002 . . . . Y-02	Kyne, Peter B. 1880-1957 . . . . DLB-78	Lambert, Anne-Thérèse de (Anne-Thérèse de Marguenat de Courcelles, marquise de Lambert) 1647-1733 . . . . DLB-313
Krivulin, Viktor Borisovich 1944-2001 . . DLB-285	Kyōgoku Tamekane 1254-1332 . . . . DLB-203	
Krleža, Miroslav 1893-1981 . . . . DLB-147; CDWLB-4	Kyrklund, Willy 1921- DLB-257	
		Lambert, Betty 1933-1983 . . . . DLB-60
Krock, Arthur 1886-1974 . . . . DLB-29	# L	La Mettrie, Julien Offroy de 1709-1751 . . . . DLB-313
Kroetsch, Robert 1927- DLB-53	L. E. L. (see Landon, Letitia Elizabeth)	
Kropotkin, Petr Alekseevich 1842-1921 . . DLB-277	Laberge, Albert 1871-1960 . . . . DLB-68	Lamm, Donald Goodbye, Gutenberg? A Lecture at the New York Public Library, 18 April 1995 . . . . Y-95
Kross, Jaan 1920- DLB-232	Laberge, Marie 1950- DLB-60	
Kruchenykh, Aleksei Eliseevich 1886-1968 . . . . DLB-295	Labiche, Eugène 1815-1888 . . . . DLB-192	
	Labrunie, Gerard (see Nerval, Gerard de)	Lamming, George 1927- DLB-125; CDWLB-3
Krúdy, Gyula 1878-1933 . . . . DLB-215	La Bruyère, Jean de 1645-1696 . . . . DLB-268	
Krutch, Joseph Wood 1893-1970 . . . . DLB-63, 206, 275	La Calprenède 1609?-1663 . . . . DLB-268	La Mothe Le Vayer, François de 1588-1672 . . . . DLB-268
	Lacan, Jacques 1901-1981 . . . . DLB-296	
Krylov, Ivan Andreevich 1769-1844 . . . . . DLB-150	La Capria, Raffaele 1922- DLB-196	L'Amour, Louis 1908-1988 . . . . DLB-206; Y-80
Krymov, Iurii Solomonovich (Iurii Solomonovich Beklemishev) 1908-1941 . . . . DLB-272	La Chaussée, Pierre-Claude Nivelle de 1692-1754 . . . . DLB-313	Lampman, Archibald 1861-1899 . . . . DLB-92
		Lamson, Wolffe and Company DLB-49
Kubin, Alfred 1877-1959 . . . . DLB-81	Laclos, Pierre-Ambroise-François Choderlos de 1741-1803 . . . . DLB-313	Lancer Books DLB-46
Kubrick, Stanley 1928-1999 . . . . DLB-26		Lanchester, John 1962- DLB-267
Kudrun circa 1230-1240 . . . . DLB-138	Lacombe, Patrice (see Trullier-Lacombe, Joseph Patrice)	Lander, Peter (see Cunningham, Peter)
Kuffstein, Hans Ludwig von 1582-1656 . . DLB-164		Landesman, Jay 1919- and Landesman, Fran 1927- DLB-16
Kuhlmann, Quirinus 1651-1689 . . . . DLB-168	Lacretelle, Jacques de 1888-1985 . . . . DLB-65	
Kuhn, Thomas S. 1922-1996 . . . . DLB-279	Lacy, Ed 1911-1968 . . . . DLB-226	Landolfi, Tommaso 1908-1979 . . . . DLB-177
Kuhnau, Johann 1660-1722 . . . . DLB-168	Lacy, Sam 1903- DLB-171	Landon, Letitia Elizabeth 1802-1838 . . . . . DLB-96
Kukol'nik, Nestor Vasil'evich 1809-1868 . . . . DLB-205	Ladd, Joseph Brown 1764-1786 . . . . DLB-37	Landor, Walter Savage 1775-1864 . . . . DLB-93, 107
	La Farge, Oliver 1901-1963 . . . . DLB-9	Landry, Napoléon-P. 1884-1956 . . . . DLB-92
Kukučín, Martin 1860-1928 . . . . DLB-215; CDWLB-4	Lafayette, Marie-Madeleine, comtesse de 1634-1693 . . . . DLB-268	Landvik, Lorna 1954- DLB-292
		Lane, Charles 1800-1870 . . . . DLB-1, 223; DS-5
Kumin, Maxine 1925- DLB-5	Laffan, Mrs. R. S. de Courcy (see Adams, Bertha Leith)	Lane, F. C. 1885-1984 . . . . DLB-241
Kuncewicz, Maria 1895-1989 . . . . DLB-215		Lane, Laurence W. 1890-1967 . . . . DLB-91
Kundera, Milan 1929- DLB-232; CDWLB-4	Lafferty, R. A. 1914-2002 . . . . DLB-8	Lane, M. Travis 1934- DLB-60
Kunene, Mazisi 1930- DLB-117	La Flesche, Francis 1857-1932 . . . . DLB-175	Lane, Patrick 1939- DLB-53
Kunikida Doppo 1869-1908 . . . . DLB-180	La Fontaine, Jean de 1621-1695 . . . . DLB-268	Lane, Pinkie Gordon 1923- DLB-41
Kunitz, Stanley 1905- DLB-48	Laforge, Jules 1860-1887 . . . . DLB-217	
Kunjufu, Johari M. (see Amini, Johari M.)	Lagerkvist, Pär 1891-1974 . . . . DLB-259	John Lane Company DLB-49

Laney, Al 1896-1988 . . . . DLB-4, 171
Lang, Andrew 1844-1912 . . . . . . DLB-98, 141, 184
Langer, Susanne K. 1895-1985 . . . . DLB-270
Langevin, André 1927- DLB-60
Langford, David 1953- DLB-261
Langgässer, Elisabeth 1899-1950 . . . . DLB-69
Langhorne, John 1735-1779 . . . . DLB-109
Langland, William circa 1330-circa 1400. . DLB-146
Langton, Anna 1804-1893 . . . . DLB-99
Lanham, Edwin 1904-1979 . . . . DLB-4
Lanier, Sidney 1842-1881 . . . . DLB-64; DS-13
Lanyer, Aemilia 1569-1645 . . . . DLB-121
Lapointe, Gatien 1931-1983 . . . . DLB-88
Lapointe, Paul-Marie 1929- DLB-88
Larcom, Lucy 1824-1893 . . . . DLB-221, 243
Lardner, John 1912-1960 . . . . DLB-171
Lardner, Ring 1885-1933
 . . . . . DLB-11, 25, 86, 171; DS-16; CDALB-4
 Lardner 100: Ring Lardner
 Centennial Symposium Y-85
Lardner, Ring, Jr. 1915-2000 . . . . . . DLB-26, Y-00
Larkin, Philip 1922-1985 . . . . . DLB-27; CDBLB-8
 The Philip Larkin Society Y-99
La Roche, Sophie von 1730-1807 . . . . DLB-94
La Rochefoucauld, François duc de
 1613-1680 . . . . DLB-268
La Rocque, Gilbert 1943-1984 . . . . DLB-60
Laroque de Roquebrune, Robert
 (see Roquebrune, Robert de)
Larrick, Nancy 1910- DLB-61
Lars, Claudia 1899-1974 . . . . DLB-283
Larsen, Nella 1893-1964 . . . . DLB-51
Larsen, Thøger 1875-1928 . . . . DLB-300
Larson, Clinton F. 1919-1994 . . . . DLB-256
La Sale, Antoine de
 circa 1386-1460/1467 . . . . DLB-208
Lasch, Christopher 1932-1994 . . . . DLB-246
Lasker-Schüler, Else 1869-1945 . . . . . DLB-66, 124
Lasnier, Rina 1915-1997 . . . . DLB-88
Lassalle, Ferdinand 1825-1864 . . . . DLB-129
Late-Medieval Castilian Theater DLB-286
Latham, Robert 1912-1995 . . . . DLB-201
Lathan, Emma (Mary Jane Latsis [1927-1997] and
 Martha Henissart [1929-]) DLB-306
Lathrop, Dorothy P. 1891-1980 . . . . DLB-22
Lathrop, George Parsons 1851-1898 . . . . . . DLB-71
Lathrop, John, Jr. 1772-1820 . . . . DLB-37
Latimer, Hugh 1492?-1555 . . . . DLB-136
Latimore, Jewel Christine McLawler
 (see Amini, Johari M.)
Latin Literature, The Uniqueness of DLB-211
La Tour du Pin, Patrice de 1911-1975 . . . . DLB-258
Latymer, William 1498-1583 . . . . DLB-132
Laube, Heinrich 1806-1884 . . . . DLB-133
Laud, William 1573-1645 . . . . DLB-213
Laughlin, James 1914-1997 . . . . . DLB-48; Y-96, 97

A Tribute [to Henry Miller] Y-80
Tribute to Albert Erskine Y-93
Tribute to Kenneth Rexroth Y-82
Tribute to Malcolm Cowley Y-89
Laumer, Keith 1925-1993 . . . . DLB-8
Lauremberg, Johann 1590-1658 . . . . DLB-164
Laurence, Margaret 1926-1987 . . . . DLB-53
Laurentius von Schnüffis 1633-1702 . . . . . DLB-168
Laurents, Arthur 1918- DLB-26
Laurie, Annie (see Black, Winifred)
Laut, Agnes Christiana 1871-1936 . . . . DLB-92
Lauterbach, Ann 1942- DLB-193
Lautréamont, Isidore Lucien Ducasse,
 Comte de 1846-1870 . . . . DLB-217
Lavater, Johann Kaspar 1741-1801 . . . . DLB-97
Lavin, Mary 1912-1996 . . . . DLB-15
Law, John (see Harkness, Margaret)
Lawes, Henry 1596-1662 . . . . DLB-126
Lawler, Ray 1921- DLB-289
Lawless, Anthony (see MacDonald, Philip)
Lawless, Emily (The Hon. Emily Lawless)
 1845-1913 . . . . DLB-240
Lawrence, D. H. 1885-1930
 . . . . . DLB-10, 19, 36, 98, 162, 195; CDBLB-6
 The D. H. Lawrence Society of
 North America Y-00
Lawrence, David 1888-1973 . . . . DLB-29
Lawrence, Jerome 1915- DLB-228
Lawrence, Seymour 1926-1994 . . . . Y-94
 Tribute to Richard Yates Y-92
Lawrence, T. E. 1888-1935 . . . . DLB-195
 The T. E. Lawrence Society Y-98
Lawson, George 1598-1678 . . . . DLB-213
Lawson, Henry 1867-1922 . . . . DLB-230
Lawson, John ?-1711 . . . . DLB-24
Lawson, John Howard 1894-1977 . . . . DLB-228
Lawson, Louisa Albury 1848-1920 . . . . . . DLB-230
Lawson, Robert 1892-1957 . . . . DLB-22
Lawson, Victor F. 1850-1925 . . . . DLB-25
Layard, Austen Henry 1817-1894 . . . . DLB-166
Layton, Irving 1912- DLB-88
LaZamon flourished circa 1200 . . . . DLB-146
Lazarević, Laza K. 1851-1890 . . . . DLB-147
Lazarus, George 1904-1997 . . . . DLB-201
Lazhechnikov, Ivan Ivanovich
 1792-1869 . . . . DLB-198
Lea, Henry Charles 1825-1909 . . . . DLB-47
Lea, Sydney 1942- DLB-120, 282
Lea, Tom 1907-2001 . . . . DLB-6
Leacock, John 1729-1802 . . . . DLB-31
Leacock, Stephen 1869-1944 . . . . DLB-92
Lead, Jane Ward 1623-1704 . . . . DLB-131
Leadenhall Press DLB-106
"The Greatness of Southern Literature":
 League of the South Institute for the
 Study of Southern Culture and History
 . . . . Y-02

Leakey, Caroline Woolmer 1827-1881 . . . . DLB-230
Leapor, Mary 1722-1746 . . . . DLB-109
Lear, Edward 1812-1888 . . . . DLB-32, 163, 166
Leary, Timothy 1920-1996 . . . . DLB-16
W. A. Leary and Company DLB-49
Léautaud, Paul 1872-1956 . . . . DLB-65
Leavis, F. R. 1895-1978 . . . . DLB-242
Leavitt, David 1961- DLB-130
Leavitt and Allen DLB-49
Le Blond, Mrs. Aubrey 1861-1934 . . . . . . DLB-174
le Carré, John (David John Moore Cornwell)
 1931- DLB-87; CDBLB-8
 Tribute to Graham Greene Y-91
 Tribute to George Greenfield Y-00
Lécavelé, Roland (see Dorgeles, Roland)
Lechlitner, Ruth 1901- DLB-48
Leclerc, Félix 1914-1988 . . . . DLB-60
Le Clézio, J. M. G. 1940- DLB-83
Leder, Rudolf (see Hermlin, Stephan)
Lederer, Charles 1910-1976 . . . . DLB-26
Ledwidge, Francis 1887-1917 . . . . DLB-20
Lee, Chang-rae 1965- DLB-312
Lee, Cherylene 1953- DLB-312
Lee, Dennis 1939- DLB-53
Lee, Don L. (see Madhubuti, Haki R.)
Lee, George W. 1894-1976 . . . . DLB-51
Lee, Gus 1946- DLB-312
Lee, Harper 1926- DLB-6; CDALB-1
Lee, Harriet 1757-1851 and
 Lee, Sophia 1750-1824 . . . . DLB-39
Lee, Laurie 1914-1997 . . . . DLB-27
Lee, Leslie 1935- DLB-266
Lee, Li-Young 1957- DLB-165, 312
Lee, Manfred B. 1905-1971 . . . . DLB-137
Lee, Nathaniel circa 1645-1692 . . . . DLB-80
Lee, Robert E. 1918-1994 . . . . DLB-228
Lee, Sir Sidney 1859-1926 . . . . DLB-149, 184
 "Principles of Biography," in
 Elizabethan and Other Essays DLB-149
Lee, Tanith 1947- DLB-261
Lee, Vernon
 1856-1935 . . . . DLB-57, 153, 156, 174, 178
Lee and Shepard DLB-49
Le Fanu, Joseph Sheridan
 1814-1873 . . . . DLB-21, 70, 159, 178
Leffland, Ella 1931- Y-84
le Fort, Gertrud von 1876-1971 . . . . DLB-66
Le Gallienne, Richard 1866-1947 . . . . DLB-4
Legaré, Hugh Swinton
 1797-1843 . . . . DLB-3, 59, 73, 248
Legaré, James Mathewes 1823-1859 . . . DLB-3, 248
Léger, Antoine-J. 1880-1950 . . . . DLB-88
Leggett, William 1801-1839 . . . . DLB-250
Le Guin, Ursula K.
 1929- DLB-8, 52, 256, 275; CDALB-6
Lehman, Ernest 1920- DLB-44

Lehmann, John 1907-1989 . . . . DLB-27, 100	Lescarbot, Marc circa 1570-1642 . . . . DLB-99	Lewis, Charles B. 1842-1924 . . . . DLB-11
John Lehmann Limited. DLB-112	LeSeur, William Dawson 1840-1917 . . . . . DLB-92	Lewis, David 1941-2001. . . . . .DLB-279
Lehmann, Rosamond 1901-1990 . . . . DLB-15	LeSieg, Theo. (see Geisel, Theodor Seuss)	Lewis, Henry Clay 1825-1850 . . . . DLB-3, 248
Lehmann, Wilhelm 1882-1968. . . . . DLB-56	Leskov, Nikolai Semenovich 1831-1895 . . . . DLB-238	Lewis, Janet 1899-1999. . . . . Y-87
Leiber, Fritz 1910-1992. . . . . DLB-8	Leslie, Doris before 1902-1982 . . . . DLB-191	Tribute to Katherine Anne Porter Y-80
Leibniz, Gottfried Wilhelm 1646-1716 . . . DLB-168	Leslie, Eliza 1787-1858 . . . . DLB-202	Lewis, Matthew Gregory 1775-1818. . . . . .DLB-39, 158, 178
Leicester University Press. DLB-112	Leslie, Frank (Henry Carter) 1821-1880 . . . . DLB-43, 79	Lewis, Meriwether 1774-1809. . . . . . DLB-183, 186
Leigh, Carolyn 1926-1983 . . . . DLB-265	Frank Leslie [publishing house] DLB-49	Lewis, Norman 1908- DLB-204
Leigh, W. R. 1866-1955 . . . . DLB-188	Leśmian, Bolesław 1878-1937 . . . . DLB-215	Lewis, R. W. B. 1917- DLB-111
Leinster, Murray 1896-1975 . . . . DLB-8	Lesperance, John 1835?-1891 . . . . DLB-99	Lewis, Richard circa 1700-1734 . . . . DLB-24
Leiser, Bill 1898-1965. . . . . DLB-241	Lespinasse, Julie de 1732-1776 . . . . DLB-313	Lewis, Saunders 1893-1985 . . . . DLB-310
Leisewitz, Johann Anton 1752-1806 . . . . . . DLB-94	Lessing, Bruno 1870-1940. . . . . DLB-28	Lewis, Sinclair 1885-1951 . . . . . DLB-9, 102; DS-1; CDALB-4
Leitch, Maurice 1933- DLB-14	Lessing, Doris 1919- DLB-15, 139; Y-85; CDBLB-8	Sinclair Lewis Centennial Conference. . . . Y-85
Leithauser, Brad 1943- DLB-120, 282	Lessing, Gotthold Ephraim 1729-1781 . . . . .DLB-97; CDWLB-2	The Sinclair Lewis Society. Y-99
Leland, Charles G. 1824-1903 . . . . DLB-11	The Lessing Society Y-00	Lewis, Wilmarth Sheldon 1895-1979 . . . . DLB-140
Leland, John 1503?-1552 . . . . DLB-136	Le Sueur, Meridel 1900-1996 . . . . DLB-303	Lewis, Wyndham 1882-1957 . . . . DLB-15
Lemay, Pamphile 1837-1918 . . . . DLB-99	Lettau, Reinhard 1929-1996. . . . . DLB-75	*Time and Western Man* [excerpt] (1927) DLB-36
Lemelin, Roger 1919-1992 . . . . DLB-88	The Hemingway Letters Project Finds an Editor Y-02	Lewisohn, Ludwig 1882-1955 . . .DLB-4, 9, 28, 102
Lemercier, Louis-Jean-Népomucène 1771-1840. . . . . DLB-192	Lever, Charles 1806-1872. . . . . DLB-21	Leyendecker, J. C. 1874-1951 . . . . DLB-188
Le Moine, James MacPherson 1825-1912 . DLB-99	Lever, Ralph ca. 1527-1585 . . . . DLB-236	Leyner, Mark 1956- DLB-292
Lemon, Mark 1809-1870 . . . . DLB-163	Leverson, Ada 1862-1933. . . . . DLB-153	Lezama Lima, José 1910-1976. . . . . . DLB-113, 283
Le Moyne, Jean 1913-1996. . . . . DLB-88	Levertov, Denise 1923-1997. . . . . DLB-5, 165; CDALB-7	Lézardière, Marie-Charlotte-Pauline Robert de 1754-1835. . . . . DLB-313
Lemperly, Paul 1858-1939 . . . . DLB-187	Levi, Peter 1931-2000. . . . . DLB-40	L'Heureux, John 1934- DLB-244
Leñero, Vicente 1933- DLB-305	Levi, Primo 1919-1987 . . . . DLB-177, 299	Libbey, Laura Jean 1862-1924 . . . . DLB-221
L'Engle, Madeleine 1918- DLB-52	Levien, Sonya 1888-1960 . . . . DLB-44	Libedinsky, Iurii Nikolaevich 1898-1959 . . . . .DLB-272
Lennart, Isobel 1915-1971 . . . . DLB-44	Levin, Meyer 1905-1981 . . . . . . .DLB-9, 28; Y-81	*The Liberator* DLB-303
Lennox, Charlotte 1729 or 1730-1804 . . . . DLB-39	Levin, Phillis 1954- DLB-282	Library History Group. Y-01
Lenox, James 1800-1880. . . . . DLB-140	Lévinas, Emmanuel 1906-1995 . . . . DLB-296	E-Books' Second Act in Libraries Y-02
Lenski, Lois 1893-1974 . . . . DLB-22	Levine, Norman 1923- DLB-88	The Library of America DLB-46
Lentricchia, Frank 1940- DLB-246	Levine, Philip 1928- DLB-5	The Library of America: An Assessment After Two Decades Y-02
Lenz, Hermann 1913-1998 . . . . DLB-69	Levis, Larry 1946- DLB-120	Licensing Act of 1737 . . . . DLB-84
Lenz, J. M. R. 1751-1792. . . . . DLB-94	Lévi-Strauss, Claude 1908- DLB-242	Leonard Lichfield I [publishing house]. . . .DLB-170
Lenz, Siegfried 1926- DLB-75	Levitov, Aleksandr Ivanovich 1835?-1877 . . . . .DLB-277	Lichtenberg, Georg Christoph 1742-1799 . . . . DLB-94
Leonard, Elmore 1925- DLB-173, 226	Levy, Amy 1861-1889 . . . . DLB-156, 240	The Liddle Collection Y-97
Leonard, Hugh 1926- DLB-13	Levy, Benn Wolfe 1900-1973 . . . . . . .DLB-13; Y-81	Lidman, Sara 1923- DLB-257
Leonard, William Ellery 1876-1944 . . . . . DLB-54	Levy, Deborah 1959- DLB-310	Lieb, Fred 1888-1980 . . . . .DLB-171
Leong, Russell C. 1950- DLB-312	Lewald, Fanny 1811-1889 . . . . DLB-129	Liebling, A. J. 1904-1963 . . . . .DLB-4, 171
Leonov, Leonid Maksimovich 1899-1994 . . . . DLB-272	Lewes, George Henry 1817-1878 . . . . DLB-55, 144	Lieutenant Murray (see Ballou, Maturin Murray)
Leonowens, Anna 1834-1914 . . . . DLB-99, 166	"Criticism in Relation to Novels" (1863) DLB-21	Lighthall, William Douw 1857-1954. . . . . . DLB-92
Leont'ev, Konstantin Nikolaevich 1831-1891 . . . . .DLB-277	*The Principles of Success in Literature* (1865) [excerpt] DLB-57	Lihn, Enrique 1929-1988 . . . . DLB-283
Leopold, Aldo 1887-1948 . . . . .DLB-275	Lewis, Agnes Smith 1843-1926. . . . . .DLB-174	Lilar, Françoise (see Mallet-Joris, Françoise)
LePan, Douglas 1914-1998 . . . . DLB-88	Lewis, Alfred H. 1857-1914 . . . . DLB-25, 186	Lili'uokalani, Queen 1838-1917 . . . . DLB-221
Lepik, Kalju 1920-1999. . . . . DLB-232	Lewis, Alun 1915-1944 . . . . DLB-20, 162	Lillo, George 1691-1739 . . . . DLB-84
Leprohon, Rosanna Eleanor 1829-1879 . . . DLB-99	Lewis, C. Day (see Day Lewis, C.)	Lilly, J. K., Jr. 1893-1966 . . . . DLB-140
Le Queux, William 1864-1927 . . . . DLB-70	Lewis, C. I. 1883-1964 . . . . .DLB-270	Lilly, Wait and Company DLB-49
Lermontov, Mikhail Iur'evich 1814-1841. . . . . DLB-205	Lewis, C. S. 1898-1963 . . . . DLB-15, 100, 160, 255; CDBLB-7	Lily, William circa 1468-1522 . . . . DLB-132
Lerner, Alan Jay 1918-1986 . . . . DLB-265	The New York C. S. Lewis Society Y-99	Lim, Shirley Geok-lin 1944- DLB-312
Lerner, Max 1902-1992 . . . . DLB-29		Lima, Jorge de 1893-1953 . . . . DLB-307
Lernet-Holenia, Alexander 1897-1976. . . . . DLB-85		Lima Barreto, Afonso Henriques de 1881-1922 . . . . DLB-307
Le Rossignol, James 1866-1969 . . . . DLB-92		
Lesage, Alain-René 1668-1747 . . . . DLB-313		

Limited Editions Club DLB-46
Limón, Graciela 1938- DLB-209
Lincoln and Edmands DLB-49
Lind, Jakov 1927- DLB-299
Linda Vilhjálmsdóttir 1958- DLB-293
Lindesay, Ethel Forence
  (see Richardson, Henry Handel)
Lindgren, Astrid 1907-2002 . . . . DLB-257
Lindgren, Torgny 1938- DLB-257
Lindsay, Alexander William, Twenty-fifth
  Earl of Crawford 1812-1880 . . . . DLB-184
Lindsay, Sir David circa 1485-1555 . . . . . . DLB-132
Lindsay, David 1878-1945 . . . . DLB-255
Lindsay, Jack 1900-1990 . . . . Y-84
Lindsay, Lady (Caroline Blanche
  Elizabeth Fitzroy Lindsay)
  1844-1912 . . . . DLB-199
Lindsay, Norman 1879-1969 . . . . DLB-260
Lindsay, Vachel
  1879-1931 . . . . DLB-54; CDALB-3
Linebarger, Paul Myron Anthony
  (see Smith, Cordwainer)
Link, Arthur S. 1920-1998 . . . . DLB-17
Linn, Ed 1922-2000 . . . . DLB-241
Linn, John Blair 1777-1804 . . . . DLB-37
Lins, Osman 1924-1978 . . . . DLB-145, 307
Linton, Eliza Lynn 1822-1898 . . . . DLB-18
Linton, William James 1812-1897 . . . . DLB-32
Barnaby Bernard Lintot
  [publishing house] DLB-170
Lion Books DLB-46
Lionni, Leo 1910-1999 . . . . DLB-61
Lippard, George 1822-1854 . . . . DLB-202
Lippincott, Sara Jane Clarke
  1823-1904 . . . . DLB-43
J. B. Lippincott Company DLB-49
Lippmann, Walter 1889-1974 . . . . DLB-29
Lipton, Lawrence 1898-1975 . . . . DLB-16
Lisboa, Irene 1892-1958 . . . . DLB-287
Liscow, Christian Ludwig
  1701-1760 . . . . DLB-97
Lish, Gordon 1934- DLB-130
  Tribute to Donald Barthelme Y-89
  Tribute to James Dickey Y-97
Lisle, Charles-Marie-René Leconte de
  1818-1894 . . . . DLB-217
Lispector, Clarice
  1925?-1977 . . . . DLB-113, 307; CDWLB-3
LitCheck Website Y-01
Literary Awards and Honors Y-81-02
  Booker Prize Y-86, 96-98
  The Drue Heinz Literature Prize Y-82
  The Elmer Holmes Bobst Awards
    in Arts and Letters Y-87
  The Griffin Poetry Prize Y-00
  Literary Prizes [British] DLB-15, 207
  National Book Critics Circle
    Awards Y-00-01

The National Jewish
  Book Awards Y-85
Nobel Prize Y-80-02
Winning an Edgar Y-98
The Literary Chronicle and Weekly Review
  1819-1828 . . . . DLB-110
Literary Periodicals:
  Callaloo Y-87
  Expatriates in Paris DS-15
  New Literary Periodicals:
    A Report for 1987 . . . . Y-87
  A Report for 1988 . . . . Y-88
  A Report for 1989 . . . . Y-89
  A Report for 1990 . . . . Y-90
  A Report for 1991 . . . . Y-91
  A Report for 1992 . . . . Y-92
  A Report for 1993 . . . . Y-93
Literary Research Archives
  The Anthony Burgess Archive at
    the Harry Ransom Humanities
    Research Center Y-98
  Archives of Charles Scribner's Sons DS-17
  Berg Collection of English and
    American Literature of the
    New York Public Library Y-83
  The Bobbs-Merrill Archive at the
    Lilly Library, Indiana University Y-90
  Die Fürstliche Bibliothek Corvey Y-96
  Guide to the Archives of Publishers,
    Journals, and Literary Agents in
    North American Libraries Y-93
  The Henry E. Huntington Library Y-92
  The Humanities Research Center,
    University of Texas Y-82
  The John Carter Brown Library Y-85
  Kent State Special Collections Y-86
  The Lilly Library Y-84
  The Modern Literary Manuscripts
    Collection in the Special
    Collections of the Washington
    University Libraries Y-87
  A Publisher's Archives: G. P. Putnam . . . Y-92
  Special Collections at Boston
    University Y-99
  The University of Virginia Libraries Y-91
  The William Charvat American Fiction
    Collection at the Ohio State
    University Libraries Y-92
Literary Societies Y-98-02
  The Margery Allingham Society Y-98
  The American Studies Association
    of Norway Y-00
  The Arnold Bennett Society Y-98
  The Association for the Study of
    Literature and Environment
    (ASLE) Y-99
  Belgian Luxembourg American Studies
    Association Y-01
  The E. F. Benson Society Y-98
  The Elizabeth Bishop Society Y-01
  The [Edgar Rice] Burroughs
    Bibliophiles Y-98

The Byron Society of America Y-00
The Lewis Carroll Society
  of North America Y-00
The Willa Cather Pioneer Memorial
  and Education Foundation Y-00
New Chaucer Society Y-00
The Wilkie Collins Society Y-98
The James Fenimore Cooper Society Y-01
The Stephen Crane Society Y-98, 01
The E. E. Cummings Society Y-01
The James Dickey Society Y-99
John Dos Passos Newsletter Y-00
The Priory Scholars [Sir Arthur Conan
  Doyle] of New York Y-99
The International Theodore Dreiser
  Society Y-01
The Friends of the Dymock Poets Y-00
The George Eliot Fellowship Y-99
The T. S. Eliot Society: Celebration and
  Scholarship, 1980-1999 . . . . Y-99
The Ralph Waldo Emerson Society Y-99
The William Faulkner Society Y-99
The C. S. Forester Society Y-00
The Hamlin Garland Society Y-01
The [Elizabeth] Gaskell Society Y-98
The Charlotte Perkins Gilman Society . . . Y-99
The Ellen Glasgow Society Y-01
Zane Grey's West Society Y-00
The Ivor Gurney Society Y-98
The Joel Chandler Harris Association . . . Y-99
The Nathaniel Hawthorne Society Y-00
The [George Alfred] Henty Society Y-98
George Moses Horton Society Y-99
The William Dean Howells Society Y-01
WW2 HMSO Paperbacks Society Y-98
American Humor Studies Association . . . Y-99
International Society for Humor Studies . . . Y-99
The W. W. Jacobs Appreciation Society . . Y-98
The Richard Jefferies Society Y-98
The Jerome K. Jerome Society Y-98
The D. H. Lawrence Society of
  North America Y-00
The T. E. Lawrence Society Y-98
The [Gotthold] Lessing Society Y-00
The New York C. S. Lewis Society Y-99
The Sinclair Lewis Society Y-99
The Jack London Research Center Y-00
The Jack London Society Y-99
The Cormac McCarthy Society Y-99
The Melville Society Y-01
The Arthur Miller Society Y-01
The Milton Society of America Y-00
International Marianne Moore Society . . . Y-98
International Nabokov Society Y-99
The Vladimir Nabokov Society Y-01
The Flannery O'Connor Society Y-99

Cumulative Index

The Wilfred Owen Association Y-98

Penguin Collectors' Society Y-98

The [E. A.] Poe Studies Association Y-99

The Katherine Anne Porter Society Y-01

The Beatrix Potter Society Y-98

The Ezra Pound Society Y-01

The Powys Society Y-98

Proust Society of America Y-00

The Dorothy L. Sayers Society Y-98

The Bernard Shaw Society Y-99

The Society for the Study of
Southern Literature Y-00

The Wallace Stevens Society Y-99

The Harriet Beecher Stowe Center Y-00

The R. S. Surtees Society Y-98

The Thoreau Society Y-99

The Tilling [E. F. Benson] Society Y-98

The Trollope Societies Y-00

H. G. Wells Society Y-98

The Western Literature Association Y-99

The William Carlos Williams Society Y-99

The Henry Williamson Society Y-98

The [Nero] Wolfe Pack Y-99

The Thomas Wolfe Society Y-99

Worldwide Wodehouse Societies Y-98

The W. B. Yeats Society of N.Y. Y-99

The Charlotte M. Yonge Fellowship Y-98

Literary Theory
The Year in Literary Theory Y-92–Y-93

Literature at Nurse, or Circulating Morals (1885),
by George Moore DLB-18

Litt, Toby 1968- DLB-267

Littell, Eliakim 1797-1870 . . . . DLB-79

Littell, Robert S. 1831-1896 . . . . DLB-79

Little, Brown and Company DLB-49

Little Magazines and Newspapers DS-15

Selected English-Language Little
Magazines and Newspapers
[France, 1920-1939] DLB-4

The Little Magazines of the
New Formalism DLB-282

The Little Review 1914-1929 . . . . DS-15

Littlewood, Joan 1914-2002 . . . . DLB-13

Liu, Aimee E. 1953- DLB-312

Lively, Penelope 1933- DLB-14, 161, 207

Liverpool University Press DLB-112

The Lives of the Poets (1753) DLB-142

Livesay, Dorothy 1909-1996 . . . . DLB-68

Livesay, Florence Randal 1874-1953 . . . . . DLB-92

Livings, Henry 1929-1998 . . . . DLB-13

Livingston, Anne Howe 1763-1841 . . . DLB-37, 200

Livingston, Jay 1915-2001 . . . . DLB-265

Livingston, Myra Cohn 1926-1996 . . . . . DLB-61

Livingston, William 1723-1790 . . . . DLB-31

Livingstone, David 1813-1873 . . . . DLB-166

Livingstone, Douglas 1932-1996 . . . . DLB-225

Livshits, Benedikt Konstantinovich
1886-1938 or 1939 . . . . DLB-295

Livy 59 B.C.-A.D. 17 . . . . DLB-211; CDWLB-1

Liyong, Taban lo (see Taban lo Liyong)

Lizárraga, Sylvia S. 1925- DLB-82

Llewellyn, Richard 1906-1983 . . . . DLB-15

Lloréns Torres, Luis 1876-1944 . . . . DLB-290

Edward Lloyd [publishing house] DLB-106

Lobato, José Bento Monteiro
1882-1948 . . . . DLB-307

Lobel, Arnold 1933- DLB-61

Lochhead, Liz 1947- DLB-310

Lochridge, Betsy Hopkins (see Fancher, Betsy)

Locke, Alain 1886-1954 . . . . DLB-51

Locke, David Ross 1833-1888 . . . . . . DLB-11, 23

Locke, John 1632-1704 . . . . . DLB-31, 101, 213, 252

Locke, Richard Adams 1800-1871 . . . . . . DLB-43

Locker-Lampson, Frederick
1821-1895 . . . . DLB-35, 184

Lockhart, John Gibson
1794-1854 . . . . DLB-110, 116 144

Lockridge, Francis 1896-1963 . . . . DLB-306

Lockridge, Richard 1898-1982 . . . . DLB-306

Lockridge, Ross, Jr. 1914-1948 . . . . . DLB-143; Y-80

Locrine and Selimus DLB-62

Lodge, David 1935- DLB-14, 194

Lodge, George Cabot 1873-1909 . . . . . . DLB-54

Lodge, Henry Cabot 1850-1924 . . . . DLB-47

Lodge, Thomas 1558-1625 . . . . DLB-172

Defence of Poetry (1579) [excerpt] DLB-172

Loeb, Harold 1891-1974 . . . . DLB-4; DS-15

Loeb, William 1905-1981 . . . . DLB-127

Loesser, Frank 1910-1969 . . . . DLB-265

Lofting, Hugh 1886-1947 . . . . DLB-160

Logan, Deborah Norris 1761-1839 . . . . . DLB-200

Logan, James 1674-1751 . . . . DLB-24, 140

Logan, John 1923-1987 . . . . DLB-5

Logan, Martha Daniell 1704?-1779 . . . . . DLB-200

Logan, William 1950- DLB-120

Logau, Friedrich von 1605-1655 . . . . DLB-164

Logue, Christopher 1926- DLB-27

Lohenstein, Daniel Casper von
1635-1683 . . . . DLB-168

Lo-Johansson, Ivar 1901-1990 . . . . DLB-259

Lokert, George (or Lockhart)
circa 1485-1547 . . . . DLB-281

Lomonosov, Mikhail Vasil'evich
1711-1765 . . . . DLB-150

London, Jack
1876-1916 . . . . . DLB-8, 12, 78, 212; CDALB-3

The Jack London Research Center Y-00

The Jack London Society Y-99

The London Magazine 1820-1829 . . . . DLB-110

Long, David 1948- DLB-244

Long, H., and Brother DLB-49

Long, Haniel 1888-1956 . . . . DLB-45

Long, Ray 1878-1935 . . . . DLB-137

Longfellow, Henry Wadsworth
1807-1882 . . . . DLB-1, 59, 235; CDALB-2

Longfellow, Samuel 1819-1892 . . . . DLB-1

Longford, Elizabeth 1906-2002 . . . . DLB-155

Tribute to Alfred A. Knopf Y-84

Longinus circa first century DLB-176

Longley, Michael 1939- DLB-40

T. Longman [publishing house] DLB-154

Longmans, Green and Company DLB-49

Longmore, George 1793?-1867 . . . . DLB-99

Longstreet, Augustus Baldwin
1790-1870 . . . . DLB-3, 11, 74, 248

D. Longworth [publishing house] DLB-49

Lønn, Øystein 1936- DLB-297

Lonsdale, Frederick 1881-1954 . . . . DLB-10

Loos, Anita 1893-1981 . . . . . DLB-11, 26, 228; Y-81

Lopate, Phillip 1943- Y-80

Lopes, Fernão 1380/1390?-1460? DLB-287

Lopez, Barry 1945- DLB-256, 275

López, Diana (see Isabella, Ríos)

López, Josefina 1969- DLB-209

López de Mendoza, Íñigo
(see Santillana, Marqués de)

López Velarde, Ramón 1888-1921 . . . . . DLB-290

Loranger, Jean-Aubert 1896-1942 . . . . . . DLB-92

Lorca, Federico García 1898-1936 . . . . . DLB-108

Lord, John Keast 1818-1872 . . . . DLB-99

Lorde, Audre 1934-1992 . . . . DLB-41

Lorimer, George Horace 1867-1937 . . . . DLB-91

A. K. Loring [publishing house] DLB-49

Loring and Mussey DLB-46

Lorris, Guillaume de (see *Roman de la Rose*)

Lossing, Benson J. 1813-1891 . . . . DLB-30

Lothar, Ernst 1890-1974 . . . . DLB-81

D. Lothrop and Company DLB-49

Lothrop, Harriet M. 1844-1924 . . . . DLB-42

Loti, Pierre 1850-1923 . . . . DLB-123

Lotichius Secundus, Petrus 1528-1560 . . . DLB-179

Lott, Emmeline ?-? DLB-166

Louisiana State University Press Y-97

Lounsbury, Thomas R. 1838-1915 . . . . . . DLB-71

Louÿs, Pierre 1870-1925 . . . . DLB-123

Løveid, Cecile 1951- DLB-297

Lovejoy, Arthur O. 1873-1962 . . . . DLB-270

Lovelace, Earl 1935- DLB-125; CDWLB-3

Lovelace, Richard 1618-1657 . . . . DLB-131

John W. Lovell Company DLB-49

Lovell, Coryell and Company DLB-49

Lover, Samuel 1797-1868 . . . . DLB-159, 190

Lovesey, Peter 1936- DLB-87

Tribute to Georges Simenon Y-89

Lovinescu, Eugen
1881-1943 . . . . DLB-220; CDWLB-4

Lovingood, Sut
(see Harris, George Washington)

Low, Samuel 1765-? DLB-37

Lowell, Amy 1874-1925..............DLB-54, 140

Lowell, James Russell 1819-1891
......DLB-1, 11, 64, 79, 189, 235; CDALB-2

Lowell, Robert
1917-1977............DLB-5, 169; CDALB-7

Lowenfels, Walter 1897-1976...............DLB-4

Lowndes, Marie Belloc 1868-1947.........DLB-70

Lowndes, William Thomas 1798-1843...DLB-184

Humphrey Lownes [publishing house]...DLB-170

Lowry, Lois 1937- DLB-52

Lowry, Malcolm 1909-1957...DLB-15; CDBLB-7

Lowther, Pat 1935-1975..................DLB-53

Loy, Mina 1882-1966................DLB-4, 54

Loynaz, Dulce María 1902-1997.........DLB-283

Lozeau, Albert 1878-1924...............DLB-92

Lubbock, Percy 1879-1965..............DLB-149

Lucan A.D. 39-A.D. 65..................DLB-211

Lucas, E. V. 1868-1938........DLB-98, 149, 153

Fielding Lucas Jr. [publishing house]......DLB-49

Luce, Clare Booth 1903-1987...........DLB-228

Luce, Henry R. 1898-1967...............DLB-91

John W. Luce and Company..............DLB-46

Lucena, Juan de ca. 1430-1501..........DLB-286

Lucian circa 120-180..................DLB-176

Lucie-Smith, Edward 1933- DLB-40

Lucilius circa 180 B.C.-102/101 B.C......DLB-211

Lucini, Gian Pietro 1867-1914..........DLB-114

Luco Cruchaga, Germán 1894-1936.....DLB-305

Lucretius circa 94 B.C.-circa 49 B.C.
....................DLB-211; CDWLB-1

Luder, Peter circa 1415-1472...........DLB-179

Ludlam, Charles 1943-1987.............DLB-266

Ludlum, Robert 1927-2001 ....Y-82

Ludus de Antichristo circa 1160..........DLB-148

Ludvigson, Susan 1942- DLB-120

Ludwig, Jack 1922- DLB-60

Ludwig, Otto 1813-1865................DLB-129

Ludwigslied 881 or 882..................DLB-148

Luera, Yolanda 1953- DLB-122

Luft, Lya 1938- DLB-145

Lugansky, Kazak Vladimir
(see Dal', Vladimir Ivanovich)

Lugn, Kristina 1948- DLB-257

Lugones, Leopoldo 1874-1938..........DLB-283

Luhan, Mabel Dodge 1879-1962.........DLB-303

Lukács, Georg (see Lukács, György)

Lukács, György
1885-1971........DLB-215, 242; CDWLB-4

Luke, Peter 1919- DLB-13

Lummis, Charles F. 1859-1928..........DLB-186

Lundkvist, Artur 1906-1991............DLB-259

Lunts, Lev Natanovich 1901-1924........DLB-272

F. M. Lupton Company..................DLB-49

Lupus of Ferrières circa 805-circa 862....DLB-148

Lurie, Alison 1926- DLB-2

Lussu, Emilio 1890-1975................DLB-264

Lustig, Arnošt 1926- DLB-232, 299

Luther, Martin
1483-1546.........DLB-179; CDWLB-2

Luzi, Mario 1914- DLB-128

L'vov, Nikolai Aleksandrovich
1751-1803........................DLB-150

Lyall, Gavin 1932- DLB-87

Lydgate, John circa 1370-1450..........DLB-146

Lyly, John circa 1554-1606.........DLB-62, 167

Lynch, Martin 1950-...................DLB-310

Lynch, Patricia 1898-1972..............DLB-160

Lynch, Richard flourished 1596-1601....DLB-172

Lynd, Robert 1879-1949.................DLB-98

Lynds, Dennis (Michael Collins)
1924- DLB-306

Tribute to John D. MacDonald..........Y-86

Tribute to Kenneth Millar..............Y-83

Why I Write Mysteries: Night and Day..Y-85

Lyon, Matthew 1749-1822...............DLB-43

Lyotard, Jean-François 1924-1998.......DLB-242

Lyricists
Additional Lyricists: 1920-1960......DLB-265

Lysias circa 459 B.C.-circa 380 B.C.......DLB-176

Lytle, Andrew 1902-1995..........DLB-6; Y-95

Tribute to Caroline Gordon............Y-81

Tribute to Katherine Anne Porter.......Y-80

Lytton, Edward
(see Bulwer-Lytton, Edward)

Lytton, Edward Robert Bulwer
1831-1891........................DLB-32

M

Maass, Joachim 1901-1972...............DLB-69

Mabie, Hamilton Wright 1845-1916.......DLB-71

Mac A'Ghobhainn, Iain (see Smith, Iain Crichton)

MacArthur, Charles 1895-1956......DLB-7, 25, 44

Macaulay, Catherine 1731-1791.........DLB-104

Macaulay, David 1945- DLB-61

Macaulay, Rose 1881-1958...............DLB-36

Macaulay, Thomas Babington
1800-1859............DLB-32, 55; CDBLB-4

Macaulay Company......................DLB-46

MacBeth, George 1932-1992..............DLB-40

Macbeth, Madge 1880-1965...............DLB-92

MacCaig, Norman 1910-1996.............DLB-27

MacDiarmid, Hugh
1892-1978..............DLB-20; CDBLB-7

MacDonald, Cynthia 1928- DLB-105

MacDonald, George 1824-1905....DLB-18, 163, 178

MacDonald, John D.
1916-1986.................DLB-8, 306; Y-86

MacDonald, Philip 1899?-1980...........DLB-77

Macdonald, Ross (see Millar, Kenneth)

Macdonald, Sharman 1951- DLB-245

MacDonald, Wilson 1880-1967...........DLB-92

Macdonald and Company (Publishers)...DLB-112

MacEwen, Gwendolyn 1941-1987....DLB-53, 251

Macfadden, Bernarr 1868-1955.......DLB-25, 91

MacGregor, John 1825-1892............DLB-166

MacGregor, Mary Esther (see Keith, Marian)

Macherey, Pierre 1938- DLB-296

Machado, Antonio 1875-1939...........DLB-108

Machado, Manuel 1874-1947...........DLB-108

Machado de Assis, Joaquim Maria
1839-1908......................DLB-307

Machar, Agnes Maule 1837-1927.........DLB-92

Machaut, Guillaume de
circa 1300-1377..................DLB-208

Machen, Arthur Llewelyn Jones
1863-1947..............DLB-36, 156, 178

MacIlmaine, Roland fl. 1574...........DLB-281

MacInnes, Colin 1914-1976..............DLB-14

MacInnes, Helen 1907-1985..............DLB-87

Mac Intyre, Tom 1931- DLB-245

Mačiulis, Jonas (see Maironis, Jonas)

Mack, Maynard 1909- DLB-111

Mackall, Leonard L. 1879-1937.........DLB-140

MacKay, Isabel Ecclestone 1875-1928.....DLB-92

MacKaye, Percy 1875-1956...............DLB-54

Macken, Walter 1915-1967...............DLB-13

Mackenzie, Alexander 1763-1820.........DLB-99

Mackenzie, Alexander Slidell
1803-1848......................DLB-183

Mackenzie, Compton 1883-1972....DLB-34, 100

Mackenzie, Henry 1745-1831............DLB-39

The Lounger, no. 20 (1785)..........DLB-39

Mackenzie, Kenneth (Seaforth Mackenzie)
1913-1955......................DLB-260

Mackenzie, William 1758-1828.........DLB-187

Mackey, Nathaniel 1947- DLB-169

Mackey, Shena 1944- DLB-231

Mackey, William Wellington 1937- DLB-38

Mackintosh, Elizabeth (see Tey, Josephine)

Mackintosh, Sir James 1765-1832.......DLB-158

Macklin, Charles 1699-1797.............DLB-89

Maclaren, Ian (see Watson, John)

MacLaverty, Bernard 1942- DLB-267

MacLean, Alistair 1922-1987...........DLB-276

MacLean, Katherine Anne 1925- DLB-8

Maclean, Norman 1902-1990...........DLB-206

MacLeish, Archibald 1892-1982
......DLB-4, 7, 45; Y-82; DS-15; CDALB-7

MacLennan, Hugh 1907-1990............DLB-68

MacLeod, Alistair 1936- DLB-60

Macleod, Fiona (see Sharp, William)

Macleod, Norman 1906-1985..............DLB-4

Mac Low, Jackson 1922- DLB-193

Macmillan and Company...............DLB-106

The Macmillan Company................DLB-49

Macmillan's English Men of Letters,
First Series (1878-1892)............DLB-144

MacNamara, Brinsley 1890-1963.........DLB-10

MacNeice, Louis 1907-1963.........DLB-10, 20

Cumulative Index

Macphail, Andrew 1864-1938 .... DLB-92

Macpherson, James 1736-1796 .... DLB-109

Macpherson, Jay 1931- DLB-53

Macpherson, Jeanie 1884-1946 .... DLB-44

Macrae Smith Company DLB-46

MacRaye, Lucy Betty (see Webling, Lucy)

John Macrone [publishing house] DLB-106

MacShane, Frank 1927-1999 .... DLB-111

Macy-Masius DLB-46

Madden, David 1933- DLB-6

Madden, Sir Frederic 1801-1873 .... DLB-184

Maddow, Ben 1909-1992 .... DLB-44

Maddux, Rachel 1912-1983 ...... DLB-234; Y-93

Madgett, Naomi Long 1923- DLB-76

Madhubuti, Haki R. 1942- DLB-5, 41; DS-8

Madison, James 1751-1836 .... DLB-37

Madsen, Svend Åge 1939- DLB-214

Madrigal, Alfonso Fernández de (El Tostado)
ca. 1405-1455 .... DLB-286

Maeterlinck, Maurice 1862-1949 .... DLB-192

Mafūz, Najīb 1911- Y-88

  Nobel Lecture 1988 .... Y-88

The Little Magazines of the
  New Formalism DLB-282

Magee, David 1905-1977 .... DLB-187

Maginn, William 1794-1842 .... DLB-110, 159

Magoffin, Susan Shelby 1827-1855 ...... DLB-239

Mahan, Alfred Thayer 1840-1914 .... DLB-47

Maheux-Forcier, Louise 1929- DLB-60

Mahin, John Lee 1902-1984 .... DLB-44

Mahon, Derek 1941- DLB-40

Maiakovsky, Vladimir Vladimirovich
1893-1930 .... DLB-295

Maikov, Apollon Nikolaevich
1821-1897 .... DLB-277

Maikov, Vasilii Ivanovich 1728-1778 .... DLB-150

Mailer, Norman 1923-
......DLB-2, 16, 28, 185, 278; Y-80, 83, 97;
                           DS-3; CDALB-6

  Tribute to Isaac Bashevis Singer Y-91

  Tribute to Meyer Levin Y-81

Maillart, Ella 1903-1997 .... DLB-195

Maillet, Adrienne 1885-1963 .... DLB-68

Maillet, Antonine 1929- DLB-60

Maillu, David G. 1939- DLB-157

Maimonides, Moses 1138-1204 .... DLB-115

Main Selections of the Book-of-the-Month
  Club, 1926-1945 .... DLB-9

Mainwaring, Daniel 1902-1977 .... DLB-44

Mair, Charles 1838-1927 .... DLB-99

Mair, John circa 1467-1550 .... DLB-281

Maironis, Jonas 1862-1932 .. DLB-220; CDWLB-4

Mais, Roger 1905-1955 ..... DLB-125; CDWLB-3

Maitland, Sara 1950- DLB-271

Major, Andre 1942- DLB-60

Major, Charles 1856-1913 .... DLB-202

Major, Clarence 1936- DLB-33

Major, Kevin 1949- DLB-60

Major Books DLB-46

Makanin, Vladimir Semenovich
1937- DLB-285

Makarenko, Anton Semenovich
1888-1939 .... DLB-272

Makemie, Francis circa 1658-1708 ...... DLB-24

The Making of Americans Contract Y-98

Maksimov, Vladimir Emel'ianovich
1930-1995 .... DLB-302

Maksimović, Desanka
1898-1993 .... DLB-147; CDWLB-4

Malamud, Bernard 1914-1986
.... DLB-2, 28, 152; Y-80, 86; CDALB-1

  Bernard Malamud Archive at the
    Harry Ransom Humanities
    Research Center Y-00

Mălăncioiu, Ileana 1940- DLB-232

Malaparte, Curzio
(Kurt Erich Suckert) 1898-1957 ..... DLB-264

Malerba, Luigi 1927- DLB-196

Malet, Lucas 1852-1931 .... DLB-153

Mallarmé, Stéphane 1842-1898 .... DLB-217

Malleson, Lucy Beatrice (see Gilbert, Anthony)

Mallet-Joris, Françoise (Françoise Lilar)
1930- DLB-83

Mallock, W. H. 1849-1923 .... DLB-18, 57

  "Every Man His Own Poet; or,
    The Inspired Singer's Recipe
    Book" (1877) DLB-35

  "Le Style c'est l'homme" (1892) DLB-57

  Memoirs of Life and Literature (1920),
    [excerpt] DLB-57

Malone, Dumas 1892-1986 .... DLB-17

Malone, Edmond 1741-1812 .... DLB-142

Malory, Sir Thomas
circa 1400-1410 - 1471 ... DLB-146; CDBLB-1

Malouf, David 1934- DLB-289

Malpede, Karen 1945- DLB-249

Malraux, André 1901-1976 .... DLB-72

The Maltese Falcon (Documentary) DLB-280

Malthus, Thomas Robert
1766-1834 .... DLB-107, 158

Maltz, Albert 1908-1985 .... DLB-102

Malzberg, Barry N. 1939- DLB-8

Mamet, David 1947- DLB-7

Mamin, Dmitrii Narkisovich
1852-1912 .... DLB-238

Manaka, Matsemela 1956- DLB-157

Manchester University Press DLB-112

Mandel, Eli 1922-1992 .... DLB-53

Mandel'shtam, Nadezhda Iakovlevna
1899-1980 .... DLB-302

Mandel'shtam, Osip Emil'evich
1891-1938 .... DLB-295

Mandeville, Bernard 1670-1733 .... DLB-101

Mandeville, Sir John
mid fourteenth century DLB-146

Mandiargues, André Pieyre de
1909-1991 .... DLB-83

Manea, Norman 1936- DLB-232

Manfred, Frederick 1912-1994 .... DLB-6, 212, 227

Manfredi, Gianfranco 1948- DLB-196

Mangan, Sherry 1904-1961 .... DLB-4

Manganelli, Giorgio 1922-1990 .... DLB-196

Manilius fl. first century A.D. DLB-211

Mankiewicz, Herman 1897-1953 .... DLB-26

Mankiewicz, Joseph L. 1909-1993 ...... DLB-44

Mankowitz, Wolf 1924-1998 .... DLB-15

Manley, Delarivière 1672?-1724 ..... DLB-39, 80

  Preface to The Secret History, of Queen
    Zarah, and the Zarazians (1705) DLB-39

Mann, Abby 1927- DLB-44

Mann, Charles 1929-1998 .... Y-98

Mann, Emily 1952- DLB-266

Mann, Heinrich 1871-1950 .... DLB-66, 118

Mann, Horace 1796-1859 .... DLB-1, 235

Mann, Klaus 1906-1949 .... DLB-56

Mann, Mary Peabody 1806-1887 .... DLB-239

Mann, Thomas 1875-1955 ... DLB-66; CDWLB-2

Mann, William D'Alton 1839-1920 ..... DLB-137

Mannin, Ethel 1900-1984 .... DLB-191, 195

Manning, Emily (see Australie)

Manning, Frederic 1882-1935 .... DLB-260

Manning, Laurence 1899-1972 .... DLB-251

Manning, Marie 1873?-1945 .... DLB-29

Manning and Loring DLB-49

Mannyng, Robert flourished
1303-1338 .... DLB-146

Mano, D. Keith 1942- DLB-6

Manor Books DLB-46

Manrique, Gómez 1412?-1490 .... DLB-286

Manrique, Jorge ca. 1440-1479 .... DLB-286

Mansfield, Katherine 1888-1923 .... DLB-162

Mantel, Hilary 1952- DLB-271

Manuel, Niklaus circa 1484-1530 ...... DLB-179

Manzini, Gianna 1896-1974 .... DLB-177

Mapanje, Jack 1944- DLB-157

Maraini, Dacia 1936- DLB-196

Maramzin, Vladimir Rafailovich
1934- DLB-302

March, William (William Edward Campbell)
1893-1954 .... DLB-9, 86

Marchand, Leslie A. 1900-1999 .... DLB-103

Marchant, Bessie 1862-1941 .... DLB-160

Marchant, Tony 1959- DLB-245

Marchenko, Anastasiia Iakovlevna
1830-1880 .... DLB-238

Marchessault, Jovette 1938- DLB-60

Marcinkevičius, Justinas 1930- DLB-232

Marcos, Plínio (Plínio Marcos de Barros)
1935-1999 .... DLB-307

Marcus, Frank 1928- DLB-13

Marcuse, Herbert 1898-1979 .... DLB-242

Marden, Orison Swett 1850-1924 . . . . DLB-137
Marechera, Dambudzo 1952-1987. . . . . . . DLB-157
Marek, Richard, Books DLB-46
Mares, E. A. 1938- DLB-122
Margulies, Donald 1954- DLB-228
Mariani, Paul 1940- DLB-111
Marie de France flourished 1160-1178 . . . . DLB-208
Marie-Victorin, Frère (Conrad Kirouac) 1885-1944 . . . . DLB-92
Marin, Biagio 1891-1985 . . . . DLB-128
Marinetti, Filippo Tommaso 1876-1944 . . . . DLB-114, 264
Marinina, Aleksandra (Marina Anatol'evna Alekseeva) 1957- DLB-285
Marinković, Ranko 1913- DLB-147; CDWLB-4
Marion, Frances 1886-1973 . . . . DLB-44
Marius, Richard C. 1933-1999 . . . . Y-85
Markevich, Boleslav Mikhailovich 1822-1884 . . . . DLB-238
Markfield, Wallace 1926-2002 . . . . DLB-2, 28
Markham, Edwin 1852-1940 . . . . DLB-54, 186
Markle, Fletcher 1921-1991 . . . . DLB-68; Y-91
Marlatt, Daphne 1942- DLB-60
Marlitt, E. 1825-1887 . . . . DLB-129
Marlowe, Christopher 1564-1593 . . . . DLB-62; CDBLB-1
Marlyn, John 1912- DLB-88
Marmion, Shakerley 1603-1639 . . . . DLB-58
Der Marner before 1230-circa 1287 . . . . . DLB-138
Marnham, Patrick 1943- DLB-204
The *Marprelate Tracts* 1588-1589 . . . . DLB-132
Marquand, John P. 1893-1960 . . . . DLB-9, 102
Marques, Helena 1935- DLB-287
Marqués, René 1919-1979 . . . . DLB-113, 305
Marquis, Don 1878-1937 . . . . DLB-11, 25
Marriott, Anne 1913-1997 . . . . DLB-68
Marryat, Frederick 1792-1848 . . . . DLB-21, 163
Marsh, Capen, Lyon and Webb DLB-49
Marsh, George Perkins 1801-1882 . . . . DLB-1, 64, 243
Marsh, James 1794-1842 . . . . DLB-1, 59
Marsh, Narcissus 1638-1713 . . . . DLB-213
Marsh, Ngaio 1899-1982 . . . . DLB-77
Marshall, Alan 1902-1984 . . . . DLB-260
Marshall, Edison 1894-1967 . . . . DLB-102
Marshall, Edward 1932- DLB-16
Marshall, Emma 1828-1899 . . . . DLB-163
Marshall, James 1942-1992 . . . . DLB-61
Marshall, Joyce 1913- DLB-88
Marshall, Paule 1929- DLB-33, 157, 227
Marshall, Tom 1938-1993 . . . . DLB-60
Marsilius of Padua circa 1275-circa 1342 . . . . DLB-115
Mars-Jones, Adam 1954- DLB-207
Marson, Una 1905-1965 . . . . DLB-157
Marston, John 1576-1634 . . . . DLB-58, 172

Marston, Philip Bourke 1850-1887 . . . . . . DLB-35
Martens, Kurt 1870-1945 . . . . DLB-66
Martí, José 1853-1895 . . . . DLB-290
Martial circa A.D. 40-circa A.D. 103 . . . . DLB-211; CDWLB-1
William S. Martien [publishing house] DLB-49
Martin, Abe (see Hubbard, Kin)
Martin, Catherine ca. 1847-1937 . . . . DLB-230
Martin, Charles 1942- DLB-120, 282
Martin, Claire 1914- DLB-60
Martin, David 1915-1997 . . . . DLB-260
Martin, Jay 1935- DLB-111
Martin, Johann (see Laurentius von Schnüffis)
Martin, Thomas 1696-1771 . . . . DLB-213
Martin, Violet Florence (see Ross, Martin)
Martin du Gard, Roger 1881-1958 . . . . . . DLB-65
Martineau, Harriet 1802-1876 . . . . DLB-21, 55, 159, 163, 166, 190
Martínez, Demetria 1960- DLB-209
Martínez de Toledo, Alfonso 1398?-1468 . . . . DLB-286
Martínez, Eliud 1935- DLB-122
Martínez, Max 1943- DLB-82
Martínez, Rubén 1962- DLB-209
Martinson, Harry 1904-1978 . . . . DLB-259
Martinson, Moa 1890-1964 . . . . DLB-259
Martone, Michael 1955- DLB-218
Martyn, Edward 1859-1923 . . . . DLB-10
Marvell, Andrew 1621-1678 . . . . DLB-131; CDBLB-2
Marvin X 1944- DLB-38
Marx, Karl 1818-1883 . . . . DLB-129
Marzials, Theo 1850-1920 . . . . DLB-35
Masefield, John 1878-1967 . . . . DLB-10, 19, 153, 160; CDBLB-5
Masham, Damaris Cudworth, Lady 1659-1708 . . . . DLB-252
Masino, Paola 1908-1989 . . . . DLB-264
Mason, A. E. W. 1865-1948 . . . . DLB-70
Mason, Bobbie Ann 1940- DLB-173; Y-87; CDALB-7
Mason, F. van Wyck (Geoffrey Coffin, Frank W. Mason, Ward Weaver) 1901-1978 . . . . DLB-306
Mason, William 1725-1797 . . . . DLB-142
Mason Brothers DLB-49
The Massachusetts Quarterly Review 1847-1850 . . . . DLB-1
The Masses DLB-303
Massey, Gerald 1828-1907 . . . . DLB-32
Massey, Linton R. 1900-1974 . . . . DLB-187
Massie, Allan 1938- DLB-271
Massinger, Philip 1583-1640 . . . . DLB-58
Masson, David 1822-1907 . . . . DLB-144
Masters, Edgar Lee 1868-1950 . . . . DLB-54; CDALB-3
Masters, Hilary 1928- DLB-244
Mastronardi, Lucio 1930-1979 . . . . DLB-177

Matevski, Mateja 1929- . . . DLB-181; CDWLB-4
Mather, Cotton 1663-1728 . . . . DLB-24, 30, 140; CDALB-2
Mather, Increase 1639-1723 . . . . DLB-24
Mather, Richard 1596-1669 . . . . DLB-24
Matheson, Annie 1853-1924 . . . . DLB-240
Matheson, Richard 1926- DLB-8, 44
Matheus, John F. 1887- DLB-51
Mathews, Cornelius 1817?-1889 . . . DLB-3, 64, 250
Elkin Mathews [publishing house] DLB-112
Mathews, John Joseph 1894-1979 . . . . . . DLB-175
Mathias, Roland 1915- DLB-27
Mathis, June 1892-1927 . . . . DLB-44
Mathis, Sharon Bell 1937- DLB-33
Matković, Marijan 1915-1985 . . . . DLB-181
Matoš, Antun Gustav 1873-1914 . . . . DLB-147
Matos Paoli, Francisco 1915-2000 . . . . DLB-290
Matsumoto Seichō 1909-1992 . . . . DLB-182
The Matter of England 1240-1400 . . . . . DLB-146
The Matter of Rome early twelfth to late fifteenth century DLB-146
Matthew of Vendôme circa 1130-circa 1200 . . . . DLB-208
Matthews, Brander 1852-1929 . . DLB-71, 78; DS-13
Matthews, Jack 1925- DLB-6
Matthews, Victoria Earle 1861-1907 . . . . DLB-221
Matthews, William 1942-1997 . . . . DLB-5
Matthías Jochumsson 1835-1920 . . . . DLB-293
Matthías Johannessen 1930- DLB-293
Matthiessen, F. O. 1902-1950 . . . . DLB-63
Matthiessen, Peter 1927- DLB-6, 173, 275
Maturin, Charles Robert 1780-1824 . . . . . DLB-178
Maugham, W. Somerset 1874-1965 . . . . DLB-10, 36, 77, 100, 162, 195; CDBLB-6
Maupassant, Guy de 1850-1893 . . . . DLB-123
Maupin, Armistead 1944- DLB-278
Mauriac, Claude 1914-1996 . . . . DLB-83
Mauriac, François 1885-1970 . . . . DLB-65
Maurice, Frederick Denison 1805-1872 . . . . DLB-55
Maurois, André 1885-1967 . . . . DLB-65
Maury, James 1718-1769 . . . . DLB-31
Mavor, Elizabeth 1927- DLB-14
Mavor, Osborne Henry (see Bridie, James)
Maxwell, Gavin 1914-1969 . . . . DLB-204
Maxwell, William 1908-2000 . . . . DLB-218, 278; Y-80
Tribute to Nancy Hale Y-88
H. Maxwell [publishing house] DLB-49
John Maxwell [publishing house] DLB-106
May, Elaine 1932- DLB-44
May, Karl 1842-1912 . . . . DLB-129
May, Thomas 1595/1596-1650 . . . . DLB-58
Mayer, Bernadette 1945- DLB-165
Mayer, Mercer 1943- DLB-61
Mayer, O. B. 1818-1891 . . . . DLB-3, 248
Mayes, Herbert R. 1900-1987 . . . . DLB-137

Mayes, Wendell 1919-1992 . . . . DLB-26	McCullagh, Joseph B. 1842-1896 . . . . DLB-23	McKnight, Reginald 1956- DLB-234
Mayfield, Julian 1928-1984. . . . . . . DLB-33; Y-84	McCullers, Carson 1917-1967 . . . . . . DLB-2, 7, 173, 228; CDALB-1	McLachlan, Alexander 1818-1896 . . . . DLB-99
Mayhew, Henry 1812-1887 . . . . . DLB-18, 55, 190	McCulloch, Thomas 1776-1843 . . . . DLB-99	McLaren, Floris Clark 1904-1978 . . . . DLB-68
Mayhew, Jonathan 1720-1766 . . . . DLB-31	McCunn, Ruthanne Lum 1946- DLB-312	McLaverty, Michael 1907- DLB-15
Mayne, Ethel Colburn 1865-1941 . . . . . . DLB-197	McDermott, Alice 1953- DLB-292	McLean, Duncan 1964- DLB-267
Mayne, Jasper 1604-1672 . . . . DLB-126	McDonald, Forrest 1927- DLB-17	McLean, John R. 1848-1916 . . . . DLB-23
Mayne, Seymour 1944- DLB-60	McDonald, Walter 1934- DLB-105, DS-9	McLean, William L. 1852-1931 . . . . DLB-25
Mayor, Flora Macdonald 1872-1932 . . . . . DLB-36	"Getting Started: Accepting the Regions You Own—or Which Own You" DLB-105	McLennan, William 1856-1904 . . . . DLB-92
Mayröcker, Friederike 1924- DLB-85		McLoughlin Brothers DLB-49
Mazrui, Ali A. 1933- DLB-125		McLuhan, Marshall 1911-1980 . . . . DLB-88
Mažuranić, Ivan 1814-1890 . . . . DLB-147	Tribute to James Dickey Y-97	McMaster, John Bach 1852-1932 . . . . DLB-47
Mazursky, Paul 1930- DLB-44	McDougall, Colin 1917-1984 . . . . DLB-68	McMillan, Terri 1951- DLB-292
McAlmon, Robert 1896-1956 . . . DLB-4, 45; DS-15	McDowell, Katharine Sherwood Bonner 1849-1883 . . . . DLB-202, 239	McMurtry, Larry 1936- DLB-2, 143, 256; Y-80, 87; CDALB-6
"A Night at Bricktop's" Y-01		
McArthur, Peter 1866-1924 . . . . DLB-92	Obolensky McDowell [publishing house] DLB-46	McNally, Terrence 1939- DLB-7, 249
McAuley, James 1917-1976 . . . . DLB-260		McNeil, Florence 1937- DLB-60
Robert M. McBride and Company DLB-46	McEwan, Ian 1948- DLB-14, 194	McNeile, Herman Cyril 1888-1937 . . . . . . DLB-77
McCabe, Patrick 1955- DLB-194	McFadden, David 1940- DLB-60	McNickle, D'Arcy 1904-1977 . . . . DLB-175, 212
McCafferty, Owen 1961- DLB-310	McFall, Frances Elizabeth Clarke (see Grand, Sarah)	McPhee, John 1931- DLB-185, 275
McCaffrey, Anne 1926- DLB-8		McPherson, James Alan 1943- DLB-38, 244
McCann, Colum 1965- DLB-267	McFarland, Ron 1942- DLB-256	McPherson, Sandra 1943- Y-86
McCarthy, Cormac 1933- DLB-6, 143, 256	McFarlane, Leslie 1902-1977 . . . . DLB-88	McTaggart, J. M. E. 1866-1925 . . . . DLB-262
The Cormac McCarthy Society Y-99	McFee, William 1881-1966 . . . . DLB-153	McWhirter, George 1939- DLB-60
McCarthy, Mary 1912-1989 . . . . DLB-2; Y-81	McGahern, John 1934- DLB-14, 231	McWilliam, Candia 1955- DLB-267
McCarthy, Shaun Lloyd (see Cory, Desmond)	McGee, Thomas D'Arcy 1825-1868 . . . . . DLB-99	McWilliams, Carey 1905-1980 . . . . DLB-137
McCay, Winsor 1871-1934 . . . . DLB-22	McGeehan, W. O. 1879-1933 . . . . DLB-25, 171	"*The Nation's* Future," Carey McWilliams's Editorial Policy in *Nation*. DLB-137
McClane, Albert Jules 1922-1991 . . . . DLB-171	McGill, Ralph 1898-1969 . . . . DLB-29	
McClatchy, C. K. 1858-1936 . . . . DLB-25	McGinley, Phyllis 1905-1978 . . . . DLB-11, 48	
McClellan, George Marion 1860-1934 . . . . DLB-50	McGinniss, Joe 1942- DLB-185	Mda, Zakes 1948- DLB-225
"The Negro as a Writer" DLB-50	McGirt, James E. 1874-1930 . . . . DLB-50	Mead, George Herbert 1863-1931 . . . . DLB-270
McCloskey, Robert 1914- DLB-22	McGlashan and Gill DLB-106	Mead, L. T. 1844-1914 . . . . DLB-141
McCloy, Helen 1904-1992 . . . . DLB-306	McGough, Roger 1937- DLB-40	Mead, Matthew 1924- DLB-40
McClung, Nellie Letitia 1873-1951 . . . . . . DLB-92	McGrath, John 1935- DLB-233	Mead, Taylor ?- DLB-16
McClure, James 1939- DLB-276	McGrath, Patrick 1950- DLB-231	Meany, Tom 1903-1964 . . . . DLB-171
McClure, Joanna 1930- DLB-16	McGraw-Hill DLB-46	Mechthild von Magdeburg circa 1207-circa 1282 . . . . DLB-138
McClure, Michael 1932- DLB-16	McGuane, Thomas 1939- DLB-2, 212; Y-80	
McClure, Phillips and Company DLB-46	Tribute to Seymour Lawrence Y-94	Medieval Galician-Portuguese Poetry DLB-287
McClure, S. S. 1857-1949 . . . . DLB-91	McGuckian, Medbh 1950- DLB-40	Medill, Joseph 1823-1899 . . . . DLB-43
A. C. McClurg and Company DLB-49	McGuffey, William Holmes 1800-1873 . . . DLB-42	Medoff, Mark 1940- DLB-7
McCluskey, John A., Jr. 1944- DLB-33	McGuinness, Frank 1953- DLB-245	Meek, Alexander Beaufort 1814-1865 . . . . DLB-3, 248
McCollum, Michael A. 1946- Y-87	McHenry, James 1785-1845 . . . . DLB-202	
McConnell, William C. 1917- DLB-88	McIlvanney, William 1936- DLB-14, 207	Meeke, Mary ?-1816? DLB-116
McCord, David 1897-1997 . . . . DLB-61	McIlwraith, Jean Newton 1859-1938 . . . . . DLB-92	Mei, Lev Aleksandrovich 1822-1862 . . . . . DLB-277
McCord, Louisa S. 1810-1879 . . . . DLB-248	McInerney, Jay 1955- DLB-292	Meinke, Peter 1932- DLB-5
McCorkle, Jill 1958- DLB-234; Y-87	McInerny, Ralph 1929- DLB-306	Meireles, Cecília 1901-1964 . . . . DLB-307
McCorkle, Samuel Eusebius 1746-1811 . . . DLB-37	McIntosh, Maria Jane 1803-1878 . . . DLB-239, 248	Mejia Vallejo, Manuel 1923- DLB-113
McCormick, Anne O'Hare 1880-1954 . . . . DLB-29	McIntyre, James 1827-1906 . . . . DLB-99	Melanchthon, Philipp 1497-1560 . . . . DLB-179
McCormick, Kenneth Dale 1906-1997 . . . . . Y-97	McIntyre, O. O. 1884-1938 . . . . DLB-25	Melançon, Robert 1947- DLB-60
McCormick, Robert R. 1880-1955 . . . . . . DLB-29	McKay, Claude 1889-1948 . . . . . DLB-4, 45, 51, 117	Mell, Max 1882-1971 . . . . DLB-81, 124
McCourt, Edward 1907-1972 . . . . DLB-88	The David McKay Company DLB-49	Mellow, James R. 1926-1997 . . . . DLB-111
McCoy, Horace 1897-1955 . . . . DLB-9	McKean, William V. 1820-1903 . . . . DLB-23	Mel'nikov, Pavel Ivanovich 1818-1883 . . DLB-238
McCrae, Hugh 1876-1958 . . . . DLB-260	McKenna, Stephen 1888-1967 . . . . DLB-197	Meltzer, David 1937- DLB-16
McCrae, John 1872-1918 . . . . DLB-92	The McKenzie Trust Y-96	Meltzer, Milton 1915- DLB-61
McCrumb, Sharyn 1948- DLB-306	McKerrow, R. B. 1872-1940 . . . . DLB-201	Melville, Elizabeth, Lady Culross circa 1585-1640 . . . . DLB-172
	McKinley, Robin 1952- DLB-52	

Melville, Herman 1819-1891 . . . . DLB-3, 74, 250; CDALB-2
    The Melville Society Y-01
Melville, James (Roy Peter Martin) 1931- DLB-276
Mena, Juan de 1411-1456 . . . . DLB-286
Mena, María Cristina 1893-1965. . . . DLB-209, 221
Menander 342-341 B.C.-circa 292-291 B.C. DLB-176; CDWLB-1
Menantes (see Hunold, Christian Friedrich)
Mencke, Johann Burckhard 1674-1732 . . . DLB-168
Mencken, H. L. 1880-1956 . . . . DLB-11, 29, 63, 137, 222; CDALB-4
    "Berlin, February, 1917" Y-00
    From the Initial Issue of *American Mercury* (January 1924) DLB-137
    Mencken and Nietzsche: An Unpublished Excerpt from H. L. Mencken's *My Life as Author and Editor* Y-93
Mendelssohn, Moses 1729-1786. . . . . DLB-97
Mendes, Catulle 1841-1909 . . . . DLB-217
Méndez M., Miguel 1930- DLB-82
The Mercantile Library of New York Y-96
Mercer, Cecil William (see Yates, Dornford)
Mercer, David 1928-1980 . . . . DLB-13, 310
Mercer, John 1704-1768 . . . . DLB-31
Mercer, Johnny 1909-1976. . . . . DLB-265
Meredith, George 1828-1909 . . . . DLB-18, 35, 57, 159; CDBLB-4
Meredith, Louisa Anne 1812-1895 . . DLB-166, 230
Meredith, Owen (see Lytton, Edward Robert Bulwer)
Meredith, William 1919- DLB-5
Meres, Francis *Palladis Tamia, Wits Treasurie* (1598) [excerpt] DLB-172
Merezhkovsky, Dmitrii Sergeevich 1865-1941 . . . . DLB-295
Mergerle, Johann Ulrich (see Abraham a Sancta Clara)
Mérimée, Prosper 1803-1870 . . . . DLB-119, 192
Merivale, John Herman 1779-1844 . . . . DLB-96
Meriwether, Louise 1923- DLB-33
Merleau-Ponty, Maurice 1908-1961 . . . . DLB-296
Merlin Press DLB-112
Merriam, Eve 1916-1992 . . . . DLB-61
The Merriam Company DLB-49
Merril, Judith 1923-1997 . . . . DLB-251
    Tribute to Theodore Sturgeon Y-85
Merrill, James 1926-1995 . . . . . . DLB-5, 165; Y-85
Merrill and Baker DLB-49
The Mershon Company DLB-49
Merton, Thomas 1915-1968 . . . . DLB-48; Y-81
Merwin, W. S. 1927- DLB-5, 169
Julian Messner [publishing house] DLB-46
Mészöly, Miklós 1921- DLB-232
J. Metcalf [publishing house] DLB-49
Metcalf, John 1938- DLB-60

The Methodist Book Concern DLB-49
Methuen and Company DLB-112
Meun, Jean de (see *Roman de la Rose*)
Mew, Charlotte 1869-1928 . . . . DLB-19, 135
Mewshaw, Michael 1943- Y-80
    Tribute to Albert Erskine Y-93
Meyer, Conrad Ferdinand 1825-1898. . . . DLB-129
Meyer, E. Y. 1946- DLB-75
Meyer, Eugene 1875-1959 . . . . DLB-29
Meyer, Michael 1921-2000 . . . . DLB-155
Meyers, Jeffrey 1939- DLB-111
Meynell, Alice 1847-1922 . . . . DLB-19, 98
Meynell, Viola 1885-1956 . . . . DLB-153
Meyrink, Gustav 1868-1932 . . . . DLB-81
Mézières, Philipe de circa 1327-1405 . . . . DLB-208
Michael, Ib 1945- DLB-214
Michael, Livi 1960- DLB-267
Michaëlis, Karen 1872-1950 . . . . DLB-214
Michaels, Anne 1958- DLB-299
Michaels, Leonard 1933- DLB-130
Michaux, Henri 1899-1984 . . . . DLB-258
Micheaux, Oscar 1884-1951 . . . . DLB-50
Michel of Northgate, Dan circa 1265-circa 1340. . . . . DLB-146
Micheline, Jack 1929-1998 . . . . DLB-16
Michener, James A. 1907?-1997. . . . . DLB-6
Micklejohn, George circa 1717-1818 . . . . . . DLB-31
Middle Hill Press DLB-106
Middleton, Christopher 1926- DLB-40
Middleton, Richard 1882-1911 . . . . DLB-156
Middleton, Stanley 1919- DLB-14
Middleton, Thomas 1580-1627 . . . . DLB-58
Miegel, Agnes 1879-1964 . . . . DLB-56
Miežélaitis, Eduardas 1919-1997 . . . . DLB-220
Miguéis, José Rodrigues 1901-1980. . . . . . DLB-287
Mihailović, Dragoslav 1930- DLB-181
Mihalić, Slavko 1928- DLB-181
Mikhailov, A. (see Sheller, Aleksandr Konstantinovich)
Mikhailov, Mikhail Larionovich 1829-1865 . . . . DLB-238
Mikhailovsky, Nikolai Konstantinovich 1842-1904 . . . . DLB-277
Miles, Josephine 1911-1985 . . . . DLB-48
Miles, Susan (Ursula Wyllie Roberts) 1888-1975 . . . . DLB-240
Miliković, Branko 1934-1961 . . . . DLB-181
Milius, John 1944- DLB-44
Mill, James 1773-1836 . . . . DLB-107, 158, 262
Mill, John Stuart 1806-1873 . . . . . . DLB-55, 190, 262; CDBLB-4
    Thoughts on Poetry and Its Varieties (1833) DLB-32
Andrew Millar [publishing house] DLB-154
Millar, Kenneth 1915-1983 . . . . DLB-2, 226; Y-83; DS-6

Millay, Edna St. Vincent 1892-1950 . . . . DLB-45, 249; CDALB-4
Millen, Sarah Gertrude 1888-1968 . . . . . DLB-225
Miller, Andrew 1960- DLB-267
Miller, Arthur 1915-2005. . . DLB-7, 266; CDALB-1
    The Arthur Miller Society. Y-01
Miller, Caroline 1903-1992 . . . . DLB-9
Miller, Eugene Ethelbert 1950- DLB-41
    Tribute to Julian Mayfield. Y-84
Miller, Heather Ross 1939- DLB-120
Miller, Henry 1891-1980 . . . . DLB-4, 9; Y-80; CDALB-5
Miller, Hugh 1802-1856 . . . . DLB-190
Miller, J. Hillis 1928- DLB-67
Miller, Jason 1939- DLB-7
Miller, Joaquin 1839-1913 . . . . DLB-186
Miller, May 1899-1995 . . . . DLB-41
Miller, Paul 1906-1991 . . . . DLB-127
Miller, Perry 1905-1963. . . . . DLB-17, 63
Miller, Sue 1943- DLB-143
Miller, Vassar 1924-1998. . . . . DLB-105
Miller, Walter M., Jr. 1923-1996 . . . . DLB-8
Miller, Webb 1892-1940 . . . . DLB-29
James Miller [publishing house] DLB-49
Millett, Kate 1934- DLB-246
Millhauser, Steven 1943- DLB-2
Millican, Arthenia J. Bates 1920- DLB-38
Milligan, Alice 1866-1953 . . . . DLB-240
Mills, Magnus 1954- DLB-267
Mills and Boon DLB-112
Milman, Henry Hart 1796-1868 . . . . DLB-96
Milne, A. A. 1882-1956 . . . . . . DLB-10, 77, 100, 160
Milner, Ron 1938- DLB-38
William Milner [publishing house] DLB-106
Milnes, Richard Monckton (Lord Houghton) 1809-1885 . . . . DLB-32, 184
Milton, John 1608-1674 . . . . . DLB-131, 151, 281; CDBLB-2
    The Milton Society of America. Y-00
Miłosz, Czesław 1911- DLB-215; CDWLB-4
Minakami Tsutomu 1919- DLB-182
Minamoto no Sanetomo 1192-1219. . . . . . DLB-203
Minco, Marga 1920- DLB-299
The Minerva Press DLB-154
Minnesang circa 1150-1280 . . . . DLB-138
    The Music of *Minnesang* DLB-138
Minns, Susan 1839-1938 . . . . DLB-140
Minton, Balch and Company DLB-46
Mirbeau, Octave 1848-1917. . . . . DLB-123, 192
Mirikitani, Janice 1941- DLB-312
Mirk, John died after 1414? DLB-146
Miró, Ricardo 1883-1940 . . . . DLB-290
Miron, Gaston 1928-1996 . . . . DLB-60
A Mirror for Magistrates DLB-167
Mishima Yukio 1925-1970 . . . . DLB-182

Cumulative Index

Mistral, Gabriela 1889-1957 . . . . DLB-283

Mitchel, Jonathan 1624-1668 . . . . DLB-24

Mitchell, Adrian 1932- DLB-40

Mitchell, Donald Grant
   1822-1908 . . . . DLB-1, 243; DS-13

Mitchell, Gladys 1901-1983 . . . . DLB-77

Mitchell, James Leslie 1901-1935 . . . . DLB-15

Mitchell, John (see Slater, Patrick)

Mitchell, John Ames 1845-1918 . . . . DLB-79

Mitchell, Joseph 1908-1996. . . . . . . .DLB-185; Y-96

Mitchell, Julian 1935- DLB-14

Mitchell, Ken 1940- DLB-60

Mitchell, Langdon 1862-1935. . . . . DLB-7

Mitchell, Loften 1919- DLB-38

Mitchell, Margaret 1900-1949 . . DLB-9; CDALB-7

Mitchell, S. Weir 1829-1914. . . . . DLB-202

Mitchell, W. J. T. 1942- DLB-246

Mitchell, W. O. 1914-1998 . . . . DLB-88

Mitchison, Naomi Margaret (Haldane)
   1897-1999 . . . . DLB-160, 191, 255

Mitford, Mary Russell 1787-1855 . . . .DLB-110, 116

Mitford, Nancy 1904-1973 . . . . DLB-191

Mittelholzer, Edgar
   1909-1965 . . . . .DLB-117; CDWLB-3

Mitterer, Erika 1906- DLB-85

Mitterer, Felix 1948- DLB-124

Mitternacht, Johann Sebastian
   1613-1679. DLB-168

Miyamoto Yuriko 1899-1951 . . . . DLB-180

Mizener, Arthur 1907-1988. . . . . DLB-103

Mo, Timothy 1950- DLB-194

Moberg, Vilhelm 1898-1973 . . . . DLB-259

Modern Age Books. DLB-46

Modern Language Association of America
   The Modern Language Association of
    America Celebrates Its Centennial . . . Y-84

The Modern Library DLB-46

Modiano, Patrick 1945- DLB-83, 299

Moffat, Yard and Company DLB-46

Moffet, Thomas 1553-1604 . . . . DLB-136

Mofolo, Thomas 1876-1948 . . . . DLB-225

Mohr, Nicholasa 1938- DLB-145

Moix, Ana María 1947- DLB-134

Molesworth, Louisa 1839-1921 . . . . DLB-135

Molière (Jean-Baptiste Poquelin)
   1622-1673 . . . . DLB-268

Møller, Poul Martin 1794-1838. . . . . DLB-300

Möllhausen, Balduin 1825-1905 . . . . DLB-129

Molnár, Ferenc 1878-1952 . . DLB-215; CDWLB-4

Molnár, Miklós (see Mészöly, Miklós)

Momaday, N. Scott
   1934- DLB-143, 175, 256; CDALB-7

Monkhouse, Allan 1858-1936. . . . . DLB-10

Monro, Harold 1879-1932 . . . . DLB-19

Monroe, Harriet 1860-1936 . . . . DLB-54, 91

Monsarrat, Nicholas 1910-1979 . . . . DLB-15

Montagu, Lady Mary Wortley
   1689-1762. . . . . DLB-95, 101

Montague, C. E. 1867-1928 . . . . DLB-197

Montague, John 1929- DLB-40

Montale, Eugenio 1896-1981 . . . . DLB-114

Montalvo, Garci Rodríguez de
   ca. 1450?-before 1505 . . . . DLB-286

Montalvo, José 1946-1994 . . . . DLB-209

Monterroso, Augusto 1921-2003 . . . . DLB-145

Montesquiou, Robert de 1855-1921 . . . . . DLB-217

Montgomerie, Alexander
   circa 1550?-1598 . . . . DLB-167

Montgomery, James 1771-1854. . . . . . DLB-93, 158

Montgomery, John 1919- DLB-16

Montgomery, Lucy Maud
   1874-1942. . . . . DLB-92; DS-14

Montgomery, Marion 1925- DLB-6

Montgomery, Robert Bruce (see Crispin, Edmund)

Montherlant, Henry de 1896-1972 . . . . . . DLB-72

The Monthly Review 1749-1844 . . . . DLB-110

Monti, Ricardo 1944- DLB-305

Montigny, Louvigny de 1876-1955. . . . . . DLB-92

Montoya, José 1932- DLB-122

Moodie, John Wedderburn Dunbar
   1797-1869 . . . . DLB-99

Moodie, Susanna 1803-1885 . . . . DLB-99

Moody, Joshua circa 1633-1697 . . . . DLB-24

Moody, William Vaughn 1869-1910 . . . .DLB-7, 54

Moorcock, Michael 1939- DLB-14, 231, 261

Moore, Alan 1953- DLB-261

Moore, Brian 1921-1999. . . . . DLB-251

Moore, Catherine L. 1911-1987 . . . . DLB-8

Moore, Clement Clarke 1779-1863. . . . . . DLB-42

Moore, Dora Mavor 1888-1979 . . . . DLB-92

Moore, G. E. 1873-1958 . . . . DLB-262

Moore, George 1852-1933 . . . . DLB-10, 18, 57, 135

   Literature at Nurse, or Circulating Morals
   (1885) DLB-18

Moore, Lorrie 1957- DLB-234

Moore, Marianne
   1887-1972 . . . . DLB-45; DS-7; CDALB-5

   International Marianne Moore Society . . . Y-98

Moore, Mavor 1919- DLB-88

Moore, Richard 1927- DLB-105

   "The No Self, the Little Self, and
    the Poets" DLB-105

Moore, T. Sturge 1870-1944. . . . . DLB-19

Moore, Thomas 1779-1852. . . . . DLB-96, 144

Moore, Ward 1903-1978 . . . . DLB-8

Moore, Wilstach, Keys and Company DLB-49

Moorehead, Alan 1901-1983 . . . . DLB-204

Moorhouse, Frank 1938- DLB-289

Moorhouse, Geoffrey 1931- DLB-204

The Moorland-Spingarn Research
   Center DLB-76

Moorman, Mary C. 1905-1994 . . . . DLB-155

Mora, Pat 1942- DLB-209

Moraes, Vinicius de 1913-1980 . . . . DLB-307

Moraga, Cherríe 1952- DLB-82, 249

Morales, Alejandro 1944- DLB-82

Morales, Mario Roberto 1947- DLB-145

Morales, Rafael 1919- DLB-108

Morality Plays: *Mankind* circa 1450-1500
   and *Everyman* circa 1500. . . . . DLB-146

Morand, Paul (1888-1976) DLB-65

Morante, Elsa 1912-1985 . . . . .DLB-177

Morata, Olympia Fulvia 1526-1555 . . . . . .DLB-179

Moravia, Alberto 1907-1990 . . . . .DLB-177

Mordaunt, Elinor 1872-1942 . . . . .DLB-174

Mordovtsev, Daniil Lukich 1830-1905. . . DLB-238

More, Hannah
   1745-1833. . . . . DLB-107, 109, 116, 158

More, Henry 1614-1687 . . . . DLB-126, 252

More, Sir Thomas
   1477/1478-1535 . . . . DLB-136, 281

Morejón, Nancy 1944- DLB-283

Morency, Pierre 1942- DLB-60

Moreno, Dorinda 1939- DLB-122

Moretti, Marino 1885-1979. . . . . DLB-114, 264

Morgan, Berry 1919- DLB-6

Morgan, Charles 1894-1958. . . . . . . .DLB-34, 100

Morgan, Edmund S. 1916- DLB-17

Morgan, Edwin 1920- DLB-27

Morgan, John Pierpont 1837-1913 . . . . . . DLB-140

Morgan, John Pierpont, Jr. 1867-1943 . . . DLB-140

Morgan, Robert 1944- DLB-120, 292

Morgan, Sydney Owenson, Lady
   1776?-1859 . . . . .DLB-116, 158

Morgner, Irmtraud 1933-1990 . . . . DLB-75

Morhof, Daniel Georg 1639-1691 . . . . . . DLB-164

Mori, Kyoko 1957- DLB-312

Mori Ōgai 1862-1922 . . . . DLB-180

Mori, Toshio 1910-1980 . . . . DLB-312

Móricz, Zsigmond 1879-1942 . . . . DLB-215

Morier, James Justinian
   1782 or 1783?-1849 . . . . DLB-116

Mörike, Eduard 1804-1875. . . . . DLB-133

Morin, Paul 1889-1963. . . . . DLB-92

Morison, Richard 1514?-1556 . . . . DLB-136

Morison, Samuel Eliot 1887-1976 . . . . . . .DLB-17

Morison, Stanley 1889-1967. . . . . DLB-201

Moritz, Karl Philipp 1756-1793 . . . . DLB-94

Moriz von Craûn circa 1220-1230 . . . . DLB-138

Morley, Christopher 1890-1957 . . . . DLB-9

Morley, John 1838-1923 . . . . .DLB-57, 144, 190

Moro, César 1903-1956 . . . . DLB-290

Morris, George Pope 1802-1864 . . . . DLB-73

Morris, James Humphrey (see Morris, Jan)

Morris, Jan 1926- DLB-204

Morris, Lewis 1833-1907 . . . . DLB-35

Morris, Margaret 1737-1816 . . . . DLB-200

Morris, Mary McGarry 1943- DLB-292

Morris, Richard B. 1904-1989 . . . . .DLB-17

Morris, William 1834-1896
....DLB-18, 35, 57, 156, 178, 184; CDBLB-4

Morris, Willie 1934-1999................Y-80

 Tribute to Irwin Shaw................Y-84

 Tribute to James Dickey..............Y-97

Morris, Wright
1910-1998..........DLB-2, 206, 218; Y-81

Morrison, Arthur 1863-1945....DLB-70, 135, 197

Morrison, Charles Clayton 1874-1966.....DLB-91

Morrison, John 1904-1998.............DLB-260

Morrison, Toni 1931-
........DLB-6, 33, 143; Y-81, 93; CDALB-6

 Nobel Lecture 1993..................Y-93

Morrissy, Mary 1957-.................DLB-267

William Morrow and Company..........DLB-46

Morse, James Herbert 1841-1923.........DLB-71

Morse, Jedidiah 1761-1826..............DLB-37

Morse, John T., Jr. 1840-1937...........DLB-47

Morselli, Guido 1912-1973.............DLB-177

Morte Arthure, the *Alliterative* and the
Stanzaic circa 1350-1400............DLB-146

Mortimer, Favell Lee 1802-1878........DLB-163

Mortimer, John
1923-.........DLB-13, 245, 271; CDBLB-8

Morton, Carlos 1942-.................DLB-122

Morton, H. V. 1892-1979..............DLB-195

John P. Morton and Company..........DLB-49

Morton, Nathaniel 1613-1685...........DLB-24

Morton, Sarah Wentworth 1759-1846.....DLB-37

Morton, Thomas circa 1579-circa 1647....DLB-24

Moscherosch, Johann Michael
1601-1669.......................DLB-164

Humphrey Moseley
[publishing house]................DLB-170

Möser, Justus 1720-1794................DLB-97

Mosley, Nicholas 1923-..........DLB-14, 207

Mosley, Walter 1952-.................DLB-306

Moss, Arthur 1889-1969.................DLB-4

Moss, Howard 1922-1987................DLB-5

Moss, Thylias 1954-..................DLB-120

Motion, Andrew 1952-.................DLB-40

Motley, John Lothrop
1814-1877..........DLB-1, 30, 59, 235

Motley, Willard 1909-1965.........DLB-76, 143

Mott, Lucretia 1793-1880.............DLB-239

Benjamin Motte Jr.
[publishing house]................DLB-154

Motteux, Peter Anthony 1663-1718......DLB-80

Mottram, R. H. 1883-1971..............DLB-36

Mount, Ferdinand 1939-...............DLB-231

Mouré, Erin 1955-....................DLB-60

Mourning Dove (Humishuma) between
1882 and 1888?-1936..........DLB-175, 221

Movies
 Fiction into Film, 1928-1975: A List
 of Movies Based on the Works
 of Authors in British Novelists,
 1930-1959.....................DLB-15

 Movies from Books, 1920-1974........DLB-9

Mowat, Farley 1921-..................DLB-68

A. R. Mowbray and Company,
Limited.........................DLB-106

Mowrer, Edgar Ansel 1892-1977..........DLB-29

Mowrer, Paul Scott 1887-1971...........DLB-29

Edward Moxon [publishing house].......DLB-106

Joseph Moxon [publishing house].......DLB-170

Moyes, Patricia 1923-2000.............DLB-276

Mphahlele, Es'kia (Ezekiel)
1919-..........DLB-125, 225; CDWLB-3

Mrożek, Sławomir 1930-...DLB-232; CDWLB-4

Mtshali, Oswald Mbuyiseni
1940-........................DLB-125, 225

al-Mubarrad 826-898 or 899............DLB-311

Mucedorus...........................DLB-62

Mudford, William 1782-1848............DLB-159

Mudrooroo (see Johnson, Colin)

Mueller, Lisel 1924-..................DLB-105

Muhajir, El (see Marvin X)

Muhajir, Nazzam Al Fitnah (see Marvin X)

Muhammad the Prophet circa 570-632...DLB-311

Mühlbach, Luise 1814-1873.............DLB-133

Muir, Edwin 1887-1959........DLB-20, 100, 191

Muir, Helen 1937-.....................DLB-14

Muir, John 1838-1914...........DLB-186, 275

Muir, Percy 1894-1979.................DLB-201

Mujū Ichien 1226-1312.................DLB-203

Mukherjee, Bharati 1940-.........DLB-60, 218

Mulcaster, Richard 1531 or 1532-1611...DLB-167

Muldoon, Paul 1951-..................DLB-40

Mulisch, Harry 1927-.................DLB-299

Müller, Friedrich (see Müller, Maler)

Müller, Heiner 1929-1995..............DLB-124

Müller, Maler 1749-1825................DLB-94

Muller, Marcia 1944-..................DLB-226

Muller, Wilhelm 1794-1827..............DLB-90

Mumford, Lewis 1895-1990..............DLB-63

Munby, A. N. L. 1913-1974.............DLB-201

Munby, Arthur Joseph 1828-1910........DLB-35

Munday, Anthony 1560-1633.......DLB-62, 172

Mundt, Clara (see Mühlbach, Luise)

Mundt, Theodore 1808-1861............DLB-133

Munford, Robert circa 1737-1783........DLB-31

Mungoshi, Charles 1947-..............DLB-157

Munk, Kaj 1898-1944..................DLB-214

Munonye, John 1929-..................DLB-117

Munro, Alice 1931-....................DLB-53

George Munro [publishing house].......DLB-49

Munro, H. H.
1870-1916.........DLB-34, 162; CDBLB-5

Munro, Neil 1864-1930.................DLB-156

Norman L. Munro [publishing house].....DLB-49

Munroe, Kirk 1850-1930................DLB-42

Munroe and Francis....................DLB-49

James Munroe and Company............DLB-49

Joel Munsell [publishing house]........DLB-49

Munsey, Frank A. 1854-1925.........DLB-25, 91

Frank A. Munsey and Company.........DLB-49

Mura, David 1952-....................DLB-312

Murakami Haruki 1949-...............DLB-182

Murayama, Milton 1923-...............DLB-312

Murav'ev, Mikhail Nikitich 1757-1807....DLB-150

Murdoch, Iris 1919-1999
..............DLB-14, 194, 233; CDBLB-8

Murdock, James
 From *Sketches of Modern Philosophy*.......DS-5

Murdoch, Rupert 1931-...............DLB-127

Murfree, Mary N. 1850-1922........DLB-12, 74

Murger, Henry 1822-1861..............DLB-119

Murger, Louis-Henri (see Murger, Henry)

Murnane, Gerald 1939-...............DLB-289

Murner, Thomas 1475-1537............DLB-179

Muro, Amado 1915-1971...............DLB-82

Murphy, Arthur 1727-1805.........DLB-89, 142

Murphy, Beatrice M. 1908-1992.........DLB-76

Murphy, Dervla 1931-................DLB-204

Murphy, Emily 1868-1933..............DLB-99

Murphy, Jack 1923-1980...............DLB-241

John Murphy and Company............DLB-49

Murphy, John H., III 1916-...........DLB-127

Murphy, Richard 1927-1993............DLB-40

Murphy, Tom 1935-..................DLB-310

Murray, Albert L. 1916-..............DLB-38

Murray, Gilbert 1866-1957.............DLB-10

Murray, Jim 1919-1998...............DLB-241

John Murray [publishing house].......DLB-154

Murray, Judith Sargent 1751-1820....DLB-37, 200

Murray, Les 1938-...................DLB-289

Murray, Pauli 1910-1985..............DLB-41

Murry, John Middleton 1889-1957......DLB-149

 "The Break-Up of the Novel"
 (1922)........................DLB-36

Murry, John Middleton, Jr. (see Cowper, Richard)

Musäus, Johann Karl August 1735-1787...DLB-97

Muschg, Adolf 1934-..................DLB-75

Musil, Robert
1880-1942........DLB-81, 124; CDWLB-2

Muspilli circa 790-circa 850...........DLB-148

Musset, Alfred de 1810-1857.......DLB-192, 217

Benjamin B. Mussey
and Company....................DLB-49

Muste, A. J. 1885-1967................DLB-303

Mutafchieva, Vera 1929-..............DLB-181

Mutis, Alvaro 1923-..................DLB-283

Mwangi, Meja 1948-..................DLB-125

Myers, Frederic W. H.
1843-1901.......................DLB-190

Myers, Gustavus 1872-1942............DLB-47

Myers, L. H. 1881-1944...............DLB-15

Myers, Walter Dean 1937-.............DLB-33

Myerson, Julie 1960-.................DLB-267

Mykle, Agnar 1915-1994 . . . . DLB-297

Mykolaitis-Putinas,
    Vincas 1893-1967 . . . . DLB-220

Myles, Eileen 1949- DLB-193

Myrdal, Jan 1927- DLB-257

Mystery
    1985: The Year of the Mystery:
        A Symposium Y-85

    Comments from Other Writers Y-85

    The Second Annual New York Festival
        of Mystery Y-00

    Why I Read Mysteries Y-85

    Why I Write Mysteries: Night and Day,
        by Michael Collins Y-85

N

Na Prous Boneta circa 1296-1328 . . . . DLB-208

Nabl, Franz 1883-1974 . . . . DLB-81

Nabakov, Véra 1902-1991 . . . . Y-91

Nabokov, Vladimir 1899-1977 . . DLB-2, 244, 278;
    Y-80, 91; DS-3; CDALB-1

    International Nabokov Society Y-99

    An Interview [On Nabokov], by
        Fredson Bowers Y-80

    Nabokov Festival at Cornell Y-83

    The Vladimir Nabokov Archive in the
        Berg Collection of the New York
        Public Library: An Overview Y-91

    The Vladimir Nabokov Society Y-01

Nádaši, Ladislav (see Jégé)

Naden, Constance 1858-1889 . . . . DLB-199

Nadezhdin, Nikolai Ivanovich
    1804-1856 . . . . DLB-198

Nadson, Semen Iakovlevich 1862-1887 . . . DLB-277

Naevius circa 265 B.C.-201 B.C. DLB-211

Nafis and Cornish DLB-49

Nagai Kafū 1879-1959 . . . . DLB-180

Nagel, Ernest 1901-1985 . . . . DLB-279

Nagibin, Iurii Markovich 1920-1994 . . . . DLB-302

Nagrodskaia, Evdokiia Apollonovna
    1866-1930 . . . . DLB-295

Naipaul, Shiva 1945-1985 . . . . DLB-157; Y-85

Naipaul, V. S. 1932- DLB-125, 204, 207;
    Y-85, Y-01; CDBLB-8; CDWLB-3

    Nobel Lecture 2001: "Two Worlds" Y-01

Nakagami Kenji 1946-1992 . . . . DLB-182

Nakano-in Masatada no Musume (see Nijō, Lady)

Nałkowska, Zofia 1884-1954 . . . . DLB-215

Namora, Fernando 1919-1989 . . . . DLB-287

Joseph Nancrede [publishing house] DLB-49

Naranjo, Carmen 1930- DLB-145

Narbikova, Valeriia Spartakovna
    1958- DLB-285

Narezhny, Vasilii Trofimovich
    1780-1825 . . . . DLB-198

Narrache, Jean (Emile Coderre)
    1893-1970 . . . . DLB-92

Nasby, Petroleum Vesuvius (see Locke, David Ross)

Eveleigh Nash [publishing house] DLB-112

Nash, Ogden 1902-1971 . . . . DLB-11

Nashe, Thomas 1567-1601? DLB-167

Nason, Jerry 1910-1986 . . . . DLB-241

Nasr, Seyyed Hossein 1933- DLB-279

Nast, Condé 1873-1942 . . . . DLB-91

Nast, Thomas 1840-1902 . . . . DLB-188

Nastasijević, Momčilo 1894-1938 . . . . DLB-147

Nathan, George Jean 1882-1958 . . . . DLB-137

Nathan, Robert 1894-1985 . . . . DLB-9

Nation, Carry A. 1846-1911 . . . . DLB-303

National Book Critics Circle Awards Y-00–01

The National Jewish Book Awards Y-85

Natsume Sōseki 1867-1916 . . . . DLB-180

Naughton, Bill 1910-1992 . . . . DLB-13

Nava, Michael 1954- DLB-306

Navarro, Joe 1953- DLB-209

Naylor, Gloria 1950- DLB-173

Nazor, Vladimir 1876-1949 . . . . DLB-147

Ndebele, Njabulo 1948- DLB-157, 225

Neagoe, Peter 1881-1960 . . . . DLB-4

Neal, John 1793-1876 . . . . DLB-1, 59, 243

Neal, Joseph C. 1807-1847 . . . . DLB-11

Neal, Larry 1937-1981 . . . . DLB-38

The Neale Publishing Company DLB-49

Nearing, Scott 1883-1983 . . . . DLB-303

Nebel, Frederick 1903-1967 . . . . DLB-226

Nebrija, Antonio de 1442 or 1444-1522 . . DLB-286

Nedreaas, Torborg 1906-1987 . . . . DLB-297

F. Tennyson Neely [publishing house] DLB-49

Negoițescu, Ion 1921-1993 . . . . DLB-220

Negri, Ada 1870-1945 . . . . DLB-114

Neihardt, John G. 1881-1973 . . . . . DLB-9, 54, 256

Neidhart von Reuental
    circa 1185-circa 1240 . . . . DLB-138

Neilson, John Shaw 1872-1942 . . . . DLB-230

Nekrasov, Nikolai Alekseevich
    1821-1877 . . . . DLB-277

Nekrasov, Viktor Platonovich
    1911-1987 . . . . DLB-302

Neledinsky-Meletsky, Iurii Aleksandrovich
    1752-1828 . . . . DLB-150

Nelligan, Emile 1879-1941 . . . . DLB-92

Nelson, Alice Moore Dunbar 1875-1935 . . DLB-50

Nelson, Antonya 1961- DLB-244

Nelson, Kent 1943- DLB-234

Nelson, Richard K. 1941- DLB-275

Nelson, Thomas, and Sons [U.K.] DLB-106

Nelson, Thomas, and Sons [U.S.] DLB-49

Nelson, William 1908-1978 . . . . DLB-103

Nelson, William Rockhill 1841-1915 . . . . . DLB-23

Nemerov, Howard 1920-1991 . . . . . DLB-5, 6; Y-83

Németh, László 1901-1975 . . . . DLB-215

Nepos circa 100 B.C.-post 27 B.C. DLB-211

Nėris, Salomėja 1904-1945 . . DLB-220; CDWLB-4

Neruda, Pablo 1904-1973 . . . . DLB-283

Nerval, Gérard de 1808-1855 . . . . DLB-217

Nervo, Amado 1870-1919 . . . . DLB-290

Nesbit, E. 1858-1924 . . . . DLB-141, 153, 178

Ness, Evaline 1911-1986 . . . . DLB-61

Nestroy, Johann 1801-1862 . . . . DLB-133

Nettleship, R. L. 1846-1892 . . . . DLB-262

Neugeboren, Jay 1938- DLB-28

Neukirch, Benjamin 1655-1729 . . . . DLB-168

Neumann, Alfred 1895-1952 . . . . DLB-56

Neumann, Ferenc (see Molnár, Ferenc)

Neumark, Georg 1621-1681 . . . . DLB-164

Neumeister, Erdmann 1671-1756 . . . . . . DLB-168

Nevins, Allan 1890-1971 . . . . DLB-17; DS-17

Nevinson, Henry Woodd 1856-1941 . . . . DLB-135

The New American Library DLB-46

New Directions Publishing Corporation . . DLB-46

The New Monthly Magazine 1814-1884 . . . . DLB-110

New York Times Book Review Y-82

John Newbery [publishing house] DLB-154

Newbolt, Henry 1862-1938 . . . . DLB-19

Newbound, Bernard Slade (see Slade, Bernard)

Newby, Eric 1919- DLB-204

Newby, P. H. 1918- DLB-15

Thomas Cautley Newby
    [publishing house] DLB-106

Newcomb, Charles King 1820-1894 . . . DLB-1, 223

Newell, Peter 1862-1924 . . . . DLB-42

Newell, Robert Henry 1836-1901 . . . . DLB-11

Newhouse, Samuel I. 1895-1979 . . . . DLB-127

Newman, Cecil Earl 1903-1976 . . . . DLB-127

Newman, David 1937- DLB-44

Newman, Frances 1883-1928 . . . . Y-80

Newman, Francis William 1805-1897 . . . . DLB-190

Newman, G. F. 1946- DLB-310

Newman, John Henry
    1801-1890 . . . . DLB-18, 32, 55

Mark Newman [publishing house] DLB-49

Newmarch, Rosa Harriet 1857-1940 . . . . . DLB-240

George Newnes Limited DLB-112

Newsome, Effie Lee 1885-1979 . . . . DLB-76

Newton, A. Edward 1864-1940 . . . . DLB-140

Newton, Sir Isaac 1642-1727 . . . . DLB-252

Nexø, Martin Andersen 1869-1954 . . . . . DLB-214

Nezval, Vítěslav
    1900-1958 . . . . DLB-215; CDWLB-4

Ngugi wa Thiong'o
    1938- DLB-125; CDWLB-3

Niatum, Duane 1938- DLB-175

The *Nibelungenlied* and the *Klage*
    circa 1200 . . . . DLB-138

Nichol, B. P. 1944-1988 . . . . DLB-53

Nicholas of Cusa 1401-1464 . . . . DLB-115

Nichols, Ann 1891?-1966 . . . . DLB-249

Nichols, Beverly 1898-1983 . . . . DLB-191

Nichols, Dudley 1895-1960 . . . . DLB-26

Nichols, Grace 1950- DLB-157

Nichols, John 1940- Y-82
Nichols, Mary Sargeant (Neal) Gove
    1810-1884 .... DLB-1, 243
Nichols, Peter 1927- DLB-13, 245
Nichols, Roy F. 1896-1973 .... DLB-17
Nichols, Ruth 1948- DLB-60
Nicholson, Edward Williams Byron
    1849-1912 .... DLB-184
Nicholson, Geoff 1953- DLB-271
Nicholson, Norman 1914- DLB-27
Nicholson, William 1872-1949 .... DLB-141
Ní Chuilleanáin, Eiléan 1942- DLB-40
Nicol, Eric 1919- DLB-68
Nicolai, Friedrich 1733-1811 .... DLB-97
Nicolas de Clamanges circa 1363-1437 ... DLB-208
Nicolay, John G. 1832-1901 and
    Hay, John 1838-1905 .... DLB-47
Nicole, Pierre 1625-1695 .... DLB-268
Nicolson, Adela Florence Cory (see Hope, Laurence)
Nicolson, Harold 1886-1968 .... DLB-100, 149
    "The Practice of Biography," in
    *The English Sense of Humour and
    Other Essays* DLB-149
Nicolson, Nigel 1917- DLB-155
Niebuhr, Reinhold 1892-1971 ..... DLB-17; DS-17
Niedecker, Lorine 1903-1970 .... DLB-48
Nieman, Lucius W. 1857-1935 .... DLB-25
Nietzsche, Friedrich
    1844-1900 .... DLB-129; CDWLB-2
    Mencken and Nietzsche: An Unpublished
    Excerpt from H. L. Mencken's *My Life
    as Author and Editor* Y-93
Nievo, Stanislao 1928- DLB-196
Niggli, Josefina 1910-1983 .... Y-80
Nightingale, Florence 1820-1910 .... DLB-166
Nijō, Lady (Nakano-in Masatada no Musume)
    1258-after 1306 .... DLB-203
Nijo Yoshimoto 1320-1388 .... DLB-203
Nikitin, Ivan Savvich 1824-1861 .... DLB-277
Nikitin, Nikolai Nikolaevich 1895-1963 ... DLB-272
Nikolev, Nikolai Petrovich 1758-1815 .... DLB-150
Niles, Hezekiah 1777-1839 .... DLB-43
Nims, John Frederick 1913-1999 .... DLB-5
    Tribute to Nancy Hale Y-88
Nin, Anaïs 1903-1977 .... DLB-2, 4, 152
Nína Björk Árnadóttir 1941-2000 .... DLB-293
Niño, Raúl 1961- DLB-209
Nissenson, Hugh 1933- DLB-28
Niven, Frederick John 1878-1944 .... DLB-92
Niven, Larry 1938- DLB-8
Nixon, Howard M. 1909-1983 .... DLB-201
Nizan, Paul 1905-1940 .... DLB-72
Njegoš, Petar II Petrović
    1813-1851 .... DLB-147; CDWLB-4
Nkosi, Lewis 1936- DLB-157, 225
Noah, Mordecai M. 1785-1851 .... DLB-250
Noailles, Anna de 1876-1933 .... DLB-258

Nobel Peace Prize
    The Nobel Prize and Literary Politics Y-88
    Elie Wiesel Y-86
Nobel Prize in Literature
    Joseph Brodsky Y-87
    Camilo José Cela Y-89
    Dario Fo Y-97
    Gabriel García Márquez Y-82
    William Golding Y-83
    Nadine Gordimer Y-91
    Günter Grass Y-99
    Seamus Heaney Y-95
    Imre Kertész Y-02
    Najīb Maḥfūẓ Y-88
    Toni Morrison Y-93
    V. S. Naipaul Y-01
    Kenzaburō Ōe Y-94
    Octavio Paz Y-90
    José Saramago Y-98
    Jaroslav Seifert Y-84
    Claude Simon Y-85
    Wole Soyinka Y-86
    Wisława Szymborska Y-96
    Derek Walcott Y-92
    Gao Xingjian Y-00
Nobre, António 1867-1900 .... DLB-287
Nodier, Charles 1780-1844 .... DLB-119
Noël, Marie (Marie Mélanie Rouget)
    1883-1967 .... DLB-258
Noel, Roden 1834-1894 .... DLB-35
Nogami Yaeko 1885-1985 .... DLB-180
Nogo, Rajko Petrov 1945- DLB-181
Nolan, William F. 1928- DLB-8
    Tribute to Raymond Chandler Y-88
Noland, C. F. M. 1810?-1858 .... DLB-11
Noma Hiroshi 1915-1991 .... DLB-182
Nonesuch Press DLB-112
Creative Nonfiction Y-02
Nonni (Jón Stefán Sveinsson or Svensson)
    1857-1944 .... DLB-293
Noon, Jeff 1957- DLB-267
Noonan, Robert Phillipe (see Tressell, Robert)
Noonday Press DLB-46
Noone, John 1936- DLB-14
Nora, Eugenio de 1923- DLB-134
Nordan, Lewis 1939- DLB-234
Nordbrandt, Henrik 1945- DLB-214
Nordhoff, Charles 1887-1947 .... DLB-9
Norén, Lars 1944- DLB-257
Norfolk, Lawrence 1963- DLB-267
Norman, Charles 1904-1996 .... DLB-111
Norman, Marsha 1947- DLB-266; Y-84
Norris, Charles G. 1881-1945 .... DLB-9
Norris, Frank
    1870-1902 .... DLB-12, 71, 186; CDALB-3
Norris, Helen 1916- DLB-292

Norris, John 1657-1712 .... DLB-252
Norris, Leslie 1921- DLB-27, 256
Norse, Harold 1916- DLB-16
Norte, Marisela 1955- DLB-209
North, Marianne 1830-1890 .... DLB-174
North Point Press DLB-46
Nortje, Arthur 1942-1970 .... DLB-125, 225
Norton, Alice Mary (see Norton, Andre)
Norton, Andre 1912- DLB-8, 52
Norton, Andrews 1786-1853 .... DLB-1, 235; DS-5
Norton, Caroline 1808-1877 .... DLB-21, 159, 199
Norton, Charles Eliot
    1827-1908 .... DLB-1, 64, 235
Norton, John 1606-1663 .... DLB-24
Norton, Mary 1903-1992 .... DLB-160
Norton, Thomas 1532-1584 .... DLB-62
W. W. Norton and Company DLB-46
Norwood, Robert 1874-1932 .... DLB-92
Nosaka Akiyuki 1930- DLB-182
Nossack, Hans Erich 1901-1977 .... DLB-69
Notker Balbulus circa 840-912 .... DLB-148
Notker III of Saint Gall
    circa 950-1022 .... DLB-148
Notker von Zweifalten ?-1095 .... DLB-148
Nourse, Alan E. 1928- DLB-8
Novak, Slobodan 1924- DLB-181
Novak, Vjenceslav 1859-1905 .... DLB-147
Novakovich, Josip 1956- DLB-244
Novalis 1772-1801 .... DLB-90; CDWLB-2
Novaro, Mario 1868-1944 .... DLB-114
Novás Calvo, Lino 1903-1983 .... DLB-145
Novelists
    Library Journal Statements and
    Questionnaires from First Novelists Y-87
Novels
    The Columbia History of the American Novel
    A Symposium on Y-92
    The Great Modern Library Scam Y-98
    Novels for Grown-Ups Y-97
    The Proletarian Novel DLB-9
    Novel, The "Second-Generation" Holocaust
    .... DLB-299
    The Year in the Novel Y-87–88, Y-90–93
Novels, British
    "The Break-Up of the Novel" (1922),
    by John Middleton Murry DLB-36
    The Consolidation of Opinion: Critical
    Responses to the Modernists DLB-36
    "Criticism in Relation to Novels"
    (1863), by G. H. Lewes DLB-21
    "Experiment in the Novel" (1929)
    [excerpt], by John D. Beresford ... DLB-36
    "The Future of the Novel" (1899), by
    Henry James DLB-18
    The Gay Science (1866), by E. S. Dallas
    [excerpt] DLB-21
    A Haughty and Proud Generation
    (1922), by Ford Madox Hueffer ... DLB-36
    Literary Effects of World War II DLB-15

Cumulative Index

"Modern Novelists –Great and Small"
(1855), by Margaret Oliphant DLB-21

The Modernists (1932),
by Joseph Warren Beach........ DLB-36

A Note on Technique (1926), by
Elizabeth A. Drew [excerpts] DLB-36

Novel-Reading: *The Works of Charles
Dickens; The Works of W. Makepeace
Thackeray* (1879),
by Anthony Trollope DLB-21

Novels with a Purpose (1864), by
Justin M'Carthy............... DLB-21

"On Art in Fiction" (1838),
by Edward Bulwer DLB-21

The Present State of the English Novel
(1892), by George Saintsbury DLB-18

Representative Men and Women:
A Historical Perspective on
the British Novel, 1930-1960..... DLB-15

"The Revolt" (1937), by Mary Colum
[excerpts] DLB-36

"Sensation Novels" (1863), by
H. L. Manse DLB-21

Sex, Class, Politics, and Religion [in
the British Novel, 1930-1959] DLB-15

Time and Western Man (1927),
by Wyndham Lewis [excerpts] ... DLB-36

Noventa, Giacomo 1898-1960 .... DLB-114

Novikov, Nikolai Ivanovich
1744-1818..................... DLB-150

Novomeský, Laco 1904-1976 .... DLB-215

Nowlan, Alden 1933-1983 .... DLB-53

Noyes, Alfred 1880-1958 .... DLB-20

Noyes, Crosby S. 1825-1908 .... DLB-23

Noyes, Nicholas 1647-1717 .... DLB-24

Noyes, Theodore W. 1858-1946 .... DLB-29

Nozick, Robert 1938-2002 ....DLB-279

N-Town Plays circa 1468 to early
sixteenth century................ DLB-146

Nugent, Frank 1908-1965.............. DLB-44

Nunez, Sigrid 1951- DLB-312

Nušić, Branislav
1864-1938 .... DLB-147; CDWLB-4

David Nutt [publishing house] DLB-106

Nwapa, Flora
1931-1993 .... DLB-125; CDWLB-3

Nye, Edgar Wilson (Bill)
1850-1896 .... DLB-11, 23, 186

Nye, Naomi Shihab 1952- DLB-120

Nye, Robert 1939- DLB-14, 271

Nyka-Niliūnas, Alfonsas 1919- DLB-220

O

Oakes, Urian circa 1631-1681 .... DLB-24

Oakes Smith, Elizabeth
1806-1893 .... DLB-1, 239, 243

Oakley, Violet 1874-1961............. DLB-188

Oates, Joyce Carol 1938-
.... DLB-2, 5, 130; Y-81; CDALB-6

Tribute to Michael M. Rea Y-97

Ōba Minako 1930- DLB-182

Ober, Frederick Albion 1849-1913...... DLB-189

Ober, William 1920-1993................. Y-93

Oberholtzer, Ellis Paxson 1868-1936 .... DLB-47

The Obituary as Literary Form Y-02

Obradović, Dositej 1740?-1811......... DLB-147

O'Brien, Charlotte Grace 1845-1909 .... DLB-240

O'Brien, Edna 1932- ... DLB-14, 231; CDBLB-8

O'Brien, Fitz-James 1828-1862 .... DLB-74

O'Brien, Flann (see O'Nolan, Brian)

O'Brien, Kate 1897-1974............... DLB-15

O'Brien, Tim
1946- DLB-152; Y-80; DS-9; CDALB-7

O'Casey, Sean 1880-1964..... DLB-10; CDBLB-6

Occom, Samson 1723-1792..........DLB-175

Occomy, Marita Bonner 1899-1971 ...... DLB-51

Ochs, Adolph S. 1858-1935 .... DLB-25

Ochs-Oakes, George Washington
1861-1931 .... DLB-137

O'Connor, Flannery 1925-1964
.... DLB-2, 152; Y-80; DS-12; CDALB-1

The Flannery O'Connor Society Y-99

O'Connor, Frank 1903-1966 .... DLB-162

O'Connor, Joseph 1963- DLB-267

Octopus Publishing Group........... DLB-112

Oda Sakunosuke 1913-1947 .... DLB-182

Odell, Jonathan 1737-1818 .... DLB-31, 99

O'Dell, Scott 1903-1989 .... DLB-52

Odets, Clifford 1906-1963 ....DLB-7, 26

Odhams Press Limited DLB-112

Odio, Eunice 1922-1974 .... DLB-283

Odoevsky, Aleksandr Ivanovich
1802-1839 .... DLB-205

Odoevsky, Vladimir Fedorovich
1804 or 1803-1869.............. DLB-198

O'Donnell, Peter 1920- DLB-87

O'Donovan, Michael (see O'Connor, Frank)

O'Dowd, Bernard 1866-1953.......... DLB-230

Ōe, Kenzaburō 1935- DLB-182; Y-94

Nobel Lecture 1994: Japan, the
Ambiguous, and Myself Y-94

Oehlenschläger, Adam 1779-1850....... DLB-300

O'Faolain, Julia 1932- DLB-14, 231

O'Faolain, Sean 1900-1991 .... DLB-15, 162

Off-Loop Theatres DLB-7

Offord, Carl Ruthven 1910- DLB-76

O'Flaherty, Liam 1896-1984....DLB-36, 162; Y-84

Ogarev, Nikolai Platonovich 1813-1877 ...DLB-277

J. S. Ogilvie and Company DLB-49

Ogilvy, Eliza 1822-1912 .... DLB-199

Ogot, Grace 1930- DLB-125

O'Grady, Desmond 1935- DLB-40

Ogunyemi, Wale 1939- DLB-157

O'Hagan, Howard 1902-1982 .... DLB-68

O'Hara, Frank 1926-1966 .... DLB-5, 16, 193

O'Hara, John
1905-1970...... DLB-9, 86; DS-2; CDALB-5

John O'Hara's Pottsville Journalism Y-88

O'Hare, Kate Richards 1876-1948 .... DLB-303

O'Hegarty, P. S. 1879-1955 .... DLB-201

Ohio State University
The William Charvat American Fiction
Collection at the Ohio State
University Libraries Y-92

Okada, John 1923-1971 .... DLB-312

Okara, Gabriel 1921- DLB-125; CDWLB-3

O'Keeffe, John 1747-1833 .... DLB-89

Nicholas Okes [publishing house]........DLB-170

Okigbo, Christopher
1930-1967 ....DLB-125; CDWLB-3

Okot p'Bitek 1931-1982 .....DLB-125; CDWLB-3

Okpewho, Isidore 1941- DLB-157

Okri, Ben 1959- DLB-157, 231

Ólafur Jóhann Sigurðsson 1918-1988.... DLB-293

Old Dogs / New Tricks? New Technologies,
the Canon, and the Structure of
the Profession...................... Y-02

Old Franklin Publishing House DLB-49

Old German Genesis and *Old German Exodus*
circa 1050-circa 1130 .... DLB-148

The *Old High German Isidor*
circa 790-800 .... DLB-148

Older, Fremont 1856-1935............. DLB-25

Oldham, John 1653-1683 .... DLB-131

Oldman, C. B. 1894-1969 .... DLB-201

Olds, Sharon 1942- DLB-120

Olearius, Adam 1599-1671 .... DLB-164

O'Leary, Ellen 1831-1889 .... DLB-240

O'Leary, Juan E. 1879-1969 .... DLB-290

Olesha, Iurii Karlovich 1899-1960 ....DLB-272

Oliphant, Laurence 1829?-1888..... DLB-18, 166

Oliphant, Margaret 1828-1897 ...DLB-18, 159, 190

"Modern Novelists–Great and Small"
(1855) DLB-21

Oliveira, Carlos de 1921-1981 .... DLB-287

Oliver, Chad 1928-1993................. DLB-8

Oliver, Mary 1935- DLB-5, 193

Ollier, Claude 1922- DLB-83

Olsen, Tillie 1912/1913-
.... DLB-28, 206; Y-80; CDALB-7

Olson, Charles 1910-1970........DLB-5, 16, 193

Olson, Elder 1909- DLB-48, 63

Olson, Sigurd F. 1899-1982 ....DLB-275

The Omega Workshops.................DS-10

Omotoso, Kole 1943- DLB-125

Omulevsky, Innokentii Vasil'evich
1836 [or 1837]-1883.............. DLB-238

Ondaatje, Michael 1943- DLB-60

O'Neill, Eugene 1888-1953 .... DLB-7; CDALB-5

Eugene O'Neill Memorial Theater
Center DLB-7

Eugene O'Neill's Letters: A Review Y-88

Onetti, Juan Carlos
1909-1994 ....DLB-113; CDWLB-3

Onions, George Oliver 1872-1961 ...... DLB-153

Onofri, Arturo 1885-1928 . . . . DLB-114	Otero, Blas de 1916-1979 . . . . DLB-134	Page, Thomas Nelson 1853-1922 . . . . DLB-12, 78; DS-13
O'Nolan, Brian 1911-1966 . . . . DLB-231	Otero, Miguel Antonio 1859-1944 . . . . DLB-82	Page, Walter Hines 1855-1918 . . . . DLB-71, 91
Oodgeroo of the Tribe Noonuccal (Kath Walker) 1920-1993 . . . . DLB-289	Otero, Nina 1881-1965 . . . . DLB-209	Paget, Francis Edward 1806-1882 . . . . DLB-163
Opie, Amelia 1769-1853 . . . . DLB-116, 159	Otero Silva, Miguel 1908-1985 . . . . DLB-145	Paget, Violet (see Lee, Vernon)
Opitz, Martin 1597-1639 . . . . DLB-164	Otfried von Weißenburg circa 800-circa 875? DLB-148	Pagliarani, Elio 1927- DLB-128
Oppen, George 1908-1984 . . . . DLB-5, 165	Otis, Broaders and Company DLB-49	Pain, Barry 1864-1928 . . . . DLB-135, 197
Oppenheim, E. Phillips 1866-1946 . . . . DLB-70	Otis, James (see Kaler, James Otis)	Pain, Philip ?-circa 1666 . . . . DLB-24
Oppenheim, James 1882-1932 . . . . DLB-28	Otis, James, Jr. 1725-1783 . . . . DLB-31	Paine, Robert Treat, Jr. 1773-1811 . . . . DLB-37
Oppenheimer, Joel 1930-1988 . . . . DLB-5, 193	Ottaway, James 1911-2000 . . . . DLB-127	Paine, Thomas 1737-1809 . . . . DLB-31, 43, 73, 158; CDALB-2
Optic, Oliver (see Adams, William Taylor)	Ottendorfer, Oswald 1826-1900 . . . . DLB-23	Painter, George D. 1914- DLB-155
Orczy, Emma, Baroness 1865-1947 . . . . DLB-70	Ottieri, Ottiero 1924- DLB-177	Painter, William 1540?-1594 . . . . DLB-136
Oregon Shakespeare Festival Y-00	Otto-Peters, Louise 1819-1895 . . . . DLB-129	Palazzeschi, Aldo 1885-1974 . . . . DLB-114, 264
Origo, Iris 1902-1988 . . . . DLB-155	Otway, Thomas 1652-1685 . . . . DLB-80	Palei, Marina Anatol'evna 1955- DLB-285
O'Riordan, Kate 1960- DLB-267	Ouellette, Fernand 1930- DLB-60	Palencia, Alfonso de 1424-1492 . . . . DLB-286
Orlovitz, Gil 1918-1973 . . . . DLB-2, 5	Ouida 1839-1908 . . . . DLB-18, 156	Palés Matos, Luis 1898-1959 . . . . DLB-290
Orlovsky, Peter 1933- DLB-16	Outing Publishing Company DLB-46	Paley, Grace 1922- DLB-28, 218
Ormond, John 1923- DLB-27	Overbury, Sir Thomas circa 1581-1613 . . . . DLB-151	Paley, William 1743-1805 . . . . DLB-252
Ornitz, Samuel 1890-1957 . . . . DLB-28, 44	The Overlook Press DLB-46	Palfrey, John Gorham 1796-1881 . . . . DLB-1, 30, 235
O'Rourke, P. J. 1947- DLB-185	Ovid 43 B.C.-A.D. 17 . . . . DLB-211; CDWLB-1	Palgrave, Francis Turner 1824-1897 . . . . . . DLB-35
Orozco, Olga 1920-1999 . . . . DLB-283	Owen, Guy 1925- DLB-5	Palmer, Joe H. 1904-1952 . . . . DLB-171
Orten, Jiří 1919-1941 . . . . DLB-215	Owen, John 1564-1622 . . . . DLB-121	Palmer, Michael 1943- DLB-169
Ortese, Anna Maria 1914- DLB-177	John Owen [publishing house] DLB-49	Palmer, Nettie 1885-1964 . . . . DLB-260
Ortiz, Simon J. 1941- DLB-120, 175, 256	Peter Owen Limited DLB-112	Palmer, Vance 1885-1959 . . . . DLB-260
Ortnit and Wolfdietrich circa 1225-1250 . . . . DLB-138	Owen, Robert 1771-1858 . . . . DLB-107, 158	Paltock, Robert 1697-1767 . . . . DLB-39
Orton, Joe 1933-1967 . . . . . DLB-13, 310; CDBLB-8	Owen, Wilfred 1893-1918 . . . . DLB-20; DS-18; CDBLB-6	Paludan, Jacob 1896-1975 . . . . DLB-214
Orwell, George (Eric Arthur Blair) 1903-1950 . . . DLB-15, 98, 195, 255; CDBLB-7	A Centenary Celebration Y-93	Paludin-Müller, Frederik 1809-1876 . . . . . DLB-300
The Orwell Year Y-84	The Wilfred Owen Association Y-98	Pan Books Limited DLB-112
(Re-)Publishing Orwell Y-86	The Owl and the Nightingale circa 1189-1199 . . . . DLB-146	Panaev, Ivan Ivanovich 1812-1862 . . . . . DLB-198
Ory, Carlos Edmundo de 1923- DLB-134	Owsley, Frank L. 1890-1956 . . . . DLB-17	Panaeva, Avdot'ia Iakovlevna 1820-1893 . . . . DLB-238
Osbey, Brenda Marie 1957- DLB-120	Oxford, Seventeenth Earl of, Edward de Vere 1550-1604 . . . . DLB-172	Panama, Norman 1914- and Frank, Melvin 1913-1988 . . . . DLB-26
Osbon, B. S. 1827-1912 . . . . DLB-43	OyamO (Charles F. Gordon) 1943- DLB-266	Pancake, Breece D'J 1952-1979 . . . . DLB-130
Osborn, Sarah 1714-1796 . . . . DLB-200	Ozerov, Vladislav Aleksandrovich 1769-1816 . . . . DLB-150	Panduro, Leif 1923-1977 . . . . DLB-214
Osborne, John 1929-1994 . . . . DLB-13; CDBLB-7	Ozick, Cynthia 1928- . . . DLB-28, 152, 299; Y-82	Panero, Leopoldo 1909-1962 . . . . DLB-108
Osgood, Frances Sargent 1811-1850 . . . . . DLB-250	First Strauss "Livings" Awarded to Cynthia Ozick and Raymond Carver An Interview with Cynthia Ozick Y-83	Pangborn, Edgar 1909-1976 . . . . DLB-8
Osgood, Herbert L. 1855-1918 . . . . DLB-47		Panizzi, Sir Anthony 1797-1879 . . . . DLB-184
James R. Osgood and Company DLB-49		Panneton, Philippe (see Ringuet)
Osgood, McIlvaine and Company DLB-112		Panova, Vera Fedorovna 1905-1973 . . . . . DLB-302
O'Shaughnessy, Arthur 1844-1881 . . . . DLB-35	Tribute to Michael M. Rea Y-97	Panshin, Alexei 1940- DLB-8
Patrick O'Shea [publishing house] DLB-49	# P	Pansy (see Alden, Isabella)
Osipov, Nikolai Petrovich 1751-1799 . . . . . DLB-150		Pantheon Books DLB-46
Oskison, John Milton 1879-1947 . . . . DLB-175	Pace, Richard 1482?-1536 . . . . DLB-167	Papadat-Bengescu, Hortensia 1876-1955 . . . . DLB-220
Osler, Sir William 1849-1919 . . . . DLB-184	Pacey, Desmond 1917-1975 . . . . DLB-88	Papantonio, Michael 1907-1976 . . . . DLB-187
Osofisan, Femi 1946- DLB-125; CDWLB-3	Pacheco, José Emilio 1939- DLB-290	Paperback Library DLB-46
Ostenso, Martha 1900-1963 . . . . DLB-92	Pack, Robert 1929- DLB-5	Paperback Science Fiction DLB-8
Ostrauskas, Kostas 1926- DLB-232	Padell Publishing Company DLB-46	Papini, Giovanni 1881-1956 . . . . DLB-264
Ostriker, Alicia 1937- DLB-120	Padgett, Ron 1942- DLB-5	Paquet, Alfons 1881-1944 . . . . DLB-66
Ostrovsky, Aleksandr Nikolaevich 1823-1886 . . . . DLB-277	Padilla, Ernesto Chávez 1944- DLB-122	Paracelsus 1493-1541 . . . . DLB-179
Ostrovsky, Nikolai Alekseevich 1904-1936 . . . . DLB-272	L. C. Page and Company DLB-49	Paradis, Suzanne 1936- DLB-53
Osundare, Niyi 1947- DLB-157; CDWLB-3	Page, Louise 1955- DLB-233	Páral, Vladimír, 1932- DLB-232
Oswald, Eleazer 1755-1795 . . . . DLB-43	Page, P. K. 1916- DLB-68	Pardoe, Julia 1804-1862 . . . . DLB-166
Oswald von Wolkenstein 1376 or 1377-1445 . . . . DLB-179		

Cumulative Index

Paredes, Américo 1915-1999 . . . . DLB-209
Pareja Diezcanseco, Alfredo 1908-1993 . . DLB-145
Parents' Magazine Press DLB-46
Paretsky, Sara 1947- DLB-306
Parfit, Derek 1942- DLB-262
Parise, Goffredo 1929-1986 . . . . DLB-177
Parish, Mitchell 1900-1993 . . . . DLB-265
Parizeau, Alice 1930-1990 . . . . DLB-60
Park, Ruth 1923?- DLB-260
Parke, John 1754-1789 . . . . DLB-31
Parker, Dan 1893-1967 . . . . DLB-241
Parker, Dorothy 1893-1967 . . . . . . DLB-11, 45, 86
Parker, Gilbert 1860-1932 . . . . DLB-99
Parker, James 1714-1770 . . . . DLB-43
Parker, John [publishing house] DLB-106
Parker, Matthew 1504-1575 . . . . DLB-213
Parker, Robert B. 1932- DLB-306
Parker, Stewart 1941-1988 . . . . DLB-245
Parker, Theodore 1810-1860 . . . DLB-1, 235; DS-5
Parker, William Riley 1906-1968 . . . . DLB-103
J. H. Parker [publishing house] DLB-106
Parkes, Bessie Rayner (Madame Belloc)
  1829-1925 . . . . DLB-240
Parkman, Francis
  1823-1893 . . . . DLB-1, 30, 183, 186, 235
Parks, Gordon 1912- DLB-33
Parks, Tim 1954- DLB-231
Parks, William 1698-1750 . . . . DLB-43
William Parks [publishing house] DLB-49
Parley, Peter (see Goodrich, Samuel Griswold)
Parmenides late sixth-fifth century B.C. . . . DLB-176
Parnell, Thomas 1679-1718 . . . . DLB-95
Parnicki, Teodor 1908-1988 . . . . DLB-215
Parnok, Sofiia Iakovlevna (Parnokh)
  1885-1933 . . . . DLB-295
Parr, Catherine 1513?-1548 . . . . DLB-136
Parra, Nicanor 1914- DLB-283
Parrington, Vernon L. 1871-1929 . . . . . DLB-17, 63
Parrish, Maxfield 1870-1966 . . . . DLB-188
Parronchi, Alessandro 1914- DLB-128
Parshchikov, Aleksei Maksimovich
  (Raiderman) 1954- DLB-285
Partisan Review DLB-303
Parton, James 1822-1891 . . . . DLB-30
Parton, Sara Payson Willis
  1811-1872 . . . . DLB-43, 74, 239
S. W. Partridge and Company DLB-106
Parun, Vesna 1922- DLB-181; CDWLB-4
Pascal, Blaise 1623-1662 . . . . DLB-268
Pasinetti, Pier Maria 1913- DLB-177
  Tribute to Albert Erskine Y-93
Pasolini, Pier Paolo 1922-1975 . . . . . DLB-128, 177
Pastan, Linda 1932- DLB-5
Pasternak, Boris
  1890-1960 . . . . DLB-302

Paston, George (Emily Morse Symonds)
  1860-1936 . . . . DLB-149, 197
The Paston Letters 1422-1509 . . . . DLB-146
Pastorius, Francis Daniel
  1651-circa 1720 . . . . DLB-24
Patchen, Kenneth 1911-1972 . . . . DLB-16, 48
Pater, Walter 1839-1894 . . . DLB-57, 156; CDBLB-4
  Aesthetic Poetry (1873) DLB-35
  "Style" (1888) [excerpt] DLB-57
Paterson, A. B. "Banjo" 1864-1941 . . . . . . DLB-230
Paterson, Katherine 1932- DLB-52
Patmore, Coventry 1823-1896 . . . . DLB-35, 98
Paton, Alan 1903-1988 . . . . DLB-225; DS-17
Paton, Joseph Noel 1821-1901 . . . . DLB-35
Paton Walsh, Jill 1937- DLB-161
Patrick, Edwin Hill ("Ted") 1901-1964 . . DLB-137
Patrick, John 1906-1995 . . . . DLB-7
Pattee, Fred Lewis 1863-1950 . . . . DLB-71
Patterson, Alicia 1906-1963 . . . . DLB-127
Patterson, Eleanor Medill 1881-1948 . . . . . DLB-29
Patterson, Eugene 1923- DLB-127
Patterson, Joseph Medill 1879-1946 . . . . . DLB-29
Pattillo, Henry 1726-1801 . . . . DLB-37
Paul, Elliot 1891-1958 . . . . DLB-4; DS-15
Paul, Jean (see Richter, Johann Paul Friedrich)
Paul, Kegan, Trench, Trubner and
  Company Limited DLB-106
Peter Paul Book Company DLB-49
Stanley Paul and Company Limited DLB-112
Paulding, James Kirke
  1778-1860 . . . . DLB-3, 59, 74, 250
Paulin, Tom 1949- DLB-40
Pauper, Peter, Press DLB-46
Paustovsky, Konstantin Georgievich
  1892-1968 . . . . DLB-272
Pavese, Cesare 1908-1950 . . . . DLB-128, 177
Pavić, Milorad 1929- DLB-181; CDWLB-4
Pavlov, Konstantin 1933- DLB-181
Pavlov, Nikolai Filippovich 1803-1864 . . . DLB-198
Pavlova, Karolina Karlovna 1807-1893 . . . DLB-205
Pavlović, Miodrag
  1928- DLB-181; CDWLB-4
Pavlovsky, Eduardo 1933- DLB-305
Paxton, John 1911-1985 . . . . DLB-44
Payn, James 1830-1898 . . . . DLB-18
Payne, John 1842-1916 . . . . DLB-35
Payne, John Howard 1791-1852 . . . . DLB-37
Payson and Clarke DLB-46
Paz, Octavio 1914-1998 . . . . DLB-290; Y-90, 98
  Nobel Lecture 1990 . . . . Y-90
Pazzi, Roberto 1946- DLB-196
Pea, Enrico 1881-1958 . . . . DLB-264
Peabody, Elizabeth Palmer
  1804-1894 . . . . DLB-1, 223
  Preface to *Record of a School:
    Exemplifying the General Principles
    of Spiritual Culture* DS-5

Elizabeth Palmer Peabody
  [publishing house] DLB-49
Peabody, Josephine Preston 1874-1922 . . DLB-249
Peabody, Oliver William Bourn
  1799-1848 . . . . DLB-59
Peace, Roger 1899-1968 . . . . DLB-127
Peacham, Henry 1578-1644? DLB-151
Peacham, Henry, the Elder
  1547-1634 . . . . DLB-172, 236
Peachtree Publishers, Limited DLB-46
Peacock, Molly 1947- DLB-120
Peacock, Thomas Love 1785-1866 . . . DLB-96, 116
Pead, Deuel ?-1727 . . . . DLB-24
Peake, Mervyn 1911-1968 . . . . . DLB-15, 160, 255
Peale, Rembrandt 1778-1860 . . . . DLB-183
Pear Tree Press DLB-112
Pearce, Philippa 1920- DLB-161
H. B. Pearson [publishing house] DLB-49
Pearson, Hesketh 1887-1964 . . . . DLB-149
Peattie, Donald Culross 1898-1964 . . . . . . DLB-275
Pechersky, Andrei (see Mel'nikov, Pavel Ivanovich)
Peck, George W. 1840-1916 . . . . DLB-23, 42
H. C. Peck and Theo. Bliss
  [publishing house] DLB-49
Peck, Harry Thurston 1856-1914 . . . . . DLB-71, 91
Peden, William 1913-1999 . . . . DLB-234
  Tribute to William Goyen Y-83
Peele, George 1556-1596 . . . . DLB-62, 167
Pegler, Westbrook 1894-1969 . . . . DLB-171
Péguy, Charles 1873-1914 . . . . DLB-258
Peirce, Charles Sanders 1839-1914 . . . . . . DLB-270
Pekić, Borislav 1930-1992 . . . DLB-181; CDWLB-4
Pelecanos, George P. 1957- DLB-306
Pelevin, Viktor Olegovich 1962- DLB-285
Pellegrini and Cudahy DLB-46
Pelletier, Aimé (see Vac, Bertrand)
Pelletier, Francine 1959- DLB-251
Pellicer, Carlos 1897?-1977 . . . . DLB-290
Pemberton, Sir Max 1863-1950 . . . . DLB-70
de la Peña, Terri 1947- DLB-209
Penfield, Edward 1866-1925 . . . . DLB-188
Penguin Books [U.K.] DLB-112
  Fifty Penguin Years Y-85
  Penguin Collectors' Society Y-98
Penguin Books [U.S.] DLB-46
Penn, William 1644-1718 . . . . DLB-24
Penn Publishing Company DLB-49
Penna, Sandro 1906-1977 . . . . DLB-114
Pennell, Joseph 1857-1926 . . . . DLB-188
Penner, Jonathan 1940- Y-83
Pennington, Lee 1939- Y-82
Penton, Brian 1904-1951 . . . . DLB-260
Pepper, Stephen C. 1891-1972 . . . . DLB-270
Pepys, Samuel
  1633-1703 . . . . DLB-101, 213; CDBLB-2
Percy, Thomas 1729-1811 . . . . DLB-104

Percy, Walker 1916-1990 . . . . DLB-2; Y-80, 90
    Tribute to Caroline Gordon Y-81
Percy, William 1575-1648 . . . . DLB-172
Perec, Georges 1936-1982 . . . . DLB-83, 299
Perelman, Bob 1947- DLB-193
Perelman, S. J. 1904-1979 . . . . DLB-11, 44
Pérez de Guzmán, Fernán
    ca. 1377-ca. 1460 . . . . DLB-286
Perez, Raymundo "Tigre"
    1946- DLB-122
Peri Rossi, Cristina 1941- DLB-145, 290
Perkins, Eugene 1932- DLB-41
Perkins, Maxwell
    The Claims of Business and Literature:
    An Undergraduate Essay Y-01
Perkins, William 1558-1602 . . . . DLB-281
Perkoff, Stuart Z. 1930-1974 . . . . DLB-16
Perley, Moses Henry 1804-1862 . . . . DLB-99
Permabooks DLB-46
Perovsky, Aleksei Alekseevich
    (Antonii Pogorel'sky) 1787-1836 . . . . . DLB-198
Perrault, Charles 1628-1703 . . . . DLB-268
Perri, Henry 1561-1617 . . . . DLB-236
Perrin, Alice 1867-1934 . . . . DLB-156
Perry, Anne 1938- DLB-276
Perry, Bliss 1860-1954 . . . . DLB-71
Perry, Eleanor 1915-1981 . . . . DLB-44
Perry, Henry (see Perri, Henry)
Perry, Matthew 1794-1858 . . . . DLB-183
Perry, Sampson 1747-1823 . . . . DLB-158
Perse, Saint-John 1887-1975 . . . . DLB-258
Persius A.D. 34-A.D. 62 . . . . DLB-211
Perutz, Leo 1882-1957 . . . . DLB-81
Pesetsky, Bette 1932- DLB-130
Pessanha, Camilo 1867-1926 . . . . DLB-287
Pessoa, Fernando 1888-1935 . . . . DLB-287
Pestalozzi, Johann Heinrich 1746-1827 . . . . DLD-94
Peter, Laurence J. 1919-1990 . . . . DLB-53
Peter of Spain circa 1205-1277 . . . . DLB-115
Peterkin, Julia 1880-1961 . . . . DLB-9
Peters, Ellis (Edith Pargeter)
    1913-1995 . . . . DLB-276
Peters, Lenrie 1932- DLB-117
Peters, Robert 1924- DLB-105
    "Foreword to *Ludwig of Baviria*" DLB-105
Petersham, Maud 1889-1971 and
    Petersham, Miska 1888-1960 . . . . DLB-22
Peterson, Charles Jacobs 1819-1887 . . . . . . DLB-79
Peterson, Len 1917- DLB-88
Peterson, Levi S. 1933- DLB-206
Peterson, Louis 1922-1998 . . . . DLB-76
Peterson, T. B., and Brothers DLB-49
Petitclair, Pierre 1813-1860 . . . . DLB-99
Petrescu, Camil 1894-1957 . . . . DLB-220
Petronius circa A.D. 20-A.D. 66
    . . . . DLB-211; CDWLB-1

Petrov, Aleksandar 1938- DLB-181
Petrov, Evgenii (Evgenii Petrovich Kataev)
    1903-1942 . . . . DLB-272
Petrov, Gavriil 1730-1801 . . . . DLB-150
Petrov, Valeri 1920- DLB-181
Petrov, Vasilii Petrovich 1736-1799 . . . . . . DLB-150
Petrović, Rastko
    1898-1949 . . . . DLB-147; CDWLB-4
Petrushevskaia, Liudmila Stefanovna
    1938- DLB-285
Petruslied circa 854? DLB-148
Petry, Ann 1908-1997 . . . . DLB-76
Pettie, George circa 1548-1589 . . . . DLB-136
Pétur Gunnarsson 1947- DLB-293
Peyton, K. M. 1929- DLB-161
Pfaffe Konrad flourished circa 1172 . . . . . . DLB-148
Pfaffe Lamprecht flourished circa 1150 . . . DLB-148
Pfeiffer, Emily 1827-1890 . . . . DLB-199
Pforzheimer, Carl H. 1879-1957 . . . . DLB-140
Phaedrus circa 18 B.C.-circa A.D. 50 . . . . . DLB-211
Phaer, Thomas 1510?-1560 . . . . DLB-167
Phaidon Press Limited DLB-112
Pharr, Robert Deane 1916-1992 . . . . DLB-33
Phelps, Elizabeth Stuart 1815-1852 . . . . . . DLB-202
Phelps, Elizabeth Stuart 1844-1911 . . . DLB-74, 221
Philander von der Linde
    (see Mencke, Johann Burckhard)
Philby, H. St. John B. 1885-1960 . . . . DLB-195
Philip, Marlene Nourbese 1947- DLB-157
Philippe, Charles-Louis 1874-1909 . . . . DLB-65
Philips, John 1676-1708 . . . . DLB-95
Philips, Katherine 1632-1664 . . . . DLB-131
Phillipps, Sir Thomas 1792-1872 . . . . DLB-184
Phillips, Caryl 1958- DLB-157
Phillips, David Graham
    1867-1911 . . . . DLB-9, 12, 303
Phillips, Jayne Anne 1952- . . . . . . DLB-292; Y 80
    Tribute to Seymour Lawrence Y-94
Phillips, Robert 1938- DLB-105
    "Finding, Losing, Reclaiming: A Note
    on My Poems" DLB-105
    Tribute to William Goyen Y-83
Phillips, Stephen 1864-1915 . . . . DLB-10
Phillips, Ulrich B. 1877-1934 . . . . DLB-17
Phillips, Wendell 1811-1884 . . . . DLB-235
Phillips, Willard 1784-1873 . . . . DLB-59
Phillips, William 1907-2002 . . . . DLB-137
Phillips, Sampson and Company DLB-49
Phillpotts, Adelaide Eden (Adelaide Ross)
    1896-1993 . . . . DLB-191
Phillpotts, Eden 1862-1960 . . DLB-10, 70, 135, 153
Philo circa 20-15 B.C.-circa A.D. 50 . . . . . DLB-176
Philosophical Library DLB-46
Philosophy
    Eighteenth-Century Philosophical
    Background DLB-31
    Philosophic Thought in Boston DLB-235

    Translators of the Twelfth Century:
    Literary Issues Raised and
    Impact Created DLB-115
Elihu Phinney [publishing house] DLB-49
Phoenix, John (see Derby, George Horatio)
PHYLON (Fourth Quarter, 1950),
    The Negro in Literature:
    The Current Scene DLB-76
Physiologus circa 1070-circa 1150 . . . . DLB-148
Piccolo, Lucio 1903-1969 . . . . DLB-114
Pickard, Tom 1946- DLB-40
William Pickering [publishing house] DLB-106
Pickthall, Marjorie 1883-1922 . . . . DLB-92
Picoult, Jodi 1966- DLB-292
Pictorial Printing Company DLB-49
Piel, Gerard 1915- DLB-137
    "An Announcement to Our Readers,"
    Gerard Piel's Statement in *Scientific
    American* (April 1948) DLB-137
Pielmeier, John 1949- DLB-266
Piercy, Marge 1936- DLB-120, 227
Pierro, Albino 1916-1995 . . . . DLB-128
Pignotti, Lamberto 1926- DLB-128
Pike, Albert 1809-1891 . . . . DLB-74
Pike, Zebulon Montgomery 1779-1813 . . . DLB-183
Pillat, Ion 1891-1945 . . . . DLB-220
Pil'niak, Boris Andreevich (Boris Andreevich
    Vogau) 1894-1938 . . . . DLB-272
Pilon, Jean-Guy 1930- DLB-60
Pinar, Florencia fl. ca. late
    fifteenth century DLB-286
Pinckney, Eliza Lucas 1722-1793 . . . . DLB-200
Pinckney, Josephine 1895-1957 . . . . DLB-6
Pindar circa 518 B.C.-circa 438 B.C.
    . . . . DLB-176; CDWLB-1
Pindar, Peter (see Wolcot, John)
Pineda, Cecile 1942- DLB-209
Pinero, Arthur Wing 1855-1934 . . . . DLB-10
Piñero, Miguel 1946-1988 . . . . DLB-266
Pinget, Robert 1919-1997 . . . . DLB-83
Pinkney, Edward Coote 1802-1828 . . . . . . DLB-248
Pinnacle Books DLB-46
Piñon, Nélida 1935- DLB-145, 307
Pinsky, Robert 1940- Y-82
    Reappointed Poet Laureate Y-98
Pinter, Harold 1930- . . . DLB-13, 310; CDBLB-8
    Writing for the Theatre DLB-13
Pinto, Fernão Mendes 1509/1511?-1583 . . DLB-287
Piontek, Heinz 1925- DLB-75
Piozzi, Hester Lynch [Thrale]
    1741-1821 . . . . DLB-104, 142
Piper, H. Beam 1904-1964 . . . . DLB-8
Piper, Watty DLB-22
Pirandello, Luigi 1867-1936 . . . . DLB-264
Pirckheimer, Caritas 1467-1532 . . . . DLB-179
Pirckheimer, Willibald 1470-1530 . . . . DLB-179
Pires, José Cardoso 1925-1998 . . . . DLB-287

Pisar, Samuel 1929- Y-83

Pisarev, Dmitrii Ivanovich 1840-1868 ....DLB-277

Pisemsky, Aleksei Feofilaktovich
  1821-1881 .... DLB-238

Pitkin, Timothy 1766-1847 .... DLB-30

Pitter, Ruth 1897- DLB-20

Pix, Mary 1666-1709 .... DLB-80

Pixerécourt, René Charles Guilbert de
  1773-1844 .... DLB-192

Pizarnik, Alejandra 1936-1972 .... DLB-283

Plá, Josefina 1909-1999 .... DLB-290

Plaatje, Sol T. 1876-1932 .... DLB-125, 225

Plante, David 1940- Y-83

Platen, August von 1796-1835 .... DLB-90

Plantinga, Alvin 1932- DLB-279

Plath, Sylvia
  1932-1963 .... DLB-5, 6, 152; CDALB-1

Plato circa 428 B.C.-348-347 B.C.
  ....DLB-176; CDWLB-1

Plato, Ann 1824?-? DLB-239

Platon 1737-1812 .... DLB-150

Platonov, Andrei Platonovich (Andrei
  Platonovich Klimentev) 1899-1951 .. DLB-272

Platt, Charles 1945- DLB-261

Platt and Munk Company DLB-46

Plautus circa 254 B.C.-184 B.C.
  .... DLB-211; CDWLB-1

Playboy Press DLB-46

John Playford [publishing house] DLB-170

Der Pleier flourished circa 1250 .... DLB-138

Pleijel, Agneta 1940- DLB-257

Plenzdorf, Ulrich 1934- DLB-75

Pleshcheev, Aleksei Nikolaevich
  1825?-1893 ....DLB-277

Plessen, Elizabeth 1944- DLB-75

Pletnev, Petr Aleksandrovich
  1792-1865 .... DLB-205

Pliekšāne, Elza Rozenberga (see Aspazija)

Pliekšāns, Jānis (see Rainis, Jānis)

Plievier, Theodor 1892-1955 .... DLB-69

Plimpton, George 1927-2003...DLB-185, 241; Y-99

Pliny the Elder A.D. 23/24-A.D. 79 ...... DLB-211

Pliny the Younger
  circa A.D. 61-A.D. 112 .... DLB-211

Plomer, William
  1903-1973 .... DLB-20, 162, 191, 225

Plotinus 204-270 ....DLB-176; CDWLB-1

Plowright, Teresa 1952- DLB-251

Plume, Thomas 1630-1704 .... DLB-213

Plumly, Stanley 1939- DLB-5, 193

Plumpp, Sterling D. 1940- DLB-41

Plunkett, James 1920- DLB-14

Plutarch
  circa 46-circa 120 ....DLB-176; CDWLB-1

Plymell, Charles 1935- DLB-16

Pocket Books DLB-46

Podestá, José J. 1858-1937 .... DLB-305

Poe, Edgar Allan 1809-1849
  .... DLB-3, 59, 73, 74, 248; CDALB-2

The Poe Studies Association Y-99

Poe, James 1921-1980................. DLB-44

The Poet Laureate of the United States Y-86

Statements from Former Consultants
  in Poetry Y-86

Poetry
  Aesthetic Poetry (1873) DLB-35

  A Century of Poetry, a Lifetime of
    Collecting: J. M. Edelstein's
    Collection of Twentieth-
    Century American Poetry Y-02

  "Certain Gifts," by Betty Adcock.... DLB-105

  Concrete Poetry................. DLB-307

  Contempo Caravan: Kites in a
    Windstorm Y-85

  "Contemporary Verse Story-telling,"
    by Jonathan Holden DLB-105

  "A Detail in a Poem," by Fred
    Chappell DLB-105

  "The English Renaissance of Art"
    (1908), by Oscar Wilde......... DLB-35

  "Every Man His Own Poet; or,
    The Inspired Singer's Recipe
    Book" (1877), by
    H. W. Mallock DLB-35

  "Eyes Across Centuries: Contemporary
    Poetry and 'That Vision Thing,'"
    by Philip Dacey DLB-105

  A Field Guide to Recent Schools
    of American Poetry Y-86

  "Finding, Losing, Reclaiming:
    A Note on My Poems,
    by Robert Phillips" DLB-105

  "The Fleshly School of Poetry and Other
    Phenomena of the Day" (1872) ... DLB-35

  "The Fleshly School of Poetry:
    Mr. D. G. Rossetti" (1871) DLB-35

  The G. Ross Roy Scottish Poetry Collection
    at the University of South Carolina .. Y-89

  "Getting Started: Accepting the Regions
    You Own–or Which Own You,"
    by Walter McDonald DLB-105

  "The Good, The Not So Good," by
    Stephen Dunn DLB-105

  The Griffin Poetry Prize Y-00

  The Hero as Poet. Dante; Shakspeare
    (1841), by Thomas Carlyle...... DLB-32

  "Images and 'Images,'" by Charles
    Simic DLB-105

  "Into the Mirror," by Peter Cooley .. DLB-105

  "Knots into Webs: Some Autobiographical
    Sources," by Dabney Stuart..... DLB-105

  "L'Envoi" (1882), by Oscar Wilde ... DLB-35

  "Living in Ruin," by Gerald Stern ... DLB-105

  Looking for the Golden Mountain:
    Poetry Reviewing Y-89

  Lyric Poetry (French) DLB-268

  Medieval Galician-Portuguese
    Poetry DLB-287

  "The No Self, the Little Self, and the
    Poets," by Richard Moore...... DLB-105

  On Some of the Characteristics of Modern
    Poetry and On the Lyrical Poems of
    Alfred Tennyson (1831) DLB-32

  The Pitt Poetry Series: Poetry Publishing
    Today Y-85

  "The Poetry File," by Edward
    Field...................... DLB-105

  Poetry in Nineteenth-Century France:
    Cultural Background and Critical
    Commentary.................DLB-217

  The Poetry of Jorge Luis Borges Y-86

  "The Poet's Kaleidoscope: The Element
    of Surprise in the Making of the
    Poem" by Madeline DeFrees.... DLB-105

  The Pre-Raphaelite Controversy DLB-35

  Protest Poetry in Castile DLB-286

  "Reflections: After a Tornado,"
    by Judson Jerome DLB-105

  Statements from Former Consultants
    in Poetry Y-86

  Statements on the Art of Poetry...... DLB-54

  The Study of Poetry (1880), by
    Matthew Arnold DLB-35

  A Survey of Poetry Anthologies,
    1879-1960 .... DLB-54

  Thoughts on Poetry and Its Varieties
    (1833), by John Stuart Mill DLB-32

  Under the Microscope (1872), by
    A. C. Swinburne DLB-35

  The Unterberg Poetry Center of the
    92nd Street Y.................... Y-98

  Victorian Poetry: Five Critical
    Views DLBV-35

  Year in Poetry Y-83–92, 94–01

  Year's Work in American Poetry........ Y-82

Poets
  The Lives of the Poets (1753) DLB-142

  Minor Poets of the Earlier
    Seventeenth Century.......... DLB-121

  Other British Poets Who Fell
    in the Great War............. DLB-216

  Other Poets [French] DLB-217

  Second-Generation Minor Poets of
    the Seventeenth Century....... DLB-126

  Third-Generation Minor Poets of
    the Seventeenth Century....... DLB-131

Pogodin, Mikhail Petrovich 1800-1875... DLB-198

Pogorel'sky, Antonii
  (see Perovsky, Aleksei Alekseevich)

Pohl, Frederik 1919- DLB-8

  Tribute to Isaac Asimov................ Y-92

  Tribute to Theodore Sturgeon.......... Y-85

Poirier, Louis (see Gracq, Julien)

Poláček, Karel 1892-1945....DLB-215; CDWLB-4

Polanyi, Michael 1891-1976 .... DLB-100

Pole, Reginald 1500-1558............. DLB-132

Polevoi, Nikolai Alekseevich 1796-1846.. DLB-198

Polezhaev, Aleksandr Ivanovich
  1804-1838 .... DLB-205

Poliakoff, Stephen 1952- DLB-13

Polidori, John William 1795-1821 ..... DLB-116

Polite, Carlene Hatcher 1932- DLB-33

Pollard, Alfred W. 1859-1944 . . . . .DLB-201

Pollard, Edward A. 1832-1872. . . . . .DLB-30

Pollard, Graham 1903-1976. . . . . .DLB-201

Pollard, Percival 1869-1911 . . . . .DLB-71

Pollard and Moss. .DLB-49

Pollock, Sharon 1936- DLB-60

Polonsky, Abraham 1910-1999 . . . . .DLB-26

Polonsky, Iakov Petrovich 1819-1898. . . . .DLB-277

Polotsky, Simeon 1629-1680 . . . . .DLB-150

Polybius circa 200 B.C.-118 B.C. DLB-176

Pomialovsky, Nikolai Gerasimovich
1835-1863 . . . . .DLB-238

Pomilio, Mario 1921-1990 . . . . .DLB-177

Pompéia, Raul (Raul d'Avila Pompéia)
1863-1895 . . . . .DLB-307

Ponce, Mary Helen 1938- DLB-122

Ponce-Montoya, Juanita 1949- DLB-122

Ponet, John 1516?-1556. . . . . .DLB-132

Ponge, Francis 1899-1988 . . . . .DLB-258; Y-02

Poniatowska, Elena
1933- DLB-113; CDWLB-3

Ponsard, François 1814-1867 . . . . .DLB-192

William Ponsonby [publishing house] DLB-170

Pontiggia, Giuseppe 1934- DLB-196

Pontoppidan, Henrik 1857-1943 . . . . .DLB-300

Pony Stories, Omnibus Essay on DLB-160

Poole, Ernest 1880-1950 . . . . .DLB-9

Poole, Sophia 1804-1891 . . . . .DLB-166

Poore, Benjamin Perley 1820-1887 . . . . . . .DLB-23

Popa, Vasko 1922-1991 . . . . . .DLB-181; CDWLB-4

Pope, Abbie Hanscom 1858-1894 . . . . . . .DLB-140

Pope, Alexander
1688-1744 . . . . . .DLB-95, 101, 213; CDBLB-2

Popov, Aleksandr Serafimovich
(see Serafimovich, Aleksandr Serafimovich)

Popov, Evgenii Anatol'evich 1946- DLB-285

Popov, Mikhail Ivanovich
1742-circa 1790 . . . . .DLB-150

Popović, Aleksandar 1929-1996. . . . . .DLB-181

Popper, Karl 1902-1994. . . . . .DLB-262

Popular Culture Association/
American Culture Association. Y-99

Popular Library. DLB-46

Poquelin, Jean-Baptiste (see Molière)

Porete, Marguerite ?-1310 . . . . .DLB-208

Porlock, Martin (see MacDonald, Philip)

Porpoise Press DLB-112

Porta, Antonio 1935-1989 . . . . .DLB-128

Porter, Anna Maria 1780-1832. . . . . .DLB-116, 159

Porter, Cole 1891-1964 . . . . .DLB-265

Porter, David 1780-1843 . . . . .DLB-183

Porter, Eleanor H. 1868-1920 . . . . .DLB-9

Porter, Gene Stratton (see Stratton-Porter, Gene)

Porter, Hal 1911-1984 . . . . .DLB-260

Porter, Henry ?-? DLB-62

Porter, Jane 1776-1850 . . . . .DLB-116, 159

Porter, Katherine Anne 1890-1980
. . . . . . .DLB-4, 9, 102; Y-80; DS-12; CDALB-7

The Katherine Anne Porter Society Y-01

Porter, Peter 1929- DLB-40, 289

Porter, William Sydney (O. Henry)
1862-1910 . . . . .DLB-12, 78, 79; CDALB-3

Porter, William T. 1809-1858 . . . . .DLB-3, 43, 250

Porter and Coates DLB-49

Portillo Trambley, Estela 1927-1998 . . . . .DLB-209

Portis, Charles 1933- DLB-6

Medieval Galician-Portuguese Poetry DLB-287

Posey, Alexander 1873-1908 . . . . .DLB-175

Postans, Marianne circa 1810-1865. . . . . . .DLB-166

Postgate, Raymond 1896-1971. . . . . .DLB-276

Postl, Carl (see Sealsfield, Carl)

Postmodern Holocaust Fiction. DLB-299

Poston, Ted 1906-1974 . . . . .DLB-51

Potekhin, Aleksei Antipovich
1829-1908 . . . . .DLB-238

Potok, Chaim 1929-2002. . . . . .DLB-28, 152

A Conversation with Chaim Potok. Y-84

Tribute to Bernard Malamud Y-86

Potter, Beatrix 1866-1943 . . . . .DLB-141

The Beatrix Potter Society Y-98

Potter, David M. 1910-1971 . . . . .DLB-17

Potter, Dennis 1935-1994 . . . . .DLB-233

John E. Potter and Company. DLB-49

Pottle, Frederick A. 1897-1987 . . . . .DLB-103; Y-87

Poulin, Jacques 1937- DLB-60

Pound, Ezra 1885-1972
. . . . .DLB-4, 45, 63; DS-15; CDALB-4

The Cost of the Cantos: William Bird
to Ezra Pound. Y-01

The Ezra Pound Society Y-01

Poverman, C. E. 1944- DLB-234

Povey, Meic 1950- DLB-310

Povich, Shirley 1905-1998 . . . . .DLB-171

Powell, Anthony 1905-2000 . . .DLB-15; CDBLB-7

The Anthony Powell Society: Powell and
the First Biennial Conference Y-01

Powell, Dawn 1897-1965
Dawn Powell, Where Have You Been
All Our Lives? Y-97

Powell, John Wesley 1834-1902 . . . . .DLB-186

Powell, Padgett 1952- DLB-234

Powers, J. F. 1917-1999 . . . . .DLB-130

Powers, Jimmy 1903-1995. . . . . .DLB-241

Pownall, David 1938- DLB-14

Powys, John Cowper 1872-1963 . . . . .DLB-15, 255

Powys, Llewelyn 1884-1939 . . . . .DLB-98

Powys, T. F. 1875-1953 . . . . .DLB-36, 162

The Powys Society Y-98

Poynter, Nelson 1903-1978 . . . . .DLB-127

Prado, Adélia 1935- DLB-307

Prado, Pedro 1886-1952 . . . . .DLB-283

Prados, Emilio 1899-1962 . . . . .DLB-134

Praed, Mrs. Caroline (see Praed, Rosa)

Praed, Rosa (Mrs. Caroline Praed)
1851-1935 . . . . .DLB-230

Praed, Winthrop Mackworth 1802-1839. . .DLB-96

Praeger Publishers DLB-46

Praetorius, Johannes 1630-1680. . . . . .DLB-168

Pratolini, Vasco 1913-1991 . . . . .DLB-177

Pratt, E. J. 1882-1964. . . . . .DLB-92

Pratt, Samuel Jackson 1749-1814 . . . . .DLB-39

Preciado Martin, Patricia 1939- DLB-209

Préfontaine, Yves 1937- DLB-53

Prelutsky, Jack 1940- DLB-61

Prentice, George D. 1802-1870 . . . . .DLB-43

Prentice-Hall DLB-46

Prescott, Orville 1906-1996. . . . . Y-96

Prescott, William Hickling
1796-1859 . . . . .DLB-1, 30, 59, 235

Prešeren, Francè
1800-1849 . . . . .DLB-147; CDWLB-4

Presses (See also Publishing)
Small Presses in Great Britain and
Ireland, 1960-1985 . . . . .DLB-40

Small Presses I: Jargon Society Y-84

Small Presses II: The Spirit That Moves
Us Press Y-85

Small Presses III: Pushcart Press Y-87

Preston, Margaret Junkin
1820-1897 . . . . .DLB-239, 248

Preston, May Wilson 1873-1949 . . . . .DLB-188

Preston, Thomas 1537-1598 . . . . .DLB-62

Prévert, Jacques 1900-1977 . . . . .DLB-258

Price, Anthony 1928- DLB-276

Price, Reynolds 1933- DLB-2, 218, 278

Price, Richard 1723-1791 . . . . .DLB-158

Price, Richard 1949- Y-81

Prichard, Katharine Susannah
1883-1969 . . . . .DLB-260

Prideaux, John 1578-1650 . . . . .DLB-236

Priest, Christopher 1943- . . . . . DLB 14, 207, 261

Priestley, J. B. 1894-1984
. . . .DLB-10, 34, 77, 100, 139; Y-84; CDBLB-6

Priestley, Joseph 1733-1804 . . . . .DLB-252

Prigov, Dmitrii Aleksandrovich 1940- . . .DLB-285

Prime, Benjamin Young 1733-1791 . . . . . .DLB-31

Primrose, Diana floruit circa 1630. . . . . . .DLB-126

Prince, F. T. 1912- DLB-20

Prince, Nancy Gardner 1799-? DLB-239

Prince, Thomas 1687-1758 . . . . .DLB-24, 140

Pringle, Thomas 1789-1834 . . . . .DLB-225

Printz, Wolfgang Casper 1641-1717. . . . . .DLB-168

Prior, Matthew 1664-1721 . . . . .DLB-95

Prisco, Michele 1920- DLB-177

Prishvin, Mikhail Mikhailovich
1873-1954 . . . . .DLB-272

Pritchard, William H. 1932- DLB-111

Pritchett, V. S. 1900-1997 . . . . .DLB-15, 139

Probyn, May 1856 or 1857-1909. . . . . . . .DLB-199

Procter, Adelaide Anne 1825-1864 . . .DLB-32, 199

Cumulative Index

Procter, Bryan Waller 1787-1874 .... DLB-96, 144
Proctor, Robert 1868-1903............ DLB-184
Prokopovich, Feofan 1681?-1736 .... DLB-150
Prokosch, Frederic 1906-1989 .... DLB-48
Pronzini, Bill 1943- DLB-226
Propertius circa 50 B.C.-post 16 B.C.
.... DLB-211; CDWLB-1
Propper, Dan 1937- DLB-16
Prose, Francine 1947- DLB-234
Protagoras circa 490 B.C.-420 B.C. DLB-176
Protest Poetry in Castile
ca. 1445-ca. 1506 .... DLB-286
Proud, Robert 1728-1813 .... DLB-30
Proust, Marcel 1871-1922............. DLB-65
   Marcel Proust at 129 and the Proust
     Society of America............... Y-00
   Marcel Proust's *Remembrance of Things Past*:
     The Rediscovered Galley Proofs..... Y-00
Prutkov, Koz'ma Petrovich
1803-1863 .... DLB-277
Prynne, J. H. 1936- DLB-40
Przybyszewski, Stanislaw 1868-1927 ..... DLB-66
Pseudo-Dionysius the Areopagite floruit
circa 500....................... DLB-115
Public Lending Right in America
   PLR and the Meaning of Literary
     Property....................... Y-83
   Statement by Sen. Charles
     McC. Mathias, Jr. PLR Y-83
   Statements on PLR by American Writers ... Y-83
Public Lending Right in the United Kingdom
   The First Year in the United Kingdom ... Y-83
Publishers [listed by individual names]
   Publishers, Conversations with:
     An Interview with Charles Scribner III... Y-94
     An Interview with Donald Lamm Y-95
     An Interview with James Laughlin....... Y-96
     An Interview with Patrick O'Connor Y-84
Publishing
   The Art and Mystery of Publishing:
     Interviews Y-97
   Book Publishing Accounting: Some Basic
     Concepts Y-98
   1873 Publishers' Catalogues......... DLB-49
   The Literary Scene 2002: Publishing, Book
     Reviewing, and Literary Journalism ... Y-02
   Main Trends in Twentieth-Century
     Book Clubs DLB-46
   Overview of U.S. Book Publishing,
     1910-1945 .... DLB-9
   The Pitt Poetry Series: Poetry Publishing
     Today Y-85
   Publishing Fiction at LSU Press........ Y-87
   The Publishing Industry in 1998:
     Sturm-und-drang.com.............. Y-98
   The Publishing Industry in 1999 .... Y-99
   Publishers and Agents: The Columbia
     Connection Y-87
   Responses to Ken Auletta Y-97
   Southern Writers Between the Wars ... DLB-9
   The State of Publishing Y-97
   Trends in Twentieth-Century
     Mass Market Publishing DLB-46
   The Year in Book Publishing.......... Y-86
Pückler-Muskau, Hermann von
1785-1871 .... DLB-133
Pufendorf, Samuel von 1632-1694 ...... DLB-168
Pugh, Edwin William 1874-1930 .... DLB-135
Pugin, A. Welby 1812-1852 .... DLB-55
Puig, Manuel 1932-1990.....DLB-113; CDWLB-3
Pulgar, Hernando del (Fernando del Pulgar)
ca. 1436-ca. 1492 .... DLB-286
Pulitzer, Joseph 1847-1911 .... DLB-23
Pulitzer, Joseph, Jr. 1885-1955 .... DLB-29
Pulitzer Prizes for the Novel, 1917-1945.... DLB-9
Pulliam, Eugene 1889-1975............ DLB-127
Purcell, Deirdre 1945- DLB-267
Purchas, Samuel 1577?-1626........... DLB-151
Purdy, Al 1918-2000................. DLB-88
Purdy, James 1923- DLB-2, 218
Purdy, Ken W. 1913-1972 .... DLB-137
Pusey, Edward Bouverie 1800-1882...... DLB-55
Pushkin, Aleksandr Sergeevich
1799-1837..................... DLB-205
Pushkin, Vasilii L'vovich
1766-1830..................... DLB-205
Putnam, George Palmer
1814-1872............DLB-3, 79, 250, 254
G. P. Putnam [publishing house] DLB-254
G. P. Putnam's Sons [U.K.] DLB-106
G. P. Putnam's Sons [U.S.]............. DLB-49
   A Publisher's Archives: G. P. Putnam Y-92
Putnam, Hilary 1926- DLB-279
Putnam, Samuel 1892-1950 .... DLB-4; DS-15
Puttenham, George 1529?-1590 .... DLB-281
Puzo, Mario 1920-1999 .... DLB-6
Pyle, Ernie 1900-1945................. DLB-29
Pyle, Howard
1853-1911 .... DLB-42, 188; DS-13
Pyle, Robert Michael 1947- DLB-275
Pym, Barbara 1913-1980 ......DLB-14, 207; Y-87
Pynchon, Thomas 1937- DLB-2, 173
Pyramid Books..................... DLB-46
Pyrnelle, Louise-Clarke 1850-1907....... DLB-42
Pythagoras circa 570 B.C.-? DLB-176

Q

Qays ibn al-Mulawwah circa 680-710.... DLB-311
Quad, M. (see Lewis, Charles B.)
Quaritch, Bernard 1819-1899........... DLB-184
Quarles, Francis 1592-1644 .... DLB-126
The Quarterly Review 1809-1967 .... DLB-110
Quasimodo, Salvatore 1901-1968....... DLB-114
Queen, Ellery (see Dannay, Frederic, and
Manfred B. Lee)
Queen, Frank 1822-1882 .... DLB-241
The Queen City Publishing House DLB-49
Queirós, Eça de 1845-1900............ DLB-287
Queneau, Raymond 1903-1976 ..... DLB-72, 258
Quennell, Peter 1905-1993......... DLB-155, 195
Quental, Antero de
1842-1891 .... DLB-287
Quesada, José Luis 1948- DLB-290
Quesnel, Joseph 1746-1809............. DLB-99
Quiller-Couch, Sir Arthur Thomas
1863-1944 ....DLB-135, 153, 190
Quin, Ann 1936-1973............. DLB-14, 231
Quinault, Philippe 1635-1688 ....DLB-268
Quincy, Samuel, of Georgia ?-? DLB-31
Quincy, Samuel, of Massachusetts
1734-1789.................... DLB-31
Quindlen, Anna 1952- DLB-292
Quine, W. V. 1908-2000 ....DLB-279
Quinn, Anthony 1915-2001 .... DLB-122
Quinn, John 1870-1924................DLB-187
Quiñónez, Naomi 1951- DLB-209
Quintana, Leroy V. 1944- DLB-82
Quintana, Miguel de 1671-1748
   A Forerunner of Chicano
     Literature.................... DLB-122
Quintilian
circa A.D. 40-circa A.D. 96 .... DLB-211
Quintus Curtius Rufus
fl. A.D. 35 .... DLB-211
Harlin Quist Books.................... DLB-46
Quoirez, Françoise (see Sagan, Françoise)

R

Raabe, Wilhelm 1831-1910 .... DLB-129
Raban, Jonathan 1942- DLB-204
Rabe, David 1940- DLB-7, 228; Y-91
Rabi'ah al-'Adawiyyah circa 720-801 .... DLB-311
Raboni, Giovanni 1932- DLB-128
Rachilde 1860-1953 .... DLB-123, 192
Racin, Kočo 1908-1943 ....DLB-147
Racine, Jean 1639-1699................DLB-268
Rackham, Arthur 1867-1939 .... DLB-141
Raczymow, Henri 1948- DLB-299
Radauskas, Henrikas
1910-1970............ DLB-220; CDWLB-4
Radcliffe, Ann 1764-1823 ....DLB-39, 178
Raddall, Thomas 1903-1994 .... DLB-68
Radford, Dollie 1858-1920............ DLB-240
Radichkov, Yordan 1929- DLB-181
Radiguet, Raymond 1903-1923 .... DLB-65
Radishchev, Aleksandr Nikolaevich
1749-1802..................... DLB-150
Radnóti, Miklós
1909-1944 ....DLB-215; CDWLB-4
Radrigán, Juan 1937- DLB-305
Radványi, Netty Reiling (see Seghers, Anna)
Rahv, Philip 1908-1973 ....DLB-137
Raich, Semen Egorovich 1792-1855..... DLB-205
Raičković, Stevan 1928- DLB-181
Raiderman (see Parshchikov, Aleksei Maksimovich)

Raimund, Ferdinand Jakob 1790-1836.....DLB-90
Raine, Craig 1944- DLB-40
Raine, Kathleen 1908- DLB-20
Rainis, Jānis 1865-1929 .....DLB-220; CDWLB-4
Rainolde, Richard
  circa 1530-1606..............DLB-136, 236
Rainolds, John 1549-1607 ....DLB-281
Rakić, Milan 1876-1938.....DLB-147; CDWLB-4
Rakosi, Carl 1903- DLB-193
Ralegh, Sir Walter
  1554?-1618 ....DLB-172; CDBLB-1
Raleigh, Walter
  Style (1897) [excerpt] DLB-57
Ralin, Radoy 1923- DLB-181
Ralph, Julian 1853-1903................DLB-23
Ramat, Silvio 1939-..................DLB-128
Ramée, Marie Louise de la (see Ouida)
Ramírez, Sergío 1942- DLB-145
Ramke, Bin 1947- DLB-120
Ramler, Karl Wilhelm 1725-1798.........DLB-97
Ramon Ribeyro, Julio 1929-1994 ....DLB-145
Ramos, Graciliano 1892-1953 ....DLB-307
Ramos, Manuel 1948- DLB-209
Ramos Sucre, José Antonio 1890-1930 ...DLB-290
Ramous, Mario 1924-..................DLB-128
Rampersad, Arnold 1941- DLB-111
Ramsay, Allan 1684 or 1685-1758........DLB-95
Ramsay, David 1749-1815...............DLB-30
Ramsay, Martha Laurens 1759-1811.....DLB-200
Ramsey, Frank P. 1903-1930............DLB-262
Ranch, Hieronimus Justesen
  1539-1607........................DLB-300
Ranck, Katherine Quintana 1942- DLB-122
Rand, Avery and Company.............DLB-49
Rand, Ayn 1905-1982 ... DLB-227, 279; CDALB-7
Rand McNally and Company DLB-49
Randall, David Anton 1905-1975.......DLB-140
Randall, Dudley 1914- DLB-41
Randall, Henry S. 1811-1876............DLB-30
Randall, James G. 1881-1953 ....DLB-17
The Randall Jarrell Symposium: A Small
  Collection of Randall Jarrells Y-86
Excerpts From Papers Delivered at the
  Randall Jarrel Symposium Y-86
Randall, John Herman, Jr. 1899-1980 ....DLB-279
Randolph, A. Philip 1889-1979 ....DLB-91
Anson D. F. Randolph
  [publishing house]...............DLB-49
Randolph, Thomas 1605-1635 ......DLB-58, 126
Random House DLB-46
Rankin, Ian (Jack Harvey) 1960- DLB-267
Henry Ranlet [publishing house] DLB-49
Ransom, Harry 1908-1976..............DLB-187
Ransom, John Crowe
  1888-1974 ....DLB-45, 63; CDALB-7
Ransome, Arthur 1884-1967 ....DLB-160
Raphael, Frederic 1931- DLB-14

Raphaelson, Samson 1896-1983 ....DLB-44
Rare Book Dealers
  Bertram Rota and His Bookshop Y-91
  An Interview with Glenn Horowitz Y-90
  An Interview with Otto Penzler Y-96
  An Interview with Ralph Sipper Y-94
  New York City Bookshops in the
    1930s and 1940s: The Recollections
    of Walter Goldwater.............Y-93
Rare Books
  Research in the American Antiquarian
    Book Trade Y-97
  Two Hundred Years of Rare Books and
    Literary Collections at the
    University of South Carolina Y-00
Rascón Banda, Víctor Hugo 1948- DLB-305
Rashi circa 1040-1105 ....DLB-208
Raskin, Ellen 1928-1984 ....DLB-52
Rasputin, Valentin Grigor'evich
  1937- DLB-302
Rastell, John 1475?-1536 .... DLB-136, 170
Rattigan, Terence
  1911-1977 ....DLB-13; CDBLB-7
Raven, Simon 1927-2001 .... DLB-271
Ravenhill, Mark 1966- DLB-310
Ravnkilde, Adda 1862-1883 ....DLB-300
Rawicz, Piotr 1919-1982 ....DLB-299
Rawlings, Marjorie Kinnan 1896-1953
  ....DLB-9, 22, 102; DS-17; CDALB-7
Rawlinson, Richard 1690-1755 ....DLB-213
Rawlinson, Thomas 1681-1725 ....DLB-213
Rawls, John 1921-2002 ....DLB-279
Raworth, Tom 1938- DLB-40
Ray, David 1932- DLB-5
Ray, Gordon Norton 1915-1986 ....DLB-103, 140
Ray, Henrietta Cordelia 1849-1916.......DLB-50
Raymond, Ernest 1888-1974 ....DLB-191
Raymond, Henry J. 1820-1869 .... DLB-43, 79
Raymond, René (see Chase, James Hadley)
Razaf, Andy 1895-1973 ....DLB-265
al-Razi 865?-925?......................DLB-311
Rea, Michael 1927-1996................ Y-97
  Michael M. Rea and the Rea Award for
    the Short Story Y-97
Reach, Angus 1821-1856 ....DLB-70
Read, Herbert 1893-1968 ....DLB-20, 149
Read, Martha Meredith.................DLB-200
Read, Opie 1852-1939..................DLB-23
Read, Piers Paul 1941- DLB-14
Reade, Charles 1814-1884...............DLB-21
Reader's Digest Condensed Books DLB-46
Readers Ulysses Symposium Y-97
Reading, Peter 1946- DLB-40
Reading Series in New York City Y-96
Reaney, James 1926- DLB-68
Rebhun, Paul 1500?-1546 ....DLB-179
Rèbora, Clemente 1885-1957 ....DLB-114
Rebreanu, Liviu 1885-1944............DLB-220

Rechy, John 1931- DLB-122, 278; Y-82
Redding, J. Saunders 1906-1988 ...... DLB-63, 76
J. S. Redfield [publishing house] DLB-49
Redgrove, Peter 1932- DLB-40
Redmon, Anne 1943- Y-86
Redmond, Eugene B. 1937- DLB-41
Redol, Alves 1911-1969................DLB-287
James Redpath [publishing house]........DLB-49
Reed, Henry 1808-1854................DLB-59
Reed, Henry 1914-1986................DLB-27
Reed, Ishmael
  1938- DLB-2, 5, 33, 169, 227; DS-8
Reed, Rex 1938- DLB-185
Reed, Sampson 1800-1880..........DLB-1, 235
Reed, Talbot Baines 1852-1893.........DLB-141
Reedy, William Marion 1862-1920.......DLB-91
Reese, Lizette Woodworth 1856-1935.....DLB-54
Reese, Thomas 1742-1796 ....DLB-37
Reeve, Clara 1729-1807................DLB-39
  Preface to *The Old English Baron*
    (1778) DLB-39
  The Progress of Romance (1785)
    [excerpt] DLB-39
Reeves, James 1909-1978...............DLB-161
Reeves, John 1926- DLB-88
Reeves-Stevens, Garfield 1953- DLB-251
Régio, José (José Maria dos Reis Pereira)
  1901-1969 ....DLB-287
Henry Regnery Company DLB-46
Rêgo, José Lins do 1901-1957 ....DLB-307
Rehberg, Hans 1901-1963...............DLB-124
Rehfisch, Hans José 1891-1960 ....DLB-124
Reich, Ebbe Kløvedal 1940- DLB-214
Reid, Alastair 1926- DLB-27
Reid, B. L. 1918-1990 ....DLB-111
Reid, Christopher 1949- DLB-40
Reid, Forrest 1875-1947................DLB-153
Reid, Helen Rogers 1882-1970 ....DLB-29
Reid, James ?-?........................DLB-31
Reid, Mayne 1818-1883.............DLB-21, 163
Reid, Thomas 1710-1796............DLB-31, 252
Reid, V. S. (Vic) 1913-1987.............DLB-125
Reid, Whitelaw 1837-1912...............DLB-23
Reilly and Lee Publishing Company......DLB-46
Reimann, Brigitte 1933-1973 ....DLB-75
Reinmar der Alte circa 1165-circa 1205...DLB-138
Reinmar von Zweter
  circa 1200-circa 1250................DLB-138
Reisch, Walter 1903-1983 ....DLB-44
Reizei Family.........................DLB-203
Religion
  A Crisis of Culture: The Changing
    Role of Religion in the
    New Republic...................DLB-37
Remarque, Erich Maria
  1898-1970 ....DLB-56; CDWLB-2

Remington, Frederic 1861-1909 .... DLB-12, 186, 188

Remizov, Aleksei Mikhailovich 1877-1957 .... DLB-295

Renaud, Jacques 1943- DLB-60

Renault, Mary 1905-1983................. Y-83

Rendell, Ruth (Barbara Vine) 1930- DLB-87, 276

Rensselaer, Maria van Cortlandt van 1645-1689 .... DLB-200

Repplier, Agnes 1855-1950........... DLB-221

Reshetnikov, Fedor Mikhailovich 1841-1871..................... DLB-238

Rettenbacher, Simon 1634-1706 .... DLB-168

Retz, Jean-François-Paul de Gondi, cardinal de 1613-1679 .... DLB-268

Reuchlin, Johannes 1455-1522 ....DLB-179

Reuter, Christian 1665-after 1712....... DLB-168

Fleming H. Revell Company DLB-49

Reverdy, Pierre 1889-1960........... DLB-258

Reuter, Fritz 1810-1874............. DLB-129

Reuter, Gabriele 1859-1941 .... DLB-66

Reventlow, Franziska Gräfin zu 1871-1918..................... DLB-66

Review of Reviews Office............ DLB-112

Rexroth, Kenneth 1905-1982 ....DLB-16, 48, 165, 212; Y-82; CDALB-1

The Commercialization of the Image of Revolt DLB-16

Rey, H. A. 1898-1977................. DLB-22

Reyes, Carlos José 1941- DLB-305

Reynal and Hitchcock DLB-46

Reynolds, G. W. M. 1814-1879 .... DLB-21

Reynolds, John Hamilton 1794-1852..................... DLB-96

Reynolds, Sir Joshua 1723-1792 .... DLB-104

Reynolds, Mack 1917-1983.............. DLB-8

Reznikoff, Charles 1894-1976........ DLB-28, 45

Rhetoric
Continental European Rhetoricians, 1400-1600, and Their Influence in Reaissance England DLB-236

A Finding Guide to Key Works on Microfilm................ DLB-236

Glossary of Terms and Definitions of Rhetoic and Logic DLB-236

Rhett, Robert Barnwell 1800-1876 .... DLB-43

Rhode, John 1884-1964 .... DLB-77

Rhodes, Eugene Manlove 1869-1934.... DLB-256

Rhodes, James Ford 1848-1927......... DLB-47

Rhodes, Richard 1937- DLB-185

Rhys, Jean 1890-1979 .....DLB-36, 117, 162; CDBLB-7; CDWLB-3

Ribeiro, Bernadim fl. ca. 1475/1482-1526/1544 .... DLB-287

Ricardo, David 1772-1823 ....DLB-107, 158

Ricardou, Jean 1932- DLB-83

Rice, Anne (A. N. Roquelare, Anne Rampling) 1941- DLB-292

Rice, Christopher 1978- DLB-292

Rice, Elmer 1892-1967 .... DLB-4, 7

Rice, Grantland 1880-1954..........DLB-29, 171

Rich, Adrienne 1929- DLB-5, 67; CDALB-7

Richard, Mark 1955- DLB-234

Richard de Fournival 1201-1259 or 1260................ DLB-208

Richards, David Adams 1950- DLB-53

Richards, George circa 1760-1814 .... DLB-37

Richards, I. A. 1893-1979 .... DLB-27

Richards, Laura E. 1850-1943 .... DLB-42

Richards, William Carey 1818-1892 ..... DLB-73

Grant Richards [publishing house]...... DLB-112

Richardson, Charles F. 1851-1913 .... DLB-71

Richardson, Dorothy M. 1873-1957 ...... DLB-36

The Novels of Dorothy Richardson (1918), by May Sinclair DLB-36

Richardson, Henry Handel (Ethel Florence Lindesay Robertson) 1870-1946................ DLB-197, 230

Richardson, Jack 1935- DLB-7

Richardson, John 1796-1852............ DLB-99

Richardson, Samuel 1689-1761.......... DLB-39, 154; CDBLB-2

Introductory Letters from the Second Edition of *Pamela* (1741)......... DLB-39

Postscript to [the Third Edition of] *Clarissa* (1751)............. DLB-39

Preface to the First Edition of *Pamela* (1740) DLB-39

Preface to the Third Edition of *Clarissa* (1751) [excerpt] DLB-39

Preface to Volume 1 of *Clarissa* (1747)..................... DLB-39

Preface to Volume 3 of *Clarissa* (1748)..................... DLB-39

Richardson, Willis 1889-1977........... DLB-51

Riche, Barnabe 1542-1617 .... DLB-136

Richepin, Jean 1849-1926............ DLB-192

Richler, Mordecai 1931-2001 .... DLB-53

Richter, Conrad 1890-1968 .... DLB-9, 212

Richter, Hans Werner 1908-1993 .... DLB-69

Richter, Johann Paul Friedrich 1763-1825............. DLB-94; CDWLB-2

Joseph Rickerby [publishing house] DLB-106

Rickword, Edgell 1898-1982 .... DLB-20

Riddell, Charlotte 1832-1906 .... DLB-156

Riddell, John (see Ford, Corey)

Ridge, John Rollin 1827-1867 ....DLB-175

Ridge, Lola 1873-1941 .... DLB-54

Ridge, William Pett 1859-1930......... DLB-135

Riding, Laura (see Jackson, Laura Riding)

Ridler, Anne 1912- DLB-27

Ridruego, Dionisio 1912-1975 .... DLB-108

Riel, Louis 1844-1885................ DLB-99

Riemer, Johannes 1648-1714............ DLB-168

Rifbjerg, Klaus 1931- DLB-214

Riffaterre, Michael 1924- DLB-67

A Conversation between William Riggan and Janette Turner Hospital Y-02

Riggs, Lynn 1899-1954 .... DLB-175

Riis, Jacob 1849-1914............... DLB-23

John C. Riker [publishing house] DLB-49

Riley, James 1777-1840 .... DLB-183

Riley, John 1938-1978................ DLB-40

Rilke, Rainer Maria 1875-1926............. DLB-81; CDWLB-2

Rimanelli, Giose 1926- DLB-177

Rimbaud, Jean-Nicolas-Arthur 1854-1891 .... DLB-217

Rinehart and Company DLB-46

Ringuet 1895-1960 .... DLB-68

Ringwood, Gwen Pharis 1910-1984 ..... DLB-88

Rinser, Luise 1911- DLB-69

Ríos, Alberto 1952- DLB-122

Ríos, Isabella 1948- DLB-82

Ripley, Arthur 1895-1961.............. DLB-44

Ripley, George 1802-1880 .....DLB-1, 64, 73, 235

The Rising Glory of America: Three Poems DLB-37

The Rising Glory of America: Written in 1771 (1786), by Hugh Henry Brackenridge and Philip Freneau DLB-37

Riskin, Robert 1897-1955 .... DLB-26

Risse, Heinz 1898- DLB-69

Rist, Johann 1607-1667 .... DLB-164

Ristikivi, Karl 1912-1977 .... DLB-220

Ritchie, Anna Mowatt 1819-1870..... DLB-3, 250

Ritchie, Anne Thackeray 1837-1919...... DLB-18

Ritchie, Thomas 1778-1854 .... DLB-43

The Ritz Paris Hemingway Award.......... Y-85

Mario Varga Llosa's Acceptance Speech .. Y-85

Rivard, Adjutor 1868-1945............. DLB-92

Rive, Richard 1931-1989 .... DLB-125, 225

Rivera, José 1955- DLB-249

Rivera, Marina 1942- DLB-122

Rivera, Tomás 1935-1984 .... DLB-82

Rivers, Conrad Kent 1933-1968........ DLB-41

Riverside Press DLB-49

Rivington, James circa 1724-1802......... DLB-43

Charles Rivington [publishing house]. ... DLB-154

Rivkin, Allen 1903-1990 .... DLB-26

Roa Bastos, Augusto 1917- DLB-113

Robbe-Grillet, Alain 1922- DLB-83

Robbins, Tom 1936- Y-80

Roberts, Charles G. D. 1860-1943....... DLB-92

Roberts, Dorothy 1906-1993 .... DLB-88

Roberts, Elizabeth Madox 1881-1941 ....DLB-9, 54, 102

Roberts, John (see Swynnerton, Thomas)

Roberts, Keith 1935-2000............ DLB-261

Roberts, Kenneth 1885-1957 .... DLB-9

Roberts, Michèle 1949- DLB-231

Roberts, Theodore Goodridge 1877-1953..................... DLB-92

Roberts, Ursula Wyllie (see Miles, Susan)

Roberts, William 1767-1849............DLB-142

James Roberts [publishing house] DLB-154

Roberts Brothers DLB-49

A. M. Robertson and Company DLB-49

Robertson, Ethel Florence Lindesay
(see Richardson, Henry Handel)

Robertson, William 1721-1793..........DLB-104

Robin, Leo 1895-1984.................DLB-265

Robins, Elizabeth 1862-1952 ....DLB-197

Robinson, A. Mary F. (Madame James
Darmesteter, Madame Mary
Duclaux) 1857-1944................DLB-240

Robinson, Casey 1903-1979.............DLB-44

Robinson, Derek Y-02

Robinson, Edwin Arlington
1869-1935 ....DLB-54; CDALB-3

Review by Derek Robinson of George
Greenfield's *Rich Dust* Y-02

Robinson, Henry Crabb 1775-1867 ......DLB-107

Robinson, James Harvey 1863-1936 ......DLB-47

Robinson, Lennox 1886-1958 ....DLB-10

Robinson, Mabel Louise 1874-1962.......DLB-22

Robinson, Marilynne 1943- DLB-206

Robinson, Mary 1758-1800 ....DLB-158

Robinson, Richard circa 1545-1607.......DLB-167

Robinson, Therese 1797-1870........DLB-59, 133

Robison, Mary 1949- DLB-130

Roblès, Emmanuel 1914-1995 ....DLB-83

Roccatagliata Ceccardi, Ceccardo
1871-1919 ....DLB-114

Rocha, Adolfo Correira da (see Torga, Miguel)

Roche, Billy 1949- DLB-233

Rochester, John Wilmot, Earl of
1647-1680 ....DLB-131

Rochon, Esther 1948- DLB-251

Rock, Howard 1911-1976 ....DLB-127

Rockwell, Norman Perceval 1894-1978...DLB-188

Rodgers, Carolyn M. 1945- DLB-41

Rodgers, W. R. 1909-1969 ....DLB-20

Rodney, Lester 1911- DLB-241

Rodrigues, Nelson 1912-1980 ....DLB-307

Rodríguez, Claudio 1934-1999 ....DLB-134

Rodríguez, Joe D. 1943- DLB-209

Rodríguez, Luis J. 1954- DLB-209

Rodriguez, Richard 1944- DLB-82, 256

Rodríguez Julia, Edgardo 1946- DLB-145

Roe, E. P. 1838-1888...................DLB-202

Roethke, Theodore
1908-1963 ....DLB-5, 206; CDALB-1

Rogers, Jane 1952- DLB-194

Rogers, Pattiann 1940- DLB-105

Rogers, Samuel 1763-1855..............DLB-93

Rogers, Will 1879-1935.................DLB-11

Rohmer, Sax 1883-1959 ....DLB-70

Roiphe, Anne 1935- Y-80

Rojas, Arnold R. 1896-1988 ....DLB-82

Rojas, Fernando de ca. 1475-1541 ....DLB-286

Rolfe, Edwin (Solomon Fishman)
1909-1954 ....DLB-303

Rolfe, Frederick William
1860-1913 ....DLB-34, 156

Rolland, Romain 1866-1944 ....DLB-65

Rolle, Richard circa 1290-1300 - 1340....DLB-146

Rölvaag, O. E. 1876-1931 ....DLB-9, 212

Romains, Jules 1885-1972 ....DLB-65

A. Roman and Company................DLB-49

Roman de la Rose: Guillaume de Lorris
1200/1205-circa 1230, Jean de
Meun 1235-1240-circa 1305 ....DLB-208

Romano, Lalla 1906-2001 ....DLB-177

Romano, Octavio 1923- DLB-122

Rome, Harold 1908-1993 ....DLB-265

Romero, Leo 1950- DLB-122

Romero, Lin 1947- DLB-122

Romero, Orlando 1945- DLB-82

Rook, Clarence 1863-1915 ....DLB-135

Roosevelt, Theodore
1858-1919 ....DLB-47, 186, 275

Root, Waverley 1903-1982 ....DLB-4

Root, William Pitt 1941- DLB-120

Roquebrune, Robert de 1889-1978 ....DLB-68

Rorty, Richard 1931- DLB-246, 279

Rosa, João Guimarães 1908-1967...DLB-113, 307

Rosales, Luis 1910-1992 ....DLB-134

Roscoe, William 1753-1831 ....DLB-163

Rose, Reginald 1920-2002..............DLB-26

Rose, Wendy 1948- DLB-175

Rosegger, Peter 1843-1918 ....DLB-129

Rosei, Peter 1946- DLB-85

Rosen, Norma 1925- DLB-28

Rosenbach, A. S. W. 1876-1952.........DLB-140

Rosenbaum, Ron 1946- DLB-185

Rosenbaum, Thane 1960- DLB-299

Rosenberg, Isaac 1890-1918 ....DLB-20, 216

Rosenfeld, Isaac 1918-1956 ....DLB-28

Rosenthal, Harold 1914-1999 ....DLB-241

Jimmy, Red, and Others: Harold
Rosenthal Remembers the Stars of
the Press Box Y-01

Rosenthal, M. L. 1917-1996..............DLB-5

Rosenwald, Lessing J. 1891-1979.........DLB-187

Ross, Alexander 1591-1654.............DLB-151

Ross, Harold 1892-1951 ....DLB-137

Ross, Jerry 1926-1955 ....DLB-265

Ross, Leonard Q. (see Rosten, Leo)

Ross, Lillian 1927- DLB-185

Ross, Martin 1862-1915................DLB-135

Ross, Sinclair 1908-1996 ....DLB-88

Ross, W. W. E. 1894-1966 ....DLB-88

Rosselli, Amelia 1930-1996 ....DLB-128

Rossen, Robert 1908-1966 ....DLB-26

Rosset, Barney.......................Y-02

Rossetti, Christina 1830-1894 ...DLB-35, 163, 240

Rossetti, Dante Gabriel
1828-1882 ....DLB-35; CDBLB-4

The Stealthy School of
Criticism (1871) DLB-35

Rossner, Judith 1935- DLB-6

Rostand, Edmond 1868-1918 ....DLB-192

Rosten, Leo 1908-1997 ....DLB-11

Rostenberg, Leona 1908- DLB-140

Rostopchina, Evdokiia Petrovna
1811-1858 ....DLB-205

Rostovsky, Dimitrii 1651-1709 ....DLB-150

Rota, Bertram 1903-1966 ....DLB-201

Bertram Rota and His Bookshop Y-91

Roth, Gerhard 1942- DLB-85, 124

Roth, Henry 1906?-1995................DLB-28

Roth, Joseph 1894-1939................DLB-85

Roth, Philip
1933- DLB-2, 28, 173; Y-82; CDALB-6

Rothenberg, Jerome 1931- DLB-5, 193

Rothschild Family DLB-184

Rotimi, Ola 1938- DLB-125

Rotrou, Jean 1609-1650 ....DLB-268

Routhier, Adolphe-Basile 1839-1920......DLB-99

Routier, Simone 1901-1987 ....DLB-88

George Routledge and Sons DLB-106

Roversi, Roberto 1923- DLB-128

Rowe, Elizabeth Singer 1674-1737 .....DLB-39, 95

Rowe, Nicholas 1674-1718...............DLB-84

Rowlands, Ian 1964- DLB-310

Rowlands, Samuel circa 1570-1630 ......DLB-121

Rowlandson, Mary
circa 1637-circa 1711 ....DLB-24, 200

Rowley, William circa 1585-1626 ....DLB-58

Rowling, J. K.
The Harry Potter Phenomenon Y-99

Rowse, A. L. 1903-1997................DLB-155

Rowson, Susanna Haswell
circa 1762-1824 ....DLB-37, 200

Roy, Camille 1870-1943 ....DLB-92

The G. Ross Roy Scottish Poetry Collection
at the University of South Carolina Y-89

Roy, Gabrielle 1909-1983 ....DLB-68

Roy, Jules 1907-2000 ....DLB-83

The Royal Court Theatre and the English
Stage Company..................DLB-13

The Royal Court Theatre and the New
Drama........................DLB-10

The Royal Shakespeare Company
at the Swan Y-88

Royall, Anne Newport 1769-1854 ....DLB-43, 248

Royce, Josiah 1855-1916 ....DLB-270

The Roycroft Printing Shop DLB-49

Royde-Smith, Naomi 1875-1964 ....DLB-191

Royster, Vermont 1914-1996 ....DLB-127

Richard Royston [publishing house] DLB-170

Rozanov, Vasilii Vasil'evich
1856-1919 ....DLB-295

Różewicz, Tadeusz 1921- DLB-232	Ryder, Jack 1871-1936 ....DLB-241	St. John, J. Allen 1872-1957............DLB-188
Ruark, Gibbons 1941- DLB-120	Ryga, George 1932-1987 ....DLB-60	St John, Madeleine 1942- DLB-267
Ruban, Vasilii Grigorevich 1742-1795 ...DLB-150	Rylands, Enriqueta Augustina Tennant 1843-1908 ....DLB-184	St. Johns, Adela Rogers 1894-1988........DLB-29
Rubens, Bernice 1928- DLB-14, 207		St. Omer, Garth 1931- DLB-117
Rubião, Murilo 1916-1991 ....DLB-307	Rylands, John 1801-1888 ....DLB-184	Saint Pierre, Michel de 1916-1987 ....DLB-83
Rubina, Dina Il'inichna 1953- DLB-285	Ryle, Gilbert 1900-1976 ....DLB-262	St. Dominic's Press..................DLB-112
Rubinshtein, Lev Semenovich 1947- ...DLB-285	Ryleev, Kondratii Fedorovich 1795-1826.................DLB-205	The St. John's College Robert Graves Trust ..Y-96
Rudd and Carleton..................DLB-49	Rymer, Thomas 1643?-1713...........DLB-101	St. Martin's Press DLB-46
Rudd, Steele (Arthur Hoey Davis) DLB-230	Ryskind, Morrie 1895-1985 ....DLB-26	*St. Nicholas* 1873-1881 ....DS-13
Rudkin, David 1936- DLB-13	Rzhevsky, Aleksei Andreevich 1737-1804.................DLB-150	Saintsbury, George 1845-1933.......DLB-57, 149
Rudnick, Paul 1957- DLB-266		"Modern English Prose" (1876)......DLB-57
Rudnicki, Adolf 1909-1990............DLB-299	# S	The Present State of the English Novel (1892), ...DLB-18
Rudolf von Ems circa 1200-circa 1254 ...DLB-138	The Saalfield Publishing Company DLB-46	Saiokuken Sōchō 1448-1532...........DLB-203
Ruffin, Josephine St. Pierre 1842-1924....DLB-79	Saba, Umberto 1883-1957 ....DLB-114	Saki (see Munro, H. H.)
Ruganda, John 1941- DLB-157	Sábato, Ernesto 1911- DLB-145; CDWLB-3	Salaam, Kalamu ya 1947- DLB-38
Ruggles, Henry Joseph 1813-1906 ....DLB-64	Saberhagen, Fred 1930- DLB-8	Šalamun, Tomaž 1941- DLB-181; CDWLB-4
Ruiz de Burton, María Amparo 1832-1895 ....DLB-209, 221	Sabin, Joseph 1821-1881...............DLB-187	Salas, Floyd 1931- DLB-82
	Sabino, Fernando (Fernando Tavares Sabino) 1923- DLB-307	Sálaz-Marquez, Rubén 1935- DLB-122
Rukeyser, Muriel 1913-1980 ....DLB-48		Salcedo, Hugo 1964- DLB-305
Rule, Jane 1931- DLB-60	Sacer, Gottfried Wilhelm 1635-1699 ....DLB-168	Salemson, Harold J. 1910-1988 ....DLB-4
Rulfo, Juan 1918-1986 .....DLB-113; CDWLB-3	Sachs, Hans 1494-1576......DLB-179; CDWLB-2	Salesbury, William 1520?-1584? DLB-281
Rumaker, Michael 1932- DLB-16	Sá-Carneiro, Mário de 1890-1916 ......DLB-287	Salinas, Luis Omar 1937- DLB-82
Rumens, Carol 1944- DLB-40	Sack, John 1930- DLB-185	Salinas, Pedro 1891-1951 ....DLB-134
Rummo, Paul-Eerik 1942- DLB-232	Sackler, Howard 1929-1982 ....DLB-7	Salinger, J. D. 1919- DLB-2, 102, 173; CDALB-1
Runyon, Damon 1880-1946 ....DLB-11, 86, 171	Sackville, Lady Margaret 1881-1963 ....DLB-240	
	Sackville, Thomas 1536-1608 and Norton, Thomas 1532-1584.........DLB-62	Salkey, Andrew 1928- DLB-125
Ruodlieb circa 1050-1075 ....DLB-148		Sallust circa 86 B.C.-35 B.C. DLB-211; CDWLB-1
Rush, Benjamin 1746-1813..............DLB-37	Sackville, Thomas 1536-1608...........DLB-132	
Rush, Rebecca 1779-? DLB-200	Sackville-West, Edward 1901-1965 .....DLB-191	Salt, Waldo 1914-1987 ....DLB-44
Rushdie, Salman 1947- DLB-194	Sackville-West, Vita 1892-1962 .....DLB-34, 195	Salter, James 1925- DLB-130
Rusk, Ralph L. 1888-1962 ....DLB-103	Sá de Miranda, Francisco de 1481-1588?.................DLB-287	Salter, Mary Jo 1954- DLB-120
Ruskin, John 1819-1900......DLB-55, 163, 190; CDBLB-4		Saltus, Edgar 1855-1921...............DLB-202
	Sadlier, Mary Anne 1820-1903..........DLB-99	Saltykov, Mikhail Evgrafovich 1826-1889 ....DLB-238
Russ, Joanna 1937- DLB-8	D. and J. Sadlier and Company DLB-49	
Russell, Benjamin 1761-1845 ....DLB-43	Sadoff, Ira 1945- DLB-120	Salustri, Carlo Alberto (see Trilussa)
Russell, Bertrand 1872-1970 ....DLB-100, 262	Sadoveanu, Mihail 1880-1961 ....DLB-220	Salverson, Laura Goodman 1890-1970....DLB-92
Russell, Charles Edward 1860-1941......DLB-25	Sadur, Nina Nikolaevna 1950- DLB-285	Samain, Albert 1858-1900 ....DLB-217
Russell, Charles M. 1864-1926.........DLB-188	Sáenz, Benjamin Alire 1954- DLB-209	Sampson, Richard Henry (see Hull, Richard)
Russell, Eric Frank 1905-1978 ....DLB-255	Saenz, Jaime 1921-1986 ....DLB-145, 283	Samuels, Ernest 1903-1996............DLB-111
Russell, Fred 1906-2003 ....DLB-241	Saffin, John circa 1626-1710 ....DLB-24	Sanborn, Franklin Benjamin 1831-1917....................DLB-1, 223
Russell, George William (see AE)	Sagan, Françoise 1935- DLB-83	
Russell, Countess Mary Annette Beauchamp (see Arnim, Elizabeth von)	Sage, Robert 1899-1962 ....DLB-4	Sánchez, Luis Rafael 1936- DLB-145, 305
	Sagel, Jim 1947- DLB-82	Sánchez, Philomeno "Phil" 1917- DLB-122
Russell, Willy 1947- DLB-233	Sagendorph, Robb Hansell 1900-1970 ...DLB-137	Sánchez, Ricardo 1941-1995............DLB-82
B. B. Russell and Company DLB-49	Sahagún, Carlos 1938- DLB-108	Sánchez, Saúl 1943- DLB-209
R. H. Russell and Son................DLB-49	Sahkomaapii, Piitai (see Highwater, Jamake)	Sanchez, Sonia 1934- DLB-41; DS-8
Rutebeuf flourished 1249-1277 ....DLB-208	Sahl, Hans 1902-1993................DLB-69	Sánchez de Arévalo, Rodrigo 1404-1470...................DLB-286
Rutherford, Mark 1831-1913 ....DLB-18	Said, Edward W. 1935- DLB-67	
Ruxton, George Frederick 1821-1848 ....DLB-186	Saigyō 1118-1190 ....DLB-203	Sánchez, Florencio 1875-1910..........DLB-305
	Saijo, Albert 1926- DLB-312	Sand, George 1804-1876..........DLB-119, 192
R-va, Zeneida (see Gan, Elena Andreevna)	Saiko, George 1892-1962 ....DLB-85	Sandburg, Carl 1878-1967............DLB-17, 54; CDALB-3
Ryan, James 1952- DLB-267	Sainte-Beuve, Charles-Augustin 1804-1869 ....DLB-217	
Ryan, Michael 1946- Y-82		Sandel, Cora (Sara Fabricius) 1880-1974 ....DLB-297
Ryan, Oscar 1904- DLB-68	Saint-Exupéry, Antoine de 1900-1944 ....DLB-72	
Rybakov, Anatolii Naumovich 1911-1994......................DLB-302		Sandemose, Aksel 1899-1965 ....DLB-297
		Sanders, Edward 1939- DLB-16, 244

Sanderson, Robert 1587-1663 . . . . .DLB-281

Sandoz, Mari 1896-1966 . . . . .DLB-9, 212

Sandwell, B. K. 1876-1954 . . . . .DLB-92

Sandy, Stephen 1934- DLB-165

Sandys, George 1578-1644 . . . . .DLB-24, 121

Sangster, Charles 1822-1893 . . . . .DLB-99

Sanguineti, Edoardo 1930- DLB-128

Sanjōnishi Sanetaka 1455-1537 . . . . .DLB-203

San Pedro, Diego de fl. ca. 1492 . . . . .DLB-286

Sansay, Leonora ?-after 1823 . . . . .DLB-200

Sansom, William 1912-1976 . . . . .DLB-139

Sant'Anna, Affonso Romano de
   1937- DLB-307

Santayana, George
   1863-1952 . . . . . . DLB-54, 71, 246, 270; DS-13

Santiago, Danny 1911-1988 . . . . .DLB-122

Santillana, Marqués de (Íñigo López de Mendoza)
   1398-1458 .DLB-286

Santmyer, Helen Hooven 1895-1986 . . . . .Y-84

Santos, Bienvenido 1911-1996 . . . . .DLB-312

Sanvitale, Francesca 1928- DLB-196

Sapidus, Joannes 1490-1561 . . . . .DLB-179

Sapir, Edward 1884-1939 . . . . .DLB-92

Sapper (see McNeile, Herman Cyril)

Sappho circa 620 B.C.-circa 550 B.C.
   . . . . .DLB-176; CDWLB-1

Saramago, José 1922- DLB-287; Y-98

   Nobel Lecture 1998: How Characters
   Became the Masters and the Author
   Their Apprentice Y-98

Sarban (John W. Wall) 1910-1989 . . . . . .DLB-255

Sardou, Victorien 1831-1908 . . . . .DLB-192

Sarduy, Severo 1937-1993 . . . . .DLB-113

Sargent, Pamela 1948- DLB-8

Saro-Wiwa, Ken 1941- DLB-157

Saroyan, Aram
   Rites of Passage [on William Saroyan] . . . Y-83

Saroyan, William
   1908-1981 . . . . . DLB-7, 9, 86; Y-81; CDALB-7

Sarraute, Nathalie 1900-1999 . . . . .DLB-83

Sarrazin, Albertine 1937-1967 . . . . .DLB-83

Sarris, Greg 1952- DLB-175

Sarton, May 1912-1995 . . . . .DLB-48; Y-81

Sartre, Jean-Paul 1905-1980 . . . . .DLB-72, 296

Sassoon, Siegfried
   1886-1967 . . . . .DLB-20, 191; DS-18

   A Centenary Essay Y-86

   Tributes from Vivien F. Clarke and
   Michael Thorpe Y-86

Sata Ineko 1904- DLB-180

Saturday Review Press DLB-46

Saunders, James 1925- DLB-13

Saunders, John Monk 1897-1940 . . . . .DLB-26

Saunders, Margaret Marshall
   1861-1947 .DLB-92

Saunders and Otley DLB-106

Saussure, Ferdinand de 1857-1913 . . . . . . .DLB-242

Savage, James 1784-1873 . . . . .DLB-30

Savage, Marmion W. 1803?-1872 . . . . .DLB-21

Savage, Richard 1697?-1743 . . . . .DLB-95

Savard, Félix-Antoine 1896-1982 . . . . .DLB-68

Savery, Henry 1791-1842 . . . . .DLB-230

Saville, (Leonard) Malcolm 1901-1982 . . .DLB-160

Savinio, Alberto 1891-1952 . . . . .DLB-264

Sawyer, Robert J. 1960- DLB-251

Sawyer, Ruth 1880-1970 . . . . .DLB-22

Sayers, Dorothy L.
   1893-1957 . . . . DLB-10, 36, 77, 100; CDBLB-6

   The Dorothy L. Sayers Society Y-98

Sayle, Charles Edward 1864-1924 . . . . . . .DLB-184

Sayles, John Thomas 1950- DLB-44

Sbarbaro, Camillo 1888-1967 . . . . .DLB-114

Scalapino, Leslie 1947- DLB-193

Scannell, Vernon 1922- DLB-27

Scarry, Richard 1919-1994 . . . . .DLB-61

Schack, Hans Egede 1820-1859 . . . . .DLB-300

Schaefer, Jack 1907-1991 . . . . .DLB-212

Schaeffer, Albrecht 1885-1950 . . . . .DLB-66

Schaeffer, Susan Fromberg 1941- . . .DLB-28, 299

Schaff, Philip 1819-1893 . . . . DS-13

Schaper, Edzard 1908-1984 . . . . .DLB-69

Scharf, J. Thomas 1843-1898 . . . . .DLB-47

Schede, Paul Melissus 1539-1602 . . . . . . .DLB-179

Scheffel, Joseph Viktor von 1826-1886 . . .DLB-129

Scheffler, Johann 1624-1677 . . . . .DLB-164

Schelling, Friedrich Wilhelm Joseph von
   1775-1854 .DLB-90

Scherer, Wilhelm 1841-1886 . . . . .DLB-129

Scherfig, Hans 1905-1979 . . . . .DLB-214

Schickele, René 1883-1940 . . . . .DLB-66

Schiff, Dorothy 1903-1989 . . . . .DLB-127

Schiller, Friedrich
   1759-1805 . . . . .DLB-94; CDWLB-2

Schirmer, David 1623-1687 . . . . .DLB-164

Schlaf, Johannes 1862-1941 . . . . .DLB-118

Schlegel, August Wilhelm 1767-1845 . . . . .DLB-94

Schlegel, Dorothea 1763-1839 . . . . .DLB-90

Schlegel, Friedrich 1772-1829 . . . . .DLB-90

Schleiermacher, Friedrich 1768-1834 . . . . .DLB-90

Schlesinger, Arthur M., Jr. 1917- DLB-17

Schlumberger, Jean 1877-1968 . . . . .DLB-65

Schmid, Eduard Hermann Wilhelm
   (see Edschmid, Kasimir)

Schmidt, Arno 1914-1979 . . . . .DLB-69

Schmidt, Johann Kaspar (see Stirner, Max)

Schmidt, Michael 1947- DLB-40

Schmidtbonn, Wilhelm August
   1876-1952 .DLB-118

Schmitz, Aron Hector (see Svevo, Italo)

Schmitz, James H. 1911-1981 . . . . .DLB-8

Schnabel, Johann Gottfried 1692-1760 . . . .DLB-168

Schnackenberg, Gjertrud 1953- DLB-120

Schnitzler, Arthur
   1862-1931 . . . . .DLB-81, 118; CDWLB-2

Schnurre, Wolfdietrich 1920-1989 . . . . .DLB-69

Schocken Books .DLB-46

Scholartis Press .DLB-112

Scholderer, Victor 1880-1971 . . . . .DLB-201

The Schomburg Center for Research
   in Black Culture DLB-76

Schönbeck, Virgilio (see Giotti, Virgilio)

Schönherr, Karl 1867-1943 . . . . .DLB-118

Schoolcraft, Jane Johnston 1800-1841 . . . .DLB-175

School Stories, 1914-1960 . . . . .DLB-160

Schopenhauer, Arthur 1788-1860 . . . . .DLB-90

Schopenhauer, Johanna 1766-1838 . . . . . . .DLB-90

Schorer, Mark 1908-1977 . . . . .DLB-103

Schottelius, Justus Georg 1612-1676 . . . . .DLB-164

Schouler, James 1839-1920 . . . . .DLB-47

Schoultz, Solveig von 1907-1996 . . . . .DLB-259

Schrader, Paul 1946- DLB-44

Schreiner, Olive
   1855-1920 . . . . .DLB-18, 156, 190, 225

Schroeder, Andreas 1946- DLB-53

Schubart, Christian Friedrich Daniel
   1739-1791 .DLB-97

Schubert, Gotthilf Heinrich 1780-1860 . . . .DLB-90

Schücking, Levin 1814-1883 . . . . .DLB-133

Schulberg, Budd 1914- DLB-6, 26, 28; Y-81

   Excerpts from USC Presentation
   [on F. Scott Fitzgerald] Y-96

F. J. Schulte and Company DLB-49

Schulz, Bruno 1892-1942 . . . . .DLB-215; CDWLB-4

Schulze, Hans (see Praetorius, Johannes)

Schupp, Johann Balthasar 1610-1661 . . . . .DLB-164

Schurz, Carl 1829-1906 . . . . .DLB-23

Schuyler, George S. 1895-1977 . . . . . . .DLB-29, 51

Schuyler, James 1923-1991 . . . . .DLB-5, 169

Schwartz, Delmore 1913-1966 . . . . .DLB-28, 48

Schwartz, Jonathan 1938- Y-82

Schwartz, Lynne Sharon 1939- DLB-218

Schwarz, Sibylle 1621-1638 . . . . .DLB-164

Schwarz-Bart, Andre 1928- DLB-299

Schwerner, Armand 1927-1999 . . . . .DLB-165

Schwob, Marcel 1867-1905 . . . . .DLB-123

Sciascia, Leonardo 1921-1989 . . . . .DLB-177

Science Fiction and Fantasy
   Documents in British Fantasy and
   Science Fiction DLB-178

   Hugo Awards and Nebula Awards DLB-8

   The Iconography of Science-Fiction
   Art DLB-8

   The New Wave DLB-8

   Paperback Science Fiction DLB-8

   Science Fantasy DLB-8

   Science-Fiction Fandom and
   Conventions DLB-8

   Science-Fiction Fanzines: The Time
   Binders DLB-8

   Science-Fiction Films DLB-8

Science Fiction Writers of America
 and the Nebula Award..........DLB-8
Selected Science-Fiction Magazines and
 Anthologies.................DLB-8
A World Chronology of Important Science
 Fiction Works (1818-1979).......DLB-8
The Year in Science Fiction
 and Fantasy.................Y-00, 01
Scot, Reginald circa 1538-1599........DLB-136
Scotellaro, Rocco 1923-1953..........DLB-128
Scott, Alicia Anne (Lady John Scott)
 1810-1900...................DLB-240
Scott, Catharine Amy Dawson
 1865-1934...................DLB-240
Scott, Dennis 1939-1991..............DLB-125
Scott, Dixon 1881-1915..............DLB-98
Scott, Duncan Campbell 1862-1947......DLB-92
Scott, Evelyn 1893-1963.............DLB-9, 48
Scott, F. R. 1899-1985..............DLB-88
Scott, Frederick George 1861-1944......DLB-92
Scott, Geoffrey 1884-1929...........DLB-149
Scott, Harvey W. 1838-1910..........DLB-23
Scott, Lady Jane (see Scott, Alicia Anne)
Scott, Paul 1920-1978............DLB-14, 207
Scott, Sarah 1723-1795..............DLB-39
Scott, Tom 1918-..................DLB-27
Scott, Sir Walter 1771-1832
 ......DLB-93, 107, 116, 144, 159; CDBLB-3
Scott, William Bell 1811-1890..........DLB-32
Walter Scott Publishing Company
 Limited......................DLB-112
William R. Scott [publishing house]......DLB-46
Scott-Heron, Gil 1949-..............DLB-41
Scribe, Eugene 1791-1861............DLB-192
Scribner, Arthur Hawley 1859-1932.....DS-13, 16
Scribner, Charles 1854-1930..........DS-13, 16
Scribner, Charles, Jr. 1921-1995........Y-95
 Reminiscences....................DS-17
Charles Scribner's Sons DLB-49; DS-13, 16, 17
 Archives of Charles Scribner's Sons.....DS-17
Scribner's Magazine....................DS-13
Scribner's Monthly....................DS-13
Scripps, E. W. 1854-1926............DLB-25
Scudder, Horace Elisha 1838-1902....DLB-42, 71
Scudder, Vida Dutton 1861-1954........DLB-71
Scudéry, Madeleine de 1607-1701.......DLB-268
Scupham, Peter 1933-...............DLB-40
Seabrook, William 1886-1945..........DLB-4
Seabury, Samuel 1729-1796...........DLB-31
Seacole, Mary Jane Grant 1805-1881....DLB-166
The Seafarer circa 970................DLB-146
Sealsfield, Charles (Carl Postl)
 1793-1864..................DLB-133, 186
Searle, John R. 1932-................DLB-279
Sears, Edward I. 1819?-1876..........DLB-79
Sears Publishing Company............DLB-46
Seaton, George 1911-1979............DLB-44

Seaton, William Winston 1785-1866......DLB-43
Martin Secker [publishing house].......DLB-112
Martin Secker, and Warburg Limited ...DLB-112
The "Second Generation" Holocaust
 Novel.......................DLB-299
Sedgwick, Arthur George 1844-1915.....DLB-64
Sedgwick, Catharine Maria
 1789-1867..........DLB-1, 74, 183, 239, 243
Sedgwick, Ellery 1872-1960............DLB-91
Sedgwick, Eve Kosofsky 1950-.......DLB-246
Sedley, Sir Charles 1639-1701.........DLB-131
Seeberg, Peter 1925-1999.............DLB-214
Seeger, Alan 1888-1916...............DLB-45
Seers, Eugene (see Dantin, Louis)
Segal, Erich 1937-....................Y-86
Segal, Lore 1928-..................DLB-299
Šegedin, Petar 1909-................DLB-181
Seghers, Anna 1900-1983....DLB-69; CDWLB-2
Seid, Ruth (see Sinclair, Jo)
Seidel, Frederick Lewis 1936-..........Y-84
Seidel, Ina 1885-1974................DLB-56
Seifert, Jaroslav
 1901-1986.......DLB-215; Y-84; CDWLB-4
 Jaroslav Seifert Through the Eyes of
  the English-Speaking Reader........Y-84
 Three Poems by Jaroslav Seifert........Y-84
Seifullina, Lidiia Nikolaevna 1889-1954...DLB-272
Seigenthaler, John 1927-.............DLB-127
Seizin Press......................DLB-112
Séjour, Victor 1817-1874..............DLB-50
Séjour Marcou et Ferrand, Juan Victor
 (see Séjour, Victor)
Sekowski, Józef-Julian, Baron Brambeus
 (see Senkovsky, Osip Ivanovich)
Selby, Bettina 1934-................DLB-204
Selby, Hubert, Jr. 1928-..........DLB-2, 227
Selden, George 1929-1989.............DLB-52
Selden, John 1584-1654..............DLB-213
Selenić, Slobodan 1933-1995..........DLB-181
Self, Edwin F. 1920-...............DLB-137
Self, Will 1961-...................DLB-207
Seligman, Edwin R. A. 1861-1939.......DLB-47
Selimović, Meša
 1910-1982...........DLB-181; CDWLB-4
Sellars, Wilfrid 1912-1989............DLB-279
Sellings, Arthur (Arthur Gordon Ley)
 1911-1968....................DLB-261
Selous, Frederick Courteney 1851-1917...DLB-174
Seltzer, Chester E. (see Muro, Amado)
Thomas Seltzer [publishing house].......DLB-46
Selvon, Sam 1923-1994 ....DLB-125; CDWLB-3
Semel, Nava 1954-.................DLB-299
Semmes, Raphael 1809-1877..........DLB-189
Senancour, Etienne de 1770-1846......DLB-119
Sena, Jorge de 1919-1978............DLB-287
Sendak, Maurice 1928-...............DLB-61

Seneca the Elder
 circa 54 B.C.-circa A.D. 40.........DLB-211
Seneca the Younger
 circa 1 B.C.-A.D. 65.....DLB-211; CDWLB-1
Senécal, Eva 1905-.................DLB-92
Sengstacke, John 1912-1997...........DLB-127
Senior, Olive 1941-.................DLB-157
Senkovsky, Osip Ivanovich
 (Józef-Julian Sekowski, Baron Brambeus)
 1800-1858....................DLB-198
Šenoa, August 1838-1881....DLB-147; CDWLB-4
Sepamla, Sipho 1932-............DLB-157, 225
Serafimovich, Aleksandr Serafimovich
 (Aleksandr Serafimovich Popov)
 1863-1949....................DLB-272
Serao, Matilde 1856-1927............DLB-264
Seredy, Kate 1899-1975..............DLB-22
Sereni, Vittorio 1913-1983...........DLB-128
William Seres [publishing house].......DLB-170
Sergeev-Tsensky, Sergei Nikolaevich (Sergei
 Nikolaevich Sergeev) 1875-1958.....DLB-272
Serling, Rod 1924-1975...............DLB-26
Sernine, Daniel 1955-...............DLB-251
Serote, Mongane Wally 1944-....DLB-125, 225
Serraillier, Ian 1912-1994............DLB-161
Serrano, Nina 1934-................DLB-122
Service, Robert 1874-1958............DLB-92
Sessler, Charles 1854-1935............DLB-187
Seth, Vikram 1952-..............DLB-120, 271
Seton, Elizabeth Ann 1774-1821........DLB-200
Seton, Ernest Thompson
 1860-1942................DLB-92; DS-13
Seton, John circa 1509-1567..........DLB-281
Setouchi Harumi 1922-..............DLB-182
Settle, Mary Lee 1918-...............DLB-6
Seume, Johann Gottfried 1763-1810......DLB-94
Seuse, Heinrich 1295?-1366...........DLB-179
Seuss, Dr. (see Geisel, Theodor Seuss)
Severianin, Igor' 1887-1941..........DLB-295
Severin, Timothy 1940-.............DLB-204
Sévigné, Marie de Rabutin Chantal,
 Madame de 1626-1696............DLB-268
Sewall, Joseph 1688-1769.............DLB-24
Sewall, Richard B. 1908-............DLB-111
Sewall, Samuel 1652-1730.............DLB-24
Sewell, Anna 1820-1878..............DLB-163
Sexton, Anne 1928-1974...DLB-5, 169; CDALB-1
Seymour-Smith, Martin 1928-1998.....DLB-155
Sgorlon, Carlo 1930-...............DLB-196
Shaara, Michael 1929-1988.............Y-83
Shabel'skaia, Aleksandra Stanislavovna
 1845-1921....................DLB-238
Shadwell, Thomas 1641?-1692.........DLB-80
Shaffer, Anthony 1926-...............DLB-13
Shaffer, Peter 1926- DLB-13, 233; CDBLB-8
Muhammad ibn Idris al-Shafi'i 767-820 ..DLB-311
Shaftesbury, Anthony Ashley Cooper,
 Third Earl of 1671-1713...........DLB-101

Shaginian, Marietta Sergeevna
1888-1982 . . . . DLB-272

Shairp, Mordaunt 1887-1939 . . . . DLB-10

Shakespeare, Nicholas 1957- DLB-231

Shakespeare, William
1564-1616 . . . . . . DLB-62, 172, 263; CDBLB-1

    The New Variorum Shakespeare Y-85

    Shakespeare and Montaigne: A Symposium
by Jules Furthman. Y-02

    $6,166,000 for a *Book!* Observations on
*The Shakespeare First Folio: The History
of the Book* Y-01

    Taylor-Made Shakespeare? Or Is
"Shall I Die?" the Long-Lost Text
of Bottom's Dream? Y-85

The Shakespeare Globe Trust Y-93

Shakespeare Head Press DLB-112

Shakhova, Elisaveta Nikitichna
1822-1899 . . . . DLB-277

Shakhovskoi, Aleksandr Aleksandrovich
1777-1846. . . . . .DLB-150

Shalamov, Varlam Tikhonovich
1907-1982 . . . . DLB-302

al-Shanfara flourished sixth century DLB-311

Shange, Ntozake 1948- DLB-38, 249

Shapcott, Thomas W. 1935- DLB-289

Shapir, Ol'ga Andreevna 1850-1916 . . . . .DLB-295

Shapiro, Karl 1913-2000 . . . . .DLB-48

Sharon Publications DLB-46

Sharov, Vladimir Aleksandrovich
1952- DLB-285

Sharp, Margery 1905-1991 . . . . DLB-161

Sharp, William 1855-1905 . . . . DLB-156

Sharpe, Tom 1928- DLB-14, 231

Shaw, Albert 1857-1947 . . . . DLB-91

Shaw, George Bernard
1856-1950 . . . . . . DLB-10, 57, 190, CDBLB-6

    The Bernard Shaw Society Y-99

    "Stage Censorship: The Rejected
Statement" (1911) [excerpts] DLB-10

Shaw, Henry Wheeler 1818-1885 . . . . DLB-11

Shaw, Irwin
1913-1984 . . . . . . DLB-6, 102; Y-84; CDALB-1

Shaw, Joseph T. 1874-1952 . . . . .DLB-137

    "As I Was Saying," Joseph T. Shaw's
Editorial Rationale in *Black Mask*
(January 1927) DLB-137

Shaw, Mary 1854-1929 . . . . .DLB-228

Shaw, Robert 1927-1978 . . . . .DLB-13, 14

Shaw, Robert B. 1947- DLB-120

Shawn, Wallace 1943- DLB-266

Shawn, William 1907-1992 . . . . .DLB-137

Frank Shay [publishing house] DLB-46

Shchedrin, N. (see Saltykov, Mikhail Evgrafovich)

Shcherbakova, Galina Nikolaevna
1932- DLB-285

Shcherbina, Nikolai Fedorovich
1821-1869 . . . . DLB-277

Shea, John Gilmary 1824-1892 . . . . DLB-30

Sheaffer, Louis 1912-1993 . . . . .DLB-103

Sheahan, Henry Beston (see Beston, Henry)

Shearing, Joseph 1886-1952 . . . . .DLB-70

Shebbeare, John 1709-1788 . . . . .DLB-39

Sheckley, Robert 1928- DLB-8

Shedd, William G. T. 1820-1894 . . . . DLB-64

Sheed, Wilfrid 1930- DLB-6

Sheed and Ward [U.S.] DLB-46

Sheed and Ward Limited [U.K.] DLB-112

Sheldon, Alice B. (see Tiptree, James, Jr.)

Sheldon, Edward 1886-1946 . . . . DLB-7

Sheldon and Company DLB-49

Sheller, Aleksandr Konstantinovich
1838-1900 . . . . DLB-238

Shelley, Mary Wollstonecraft 1797-1851
. . . . DLB-110, 116, 159, 178; CDBLB-3

    Preface to *Frankenstein; or, The
Modern Prometheus* (1818) DLB-178

Shelley, Percy Bysshe
1792-1822 . . . . . . DLB-96, 110, 158; CDBLB-3

Shelnutt, Eve 1941- DLB-130

Shenshin (see Fet, Afanasii Afanas'evich)

Shenstone, William 1714-1763 . . . . DLB-95

Shepard, Clark and Brown DLB-49

Shepard, Ernest Howard 1879-1976. . . . . .DLB-160

Shepard, Sam 1943- DLB-7, 212

Shepard, Thomas I, 1604 or 1605-1649 . . .DLB-24

Shepard, Thomas, II, 1635-1677 . . . . DLB-24

Shepherd, Luke flourished 1547-1554 . . . .DLB-136

Sherburne, Edward 1616-1702 . . . . DLB-131

Sheridan, Frances 1724-1766 . . . . .DLB-39, 84

Sheridan, Richard Brinsley
1751-1816 . . . . DLB-89; CDBLB-2

Sherman, Francis 1871-1926 . . . . DLB-92

Sherman, Martin 1938- DLB-228

Sherriff, R. C. 1896-1975 . . . . DLB-10, 191, 233

Sherrod, Blackie 1919- DLB-241

Sherry, Norman 1935- DLB-155

    Tribute to Graham Greene Y-91

Sherry, Richard 1506-1551 or 1555 . . . . . .DLB-236

Sherwood, Mary Martha 1775-1851 . . . . .DLB-163

Sherwood, Robert E. 1896-1955 . . . DLB-7, 26, 249

Shevyrev, Stepan Petrovich
1806-1864 . . . . DLB-205

Shiel, M. P. 1865-1947 . . . . .DLB-153

Shiels, George 1886-1949 . . . . .DLB-10

Shiga Naoya 1883-1971 . . . . .DLB-180

Shiina Rinzō 1911-1973 . . . . .DLB-182

Shikishi Naishinnō 1153?-1201 . . . . .DLB-203

Shillaber, Benjamin Penhallow
1814-1890 . . . . DLB-1, 11, 235

Shimao Toshio 1917-1986 . . . . .DLB-182

Shimazaki Tōson 1872-1943 . . . . .DLB-180

Shimose, Pedro 1940- DLB-283

Shine, Ted 1931- DLB-38

Shinkei 1406-1475 . . . . DLB-203

Ship, Reuben 1915-1975 . . . . .DLB-88

Shirer, William L. 1904-1993 . . . . DLB-4

Shirinsky-Shikhmatov, Sergii Aleksandrovich
1783-1837 . . . . DLB-150

Shirley, James 1596-1666 . . . . .DLB-58

Shishkov, Aleksandr Semenovich
1753-1841 . . . . DLB-150

Shockley, Ann Allen 1927- DLB-33

Sholokhov, Mikhail Aleksandrovich
1905-1984 . . . . DLB-272

Shōno Junzō 1921- DLB-182

Shore, Arabella 1820?-1901 . . . . .DLB-199

Shore, Louisa 1824-1895 . . . . DLB-199

Short, Luke (see Glidden, Frederick Dilley)

Peter Short [publishing house] DLB-170

Shorter, Dora Sigerson 1866-1918 . . . . . . .DLB-240

Shorthouse, Joseph Henry 1834-1903 . . . . DLB-18

Short Stories
    Michael M. Rea and the Rea Award
for the Short Story Y-97

    The Year in Short Stories Y-87

    The Year in the Short Story Y-88, 90–93

Shōtetsu 1381-1459 . . . . DLB-203

Showalter, Elaine 1941- DLB-67

Shreve, Anita 1946- DLB-292

Shukshin, Vasilii Makarovich
1929-1974 . . . . DLB-302

Shulevitz, Uri 1935- DLB-61

Shulman, Max 1919-1988 . . . . .DLB-11

Shute, Henry A. 1856-1943 . . . . DLB-9

Shute, Nevil (Nevil Shute Norway)
1899-1960 . . . . DLB-255

Shuttle, Penelope 1947- DLB-14, 40

Shvarts, Evgenii L'vovich 1896-1958 . . . . .DLB-272

Sibawayhi circa 750-circa 795 . . . . .DLB-311

Sibbes, Richard 1577-1635 . . . . .DLB-151

Sibiriak, D. (see Mamin, Dmitrii Narkisovich)

Siddal, Elizabeth Eleanor 1829-1862 . . . . .DLB-199

Sidgwick, Ethel 1877-1970 . . . . .DLB-197

Sidgwick, Henry 1838-1900 . . . . .DLB-262

Sidgwick and Jackson Limited DLB-112

Sidney, Margaret (see Lothrop, Harriet M.)

Sidney, Mary 1561-1621 . . . . .DLB-167

Sidney, Sir Philip
1554-1586 . . . . DLB-167; CDBLB-1

    An Apologie for Poetrie (the Olney edition,
1595, of *Defence of Poesie*) DLB-167

Sidney's Press DLB-49

Sierra, Rubén 1946- DLB-122

Sierra Club Books DLB-49

Siger of Brabant circa 1240-circa 1284 . . . .DLB-115

Sigourney, Lydia Huntley
1791-1865 . . . . . . DLB-1, 42, 73, 183, 239, 243

Silkin, Jon 1930-1997 . . . . DLB-27

Silko, Leslie Marmon
1948- DLB-143, 175, 256, 275

Silliman, Benjamin 1779-1864 . . . . .DLB-183

Silliman, Ron 1946- DLB-169

Silliphant, Stirling 1918-1996 . . . . DLB-26

Sillitoe, Alan 1928- DLB-14, 139; CDBLB-8
   Tribute to J. B. Priestly Y-84
Silman, Roberta 1934- DLB-28
Silone, Ignazio (Secondino Tranquilli) 1900-1978..................... DLB-264
Silva, Beverly 1930- DLB-122
Silva, Clara 1905-1976 .... DLB-290
Silva, José Asunció 1865-1896 .... DLB-283
Silverberg, Robert 1935- DLB-8
Silverman, Kaja 1947- DLB-246
Silverman, Kenneth 1936- DLB-111
Simak, Clifford D. 1904-1988........... DLB-8
Simcoe, Elizabeth 1762-1850........... DLB-99
Simcox, Edith Jemima 1844-1901....... DLB-190
Simcox, George Augustus 1841-1905..... DLB-35
Sime, Jessie Georgina 1868-1958 .... DLB-92
Simenon, Georges 1903-1989....... DLB-72; Y-89
Simic, Charles 1938- DLB-105
   "Images and 'Images'" DLB-105
Simionescu, Mircea Horia 1928- DLB-232
Simmel, Georg 1858-1918 .... DLB-296
Simmel, Johannes Mario 1924- DLB-69
Valentine Simmes [publishing house].....DLB-170
Simmons, Ernest J. 1903-1972 .... DLB-103
Simmons, Herbert Alfred 1930- DLB-33
Simmons, James 1933- DLB-40
Simms, William Gilmore 1806-1870............DLB-3, 30, 59, 73, 248
Simms and M'Intyre................. DLB-106
Simon, Claude 1913- DLB-83; Y-85
   Nobel Lecture Y-85
Simon, Neil 1927- DLB-7, 266
Simon and Schuster DLB-46
Simonov, Konstantin Mikhailovich 1915-1979..................... DLB-302
Simons, Katherine Drayton Mayrant 1890-1969 .... Y-83
Simović, Ljubomir 1935- DLB-181
Simpkin and Marshall [publishing house] DLB-154
Simpson, Helen 1897-1940 .... DLB-77
Simpson, Louis 1923- DLB-5
Simpson, N. F. 1919- DLB-13
Sims, George 1923- DLB-87; Y-99
Sims, George Robert 1847-1922 ...DLB-35, 70, 135
Sinán, Rogelio 1902-1994........ DLB-145, 290
Sinclair, Andrew 1935- DLB-14
Sinclair, Bertrand William 1881-1972..... DLB-92
Sinclair, Catherine 1800-1864........... DLB-163
Sinclair, Jo 1913-1995................ DLB-28
Sinclair, Lister 1921- DLB-88
Sinclair, May 1863-1946........... DLB-36, 135
   The Novels of Dorothy Richardson (1918) DLB-36
Sinclair, Upton 1878-1968 ..... DLB-9; CDALB-5
Upton Sinclair [publishing house]....... DLB-46

Singer, Isaac Bashevis 1904-1991 ....DLB-6, 28, 52, 278; Y-91; CDALB-1
Singer, Mark 1950- DLB-185
Singmaster, Elsie 1879-1958 .... DLB-9
Siniavsky, Andrei (Abram Tertz) 1925-1997..................... DLB-302
Sinisgalli, Leonardo 1908-1981........ DLB-114
Siodmak, Curt 1902-2000.............. DLB-44
Sîrbu, Ion D. 1919-1989............... DLB-232
Siringo, Charles A. 1855-1928 .... DLB-186
Sissman, L. E. 1928-1976 .... DLB-5
Sisson, C. H. 1914- DLB-27
Sitwell, Edith 1887-1964 ...... DLB-20; CDBLB-7
Sitwell, Osbert 1892-1969.........DLB-100, 195
Skácel, Jan 1922-1989............. DLB-232
Skalbe, Kārlis 1879-1945............. DLB-220
Skármeta, Antonio 1940- DLB-145; CDWLB-3
Skavronsky, A. (see Danilevsky, Grigorii Petrovich)
Skeat, Walter W. 1835-1912 .... DLB-184
William Skeffington [publishing house] .. DLB-106
Skelton, John 1463-1529............. DLB-136
Skelton, Robin 1925-1997.........DLB-27, 53
Škėma, Antanas 1910-1961........... DLB-220
Skinner, Constance Lindsay 1877-1939...................... DLB-92
Skinner, John Stuart 1788-1851 .... DLB-73
Skipsey, Joseph 1832-1903 .... DLB-35
Skou-Hansen, Tage 1925- DLB-214
Skrzynecki, Peter 1945- DLB-289
Škvorecký, Josef 1924- DLB-232; CDWLB-4
Slade, Bernard 1930- DLB-53
Slamnig, Ivan 1930- DLB-181
Slančeková, Božena (see Timrava)
Slataper, Scipio 1888-1915 .... DLB-264
Slater, Patrick 1880-1951 .... DLB-68
Slaveykov, Pencho 1866-1912 .... DLB-147
Slaviček, Milivoj 1929- DLB-181
Slavitt, David 1935- DLB-5, 6
Sleigh, Burrows Willcocks Arthur 1821-1869 .... DLB-99
Sleptsov, Vasilii Alekseevich 1836-1878 ...DLB-277
Slesinger, Tess 1905-1945.............. DLB-102
Slessor, Kenneth 1901-1971 .... DLB-260
Slick, Sam (see Haliburton, Thomas Chandler)
Sloan, John 1871-1951 .... DLB-188
Sloane, William, Associates DLB-46
Slonimsky, Mikhail Leonidovich 1897-1972.....................DLB-272
Sluchevsky, Konstantin Konstantinovich 1837-1904.....................DLB-277
Small, Maynard and Company DLB-49
Smart, Christopher 1722-1771.......... DLB-109
Smart, David A. 1892-1957 .... DLB-137
Smart, Elizabeth 1913-1986 .... DLB-88
Smart, J. J. C. 1920- DLB-262

Smedley, Menella Bute 1820?-1877 ..... DLB-199
William Smellie [publishing house]...... DLB-154
Smiles, Samuel 1812-1904 .... DLB-55
Smiley, Jane 1949- DLB-227, 234
Smith, A. J. M. 1902-1980 .... DLB-88
Smith, Adam 1723-1790 .... DLB-104, 252
Smith, Adam (George Jerome Waldo Goodman) 1930- DLB-185
Smith, Alexander 1829-1867 .... DLB-32, 55
   "On the Writing of Essays" (1862) ... DLB-57
Smith, Amanda 1837-1915 .... DLB-221
Smith, Betty 1896-1972................ Y-82
Smith, Carol Sturm 1938- Y-81
Smith, Charles Henry 1826-1903........ DLB-11
Smith, Charlotte 1749-1806 .... DLB-39, 109
Smith, Chet 1899-1973................DLB-171
Smith, Cordwainer 1913-1966 .... DLB-8
Smith, Dave 1942- DLB-5
   Tribute to James Dickey Y-97
   Tribute to John Gardner Y-82
Smith, Dodie 1896- DLB-10
Smith, Doris Buchanan 1934- DLB-52
Smith, E. E. 1890-1965 .... DLB-8
Smith, Elihu Hubbard 1771-1798 .... DLB-37
Smith, Elizabeth Oakes (Prince) (see Oakes Smith, Elizabeth)
Smith, Eunice 1757-1823............. DLB-200
Smith, F. Hopkinson 1838-1915............DS-13
Smith, George D. 1870-1920............ DLB-140
Smith, George O. 1911-1981 .... DLB-8
Smith, Goldwin 1823-1910............. DLB-99
Smith, H. Allen 1907-1976 .... DLB-11, 29
Smith, Harry B. 1860-1936 ....DLB-187
Smith, Hazel Brannon 1914-1994........DLB-127
Smith, Henry circa 1560-circa 1591 ..... DLB-136
Smith, Horatio (Horace) 1779-1849................... DLB-96, 116
Smith, Iain Crichton 1928-1998..... DLB-40, 139
Smith, J. Allen 1860-1924............. DLB-47
Smith, James 1775-1839............. DLB-96
Smith, Jessie Willcox 1863-1935........ DLB-188
Smith, John 1580-1631............. DLB-24, 30
Smith, John 1618-1652 .... DLB-252
Smith, Josiah 1704-1781 .... DLB-24
Smith, Ken 1938- DLB-40
Smith, Lee 1944- DLB-143; Y-83
Smith, Logan Pearsall 1865-1946 .... DLB-98
Smith, Margaret Bayard 1778-1844 ..... DLB-248
Smith, Mark 1935- Y-82
Smith, Michael 1698-circa 1771 .... DLB-31
Smith, Pauline 1882-1959............. DLB-225
Smith, Red 1905-1982 ....DLB-29, 171
Smith, Roswell 1829-1892 .... DLB-79
Smith, Samuel Harrison 1772-1845 ..... DLB-43
Smith, Samuel Stanhope 1751-1819 ..... DLB-37

Smith, Sarah (see Stretton, Hesba)

Smith, Sarah Pogson 1774-1870 .... DLB-200

Smith, Seba 1792-1868 .... DLB-1, 11, 243

Smith, Stevie 1902-1971 .... DLB-20

Smith, Sydney 1771-1845 .... DLB-107

Smith, Sydney Goodsir 1915-1975 .... DLB-27

Smith, Sir Thomas 1513-1577 .... DLB-132

Smith, W. Gordon 1928-1996 .... DLB-310

Smith, Wendell 1914-1972 .... DLB-171

Smith, William flourished 1595-1597 .... DLB-136

Smith, William 1727-1803 .... DLB-31

   A General Idea of the College of Mirania (1753) [excerpts] DLB-31

Smith, William 1728-1793 .... DLB-30

Smith, William Gardner 1927-1974 .... DLB-76

Smith, William Henry 1808-1872 .... DLB-159

Smith, William Jay 1918- DLB-5

Smith, Elder and Company DLB-154

Harrison Smith and Robert Haas [publishing house] DLB-46

J. Stilman Smith and Company DLB-49

W. B. Smith and Company DLB-49

W. H. Smith and Son DLB-106

Leonard Smithers [publishing house] DLB-112

Smollett, Tobias 1721-1771 .... DLB-39, 104; CDBLB-2

   Dedication to *Ferdinand Count Fathom* (1753) DLB-39

   Preface to *Ferdinand Count Fathom* (1753) DLB-39

   Preface to *Roderick Random* (1748) DLB-39

Smythe, Francis Sydney 1900-1949 ...... DLB-195

Snelling, William Joseph 1804-1848 ..... DLB-202

Snellings, Rolland (see Touré, Askia Muhammad)

Snodgrass, W. D. 1926- DLB-5

Snorri Hjartarson 1906-1986 .... DLB-293

Snow, C. P. 1905-1980 ..... DLB-15, 77; DS-17; CDBLB-7

Snyder, Gary 1930- DLB-5, 16, 165, 212, 237, 275

Sobiloff, Hy 1912-1970 .... DLB-48

The Society for Textual Scholarship and *TEXT* Y-87

The Society for the History of Authorship, Reading and Publishing Y-92

Söderberg, Hjalmar 1869-1941 .... DLB-259

Södergran, Edith 1892-1923 .... DLB-259

Soffici, Ardengo 1879-1964 .... DLB-114, 264

Sofola, 'Zulu 1938- DLB-157

Sokhanskaia, Nadezhda Stepanovna (Kokhanovskaia) 1823?-1884 .... DLB-277

Sokolov, Sasha (Aleksandr Vsevolodovich Sokolov) 1943- DLB-285

Solano, Solita 1888-1975 .... DLB-4

Soldati, Mario 1906-1999 .... DLB-177

Soledad (see Zamudio, Adela)

Šoljan, Antun 1932-1993 .... DLB-181

Sollers, Philippe (Philippe Joyaux) 1936- DLB-83

Sollogub, Vladimir Aleksandrovich 1813-1882 .... DLB-198

Sollors, Werner 1943- DBL-246

Solmi, Sergio 1899-1981 .... DLB-114

Sologub, Fedor 1863-1927 .... DLB-295

Solomon, Carl 1928- DLB-16

Solórzano, Carlos 1922- DLB-305

Soloukhin, Vladimir Alekseevich 1924-1997 .... DLB-302

Solov'ev, Sergei Mikhailovich 1885-1942 .... DLB-295

Solov'ev, Vladimir Sergeevich 1853-1900 .... DLB-295

Solstad, Dag 1941- DLB-297

Solway, David 1941- DLB-53

Solzhenitsyn, Aleksandr 1918- DLB-302

   Solzhenitsyn and America Y-85

Some Basic Notes on Three Modern Genres: Interview, Blurb, and Obituary Y-02

Somerville, Edith Œnone 1858-1949 ..... DLB-135

Somov, Orest Mikhailovich 1793-1833 ... DLB-198

Sønderby, Knud 1909-1966 .... DLB-214

Sone, Monica 1919- DLB-312

Song, Cathy 1955- DLB-169, 312

Sonnevi, Göran 1939- DLB-257

Sono Ayako 1931- DLB-182

Sontag, Susan 1933-2004 .... DLB-2, 67

Sophocles 497/496 B.C.-406/405 B.C. DLB-176; CDWLB-1

Šopov, Aco 1923-1982 .... DLB-181

Sorel, Charles ca.1600-1674 .... DLB-268

Sørensen, Villy 1929- DLB-214

Sorensen, Virginia 1912-1991 .... DLB-206

Sorge, Reinhard Johannes 1892-1916 .... DLB-118

Sorokin, Vladimir Georgievich 1955- DLB-285

Sorrentino, Gilbert 1929- DLB-5, 173; Y-80

Sosa, Roberto 1930- DLB-290

Sotheby, James 1682-1742 .... DLB-213

Sotheby, John 1740-1807 .... DLB-213

Sotheby, Samuel 1771-1842 .... DLB-213

Sotheby, Samuel Leigh 1805-1861 ...... DLB-213

Sotheby, William 1757-1833 .... DLB-93, 213

Soto, Gary 1952- DLB-82

Soueif, Ahdaf 1950- DLB-267

Souster, Raymond 1921- DLB-88

The *South English Legendary* circa thirteenth-fifteenth centuries DLB-146

Southerland, Ellease 1943- DLB-33

Southern, Terry 1924-1995 .... DLB-2

Southern Illinois University Press Y-95

Southern Literature Fellowship of Southern Writers Y-98

   The Fugitives and the Agrarians: The First Exhibition Y-85

"The Greatness of Southern Literature": League of the South Institute for the Study of Southern Culture and History Y-02

The Society for the Study of Southern Literature Y-00

Southern Writers Between the Wars ... DLB-9

Southerne, Thomas 1659-1746 .... DLB-80

Southey, Caroline Anne Bowles 1786-1854 .... DLB-116

Southey, Robert 1774-1843 ..... DLB-93, 107, 142

Southwell, Robert 1561?-1595 .... DLB-167

Southworth, E. D. E. N. 1819-1899 ...... DLB-239

Sowande, Bode 1948- DLB-157

Tace Sowle [publishing house] DLB-170

Soyfer, Jura 1912-1939 .... DLB-124

Soyinka, Wole 1934- DLB-125; Y-86, Y-87; CDWLB-3

   Nobel Lecture 1986: This Past Must Address Its Present Y-86

Spacks, Barry 1931- DLB-105

Spalding, Frances 1950- DLB-155

Spanish Travel Writers of the Late Middle Ages DLB-286

Spark, Muriel 1918- DLB-15, 139; CDBLB-7

Michael Sparke [publishing house] DLB-170

Sparks, Jared 1789-1866 .... DLB-1, 30, 235

Sparshott, Francis 1926- DLB-60

Späth, Gerold 1939- DLB-75

Spatola, Adriano 1941-1988 .... DLB-128

Spaziani, Maria Luisa 1924- DLB-128

Specimens of Foreign Standard Literature 1838-1842 .... DLB-1

The Spectator 1828- DLB-110

Spedding, James 1808-1881 .... DLB-144

Spee von Langenfeld, Friedrich 1591-1635 .... DLB-164

Speght, Rachel 1597-after 1630 .... DLB-126

Speke, John Hanning 1827-1864 .... DLB-166

Spellman, A. B. 1935- DLB-41

Spence, Catherine Helen 1825-1910 ..... DLB-230

Spence, Thomas 1750-1814 .... DLB-158

Spencer, Anne 1882-1975 .... DLB-51, 54

Spencer, Charles, third Earl of Sunderland 1674-1722 .... DLB-213

Spencer, Elizabeth 1921- DLB-6, 218

Spencer, George John, Second Earl Spencer 1758-1834 .... DLB-184

Spencer, Herbert 1820-1903 .... DLB-57, 262

   "The Philosophy of Style" (1852) DLB-57

Spencer, Scott 1945- Y-86

Spender, J. A. 1862-1942 .... DLB-98

Spender, Stephen 1909-1995 ... DLB-20; CDBLB-7

Spener, Philipp Jakob 1635-1705 .... DLB-164

Spenser, Edmund circa 1552-1599 .... DLB-167; CDBLB-1

   Envoy from *The Shepheardes Calender* DLB-167

"The Generall Argument of the
 Whole Booke," from
 The Shepheardes Calender DLB-167

"A Letter of the Authors Expounding
 His Whole Intention in the Course
 of this Worke: Which for that It
 Giueth Great Light to the Reader,
 for the Better Vnderstanding
 Is Hereunto Annexed,"
 from *The Faerie Queene* (1590) DLB-167

"To His Booke," from
 The Shepheardes Calender (1579) . . . DLB-167

"To the Most Excellent and Learned
 Both Orator and Poete, Mayster
 Gabriell Haruey, His Verie Special
 and Singular Good Frend E. K.
 Commendeth the Good Lyking of
 This His Labour, and the Patronage
 of the New Poete," from
 The Shepheardes Calender DLB-167

Sperr, Martin 1944- DLB-124

Spewack, Bella Cowen 1899-1990 . . . . . DLB-266

Spewack, Samuel 1899-1971 . . . . DLB-266

Spicer, Jack 1925-1965 . . . . DLB-5, 16, 193

Spiegelman, Art 1948- DLB-299

Spielberg, Peter 1929- Y-81

Spielhagen, Friedrich 1829-1911 . . . . DLB-129

"Spielmannsepen" (circa 1152-circa 1500) . . DLB-148

Spier, Peter 1927- DLB-61

Spillane, Mickey 1918- DLB-226

Spink, J. G. Taylor 1888-1962 . . . . DLB-241

Spinrad, Norman 1940- DLB-8

Tribute to Isaac Asimov. Y-92

Spires, Elizabeth 1952- DLB-120

Spitteler, Carl 1845-1924 . . . . DLB-129

Spivak, Lawrence E. 1900- DLB-137

Spofford, Harriet Prescott
 1835-1921 . . . . DLB-74, 221

Sports
 Jimmy, Red, and Others: Harold
 Rosenthal Remembers the Stars
 of the Press Box. Y-01

The Literature of Boxing in England
 through Arthur Conan Doyle Y-01

Notable Twentieth-Century Books
 about Sports. DLB-241

Sprigge, Timothy L. S. 1932- DLB-262

Spring, Howard 1889-1965. . . . . DLB-191

Squibob (see Derby, George Horatio)

Squier, E. G. 1821-1888 . . . . DLB-189

Stableford, Brian 1948- DLB-261

Stacpoole, H. de Vere 1863-1951 . . . . . . DLB-153

Staël, Germaine de 1766-1817 . . . . . . DLB-119, 192

Staël-Holstein, Anne-Louise Germaine de
 (see Staël, Germaine de)

Staffeldt, Schack 1769-1826 . . . . DLB-300

Stafford, Jean 1915-1979 . . . . DLB-2, 173

Stafford, William 1914-1993 . . . . DLB-5, 206

Stallings, Laurence 1894-1968 . . . . DLB-7, 44

Stallworthy, Jon 1935- DLB-40

Stampp, Kenneth M. 1912- DLB-17

Stănescu, Nichita 1933-1983 . . . . DLB-232

Stanev, Emiliyan 1907-1979 . . . . DLB-181

Stanford, Ann 1916- DLB-5

Stangerup, Henrik 1937-1998 . . . . DLB-214

Stanihurst, Richard 1547-1618 . . . . DLB-281

Stanitsky, N. (see Panaeva, Avdot'ia Iakovlevna)

Stankevich, Nikolai Vladimirovich
 1813-1840 . . . . DLB-198

Stanković, Borisav ("Bora")
 1876-1927 . . . . DLB-147; CDWLB-4

Stanley, Henry M. 1841-1904 . . . DLB-189; DS-13

Stanley, Thomas 1625-1678 . . . . DLB-131

Stannard, Martin 1947- DLB-155

William Stansby [publishing house] DLB-170

Stanton, Elizabeth Cady 1815-1902 . . . . . DLB-79

Stanton, Frank L. 1857-1927 . . . . DLB-25

Stanton, Maura 1946- DLB-120

Stapledon, Olaf 1886-1950 . . . . DLB-15, 255

Star Spangled Banner Office. DLB-49

Stark, Freya 1893-1993 . . . . DLB-195

Starkey, Thomas circa 1499-1538 . . . . . . DLB-132

Starkie, Walter 1894-1976 . . . . DLB-195

Starkweather, David 1935- DLB-7

Starrett, Vincent 1886-1974 . . . . DLB-187

Stationers' Company of London, The DLB-170

Statius circa A.D. 45-A.D. 96 . . . . DLB-211

Stead, Christina 1902-1983 . . . . DLB-260

Stead, Robert J. C. 1880-1959 . . . . DLB-92

Steadman, Mark 1930- DLB-6

Stearns, Harold E. 1891-1943 . . . . . . DLB-4; DS-15

Stebnitsky, M. (see Leskov, Nikolai Semenovich)

Stedman, Edmund Clarence 1833-1908 . . . DLB-64

Steegmuller, Francis 1906-1994 . . . . DLB-111

Steel, Flora Annie 1847-1929 . . . . . . DLB-153, 156

Steele, Max 1922- Y-80

Steele, Richard
 1672-1729 . . . . DLB-84, 101; CDBLB-2

Steele, Timothy 1948- DLB-120

Steele, Wilbur Daniel 1886-1970 . . . . DLB-86

Wallace Markfield's "Steeplechase" Y-02

Steere, Richard circa 1643-1721 . . . . DLB-24

Stefán frá Hvítadal (Stefán Sigurðsson)
 1887-1933 . . . . DLB-293

Stefán Guðmundsson (see Stephan G. Stephansson)

Stefán Hörður Grímsson
 1919 or 1920-2002 . . . . DLB-293

Steffens, Lincoln 1866-1936 . . . . DLB-303

Stefanovski, Goran 1952- DLB-181

Stegner, Wallace
 1909-1993 . . . . DLB-9, 206, 275; Y-93

Stehr, Hermann 1864-1940 . . . . DLB-66

Steig, William 1907- DLB-61

Stein, Gertrude 1874-1946
 . . . . DLB-4, 54, 86, 228; DS-15; CDALB-4

Stein, Leo 1872-1947 . . . . DLB-4

Stein and Day Publishers DLB-46

Steinbeck, John 1902-1968
 . . . . DLB-7, 9, 212, 275, 309; DS-2; CDALB-5

John Steinbeck Research Center,
 San Jose State University. Y-85

The Steinbeck Centennial Y-02

Steinem, Gloria 1934- DLB-246

Steiner, George 1929- DLB-67, 299

Steinhoewel, Heinrich 1411/1412-1479. . . . DLB-179

Steinn Steinarr (Aðalsteinn Kristmundsson)
 1908-1958 . . . . DLB-293

Steinunn Sigurðardóttir 1950- DLB-293

Steloff, Ida Frances 1887-1989 . . . . DLB-187

Stendhal 1783-1842. . . . . DLB-119

Stephan G. Stephansson (Stefán Guðmundsson)
 1853-1927 . . . . DLB-293

Stephen, Leslie 1832-1904 . . . . . . DLB-57, 144, 190

Stephen Family (Bloomsbury Group) DS-10

Stephens, A. G. 1865-1933 . . . . DLB-230

Stephens, Alexander H. 1812-1883 . . . . . . DLB-47

Stephens, Alice Barber 1858-1932 . . . . . . DLB-188

Stephens, Ann 1810-1886 . . . . DLB-3, 73, 250

Stephens, Charles Asbury 1844?-1931 . . . . DLB-42

Stephens, James 1882?-1950 . . . . . DLB-19, 153, 162

Stephens, John Lloyd 1805-1852 . . . DLB-183, 250

Stephens, Michael 1946- DLB-234

Stephensen, P. R. 1901-1965 . . . . DLB-260

Sterling, George 1869-1926 . . . . DLB-54

Sterling, James 1701-1763 . . . . DLB-24

Sterling, John 1806-1844 . . . . DLB-116

Stern, Gerald 1925- DLB-105

"Living in Ruin" DLB-105

Stern, Gladys B. 1890-1973 . . . . DLB-197

Stern, Madeleine B. 1912- DLB-111, 140

Stern, Richard 1928- DLB-218; Y-87

Stern, Stewart 1922- DLB-26

Sterne, Laurence 1713-1768 . . . DLB-39; CDBLB-2

Sternheim, Carl 1878-1942 . . . . DLB-56, 118

Sternhold, Thomas ?-1549 . . . . DLB-132

Steuart, David 1747-1824 . . . . DLB-213

Stevens, Henry 1819-1886 . . . . DLB-140

Stevens, Wallace 1879-1955 . . . DLB-54; CDALB-5

The Wallace Stevens Society Y-99

Stevenson, Anne 1933- DLB-40

Stevenson, D. E. 1892-1973 . . . . DLB-191

Stevenson, Lionel 1902-1973 . . . . DLB-155

Stevenson, Robert Louis
 1850-1894 . . . . . . DLB-18, 57, 141, 156, 174;
 DS-13; CDBLB-5

"On Style in Literature:
 Its Technical Elements" (1885) . . . DLB-57

Stewart, Donald Ogden
 1894-1980 . . . . DLB-4, 11, 26; DS-15

Stewart, Douglas 1913-1985 . . . . DLB-260

Stewart, Dugald 1753-1828 . . . . DLB-31

Stewart, George, Jr. 1848-1906 . . . . DLB-99

Stewart, George R. 1895-1980 . . . . DLB-8

Stewart, Harold 1916-1995 . . . . DLB-260

Stewart, J. I. M. (see Innes, Michael)

Stewart, Maria W. 1803?-1879 . . . . DLB-239

Stewart, Randall 1896-1964...........DLB-103
Stewart, Sean 1965- DLB-251
Stewart and Kidd Company DLB-46
Sthen, Hans Christensen 1544-1610 .....DLB-300
Stickney, Trumbull 1874-1904...........DLB-54
Stieler, Caspar 1632-1707..............DLB-164
Stifter, Adalbert
   1805-1868 ....DLB-133; CDWLB-2
Stiles, Ezra 1727-1795 ....DLB-31
Still, James 1906-2001 ....DLB-9; Y-01
Stirling, S. M. 1953- DLB-251
Stirner, Max 1806-1856................DLB-129
Stith, William 1707-1755................DLB-31
Stivens, Dal 1911-1997................DLB-260
Elliot Stock [publishing house]...........DLB-106
Stockton, Annis Boudinot 1736-1801.....DLB-200
Stockton, Frank R.
   1834-1902 ....DLB-42, 74; DS-13
Stockton, J. Roy 1892-1972 ....DLB-241
Ashbel Stoddard [publishing house].......DLB-49
Stoddard, Charles Warren 1843-1909....DLB-186
Stoddard, Elizabeth 1823-1902 ....DLB-202
Stoddard, Richard Henry
   1825-1903 ....DLB-3, 64, 250; DS-13
Stoddard, Solomon 1643-1729..........DLB-24
Stoker, Bram
   1847-1912 ....DLB-36, 70, 178; CDBLB-5
   On Writing *Dracula,* from the
     Introduction to *Dracula* (1897) ...DLB-178
   Dracula (Documentary) DLB-304
Frederick A. Stokes Company...........DLB-49
Stokes, Thomas L. 1898-1958 ....DLB-29
Stokesbury, Leon 1945- DLB-120
Stolberg, Christian Graf zu 1748-1821.....DLB-94
Stolberg, Friedrich Leopold Graf zu
   1750-1819 ....DLB-94
Stone, Lucy 1818-1893 ....DLB-79, 239
Stone, Melville 1848-1929 ....DLB-25
Stone, Robert 1937- DLB-152
Stone, Ruth 1915- DLB-105
Stone, Samuel 1602-1663..............DLB-24
Stone, William Leete 1792-1844 ....DLB-202
Herbert S. Stone and Company..........DLB-49
Stone and Kimball DLB-49
Stoppard, Tom
   1937- DLB-13, 233; Y-85; CDBLB-8
   Playwrights and Professors DLB-13
Storey, Anthony 1928- DLB-14
Storey, David 1933- DLB-13, 14, 207, 245
Storm, Theodor
   1817-1888 ....DLB-129; CDWLB-2
Storni, Alfonsina 1892-1938............DLB-283
Story, Thomas circa 1670-1742 ....DLB-31
Story, William Wetmore 1819-1895 ...DLB-1, 235
Storytelling: A Contemporary Renaissance... Y-84
Stoughton, William 1631-1701..........DLB-24
Stout, Rex 1886-1975................DLB-306

Stow, John 1525-1605 ....DLB-132
Stow, Randolph 1935- DLB-260
Stowe, Harriet Beecher 1811-1896......DLB-1,12,
     42, 74, 189, 239, 243; CDALB-3
   The Harriet Beecher Stowe Center...... Y-00
Stowe, Leland 1899-1994...............DLB-29
Stoyanov, Dimitr Ivanov (see Elin Pelin)
Strabo 64/63 B.C.-circa A.D. 25..........DLB-176
Strachey, Lytton 1880-1932......DLB-149; DS-10
   Preface to *Eminent Victorians* DLB-149
William Strahan [publishing house]......DLB-154
Strahan and Company.................DLB-106
Strand, Mark 1934- DLB-5
The Strasbourg Oaths 842.............DLB-148
Stratemeyer, Edward 1862-1930 ....DLB-42
Strati, Saverio 1924- DLB-177
Stratton and Barnard DLB-49
Stratton-Porter, Gene
   1863-1924 ....DLB-221; DS-14
Straub, Peter 1943- Y-84
Strauß, Botho 1944- DLB-124
Strauß, David Friedrich 1808-1874 ......DLB-133
The Strawberry Hill Press.............DLB-154
Strawson, P. F. 1919- DLB-262
Streatfeild, Noel 1895-1986 ....DLB-160
Street, Cecil John Charles (see Rhode, John)
Street, G. S. 1867-1936................DLB-135
Street and Smith.....................DLB-49
Streeter, Edward 1891-1976............DLB-11
Streeter, Thomas Winthrop 1883-1965...DLB-140
Stretton, Hesba 1832-1911.........DLB-163, 190
Stribling, T. S. 1881-1965 ....DLB-9
Der Stricker circa 1190-circa 1250.......DLB-138
Strickland, Samuel 1804-1867 ....DLB-99
Strindberg, August 1849-1912..........DLB-259
Stringer, Arthur 1874-1950 ....DLB-92
Stringer and Townsend DLB-49
Strittmatter, Erwin 1912-1994 ....DLB-69
Strniša, Gregor 1930-1987 ....DLB-181
Strode, William 1630-1645 ....DLB-126
Strong, L. A. G. 1896-1958 ....DLB-191
Strother, David Hunter (Porte Crayon)
   1816-1888 ....DLB-3, 248
Strouse, Jean 1945- DLB-111
Strugatsky, Arkadii Natanovich
   1925- DLB-302
Strugatsky, Boris Natanovich 1933- DLB-302
Stuart, Dabney 1937- DLB-105
   "Knots into Webs: Some
     Autobiographical Sources" DLB-105
Stuart, Jesse 1906-1984 ..... DLB-9, 48, 102; Y-84
Lyle Stuart [publishing house]..........DLB-46
Stuart, Ruth McEnery 1849?-1917 ....DLB-202
Stub, Ambrosius 1705-1758 ....DLB-300
Stubbs, Harry Clement (see Clement, Hal)

Stubenberg, Johann Wilhelm von
   1619-1663 ....DLB-164
Stuckenberg, Viggo 1763-1905 ....DLB-300
Studebaker, William V. 1947- DLB-256
Studies in American Jewish Literature........ Y-02
Studio.............................DLB-112
Stump, Al 1916-1995 ....DLB-241
Sturgeon, Theodore
   1918-1985 ....DLB-8; Y-85
Sturges, Preston 1898-1959 ....DLB-26
Styron, William
   1925- DLB-2, 143, 299; Y-80; CDALB-6
   Tribute to James Dickey Y-97
Suárez, Clementina 1902-1991 ....DLB-290
Suárez, Mario 1925- DLB-82
Suassuna, Ariano 1927- DLB-307
Such, Peter 1939- DLB-60
Suckling, Sir John 1609-1641?........DLB-58, 126
Suckow, Ruth 1892-1960...........DLB-9, 102
Sudermann, Hermann 1857-1928 ....DLB-118
Sue, Eugène 1804-1857 ....DLB-119
Sue, Marie-Joseph (see Sue, Eugène)
Suetonius circa A.D. 69-post A.D. 122.....DLB-211
Suggs, Simon (see Hooper, Johnson Jones)
Sui Sin Far (see Eaton, Edith Maude)
Suits, Gustav 1883-1956 ....DLB-220; CDWLB-4
Sukenick, Ronald 1932- DLB-173; Y-81
   An Author's Response Y-82
Sukhovo-Kobylin, Aleksandr Vasil'evich
   1817-1903 ....DLB-277
Suknaski, Andrew 1942- DLB-53
Sullivan, Alan 1868-1947 ....DLB-92
Sullivan, C. Gardner 1886-1965 ....DLB-26
Sullivan, Frank 1892-1976 ....DLB-11
Sulte, Benjamin 1841-1923 ....DLB-99
Sulzberger, Arthur Hays 1891-1968 .....DLB-127
Sulzberger, Arthur Ochs 1926- DLB-127
Sulzer, Johann Georg 1720-1779 ....DLB-97
Sumarokov, Aleksandr Petrovich
   1717-1777 ....DLB-150
Summers, Hollis 1916- DLB-6
Sumner, Charles 1811-1874.............DLB-235
Sumner, William Graham 1840-1910 ....DLB-270
Henry A. Sumner
   [publishing house].................DLB-49
Sundman, Per Olof 1922-1992 ....DLB-257
Supervielle, Jules 1884-1960 ....DLB-258
Surtees, Robert Smith 1803-1864 ....DLB-21
   The R. S. Surtees Society Y-98
Sutcliffe, Matthew 1550?-1629..........DLB-281
Sutcliffe, William 1971- DLB-271
Sutherland, Efua Theodora 1924-1996 ...DLB-117
Sutherland, John 1919-1956 ....DLB-68
Sutro, Alfred 1863-1933................DLB-10
Svava Jakobsdóttir 1930- DLB-293
Svendsen, Hanne Marie 1933- DLB-214

Cumulative Index

Svevo, Italo (Ettore Schmitz) 1861-1928 .... DLB-264

Swados, Harvey 1920-1972 .... DLB-2

Swain, Charles 1801-1874 .... DLB-32

Swallow Press DLB-46

Swan Sonnenschein Limited DLB-106

Swanberg, W. A. 1907-1992 .... DLB-103

Swedish Literature
    The Literature of the Modern Breakthrough DLB-259

Swenson, May 1919-1989 .... DLB-5

Swerling, Jo 1897- DLB-44

Swift, Graham 1949- DLB-194

Swift, Jonathan 1667-1745 .... DLB-39, 95, 101; CDBLB-2

Swinburne, A. C. 1837-1909 .... DLB-35, 57; CDBLB-4
    Under the Microscope (1872) DLB-35

Swineshead, Richard floruit circa 1350... DLB-115

Swinnerton, Frank 1884-1982 .... DLB-34

Swisshelm, Jane Grey 1815-1884 .... DLB-43

Swope, Herbert Bayard 1882-1958 ...... DLB-25

Swords, James ?-1844 .... DLB-73

Swords, Thomas 1763-1843 .... DLB-73

T. and J. Swords and Company DLB-49

Swynnerton, Thomas (John Roberts) circa 1500-1554 .... DLB-281

Sykes, Ella C. ?-1939 .... DLB-174

Sylvester, Josuah 1562 or 1563-1618 .... DLB-121

Symonds, Emily Morse (see Paston, George)

Symonds, John Addington 1840-1893 .... DLB-57, 144
    "Personal Style" (1890) DLB-57

Symons, A. J. A. 1900-1941 .... DLB-149

Symons, Arthur 1865-1945 .... DLB-19, 57, 149

Symons, Julian 1912-1994 ..... DLB-87, 155; Y-92
    Julian Symons at Eighty Y-92

Symons, Scott 1933- DLB-53

Synge, John Millington 1871-1909 .... DLB-10, 19; CDBLB-5
    Synge Summer School: J. M. Synge and the Irish Theater, Rathdrum, County Wiclow, Ireland Y-93

Syrett, Netta 1865-1943 .... DLB-135, 197

Szabó, Lőrinc 1900-1957 .... DLB-215

Szabó, Magda 1917- DLB-215

Szymborska, Wisława 1923- DLB-232, Y-96; CDWLB-4
    Nobel Lecture 1996: The Poet and the World Y-96

T

Taban lo Liyong 1939?- DLB-125

al-Tabari 839-923 .... DLB-311

Tablada, José Juan 1871-1945 .... DLB-290

Tabori, George 1914- DLB-245

Tabucchi, Antonio 1943- DLB-196

Taché, Joseph-Charles 1820-1894 ...... DLB-99

Tachihara Masaaki 1926-1980 .... DLB-182

Tacitus circa A.D. 55-circa A.D. 117 .... DLB-211; CDWLB-1

Tadijanović, Dragutin 1905- DLB-181

Tafdrup, Pia 1952- DLB-214

Tafolla, Carmen 1951- DLB-82

Taggard, Genevieve 1894-1948 .... DLB-45

Taggart, John 1942- DLB-193

Tagger, Theodor (see Bruckner, Ferdinand)

Taiheiki late fourteenth century DLB-203

Tait, J. Selwin, and Sons DLB-49

Tait's Edinburgh Magazine 1832-1861 ..... DLB-110

The Takarazaka Revue Company Y-91

Talander (see Bohse, August)

Talese, Gay 1932- DLB-185
    Tribute to Irwin Shaw Y-84

Talev, Dimitr 1898-1966 .... DLB-181

Taliaferro, H. E. 1811-1875 .... DLB-202

Tallent, Elizabeth 1954- DLB-130

TallMountain, Mary 1918-1994 .... DLB-193

Talvj 1797-1870 .... DLB-59, 133

Tamási, Áron 1897-1966 .... DLB-215

Tammsaare, A. H. 1878-1940 .... DLB-220; CDWLB-4

Tan, Amy 1952- DLB-173, 312; CDALB-7

Tandori, Dezső 1938- DLB-232

Tanner, Thomas 1673/1674-1735 .... DLB-213

Tanizaki Jun'ichirō 1886-1965 .... DLB-180

Tapahonso, Luci 1953- DLB-175

The Mark Taper Forum DLB-7

Taradash, Daniel 1913- DLB-44

Tarasov-Rodionov, Aleksandr Ignat'evich 1885-1938 .... DLB-272

Tarbell, Ida M. 1857-1944 .... DLB-47

Tardivel, Jules-Paul 1851-1905 .... DLB-99

Targan, Barry 1932- DLB-130
    Tribute to John Gardner Y-82

Tarkington, Booth 1869-1946 ...... DLB-9, 102

Tashlin, Frank 1913-1972 .... DLB-44

Tasma (Jessie Couvreur) 1848-1897 .... DLB-230

Tate, Allen 1899-1979 .... DLB-4, 45, 63; DS-17

Tate, James 1943- DLB-5, 169

Tate, Nahum circa 1652-1715 .... DLB-80

Tatian circa 830 .... DLB-148

Taufer, Veno 1933- DLB-181

Tauler, Johannes circa 1300-1361 ..... DLB-179

Tavares, Salette 1922-1994 .... DLB-287

Tavčar, Ivan 1851-1923 .... DLB-147

Taverner, Richard ca. 1505-1575 ...... DLB-236

Taylor, Ann 1782-1866 .... DLB-163

Taylor, Bayard 1825-1878 ...... DLB-3, 189, 250

Taylor, Bert Leston 1866-1921 .... DLB-25

Taylor, Charles H. 1846-1921 .... DLB-25

Taylor, Edward circa 1642-1729 .... DLB-24

Taylor, Elizabeth 1912-1975 .... DLB-139

Taylor, Sir Henry 1800-1886 .... DLB-32

Taylor, Henry 1942- DLB-5
    Who Owns American Literature Y-94

Taylor, Jane 1783-1824 .... DLB-163

Taylor, Jeremy circa 1613-1667 .... DLB-151

Taylor, John 1577 or 1578 - 1653 ..... DLB-121

Taylor, Mildred D. 1943- DLB-52

Taylor, Peter 1917-1994 ... DLB-218, 278; Y-81, 94

Taylor, Susie King 1848-1912 .... DLB-221

Taylor, William Howland 1901-1966 ... DLB-241

William Taylor and Company DLB-49

Teale, Edwin Way 1899-1980 .... DLB-275

Teasdale, Sara 1884-1933 .... DLB-45

Teillier, Jorge 1935-1996 .... DLB-283

Telles, Lygia Fagundes 1924- DLB-113, 307

The Temper of the West: William Jovanovich ... Y-02

Temple, Sir William 1555?-1627 .... DLB-281

Temple, Sir William 1628-1699 .... DLB-101

Temple, William F. 1914-1989 .... DLB-255

Temrizov, A. (see Marchenko, Anastasia Iakovlevna)

Tench, Watkin ca. 1758-1833 .... DLB-230

Tender Is the Night (Documentary) DLB-273

Tendriakov, Vladimir Fedorovich 1923-1984 .... DLB-302

Tenn, William 1919- DLB-8

Tennant, Emma 1937- DLB-14

Tenney, Tabitha Gilman 1762-1837... DLB-37, 200

Tennyson, Alfred 1809-1892 .. DLB-32; CDBLB-4
    On Some of the Characteristics of Modern Poetry and On the Lyrical Poems of Alfred Tennyson (1831) DLB-32

Tennyson, Frederick 1807-1898 .... DLB-32

Tenorio, Arthur 1924- DLB-209

Tepl, Johannes von circa 1350-1414/1415 .... DLB-179

Tepliakov, Viktor Grigor'evich 1804-1842 .... DLB-205

Terence circa 184 B.C.-159 B.C. or after DLB-211; CDWLB-1

Terhune, Albert Payson 1872-1942 ..... DLB-9

Terhune, Mary Virginia 1830-1922 ..... DS-13

Terpigorev, Sergei Nikolaevich (S. Atava) 1841-1895 .... DLB-277

Terry, Megan 1932- DLB-7, 249

Terson, Peter 1932- DLB-13

Tesich, Steve 1943-1996 .... Y-83

Tessa, Delio 1886-1939 .... DLB-114

Testori, Giovanni 1923-1993 .... DLB-128, 177

Texas
    The Year in Texas Literature Y-98

Tey, Josephine 1896?-1952 .... DLB-77

Thacher, James 1754-1844 .... DLB-37

Thacher, John Boyd 1847-1909 .... DLB-187

Thackeray, William Makepeace 1811-1863 .. DLB-21, 55, 159, 163; CDBLB-4

Thames and Hudson Limited DLB-112

Thanet, Octave (see French, Alice)

Thaxter, Celia Laighton 1835-1894 .... DLB-239

Thayer, Caroline Matilda Warren 1785-1844 .... DLB-200

Thayer, Douglas H. 1929- DLB-256

Theater
   Black Theatre: A Forum [excerpts] DLB-38
   Community and Commentators: Black Theatre and Its Critics DLB-38
   German Drama from Naturalism to Fascism: 1889-1933 .... DLB-118
   A Look at the Contemporary Black Theatre Movement............. DLB-38
   The Lord Chamberlain's Office and Stage Censorship in England DLB-10
   New Forces at Work in the American Theatre: 1915-1925 .... DLB-7
   Off Broadway and Off-Off Broadway .. DLB-7
   Oregon Shakespeare Festival............ Y-00
   Plays, Playwrights, and Playgoers..... DLB-84
   Playwrights on the Theater......... DLB-80
   Playwrights and Professors DLB-13
   Producing *Dear Bunny, Dear Volodya*: The Friendship and the Feud Y-97
   Viewpoint: Politics and Performance, by David Edgar DLB-13
   Writing for the Theatre, by Harold Pinter................ DLB-13
   The Year in Drama Y-82–85, 87–98
   The Year in U.S. Drama Y-00

Theater, English and Irish
   Anti-Theatrical Tracts DLB-263
   The Chester Plays circa 1505-1532; revisions until 1575............. DLB-146
   Dangerous Years: London Theater, 1939-1945.................... DLB-10
   A Defense of Actors DLB-263
   The Development of Lighting in the Staging of Drama, 1900-1945 .... DLB-10
   Education DLB-263
   The End of English Stage Censorship, 1945-1968.................... DLB-13
   Epigrams and Satires............. DLB-263
   Eyewitnesses and Historians DLB-263
   Fringe and Alternative Theater in Great Britain.................. DLB-13
   The Great War and the Theater, 1914-1918 [Great Britain] DLB-10
   Licensing Act of 1737 .... DLB-84
   Morality Plays: *Mankind* circa 1450-1500 and *Everyman* circa 1500 .... DLB-146
   The New Variorum Shakespeare Y-85
   N-Town Plays circa 1468 to early sixteenth century DLB-146
   Politics and the Theater DLB-263
   Practical Matters DLB-263
   Prologues, Epilogues, Epistles to Readers, and Excerpts from Plays..................... DLB-263
   The Publication of English Renaissance Plays............. DLB-62
   Regulations for the Theater DLB-263
   Sources for the Study of Tudor and Stuart Drama DLB-62
   Stage Censorship: "The Rejected Statement" (1911), by Bernard Shaw [excerpts]................ DLB-10
   Synge Summer School: J. M. Synge and the Irish Theater, Rathdrum, County Wiclow, Ireland.......... Y-93
   The Theater in Shakespeare's Time ... DLB-62
   The Theatre Guild DLB-7
   The Townely Plays fifteenth and sixteenth centuries DLB-146
   The Year in British Drama Y-99–01
   The Year in Drama: London Y-90
   The Year in London Theatre Y-92
   A Yorkshire Tragedy................. DLB-58

Theaters
   The Abbey Theatre and Irish Drama, 1900-1945.................... DLB-10
   Actors Theatre of Louisville DLB-7
   American Conservatory Theatre DLB-7
   Arena Stage..................... DLB-7
   Black Theaters and Theater Organizations in America, 1961-1982: A Research List DLB-38
   The Dallas Theater Center DLB-7
   Eugene O'Neill Memorial Theater Center.................... DLB-7
   The Goodman Theatre.............. DLB-7
   The Guthrie Theater DLB-7
   The Mark Taper Forum DLB-7
   The National Theatre and the Royal Shakespeare Company: The National Companies............ DLB-13
   Off-Loop Theatres DLB-7
   The Royal Court Theatre and the English Stage Company DLB-13
   The Royal Court Theatre and the New Drama DLB-10
   The Takarazaka Revue Company Y-91

Thegan and the Astronomer flourished circa 850................ DLB-148

Thelwall, John 1764-1834 .... DLB-93, 158

Theocritus circa 300 B.C.-260 B.C........ DLB-176

Theodorescu, Ion N. (see Arghezi, Tudor)

Theodulf circa 760-circa 821 .... DLB-148

Theophrastus circa 371 B.C.-287 B.C...... DLB-176

Thériault, Yves 1915-1983................ DLB-88

Thério, Adrien 1925- DLB-53

Theroux, Paul 1941- DLB-2, 218; CDALB-7

Thesiger, Wilfred 1910- DLB-204

They All Came to Paris.................. DS-15

Thibaudeau, Colleen 1925- DLB-88

Thiele, Colin 1920- DLB-289

Thielen, Benedict 1903-1965........... DLB-102

Thiong'o Ngugi wa (see Ngugi wa Thiong'o)

This Quarter 1925-1927, 1929-1932 .... DS-15

Thoma, Ludwig 1867-1921 .... DLB-66

Thoma, Richard 1902- DLB-4

Thomas, Audrey 1935- DLB-60

Thomas, D. M. 1935- ... DLB-40, 207, 299; Y-82; CDBLB-8
   The Plagiarism Controversy........... Y-82

Thomas, Dylan 1914-1953 .... DLB-13, 20, 139; CDBLB-7
   The Dylan Thomas Celebration........ Y-99

Thomas, Ed 1961- DLB-310

Thomas, Edward 1878-1917 .... DLB-19, 98, 156, 216
   The Friends of the Dymock Poets Y-00

Thomas, Frederick William 1806-1866... DLB-202

Thomas, Gwyn 1913-1981 .... DLB-15, 245

Thomas, Isaiah 1750-1831....... DLB-43, 73, 187

Thomas, Johann 1624-1679............ DLB-168

Thomas, John 1900-1932............... DLB-4

Thomas, Joyce Carol 1938- DLB-33

Thomas, Lewis 1913-1993............. DLB-275

Thomas, Lorenzo 1944- DLB-41

Thomas, Norman 1884-1968 .... DLB-303

Thomas, R. S. 1915-2000 ..... DLB-27; CDBLB-8

Isaiah Thomas [publishing house] DLB-49

Thomasîn von Zerclære circa 1186-circa 1259.............. DLB-138

Thomason, George 1602?-1666 .... DLB-213

Thomasius, Christian 1655-1728........ DLB-168

Thompson, Daniel Pierce 1795-1868..... DLB-202

Thompson, David 1770-1857............ DLB-99

Thompson, Dorothy 1893-1961 .... DLB-29

Thompson, E. P. 1924-1993 .... DLB-242

Thompson, Flora 1876-1947 .... DLB-240

Thompson, Francis 1859-1907 .... DLB-19; CDBLB-5

Thompson, George Selden (see Selden, George)

Thompson, Henry Yates 1838-1928 ..... DLB-184

Thompson, Hunter S. 1939-2005 .... DLB-185

Thompson, Jim 1906-1977............. DLB-226

Thompson, John 1938-1976............. DLB-60

Thompson, John R. 1823-1873 .... DLB-3, 73, 248

Thompson, Lawrance 1906-1973 .... DLB-103

Thompson, Maurice 1844-1901 ...... DLB-71, 74

Thompson, Ruth Plumly 1891-1976 ...... DLB-22

Thompson, Thomas Phillips 1843-1933 ... DLB-99

Thompson, William 1775-1833 .... DLB-158

Thompson, William Tappan 1812-1882 .... DLB-3, 11, 248

Thomson, Cockburn "Modern Style" (1857) [excerpt]...... DLB-57

Thomson, Edward William 1849-1924.... DLB-92

Thomson, James 1700-1748 .... DLB-95

Thomson, James 1834-1882 .... DLB-35

Thomson, Joseph 1858-1895........... DLB-174

Thomson, Mortimer 1831-1875......... DLB-11

Thomson, Rupert 1955- DLB-267

Thon, Melanie Rae 1957- DLB-244

Thor Vilhjálmsson 1925- DLB-293

Þórarinn Eldjárn 1949- DLB-293

Þórbergur Þórðarson 1888-1974 .... DLB-293

Thoreau, Henry David 1817-1862 .... DLB-1, 183, 223, 270, 298; DS-5; CDALB-2

    The Thoreau Society Y-99

    The Thoreauvian Pilgrimage: The Structure of an American Cult .. DLB-223

Thorne, William 1568?-1630 .... DLB-281

Thornton, John F. [Repsonse to Ken Auletta] Y-97

Thorpe, Adam 1956- DLB-231

Thorpe, Thomas Bangs 1815-1878 .... DLB-3, 11, 248

Thorup, Kirsten 1942- DLB-214

Thotl, Birgitte 1610-1662 .... DLB-300

Thrale, Hester Lynch (see Piozzi, Hester Lynch [Thrale])

The Three Marias: A Landmark Case in Portuguese Literary History (Maria Isabel Barreno, 1939- ; Maria Teresa Horta, 1937- ; Maria Velho da Costa, 1938-) DLB-287

Thubron, Colin 1939- DLB-204, 231

Thucydides circa 455 B.C.-circa 395 B.C. DLB-176

Thulstrup, Thure de 1848-1930 .... DLB-188

Thümmel, Moritz August von 1738-1817 .... DLB-97

Thurber, James 1894-1961 .... DLB-4, 11, 22, 102; CDALB-5

Thurman, Wallace 1902-1934 .... DLB-51

    "Negro Poets and Their Poetry" DLB-50

Thwaite, Anthony 1930- DLB-40

    The Booker Prize, Address Y-86

Thwaites, Reuben Gold 1853-1913 ...... DLB-47

Tibullus circa 54 B.C.-circa 19 B.C. DLB-211

Ticknor, George 1791-1871 ....DLB-1, 59, 140, 235

Ticknor and Fields DLB-49

Ticknor and Fields (revived) DLB-46

Tieck, Ludwig 1773-1853 .... DLB-90; CDWLB-2

Tietjens, Eunice 1884-1944 .... DLB-54

Tikkanen, Märta 1935- DLB-257

Tilghman, Christopher circa 1948 ...... DLB-244

Tilney, Edmund circa 1536-1610 .... DLB-136

Charles Tilt [publishing house] DLB-106

J. E. Tilton and Company DLB-49

Time-Life Books DLB-46

Times Books DLB-46

Timothy, Peter circa 1725-1782 .... DLB-43

Timrava 1867-1951 .... DLB-215

Timrod, Henry 1828-1867 .... DLB-3, 248

Tindal, Henrietta 1818?-1879 .... DLB-199

Tinker, Chauncey Brewster 1876-1963 ....DLB-140

Tinsley Brothers DLB-106

Tiptree, James, Jr. 1915-1987 .... DLB-8

Tišma, Aleksandar 1924- DLB-181

Titus, Edward William 1870-1952 .... DLB-4; DS-15

Tiutchev, Fedor Ivanovich 1803-1873 ... DLB-205

Tlali, Miriam 1933- DLB-157, 225

Todd, Barbara Euphan 1890-1976 ...... DLB-160

Todorov, Tzvetan 1939- DLB-242

Tofte, Robert 1561 or 1562-1619 or 1620 .... DLB-172

Tóibín, Colm 1955- DLB-271

Toklas, Alice B. 1877-1967 .... DLB-4; DS-15

Tokuda Shūsei 1872-1943 .... DLB-180

Toland, John 1670-1722 .... DLB-252

Tolkien, J. R. R. 1892-1973 ...... DLB-15, 160, 255; CDBLB-6

Toller, Ernst 1893-1939 .... DLB-124

Tollet, Elizabeth 1694-1754 .... DLB-95

Tolson, Melvin B. 1898-1966 .... DLB-48, 76

Tolstaya, Tatyana 1951- DLB-285

Tolstoy, Aleksei Konstantinovich 1817-1875 .... DLB-238

Tolstoy, Aleksei Nikolaevich 1883-1945 ..DLB-272

Tolstoy, Leo 1828-1910 .... DLB-238

Tomalin, Claire 1933- DLB-155

Tómas Guðmundsson 1901-1983 .... DLB-293

Tomasi di Lampedusa, Giuseppe 1896-1957 ....DLB-177

Tomlinson, Charles 1927- DLB-40

Tomlinson, H. M. 1873-1958 ....DLB-36, 100, 195

Abel Tompkins [publishing house] DLB-49

Tompson, Benjamin 1642-1714 .... DLB-24

Tomson, Graham R. (see Watson, Rosamund Marriott)

Ton'a 1289-1372 .... DLB-203

Tondelli, Pier Vittorio 1955-1991 .... DLB-196

Tonks, Rosemary 1932- DLB-14, 207

Tonna, Charlotte Elizabeth 1790-1846 ... DLB-163

Jacob Tonson the Elder [publishing house] DLB-170

Toole, John Kennedy 1937-1969 .... Y-81

Toomer, Jean 1894-1967 .... DLB-45, 51; CDALB-4

Topsoe, Vilhelm 1840-1881 .... DLB-300

Tor Books DLB-46

Torberg, Friedrich 1908-1979 .... DLB-85

Torga, Miguel (Adolfo Correira da Rocha) 1907-1995 .... DLB-287

Torrence, Ridgely 1874-1950 .... DLB-54, 249

Torres-Metzger, Joseph V. 1933- DLB-122

El Tostado (see Madrigal, Alfonso Fernández de)

Toth, Susan Allen 1940- Y-86

Richard Tottell [publishing house] DLB-170

    "The Printer to the Reader," (1557) DLB-167

Tough-Guy Literature DLB-9

Touré, Askia Muhammad 1938- DLB-41

Tourgée, Albion W. 1838-1905 .... DLB-79

Tournemir, Elizaveta Sailhas de (see Tur, Evgeniia)

Tourneur, Cyril circa 1580-1626 .... DLB-58

Tournier, Michel 1924- DLB-83

Frank Tousey [publishing house] DLB-49

Tower Publications DLB-46

Towne, Benjamin circa 1740-1793 .... DLB-43

Towne, Robert 1936- DLB-44

The Townely Plays fifteenth and sixteenth centuries DLB-146

Townsend, Sue 1946- DLB-271

Townshend, Aurelian by 1583-circa 1651 .... DLB-121

Toy, Barbara 1908-2001 .... DLB-204

Tozzi, Federigo 1883-1920 .... DLB-264

Tracy, Honor 1913-1989 .... DLB-15

Traherne, Thomas 1637?-1674 .... DLB-131

Traill, Catharine Parr 1802-1899 .... DLB-99

Train, Arthur 1875-1945 .... DLB-86; DS-16

Tranquilli, Secondino (see Silone, Ignazio)

The Transatlantic Publishing Company .. DLB-49

The Transatlantic Review 1924-1925 .... DS-15

The Transcendental Club 1836-1840 ....DLB-1; DLB-223

Transcendentalism DLB-1; DLB-223; DS-5

    "A Response from America," by John A. Heraud DS-5

    Publications and Social Movements DLB-1

    The Rise of Transcendentalism, 1815-1860 .... DS-5

    Transcendentalists, American DS-5

    "What Is Transcendentalism? By a Thinking Man," by James Kinnard Jr. DS-5

transition 1927-1938 .... DS-15

Translations (Vernacular) in the Crowns of Castile and Aragon 1352-1515 ...... DLB-286

Tranströmer, Tomas 1931- DLB-257

Tranter, John 1943- DLB-289

Travel Writing

    American Travel Writing, 1776-1864 (checklist) DLB-183

    British Travel Writing, 1940-1997 (checklist) DLB-204

    Travel Writers of the Late Middle Ages DLB-286

    (1876-1909) DLB-174

    (1837-1875) DLB-166

    (1910-1939) DLB-195

Traven, B. 1882?/1890?-1969? DLB-9, 56

Travers, Ben 1886-1980 .... DLB-10, 233

Travers, P. L. (Pamela Lyndon) 1899-1996 .... DLB-160

Trediakovsky, Vasilii Kirillovich 1703-1769 .... DLB-150

Treece, Henry 1911-1966 .... DLB-160

Treitel, Jonathan 1959- DLB-267

Trejo, Ernesto 1950-1991 .... DLB-122

Trelawny, Edward John 1792-1881 ....DLB-110, 116, 144

Tremain, Rose 1943- DLB-14, 271

Tremblay, Michel 1942- DLB-60

Trent, William P. 1862-1939......... DLB-47, 71

Trescot, William Henry 1822-1898.......DLB-30

Tressell, Robert (Robert Phillipe Noonan)
1870-1911 ....DLB-197

Trevelyan, Sir George Otto
1838-1928 ....DLB-144

Trevisa, John circa 1342-circa 1402......DLB-146

Trevisan, Dalton 1925- DLB-307

Trevor, William 1928- DLB-14, 139

Triana, José 1931- DLB-305

Trierer Floyris circa 1170-1180 ....DLB-138

Trifonov, Iurii Valentinovich
1925-1981 ....DLB-302

Trillin, Calvin 1935- DLB-185

Trilling, Lionel 1905-1975 ....DLB-28, 63

Trilussa 1871-1950.................DLB-114

Trimmer, Sarah 1741-1810 ....DLB-158

Triolet, Elsa 1896-1970 ....DLB-72

Tripp, John 1927- DLB-40

Trocchi, Alexander 1925-1984 ....DLB-15

Troisi, Dante 1920-1989 ....DLB-196

Trollope, Anthony
1815-1882 .... DLB-21, 57, 159; CDBLB-4

Novel-Reading: *The Works of Charles Dickens; The Works of W. Makepeace Thackeray* (1879) DLB-21

The Trollope Societies Y-00

Trollope, Frances 1779-1863 ....DLB-21, 166

Trollope, Joanna 1943- DLB-207

Troop, Elizabeth 1931- DLB-14

Tropicália.....................DLB-307

Trotter, Catharine 1679-1749........DLB-84, 252

Trotti, Lamar 1898-1952...............DLB-44

Trottier, Pierre 1925- DLB-60

Trotzig, Birgitta 1929- DLB-257

Troupe, Quincy Thomas, Jr. 1943 ......DLB-41

John F. Trow and Company DLB-49

Trowbridge, John Townsend 1827-1916 ..DLB-202

Trudel, Jean-Louis 1967- DLB-251

Truillier-Lacombe, Joseph-Patrice
1807-1863 ....DLB-99

Trumbo, Dalton 1905-1976.............DLB-26

Trumbull, Benjamin 1735-1820..........DLB-30

Trumbull, John 1750-1831..............DLB-31

Trumbull, John 1756-1843.............DLB-183

Truth, Sojourner 1797?-1883...........DLB-239

Tscherning, Andreas 1611-1659 ....DLB-164

Tsubouchi Shōyō 1859-1935...........DLB-180

Tsvetaeva, Marina Ivanovna
1892-1941 ....DLB-295

Tuchman, Barbara W.
Tribute to Alfred A. Knopf Y-84

Tucholsky, Kurt 1890-1935............DLB-56

Tucker, Charlotte Maria
1821-1893 ....DLB-163, 190

Tucker, George 1775-1861........DLB-3, 30, 248

Tucker, James 1808?-1866?............DLB-230

Tucker, Nathaniel Beverley
1784-1851 ....DLB-3, 248

Tucker, St. George 1752-1827 ....DLB-37

Tuckerman, Frederick Goddard
1821-1873 ....DLB-243

Tuckerman, Henry Theodore 1813-1871....DLB-64

Tumas, Juozas (see Vaizgantas)

Tunis, John R. 1889-1975 ....DLB-22, 171

Tunstall, Cuthbert 1474-1559 ....DLB-132

Tunström, Göran 1937-2000 ....DLB-257

Tuohy, Frank 1925- DLB-14, 139

Tupper, Martin F. 1810-1889 ....DLB-32

Tur, Evgeniia 1815-1892 ....DLB-238

Turbyfill, Mark 1896-1991 ....DLB-45

Turco, Lewis 1934- Y-84

Tribute to John Ciardi Y-86

Turgenev, Aleksandr Ivanovich
1784-1845 ....DLB-198

Turgenev, Ivan Sergeevich
1818-1883 ....DLB-238

Turnbull, Alexander H. 1868-1918......DLB-184

Turnbull, Andrew 1921-1970 ....DLB-103

Turnbull, Gael 1928- DLB-40

Turner, Arlin 1909-1980 ....DLB-103

Turner, Charles (Tennyson)
1808-1879 ....DLB-32

Turner, Ethel 1872-1958 ....DLB-230

Turner, Frederick 1943- DLB-40

Turner, Frederick Jackson
1861-1932 .... DLB-17, 186

A Conversation between William Riggan
and Janette Turner Hospital Y-02

Turner, Joseph Addison 1826-1868........DLB-79

Turpin, Waters Edward 1910-1968........DLB-51

Turrini, Peter 1944- DLB-124

Tutuola, Amos 1920-1997 ... DLB-125; CDWLB-3

Twain, Mark (see Clemens, Samuel Langhorne)

Tweedie, Ethel Brilliana
circa 1860-1940 ....DLB-174

A Century of Poetry, a Lifetime of
Collecting: J. M. Edelstein's
Collection of Twentieth-
Century American Poetry........... YB-02

Twombly, Wells 1935-1977............DLB-241

Twysden, Sir Roger 1597-1672 ....DLB-213

Ty-Casper, Linda 1931- DLB-312

Tyler, Anne 1941- .. DLB-6, 143; Y-82; CDALB-7

Tyler, Mary Palmer 1775-1866 ....DLB-200

Tyler, Moses Coit 1835-1900 .... DLB-47, 64

Tyler, Royall 1757-1826 ....DLB-37

Tylor, Edward Burnett 1832-1917 ....DLB-57

Tynan, Katharine 1861-1931........DLB-153, 240

Tyndale, William circa 1494-1536........DLB-132

Tyree, Omar 1969- DLB-292

U

Uchida, Yoshiko 1921-1992 ..DLB-312; CDALB-7

Udall, Nicholas 1504-1556 ....DLB-62

Ugrêsić, Dubravka 1949- DLB-181

Uhland, Ludwig 1787-1862 ....DLB-90

Uhse, Bodo 1904-1963 ....DLB-69

Ujević, Augustin "Tin"
1891-1955 ....DLB-147

Ulenhart, Niclas flourished circa 1600....DLB-164

Ulfeldt, Leonora Christina 1621-1698....DLB-300

Ulibarrí, Sabine R. 1919- DLB-82

Ulica, Jorge 1870-1926................DLB-82

Ulitskaya, Liudmila Evgen'evna
1943- DLB-285

Ulivi, Ferruccio 1912- DLB-196

Ulizio, B. George 1889-1969 ....DLB-140

Ulrich von Liechtenstein
circa 1200-circa 1275...............DLB-138

Ulrich von Zatzikhoven
before 1194-after 1214 ....DLB-138

'Umar ibn Abi Rabi'ah 644-712 or 721 ...DLB-311

Unaipon, David 1872-1967 ....DLB-230

Unamuno, Miguel de 1864-1936........DLB-108

Under, Marie 1883-1980 ... DLB-220; CDWLB-4

Underhill, Evelyn 1875-1941 ....DLB-240

Undset, Sigrid 1882-1949 ....DLB-297

Ungaretti, Giuseppe 1888-1970 ....DLB-114

Unger, Friederike Helene 1741-1813......DLB-94

United States Book Company DLB-49

Universal Publishing and Distributing
Corporation DLB-46

University of Colorado
Special Collections at the University of
Colorado at Boulder.............. Y-98

Indiana University Press Y-02

The University of Iowa
Writers' Workshop Golden Jubilee Y-86

University of Missouri Press Y-01

University of South Carolina
The G. Ross Roy Scottish
Poetry Collection Y-89

Two Hundred Years of Rare Books and
Literary Collections at the
University of South Carolina Y-00

The University of South Carolina Press Y-94

University of Virginia
The Book Arts Press at the University
of Virginia Y-96

The Electronic Text Center and the
Electronic Archive of Early American
Fiction at the University of Virginia
Library...................... Y-98

University of Virginia Libraries Y-91

University of Wales Press DLB-112

University Press of Florida Y-00

University Press of Kansas Y-98

University Press of Mississippi Y-99

Unnur Benediktsdóttir Bjarklind (see Hulda)

Uno Chiyo 1897-1996 ....DLB-180

Unruh, Fritz von 1885-1970.........DLB-56, 118

Unsworth, Barry 1930- DLB-194

Unt, Mati 1944- DLB-232

Cumulative Index

The Unterberg Poetry Center of the
   92nd Street Y Y-98
Untermeyer, Louis 1885-1977 .... DLB-303
T. Fisher Unwin [publishing house] DLB-106
Upchurch, Boyd B. (see Boyd, John)
Updike, John 1932- DLB-2, 5, 143, 218, 227;
                             Y-80, 82; DS-3; CDALB-6
   John Updike on the Internet Y-97
   Tribute to Alfred A. Knopf Y-84
   Tribute to John Ciardi Y-86
Upīts, Andrejs 1877-1970 .... DLB-220
Uppdal, Kristofer 1878-1961........... DLB-297
Upton, Bertha 1849-1912.............. DLB-141
Upton, Charles 1948- DLB-16
Upton, Florence K. 1873-1922 .... DLB-141
Upward, Allen 1863-1926 .... DLB-36
Urban, Milo 1904-1982 .... DLB-215
Ureña de Henríquez, Salomé 1850-1897 . DLB-283
Urfé, Honoré d' 1567-1625 .... DLB-268
Urista, Alberto Baltazar (see Alurista)
Urquhart, Fred 1912-1995 .... DLB-139
Urrea, Luis Alberto 1955- DLB-209
Urzidil, Johannes 1896-1970........... DLB-85
U.S.A. (Documentary) DLB-274
Usigli, Rodolfo 1905-1979 .... DLB-305
Usk, Thomas died 1388............... DLB-146
Uslar Pietri, Arturo 1906-2001 .... DLB-113
Uspensky, Gleb Ivanovich
   1843-1902 ....DLB-277
Ussher, James 1581-1656 .... DLB-213
Ustinov, Peter 1921- DLB-13
Uttley, Alison
   1884-1976.................... DLB-160
Uz, Johann Peter 1720-1796 .... DLB-97

V

Vadianus, Joachim 1484-1551 ....DLB-179
Vac, Bertrand (Aimé Pelletier) 1914- DLB-88
Vācietis, Ojārs 1933-1983............. DLB-232
Vaculík, Ludvík 1926- DLB-232
Vaičiulaitis, Antanas 1906-1992 .... DLB-220
Vaičiūnaite, Judita 1937- DLB-232
Vail, Laurence 1891-1968............... DLB-4
Vail, Petr L'vovich 1949- DLB-285
Vailland, Roger 1907-1965 .... DLB-83
Vaižgantas 1869-1933................. DLB-220
Vajda, Ernest 1887-1954.............. DLB-44
Valdés, Gina 1943- DLB-122
Valdez, Luis Miguel 1940- DLB-122
Valduga, Patrizia 1953- DLB-128
Vale Press........................ DLB-112
Valente, José Angel 1929-2000 .... DLB-108
Valenzuela, Luisa 1938- .. DLB-113; CDWLB-3
Valera, Diego de 1412-1488 .... DLB-286
Valeri, Diego 1887-1976 .... DLB-128

Valerius Flaccus fl. circa A.D. 92........ DLB-211
Valerius Maximus fl. circa A.D. 31 ...... DLB-211
Valéry, Paul 1871-1945............... DLB-258
Valesio, Paolo 1939- DLB-196
Valgardson, W. D. 1939- DLB-60
Valle, Luz 1899-1971 .... DLB-290
Valle, Víctor Manuel 1950- DLB-122
Valle-Inclán, Ramón del 1866-1936..... DLB-134
Vallejo, Armando 1949- DLB-122
Vallejo, César Abraham 1892-1938 .... DLB-290
Vallès, Jules 1832-1885................ DLB-123
Vallette, Marguerite Eymery (see Rachilde)
Valverde, José María 1926-1996 .... DLB-108
Vampilov, Aleksandr Valentinovich (A. Sanin)
   1937-1972..................... DLB-302
Van Allsburg, Chris 1949- DLB-61
Van Anda, Carr 1864-1945 .... DLB-25
Vanbrugh, Sir John 1664-1726 .... DLB-80
Vance, Jack 1916?- DLB-8
Vančura, Vladislav
   1891-1942 .... DLB-215; CDWLB-4
van der Post, Laurens 1906-1996 ...... DLB-204
Van Dine, S. S. (see Wright, Williard Huntington)
Van Doren, Mark 1894-1972 .... DLB-45
van Druten, John 1901-1957........... DLB-10
Van Duyn, Mona 1921- DLB-5
   Tribute to James Dickey Y-97
Van Dyke, Henry 1852-1933 ..... DLB-71; DS-13
Van Dyke, Henry 1928- DLB-33
Van Dyke, John C. 1856-1932......... DLB-186
Vane, Sutton 1888-1963.............. DLB-10
Van Gieson, Judith 1941- DLB-306
Vanguard Press DLB-46
van Gulik, Robert Hans 1910-1967 ...... DS-17
van Itallie, Jean-Claude 1936- DLB-7
Van Loan, Charles E. 1876-1919 .....DLB-171
Vann, Robert L. 1879-1940 .... DLB-29
Van Rensselaer, Mariana Griswold
   1851-1934 .... DLB-47
Van Rensselaer, Mrs. Schuyler
   (see Van Rensselaer, Mariana Griswold)
Van Vechten, Carl 1880-1964 ..... DLB-4, 9, 51
van Vogt, A. E. 1912-2000.......... DLB-8, 251
Varela, Blanca 1926- DLB-290
Vargas Llosa, Mario
   1936- DLB-145; CDWLB-3
   Acceptance Speech for the Ritz Paris
      Hemingway Award Y-85
Varley, John 1947- Y-81
Varnhagen von Ense, Karl August
   1785-1858..................... DLB-90
Varnhagen von Ense, Rahel
   1771-1833 .... DLB-90
Varro 116 B.C.-27 B.C. DLB-211
Vasilenko, Svetlana Vladimirovna
   1956- DLB-285
Vasiliu, George (see Bacovia, George)

Vásquez, Richard 1928- DLB-209
Vásquez Montalbán, Manuel 1939- ... DLB-134
Vassa, Gustavus (see Equiano, Olaudah)
Vassalli, Sebastiano 1941- DLB-128, 196
Vaugelas, Claude Favre de 1585-1650 ....DLB-268
Vaughan, Henry 1621-1695........... DLB-131
Vaughan, Thomas 1621-1666 .... DLB-131
Vaughn, Robert 1592?-1667........... DLB-213
Vaux, Thomas, Lord 1509-1556 .... DLB-132
Vazov, Ivan 1850-1921.......DLB-147; CDWLB-4
Véa, Alfredo, Jr. 1950- DLB-209
Veblen, Thorstein 1857-1929 .... DLB-246
Vedel, Anders Sørensen 1542-1616 ..... DLB-300
Vega, Janine Pommy 1942- DLB-16
Veiller, Anthony 1903-1965 .... DLB-44
Velásquez-Trevino, Gloria 1949- DLB-122
Veley, Margaret 1843-1887 .... DLB-199
Velleius Paterculus
   circa 20 B.C.-circa A.D. 30......... DLB-211
Veloz Maggiolo, Marcio 1936- DLB-145
Vel'tman, Aleksandr Fomich
   1800-1870..................... DLB-198
Venegas, Daniel ?-? DLB-82
Venevitinov, Dmitrii Vladimirovich
   1805-1827 .... DLB-205
Verbitskaia, Anastasiia Alekseevna
   1861-1928 .... DLB-295
Verde, Cesário 1855-1886 .... DLB-287
Vergil, Polydore circa 1470-1555 .... DLB-132
Veríssimo, Erico 1905-1975 ....DLB-145, 307
Verlaine, Paul 1844-1896............DLB-217
Vernacular Translations in the Crowns of
   Castile and Aragon 1352-1515...... DLB-286
Verne, Jules 1828-1905............... DLB-123
Verplanck, Gulian C. 1786-1870........ DLB-59
Very, Jones 1813-1880 .... DLB-1, 243; DS-5
Vesaas, Halldis Moren 1907-1995 ...... DLB-297
Vesaas, Tarjei 1897-1970 .... DLB-297
Vian, Boris 1920-1959 .... DLB-72
Viazemsky, Petr Andreevich
   1792-1878 .... DLB-205
Vicars, Thomas 1591-1638 .... DLB-236
Vicente, Gil 1465-1536/1540? DLB-287
Vickers, Roy 1888?-1965 .... DLB-77
Vickery, Sukey 1779-1821 .... DLB-200
Victoria 1819-1901 .... DLB-55
Victoria Press..................... DLB-106
Vidal, Gore 1925- DLB-6, 152; CDALB-7
Vidal, Mary Theresa 1815-1873........ DLB-230
Vidmer, Richards 1898-1978 .... DLB-241
Viebig, Clara 1860-1952 .... DLB-66
Vieira, António, S. J. (Antonio Vieyra)
   1608-1697 .... DLB-307
Viereck, George Sylvester 1884-1962..... DLB-54
Viereck, Peter 1916- DLB-5
Vietnam War (ended 1975)

Resources for the Study of Vietnam War
    Literature DLB-9

Viets, Roger 1738-1811 . . . . DLB-99

Vigil-Piñon, Evangelina 1949- DLB-122

Vigneault, Gilles 1928- DLB-60

Vigny, Alfred de 1797-1863 . . . . DLB-119, 192, 217

Vigolo, Giorgio 1894-1983 . . . . DLB-114

Vik, Bjorg 1935- DLB-297

The Viking Press DLB-46

Vilde, Eduard 1865-1933. . . . . DLB-220

Vilinskaia, Mariia Aleksandrovna
    (see Vovchok, Marko)

Villa, José García 1908-1997 . . . . DLB-312

Villanueva, Alma Luz 1944- DLB-122

Villanueva, Tino 1941- DLB-82

Villard, Henry 1835-1900 . . . . DLB-23

Villard, Oswald Garrison 1872-1949 . . . DLB-25, 91

Villarreal, Edit 1944- DLB-209

Villarreal, José Antonio 1924- DLB-82

Villaseñor, Victor 1940- DLB-209

Villedieu, Madame de (Marie-Catherine
    Desjardins) 1640?-1683 . . . . DLB-268

Villegas de Magnón, Leonor
    1876-1955 . . . . DLB-122

Villehardouin, Geoffroi de
    circa 1150-1215 . . . . DLB-208

Villemaire, Yolande 1949- DLB-60

Villena, Enrique de
    ca. 1382/84-1432 . . . . DLB-286

Villena, Luis Antonio de 1951- DLB-134

Villiers, George, Second Duke
    of Buckingham 1628-1687 . . . . DLB-80

Villiers de l'Isle-Adam, Jean-Marie
    Mathias Philippe-Auguste,
    Comte de 1838-1889 . . . . DLB-123, 192

Villon, François 1431-circa 1463? DLB-208

Vine Press DLB-112

Viorst, Judith ?- DLB-52

Vipont, Elfrida (Elfrida Vipont Foulds,
    Charles Vipont) 1902-1992 . . . . DLB-160

Viramontes, Helena María 1954- DLB-122

Virgil 70 B.C.-19 B.C. DLB-211; CDWLB-1

Vischer, Friedrich Theodor
    1807-1887 . . . . DLB-133

Vitier, Cintio 1921- DLB-283

Vitruvius circa 85 B.C.-circa 15 B.C. DLB-211

Vitry, Philippe de 1291-1361 . . . . DLB-208

Vittorini, Elio 1908-1966 . . . . DLB-264

Vivanco, Luis Felipe 1907-1975 . . . . DLB-108

Vivian, E. Charles (Charles Henry Cannell,
    Charles Henry Vivian, Jack Mann,
    Barry Lynd) 1882-1947 . . . . DLB-255

Viviani, Cesare 1947- DLB-128

Vivien, Renée 1877-1909 . . . . DLB-217

Vizenor, Gerald 1934- DLB-175, 227

Vizetelly and Company DLB-106

Vladimov, Georgii
    1931-2003 . . . . DLB-302

Voaden, Herman 1903-1991 . . . . DLB-88

Voß, Johann Heinrich 1751-1826 . . . . DLB-90

Vogau, Boris Andreevich
    (see Pil'niak, Boris Andreevich)

Voigt, Ellen Bryant 1943- DLB-120

Voinovich, Vladimir Nikolaevich
    1932- DLB-302

Vojnović, Ivo 1857-1929 . . . . DLB-147; CDWLB-4

Vold, Jan Erik 1939- DLB-297

Volkoff, Vladimir 1932- DLB-83

P. F. Volland Company DLB-46

Vollbehr, Otto H. F.
    1872?-1945 or 1946 . . . . DLB-187

Vologdin (see Zasodimsky, Pavel Vladimirovich)

Voloshin, Maksimilian Aleksandrovich
    1877-1932 . . . . DLB-295

Volponi, Paolo 1924-1994 . . . . DLB-177

Vonarburg, Élisabeth 1947- DLB-251

von der Grün, Max 1926- DLB-75

Vonnegut, Kurt 1922- DLB-2, 8, 152;
                                Y-80; DS-3; CDALB-6

    Tribute to Isaac Asimov Y-92

    Tribute to Richard Brautigan Y-84

Voranc, Prežihov 1893-1950 . . . . DLB-147

Voronsky, Aleksandr Konstantinovich
    1884-1937 . . . . DLB-272

Vorse, Mary Heaton 1874-1966 . . . . DLB-303

Vovchok, Marko 1833-1907 . . . . DLB-238

Voynich, E. L. 1864-1960 . . . . DLB-197

Vroman, Mary Elizabeth
    circa 1924-1967 . . . . DLB-33

W

Wace, Robert ("Maistre")
    circa 1100-circa 1175 . . . . DLB-146

Wackenroder, Wilhelm Heinrich
    1773-1798 . . . . DLB-90

Wackernagel, Wilhelm 1806-1869 . . . . . . DLB-133

Waddell, Helen 1889-1965 . . . . DLB-240

Waddington, Miriam 1917- DLB-68

Wade, Henry 1887-1969 . . . . DLB-77

Wagenknecht, Edward 1900- DLB-103

Wägner, Elin 1882-1949 . . . . DLB-259

Wagner, Heinrich Leopold 1747-1779 . . . . DLB-94

Wagner, Henry R. 1862-1957 . . . . DLB-140

Wagner, Richard 1813-1883 . . . . DLB-129

Wagoner, David 1926- DLB-5, 256

Wah, Fred 1939- DLB-60

Waiblinger, Wilhelm 1804-1830 . . . . DLB-90

Wain, John
    1925-1994 . . . DLB-15, 27, 139, 155; CDBLB-8
    Tribute to J. B. Priestly Y-84

Wainwright, Jeffrey 1944- DLB-40

Waite, Peirce and Company DLB-49

Wakeman, Stephen H. 1859-1924 . . . . DLB-187

Wakoski, Diane 1937- DLB-5

Walahfrid Strabo circa 808-849 . . . . DLB-148

Henry Z. Walck [publishing house] DLB-46

Walcott, Derek
    1930- DLB-117; Y-81, 92; CDWLB-3
    Nobel Lecture 1992: The Antilles:
        Fragments of Epic Memory Y-92

Robert Waldegrave [publishing house] . . . DLB-170

Waldis, Burkhard circa 1490-1556? DLB-179

Waldman, Anne 1945- DLB-16

Waldrop, Rosmarie 1935- DLB-169

Walker, Alice 1900-1982 . . . . DLB-201

Walker, Alice
    1944- DLB-6, 33, 143; CDALB-6

Walker, Annie Louisa (Mrs. Harry Coghill)
    circa 1836-1907 . . . . DLB-240

Walker, George F. 1947- DLB-60

Walker, John Brisben 1847-1931 . . . . DLB-79

Walker, Joseph A. 1935- DLB-38

Walker, Kath (see Oodgeroo of the Tribe Noonuccal)

Walker, Margaret 1915-1998. . . . . . . DLB-76, 152

Walker, Obadiah 1616-1699 . . . . DLB-281

Walker, Ted 1934- DLB-40

Walker, Evans and Cogswell Company . . . DLB-49

Wall, John F. (see Sarban)

Wallace, Alfred Russel 1823-1913 . . . . DLB-190

Wallace, Dewitt 1889-1981 . . . . DLB-137

Wallace, Edgar 1875-1932 . . . . DLB-70

Wallace, Lew 1827-1905 . . . . DLB-202

Wallace, Lila Acheson 1889-1984 . . . . DLB-137

"A Word of Thanks," From the Initial
    Issue of *Reader's Digest*
    (February 1922) DLB-137

Wallace, Naomi 1960- DLB-249

Wallace Markfield's "Steeplechase" Y-02

Wallace-Crabbe, Chris 1934- DLB-289

Wallant, Edward Lewis
    1926-1962 . . . . DLB-2, 28, 143, 299

Waller, Edmund 1606-1687 . . . . DLB-126

Walpole, Horace 1717-1797 . . . . . DLB-39, 104, 213

    Preface to the First Edition of
       The Castle of Otranto (1764) DLB-39, 178

    Preface to the Second Edition of
       The Castle of Otranto (1765) DLB-39, 178

Walpole, Hugh 1884-1941 . . . . DLB-34

Walrond, Eric 1898-1966 . . . . DLB-51

Walser, Martin 1927- DLB-75, 124

Walser, Robert 1878-1956 . . . . DLB-66

Walsh, Ernest 1895-1926 . . . . DLB-4, 45

Walsh, Robert 1784-1859 . . . . DLB-59

Walters, Henry 1848-1931 . . . . DLB-140

Waltharius circa 825 . . . . DLB-148

Walther von der Vogelweide
    circa 1170-circa 1230 . . . . DLB-138

Walton, Izaak
    1593-1683 . . . . DLB-151, 213; CDBLB-1

Wambaugh, Joseph 1937- DLB-6; Y-83

Wand, Alfred Rudolph 1828-1891 . . . . . . DLB-188

Wandor, Micheline 1940- DLB-310

Waniek, Marilyn Nelson 1946- DLB-120

Wanley, Humphrey 1672-1726 . . . . DLB-213

Cumulative Index

War of the Words (and Pictures):
 The Creation of a Graphic Novel Y-02
Warburton, William 1698-1779 .... DLB-104
Ward, Aileen 1919- DLB-111
Ward, Artemus (see Browne, Charles Farrar)
Ward, Arthur Henry Sarsfield (see Rohmer, Sax)
Ward, Douglas Turner 1930- DLB-7, 38
Ward, Mrs. Humphry 1851-1920 .... DLB-18
Ward, James 1843-1925 .... DLB-262
Ward, Lynd 1905-1985 .... DLB-22
Ward, Lock and Company DLB-106
Ward, Nathaniel circa 1578-1652 .... DLB-24
Ward, Theodore 1902-1983 .... DLB-76
Wardle, Ralph 1909-1988 .... DLB-103
Ware, Henry, Jr. 1794-1843 .... DLB-235
Ware, William 1797-1852 .... DLB-1, 235
Warfield, Catherine Ann 1816-1877 ...... DLB-248
Waring, Anna Letitia 1823-1910 .... DLB-240
Frederick Warne and Company [U.K.] DLB-106
Frederick Warne and Company [U.S.] DLB-49
Warner, Anne 1869-1913 .... DLB-202
Warner, Charles Dudley 1829-1900 ..... DLB-64
Warner, Marina 1946- DLB-194
Warner, Rex 1905-1986 .... DLB-15
Warner, Susan 1819-1885 ... DLB-3, 42, 239, 250
Warner, Sylvia Townsend
 1893-1978 .... DLB-34, 139
Warner, William 1558-1609 .... DLB-172
Warner Books DLB-46
Warr, Bertram 1917-1943 .... DLB-88
Warren, John Byrne Leicester
 (see De Tabley, Lord)
Warren, Lella 1899-1982 .... Y-83
Warren, Mercy Otis 1728-1814 ..... DLB-31, 200
Warren, Robert Penn 1905-1989 ..... DLB-2, 48,
 152; Y-80, 89; CDALB-6
 Tribute to Katherine Anne Porter Y-80
Warren, Samuel 1807-1877 .... DLB-190
Die Wartburgkrieg circa 1230-circa 1280 ... DLB-138
Warton, Joseph 1722-1800 .... DLB-104, 109
Warton, Thomas 1728-1790 .... DLB-104, 109
Warung, Price (William Astley)
 1855-1911 .... DLB-230
Washington, George 1732-1799 .... DLB-31
Washington, Ned 1901-1976 .... DLB-265
Wassermann, Jakob 1873-1934 .... DLB-66
Wasserstein, Wendy 1950- DLB-228
Wassmo, Herbjorg 1942- DLB-297
Wasson, David Atwood 1823-1887 ..... DLB-1, 223
Watanna, Onoto (see Eaton, Winnifred)
Waten, Judah 1911?-1985 .... DLB-289
Waterhouse, Keith 1929- DLB-13, 15
Waterman, Andrew 1940- DLB-40
Waters, Frank 1902-1995 ....DLB-212; Y-86
Waters, Michael 1949- DLB-120
Watkins, Tobias 1780-1855 .... DLB-73

Watkins, Vernon 1906-1967 .... DLB-20
Watmough, David 1926- DLB-53
Watson, Colin 1920-1983 ....DLB-276
Watson, Ian 1943- DLB-261
Watson, James Wreford (see Wreford, James)
Watson, John 1850-1907 .... DLB-156
Watson, Rosamund Marriott
 (Graham R. Tomson) 1860-1911 .... DLB-240
Watson, Sheila 1909-1998 .... DLB-60
Watson, Thomas 1545?-1592 .... DLB-132
Watson, Wilfred 1911- DLB-60
W. J. Watt and Company DLB-46
Watten, Barrett 1948- DLB-193
Watterson, Henry 1840-1921 .... DLB-25
Watts, Alan 1915-1973 .... DLB-16
Watts, Isaac 1674-1748 .... DLB-95
Franklin Watts [publishing house] DLB-46
Waugh, Alec 1898-1981 .... DLB-191
Waugh, Auberon 1939-2000 ...DLB-14, 194; Y-00
Waugh, Evelyn 1903-1966..... DLB-15, 162, 195;
 CDBLB-6
Way and Williams DLB-49
Wayman, Tom 1945- DLB-53
Weatherly, Tom 1942- DLB-41
Weaver, Gordon 1937- DLB-130
Weaver, Robert 1921- DLB-88
Webb, Beatrice 1858-1943 .... DLB-190
Webb, Francis 1925-1973 .... DLB-260
Webb, Frank J. ?-? DLB-50
Webb, James Watson 1802-1884 .... DLB-43
Webb, Mary 1881-1927 .... DLB-34
Webb, Phyllis 1927- DLB-53
Webb, Sidney 1859-1947 .... DLB-190
Webb, Walter Prescott 1888-1963 .... DLB-17
Webbe, William ?-1591 .... DLB-132
Webber, Charles Wilkins 1819-1856? ... DLB-202
Weber, Max 1864-1920 .... DLB-296
Webling, Lucy (Lucy Betty MacRaye)
 1877-1952 .... DLB-240
Webling, Peggy (Arthur Weston)
 1871-1949 .... DLB-240
Webster, Augusta 1837-1894 ...... DLB-35, 240
Webster, John
 1579 or 1580-1634? DLB-58; CDBLB-1
 The Melbourne Manuscript........... Y-86
Webster, Noah
 1758-1843 .... DLB-1, 37, 42, 43, 73, 243
Webster, Paul Francis 1907-1984 .... DLB-265
Charles L. Webster and Company....... DLB-49
Weckherlin, Georg Rodolf 1584-1653 ... DLB-164
Wedekind, Frank
 1864-1918 ....DLB-118; CDWLB-2
Weeks, Edward Augustus, Jr.
 1898-1989 .... DLB-137
Weeks, Stephen B. 1865-1918 .... DLB-187
Weems, Mason Locke 1759-1825...DLB-30, 37, 42
Weerth, Georg 1822-1856 .... DLB-129

Weidenfeld and Nicolson............ DLB-112
Weidman, Jerome 1913-1998 .... DLB-28
Weigl, Bruce 1949- DLB-120
Weil, Jiří 1900-1959 .... DLB-299
Weinbaum, Stanley Grauman
 1902-1935 ....DLB-8
Weiner, Andrew 1949- DLB-251
Weintraub, Stanley 1929- DLB-111; Y82
Weise, Christian 1642-1708 .... DLB-168
Weisenborn, Gunther 1902-1969.... DLB-69, 124
Weiss, John 1818-1879 .... DLB-1, 243
Weiss, Paul 1901-2002 ....DLB-279
Weiss, Peter 1916-1982 .... DLB-69, 124
Weiss, Theodore 1916- DLB-5
Weiß, Ernst 1882-1940.............. DLB-81
Weiße, Christian Felix 1726-1804........ DLB-97
Weitling, Wilhelm 1808-1871........ DLB-129
Welch, James 1940- DLB-175, 256
Welch, Lew 1926-1971? DLB-16
Weldon, Fay 1931- DLB-14, 194; CDBLB-8
Wellek, René 1903-1995 .... DLB-63
Wells, Carolyn 1862-1942 .... DLB-11
Wells, Charles Jeremiah
 circa 1800-1879 .... DLB-32
Wells, Gabriel 1862-1946............ DLB-140
Wells, H. G. 1866-1946
 ....DLB-34, 70, 156, 178; CDBLB-6
 H. G. Wells Society Y-98
 Preface to The Scientific Romances of
  H. G. Wells (1933) DLB-178
Wells, Helena 1758?-1824 .... DLB-200
Wells, Rebecca 1952- DLB-292
Wells, Robert 1947- DLB-40
Wells-Barnett, Ida B. 1862-1931..... DLB-23, 221
Welsh, Irvine 1958- DLB-271
Welty, Eudora 1909-2001 ...... DLB-2, 102, 143;
 Y-87, 01; DS-12; CDALB-1
 Eudora Welty: Eye of the Storyteller..... Y-87
 Eudora Welty Newsletter Y-99
 Eudora Welty's Funeral............. Y-01
 Eudora Welty's Ninetieth Birthday Y-99
 Eudora Welty Remembered in
  Two Exhibits.................. Y-02
Wendell, Barrett 1855-1921 .... DLB-71
Wentworth, Patricia 1878-1961 .... DLB-77
Wentworth, William Charles
 1790-1872 .... DLB-230
Werder, Diederich von dem 1584-1657 .. DLB-164
Werfel, Franz 1890-1945 .... DLB-81, 124
Werner, Zacharias 1768-1823........... DLB-94
The Werner Company.............. DLB-49
Wersba, Barbara 1932- DLB-52
Wescott, Glenway
 1901-1987 ....DLB-4, 9, 102; DS-15
Wesker, Arnold 1932- ... DLB-13, 310; CDBLB-8
Wesley, Charles 1707-1788 .... DLB-95
Wesley, John 1703-1791 .... DLB-104

Wesley, Mary 1912-2002. . . . . .DLB-231

Wesley, Richard 1945- DLB-38

Wessel, Johan Herman 1742-1785 . . . . . . .DLB-300

A. Wessels and Company DLB-46

Wessobrunner Gebet circa 787-815 . . . . . . .DLB-148

West, Anthony 1914-1988. . . . . .DLB-15

    Tribute to Liam O'Flaherty. Y-84

West, Cheryl L. 1957- DLB-266

West, Cornel 1953- DLB-246

West, Dorothy 1907-1998 . . . . .DLB-76

West, Jessamyn 1902-1984 . . . . .DLB-6; Y-84

West, Mae 1892-1980 . . . . .DLB-44

West, Michael Lee 1953- DLB-292

West, Michelle Sagara 1963- DLB-251

West, Morris 1916-1999 . . . . .DLB-289

West, Nathanael
    1903-1940 . . . . .DLB-4, 9, 28; CDALB-5

West, Paul 1930- DLB-14

West, Rebecca 1892-1983 . . . . .DLB-36; Y-83

West, Richard 1941- DLB-185

West and Johnson DLB-49

Westcott, Edward Noyes 1846-1898 . . . . .DLB-202

The Western Literature Association Y-99

The Western Messenger
    1835-1841 . . . . DLB-1; DLB-223

Western Publishing Company. DLB-46

Western Writers of America Y-99

The Westminster Review 1824-1914 . . . . . . .DLB-110

Weston, Arthur (see Webling, Peggy)

Weston, Elizabeth Jane circa 1582-1612 . .DLB-172

Wetherald, Agnes Ethelwyn 1857-1940. . . .DLB-99

Wetherell, Elizabeth (see Warner, Susan)

Wetherell, W. D. 1948- DLB-234

Wetzel, Friedrich Gottlob 1779-1819 . . . . . .DLB-90

Weyman, Stanley J. 1855-1928 . . . . .DLB-141, 156

Wezel, Johann Karl 1747-1819 . . . . .DLB-94

Whalen, Philip 1923-2002. . . . . .DLB-16

Whalley, George 1915-1983 . . . . .DLB-88

Wharton, Edith 1862-1937 . . . . DLB-4, 9, 12,
    78, 189; DS-13; CDALB-3

Wharton, William 1920s?- Y-80

Whately, Mary Louisa 1824-1889. . . . . . .DLB-166

Whately, Richard 1787-1863 . . . . .DLB-190

    Elements of Rhetoric (1828;
    revised, 1846) [excerpt]. DLB-57

Wheatley, Dennis 1897-1977 . . . . DLB-77, 255

Wheatley, Phillis
    circa 1754-1784. . . . . . .DLB-31, 50; CDALB-2

Wheeler, Anna Doyle 1785-1848?. DLB-158

Wheeler, Charles Stearns 1816-1843 . . .DLB-1, 223

Wheeler, Monroe 1900-1988. . . . . .DLB-4

Wheelock, John Hall 1886-1978 . . . . .DLB-45

    From John Hall Wheelock's
    Oral Memoir. Y-01

Wheelwright, J. B. 1897-1940. . . . . .DLB-45

Wheelwright, John circa 1592-1679 . . . . . .DLB-24

Whetstone, George 1550-1587 . . . . .DLB-136

Whetstone, Colonel Pete (see Noland, C. F. M.)

Whewell, William 1794-1866. . . . . .DLB-262

Whichcote, Benjamin 1609?-1683 . . . . . . .DLB-252

Whicher, Stephen E. 1915-1961 . . . . .DLB-111

Whipple, Edwin Percy 1819-1886 . . . . . .DLB-1, 64

Whitaker, Alexander 1585-1617 . . . . .DLB-24

Whitaker, Daniel K. 1801-1881. . . . . .DLB-73

Whitcher, Frances Miriam
    1812-1852 . . . . DLB-11, 202

White, Andrew 1579-1656. . . . . .DLB-24

White, Andrew Dickson 1832-1918 . . . . . .DLB-47

White, E. B. 1899-1985 . . . .DLB-11, 22; CDALB-7

White, Edgar B. 1947- DLB-38

White, Edmund 1940- DLB-227

White, Ethel Lina 1887-1944 . . . . .DLB-77

White, Hayden V. 1928- DLB-246

White, Henry Kirke 1785-1806 . . . . .DLB-96

White, Horace 1834-1916 . . . . .DLB-23

White, James 1928-1999 . . . . .DLB-261

White, Patrick 1912-1990 . . . . .DLB-260

White, Phyllis Dorothy James (see James, P. D.)

White, Richard Grant 1821-1885 . . . . .DLB-64

White, T. H. 1906-1964 . . . . .DLB-160, 255

White, Walter 1893-1955 . . . . .DLB-51

Wilcox, James 1949- DLB-292

William White and Company. DLB-49

White, William Allen 1868-1944. . . . . . .DLB-9, 25

White, William Anthony Parker
    (see Boucher, Anthony)

White, William Hale (see Rutherford, Mark)

Whitchurch, Victor L. 1868-1933 . . . . .DLB-70

Whitehead, Alfred North
    1861-1947 . . . . DLB-100, 262

Whitehead, E. A. (Ted Whitehead)
    1933- .DLB-310

Whitehead, James 1936- Y-81

Whitehead, William 1715-1785 . . . . . .DLB-84, 109

Whitfield, James Monroe 1822-1871 . . . . . .DLB-50

Whitfield, Raoul 1898-1945. . . . . .DLB-226

Whitgift, John circa 1533-1604 . . . . .DLB-132

Whiting, John 1917-1963 . . . . .DLB-13

Whiting, Samuel 1597-1679 . . . . .DLB-24

Whitlock, Brand 1869-1934. . . . . .DLB-12

Whitman, Albery Allson 1851-1901 . . . . . .DLB-50

Whitman, Alden 1913-1990. . . . . Y-91

Whitman, Sarah Helen (Power)
    1803-1878 . . . . DLB-1, 243

Whitman, Walt
    1819-1892 . . . .DLB-3, 64, 224, 250; CDALB-2

Albert Whitman and Company. DLB-46

Whitman Publishing Company. DLB-46

Whitney, Geoffrey
    1548 or 1552?-1601 . . . . .DLB-136

Whitney, Isabella flourished 1566-1573. . .DLB-136

Whitney, John Hay 1904-1982 . . . . .DLB-127

Whittemore, Reed 1919-1995 . . . . .DLB-5

Whittier, John Greenleaf
    1807-1892 . . . . DLB-1, 243; CDALB-2

Whittlesey House DLB-46

Wickham, Anna (Edith Alice Mary Harper)
    1884-1947 . . . . .DLB-240

Wickram, Georg circa 1505-circa 1561 . . .DLB-179

Wicomb, Zoë 1948- DLB-225

Wideman, John Edgar 1941- DLB-33, 143

Widener, Harry Elkins 1885-1912 . . . . . .DLB-140

Wiebe, Rudy 1934- DLB-60

Wiechert, Ernst 1887-1950. . . . . .DLB-56

Wied, Gustav 1858-1914. . . . . .DLB-300

Wied, Martina 1882-1957 . . . . .DLB-85

Wiehe, Evelyn May Clowes (see Mordaunt, Elinor)

Wieland, Christoph Martin 1733-1813 . . . .DLB-97

Wienbarg, Ludolf 1802-1872. . . . . .DLB-133

Wieners, John 1934- DLB-16

Wier, Ester 1910- DLB-52

Wiesel, Elie
    1928- DLB-83, 299; Y-86, 87; CDALB-7

    Nobel Lecture 1986: Hope, Despair and
    Memory Y-86

Wiggin, Kate Douglas 1856-1923 . . . . . . .DLB-42

Wigglesworth, Michael 1631-1705. . . . . . . .DLB-24

Wilberforce, William 1759-1833 . . . . . . .DLB-158

Wilbrandt, Adolf 1837-1911 . . . . .DLB-129

Wilbur, Richard 1921- . . .DLB-5, 169; CDALB-7

    Tribute to Robert Penn Warren Y-89

Wilcox, James 1949- DLB-292

Wild, Peter 1940- DLB-5

Wilde, Lady Jane Francesca Elgee
    1821?-1896 . . . . .DLB-199

Wilde, Oscar 1854-1900
    . DLB-10, 19, 34, 57, 141, 156, 190; CDBLB-5

    "The Critic as Artist" (1891). DLB-57

    "The Decay of Lying" (1889) DLB-18

    "The English Renaissance of
    Art" (1908) DLB-35

    "L'Envoi" (1882). DLB-35

    Oscar Wilde Conference at Hofstra
    University. Y-00

Wilde, Richard Henry 1789-1847 . . . . . .DLB-3, 59

W. A. Wilde Company DLB-49

Wilder, Billy 1906- DLB-26

Wilder, Laura Ingalls 1867-1957 . . . . .DLB-22, 256

Wilder, Thornton
    1897-1975. . . . . . . .DLB-4, 7, 9, 228; CDALB-7

    Thornton Wilder Centenary at Yale. Y-97

Wildgans, Anton 1881-1932 . . . . .DLB-118

Wiley, Bell Irvin 1906-1980. . . . . .DLB-17

John Wiley and Sons. DLB-49

Wilhelm, Kate 1928- DLB-8

Wilkes, Charles 1798-1877. . . . . .DLB-183

Wilkes, George 1817-1885. . . . . .DLB-79

Wilkins, John 1614-1672 . . . . .DLB-236

Wilkinson, Anne 1910-1961 . . . . .DLB-88

Wilkinson, Christopher 1941- DLB-310

Wilkinson, Eliza Yonge
    1757-circa 1813 . . . . .DLB-200

Wilkinson, Sylvia 1940- Y-86

Cumulative Index

Wilkinson, William Cleaver 1833-1920 ... DLB-71

Willard, Barbara 1909-1994 ... DLB-161

Willard, Emma 1787-1870 ... DLB-239

Willard, Frances E. 1839-1898 ... DLB-221

Willard, Nancy 1936- ... DLB-5, 52

Willard, Samuel 1640-1707 ... DLB-24

L. Willard [publishing house] ... DLB-49

Willeford, Charles 1919-1988 ... DLB-226

William of Auvergne 1190-1249 ... DLB-115

William of Conches circa 1090-circa 1154 ... DLB-115

William of Ockham circa 1285-1347 ... DLB-115

William of Sherwood 1200/1205-1266/1271 ... DLB-115

The William Charvat American Fiction Collection at the Ohio State University Libraries ... Y-92

Williams, Ben Ames 1889-1953 ... DLB-102

Williams, C. K. 1936- ... DLB-5

Williams, Chancellor 1905-1992 ... DLB-76

Williams, Charles 1886-1945 ... DLB-100, 153, 255

Williams, Denis 1923-1998 ... DLB-117

Williams, Emlyn 1905-1987 ... DLB-10, 77

Williams, Garth 1912-1996 ... DLB-22

Williams, George Washington 1849-1891 ... DLB-47

Williams, Heathcote 1941- ... DLB-13

Williams, Helen Maria 1761-1827 ... DLB-158

Williams, Hugo 1942- ... DLB-40

Williams, Isaac 1802-1865 ... DLB-32

Williams, Joan 1928- ... DLB-6

Williams, Joe 1889-1972 ... DLB-241

Williams, John A. 1925- ... DLB-2, 33

Williams, John E. 1922-1994 ... DLB-6

Williams, Jonathan 1929- ... DLB-5

Williams, Miller 1930- ... DLB-105

Williams, Nigel 1948- ... DLB-231

Williams, Raymond 1921-1988 ... DLB-14, 231, 242

Williams, Roger circa 1603-1683 ... DLB-24

Williams, Rowland 1817-1870 ... DLB-184

Williams, Samm-Art 1946- ... DLB-38

Williams, Sherley Anne 1944-1999 ... DLB-41

Williams, T. Harry 1909-1979 ... DLB-17

Williams, Tennessee 1911-1983 ... DLB-7; Y-83; DS-4; CDALB-1

Williams, Terry Tempest 1955- ... DLB-206, 275

Williams, Ursula Moray 1911- ... DLB-160

Williams, Valentine 1883-1946 ... DLB-77

Williams, William Appleman 1921- ... DLB-17

Williams, William Carlos 1883-1963 ... DLB-4, 16, 54, 86; CDALB-4

The William Carlos Williams Society ... Y-99

Williams, Wirt 1921- ... DLB-6

A. Williams and Company ... DLB-49

Williams Brothers ... DLB-49

Wililiamson, David 1942- ... DLB-289

Williamson, Henry 1895-1977 ... DLB-191

The Henry Williamson Society ... Y-98

Williamson, Jack 1908- ... DLB-8

Willingham, Calder Baynard, Jr. 1922-1995 ... DLB-2, 44

Williram of Ebersberg circa 1020-1085 ... DLB-148

Willis, John circa 1572-1625 ... DLB-281

Willis, Nathaniel Parker 1806-1867 ... DLB-3, 59, 73, 74, 183, 250; DS-13

Willis, Ted 1918-1992 ... DLB-310

Willkomm, Ernst 1810-1886 ... DLB-133

Wills, Garry 1934- ... DLB-246

Tribute to Kenneth Dale McCormick ... Y-97

Willson, Meredith 1902-1984 ... DLB-265

Willumsen, Dorrit 1940- ... DLB-214

Wilmer, Clive 1945- ... DLB-40

Wilson, A. N. 1950- ... DLB-14, 155, 194

Wilson, Angus 1913-1991 ... DLB-15, 139, 155

Wilson, Arthur 1595-1652 ... DLB-58

Wilson, August 1945- ... DLB-228

Wilson, Augusta Jane Evans 1835-1909 ... DLB-42

Wilson, Colin 1931- ... DLB-14, 194

Tribute to J. B. Priestly ... Y-84

Wilson, Edmund 1895-1972 ... DLB-63

Wilson, Ethel 1888-1980 ... DLB-68

Wilson, F. P. 1889-1963 ... DLB-201

Wilson, Harriet E. 1827/1828?-1863? ... DLB-50, 239, 243

Wilson, Harry Leon 1867-1939 ... DLB-9

Wilson, John 1588-1667 ... DLB-24

Wilson, John 1785-1854 ... DLB-110

Wilson, John Anthony Burgess (see Burgess, Anthony)

Wilson, John Dover 1881-1969 ... DLB-201

Wilson, Lanford 1937- ... DLB-7

Wilson, Margaret 1882-1973 ... DLB-9

Wilson, Michael 1914-1978 ... DLB-44

Wilson, Mona 1872-1954 ... DLB-149

Wilson, Robert Charles 1953- ... DLB-251

Wilson, Robert McLiam 1964- ... DLB-267

Wilson, Robley 1930- ... DLB-218

Wilson, Romer 1891-1930 ... DLB-191

Wilson, Thomas 1524-1581 ... DLB-132, 236

Wilson, Woodrow 1856-1924 ... DLB-47

Effingham Wilson [publishing house] ... DLB-154

Wimpfeling, Jakob 1450-1528 ... DLB-179

Wimsatt, William K., Jr. 1907-1975 ... DLB-63

Winchell, Walter 1897-1972 ... DLB-29

J. Winchester [publishing house] ... DLB-49

Winckelmann, Johann Joachim 1717-1768 ... DLB-97

Winckler, Paul 1630-1686 ... DLB-164

Wind, Herbert Warren 1916- ... DLB-171

John Windet [publishing house] ... DLB-170

Windham, Donald 1920- ... DLB-6

Wing, Donald Goddard 1904-1972 ... DLB-187

Wing, John M. 1844-1917 ... DLB-187

Allan Wingate [publishing house] ... DLB-112

Winnemucca, Sarah 1844-1921 ... DLB-175

Winnifrith, Tom 1938- ... DLB-155

Winsloe, Christa 1888-1944 ... DLB-124

Winslow, Anna Green 1759-1780 ... DLB-200

Winsor, Justin 1831-1897 ... DLB-47

John C. Winston Company ... DLB-49

Winters, Yvor 1900-1968 ... DLB-48

Winterson, Jeanette 1959- ... DLB-207, 261

Winther, Christian 1796-1876 ... DLB-300

Winthrop, John 1588-1649 ... DLB-24, 30

Winthrop, John, Jr. 1606-1676 ... DLB-24

Winthrop, Margaret Tyndal 1591-1647 ... DLB-200

Winthrop, Theodore 1828-1861 ... DLB-202

Wirt, William 1772-1834 ... DLB-37

Wise, John 1652-1725 ... DLB-24

Wise, Thomas James 1859-1937 ... DLB-184

Wiseman, Adele 1928-1992 ... DLB-88

Wishart and Company ... DLB-112

Wisner, George 1812-1849 ... DLB-43

Wister, Owen 1860-1938 ... DLB-9, 78, 186

Wister, Sarah 1761-1804 ... DLB-200

Wither, George 1588-1667 ... DLB-121

Witherspoon, John 1723-1794 ... DLB-31

The Works of the Rev. John Witherspoon (1800-1801) [excerpts] ... DLB-31

Withrow, William Henry 1839-1908 ... DLB-99

Witkacy (see Witkiewicz, Stanisław Ignacy)

Witkiewicz, Stanisław Ignacy 1885-1939 ... DLB-215; CDWLB-4

Wittenwiler, Heinrich before 1387-circa 1414? ... DLB-179

Wittgenstein, Ludwig 1889-1951 ... DLB-262

Wittig, Monique 1935- ... DLB-83

Wodehouse, P. G. 1881-1975 ... DLB-34, 162; CDBLB-6

Worldwide Wodehouse Societies ... Y-98

Wohmann, Gabriele 1932- ... DLB-75

Woiwode, Larry 1941- ... DLB-6

Tribute to John Gardner ... Y-82

Wolcot, John 1738-1819 ... DLB-109

Wolcott, Roger 1679-1767 ... DLB-24

Wolf, Christa 1929- ... DLB-75; CDWLB-2

Wolf, Friedrich 1888-1953 ... DLB-124

Wolfe, Gene 1931- ... DLB-8

Wolfe, Thomas 1900-1938 ... DLB-9, 102, 229; Y-85; DS-2, DS-16; CDALB-5

"All the Faults of Youth and Inexperience": A Reader's Report on Thomas Wolfe's *O Lost* ... Y-01

Emendations for *Look Homeward, Angel* ... Y-00

Eugene Gant's Projected Works ... Y-01

Fire at the Old Kentucky Home [Thomas Wolfe Memorial] ... Y-98

Thomas Wolfe Centennial Celebration in Asheville ... Y-00

The Thomas Wolfe Collection at the University of North Carolina at Chapel Hill ... Y-97

The Thomas Wolfe Society Y-97, 99
Wolfe, Tom 1931- DLB-152, 185
John Wolfe [publishing house]. DLB-170
Reyner (Reginald) Wolfe
 [publishing house] DLB-170
Wolfenstein, Martha 1869-1906 . . . . .DLB-221
Wolff, David (see Maddow, Ben)
Wolff, Egon 1926- DLB-305
Wolff, Helen 1906-1994 . . . . Y-94
Wolff, Tobias 1945- DLB-130
 Tribute to Michael M. Rea Y-97
 Tribute to Raymond Carver Y-88
Wolfram von Eschenbach
 circa 1170-after 1220 . . . . DLB-138; CDWLB-2
 Wolfram von Eschenbach's *Parzival*:
  Prologue and Book 3 . . . . DLB-138
Wolker, Jiří 1900-1924 . . . . DLB-215
Wollstonecraft, Mary 1759-1797
 . . . . DLB-39, 104, 158, 252; CDBLB-3
Women
 Women's Work, Women's Sphere:
  Selected Comments from Women
  Writers DLB-200
Wondratschek, Wolf 1943- DLB-75
Wong, Elizabeth 1958- DLB-266
Wong, Nellie 1934- DLB-312
Wong, Shawn 1949- DLB-312
Wood, Anthony à 1632-1695 . . . . .DLB-213
Wood, Benjamin 1820-1900 . . . . DLB-23
Wood, Charles 1932-1980. . . . . DLB-13
 The Charles Wood Affair:
  A Playwright Revived. Y-83
Wood, Mrs. Henry 1814-1887. . . . . DLB-18
Wood, Joanna E. 1867-1927. . . . . DLB-92
Wood, Sally Sayward Barrell Keating
 1759-1855 . . . . DLB-200
Wood, William ?-? DLB-24
Samuel Wood [publishing house] DLB-49
Woodberry, George Edward
 1855-1930 . . . . DLB-71, 103
Woodbridge, Benjamin 1622-1684 . . . . . . DLB-24
Woodbridge, Frederick J. E. 1867-1940 . . . DLB-270
Woodcock, George 1912-1995 . . . . DLB-88
Woodhull, Victoria C. 1838-1927 . . . . DLB-79
Woodmason, Charles circa 1720-? DLB-31
Woodress, James Leslie, Jr. 1916- DLB-111
Woods, Margaret L. 1855-1945. . . . . . . .DLB-240
Woodson, Carter G. 1875-1950. . . . . DLB-17
Woodward, C. Vann 1908-1999 . . . . DLB-17
Woodward, Stanley 1895-1965 . . . . DLB-171
Woodworth, Samuel 1785-1842. . . . . . . .DLB-250
Wooler, Thomas 1785 or 1786-1853 . . . . .DLB-158
Woolf, David (see Maddow, Ben)
Woolf, Douglas 1922-1992 . . . . .DLB-244
Woolf, Leonard 1880-1969 . . . . . . DLB-100; DS-10
Woolf, Virginia 1882-1941
 . . . . DLB-36, 100, 162; DS-10; CDBLB-6
 "The New Biography," *New York Herald
  Tribune*, 30 October 1927 . . . . DLB-149

Woollcott, Alexander 1887-1943 . . . . DLB-29
Woolman, John 1720-1772. . . . . DLB-31
Woolner, Thomas 1825-1892 . . . . DLB-35
Woolrich, Cornell 1903-1968 . . . . .DLB-226
Woolsey, Sarah Chauncy 1835-1905 . . . . . DLB-42
Woolson, Constance Fenimore
 1840-1894 . . . . DLB-12, 74, 189, 221
Worcester, Joseph Emerson
 1784-1865 . . . . DLB-1, 235
Wynkyn de Worde [publishing house] . . . DLB-170
Wordsworth, Christopher 1807-1885 . . . . DLB-166
Wordsworth, Dorothy 1771-1855 . . . . . . .DLB-107
Wordsworth, Elizabeth
 1840-1932 . . . . DLB-98
Wordsworth, William
 1770-1850 . . . . DLB-93, 107; CDBLB-3
Workman, Fanny Bullock
 1859-1925 . . . . DLB-189
World Literatue Today: A Journal for the
 New Millennium Y-01
World Publishing Company DLB-46
World War I (1914-1918) DS-18
 The Great War Exhibit and Symposium
  at the University of South Carolina . . Y-97
 The Liddle Collection and First World
  War Research. Y-97
 Other British Poets Who Fell
  in the Great War DLB-216
 The Seventy-Fifth Anniversary of
  the Armistice: The Wilfred Owen
  Centenary and the Great War Exhibit
  at the University of Virginia. Y-93
World War II (1939–1945)
 Literary Effects of World War II DLB-15
 World War II Writers Symposium
  at the University of South Carolina,
  12–14 April 1995 . . . . Y-95
 WW2 HMSO Paperbacks Society Y-98
R. Worthington and Company DLB-49
Wotton, Sir Henry 1568-1639 . . . . .DLB-121
Wouk, Herman 1915- Y-82; CDALB-7
 Tribute to James Dickey Y-97
Wreford, James 1915- DLB-88
Wren, Sir Christopher 1632-1723 . . . . . . .DLB-213
Wren, Percival Christopher 1885-1941. . .DLB-153
Wrenn, John Henry 1841-1911 . . . . .DLB-140
Wright, C. D. 1949- DLB-120
Wright, Charles 1935- DLB-165; Y-82
Wright, Charles Stevenson 1932- DLB-33
Wright, Chauncey 1830-1875 . . . . .DLB-270
Wright, Frances 1795-1852 . . . . DLB-73
Wright, Harold Bell 1872-1944 . . . . DLB-9
Wright, James 1927-1980
 . . . . DLB-5, 169; CDALB-7
Wright, Jay 1935- DLB-41
Wright, Judith 1915-2000 . . . . .DLB-260
Wright, Louis B. 1899-1984 . . . . DLB-17
Wright, Richard
 1908-1960 . . . . DLB-76, 102; DS-2; CDALB-5
Wright, Richard B. 1937- DLB-53
Wright, S. Fowler 1874-1965 . . . . .DLB-255
Wright, Sarah Elizabeth 1928- DLB-33

Wright, T. H. "Style" (1877) [excerpt]. DLB-57
Wright, Willard Huntington (S. S. Van Dine)
 1887-1939 . . . . DLB-306; DS-16
Wrightson, Patricia 1921- DLB-289
Wrigley, Robert 1951- DLB-256
Writers' Forum Y-85
Writing
 A Writing Life. Y-02
 On Learning to Write Y-88
 The Profession of Authorship:
  Scribblers for Bread Y-89
 A Writer Talking: A Collage Y-00
Wroth, Lawrence C. 1884-1970 . . . . .DLB-187
Wroth, Lady Mary 1587-1653 . . . . .DLB-121
Wurlitzer, Rudolph 1937- DLB-173
Wyatt, Sir Thomas circa 1503-1542 . . . . .DLB-132
Wycherley, William
 1641-1715 . . . . .DLB-80; CDBLB-2
Wyclif, John circa 1335-1384. . . . . .DLB-146
Wyeth, N. C. 1882-1945 . . . . .DLB-188; DS-16
Wyle, Niklas von circa 1415-1479 . . . . . . .DLB-179
Wylie, Elinor 1885-1928 . . . . DLB-9, 45
Wylie, Philip 1902-1971. . . . . DLB-9
Wyllie, John Cook 1908-1968 . . . . .DLB-140
Wyman, Lillie Buffum Chace
 1847-1929 .DLB-202
Wymark, Olwen 1934- DLB-233
Wynd, Oswald Morris (see Black, Gavin)
Wyndham, John (John Wyndham Parkes
 Lucas Beynon Harris) 1903-1969 . . . .DLB-255
Wynne-Tyson, Esmé 1898-1972 . . . . .DLB-191

X

Xenophon circa 430 B.C.-circa 356 B.C. DLB-176

Y

Yamamoto, Hisaye 1921- DLB-312
Yamanaka, Lois-Ann 1961- DLB-312
Yamashita, Karen Tei 1951- DLB-312
Yamauchi, Wakako 1924- DLB-312
Yasuoka Shōtarō 1920- DLB-182
Yates, Dornford 1885-1960 . . . . DLB-77, 153
Yates, J. Michael 1938- DLB-60
Yates, Richard 1926-1992 . . . DLB-2, 234; Y-81, 92
Yau, John 1950- DLB-234, 312
Yavorov, Peyo 1878-1914 . . . . .DLB-147
Yearsley, Ann 1753-1806 . . . . .DLB-109
Yeats, William Butler
 1865-1939 . . . . DLB-10, 19, 98, 156; CDBLB-5
 The W. B. Yeats Society of N.Y. Y-99
Yellen, Jack 1892-1991. . . . . .DLB-265
Yep, Laurence 1948- DLB-52, 312
Yerby, Frank 1916-1991 . . . . DLB-76
Yezierska, Anzia 1880-1970 . . . . DLB-28, 221
Yolen, Jane 1939- DLB-52
Yonge, Charlotte Mary 1823-1901 . . . DLB-18, 163
 The Charlotte M. Yonge Fellowship. . . . Y-98
The York Cycle circa 1376-circa 1569 . . . .DLB-146
A Yorkshire Tragedy DLB-58
Thomas Yoseloff [publishing house] DLB-46

Cumulative Index

Youd, Sam (see Christopher, John)
Young, A. S. "Doc" 1919-1996 .... DLB-241
Young, Al 1939- DLB-33
Young, Arthur 1741-1820 .... DLB-158
Young, Dick 1917 or 1918-1987 .... DLB-171
Young, Edward 1683-1765 .... DLB-95
Young, Frank A. "Fay" 1884-1957 ...... DLB-241
Young, Francis Brett 1884-1954 .... DLB-191
Young, Gavin 1928- DLB-204
Young, Stark 1881-1963 ...... DLB-9, 102; DS-16
Young, Waldeman 1880-1938 .... DLB-26
William Young [publishing house] DLB-49
Young Bear, Ray A. 1950- DLB-175
Yourcenar, Marguerite 1903-1987 ...DLB-72; Y-88
Yovkov, Yordan 1880-1937 ...DLB-147; CDWLB-4

Z

Zachariä, Friedrich Wilhelm 1726-1777 ... DLB-97
Zagajewski, Adam 1945- DLB-232
Zagoskin, Mikhail Nikolaevich
 1789-1852.................... DLB-198
Zajc, Dane 1929- DLB-181
Zālīte, Māra 1952- DLB-232
Zalygin, Sergei Pavlovich 1913-2000 .... DLB-302
Zamiatin, Evgenii Ivanovich 1884-1937 .. DLB-272
Zamora, Bernice 1938- DLB-82
Zamudio, Adela (Soledad) 1854-1928 ... DLB-283
Zand, Herbert 1923-1970 .... DLB-85
Zangwill, Israel 1864-1926 ...... DLB-10, 135, 197
Zanzotto, Andrea 1921- DLB-128
Zapata Olivella, Manuel 1920- DLB-113

Zapoev, Timur Iur'evich
 (see Kibirov, Timur Iur'evich)
Zasodimsky, Pavel Vladimirovich
 1843-1912 .... DLB-238
Zebra Books DLB-46
Zebrowski, George 1945- DLB-8
Zech, Paul 1881-1946................. DLB-56
Zeidner, Lisa 1955- DLB-120
Zeidonis, Imants 1933- DLB-232
Zeimi (Kanze Motokiyo) 1363-1443..... DLB-203
Zelazny, Roger 1937-1995 .... DLB-8
Zenger, John Peter 1697-1746 .... DLB-24, 43
Zepheria DLB-172
Zesen, Philipp von 1619-1689 .... DLB-164
Zhadovskaia, Iuliia Valerianovna
 1824-1883 .... DLB-277
Zhukova, Mar'ia Semenovna
 1805-1855 .... DLB-277
Zhukovsky, Vasilii Andreevich
 1783-1852 .... DLB-205
Zhvanetsky, Mikhail Mikhailovich
 1934- DLB-285
G. B. Zieber and Company DLB-49
Ziedonis, Imants 1933- CDWLB-4
Zieroth, Dale 1946- DLB-60
Zigler und Kliphausen, Heinrich
 Anshelm von 1663-1697 .... DLB-168
Zil'ber, Veniamin Aleksandrovich
 (see Kaverin, Veniamin Aleksandrovich)
Zimmer, Paul 1934- DLB-5
Zinberg, Len (see Lacy, Ed)
Zincgref, Julius Wilhelm 1591-1635..... DLB-164

Zindel, Paul 1936- DLB-7, 52; CDALB-7
Zinnes, Harriet 1919- DLB-193
Zinov'ev, Aleksandr Aleksandrovich
 1922- DLB-302
Zinov'eva-Annibal, Lidiia Dmitrievna
 1865 or 1866-1907 .... DLB-295
Zinzendorf, Nikolaus Ludwig von
 1700-1760 .... DLB-168
Zitkala-Ša 1876-1938................. DLB-175
Zīverts, Mārtiņš 1903-1990 .... DLB-220
Zlatovratsky, Nikolai Nikolaevich
 1845-1911 .... DLB-238
Zola, Emile 1840-1902 .... DLB-123
Zolla, Elémire 1926- DLB-196
Zolotow, Charlotte 1915- DLB-52
Zoshchenko, Mikhail Mikhailovich
 1895-1958 .... DLB-272
Zschokke, Heinrich 1771-1848 .... DLB-94
Zubly, John Joachim 1724-1781 .... DLB-31
Zu-Bolton, Ahmos, II 1936- DLB-41
Zuckmayer, Carl 1896-1977 ...... DLB-56, 124
Zukofsky, Louis 1904-1978 .... DLB-5, 165
Zupan, Vitomil 1914-1987 .... DLB-181
Župančič, Oton 1878-1949 ...DLB-147; CDWLB-4
zur Mühlen, Hermynia 1883-1951....... DLB-56
Zweig, Arnold 1887-1968 .... DLB-66
Zweig, Stefan 1881-1942 .... DLB-81, 118
Zwinger, Ann 1925- DLB-275
Zwingli, Huldrych 1484-1531 .... DLB-179

Ø

Øverland, Arnulf 1889-1968 .... DLB-297

ISBN 0-7876-8131-8

90000